LET'S GO:
India & Nepal

"Its yearly revision by a new crop of Harvard students makes it as valuable as ever." **—The New York Times**

"Value-packed, unbeatable, accurate, and comprehensive." **—The Los Angeles Times**

"A world-wise traveling companion—always ready with friendly advice and helpful hints, all sprinkled with a bit of wit." **—The Philadelphia Inquirer**

"Lighthearted and sophisticated, informative and fun to read. [Let's Go] helps the novice traveler navigate like a knowledgeable old hand." **—Atlanta Journal-Constitution**

"All the essential information you need, from making a phone call to exchanging money to contacting your embassy. [Let's Go] provides maps to help you find your way from every train station to a full range of youth hostels and hotels." **—Minneapolis Star Tribune**

"Unbeatable: good sight-seeing advice; up-to-date info on restaurants, hotels, and inns; a commitment to money-saving travel; and a wry style that brightens nearly every page." **—The Washington Post**

▓ Let's Go researchers have to make it on their own.

"The writers seem to have experienced every rooster-packed bus and lunar-surfaced mattress about which they write." **—The New York Times**

"Retains the spirit of the student-written publication it is: candid, opinionated, resourceful, amusing info for the traveler of limited means but broad curiosity." **—Mademoiselle**

▓ No other guidebook is as comprehensive.

"Whether you're touring the United States, Europe, Southeast Asia, or Central America, a Let's Go guide will clue you in to the cheapest, yet safe, hotels and hostels, food and transportation. Going beyond the call of duty, the guides reveal a country's latest news, cultural hints, and off-beat information that any tourist is likely to miss." **—Tulsa World**

▓ Let's Go is completely revised each year.

"Up-to-date travel tips for touring four continents on skimpy budgets." **—Time**

"Inimitable.... Let's Go's 24 guides are updated yearly (as opposed to the general guidebook standard of every two to three years), and in a marvelously spunky way." **—The New York Times**

LET'S GO

The Budget Guide to
India
& Nepal

1997

Derek McKee
Editor

Mary B. Lawless
Associate Editor

Anna C. Portnoy
Associate Editor

St. Martin's Press ≉ New York

HELPING LET'S GO

If you want to share your discoveries, suggestions, or corrections, please drop us a line. We read every piece of correspondence, whether a postcard, a 10-page e-mail, or a coconut. All suggestions are passed along to our researcher-writers. Please note that mail received after May 1997 may be too late for the 1998 book, but will be retained for the following edition. **Address mail to:**

**Let's Go: India & Nepal
67 Mt. Auburn Street
Cambridge, MA 02138
USA**

Visit Let's Go at **http://www.letsgo.com,** or send e-mail to:

**Fanmail@letsgo.com
Subject: "Let's Go: India & Nepal"**

In addition to the invaluable travel advice our readers share with us, many are kind enough to offer their services as researchers or editors. Unfortunately, the charter of Let's Go, Inc. enables us to employ only currently enrolled Harvard-Radcliffe students.

Contents

Maps

About Let's Go

THIRTY-SIX YEARS OF WISDOM

Back in 1960, a few students at Harvard University banded together to produce a 20-page pamphlet offering a collection of tips on budget travel in Europe. This modest, mimeographed packet, offered as an extra to passengers on student charter flights to Europe, met with instant popularity. The following year, students traveling to Europe researched the first, full-fledged edition of *Let's Go: Europe*, a pocket-sized book featuring honest, irreverent writing and a decidedly youthful outlook on the world. Throughout the 60s, our guides reflected the times; the 1969 guide to America led off by inviting travelers to "dig the scene" at San Francisco's Haight-Ashbury. During the 70s and 80s, we gradually added regional guides and expanded coverage into the Middle East and Central America. With the addition of our in-depth city guides, handy map guides, and extensive coverage of Asia, the 90s are also proving to be a time of explosive growth for Let's Go, and there's certainly no end in sight. The first editions of *Let's Go: India & Nepal* and *Let's Go: Ecuador & The Galápagos Islands* hit the shelves this year, and research for next year's series has already begun.

We've seen a lot in 37 years. *Let's Go: Europe* is now the world's bestselling international guide, translated into seven languages. And our new guides bring Let's Go's total number of titles, with their spirit of adventure and their reputation for honesty, accuracy, and editorial integrity, to 30. But some things never change: our guides are still researched, written, and produced entirely by students who know first-hand how to see the world on the cheap.

HOW WE DO IT

Each guide is completely revised and thoroughly updated every year by a well-traveled set of 200 students. Every winter, we recruit over 120 researchers and 60 editors to write the books anew. After several months of training, Researcher-Writers hit the road for seven weeks of exploration, from Anchorage to Ankara, Estonia to El Salvador, Iceland to Indonesia. Hired for their rare combination of budget travel sense, writing ability, stamina, and courage, these adventurous travelers know that train strikes, stolen luggage, food poisoning, and marriage proposals are all part of a day's work. Back at our offices, editors work from spring to fall, massaging copy written on Himalayan bus rides into witty yet informative prose. A student staff of typesetters, cartographers, publicists, and managers keeps our lively team together. In September, the collected efforts of the summer are delivered to our printer, who turns them into books in record time, so that you have the most up-to-date information available for *your* vacation. And even as you read this, work on next year's editions is well underway.

WHY WE DO IT

At Let's Go, our goal is to give you a great vacation. We don't think of budget travel as the last recourse of the destitute; we believe that it's the only way to travel. Living cheaply and simply brings you closer to the people and places you've been saving up to visit. Our books will ease your anxieties and answer your questions about the basics—so you can get off the beaten track and explore. Once you learn the ropes, we encourage you to put Let's Go away now and then to strike out on your own. As any seasoned traveler will tell you, the best discoveries are often those you make yourself. When you find something worth sharing, drop us a line. We're Let's Go Publications, 67 Mt. Auburn St., Cambridge, MA 02138, USA (e-mail: fanmail@letsgo.com).

HAPPY TRAVELS!

Acknowledgements

First thanks to Steve for his support through each and every crisis, and to Mary and Anna for sticking with it to the end, and to all you wonderful R/Ws. Thanks to Mike F. for his tutelage and trailblazing, to Neela for provocative debates and company during late nights at the office. Many thanks to Sandhya Rao, Eric Unverzagt, Jonathan Lawson, and Lisa Cloutier for their many contributions. Thanks to Pai, Anne E., Sam, Timur, Jesse G., Krysztof, Jay, Alex T., SoRelle, and Gene for office sanity. Thanks to Amanda and Michelle for all their patience. For help on the road thanks to T.P. Das, Unicef Patna, Pablo, Anu S., Claudia Huang, and Vikas Swarnakar. Thanks to Pusey Library, T.R. Pattabiraman, Carol Weiss, Nina Davenport, Beatrice Chrystall, Café of India, Ashutosh Varshney, and the GOI Tourist Office in New York. Thanks to my teachers Isabel, Lida, JRS, Douglas, Sarah L. Thanks to my family: mum, dad, Ruth. Thanks to my friends Ananda, Tahmima, Matt, Chris, Ryan, Mike C., Sonia, Becca, Bruce, Jason, Mike E., and to the Center for High-Energy Metaphysics. And for love, support, and enthusiasm, endless thanks to Nina. **—DDM**

Many thanks to Derek and Anna for hard work and good cheer into the wee small hours and to Steve for support and candy. I dedicate this book to Ken, my favorite author, and to Nan. Love to everyone at 223 Highland #2 and 43 DeWolfe. **—MBL**

Much thanks to...Derek: for taking on this project with courage and commitment. Congrats! Derek, Mary, and Steve: for making the final I&N team a working success. Susan Harper and Ashutosh Varshney: for introducing me to India. One Story Street: for food fests, smokey treats, a cozy couch, witicisms, late nights, and a memorable summer. David: for your amusing musings. Anand: for Anandisms. Dad: for progress. Mom: for your invaluable insight, guidance, and faith this summer. Eliza, Nate, Penny, Sarah: for knowing where (Watertown) and being there. **—ACP**

Editor	Derek McKee
Associate Editor	Mary B. Lawless
Associate Editor	Anna C. Portnoy
Managing Editor	Stephen P. Janiak
Publishing Director	Michelle C. Sullivan
Production Manager	Daniel O. Williams
Associate Production Manager	Michael S. Campbell
Cartography Manager	Amanda K. Bean
Editorial Manager	John R. Brooks
Editorial Manager	Allison Crapo
Financial Manager	Stephen P. Janiak
Personnel Manager	Alexander H. Travelli
Publicity Manager	SoRelle B. Braun
Associate Publicity Manager	David Fagundes
Associate Publicity Manager	Elisabeth Mayer
Assistant Cartographer	Jonathan D. Kibera
Assistant Cartographer	Mark C. Staloff
Office Coordinator	Jennifer L. Schuberth
Director of Advertising and Sales	Amit Tiwari
Senior Sales Executives	Andrew T. Rourke
	Nicholas A. Valtz, Charles E. Varner
General Manager	Richard Olken
Assistant General Manager	Anne E. Chisholm

Researcher-Writers

Wendy R. Anderson *Orissa*
Returning to eastern India after an earlier stay as a volunteer in Calcutta, Wendy brought an extensive religion background to Orissa's temples and sandy beaches. Wendy's research *juggernaut* was stopped in its tracks when her moped ran off the road, but not before she provided us with spectacular coverage of Bhubaneswar and Puri. *Let's Go* hopes Wendy will return next year to pick up where she left off.

Pooja A. Bhatia *Karnataka, Andhra Pradesh*
Pooja left no stone unturned as she cruised through Karnataka, decolonizing the Deccan with her prodigious pen. Whether bar-hopping in Bangalore or gazing at idyllic rural scenes, Pooja provided prose descriptions worthy of an aquatint by the Daniells. Her sense of wide-eyed excitement pervaded every situation, and, conveyed in her writing, it helped keep us healthy, too.

Ravi Chhatpar *Rajasthan, Gujarat*
A cool breeze in the Rajasthani desert, Ravi scooped out travel facts with the suicidal determination of a Rajput warrior. Uncovering smuggling scams and discovering desert delicacies, Ravi helped us think about local life from the viewpoint of his many friends and contacts. His long, wistful letters and phone calls kept us entertained; his precise research made our lives easier.

Jishnu Das *Himachal Pradesh, Jammu and Kashmir*
Jishnu brought native savvy and years of hilly travel wisdom to *Let's Go*'s first venture into the Indian Himalaya. Straying far from any predictable schedule, Jishnu racked up hundreds of hours of bus travel, still finding time to sort through issues of mountain economics and ecology. Jishnu's informed prose and stunning slides helped us feel every glacial stream and taste every morsel of *momo*.

Charles Kapelke *Delhi, Punjab, Haryana, Western U.P.*
The editor of *Let's Go*'s first Central America guidebook brought his flashy writing to India for the first time, where he immersed himself in Hindi, Sikhism, modern art, and Bollywood films, all the while giving us copious tips on *chillum*-toting tourist culture. The last we heard from Chuck he was sprawled out on the beach in Puri, after a spell studying tabla in Varanasi. *Let's Go* thanks Chuck for three years of devoted service, and Amitabh postcards, too.

Edward McBride *Maharashtra, Madhya Pradesh*
A veteran of the *Let's Go* trail in Thailand and Egypt, Edward showed on this assignment that he is truly "Indian at heart." Bal Thackeray quaked in his *chappals* as Edward blazed through Bombay (Mumbai), where he had earlier worked as a reporter for *The Times of India*. Moving on to M.P., Edward babysat a camera crew for a section of his trip as they struggled to maintain his pace. As always, Edward's writing was a literary *mela; Let's Go* bids him a sad farewell.

Larry Myer *Eastern U.P., Bihar, Northeast India*
Equipped with Sanskrit skills and a zest for bizarre adventures, Larry stomped through the Doab befriending locals left and right, and then blazed *Let's Go*'s trail through the northeast. Dedicated and meticulous, Larry contributed reams of terrific coverage, always infused with enigmatic wit. We wish him luck as he plans for his honeymoon in Ayodhya.

Kanaka Pattabiraman *Tamil Nadu*

Flown by *Let's Go* back to her native Madras, Kanaka revisited her childhood as the daughter of a railroad man, chugging through her home state, braving cyclones and high sari prices. Touring the temples of Tamilnad, Kanaka collected *karma* constantly. Her clean and pristine pages of writing let us in on the secrets of shopping, *darshan* bribery, and obscure Hindu legends.

Karin Lynn Riley *Goa, Kerala*

Karin moved down the Malabar Coast with the grace of a Kathakali dancer, soaking in the country's oozing smells and overpowering mellowness. In Goa and the Land of Green Magic, Karin kept the spirit of hippiedom alive, helping her friends spy for environmental groups and filling us with *feni* facts. "You like India?" Karin loved it, and her blissful delight shone through in her work at every turn.

Sanjaya K. Shrestha *Western Nepal, Nepal Treks*

Sanjaya returned to his native land this year to explore its winding trails. Despite long bus rides, road washouts, and inconclusive helicopter trips, Sanjaya never despaired. Patriotism and tenacity kept him going, and when he wasn't out becoming one with the mountains, he typed up voluminous amounts of information from his base in Kathmandu.

Samuel P. Trumbull *West Bengal, Sikkim*

The managing editor of *Let's Go: India & Nepal* in its first stage, Sam stepped in to research when he was most needed, carrying his cartographer's eye and ice cream cravings to Calcutta, before heading to the hills in an effort to cool down. *Let's Go* toasts his brilliant three-year career.

Marta R. Weiss *Kathmandu Valley, Eastern Tarai*

After an earlier stay during which she taught English at a school in Thimi, Marta returned to the Kathmandu Valley this year to drink in its balmy atmosphere and turn her artistic eye on its monuments, scenery, and people. Devoted to her work and to the residents of the places she visited, Marta provided the book with insightful coverage and extravagantly exact descriptions.

Other Contributors

Lisa Cloutier

Working in the office for a large part of this year, Lisa helped out with her Grecian researcher-writer experience and her extensive knowledge of Indian culture. Whether writing essays for the Life and Times sections or encouraging researchers on the road, Lisa's sensitive disposition benefitted us all.

Michael E. Farbiarz

A veteran *Let's Go*er, editor of *Let's Go: Mexico 1995,* Mike helped kick off this Sub-continental effort with his work on the Indian history section and large chunks of the sights in central North India and Tamil Nadu. Mike provided grim chuckles for the home office with his tales of being pulled off a train and hospitalized in Nagpur, and warm encouragement for the rest of the staff with his clear vision, which lasted through both stages of the project.

Neelima Pania

Unearthing her Marwari roots, exploring big-city nightlife, and motorbiking around back roads, Neela skirted down the western edge of India during the first stage of this project. Neela's hardcore determination and motherly advice helped shape the book's direction.

How to Use This Book

Armed with a few rupees, some maps, and a genuine love and knowledge of South Asia, the inaugural team of India and Nepal researcher-writers set out to find the important practical information and the best budget deals you need for your trip. The result: an up-to-date, and knowledgeable yellow companion for your trip. *Let's Go* provides you with the tools you need to navigate India and Nepal.

The first section is **Essentials.** Peruse information on passports, packing, and padlocks. Look here for advice on planning your trip—what to do before you leave and what to do after you arrive. There are two more country-specific essentials sections. In addition to practical matters like money and hotels, these sections contain essays about history, religion, politics, and art. They are intended to provide background to the extraordinary sights, sounds, and smells of India and Nepal.

Regional coverage begins with **India.** You'll find chapters on North, East, South, and West India. Each of these chapters is divided into states radiating from the regional hubs of Delhi, Calcutta, Madras, and Bombay. Within states, cities and towns tend to be presented in a clockwise direction starting from the state's largest and most important destination. **Nepal** coverage commences with the Kathmandu Valley and then radiates out through the rest of the country.

Each city begins with an introduction, followed by an **Orientation** section to help you get your bearings, and a **Practical Information** section (where to change money, get medical help, catch a bus, etc.). Transportation listings are, when possible, arranged with the destination followed by the departure time, duration, and cost of the trip. The **Accommodations** and **Food** sections are listed in order of value based on price, location, and comfort. **Sights** sections allow you to guide yourself through sometimes daunting cities, towns, hill stations, and national parks. **Entertainment** provides coverage of bars, clubs and other diversions, while **Shopping** aims to direct you to and through bazaars and markets.

Trekking is covered in two ways: there is a general section with advice and ideas in the Essentials section; individual treks are arranged geographically. The specific treks we cover are indexed under "trekking" for quick and easy access. The appendix at the back of the book contains a **glossary** of Indian and Nepalese words you'll commonly encounter in this book or on your trip, a **phrasebook** with useful phrases in five languages and a list of **festivals and holidays for 1997** to help you plan your trip.

The **white boxes** in the guide warn you of danger—both physical and social. We want you to be aware of the hazards associated with bus travel as well as those associated with eating with your left hand. The cute and cuddly **gray boxes** offer bits of spicy prose about historical (and trivial) items of note.

Finally, a note on how *not* to use this book. Though you could easily spend your time in India and Nepal visiting only the places and things we've covered, don't allow *Let's Go* to restrain you from searching out new and challenging experiences. Rather, use this book as a starting point for your own adventures.

A NOTE TO OUR READERS

The information for this book is gathered by *Let's Go*'s researchers during the late spring and summer months. Each listing is derived from the assigned researcher's opinion based upon his or her visit at a particular time. The opinions are expressed in a candid and forthright manner. Other travelers might disagree. Those traveling at a different time may have different experiences since prices, dates, hours, and conditions are always subject to change. You are urged to check beforehand to avoid inconvenience and surprises. Travel always involves a certain degree of risk, especially in low-cost areas. When traveling, especially on a budget, always take particular care to ensure your safety.

ESSENTIALS

PLANNING YOUR TRIP

▓ When to Go

Although South Asians count six seasons in their calendar, the Indian Subcontinent essentially has three seasons—the heat, the rains, and the winter. The hot season lasts from March through May, during which dry heat builds in anticipation of the monsoon, which lasts from June to September, pounding South Asia with torrents of rain. Road wash-outs and flooding can make travel difficult during the monsoon. When the monsoon ends in September, some of the earlier heat returns, but this gradually dissipates by December and January, when India and Nepal are at their coolest. Winter is acknowledged to be the best time for visiting the Subcontinent, although there are regional exceptions. Those headed for Nepal and the Indian hills might find the winter too chilly—spring and fall (March, April, October, and November) are the most popular time to visit. Some mountain regions are only accessible by road during the summer. For more information, see **India: Climate** (p. 79), **Nepal: Climate** (p. 660), and **Climate** (p. 755).

Another consideration for the traveler is tourist season; India and Nepal have both high and low periods for tourism. These mainly depend on the weather, but also on school vacations and holidays in India, Nepal, and abroad. Low season (which coincides with the monsoon in most of the Subcontinent) means reduced services and reduced traffic at reduced prices. But certain tourist towns may close down altogether during this time. The high season brings floods of people to every popular beach or hill station and inflates prices. On the other hand, more services are available for the traveler at peak times. Certain Indian resorts have different peak seasons for domestic and foreign tourists—hill stations are typically swarmed by Indian tourists during the monsoon.

It might also be worth timing your trip to witness festivals in India or Nepal. Due to the cultural diversity in these countries, there is almost always a festival happening somewhere. For more information, see **Holidays and Festivals for 1997** (p. 769).

▓ Information

GOVERNMENT INFORMATION OFFICES

India Tourist Office: U.S.: East: 30 Rockefeller Plaza, Suite 15, N. Mezzanine, New York, NY 10012 (tel. 1 (212) 586 4901); **West:** 3550 Wilshire Blvd., Suite 204, Los Angeles, CA 90010-2485 (tel. 1 (213) 380 8855). **Canada:** 60 Bloor St. West, Suite 1003, Toronto, Ontario M4W 3B8 (tel. 1 (416) 962 6279). **U.K.:** 7 Cort St., London W1X 2AB (tel. 44 (181) 734 6613). **Australia:** Level 1, 17 Castlereagh St., Sydney NSW 2000 (tel. 61 (2) 232 1600).

Nepal tourism offices are located in Nepalese embassies and/or consulates. For more information, see **Foreign Diplomatic Missions in Nepal** (p. 47).

USEFUL PUBLICATIONS

Travelers can pick up etiquette and plumb the national psyches of India and Nepal with the *Culture Shock!* series, available at bookstores, or from Graphic Arts Center Publishing Company, P.O. Box 10306, Portland, OR 97210, USA.

Bon Voyage!, 2069 W. Bullard Ave., Fresno, CA 93711-1200 (in the U.S. tel. 1 (800) 995 9716, from everywhere else 1 (209) 447 8441; e-mail 70754.3511@compuserve.com). Annual mail order catalog offers a range of products for everyone from the luxury traveler to the diehard trekker. Books, travel accessories, luggage, electrical converters, maps, videos, and more. All merchandise may be returned for exchange or refund within 30 days of purchase, and prices are guaranteed. (Lower advertised prices will be matched and merchandise shipped free.)

Culturgrams, from the Publications Division of the David M. Kennedy Center for International Studies, Brigham Young University, PO Box 24538, Provo, UT 84602-4538, are country-specific pamphlets that clue you in on the culture of the country you'll be visiting. History and society sections are interesting but the most useful feature is the "Culture and Courtesies" section which will help you avoid giving offense.

Hippocrene Books, Inc., 171 Madison Ave., New York, NY 10016 (tel. 1 (212) 685 4371; orders 1 (718) 454 2366; fax 1 (718) 454 1391). Free catalog. Publishes travel reference books, travel guides, foreign language dictionaries, and language learning guides which cover over 100 languages. No India-specific guide books here, but great language books that can teach you handy phrases like "Pass me the hedgehog," in Marathi.

Specialty Travel Index, 305 San Anselmo Avenue, Suite 313, San Anselmo, CA 94960 (tel. 1 (415) 459 4900; fax 1 (415) 459 4974; e-mail spectrav@ix.netcom.com; http://www.spectrav.com). Published twice yearly, this is an extensive listing of "off the beaten track" and specialty travel opportunities. One copy US$6, one-year subscription (2 copies) US$10.

Superintendent of Documents, U.S. Government Printing Office, P.O. Box 371954, Pittsburgh, PA 15250-7954 (tel. 1 (202) 512 1800; fax 1 (202) 512 2250). Open Mon.-Fri. 7:30am-4:30pm. Publishes *Your Trip Abroad* (US$1.25), *Health Information for International Travel* (US$14), and "Background Notes" on all countries (US$1 each). Postage is included in the prices.

Travel Books & Language Center, Inc., 4931 Cordell Ave., Bethesda, MD 20814 (tel. 1 (800) 220-2665; fax 1 (301) 951 8546; e-mail travelbks@aol.com). Sells over 75,000 items, including books, cassettes, atlases, dictionaries, and a wide range of specialty travel maps. Free comprehensive catalogue upon request.

Ten Speed Press, P.O. Box 7123, Berkeley, CA 94707 (tel. 1 (800) 841 2665; order dept. 1 (510) 559 1629). *The Packing Book* (US$8) provides various checklists and suggested wardrobes, addresses safety concerns, imparts packing wisdom, and more.

U.S. Customs Service, P.O. Box 7407, Washington, D.C., 20044 (tel. 1 (202) 927 5580). Publishes 35 books, booklets, leaflets, and flyers on various aspects of customs. *Know Before You Go* tells everything the international traveler needs to know about customs requirements; *Pockets Hints* summarizes the most important data from KBYG.

Wide World Books and Maps, 1911 N. 45th St., Seattle, WA 98103 (tel. 1 (206) 634 3453; fax 1 (206) 634 0558; e-mail travelbk@mail.nwlink.com; http://nwlink.com/travelbk). A good selection of travel guides, travel accessories, and hard-to-find maps.

ON-LINE

The Web

The World Wide Web offers a plethora of information about traveling in India and Nepal. A standard search using one of the default search engines will turn up so much information that reading it all would mean foregoing school, work, and life, not to mention travel. Some particularly useful or interesting sites with links to other sources of information (and pretty pictures of the Taj Mahal, Mt. Everest, etc.) include http://www.internationalist.com/travel/india.html (which provides links to everything from travel and disease advisories to recipes for cool, tasty *raita*). Another site listing opportunities for charity and volunteer work, as well as more general information, is http://hulk.bu.edu/misc/india/misc.html. Check out http://www.ccil.org/

~jkrish/hindu.html for pretty pictures. Up-to-date basic facts can be found on the CIA information page, which lists information on every country imaginable, including India and Nepal. That address is http://www.odci.gov/cia/publications/95fact. Several newsgroups (accessible from most web browsers) offer fascinating insights into cultural issues and debates. Read through soc.culture.tamil for information on Tamil culture and politics (as well as India in general) and to see complete strangers (to each other as well as to you) getting all riled up about issues you'd never heard of. Other newsgroups include soc.culture.indian, soc.culture.indian.delhi, soc.culture.indian.kerala, soc.culture.indian.info, soc.culture.nepal and rec.travel.asia.

News and updates on India can be found at http://www.genius.net/indolink/IND-News/index.html, links galore await at http://www.webhead.com/WWWL/India/india2.html. A great page on Nepal is http://www.catmando.com/urstguit.htm; the Nepal Home Page (http://cen.uiuc.edu/~rshresth/Nepal.html) is good but seems to be down more often than not.

■ Documents and Formalities

Apply for travel documents early—processing may take several weeks or even months. Don't let your trip fall victim to the inevitable delays and bureaucratic snarls of passport agencies.

Before you depart, **photocopy all important documents and credit cards;** leave these with someone you can contact easily. **Never carry your passport, travel ticket, identification documents, money, traveler's checks, insurance, and credit cards all together,** or you'll be left high and dry in case of theft or loss.

When you travel in India or Nepal, **always carry your passport on your person,** and probably another form of ID as well. Many establishments, especially banks, require several IDs before cashing traveler's checks. Carry extra passport-size photos that you can attach to the sundry IDs you will eventually acquire.

Discounts for foreign students in India and Nepal are rare, so there's little point in carrying student ID, except for insurance and plane ticket discounts. For more information, see **Youth, Student, & Teacher Identification** (p. 10).

DIPLOMATIC MISSIONS

India

U.S.: 2107 Massachusetts Ave. NW, Washington, D.C. (tel. 1 (202) 939 7000). Visa and passport division for the southeastern U.S.: 2536 Massachusetts Ave. NW, Washington, D.C. 20008 (tel. 1 (202) 939 7000, 939 9839). **Consulates: Northeast:** Consulate of India, 3 East 64th St., New York, NY 10021 (tel. 1 (212) 879 7800). **West:** Consulate General of India, 540 Arguello Blvd., San Francisco CA 94118 (tel. 1 (415) 668 0683). **Midwest:** Consulate General of India, 150 North Michigan Ave. 1100, Chicago, IL 60601 (tel. 1 (312) 781 6280).

Canada: 10 Springfield Rd., Ottawa, Ontario K1M 1C9 (tel. 1 (613) 744 0913).

U.K.: India House, Aldwych, London, WC2B 4NA (tel. 44 (171) 836 8484). **Consulate:** 82 New St., Birmingham B2 4BA (tel. 44 (121) 643 0366).

Ireland: 6 Leeson Park, Dublin 6 (tel. 353 (1) 497 0842).

Australia: 3-5 Moonah Place, Yarralumla, Canberra ACT 2600 (tel. 61 (6) 273 3999). **Consulates:** 153 Walker St., 11th Floor, North Syndey NSW 2060 (tel. 61 (2) 273 3999); 13 Munro St., Coburg, Vic 3058 (tel. 61 (3) 384 0141; c/o Magic Carpet Tours and Travels Ltd., 4th Floor, 195 Adelaide Terrace, East Perth, WA 6004 (tel. 61 (9) 221 1207).

New Zealand: 10th Floor, 180 Molesworth St., P.O. Box 4045, Wellington 1 (tel. (64) 473 6390).

South Africa: Salam Centre, Johannesburg (tel. 27 (11) 333 1525).

ESSENTIALS

Nepal

Would-be wanderers from Ireland should contact the embassy in London, while New Zealanders are served via the Sydney office. There is no embassy in South Africa. For more information, see **Visas** (p. 5).

U.S.: 2131 Leroy Place NW, Washington, D.C. 20008 (tel. 1 (202) 667 4550; fax 1 (202) 667 5534). **Consulate: U.S.:** Royal Nepalese Consulate General, 820 Second Ave., Suite 202, New York, NY 10017 (tel. 1 (212) 370-4188).

Canada: 2 Sheppard Ave. East, Suite 1700, Toronto, Ontario M2N 5Y7 (tel. 1 (416) 226 8722).

U.K.: 12a Kensington Palace Gardens, London W8 4QU (tel. 44 (171) 229 1594).

Australia: 377 Sussex St., Sydney 2000 (tel. 61 (2) 264 7197); 18-20 Bank Pl., Melbourne 3000 (tel. 61 (3) 602 1271); 195 Adelaide Tce., Perth 6000 (tel. 61 (9) 221 1207).

PASSPORTS

Foreign travelers in India and Nepal must have a valid passport. **Photocopy the page of your passport that contains your photograph and identifying information.** Carry this photocopy in a safe place apart from your passport, perhaps with a traveling companion, and leave another copy at home. These measures will help prove your citizenship and facilitate the issuing of a new passport in case of loss of theft. Consulates also recommend that you carry an expired passport or an official copy of your birth certificate in a part of your baggage separate from other documents.

Losing your passport can be a nightmare. It may take weeks to process a replacement, and your new passport may be valid only for a limited time. Any visas stamped in your old passport will be irretrievably lost. If it is lost or stolen, immediately notify the local police and the nearest diplomatic mission of your home government. To expedite the replacement of your passport, you will need to know all the information that you had previously recorded and photocopied, and to show identification and proof of citizenship. Some consulates can issue new passports within two days if you give them proof of citizenship. In an emergency, ask for immediate temporary traveling papers that permit you to return to your country.

Your passport is a public document belonging to your nation's government. You may have to surrender it to a foreign government official; if you don't get it back in a reasonable time, inform the nearest diplomatic mission of your home country.

U.S.: Locations in Boston, Chicago, Honolulu, Houston, Los Angeles, Miami, New Orleans, New York, Philadelphia, San Francisco, Seattle, Stamford, and Washington, D.C. Contact the U.S. Passport Information's 24-hr. recording (tel. 1 (202) 647 0518), which offers general information, agency locations, etc. Issues and renews passports (US$65 and US$55 respectively), which are valid 10 years. Processing may take 4 weeks. Rush service US$30. For first passports, or renewing passports over 12 years old, applicants must appear in person. U.S. embassies or consulates abroad can replace lost passports, given proof of citizenship. For information about international formalities, get the booklet *Your Trip Abroad* (US$1.25) from the Superintendent of Documents, U.S. Government Printing Office, Washington, D.C. 20402 (tel. 1 (202) 783 3238). For more information, the U.S. Department of State publishes two helpful booklets: *Passports: Applying For Them the Easy Way* (item 356A, 50¢), and *Foreign Entry Requirements* (item 354A, 50¢). Send a check to R. Woods, Consumer Information Center, Pueblo, CO 81009.

Canada: 28 regional offices across Canada. Head Office, Foreign Affairs, Ottawa, Ontario, K1A OG3 (tel. 1 (613) 996 8885). Applications available in English and French at all passport offices, post offices, and most travel agencies (CDN$35). Valid 5 years, non-renewable. Takes 3 weeks, or 5 days if in person. For additional information, call the 24-hr. number (tel. 1 (800) 567 6868 in Canada; in Toronto 973 3251; in Montréal 283 2152), or refer to *Bon Voyage, But...* with a list of embassies and consulates abroad. Free from any passport office or Info-Export (BPTE), External Affairs, Ottawa, Ontario, K1A OG2.

U.K.: Offices in London, Liverpool, Newport, Peterborough, Glasgow, and Belfast. Application forms also available in post offices. Passports valid 10 years (UK£18). Takes 4-6 weeks. London office offers same-day, walk-in service; arrive early.

Ireland: Apply by mail to either the Department of Foreign Affairs, Passport Office, Setanta Centre, Molesworth St., Dublin 2 (tel. 353 (1) 671 1633), or the Passport Office, 1A South Mall, Cork (tel. 1 (21) 627 2525). The new Passport Express service offers a 2-week turn-around, available through post offices for an extra IR£3. Applications at local Garda stations or from a passport office. Passports are valid for 10 years (IR£45). Citizens under 18 or over 65 can request a 3-year passport IR£10.

Australia: Offices in Adelaide, Brisbane, Canberra, Darwin, Hobart, Melbourne, Newcastle, Perth, and Sydney. Must apply in person at a post office, Passport Office, or Australian diplomatic mission overseas. Fees are adjusted frequently. For more information, call toll free (in Australia): tel. 131232.

New Zealand: Contact local Link Centre, travel agent, or representative for an application form. Return to the New Zealand Passport Office, Documents of National Identity Division, Department of Internal Affairs, Box 10-526, Wellington (tel. 64 (4) 474 8100). The fee is NZ$80 for an application submitted in New Zealand and varies greatly overseas. Standard processing is 10 working days.

South Africa: Applications available at any Department of Home Affairs Office.

VISAS

A visa is permission for you to stay in a country for a specific purpose and a specific amount of time; it usually must be stamped in your passport. All travelers to India and Nepal (except citizens of India going to Nepal, and vice versa) must have visas.

India

Tourist visas are available for three months or six months, and are rarely extendable. Visas normally allow for multiple entries (important for side-trips to Nepal and other countries). Other options include a one year visa for students, journalists or business people, or five years for Indian nationals living abroad.

It is always faster to apply through the embassy in the country where you are a citizen. You'll need to fill out an application form and provide your current passport. Applications can be made by mail with payment in the form of money orders; no cash or checks will be accepted. How much getting the visa will cost and how long it will take varies from country to country. **U.S.:** US$40 for three months, US$60 for six months. Residents should contact the Indian Embassy in Washington or the consulate appropriate for their area (see **Embassies and Consulates,** p. 47). **Canada:** CDN$30 for three months, CDN$55 for six months. **U.K.:** UK£13 for three months, UK£26 for six months. Processing takes about three weeks except in the busy tourist season (Nov.-Jan.) when it will take about six weeks. **Ireland:** IR£14 for three months, IR£25 for six months. Irish passport holders should send a stamped, self-addressed envelope to the embassy to get an application, which will be completed and returned with your passport from 9:30am to 12:15pm Monday-Friday at the embassy. **Australia:** AUS$20 for three months, AUS$60 for six months. Each applicants must submit a copy of his or her passport, a photograph, and a travel itinerary. Applicants who come in person must pay in cash; no checks will be accepted. **New Zealand:** NZ$35 for three months; NZ$70 for six months. **South Africa:** There is no fee for a visa to visit India from South Africa. Contact the embassy for more information.

Special Permits

Certain areas of India require a special permit in addition an Indian visa. Permits can be issued by Indian diplomatic missions abroad, by the Ministry of Home Affairs in Delhi, or by Foreigners' Registration Offices in various Indian cities. Bear in mind that there is usually a reason for the extra requirements—some of these areas are unstable.

Northeast India: In the words of the Government of India Tourist Department, "Assam, Meghalaya, and Tripura states have been thrown open for tourism." A per-

mit is no longer needed for these three states, but consult your embassy about the political situation there, especially in Assam, before visiting. Due to tribal insurgencies and fears of a conflict with China, the other four states of the northeast (Arunachal Pradesh, Nagaland, Manipur, and Mizoram) require restricted area permits. These are difficult to obtain, and are usually only granted to organized tour groups of four or more. Permits are good for 15 days and renewable for 15 days at the Foreigners' Registration Office in each state's capital city. These restrictions are bound to be abolished in the near future, except in the case of Arunachal Pradesh, which borders China and is politically sensitive (though peaceful in recent years). Restricted area permits can only be obtained at the Ministry of Home Affairs, Lok Nayak Bhawan, Khan Market, New Delhi (open Mon.-Fri. 10am-5pm). Plan your trip well in advance. Permits take 2 days to 2 months, depending on the state.
Arunachal Pradesh: Applications for restricted area permits can be tendered to the Ministry of Home Affairs (8 weeks to process) or directly to the State Government (4 weeks). In the latter case, pick up an application at the Ministry of Home Affairs, send one copy to the Secretary of Tourism, Itanagar, 791111 (fax 91 (36) 022446), and bring one copy to the Resident Commissioner, Arunachal Bhawan, Kautilya Marg, New Delhi. In addition, Arunachal Pradesh charges foreign tourists US$50 per day for permits, making it prohibitively expensive for budget travelers.
Nagaland: Submit your application for a restricted area permit to the Ministry of Home Affairs; it takes one to two weeks to process, and sponsorship by the resident commissioner in Delhi is helpful. The permits are good for 15 days and can be renewed in Kohima; permits are free. Further information can be sought at Nagaland House, 29 Aurangzeb Rd., New Delhi (tel. 91 (11) 301 5638). **Manipur:** Restricted area permits for Manipur are processed in a few days by the Ministry of Home Affairs. The tourist office in New Delhi is located at the Manipur State Emporium, but they are not very helpful. **Mizoram:** Applications for restricted area permits should be submitted to the Ministry of Home Affairs; the state government always issues a Non-Objection Certificate; and applications take one week to process.
Sikkim: Sikkim borders China and is treated by the Indian government as a military buffer. Foreigners need a permit to enter Sikkim and can only remain there 15 days per year. Permits are free and readily available in the major Indian cities; the red tape is thickest in Darjeeling, where the process takes an hour; elsewhere it takes only a few moments. Permits allow travel as far north as Phodang and Yuksam. Permits can be extended at the Commissioner's Office in Gangtok in special circumstances, but then only for 3-5 days, and only once. For North Sikkim, an inner line permit is required. It is only issued through tour companies to groups of four or more. A guide must accompany the group and the minimum charge is US$30-50 per day, including guide. It takes a solid work day to procure such a permit, available only in Gangtok.
Andaman and Nicobar Islands: A permit must be obtained in advance before sailing to the Andamans. Leave plenty of time if applying for a permit from the Ministry of Home Affairs or from Indian missions abroad. Those arriving by air can obtain permits on arrival in Port Blair. The Nicobar Islands are off-limits.
Lakshadweep: Only one island of this archipelago is open to foreigners. The necessary free permit to visit this island (Bangaram) can be obtained through the Liaison Officer, Lakshadweep, 202 Kasturba Gandhi Marg, New Delhi 110001 (tel. 91 (11) 386807) or at some nice hotels in Cochin. You'll need four passport photos and a day or two to spare.
Bhutan: Officially an independent country, Bhutan's foreign policy and immigration procedures are controlled by India. The number of visas to Bhutan is limited by a quota system, and those who receive them must be on group tours of at least six and are required to spend *at least US$220 per day.* To apply for a visa, contact the Director of Tourism, Ministry of Finance, Tachichho Dzong, Thimpu, Bhutan or the Bhutan Foreign Mission, Chandra Gupta Marg, New Delhi 110021 (tel. 91 (11) 609217). The odds are similar to the odds of winning the lottery.

Nepal

Anybody with a passport can get a Nepalese visa upon arrival at the airport in Kathmandu or at any of the land border crossings from India; it's really not worth fussing over ahead of time unless you're looking for something to fuss over. The fee is the same either way; at the border it must be paid in U.S. dollars. Any Nepalese consulate or embassy can issue visas for up to sixty days, although this time can be extended once you're in Nepal. The Department of Immigration, Keshar Mahal, Thamel, Kathmandu (tel. 977 (1) 412337, 418573) grants extensions for up to five months. Apply for a visa extension a day or two before you really need it. It costs everyone US$1 per day to extend visas. **U.S.:** US$15 for 15 days (single entry), US$25 for 30 days (single entry), US$40 for 30 days (multiple entry), and US$60 for 60 days (multiple entry). Fill out an application and submit a passport to the embassy in person or in writing. Payment should be a money order, cashier's check or cash. **Canada:** CDN$24 for 15 days (single entry), CDN$40 for 30 days (single entry), CDN$64 for a 30 days (multiple entry), and CDN$96 for 60 days (multiple entry). **U.K./Ireland:** UK£20 for 30 days (single entry), UK£45 for 60 days (multiple entry). Passport holders from either country should contact the Royal Nepalese Embassy in London for an application. **Australia/New Zealand:** AUS$35 for 15 days (single entry), AUS$50 for 30 days (single entry), AUS$70 for 30 days (multiple entry), and AUS$100 for 60 days (multiple entry). Submit three passport photos, a passport and three application forms (available from travel agents) by mail or in person. Visas are processed on the spot for applicants who come in person, or mailed the same day for those who apply by post. **South Africa:** There is no Nepalese embassy in South Africa, which makes getting visa information a little trickier. Contact the Department of Immigration in Kathmandu, Tridevi Marg (tel. 412337, 418573) for more information on how to proceed. **Trekking permits** are also required for all trekking **areas** in Nepal. For more information, see **Trekking,** p. 55.

Surrounding Countries

It isn't easy to travel to many of the countries that surround India and Nepal. Burma and China, in particular, present massive amounts of red tape and restrictions. In addition, a few of these countries are politically unstable, so it is important to check for up-to-date information before embarking. The following general information is intended as a starting point.

Bangladesh: Citizens of Australia and the United Kingdom don't need visas to stay for 15 days. All others need to contact a Bangladeshi embassy or high commission; visa rules change frequently. In any event, 72 hour permits to cross the border are easy to obtain and they can validated and upgraded at the Department of Immigration Office in Dhaka. The high commission's address is 56 Ring Rd., Lajpat Nagar III, Delhi (tel. 91 (11) 683 4668); 9 Circus Ave., Park Circus, Calcutta (tel. 91 (33) 247 5208); in Nepal the embassy is located on Chakrapath, Maharajgunj, Kathmandu (tel. 977 (1) 414943).

Burma (Myanmar): For a Burmese visa, be prepared to fill out forms, write letters, and show proof that you have already set up a place to stay. Visas last 28 days and barely get you into the country. To go very far beyond Rangoon or Mandalay, more permits or a licensed guide are required. The Burmese embassy in India is located at 3/50-F Shantipath, Chanakyapuri, Delhi (tel. 91 (11) 688 9007) and in Nepal at Chakupat, Patan City Gate, Patan (tel. 977 (1) 521788).

China: To travel into Tibet from Nepal, a Chinese travel visa is required. Such visas are almost impossible to get at the embassy in Kathmandu (it's easier in Hong Kong). Visas are valid for 30 days and can be extended twice by 15 days per extension. Some travelers have also entered China by signing up for a short "mini-tour," a semi-legal group tour that disbands soon after crossing the border. Under this system, travelers can have a two- or three-day tast of Tibet and decide if they want to apply to go back for a longer time. Many travel agents in Kathmandu can arrange mini-tours. The Chinese embassy in India is at 50-D Shantipath, Chanakyapuri,

Delhi (tel. 91 (11) 600328) and in Nepal, Baluwater, Kathmandu (tel. 977 (1) 411740, visa services 977 (1) 419053.

Pakistan: Visitors to Pakistan need a visa prior to entry. The visa can be used for six months after the date of issue and is valid for three months after date of issue. After 30 days, however, foreign visitors must register at the Foreigners' Registration Office which has branches in all major cities and towns. In Delhi, 2/50-G Shantipath, Chanakyapuri (tel. 91 (11) 600603), and in Kathmandu, Pani Pokhari (tel. 977 (1) 441421).

Sri Lanka: No visas are required prior to entry into Sri Lanka. Permission to stay from 30 to 90 days is granted upon arrival.

Thailand: Citizens from certain countries, including the U.S., Canada, Australia, and most European countries, need not obtain visas if they plan to be in Thailand for less than 1 month and if they have a confirmed ticket as proof of departure. For travelers who wish to spend more time in the country, Thailand issues two main types of visas: **tourist visas** (up to 60 days, US$15) and **non-immigrant visas** for business or employment (up to 90 days, US$20). Every visa is valid for entry up to 90 days from its date of issue. To stay in Thailand for a longer period than specified by your visa, apply for an extension. The fee to apply for an extension is about US$25. Thirty-day transit visas may not be extended. For those who want to pop back to Thailand repeatedly, a **re-entry permit** is required to return. Applications should be made at the main Immigration Office well before departure. No **exit visa** is required to leave the country. The Thai embassy in India's address is 56 N Nyaya Marg, Chanakyapuri, Delhi (tel. 91 (11) 605679) and in Nepal, Bansbari, Kathmandu (tel. 977 (1) 420411).

CUSTOMS: INDIA AND NEPAL

India

All personal belongings necessary for your stay can be imported duty-free. Personal jewelry, one camera with 12 film magazines or five rolls of film, one video camera, presents valued up to Rs.500, 200 cigarettes or 50 cigars or 250 grams of tobacco and one liter of liquor are all duty free. Expensive electronic items may have to be noted in your passport to ensure that you take them with you when you leave rather than selling them. The import of gold coins, gold bullion, and silver bullion is illegal. Certain types of weapons are prohibited and all weapons being brought into the country require a possession license. Indian rupees cannot enter or leave the country. If your baggage was mishandled and you lost any of your belongings, get a certificate from the airline and get it countersigned by customs officials indicating how much of your duty free allowance you didn't use. Any cash or traveler's checks over US$10,000 or equivalent must be declared upon arrival.

Nepal

Duty-free allowance includes 1.15 liters of alcohol, 200 cigarettes, 15 rolls of film, one video camera, one radio, and one tape recorder. Drugs, arms, and ammo can't come across under any circumstances. Any money over US$2000 must be declared upon entry and only Indian nationals can import or export Indian rupees.

CUSTOMS: HOMEWARD BOUND

India: No gold jewelry valued at over Rs.2000 or other jewelry valued over Rs. 10,000 (including precious stones) may leave the country. No antiques (defined as anything over 100 years old), animal skins, or animal skin products may be taken out of India. Visitors leaving India after a stay of less than six months are exempt from income tax clearance procedures (in order to prove that you didn't earn any money illegally), but hang on to your exchange receipts nonetheless. Indian rupees may not leave the country. If you are flying to a neighboring country (Nepal, Pakistan, Sri Lanka, or Bangladesh), the **airport tax** is Rs.100; to all other countries it is Rs.300.

Nepal: Gifts and souvenirs may be brought out of Nepal but permission is required from the Department of Archaeology to export antiques. Their address is Department of Archaeology, National Archive Building, Ran Shah Path, Kathmandu (tel. 977 (1) 215358). In general, nothing over 100 years old can leave the country. Exporting gold, silver, drugs, animals, or animal parts and products is forbidden. There is a **airport tax** of Rs.500 for those flying to India, Bangladesh, Bhutan, the Maldives, Pakistan, or Sri Lanka and of Rs.600 for those going further afield.

Home Countries

United States: Citizens returning home may bring US$400 worth of accompanying goods duty-free and must pay a 10% tax on the next US$1000. Goods are considered duty-free if they are for personal or household use (this includes gifts) and cannot include more than 100 cigars, 200 cigarettes (1 carton), and 1L of wine or liquor. You must be over 21 years of age to bring liquor into the U.S. If it is necessary to mail home personal goods from the U.S., duty charges can be avoided if the package is marked "American goods returned." For more information, consult the brochure *Know Before You Go,* available from the U.S. Customs Service, Box 7407, Washington, D.C. 20044 (tel. 1 (202) 927 6724).

Canada: Citizens who remain abroad for at least one week may bring back up to CDN$500 worth of goods duty-free once per calendar year. Citizens may ship goods except tobacco and alcohol home under this exemption as long as they declare them upon arrival. Citizens of legal age (which varies by province) may import in-person up to 200 cigarettes, 50 cigars, 400g loose tobacco, 400 tobacco sticks, 1.14L wine or alcohol, and 24 355mL cans/bottles of beer; the value of these products is included in the CDN$500. For more information, write to Canadian Customs, 2265 St. Laurent Blvd., Ottawa, Ontario K1G 4K3 (tel. 1 (613) 993 0534).

United Kingdom: Citizens or visitors must declare any goods in excess of the following allowances: 200 cigarettes, 100 cigarillos, 50 cigars, or 250g tobacco; still table wine (2L); strong liqueurs over 22% volume (1L), or fortified or sparkling wine, other liqueurs (2L); perfume (60mL); toilet water (250mL); and UK£136 worth of all other goods including gifts and souvenirs. You must be over 17 to import liquor or tobacco. For more info about U.K. customs, contact Her Majesty's Customs and Excise, Custom House, Nettleton Road, Heathrow Airport, Hounslow, Middlesex TW6 2LA (tel. 44 (181) 910 3744; fax 910 3765).

Ireland: Citizens must declare everything in excess of IR£34 (IR£17 per traveler under 15 years of age) above the following allowances: 200 cigarettes; 100 cigarillos; 50 cigars; or 250g tobacco; 1L liquor or 2L wine; 2L still wine; 50g perfume; and 250mL toilet water. Travelers under 17 are not entitled to any allowance for tobacco or alcoholic products. For more information, contact The Revenue Commissioners, Dublin Castle (tel. 353 (1) 679 2777; fax 671 2021; e-mail taxes@ior.ie; http://www.revenue.ie) or The Collector of Customs and Excise, The Custom House, Dublin 1.

Australia: Citizens may import AUS$400 (under 18 AUS$200) of goods duty-free, in addition to the allowance of 1.125L alcohol and 250 cigarettes or 250g tobacco. You must be over 18 to import either of these. There is no limit to the amount of Australian and/or foreign cash that may be brought into or taken out of the country. However, amounts of AUS$5000 or more, or the equivalent in foreign currency, must be reported. All foodstuffs and animal products must be declared on arrival. For information, contact the Regional Director, Australian Customs Service, GPO Box 8, Sydney NSW 2001 (tel. 61 (2) 213 2000; fax 213 4000).

New Zealand: Citizens may bring home up to NZ$700 worth of goods duty-free if they are intended for personal use or are unsolicited gifts. The concession is 200 cigarettes (1 carton) or 250g tobacco or 50 cigars or a combination of all three not to exceed 250g. You may also bring in 4.5L of beer or wine and 1.125L of liquor. Only travelers over 17 may bring tobacco or alcoholic beverages into the country. For more information, consult the *New Zealand Customs Guide for Travelers,* available from customs offices, or contact New Zealand Customs, 50 Anzac Ave., Box 29, Auckland (tel. 64 (9) 377 3520; fax 309 2978).

South Africa: Citizens may import duty-free: 400 cigarettes; 50 cigars; 250g tobacco; 2L wine; 1L of spirits; 250mL toilet water; and 50mL perfume; and other items up to a value of SAR500. Amounts exceeding this limit but not SAR10,000 are dutiable at 20%. Certain items such as golf clubs and firearms require a duty higher than the standard 20%. Goods acquired abroad and sent to the Republic as unaccompanied baggage do not qualify for any allowances. You may not export or import South African bank notes in excess of SAR500. Persons who require specific information or advice concerning customs and excise duties can address their inquiries to the Commissioner for Customs and Excise, Private Bag X47, Pretoria 0001. This agency distributes the pamphlet *South African Customs Information,* for visitors and residents who travel abroad. South Africans residing in the U.S. should contact the Embassy of South Africa, 3051 Massachusetts Ave., NW, Washington, D.C. 20008 (tel. 1 (202) 232 4400; fax 244 9417) or the South African Home Annex, 3201 New Mexico Ave. #380, NW, Washington, D.C. 20016 (tel. 1 (202) 966 1650)

YOUTH, STUDENT, & TEACHER IDENTIFICATION

The **International Student Identity Card (ISIC)** is the most widely accepted form of student identification. Although invaluable in developed areas like Western Europe, its usefulness is very limited in South Asia. But it may still be worth getting simply to get a discount fare on your plane ticket (some budget travel agencies require an ISIC for student fares). Another benefit that the card provides is **accident insurance of up to US$3000** with no daily limit. In addition, cardholders have access to a toll-free Traveler's Assistance hotline whose multilingual staff can provide help in medical, legal, and financial emergencies overseas.

Many student travel offices issue ISICs, including Council Travel, Let's Go Travel, and STA Travel in the U.S.; Travel CUTS in Canada; and any of the organizations under the auspices of the International Student Travel Confederation (ISTC) around the world. When you apply for the card, request a copy of the *International Student Identity Card Handbook,* which lists by country some of the available discounts. You can also write to Council for a copy. The card is valid from September to December of the following year. The fee is US$18. Applicants must be at least 12 years old and degree-seeking students of a secondary or post-secondary school. Because of the proliferation of phony ISICs, many airlines and some other services require other proof of student identity: a signed letter from the registrar attesting to your student status and stamped with the school seal and/or your school ID card. The US$19 **International Teacher Identity Card (ITIC)** offers similar but limited discounts, as well as medical insurance coverage. For more information on these cards consult the organization's new web site (http://www.istc.org).

Federation of International Youth Travel Organizations (FIYTO) issues a discount card to travelers who are under 26 but not students. Known as the **GO25 Card,** this one-year card offers many of the same benefits as the ISIC, and most organizations that sell the ISIC also sell the GO25 Card. A brochure that lists discounts is free when you purchase the card. To apply, you will need a passport, valid driver's license, or copy of a birth certificate; and a passport-sized photo with your name printed on the back. The fee is US$16, CDN$15, or UK£5. For information, contact Council in the U.S. or FIYTO in Denmark.

IF YOU ARE PLANNING TO DRIVE...

For an **International Driving Permit** you must be over 18. Submit an application, two recent passport-size photos, and a U.S. driver's license. The one-year permit (US$10) is available from any local office of the **American Automobile Association (AAA),** or at the main office, American Automobile Association, 1000 AAA Drive, Heathrow, FL 32746 5080 (tel. 1 (407) 444 4245; fax 444 7823). For further information, contact a local AAA office. You can also get an IDP from the **American Automobile Touring Alliance,** Bayside Plaza, 188 The Embarcadero, San Francisco, CA 94105 (tel. 1 (415) 777 4000; fax 882 2141). Canadian license holders can obtain an IDP (CDN$10) through any **Canadian Automobile Association (CAA)** office, or by writing to CAA Ottawa, 2525 Carling Ave., Lincoln Hts., Ottawa, Ontario K2B 7Z2 (tel. 1 (613) 820 1890; fax 771 3046). Complete an application form and provide two passport-size photos and a valid driver's license. You also have to have your registration, insurance and domestic license, as well as a *carnet*, which is basically like a passport for your car. Your local automobile association is the best place to go for help sorting out these documents. For more information on the trials and tribulations associated with taking your car, For more information, see **Getting Around** (p. 48).

■ Money Matters

Once you get there, travel in India or Nepal is unbelievably cheap. The income and the cost of living in these countries are so low that it's not unusual to pay less than US$2 for a night's accommodation, or less than US$1 for a restaurant meal. Train and bus fares are a pittance when measured in foreign currency. Nevertheless, two distinct attitudes about money seem to prevail among travelers with hard currency in South Asia. Some people see an incredible opportunity to live on the very, very cheap, to stay in the cheapest lodgings no matter how miserable, to eat nothing but tasteless gruel, and make each day's goal to spend fewer rupees than yesterday. Others seem to revel in the fact that with their dollars or pounds they can afford things in India that they could never afford at home: eating lunch at a five-star hotel, or hiring a car and driver for a day. How much money you bring should depend on your style. However, even those inclined to be thrifty should budget for the occasional splurge. When you hit the travel doldrums, money can cushion the shocks. Don't sacrifice your health or safety for a few rupees.

Avoid exchanging money at luxury hotels and restaurants, which will likely gouge you on both exchange rates and commission rates; the best deal is usually found at major banks. In rural areas, look for branches of banks you recognize from larger cities. In India, the State Bank of India is usually the easiest place to change money. In major cities of India, currency exchange booths controlled by major banks are common. Although commission rates at the booths may be slightly higher, they are convenient and keep longer hours than the banks. It may be wise to keep some U.S. dollars or pounds sterling on hand in case smaller banks and exchange booths refuse to accept other currencies. If you exchange your money legally, get an encashment certificate as proof. This is sometimes demanded when paying for plane tickets or large hotel bills in rupees.

Remember that unless a commission rate is charged, service charges will eat up a chunk of your money each time you convert. To minimize your losses, exchange large sums of money at once, but never more than you can safely carry. It helps to plan ahead; if caught without local currency in an area with no convenient currency exchange center, you may be forced into a particularly disadvantageous deal.

Both India and Nepal have recently made their currencies fully convertible and subject to market rates, so there's not much to be gained from changing money on the **black market.** Those who are still willing to risk confiscation of their money for the small premium (and speedier service) the black market offers must change their money discreetly, with shopkeepers, out of public view, rather than with touts in the street. It is also worth remembering that changing money on the black market contributes to a cycle of illegal transactions, especially the smuggling of gold, gems, and electronic goods, hurting the government's ability to regulate the economy.

TRAVELER'S CHECKS

Traveler's checks are the safest and least troublesome means of carrying funds. Several agencies and many banks sell them, usually for face value plus a 1% commission. American Express and Thomas Cook are the most widely recognized in India and Nepal. Other major checks are normally exchanged with almost equal ease, although each bank seems to have its own rules about this. Banks in small towns are less likely to accept traveler's checks than banks in cities with large tourist industries. Nonetheless, there will probably be at least one place in most towns where you can exchange them for local currency; just be prepared for a long wait.

Each agency provides refunds if your checks are lost or stolen, and many provide additional services. (Note that you may need a police report verifying the loss or theft.) Expect red tape and delay in the event of theft or loss of traveler's checks. To expedite the refund process, keep your check receipts separate from your checks and store them in a safe place or with a traveling companion, leave a list of check numbers with someone at home and record these when you cash them, and ask for a list of refund centers when you buy your checks. American Express and Thomas Cook have offices in Kathmandu and in the major cities of India. Keep a separate supply of cash or traveler's checks for emergencies. Never countersign your checks until you're prepared to cash them. And always bring your passport with you when you plan to use the checks.

American Express: Call 1 (800) 221 7282 in the U.S. and Canada; in the U.K. 44 (800) 521313; in New Zealand 64 (800) 441068; in Australia 61 (8) 251902. Elsewhere, call U.S. collect 1 (801) 964 6665. American Express traveler's cheques are now available in 11 currencies: Australian, British, Canadian, Dutch, French, German, Japanese, Saudi Arabian, Spanish, Swiss, and U.S. They are the most widely recognized worldwide and the easiest to replace if lost or stolen. Checks can be purchased for a small fee at American Express Travel Service Offices, banks, and American Automobile Association offices. (AAA members can buy the checks commission-free.) Cardmembers can also purchase cheques at American Express Dispensers at Travel Service Offices at airports and by ordering them via phone (tel. 1 (800) ORDERTC. American Express offices cash their cheques commission-free, although they often offer slightly worse rates than banks. You can also buy *Cheques for Two* which can be signed by either of two people traveling together. Request the American Express booklet "Traveler's Companion," listing travel office addresses and stolen check hotlines for each European country. Traveler's checks are also available over America Online.

Citicorp: Call 1 (800) 645 6556 in the U.S. and Canada; in the U.K. 44 (181) 297 4781; from elsewhere call U.S. collect 1 (813) 623 1709. Sells both Citicorp and Citicorp Visa traveler's checks in U.S., Australian, and Canadian dollars, British pounds, German marks, Spanish pesetas, and Japanese yen. Commission is 1-2% on check purchases. Citicorp's World Courier Service guarantees hand-delivery of traveler's checks when a refund location is not convenient. Call 24hr. a day, seven days a week.

Thomas Cook MasterCard: Call 1 (800) 223 9920 in the U.S. and Canada; elsewhere call U.S. collect 1 (609) 987 7300; for the U.K. call 44 (800) 622101 free or 44 (1733) 502995 collect or 44 (1733) 318950 collect. Offers checks in U.S., Canadian, Australian, and dollars, British and Cypriot pounds, French and Swiss francs, German marks, Japanese yen, Dutch guilders, Spanish pesetas, and ECUs. Commission 1-2% for purchases. Try buying the checks at a Thomas Cook office for potentially lower commissions. If you cash your checks at a Thomas Cook Office they will not charge you a commission (whereas most banks will).

Visa: Call 1 (800) 227 6811 in the U.S.; in the U.K. 44 (800) 895492. Call any of the above numbers, if you give them your zip code, they will tell you where the closest office to you is to purchase their traveler's checks. Any kind of Visa traveler's checks can be reported lost at the Visa number.

CREDIT CARDS

Credit cards are of limited use to the penniless pilgrim because low-cost budget establishments, particularly outside the more traveled sections of the most traveled cities, rarely honor them. Occasionally, however, they can be a useful backup to your travelers' checks. There is still a great deal of variation in credit card acceptance. Sometimes a high-class restaurant may refuse credit cards while some small shop accepts all cards under the sun. Sometimes a fee is added if you use a credit card, but if you're buying carpets or crafts, using a credit card doesn't mean you can't bargain the price down. Generally, plastic is accepted at major hotels, expensive boutiques, and fine restaurants. **American Express, MasterCard,** and **Visa** are the most commonly accepted. You can often reduce conversion fees by charging a purchase instead of changing traveler's checks.

With credit cards such as American Express, Visa, and MasterCard, a few banks will give you an instant cash advance in local currency as large as your remaining credit line. The Bank of Baroda offers advances in Indian rupees to Visa card holders. Sometimes it can take a while for this to appear on your bill, so you might avoid paying mortifying interest rates.

American Express (tel. 1 (800) CASH-NOW) has a hefty annual fee (US$55) but offers a number of services. AmEx cardholders can cash personal checks at AmEx offices abroad. **Global Assist,** a 24-hr. hotline offering information. Legal assistance in emergencies is also available (tel. 1 (800) 554 2639) in U.S. and Canada; from abroad call U.S. collect (tel. 1 (301) 214 8228). Cardholders can take advantage of the American Express Travel Service; benefits include assistance in changing airline, hotel, and car rental reservations, sending mailgrams and international cables, and holding your mail at one of the more than 1700 AmEx offices around the world.

MasterCard (tel. 1 (800) 999 0454) and **Visa** (tel. 1 (800) 336 8472) credit cards are sold by individual banks. Benefits depend on the type of card. If obtaining a MasterCard or Visa for travel purposes, ask bankers about specific travel services.

Credit cards require extra vigilance. Report lost or stolen cards immediately, or you may be held responsible for forged charges. Write down the card cancellation phone numbers for your bank and keep them separate from your cards. Be sure that carbons have been torn to pieces, and ask to watch your card be imprinted; an imprint onto a blank slip can be used later to charge merchandise in your name, eventually resulting in a pitched battle with your credit card company.

GETTING MONEY FROM HOME

Having money wired to India or Nepal can be a bureaucratic fuss, subject to long delays; most travelers wisely avoid it. If you really need money sent from home, it should take about 2-3 working days. Foreign banks such as ANZ Grindlays are the most reliable; be precise about the bank branch you want the money sent to. **Western Union** (tel. 1 (800) 325 6000 in the United States) operates an international money transfer service. The sender must pay in cash at one of their offices; the recipient can pick up the cash at any overseas office (fee about US$29 to send US$250, US$70 to send US$1000).

An cheaper and easier way to get money from home is to bring an **American Express** card. AmEx allows cardholders to draw cash from their checking accounts at any of its offices and many of its representatives' offices, up to US$1000 every 21 days (no service charge, no interest). With someone feeding money into your account at home, you'll be set.

If you are an American citizen in a life-or-death situation, you can have money sent via the State Department's **Overseas Citizens Service, American Citizens Services,** Consular Affairs, Public Affairs Staff, Room 4831, U.S. Department of States, Washington, D.C. 20520 (tel. 1 (202) 647 5225; at night and on Sundays and holidays 647 4000) fax 647 3000; http://travel.state.gov). For a fee of US$15, the State Department will forward money within hours to the nearest consular office, which will then disburse it according to instructions. The office serves only Americans in the direst of straits abroad. The quickest way to have the money sent is to cable the State Department through Western Union.

■ Safety and Security

SAFETY

India and Nepal are generally safe countries to travel in; rates of crime, especially violent crime, are extremely low. The sheer mass of population in India means that you will almost always be surrounded by people, and most Indians and Nepalis are well-meaning people who will go out of their way to help a foreigner in trouble if they can. There is safety in the crowd; whenever you're around a large group of people, rest assured that they wouldn't just stand back and let someone attack you. What goes on in public is everyone's business.

Still, any would-be attacker knows that tourists carry large amounts of cash and are not as street savvy as locals, so foreigners are particularly vulnerable to crime. To avoid such unwanted attention, try to **blend in** as much as you can. Dress modestly—wear local clothes, if possible. Unless you have the right color skin, you won't be able to pass for a local, but you can at least act like a foreigner who knows what he or she is doing. The gawking camera-toter is a more obvious target than the low-profile local look-alike. Do not flaunt your money, income, or nationality in public places. Try to memorize your map and organize your pack while you're still in your hotel room and if you must do one of these things while out and about, step into a shop or restaurant and be casual. Watch out for people who grope in crowds—that goes for both men and women!

Familiarity with the language is another important identifier. If you are able to speak even a few words of the local language, this may help you seem confident, and it can gain the confidence of someone who is otherwise not likely to notice you. Even if you are struggling, you will be seen as less of an outsider for trying. It is also important to be aware of the laws and customs in the specific area where you are wandering. Be aware of how others are behaving and follow their lead. If no one else has their feet on the table or is touching the statue or jaywalking in a mini skirt, you probably shouldn't be the one to start the trend. For more information, see **Customs and Etiquette** (p. 67).

Find out about unsafe neighborhoods from tourist information, from the manager of your hotel, or from a local whom you trust. Whenever possible, *Let's Go* warns of unsafe areas, but only your eyes can tell you for sure if you've wandered into one. General desertedness is a bad sign. If you feel uncomfortable, leave as quickly and directly as you can, but don't allow your fear of the new to close off whole worlds to you. Careful, persistent exploration will build confidence and make your stay in an area much more rewarding.

India and Nepal can be more dangerous at night simply because the crowds of people, the usual safety net, will not be around. When walking at night, stick to main roads and avoid dark alleyways. Unless you are in a neighborhood that is very active at night, it is best not to go out alone. Do not let rickshaws or auto-rickshaws take you down roads you don't know at night. Do not attempt to cross through parks or any other large, deserted areas. A blissfully isolated beach can become a treacherous nightmare as soon as night falls.

If you should ever encounter any uncomfortable situations, such as someone following you and asking for something, walk away. **Con artists** are a major problem in the main tourist centers. You may be "befriended" by someone who ends up pressuring you to smuggle jewels out of the country (don't even think about it) or who wants you to buy silk from his brother's store at outrageous prices. You'll hear sob stories that end with requests for large amounts of money. Be especially alert in these situations. Do not respond, walk quickly away, and keep a grip on your belongings. Contact the police—or simply threaten to—if a hustler is particularly insistent or aggressive. **It is best to avoid anyone asking you to go somewhere that you haven't asked to go, or to do something you haven't asked to do.** It is also important never to accept food or drinks from a stranger. There have been reports of con men who drug travelers with sleeping pills in tea and rob them. Most touts—those young men who mob travelers at bus and train stations, acting as if they want to help—are only after *baksheesh* and don't mean any harm in a violent way, but if you allow them to take you somewhere you could be getting into danger. Many decent Indians and Nepalis will simply want to help you get to wherever you are going, but they will not ask anything from you.

Watch out for stray animals in India and Nepal; rabies is much more prevalent here than in Western countries. The rhesus **monkeys** that hover in the treetops above temples are sometimes aggressive, and they will snatch food and bite. If a stray **dog** growls at you, pick up a stone and act like you're about to throw it—it is truly amazing how South Asian dogs fall for this trick. Even if you can't find a stone, just bending down and pretending to pick one up usually scares dogs away.

Be careful of Indian and Nepalese **traffic,** which is very chaotic. **Rickshaws and buses will not stop if you are in the way.** *Let's Go* does not recommend **hitchhiking,** particularly for women. For more information, see **Getting Around** (p. 48).

Political violence is another problem in parts of India and Nepal. Punjab and Assam, which were big problems in the 1980s and early 1990s, appear to have calmed down for now, but the **western part of the state of Jammu and Kashmir is not in this book because tourists should not go there.** Threats to foreigners are usually incidental, but in 1995 five western tourists were taken hostage by a militant group in Kashmir. One, a Norwegian, was beheaded. Even when there's not a war for secession going on, law and order can be sketchy in remote parts of India and Nepal where political parties or organized thugs rule the countryside. The best place to get advice about unsafe areas is your own country's embassy or high commission, but you should read the newspapers while you're in India or Nepal too to keep abreast of what's going on.

The most important thing to remember when you get to India or Nepal after reading all of these horrible warnings, is to just relax and be aware of your environment. No single other factor can be as helpful as simply maintaining a watchful eye wherever you go. Generally, people will be friendly and some will even go out of their way to see that you are accommodated safely and comfortably. The people of India and Nepal are proud of their culture, and more often than not will want to project the best of it to you. This is one of the factors which can make traveling in India and Nepal all the more special. There are few countries in the world with such ancient cultural traditions still around today. Take advantage of this fact. Learn from it. Let it affect you. There are certain ways of living which will outlast others.

There is no surefire set of precautions that will protect you from all situations you might encounter when you travel. A good self-defense course will give you more concrete ways to react to different types of aggression. **Model Mugging** (East Coast 1 (617) 232 7900; Midwest 1 (312) 338 4545; West Coast 1 (415) 592 7300), an American organization with offices in several major cities, teaches a comprehensive self-defense course. (Courses US$400-500. Women's and men's courses offered.)

SECURITY

Don't put money in a wallet in your back pocket. Never count your money in public and carry as little as possible. If you carry a purse, consider leaving it at home, or buy a sturdy one with a secure clasp, and carry it crosswise on the side, away from the street with the clasp against you. For your backpack, buy a small combination padlock which slips through the two zippers, securing the pack. A **money belt** is the safest way to carry cash; you can buy one at most camping supply stores or through the Forsyth Travel Library (see **Useful Publications,** p. 1). The best combination of convenience and invulnerability is the nylon, zippered pouch with belt that should sit inside the waist of your pants or skirt. A **neck pouch** is equally safe, although less accessbile. Refrain from pulling out your neck pouch in public; if you must, be very discreet. Do avoid keeping anything precious in a fanny-pack (even if it's worn on your stomach): your valuables will be highly visible and easy to steal. In city crowds and especially on public transportation, pick-pockets are amazingly deft at their craft. Rush hour is no excuse for strangers to press up against you.

Do not under any circumstances trust any strangers with your money, passport, or other valuables. Carry a combination padlock with you, as it may be of use in securing hotel room doors while you are out seeing the sights. You will also be able to buy locks of varying sizes and qualities in India and Nepal. You should carry your **passport, traveler's checks,** and **plane ticket** on you at all times. Make **photocopies** of such important documents and store them separately. This will help you replace them in case they are lost or filched. Keep some money separate from the rest to use in an emergency or in case of theft. It is a good idea to always have US$100 in cash on hand in case of emergencies.

Be watchful of your belongings on **buses and trains,** especially when passengers are getting on and off frequently. Keep everything close to you if you can. On trains, some people use the effective technique of padlocking their bags to the luggage rack. If your bag is going on a bus roof rack, make sure it's tied down securely so someone couldn't jump off with it in a hurry. The best policy is to talk to the other travelers in your seat or compartment and ask them where you can safely put your bag. If you let people help you, they will look out for you.

You might want to leave your luggage at a guest house while you are trekking, but don't leave your valuables there, and make sure what you do leave is locked. Never leave your belongings unlocked and unattended in a hotel; depressing as it might seem, there have been many cases of theft by other travelers. When possible, leave expensive jewelry, valuables, and anything you couldn't bear to part with at home.

If your belongings are stolen in India or Nepal you should go to the police. While there is virtually no chance you'll ever see your camera again, you can at least get an official **police report** which you'll need for an insurance claim. Dress well and be prepared for unsympathetic, suspicious policemen, but persistence usually pays off.

Travel Assistance International by Worldwide Assistance Services, Inc. in the U.S. provides its members with a 24-hr. hotline for emergencies and referrals. Their year-long frequent traveler package (US$226) includes medical and travel insurance, financial assistance, and help in replacing lost documents. Call 1 (800) 821 2828, 1 (202) 828 5894), or write them at 1133 15th St. NW, Suite 400, Washington, D.C. 20005-2710. More complete information on safety while traveling for U.S. residents may be found in *Americans Traveling Abroad: What You Should Know Before You Go,* available at Barnes and Noble booksellers across the United States. More complete information on safety while traveling may be found in *Travel Safety: Security and Safeguards at Home and Abroad,* from Hippocrene Books, Inc., 171 Madison Ave., New York, NY 10016 (tel. 1 (212) 685 4371; orders 1 (718) 454 2366).

DRUGS AND ALCOHOL

In the 1960s India and Nepal earned reputations as places where one could go and stare at the mountains or the ocean for days on end while achieving a pot-induced version of *nirvana* or at least a cosmic state of unity with the vegetable kingdom. Many travelers did just that in places like Kathmandu, Manali, Goa, Pushkar, or Kovalam. Many travelers have conveniently adopted one aspect of Shiva worship, smoking *ganja* in groups out of a *chillum,* lighting it with a match and chanting *"bam"* as the flame is lit, then bringing the *chillum* to their foreheads before and after smoking to pay homage to the "third eye." But while marijuana *(ganja)* and hashish *(charas)* are grown throughout the Himalaya, and are extremely cheap everywhere in India and Nepal, travelers should understand that these drugs are illegal and considered socially unacceptable by most Indians and Nepalis. An exception is made for *sadhus* (Hindu holy men), since *ganja* is associated with Shiva, and a few ethnic groups in the Himalaya use *ganja* and *charas,* although such reports have been exaggerated. In general, drug use is one of those activities that have earned foreign travelers a bad name in India and Nepal—it's better not to get mixed up in it.

India has a 10-year minimum sentence for drug possession or trafficking, but those caught with only a minute amount of *ganja* tend to get off lighter. If charged with drug possession, you are likely to find yourself required to prove your innocence in a corrupt justice system whose rules you don't understand. An "out-of-court settlement" with the police officer at the time of arrest is not unheard of, but the police do not go around making drug busts just to get bribes. Those who attempt to "influence" a police officer must do so discreetly and euphemistically. Drug law enforcement in Nepal is a bit more lax, but sentences are still stiff, and you probably don't want to spend any time in a Nepalese prison anyway.

If you get into trouble with the law, contact your country's diplomatic mission. Bear in mind that if you are arrested, diplomats from your country can visit you, provide a list of lawyers, inform family and friends, and lend you a shoulder to cry on, but they cannot get you out of jail.

The more touristy places in India and Nepal, like Kathmandu, Pokhara, and Goa, have an abundance of alcohol. Beer is popular and, oddly enough, many Indian state Tourist Development Corporation offices, such as the one in Rajasthan, host their own tin shack "Beer Bars" usually decorating the adjoining parking lots. Beer is pretty safe at these stalls but nighttime local crowds may not be. India and Nepal both produce drinkable vodka, gin, rum, whisky and other liquors; in India these are classified as IMFL (Indian-Made Foreign Liquor). Beware of homebrewed concoctions in India and Nepal, however; the Indian press is full of stories of revelers wiped out by the dozens by bad batches of toddy. The Indian state of Gujarat has been officially dry since 1947, and its prohibitive efforts have recently been copied by Andhra Pradesh, Haryana, and Manipur. But illegal, bootlegged alcohol can still be found in so-called "dry" states. Other states, like Tamil Nadu and Delhi, have dry days. Liquor permits, available at embassies, consulates, and tourist offices in Delhi, Madras, Bombay, and Calcutta, aren't essential but may help you get more booze with less difficulty in dry areas (see **Toddies for Tourists,** p. 576). There is no drinking age in India or Nepal.

UNUSUAL LAWS AND REGULATIONS

Each country has its own rules that may not be readily apparent to the visitor. *Let's Go* attempts to list some of these in the specific country listings, but there are inevitably ones that we miss. What is most important to remember is that you are a visitor in someone else's country, and must respect their culture and customs. If you do not, hassles and potentially much worse may result. Think carefully about your actions within the context of what is and is not accepted in the culture you are in.

Common throughout India and Nepal is the practice of bribery, informally known as *baksheesh*. Those who find themselves in trouble with some aspect of the law may be able to get out of it with some money and a little bit of finesse, depending on the nature of the offense. Contrary to western notions of legality, "smoothing over" problems with a little cash is not only common but even expected in India and Nepal. For such incursions as a traffic offense, or a minor customs violations, an offer of money or foreign-made goods may suddenly shed new light on the situation. Some liquor, a shirt, or cash can work equally well depending on the scenario. While bribery is common, and sometimes expected, there are risks involved with it, as with anything illegal. Honest officials may take offense, which would only aggravate problems for the would-be briber. Those who attempt to bribe officials must do so discreetly, with plenty of excuses. It is never wise to call a bribe a bribe.

Visitors to Nepal (especially those who plan to drive) should also be aware that killing a cow in the world's only Hindu kingdom is a major offense, punishable by long prison terms. It is also illegal to actively proselytize on behalf of any religion in Nepal, with both the convert and converter eligible for long prison terms.

▓ Health

A hectic vacation can take its toll on your health, especially in a tropical climate; India and Nepal can often seem like petri dishes for every kind of bug imaginable. Keeping your body strong will help ward off serious maladies; eat properly (protein and carbohydrates), drink lots of fluids, get plenty of sleep, and don't overexert yourself. To minimize the effects of jet lag, adjust to the region's schedule as soon as possible— stay in a hotel room with windows so you know when it's night. During the hot season, take precautions against heatstroke and sunburn: drink lots of liquids, wear a hat and sunscreen, and stay inside during midday.

BEFORE YOU GO

You may want to assemble a **first-aid kit,** including: antiseptic soap, aspirin, decongestant, antihistamine, acetaminophen to lower fever, diarrhea medicine (for the most common medical complaint of travelers in India and Nepal), motion sickness medicine, pink pismuth, anti-bacterial ointment, a thermometer, bandages, insect repellent, and a Swiss Army knife with tweezers and scissors.

It is a good idea to know your **blood type** and any other essential information about your blood in case an emergency transfusion is necessary.

Bring an up-to-date, detailed copy of any **medical prescriptions** you require (in legible form, stating the medication's trade name, manufacturer, chemical name, and dosage), and carry an ample supply of all medication—matching your prescription with a foreign equivalent is not always economical, easy, or safe. Distribute medication between carry-on and checked baggage in case one goes astray. Travelers with a chronic medical condition requiring regular treatment should consult their doctors before leaving. Bring a statement describing any pre-existing medical conditions, especially if you will be bringing insulin, syringes, or any narcotics.

Travelers with **corrective lenses** should bring an extra pair, or at least a copy of their prescription. If you wear contact lenses, carry a pair of glasses in case your eyes are tired or you lose a lens. Bring extra solutions, enzyme tablets, and eyedrops, as prices can be sky-high and availability is restricted to bigger cities. For heat disinfection, you'll need outlet and perhaps voltage adapters; you may want to switch to chemical cleansers. Traveling does not always provide sanitary conditions for contact lens care—think ahead to avoid taking them out on a lurching, crowded bus. In your passport, write the names of any people to be contacted in case of a medical emergency, and list any allergies or medical conditions to alert foreign doctors.

Innoculations

No innoculations are required for entry into India or Nepal, but that doesn't mean they're not a seriously good idea. (Visitors who have been in Africa, South America, or Papua New Guinea within the six days prior to their arrival in India must have a certificate of vaccination against yellow fever.) Ask your physican for advice on what shots you'll need; the following is general information that differs from case to case. Most travelers to India or Nepal need shots against hepatitis A, typhoid, and meningitis. A fairly new hepatitis A vaccine called Havrix is available; though expensive, it lasts up to ten years. The more traditional protection is a human gammaglobulin injection which is very effective but wears off after only a few months. Those who get the gammaglobulin should wait until right before their departure. Typhoid immunity (which lasts for 3-5 years) can require a painful, protracted series of jabs in the arm; fortunately an oral form is also available. Meningitis, an often fatal disease that causes a swelling of the lining around the brain, breaks out now and then in India and Nepal; it is a good idea to be protected.

It is equally important to make sure you are immune to such diseases as diptheria, polio, tetanus, measles, mumps, and rubella. Most people in western countries are innoculated against these in childhood, but adults need an oral polio booster at some point, and a tetanus booster is necessary every 10 years.

There are also vaccines available for rabies and cholera, but neither of these are very effective; the rabies vaccine in particular does not actually prevent rabies, it only reduces the number of shots necessary you need if you get it. Many doctors will not dispense either of these shots, since they can delude people into thinking they are protected.

Useful Organizations

The United States **Centers for Disease Control (CDC)** is an excellent source of general information on health for travelers around the world, and maintains an international travelers' hotline (tel. 1 (404) 332 4559; fax 332 4565; http://www.cdc.gov). The center also offers up-to-date information on recommended vaccinations. If you have access to a fax, you can request printed information from the CDC fax information service; call the hotline from a phone and follow the prompts. (You will need the document code for the "disease directory," which provides the codes for information on a variety of diseases and on travelers' health; it is 000004; the code for advice

The best places to travel may be the best places to get hepatitis A.

You can pick up hepatitis A when traveling to high-risk areas outside of the United States. From raw shellfish or water you don't think is contaminated. Or from uncooked foods—like salad—prepared by people who don't know they're infected. At even the best places.

Symptoms of hepatitis A include jaundice, abdominal pain, fever, vomiting and diarrhea. And can cause discomfort, time away from work and memories you'd like to forget.

The U.S. Centers for Disease Control and Prevention (CDC) recommends immunization for travelers to high-risk areas. *Havrix*, available in over 45 countries, can protect you from hepatitis A. *Havrix* may cause some soreness in your arm or a slight headache.

Ask your physician about vaccination with *Havrix* at your next visit or at least 2 weeks before you travel. And have a great trip.

Please see important patient information adjacent to this ad.

Havrix®
Hepatitis A Vaccine, Inactivated

The world's first hepatitis A vaccine

For more information on how to protect yourself against hepatitis A, call

1-800-HEP-A-VAX (1-800-437-2829)

Hepatitis A Vaccine, Inactivated
Havrix®

See complete prescribing information in SmithKline Beecham Pharmaceuticals literature. The following is a brief summary.

INDICATIONS AND USAGE: *Havrix* is indicated for active immunization of persons ≥ 2 years of age against disease caused by hepatitis A virus (HAV).

CONTRAINDICATIONS: *Havrix* is contraindicated in people with known hypersensitivity to any component of the vaccine.

WARNINGS: Do not give additional injections to patients experiencing hypersensitivity reactions after a *Havrix* injection. (See CONTRAINDICATIONS.)

Hepatitis A has a relatively long incubation period. Hepatitis A vaccine may not prevent hepatitis A infection in those who have an unrecognized hepatitis A infection at the time of vaccination. Additionally, it may not prevent infection in those who do not achieve protective antibody titers (although the lowest titer needed to confer protection has not been determined).

PRECAUTIONS: As with any parenteral vaccine (1) keep epinephrine available for use in case of anaphylaxis or anaphylactoid reaction; (2) delay administration, if possible, in people with any febrile illness or active infection, except when the physican believes withholding vaccine entails the greater risk; (3) take all known precautions to prevent adverse reactions, including reviewing patients' history for hypersensitivity to this or similar vaccines.

Administer with caution to people with thrombocytopenia or a bleeding disorder, or people taking anticoagulants. Do not inject into a blood vessel. Use a separate, sterile needle or prefilled syringe for every patient. When giving concomitantly with other vaccines or IG, use separate needles and different injection sites.

As with any vaccine, if administered to immunosuppressed persons or persons receiving immunosuppressive therapy, the expected immune response may not be obtained.

Carcinogenesis, Mutagenesis, Impairment of Fertility: *Havrix* has not been evaluated for its carcinogenic potential, mutagenic potential or potential for impairment of fertility.

Pregnancy Category C: Animal reproduction studies have not been conducted with *Havrix*. It is also not known whether *Havrix* can cause fetal harm when administered to a pregnant woman or can affect reproduction capacity. Give *Havrix* to a pregnant woman only if clearly needed. It is not known whether *Havrix* is excreted in human milk. Because many drugs are excreted in human milk, use caution when administering *Havrix* to a nursing woman.

Havrix is well tolerated and highly immunogenic and effective in children.

Fully inform patients, parents or guardians of the benefits and risks of immunization with *Havrix*. For persons traveling to endemic or epidemic areas, consult current CDC advisories regarding specific locales. Travelers should take all necessary precautions to avoid contact with, or ingestion of, contaminated food or water. Duration of immunity following a complete vaccination schedule has not been established.

ADVERSE REACTIONS: *Havrix* has been generally well tolerated. As with all pharmaceuticals, however, it is possible that expanded commercial use of the vaccine could reveal rare adverse events.

The most frequently reported by volunteers in clinical trials was injection-site soreness (56% of adults; 21% of children); headache (14% of adults; less than 9% of children). Other solicited and unsolicited events are listed below:

Incidence 1% to 10% of Injections: Induration, redness, swelling; fatigue, fever (>37.5°C), malaise; anorexia, nausea.

Incidence <1% of Injections: Hematoma; pruritus, rash, urticaria; pharyngitis, other upper respiratory tract infections; abdominal pain, diarrhea, dysgeusia, vomiting; arthralgia, elevation of creatine phosphokinase, myalgia; lymphadenopathy; hypertonic episode, insomnia, photophobia, vertigo.

Additional safety data

Safety data were obtained from two additional sources in which large populations were vaccinated. In an outbreak setting in which 4,930 individuals were immunized with a single dose of either 720 EL.U. or 1440 EL.U. of *Havrix*, the vaccine was well-tolerated and no serious adverse events due to vaccination were reported. Overall, less than 10% of vaccinees reported solicited general adverse events following the vaccine. The most common solicited local adverse event was pain at the injection site, reported in 22.3% of subjects at 24 hours and decreasing to 2.4% by 72 hours.

In a field efficacy trial, 19,037 children received the 360 EL.U. dose of *Havrix*. The most commonly reported adverse events were injection-site pain (9.5%) and tenderness (8.1%), reported following first doses of *Havrix*. Other adverse events were infrequent and comparable to the control vaccine Engerix-B® (Hepatitis B Vaccine, Recombinant).

Postmarketing Reports: Rare voluntary reports of adverse events in people receiving *Havrix* since market introduction include the following: localized edema; anaphylaxis/anaphylactoid reactions, somnolence; syncope; jaundice, hepatitis; erythema multiforme, hyperhydrosis, angioedema; dyspnea; lymphadenopathy; convulsions, encephalopathy, dizziness, neuropathy, myelitis, paresthesia, Guillain-Barré syndrome, multiple sclerosis; congenital abnormality.

The U.S. Department of Health and Human Services has established the Vaccine Adverse Events Reporting System (VAERS) to accept reports of suspected adverse events after the administration of any vaccine, including, but not limited to, the reporting of events required by the National Childhood Vaccine Injury Act of 1986. The toll-free number for VAERS forms and information is 1-800-822-7967.

HOW SUPPLIED: 360 EL.U./0.5 mL: NDC 58160-836-01 Package of 1 single-dose vial.

720 EL.U./0.5 mL: NDC 58160-837-01 Package of 1 single-dose vial; NDC 58160-837-02 Package of 1 prefilled syringe.

1440 EL.U./mL: NDC 58160-835-01 Package of 1 single-dose vial; NDC 58160-835-02 Package of 1 prefilled syringe.

Manufactured by **SmithKline Beecham Biologicals**
Rixensart, Belgium
Distributed by **SmithKline Beecham Pharmaceuticals**
Philadelphia, PA 19101
BRS–HA:L5A

Havrix is a registered trademark of SmithKline Beecham.

and advisories for the Indian subcontinent is 220220). Or write directly to the Centers for Disease Control and Prevention, 1600 Clifton Rd. NE, Atlanta, GA 30333. To talk, call 1 (404) 639 3311. The CDC publishes the booklet *Health Information for International Travelers* (publication HHS-CDC 90 8280, US$6), an annual global rundown on disease, immunization, and general health advice, including risks in particular countries.

The **U.S. State Department** compiles Consular Information Sheets on health, entry requirements, and other issues for all countries. U.S. citizens can call Overseas Citizens' Services (tel. 1 (202) 647 5225) for travel health warnings. To receive the same information by fax, dial 1 (202) 647 3000 directly from a fax machine and follow the recorded instructions. The same information can be obtained from U.S. embassies and consulates abroad, or by sending a self-addressed, stamped envelope to Overseas Citizens' Services, Bureau of Consular Affairs, Room 4811, U.S. Department of State, Washington, D.C. 20520. For more general health information, contact the **American Red Cross.** The ARC publishes a First-Aid and Safety Handbook (US$15) available for purchase by calling or writing to the American Red Cross, 285 Columbus Ave., Boston, MA 02116-5114 (tel. 1 (800) 564 1234). In the U.S., the American Red Cross also offers inexpensive first-aid and CPR courses.

Those with medical conditions (e.g. diabetes, allergies to antibiotics, epilepsy, heart conditions) may want to obtain a stainless steel **Medic Alert** identification tag (US$35 the first year, and US$15 annually thereafter), which identifies the disease and gives a 24-hour collect-call information number. Contact Medic Alert at 1 (800) 825 3785, or write to Medic Alert Foundation, 2323 Colorado Avenue, Turlock, CA 95382. Diabetics can contact the **American Diabetes Association,** 1660 Duke St., Alexandria, VA 22314 (tel. 1 (800) 232 3472) to receive copies of the article "Travel and Diabetes" and a diabetic ID card.

Global Emergency Medical Services (GEMS) provides 24-hour international medical assistance and support coordinated through registered nurses who have on-line access to your medical information, your primary physician, and a worldwide network of English-speaking doctors and hospitals. Subscribers also receive a pocket-sized personal medical record that contains vital information in case of emergencies. For more information call 1 (800) 860 1111; fax 1 (770) 475 0058; or write: 2001 Westside Drive, Suite 120, Alpharetta, GA 30201. The **International Association for Medical Assistance to Travelers (IAMAT)** offers a membership ID card and a directory of English-speaking doctors around the world. Membership is free, though donations are appreciated and used for further research. Contact chapters in the **U.S.,** 417 Center St., Lewiston, NY 14092 (tel. 1 (716) 754 4883; fax 1 (519) 836 3412; e-mail iamat@sentex.net; http://www.sentex.net/iamat), **Canada,** 40 Regal Road, Guelph, Ontario, N1K 1B5 (tel. 1 (519) 836 0102) or 1287 St. Clair Avenue West, Toronto, M6E 1B8 (tel. 1 (416) 652 0137; fax 1 (519) 836 3412), or **New Zealand,** P.O. Box 5049, Christchurch 5.

HEALTH WHILE TRAVELING

Pay attention to the warning signals that your body may send you. You may feel fatigue and discomfort, not because of any specific illness, but simply because your body is adapting to a new climate, food, water quality, or pace when you arrive. Once you get going, some of the milder symptoms that you may safely ignore at home may be signs of something more serious; your increased exertion may wear you out and make you more susceptible to illness.

Learn of regional hazards for forests and always be aware of snakes and other dangerous animals in the wild, even in well-traveled areas. A more common problem is insects. **Insect bites,** particularly from mosquitoes, can plague your visit to India and Nepal. Many (notably mosquitoes) are most active at night, and carry dangerous diseases (malaria and others—see below). Be sure to wear repellent, long sleeves, long pants, and socks. The most you can do for prevention is use an insect repellent containing **DEET** and wear pants and long-sleeved shirts, especially in wet or forested areas or while hiking and camping. The **CDC (Centers for Disease Control)** recom-

Ayurvedic Medicine

The predominant medical tradition of Hindu culture is associated with the *Aryu-Veda*, which translates literally to the "knowledge of long life." Beholders and practitioners of this wisdom are called *vaidyas*. Ayurvedic medicine takes a holistic approach to diagnosis—a broken heart is as much an ailment as a broken leg—and to treatment—a combination of herbal potions and life notions. The earliest known herbal prescriptions date back to the Atharva Veda (c. 1000 BC), which reveals the precocity of Indian medical thought. *Vaidyas* were performing surgery on external wounds long before contact with Western systems of medicine. Ayurvedic medicine, however, is primarily associated with maintaining a balance of the three bodily essences or *doshas: vatta* (wind), *pitta* (bile), and *kapha* (phlegm). *Vatta* represents the force of kinetic energy and is associated with the nervous system and the movement of muscles and the heart. *Kapha*, which opposes *vatta*, is seat of potential energy and is associated with lymph and mucous. Finally, *pitta* mediates these two forces, governing digestive and metabolic processes and utilizing both sources of energy. Balance between the three *doshas* creates a healthy condition; but a decadent *doshas* develop distortions. So don't O.D. on *dosha*. Take your wind, bile, and phlegm in moderation and a long life awaits.

mends using flying-insect-killing spray in sleeping quarters at night, and, for greater protection, spraying clothing and bedding with **permethrin,** an insect repellent licensed for use on clothing. Apply calamine lotion to insect bites to soothe the itching. More soothing, but harder to get on the road, is a bath with baking soda or oatmeal. (Aveeno packages several oatmeal mixtures; just dump a half-cup or so of baking soda into a lukewarm bath.) **Tiger balm** is a favorite Chinese method, and is readily available in pharmacies or from street vendors.

A fairly uncommon but irksome affliction are **parasites** (hookworms, tapeworms, etc.). Some can enter your body through your feet, so don't walk around barefoot outside. They can also find their way into your stomach through undercooked meat or dirty vegetables. **Giardia** is a serious parasitic disease contracted by ingesting untreated water from lakes or streams. A stool test from a doctor will uncover these critters, which can be flushed away with the help of medicine. Symptoms of general parasitic infections include swollen glands or lymph nodes, fever, rashes, itchiness, digestive complications, eye problems, and anemia. Don't let these nasty creatures shrivel you from the inside out—wear shoes, drink purified water, and avoid uncooked food.

The Heat

Overwhelming heat can stop even the most ambitious adventurers dead in their tracks. It is very important to avoid heat exhaustion and heat stroke. The symptoms of **heat exhaustion** include fatigue, dizziness, headaches, and a feeling of lightness. The cause of heat exhaustion is, not surprisingly, dehydration. If you think you are suffering from heat exhaustion, get out of the sun and sit down in a cool area. Drink cool fluids and avoid physical exertion.

Heat stroke, which is very serious and sometimes fatal, takes heat exhaustion to a more dangerous level: high temperature, little or no sweating, flushed skin, unbearable headaches, delirium, convulsions, and unconsciousness. It is vital to get the victim of heat stroke to a hospital, but in the meantime, make sure to place wet towels on the victim and place him or her in a cool area; if that is absolutely impossible, at least be sure to continually fan the victim.

To prevent yourself from getting heat exhaustion or heat stroke, drink plenty of fluids; drinking the recommended eight glasses of water per day (minimum) should become second nature. Stay away from diuretics such as alcohol, coffee, and tea, which increase the fluids lost through urination.

Less debilitating than heatstroke, but still dangerous, is **sunburn.** Many outdoor wanderers are shocked to find themselves toasted to a crisp even though there is a thick cloud cover in their area. If you're prone to burning, carry sunscreen with you, and apply it liberally and often. Be wary of sunscreens of SPF (sun protection factor) higher than 15 or 20; higher ratings won't be of extra help, but will cost more. Wear a hat and sunglasses and a lightweight long-sleeved shirt. If you do get burned, drink lots of liquids; it'll cool you down and help your skin recover faster.

For some travelers, their visit to India and Nepal will mean an introduction to **prickly heat,** a rash that develops when sweat is trapped under the skin. Particularly in men, the groin area is very susceptible to this rash. To alleviate itchiness, try showering with mango neem soap or sprinkle talcum powder on the affected area just after bathing.

Moist, hot weather can irritate the skin in other ways as well. Various **fungal infections** (athlete's foot, jock itch, etc.) can be prevented by washing often and drying thoroughly. Wear loose-fitting clothes made of natural, absorbent fibers like cotton.

Water and Food

Don't drink the water! At least not from the tap. Nowhere in India or Nepal is tapwater safe for drinking, and streams and wells are just as dangerous. If locals seem to be doing fine, remember that they have built up lifelong immunities which you lack. Brushing teeth with tapwater is an acceptable risk for some, but don't swallow. Also be careful not to swallow water from the shower. **Drink only boiled or filtered water and avoid ice.** You will quickly become familiar with Bisleri bottled water and other brands.

The most effective method of purification is to **boil** water. Presumably, you won't be carrying a kitchen stove, however, so the simplest way to treat water is with **iodine,** either in drops (tincture of iodine) or tablets. Chlorine tablets are also available, but they don't kill absloutely everything. After treating water with iodine or chlorine wait 20 minutes for the chemical to burn off and for the parasites to die. An easy alternative to boiling and chemical treatments is to buy **mineral water,** which is available almost everywhere in India and Nepal. Stick to bottles of Bisleri, Yes, or other such labels that wrap a clear plastic seal around the cap; these are more difficult to fake. Bottles that are "sealed" with a plastic ring around the bottom of the cap are frequently refilled with tapwater and resold. Don't expect great water when you get the real thing, though. In India there are no standards defining what can be called "mineral water," and what you're usually getting is big-city tapwater sterilized with ozone gas or ultraviolet radiation. It's also worth contemplating the immense waste problem caused by all those empty plastic bottles.

Carbonated drinks ("cold drinks") are also safe—they must be carbonated in factories which use clean water, and they are sealed to keep in the fizz. If a carbonated drink is flat, don't drink it. There have been incidents of "fake" Coca-cola in India, but if you taste it, you'll know. Remember, however, that caffeine (contained in cola drinks) is a diuretic, and therefore can be bad for rehydration. Fresh lime soda, a mixture of club soda, lime juice, and sugar, is a refreshing, mineral-rich alternative. **Coconut water,** sold on street corners all over India, is excellent for replacing fluids and minerals. **Coffee** and **tea,** which are boiled in preparation, are also usually safe, although some of the toughest parasites are not killed by simple boiling. Avoid drinks such as *lassis* or *nimbu pani* (lemonade) except in the best restaurants; these are made with water, and it usually isn't purified. **Insist on beverages without ice,** even if that means desert temperatures can only be combatted with lukewarm Thums-Up Cola. The water used to make ice is rarely clean. Many restaurants use "Aquaguard" filters however, which make their water safe to drink.

Water safety is also seasonal, and it's much more risky to drink the water in the **monsoon,** when all the year's crud seeps into the water supply, than in the dry season. If you visit South Asia during the monsoon be especially careful about water.

Any food that is cooked immediately before serving is safe. To be extra safe, however, **avoid food that is cooked on the street.** This is one rule that most foreigners living in India and Nepal follow. Street vendors are rarely sanitary, and their equipment is open to disease-carrying flies. The same is true of juice stands. If possible, eat in restaurants that serve local food and are popular with locals. Indians and Nepalis know what they're doing when they prepare their own cuisine, and busy kitchens are likely to be cleaner. Tourist restaurants that serve shoddy imitations of Western food are often less sanitary than *dhabas* that dish out *dal bhat* to truckers all day. Everything will be much easier, in fact, if you eat at regular times and eat the same sort of foods regularly every day. Eating in different places all the time can be disturbing to your body.

The biggest risk to travelers usually comes from **fruit, vegetables, and dairy products.** With fruit, if you can peel it, you can eat it. If you crave a salad, make sure the restaurant soaks its vegetables in iodine. Take dairy products only from clean-looking establishments. Beware of some juice stands and sugar-cane juice stands; their equipment is not always kept clean.

Other than that, the spiciness of the food and the variation in ingredients can also put a strain on your stomach. Adjust to the region's cooking slowly. Have high-energy, non-sugary foods with you to keep your strength up; you'll need plenty of protein and carbohydrates. **Washing your hands before you eat** is a sensible rule that you should not forget while you travel; in fact, it's especially important at times like this. Bring a few packs of handi-wipes or diaper wipes (or even alcohol pads), since sinks and soap may not always be available.

Diarrhea

Few travelers to India and Nepal get away without at least one bout of **diarrhea.** It has many causes, including parasites, bacteria, food poisoning, viruses, and simply adjusting to new kinds of food. To prevent it, drink safe water, wash your hands before eating, and stay away from street food. **The biggest danger from diarrhea is dehydration. If you get diarrhea, drink liquids constantly in order to keep yourself hydrated.** Water is good for starters, but it is also important to replace the minerals you lose. **Adding 60ml (4 tablespoons) of sugar and 3ml (½ teaspoon) of salt to a liter of pure water makes an effective rehydration drink.** If you can't find these ingredients, prepared mixtures of oral rehydration salts (ORS) are available at all pharmacies. (Electral is the most common brand in India.) Non-caffeinated soft drinks such as Sprite, allowed to go flat, are also good. Down large amounts of these mixtures daily. People with diarrhea should also eat simple, starchy foods, like bananas or plain boiled rice. Anti-diarrheals like Immodium AD or Lomotil can help to stop the diarrhea, but such drugs can also complicate serious infections. Remember that diarrhea is your body's attempt to expel the bacteria or parasite. You don't necessarily want to stop that. Avoid anti-diarrheals if you suspect you have been exposed to contaminated food or water, which puts you at risk for cholera, typhoid fever, and other diseases. Get lots of rest and wait for the illness to run its course. If you develop a fever or your symptoms don't go away after four or five days, consult a doctor.

Food- and Water-Borne Diseases

Dysentery

One of the most common forms of diarrhea is dysentery, which is caused when bacteria or amoebas infect the mucous lining of the large intestine. The most common symptoms of dysentery are diarrhea (often containing mucus) and gripping abdominal pain. If bacteria are the cause, the dysentery usually comes on suddenly and exhausts itself; amoebas on the other hand cause a long and intermittent illness that will recur if not treated. Pepto-Bismol is ineffective against dysentery, but other drugs can be used to kill the intruders and restore the normal intestinal bacteria. Terramycin (tetracycline) is an antibiotic that kills dysentery bacteria. Metronidazole (known as Flagyl or Metrogyl in India) is commonly used to kill amoebic parasites. Nutrolin B (a combination of lactobacillus acidophilus and vitamin B complex) helps restore the intestinal flora, and is essential to take with any antibiotic. It is a good preventitive medicine as well.

Cholera

Cholera is still a perennial problem in India and Nepal, breaking out now and then in deadly local epidemics. Cholera is an acute intestinal bacteria-borne infection that works quickly and with murderous intent. The symptoms—explosive and interminable diarrhea, unstoppable vomiting, dehydration, muscle cramps, and lethargy—come suddenly, and unless quickly treated, prove fatal in a short time. It is vital for the cholera-infected to immediately find a hospital. In the meantime, the patient should guzzle liquids to battle dehydration. Cholera is passed from person to person like wildfire through contaminated food or water, human waste, and unsanitary cooking methods. The best way to prevent cholera is to drink clean water, peel your own fruit, and eat only thoroughly cooked food.

Vaccinations are available for cholera (and typhoid fever in one shot), but they are only 50% effective in preventing illness for the first three to six months after vaccination. The CDC recommends vaccination for people with stomach ulcers, those who use anti-acid therapy, and those who will be living in unsanitary conditions in epidemic areas.

Typhoid Fever

Caused by a bacterium, typhoid is spread through contaminated food, water, and human waste, and through contact with an infected person. Symptoms of the disease gradually creep up on the victim. For the first week or so, a fever slowly rises, sometimes accompanied by vomiting and diarrhea. Next, a rash may appear, and delirium and dehydration seize the victim. Headaches, fatigue, loss of appetite, and constipation are also associated symptoms. Untreated, the patient may develop life-threatening pneumonia. As with other dangerous, communicable diseases, it is imperative to find quick medical care.

Typhoid fever is treatable with antibiotics, and a vaccine is available, although it is only 70% effective. The CDC recommends vaccination for those traveling off the beaten tourist paths, that is, those going to small cities or towns, or those staying longer than six weeks. It is also important, of course, to drink only bottled or boiled water and eat only thoroughly cooked food to lower the risk of infection.

Hepatitis

Prevalent in areas with poor sanitation, **hepatitis A** and **hepatitis B** are both caused by viruses attacking the liver. Hepatitis A, like typhoid fever, is spread through the contamination of water and food with viruses present in human feces. It is therefore important to be wary of uncooked foods that may have been contaminated during handling, such as fresh fruits and vegetables. It can also be transmitted from direct person-to-person contact. Fatigue, vomiting, nausea, fever, loss of appetite, dark urine, jaundice, light stools, and aches and pains are among the symptoms. At particular risk are travelers, especially those visiting rural areas, coming into close contact with local people, or eating in settings with poor sanitation. Hepatitis B, in contrast, is spread through the transfer of bodily fluids, such as blood, semen, and saliva, from one person to another. Its incubation period varies and can be much longer than the 30-day incubation period of hepatitis A. Thus, a person may not begin having symptoms until many years after infection.

Hepatitis has no known cure, but vaccinations are available to protect travelers against both types of hepatitis. Protection from hepatitis A requires a shot of immune globulin, which is given about a week before departure and after all other immunizations have been completed. Ask your doctor about a new vaccine for Hepatitis A called Havrix which lasts up to ten years. For protection against hepatitis B, a three-shot series given in six months is required. The CDC recommends the hepatitis B vaccinations for health-care workers, sexually active travelers, long-term visitors who will have extensive contact with the local population, and anyone planning on seeking any medical treatment while in India and Nepal, as there is a high risk for hepatitis B in the region.

Malaria and Other Insect-Borne Diseases

Malaria is the most serious disease that travelers to India and Nepal are likely to contract. It is caused by a parasite carried by the female *Anopheles* mosquito. The disease is prevalent in most tropical areas of the world. Because the incubation period for the disease varies, it could take up to weeks or months for an infected person to show any symptoms. When the disease does hit, the first symptoms include headaches, chills, general achiness, and fatigue. Next comes a very high fever and sweating. In some cases, vomiting and diarrhea also show up. If you think you may have malaria, go to the nearest hospital immediately and have a blood test. No precautions can fully protect you from contracting malaria. While traveling and for up to a year later, seek medical attention to treat any flu-like symptoms. Malaria can be fatal. Anemia, kidney failure, coma, and death can result if it goes untreated.

Malaria is generally found in heavily forested areas. It is virtually but not entirely impossible to get malaria in big cities and towns. The CDC says that preventative medication against malaria is not necessary if you only visit urban areas; however, as mentioned above, precautions should be taken to avoid being bitten by mosquitoes and to treat flu-like symptoms. Malaria is only found below 1200m in altitude, so the mountainous areas of Nepal and northern India are relatively safe.

Various forms of medication can be taken to prevent malaria (no shots are available). Some doctors may prescribe mefloquine (sold under the name Lariam), taken in a 250mg tablet once a week, one week before leaving until four weeks after leaving. Mefloquine is a drug approved by the Centers for Disease Control, with the reservation that it should not be taken by pregnant women, children under 30 pounds, or people with a history of epilepsy, psychiatric disorder, or a known hypersensitivity to mefloquine. Carrying the drug Fansidar is often recommended, but it should only be used in the case of serious illness and when medical care is not readily available. The best way to combat malaria is to wear insect repellent containing DEET, sleep under bednets, and stay away from uninhabited jungle areas. Also, to combat mosquitoes, you can use mosquito coils or "Good Knight," an electric device that cooks little cakes, sending anti-mosquito gases into the air.

Mosquitoes also carry a virus that causes **dengue fever.** Dengue fever, found in most of the region, tends to be an urban malady. It exhibits symptoms similar to malaria, but certain characteristics differentiate it from its more famous cousin. Dengue fever has two stages and is characterized by its sudden onset. Stage one lasts from two to four days, and its symptoms include chills, high fever, severe headaches, swollen lymph nodes, muscle aches, and in some instances, a pink rash on the face. Then the fever quickly disappears, and profuse sweating follows. For 24 hours there is no fever, but then it suddenly appears with a rash all over the body. If you think you have contracted dengue fever, see a doctor, drink plenty of liquids, and remain in bed. It is also important to take acetaminophen (Tylenol) or ibuprofen (Advil) for dengue fever; do not take aspirin. Unfortunately, the only prevention for dengue fever is avoiding mosquitoes. Dengue mosquitoes bite during the day, unlike their nocturnal blood-sucking colleagues.

Rounding out the list of communicable diseases carried by mosquitoes is **Japanese encephalitis.** The Culex mosquito carries the virus for this nasty ailment, which is most prevalent in rural areas, from July to December. Symptoms include flu-like symptoms—chills, headache, fever, vomiting, muscle fatigue—and delirium. Symptoms are similar to malaria, but the fatality rate of Japanese encephalitis is much higher, so it is vital to get medical help as soon as symptoms arise. A vaccine, JE-VAX, is available; you can be vaccinated against this disease with a three-shot series given a week apart or on a longer, safer schedule. The vaccine is effective for about a year. Serious side-effects have been associated with the vaccine, and so travelers should seriously consider whether it is necessary. The CDC claims that there is a very low chance that a traveler will be infected if proper precautions are taken (using mosquito repellents containing DEET, sleeping under nets, etc.).

Other Serious Infectious Diseases

Meningococcal meningitis is an inflammation of the lining surrounding the brain and spinal cord. The bacteria are carried in the nose and throat and so they are often spread through coughs and sneezes. Meningitis is less common in India than in Nepal where there have been several recent outbreaks. The first symptom of meningitis is a rash, then fever, sensitivity to light, stiffness of the neck, and headache. Consult a doctor immediately if you have these symptoms; meningitis can kill in hours. Fortunately a vaccine exists. For more information, see **Innoculations** (p. 18).

Rabies is common in India and even more so in Nepal. Transmitted through the saliva of infected animals, it is fatal if not treated. The best policy is to stay away from dogs and monkeys. If you are bitten by an animal, washing the wound thoroughly with soap and water may reduce the chance of infection. If you suspect the animal is rabid, see a doctor immediately. Once you begin having symptoms of rabies (thirst, muscle spasms), the disease is in its terminal stage, so it is absolutely necessary to act quickly. If the animal can be found, tests can ascertain whether the animal does indeed have rabies. You should be admitted to a hospital, where doctors can begin giving you the six shots that will protect you from getting the disease. A rabies vaccine is available but it is only semi-effective; however, if you plan to be in close contact with animals in India or Nepal they are probably a good idea. Three shots are necessary; it takes one year to receive them in series.

Schistosomiasis is another common infection caused by the larvae of a flatworm that can penetrate the skin. The larvae are found in fresh water, so swimming in fresh water, especially in rural areas, should be avoided. If your skin is exposed to untreated water, the CDC recommends immediate and vigorous rubbing with a towel and/or the application of rubbing alcohol to reduce the risk of infection. If infected, you may notice an itchy localized rash; later symptoms include fever, fatigue, painful urination, diarrhea, loss of appetite, night sweats, and a hive-like rash on the body. Schistosomiasis can be treated with drugs.

AIDS, HIV, STDS

Acquired Immune Deficiency Syndrome (AIDS) is a term used to describe people who have the human immunodeficiency virus (HIV) and whose immune systems are severely impaired. People with AIDS have difficulty fighting off even minor illnesses (like the common cold), and frequently catch diseases from which people with normally functioning immune systems are protected. While not everyone who is HIV positive has AIDS, any person who is HIV positive can transmit this virus, which impairs the immune system and ultimately leads to death. Due to an active prostitution industry and drug subculture, as well as large-scale denial, HIV and AIDS are proliferating at an alarming rate in India and Nepal. Only a few thousand full-blown AIDS cases have been officially counted in India and only a few dozen in Nepal, but this is largely due to inconsistent reporting. The World Health Organization estimates that there are over four million HIV-infected persons in South and Southeast Asia; the majority of these are in Thailand and India. The governments of India and Nepal are now beginning to recognize AIDS as a problem.

The best advice is to follow all the precautions you should follow at home: avoid sex without a condom and never share needles of any sort. It may not always be easy to buy condoms in India or Nepal, and when it is, they may not be of a high quality. If you plan on being sexually active while traveling, it's a good idea to take a supply of good-quality Western-made condoms with you before you depart.

Although heterosexual sex is the most common method of HIV transmission in India and Nepal, there are other risks as well. Since many hospitals lack money and resources, they may re-use needles and other instruments without sterilizing them. The risk of obtaining HIV this way is slight, however, so it should never cause one to refuse medical care in an emergency. If you need an injection, make sure the needle has been sterilized; to be extra safe, carry your own syringes with you and insist that these be used. Avoid any other contact with needles (tattooing, piercing, acupuncture, etc.) unless you can be absolutely sure the needles have been sterilized. If you get a shave from a barber make sure he uses a new blade.

For more information on AIDS, call the **U.S. Center for Disease Control's 24-hour Hotline** at 1 (800) 342 2437 (TTY 1 (800) 243 7889, Mon-Fri 10am-10pm). The **World Health Organization** (tel. 1 (202) 861 3200) provides statistics on AIDS.

Sexually Transmitted Diseases are spread through sexual contact with an infected person. Hepatitis B is discussed above; see **Hepatitis** (p. 23). Syphilis is a common STD which can go through three stages, finally resulting in inflammation of the heart and central nervous system and death if left untreated. If syphilis is caught early enough however, when soft cankers appear on the genitals about three weeks after infection, it can be treated and cured with penicillin. Gonorrhea is another STD whose incubation period is shorter than that of syphilis, lasting anywhere from three to seven days. Symptoms include a discharge of pus and infection of the urethra. If left untreated, gonorrhea causes considerable discomfort. The disease can be treated with penicillin. Another STD, chlamydia, has symptoms identical to those of gonorrhea, but is resistant to penicillin treatment. Herpes, caused by a virus, is a terribly discomforting STD for which there is no known cure. At the end of the 2-10-day incubation period, lesions begin to form at the site of the infection, whether it be the genital area, the mouth, or the hand. Protected sex does not necessarily keep contact with infected areas from occurring. The only way to be sure is to check for sores before touching the other individual and to pick sexual partners carefully. Lesions will eventually go away, but often recur throughout one's lifetime. For more information, call the U.S. Center for Disease Control's STDs Hotline, 1 (800) 227 8922. Open Mon.-Fri. 8am-11pm, Eastern Time. Council's brochure, *Travel Safe: AIDS and International Travel,* is available at all Council Travel offices (see p. 43).

WOMEN'S HEALTH

Women traveling in unsanitary conditions are vulnerable to **urinary tract** and **bladder infection**s (cystitis), common and severely uncomfortable bacterial diseases that cause a burning sensation and painful (sometimes frequent) urination. A strong antibiotic usually gets rid of the symptoms within a couple of days. Other recommendations are to drink enormous amounts of vitamin C-rich juice and plenty of water, and to urinate frequently. Untreated bladder infections can become very serious, leading to kidney infections or pelvic inflammatory disease. Treat an infection the best you can while on the road; if it persists, see a doctor and definitely check with one when you get home. If you are prone to vaginal **yeast infections** or thrush, take an over-the-counter medication along with you, as treatments may not be readily available elsewhere.

Sanitary napkins and tampons are sometimes hard to find overseas; your preferred brands may not be available, so it is advisable to bring your own. O.B. brand tampons have minimal packaging and occupy less space in baggage. Refer to *The Handbook for Women Travellers* by Maggie and Gemma Moss or see the women's health guide *Our Bodies, Our Selves,* published by the Boston Women's Health Collective, for more extensive information specific to women's health on the road.

GETTING HELP

Tourist centers are full of **pharmacies,** and many pharmacists speak enough English to understand what you need. Most pharmacies will fill a prescription with a note from a doctor. Few are open 24 hours. In an emergency, head to the nearest major hospital, which is almost certainly open all night and has an in-house pharmacy. Outside the major tourist centers, the going is a bit rougher, although every major town should have at least one pharmacy.

Both India and Nepal suffer from a lack of doctors and medical equipment. In India, there is only one doctor for every 2440 people; in Nepal, only one for every 16,829 people. **Public hospitals** are overcrowded, short on staff and supplies, and rarely have English-speaking staff. In many places in India, "hospitals" function essentially as hospices—homes for the dying. In cases of serious medical problems most foreign visitors to India go to more expensive **private hospitals.** Although these are mainly located in the big cities, where they are found elsewhere they are usually known as "nursing homes." The best are often run by medical schools or Christian missionary organizations. Small private **clinics,** usually operated by a single physician, are also widely available. In Kathmandu, a number of tourist-oriented clinics offer care up to western standards. For serious medical problems, however, those who can afford it have themselves evacuated to better facilities in Bangkok, Singapore, or Europe.

Another suggestion is to contact your **diplomatic mission** upon arrival and inquire as to their suggested **list of doctors.** Carry these names around with other medical documents. To be admitted to many hospitals or nursing homes one must have a doctor who will take your case. If a **blood transfusion** is necessary, inquire as to whether someone from your diplomatic mission can donate blood, or whether family members at home can send blood by air. Also ask whether your diplomatic mission can help arrange emergency evacuation.

Travel insurance (such as that offered with the ISIC and ITIC cards) is enough to cover most **medical expenses** in India or Nepal. Even for long-term stays and major surgery at top hospitals, costs are exponentially lower than what they would be in developed countries. Nevertheless, it is a good idea to carry a credit card for immediate payment. Westerners do not have good reputations for paying their bills fairly and squarely, and many hospitals are hesitant to trust them with outstanding payments.

■ Insurance

Insurance is like contraception—you only really want it when it's too late. Beware of buying unnecessary travel coverage. Your regular policies may well extend while you're away. **Medical insurance** often covers costs incurred abroad; check with your provider. U.S. Medicare's foreign travel coverage is valid only in Canada and Mexico. Canadians are protected by their home province's health insurance plan for up to 90 days after leaving the country; check with the provincial Ministry of Health or Health Plan Headquarters for details. Australia has Reciprocal Health Care Agreements (RHCAs) with several countries; when traveling in these nations Australians are entitled to many of the services that they would receive at home. The Commonwealth Department of Human Services and Health can provide more information. **Homeowners' insurance** often covers theft during travel, especially for loss of travel documents (passport, plane ticket, railpass, etc.) up to US$500.

Among the most convenient forms of insurance, **ISIC** and **ITIC** provide US$3000 worth of accident and illness insurance and US$100 per day up to 60 days of hospitalization. They also offer up to US$1000 for accidental death or dismemberment, and up to US$25,000 for emergency evacuation due to an illness. Just by buying the card, you're covered in these important ways. The cards also give access to a helpful toll-free Traveler's Assistance hotline (tel. 1 (713) 267 2525) whose multilingual staff can provide help in emergencies overseas. To supplement ISIC's insurance, **Council** (see p. 43) offers the inexpensive Trip-Safe plan with options covering medical treatment and hospitalization, accidents, baggage loss, and charter flights missed due to illness; they and **STA** also offer more comprehensive and expensive policies. **American Express** cardholders receive automatic car rental and travel accident insurance on flight purchases made with the card. Inquire through customer service (tel. 1 (800) 528 4800).

Remember that insurance companies usually require a copy of the police report for thefts, or evidence of having paid medical expenses (doctor's statements, receipts) before they will honor a claim and may have time limits on filing for reimbursement. Always carry policy numbers and proof of insurance. Check with each insurance carrier for specific restrictions.

Access America, 6600 West Broad St., PO Box 11188, Richmond, VA 23230 (tel. 1 (800) 284 8300; fax 1 (804) 673 1491). Covers trip cancellation/interruption, on-

the-spot hospital admittance costs, emergency medical evacuation, sickness, and baggage loss. 24-hr. hotline.

The Berkley Group/Carefree Travel Insurance, 100 Garden City Plaza, P.O. Box 9366, Garden City, NY 11530-9366 (tel. 1 (800) 323 3149, 1 (516) 294 0220; fax 1 (516) 294 1096). Offers two comprehensive packages including coverage for trip cancellation/interruption/delay, accident and sickness, medical, baggage loss, bag delay, accidental death and dismemberment, and travel supplier insolvency. Trip cancellation/interruption may be purchased separately at a rate of US$5.50 per US$100 of coverage. 24-hr. worldwide emergency assistance hotline.

Columbus Travel Insurance Services Ltd., 17 Devonshire Sq., London EC2M 4SQ (tel. 44 (171) 436 4451) offers two Globetrotter packages, one standard, one super. Rates begin at £15 for five days of standard coverage all the way up to £299 for a full year of super coverage. They also offer special insurance for backpackers—you don't have to insure your luggage if you don't really have any.

Cover More, Private Bank, 913 North Sydney, Australia 2059 (tel. 61 (2) 202 8000). Cover More offers competitive rates on medical, ticket cancellation, additional expenses, belongings, and personal liability insurance. There's also a special hijacking allowance —how comforting. The same package is offered to business travelers although the costs and rewards are a little higher.

Endsleigh, 97-107 Southhampton Row, London WC1B 4A6 (tel. 44 (171) 436 4451), offers two comprehensive world travelers insurance packages. The differences between the two involve price and coverage but both are a good deal.

Globalcare Travel Insurance, 220 Broadway, Lynnfield, MA 01940 (tel. 1 (800) 821 2488; fax 1 (617) 592 7720); e-mail global@nebc.mv.com; http://nebc.mv.com/globalcare). Complete medical, legal, emergency, and travel-related services. On-the-spot payments and special student programs, including benefits for trip cancellation and interruption. GTI waives pre-existing medical conditions with their Globalcare Economy Plan for cruise and travel, and provides coverage for the bankruptcy or default of cruiselines, airlines, or tour operators.

Travel Assistance International, by Worldwide Assistance Services, Inc., 1133 15th St. NW, Suite 400, Washington, D.C. 20005-2710 (tel. 1 (800) 821 2828, 1 (202) 828 5894; fax 1 (202) 828 5896); e-mail wassist@aol.com). TAI provides its members with a 24-hr. free hotline for travel emergencies and referrals. Their Per-Trip (starting at US$52) and Frequent Traveler (starting at US$226) plans include medical, travel, and financial insurance, translation, and lost document/item assistance.

Travel Guard International, 1145 Clark St., Stevens Point, WI 54481 (tel. 1 (800) 826 1300, 1 (715) 345 0505; fax 1 (715) 345 0525). Comprehensive insurance programs starting at US$44. Programs cover trip cancellation and interruption, bankruptcy and financial default, lost luggage, medical coverage abroad, emergency assistance, accidental death. 24-hr. hotline.

Travel Insured International, Inc., 52-S Oakland Ave., P.O. Box 280568, East Hartford, CT 06128-0568 (tel. 1 (800) 243 3174; fax 1 (203) 528 8005). Insurance against accident, baggage loss, sickness, trip cancellation and interruption, travel delay, and default. Covers emergency medical evacuation and automatic flight insurance.

Wallach and Company, Inc., 107 West Federal St., P.O. Box 480, Middleburg, VA 20118-0480 (tel. 1 (800) 237 6615; fax 1 (540) 687 3172) or e-mail wallach.r@mediasoft.net). Comprehensive medical insurance including evacuation and repatriation of remains and direct payment of claims to providers of services. Other optional coverages available. 24-hr. toll-free international assistance.

■ Alternatives to Tourism

Opportunities for work, study, or other activities conducive to personal growth abound in India and Nepal. Many foreigners go to teach English, to study Indian and Nepalese languages, or to volunteer at health clinics and rural development projects. Foreign tourists often get tired of the routine of zipping from place to place and find that what they'd really like is to settle down and get to know one city or village more intimately. What follows is a list of organized study and work programs and resources for finding out more information. However, don't stop here. India and Nepal are good places to go and see what happens. A surprising number of alternatives can be arranged informally in India and Nepal. Foreigners, who are usually rich compared to Indians and Nepalis, have an advantage because the cost of living is so low. If you're willing to work for room and board, you will find many possibilities open to you. We list such out-of-the-way opportunities in the specific country sections when we can, but the best advice is to look around and ask around—other foreigners are particularly helpful.

STUDY

Foreign study programs vary tremendously in expense, academic quality, living conditions, degree of contact with local students, and exposure to the local culture and language. Most American undergraduates enroll in programs sponsored by U.S. universities, and many colleges give academic information about study abroad programs. Local libraries and bookstores are also helpful sources for current information on study abroad. The Internet has a study abroad website at **http://www.study-abroad.com/liteimage.html.**

Association of Commonwealth Universities, John Foster House, 36 Gordon Square, London WC1H 0PF (tel. 44 (171) 387 8572; fax 387 2655). Administers scholarship programs such as the British Marshall Scholarships and publishes information about Commonwealth universities. A good place to look for information about study in India as they have a big library and a lot of contacts.

College Consortium for International Studies, 2000 P St., NW, Suite 503, Washington, D.C. 20036 (tel. 1 (800) 453 6956, 1 (202) 223 0330). Programs in Delhi, Bangalore, and Madras.

Cornell University, 474 Uris Hall, Ithica, NY 14853 7601 (tel. 1 (607) 255 6224). Has a program in Kirtipur, Nepal.

Council sponsors over 40 study abroad programs throughout the world. Contact them for more information (see p. 43).

Friends World Program, 239 Montauk Highway, Southampton, NY 11968 (tel. 1 (516) 287 8466). Has a programs in Bangalore.

International Schools Services, Educational Staffing Program, 15 Roszel Road, P.O. Box 5910, Princeton, NJ 08543 (tel. 1 (609) 452 0990; fax 452 2690; e-mail: edustaffing%ISS@mcimail.com). Recruits teachers and administrators for the Lincoln School in Kathmandu in addition to its hundreds of schools in Africa, Asia, Central and South America, Europe, and the Middle East. All instruction in English. Applicants must have a bachelor's degree and 2 years of relevant experience. Nonrefundable US$75 application processing fee.

Naropa Institute, 2130 Arapahoe Ave., Boulder, CO 80302 (tel. 1 (303) 444 0202). Has a program in Kathmandu.

Partnership for Service Learning, 815 Second Ave., Suite 315, New York, NY 10017 (tel. 1 (212) 986 0989, offers two programs—an intersession or a full semester including intersession—that combine volunteer social work with intensive study of language and culture. The cost of the intersession program is US$3600 (airfare included) and the semester-long program is US$7500 (including airfare and intersession). Time is spent in Calcutta (in hotels during intersession, homestays during the semester), with trips to Agra and Delhi.

Peterson's, P.O. Box 2123, Princeton, NJ 08543-2123, (tel. 1 (800) 338 3282; fax 1 (609) 243 9150; http://www.petersons.com) publishes *Peterson's Study Abroad,* a guide listing many foreign and domestic study programs for undergraduates interested in foreign study. Cross-indexed by subject, duration and cost, it lists many programs in India and several in Nepal. (US$27).

Pitzer College, External Studies, 1050 N. Mills Ave., Claremont, CA 91711-6110 (tel. 1 (909) 621 8104). Has a program in Kathmandu.

School for International Training, College Semester Abroad Admissions. Kipling Rd., P.O. Box 676. Brattleboro, VT 05302. (tel. 1 (800) 336 1616, 1 (802) 258 3279). Offers semester long programs during which you travel through Delhi and Udaipur in India and Kathmandu and surrounding villages in Nepal that include a homestay, language and cultural instruction, classes in history, politics, arts and humanities and field study opportunities. The cost of the India program is US$8600, including airfare, room and board, and the Nepal program costs US$9300. Financial aid is available and U.S. financial aid is transferable. Many U.S. colleges will transfer credit for semester work done abroad.

University of Wisconsin-Madison, 261 Bascom Hall, Madison, WI 53706 (tel. (1 608) 262 2851). Has programs in Kathmandu and Varanasi.

World College Institute of New College of California, 25 14th St., San Francisco, CA 94103 (tel. (1 415) 431 2491). Has a program in Kathmandu.

WORK

Working in another country can allow you much more intimate contact with the people and their language and culture. Work visas for India and Nepal are seldom granted to foreigners, but volunteering is always possible on a tourist visa.

Paid Work

There's no better way to submerge yourself in a foreign culture than to become part of its economy. The good news is that it's easy to find a temporary job in Indian and Nepal; native speakers of English often find that their skills are in high demand. The bad news is that unless you have connections, it will rarely be lucrative or glamorous, and it is very difficult to get permission to work at all (both India and Nepal are exporters of labor, with many going to earn a living in the Middle East).

Many books exist which list work-abroad opportunities. Note especially the excellent guides put out by **Vacation Work.** In order to avoid scams from fraudulent employment agencies which demand large fees and provide no results, educate yourself using publications from the following sources.

Council publishes *Work, Study, Travel Abroad: The Whole World Handbook,* which covers specific programs on all continents. Includes both summer and long-term work abroad. Published by St. Martin's Press (US$14). Also offers *The High School Student's Guide to Study, Travel and Adventure Abroad* (US$14). Write to Council, Marketing Services Dept., 205 E. 42nd St., New York, NY 10017 5706 (tel. (1 888) COUNCIL; fax (1 212) 822 2699; e-mail books@ciee.org; http://www.ciee.org).

Office of Overseas Schools, A/OS Room 245, SA-29, Dept. of State, Washington, D.C. 20522-2902 (tel. (1 703) 875 7800). Teaching jobs abroad.

Transitions Abroad Publishing, Inc., 18 Hulst Rd., P.O. Box 1300, Amherst, MA 01004-1300 (tel. (1 800) 293 0373; fax (1 413) 256 0373; e-mail tra-broad@aol.com). Publishes a bimonthly magazine listing all kinds of opportunities and printed resources for those seeking to study, work, or travel abroad. They also publish *The Alternative Travel Directory,* an exhaustive listing of information for the "active international traveler." For subscriptions (USA US$20 for 6 issues, Canada US$26, other countries US$38), contact them at *Transitions Abroad,* Dept. TRA, Box 3000, Denville, NJ 07834.

Vacation Work Publications, 9 Park End St., Oxford OX1 1HJ (tel. 44 (1865) 241978; fax 790885). Publishes a variety of guides and directories with job listings and information for the working traveler. Opportunities for summer or full-time work in countries all over the world. Write for a catalogue.

Volunteering

Many travelers to India and Nepal end up wanting to repay the country they're visiting and alleviate its poverty. Volunteer work is a good way to examine your conscience and help out the country while learning more about it too. The cost of living in India and Nepal is low enough that volunteering is not a great financial setback. It is often possible to receive room and board in exchange for your efforts.

Australian Volunteers Abroad: Overseas Service Bureau Program, PO Box 350, Fitzroy Vic 3065, Australia (tel. 61 (3) 9279 1788); fax 9416 1619).

Council organizes Council International Volunteer Projects, 205 E. 42nd St., New York, NY 10017 (tel. 1 (888) COUNCIL; fax 1 (212) 822 2699: http://www.ciee.org). From Europe, write to Council, 28A Poland St., Oxford Circus, London W1V 3DD (tel. 44 (171) 287 3337 from the U.K., 44 (171) 437 7767 from the rest of the world). Participants must be at least 18 years of age and must submit a special application. US$195 placement fee, plus a fee of US$250-300 to the host organization in India. You are responsible for travel, insurance and immunization costs. They have four three- to four-week programs in Jan., Feb., April, and Oct. and the application deadline is two months prior to the start of the program. The number to call for information on the India program is 1 (212) 822 2695; e-mail ivp-brochure@ciee.org. This contact information applies to U.S. residents only—others should e-mail the Coordinating Committee of International Voluntary Service at UNESCO in Paris at ccivs@sytek.fr. For more information on Council, see p. 43.

Missionaries of Charity, International Committee of Co-Workers, 41 Villiers Road, Southal, Middlesex (tel. 44 (181) 574 1892).

Peace Corps, 1990 K St. NW, Washington, D.C. 20526 (tel. 1 (800) 424 8580; fax 1 (202) 606 4469; http://www.peacecorps.gov). Write for their "blue" brochure, which details applicant requirements. Opportunities in a variety of fields (from agriculture to business) in Nepal. Volunteers must be U.S. citizens willing to make a two-year commitment.

Voluntary Service Overseas (VSO), 317 Putney Bridge Rd., London SW15 2PN (tel. 44 (181) 780 2266; fax 780 1326).

SPIRITUAL INTERESTS

The birthplace of several major world religions, South Asia remains a land of serious spirituality. In a recent international poll, 98% of Indians reported that they believe in some form of God, a higher number than in most other countries. It is no wonder that India and Nepal attract many travelers wishing to throw off their old assumptions and try out other approaches to life's questions. Aside from the mainstream traditions in India and Nepal (see **India: Religion,** p. 96, and **Nepal: Religion,** p. 666), certain religious communities are particularly open to initiates from abroad.

For **Hinduism,** these mostly take the form of ashrams (retreats), many of which are under the leadership of a modern-day guru—those who have attracted many foreign devotees are often referred to as "export gurus." Some of the most famous ashrams in India include that of the late Sri Aurobindo in Pondicherry, and the Osho Commune in Pune, dedicated to the memory of Bhagwan Shree Rajneesh. Rishikesh is a major center for gurus and students of yoga. There are literally hundreds of ashrams across India, with bigger and smaller followings. If you have trouble finding a guru to your liking, don't hesitate to talk to other travelers, ask the teacher at the outset what his philosophy is, or simply try a few out. However, what any expert in the world will tell you is that it doesn't matter how many teachers you jump around to, but how much you practice on your own time that counts. Self-fulfillment is a big thing to promise, and while some spiritualists tend to liberally brag about the virtues of their teachings, it really comes down to personal effort. Those who stay in an ashram are normally required to avoid meat and smelly food as well as alcohol, tobacco, *pan* (betel), or any drugs. Ashram-dwellers must also usually stay clean and quiet.

Since the 1959 Chinese crackdown in Tibet, India and Nepal have also become the most accessible places in the world to study **Tibetan Buddhism.** The most popular place is Dharamsala in India, the home of the Dalai Lama and the Tibetan government-in-exile. Nepal's foremost Tibetan Buddhist center is located at Boudha outside of Kathmandu. Unlike Tibetan *lamas* (monks), Western students of Tibetan Buddhism do not usually live in monasteries, although they are expected to live austerely. Public lectures (sometimes in English) and meditation courses are offered at the major Tibetan Buddhist centers. The most thoroughly connected source for information on Tibet is the International Campaign for Tibet, based in Washington, D.C., which provides information about Tibetan organizations in India, Nepal, and worldwide in the *International Tibet Resources Directory* (US$7). Contact the International Campaign for Tibet, 1735 Eye St. NW, Suite 615, Washington, D.C. 20006 (tel. 1 (202) 785-1515; fax 785-4343).

■ Specific Concerns

TRAVELING ALONE

There are many benefits to traveling alone, among them greater independence and challenge. As a lone traveler, you have all the more incentive to meet and interact with natives, and without the distraction of company you can write a great travel log, in the grand tradition of Fa-Hsien, Alberuni, or Mark Twain. On the other hand, you may also be a more visible target for robbery and harassment. Lone travelers need to be well-organized and look confident at all times. Try not to stand out as a tourist. Try to maintain regular contact with someone at home who knows your itinerary.

Some travelers like to meet up with other foreigners on the road. This not only provides much-longed-for company, but a way to share news of interesting places and events. India and Nepal are magical in the bonds they can create between travelers. Yet be careful not to let a comfortable "travelers' scene" insulate you from local life.

A Foxy Old Woman's Guide to Traveling Alone by Jay Ben-Lesser. Encompasses practically every specific concern, offering anecdotes and tips for anyone interested in solitary adventure. No experience necessary. Crossing Press, US$11.

WOMEN TRAVELERS

Due to sheer biological differences, women exploring on their own face additional safety concerns, but India and Nepal are not particularly difficult countries for women travelers. A great amount of respect is given to women in South Asian culture. On the other hand, South Asian women are seldom given much independence, and are often seen as people to be looked after. Women traveling alone will be seen as curiosities but also as objects of pity, since they have no one to take care of them. Don't be scared when locals ask if you are married—this is almost always an expression of concern, not a come-on. Foreign women might notice that the culture of India or Nepal does not allow them the same freedom it would allow a foreign male traveler; at ticket counters, hotel reception desks, and shops, the (mostly male) staff will be puzzled at the fact that women don't have a man with them to arrange everything. This can make it difficult to communicate. Women traveling *with* men often have difficulties as well, for they will seldom get to meet people; any man their companion meets might address himself only to him, ignoring the woman completely.

Incidents of **sexual harassment** are common but seldom serious. Especially in northern India, single women may be subject to verbal advances or groping. This is partly due to stereotypes from American television and movies that have made some Indians and Nepalis believe all white women are loose. The slightest bit of resistance usually stops such abuse, since most harassers have encountered few foreign women before and are unsure of themselves. On the other hand, sometimes harassment results when women are seen to be flaunting their independence, which is associated with promiscuity. Women traveling alone should always stay inconspicuous, and should not set out to overturn the patriarchal social order. If need be, turn to an older woman for help in an uncomfortable situation; her stern rebukes will usually be enough to embarrass the most persistent jerks. Don't hesitate to get the attention of **passersby** if you are being harassed. The crowds are your biggest asset in India and Nepal. People have a strong sense of public morality and will not let anyone hurt someone else in plain view. On the other hand, small-town policemen are sometimes not terribly enlightened about women. They, like other men, may assume that a women traveling alone is looking for sex. Don't hesitate to call the police in an emergency, but don't place all your trust in them, particularly in untouristed areas.

The less you look like a tourist, the better off you'll be. Look as if you know where you're going (even when you don't) and **approach women** (or couples) if you need help or directions. **Dress conservatively, covering legs and shoulders, and always wear a bra.** Wearing a *salwar kameez,* Indian baggy pants with a loose long-sleeved shirt, can help as well.

Always trust your instincts: if you'd feel better somewhere else, move on. Invest in secure accommodations, particularly family-run guest houses with doors that lock from the inside. Stay in central locations and avoid late-night walks. In major cities of India, the **YWCAs** sometimes accept only female guests or married couples. **Hitching** is never safe for solo women, or even for two or more women traveling together. On trains, try to get into a **ladies' compartment.** On buses, you should be allowed to sit near the front.

All this advice varies from region to region. South India is said to be safer for women than the north. Bihar and eastern Uttar Pradesh, where law and order are thin, are some of the most dangerous areas; there have even been cases of foreign women being raped here. The Himalayan regions however, from Himachal Pradesh to Nepal to Sikkim, are among the safest areas; attitudes toward women are much more liberated among many mountain ethnic groups. And of course in the cosmopolitan, Westernized circles in major cities (especially in Bombay) women can usually expect equal treatment.

A **Model Mugging** course will not only prepare you for a potential mugging, but will also raise your level of awareness of your surroundings as well as your confidence (see **Safety and Security,** p. 13). Women also face additional health concerns when traveling (see **Health,** p. 17). All of these warnings and suggestions should not discourage women from traveling alone. Don't take unnecessary risks, but don't lose your spirit of adventure either, and don't think you have to avoid all local men.

Handbook For Women Travelers by Maggie and Gemma Moss (UK£9). Encyclopedic and well-written. From Piaktus Books, 5 Windmill St., London W1P 1HF (tel. 44 (171) 631 07 10).

Directory of Women's Media is available from the National Council for Research on Women, 530 Broadway, 10th Floor, New York, NY 10012 (tel. 1 (212) 274 0730; fax 274 0821). The publication lists women's publishers, bookstores, theaters, and news organizations (mail orders, US$30).

A Journey of One's Own, by Thalia Zepatos, (Eighth Mountain Press US$17), The latest thing on the market, interesting and full of good advice, plus a specific and manageable bibliography of books and resources.

Women Travel: Adventures, Advice & Experience by Miranda Davies and Natania Jansz (Penguin, US$13). Info on specific foreign countries plus a decent bibliography and resource index. *More Women Travel,* the sequel, is US$15.

Women Going Places, a women's travel and resource guide emphasizing women-owned enterprises. Geared towards lesbians, but offers advice appropriate for all women. US$14 from Inland Book Company, 1436 W. Randolph St. Chicago, IL 60607 (tel. 1 (800) 243 0138), or order from a local bookstore.

OLDER TRAVELERS

Senior citizens are rarely offered discounts in India or Nepal, which is fine since prices are so low already. Some of the following books and organizations offer tips for older people undertaking journeys to distant places:

Elderhostel, 75 Federal St., 3rd Fl., Boston, MA 02110-1941 (tel. 1 (617) 426 7788; fax 1 (617) 426 8351; http://www.elderhostel.org). For those 55 or over (spouse of any age). Programs lasting one to four weeks at colleges, universities, and other learning centers in over 50 countries on varied subjects.

Pilot Books, 103 Cooper St., Babylon, NY 11702 (tel. 1 (516) 422 2225). Publishes a large number of helpful guides including *The International Health Guide for Senior Citizens* (US$5, postage US$2). Call or write for a complete list of titles.

BISEXUAL, GAY, AND LESBIAN TRAVELERS

Homosexuality is a taboo topic in India and Nepal, and in India, male homosexual sex is illegal. *Hijras* (male eunuchs) form a subculture of prostitutes in the big cites, especially Bombay, but this shady scene is not open to foreigners. Most gays and lesbians in India and Nepal stay closeted. Heterosexual marriage is expected of just about everyone, so occasional sexual encounters are much more common than long-term relationships. However, friends of the same sex commonly hold hands or hug in public, and nothing is seen as sexual about this. In fact, such behavior is much more acceptable than heterosexual public displays of affection.

There are only a handful specifically gay clubs or cruising areas in India and Nepal, although solo male travelers can expect to be propositioned in public places now and then. Gay organizations tend to stay underground. In the United States, Aero Travel, Inc., 4001 N. 9th St., Suite 217, Arlington, VA 22203 (tel. 1 (800) 356 1109, 1 (703) 807 1172), is a travel agency specializing in travel to India *and* travel for gay couples. The following books contain gay and lesbian listings worldwide, although their information on India and Nepal is minimal.

Ferrari Guides, PO Box 37887, Phoenix, AZ 85069 (tel. 1 (602) 863 2408; fax 439 3952; e-mail ferrari@q-net.com). Gay and lesbian travel guides: *Gay Travel A to Z* (US$16), *Men's Travel in Your Pocke*t (US$14), *Women's Travel in Your Pocket* (US$14). Available in bookstores or by mail order. (Postage/handling US$4.50 for the first item, US$1 for each additional item mailed within the U.S.)

Gay's the Word, 66 Marchmont St., London WC1N 1AB (tel. 44 (171) 278 7654). The largest gay and lesbian bookshop in the U.K. Mail order service available. No catalog of listings, but they will provide a list of titles on a given subject. Open Mon.-Sat. 10am-6pm, Thurs. 10am-7pm and Sun. 2-6pm.

Giovanni's Room, 345 S. 12th St., Philadelphia, PA 19107 (tel. 1 (215) 923 2960; fax 923 0813; e-mail gilphilp@netaxs.com). An international feminist, lesbian, and gay bookstore with mail-order service. Carries many of the books listed here.

International Gay Travel Association, Box 4974, Key West, FL 33041 (tel. 1 (800) 448 8550; fax 1 (305) 296 6633; e-mail IGTA@aol.com; http://www.rainbow-mall.com/igta. An organization of over 1100 companies serving gay and lesbian travelers. Call for lists of travel agents, accommodations, and events.

International Lesbian and Gay Association (ILGA), 81 rue Marché-au-Charbon, B-1000 Bruxelles, Belgium (tel./fax 32 (2) 502 2471). Not a travel service. Provides political information, such as homosexuality laws of individual countries.

Spartacus International Gay Guides (US$32.95), published by Bruno Gmunder, Postfach 110729, D-10837 Berlin, Germany (tel. 49 (30) 615 0030; fax 615 9134). Lists bars, restaurants, hotels, and bookstores around the world catering to gays. Also lists hotlines for gays in various countries and homosexuality laws for each country. Available in bookstores and by mail.

DISABLED TRAVELERS

Call ahead to make arrangements with airlines and make sure adequate facilities are available. Most of South Asia is ill-equipped to deal with disabled travelers. Hospitals cannot be relied upon to replace broken braces or prostheses successfully; their orthopedic materials, even in major cities, are faulty at best. Facilities for disabled travelers are generally nonexistent. Public transportation (trains, buses, rickshaws, etc.) is completely inaccessible. While the classier hotels often have elevators (which may not be wheelchair accessible), most budget accommodations don't. Most cities have no sidewalks, let alone ramps, and larger cities are packed with curbs and steps. Many sights require climbing long staircases or hiking.

Call or write to the **World Institute on Disability** at 510 16th St., Suite 100, Oakland, CA 94612 (tel. 1 (510) 763 4100; fax 1 (510) 763 4109) for information on disability rights advocates around the world. Contact the **tourism office** nearest you for more information (see **Information,** p. 1). Another option worth considering is a "custom vacation" from **Flying Wheels Travel Service,** 143 W. Bridge St., Owatonne, MN 55060 (tel. 1 (800) 535 6790; fax 451 1685). They arrange and organize trips for the disabled and you pick the destination. It's a tour or cruise made especially for you and your friends. You can also root around in a number of more general books helpful to travelers with disabilities. The following organizations provide information or publications that might be of assistance.

Mobility International, USA (MIUSA), P.O. Box 10767, Eugene, OR 97440 (tel. 1 (514) 343 1284 voice and TDD; fax 1 (514) 343 6812). International Headquarters, Rue de Manchester 25, Brussels, Belgium, B-1070 (tel. 32 (2) 410 6297; fax 410 6874). Contacts in 30 countries. Information on travel programs, international work camps, accommodations, access guides, and organized tours for those with physical disabilities. Membership US$25 per year, newsletter US$15. Sells the periodically updated and expanded *A World of Options: A Guide to International Educational Exchange, Community Service, and Travel for Persons with Disabilities* (US$14, nonmembers US$16). In addition, MIUSA offers a series of courses that teach strategies helpful for travelers with disabilities. Call for details.

Moss Rehab Hospital Travel Information Service, (tel. 1 (215) 456 9600, TDD 456 9602)). A telephone information resource center on international travel accessibility and other travel-related concerns for those with disabilities.

Twin Peaks Press, PO Box 129, Vancouver, WA 98666 0129 (tel. 1 (360) 694 2462, orders only MC and Visa 1 (800) 637 2256; fax 1 (360) 696 3210). Publishers of *Travel for the Disabled,* which provides travel tips, lists of accessible tourist attractions, and advice on other resources for disabled travelers (US$20). Also publishes *Directory for Travel Agencies of the Disabled* (US$20), *Wheelchair Vagabond* (US$15), and *Directory of Accessible Van Rentals* (US$10). Postage US$3 for first book, US$1.50 for each additional book.

TRAVELERS WITH CHILDREN

Traveling in India or Nepal with children can be a difficult adventure, as even seasoned adults have difficulty adjusting to the transportation and amenities. However, the friendliness Indians and Nepalis show towards children can often help you meet people and can lead to a more interesting trip. If you are traveling with small children, it is particularly crucial to follow the health advice and protect them from sunburn, excessive heat, insect bites, and especially diarrhea, which can be very dangerous for children. Older children should carry some sort of ID in case of an emergency. Arrange a reunion spot in case of separation when sight-seeing.

Children under two generally fly for 10% of the adult airfare on international flights (this does not necessarily include a seat). International fares are usually discounted 25% for children from two to eleven.

The following publications offer tips for adults traveling with children or distractions for the kids themselves. You can also contact the publishers to see if they have other related publications that you might find useful.

Backpacking with Babies and Small Children (US$10). Published by Wilderness Press, 2440 Bancroft Way, Berkeley, CA 94704 (tel. 1 (800) 443 7227, 1 (510) 843 8080; fax 548 1355).

Travel with Children by Maureen Wheeler (US$11.95, postage US$1.50). Published by Lonely Planet Publications, Embarcadero West, 155 Filbert St., #251, Oakland, CA 94607 (tel. 1 (800) 275 8555, 1 (510) 893 8555; fax 893 8563; e-mail info@lonelyplanet.com; http://www.lonelyplanet.com). Also P.O. Box 617, Hawthorn, Victoria 3122, Australia.

TRAVELERS WITH SPECIAL DIETS

India and Nepal are paradise for vegetarians. The staple foods of a budget-minded connoisseur (rice and *dal*) will meet the most stringent vegetarian standards. Those opposed to consuming any animal products, however, should be warned that *ghee* (clarified butter) is widely used Indian cooking, and that cheese often appears in otherwise vegetarian entrees. While **kosher** meals are next to nonexistent in India and Nepal, the Muslim presence makes **halal** food a large part of the cuisine. The *Jewish Travel Guide,* published by Ballantine-Mitchell, Newbury House 890-900, Eastern Ave., Newbury Park, Ilford, Essex IG2 7HH (tel. 44 (181) 599 8866; fax 599 0984), lists synagogues, kosher restaurants, and Jewish institutions in over 80 countries, though it contains minimal information for India and none for Nepal.

■ Pack Light

Pack light. This means you. Your backpack or suitcase may be feather-light when you buy it or drag it out of storage and as buoyant as your enthusiasm all the way to the airport, but as soon as the plane lands it will become a ponderous, hot, uncomfortable nuisance. Before you leave, pack your bag and take it for a walk. Try to convince yourself that you're in Nepal already, sweltering in the high heat and humidity. You're hiking up mountains, diving to grab onto a bus, sprinting for shelter in a monsoon downpour. At the slightest sign of heaviness, curb your vanity and unpack something. As a general rule, pack only what you absolutely need, then take half the clothes and twice the money. A *New York Times* correspondent recommends that you take "no more than you can carry for half a mile at a dead run." This may be extreme, but you get the idea. That said, it is important to remember to pack the stuff you'll need. Leave the mini-skirts and tank tops at home; even shorts are a bad idea unless you'll be spending all of your time in a major city. It is considered disrespectful for women and juvenile for men to wear shorts. Even if you're in the middle of nowhere on a trek, shorts are still a bad idea—you don't want to make it easy for insects and leeches to bite. Picking out what to bring on your voyage, consider the time of year you are going as well as your regional destination. Early morning in a tent in Nepal in February will require very different attire than a beach in Goa on a hot May day.

Comfortable **walking shoes** are essential. This is not the place to cut corners, because your feet are going to take a beating. Blisters, corns, and sharp, shooting pains in your feet will be obvious obstacles to your enjoyment of the trip. Try to break them in before you leave. For heavy-duty trekking, a pair of sturdy lace-up **hiking boots** will help out. A double pair of socks—light, absorbent cotton inside and thick wool outside—will cushion feet and keep them dry. Break in your shoes before you go, but if you do get plagued by blisters, moleskin (sold at camping/sporting goods stores) helps protect the tender area. If you only want one pair of shoes, that evolutionary cross-breed the "sneaker-hiking boot" can serve as well as a hard-core boot for most trekking and may be more comfortable for the rest of your trip's activities. Bring a pair of flip-flops for protection against the foliage and fungi that lurk in some hotel showers.

Don't forget—rain gear is essential. A waterproof jacket and a backpack cover will take care of you and your stuff at a moment's notice, which is often all you'll get. A little more cumbersome, a lightweight poncho will cover your back and pack well and serve as a ground cloth. Gore-Tex, that miracle fabric that's both waterproof and breathable, is helpful if you plan on hiking.

LUGGAGE

Backpack: If you plan to cover most of your itinerary by foot or will be riding on a great deal of buses and trains (and you probably will), the unbeatable baggage is a sturdy backpack with several external compartments. Some convert into a more normal-looking suitcase. In general, **internal-frame** packs are easier to carry and

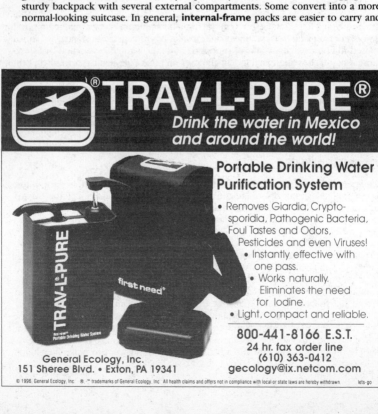

more efficient for general traveling purposes. If you'll be doing extensive camping or hiking, you may want to consider an **external-frame** pack, which offers added support, distributes weight better, and allows for a sleeping bag to be strapped on. External-frame packs have been known to get caught and mangled in baggage conveyors; tie down loose parts to minimize risk. In any case, get a pack with a strong, padded hip belt to transfer weight from your shoulders to your legs. Whichever style you choose, avoid excessively low-end prices—you get what you pay for. Quality packs cost anywhere from US$125 to US$300. Packs with several compartments are best, but beware of ones with many outside zippers or flaps that could make a pickpocket's dream come true. If checking a backpack on a flight, tape down loose straps that can catch in the conveyer belt and rip your bag apart. An empty **lightweight duffel bag** packed inside your luggage will be useful: once abroad you can fill your luggage with purchases and keep your dirty clothes in the duffel.

Light suitcase/large duffel bag: These are OK if you are going to do your exploring in a large and relatively luxurious city. Those striving for a more casual, unobtrusive look should take a large shoulder bag that closes securely.

Daypack or courier bag: A smaller bag, in addition to your pack, is indispensable for plane flights, sight-seeing, a picnic on the beach and keeping some of your valuables on you. Make sure it's big enough to hold lunch, a camera, a water bottle, and this book. Get one with secure zippers and closures.

Moneybelt or neck pouch: Guard your money, passport, and other important articles in either one of these, and keep it with you *at all times*. The best combination of convenience and invulnerability is the nylon, zippered pouch with belt that should sit *inside* the waist of your pants or skirt (though not too inconveniently). Neck pouches should be worn under at least one layer of clothing. Money belts and neck pouches are available at any good camping store. **Avoid the oh-so-popular "fanny pack":** it's an invitation to thieves, even worn in front. For more information, see **Safety and Security** (p. 13).

PACKING LIST

The following is not an exhaustive list, but you'll find these miscellaneous items valuable.

small umbrella	Ziploc bags (for damp clothes, soap, food, pens)
petite alarm clock	waterproof matches
sun hat	moleskin (for blisters)
needle and thread	safety pins
good sunglasses	maps
pocketknife	notebook and pens
plastic water bottle	pocket phrasebook
small flashlight	string (makeshift clothesline and lashing material)
towel	padlock
whistle	rubber bands
cold-water soap	earplugs
tweezers	insect repellent (with DEET)
bungee cord	squash ball (to use as a sink plug for washing clothes)
sunscreen	garbage bags
toilet paper	clothespins
compass	electrical tape (for patching tears)

Some items are not always available on the road:

deodorant	tampons
condoms	razors

ESSENTIALS

Most toiletries are available in cities, so don't panic if you happen to forget your toothbrush. Don't forget deodorant, though, since something comparable may be hard to come by. Keep in mind that fragrant deodorants, shampoos, and soaps attract insects and other unwelcome forest creatures with reckless abandon. Finding a non-scented shampoo, etc., is your best bet. For cold-water soap, all-natural **Dr. Bronner's Castile Soap,** sold at camping and health food stores, is usable for anything from washing clothes, bathing, and shampooing to brushing your teeth, (although it tastes disgusting). Rare, expensive, or of questionable quality in India and Nepal are contraceptives, contact-lens fluid, and tampons. If you are heterosexual and sexually active, you will need to worry about contraception. Women on the Pill should bring enough to allow for possible loss or extended stays, and should bring a prescription, since forms of the Pill vary a good deal. If you use a diaphragm, be sure that you have a supply of contraceptive jelly as well. Carry your own towel and sheets for very cheap hotels. Toilet paper is not found in most Indian and Nepali bathrooms, but it is widely available in pharmacies, so there's no need to pack it. To be safe, buy anything you forgot to bring as soon as you arrive, so you don't find yourself in a small village at a loss for insect repellent (see **Trekking,** p. 54).

■ Electricity

In India and Nepal electricity is 220V AC, enough to fry any North American machine. Plugs are European round-pin style of various sizes. British, Irish, and Australian plugs will need adaptors, and American and Canadian plugs will require a transformer, too. You might want to consider a circuit breaker (like a power strip) or a voltage stabilizer, especially if you're using something valuable and sensitive, like a laptop computer. Power cuts and surges are quite common, so don't count on elec-

tricity, especially in rural areas. Bring a flashlight, and leave the hair dryer and electric razor at home.

GETTING THERE

The first challenge to the budget traveler is getting there. Most foreign travelers fly into India or Nepal (or at least into the general area), since getting into and through some of the countries surrounding India and Nepal is difficult.

■ By Plane

The airline industry attempts to squeeze every dollar from customers; finding a cheap airfare in their deliberately mysterious and confusing jungle will be easier if you understand the airlines' systems better than most people do. Call every toll-free number and don't be afraid to ask about discounts. Have several knowledgeable **travel agents** guide you; better yet, have an agent who specializes in the region(s) you will be traveling to guide you. An agent whose clients fly mostly to Bermuda is most likely not the best person to hunt down a bargain flight to Bombay. Travel agents may not want to spend time finding the cheapest fares (for which they receive the lowest commissions), but if you travel often, you should definitely find an agent who will cater to you and your needs, tracking down deals in exchange for your frequent business. **TravelHUB** (http://www.travelhub.com) will help you search for travel agencies on the web.

Students and people under 26 ("youth") with proper identification qualify for reduced airfares. These are rarely available from airlines or travel agents, but instead from student travel agencies like **Let's Go Travel, STA, Travel CUTS, USTN,** and **Council Travel**. These agencies negotiate special reduced-rate bulk purchases with the airlines, then resell them to the youth market. Return-date change fees also tend to be low (around US$25 per segment through Council or Let's Go Travel). Most flights are on major airlines, though in peak season some agencies may sell seats on less reliable chartered aircraft. Student travel agencies can also help non-students and people over 26, but probably won't be able to get the same low fares.

Seniors can also get great deals; many airlines offer senior traveler clubs or airline passes and discounts for their companions as well. Sunday newspapers often have travel sections that list bargain fares from the local airport. Australians should consult the Saturday travel section of the *Sydney Morning Herald*, as well as the ethnic press, where special deals may be advertised. *The Airline Passenger's Guerrilla Handbook* (US$15; last published in 1990) is a more renegade resource. On the web, try **Air Traveler's Handbook** (http://www.cis.ohio-state.edu/hypertext/faq/ usenet/travel/air/handbook/top.html), for thorough information on air travel.

Airfares to India and Nepal peak in December and January. Traveling from hubs such as New York, Los Angeles, London, or Sydney will win more competitive fare than from smaller cities. Return-date flexibility is usually not an option for the budget traveler; traveling with an "open return" ticket can be pricier than fixing a return date and paying to change it. Whenever flying internationally, pick up your ticket well in advance of the departure date, have the flight confirmed within 72 hours of departure, and arrive at the airport at least three hours before your flight.

There are four major international airport in India: Anna International Airport in Madras (see p. 447), Dum Dum Airport in Calcutta (see p. 370), Indira Gandhi International Airport in Delhi (see p. 121), and Sahar International Airport in Bombay (see p. 585). Tribhuvan International Airport (see p. 677) in Kathmandu serves Nepal. Many airlines offer service into India, and Royal Nepal Airlines, Aeroflot, Biman Bangladesh Airlines, Burma Airways Corporation, Civil Aviation Administration of China, Dragon Air, Druk Airlines, Indian Airlines, Lufthansa, Pakistan International Airlines, Singapore Airlines and Thai International all offer flights into Nepal. Flights takes

about nine hours from London, or 17 hours from the east coast of the United States, with a layover in Europe and possibly in the Middle East.

If you only plan to stay in India for a little while (but you should really stay longer!), consider getting a "Round the World" ticket. These tickets are combos that usually offer stops in cities like Delhi or Bombay, as well as other major cities in South and Southeast Asia. These tickets can be cheap and flexible, so shop around.

COMMERCIAL AIRLINES

The commercial airlines' lowest regular offer is the **APEX** (Advance Purchase Excursion Fare); specials advertised in newspapers may be cheaper, but have more restrictions and fewer available seats. APEX fares provide you with confirmed reservations and allow "open-jaw" tickets (landing in and returning from different cities). Generally, reservations must be made seven to 21 days in advance, with seven- to 14-day minimum and up to 90-day maximum stay limits, and hefty cancellation and change penalties. Book APEX fares well ahead for flights in peak season.

Even if you pay an airline's lowest published fare, you may waste hundreds of dollars. For the adventurous or the bargain-hungry, there are other, perhaps more inconvenient or time-consuming options, but before shopping around it is a good idea to find out the average commercial price in order to measure just how great a "bargain" you are being offered. Consult the Official Airline Guide, 2000 Clearwater Dr., Oakbrook, IL 60521 (tel. 1 (800) 323 3537; available in many libraries and that's a good thing—it costs US$397). The OAG is published monthly and lists every flight and connection on nearly every carrier.

BUDGET TRAVEL AGENCIES

Fortunately, you can take advantage of the numerous **discount travel agencies.** These agencies sell regular airline tickets at wholesale prices. Even though the prices are low, your seat is guaranteed and you can usually cancel your ticket and still receive a fairly sizeable refund. Student-oriented travel agencies such as Council Travel, STA Travel, and Travel CUTS sometimes have special deals that regular travel agents can't offer. Even if they don't, though, their ticket prices are usually among the lowest to be found. A survey of travel agents can be found on the World Wide Web at http://www.cc.gatech.edu/grads.k.prince.kohli, on every soc.culture site relevant to India, or can be requested by sending mail to pkohli@prism.gatech.edu with the subject listed as "travel survey." For more information on discount travel agencies, scan the weekend travel section of major newspapers (especially *The New York Times*). Some discount travel organizations don't deal with the cheapest airlines, such as Kuwait Air and AeroFlot. It's a good idea to get a travel agent who specializes in flights to South Asia and deals with many South Asian clients.

Council Travel (http://www.ciee.org/cts/ctshome.htm), the travel division of Council, is a full-service travel agency specializing in youth and budget travel. Council offers railpasses, discount airfares, hosteling cards, guidebooks, budget tours, travel gear, and student (ISIC), youth (GO25), and teacher (ITIC) identity cards. U.S. offices include: Emory Village, 1561 N. Decatur Rd., **Atlanta,** GA 30307 (tel. 1 (404) 377 9997); 2000 Guadalupe, **Austin,** TX 78705 (tel. 1 (512) 472 4931); 273 Newbury St., **Boston,** MA 02116 (tel. 1 (617) 266 1926); 1138 13th St., **Boulder,** CO 80302 (tel. 1 (303) 447 8101); 1153 N. Dearborn, **Chicago,** IL 60610 (tel. 1 (312) 951 0585); 10904 Lindbrook Dr., **Los Angeles,** CA 90024 (tel. 1 (310) 208 3551); 1501 University Ave. SE, **Minneapolis,** MN 55414 (tel. 1 (612) 379 2323); 205 E. 42nd St., **New York,** NY 10017 (tel. 1 (212) 822 2700); 953 Garnet Ave., **San Diego,** CA 92109 (tel. 1 (619) 270 6401); 530 Bush St., **San Francisco,** CA 94108 (tel. 1 (415) 421 3473); 4311½ University Way, **Seattle,** WA 98105 (tel. 1 (206) 632 2448); 3300 M St. NW, **Washington, D.C.** 20007 (tel. 1 (202) 337 6464). **For U.S. cities not listed,** call 1 (800) 2COUNCIL. Also 28A Poland St. (Oxford Circus), **London,** W1V 3DB (tel. 44 (171) 437 7767).

ESSENTIALS

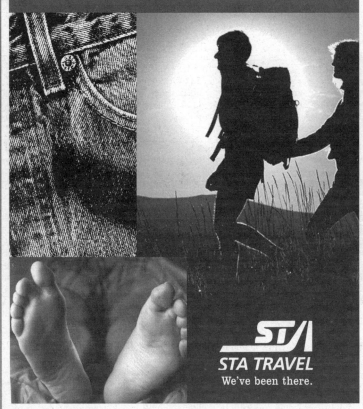

STA Travel, 6560 North Scottsdale Rd. #F100, Scottsdale, AZ 85253 (tel. 1 (800) 777 0112 anywhere in the U.S.). A student and youth travel organization with over 100 offices around the world and 14 U.S. locations offering discount airfares (for travelers under 26 and full-time students under 32), railpasses, accommodations, tours, insurance, and ISICs. In the U.S.: 297 Newbury St., **Boston,** MA 02115 (tel. 1 (617) 266 6014); 429 S. Dearborn St., **Chicago,** IL 60605 (tel. 1 (312) 786 9050); 7202 Melrose Ave., **Los Angeles,** CA 90046 (tel. 1 (213) 934 8722); 10 Downing St., **New York,** NY 10014 (tel. 1 (212) 477 7166); 3730 Walnut St. **Philadelphia,** PA 19104 (tel. 1 (215) 382 2928); 51 Grant Ave., **San Francisco,** CA 94108 (tel. 1 (415) 391 8407); 4341 University Way NE, **Seattle,** WA 98105 (tel. 1 (206) 633 5000); 2401 Pennsylvania Ave., Suite G, **Washington, D.C.** 20037 (tel. 1 (202) 887 0912). In the U.K.: Priory House, 6 Wrights Ln., **London** W8 6TA (tel. 44 (171) 938 4711). In New Zealand: 10 High St., **Auckland** (tel. 64 (9) 309 9723). In Australia: 224 Faraday St., Carlton, **Melbourne** VIC 3050 (tel. 61 (3) 347 6911).

Let's Go Travel, Harvard Student Agencies, 67 Mt. Auburn St., Cambridge, MA 02138 1 (800) 5LETSGO, 1 (617) 495 9649). Let's Go offers railpasses, HI-AYH memberships, ISICs, International Teacher ID cards, GO 25 cards, guidebooks (including all *Let's Go* titles), maps, bargain flights, and a complete line of budget travel gear. All items available by mail; call or write for a catalog (or see catalog in center of this publication).

International Student Exchange Flights (ISE), 5010 East Shea Blvd., #A104, Scottsdale, AZ 85254 (tel. 1 (602) 951 1177). Offers budget student flights to Europe and Asia, Eurail, HI-AYH memberships, the International Student Exchange Identity Card, and travel guides. Free catalog.

Travel Management International (TMI), Grand Ave., Minneapolis, MN 55409 (tel. 1 (800) 245 3672). Travel service specializing in customized international trip planning; offers student fares and railpasses.

Travel CUTS (Canadian University Travel Services, Ltd.), 187 College St., Toronto, Ontario M5T 1P7 (tel. 1 (416) 798CUTS; fax 1 (416) 979 8167). Offices across Canada. Also, in the U.K., 295-A Regent St., London W1R 7YA (tel. 44 (171) 637 3161). Discounted European, South Pacific, and domestic flights; ISIC, GO 25, and HI hostel cards; and discount travel passes. Special fares with valid ISIC or FIYTO cards. Offers free *Student Traveller* magazine, and info on Student Work Abroad Program (SWAP).

Unitravel, 1177 North Warson Rd., St. Louis, MO 63132 (tel. 1 (800) 325 2222; fax 1 (314) 569 2503). Offers discounted airfares on major airlines worldwide.

Campus Travel, 52 Grosvenor Gardens, London W1. Campus is a large supplier of student travel products in the U.K., with 37 branches throughout the country. Arranges for student cards, flights, trains, boats, and a range of related products and services. In London, (tel. 44 (171) 730 8111). In Manchester (tel. 44 (161) 273 1721). In Scotland (tel. 44 (131) 668 33 03).

CTS Travel, 220 Kensington High St., London W8 (tel. 44 (171) 937 3388). Specializes in student/youth travel and discount flights. Open Mon.-Fri. 9:30am-6pm, Sat. 10am-5pm. Also at 44 Goodge St., London W1.

TICKET CONSOLIDATORS

Ticket consolidators resell unsold tickets on commercial and charter airlines at unpublished fares. Consolidator flights are the best deals if you are traveling on short notice (you bypass advance purchase requirements, since you aren't tangled in airline bureaucracy), on a high-priced trip, to an offbeat destination, or in the peak season, when published fares are jacked way up. There is rarely a maximum age or stay limit, but unlike tickets bought through an airline, you won't be able to use your tickets on another flight if you miss yours, and you will have to go back to the consolidator to get a refund, rather than the airline. Keep in mind that these tickets are often for coach seats on connecting (not direct) flights, and that frequent-flyer miles may not be credited. Decide what you can and can't live with(out) before shopping.

Consolidators come in three varieties: wholesale only, who sell only to travel agencies; specialty agencies (both wholesale and retail); and **"bucket shops"** or discount retail agencies. Private consumers can deal directly only with the latter, but can have access to a larger market through a travel agent, who can also get tickets from wholesale consolidators. Look for bucket shops' tiny ads in weekend papers (in the U.S., the *Sunday New York Times* is best). In London, the real bucket shop center, the Air Travel Advisory Bureau (tel. 44 (171) 636 5000) provides a list of consolidators. Many ticket consolidators specialize in flights to a single destination. Ask also about accommodations and car rental discounts; some consolidators have fingers in many pies.

But among the many reputable and trustworthy companies are some shady wheeler-dealers. It is preferable to deal with consolidators close to home so you can visit in person. Ask to receive your tickets as quickly as possible so you have time to fix any problems. Get the company's policy in writing—insist on a receipt that gives full details about the tickets, refunds, and restrictions, and record who you talked to and when. It may be worth paying with a credit card (despite the 2-5% fee) so you can stop payment if you never receive your tickets. Beware the "bait and switch" gag: shyster firms will advertise a super-low fare and then tell a caller that it has been sold. Although this can be a legitimate excuse, if they can't offer you a price near the advertised fare on *any* date, it is a scam to lure in customers.

For destinations worldwide, try **Airfare Busters,** with offices in Washington, D.C. (tel. 1 (800) 776 0481), Boca Raton, FL (tel. 1 (800) 881 3273), and Houston, TX (tel. (232 8783); **Pennsylvania Travel,** Paoli, PA (tel. 1 (800) 331 0947); **Cheap Tickets,** offices in Los Angeles, CA, San Francisco, CA, Honolulu, HI, Overland Park, KS, and New York, NY, (tel. 1 (800) 377 1000); and **Moment's Notice,** New York, NY (tel. 1 (718) 234 6295; fax 234 6450), for air tickets, tours, and hotels; US$25 annual fee. For a processing fee, depending on the number of travelers and the itinerary, **Travel Avenue,** Chicago, IL (tel. 1 (800) 333 3335), will search for the lowest international airfare available and even give you a rebate on fares over US$300. Some consolidators specializing in travel to South Asia include: **Am-Jet,** New York, NY (tel. 1 (800) 414 4147, 1 (212) 697 5332), **Skybird Tours,** Southfield, MI (tel. 1 (810) 559 0900), and **Trek Holidays,** Edmonton, Alberta (tel. 1 (800) 661 7265, 1 (403) 439 9118).

Kelly Monaghan's *Consolidators: Air Travel's Bargain Basement* (US$7) from the Intrepid Traveler, P.O. Box 438, New York, NY 10034 (e-mail intreptrav@aol.com), is a valuable source for more information, with lists of consolidators by destination. Cyber-resources include **World Wide Wanderer** (http://www.tmn.com/wwwanderer/wwwa) and Edward Hasbrouck's **Airline ticket consolidators and bucket shops** (http://www.gnn.com/gnn/wic/wics/trav.97.html).

CHARTER FLIGHTS

The theory behind a charter is that a tour operator contracts with an airline (usually one specializing in charters) to fly extra loads of passengers to peak-season destinations. Charter flights fly less frequently than major airlines and have more restrictions, particularly on refunds. They are also almost always fully booked, and schedules and itineraries may change or be cancelled at the last moment (as late as 48 hours before the trip, and without a full refund); you'll be much better off purchasing a ticket on a regularly scheduled airline. As always, pay with a credit card if you can; consider travelers insurance against trip interruption.

Try **Interworld** (tel. 1 (305) 443 4929); **Travac** (tel. 1 (800) 872 8800); or **Rebel,** Valencia, CA (tel. 1 (800) 227 3235) or Orlando, FL (tel. 1 (800) 732 3588). Don't be afraid to call every number and hunt for the best deal. Many companies offer charters to vacations spots like Goa.

■ By Land

Driving a car (or better yet a bus) across Asia was a classic 1960s hippie expedition. From İstanbul, the route would pass through Turkey and Iran to Kabul, Afghanistan, and from there through Pakistan to India. U.S. passport holders cannot go through Iran now, but the overland route is still an option for citizens of other countries, although Afghanistan is off-limits. The only border crossing open from Pakistan to

India is between Lahore and Amritsar. There are no borders open between India and China or Burma.

Selling your car in India or Nepal was once a good way to finance a trip, but hefty duties on car imports have now stolen any hope of profit from such ventures. You must have a *carnet*, an automotive passport, to prove that you'll take your car out with you and not sell it on the black market. For more information, see **Documents and Formalities** (p. 3).

Bear in mind that road conditions in India and Nepal are unsafe, unleaded petrol is not widely available in India or Nepal, and that it may be difficult or impossible to find parts, fluids, or qualified repair people.

ONCE THERE

■ Foreign Diplomatic Missions in India

The following is an incomplete list of embassies and consulates, and high commissions in India. More information is listed geographically in the book.

United States: Shantipath, Chanakyapuri, Delhi (tel. 91 (11) 688 9033, 611 3033); Lincoln House, 78 Bhulabhai Desai Rd., Bombay (tel. 91 (22) 363 3611); 5/1 Ho Chi Minh Sarani, Calcutta (tel. 91 (33) 242 3611). Open Mon.-Fri. 8:30am-12:30pm and 2-4pm; 220 Mount Rd., Madras (tel. 827 3040).

Canada: 7/8 Shantipath, Chanakyapuri, Delhi (tel. 91 (11) 687 6500; fax 687 6579); 41/42 Makers Chambers VI, Nariman Point, Bombay (tel. 91 (22) 287 6027).

United Kingdom: 50 Shantipath, Chanakyapuri, Delhi (tel. 91 (11) 687 2161; fax 687 2882); Maker Chambers IV, 1st fl., 222 Jamhalal Bajaj Marg, Nariman Point, Bombay (tel. 91 (22) 283 3602, 283 0517); 24 Anderson Rd., Madras (tel. 91 (44) 827 3136); 1 Ho Chi Minh Sarani, Calcutta (tel. 91 (33) 242 5171). Open Mon.-Fri. 9am-noon.

Ireland: 230 Jor Bagh Rd., Delhi (tel. 91 (11) 462 6733; fax 469 7053); Royal Bombay Yacht Club, Apollo Bunder, Colaba, Bombay (tel. 91 (22) 287 2045, 495 1870).

Australia: 1/50G Shantipath, Chanakyapuri, Delhi (tel. 91 (11) 688 8223; fax 688 7530); Maker Towers, 16th Floor, E. Block, Cuffe Parade, Bombay (tel. 91 (22) 218 1071); 114-115 M.G. Rd., Madras (tel. 91 (44) 827 6036).

New Zealand: 50-N Nyaya Marg, Chanakyapuri, Delhi (tel. 91 (11) 688 3170; fax 687 2317).

South Africa: Consulate, Gandhi Museum, Altamount Rt., near Kemp's Corner, Bombay (tel. 91 (22) 389 3725).

■ Foreign Diplomatic Missions in Nepal

For more information on embassies, consulates, and high commissions in Nepal, and on visa procedures for individual countries, see p. 683.

U.S.: Pani Pokhari, Kathmandu (tel. 977 (1) 411179). Open Mon.-Fri. 8am-5pm. Consular services Mon., Wed., Fri. 2-4:40pm, Tues., Thurs. 8:30-11:30am.

Canada: Lazmipath, Kathmandu (tel. 977 (1) 415193), down the lane opposite Navin Books stationery shop. Open Mon.-Fri. 9am-5pm.

Australia: Bansbari, Kathmandu (tel. 977 (1) 417566), on Maharaganj, just past Ring Rd. Consular services open Mon.-Thurs. 10am-12:30pm.

U.K.: Lazimpath, Kathmandu (tel. 977 (1) 414588). Open Mon.-Fri. 8:15am-5pm. Consular services 9am-noon.

China: Baluwatar, Kathmandu (tel. 977 (1) 411740, visa services tel. 419053). Bring plane tickets and one photo. Visas ready the same day. Visas to Tibet are available only to tour groups, although some travelers (legally) enter with groups and then (illegally) go it alone. Those who plan do this needn't warn the Chinese embassy officials. Visa dept. open Mon.-Fri. 10am-noon.

India: Lainchaur (tel. 977 (1) 410900). Off Lazimpath just before the Hotel Ambassador. Put yourself through the week-long visa ordeal Mon.-Fri.: telex forms issued at counter B from 9:30-11am, accepted 9:30am-noon.

■ Getting Around

Moving around in India and Nepal can be harder than it looks, despite the common view of herds of men crowded onto the backs of trucks, attached only by the loose ligaments of a single arm and what must be a penchant for danger. You'll be confronted by strange ticket terminology, rigid-sounding departure schedules that get improvised for the strangest reasons, and unfamiliar squishy situations that will test your etiquette sense.

BY PLANE

India and Nepal both have extensive air networks serving every corner of their countries at reasonably cheap fares. In the last few years both countries have opened up the skies to private companies, but the government-run Indian Airlines and Royal Nepal Airlines Corporation (RNAC), which once had monopolies, still have the most extensive schedules and fly subsidized routes to less popular destinations. However, air travel is much more expensive than surface travel, and it will not always save you time. Waiting in airport-office queues, traveling to and from airports (which are usually far outside of town), and checking in can slow you down, but most of all, Indian and Nepalese airports love to subject passengers to purgatorial delays. It is best to fly only to escape unbearable cross-country bus or train rides. In Nepal, where the terrain is so hilly and the roads are so bad, the balance might be shifted slightly in favor of air travel.

Air travel is generally safe even though the planes are usually hand-me-downs from European or East Asian airlines, and flights are often bumpy. Be prepared for spontaneously opening luggage storage bins and cardboard boxes filled with cardboard-tasting ketchup sandwiches.

BY TRAIN

The Indian rail network, one of the few things Indians will readily thank their British colonial masters for, is incredibly extensive. For budget travelers rail is really the best way to get around India. For more information, see **Getting Around** (p. 74). Due to its mountains and its freedom from colonization, Nepal has no trains except for one that runs across the Indian border to Janakpur.

BY BUS

Extensive networks of bus routes cover all of India and Nepal. In Nepal buses are the most popular mode of long-distance transportation, while in India they finish a close second to the trains. Buses also go to the hilly areas of India where trains cannot go. Buses involve less pre-departure hassle than trains. For short trips, advance bookings are rarely necessary—just show up at the bus stand and climb aboard; you can pay the conductor somewhere along the way. Supply meets demand in the bus industry. For longer trips (over 10hr.) it might be necessary to book a day in advance. Do this directly at the bus stand rather than through a travel agent.

The main drawback to bus travel in India and Nepal is its extreme discomfort. Seats are usually narrower than an adult's shoulder span, with very little cushioning, and they are spaced to allow for absolutely no legroom (and then you find yourself assigned to the seat next to a woman carrying two babies in her lap, or a man who keeps nodding off to sleep on your shoulder). For people with long arms and legs, bus travel can be prohibitively uncomfortable. But at least you'll have a seat—there are often more passengers than seats, and many make the same trips standing up. Buses also tend to make frequent, extended stops for snacks and tea, which slow down the journey, but offer much-needed chances to stretch. At scheduled rest stops, women might have a hard time finding a place to use as a toilet; they should ask the conductor to wait longer for them. To avoid bumps, stay away from the back seats of the bus. There is also some risk involved in bus travel, as in all road travel in South Asia (see **Getting Around: By Car,** below). Road conditions are usually poor and traffic unpredictable. Most people expect their bus drivers to get from point A to point B as fast as possible—and the driver usually tries to accommodate the wishes of his passengers. Expect to hear much grinding of gears and blaring of horns, and to feel sudden lurches. **Never ride on the roof of a bus,** no matter how cool the breeze and the scenery. This is illegal and terribly dangerous.

Among the different of types of buses available, **tourist buses** or **"luxury" buses** have cushioned seats and more space than other buses; although they are certainly not luxurious by Western standards, they usually seat four passengers abreast rather than five. Tourist buses usually have fans, or even air conditioning. Tourist buses are usually only available on very popular tourist routes, however. For other journeys, **express buses** are the norm. Express buses still have padded seats, but they are much more crowded, and they stop for anyone who wants to get on. **Night buses,** which usually leave for long journeys in the early evening to arrive the next morning, have reclining seats and a bit more legroom, but you shouldn't count on getting any sleep. They stop for *chai* endlessly (just be glad the driver is getting his caffeine). At all costs avoid **video coaches,** which show Hindi films and play their music at speaker-distorting volumes.

Luggage on the roof rack of a bus is usually safe, but bags have been known to disappear at intermediate stops in a flurry of untrackable movement. This is especially a problem at night. Make sure your pack is tied down, and ask if you can put it elsewhere—in a compartment at the back, or at the front of the bus with the driver where you can keep an eye on it. If your luggage goes on the roof, give *baksheesh* to the person who put it up there.

Local buses in big cities have their destinations inscribed in the local language. In a hurry to wedge themselves into city traffic, bus drivers tend to roll-stop without really coming to rest at all, so you may want to learn the skill of leaping on and off the back entrance stairs. Take notice of the convenient side handle bars. Once safely in, sit or stand until the bus-*wallah*, with his little bus satchel, comes by and clicks a small metal contraption in your face. That means pay-up time—ask how many rupees it is to your destination, since ticket prices vary by distance. Women on city buses tend to get preferential seating, so male passengers may be expected to politely give up their seats to female passengers.

> **Warning:** Due to poor road conditions and aggressive driving, road travel in India and Nepal is dangerous.

BY CAR

Driving a car in India or Nepal is not for the faint of heart. Besides swerving to avoid cars and motorcycles, travelers have to remember to drive on the left in most places and learn to dodge rickshaws, people, and cows. There is a general disregard for anything resembling traffic regulations. The unwritten rule is that the bigger the vehicle, the greater amount of respect it should be accorded. Drivers are reckless and aggressive, constrained only by the general dilapidation of the roads and their vehicles. Many pedestrians who have just arrived from villages lack a basic traffic sense. Not surprisingly, India and Nepal have high rates of road accidents—although these seem to result in remarkably few fatalities. As with all adversity here, people seem to recover, move on, and clear things up remarkably quickly.

If you get into a traffic accident in India or Nepal, **leave the scene of the accident immediately and go to the nearest police station.** If people are injured or killed, mobs can gather, thirsting for revenge, and you don't want to be caught in one.

A car is entirely unnecessary in a large city; efficient transportation abounds, and taxis are ubiquitous. Also, some rental companies do not offer insurance; a serious accident may mean spending some time in jail or the hospital, and shelling out a large sum of money to cover damages. If you absolutely must have a car, keep your international driver's license handy, as well as a substantial amount of money.

The cost of renting a four-door sedan is many times the cost of a night's stay at a guest house. It is more common to hire a car with a **driver,** who should look after petrol costs and repairs, and who will take responsibility for any problems. Some foreign rental agencies such as Budget and Hertz now have branches in the major Indian cities, but it is normally much cheaper to hire a taxi for the day or for a specific journey; fares vary by distance. With enough passengers to split the costs, this is usually within the price range of a budget traveler.

Drivers in India and Nepal also need detailed **road maps;** while *Let's Go* includes highways and roads on maps whenever possible, rural roads are sometimes closed or washed-out during monsoon season. The *India and Bangladesh Travel Atlas* published by Lonely Planet Publications contains large-scale maps of Indian highways in a portable package.

Hitchhiking is unheard of and unnecessary in most parts of India and Nepal, since public transportation networks are extensive and cheap. In mountain areas, where traffic is sparse, cargo trucks sometimes take on passengers for a small charge. *Let's Go* does not recommend hitchhiking, and women should absolutely never hitchhike without a male companion.

BY TAXI

Taxis are found in the larger cities of India and Nepal; in some cities, such as Bombay, *only* taxis and not rickshaws or auto-rickshaws are allowed within the metropolitan limits. Taxis are supposed to have meters, but these are sometimes out of date, so the driver will add a percentage or wield an official-looking "fare adjustment card" with up-to-date prices. All this varies from city to city; there are no hard-and-fast rules, but in general you should insist on using the meter rather than negotiating a price. Private taxi companies exist to rent out taxis and drivers for longer hours, short trips, or even days; enquire at train stations, airports, or tourist offices.

BY TEMPO AND AUTO-RICKSHAW

To some, these hooded three-wheelers are a symbol of the Asian experience; to others, they are diesel fume-belching beasts. Fans argue that they are cheap compared to taxis, more convenient than buses, and small enough to dart through heavy traffic. Much of this, of course, depends upon the driver. Their acrobatic abilities are matched only by their tendency to flip over. Detractors criticize them for the damage they do to the environment and human ears. Auto-rickshaws seat one to three, depending upon the size of the passengers. Low ceilings, minimal legroom, and narrow seats (not to mention a vibrating action that threatens to dismantle the vehicle's slipshod frame) could make a six-foot person forgo an auto-rickshaw ride forever.

While the auto-rickshaw-*wallah* will insist that the meter is most definitely "broken," push for its use. Payment will inevitably entail negotiation, haggling, and flat-out struggle. Avoid pushy drivers, and always scoff at the first price demanded—let a driver come down to about 30-40% of his original price before getting in. Be aware of local specifics: depending on the town, some drivers may add a surcharge to the meter or display a price increase card, because the meters are outdated and the price of fuel has risen.

Tempos are larger, seating about six, and some designs resemble elongated auto-rickshaws gone wheelbarrow. Tempos follow fixed routes and have fixed fees; they are of limited use to foreigners however because their destinations are never marked.

BY RICKSHAW

Except for the hand-pulled carts of downtown Calcutta, rickshaws in India and Nepal are tricycle rickshaws: the driver pedals in front while his trusting passengers sit on a cushioned box above the rear axle. Many rickshaw-*wallahs* have been driving for years, scraping out a living from day to day; few of them own their rickshaws, and most of their earnings go to the machine's owner as rent. Rickshaws are not always found in metropolitan areas, such as Bombay, but they are found in the countryside wherever there is flat terrain. In Nepal rickshaws are limited to the Tarai and to parts of Kathmandu where they mainly cater to tourists. The main benefit of riding in a rickshaw is the fresh breeze and the open view; negatives include the longer traveling time and the sorrow of seeing an old man labor away. Pay attention to terrain when hiring rickshaws. On even the most gentle gradient the rickshaw-*wallah* won't be able to pedal. If he jumps out and starts pushing you up the hill, it's polite to lend a hand.

Make sure your rickshaw-wallah is not intoxicated. Many rickshaw-*wallahs* spend the day drunk or stoned; if your driver is unable to follow clear directions, jump out and find a new one.

The worst part about a rickshaw ride is settling the price, which is highly negotiable. Foreigners usually pay about Rs.10 per kilometer in India, but rickshaw-*wallahs* in touristy places ask for more, and in villages they ask for less. Haggling can be fierce, and you might have to bluff by walking away repeatedly. Some travelers prefer to settle on a price at the outset to prevent disagreements later. But on the other hand, if you don't ask the fare when you climb on, many rickshaw-*wallahs* will assume you know the correct fare, and you can just pay what you think it is when you get off.

Rickshaw-*wallahs* have the annoying habit of getting in commission cahoots with hotels and will inform you that your choice has been shut down or that its staff is on strike. Chances are that the "insider info" is incorrect and your driver simply wants his cut. If a driver taking you home asks if you need a ride the next day, know that if you flippantly agree he will probably sleep in his rickshaw that night waiting for you (many drivers sleep in their rickshaws anyway).

BY MOTORCYCLE, MOPED, AND SCOOTER

Motorcycles, mopeds, and scooters are probably more useful for travelers than cars. A motorcycle can liberate you to explore rural roads not accessible by public transportation; although you might get lost, this can lead to memorable adventures. Unfortunately, motorcycles, mopeds, and scooters are very dangerous in India and Nepal. *Let's Go* researchers have consistent track records of two-wheeled misfortune. Helmets are rarely provided, but unless you have a death wish, you shouldn't get on a motorcycle or motorbike without one; traffic fatalities on motorcycles are frighteningly high. As with cars, motorcycle drivers in India and Nepal find themselves dodging new and exciting obstacles, and on motorcycles they have less protection. Remember that larger vehicles have the right of way. Motorcycle rental shops are abundant near major tourist stops. An international driver's permit is legally required for you to rent a scooter or motorcycle, but it is rarely checked. Motorcycle and scooter engines in India and Nepal are usually only 100cc, so they are not very good for long trips. **Mopeds,** or "Lunas" as they are often called, are easy to operate but dangerous to take into any sort of traffic. **Scooters** have a high center of gravity and small wheels, which make them very dangerous; most scooters are also very difficult to operate and must be manually shifted from gear to gear. A popular alternative for tourists in some areas is to rent Kinetic-Hondas, automatic shifting scooters that are easy to operate and a bit safer on the road. If you are considering renting a motorcycle, remember also the disproportionate amount of air pollution they cause.

BY BICYCLE

Since the largest vehicles can crush all smaller ones in their path, is it usually useless to try to ride a bicycle in the big Indian cities. But on backroads through rural towns, and in much of Nepal, bicycles really become worth the small change they're rented for. However, most bikes in India and Nepal don't have gears, so hills are hellacious. In many tourist centers like Kathmandu and Pokhara, bikes can be rented very cheaply, usually on a daily basis. Clunking Indian bikes are also very cheap to buy and resell.

■ Border Crossings

India-Nepal: There are six overland border crossings between India and Nepal: Mahendranagar, Dhangadi, Nepalganj, Sunauli, Raxaul/Birganj, and Kakarbhitta. Sunauli is a 3 hr. bus ride from Gorakhpur in Uttar Pradesh; from there you can catch a 10-hr. bus to Pokhara or a 12-hr. bus to Kathmandu. Raxaul is a 5-hr. bus ride from Patna in Bihar; from Birganj, across the border, it's a 12-hr. bus ride to Kathmandu. The Kakarbhitta crossing, at the eastern end of Nepal, is easily accessible from Siliguri, which is a transit point for Darjeeling. It is not usually necessary to get a Nepalese visa before you arrive at the border, but you must get your Indian visa ahead of time if you're going from Nepal to India. Visitors are also allowed to drive across the border, so long as they possess an international *carnet*. For more information see **Raxaul,** p. 443; **Birganj,** p. 749; **Sunauli,** p. 741; and **Kakarbhitta,** p. 753.

India-Bangladesh: Trains and buses run from Calcutta to Bangaon in West Bengal. From there it is only a rickshaw ride across the border to Benapol in Bangladesh, with connections via Khulna or Jessore to Dhaka. The border in the north, near Darjeeling, from Jalpaiguri to Haldibari, is only periodically open and requires an exit permit.

India-Burma: No land frontier open.

India-Bhutan: If you are lucky enough to get a Bhutanese visa, you must cross the border at Puntsholing, a 3-4 hr. bus ride from Siliguri in West Bengal. Make sure you also have a "transit permit" from the Indian ministry of External Affairs.

India-China: No land frontier open.

India-Pakistan: Due to the Kashmiri-cool relations between India and Pakistan, only one crossing is open along the entire length of the two countries' 2000-km border. A daily train runs from Amritsar in the Indian Punjab to Attari, the border town (still in India); from there you catch another train to Lahore in the Pakistani Punjab. For more information see **Pakistan Border,** p. 338

India-Sri Lanka: The boat service from Rameswaram in Tamil Nadu to Talaimannar in Sri Lanka has been indefinitely suspended due to the war in northern Sri Lanka. Travelers must fly to Sri Lanka.

Nepal-China: The Arniko Rajmarg (Kathmandu-Kodari Highway) links Kathmandu with the Tibet Autonomous Region of China via the exit point of Kodari. The border is currently open only to travelers on organized tours. Before crossing into Tibet, check in with your embassy in Kathmandu to make sure that the border situation is stable, as there have occasionally been difficulties for tourists crossing overland into Tibet.

■ Accommodations

Cheap accommodations in India and Nepal are plentiful. You can easily stay here without spending more than US$2 or US$3 per night, as long as you don't mind life without air conditioning. Even posh hotels are much cheaper here than they would be at home. Rates often vary according to the season, however, and in cheaper hotels they're often negotiable. The prices listed in this book represent our best research efforts, but often we cannot predict the ups and downs of Indian and Nepali hotel prices—all prices listed in this book should be taken only as a relative index.

BUDGET HOTELS

The main tourist centers nurture **ghettoes** of shabbily built hotels, which exist to give most budget travelers their first taste of Eastern asceticism—bare concrete cells with hard beds and a ceiling fan on overdrive. They are, nevertheless, all you really need, and compared to hotels in richer countries their rates are unbelievably cheap. The architects who built them seem to have been blind to the dangers of fire and earthquake, and their structure is often as haphazard as the layout of the city streets around them, squeezing in a range of singles, doubles, and triples, with or without attached bath. Dorm beds are also sometimes available. These hotels often have restaurants, and managers are happy to arrange to provide any service rupees can buy. Where tourist ghettoes have developed and most of the clientele is foreign, competition has made hotels much cheaper, cleaner, and more comfortable. It is rarely necessary to make **reservations** at such hotels, except at major peak times (such as festivals). However, it can be difficult to get accommodation in big cities that see few foreign tourists—the hotels may be full of Indian or Nepali businessmen, or they may lack the paperwork to accept foreigners.

One thing to look out for when choosing a hotel is the **checkout time**—many cheap hotels have a 24-hour rule, which means if you arrive in town in the morning after an overnight train you'll be expected to leave as early as when you check out. Above all, don't let touts or rickshaw-*wallahs* make your lodging plans. These shady characters often suck up tourists from train and bus stations and cart them off to whichever hotel is paying the biggest **commission,** and that commission sooner or later adds to your room price. Touts will fervently insist that the hotel where you wanted to stay is "closed" or "full," and they will continue to lie even as you walk up to the hotel door to discover the truth.

Many budget travelers prefer to bring their own **padlock** for budget hotels, since the locally-made padlocks they provide are often suspect. Sheets (if desired), towels, soap, and toilet paper also need to be carried. It is good to ask about utilities before choosing a hotel. Many have **hot water** only at certain hours of the day, or only in buckets. Since the power supply is erratic everywhere in India, **generators** are a plus—although these often create terrifying noises. Although no self-respecting budget hotel has air-conditioning, **air-cooling,** a system by which air is blown by a fan over the surface of water, is common.

Prices fluctuate wildly according to the season. In the high season (generally from November to March, although this varies by region) prices are frequently three or four times the off-season rates, and prices can also vary depending on perceived ability to pay—foreigners are charged more. Off-season travelers can often swing special deals.

Another important aspect of accommodations in India and Nepal is the existence of a **travelers' scene.** Some hotels in various towns have built reputations as places for foreign travelers to hang out and share stories. This can be an invaluable way of grappling with your travel experiences, and it is something to look out for. On the other hand, hobnobbing with other travelers too much leads some people to insulate themselves from the locals. In a particularly sad twist, some budget hotels in India have even instituted discriminatory **no-Indians policies** in order to create sanitized, foreigners-only environments for their clients.

Budget hotels frequently have **restaurants** attached, and even Star TV and air-conditioning in some of the nicer places. One attractive feature of budget hotels in India is **room service,** which usually costs no more than food in the restaurant. If you are a lazy **launderer,** you can sacrifice your clothes for one day's worth of purificatory libations. It is guaranteed that your clothes will return cleaner than they ever were back home. Since laundry is generally charged by the piece, items like underwear and socks can add up, and it could pay to wash some yourself. But it is said that Indian laundry services promise that with each garment washed, the mind is cleansed also.

UPSCALE HOTELS

Pricier accommodations are certainly available almost anywhere in India, offering such amenities as air conditioning, hot water, and televisions, which you won't find in budget hotels. Although these hotels' rates seem exorbitant when compared to those of budget hotels, they are really nothing compared to hotel rates at home. Before you check into a more expensive hotel, however, ask yourself whether you'll really be more comfortable. Many mid-range hotels are all show, and upstairs from a spacious, carpeted lobby decorated with hotel logos the rooms are only marginally better than those in budget hotels. Large, expensive hotels such as the Taj, Sheraton, and Oberoi chains and the ITDC's line of Ashoks are also present in the main cities and tourist centers. Such starry wonders are usually much more affordable in India and Nepal than their counterparts elsewhere, but if a night's stay is out of the question, the bookstores, restaurants, and pools at these places are often a great resource. Again, ask yourself if you'd really be more comfortable in a place that lavished luxury on you than in a simple room with the bare necessities; the answer for many travelers is no. These large hotels usually require payment in foreign exchange; this rule extends even further down the price scale in Nepal.

RELIGIOUS REST HOUSES

Traditional rest houses for Hindu pilgrims known as *dharamshalas* are sometimes open to foreign guests as well, providing the most Spartan accommodations free of charge, although it is kind to give a donation. Sikh *gurudwaras* also have a tradition of hospitality. Be on your best behavior if you stay in such religious places; usually smoking and drinking are not allowed.

■ Trekking

The Himalaya rise majestically from the landscape, cradling the Indian subcontinent in the arms of Eurasia. Their lofty peaks, including that of Mt. Everest, the world's highest mountain, have been long been revered by hill communities, which are as varied as the landscape they inhabit. Early Tibetan scripts and Hindu epics reveal the wondrous Himalaya as the site of meditation and sacrifice. The Himalaya have a magnetic energy that lately seems to be attracting tourists from around the world, for vacations that appear to be a respite from the ever-quickening pace of modern life. Trekking has become a flourishing industry in Nepal and parts of India. Mountain tourism provides seasonal jobs to skilled guides, porters, cooks, village lodgers, and shop owners. The trekking experience provides opportunity to interact with the people of the diverse hill communities and appreciate their simple and arduous lifestyle.

Trekking is not mountaineering. Trekking through the Himalaya means walking from destination to destination, following trails, many of which are also used for communication and trade. A trek can be a day, a week, a month, or if it suits you, a lifelong journey (although visa regulations might prohibit this!). The trails are often steep and taxing, but the popular routes are well-maintained. Most treks follow trails through populated areas at elevations of 1000m to 3000m, but some extend over 5000m. A typical day's walk lasts from five to seven hours and involves a number of ascents and descents, repaid with beautiful scenery as well as aching muscles.

Some trekkers bring medicines such as aspirin to give to villagers along the trail. Such gifts will make you popular and will help people out, but don't give presents too liberally—this can encourage a beggar mentality. Some of the main trails in Nepal are now veritable gauntlets of children asking for candies, pens, and rupees, thanks to the legacy of over-generous trekkers.

WHEN TO GO

The post-monsoon reprieve, October through November, is the favored trekking season in Nepal and the monsoonal hill regions of Kangra, Kulu, Shimla, Garhwal, and Kumaon in India. The afternoon haze gives way to bright sunshine, and crisp, clear air. The temperatures are comfortably warm, even balmy in October. These ideal climatic conditions make October and November the high season for trekking. You may have more company than you wanted on the more popular trails. From December to February, it may be too cold for trekking at high altitudes. The temperatures drop in March and April, making trekking more feasible, but the air is characteristically dusty, dry, and hazy. And, as ever in the mountains, extreme weather conditions of all kinds can arise unexpectedly. But rhododendrons, magnolias, and orchids shower magnificent color over the landscape during March and April. Come May—the hottest, yet least predictable of months climatically—the monsoon is just around the corner and most trekking activities taper off, or retreat to higher regions. Few trekkers choose to endure the cloud-bound, slippery, and leech-beleaguered trail conditions of the monsoon. But for the persistent and enterprising, trekking during the summer season has the benefit of the virtual absence of western tourists.

The two main trekking seasons in India are pre-monsoon (May and June) and post-monsoon (Sept.-Nov.). The treks in India usually ascend to heights of 4000m, where the temperatures drop. The areas of Upper Kinnaur, Lahaul, Spiti, Ladakh, and Anskar are in rain shadow, meaning they get none of the monsoon rains.

PLANNING A TREK

There are two possible ways of organizing a trek in the Indian or Nepalese Himayala. Trekking independently saves money and allows you the control to individualize your experience to suit your interests. You set the pace, choose your trekking companions, plan rest days and side trips of interest in your own personalized adventure. Arranging your own trek also entails obtaining permits, renting equipment, buying supplies, and hiring porters or guides. If you are blessed with the virtue of patience and the asset of time, then planning an independent trek may be the way to go. Otherwise, a trekking agency can take care of all the preparations for you, minimizing hassle, and their expertise may make it possible to trek through more remote backcountry. But the ease and comfort come with a pricetag.

Trekking Permits and Other Fees

Permits are required for all trekking areas in Nepal and can be obtained in Thamel at the Department of Immigration (tel. 977 (1) 412337). You can complete the process in one day, but at the height of the trekking season, the long lines could extend the process to two or even three days. **Always carry your trekking permit on the way to the trek and while on the trek,** so that registering at the police posts will be a mere formality, and moving along will be easier. If your trek enters a national park (Everest and Langtang) or a conservation area (Annapurna), you will have to pay a fee of NRs.650, about US$12.

Except in North Sikkim, a trekking permit is not required in India. Area permits give access to all trekking areas as well, but no overnight camping is allowed in mountain national parks.

Tea Houses in Nepal and Tents in India

Villages along Nepal's most popular trek routes have outdone themselves to accommodate passing foreigners, and are filled with small lodges referred to as "tea houses." There are enough tea houses along the way and enough people who speak passable English for you to do the trek yourself, with the help of a trekking map and a trekking guidebook. For the adventure-seeking and budget-minded, this is the way to trek. Stan Armington's *Trekking in the Nepal Himalaya* (US$14.95, published by Lonely Planet Publications) is the authoritative trekking guidebook for Nepal. Making an effort to learn about the trek before setting off is helpful—some trekking agencies will offer free advice and information. The officials you will come across while securing a trekking permit and paying entry fees will be able to answer additional questions.

On the trek, use a map and ask people for directions. The simplest and perhaps the most helpful question to ask is the way to the next village on the map. Every day you need to have an idea of the village where you want to spend the night. A question which causes more confusion is how long it takes to get to the next village. You will get a half dozen different answers. Ask the people on the paths this question, rather than tea house owners, who have been known to exaggerate distances to trick you into staying at their place. The key for trekking by yourself is going day by day and being flexible. It might rain, you might realize that you aren't as fit as you thought, and of course, you need time for your body to acclimatize.

English signs advertise lodging and food at a bargain budget—usually under NRs.20—and often an English-speaking manager will greet the guests. Increasingly, private rooms are becoming available along the most popular routes in Nepal, but dormitory-style accommodations predominate in the backcountry and at high-elevations. Tea houses, also called inns, guest houses, or trekking lodges, are bustling with activity and noise, and although the physical exertion of trekking can make for sound sleeping, you may want to invest in a pair of earplugs. But the tea house social scene can be an enlivening experience and the tea houses are full of potential trekking companions. Many of the lodges have been converted from homes and reveal the charm of Nepalese village life. The menu (this, too, is usually in English) may advertise enticing cuisine, which is often permanently unavailable. The staple trekking lodge meal is *dal bhat,* and Tibetan dishes are usually available. Along the most popular routes, you may be willing to shovel out a few more rupees for the familiar taste of apple pie and for a cold beer to wash it down.

The extensive food and lodging industries that enable trekkers to carry minimal equipment are not available everywhere in Nepal however, especially in the high mountains above 4500m. India has no equivalent for the tea houses either. In certain areas, there may be the occasional rest house, but they are often out of the way and food supplies en route are unreliable. Beginner and expert trekkers alike should be accompanied by someone who knows the specific trails. Getting lost in the Indian Himalaya is very easy, and often trekkers see no one but their own partners for three or four days at a time. In addition, trekkers in the Indian Himalaya must be prepared to be more self-sufficient. Tents are essential for shelter, and the stock of supplies and equipment are considerably greater. For more information, see **Packing and Equipment** (p. 57). Because of the heavier load, porters or horsemen are needed more often than in Nepal. Backpacks become a weighty burden on treks longer than a few days.

Porters and Guides

One variation on individual trekking is to hire your own porters and guides. You will have a knowledgeable local with you, you will not have to carry as much, and you will give a boost to the Himalayan economy. Porters carry most of your gear, allowing you the comfort of walking with only a small pack with the items you'll need during the day. You will have to constantly make sure that your porter understands what you want him to do and where you want to go each day. There is a small chance that your porter will disappear, leaving you with a heavy bag, or worse still, just the items on your person. So choose your porter carefully. In Nepal, porters can often be hired on the spot, even in the most unlikely of places. The trekking service industry in the Indian Himalaya is not as widespread, but you can arrange your own equipment, food, and staff at most hill stations or trailheads.

Guides, who usually speak English, are not necessary for the most well-known routes, where it is easy to find your way. Having someone who knows English and who is relatively educated might prove helpful in negotiations and pre-trek planning, however. A guide can color your experience with their knowledge of the land and culture. Often, guides will take trekkers on unusual side trips to visit friends and family. Guides are generally reluctant to carry anything.

Although porters and guides are easy to find, you'll want to investigate their honesty and experience. Spending some time in choosing a good guide is well worth the effort. Ask to see letters of recommendation from previous employer-trekkers. You can be almost certain to get reputable workers through a guest house or trekking agency. Guides and porters hired through companies are slightly more expensive but are, in most cases, more reliable and better qualified than those that you would find yourself. In the unlikely but still possible event that your guide or porter disappears, you have a company to hold responsible—an insurance that is worth the extra couple of dollars per day. If you do hire your own guides and porters, make sure you know exactly what services are covered in the wage, where you will go, and what supplies you will be obliged to supply along the way. Most agreements stipulate that guides and porters pay for their food and accommodations out of their wages. As a responsible employer, you should make sure that porters and guides are adequately clothed when trekking at high altitudes by outfitting them with good shoes, a parka, sunglasses, mittens, and a sleeping bag. Establish beforehand if you expect them to return anything. The standard salary for a porter carrying 20 kilos is about US$10 per day Nepal, US$5 per day in India; the salary for guides is higher (US$12-20 per day in India). In addition to these fees, you are expected to tip your staff generously at the end of a trek. Trekking in India tends to be a lot cheaper than in Nepal, mostly because tents and sleeping bags replace the cost of trail accommodations. A trek in Gurhwal, for example, might cost US$8 per person per day, while a trek in India can be as low as IRs.500 per person per day.

Organized Trekking

Many tourists do not want to spend their precious vacation time planning their trek, buying equipment, and hiring a staff. For a fee, trekking agencies in Kathmandu and other major hill towns will take care of the logistics of your trek for you. The agent makes reservations for hotels and flights well in advance and provides a complete staff—a guide, porters, and cooks—for the trek. While you don't need to worry about arrangements, you must commit to the prearranged itinerary—you can't decide on your own to take a day off or cultivate your soon-to-be-discovered skills as a nature photographer. And you may be trekking alongside people you have never met before. Organized treks can usually veer off from the crowded routes into more remote areas, however. The group carries its own food, which is prepared by cooks skilled in the art of cooking by kerosene. Porters carry tents for the group. Although tents can be colder and more cramped, they do offer a quiet night and the conve-nience of setting your own bedtime. The comforts of trekking through an agency may also include tables, chairs, dining tents, toilet tents, and other modern luxuries. But for all this comfort and convenience, there is a price, which can range from US$15 to US$150 (usually US$40-50) per person per day. And almost none of this money ever reaches the people who live in the trekking region; instead it goes to pad the wallet of the middleman in the city.

You can book through a big international adventure travel company from your home country, in which case everything is organized and arranged before you even touch down in South Asia. If you wait until you arrive, you can book through a local trekking agency, which usually require one week's advance notice. Organized treks may suit those with limited time to plan their trek, or those not wishing to trouble their tired bodies by having to find good tea houses and lodges at the end of the day. Organized treks are also recommended for the physically disabled and those seeking to live in luxury all the way to the top of the world. See the chapters on each trekking region for more details.

PACKING AND EQUIPMENT

What you carry with you on your trek will depend greatly on where you go, the style of trekking you choose and, if you have arranged a trek through an agency, what they provide. In Nepal, tea house trekking relieves you of having to carry food, cooking supplies, and tents. If you are traveling at high elevations in Nepal, or virtually any-where in the Indian Himalayas, you will need to take these with you. In addition, if going on a popular trek, during high season, there is the possibility that you will not be able to find a bed in a village and will need a sleeping bag.

High-tech gear is not necessary for most trekking. Aim to keep the weight of your luggage to a minimum, Good used and new equipment is available in Nepal, but not in India. In Nepal, the largest number of rental stores are in Kathmandu, but rental stores can also be found in Pokhara and stations along the Everest trek such as Lukla and Namche Bazaar. Many rental shops will also sell equipment. If you don't have your own equipment, you'll have to go from shop to shop until you find the size, quality, and to a limited extent, price, you want. Spend a lot of time (an entire day) finding the right gear. In Nepal, most of the gear you will come across was left behind by mountaineering or trekking expeditions. So organized inventories and a huge selection of sizes don't exist. Deposits are required. When renting equipment, be sure to inspect clothing and sleeping bags for fleas and broken zippers. Be aware that rental agencies often require a hefty deposit of US$50 or more. Because it is particularly important to get footwear that fits and is comfortable, break in running shoes or boots before you leave. For most treks, running shoes are adequate. However, boots provide ankle protection and have stiffer soles. Boots are necessary wherever there is snow. Clothing should be lightweight and versatile, to accommodate the variations in the weather. If you are going on any trek that will take you more than 1km from civilization, you should pack enough equipment to keep you alive should disaster befall you. This includes raingear, warm layers (not cotton!), especially hat and mittens, a first-aid kit, high energy food, and water. In much of Nepal, the price of food is fixed by the Annapurna Conservation Area Project, so bargaining is a futile exercise. The price of food and bottled drinks rises with the elevation. Lodge management committees that set up standard prices are active in many trekking areas and get rid of the bargaining element. Souvenir vendors are the people to bargain with.

Clothing	Equipment
boots or running shoes	sleeping bag
camp shoes or thongs	water bottle
socks - polypropylene	flashlight, batteries
down jacket	insulated mat
wool shirt	backpack
hiking shorts	toilet paper
long pants	matches
poncho or umbrella	sunblock
cotton T-shirts or blouses	towel
thermal underwear	laundry soap
gloves	sewing kit
sunhat	small knife
snow gaiters	first aid kit
snow goggles/sunglasses	

HEALTH AND SAFETY

The three most important things to remember when trekking are to stay warm, stay dry, and stay hydrated. Trekking takes a certain amount of physical exertion, but there is no need for overexertion. Go at a comfortable pace and take rest days when necessary.

As you would anywhere in South Asia, make sure your water is safe. Unfortunately, the food and water served at inns and tea houses is not always properly prepared. Lapses in kitchen hygiene increase the risk of stomach illness. Eat in the inns that appear most sanitary. Washing your hands before eating will reduce the chance of contaminating your food and inducing stomach sickness. For more information, see **Health** (p. 17).

Knee and ankle strains are common trekking injuries. Knees can become painfully inflamed, especially when carrying a heavy load or walking downhill. If you think you're susceptible to knee injuries, bind them with an ace bandage as a preventive measure. Sprained ankles can be serious, and could keep you from walking for hours or days. Good footwear with ankle support is the best prevention. Be sure that boots are broken in. A bad blister will ruin your trek. If you feel a "hot-spot" coming on, cover it with moleskin immediately.

If you are trekking to altitudes above 3500m, you will probably experience mild symptoms of altitude sickness, which can worsen into **acute mountain sickness (AMS)**. Serious cases of AMS are rare but can be fatal if left untreated. At high altitudes, there is less oxygen and lower atmospheric pressure, which can take their toll on the body—even the Sherpas aren't immune to elevation changes. It is important to allow time for acclimatization. Most people are capable of adjusting to very high elevations, but the process must be done in stages. Don't go too high too fast. Trekkers who fly directly to high altitudes are more likely to be affected by AMS and should be especially careful to acclimatize. The best cure is prevention. Be sure to increase your intake of liquids, eat well, keep warm, get plenty of sleep, and avoid alcohol. Even if you take these precautions, don't panic if you experience headaches, dizziness, insomnia, nausea, loss of appetite, shortness of breath, or swelling of the hands and feet—all minor symptoms of AMS. This is your body sending you a message that it hasn't yet adjusted to the elevation. Take heed. You shouldn't ascend further until you start feeling better. It is also recommended that you sleep at a lower altitude than the greatest height reached during the day. It is also necessary to stop for a few days to acclimatize when you reach 3500m, and again when you reach 4500m. Allow some flexibility in your schedule; it will be easier to turn back or spend a day at one elevation if your plan allows for such contingencies. Also keep in mind that not everyone in your group will acclimatize at the same rate. The group might have to break up or stop entirely in response to the needs of a group member. The minor discomforts of AMS generally abate after a day or so but if they persist or worsen, **the only effective treatment is descent.** Anyone experiencing serious symptoms—vomiting, delirium, lack of coordination and balance, rapid heart rate, breathlessness, bloody sputum, or blueness in the face—should be taken downhill immediately. These symptoms can develop within hours, but dramatic recovery can occur with the descent of only a few hundred vertical meters.

Frostbite and **hypothermia** are other altitude-related dangers, because the weather in the Himalaya can be capricious. To prevent exposure, dress warmly and in layers, keep dry, cover any exposed extremities (wear a hat and mittens), eat well, and drink warm liquids. Make for shelter if conditions become severe. A good pair of sunglasses can protect you from snow blindness, a condition which is caused by ultraviolet light reflected from snow or ice. Ultraviolet light is much stronger at higher altitudes, so it is wise to protect against sunburn with sunblock and a sunhat.

Leeches are rampant during monsoon season and a common annoyance during damp rainforest conditions. Trekkers often get these blood-sucking leeches on their legs or in their boots. Carry salt with you in a small container (a film container works well) for a chemical attack on leeches. Carefully applying a burning cigarette is another effective way of forcing a leech off your skin. Unlike ticks, they do not leave any part of themselves behind, so it is safe to pull them off if you're not too squeamish. Unfortunately, this could leave the bite open to infection. If you feel a leech has entered your shoes, the best thing might be to keep walking until the next village, because stopping will only give other leeches an opportunity to stick to you. A leech bite isn't painful; the effect is more psychological—thinking about the blood that slimy sucker is stealing from your body! Leeches are not known to transmit diseases.

Carry a **first-aid kit** for minor injuries. For suggestion for what to include in a first aid kit, see **Health,** p. 17. Cuts to the skin should be cleaned with Dettol, clean water, or Betadine solutions, and covered with a firm bandage. Clean and dress the wound daily. If the wound becomes infected, you can apply an antibiotic ointment. Broken bones should be realigned, and stablized with a padded splint. Check frequently to make sure the splint is not cutting off circulation. Compound fractures, where the bone is exposed to the air through the wound, require more urgent medical treatment.

Although trekkers do not often need serious medical attention, trekking mishaps do happen. In non-urgent cases, find some kind of animal (horse, pony, yak) to help transport a sick or injured trekker to the nearest hospital or airstrip. If urgent medical attention is needed, **emergency rescue** request messages can be sent through radio at police, army, national park, and other official offices. Helicopter rescue is very expensive (usually US$1000-2000). In Nepal, money must be deposited or guaranteed in Kathmandu before the helicopter will fly. For people on agency treks, the agency will advance the money. This process is often made easier if you are registered with your national embassy.

Individuals, particularly women, are not advised to trek alone. It is better to find a group, either on your own, through noticeboards, or through a trekking agency. For women trekking alone, it might be better to have a porter than a guide. In the few unfortunate cases in the past, many more guides than porters have tried to take advantage of single women trekkers.

Responsible Trekking

Trekking can enhance the local economy, but it can it can burden and degrade the environment. Cultivate a respectful relationship with the land on which you tread. The delicate ecological balance in the Himalaya is at risk. Some of the most pressing problems include deforestation, overgrazing, landslides, and sanitation problems. Trekkers can put additional strain on the local wood supplies. When at all possible, eat at teahouses that cook with kerosene or electricity instead of wood. Treat your water with iodine instead of asking innkeepers for boiled water. If trekking with an agency, request that kerosene or gas be used for cooking and heating water. Blazing campfire hearths are taboo where deforestation is a problem. Outfit yourself and your porters with warm clothes so as to reduce your reliance on wood fires for warmth. Limit hot showers to those heated by electricity, solar energy, or back-boilers. Such industrious and innovative shower suppliers deserve encouragement.

In addition, trekkers contribute to litter, sanitation, and water pollution problems with their waste. Pink and white toilet paper streamers are an especially sore sight when set against the beautiful Himalayan landscape. The rule to follow is: burn it, bury it, or carry it out. Toilet paper is generally burned, biodegradables such as food wastes are buried, and non-disposables (plastics, aluminum foil, batteries, glass, cans, etc.) are packed up and carried to a suitable waste treatment site. All excrement should be buried in a 40cm-deep hole in a spot well away from water sources, religious sites, village compounds, and cropfields. Use biodegradable soap and shampoo, and don't rinse directly in streams. If you can't leave the area clean, don't go. On organized treks, make sure that a person from your team is the last to leave camp; guided tour operators seldom do what they promise about camp garbage disposal.

Waste, its accumulation, and its disposal in the Himalaya has fortunately received media attention lately. The result has been greater awareness and several expeditions to clean up the treks, mostly in Nepal. If you hear of a clean trek being organized, jump at the opportunity, or at least write to *Let's Go* about it.

Flora and fauna are also threatened in the Himalaya. Terraced farming is causing widespread erosion. Trekkers shouldn't ever cut vegetation or clear new campsites. Loss of vegetation contributes to erosion, which is already widespread because of terraced farming. Feeding wild animals may be exciting, but it only weakens their defenses.

INFORMATION SOURCES

Himalayan Rescue Association (HRA) is located near the Department of Immigration in Thamel on the first floor of Hotel Tibicho. P.O. Box 4944, Kathmandu, Nepal (tel. 977 (1) 418755). A voluntary non-profit organization providing information for trekkers on where and how to trek, trekking hazards, altitude sickness, and how to protect the Himalayan environment. During the trekking season (Oct.-Dec. and March-May) they have free talks and slide shows on altitude sickness daily at 2pm. They also have in-season clinics during the trekking season in Pheriche on the Everest trek and in Marang on the Annapurna Circuit with volunteer Western doctors. Open Sun.-Fri. 10am-5pm.

Kathmandu Environmental Education Project (KEEP). Take a right past Hotel Tilicho to Potala Tourist Home, P.O. Box 9178, Kathmandu. (tel. 977 (1) 410303). A non-profit organization that provides information on minimizing your impact on the environment and culture. They offer free advice to trekkers and trekking staff. During the trekking season (Oct.-Dec. and Feb.-May) they have a free talk on eco-tourism at their office at 4pm every Friday. Open Sun.-Fri. 10am-5pm.

Annapurna Conservation Area Project, c/o KMTMC, P.O. Box 3712, Kathmandu (tel. 977 (1) 526571; fax 625570). The most authoritative source of information on the Annapurna region of Nepal, ACAP promotes environmentally sound practices among trekkers.

Nepal Mountaineering Association (NMA) is located in Hatisar in Kathmandu (tel. 977 (1) 411525). The NMA issues all permits for trekking peaks.

Indian Mountaineering Foundation, Benito Juarez Marg, Anand Niketan (tel. 91 (11) 602245, 671211). Information on treks, and especially climbs over 6000m.

■ River Rafting and Adventure Activities

Aqua-Terra Adventures, Suite 309, Oriental House, Gudmohar Enclave Commercial Complex, New Delhi (tel. 91 (11) 651 8625; fax 686 4771). Conducts cultural tours, river rafting and trekking in the Himalayas. Offers whitewater runs ranging from a few hours to two weeks or more. White water rafting in India is a relatively new sport, but the rafters rank with the best in the world—expeditions are organized on the Zanskar, Beas, Sutlej, Indus, and Ganga Rivers. Alaknandu River Expedition: 7 days, Rudraprayag-Rishikesh, US$185 per person. Bhagirathi River Expedition: 6 days, Tehri-Rishikesh, US$245 per person. Zanskar River Expedition: Padum-Leh, 13 days, US$1100. The group also organizes treks, jeep safaris and wildlife tours, and is friendly and open to new ideas.

Himalayan Riverrunners, F-5 Hauz Khas Enclave, New Delhi (tel. 91 (11) 685 2602; fax (011) 686 5604). A reliable company, run by Yousuf Zaheer, one of the pioneers of the sport in India, who has been rafting for over 15 years. Apart from the trips mentioned above (prices are equivalent), a quick 2-day run down the upper Ganga is offered for US$501. The company also conducts only a few treks in the Garhwal region.

Easy Rider Tours, B-33, 1st Floor, Sector 15, Noida, UP (tel. 91 (11) 853 0861). A relatively new venture, this company organizes motorbike tours both in the Himalayas and in South India, on the workhorse of Indian bikes, the 350cc Enfield Bullet. An amazing experience, one can also hire bikes at Rs.500 a day, and a mechanic for Rs.600 per day (split between the number of bikes).

■ Keeping in Touch

MAIL

Mail can be sent internationally through **Poste Restante** to any city or town; it's well worth using and quite reliable. Mark the envelope "HOLD" and address it legibly, and in english to the addressee's legal name. For example, "Michelle SULLIVAN, *Poste Restante*, GPO, City, Country." The last name should be capitalized and underlined. The mail will go to a special desk in the central post office, unless you specify another post office by street address or postal code. As a rule, it is best to use the largest post office in the area—usually called the General Post Office (GPO) in major cities and towns in India and Nepal; sometimes mail will be sent there regardless of what you write on the envelope. When possible, it is usually safer and quicker to send mail express or registered, since the reliability of mail service varies drastically across the region. When picking up your mail, bring your passport or another ID. Have the clerks check under both your first and last name; confusion abounds on the issue of how to alphabetize Western names. The word *Poste Restante* is also not understood everywhere; if it doesn't work, try asking for mail sent "in care of the postmaster." *Let's Go* lists post offices in the Practical Information section for each town.

Aerogrammes, printed sheets that fold into envelopes and travel via airmail, are available at post offices. It helps to mark "airmail" in the appropriate language if possible, though *par avion* is universally understood. Most post offices will charge exorbitant fees or simply refuse to send Aerogrammes with enclosures. Allow *at least* two weeks for mail delivery to or from South Asia. Much depends on the national post office involved.

If regular airmail is too slow, there are a few faster, more expensive, options. Both **Federal Express** (tel. 1 (800) 238 5355) and **DHL** (tel. 1 (800) 225 5345) operate throughout South Asia; Federal Express operates in India as a joint venture with an Indian company, **Blue Dart.** Federal Express packages from the U.S. to India or Nepal cost about US$55. Delivery takes 4 business days. **DHL** costs about US$71 to India or Nepal. Delivery takes 5 business days. DHL packages sent from India to the U.S. cost US$30-40.

Surface mail is by far the cheapest and slowest way to send mail. It is really only appropriate for sending large quantities of items you won't need to see for a while. It is vital, therefore, to distinguish your airmail from surface mail by explicitly labeling "airmail" in the appropriate language. When ordering books and materials from abroad, always include one or two **International Reply Coupons (IRCs)**—a way of providing the postage to cover delivery. IRCs should be available from your local post office (US$1.05).

American Express offices throughout the world will act as a mail service for cardholders if contacted in advance. Under this free **"Client Letter Service,"** they will hold mail for 30 days, forward upon request, and accept telegrams. Just like *Poste Restante*, the last name of the person to whom the mail is addressed should be capitalized and underlined. Some offices will offer these services to non-cardholders (especially those who have purchased AmEx Travellers' Cheques), but you must call ahead to make sure. Check the Practical Information section of the countries you plan to visit; *Let's Go* lists AmEx office locations for most large cities. A complete list is available free from AmEx (tel. 1 (800) 528 4800) in the booklet *Traveler's Companion*.

TELEPHONES

The easiest way to make international phone calls in India and Nepal, thanks to the recent arrival of satellites and fiber optics, is through the yellow STD/ISD phone "booths" (really phone shops) that dot the landscape of every major Indian street. **International Subscriber Dialing (ISD)** calls can be made with or without the help of an operator. Without operator assistance, an ISD call may be made from phone booths by dialing "00" followed by the country code, the city or area code, and the local number. Most of these booths also send and receive **faxes** for customers.

English-speaking operators are often available for both local and international assistance, but international collect calls cannot be made from India or Nepal to some countries. It's usually cheaper to find a phone booth and call just long enough to be able to say "call me" and give your number. Discuss this with the booth operator in advance before you try it. The rate for an incoming call should be between nothing and the cost of a local call. However, most STD/ISD booth operators will not allow incoming return calls because they don't make any money this way. An alternative is to have your friend call you back at your hotel or some other place with a reliable phone. But travelers should budget enough to pay for all overseas calls on the spot if necessary.

A **calling card** is another alternative; your local long-distance phone company will have a number for you to dial while traveling (either toll-free or charged as a local call) to connect instantly to an operator in your home country. The calls (plus a small surcharge) are then billed either collect or to a calling card. For more information, call **AT&T** about its **USADirect** and **World Connect** services (tel. 1 (800) 331 1140, from abroad 1 (412) 553 7458), **Sprint** (tel. 1 (800) 877 4646), or **MCI WorldPhone** and **World Reach** (tel. 1 (800) 996 7535). MCI's WorldPhone also provides access to MCI's Traveler's Assist, which gives legal and medical advice, exchange rate information, and translation services. In Canada, contact Bell Canada **Canada Direct** (tel. 1 (800) 565 4708); in the U.K., British Telecom **BT Direct** (tel. 44 (800) 345144); in Ireland, Telecom Éireann **Ireland Direct** (tel. 353 (800) 250250); in Australia, Telstra **Australia Direct** (tel. 132200); in New Zealand, **Telecom New Zealand** (tel. 123); and in South Africa, **Telkom South Africa** (tel. 0903). We have very little information on how well these services work from India or Nepal, however; it is likely that many of them won't work outside major cities. And even those that work in theory are often disallowed by greedy STD/ISD booth owners.

Rates for international calls from India are the same around the clock, but long-distance calls within India are half-price after 6pm, and one-quarter price after 9pm. When calling home, remember **time zones**. South Asian countries have no daylight savings time.

OTHER COMMUNICATION

Domestic and international **telegrams** are slower than telephones but faster than post. In India, Central Telegraph Offices (CTOs) in many cities offer telegraph service to Europe or Australasia for Rs.2 per word, or to North America for Rs.2.50 per word. Central Telegraph Offices also frequently have 24-hour STD/ISD phone services. **Faxes** are available at many STD/ISD booths.

If you're addicted to the blinking cursor of the cyber-world, **electronic mail (e-mail)** is an attractive option. With a minimum of computer knowledge and a little planning, you can beam messages anywhere for only a small charge. Look for bureaus that offer access to e-mail for sending individual messages; these are now widely available in places like Kathmandu.

■ Economics and Ethics

For foreigners, the shock of entering a new culture in India or Nepal is often compounded with an equal shock caused by the poverty of those around them. Bony rickshaw-*wallahs* wince as they pedal down flooded roads, cows graze on any available tuft of urban vegetation, and street children roam in tattered clothes. The poverty in these countries is also evident in the poorly paved roads and the piles of household garbage that no one can afford to dispose of. Due to their relative wealth, foreigners are mobbed by touts, assailed by armies of beggars, accosted by slippery con men, and they are often charged more than locals as a matter of official policy. For budget travelers, these shenanigans can be exhausting and infuriating. Inequality does not excuse the lack of respect with which touts and some other people working in the tourism industry treat their customers. After a tout has lied to you about a hotel in order to get you into one that would pay a commission, or after a rickshaw-*wallah* has asked you for five times the real fare in hopes that you might be stupid enough to pay, you may find yourself arguing over small differences in money not because of the amount, but as a matter of principle.

However, Western travelers trying to pinch paise should remember how much their money really means to the people they deal with. Foreigners are wealthy compared to most Indians and Nepalis—no budget travel excuses are acceptable here. Even the most austere budget travelers frequently spend as much in a day as their hotel watchman or rickshaw-*wallah* earns in a month. Budget travelers have also paid for a roundtrip plane ticket to India and Nepal, an unimaginable sum of money for most Indians and Nepalis.

It is also important to remember that not everyone shares a rational Western view of buying and selling as simple transactions. In many countries, economics are heavily mixed with other cultural patterns; business dealings are founded on long-term social relationships. For strangers to waltz in and demand certain services in exchange for dollars can upset older ways of doing business. It is important to accept your status as an outsider and to be prepared to pay more. In the Indian and Nepali economic system, "fair" doesn't necessarily mean a set price for everyone. Tourists are not members of Indian or Nepali society, and must reconcile themselves to this. It's annoying to see rickshaw-*wallahs* who ask for inflated prices (and clueless tourists who pay whatever they're asked), but it is equally annoying to see Westerners who haggle fiercely over one or two rupees. Travelers must be willing to pay slightly more than the "local" price.

Many foreigners come to India and Nepal with a preset idea of what they want to find—grand architecture, soaring mountains, or gobs and gobs of *karma*. But staying in air-conditioned hotels and touring in private cars, their money becomes a shield, bringing fawning treatment as well as an ego boost. When people don't behave as they expect, and their trip doesn't work out just as planned, they start to see people as obstructive to their experience. They feel they haven't gotten their "money's worth." Although budget travelers are usually much better about this, one shouldn't assume that because one is spending next to nothing one is really coping better with India or Nepal. Budget travelers have ways of insulating themselves as well, often by staying in social circles with other foreign travelers rather than meeting natives.

The best advice is to come to India or Nepal without expectations. Travel is at its best when it is spontaneous and unplanned. You might find your best experiences happen the time the plane gets cancelled and you're stuck in a city with "nothing to do" for a while, and you find that there is lots to do. Meeting natives of the countries you're visiting is what it's all about, so don't miss such opportunities when they come up. Indians and Nepalis are wonderful hosts if you allow them to be hosts on their own terms. Let yourself be vulnerable to new experiences, and ask people to help you. As a foreigner, unfamiliar with the terrain, you will merit gushing hospitality.

Try to avoid the trap of imagining a "real" India or Nepal and trying to discover it. Each country contains millions of people, each with a life as interesting as yours. Many westerners long to visit an India or a Nepal that is "traditional," or "spiritual." As you'll see upon arrival, India contains tradition and spirituality, but much more. These stereotypes have been created by Westerners questioning their own fast-paced, technologically advanced lifestyle and looking for something opposite. Life is much more complicated than that, and Indians and Nepalis have their own interests as well; they don't exist just to be part of an "experience" for tourists. Rather than looking for an "unspoiled" India or Nepal (which never existed in the first place) try to immerse yourself in the much more interesting topic of what these countries are like today.

You might find that chasing after a country's history or religion or architecture, zipping from sight to sight, prevents you from having really meaningful contact with the locals. In that case, don't hesitate to settle down for a while. Ask about opportunities for study or volunteer work. By getting involved in some longer, more stable activity, you will have more exposure to individual Indians and Nepalis, and a much more enriching time. Although most Indians and Nepalis will never be able to afford a plane ticket to your home country, you will often find that they are just as curious about your country as you are about theirs. By meeting local people and talking to them about your experiences, you can make the cross-cultural exchange go both ways. For more information, see **Alternatives to Tourism** (p. 29).

The following sections describe some of the issues foreign travelers in India and Nepal face when they deal with money.

TOUTS, MIDDLEMEN, AND SCAMS

Touts are the scruffy-looking men who surround travelers at bus stands and train stations, or accost them in streets of tourist ghettos, offering deals on transportation, currency exchange, magic from the plant kingdom, or any service rupees can buy. If you have trouble finding something, a tout will probably be able to help you for a little *baksheesh,* but what really distinguishes touts is their unhelpfulness. They are pushy and will try to trap you into paying for something you don't really want. They count on foreigners to be naive enough to follow along.

It is hard to **find a hotel** without a tout getting involved; you'll be approached as soon as you get off the bus or train. Touts (and taxi drivers and rickshaw-*wallahs* too) are paid commissions by hotels to gather tourists, and these commissions are usually added to the hotel bill. The best policy is to be firm. Decide where you want to go and have someone take you there. If the hotel isn't paying commissions, touts will tell you it's full or closed; don't believe it. If no one will take you there, find someone who doesn't speak English, or have someone take you to a general area from where you can hunt for a good place to stay. A traveler wearing a big backpack in a tourist ghetto will attract touts like flies to a rotting mango, so try to find a safe place (often a restaurant) where you can put down your pack while you search.

> ## If You Can't Beat 'Em, Join 'Em
> One *Let's Go* researcher-writer tell us, "If a cab driver or someone pisses me off, I settle down, smile at them, they know we're both full of shit, and then I hit 'em up for a cigarette."

In major tourist centers you'll often meet people who want you to visit their home or their workplace or to take you for tours. You may be told some story as an excuse for them to take you somewhere to look at jewels, gifts, or other supposedly rare and hard to get export items. Unless you have asked to go somewhere, you are under no obligation to follow them or to pay them for being taken to a place in which you have no interest. Don't give them money when they ask you for it, regardless of what they say they will do for you. This is especially important to remember upon arrival when you will be at your most vulnerable.

Travel agents in the major tourist centers frequently resemble touts with desks and telephones. They are known to give false information, charge hefty commissions, and they even sometimes sell bogus tickets. Unless they have a peon to do it for them, most Indians buy train tickets directly from the station. It's best to do this yourself too. **Eliminating the middleman** will give you more control over your travels, will save you money, and will get you more acquainted with the way things work in the country you're visiting.

Another hassle at many monuments and temples are the unofficial **"guides"** who won't allow travelers to peacefully enjoy the sights but spew ignorant drivel, later demanding *baksheesh*. Be forceful with these people and they will usually back off— don't hesitate to push your way through. However, some historical sites have sophisticated and informative guides. It is usually better to book a guide through a tourist office or other government organization than to wait to be approached by some strange man.

When ignored, many touts are equipped with a guilt-trip line, tailored to your demographic group, for example: "Excuse me sir, one question: Why don't you white Americans like to talk to us Indians?" Don't let these attacks on your insecurities get to you. There are better ways of meeting Indians and Nepalis than letting them cheat you.

BEGGING

From lines of beggars outside temples to children weaving through traffic to beg at car windows, the sad phenomenon of begging is impossible to ignore in India and Nepal. Nothing can prepare a traveler for the all-too-common sight of children and impoverished women holding starving babies while begging for food and money. It is said that some children are even maimed by family members in order to increase sympathy and hence, charity. While giving may temporarily ease your conscience, it is not always the best choice. Sometimes a person seen giving charity may be singled out by other beggars and quickly approached. Giving can also encourage a cycle of poverty—some children avoid attending school because they can earn money by begging. It is, however, customary to give to beggars at pilgrimage sites and to *sadhus,* wandering Hindu holy men who survive by begging. If you give to beggars, a small donation like one or two rupees is considered enough. **Don't give** to cute, healthy kids who cheerfully approach tourists with requests for rupees, coins, or pens. These are not beggars, but regular schoolchildren having fun trying their luck to see what they can get from foreigners. This encourages a begging mentality, and their parents usually find this behavior embarrassing. A quick "Begging is bad" or "Don't you have anything better to do?" is a more appropriate response.

BARGAINING

India and Nepal are wonderful places to practice your bargaining skills. Taxi and auto-rickshaw fares (when not metered) and items in outdoor markets are fair game for haggling. Don't bargain on prepared or packaged foods (on the street or in restaurants) or on items marked with a price tag. But in smaller, family-run stores it might not hurt to try. Be prepared to pay what you offer; it is considered outrageous to refuse to purchase something after settling on a price. Start by offering half the stated price and let your charismatic powers do the rest.

Bargaining requires patience and cooperation from both parties. If you seem stubborn and grouchy, the vendor is less likely to want to come down. Chat with him or her a little. Strike up a conversation if you have any language in common. You'll find that the personal touch goes a long way. You should feel right to refuse any vendor or rickshaw-*wallah* who bargains rudely or aggressively.

BAKSHEESH

The word *baksheesh* is usually translated as a "tip," but the concept really includes a whole range of exchanges. Bribing a railway porter to find a seat on a "full" train is *baksheesh;* so is giving small change to beggars. *Baksheesh* can work wonders— Rs.20 *baksheesh* given to an Indian traffic policeman has been known to make moving violations disappear forever, and foreigners visiting some Hindu temples have been surprised to be asked for a donation with the phrase "*baksheesh* for God." Small tips are expected for restaurant service, train "coolie" porter service, and unofficial tour guides. There is no need to tip taxi drivers; they overcharge as it is. Tips depend on your level of satisfaction or gratitude, and usually run between Rs.1 and Rs.20, not following any particular percentage rule. Alternatively, a pack of cigarettes or some other small gift is often appreciated. Most Indians and Nepalis expect great tips from foreigners, but don't be swayed by groans and protests. If your first offer is met with a quick roll of the head signifying "OK," then you have done well. Another good guideline for *baksheesh* is to watch what wealthy Indians and Nepalis do. They almost always give something, but it's usually not more than a rupee or two.

■ Environmentally Responsible Tourism

Travel to another country inevitably affects that country's ecology, especially in poor countries where so much development has taken place in order to build up the tourism industry. Nevertheless, there is not a list somewhere of activities which do or do not make you an environmentally responsible tourist, and no objective criteria exists that can be used to judge your fellow traveler's guilt or innocence. Being responsible does not mean never going on a trek or only using biodegradable shampoo. Rather, responsible tourism means understanding the short- and long-term effects of your actions, seriously considering these effects, and realizing you are responsible for them. Only looking at part of the picture does not lead to a responsible decision. This is especially true with spending your money. When purchasing a good or service, a rupee does much more than simply provide for you—it influences the growth of industries and the lives of those who work in them. Responsible tourism means being aware of these factors and weighing them in order to make a responsible decision.

As a traveler, there are certain measures you can take to minimize your impact on the countries you visit. Always turn off the lights and the air conditioning when you leave a room, and make sure that the doors and windows are shut when the air conditioning is on. Better yet, stay in a place without air conditioning; most Indians and Nepalis do this their entire lives. Don't accept excess packaging, particularly styrofoam boxes as they are not biodegradable. Even using refillable ballpoint pens available at almost all stationery shops will make that small difference. If you are a woman, buy feminine hygiene products with minimal packaging; O.B. brand tampons have no applicator and come in small, discreet boxes. Choose glass soda bottles over drinking boxes, or marginally recyclable aluminum cans. Reuse plastic bags. It's hard to convince Indian and Nepali market vendors not to give you 3 plastic bags where one would suffice, but with a little extra effort, you'll surely succeed.

After some time in this part of the world, you will undoubtedly realize that the bucket showers and squat toilets are significantly more water-efficient than their Western counterparts. To be further water-friendly, carry a refillable water bottle or canteen. While the water in India and Nepal does present a credible health hazard, you can bring purifying tablets or iodine drops from home to treat it. This method will save you buying countless plastic water bottles which will probably end up floating down the Yamuna or decomposing next to the railroad tracks. Not a pretty sight.

One of the best ways to undo some of the effects of environmental destruction in India or Nepal and to minimize your own impact is to volunteer for one of the many environmental organizations there (see **Alternatives to Tourism,** p. 29). There remains little information regarding responsible tourism in India and Nepal. Should you happen to uncover a great "ecotourism" operator or have further ideas on how to be a low-impact tourist, we at *Let's Go* would love to hear of them. Please do not hesitate to call or write to us.

■ Customs and Etiquette

Try to adapt your behavior to India and Nepal while you travel. It will be much easier and safer for you to move around if you do not stand out in any way that may be seen as rude or offensive.

CLOTHING

Dress modestly. Clothing can elicit reactions as polarized as a warm welcome and a nasty jeer. While exhibiting sleek, tan shoulders or long, lean legs is a matter of pride and envy in the West, most Indians and Nepalese find it distasteful and even disrespectful. In some areas, a man walking down the street sporting shorts will be giggled at, since only little boys wear shorts and panthood is synonymous with manhood. Similarly, but for different reasons, women should try to keep legs covered, at least to the knee. Try to think of this as much for your own comfort, as a shield from greedy or disapproving eyes, as for cultural sensitivity points. Bare shoulders are another sure sign of immorality (and a quick way to sunburn). Ragged clothes will also draw attention to you. In India, many women will find they are treated more respectfully when they wear a *salwar kameez*. While men's clothing in India is typically more westernized, men might want to buy a thin cotton *kurta pajama*—these garments will cover you up while keeping you cool. If you are well-dressed, this will certainly affect the way that people respond to you as a foreigner. Like everything in South Asia, these rules vary by region. Clothing taboos are looser in Nepal and throughout the Himalaya, and also in cosmopolitan centers like Bombay.

FOOD

Most Indian and Nepalis eat with their hands, a skill many foreigners have trouble picking up. While restaurants usually give cutlery to foreigners, you may have to eat with your hands if you are invited to someone's home. The most important thing is to **eat with your right hand only.** The left hand is used for cleaning after defecation, so it is seen as polluted. Keep your left hand in your lap throughout the meal. You can use your left hand to hold a fork or a glass or to pass a dish (and you'll need to do this, because your right hand will be awfully mucky) but it can never touch food or your lips directly. With the tips of the fingers of your right hand held together like a scoop, pick up a bite of food. Lift it up and push it into your mouth with your thumb. Sound easy? If this is done right, in theory, the food should never touch higher than the first joint of your fingers.

Any food that comes into contact with one person's saliva is unclean for anyone else. Indians and Nepalis will not usually take bites of each other's food, or drink from the same cup; watch how locals drink from water bottles, pouring the drink in without touching their lips. Besides being culturally correct this is a good rule to follow in South Asia for health reasons.

In Hindu houses, the family **hearth** is sacred, so if food is cooked before you on a fire (as it frequently is in trekking lodges) never play with the fire or throw garbage in it.

Food in India or Nepal usually begins with a staple dish: usually rice in southern and eastern India, wheat bread in the north. Many foreigners are amazed at the masses of starch consumed. For many people it is the only food they eat on a regular basis. Almost all Jains and many Hindus (especially in South India) are **vegetarian,** and besides, for many non-vegetarians, meat is an expensive luxury. Due to the cow's sacred status in Hinduism, beef is scarce in India and unavailable in Nepal. Muslims do not eat pork and are supposed to shun alcohol; this latter restriction is not always observed. Only the most modernized, Westernized women of any religion drink alcohol.

HYGIENE

Westerners, brought up with to believe their hygiene is "scientific," are often amazed at how Indians and Nepalis can have so many rules about bodily purity even while they practice such unhygienic customs as bathing and drinking from rivers filled with decaying garbage and excrement. The truth is that many Western hygiene customs are just as irrational and ritualistic, even if we tell ourselves we're combating "germs." There is no scientific justification for sharing a glass with a friend but not with a stranger, for example; it has more to do with culture.

All **bodily secretions** and products are considered polluting in South Asian culture, and the people who come into contact with them—laundrymen, barbers, latrine cleaners—have historically formed the lowest ranks of the caste system.

The **head** is the most sacred part of the body, and purity decreases all the way to the toes. To **touch something with your feet** is a grave insult, and you should never touch a person with your feet, or step over a seated person's outstretched legs, or even point at someone with your foot. Never put your feet on a table, or any other surface used for eating or studying. To touch someone else's feet, on the other hand, is an act of veneration. If you accidentally touch someone else with your foot, touch your forehead and then their knee or foot, whichever is more accessible.

The **left hand** is also polluted because it comes into contact with feces. Always use your right hand to eat, give, take, or point. However, the left hand should be used to put on shoes.

COMMUNICATION AND BODY LANGUAGE

A quick **sideways roll of the head,** similar to shaking one's head but more like a sideways nod, means "OK," or "I understand." Many foreigners are baffled by this gesture, thinking their hosts are answering their most innocent comments and requests with a firm "no." It is actually much easier to get a **"yes"** from Indians and Nepalis—sometimes too easy. South Asians are often embarrassed to give a negative answer, and will occasionally describe a totally fictional set of directions to the river or the post office rather than admit they don't know the way. Avoid asking yes-or-no questions; phrase questions so that you'll know whether your respondent really knew what he or she was talking about.

When you meet people, be prepared for **questions** about your nationality, age, marital status, family, education, employment, and income. There's nothing threatening about this. None of these are seen as private matters. It's just innocent curiosity. Ask people the same questions back; they'll be glad to chat.

Indian English, especially when written, is full of colorful and antique-sounding phrases. You may be surprised to hear people address you as "madame" or "good gentleman," or to read letters asking you to "kindly do the needful" and signed "your most humble servant." For some useful phrases as well as words that commonly appear in English, see the **Appendix,** p. 755.

Many foreigners have trouble adjusting to the constant **stares** they get in India and Nepal. There's no solution but to adjust. Don't stare back—this will only confuse and anger people. There's no taboo about staring in South Asian culture and most staring is done out of innocent curiosity. Bask in the attention, and remember that people's curiosity about you is due to the limited chance they have for contact with different people; don't deny them an opportunity.

WOMEN AND MEN

Although big city parks are filled with couples courting, nothing ever happens between them in plain view. Displays of **physical affection** between women and men are rare, so stay tame when in public. Some affection is considered completely natural and acceptable, such as that between men. Everywhere, men walk comfortably down the street clasping hands.

Except in Westernized circles and among some groups high in the mountains, most Indian and Nepali women appear quite meek and quiet in public. It is difficult for strange men to talk to them, and probably best not to try. Women travelers also might have a hard time meeting Indian and Nepali women, although women should try to find other women to help out in emergencies (see **Women Travelers,** p. 33).

TIME

Nothing runs quite on schedule in India and Nepal as foreigners might expect. Buses leave late, offices open late, dinner parties start late. South Asia operates on a very different conception of time from most Western countries, requiring infinite patience. The only real solution is to set your clock this way too; if you allow yourself to get annoyed at every delay, you'll be a basket case by the end of your trip. As infuriated as you might want to be, take the time to look around you and enjoy the little things—isn't that what you came for anyway?

In response to your requests in banks, phone booths, and other places you'll commonly be told to **"sit down."** It is assumed you would rather wait and have something done for you rather than doing it yourself, even if you could do it faster. If you really need to accomplish something, it is sometimes necessary to be rude and decline the offer of a seat.

PLACES OF WORSHIP

Be especially sensitive about etiquette in places of worship. Secular visitors to sacred shrines are expected to follow customs and rituals just as perfectly as believers. **Dress conservatively,** keeping legs and shoulders covered, and **take off your shoes** before entering any mosque, *gurudwara,* or Hindu, Jain, or Buddhist temple. Visitors to Sikh *gurudwaras* must cover their heads as well—handkerchiefs are usually provided. At the entrance to popular temples, shoe-*wallahs* will guard your shoes for a few rupees' *baksheesh.* Ask before taking **photographs** in places of worship. It is normally forbidden to take pictures of images of deities in Hindu temples.

Many Hindu temples, especially those in Kerala, but also in Nepal and in pilgrimage sites such as Puri and Varanasi, ban non-Hindus from entering. In practice this rule excludes anyone who doesn't look sufficiently South Asian. Some Hindu and Jain temples forbid menstruating women to enter.

It is common practice in Hindu temples to partake of an offering of consecrated fruit and/or water called *prasad,* which is received with the right hand over the left (and no one takes seconds). It is protocol to leave a small donation at the entrance to the temple sanctuary, though this can cause some dilemmas when temple priests aggressively force *prasad* into your hands, expecting large amounts of cash in return. Usually a donation of one or two rupees will suffice.

Hinduism and Buddhism consider the right-hand side auspicious and the left-hand side inauspicious; thus it is customary to walk around Hindu temples and Buddhist *stupas* **clockwise,** with your right side toward the shrine. In fact, any circular motion, such as the turning of Tibetan Buddhist prayer wheels, must proceed in a clockwise direction.

Let's Go Picks

For this page, and this page only, we renounce our pretense of objectivity and reveal our personal faves. Pick from our picks, or pick your own favorites, and then send us a postcard so we can include your choices in a Readers' Picks 1998.

Wild Wonders: Camel safaris in Jaisalmer. You'll be blown away in the dunes of the desert (see p. 317). **Elephant rides in Chitwan.** Forget jeeps and rickshaws—elephants brave the jungle best (see p. 745). **Mudumalai Wildlife Sanctuary.** This government-protected natural wonder is safari heaven (see p. 495).

Sacred Structures: Golden Temple, Amritsar. The temple's tranquility has proved indelible despite a turbulent history (see p. 333). **Stupa,** Boudha. Nepal's oldest *stupa* stupefies with its whitewashed wonder (see p. 706).

Magnificent Monuments: Kandariya Mahadev Temple, Khajuraho. A whirling, wheeling wonder of medieval architecture (see p. 250). **Victoria Memorial,** Calcutta. The Taj Mahal of the British viceroys (see p. 379). **Changu Narayan,** Kathmandu Valley. A collection of gorgeous sculptures on a glorious hilltop perch (see p. 715). **Golconda Fort,** Hyderabad. Fantastically eerie ruins of the headquarters of the 16th-century empire (see p. 579). **Qutab Minar,** Delhi. Sandstone victory tower built by India's first Muslim kingdom (see p. 145).

Places We Hate to Leave: Mandu. A little-touristed little city infused with the romance and ruins of its golden age (see p. 242). **Udaipur.** Elegant palaces steeped in romanticism (see p. 290). **Ayodhya.** Religious fanaticism and spiritual serenity in the same spot (see p. 212). **Pushkar.** Redemption, food, and fun all rolled into one, especially at the Pushkar Fair (see p. 280).

Human-Made Wonders: Rock Garden, Chandigarh (see p. 328). Nek Chand has turned stones and scraps into sculpture for his fantasy garden world. **Janakpur Womens' Development Center.** The walls of the village are dressed to impress, thanks to the efforts of Janakpur's women (see p. 750). **Calico Museum of Textiles,** Ahmedabad. A treat for the aesthete (see p. 642).

Best For a Rest: Tranquillity Retreat, near Almora. The extra "l" in Tranquillity is for a lush landscape and a loveable lady named Armelle (see p. 187). **Jungle Hut,** Mudumulai Wildlife Sanctuary. Sunny cottages are made even brighter with batik prints and a friendly family (see p. 496).

Scenes to be Seen: Gorkha Durbar, Gorkha. This is the place to be humbled by Himalaya and sedated by the sunrise (see p. 726). **Coaker's Walk,** Kodaikanal. Stroll along this path for beautiful views of Kodai (see p. 490). **Sunrise** in Kaniyakumari—the end of India at the beginning of the day (see p. 484).

Let's Go Trek: Annapurna Sanctuary Trek. A few short steps from low-lying Pokhara right into the lap of the Himalaya (see p. 737). **Annapurna Circuit Trek.** A circuit of culture, climate, and company (see p. 738).

Sustenance in Style: Nirula's, Kathmandu. Bureaucratized ice cream on the edge of South Asia (see p. 689). **Moondance,** Pokhara. You can feast on food, move to the music, and battle a game of backgammon all in the same place (see p. 733). **Café Nyatapola,** Bhaktapur. A neat treat to eat on top of a pagoda (see p. 712). **Trishna,** Bombay. Sumptuous seafood, it's Bombay's best (see p. 597). **Tulika's Ice Cream Parlor,** Calcutta. Nothin' like Dutch chocolate in India (see p. 377). **Daily Bread,** Kodaikanal. Charming brother and sister owners, delicious coffee, and goodies galore (see p. 489).

Balmiest Beaches: Bet Dwarka, Gujarat. The island is surrounded by the solitude of the sea (see p. 653). **Anjuna Beach,** Goa. A hippie happening paradise (see p. 631). **Varkala,** Kerala. A less touristy resort town, with beautiful waves and mists (see p. 508).

Best Dancing Gods: Kathakali Dance, Cochin (see p. 525).

INDIA

On August 15, 1997, India will celebrate the 50th anniversary of its Independence from British rule, an event which, even a half-century later, continues to define how the nation sees itself. One of the world's great civilizations, "India" is often used to refer to all of South Asia, including countries now beyond the borders of the Republic of India. In the 18th and 19th centuries British colonizers glued this disparate patch of turf together, splitting off parts of it in 1947, but leaving most of the land mass intact as one immense nation, struggling to find its place in the 20th century. India is currently in the throes of rapid change, as it ponders the results of its 1991 decision to let in foreign investors, and as groups of people long at the bottom of the social ladder find new ways into power. Yet the legacy of India's ancient Sanskrit-speaking civilization lives on—to Indians, the country is still "Bharat," the land of the ancient Sanskrit-speakers, the land that gave birth to four major world religions. This heritage now threatens to divide Indians between those who identify with it and those who don't, but the tumult of the 20th century provides one point just about all Indians can rally behind.

ESSENTIALS

▓ Money

NRs.100=Rs.62.94	Rs.100=NRs.158.9
US$1=Rs.35.09	Rs.100=US$2.850
CDN$1=Rs.25.65	Rs.100=CDN$3.899
UK£1=Rs.54.16	Rs.100=UK£1.847
IR£1=Rs.55.74	Rs.100=IR£1.794
AUS$1=30.78	Rs.100=AUS$3.616
NZ$1=Rs.23.71	Rs.100=NZ$4.217
SAR=Rs.8.07	Rs.100=SAR12.393

Currency is measured in rupees (Rs.) which are divided into 100 paise (p.). Paise come in denominations of 5, 10, 20, 25, and 50p., while rupees come in Rs.1, 2, and 5 coins and bills worth Rs.1, 2, 5, 10, 20, 50, 100, and 500. Check all banknotes carefully; ripped bills will be refused by many merchants (although banks will exchange them for new ones).

The State Bank of India is the most common place to change money, but branches of other banks sometimes have foreign exchange facilities as well. Banking hours are short (Mon.-Fri. 10am-2pm, Sat. 10am-noon), although in some big tourist centers banks stay open until 5pm on weekdays. With the rapid changes in India's economy, high inflation is expected in the next year, and all prices in this book could easily go up by about 10%; on the other hand, the exchange rate is likely to change as well, meaning that prices will probably stay the same in hard currency terms.

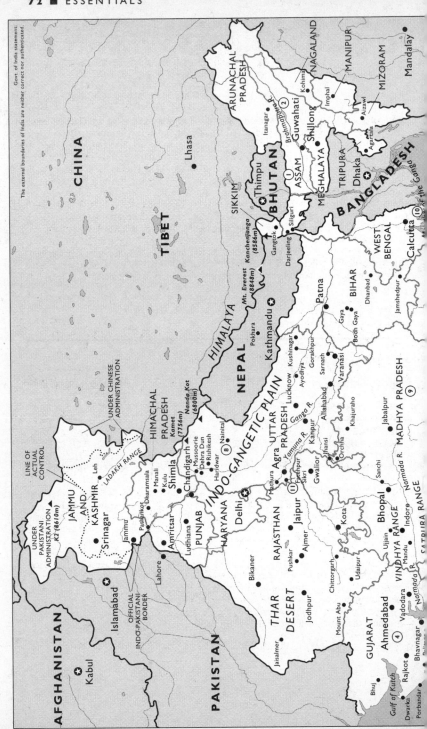

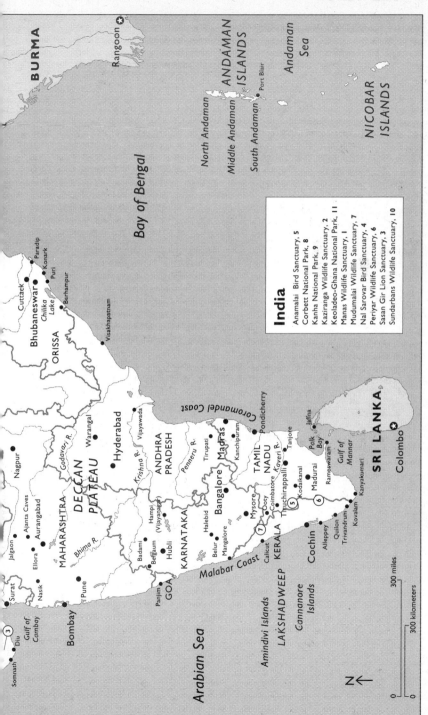

India

Anamalai Bird Sanctuary, 5
Corbett National Park, 8
Kanha National Park, 9
Kaziranga Wildlife Sanctuary, 2
Keoladeo-Ghana National Park, 11
Manas Wildlife Sanctuary, 1
Mudumalai Wildlife Sanctuary, 7
Nal Sarovar Bird Sanctuary, 4
Periyar Wildlife Sanctuary, 6
Sasan Gir Lion Sanctuary, 3
Sundarbans Wildlife Sanctuary, 10

■ Getting Around

BY PLANE

The government's domestic carrier, Indian Airlines, flies to over 50 cities in India and neighboring countries. India's airline industry has recently been opened up to small private airlines (officially called ATOs, "air taxi operators")—East West, Jet Airways, ModiLuft, Skyline NEPC, and Sahara. Indian Airlines still has the largest fleet and handles about 75% of the traffic, but it is a lumbering dinosaur, losing money heavily. The private airlines are seen as the wave of the future, although three of them (East West, Modiluft, and Skyline NEPC) were reported to be on the brink of bankruptcy in 1996.

Reservations are essential on all flights and must be made well in advance, especially during the peak seasons. Flights almost always sell out. Go to one of the airlines' offices to make a booking, or use a travel agent. If you don't get a seat, put your name on the waiting list and show up at the airport early; miracles can happen.

Indian Airlines offers **youth fares** at a 25% reduction for passengers ages 12 to 30. Children under 12 pay 50%, and infants under two pay 10%. Foreigners must buy their plane tickets with foreign currency, and any change is returned in rupees.

Indian Airlines offers a traveling package for foreign tourists called **"Discover India"** that provides for unlimited air travel for 21 days, provided that no destinations are repeated except the first and last points; only a limited number of seats on each flight are allotted to 'Discover India' subscribers. If you plan on jam-packing sights cross-country, this package is perfect, but if you want to glimpse the countryside and ingest more culture than the airport giftshop has to offer, you'll probably have to stick to the ground.

Guard your Indian Airlines ticket well—if you lose it, they will accept no responsibility. Check-in time for domestic flights is one hour before departure.

BY TRAIN

With over 1.6 million people on its payroll, the Indian Railways are the world's largest employer. Eleven million passengers are carried over its vast network daily. There is a unique culture on the Indian railways, which is quite a change from India's touristy packaging. From the landscapes rushing outside the window to the storms of clay *chai* cups whizzing inside, you're bound to get a glimpse of India on the train, or at least a glimpse of how India travels. You'll meet locals eager to chat about your country and theirs. Trains are generally the best way to cover long distances in India at a reasonable cost.

The Indian Railways might not get you there on time, but they will get you there—and "there" is just about anywhere in the country. The only exceptions are the hilly areas, mainly in the north. A few hill stations are reached by **"toy trains,"** narrow-gauge machines that run on rails two feet (0.610m) apart. Meter-gauge and broad-gauge (1.676m) trains are the norm elsewhere. These distinctions are usually irrelevant to all but train buffs however. Speeds are more important. **Express** or **mail** trains are the fast, useful ones that rush between cities. The *Shatabdi Express* and the *Rajdhani Express* are **superfast** trains which cover the main lines, such as Delhi-Bombay and Delhi-Calcutta, and even some smaller ones such as Delhi-Bhopal. Superfast trains come with full air conditioning and meals, stop only at big cities, and are more expensive. Unless you are headed to an out-of-the-way village it is probably best to avoid the local **passenger** trains, which lumber along and stop at every small-town station.

Various classes of comfort are available, from air-conditioned first class, to non-A/C first, to the many *avatars* of second class. **First class** on an Indian train is three or four times the price of second class, though still not very expensive. In first class, you won't be squeezed to your bench by an excessive crowd (which can be half the fun). Air conditioning is unnecessary on trains, because once the train gets moving you'll be cooled off anyway. First-class sleeper cars are divided into compartments, offering

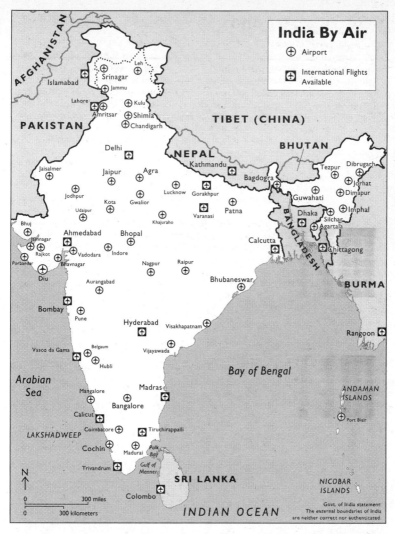

India By Air
⊕ Airport
⊞ International Flights Available

more privacy than second-class sleepers, which have rows of berths in the open. **Second class** is probably the best bet on a budget. Though crowded and dirty, second-class will certainly give you more contact with fellow passengers, and it is just as possible to get a good night's sleep in second-class **sleepers** (you're guaranteed a soft padded berth to yourself). During the day, second class is something of a free-for all, but this is tolerable for short trips.

For long trips, especially overnight ones, it's necessary to make **reservations** (usually a day or two in advance). It is safest to do this right at the station or booking office. Avoid **travel agents** if you can; they frequently charge hefty commissions and

Warning: As this book went to press, the Indian Railways announced a **fare increase** for all trains, effective October 1, 1996. The fares listed in this book do not reflect the new fare structure and may be incorrect.

have been known to give false information in order to steer you into the best deal for them. **Computers** have made bookings systematic, but there are still long, anarchic lineups. A **tourist quota** is often set aside for anyone who can show a foreign passport. A few major stations even have separate queues for tourists and many have ladies' queues or allow women to jump to the front of the line to avoid pushing and shoving. Get a reservation slip from the window, and scribble down the train you want. Each route has a **name** and a **number,** information that locals seem to have memorized at birth. For route information, arm yourself with *Trains at a Glance,* Indian Railways' "Abstract Time Table" which contains **schedules** for all mail and express trains (Rs.15). The **fares** on Indian Railways correspond to distance and class. If you have trouble finding your way at a station, try the **enquiry counter**—the people at these booths are generally well-informed and speak English.

If you fail to get a reservation, you can still get on the **waiting list** and hope. In an emergency, try to find the **stationmaster.** He will probably be busy and not thrilled to see you, but if anyone can find a seat for you on a "full" train, it's he, and with some patience you might be able to persuade him. As a last resort, *baksheesh* to porters (especially if you're getting on at the beginning of the line) has been known to turn up unreserved berths like nothing else. If you **cancel** your reservation more than 24 hours before your trip, you can still get a refund but you'll be charged Rs. 10-50 depending on the class. Up to four hours before, you'll get 75% back, and after that (even sometimes 12 hours after the train has left), you can get still get 50%.

If you have a reservation, it is fine to get to the station just a few minutes before the train arrives. Check the computer-printed list for your name and seat, and listen for announcements. If your train is delayed, the **waiting rooms** can be a good place to pass time and avoid stares. It's usually not difficult for foreigners to assume a place in the first class waiting room, regardless of what class they're traveling. The guard probably doesn't speak English, and some travelers pretend not to understand when he or she asks to see tickets. Railway station **restaurants** are also worth checking out, for their good, cheap, steel-plate *thalis.* Railway **retiring rooms** are available to anyone with a valid ticket or Indrail pass. These are usually cheaper than budget hotels and can be convenient if you arrive late or have to catch an early-morning train. Retiring rooms operate on a 24-hour basis, and most also rent for 12 hours at a stretch. But check out the noise level first. Women traveling on their own or with children should enquire about **ladies' compartments,** available on most overnight mail and express trains.

Foreign passport holders can buy **Indrail Passes,** which are available for lengths of 1, 2, 4, 7, 15, 21, 30, 60, or 90 days, in 1st class A/C, 2nd class A/C, and 2nd class non-A/C. Indrail Passes include all fares, reservation charges, and any supplementary charges, but are not really a bargain. They must be paid for in hard currency, and prices are high: a 30-day pass for 2nd class non-A/C costs US$125. To spend that much on train tickets in a month you'd have to be constantly on the move. The small advantage of Indrail Passes is that they can save you some hassle: on shorter, unreserved journeys, Indrail Pass holders can jump on the train without buying a ticket. Reservations are still necessary for longer trips, however.

BY BUS

Bus travel in India is slightly complicated by the existence of both state and private bus companies. State government buses are often crowded, so you may have to buy tickets early; get to the bus stand at least half an hour before departure. Some private bus companies offer excellent service, while others should not hold an operating license; there are so many private operators in the country that it is difficult to know the quality of an operation until you're already on a bus and screaming down the highway. As with train tickets, it is generally unwise to buy bus tickets from random travel agencies, especially for complicated trips that require changing buses; there are endless reports of scams. Avoid the video coaches unless you like watching old black-and-white Hindi films for five hours (or longer) at ear-splitting levels.

BY CAR

India's legacy of protectionist economics has left it with a freakish fleet of home-grown automobiles, from suave 1950s-style Ambassadors to putting little Marutis. Most domestic rent-a-car companies provide a driver as well as wheels; several foreign (self-driven) car rental companies including Budget and Hertz now have offices in major cities. It is also worth inquiring at government tourist offices, which frequently hire cars and drivers. For more information on cars and road conditions in India, contact the Automobile Association of India, with offices in major cities.

> **Warning:** Due to poor road conditions and aggressive driving, road travel in India is dangerous.

BY BOAT

A new ferry service has opened between Bombay and Goa, and ships travel regularly from Calcutta and Madras to Port Blair. Except for these routes, however, boats are mainly used for sight-seeing rather than transport. For more information, see **Backwater Cruises,** p. 526, 512, and 515.

■ Accommodations

Much of our accommodations wisdom applies to both India and Nepal, so be sure to consult **Essentials: Accommodations** (p. 52) for more information. Keep in mind that many Indian budget hotels, especially in the big cities, cater more to Indian travelers than to foreigners, and often the cravings of foreigners have not been well-anticipated. In tourist meccas such as Agra and Jaipur, many hotels do cater primarily to foreigners, sometimes even exclusively to foreigners.

HOSTELS

Youth hostels are scattered in various locations throughout India, especially in the far north and south. They are extremely cheap and tend to be popular with foreign visitors, their denizens crowding nearby restaurants in the evenings. YMCAs and YWCAs are only found in the big cities and are usually more expensive, although YWCAs' women-only policy makes them safer for lone women travelers. Hostels in India rarely exclude nonmembers of hosteling organizations, however, nor do they charge nonmembers extra.

TOURIST BUNGALOWS

In India, the state tourism development corporations have set up large "Tourist Bungalows" in many cities. Combining hotel with tourist office, these places may be convenient, but the slight improvement over budget hotels is seldom worth the price, and the staff can sometimes be unenthusiastic and unhelpful. The overpriced "dining halls" in Tourist Bungalows are forsaken by cost-conscious Indians, so they can be quiet places to sit and read or write—you'll seldom be disturbed by waiters.

PALACE HOTELS

Across western and central India, many former palaces of rajas and maharajas have now been turned into middle-range hotels, offering travelers the decadence of a bygone era at an affordable price. Palace hotels are sometimes still inhabited by the royal families themselves. Furniture, decorations, and facilities such as libraries give these hotels their character.

HOMESTAYS

Staying with a family provides the paying guest with the opportunity to experience the people, country, and traditions first-hand, and the Government of India Tourist

Department is aggressively promoting this concept. The "Paying Guest Scheme" is a relatively new phenomenon in India, but is gaining momentum in a number of states, particularly Tamil Nadu and Rajasthan. The Government of India Tourist Offices publish a comprehensive list of host families and information about the rooms, facilities, and meals that will be provided. Homestays are more expensive than budget hotels, but cheaper than starred hotels.

■ Keeping in Touch

Since much of the information for keeping in touch with the outside world when in India is the same as for Nepal, see **Essentials: Keeping in Touch** (p. 61).

Mail takes about two to three weeks to go between India and North America. You can mail your letters at any post office (watch it get postmarked yourself) or have your hotel take care of it for you. **Poste Restante** is like general delivery and it is the best way to get those love letters from home. Have your correspondents mark the date of your arrival on the envelope and emphasize your last name when addressing it. The letters are filed alphabetically at the post office—if you don't see that epistle under your last name, check under your first. Letters should be addressed to you, c/o *Poste Restante*, GPO, and then the city and state. Take your passport with you for identification when you go to pick up your mail. **American Express** offices will also hold mail for anyone with an American Express cards or even a single tattered US$20 AmEx Traveller's Cheque.

Trying to send a package home will involve getting it cleared by customs, taking it to a tailor to get it wrapped in cloth and sealed with wax, going to the post office to fill out the customs forms, buying stamps, and then, finally, seeing it processed and on its way. It may take a couple of months or even a couple of years to get home if you send your booty surface mail—and all packages run the risk of getting x-rayed or searched, so don't try to mail home anything illegal. If you need to receive a package from abroad, it's probably a good idea to have it registered—which will lessen the great likelihood that your toy hedgehogs will get stolen.

Phones are widespread in India, and fairly easy to use. The STD/ISD sign (Standard Trunk Dialing/International Subscriber Dialing) means that there's a phone nearby. Phones are sometimes open 24 hours a day, and there are also often private telecommunication offices that offer such modern amenities as faxes. **India's country code is 91;** the city code for Delhi is 11; Bombay is 22; Calcutta is 33; and Madras is 44—these codes must be preceded by a "0" if calling from within India. Calling home, dial the international access code (00), the country code, the city or area code and then the number. The country code is 977 for Nepal, 1 for the United States and Canada, 44 for the United Kingdom, 353 for Ireland, 61 for Australia, 64 for New Zealand, and 27 for South Africa.

■ Staying Safe

Read the headlines and ask at your country's diplomatic mission about unstable areas. Political violence in India is rarely aimed at foreigners, but there are dangers nonetheless. The state of Jammu and Kashmir, with the exception of the eastern regions of Ladakh and Zanskar, is out of the question for foreign travelers for the moment. For more information, see **Jammu and Kashmir** (p. 358). In the last few years violence has also affected northern Uttar Pradesh and parts of Assam.

■ Hours and Holidays

Most shops and offices are open from Monday to Friday 10am to 5pm, although some commercial offices and post offices are open Saturday mornings as well. Some government offices confuse things by opening alternate Saturdays. Most banks are open from 10am to 2pm during the week and until noon on Saturday. Some of these hours are extended to as early as 8am and as late as 6pm in major cities like Delhi but don't count on it.

India is 5½ hours ahead of GMT, 4½ hours behind Australian Eastern Standard Time and 10½ hours ahead of North America's Eastern Standard Time. Summer time puts the northern countries an hour closer to India.

India has many festivals on many different calendar systems, but the Gregorian calendar is used for most official purposes. For more information, see **Festivals and Holidays** (p. 769).

LIFE AND TIMES

■ Geography

By grace or coincidence, with the eternal whites of the snow-clad Himalaya, the verdant greens of dense jungle and tropical rainforest, and the earth-hewn tones of desert and arid plateau, the tripartite band of the Indian national flag finds its reflection in India's geography. Northern India is lorded over by the Himalaya, whose impenetrable heights have historically maintained the cultures of South Asia in isolation from those of Central Asia, Tibet, and China. Highest and youngest of the world's mountain ranges, the Himalaya's crescent-shaped span extends over 2000km of almost uninterrupted ups and downs. More accurately a series of mountain chains than a single range, the Himalaya's deep nesting valleys fashion the watersheds of the Subcontinent's three major river systems, the Indus, Ganga, and Brahmaputra. Fed by rainwater and glacial runoff, these rivers' networks of silt-dumping tributaries in turn nourish North India's immense Indo-Gangetic Plain, one of the most densely populated regions in the world.

A belt of stepped hills known as the Vindhyas separate the Indo-Gangetic Plain from the Deccan Plateau. This central, peninsular part of India is considered India's most ancient land surface; the Archean rocks of the Deccan Plateau are 300-500 million years old. Washed by the Arabian Sea to the west and the Bay of Bengal to the east, peninsular India tapers as it draws south, dipping into the Indian Ocean at its southernmost point, Kanyakumari. Flanking the Malabar Coast, the Western Ghats (a north-south chain of mid-sized hills) are separated from the Arabian Sea by a narrow strip of richly forested coastal plain. A broader coastal area stretches between the Bay of Bengal and the Eastern Ghats. The southern fringes of the Western and Eastern Ghats converge at the Nilgiri Hills, the southernmost tip of the Deccan Plateau. The Lakshadweep Islands, just off the Malabar coast in the Arabian Sea, and the Andaman and Nicobar Islands in the Bay of Bengal are also Indian territories.

■ Climate

Never relegated to the background, the weather in India is a beast of myth and metaphor, challenging many travelers' endurances. The monsoon regime of rain-bearing winds determines the course of seasons throughout India, with topography setting the stage for regional variations. There are basically three seasons in India (Indians may count as many as six, though few travelers will sense such subtleties). Hot season reigns February through May, with heat building up across the plains. By June, cold air masses that had accumulated over Central Asia during the winter are warmed; as this air is warmed it rises, pulling the wet winds and rains of the monsoon up over India from the Bay of Bengal and the Arabian Sea. Monsoon season runs roughly June through September, setting the country awash with frequent, often intense downpours, flooding cities and washing out roads. By September or October the monsoon has retreated, and the winter is cool and mild. For more information, see **Climate** (p. 755).

■ People

The 938 million people packed within India's borders represent a diverse array of identities. Six major religions, 18 major languages, and numerous racial groups coexist in India, sometimes harmoniously, others not. Seven out of 10 Indians live in villages, where an agricultural way of life continues, largely unaffected by the changes of the modern world. Population is densest in the north, in the valley and delta of the Ganga river, and in the extreme south, in Tamil Nadu and Kerala. India's four largest cities, Bombay (12.6 million), Calcutta (11 million), Delhi (8.4 million), and Madras (5.4 million) make up only 4% of the population. India's population is growing at just under 2% per year, which means that India should have one billion people before the year 2000.

Most Indians (83%) are Hindu, although there is a large minority of Muslims (11%), and smaller groups of Christians and Sikhs. Hindi is the national language, and although it is the mother tongue of only about 30% of the people (mostly in the central northern region of the country) it is widely spoken elsewhere too. Dozens of other languages are spoken in different regions. The ethnic origins of Indians reflect a mix between the light-skinned Aryan people, whose genes are more concentrated in the north, and the Dravidian peoples of the south. India also contains numerous "tribal" groups or *adivasis,* aboriginal peoples, many of whose ethnic origins are Tibeto-Burmese or Proto-Australoid. *Adivasis* are concentrated in the northeastern states as well as in Madhya Pradesh, Orissa, and Gujarat.

■ History

Tools and stone flakes in India date back 200,000 to 400,000 years, pointing to a long history of human activity. The geography of the subcontinent has always made India hospitable for settlement. The Himalayan mountain range in the north block out the cold winds of Central Asia and the Tibetan Plateau, making the subcontinent's overall climate disproportionately tropical. Himalayan ice trickles into the great river systems of the Indus, the Ganga, and the Brahmaputra, which spread water and fertile silt across the north Indian plains. Historically, the Himalaya have always separated the Indian Subcontinent geographically from the rest of Asia, except at the northwest frontier, where passes through the mountains lead directly onto the plains. It is here that foreign ruling powers have entered India in the past. The Indo-Gangetic plain in the North stretches across the subcontinent as a flat fertile expanse. The Vindhya hills form a barrier between north and south, dividing the Gangetic plain from the Deccan plateau.

The Indus Valley Civilization

The first known civilization in the Indian subcontinent was located in the valley of the Indus River in what is now Pakistan. This civilization arose around 2500 BC and flourished for nearly 1000 years until its decline. The two largest archeological sites from the Indus civilization are at Harappa and Mohenjo-Daro, but at least 15 other sites have also been identified as parts of this civilization, which covered an area greater than Pakistan.

The cities of the Indus civilization were planned according to rigid patterns that changed little if at all over their 1000-year history. The streets were laid out in grids and accompanied by incredibly well-designed drainage systems. Each city also had a large central bath which probably had some ritual function. The Indus dwellers were skilled farmers and had highly developed systems of irrigation, which allowed them to harvest and keep huge stores of wheat and barley. Each city had a population of about 35,000, and everything about their civilization appears to have been regimented. The Indus people traded by land and sea with the civilizations on the Nile, Tigris, and Euphrates Rivers in the Near East. Despite all of this, little is known about this ancient culture, for their script, found on numerous steatite seals, remains undeciphered. The multitude of seals left behind by the Indus people depict humans, gods, and animals. They seem to have worshiped a mother-goddess and some deity that may have been a prototype of the Hindu god Shiva.

Around 1800 BC, the Indus River changed its course, causing catastrophic flooding. This spelled chaos for a civilization that had lasted for 1000 years with little change at all. Despite the fact that the Indus Valley civilization collapsed nearly 4000 years ago, its influence still remains in the daily lives of Hindus today, in their rituals of bathing; the remnants of smashed clay cups at the sites of Indus Valley wells also call to mind the Hindu prohibition against drinking from another person's cup.

The Aryans

With the Indus culture in decline, there appeared at about the same time a new group of people in the subcontinent, the Aryans. The Aryans were nomadic, light-skinned tribal peoples who came from the Caucasus mountain region in Central Asia, establishing themselves in India around 1500 BC. From around 2000 BC they had begun to leave their homeland in southern Russia for a reason which still remains unknown, and they began migrating into Europe and the Indian subcontinent. *Arya*

The Ramayana

The epic *Ramayana,* the story of the Hindu god Rama, was first written down by the sage Valmiki about 500 BC, although it comes from still older oral traditions. The *Ramayana* remains India's best-known tale and has endured countless retellings. In 1972, introducing his own version, the novelist R.K. Narayan ventured to say that "every individual…living in India is aware of the story of the *Ramayana* in some measure or other." During the 1980s the *Ramayana* was turned into a hugely popular TV series, and during the 1990s the story hit the headlines again due to Hindu-Muslim conflict over Rama's supposed birthplace in Ayodhya. Here is a brief synopsis:

Lord Rama was crown prince of the kingdom of Kosala and lived in the capital city, Ayodhya. Beloved by all his subjects, Rama was the paragon of beauty, strength, intelligence, and virtue. He won the hand of beautiful Sita, the princess of a neighboring kingdom, by snapping in two an unbendable bow that Shiva had presented to Sita's father. Rama was all set to inherit the throne from his father, Dasaratha, when one of Dasaratha's wives tricked the king into promising to make her son Bharatha king instead. At her demand, Rama, Sita, and Rama's brother Lakshmana were exiled to the forest for 14 years to live as ascetics.

While Rama and Lakshmana hunted wild beasts and protected ascetics, Ravana, the ten-headed king of the demons, began to eye Sita. One morning one of Ravana's cronies appeared before Sita in the form of a golden stag. Sita urged Rama to go capture the creature, and while Rama was gone, Ravana abducted Sita to his island kingdom of Lanka. Rama was at a loss while Ravana kept Sita in his palace and lavished gifts on her, hoping to win her over. However, Rama and Lakshmana soon allied with the clever monkey Hanuman and won the favor of the monkey king, Sugriva, who sent huge armies of monkeys to attack Lanka. Hanuman, whose father was the wind god, led the charge across the strait, throwing down rocks for the others to use as stepping stones. After a terrifying celestial battle Ravana was slain by one of Rama's arrows.

By this time, the 14 years of exile had elapsed and it was time for Rama to reclaim his throne, which Bharatha gladly handed over to him. The whole capital erupted in celebration as Rama learned that he was in fact an *avatara* (incarnation) of Vishnu. But there was one matter left to settle—Sita had been living in Ravana's household for months, and her chastity was questioned. Rama made Sita submit to a fire-ordeal, yet she emerged unscorched by the flames. Still, rumors persisted, and when Sita became pregnant with twins, Rama was persuaded to banish her to the forest. There Sita met Valmiki, to whom she told the story of the *Ramayana.* And after her sons were born, Sita asked the earth to swallow her up. Meanwhile, in Ayodhya, Rama's kingdom decayed.

literally means "noble one" in Sanskrit. The Aryans arrived into the vacuum left by the disappearance of the Indus civilization, bringing with them their own language, religious traditions, and culture.

The Aryans were a warlike people who, although they were nomads and herders, brought with them a technology and culture that changed the course of the cultures they encountered. They belonged to different tribes, each of which was ruled by a *raja* (chieftain or king). They had domesticated the horse, and along with horses, they brought spoke-wheeled chariots. Gradually the Aryans spread from the Punjab and northern Indus, where they had first arrived, across all of northern India.

The arrival of these nomadic herdsmen marked the first of the many invasions that would shape India's history, and the Aryan influence was fundamental. Their spoken language was Sanskrit, a language related to Latin and Greek, and the root of all the North Indian languages. In their religions, they observed fire-sacrifices with oblations made to various deities. These sacrifices were performed by the Brahmins, sages of the priestly caste who chanted the hymns of the Rig Veda. The Rig Veda is a collection of Sanskrit hymns composed between 1500 and 900 BC. They were transmitted orally without a single change for several centuries until a script was developed and they were finally written down.

Along with their language, the Aryans also established their social order in India. Aryan society was divided into three classes or *varnas,* the priests, warriors, and commoners, also known as Brahmins, *kshatriyas,* and *vaishyas.* This is the basis for what later became the caste system. As they pressed farther on into new territory, they met the indigenous peoples whom they called *dasas.* Taken as slaves by the Aryans, the *dasas* became a servant class known as the *shudras.* These are thought to be the ancestors of South India's Dravidian people and the remaining survivors of the once-great Indus civilization.

The environment of India altered the culture of the Aryans. As they moved into the Doab, the fertile plain of the Ganges and Yamuna rivers, their tribes ossified into kingdoms and the people settled into villages. By the time the Aryans reached the area now called Bihar around 1000 BC they had abandoned bronze and had begun using iron. The Aryans were superb metallurgists, and the discovery of iron allowed them to clear the great forests that then covered the region.

The late 9th century BC is thought to have been the age of the great Sanskrit epics, the *Ramayana* and the *Mahabharata,* and it is also the age of development of the more highly philosophical thought expressed in the Upanishads. During this period, the myths and stories which constitute the two epics were beginning to take shape, as was a rethinking of the meaning behind the sacrifice and vision of the Vedic hymns. This was the age of great kingdoms and fantastic wars, so characteristic of the India known as "Bharat." These great epics, transmitted orally, would be written down between the 2nd century BC and the 5th century AD. The *Mahabharata* is the story of two families at war, the evil Kurus and their just cousins the Pandavas, five brothers who unfairly lose their kingdom to their cousins in a dice game and then go to war to win it back. This epic is set in a time when *dharma* is lapsing, when the world order begins to deteriorate, and so was quite characteristic of the political and religious climate of the time. The *Ramayana* recounts Lord Rama's efforts to rescue his wife Sita from the demon Ravana.

All the changes in Aryan culture at this time brought a proportional degree of alienation and rejection by the peoples in the lands they had conquered. Many thinkers became dissatisfied with the old Brahmanic religion and its corps of elite priests. A speculative ascetic movement began around the 8th century BC, which led the establishment of ascetic forest communities, the practice of *yoga,* and belief in the doctrines of *karma,* rebirth, and *moksha* (liberation). The Hindu Upanishads, were composed at this time, and in the 6th century two new faiths, Jainism and Buddhism, were founded (see **Religion,** p. 96).

The Mauryas

Although communications and trade had improved in North India by the 6th century BC, the land of the Aryans remained divided into 16 major kingdoms. In 326 BC, however, Alexander the Great arrived on India's northwest frontier intent on conquering India's riches for himself. Alexander's mutinous troops forced him to turn back, but his invasion seems to have provided the inspiration and the chaos that allowed another conqueror to take control of India. Chandragupta Maurya, an adventurer from eastern India, took control of the kingdom of Magadha, the most powerful Aryan state, located in the area of present-day Bihar. Advised by his brilliant minister Chanakya (also known as Kautilya), who reportedly met with Alexander, Chandragupta proceeded to conquer the rest of India. The Mauryan Empire was thus established, India's first forced unification. From their capital at Pataliputra (at the site of modern Patna), the Mauryas would rule for 140 years.

The Mauryan government was obsessive and strict. Each village's affairs were watched and assiduously taxed to pay for a huge bureaucracy and army. The Mauryas' military campaigns soon gave them control of all of South Asia except for the southern tip. But at the height of the empire's power its policies were changed as the result of a bloody battle. The Kalinga kingdom in Orissa put up such resistance to the Mauryas that after conquering them, the emperor Ashoka (r. 269-232 BC) decided to renounce violence and become a Buddhist. Ashoka wanted to rule by *dharma*, to be a righteous emperor as well as a pragmatic one. He organized and spread Buddhism in India and dispatched missionaries to the rest of Asia.

In India, Ashoka also spread a message of unity. Even though the Mauryan empire collapsed after Ashoka's death, the pillars he planted and the edicts he inscribed from Afghanistan to Bengal were left as reminders of the fact that India had once been a single, successful country.

Trade and Buddhism

After the fall of the Mauryas, India was again politically divided. Strong powers such as the Shakas and Kushanas entered from the north, or like the Andhras rose up in the peninsula, but these kingdoms never expanded beyond their regions. In spite of political disarray, however, this was a time of cultural ferment. A powerful system of craft guilds (related to the caste system) advanced Indian technology. Trade continued to rely on Mauryan roads and local institutions, which still linked the Indian countryside. Trade became the main cohesive force in India from the 2nd century BC to the 4th century AD. At the southern tip of the peninsula, trade ended the isolation of the Cheras, Pandyas, and Cholas, three Dravidian kingdoms that had never been part of the Mauryan sphere. Turning to the sea, these peoples gave India commercial links to China and the West, where Roman traders paid richly for Indian cloth, spices, wood, and gems.

This period also witnessed the zenith of Buddhism in South Asia. Mahayana Buddhism, a sect that placed less emphasis on monastic life and made Buddhism accessible to the layperson, spread after the 2nd century AD. Hinduism, however, was beginning to de-emphasize the old Brahmanic rituals, and a devotional movement called *bhakti* emerged, which stressed personal devotion to gods such as Vishnu and Shiva. Competing with Buddhism, *bhakti* Hinduism heated up in the south and would gradually brought back all of India into the Hindu fold. The Bhagavad Gita, a hymn containing the essence of Hindu philosophy, was also composed at this time.

Buddhism inspired many cultural achievements of the time. Sculptors reached new heights of excellence, carving stone images of the Buddha to be used in worship. At the same time, Indian medicine and astronomy got going with a push from the Greeks, who had settled down on the northwest frontier after Alexander's campaigns. India's linguistics and mathematics were far ahead of those in the West, however; a scientific system for Sanskrit grammar had been developed by Panini as early as the 4th century BC, and Indian mathematicians invented the concept of zero as well as the "Arabic" system of numerals (called "Arabic" by Europeans who learned of it from Arab merchants) during this period. Such artistic and intellectual pursuits were often hosted by Buddhist monasteries and paid for by wealthy guilds.

The Guptas: A "Golden Age"

In 319 AD, another Chandragupta came to power in the eastern kingdom of Magadha. Though he was not related to his namesake, the founder of the Maurya dynasty, Chandragupta openly sought to emulate this conqueror and soon launched an empire of his own. From their base in Pataliputra, Chandragupta and later his son, Samudragupta, expanded up and down the Ganga Valley. By the time of its peak under Chandragupta II (r. 375-415 AD), the Gupta Empire would cautiously embrace all of North India.

The Guptas get more credit for the cultural refinements of their age than for their political power, however. The Gupta era is often billed as India's "golden age" or "classical age." During this time, many of the trends of the earlier period came to their full fruition. India's affluence in overseas trade and her powerful craft guilds paid for advances in the arts and sciences. The Guptas were great patrons of all these activities. India's first stone dams and temples were built, and the great sculptures of the caves at Ajanta were executed at this time. Kalidasa, the greatest classical Sanskrit poet, was a member of the court of Chandragupta II.

The most important difference between the Guptas and the Mauryas, however, was their religion. Though they sponsored the activities of all religions, the Guptas themselves were Hindu. They lavished resources on Hindu theological studies—the six schools of Hindu philosophy date from around this time—and on the building of Hindu temples. Their law and institutions stuck to orthodox Hinduism. Social prescriptions such as the patriarchal joint family and the caste system now became fixed in North India. The Guptas have become something of a prototype for Hindu monarchs ever since.

Although South India was outside of the Gupta empire, it was an active participant in the culture of the Gupta age. Northern traders and Brahmin priests had by this point brought the south into the Hindu world, and even though the south remained politically divided, southern kings were mimicking Aryan political structures. This "Aryanization" catalyzed the south rather than stifling it. Distinct South Indian architectural styles emerged, and Tamil poet-saints (the Vaishnava Alvars and Shaiva Nayanars) and thinkers joined the ranks of the holiest Hindus, leading the *bhakti* devotional movement that would overtake the North.

Regionalism

The Gupta Empire slowly disintegrated in the 5th century under pressure from Huns attacking from Central Asia. North India curdled into small kingdoms again. Except for a fleeting half-century from 606 to 647, when the young conqueror and poet-king Harsha built an empire from his capital at Kannauj in the Ganga plain, North India remained divided for 700 years. Strong regional identities grew. A feudal system of economics came into full force at this time, measuring wealth in land rather than money; this only added to people's insularity. North India's regional languages began to develop at this time.

The Rajputs, a group of warrior clans who probably originated outside of India but claimed the noble status of *kshatriyas* in the Hindu caste system, became the major force in northwest India after the 8th century. The Rajputs set up several small kingdoms from their base in the Rajasthan desert, creating a culture of chivalry with its own literature and architecture. The Rajput clans warred with one another, however, and they never managed to put together an empire. The strongest kingdom in India at this time was the Chola dynasty from Tamil Nadu, which conquered most of the southern peninsula and even sent forces to the Maldives, Sri Lanka, and Malaysia. But the Rajputs, in the north, would have to contend with the most serious foreign challenge of the age: people from the west with new ideas that had the potential to rearrange India. Being so divided they were ill-equipped to face it.

The Arrival of Islam

After the teachings of Muhammad in the 7th century, Islam had spread from Arabia right up to Sindh on the western frontier of India. Muslims traded with India by sea, and a few settled down on the west coast, but their religion simmered peacefully for 300 years before it appeared in India in full force. A change would come with the raids of Mahmud of Ghazni, the king of a Turkish dynasty in Afghanistan. Between 997 and 1030 Mahmud's armies swarmed in to loot North India on almost an annual basis. Mahmud was a plunderer and his mission had little to do with God, but he could justify his destruction of richly endowed Hindu temples by calling it Islamic iconoclasm. Mahmud never settled in India, content to carry its wealth back into the hills.

By the end of the 12th century, another Muslim king put forth more permanent designs for India. In 1192 Muhammad of Ghur conquered the Ganges Valley and defeated a loose coalition of Rajputs. Though he quickly returned to his home in Afghanistan, he left behind his general, the slave Qutb-ud-din Aibak, to govern the conquered lands from Delhi. When Muhammad died in 1206, Qutb-ud-din seceded, proclaiming the birth of the Delhi Sultanate, India's first Muslim kingdom.

The Sultanate ruled most of North India for 300 years, and by the early 15th century, there were independent Muslim kingdoms in Bengal, Gujarat, and central India. Still, the Delhi Sultanate's hold on power was always precarious. The palace was in constant turmoil, chewing up five dynasties in three centuries, and the sultans paid for their hedonistic court life by heavily taxing Hindus. The people frequently revolted, as did provincial nobles. In another major setback, the city of Delhi was obliterated by the Central Asian conqueror Timur (Tamerlane) in 1398.

Even if the sultans had difficulty controlling their subjects, most of India was nevertheless blanketed with a new Muslim ruling class, a fact which carried with it various complications. The Muslims did not assimilate to India as invaders in the past had often done. Their ties to the Islamic communities in the Middle East and Central Asia gave them other civilizations to identify with, and the theologians they brought with them watched to make sure their Islam was pure. Only a minority of Hindus converted to Islam—most of them high-caste elites who wanted to join in Muslim power, or lower-caste farmers and artisans who were influenced by mystical Sufi saints. But the fact that the new faith accepted untouchables into its fold only tarnished its image in the eyes of most higher-caste Hindus. The segregation of Hindu and Muslim communities, which remains one of India's most controversial issues 800 years later, had begun. In parts of India, Hindu monarchs tried to resist the impact of Islam. The Vijayanagar kingdom ruled large parts of South India and the Deccan plateau from 1336 to 1565, building temples vigorously. But it was finally defeated by a coalition of Muslim sultanates from the Deccan.

Many movements attempted to unify the two faiths. In the Punjab, Guru Nanak was attracting adherents to Sikhism, a new religion that presented a synthesis of Hinduism and Islam. In Bengal, Islam became popular among the masses thanks to wandering Sufi mystics whose religion was similar to devotional movements in Hinduism. But religious fragmentation undermined the centralized political authority of the Lodis, the last of the Delhi sultanate's dynasties, and led to all sorts of regional troubles. Provincial governors seceded in Bihar, Portugese ships landed unmolested in Goa, and in central India the one-eyed, one-armed Rajput leader Rana Sanaga called for foreign intervention to vanquish the Delhi Sultanate.

The Mughals

Rana Sanaga's call was heeded by the Central Asian warlord Babur (1483-1530). Babur, descended from both Timur and Genghis Khan, was well-endowed with a warlord's pedigree. In his early years, Babur gave every indication of following in the blood-soaked footsteps of his ancestors, conquering Samarkand at age 13 and Kabul eight years later. But the great warrior didn't spend all his time fighting, and when he wasn't boozing it up Babur found time to compose poetry, indulge in gardening, and craft a wistful autobiography. Recounting his attack on the Delhi Sultanate, Babur wrote: "I placed my foot in the stirrup of resolution, and my palms I placed on the reins of confidence in Allah." Such words have a way of obscuring the horrors of combat, and the Battle of Panipat, fought outside of Delhi in the spring of 1526, was in fact gruesome. But the overmatched Babur prevailed and crushed the Lodi dynasty. There was now some doubt as to what Babur would do. Would his armies occupy and rule South Asia or would they be content to plunder the region and return home? The question was settled in 1530 when Babur's son Humayun became sick. According to legend, Babur prayed that the sickness which afflicted his son should be transferred to him; within weeks, Babur was buried in Kabul and Humayun was proclaimed emperor over territories which stretched from Bihar in the east to Kabul in the west. Sporadic raiding had given way to the Mughal dynasty.

Addicted to opium and dependent on the capricious predictions of his astrologers, Emperor Humayun had difficulty leading his ethnically diverse army, and within a decade his troops had become disloyal. In 1540, Humayun was unseated by the Afghan warlord Sher Shah, who had carved out a kingdom for himself in eastern India. Humayun was driven into the Sindh desert, where he wandered at the head of a dwindling band of followers. Back in Delhi, Sher Shah worked to secure his position, laying the groundwork for a sophisticated administration and fortifying key cities. But disaster struck in 1545, when Sher Shah was killed during a siege of a Rajput stronghold. Seeing an opportunity, Humayun acted aggressively, gaining Persian backing and recapturing Delhi. Only months after his glorious triumphs, however, Humayun slipped down the stairs of his library; injuries from the fall killed him, and in 1555, Akbar, who had been born in the Sindh desert during Humayun's wanderings, became emperor.

Though Akbar was only 13 when he succeeded his father, he quickly proved his military mettle, squashing rebellions and establishing Mughal hegemony with successful campaigns in Rajasthan, Gujarat, Orissa, Kashmir, and Bengal. As Akbar consolidated his empire through battle, he formulated policies rooted in the assumption that the Mughals were no mere flash in the pan, that their long-term future lay in South Asia, and not in the Central Asian lands from which Babur had come. Akbar worked to institutionalize policy-making, creating a centralized imperial bureaucracy in order to lend Mughal governance an aura of permanence. Moreover, the emperor and his inner circle devised an efficient revenue collection system so that new territories would not need to be conquered in order to keep the existing empire financially solvent. Most importantly, Akbar concluded that for the Mughals to dominate South Asia they could not rely on brute force and repression indefinitely—the Muslim Mughals would need to earn the trust of Hindus. To give Hindu elites a stake in the success of the Mughal regime, Akbar married a Rajput princess and appointed well-educated Hindus to important government posts; to ingratiate his regime with the masses, Akbar denounced the destruction of Hindu temples and eliminated the *jizya*, a widely despised tax levied only on non-Muslims.

Akbar's policies encouraged Hindus and Muslims to believe that they would be neighbors in South Asia for centuries. Coming to terms with this fact, Hindu and Muslim cultures began to take account of each other, and under Akbar's generous patronage a sensibility marked by the mingling of Muslim and Hindu elements emerged. North Indian music began to assimilate Persian influences, and Hindu painters began to experiment with miniature painting, a genre favored by the Mughals. Meanwhile, the Urdu language, with its Persian vocabulary and Hindi grammatical structure, gained popularity, and Muslims began the practice of pilgrimages to the tombs of holy figures, similar to Hindu pilgramges. When it came to religious mixing and matching, even Akbar got in on the game, inviting Hindus, Jains, Christians, and Zoro-astrians to discuss their faiths in his court. Eventually, Akbar developed a new religion which incorporated ideas from all the major religious systems of the region. While the religion Akbar devised did not outlive him, the pluralistic spirit which animated it did, and it was during Akbar's reign that North India made peace with itself culturally, in the process accommodating itself to Mughal political domination.

Akbar's successors Jahangir (r. 1605-27) and Shah Jahan (r. 1628-57) were content to build on Akbar's work, and their reigns were a golden era for the Mughals: the populace was well-fed, the empire's frontiers were relatively secure, and a series of staggeringly beautiful exclamation points—the marble Taj Mahal and the sandstone Red Forts—were erected in Delhi and Agra. Troubles, however, began to make themselves felt in 1657, when Shah Jahan fell sick; soon enough, the emperor's sons were at war with each other, fighting over who would succeed him. The bloody familial fighting sapped the Mughals' strength and left the empire in the hands of the uncompromisingly vicious Aurangzeb, who had murdered his older brother during the succession struggle and who ordered Shah Jahan imprisoned, lest his health improve.

For 48 years, Aurangzeb ruled South Asia as the Mughal emperor. In some respects, Aurangzeb's reign was successful—his armies, for instance, were able to conquer massive tracts of fertile land in southern and eastern India. On balance, however, Aurangzeb's rule was simply a disaster, and by adopting imperial policies which alienated and angered Hindus, Aurangzeb sowed the seeds of the empire's collapse. Deeply religious, Aurangzeb energetically rolled back a century of tolerant social policy, making it difficult for Hindus to advance through the civil service bureaucracy, forbidding the repair of Hindu temples, and, over a great deal of protest, re-introducing the discriminatory *jizya* tax. With the social contract implicit in Akbar's policies—the Mughals would rule, but they would not impose Islam on the Hindu majority—being undone by Aurangzeb's short-sighted radicalism, ordinary Hindus turned on the Mughals. The peasants of Bengal and Orissa began to support the Marathas, and in the Punjab the Sikhs became a force to be reckoned with after Aurangzeb murdered Guru Tegh Bahadur for refusing to convert to Islam. By the time the 88-year-old Aurangzeb died in the opening years of the 18th century, the Mughal empire was irreparably frayed. Over the next half century, the Mughals would rule in name only. The dynasty's weakness was repeatedly revealed—Delhi was sacked and looted by Persians in 1738 and by Afghans in 1757.

As the Mughal Empire's control over northern India slipped away, a number of groups sought to step into the power vacuum. The Maratha leader Shivaji Bhonsle posed a serious threat to the Mughals during the reign of Aurangzeb, and the Maratha Confederacy, comprised of Maharashtrian "nationalists" of different castes, stood the best chance of taking the Mughals' place in the 18th century. The Marathas' hopes were dashed in 1761, however, when they were dealt a decisive defeat outside of Delhi by an invading Afghan army. In the wake of the defeat, the Confederacy splintered. With the Marathas unable to fill the shoes of the mighty Mughals, the way was clearing for another group—perhaps a non-indigenous group—to play a politically dominant role in South Asia.

The Beginnings of British Rule

Lured by the riches of the prosperous Mughal Empire, European ships sailed the oceans throughout the 15th and 16th centuries, stumbling their way across the globe and happening upon the New World in the process. India itself, however, did not witness the arrival of substantial numbers of Europeans until the 17th century, when English, Portuguese, Dutch, and French subjects came to South Asia as agents of government-chartered trading companies. With the gradual ebbing of Portuguese sea power, the Netherlands' decision to concentrate commercial energies on the islands of Southeast Asia, and the settlement which ended the Seven Years' War, the English East India Company became the dominant firm in South Asia. From its Indian bases in the south and east—two of which would grow into Calcutta and Madras—the Company carried on a highly profitable trade, exchanging gold and silver for Indian finished goods, especially hand-crafted textiles.

As the Company carved out a commercial niche during the early 18th century, the Mughal Empire was in decline, lawlessness was unleashed on India and banditry became an increasingly serious social problem. For the Company, this banditry was especially troubling—it threatened the network of warehouses where valuable goods were stored before being shipped to Great Britain. Seeing rich possibilities in the need to defend its warehouses, the Company recruited small Indian armies and equipped them with comparatively powerful European-made weapons. Often hired out to rival Indian factions, these mercenary armies served as the wedge by which the Company became a powerful and controlling force in Bengal during the middle decades of the 18th century. From Bengal, the Company extended its domination. Led by the iron-willed Robert Clive, it aligned itself with a coalition of Muslims and Hindus and, after a series of battles which culminated with the Battle of Plassey in 1757, asserted control over vast swatches of Eastern India.

East India Company Government

As land passed under its control, the Company began to behave less like a trading firm and more like an imperial overlord. During the 1774-1793 period, when it was led first by Warren Hastings and then by Lord Cornwallis, the Company was divided into separate political and commercial units and developed a British-dominated bureaucracy for institutionalized administration of Indian territory. Moreover, the Company was increasingly relying on land and not on commerce as a source of revenue. Territory was parceled out by the Company in accord with the Permanent Settlement of 1793, which made the Mughal tax collectors, or *zamindars,* the owners of the lands they had administered. The Settlement created an elite class of powerful Indians who were loyal to the Company. The big losers in the new arrangement were the peasants. During the Mughal reign, title to the land had been theirs. Now, they worked it, their toil generating the revenue needed by Indian land-holders to pay off the Company.

In the wake of the Settlement, the Company gobbled up more and more land. By the 1820s, most of India had become for all practical purposes a post of the British Empire. In the face of this emerging reality, a debate ensued in Britain. On one side was the old guard, represented by leaders like Hastings, who believed that India should be exploited economically but left alone socially, culturally, and religiously. Opposing the old-guard was an informal alliance of Evangelicals (who sought to spread Christianity to "idolatrous" India) and humanists (who believed that progress in India was hampered by "irrational" practices). As Britain lurched away from conservatism in the 1820s and 1830s, the Evangelicals and the humanists, both of whom spoke glowingly of the "civilizing" power of imperialism, won the day. The move to transform Indian life was on.

Between the late 1820s and 1857, the Company was guided by two complementary concerns. On the one hand, Company authorities moved to eliminate practices which offended British moral sensibilities; on the other hand, the Company sought to press Indian society into a European mold. In accord with these twin concerns, railways, textile mills, and telegraphs were introduced into South Asia, and *sati,* the Hindu custom by which widows were burned on their husbands' funeral pyres, was banned. Moreover, the Company sought to transform India both linguistically and culturally–an 1835 resolution committed Company authorities to "the promotion of European literature and science." To facilitate the realization of this imperialist goal, British authorities changed the official state language from Persian to English, and funded the development of secondary schools, medical colleges, and universities where knowledge was synonymous with Western knowledge and the language of instruction was English. India's government was administered by men like Lord Macaulay, who claimed that "One shelf of a good English library has more worth than native [Indian] literature in its entirety."

Sensing that the cultural agenda of British imperialism was undermining traditional ways, millions of Indians became alienated from British rule. This alienation gave way to anger under pressure from severe economic dislocation and persistent rural poverty. In the face of seething discontent, British officials extended their authority, inventing an absurd legal fiction, the "doctrine of lapse," which allowed the British to annex any Indian kingdom whose ruler died without a direct male heir. By the 1850s, India had become a powderkeg; it would be ignited by a gun.

In 1857, the Company introduced a new rifle for use by its 200,000 Indian troops. Called the Lee-Enfield, the rifle's ammunition cartridges were lubricated with a mixture of pig and cow fat. Hindus (for whom cows are sacred) and Muslims (for whom pigs are impure) were incensed, especially when it emerged that soldiers had to bite the tip off the cartridges with their teeth before loading them. Thousands of Indian troops rose in rebellion, and in May of 1857 they raised the Mughal flag over Delhi, indiscriminately massacring Europeans as they reclaimed the city. Lucknow and Kanpur also fell under the control of leaders eager to restore the Mughal Empire. Backed by Sikh regiments, British troops returned the bloody favor four months later, re-capturing Delhi and viciously murdering vast numbers of Indians in the process. By March of 1858, the "Indian Mutiny," or the "First War of Independence," as Indian nationalists prefer to call it, had been finally and fully suppressed.

After the gory events of the revolt, British attitudes changed radically. Assuming a "White Man's Burden" marked by increasingly explicit racism, the British withdrew socially and culturally from Indian society, setting up "hill stations" remote from major Indian population centers and stoically renouncing their quest to systematically introduce "civilizing" Western learning to South Asia. Meanwhile, the British tightened their political control over India. An 1858 act of the British Parliament eliminated the governing authority of the Company; within a year, the British crown was directly administering India as a full-fledged colony of the British Empire. To ensure tight control over India, Crown authorities increased the ratio of British to Indian soldiers stationed in South Asia, forbade Indians from becoming officers of the army, and staffed the upper echelons of the burgeoning Indian Civil Service with bureaucrats of English birth.

Crown Rule and Indian Renewal

With Britain cracking down, a century-long period of religious revitalization reached its invigorating conclusion as Hindu groups such as the mystical Ramakrishna Mission and the reform-minded Arya Samaja became exceptionally popular. With their religious beliefs energized, millions of Hindus began to take a newly self-conscious pride in Indian culture. In turn, this new cultural pride made British political rule seem intolerably invasive.

Demanding reforms which would give Indians more control over their country's affairs, a group of seventy wealthy Indians met in Bombay in 1885 to form a political association, the Indian National Congress. As it attracted new members over the next 20 years, controversies rent Congress into two camps, each led by Brahmins. On the one side were the moderates, who advocated reform within the context of the British Empire. Opposing them were the extremists, who sought to replace British imperialism with homegrown self-government. The views of the extremists rose to the fore after 1905, when the British viceroy, seeking to simplify administration of the empire (but also to create divisions among Indians), partitioned Bengal into two provinces, one with a Hindu majority, the other with a Muslim majority. The anger and resentment felt by millions of Indians was articulated in 1905 by a man who had once led the moderates, Congress President Gopal Krishna Gokhale. "A cruel wrong has been inflicted on our Bengalee brethren," Gokhale proclaimed. "The scheme of partition…will always stand as a complete illustration of the worst features of the present system of bureaucratic rule—its utter contempt for public opinion, its arrogant pretensions to superior wisdom, its reckless disregard of the most cherished feelings of the people." The ground had shifted; self-rule in some form had become the objective.

In the decade following the partition of Bengal, Indians from a wide variety of backgrounds did what they could to resist British rule. Disaffected Bengali youth read Bipin Chandra Pal's radical journal, *Bande Mataram*; other young people became terrorists, turning to the bomb and founding newspapers such as *Yuganta*. Muslims concerned about Hindu domination of Congress founded the All-India Muslim League in 1906; the League threw its support to the cause of self-government in 1913. Men and women of all regions, religions, and ages boycotted British-made textiles, opting instead for the grittier, Indian-made *swadeshi* cloth, which was worn proudly as a symbol of national self-sufficiency.

Indian nationalist leaders cooperated with the British during the First World War, hoping that their loyalty in the British Empire's time of need would be rewarded by greater freedoms after the war. Instead the British announced oppressive measures in 1919, suspending civil liberties and placing India under martial law. When a group of unarmed Indians assembled in Amritsar for a peaceful protest, 400 of them were massacred by the British Indian army. There could now be no turning back from the goal of total independence.

It was against this backdrop of disaffection that Mohandas Karamchand Gandhi returned to India in 1915, having been proclaimed Mahatma ("Great Soul") by Rabindranath Tagore, the Bengali poet. Born into a Gujarati *vaishya* family in 1869, Gandhi had gone to England to study law. After completing his education, Gandhi spent twenty years in South Africa, where he devoted himself to ending the racist discrimination experienced by Indian South Africans and evolved the idea of *satyagraha*. A kind of non-violent resistance defined by Gandhi in his autobiography as "soul force," the ideal of *satyagraha* would lend the Independence movement moral credibility in the world's eyes for the next three decades.

Towards Independence

Supported by Hindus (for whom he was a true Mahatma), by Muslims (who appreciated his support for the crumbling Ottoman Empire), and by common folk (who were swayed when he renounced his fashionable European clothing for the simple cotton garb of the masses), Gandhi enjoyed amazing popularity throughout the 1920s and 1930s. Gandhi's popularity meant that the leadership of the Congress party was his; in turn, the once-elite Congress was re-made under Gandhi's leadership into a mass party supported by millions of ordinary Indians.

Encouraged by Gandhi's Congress party, millions of Indians participated in non-violent civil disobedience throughout the 1920s. These efforts were forced to a culmination in 1930, when Gandhi's thunder seemed to have been stolen by Jawaharlal Nehru, the young leader of the Congress party's radical wing, who had audaciously declared January 26, 1930 Indian Independence Day. Not wanting to be outdone by the radicals, Gandhi embarked on his famous "salt march" seven weeks after Nehru's declaration. Imperial authorities had declared it illegal for salt to be sold or manufactured except under the auspices of the heavily taxed official monopoly. Pointing to imperial salt policies as a symbol of the broadly deleterious effects of British rule, Gandhi marched to the sea, attracting crowds of supporters and media coverage as he went. Staff in hand and clothing fraying, Gandhi reached the coastal town of Dandi in April. Wading into the water, Gandhi proceeded to make salt by taking a handful of sea-water and pouring it on dry ground, as he pronounced the obvious—he was breaking the salt law.

As Gandhi thumbed his nose at their laws, British authorities cracked down. Over 60,000 Indians were arrested in 1930. But the tide could not be turned back, and the British seemed to know it. In 1932, the army began granting commissions to Indian officers; in 1935, the Government of India Act, which granted authority over provincial government to elected Indian representatives, was passed.

Meanwhile, tensions between Congress and the All-India Muslim League were becoming intense; they would rise to a fever pitch during World War II. In 1940, leaders of Congress charged that the Muslim League had opportunistically taken advantage of dislocations brought on by the war to gain power for itself. Claiming to speak for India's Muslim communities, leaders such as Muhammad Ali Jinnah retorted that aggressively seizing power was necessary, for Muslim rights could not be guaranteed in the independent, Hindu-dominated India which seemed about to materialize. In 1940, the League declared that the Muslims of India were a separate nation and demanded the creation of an independent Muslim state. The state, the League declared, should be named Pakistan.

Sapped by the fight against Nazi Germany, British authorities concluded soon after the end of World War II that India could no longer be held as a colony. While imperial authorities hoped to maintain India's territorial integrity, the vicious ethnic conflict which bloodied Calcutta, the Punjab, and the Ganga Valley in 1946 made divvying up India into two sovereign states—one Hindu-dominated, the other Muslim-dominated—seem to be the only reasonable option. Independence for India (and existence for the state of Pakistan) officially arrived when the vast territory which had been the "jewel in the crown" of the British Empire was partitioned. The date was August 15, 1947. For hundreds of millions of Indians, the world had been turned upside down.

After Independence

On the night of the 14th, Jawaharlal Nehru, the new prime minister, spoke to the people. "A moment comes," he said, "which comes but rarely in history, when we step from the old to the new, when an age ends and when the soul of a nation, long suppressed, finds utterance."

The words were stirring, but the soul of the nation would not be joyous for long. For in their rush to get into the country where they wanted to live, millions of Sikhs and Hindus streamed into India while millions of Muslims hurried toward Pakistan. The simultaneous and massive migration (probably the largest population movement in human history) touched off stampedes and inter-ethnic violence on a horrific scale. More than 500,000 people were killed. Five months later, Mahatma Gandhi was murdered, cut down by Hindu extremists angered by his attempts to appease the Muslim League. The long-awaited post-colonial period had begun on a painful note.

The first tasks for Nehru's government—forging democratic institutions and establishing a workable administrative structure for the newly free nation—did not meet much opposition. It was quickly decided that India would be ruled as a federation, with power shared between state authorities and New Delhi-based national authorities; elections would take place at least once every fifth year, and parliament would be divided between a lower house (Lok Sabha) and an upper house (Rajya Sabha). In fulfillment of a pledge Congress had made long before independence, Nehru's government passed the States Reorganization Act (1956), which re-drew India's internal boundaries so that states became "linguistic states," in which the language of local government was the language of local people.

Democratization and administrative reform were addressed competently and quickly by Nehru's government. During his reign as prime minister, however, the urbane and idealistic Nehru would ran up against problems of a more intractable nature—problems, in fact, of such magnitude and severity that they continue to haunt contemporary India.

On the economic front, Nehru's India had many difficulties, the most serious of which were massive poverty and the substantial wealth gap between the urban middle classes on the one hand and the nation's village-dwelling farmers on the other. While the socialist Nehru labored heroically to make India a more prosperous nation, embarking on five year plans and successfully soliciting foreign aid, phenomenally rapid population growth (literally) ate up most economic gains—neither per-capita productivity nor per-capita income rose as quickly as they might have. Equitably slicing up the nation's economic pie proved as difficult as coaxing expansion out of the pie. Indeed, the needs of efficient production of wealth often conflicted with the imperatives of fair distribution. An illuminating example is the case of the "Green Revolution," which began during the early years of Nehru's prime ministership and which brought high-yield crop strains, high-tech farm machinery, and chemical fertilizers to India. While the Green Revolution greatly increased India's grain production, small farmers who could not afford modern agricultural products could not successfully compete with well-off farmers who could. The result was a surge in share-cropping and tenancy and a wave of migration to the cities.

Other difficult problems encountered by Nehru concerned foreign relations. In 1962, a border dispute led to war with China; northern India was able to avoid being overrun only when U.S. and British military reinforcements were rapidly deployed to South Asia.

Under Nehru, India also struggled to build constructive relations with Pakistan and to develop a feasible policy regarding Kashmir, a sizeable area in the Himalaya approximately 400 miles north of New Delhi. Tensions arose at Independence while Kashmir—where 75% of the population was Muslim but the maharaja was Hindu—considered whether it wanted to be a part of India or Pakistan. Border skirmishes with Pakistan led the maharaja to accede to India, with Nehru promising that the people of Kashmir would eventually be able to decide their own fate by voting. A brief, undeclared war between India and Pakistan ended in 1949 with a UN-brokered cease-fire. While the war established a de facto—though still disputed—border between Pakistani Kashmir and Indian Kashmir, it did not solve difficult underlying problems. Indeed, Indian Kashmir has been the site of terrible violence since 1989. For more information, see **Jammu and Kashmir** (p. 358).

Indira's India

After Nehru died in 1964, he was succeeded by Lal Bahadur Shastri, who died of a heart attack in 1966 soon after leading India to victory in a defensive war against Pakistan. Shastri was succeeded by Nehru's soft-spoken daughter, Indira Gandhi (no relation to the Mahatma, Indira's last name came from her husband, Feroze Gandhi). During the early years of her rule, Indira's policies were marked by a lack of both patience and wisdom. In the face of a crumbling economy, Indira devalued the rupee; over mounting public pressure, Indira feuded endlessly with the "old guard" of Congress. While these rash moves alienated many of her supporters, Indira's public image was resuscitated in 1971, when she led India to victory in a large-scale war against Pakistan. The war resulted in the creation of an independent nation, Bangladesh, from what had been the eastern wing of Pakistan. With Pakistan's power reduced, there could no longer be any doubt—India was South Asia's dominant power.

In large measure because of Indira's autocratic tendencies, the post-war years were troubled ones for India. After the oil crisis of 1973, India was caught in the twin pincers of rising inflation and worsening poverty, and millions of Indians slipped toward starvation. Economic troubles rapidly gave way to social and political dislocation, as protesting students took to the streets, and India's former finance minister, the wealthy banker Morarji Desai, founded the Janata Dal, an anti-Indira party. For Indira Gandhi, events reached a crisis point in 1975, when she was found guilty of election fraud. Rather than step down as the law demanded, Indira declared a national emergency. Mrs. Gandhi endowed herself with dictatorial powers and began to govern like a tyrant, imposing sterilization on families with more than two children, aggressively censoring all national media outlets, and having her political opponents arrested.

Indira Gandhi graciously ended her tyrannical run in January 1977, and was defeated in elections by Desai two months later. Unable to hold his party together, however, Desai's fortunes quickly faded and Indira was re-elected to the prime ministership in 1980. Indira Gandhi's second term was consumed with confronting Sikh militants, who launched a campaign of terror in Punjab and Haryana as a way of pressuring India's national government into creating a sovereign Sikh nation. When in 1984 militants armed with machine guns and assault rifles seized the Golden Temple at Amritsar, the holiest site in Sikhism, Indira decided to loose the army. The temple was stormed with tragic results—hundreds of soldiers and civilians were killed during a four-day battle. And the worst was yet to come. By storming the temple, Indira had effectively desecrated it, violating India's tenuous principle of religious tolerance. On October 31, 1984, two Sikh bodyguards killed Indira at her home in New Delhi; Indira's death touched off massive rioting in the capital, and thousands of Sikhs were massacred by gangs of Hindu thugs while the police looked away. Indira's son Rajiv Gandhi, a former commercial airline pilot, rushed home to Delhi to succeed her as the next ruler of the Nehru family dynasty.

The Last 13 Years

A "sympathy vote" in the elections following Indira's assassination swept Rajiv Gandhi's Congress (I) party into an impressive majority position, with over 400 of the 500 seats in the Lok Sabha. Many Indians had high hopes that Rajiv's administration would bring about the changes India so badly needed, a solution to the problems in the Punjab and an end to India's miserable poverty. But Rajiv Gandhi's prime ministership began inauspiciously, with a tragic gas leak from the Union Carbide chemical plant in Bhopal in December 1984, which killed 2000-3000 people in their sleep before it was detected. Rajiv's government did not succeed in most of its projects. An agreement with Sikh leaders that would have ended the violence in Punjab by giving the Sikhs the city of Chandigarh was shelved by the government at the last minute, and problems continued. Rajiv's free-enterprise, trickle-down economic policies did little for the poor, helping more to bring in the foreign cars and VCRs that the rich craved. But Rajiv's biggest failing was in foreign policy.

The island nation of Sri Lanka, only 35km off the coast of southern India, is inhabited by a Buddhist Sinhalese-speaking majority, who make up about 75% of the population, and a Hindu Tamil minority, who constitute the other 25%. Since 1956, when Sinhalese had been made the island's only official language, Tamil separatists, nicknamed "Tigers," have been fighting a draining guerilla war in the northern part of the island. In 1986 the conflict began to escalate. Under the mantle of SAARC, the South Asian Association for Regional Cooperation, which India had started in 1985 to improve relations with its neighbors (especially Pakistan), Rajiv Gandhi sent Indian troops to Sri Lanka as "peacekeepers." The Sri Lankan government was happy to get its own troops out of the futile conflict, and India hoped that its armies would soon force the Tigers to the bargaining table. But India was unprepared for the lashing it would get; by the time it was forced to withdraw its troops in 1990, almost 100 Indian soldiers had been killed for every Tiger killed.

The 1989 elections transferred power to a fragile coalition led by Prime Minister V.P. Singh of the Janata Dal, and endorsed by a group of parties including the Hindu nationalist Bharatiya Janata Party (BJP). Although Singh tried to settle the Punjab crisis, the northern state of Jammu and Kashmir soon eclipsed the Punjab as India's most troubled region. Muslim militants, alleged by India to have been trained and armed by Pakistan, fought a guerilla campaign against Indian authorities. The state capital of Srinagar, once a popular tourist destination, became a war zone. But other problems would be the cause of the Singh government's downfall. Singh supported a federal commission's recommendation that 60% of university admissions and civil service jobs should be reserved for lower castes and former untouchables. Young high-caste Hindus, frightened at their bleak future under such a system, took to the streets, and a few even publicly immolated themselves in protest. Support for Singh was slipping away. The final blow to his government came when he arrested L. K. Advani, the leader of the BJP, who was trying to rally support for the building of a Hindu temple on a controversial site in Ayodhya, Uttar Pradesh. The BJP withdrew its support from the Singh, and the government fell. A new government was formed under Prime Minister Chandra Shekhar, but it lasted only a few months.

The elections of 1991 were basically settled when Rajiv Gandhi, campaigning in Tamil Nadu, was assassinated by a Tamil Tiger suicide bomber. Congress (I) returned to power on a sympathy vote, led by the veteran P.V. Narasimha Rao. An aging disciple of Nehru, seen by the party as a compromise candidate, Rao surprised everyone with his political wiles. He initiated unpopular economic reforms, which were made necessary by a national financial crisis in 1991. The government cut its spending and opened India to foreign investment.

Late 1991 brought renewed rumblings of the dispute over the Babri Masjid in Ayodhya. The mosque, built by the Mughal conqueror Babur in the 16th century, is believed by orthodox Hindus to occupy the very birthplace of the god Rama. In December 1992, with a BJP government ruling the state of Uttar Pradesh where Ayodhya is located, Hindu nationalist leaders called for volunteers to build a temple on Rama's birthplace *(Ram Janmabhumi)*. From all over India devotees converged on Ayodhya, bricks in hand, and proceeded to tear down the mosque. Hindu-Muslim violence erupted across South Asia, especially in major cities like Bombay. Rao's government banned the Hindu nationalist parties, dismissing the government of Uttar Pradesh and three other states ruled by the BJP.

Although the Rao government clung to power and continued with its program of economic liberalization, its weaknesses were becoming more and more obvious. By 1994 the Hindu nationalists had made a complete comeback, winning elections in several states. In 1995 the state of Maharashtra, which includes the industrial powerhouse of Bombay, came under the control of a particularly radical Hindu nationalist party, the Shiv Sena. Problems in Kashmir continued as well, with the government's control of the insurgency bringing accusations of human rights violations from around the world. In late 1995, as India headed for another election, a kickback scandal tarnished a large number of Rao's ministers.

The BJP won more seats than any other party in the May 1996 Lok Sabha elections, but it still had a minority, and the government it formed fell to a vote of no-confidence two weeks later. Power passed in June to a makeshift coalition of low-caste, populist, and socialist parties called the United Front, which put forward H. D. Deve Gowda as its candidate for prime minister. With the support of Congress, this precarious arrangement still holds for the time being.

▨ This Year's News

India's current government, a coalition headed by Prime Minister H.D. Deve Gowda of the Janata Dal, depends on the support of the Congress Party, led by former prime minister P.V. Narasimha Rao. The Congress Party is trying to improve its image in hopes of being re-elected, and should it decide it is ready, India could be slated for another round of national elections in 1997. However, Rao has been accused in several corruption cases which threaten to send him to prison in the coming year. If this were to happen, Rao's rivals in the Congress would be unlikely to pull out if very soon.

In the meantime, foreign investment continues to be the major buzz, as money pours into India's energy, telecommunications, and transportation industries. Car manufacturing is on a major upswing too, which promises to lead to greater traffic congestion and pollution in the major cities in the next few years.

The insurgency in Kashmir appears to be dwindling. Elections were held in the troubled state in May and September 1996, and although some voters were coerced into participating by the Indian army, most voted freely. A peaceful note sent by Benazir Bhutto has also sparked hopes of an entente between India and Pakistan. Both countries could benefit economically from better relations.

▨ Government and Politics

The largest democracy in the world with over 600 million eligible to vote, India is an important example of how democracy can work in a poor, agrarian society. India's parliamentary system is borrowed from Britain, but adapted to suit Indian needs. Its constitution, adopted in 1950, is the world's longest, with 395 articles. The architects of the constitution tried to create a federal system that would reflect India's diversity, but they also wanted a strong central government to handle poverty and religious conflicts. The result has been a highly centralized form of federalism.

At the head of India's government are the president, vice president, and a council of ministers headed by the prime minister. The president, appointed for a five-year term, is essentially a figurehead. The prime minister, chosen by the majority party in the Lok Sabha, the lower house, retains the real executive power. In the words of Jawaharlal Nehru, the prime minister is the "linchpin of government." The Lok Sabha ("House of the People") and the Rajya Sabha ("Council of States") together make up the Indian parliament. All but two of the Lok Sabha's 545 seats are elected by general suffrage; members of the Rajya Sabha are chosen by state governments. India's

Supreme Court is remarkably independent, often asserting its right to make bold decisions on controversial issues the government would rather avoid. Recently it has begun to show its teeth as well, taking up the fight against corruption at the expense of many politicians.

The governments of India's 26 states are organized similarly. Governors act as figureheads, while the real power is in the hands of the chief minister. Each state also has a legislative assembly, or Vidhan Sabha, which is elected for a term of up to five years. Although the state governments depend on the Center for financial support, the states have jurisdiction over education, agriculture, welfare, and police. State governments are divided into local administrations, with the *panchayat* or village council at the lowest level. The central government has the power to dismiss state government in cases of emergency, although this option of "President's Rule" has been abused by central governments—most notoriously by Indira Gandhi—to attack their opponents.

The Congress (I) party, which grew out of the Congress that led India to independence, has dominated Indian politics since 1947. Despite the Congress' tradition of inclusiveness, it has had difficulty incorporating all the disparate interests of ideology, caste, region, and religion. As a result, politics have become more regionalized. In the 1996 elections, no single party won a majority of seats in the Lok Sabha, so a group of parties from the political "left," including populist, lower-caste parties such as the Janata Dal, and socialist parties like the Communist Party of India (Marxist), now rule as a coalition government with the support of the Congress (I). In opposition now, on the "right" of India's political spectrum, are the Hindu nationalist parties, such as the BJP (see **Hindu Nationalism,** p. 101). Hindu nationalism and low-caste parties are the rising forces in Hinduism in the 1990s, although in many states regional parties remain supreme.

Although politics in India are often marred by corruption, and violence is used in some regions to intimidate voters, India's democracy is working smoothly on the whole. Given India's low level of literacy, its high voter participation and political consciousness represent a major achievement. The world's largest democracy has remained democratic since its birth. Voter participation in rural areas and among women has steadily increased since the 1950s. Many more parties are trying to appeal specifically to farmers and low-caste groups, and many more politicians of late have come from agricultural backgrounds (while previously politics were dominated by the educated elites).

▓ Economics

India's economy is overwhelmingly agricultural, with about 70% of the people earning a living from agriculture. Staple foods like wheat and rice are the major crops. Cash crops such as tea and cotton are important exports. Yet at the same time, India is technologically advanced. Nuclear reactors, satellites, television sets, and oil rigs are all built in India. Although such industries have not produced top-quality items for international markets, India has a diverse industrial base.

This situation was brought about by government planning during the 1950s and 60s. A series of Five Year Plans, modeled on the Soviet Union, created huge state-owned industries. Private industries were restricted by licensing, and foreign investment almost nonexistent. The aim was to build up India to self-sufficiency, in the tradition of the *swadeshi* movement in which Indians boycotted British imports.

A lack of exports, however, meant that India had to borrow in order to buy from abroad, and in 1991 a financial crisis almost forced the country to default on its foreign debt. Under pressure from the World Bank and the International Monetary Fund, India made dramatic changes in its economic policies. Now India is liberalizing its economy to encourage private investment. The government has eliminated licensing and scrapped quotas on imports. As a result, India has seen rapid industrial development in the past few years. Foreign investment has been pouring in, especially in the areas of communication, electricity, and computer technology (in addition to bringing Pepsi and Coca-cola to India for the first time). The government has been slower to sell off its money-losing public-sector industries however, because this would require massive, politically unpopular layoffs.

Big economic reforms, however, have done little so far for the vast majority of Indian people. While there is no way to calculate average incomes in a country where so many people live off the land and pay no tax, it is estimated that 40% of India's people live in poverty. Food production has increased dramatically since Independence, mainly due to improvements in irrigation, fertilizers, and pesticides, and the 1960s Green Revolution which brought in new high-yield grains. India has not experienced a famine since 1942 and by the 1980s, India achieved a food surplus. And yet the soaring population and inequalities in distribution still leave a fifth of the population undernourished.

■ Religion

HINDUISM

> *"This entire cosmos, whatever is still or moving, is pervaded by the divine."*
> *-Isa Upanishad*

Known to its many practitioners as *Sanatana Dharma* (Eternal Faith), Hinduism is one of the oldest and most versatile of all of the world's religions, claiming the largest number of followers in Asia. "Hinduism" was the name given to the religion of the people Alexander the Great called "Hindus," because they lived across the Indus River. Because India's history is so varied, Hinduism actually comprises a multitude of local and regional religions which have all been absorbed. It would be wrong to say that Hinduism is a uniform faith, but it would be equally wrong to say that the many different strains in Hinduism are not integrated in a way that accommodates them all.

Hindu beliefs are hard to define because Hinduism is so inclusive. All Hindus acknowledge the truths set forth in the books of the four Vedas. From that point, Hindus go off in their different directions, worshiping an immense number of gods in an immense variety of ways. Shiva, Vishnu, and the Goddess receive the most adulation, but there are many others as well, including local deities, some derived from the Vedic hymns of the Aryans, others from long-lost prehistoric nature cults, and others synthesized from both and then reintegrated as aspects of the major gods. Each god is surrounded by countless myths which invest him or her with a personality, and each area of the Subcontinent has its own local traditions surrounding the gods.

The Vedic Religion

The earliest existing religious influences in modern Hinduism came from the Vedic religion of the Aryans and from the religion of the Indus Valley Civilization (see **History,** p. 80). The Vedic religion was characterized by the ritual of the fire-sacrifice, which is still today performed throughout India in a form very similar to the original. The origins of the Vedic religion are found in books known as the Vedas (meaning "knowledge" or "what is known"), collections of poetic hymns in Sanskrit composed by *rishis* (sages) and addressed to different deities. The Vedic gods are all associated with certain natural phenomena or forces which existed in the "world" of the Aryans; Indra appears as the god of war, Agni is fire, Surya is the sun, Soma is the moon and a hallucinogenic drink, and Vayu is the wind. The deities in the Vedas are usually counted as 30 or 33 in number. During the fire-sacrifice, the Vedas were chanted in a particular meter by the Brahmin priest who also consumed the *soma* which was offered to the fire. Those who partook of the *soma* in this ritual were said to attain a "vision" which would make them immortal and untouched by death. This ritual was performed to maintain *rita* (the cosmic order). By making sacrifices to the Vedic gods, each was enabled to continue his function in the cosmos; any lapse in the sacrifice would result in the dissolution of *rita*. In the Vedas, there is also mention of a mystical essence called *Brahman* which pervades, binds, and maintains the cosmic *rita*. Knowledge of this *Brahman* would bring immortality to the one who perceived it. The Vedic scriptures are classified as *sruti* by the Hindus because they were "heard" by the *rishis*. Later scriptures and are known as *smrti*, (remembered). The *rishis* transmitted their "vision" in the hymns themselves, which when heard or spoken would release the power of their eternal truths.

Later as the Vedic religion entered a period of rethinking and speculation, the sacrifice, which had formerly been so central to the religion, was reinterpreted in metaphysical terms. This is the period when the Upanishads were composed, declaring the absolute principle of *advaita* (non-duality). This movement took place beginning around 800 BC and continued for about 400 years, well into the time when Buddhism was firmly established. During this period, the ritual of the fire-sacrifice, which had formerly regulated society and the cosmos, was reinterpreted in terms of a personal philosophy of *moksha* (liberation) and the doctrines of *karma* and rebirth. As a reaction against the caste order of society, many holy men began to renounce the

Caste

The ancient codes of *dharma* divided Hindu society into four ranks, each having emerged from a part of the first person, Manu: the Brahmins, the priestly and scholarly caste, who came from Manu's mouth; the *kshatriyas*, the warrior-ruler caste, who emerged from Manu's arms; the *vaishyas*, merchants, who came from Manu's thighs, and finally the *shudras*, laborers, who came from Manu's feet. These four *varnas*, or colors, form the basis of the Hindu caste system. The rules of the caste system mostly concern notions of "substance" and "purity." Hinduism grades everything in terms of its purity, especially substances associated with the body. Any transactions mix the "essences" of different people and create "pollution" between members of different castes. Brahmins must be exceptionally pure to perform religious ceremonies, so they do not mix with other castes or accept food cooked by non-Brahmins. The group formerly known as "untouchables" comprised people so low they were outside of the caste system. Their mere touch was considered polluting to upper-caste Hindus.

In practice, however, the hierarchy of the caste system has never been clearcut. More socially important than the *varnas* are *jatis*, subdivisions linked by kinship and usually sharing a very specific occupation (farming, pottery, etc.). There are thousands of these *jatis* in India, some very small and peculiar to a few villages, others numbering in the tens of millions and spread across huge regions. Due to various political and social events, such as famines, wars, mass conversions and reconversions, many of these *jatis* have split, joined, risen in status or descended, regardless of the *varna* they belong to. Some regions of India have politically dominant castes, such as the Jats in Rajasthan and Punjab and the Reddis in Andhra Pradesh, which were originally very low castes.

The Indian constitution (written by a former "untouchable," Dr. B.R. Ambedkar) and the demands of modern life have gone a long way toward abolishing the caste system. The practice of untouchability has been especially reduced; former "untouchables," now known as "Dalits" or "scheduled castes," ride on the same buses and play on the same sports teams as Brahmins. However, in India's villages (where 70% of the population lives), caste is still extremely important. Village people still normally follow their traditional caste occupation. Marriage practices also help keep caste alive. While most Hindus will now eat almost any food, no matter what the caste of the person who prepared it, most Hindu marriages still take place within *jatis*, or at least between *jatis* of equal status.

There is no surefire way to tell someone's caste, although after a while in India you'll recognize some common last names and link them to caste. Occupations are also an indicator, but never certain. In recent years affirmative action programs for lower-caste Hindus have come into effect, with a certain number of university spaces and civil service jobs reserved for scheduled castes.

world. Forest communities of ascetics became common then; yoga also arose at this time as a spiritual practice. The essence known as *Brahman* in Vedic times became identified with *atman,* the innermost Self of all beings and everything in the universe. Knowledge of the *atman* gave one liberation from the chain of rebirth. One who transcended the material world would attain a state of existence-consciousness-bliss, and would be a free soul, forever united with the Self.

Buddhism and Jainism also arose as a part of the general philosophical movement of this period. As well as developing a deep philosophical and ethical system, Buddhism developed a unified monastic order, which threatened the social structures of the time. With world-renunciation as more common than before, the Brahmin priesthood was losing power. Yet temples and devotional philosophies, partly borrowed from Buddhism, began to win converts back to Hinduism.

The Bhagavad Gita and Dharma

One of the most popular and sacred Hindu scriptures, the Bhagavad Gita, makes up the sixth chapter of the great Sanskrit epic of the *Mahabharata.* It is a dialogue between Lord Krishna, an *avatar* (incarnation) of Vishnu, and his disciple Arjuna. Heading into a great battle, Arjuna becomes despondent when he sees many friends, teachers, and elders assembled, against whom he must fight. At this point, Arjuna throws down his weapons and refuses to fight. Krishna (Arjuna's chariot-driver) then gives his disciple a lesson on *dharma* and other Hindu philosophies, including *yoga, Vedanta,* and devotionalism. One of the Gita's central philosophies is that of *karma yoga,* the *yoga* of action. Explaining that one should not seek results or be attached to the fruits of one's actions, Krishna declares that He alone is the doer and sustainer of all activity. Thus, he tells Arjuna to fulfill his *dharma* as a *kshatriya* (a member of the warrior caste) and fight, allowing himself to be an instrument of the Supreme power and not "the doer." This is the most brilliant synthesis of Hindu philosophy and teaching on *dharma.*

The concept of *dharma* is important in Hinduism. Similar to *rita, dharma* has many different meanings. Most commonly, it simply refers to the continual nature, role, and function of everything that persists in the universe. Thus, the *sanatana dharma* might also be translated as "the way things eternally are," or "the eternal religion." In Buddhism, the Buddha's teaching is referred to as the *"Buddha-Dharma,"* for this very same reason. Another example of *dharma* could be described in the image of a river. Why does a river flow downhill? Because that is its role, its nature, or its *dharma.* For the same reason, it is the *dharma* of a king to eat meat, engage in war, offer food and money to the Brahmins and rule a kingdom. *Dharma* extends to the social order as well, with a whole set of customs which are meant to maintain this order; these are set down in the *Manusmriti,* the "Laws of Manu," and in texts called *dharmashastras.* Generally there are three orders one should follow: the first is adherence to the eternal or cosmic *dharma* through religious observances, the second is adherence to one's caste *(jati) dharma,* the third is following one's *svadharma,* a personal moral code. Most often, the Hindu epics play on themes of conflict between these various duties.

Philosophy

Hindu philosophy is based on the existence of an absolute unchanging and omnipresent reality called *Brahman,* a universal soul or spirit, and *atman,* the self which is equated with *Brahman.* (The *advaita* and *dvaita* schools of thought differ on the point of whether the two are indeed one and the same or if there exists an unbridgeable gap between God and man.) The ultimate goal of existence then is to unite the *atman* with *Brahman* in the ultimate state of bliss. Unfortunately, the individual self is caught in *samsara,* all parts of the transient material world: the changing dualities of night and day, happiness and sorrow, life and death. Seeking detachment does not, however, mean a denial of life and living. Instead, Hindu thought encourages active living, along with non-attachment to the fruits of life's actions. Realization of the *atman,* the first step to liberation, can be achieved through any of the four ways of living, the *yogas* described in the *Bhagavad Gita:* action, devotion, knowledge, and psychic and physical exercises.

With a constant eye for practical living, while *dharma* and *moksha* remain the ultimate goals in life, short term goals in Hindu thought include *kama* and *artha:* sensual enjoyment and wealth. Hindu thought also divides life into four stages in which to seek these goals. The first twenty-five years should be devoted solely to knowledge, the second twenty-five to being a householder, fulfilling the duty to raise a family and future generation. The third stage rounds out the householder life and is a preparatory and slow detachment from worldly connections to enter into the fourth stage, complete renunciation to one's life as an ascetic on a spiritual quest.

Even time is cyclical in Hindu thought, enfolding the individual cycles. Periods called *yugas* constitute one breathing cycle in the life of Lord Brahma and last approximately 314 trillion years. Divided into four parts, a yuga begins in a golden era of prosperity and devolves until the *kali yuga* when *dharma* declines and the world is destroyed to be renewed again in the next *yuga*. Unfortunately, we are said to be near the tail end of a *kali yuga* at the moment.

Gods and Goddesses

To help people understand its philosophy, Hinduism includes a wealth of deities and rituals. From the central trinity of Brahma, Vishnu, and Shiva, many gods and goddesses emerge, each embodying an attribute of the eternal soul. Worshiping an attribute of *Brahman* or emulating a philosophy becomes a way to understand the whole. For example, a popular deity worshiped at the beginning of important events is Ganesh, the mythological son of Shiva. Depicted with a man's body and an elephant's head, Ganesh is worshiped for auspiciousness and as a sort of patron deity for leaders. His elephant head takes on a world of symbolic meaning: large ears to hear the voice of everyone, small eyes to not be swayed by images, a long trunk to feel out even the smallest corners—all attributes of a strong leader. Brahma, the Creator, sits upon a lotus flower emerging from the navel of Vishnu. Unbefitting of his celestial job, Brahma is rarely worshiped in modern Hinduism. Only a single temple in India is dedicated to him (see **Pushkar,** p. 280).

Vishnu, The Preserver, reclines upon a many-headed snake afloat on a sea of milk. Vishnu's ten *avataras,* or incarnations on earth, include Krishna and Rama, popular deities in North India. Rama, born a prince in what is now Ayodhya, was banished to the forest for years during which time he rescued his wife Sita from Ravana, a demon-king and evil incarnate on earth. As the epic hero of the Ramayana, Rama represents the ideal son, husband, father, and leader and is worshiped for those attributes. Krishna, the dark skinned cowherd, is known for his flute-playing and his sexual frolics with the *gopis,* or milkmaids, each of whom represents human longing for God. As charioteer to the battling prince Arjuna, Krishna also delivered the lyric verses of the *Bhagavad Gita.*

Shiva, the Destroyer, is a great ascetic who sits in meditation upon Mount Kailasha in the Himalaya, with the river Ganga spouting from his matted locks. Carrying a trident and garlanded with a snake, Shiva is the embodiment of destruction, but he also stands for creation and fertility, and he is worshiped in the form of a *linga,* originally a phallus-shaped stone. Twelve temples around India are sanctified *jyotirlingas* (*lingas* of light), where Shiva, also known as Mahadev, the "Great God," is said to have burst from the earth. Also the patron god of dance, Shiva's powerful movements are believed to have inspired the cosmos. Hindu mythology is filled with stories of Shiva's tempestuous relationship with his consort Parvati.

The various goddesses in Hinduism are often considered the consorts of the male gods, but they also have followers in their own right. All of the goddesses are worshiped as *Shakti,* the active female force of creation. Parvati, Shiva's wife, makes Shiva's power accessible to humans. Kali, also considered Shiva's consort, is the goddess of destruction, shown with black skin, a lolling red tongue, and a garland of skulls. Lakshmi, the consort of Vishnu, is the goddess of wealth and luck, both monetary and spiritual. All-powerful Durga, the demon-slayer, was created from the combined power of each of the celestial deities (beams of light emerged from the foreheads of each of the male deities and joined into one all-powerful beam). Saraswati, the consort of Brahma, is the patron of knowledge, learning and the arts. She is depicted seated on a swan with scriptures in one hand and *veena* in the other. Worship of female deities in Hinduism probably predates the worship of male gods, and is widely popular. The goddess is venerated not only as consort but as the incarnation of power and grace. One of the most popular festivals for a goddess is Navratri, nine nights dedicated to Durga, accompanying Dusshera.

The popularity of all these deities varies from North to South, village to village, and family to family. The largest distinction is between those claiming to be Vaishnava (worshipers of Vishnu) and those that are Shaiva (worshipers of Shiva). The most common Hindu ritual is *puja*, in which water and fruits are offered to the deity. After the deity has blessed these, they are distributed among the worshipers as *prasad*, consecrated food. Another important Hindu practice is *darshan*, in which worshipers gaze upon images of gods; this sight is supposed to help Hindus understand the forms of God.

Bhakti

Of all forms of Hinduism, the most popular today derive from a tradition known as *bhakti*. The *bhakti* movements, which began around the 11th century, were spread by popular poet-saints and characterized by ecstatic religious devotion. It is said that a true *bhakta* desires not to merge and become one with God, but rather to remain a devotee forever, always praising God.

Bhakti worship is filled with songs sung in local dialects and messages delivered to everyone, regardless of caste. Inspired by music and dance, the *bhakti* movement rebelled against religious orthodoxy and rituals, as well as religious intolerance. The great poet saints of the *bhakti* movement claimed that God could be realized through pure love and devotion in any form, be it poetry or song, as long as it was filled with the intoxicated and ecstatic pure love of the divine. One of the most important leaders of the bhakti movement in South India was Ramanuja, who established the Sri-Vaishnava sect. In North India, Chaitanya increased the following of Krishna. Other prominent *bhakti* figures throughout India were Mirabai, Sur Das, Tukaram, and Eknath. A great devotional figure for both Hindus and Muslims was Kabir (1440-1518). Born a Muslim weaver in Varanasi, Kabir spread a message of unity between faiths, insisting that Rama and Allah were the same God, who was worthy of devo-

Swastikas

Visitors to India with memories of the Second World War (inherited or otherwise) may be shocked to see the profusion of swastikas painted on walls and windshields, or worked into the architecture. Swastikas go a long way back in South Asia, however, and *swastika* is actually a Sanskrit word, meaning "It is well." The cross with bent arms was a widespread symbol of good luck and power in the ancient world, used by ancient Greeks, Mesopotamians, Chinese, early Christians, Mayans, and Navajos among others. The ancient Indo-Aryans also used the swastika, and it remains one of the most cherished symbols of Hindus, Jains, and Buddhists. Much like the god Ganesh, the swastika is associated with good luck and the removal of obstacles. With arms pointing clockwise it is an auspicious solar symbol, since it seems to mimic the sun's path from east to south to west across the sky. The counter-clockwise swastika, however, is a symbol of night, and is considered inauspicious. The Hindu swastika may have originated from a wheel, or from the firesticks in Vedic sacrifices, which were lain on the ground in the form of a cross. The Nazis used the swastika to symbolize "the victory of the Aryan man," leaving many people to cringe decades later at what has become the Western world's strongest symbol of hatred. This latter-day legacy has obviously failed to make a dent in India or Nepal, where Third Reich flags sometimes make it onto bumper stickers, with totally innocent intentions.

tion. The Sikh religion also emerged at this time as a blend of Hindu and Muslim beliefs.

Modern Hinduism

In the 19th century, Hinduism was reinterpreted by many thinkers who wanted to make it more rational. The Brahmo Samaj, a group founded by Ram Mohan Roy in Bengal in 1828, did away with image-worship and instead held Christian-style services with readings from the Upanishads. Another movement, the Arya Samaj, also abandoned caste and images, preaching that the Vedas were sufficient for everything in life. A great figure in the 19th-century Hindu revival was Sri Ramakrishna (1836-1886), whose message of religious unity left an indelible impression upon modern Hindu thought. As a devotee of goddess Kali from a young age, Ramakrishna meditated on the Divine until he achieved spiritual union with her. Ramakrishna proclaimed the unity of all religions. Describing God as a well, Ramakrishna suggested that each religion was a different path to the well; each found the same substance inside it. Ramakrishna believed the best religion for any person was the one in which they were raised. A disciple of Ramakrishna, Swami Vivekananda (1863-1902) introduced Hinduism and Ramakrishna's philosophy to the West during the World Parliament of Religions at the University of Chicago in 1893. Vivekananda declared the existence of God in all and encouraged self-reliance and a faith in the Self. Proclaiming the God within, he extended his philosophy to a national level, inspiring Indian patriotism and a belief in the nation's indomitable spirit. He spread the lessons of Vedanta and centuries of Hindu philosophy to a world-wide audience.

Sri Aurobindo was another reformer and Indian nationalist who, after being imprisoned for sedition by the British in 1908, underwent a series of mystical experiences while practising yoga in prison. Sri Aurobindo abandoned his political activities and devoted his life to bringing down "Supramental Consciousness" on earth, becoming one of the most prolific writers of poetry and Hindu philosophy in the 20th century. His activities were continued by his associate The Mother, a French woman who came to him to assist him in his work. Sri Aurobindo spent the rest of his life in seclusion in Pondicherry, where his center remains today.

Hindu Nationalism

The 19th-century Hindu reform movements went hand-in-hand with a popular desire to revive Indian society by reverting to traditional Hindu values. This sentiment became highly nationalistic in opposition to the British, who viewed Hinduism as an impediment to progress, and also to the Muslims, who the Hindu nationalists saw as Hindu turncoats refusing to acknowledge their true identity. The freedom fighter V.D. Savarkar developed a rallying philosophy for this movement called *Hindutva*, which asserted that all Indians, regardless of religion, must profess a certain "Hinduness" out of loyalty to the nation's primordial culture. The RSS (Rashtriya Swayamsevak Sangh, "National Volunteer Corps"), something between a scout club and a paramilitary group, founded in Nagpur in 1925, took up this ideology in its quest for a spiritual and cultural regeneration of India. The movement gathered steam until 1948, when a former RSS cadre, Nathuram Godse, assassinated Mohandas Gandhi, who he believed had been too generous to Muslims. Although many prominent Indians supported Hindu Nationalist political parties through the 50s, 60s, and 70s, the memory of the Mahatma's murder prevented any significant electoral successes.

In 1977, some Hindu Nationalists managed to join the short-lived Janata Party coalition government. After it collapsed they founded the Bharatiya Janata Party (BJP) in 1980. They have since rocketed from two seats in parliament in 1984 to 160 in the 1996 elections. As a mainstream party, they have had to moderate their most hardline policies; today they advocate only a cultural nationalism based on Hindu traditions, and even wheel out a few Muslim members for publicity's sake. But the party maintains strong ties to other radical Hindu organizations like the RSS and the Vishwa Hindu Parishad (VHP), which led the campaign to destroy the Babri Masjid in Ayodhya in 1992. The BJP's following consists mainly of upper-caste North Indian urbanites (especially civil servants and soldiers), but their following in the south and among lower-caste groups is increasing. Although their 1996 government survived less than two weeks, their increasing influence threatens to revolutionize India's largely secular politics and Hinduism's largely atomized and apolitical nature.

JAINISM

Jainism started as a rejection of Brahminical authority in the 6th century BC, at the same time as the birth of Buddhism. Its founder Vardhamana, known as Mahavira ("Great Hero"), was a follower of the ascetic saint Parshavanatha, who had lived about 200 years earlier. Mahavira abandoned his hedonistic lifestyle in favor of nudity, chastity, and asceticism, and established a new sect called the Jains (from *jina*, "conquerer"). He is venerated as the twenty-fourth in a line of *tirthankaras* (crossing-makers) the Jain equivalent to gods (Parshavanatha is the 23rd). By starving himself to death, Mahavira was the last Jain to achieve the most sublime purity and liberation from the cycle of rebirth.

At the center of Jain belief is the principle of *jiva*—all life is sacred and everything that lives possesses an immortal soul, every person, animal, plant, and insect. Even rocks have souls. Out of their respect for life, Jains developed the principle of *ahimsa* (non-violence). So as not to harm any animals, Jains must practice strict vegetarianism. The most orthodox Jain monks wear a net over their mouths and nostrils to prevent the possibility of killing an insect that might fly in. They also walk with a broom, sweeping the path before them so as not to crush any crawling animals. The occupation of agriculture was avoided, for to pull a plough through the soil would be to murder millions of tiny creatures. As a result, the Jain lay community concentrated in commerce. Liberation from the entanglement of the karmic cycle can be achieved when one gives up contact with all matter. This translates into strict ascetic practices, including chastity, lack of property, and even nudity. As with most religious orders, the Jains have become divided into sects—the Digambara ("Sky-Clad") and the Shvetambara ("White-Clad"). Of these two, the Digambara Jains have the more austere observances, wandering naked and shunning material possessions.

Jain temples are found throughout India, but are primarily seen in Western India, in Gujarat and along the west coast. The two most famous sites are at Palitana in Gujarat and Sravanabelagola in Karnataka. Today, there are estimated to be between four and five million Jains living in India.

BUDDHISM

In spite of its origins in the Ganga Valley, only traces of Buddhism remain in India today. Siddhartha Gautama, who would come to be called the Buddha, was born around 560 BC just within the modern borders of Nepal. It was an age of contemplation, and at the age of 29 Gautama fled from his plush life as a prince to wander in the forest as an ascetic. He gained enlightenment under a tree in Bodh Gaya (Bihar) and soon set off preaching his discoveries about escaping the suffering of the world by overcoming one's desires. Although Buddhism was first centered primarily in monasteries, it became the main religion in India after the 3rd century BC, when the emperor Ashoka converted. Hinduism gradually returned to supersede Buddhism during the first millennium AD. The sacking of monasteries by 12th-century Muslim invaders dealt the fatal blow to Buddhism in India.

About 7 million Buddhists are left in India, mostly at the fringes of the Hindu world, in Ladakh and Sikkim, where Buddhism never let go. Others, however, trace their belief to a recent revival: in 1956 the leader of the Hindu outcast community, Dr. B. R. Ambedkar, publicly converted to Buddhism as a political protest, and was followed by another 200,000 former "untouchables" (mainly in Maharashtra). India's central place in the Buddhist world ensures that Buddhism will not be forgotten: the holiest Buddhist pilgrimage sites are in India, drawing thousands of international visitors every year, and Buddhism has also left the country with a rich cultural legacy of cave-temples and *stupas*.

CHRISTIANITY

Since Independence, Christianity has become increasingly visible in India, drawing both adherents and political power at a pace so rapid that the Apostle Thomas would surely be pleased. In the apocryphal *Acts of the Apostles According to Thomas,* Thomas was chosen by lot to spread the Christian Gospel to India. While the book reports that he initially disliked the idea of undertaking so long a trip, Thomas is said to have arrived on the coast of Kerala in 52 AD, where he was able to attract some converts. Legend holds that twenty years after his arrival in Kerala, Thomas was killed in Tamil Nadu, his body buried in Mylapore, a suburb of modern Madras, where a shrine still exists today.

Since Thomas, ships carrying missionaries have sailed across the Arabian Sea with some frequency, pelting India's west coast with Christian ideas and values. In the 6th century AD, the Syriac Church dispatched missionaries to India, introducing Syriac customs—many of which are still alive—to South Asia. In the 16th century, it was the Portugese who sought to systematically spread Christianity to India. Soon after the arrival of the Jesuit Saint Francis Xavier in 1542, Portugese-ruled Goa became a hotbed of Catholicism. While Catholic missionaries typically focused on converting high-caste Hindus, British-backed Protestant missionaries sought to make their influence felt by building schools and hospitals, especially as the 19th century wore on and British rulers became skeptical about the possibility of "civilizing" India by changing its religion.

In the post-colonial period, the diffusion of Christianity in India has been largely due to natural increase and not to systematic missionary work. There are about 25 million Christians in today's India, 50% more than there were in 1970. India's Christians have successfully parlayed numerical growth into political power. In Kerala, where the population is 25% Christian, support for the Congress party is roused in church on Sunday. Nagaland was carved from the state of Assam in 1963, largely under pressure from the well-organized and militant Christian Nagas.

ZOROASTRIANISM

Founded in Persia between 1500 BC and 1700 BC by Zarathustra (also known as Zoroaster), Zorastrianism understands the world as starkly divided between pure good (as represented by the god Ahura Mazda) and pure evil (as represented by the god Angra Mainyu and his evil minions, *daevas*). According to Zoroastrian belief, Saoshyant, an immaculately conceived messiah, will one day establish Ahura Mazda's reign of goodness on the earth. Traditional Zoroastrians regard burial and cremation as spiritually polluting of air, earth, and fire, each of which is sacred for its purity. As such, Zoroastrians leave the bodies of their dead atop specially-designed "towers of silence," where vultures will have easy access.

Zoroastrianism was first brought to India in the middle of the 10th century, when Persian Zoroastrians arrived on the Gujarati coast ahead of the persecution and dislocation which accompanied the advance of Islam through Iran and Central Asia. Often called Parsis because of their ancient roots in Persia, today's dwindling numbers of Indian Zoroastrians—about 95,000 are left—are concentrated in western India, especially Bombay. Though few in number, the Parsis are visible because of their great wealth. One Parsi family, the Tatas, are renowned throughout India for their manufacturing industries (including India's first steel mill in 1908) and for their early financial support for India's independence movement.

ISLAM

Approximately 11% of India's population is Muslim, which amounts to about 100 million people, giving India the fourth-largest number of Muslims in the world after Indonesia, Bangladesh, and Pakistan. Muslims are spread throughout India, forming distinct communities in many places. The questions surrounding their status are the most emotionally charged issues for many Indians today.

INDIA

Muslims believe in one supreme god, Allah, and worship him through the five "pillars" of Islam: declaring their faith, praying five times daily, giving alms to the poor, fasting during the month of Ramadan, and making the *haj* pilgrimage to Mecca if they are able. A single holy book, the Qur'an, is central to Islam, and Muslims shun all use of music or images in worship—their religion appears starkly reductionistic next to Hinduism. Islam's ideas were brought forth by the Prophet Muhammad, who lived in Mecca, in Arabia, during the 7th century AD. The Prophet's role is critical in Islam, and his life is considered an example to follow. Between 610 and 622, Muhammad received revelations from the angel Gabriel. His teachings on the unity of God were received coolly at first in polytheistic Arabia, and he was driven from Mecca with his followers in the year 622 (this *hijra* (flight) marks the birth of the Muslim community and the start of the Muslim calendar). Muhammad won prestige in the northern city of Medina, and returned in triumph to Mecca in 630, becoming the temporal as well as the spiritual leader of the new Muslim empire. After Muhammad's death the Islamic community conquered Arabia and adjacent lands, and by 711 it had spread from Spain to Sindh (in western India—now part of Pakistan).

A few Muslims trickled into India: traders from Arabia, Sufi mystics from Persia, the armies of Mahmud from Afghanistan also came to raid Hindu temples. Islam's full effect was felt after 1192, however, when a Muslim kingdom took control of North India. Under the Delhi Sultanate and then the Mughal Empire, India was ruled by Muslims for 500 years. A few high-class Hindus converted to Islam in order to join the new elite, and some low-caste Hindus converted too, but the majority of the Hindu population did not convert. Large-scale conversion to Islam took place only on the eastern and western frontiers of South Asia where Hinduism's influence had been weakest. These areas have now become Pakistan and Bangladesh, but sizeable Muslim minorities remain in India.

Muslims have different customs from their Hindu neighbors: At noon on Friday, the Muslim holy day, men gather for communal prayer in the *masjid* (mosque), their place of worship, usually after an amplified call from the building's minaret. The bulbous domes of these structures can often be seen rising high above the shops around them. Many Muslim women stay secluded in their homes according to the custom of *purdah;* during the centuries of Muslim rule this practice spread among Hindu women as well. Muslims are required to avoid alcohol, pork, and shellfish. Many Muslims in India also speak their own language, Urdu, which was until recently the *lingua franca* of South Asian Islam.

Islam's two main sects are both represented in India. Most Muslims are Sunnis, following the orthodox Islam practiced throughout the Middle East. Due to the Persian influence at the Mughal court, however, India also has a sizeable number of Shi'i Muslims, members of a sect based largely in Iran. The schism between Sunnis and Shi'is originated as a dispute over the leadership of the Islamic community. Shi'is look to divinely chosen *imams* as their religious leaders, and they fervently remember the 7th-century succession dispute that caused them to branch off. The annual Shi'i festival of Muharram commemorates the martyrdom of Hussain, grandson of Muhammad and champion of the Shi'i cause.

Muslims and Hindus have repeatedly come into conflict in India, partly due to their opposing customs: Islam was born in a rage against idol-worship, and the Hindu use of divine images for *darshan* looks deceptively idolatrous. Muslims also have no compunctions about killing cows, which Hindus consider sacred, and cow-slaughter is even elevated to a religious rite at the Muslim festival of Eid-ul-Azha. Still, Muslims and Hindus have coexisted in a tense sort of peace for most of their stay together. The problems between them have been no worse than those between other religious groups. Many leaders, like the Mughal Emperor Akbar, even tried to bridge the two faiths. But events in the last few years such as the destruction of the Babri Mosque in Ayodhya (see p. 212) and the ensuing riots seem to indicate that Hindu-Muslim relations have yet to escape the 16th century. The current Hindu-Muslim antipathy really has its roots in the early 20th century, however, when Muslims became conscious of their minority status in British India. Scared about their prospects in a Hindu-dominated independent India, Muslim leaders declared their community a separate nation. This led to the controversial carving out of Pakistan in 1947, during which hundreds of thousands were killed. Muslims who have remained in India since Partition are haunted by the separatist politics of that time. Many Hindus resent their presence and accuse them of disloyalty. Unfriendly India-Pakistan relations now also mean that India's communal tensions are affected by international politics.

Most of the Muslims who remained in India after 1947 were poor, and they lost their leaders to Pakistan. India's ruling Congress Party has traditionally considered them a downtrodden minority, and eager to prove that India is a secular state, they have granted Muslims special protections. But the fact that Muslims are allowed to follow Islamic law, rather than a uniform civil code, on such matters as divorce and inheritance, angers many Hindus. In recent years the Mughal legacy of temple-breaking has also been flung back at Muslims. The Babri Mosque has already been destroyed, and Hindu nationalists have their blueprints drawn for similar sites in Varanasi and Mathura. Meanwhile the riots and massacres that began with the 1947 Partition continue to be Hindus' and Muslims' main way of airing their grievances.

SIKHISM

Guru Nanak (1469-1539), a philosopher-poet born into a Hindu family in what is today eastern Pakistan, is the venerated founder of Sikhism. After traveling to Mecca, Bengal, and many places in between, Nanak proclaimed a religious faith which brought together elements of Hinduism and Islam: Nanak rejected the image-worship and the caste system just as Islam did, but borrowed Hinduism's use of music in worship and rejected Islam's reliance on a holy book. Nanak proclaimed that there was one God, and asserted that liberation from *samsara,* the Hindu cycle of life, death, and rebirth, was possible for those who embraced God's truth. Nanak contended that bathing, donating alms to charity, and, most importantly, meditating, would erode hubris and would clear the way for individuals to accept God's truth. Nanak laid a socially egalitarian groundwork for Sikhism and attracted a community of followers, most of whom were from the Punjab.

After Nanak's death in 1539, spiritual leadership over his *sikhs* (disciples) passed to another guru, Angad. After Angad's death, guru succeeded guru, each adding new wrinkles to Sikhism. The third guru, Amar Das (1509-74), encouraged Sikhs to worship publicly in temples called *gurudwaras;* the fifth guru, Arjun Dev (1563-1606), collected more than 5000 of the previous gurus' hymns into a book called the Adi Granth and founded the magnificent Golden Temple at Amritsar. After Guru Arjun was killed by the Mughal Emperor Jahangir, an extended period of Muslim-Sikh fighting ensued. By the time the tenth and final guru, Gobind Singh, was assassinated in 1708, raids and skirmishes had become a sad fact of life throughout Punjab, the Siwalik Hills, and other parts of northern India in which large concentrations of Sikhs made their homes.

Under the leadership of this tenth guru, Guru Gobind Singh (1666-1708), Sikhism underwent a series of radical changes which left it with a visually distinctive identity. In 1699, Gobind Singh founded the Khalsa Brotherhood. Sikh men now had to undergo a kind of "baptism," pledge not to smoke tobacco or have sexual relations with Muslims, and renounce their caste names, with men taking as their name "Singh" ("Lion") and women taking the name "Kaur" ("Princess"). Moreover, the Khalsa demanded that its members adopt and abide by the "five k's": *kangah* (wooden comb), *kirpan* (sword), *kara* (steel bracelet), *kachch* (short knickers), and *kesh* (uncut hair). Gobind Singh added new hymns to the Adi Granth, re-named it the Guru Granth Sahib, and announced that the book was to be the next guru. Since Gobind Singh's death, the Guru Granth Sahib has been Sikhism's holy book, and Sikhs have become a visible minority, identifiable by the turbans they use to wrap up their uncut hair.

During the Mutiny of 1857, Sikh regiments sided with the Raj, lending support to the British at many critical junctures. The British considered the Sikhs to be naturally gifted warriors. Despite the ridiculousness of such a statement, it was perhaps due only to their skill in battle that the Sikhs survived centuries of Mughal persecution. After the Partition of 1947 divided the Punjab between Pakistan and India, millions of Sikhs crossed into India to avoid living in a Muslim state. Vicious Muslim-Sikh fighting in 1947 seemed all too similar to the violence of the past.

In 1966, India's government acceded to Sikh demands and officially carved out a Punjabi-speaking, Sikh-dominated autonomous region called Punjab. Yet the 1980s brought increasing violence, with rising fear among Sikhs of losing their independent identity. Sikh extremists led by Sant Jarnail Singh Bhindranwale demanded an independent "Khalistan." Bhindranwale transformed the Golden Temple, Sikhism's most sacred shrine, into an armory, and directed a campaign of terrorism in Punjab. The increasing violence between Sikhs and Hindus climaxed in the military siege of the Golden Temple, otherwise known as Operation Bluestar. In retaliation, two Sikh bodyguards murdered Prime Minister Indira Gandhi in 1984. What came next was gruesome, and India's Sikh community is still coming to terms with its implications: in three days of rioting in Delhi and a few other northern cities, Hindus and Muslims looted and burned Sikh-owned businesses and killed nearly 3000 Sikhs. Violence in the Punjab has since quieted.

■ Language

India is home to an astounding 1600 dialects, varying from state to state and village to village. The languages of North India, such as Hindi and Bengali, descended from Sanskrit spoken by the Aryan invaders who wandered into the area around 1500 BC. These languages are part of the greater Indo-European family, and it's not unusual to find North Indian words that resemble their counterparts in English or other European languages (the Hindi numbers 1-10 are a good example). Urdu, a language widely spoken among Muslims in India, is very similar to Hindi but also contains elements of Persian, having developed as the language of the ruling classes of the Mughal empire. The major South Indian languages, Kannada, Telugu, Malayalam and Tamil, all belong to the independent Dravidian family. They constitute a separate language family, unrelated to the North Indian languages. Indo-Aryan and Dravidian languages have inevitably influenced one another, however, and they share some features, such as retroflex consonants, in which the tongue is curled back to touch the palate. Whether the punctuated sounds of the formal and poetic Sanskrit, the regal tones of Urdu, or the frenetic roller coaster ride that is Malayalam, all Indian languages are notoriously melodic with most locals speaking with manic speed, rhythmically dotting their expressions. English spoken with an Indian accent is a classic tune to English ears.

Language has been a frightful issue in independent India. The Indian constitution (written in English) planned for Hindi to be the national language, since it is the single biggest Indian language, spoken by about 30% of the people. But most Indians identify strongly with their mother tongue, and linguistic loyalty is often linked to religion or geography. In the 1950s India was reorganized into new states to accommodate various language groups. Eighteen official languages—Assamese, Bengali, Gujarati, Hindi, Kannada, Kashmiri, Konkani, Malayalam, Manipuri, Marathi, Nepali, Oriya, Punjabi, Sanskrit, Sindhi, Tamil, Telugu, and Urdu—are recognized in the Indian constitution. Attempts to spread Hindi have met with resentment; don't be surprised to find some Indians willing to speak anything but Hindi. English controversially holds its place as a *lingua franca,* an ironically welcome vestige of British imperialism. English is the first language of many upper-class Indians, and millions more learn English in school. It is easy to get around India with English, although this might make it difficult to have more than simple conversations.

Hindi, Marathi, and Nepali are written in a script called Devanagari (the script of "the City of the Gods") which has a top line from which the letters descend, like most North Indian scripts. South Indian scripts are more exuberantly curly. Urdu is written in an Arabic-based script. For basic Hindi, Bengali, Tamil, Marathi, and Nepali vocabulary, see the **Phrasebook,** p. 762.

■ The Arts

VISUAL ARTS

India has a very old and rich artistic tradition, fed over the millennia by contact with other civilizations, yet distinctly Indian in many ways. Indian artists have commonly made their works conform to some ideal, rather than show their subjects naturalistically, or follow the properties of their materials. This is why there are so few individual portraits in Indian art, and why a temple might have been built in the same style regardless of whether wood or stone was used. The idealism of Indian art comes partly from its religious function—for hundreds of years, most art was used to decorate sacred buildings or to illustrate sacred stories. Although it is wrong to suppose that certain artistic styles are the direct functions of certain religious beliefs, one can't overlook how much Indian art has been driven by visions of the sublime and otherworldly. Art has rarely been the province of renowned individuals known for their creative knack or distinctive personal style. Instead, it has typically been produced by anonymous craftspeople and artisans employed by wealthy patrons.

Architecture

Because they built of wood and brick, we know little about the architecture of the ancient Indians. The ruins of the Indus Valley Civilization (c. 2500-1800 BC) found in Pakistan consist of functional buildings arranged in planned cities. But almost nothing remains from this time until the Maurya period (c. 324-184 BC), when builders began to make sparing use of stone. They built fortified cities and monasteries, but the most lasting structures of this time are *stupas,* huge hemispherical mounds of earth that usually contained Buddhist relics. *Stupas* could be elaborately decorated, with the mound sitting atop a terrace and surrounded by stone railings, and often capped by a stone parasol. The Great Stupa at Sanchi in Madhya Pradesh (built in the first century BC) is the most famous of these structures.

The next few centuries saw the development of the temple in India, a momentous event for architecture. Early temples (Hindu, Jain, and Buddhist) were still built of wood, but in western India some were carved into the rock of the Western Ghats. These cave-temples, or *chaityas,* usually had a projecting apse that led to a long, pillared hall, at the end of which was placed a sacred object. The greatest of the cave-temples is found at Ajanta in Maharashtra. Cave-monasteries, with each cell hewn into the rock, were also carved at this time. Even though these buildings were made of stone, they still imitated wooden forms. A change came around the 4th century AD, with the resurgence of Hinduism and the rise of the Gupta Empire. Free-standing stone Hindu temples began to appear in a new style that did not imitate wood.

The original medieval Hindu temples consisted only of a small, dark, square sanctum called the *garbhagriha* (womb chamber), which housed the deity. Soon a tall pyramidal spire, or *shikhara,* was added to this, symbolizing a connection between heaven and earth. Temples gradually became more and more elaborate, with other buildings acting as gateways for the worshiper. In the typical North Indian style, a series of up to four rooms leads to the sanctum in a straight line. Each of these outer rooms has its own *shikhara,* growing taller and taller up to the *shikhara* of the sanctum. This row of spires resembles a mountain range, symbolizing the Himalayan peaks inhabited by the gods. Unfortunately, many of the greatest North Indian medieval temples were destroyed by Islamic rulers from the 12th century onwards, but excellent examples remain in Orissa and in Khajuraho (Madhya Pradesh). In South India, the temple sanctum was expanded to a larger room, and surrounded by four rectangular entrance towers, or *gopurams,* which had *shikharas* of their own topped by barrel-vaults. These *gopurams* eventually became so exaggerated that they dwarfed the central *shikhara.* They marked a sacred area all around, creating great temple-city complexes such as those of Madurai and Srirangam in Tamil Nadu.

The conquest of India by Muslim forces in the 12th century AD brought the Islamic styles of Persia and Central Asia to India. Since Islam discourages crafting images of human or divine figures, Muslim rulers were glad to put their efforts into architecture, filling India with domes, arches, geometric patterns, and calligraphic inscriptions. The most striking monuments to the early years of the Muslim conquest were Delhi's Quwwat ul-Islam Mosque and Qutb Minar, which were built starting in 1199 AD using the remains of more than 20 Hindu and Jain temples. Most architecture under the Delhi Sultanate (1192-1526) was poor. Some of the smaller Muslim kingdoms in India, however, did not just smash Hindu temples but tried to synthesize Indian and Islamic architecture in an Indo-Saracenic style. The most successful mix occurred in Gujarat, with the construction of such buildings as the Jami Masjid at Ahmedabad. Indian Islamic architecture reached its zenith under the patronage of the Mughal emperors. The pink and red post-and-lintel buildings of Fatehpur Sikri in Uttar Pradesh, built between 1569 and 1589, testify to the elegance of Mughal architecture. Of course the Mughals also built Agra's incredible Taj Mahal, a white marble mausoleum adorned with calligraphy, studded with turquoise, jade, and coral, and surrounded by gardens laid out in the Persian *charbagh* style.

With the decline of the Mughals and the coming of European imperial control, Western architectural forms began to appear in India. The 16th-century Portuguese filled their colony of Goa with Baroque frills and ripples. In the 19th century the British imported their Neoclassical style to the metropolises of Calcutta, Madras, and Bombay, where it became fashionable among Indians as well. The British also built in neo-Gothic and neo-Saracenic styles, giving these huge cities a refreshing look. The two great architectural projects of the 20th century in India, the construction of New Delhi in the 1920s and Chandigarh in the 1950s, have both been foreign attempts to find a kind of modern architecture that would suit India. One might say that no such style has been found yet. Since Independence, Indian cities have suffered from an explosion of painfully dull concrete cubes.

Sculpture

No museum in India would be complete without a large room containing heaps of sculptures, some better, some worse, almost always poorly labeled. This abundance only shows how important sculpture has been to India's artistic traditions. At many times architecture has been little more than a vehicle for sculpture, and Indian sculpture is often inseparable from architecture, which is one reason why museum displays can look so odd. Indian sculptures almost always show religious subjects, and they are prime examples of the tendency to idealize. The forms of sculpture are seen to have inner life which allows them to emerge from the stone.

The peoples of the Indus Valley Civilization created many simple terra-cotta figurines and steatite seals with pictures of animals. As with architecture, however, there is a gap in the history of Indian sculpture from these times until the 3rd century BC, when the Mauryan emperor Ashoka planted stone columns all over India as a symbol of his rule. Many of these columns were topped with gorgeous sculptures of animals, the greatest of which is probably the lion capital found at Sarnath in Uttar Pradesh. With its four fierce lions sitting back-to-back on a lotus platform, it has become one of India's national emblems and appears on all Indian currency. The animals of the Mauryan capitals are naturalistic and muscular, showing the strength of Ashoka's political power, and they are burnished to a smooth, shiny texture. The Mauryan capitals show some influence from Persian sculptures of the time, but they also bear the marks of a native artistic style.

The first and 2nd centuries BC saw the rise of two-dimensional bas-relief sculpture, which appeared frequently on the railings of *stupas*. These reliefs often told stories from the life of the Buddha or myths about popular gods and goddesses. In the Great Stupa at Sanchi in Madhya Pradesh they reached their climax, with figures full of energy, emotion, and incredible detail. But three-dimensional sculpture continued during this period too. Several great sculptures of *yakshas* and *yakshis* (popular nature deities) were created during the first and 2nd centuries BC. The beginnings of Indian classical sculpture arrived in the first century AD when artists in Mathura (Uttar Pradesh) began to carve humanlike images of the Buddha. Unlike the earlier relief sculptures, which were primarily educational, these were sacred images used in worship, and their form was strong and sensuous.

At the same time in the Punjab (mainly in areas now belonging to Pakistan) the Gandhara school of art developed. Strongly influenced by Greek and Roman art, Gandhara artists turned out strikingly naturalistic images of the Buddha, showing intricate folds of clothing and other details. Gandharan art looks like nothing else in Indian art, but it gradually evolved to resemble more idealized forms.

During the Gupta period (4th-6th centuries AD) the sculptural school that began at Mathura reached its full flowering. Spreading throughout North India, the basic form of the Buddha image was adapted for Hindu gods with multiple pairs of arms. The Buddha-figures of this time appear to look inward, toward spiritual contemplation, and they have a more delicate appearance than the Mathura Buddhas. Distinct regional styles spun off from the Mathura style, producing great successes at Sarnath (Uttar Pradesh) and in the cave-temples of Ajanta and Elephanta in Maharashtra.

Two separate schools of sculpture emerged during the medieval period. In North India, the old sensuous and voluminous style gave way to a more elegant and rhythmic look, with more profuse decorations. This style reached its climax around the 10th century, when it was used to adorn the exteriors of the great North Indian medieval temples. In South India, a different style of stone sculpture produced the great 7th-century bas-reliefs of Mahabalipuram, and many small, light sculptures used to decorate temples in Tamil Nadu in the 9th century. Bronze sculpture in South India also reached a peak during the 9th and 10th centuries. The image of Shiva as Nataraja ("King of the Dance") surrounded by a ring of fire is one of South India's greatest contributions to Indian art. Examples of this typical image are to be found throughout Tamil Nadu, but the best is probably the one still used in worship at the Brihadishwara Temple in Tanjore.

Regional traditions also developed at this time in other areas such as Maharashtra, where large, stocky figures were created, conforming to the properties of their material; the best of these are to be found at the Kailasa Temple in Ellora. But the Islamic invasion of the 12th century effectively ended sculpture as a high art form in North India, while in the south the quality of the sculpture gradually declined.

Painting

The art of painting has deep roots in India, but due to the climate few examples have survived. The only ancient paintings that remain are those that were sheltered by rock, such as the wall-paintings at Ajanta in Maharashtra, dating from the 2nd century BC to the 5th century AD. These early paintings are similar to the relief sculpture of the time. In eastern India, miniature paintings on palm leafs were common, but few of these still exist.

The style of Indian painting best known today began in western India during the medieval period. Colorful, cluttered scenes with figures shown in profile were made to illustrate Jain manuscripts. The western Indian style gradually spread throughout India and was used for all sorts of religious pictures.

The arrival of Muslim rulers in the 12th century radically changed the course of Indian painting. The Delhi Sultans and the Mughal Emperors brought with them a taste for Persian art. Emperor Akbar (r. 1556-1605), a great patron of the arts, supervised his painters closely while they produced beautiful miniature illustrations for histories, myths, and fables. Akbar was almost singlehandedly responsible for creating the Mughal school of painting. Among other works, his court artists illuminated a magnificent Persian edition of the *Mahabharata,* which is now kept in the City Palace at Jaipur. Indian influences were infiltrating the Mughal style. During the reign of Jahangir (1605-27), fewer illustrated books were made, and the emphasis shifted to portraiture. Though not as energetic as the paintings of Akbar's reign, the images of Jahangir's reign are often deeply insightful.

The cool, delicate Mughal style influenced indigenous Indian painting as well. Under the patronage of Hindu Rajput kings in the 16th and 17th centuries, the Rajasthani school emerged, combining the abstract forms of the western Indian style with some of the naturalism of the Mughal art. Rajasthani paintings usually depicted religious subjects, especially myths about Krishna.

Both the Mughal and Rajasthani styles had declined in the 18th and 19th centuries when European art became a major influence. The first Indian attempts to copy European styles, known collectively as the Company School, were sorry, lifeless engravings and watercolors. In the late 19th and early 20th centuries, however, artists of the Calcutta-based Bengal School, led by Abanindranath Tagore, tried to combine older Indian styles with a touch of modern Western art. In the 20th century a few painters such as Jamini Roy were quite successful at mixing eastern and western influences like this. Indian painting has now become part of the worldwide museum-and-gallery scene.

MUSIC

In the Indian musical tradition, music is largely considered a spiritual activity. Rather than notes, Indian music employs *swaras,* differentiated to the most minute frequencies of sound the human ear is capable of discerning. Thus, the nuances of music are not "slurrings" of notes but practiced explorations of sound. And each *swara* is considered a door behind which stands a god—if the performer, through his or her expression, fulfills the pure dimension of that sound (possible only through devotional surrender), the door will open and the god will appear, blessing performer and audience with ecstasy and insight. Even today, training and performance in the arts is a devotional act. The refined ability to intone minute divisions of sound is considered a mark of spiritual achievement.

Modern Indian classical music, divisible between the northern Hindustani and the southern Carnatic styles, traces its origins to ancient chants. Musical form gained full exposition in the *Bharata-Natyshastra,* considered the textual source of contemporary music. Classical music styles were also introduced by Persians and Turks whose courts entertained musicians from around the Perso-Arabic world, presenting the song styles of *qawwali, khayal,* and lilting *ghazals.*

Indian classical compositions are based on *ragas* (melodic forms) which combine with specific *talas* (rhythmic cycles). Thousands of *ragas* exist, each associated with a particular moment of the day or season of the year. *Ragas* differ from one another according to the scale each employs (there are full-octave, six-note, and five-note *ragas*), and the *rasa* (mood) the composition is meant to explore. Each of the 72 parent scales has rules governing its use, but by permutations, combinations, and subtle changes, thousands of *ragas* are possible. Once the conditions of a *raga* are established and a set of given rules fixed, the artist is free to create and improvise as he or she likes, exploring the *raga*'s potential to be created anew with each performance. Likewise, while the rhythmic cycle of the *tala* repeats itself, between fixed beats there are opportunities for improvisation. *Raga* and *tala* interact expressively with one another, musicianship converging in intonation and inflection through regular and off-beat emphases of time. As a creative play, the *raga* unfolds with complexity and subtlety, yet remains as precise and accurate as a computer.

Indian classical musicians have gained a worldwide following. Ravi Shankar, who introduced Indian music to western ears in the 1960s, attracting the Beatles to study it, continues to elate on his *sitar* (a fretted, 20-stringed instrument with a long teak-

---

Rasa

The Hindustani concept of *rasa* refers to the experience of emotion that comes from listening to a piece of music. Most interestingly, each *raga* (a generative structure used as a base for a musical piece) is associated with a given *rasa,* such as wonderment, tranquility, or eroticism. If the musician and listener are both in the proper state of mind, it is thought that this one emotion will be transfered between them. Can music communicate a limited emotion or evoke a particular response, or is music open to unlimited aesthetic interpretation? Indian musicians believe the former.

wood neck fixed to a seasoned gourd). Ali Akbar Khan has achieved global acclaim for his enrapturing agility on the *sarod* (a fretless stringed instrument similar to a sitar); and Allah Rakha and his son, Zakir Hussain, mesmerize with their virtuosity on the tabla (a pressure-responsive two-piece drum capable of many tones).

Folk music is linked closely to folk dance, varying by region. From Punjabi *bhangra* to Rajasthani *langa,* folk tunes remain close to the hearts and ears of Indians, gaining an even larger audience through the recent international releases of Ila Arun and *bhangra*-rap artists in the U.K. A unique genre of Bengali music is *Rabindrasangit,* the poetic words of Rabindranath Tagore set to quasi-classical song.

Popular music ranges from the "filmi" love songs of Lata Mangeshkar to the conjugal raps of Apache Indian. Topics run the gamut from patriotic to chaotic, from ecstatic to erotic, and are always fantastic sing-alongs. Like their voiceless on-screen counterparts, movie singers are easily elevated to hallowed ground. Popular singer include the playful and prolific Kishore Kumar, whose versatile voice has filled in the melodious blanks for countless actors who have since come and gone, and Lata Mangeshkar.

DANCE

The cosmic dance of the Hindu god Shiva as Nataraja, King of the Dance, reaches into every sphere of human activity in India. Born of particular regions and interwoven with music, India's numerous dance forms, including both classical and folk styles, evolved as acts of worship, dramatizing myths and legends. Technique and philosophy, passed down from gurus to students, have carried the "visual poetry" described in the *Natya Shastra* (dating between the 2nd century BC and the 2nd century AD), into modern times. *Bharat natyam,* a major classical dance form, considered India's most ancient, originated in the temples of Tamil Nadu, and is an intricate, fluid combination of eye movement, facial expression, exacting hand gestures, and strong, rhythmic, ankle-bell-enhanced steps. The art was originally studied as worship and performed by *devadasis,* women whose lives were devoted to temple deities. *Bharat natyam* has grown to international acclaim and appreciation. *Kathak,* first performed by *nautch* (dancing courtesans) against the opulent backdrop of North India's Mughal courts, focuses on the dizzying speed and intricacy of footwork. *Kathakali,* an elaborately costumed form of dance-drama unique to Kerala, invents and presents local and mythological stories of heroes, lovers, gods, and battles. Developed from a rigorous system of yoga, the dancers, all male, must study for a minimum of 15 years to performance ripeness. A typical study regimen includes strenuous exercise and massage to increase the arch and flexibility of the spine. *Kuchipudi,* a decorative dance-drama, hails from southern Andhra Pradesh. *Odissi,* from Orissa, is considered most lyrical and erotic of all devotional temple dances. Not far from the traditions or stomping grounds of the major classical dance styles, regional folk dances, tribal martial arts, and dramatic traditions, as well as innumerable ritualistic and ceremonial dances, grace, enliven, and commemorate the walks and way-stations of daily life.

LITERATURE

The oldest known Indian literature is the writings of the Aryans, who brought Sanskrit with them to India around 1500 BC. Since the Aryans did not invent a writing system until about 800 BC, many of their tales were transmitted orally, changing from generation to generation. A remarkable exception is found in the Vedas, sacred songs composed about 1400 BC, which were ritually memorized and passed down without a flaw. The Vedas are among the world's oldest surviving texts.

During the last millennium BC, the greatest of the early Sanskrit stories, the epics *Mahabharata* and *Ramayana* were composed. Often compared to the *Iliad* and the *Odyssey* (and drawing from the same tradition), they are much more significant within their culture than the Western epics are. The *Mahabharata,* the story of the five Pandava brothers' victory over their treacherous cousins, contains the Bhagavad

Gita, the divine song with which Krishna heartened the warrior Arjuna. The *Ramayana* is probably the single best-known story in Indian culture. Ubiquitously acted out in *Ram lila* pageants, it tells the story of Lord Rama's victory over the Demon King Ravana, and his rescue of his wife Sita from Ravana's clutches (see **The Ramayana,** p. 81).

Ancient India had a secular Sanskrit literature too, which reached its climax in the work of Kalidasa, who probably lived in the 4th century AD. Kalidasa's play *Shakuntala*, about a young girl who becomes the lover of a King Dushyanta but is forgotten when he loses the ring she gave him, has had a tremendous effect on Indian literature in general. The long poem *Meghaduta* ("Cloud-Messenger"), by Kalidasa follows a cloud's journey across the Indian landscape as it carries a message from an exiled deity to his beloved.

While Sanskrit flourished in the North, the ancient Tamil language in the South developed its own literature. Anthologies of poetry were collected at great *sangams,* gathering of bards, beginning in the first century BC, and by the 6th century AD Tamil literature even had two epics of its own, *Shilappadigaram* and *Manimegalai.* Sanskrit also made inroads into the South, becoming a language of culture and learning. This pattern was echoed in North India where regional dialects emerged but Sanskrit was still used as the language of learned writing.

Foreign Muslim rulers, who consolidated their hold over India in the 13th century, brought the next infusion of culture. The Indian-born Sufi poet Amir Khusrau (1253-1325), nicknamed *Tuti-i-Hindi,* ("Parrot of India"), wrote the first great Indian literature in the Persian language, and Indians began to use Persian as a literary medium and a *lingua franca.* Amir Khusrau also wrote extensively in Hindi, however, beginning the fusion of Hindu and Muslim traditions. The broad-minded Mughal emperor Akbar was a great patron of literature in all languages, and from his reign came Tulsidas, who wrote the *Ramcharitmanas,* the Hindi version of the *Ramayana,* which is considered a masterpiece in its language. The Urdu language (and its literature of *ghazal* poems) also grew from the Hindu-Muslim synthesis.

The British invasion cast its greatest intellectual spell on Bengal, where English-language schools prepared Bengalis for service in the East India Company while introducing them to Shakespeare and Milton as well. Bankim Chandra Chatterjee combined the European genre of the novel with heady Indian patriotism in *Anandamath* ("The Abbey of Bliss," 1865). The Bengali Renaissance also produced Rabindranath Tagore, the greatest Indian artistic figure of the 20th century, whose poems, novels, songs and plays captured the Bengali spirit. His English version of his sublime book *Gitanjali* won him the Nobel prize for literature in 1913, making him the first non-European to receive that honor.

British writers in India during the colonial period left a body of work that now makes a fascinatingly confused memoir of the Raj. The "Bard of the Empire," Rudyard Kipling, was responsible for the greatest sahib literature. Born in India, Kipling left for school but returned there as an ambivalent adult, writing everything from *Kim,* the perceptive story of a half-white, half-Indian boy growing up in India, to "The White Man's Burden," an exhausted racist battle hymn. On the other side was E.M. Forster, who recorded the tragedy of misunderstandings between British and Indian cultures in his novel *A Passage to India* (1924).

The biggest trends in 20th-century Indian literature have been a shift toward humanistic concerns, a much wider use of prose, and the adoption of the English language. Among the most influential writers of the early 20th century was Mulk Raj Anand, whose small but powerful novels *Untouchable* (1935) and *Coolie* (1936) railed against the cruelty of the caste system and economic exploitation. The South Indian novelist R.K. Narayan, perhaps India's greatest English-language writer of the second half of the 20th century, has become well-known in India and worldwide for such books as *The Man-Eater of Malgudi* (1961) and *The Vendor of Sweets* (1967). Proudly distinct literatures in the various regional languages of India have also thrived in the 20th century, and have seen a great deal of experimentation with prose and other western innovations.

The surge in the popularity of "Commonwealth literature" in the past few decades has also brought to the fore several writers of Indian descent living outside of India, such as Salman Rushdie, V.S. Naipaul, and Vikram Seth. Many of their works continue to return to India and struggle with ancestral neuroses. Salman Rushdie's masterpiece *Midnight's Children* (1980), which weaves India's recent history into the magical and crazy autobiography of a man cracking into pieces, has given a generation of Indians a name for themselves.

FILM

She rises from the oasis of green, trim lawns of an Elysian garden, dotted in fuschia and rose. Effortlessly she sings a melodious love song while her curvaceous hips swing energetically to the accompanying beat. He hears her loving croon and holds her in a passionate embrace against his leather-clad body. Their bliss is interrupted by his drug-smuggling twin brother, separated from him at birth and sent by her society-minded parents to break their love asunder. A brief yet boisterous scuffle, and he emerges unscathed to return to his loving embrace. The sun sets on the suddenly mountainous backdrop. A brief vision of heaven, a perfect world, you wonder? Possibly a utopia of romance, chivalry, and kitsch? Fortunately for the common man, this bliss is available in any and every *masala* movie.

The *masala* hits, named after the eclectic spice mixture, contain a piquant pick 'n' mix combination of action, violence, comedy, romance, music, and a dash of the ridiculously impossible. The urban landscape is dominated by cinema hoardings—strident colors, dramatic gestures, and, more than a hint of erotic attraction. Film songs, which are India's pop music, command the radio waves. A vast array of film magazines trade on scandal, sex-talk, and vicious innuendo. Cinemas run shows regularly at noon, 3, 6, and 9pm to accommodate an average daily audience of 7.5 million people. While the *masala* hits captivate the masses, the educated elite criticize the puerile "formula" films and their escapism. India churns out close to a thousand feature films a year in 23 languages. Bombay is the seat of the film subculture and home to "Bollywood," the nickname for the largest movie industry in the world, while the thriving South Indian film industry has also set up shop in Madras.

It all began in 1912, when Dadasaheb Phalke produced the first Indian feature film, *Raja Harishchandra.* Its story, drawn from an episode in the ancient *Mahabharata* epic, inaugurated the distinctly Indian genre of film known as the "mythological," which became the staple of Indian cinema into the 1950s. Historicals and stunt films also made their first appearances in Indian film in the 1920s.

Sound first invaded the frames in 1931 with *Alam Ara,* directed by Irani. The first of the "talkies" was received with thunderous ovations, but sound fragmented audiences into disparate language groups. Subtitles in multiple languages were introduced to accommodate larger audiences. Hindi, followed by Tamil, emerged as the language with the widest base. Most importantly, sound meant song for Indian cinema. Filmmakers saw song as a way of overcoming the linguistic splintering and tapping into built-in emotional responses to traditional music. The songs became the main attraction of a film and critical to its success. *Indra Sabha* (1932) included nearly 70 songs and the first two decades of "talkie" film were entirely dominated by "singing stars." The musical numbers were often embellished by dances. The song-and-dance element persists even today. In 1935, P.C. Barua produced the landmark film *Devdas,* which introduced the popular themes of ineffectual manhood and unrequited love to Indian cinema. In the 1940s, the introduction of pre-recorded songs and playback singing meant that actors no longer had to be singers. The most successful playback singer was Lata Mangeshkar who holds the world record with more than 25,000 recorded songs in her career.

In the 1930s and 1940s, the "social film" was conceived by the industry to represent contemporary life. V. Shantaram's groundbreaking film *Do Aankhen Barah Hath* advocated the rehabilitation of criminals. Shantaram also introduced a preference for loudness—gaudy costumes, flighty and capricious music, exciting choreography, and implied sex—prefiguring the kind of spectacle that has become the hallmark of Bombay film. Mehboob Khan (best known for *Mother India*) specialized in Muslim costume dramas and social tragedies, with a sense of the epic and spectacular. In *Andaz* (1949), he established a new norm for Indian film immortalizing the love triangle and focusing on youth. Raj Kapoor, the "founding father" of popular cinema, introduced a casual attitude towards sex with his Chaplinesque portrayals of oh-so honest tramps, while maintaining the motif of melodramatic love.

Despite the move towards the spectacular, the decade of the 1950s belongs to the serious filmmaker. The first International Film Festival to be held in India was in 1952 and the European neo-realism demonstrated the potential for film to function as a searing political and social document. Nitin Bose and Bimal Roy made films about workers' rights, collective farming and the polarization of classes. In the 1950s and 60s, Tamil film emerged as a vehicle to promote Tamil politics. Scriptwriters like Karunanidhi and Anna Durai were key political figures as well. N.T. Rama Rao was a leading actor in Telugu cinema for 40 years before becoming the chief minister of the state of Andhra Pradesh.

This neo-realist trend contributed to the emergent art cinema, which reacted against melodrama and cheap romance, using the camera to probe issues of poverty, superstition, caste, and social and economic injustice. Satyajit Ray, the leading director of art cinema, is well known for *Pather Panchali* (1955), in which a diligently composed naturalism focuses on the isolation of rural life. Ray turns his attention to individual relationships *Pratidwanai* (1970), in which a sensitive young man can't find an answer to the angry and corrupt temper of the time. During the 70s, low-budget filmmakers like Gulzar, Hrishikesh Mukherji, and Basu Chatterji portrayed middle-class protagonists that won the hearts of the common viewer. Shyam Benegal, Mrinal Sen, Mani Kaul, and other filmmakers also made inroads in Hindi art cinema.

In the late 70s, popular film widened its mass market with a growing reliance on sex, violence, and action; it became escapist, unmindful of society. This was a fertile period for new film talent. Amitabh Bachchan became the new screen hero. His image of intelligence and rebelliousness displaced that of the romantic hero, made popular by the goody-goody, effeminate actor Rajesh Khanna. Hindi film now became mass film. The multi-starrer emerged in 1975 with *Sholay*. The movie, which ran for five years in Bombay, influenced the speech mannerisms of an entire generation: young men all over India were speaking the catchphrases of killer bandit Gabbar Singh, played by Amjad Khan.

Following the tradition of art cinema, Shyam Benegal has been awarded the unofficial badge of "India's foremost living filmmaker." His film *Manthan,* about the Gujarat Cooperative Milk Marketing Federation was funded by donations of two rupees each from 500,000 farmers. Works by Gautam Ghose, Saeed Mirza, B.V. Karanth, and Kundan Shah, among others, address social problems of landlord exploitation, urban power, untouchability, corruption, and the oppression of women. Adoor Gopalakrishnan and Aravindan, both directors from Kerala, speak specifically about their own cultures, and about the possibility of change.

Contemporary popular movies are full of images of the fraught urban scenario. Mira Nair's *Salaam Bombay!* (1988) probes the perils of urban life by visiting the street children of Bombay. Nair's realism won international acclaim and three awards at Cannes. Mani Ratnam's *Bombay* (1995) set an inter-religious love story against the backdrop of religious riots in the big city, winning the director acclaim for confronting social issues. Shekhar Kapur's factually based drama *Bandit Queen* (1995) chronicles the life of Phoolan Devi, a low-caste woman who is married off as a child, battered by her husband, and gang-raped, and responds to her abuse and humiliation by joining up with bandits in revenge. The film contained scenes of graphic violence, full-frontal nudity, and sex and was banned by the Indian censors, who operate possibly the most restrictive regime in the world. Until recently, kissing was forbidden on screen. The censors cleared the film after 10 cuts.

The arrival of the VCR and cable television in the 1980s took the wind out of the Indian film industry's sails. Commercial and art films were equally at risk at the box office. The explosion of satellite channels, with their insatiable demand for movies, is giving Bollywood a second wind. Recently, Indian cinema has explored the use of computer-generated special effects, starting in the Tamil film industry with Shankar's *Kadalan.*

The Media

Several English-language newspapers are printed in India, though their style tends to be a bit stodgy and archaic. Most newspapers are printed simultaneously in several cities and aim for a national or at least a regional audience. *The Times of India* is the nation's biggest, grandest, oldest newspaper, with good coverage of Indian news and a reputation for being pro-government. The *Times* is most popular in Delhi, Gujarat, Bombay, and the rest of Maharashtra. The *Indian Express,* another national paper, is a bit less stuffy and more widely read in South India. The most popular paper in South India is *The Hindu,* a conservative paper which covers South Indian news in more detail. The pro-Congress *Hindustan Times* is the best-selling paper in Delhi while in Calcutta and most of eastern India, *The Statesman* reigns supreme.

India Today is an excellent fortnightly news magazine with feature articles on India's culture and society. *Frontline,* published by *The Hindu,* and *Sunday Magazine* are also very good. A number of women's magazines, including *Femina* and *Woman's Era,* are now sold in India, although they tend to contain more glamor than feminism.

India's national television company, Doordarshan, operates two channels. DD1 seems to broadcast endless pictures of hydroelectric projects approaching glorious completion, but it has news in English every night at 7pm. DD2 is a bit more fun, and due to an arrangement with MTV it now broadcasts music videos from 6 to 8 every evening. Also ubiquitous is the Hong Kong-based Star TV satellite network, a package of five channels including "Channel V," TV tycoon Rupert Murdock's substitute for MTV. A crop of private channels have also opened in the last few years, relaying Hindi dramas by satellite to India and Indian workers in the Gulf states.

Sports

Sports in India run a wide gamut. While excellence is the rule in field hockey—Indian teams are consistent medal-winners at the Olympics—obsession is the rule in cricket, which is followed with joyful fanaticism by millions of Indians. Involvement with other sports is as much a function of social and regional divisions as anything else in India. Soccer and horseracing are especially popular in the east and in urban areas, while *kabadi,* an indigenous game of tag, enjoys popularity throughout the north. Tennis, polo, squash, and other games brought to India by British imperialism are primarily the province of the upper classes.

Food and Drink

In the past, protracted Vedic prose prescribed every dash and pinch, every preparation, even every plate placement to provide the therapeutic and medicinal benefits of sustenance in just the right way. Nowadays, the more casual rules of good taste and great variety have taken over India's victuals. Meals vary regionally in taste, color, and texture but universally tend to smell strong and taste spicy. A tour of India can easily become a tour of its many foods. With a myriad of colorful spices and herbs including red chili powder, yellow turmeric, green coriander, and black cumin, all elements collide to create a gastronomic extravaganza.

A typical meal for many parts of North India consists of a bread, spicy prepared vegetables, rice, and a lentil soup called *dal.* Breads come in different shapes and sizes: *chapati* is a thin whole wheat frisbee, *paratha* is a bi-layer bread, sometimes stuffed with vegetables, *naan* is a thicker chewy bread made of white flour and baked in a *tandoor,* a concave clay oven. Some rice dishes come with vegetables—try *biryani* or *pulao. Dal makhani,* a dark and thick black lentil soup, is a spicy Punjabi favorite.

Dhabas

If you take a nightlong private coach anywhere through India, you're sure to stop at one or two *dhabas,* the 24-hour truckers' stops. Here, the *parathas* and fried rice drip with grease, the *chai* comes with a kick, and a meal guaranteed to leave you sedentary for a while costs about Rs.15. Not just for truckers, these dives also cater to the affluent, car-driving, college-age set, who refuel after a night of hedonism in dance clubs, or in preparation for an all-night cram session. In the wee hours of the morning, truck drivers catch a few winks on the bamboo cots which early in the evening functioned as *sambar*-absorbent tables. Because *dhabas* serve a steady stream of hungry diners round the clock, their food is often left to boil and simmer for hours, killing any germs and making *dhabas* a generally safe place to eat.

Though *dhabas* originated in Punjab and began serving mainly Punjabi cuisine, truck drivers have disseminated the dives through all of South Asia. In Bombay and Delhi where *dhaba*-style restaurants pop up in 5-star hotels, *dhaba* culture has become something of a cult for the rich.

Needless to say, vegetarians are in luck. Meat options mostly consist of chicken and lamb dishes, since beef is considered off-limits by Hindus, and pork by Muslims. Some of the best meat dishes are those cooked in a *tandoor.* Good Indian cooking also uses *ghee* (clarified butter) as a base rather than vegetable oils.

Meals are often preceded by appetizers and followed by desserts accompanied by *masala chai,* a wonderful spicy tea with milk and sugar. Appetizers and snacks are manifold. Some gems include *samosa,* a spicy, fried potato turnover, and *bhel puri,* a sweet and sour mixture of fresh sprouts, potatoes, and yogurt. Desserts tend to be extremely sweet, many made out of boiled, sweetened milk.

South Indian cuisine employs rice and rice flour much more than the north. Instead of bread as the main carbohydrate, rice and rice-based *dosas* (thin pancakes) and *idlis* (thick steamed cakes) take center stage. These are accompanied by vegetable broths like *sambar* (a thick and spicy lentil soup), *rasam* (thinner, with tomatoes and tamarind), and *kozhambu* (sour), which are poured on the rice and mixed with it. *Dosas* are commonly stuffed with spiced potatoes to make *masala dosas.* A thicker *dosa* made with onion is called an *utthapam. Vadais* are doughnut-shaped rice cakes soaked in curd or *sambar.* Less meat is consumed in the south, but seafood dishes abound in coastal areas. A standard South Indian meal comes in the form of a *thali,* a 40-cm steel plate filled with *chapati, papadam,* rice, *sambar,* fresh yogurt, *dal,* and vegetable dishes (unlimited), while the restaurant's proprietor walks around ladling *ghee* onto your feast.

Pan is an abundant after-dinner chew and the cause of much of the distastefully crimson betel juice spatterings so surely lining every street you traverse. A *pan* leaf is filled with everything from coconut to sweetened rose petals, from fennel seeds to flavored betel nut or tobacco. If you decide to try it, ask for a sweet *pan* with no tobacco, and easy on the *kath-chuna* (a crazy limestone paste). Unsweetened *pan* is an assault for novices. Place the whole thing on one side of your soon-to-be-numb mouth and chew over a period of several minutes, the steady grind interrupted only by periodic swallows.

Drinks

India offers many delicious drinks, some of which sadly should be avoided because they are made with ice cubes of untreated water. *Lassi,* made with yogurt and sugar or salt or fruit, varies in quality and texture from smooth and delicious to watery and bland. Sugarcane juice is sold widely and is a delicious but risky drink. Although India's many varieties of tea are wonderful, coffee is also popular and delicious, especially in South India. Cold coffee with ice cream is an Indian specialty, best tried at restaurants with good ice cream, such as the Kwality chain. Thanks to its pre-1991 protectionist economy, India has also given birth to a bundle of bizarre soft drinks, referred to as "cold drinks." Thums Up is a spicy cola; Teem is a sweet, pungent lemon-limey drink; Citra has a more subdued citrus flavor. Frooti, a mango drink sold in little green drinking boxes, is excellent when cold.

Alcohol is accepted if not encouraged in some parts and frowned upon in others, where it may be hard to find (see **Drugs and Alcohol,** p. 16). Popular brands of beer are Taj Mahal and Kingfisher, while the tasty London Pilsner is not common but worth the search. Liquor is available in many bars and shops (especially in Goa), but chances are you won't get the name brand you ask for. Be careful when ordering difficult or obscure mixed drinks, as what they say is Kahlua could taste a bit like fermented Ovaltine—probably an example of Indian-Made Foreign Liquor (IMFL). Imported brands of liquor like Smirnoff are available in big cities. Not-so-good domestic wines are also available at nicer restaurants.

■ Further Sources

BOOKS

General

India, by Stanley Wolpert (1991). An easy sampler of Indian culture and history by a well known historian.

An Introduction to South Asia, by B. H. Farmer (1993). A geographical description of South Asia, its history, politics, and economics.

Culture Shock! India, by Gitanjali Kolanad (1994). A guide to Indian customs and etiquette especially aimed at those planning to live and work in India. Advice for all sorts of social situations and bureacratic hassles.

Amar Chitra Kanthas: A series of educational comic books covering stories from the *Ramayana* to the life of Vivekananda. Even though these are fun, they're crammed with common-sense knowledge about Indian history, religion, and culture.

Ancient Futures: Learning from Ladakh, by Helena Norberg-Hodge (1991). An insightful, provocative account of the effects of western modernization on Ladakhi culture.

Travel/Description

The Meghaduta, by Kalidasa (4th century AD). The great Sanskrit poet's account of a cloud's journey across India, surveying the landscape and human activity as it carries a message between separated lovers.

The Baburnama, by Babur (1530). "Hindustan…is a strange country. Compared to ours it is another world," wrote Babur, the first Mughal emperor, in his frank but maudlin autobiography. Babur painstakingly observes India's land, people, and products while longing for his cool northern homeland.

An Area of Darkness, by V.S. Naipaul (1964). A chilling account of Naipaul's journey around his ancestral homeland. Filled with insights about the country and the author.

India: A Million Mutinies Now, by V. S. Naipaul (1990). A careful, though somewhat cynical observation of the little "mutinies" of Indian life in the 1990s. Contains fascinating life-stories of the people the author met in his travels.

Arrow of the Blue-Skinned God: Retracing the Ramayana though India, by Jonah Blank (1992). A fun book comparing the culture of 1990s India to the dharmic ideals of Lord Rama, the hero of the epic *Ramayana*. Exquisitely written, though the author's presence is lacking.

The Great Railway Bazaar, by Paul Theroux (1975). This travel classic is worth rereading for its descriptions of what it feels like to be a snotty Westerner jammed on a train with hundreds of other people.

History

A Traveller's History of India, by Sinharaja Tammita-Delgoda (1995). A clear and readable introduction to Indian history for the beginner, with references to historical sites that can be visited today, and invaluable appendices.

A New History of India, by Stanley Wolpert (1993). Also a good overview of Indian history, but slightly more academic.

The Discovery of India, by Jawaharlal Nehru (1946). Indian history as seen by the founder of modern India; a classic providing insight into the way Indians understand their history.

An Autobiography, or, the Story of My Experiment with Truth, by Mohandas K. Gandhi (1927). Gandhi's personal account of the development of his beliefs, with surprisingly little attention to the political events of the time.

Politics

India: Government and Politics in a Developing Nation, by Robert L. Hardgrave, Jr. and Stanley A. Kochanek (1993). The best summary of recent Indian political issues and the government of modern India.

Operation Bluestar: The True Story, by Lt. Gen. K.S. Brar (1993). An in-depth (albeit slanted) account of the temple's recent turmoil written by an Indian commando.

Religion

Banaras: City of Light, by Diana L. Eck (1982). An explanation of the holy city, attempting to "see Kashi through Hindu eyes." A wonderful introduction to the complexities and contradictions of Hinduism in general; and many travel guidebooks are indebted to it.

Ramayana, by Valmiki, trans. William Buck (1976). An entrancing abridged account of Lord Rama's epic adventure across early India. Retold in language that brings the ancient characters to life.

What The Buddha Taught, by Walpola Rahula (1959). A Sri Lankan monk's authoritative explanation of Buddhist philosophy.

Women's Issues

May You Be the Mother of a Hundred Sons, by Elizabeth Bumiller (1990). A British journalist's exploration of sati, sex-selective abortion, and dowry deaths, always maintaining an open mind toward Indian culture.

Unveiling India, by Anees Jung (1987). A journalist who grew up in strict Muslim *purdah,* but has now cast off the veil and lives alone in New Delhi, Jung examines the apparent poverty and powerlessness of Indian women.

Fiction

Midnight's Children, by Salman Rushdie (1980). Probably the best English-language novel the 1980s, Rushdie's masterpiece tells the magical tale of children born at midnight just as India gained independence, and how the country's life and theirs evolve together.

A Passage to India, by E.M. Forster (1924). A novel of traumas and failed relationships told through the story of the friendship of an Englishman and an Indian under the British Raj. Contains observations about Indian culture (and culture shock) that hold true today.

Karma Cola, by Gita Mehta (1979). A journalistic satire about Westerners in India that will remind any overambitious tourist to take him or herself less seriously.

Poetry

Gitanjali, by Rabindranath Tagore (1913). The Nobel prize-winning work of the great Bengali poet, which uses traditional images from Indian love poetry to discuss a relationship with God.

Photography

The Ganges, by Raghubir Singh (1992). A compilation of much of the photographer's work over many years, following the course of the Ganga from source to sea, with landscapes and people snapped into amazing configurations.

FILMS

Pather Panchali, by Satyajit Ray (1955). The first and greatest film by the late master of Indian cinema. Produced on weekends with a borrowed camera and unpaid actors, its visuals capture the beauty of the Bengali landscape and the isolation of the village in which the heroine Durga lives. The score by Ravi Shankar is brilliantly matched to the picture.

Gandhi, by Richard Attenborough (1981). A somewhat romanticized tale of the life of the Mahatma, it nevertheless tells the story of the Indian Independence movement very dramatically.

Hello Photo, by Nina Davenport (1994). The next best thing to actually traveling in India, this short and visually stunning film shows one woman's experience of looking at India and being looked at.

INDIA

NORTH INDIA

Delhi

India's capital and third-largest city, Delhi is blessed with many wonders—the city offers both an array of sights that will stop your heart and a frenetic energy that will surely revive it. Unfortunately, Delhi needs to be coped with before it can be coddled, and one needs to work hard at enjoying the city. All of the contrasts familiar to travelers in India are in full force in Delhi: rich and poor, old and new, chaos and control. What distinguishes India's capital from other major cities is the polarity between its government and its people. Delhi maintains a dignified front as national capital, with the superstructures of official duties spanning eerily broad green blocks in the south-central portion of the city. Nobody sleeps on the lawns between monuments, and the billboards (in English, of course) fervently promote various welfare campaigns. But alongside this façade of control are Delhi's other streets. The inner life of a city is rarely as accessible to the casual traveler as it is in Delhi, crammed with legendary slow-churning traffic, nipped and threaded with noxious auto-rickshaws, ever striving for a tighter turn-radius, ignoring advertising campaigns that plead with drivers to stay in their lanes. It is in Delhi's streets that life happens, where the capital's ballyhooed cosmopolitanism is manufactured and displayed, where Sikhs from Chandigarh, colorfully dressed Rajasthani women, *sadhus,* and pavement-dwellers all rub shoulders, sharing space if not conversation. And it is in the streets that North India's heat and humidity are refracted through layers of filthy, polluted air, acting as a relentless social leveler, forcing the air-conditioned few and the power-thieving masses (the municipal power company claims that 40% of the electricity it produces is stolen) to sweat and suffer together. The government also plays a hand in this redistribution, bringing Delhi's throbbing chaos to periodic lulls by shutting off the power completely.

But all this is in the present, and to know Delhi one must know something of its past. The history of Delhi begins in 736 AD, with the founding of Lal Kot by the Tomara clan of Rajputs, who feuded for the next 400-odd years with the Chauhan Rajputs. The skirmishes of the Rajputs were rendered irrelevant in 1192 by Muhammad Gauri and his slave general Qutb-ud-din Aibak, who swept into North India from Central Asia and conquered the area, introducing Islam to India and founding the Delhi Sultanate. For the next 300 years North India was wracked by political instability. Delhi suffered especially when it was sacked by the mighty Turkish Central Asian warlord Timur in 1398: "for two months not a bird moved a wing in Delhi." By the early 16th century the Lodi dynasty, the Delhi Sultanate's fifth ruling family, had made its share of enemies, and the governors of Punjab and Sindh invited in the Central Asian warlord Babur. Babur battled the Lodi dynasty into submission just outside Delhi and launched the Mughal Empire, which would knit together huge swaths of South Asia for the next two centuries. The Mughal emperors continually moved their capital back and forth between Delhi and Agra, leaving each city with monumental tombs, palaces, and forts. Old Delhi, including Lal Qila and Jama Masjid, was built during the middle decades of the 17th century by the Mughal emperor Shah Jahan as a walled capital to be called Shahjahanabad. Under pressure from the Marathas and the Persian plunderer Nadir Shah, who swept into Delhi in 1739, Mughal power declined and the British stepped into the yawning power void. During the 1857 Mutiny the aging, reluctant Bahadur Shah II was proclaimed emperor in the Red Fort, and the city was badly bloodied as the British clashed with the "rebels." After the Mutiny, India was made an official part of the British Empire. In 1911, it was decided that the imperial capital would be moved to Delhi, and the city began to attract the attention of Indian nationalists who proclaimed that the flag of an Indian republic would one day fly from the Red Fort. With a speech by the Prime Minister delivered from the Red Fort and a tremendous parade in front of the city's most important British buildings, today's Delhi celebrates the vindication of the nationalists' predictions in grand style every Independence Day (Aug. 15).

As with many cities in the developing world, Delhi's population is growing rapidly; by some counts it has already topped 10 million. Waves of modern fortune-seekers, as well as poor and illiterate rural families seeking relief, have caused Delhi to swell and sprawl. South Delhi, which once seemed downright suburban, has moved to the center of the city's life. This expansion has made Delhi more diffuse and segregated—the Muslim vendors who peddle their wares in the bazaars of Old Delhi have just as little contact with the posh South Delhi-ites who work at Nehru Place as they do with the struggling South Delhi-ites who eke out a meager living in the small and mid-sized factories of Okhla.

GETTING THERE AND AWAY

By Air

Indira Gandhi International Airport serves as the main entry and departure point for international flights. The domestic terminal (tel. 329 5121, 329 5433, 329 5621) is 5km from the international terminal (tel. 565 2011, 565 2050; information 545 2050) and is closer to the city. Arrival at the airport is a piece of cake: after passing through customs, you'll proceed to the arrival hall, where across from the various tourist offices is a **State Bank of India** office (open 24hr.). This is also the place to pay for a **pre-paid taxi,** which is the least risky way to get into the center of Delhi. Pay no more than Rs.250, and never let the cab driver convince you that the hotel you ask for is burned down, full, or out of commission. Be cautious of everyone around the airport. Say where you want to go (and if it's to the train station, don't let them take you to a bogus ticketing agent), and make them go there. A taxi is safer than a rickshaw in this regard. The Government of India Tourism and Delhi Tourism offices are good places to head for initial questions and taxi-booking. Delhi Transport Corporation (DTC) and the Ex-Servicemen's Shuttle run **buses** to Connaught Place from the airport (about Rs.20). They stop near the government tourist office on Janpath; buy tickets inside. There are many daily flights from Delhi to other cities in India. Domestic Airlines: Indian Airlines (tel. 462 0566), East West (tel. 375 5167), Jagson (tel. 372 1594), Jet Airways (tel. 372 4727), Modiluft (tel. 643 0689), NEPC (tel. 332 2525), and Sahara (tel. 332 6851, 335 2771). **International airlines:** Air France, Scindia House, Janpath (tel. 331 0407); Air India, Jeevan Bharati Bldg. (tel. 331 1225); Alitalia, 16 Barakhamba Rd. (tel. 331 3777); American Airlines, 105 Indra Prakash Bldg. (332 5876); Biman Bangladesh, Babar Rd., Connaught Place (tel. 335 4401); British Airways, DLF Bldg., Sansad Marg (tel. 332 7428); Cathay Pacific, Tolstoy Marg (tel. 332 3332); Delta, Janpath (tel. 332 5222); El Al, G-57 Connaught Place (tel. 332 3960); Emirates, 18 Barakhamba Rd. (tel. 332 4665); Gulf Air (G-12, Connaught Place (tel. 332 7814); KLM, Tolstoy Marg (tel. 332 6822); Kuwait Airlines, 16 Barakhamba Rd. (tel. 331 4221); Lufthansa, 56 Janpath (tel. 332 3310); PIA, Ranjit Hotel (tel. 323 0304); Qantas, Tolstoy Marg (tel. 332 1434); RNAC, 44 Janpath (tel. 332 1164); Singapore, G-11 Connaught Place (tel. 332 6373); Swissair, Sansad Marg (tel. 332 5511); Thai, 14 Kasturba Gandhi Marg (tel. 332 3608).

To: Agra (Tues.-Thurs., Sat.-Sun. 1 per day, 40 min., US$35); Ahmedabad (4-8 per day, 1½hr., US$98); Amritsar (Mon.-Tues., Thurs., and Sat. 1-2 per day, 50min., US$69); Aurangabad (Mon., Wed., Fri., and Sun. 1 per day, 3½hr., US$127); Bangalore (4 per day, 2hr., US$195); Bagdogra (1 per day, 2hr., US$156); Bangalore (4 per day, 2hr. 40min., US$195); Bhopal (2 per day, 2hr., US$83-111); Bombay (20 per day, 1hr. 55min., US$130); Calcutta (7-10 per day, 1hr. 50min., US$151); Chandigarh (Tues., Thurs., and Sat. 1 per day, 1hr., US$72); Cochin (1 per day, 4hr., US$256); Dhaka (Mon. and Thurs. 1 per day, 2½hr., US$175); Dibrugarh (Wed., Sat.-Sun. 1 per day, 4hr., US$173); Goa (2-3 per day, 2½hr., US$179); Guwahati (2-3 per day, 2hr. 15min.,

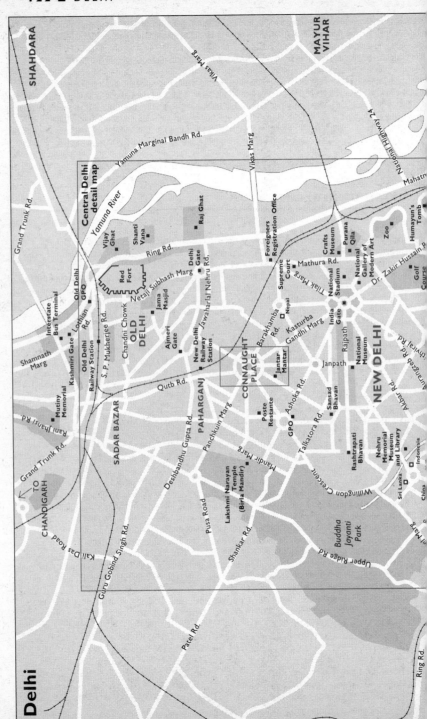

Delhi

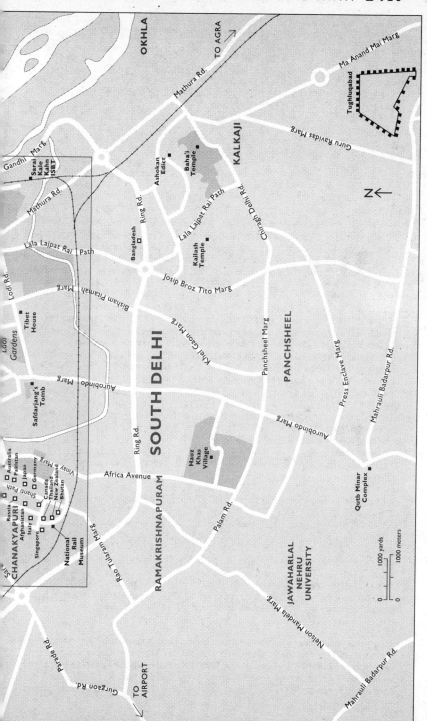

OKLA

TO AGRA

Ma Anand Mai Marg

Mathura Rd.

Tughluqabad

KALKAJI

Guru Ravidas Marg

Gandhi Marg

Sarai Kale Kahn ISBT

Ashokan Edict

Baha'i Temple

Mathura Rd.

Ring Rd.

Bangladesh

Chiragh Delhi Rd.

N

Lala Lajpat Rai Path

Lala Lajpat Rai Path

Kailash Temple

Lodi Rd.

Bisham Pitamah Marg

Josip Broz Tito Marg

Tibet House

Khel Gaon Marg

Panchsheel Marg

PANCHSHEEL

Lodi Gardens

Press Enclave Marg

Aurobindo Marg

Safdarjang's Tomb

Mahrauli Badarpur Rd.

SOUTH DELHI

Ring Rd.

Aurobindo Marg

Africa Avenue

Hauz Khas Village

Russia

Australia

Pakistan

Shanti Path

Japan

Germany

Canada

Thailand

New Zealand

Bhutan

Palam Rd.

Qutb Minar Complex

CHANAKYAPURI

Afghanistan

Italy

Singapore

Vinay Marg

RAMAKRISHNAPURAM

National Rail Museum

Rao Tularam Marg

JAWAHARLAL NEHRU UNIVERSITY

1000 yards

1000 meters

Nelson Mandela Marg

TO AIRPORT

Gurgaon Rd.

Pankha Rd.

Mahrauli Badarpur Rd.

US$182); Gwalior (Mon.-Tues., Thurs. 1 per day, 1hr., US$47); Hyderabad (3 per day, 2hr., US$154-230); Imphal (Tues. and Sat. 1 per day, 4hr., US$206); Indore (1 per day, 2hr., US$100); Jaipur (4 per day, 45min., US$43); Jammu (2 per day, 1hr., US$84); Jodhpur (Mon.-Tues., Thurs., and Sat. 1-2 per day, 1½-2hr., US$75-95); Kanpur (Mon.-Sat. 1 per day, 2hr., US$93), Kathmandu (2-4 per day, 1hr. 45min., US$142-170); Khajuraho (Tues., Thurs., Sat.-Sun. 1 per day, 2hr., US$71); Kulu (6 per day, 1hr. 20min., US$123); Leh (Mon.-Tues., Thurs., and Sat. 1 per day, 3hr., US$95-152); Lucknow (5-6 per day, 1hr., US$64-95); Ludhiana (Mon., Wed., and Fri. 1 per day, 1hr., US$80); Madras (4-5 per day, 3hr., US$197); Nagpur (1 per day, 1½hr., US$112); Paro (Mon. and Thurs. 1 per day, 4hr., US$286); Patna (2-3 per day, 1½hr., US$107); Pune (1 per day, 2hr., US$158); Raipur (2 per day, 4hr., US$147-184); Ranchi (1 per day, 4hr., US$142); Shimla (1 per day, 1hr., US$96); Srinagar (2-3 per day, 1hr. 20min., US$92-101); Trivandrum (1 per day, 4hr., US$274); Udaipur (2 per day, 2hr., US$84); Vadodara (Thurs., Sat.-Tues. 1 per day, 1½hr., US$115); Varanasi (4-5 per day, 1-2hr., US$90-134).

By Train

The **New Delhi Railway Station,** which is the main depot for trains in and out of Delhi, is north of Connaught Place, at the east end of Paharganj Main Bazaar. It is a place of great chaos, so be prepared to push your way around, and beware of theft. Foreigners' best bet is to get tickets from the **International Tourist Bureau** (tel. 373 4164) upstairs. Tickets here must be bought in foreign currency, or in rupees with encashment certificates. Expect long waits. They book reservations on tourist-quota seats and sell Indrail passes (open Mon.-Sat. 7:30am-1:30pm, 2-5pm). **Do not get sucked into one of the dodgy tourist offices around the train station.** If you don't get a ticket from the tourist bureau listed above, go to the windows in the station (for general booking) or to the **Computerised Reservation terminal,** one block south of the station along Chelmsford Rd. They have monitors that indicate available seats on popular trains days in advance. Don't listen to claims that these ticket services are "for Indians only." **"Delhi Station"** is actually in Old Delhi—some trains may leave from here or even from **Hazrat Nizamuddin Station** in the southeast part of the city. Check and plan ahead. Important phone numbers for trains in Delhi: General Enquiry (331 3535, 131), Train Arrival Enquiry (1331, 1332), Reservations (334 8686, 334 8787). To book tickets for the ultra-expensive honeymooners' dream world **Palace on Wheels,** (tel. 338 1884; fax 338 2823), go to Bikaner House, due south of India Gate across from the Children's Park.

Wherever you need to go, a train from Delhi can almost certainly take you there. The listings that follow represent only the tiniest selection from among the many trains available. Clear **timetables** for major destinations are posted in the International Tourist Bureau. To: Bhopal (*Shatabdi Exp.* 2002, 6:15am, 8hr., Rs.535 for A/C chair car); Amritsar (*Shatabdi Exp.* 2013, 4:30pm, 6hr., Rs.380 for A/C chair car); Chandigarh (*Shatabdi Exp.* 2011, 7:30am, 4hr., Rs.270 for A/C chair car; *Shatabdi Exp.* 2005, 5:15pm, 4hr., Rs.270 for A/C chair car); Lucknow (*Shatabdi Exp.* 2004, 6:20am, 6hr., Rs.405 for A/C chair car); Dehra Dun (*Shatabdi Exp.* 2017, Thurs.-Tues. 7am, 6hr., Rs.315 for A/C chair car); Bombay (*Rajdhani Exp.,* 4:05pm, 16hr., Rs.750 for A/C chair car); Patna (*Rajdhani Exp.* 2306, 5:15pm, 12hr., Rs.760 for A/C sleeper); Guwahati (*Rajdhani Exp.* 2424, 5pm, 28hr., Rs.1135 for A/C sleeper); Calcutta (*Rajdhani Exp.* 2422, 5pm, 20hr., Rs.945 for A/C sleeper); Agra (*Shatabdi Exp.* 2002, 6:15am, 2hr., Rs.250 for A/C chair car). Trains to Jaipur and elsewhere in Rajasthan often depart from **Sarai Rohila Station,** north of Sadar Bazaar.

By Bus

State buses (which include most ordinary buses) usually stop at the **Inter-State Bus Terminal (ISBT)** at Kashmiri Gate, north of Old Delhi Railway Station. Buses to Agra leave from the *other* ISBT in Delhi—the **Sarai Kale Khan ISBT,** two blocks east of the Nizamuddin Railway Station (every 30min., 5am-12:30am, 5hr., Rs.57-65). Buses also leave here for Faridabad (every 20min., 5am-9:45pm, 1hr. 15min., Rs.9) and Mathura (every 2hr., 6am-12:30am, 4hr., Rs.45). **Pre-pay a taxi** here to Paharganj (Rs.21) or Connaught Place (Rs.30); pre-paid taxi booths are outside the terminal on the street. Upstairs in this terminal is a State Bank of India branch that doesn't change foreign currency and a small post office for all major state transport companies. The circle kiosk in the middle has enquiry offices, while counters 34-40 sell tickets for common destinations. Bus companies having offices here or elsewhere in the city include: **Himachal Road Transport Company,** 1 Rajpur Rd. (tel. 251 6725); **U.P. Roadways,** Ajmeri Gate (tel. 323 5367, 251 8709); **Rajasthan Roadways,** Bikaner House (tel. 338 3469); **Punjab Roadways** (tel. 296 7842); **Haryana Roadways** (tel. 252 1262).

Ordinary and deluxe buses leave ISBT Kashmiri Gate for Amritsar (every 30min., 4:30am-10pm, 10hr., Rs.122); Almora (7:30, 8:30, and 9:15pm, 11hr., Rs.126); Ajmer (every 30min., 7-12:10am, 10hr., Rs.112) en route to Pushkar (10½hr., Rs.115); and Jodhpur (16hr., Rs.170). Other buses go to: Jaipur (every hr., 7:05am-9:05pm, 6hr., Rs.75); Udaipur (9:20am, 17hr., Rs.185); Chandigarh (every 20min., 3:30am-1:30am, 5½hr., Rs.70); Dharamsala (6:30am, 7:40, 8, and 8:45pm, Rs.158; semi-deluxe 9:30pm, Rs.232; deluxe 5:30pm, Rs.314); Jammu (8, 9pm, and midnight, 12hr., Rs.190); Nainital (7:30pm, 9hr., Rs.105; deluxe 9 and 9:30am, Rs.169); Dehra Dun (every 30min., 5am-11:30pm, 6½hr., Rs.75/130 for ordinary/deluxe); Haridwar (every 30min., 4am-12:30am, 5½hr., Rs.61); Rishikesh (every hr., 4am-11pm, 7hr., Rs.65); Mussoorie (5:30am and 10:30pm, 8hr., Rs.115); Lucknow (every hr., 5am-9pm, 13hr., Rs.147); Faizabad (every 2hr., 5:30am-5:30pm, 18hr., Rs.206); Ramnagar (near Corbett Park: 6, 7, 8 and 9am, 7hr., Rs.75); Haldwani (every hr., 6am-9:30pm, 7hr., Rs.83); Manali (10 daily, 15hr., Rs.204/231/404 for ordinary/semi-deluxe/deluxe; deluxe only at 8:30pm); Shimla (8am, 8 between 4:50-9:25pm, 10hr., Rs.117; semi-deluxe at 8:25pm, Rs.155; deluxe 9:30am, Rs.244). Bookings for deluxe buses can be made in Room 310 of the bus station, or for better deals, look for signs around Paharganj. Hare Rama Guest House posts deals for buses to Manali (Rs.200), Dharamsala, Agra, etc. Catch deluxe buses to Jaipur at Bikaner House, south of India Gate across from the Children's Park (several daily, 6:30am-10:45pm).

GETTING AROUND

Travelers have a huge array of options in Delhi: cycle-rickshaws, auto-rickshaws, horse-drawn tongas, taxis, and buses. Regardless of which method you choose, consult with trustworthy locals about appropriate fares. Cycle- and auto-rickshaw drivers in particular have a knack for overcharging, driving around in circles and *then* overcharging, or changing the fare at the end of a trip. Fluctuating petrol prices have made most meters obsolete or added a 75% surcharge to the fare. Any mishaps, cheats, etc. should be reported by calling 331 9334, or call Delhi Transport Corporation at 331 9368. Reasonable maximum fares include: Airport-Connaught, Rs.200-250; Paharganj-Connaught Rs.15; Paharganj-Old Delhi Railway Rs.20; Connaught-Chanakyapuri Rs.30. **Cycle-rickshaws** can't go through parts of New Delhi, so don't tempt them into making long detours. **Buses** are certainly cheap, but they bring long delays and big crowds. Ladies can sit on the specially marked seats on the left. Bus #620 is a good bus heading to the south (Chanakyapuri and Haus Khaz) from Connaught Place. Bus #101 goes to Connaught from the Bus Station and Old Delhi (Chandni Chowk/Red Fort). Bus #425 goes to Nizamuddin from Connaught. Bus #505 runs to Qutb Minar from the city center. Bus fares Rs.1-10. **Bicycle rental:** Mehta Cycles, 2 stores east of the Kesri Hotel on the Main Bazaar, Paharganj, rents bicycles for Rs.25 per day (plus Rs.600 deposit, Rs.5 overnight charge). Rent long-term and they'll scrap the overnight charge. **Bicycling** in Delhi is harrowing but fun. Old Delhi is congested and slow, New Delhi is a bit faster, but has broader streets. Exploring by bicycle lets you see more of the main roads, as well as some places tourists don't usually go.

ORIENTATION

Once you get the hang of it, getting around in Delhi is a breeze (and breezes are always a good thing in the sweaty, smoggy capital). Delhi is situated west of the Yamuna River and runs about 30km from north to south, and 10km from east to west. The northern two-thirds of the city are encircled by **Ring Road,** conveniently packed with buses that circumnavigate the city. The city center, commonly called **New Delhi,** centers on **Connaught Place,** a circular hub of two-story colonnaded buildings arranged around a circular swath of grass. Connaught Place is the throbbing heart (and capitalist soul) of New Delhi. Many of Connaught Place's shops provide goods and services useful to tourists, and if you're looking for an AmEx office, a copy of last Tuesday's USA Today, or the Kazakhstan Airlines reservation desk, you've come to the right place. Of course, with tourists come touts and tricksters—Connaught Place's hustlers are aggressive and exceptionally savvy; as always, a firm "no thank you" and a grin-and-bear-it attitude will serve you well. One kilometer north is the **New Delhi Railway Station.** Of the streets that break off Connaught Place, **Sansad Marg** is the most crowded; it leads to the Raj-era parliamentary buildings, 2km west of **India Gate,** straight down **Raj Path.** One kilometer south of the parliamentary buildings is **Chanakyapuri,** a neighborhood stuffed full of the consular offices of English-speaking and European countries.

South Delhi unofficially begins just south of Chanakyapuri. Aside from Ring Rd. and **Mehrauli Badarpur Road,** South Delhi's major thoroughfares run north-south. In the center is **Aurobindo Marg,** which connects Safdarjang's tomb with the Qutb Minar Complex; in the east is **Mathura Road,** which slices through **Nizamuddin** and turns into **Zakir Hussain Road** as it proceeds southeast from India Gate.

Just west of New Delhi Railway Station is **Paharganj,** a not particularly pleasant part of the city crammed with budget accommodations and backpackers. The area north of the station, is the city built by Shah Jahan; called Shahjahanabad or **Old Delhi,** it is a delightful tangle of streets and bazaars—the major thoroughfare in Old Delhi is the east-west **Chandni Chauk.**

PRACTICAL INFORMATION

> **Warning:** Delhi is full of "tourist offices" which claim to provide booking assistance, free maps, and other services. These are to be avoided—stick to the main government tourist office on Janpath, and for train tickets, to the tourist reservation office in the New Delhi Railway Station. Across from the railway are several of these offices—their bookings are likely to be fraudulent, or at least overpriced; don't believe claims that train ticketing counters are "for Indians only," etc. Almost everyone's doing something subversive in Delhi: every rickshaw driver wants to change money, and everyone wants desperately for you to buy their stuff. Con artists abound, particularly in Paharganj and other tourist hotbeds. Keep your cool and hone your street smarts.

Tourist Office: Government of India Tourist Office, 88 Janpath, between Tolstoy Marg and Connaught Circus Rd. (tel. 332 0005 or 332 0008; fax 332 0342). Perfect place to begin a trip to Delhi or other parts of India: great city map, helpful, honest staff who won't rip you off, good brochures on all of India. Open Mon.-Fri. 9am-6pm, Sat. 9am-2pm. Closed major holidays. At the International Airport, the **Delhi Tourism** and **Government of India Tourist Offices** are government-operated; "India Tourism" is private. Delhi Tourism Corporation Offices are more credible than most private agents. Delhi has tourist offices for the different states of India, so if you know where you're headed, these are good places to get information: the Chandralok Building, at 36 Janpath, south of the government office, is home to the offices for **Uttar Pradesh** (tel. 371 1296, 332 2251), **Himachal Pradesh** (tel. 332 5320), and **Haryana** (tel. 332 4911). The **Indian Mountaineering Foundation,** on Benito Juarez Marg, Anand Niketan (tel. 602245, 671211), has information on treks, and especially climbs over 6000m. The **Survey of India** has a branch in Delhi (tel. 332 2288) and provides maps of Delhi and a few trekking maps, although their main office in Dehra Dun has more. Open Mon.-Fri. 9am-1pm and 1:30-5pm.

Tours: For more information, see **Sights,** p.137.

Budget Travel: Paharganj has several agents booking buses to tourist hot spots (Manali, Dharamsala, Agra, etc.) For airline reservations and tickets, try **Gaga Travels and Tours,** at the west end of the Paharganj Main Bazaar, near the Ramakrishna Mission (tel. 751 0061; fax 753 4093). Agent Varinder Kohli is very cool, and these people aren't just out for your cash. Open daily 9:30am-7pm. The little office next to the Hare Rama Guest House, **S. G. Tours and Travels** (tel. 752 5459) is reasonably reliable, with frequent bookings to Manali (Rs.200), Dharamsala (Rs.290), and Agra (Rs.100, with A/C Rs.160). The **Thomas Cook** office (tel. 335 0562) is in the Hotel Imperial, on Janpath. The **ISTC Travels Office** (tel. 332 4789), also adjacent to the Imperial, issues and replaces International Student Identity Cards. Open Mon.-Fri. 9am-1pm and 2-5pm. For information on **tours** of Delhi, see **Sights,** p. 137.

Diplomatic Missions: Most are in the Chanakyapuri area in south-central Delhi, and are open Mon.-Fri. 8.30am-5.30pm. Most of the listed telephone numbers work 24hr. for emergencies. **U.S.,** Shantipath (tel. 688 9033, 611 3033). **Canada,** 7/8 Shantipath (tel. 687 6500; fax 687 6579). **U.K.,** Shantipath (tel. 687 2161; fax 687 2882). **Ireland,** 230 Jor Bagh (tel. 462 6733, 688 6775 (emergency); fax 469 7053). **Australia,** 1/50G Shantipath (visa dept. tel. 688 8223; fax 688 7530). Open Mon.-Fri. 9.30am-12.30pm. **New Zealand,** 50-N Nyaya Marg (tel. 688 3170; fax 687 2317). Open Mon.-Fri. 8.30am-5pm. **South Africa,** B-18 Vasant Marg, Vasant Vihar (tel. 611 9411; fax 611 3505). **European Union,** 86 Golf Links (tel. 611 9513; fax 462 9206). Open Mon.-Fri. 9am-5pm. **Germany,** 6/50-G Shantipath (tel. 687-1831; fax 687 3117). Open Mon.-Fri. 9.30am-5.30pm. **Israel,** 3 Aurangzeb Rd. (tel. 301 3238; fax 301 4298). Open Mon.-Thurs. 9am-5pm, Fri. 9am-4pm. **Netherlands,** 6/50-F Shantipath (tel. 688 4951; fax 688 4956). **Nepal,** Barakhamba Rd. (tel. 332 7361, 332 8191; fax 332 6857). Thailand, 56-N Nyaya Marg (tel. 611 8103; fax 687 8103).

Immigration Office: Unfortunately, getting a visa extension is not easy, and the process brings many travelers back to Delhi again and again. For an extension on a simple **tourist visa** (which is *not* lightly given—15 days is usually the maximum, so get your story straight ahead of time!), first head to the **Ministry of Home Affairs Foreigners Division,** in Lok Nayak Bhawan, behind Khan Market, off Subramaniya Bharati Marg around Lodi Estate. They're only open Mon.-Fri. 10am-noon, so arrive early with 4 passport photos and a letter stating your grounds for extension. If they process your application, head over to the **Foreigners Regional Registration Office** (tel. 331 9781, ext. 17), open Mon.-Fri. 9:30am-1:30pm and 2-4pm. The FRRO is also the office for getting **student visas** (with a bonafide student certificate of a recognized school/university, bank remittance certificate, and an extension application in duplicate with 2 photos), as well as **permits** for restricted parts of India. If you arrived in Delhi and need an **exit visa,** the FRRO can process it in about 20min.

Currency Exchange: Connaught Place has many banks. The American Express office in Connaught Place is probably the best place to change traveler's checks (see below). After hours, avoid changing money on the black market and head to a legitimate money changer, such as **S.G. Securities PVT Ltd.** (tel. 372 3000, 331 8000), at M-96, Middle Circle, Connaught. Open Mon.-Sat. 9:30am-8:30pm. **Bank of Baroda** (tel. 332 8230) on Sansad Marg in the big, bad building beyond the outer circle, gives cash advances on Visa and Mastercard. Open Mon.-Fri. 10am-2pm, Sat. 10am-noon. **Citibank** (tel. 371 2484), around the corner toward Connaught Place from the Bank of Baroda, has a **24-hr. ATM** (compatible with Cirrus systems), and they, too, give cash advances on Visa, Mastercard, or Diner's Club cards. Open Mon.-Fri. 10am-2pm, Sat. 10am-noon. The **State Bank of India** branch at Chandni Chowk (tel. 296 0393), 200m from the east end, changes traveler's checks. (Open Mon.-Fri. 10am-2pm, Sat. 10am-noon.) The main branch is located on Sansad Marg, near Connaught Place. For truly desperate situations, there are numerous illegal money changers along the Main Bazaar in Paharganj—just ask

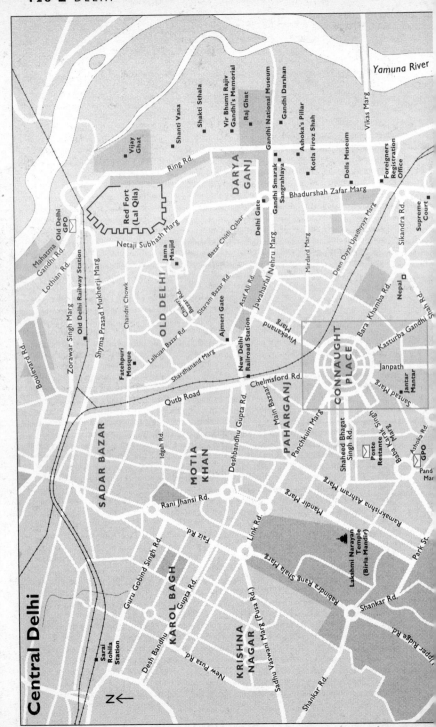

Central Delhi

Yamuna River

Vijay Ghat

Shanti Vana

Shakti Sthala

Vir Bhumi Rajiv Gandhi's Memorial

Raj Ghat

Gandhi National Museum

Gandhi Darshan

Ashoka's Pillar

Kotla Firoz Shah

Dolls Museum

Foreigners Registration Office

DARYA GANJ

Ring Rd.

Red Fort (Lal Qila)

Gandhi Smarak Sangrahalaya

Bhadurshah Zafar Marg

Vikas Marg

Sikandra Rd.

Supreme Court

Mahatma Gandhi Rd.

Old Delhi GPO

Lothian Rd.

Netaji Subhash Marg

Jama Masjid

Delhi Gate

Deen Dayal Upadhyaya Marg

Zorawar Singh Marg

Old Delhi Railway Station

Shyma Prasad Mukherji Marg

Chandni Chowk

Bazar Chitli Qabar

Jawaharlal Nehru Marg

Mirdard Marg

Nepal

Bara Khamba Rd.

Shah 'i' Rd.

Boulevard Rd.

OLD DELHI

Chawri Bazar

Sitaram Bazar Rd.

Asaf Ali Rd.

CONNAUGHT PLACE

Kasturba Gandhi Rd.

Fatehpuri Mosque

Lalkuan Bazar Rd.

Ajmeri Gate

New Delhi Railroad Station

Vivekanand Marg

Janpath

Jantar Mantar

Shardhanand Marg

Chelmsford Rd.

Sansad Marg

Qutb Road

Deshbandhu Gupta Rd.

Main Bazaar

PAHARGANJ

Panchkuin Marg

Shaheed Bhagat Singh Rd.

Poste Restante

Baba Kharak Singh Marg

Ashoka Rd.

GPO

Pand Mar

SADAR BAZAR

Idgah Rd.

MOTIA KHAN

Ramakrishna Ashram Marg

Rani Jhansi Rd.

Faiz Rd.

Mandir Marg

Link Rd.

Guru Gobind Singh Rd.

Gupta Rd.

Rabindra Rang Shala Marg

Lakshmi Narayan Temple (Birla Mandir)

Shankar Rd.

Park St.

Upper Ridge Rd.

KAROL BAGH

Desh Bandhu Rd.

New Pusa Rd.

KRISHNA NAGAR

Sadhu Vaswani Marg (Pusa Rd.)

Shankar Rd.

Sarai Rohila Station

N←

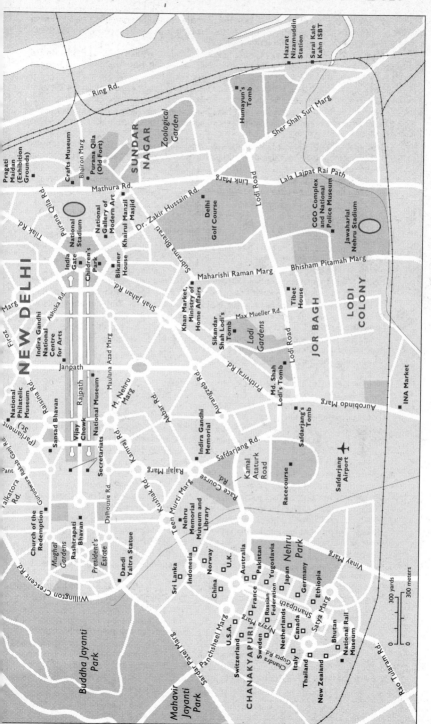

anyone on the street; they're less likely to change traveler's checks. Don't let them go off with your money promising to return with rupees, even if they leave a "friend" of theirs with you while you wait.

American Express: A-block, Connaught Place (tel. 371 2513, 332 4119), is probably the best place to change traveler's checks. They sell, buy, and change American Express checks, and cash other brands at 1% commission. There's a counter for lost/stolen cards (though the main office for 24-hr. check replacement is at Bhasant Lok (tel. 687 5929). The A-block office issues and receives American Express moneygrams, and offers usual cardmembers' services, including personal check cashing, card replacement, mail holding, and travel services. Open Mon.-Sat. 9:30am-6:30pm.

Telephones/Fax/E-Mail: STD/ISD booths are not hard to find. Many hotels will let you make local calls or can point you to the nearest office. Paharganj Main Bazaar has become a romping ground for dozens of STD/ISD offices, which now offer such services as collect and credit card calls abroad, call-backs (usually Rs.5 per min., but free at Hotel Anoop), **fax,** and **telex;** the office east of the Kesri Hotel and across the way at 1587 Main Bazaar (tel. 752 7744, 753 4151) even has **e-mail** (e-mail address: ns.delhissm1.springrpg.sprint.com). Send 25 lines for Rs.60, receive for Rs.15. Open 7:30am-midnight.

Luggage Storage: Many hotels in Paharganj store luggage, including the Galaxy Guest House on Main Bazaar. Ashok Yatra Niwas Hotel has a safer storage room, but charges about Rs.4 per day.

Market: See **Shopping,** p. 147.

Library: The **American Center Library,** 24 Kasturba Gandhi Marg (tel. 331 6841, 331 4251; fax 332 9499; e-mail library@usisdel.ernet.in), is substantial, and their CD-ROM and Internet databases are good for research. This collection includes the embassy's library. Videotapes for rent. Admission Rs.10. Open Mon.-Fri. 10am-6pm. The **British Council Library,** 17 Kasturba Gandhi Marg (tel. 371140), up the street on the other side, is less accessible. Open Tues.-Sat. 9am-5pm. The **Ramakrishna Mission,** at the west end of Paharganj Main Bazaar, has a "free" library with current periodicals. Rs.10 fee, Rs.100 deposit. Open Tues.-Sun. 8am-11am.

Cultural Centers: The American Center and British Council (see libraries, above), both have regular lectures, film screenings, and minor shindigs. **Max Mueller Bhavan,** 3 Kasturba Gandhi Marg (tel. 332 9506), has a library, and also shows films in "Siddhartha Hall." Indian cultural centers include the **Indian Council for Cultural Relations,** Azad Bhavan, 1P Estate (tel. 331 2274); the **India International Centre,** 40 Lodi Estate (tel. 461 9431); the **Indira Gandhi National Centre for the Arts,** C. V. Mess, Janpath (tel. 338 9216); and **Sangeet Natak Akademi,** Rabindra Bhavan (tel. 338 7246), which has information on classical music concerts.

English Bookstore: The inner circle of Connaught Place has several well-stocked bookstores, including the **Bookworm** (tel. 332 2260; open Mon.-Sat. 10am-7pm), the **New Book Depot** (tel. 332 0020), and the more cluttered **E.O. Galgotra and Sons,** next door, all on B-block. Vendors along the Paharganj Main Bazaar sell second-hand and new books, especially those most read by travelers. **Jackson's Books Corner** has a good supply (open daily 10am-11pm).

Pharmacy: The multi-story **Super Bazaar** (tel. 331 0163), outside of M-block of Connaught Place, is supposed to be open Mon.-Sat. 10am-7pm, but a few pharmacies here are open 24hr. Several pharmacies along Paharganj Main Bazaar cater to tourists, with tampons, toilet paper, and rolling papers.

Hospital/Medical Services: Dr. Sharwan Kumar Gupta's **Care Clinic and Laboratory,** 1468 Sangatrashan, Paharganj (tel. 751 7841, home tel. 623 3088, pager 9632-113979), 2 blocks north of the western end of the Bazaar, is convenient to Paharganj and accommodating to travelers; the staff speaks good English and is used to dealing with foreign insurance companies. Recommended by IAMAT. Open Mon.-Sat. 10am-7:30pm, Sun. 10am-1pm. For hospital service, many travelers find their way to the **East-West Medical Clinic,** 38 Golf Links Rd., Lodi area (tel. 699229). Expensive by local standards, the clinic is clean and efficient, run by an American-trained Sikh doctor and his friendly red-haired Irish wife. Other hospitals

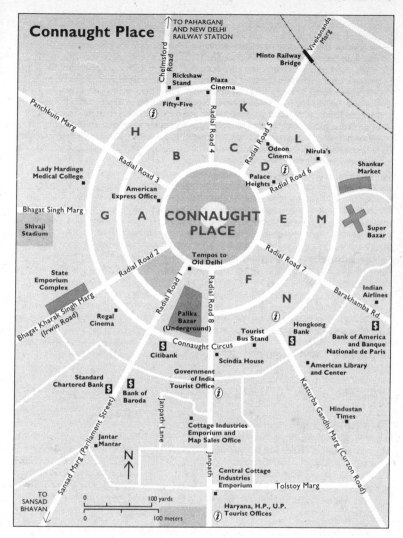

Connaught Place

TO PAHARGANJ AND NEW DELHI RAILWAY STATION

Vivekananda Marg

Chelmsford Road

Minto Railway Bridge

Rickshaw Stand

Plaza Cinema

Fifty-Five

K

Panchkuin Marg

Radial Road 4

Radial Road 5

H

B

C

Odeon Cinema

L

Nirula's

Radial Road 3

Palace Heights

D

Radial Road 6

Shankar Market

Lady Hardinge Medical College

American Express Office

Bhagat Singh Marg

G

A

CONNAUGHT PLACE

E

M

Super Bazar

Shivaji Stadium

Radial Road 2

Tempos to Old Delhi

Radial Road 7

State Emporium Complex

Radial Road 1

F

N

Indian Airlines

Bhagat Kharak Singh Marg (Irwin Road)

Regal Cinema

Palika Bazar (Underground)

Radial Road 8

Barakhamba Rd.

Tourist Bus Stand

Hongkong Bank

Bank of America and Banque Nationale de Paris

Connaught Circus

Citibank

Scindia House

American Library and Center

Standard Chartered Bank

Government of India Tourist Office

Bank of Baroda

Kasturba Gandhi Marg (Curzon Road)

Hindustan Times

Janpath Lane

Jantar Mantar

Janpath

Cottage Industries Emporium and Map Sales Office

Sansad Marg (Parliament Street)

N

Central Cottage Industries Emporium

Tolstoy Marg

TO SANSAD BHAVAN

0   100 yards

0   100 meters

Haryana, H.P., U.P. Tourist Offices

NORTH INDIA

include **Kolmet** (tel. 575 2055) and **Anand** (tel. 224126). **Emergency** service: call 1099, 102, or 545 3388.

Police: Branches all over Delhi—look for Delhi Traffic and Tourist Police kiosks at major intersections. Their motto is "for you with you always," but the booths are often deserted. Stations at Chandni Chowk next to Bahrandi Mandir (tel. 233442), Chanakyapuri, Connaught Place and many other locations.

Emergency: tel. 100.

Post Office: There are postal **branches** in nearly every part of Delhi. The **GPO** (tel. 336 4111), on Ashoka Rd. and Baba Kharak Singh Marg, is big and circular—they offer speed mail, "hybrid mail" (an inexpensive but cumbersome alternative to fax), and general parcel delivery services. Open Mon.-Fri. 10am-4:30pm, Sat. 10am-3pm for express; Mon.-Sat. 10am-5:30pm for sale of stamps. **EMS Speed Post Office,** Bhai Vir Singh Marg, a few blocks from the GPO. Open daily 9am-8pm.

Other overnight and express couriers, such as **Overnite Express** (open 24hr.) and **Blue Dart** (incorporated with Federal Express; tel. 332 4511, ext. 290; open Mon.-Sat. 10am-10pm), are located below the state tourist offices in Kanishka Shopping Plaza, next to Ashok Yatri Niwas Hotel. To receive mail by *Poste Restante* in Delhi, head to the office behind the EMS Speed Post Office on Market Rd. (Bhai Vir Singh Marg). Bring a passport to claim mail, and make sure your loved ones write to *Poste Restante*, GPO, New Delhi, 110001, India. *Poste Restante* open Mon.-Fri. 9am-5pm, Sat. 9am-1pm. For **shipping**, the Parcel Packing portion of the Sham Store (tel. 738945), in Paharganj Main Bazaar across from Galaxy Guest House, has an export license (open daily 10am-8pm). Belair Travel and Cargo (tel. 331 3985), at 10-B Scindia House, ships bulky luggage and boxes overseas. **Postal Code:** 110001.

Telephone Code: 011.

ACCOMMODATIONS

Staying in Delhi can be frustratingly expensive. Prices have been driven up, so that a room under Rs.100 is almost invariably a cesspool. Still, bargains can be found in each of three major hotel centers: Paharganj, Connaught Place, and Old Delhi.

Everybody—diplomats, movie stars, tourists, everybody!—should have to stay in **Paharganj** at least once. And if you're a budget backpacker, it's the only place to be. Paharganj is hilarious and absurd—it's easy to imagine the first bewildered hippies back in the '60s, stumbling off the train at New Delhi Station and walking up the street to the convenient string of low-end hotels. Thirty years later, Paharganj has adapted to travelers' needs, but it still retains its charming and characteristic squalor and seediness. It's no tranquil enclave, but there are dozens of STD/ISD booths, Kashmiri "travel agents" with the gift of the gab, hash dealers, money changers, and even occasional elephants walking down the Main Bazaar. It's dirty, it's decadent, and it's unadulterated Delhi. If you've just arrived in India, or are simply not into grime, **Connaught Place** has its own collection of guest houses and hotels, most of them nicer and more expensive than those in Paharganj. Many travelers do stay in Connaught, though it's less eventful than Paharganj. On the other hand, if you really want to put your nose in it, there's always **Old Delhi,** the purist's retreat. (Don't expect banana pancakes.)

Paharganj

The "heart" of Paharganj is near the center of the **Main Bazaar,** close to the west end; this is where most restaurants and popular hotels are, so head here if you crave the constant company of other travelers. Hotels nearer to the railway station often offer better deals, however, and the hike to food is not that long. Hotels with generators and good rooftop hotels are key. All of the following directions (right, left) are given from the orientation of someone walking west on Main Bazaar from the train station.

Hotel Downtown, Main Bazaar (tel. 355 5815; fax 752 0033). One-quarter of the way from the railway station. Next to Hotel Star Palace (which has a sign), set back 10m from Main Bazaar proper, left side. Friendly new hotel is still very clean; compact rooms have good fans—many have windows. Great staff, rooftop room service 24hr. Check-out noon. Mellow, quiet, and well-equipped. Singles Rs.125. Doubles with bath Rs.175.

Camran Lodge, Main Bazaar (tel. 526053). Right side. With the hands-down coolest architecture in Paharganj (it's an old mosque), the Camran is a quiet underdog among travelers. Not as sterile or as modern as other places, but rooms are large, airy, and have etched designs. Singles with bath Rs.80. Doubles Rs.120.

Vivek Hotel, 1534 Main Bazaar (tel. 523015, 753 7102). At the heart of Paharganj. Big, marble hotel with underused lobby, elevator, squat toilets, and disorientingly asymmetrical but clean rooms. Popular among backpackers. Two restaurants attached. Singles Rs.150, with air-cooling Rs.180. Doubles Rs.180, with air cooling Rs.200. Deluxe rooms with TV, telephone Rs.230-260.

Hare Krishna Guest House, Main Bazaar (tel. 753 3017, 592188). Gentle owner not as business-oriented as staff of next-door Anoop. Quieter, clean-enough rooms have tidy, elevated bathrooms, 15-cm mattresses, and a couple have interesting views (such as that of the legs of people sitting in the Anoop restaurant, to which this hotel is conveniently connected). Singles Rs.120, with bath Rs.150. Doubles Rs.150, with bath Rs.180.

Anoop Hotel, Main Bazaar (tel. 526256, 521467). Popular, multi-floor backpackers' hotel—no-Indians-allowed policy is disturbing, though. Rooms are pretty spacious, and efficiently kept-up. STD/ISD has free call-back. Toilets are not always cleaned. Singles with bath Rs.140. Doubles Rs.150, with bath Rs.180, with A/C Rs.350.

Galaxy Guest House, Main Bazaar (tel. 777 7372). Near Khanna Talkies and Anoop Hotel. Mellow and dingy, but with quiet rooftop, big doubles, and kindhearted, tolerant management, the Galaxy lives better than it looks. Take a shower while on the toilet. Check-out 24hr. Few views. Singles Rs.110, with bath Rs.140. Doubles Rs.160, with bath Rs.190.

Hare Rama Guest House, 298 Main Bazaar (tel. 751 8972, 521413). Left side from Galaxy, entrance 10m back. Discriminatory no-Indians policy doesn't really matter, since it's always filled with Israelis. Many attached services, loud, cramped rooms, and a rooftop with a consistent "scene." Singles (with bed—and that's it!) Rs.100. Doubles with bath and fan Rs.180, with A/C Rs.350.

Traveller Guest House, Main Bazaar (tel. 354 4849). Left side, not far from east end (railway station). A bit more money, but worth it for black-and-white TV, "disinfected" toilets, and air-cooler. Singles (without windows) Rs.180. Big room with front window Rs.250.

Hotel Bright, Main Bazaar (tel. 752 5852). A third of the way from the railway station on the right side. A cheapie all around—service and upkeep are not impressive, and mattresses are prehistoric. Bathrooms tight and tricky. Singles Rs.80-90. Doubles Rs.120.

Metropolis Tourist Home, Main Bazaar (tel. 525492, 355 8052; fax 752 5600). Gentle, upscale option at west end of Main Bazaar. Well-known for its restaurant, services, and clean, majestic rooms—all here in gorgeous Paharganj. Singles Rs.450. Doubles Rs.600. For an ultra-splurge, try one of the "special rooms," with carved head-board, inlaid door, black bathtub, and sitting area (Rs.1200).

Hotel Amar, Main Bazaar (tel. 524642). Near Imperial Cinema and Metropolis Hotel at west end of Main Bazaar. Go for the single. Rooms are dim, but most have TV, air-cooling, and telephone to call out for pizza. Singles Rs.125, with bath Rs.150. Doubles Rs.200, with bath Rs.300.

Arkur Guest House, opposite Hare Rama Guest House. Soft-spoken in shadow of bigger neighbors, but tiny street-side rooftop restaurant pulls in a consistent crowd. Rooms are ample and have working bathrooms. Singles Rs.125. Doubles Rs.150.

Connaught Place

Some guest lodges long popular among budget travelers have let their boosted egos lead to boosted prices and diminished quality. As a result, Connaught Place is better for mid-range and high-end hotels. For budget accommodations, hike to Paharganj.

Mr. S.C. Jain's Guesthouse, 7 Pratap Singh Bldg., Janpath Lane. Though it's a bit far from Connaught's virtuous services, it has a homey, welcoming feel of its own. The owner is a lawyer, and some rooms house musty old books. Rooms are wearing down. Dorm beds (in 4-bed dorm) Rs.100. Singles Rs.150. Doubles Rs.200, with bath Rs.250.

YWCA International Guest House, 10 Sansad Marg (tel. 336 1561, 336 1662; fax 334 1763). Just south of Jantar Mantar. A mid-range bargain with A/C, spacious rooms, several services (including AmEx check cashing), and breakfast included. Pay in foreign currency, or in rupees with encashment certificate. Singles Rs.375. Doubles Rs.625.

YWCA Blue Triangle Family Hostel, Ashoka Rd. (tel. 336 0133). Near the GPO. Peaceful part of Connaught area. Big, bright rooms in a well-oiled accommodations machine. Breakfast included. Dorm beds Rs.190. Singles Rs.325, with A/C Rs.400. Doubles Rs.500, with A/C Rs.650, executive deluxe Rs.750.

Ringo Guest House, 17 Scindia House (tel. 331 0605). Off Janpath, outside Outer Circle. Popular among travelers who come to deal with Delhi's bureaucracy—now a backpackers' retreat that's too big for its britches. Ridiculously stuffed dorm rooms, but a relaxed, pleasant atmosphere. Check-out noon. Singles Rs.90. Doubles Rs.160, with bath Rs.210.

Nirula's Hotel, L-block, Connaught Place (tel. 332 2419; fax 335 3957). The name to beat in Western-style accommodations. Off the multiplex restaurants are carpeted, Holiday Inn-style rooms, good for those who've just stumbled off the plane and are feeling freaked out by all things Indian. Singles Rs.1195. Doubles Rs.2000.

Janpath Guest House, 82 Janpath (tel. 332 1935). Near the Government Tourist Office. Businessperson's hotel has a few killer rooms and other not-so-hot ones. Central courtyard has a nice swing. Many facilities (telephones, hot and cold water, laundry, etc.). Slightly run-down. Singles Rs.325, with A/C and TV Rs.775. Doubles Rs.375.

Old Delhi

Many hotels in Old Delhi do not accept foreigners. The few that do allow foreigners tend to be run-down and feel very old, but this is a cheap and fun part of the city to stay in.

Khush-Dil Hotel, Chandni Chowk (tel. 232110), and next door **New Khush-Dil Hotel** (tel. 252 3648). At the west end of Chandni Chowk, just south of the Fatehpuri Mosque on Fatehpuri Corner. Narrow beds, dank bathrooms, feeble fans, but lovely tiled walls and excellent front-side views. Check-out 24hr. Singles Rs.100. Doubles Rs.100, with bath Rs.120.

Hotel New City Palace (tel. 327 9548), on the west side of Jama Masjid. Superb views of the mosque, complete with loud prayers. Surprisingly modern rooms have pencil-neck beds, hot water, shower, and access to a balcony. Several car parts stores on the streets below cater to late-night carburetor munchies. Singles Rs.200. Doubles Rs.250.

Bharat Hotel (tel. 235326). Just across the street, to the east of New Khush-Dil and Khush-Dil. Beyond the narrow, infernal stairs lies a small courtyard, somewhat grubby but liveable rooms, and slight respite from the chaos lurking on the street below. All 35 rooms share common baths. Singles Rs.60. Doubles Rs.120.

Hotel Vakil, 735 Jama Masjid (tel. 326 9625). On the street west of Jama Masjid, south of New City Palace. Front-side views of the mosque, excellent roof (just don't fall off!), and simple rooms with air-coolers and hot water in attached baths. Check-out 24hr. Singles Rs.200. Doubles Rs.200.

Chanakyapuri

Vishwa Yuvak Kendra International Youth Centre, Circular Rd., Chanakyapuri (tel. 301363). Across from Nehru Planetarium, in a comfortable part of town. Looks and smells uncannily like a typical youth hostel. Popular for conventions, with words of wisdom and encouragement on every wall. Rooms are big and modern. English books for sale. Singles Rs.500. Doubles Rs.570.

FOOD

It's worth shelling out a little cash for some of Delhi's excellent meals. There are countless restaurants in all price ranges, respectable Western-style fast food, superb Chinese and Middle Eastern cuisine, and even a couple of Mexican restaurants. And for those not into sampling cultural combos like "Indo-Moroccan-Mediterranean," there's plenty of knock-out Indian food as well. For a real splurge—and you have to want this *bad*—head to one of the 5-star hotels. Those in the Maurya Sheraton (on the road to the airport) and in the Ashok Frontier are considered particularly good—expect to pay up to Rs.300-350 for an entree.

Paharganj

This backpackers' ghetto has developed several hot spots for hanging out—and all of them are about five stories up. Just which hotel's rooftop restaurant will draw the crowd on any evening is unclear. The Anoop is nice and big but has poor views. The Hare Rama can get hot, but usually has something going on. The Vivek has an impressive patch of lush grass on its roof, but its service is slow, and it has lost many customers. None of these places serves particularly good food, though their breakfasts are tolerable. But the rooftops are the place to find Paharganj's pack rats sipping tea and munching curd after hours.

It's best to get off the Main Bazaar for food, though the strip's joints do offer menus that tantalize foreign tongues. The places near the Railway Station have good tea, but aren't particularly hygienic. Wander the streets north of Paharganj to see where the locals are eating.

NORTH INDIA

Malhotra Restaurant, 1833 Chuna Mandi (tel. 731849). Walk west on Main Bazaar, right at Rajguru Rd. at the Metropolis, then take the first left. Tucked down below street level, Malhotra has managed to hide from most backpackers until now, but locals know better—it's often packed. Good, clean, if not always consistent Indian and Chinese fare, with a splash of Continental. Try the excellent *kheer* with cold coffee. Open daily 6am-10:30pm.

Chawla's Relax Club. From Malhotra, walk one-half block west, then one-half block north. Look for the "restaurant" sign. Head here for breakfast—it's relaxed, filling, and fresh. Fruit and nut porridge (Rs.30) is a meal unto itself. *Prantha gobi* ("qualiflower") Rs.8. Open daily 7am-10pm.

Light Restaurant, Main Bazaar (tel. 520687). At the west end. Pronounced "Liggot" by some staff-members. Their *thalis* are only Rs.15—yes, Rs.15—and even better, you can look inside the pots and see which 2 vegetables you want with your *dal*, rice, 2 *chapatis,* and *kheer*. Big bowls of rice pudding (Rs.6) are among the best deals around.

Appetite Restaurant (tel. 753 2079). Across from Kesri Hotel. Bring yours for breakfast (Rs.30-37). This place has its act together, with music videos blaring, fans roaring, lights gleaming, and good service accompanying pizzas and burgers. Open daily 7:30am-midnight.

Restra New Lord's Café, next to the Appetite. Slow-motion service but they, too, have TV, *thalis* (Rs.30-40), and a filling "special pizza" (Rs.40). Or plow into Israeli food. Open daily 7am-11pm.

New Diamond Cafe, across from the Anoop. Narrow little room—good for meeting strangers or people-watching street-side. Decent Indian food, over-ambitious Continental. Veg. *thalis* Rs.25, Indian breakfast Rs.25, lamb with boiled potato Rs.40. Open daily 7am-midnight.

Leema Restaurant (tel. 777 7062), in Hotel Vivek, just next door. The best budget-hotel restaurant in Paharganj is not on a rooftop, but just above the street. Good A/C, fresh juices, and excellent veg. sandwiches (Rs.10). Open 7am-11pm.

Metropolis Restaurant (tel. 525492). In the Metropolis Hotel. The best restaurant on the block, with subtly prepared Chinese, Japanese, Indian, and Continental dishes. *Gosht biryani* (rice with mutton) Rs.75; Julienne of Chicken with "a touch of garlic *demiglace*" Rs.150. Subdued setting—inside, or on the rooftop. Open 8am-6pm for breakfast and snacks, 11am-11pm for lunch/dinner.

Connaught Place

Like Paharganj, Connaught has a slanted range—here, though, there are one or two good budget spots and several excellent Indian and International restaurants to delight the diplomats and business people who long for a taste of home. American-style fast-food joints such as Pizza Hut and KFC have been trying to move into the market amid great controversy.

Don't Pass Me By, 79 Scindia House (tel. 335 2942). Near Ringo and Sunny Guest Houses. With such a forthright name, how could it disappoint? Humble, budget eats are nicely prepared. Crowd into 2 tables inside, or a few more on the outside patio. Corn flakes with fruit and curd Rs.25. Tibetan bread, yummy cheese tomato omelette Rs.25.

Nirula's, L-block. (tel. 332 2419). Behemoth multi-restaurant stuffs thousands every day. Head to the ice cream bar for smooth mango scoops and shakes, or try odd Indian flavors like Zafrani Badaam Pista, 21 Love, or Gulabo (Rs.18 per scoop). Or hit the Potpourri upstairs, with lamburgers (Rs.79), a clean, mega-salad bar (Rs.80 all you can eat), or pizzas (Rs.60-100). Or eat in their classy "Chinese Room." Or sip drinks in one of 2 bars. Or, or, or—oh decisions! Additional Nirula's ice cream branch near Wimpy's on N-block.

Wimpy's, N-6 Connaught (tel. 331 3910). What Britain considers low-end fast food is all the rage in Delhi—wealthy teens clamor here for birthday parties, tourists come to sweat, and Wimpy himself stops by now and then. Maxi-, double-maxi-, lentil-burgers (Rs.18-48), keema pizza (Rs.43), and tasty shakes.

Croissants, etc., 9 Scindia House. Another recent, albeit unusual, addition to the fast food frenzy that's started to storm Delhi. Mild, basic sandwiches refresh on hot days. Ummburgers, veg. croissandwich Rs.14, chicken croissant Rs.15. Open daily 8:30am-10:30pm.

Zen Restaurant, B-block (tel. 372 4444). Elegant, but can't get its cultures straight—mostly Chinese food, a Japanese name, American 1950s music for ambience, all in the middle of India. Still, delicately prepared dishes and gracious service are worth it, particularly if the A/C is functioning. Veg. and non-veg. dishes Rs.55-200. Open 11am-noon for coffee, 12:30-10:30pm for lunch/dinner, 3-7 pm for "booze and snacks."

Parikrama, Kasturba Gandhi Marg. Delhi's revolving rooftop restaurant takes 90min. to go around once, and they won't let your meal finish before that. The floor moving against the wall induces nausea, but at least there are plaques indicating what's to be seen out the window at any given time. It's not just a gimmick; the restaurant serves good food. Come during the day to see more, or at sunset. Open daily 11am-11pm.

Mahavir Sweets, 26/2 Inner Circle, E-block (tel. 373 1762). Has "pure vegetarian sweets," and is also popular for *thalis*—fixed Rs.17, or special Rs.25. Suitable for a quick but filling bite between jaunts to the bank or bookshops.

Wenger & Co. Pastry Shop, A-block (tel. 332 4373). Next to AmEx office. Western-style sweet-tooth-pleasures such as chocolate doughnuts, strudels, and other scrumptious, if occasionally distorted, versions of European bakery fare. Open daily 10am-7:30pm.

El Arab, 13 Regal Bldg., Outer Circle. Near Gaylord's Restaurant and Regal Cinema. Lebanese cuisine, uninspired decor. Meat-laden buffet (Rs.160) has a good reputation, but a la carte options also available. Open Mon.-Sat. 11am-10pm.

Rodeo, A-block (tel. 371 3780). Near the AmEx office. For an ol' time "American West" treat, pull up a saddle to the bar—literally, since the bar stools are saddles. It'll cost you, but lasso in Mexican enchiladas and tacos (Rs.140), pollo loco (Rs.150), or classic Old West treats from the Italian and Indian menu. The waiters look like Mexicans in their cowboy hats and chaps. Mango cowboy Rs.60; pitchers of draft beer Rs.170.

Café 100, B-block (tel. 332 0663). Near Zen Restaurant. Nirula's wanna-be has a hefty buffet with salad, Indian and Chinese selections (Rs.160), pizzas and burgers, as well as "super-duper sundaes" (Rs.35 and up). Bring grandma and the rest of the clan. Open daily 10am-11pm. Buffet noon-3pm and 7-11pm.

Embassy Restaurant, D-block (tel. 332 0480). Good Indian food at not-necessarily-knuckle-breaking prices. Brain curry Rs.70, cream of asparagus soup Rs.36. Open daily 10am-11pm.

United Coffee House (tel. 332 2075). Quiet, swish setting to act snooty and snotty. Not over-the-top elegant, but not some homey café either, this coffee house serves "special soup with meatballs and spinach" (Rs.40). Veg. and non-veg. Chinese and Continental dishes Rs.45-85.

Moti Mahal Restaurant, Netaji Subhash Marg (tel. 327 3611). Outdoor patio or chandeliered dining halls pleasantly serve renowned Indian, particularly tandoori cuisine. Live music (usually singing) begins nightly (Wed.-Mon.) at 8pm. Meaty menu, and most veg. items have cheese. Chicken entrees Rs.60-200. Mineral water Rs.30. Open daily 11am-1am.

Duke's Place, Village Bistro building, Hauz Khas Village. The manager lived in Atlanta, Georgia and came to love jazz—now the music plays here nightly at 8:30pm. Swing through chocolate mousse with brandy sauce, lasagna (Rs.110), or "here comes the fudge" (Rs.45). Whether or not Ellington made it to Delhi, he'd be duly amazed. Open daily 8am-midnight.

Village Bistro, Hauz Khas Village. A complete bazaar of restaurants to treat the South Delhi elite. **Le Café** has Continental fare, **Al Capone** sells the Al Capone Burger, a tasty mutton blob on 2 buttery buns (Rs.60), and **Mohalla** has great decor and spats of live Rajasthani music to accompany their Indian menu. Open daily 10am-11pm.

SIGHTS

Like any capital city worth its salt, Delhi boasts an endless number of things to see, and what you choose to do depends on your interest and on how much time you've got. There are 1376 monuments, two of which are UNESCO sites (Qutb Minar and Humayun's tomb). If you're spending only a couple of days in Delhi, budget your time wisely! The must-sees are the Qutb Minar Complex and Old Delhi—Lal Qila, Jama Masjid, and the bazaars. Round out your time by having a look at Rashtrapati Bhavan, Humayun's Tomb, and if you need respite from the midday heat, the National Museum. If you show up first thing in the morning, chances are you'll have the place to yourself. As always, men (and occasionally a woman or two) will linger by the entrance to the various tourist attractions, flashing ID cards (often bogus) and offering their services as guides. While such guides often don't have their facts straight, or parrot information written in English on signs, some guides are quite knowledgeable. If you hire a guide, be sure to set a price in advance; don't be shy about bargaining.

Several operations run **guided tours** of Delhi. These usually hit New Delhi in the morning, stopping at Jantar Mantar, the Lakshmi Narayan Temple, Humayun's Tomb, the Baha'i Temple, driving by the more notable landmarks (such as India Gate), and jaunting south of the city to Qutb Minar. Tours of Old Delhi might include the Red Fort, Raj Ghat, Shanti Vana, and a glimpse of Jama Masjid from a distance. These tours rush you through each sight, the guides are not always informed, and a full day of bus riding, even in plush A/C comfort, is never much of a joy, but these tours are helpful if you've only got a short time in Delhi. Book through ITDC, L-block, Connaught Place (tel. 332 0331), or at Ashok Travels, near Nirula's.

Old Delhi

Red Fort (Lal Qila)

Within a year of moving the capital from Agra to Delhi, the Mughal emperor Shah Jahan ordered the construction of a massive fort and palace complex at the east end of town, on the banks of the Yamuna River. Construction of the octagonal Red Fort began on April 16, 1639, and was completed nine years later, to the day, at a cost of over 10 million rupees. Soaring to a height of 33.5m on the town side, the red sandstone rampart walls that enclose the fort cover a perimeter of 2km and are surrounded by a moat into which the Yamuna once flowed. Some of the more resplendent features of the original fort have been lost—the famed Peacock Throne was snatched away in 1739, the precious stones that once adorned the palaces have all been removed, and the canals through which the "Stream of Paradise" once gurgled are now dry. But the Red Fort remains what it has always been—an incredible monument to the power of Mughal rule and the splendor of Mughal architecture, as awe-inspiring to the citizens then as it is to visitors today.

The entrance to the fort is located toward the middle of its west wall, through the muscular, three-story **Lahore Gate,** or Lahori Gate. Next to the gate is the spot from which the Prime Minister traditionally addresses cheering throngs on Independence Day. Moreover, it was from here that the Mughal emperors would leave the fort and head west toward Jama Masjid by way of Chandni Chowk, the most crowded street in Mughal Delhi. Each time the Mughals went from Lahore Gate to Jama Masjid, they hoped to drive home the message that their rule had the force of divine sanction. Lahore Gate leads to **Chatta Chowk,** the covered passageway filled with shops which today peddle souvenirs, but which during the Mughal era provided nobles with top-quality silks, precious jewelry, and fine velvets. Chatta Chowk gives way to the rectangular, three-storied **Naubat Khana** (Drum House); five times a day, music would be played from this building, in tribute to the emperor and his court. It was also here that visitors were asked to dismount and park their elephants, and where, it is said, two early 19th-century Mughal emperors were murdered. The floral-patterned carvings adorning the walls of Naubat Khana were once painted with gold.

Naubat Khana leads into the palace area. Across the mini-courtyard behind the simple, sturdy columns stands **Diwan-i-Am** (Hall of Public Audience). It was here that the early Mughal emperors sat (everyone else was made to stand) for two hours a day, receiving visitors, chatting informally with nobles, acting as judge and jury for criminal cases, and conducting affairs of state. Against the back (west) wall of the hall, the emperor sat perched on the throne, or "Seat of the Shadow of God." The throne rested atop the canopied white marble platform now on display. Note the deeply carved floral patterns on the canopy, which curves like a Bengali-style roof. Set to the back of the platform are a series of curious panels, each adorned with red and green renderings of flowers, birds, trees, and lions. Lording over the entire scene from the central panel is the Greek god Orpheus, playing his lute to the animals. Scholars speculate that the panels, which were returned to their rightful place from the British Museum in 1903, were crafted in Florence. The low marble platform just in front of the canopied throne platform was reserved for the prime minister, who would entertain complaints within earshot of the emperor.

Beyond Diwan-i-Am were the private palaces of the Mughal emperor. Of the original six palaces, five remain; each of the palaces was connected to its neighbor by the **Nahir-i-Bihisht** (Stream of Paradise), a water-filled canal. The palaces were set in spacious formal *charbagh* gardens, repeatedly redesigned through the centuries. The southernmost of the palaces (coming from Diwan-i-Am, the palace farthest to the right) is **Mumtaz Mahal** (Palace of Jewels), used during the Mughal period by the women of the harem, and during the last half of the 19th century as a British guard house. These days, Mumtaz Mahal houses a museum (see below). North of Mumtaz Mahal is **Rang Mahal** (Palace of Colors), a white marble pavilion divided by arches into six apartments, where the emperor took his meals. During the Mughal heyday, the ceilings were decorated with silver, and the large, lotus-shaped basin, designed to collect the waters of Nahir-i-Bihisht, was once outfitted with an ornate ivory fountain. The ceilings of the northernmost and southernmost apartments are embedded with small mirrors that reflected the light of the candles set out when the emperor had a late supper. These apartments are commonly called **Shish-Mahal** (Palace of Mirrors). Just north of Rang Mahal, **Khas-Mahal** (Private Palace) is a wonder of ostentation divided into three apartments, each lavishly decorated in silk during the Mughal era. The southernmost of these is **Baithak** (Sitting Room), with a scale of justice carved in marble upon the walls. The emperor caught his beauty sleep in the center apartment, known as **Khwabagh** (Sleeping Chamber). Attached to the outer wall of the Khwabagh is a tower called **Muthamman-Burj** (Octagonal Tower), where the emperor would greet his subjects massed below, or watch animal fights staged below for his pleasure. It was on this porch that King George V and Queen Mary sat before thousands of Delhi-ites in 1911, when a *durbar* was held and the announcement was made that the Imperial Capital would be moved to Delhi from Calcutta. North of the Khwabagh is **Tasbih-Khana** (Chamber for Telling Beads), where the emperor privately prayed.

Just north of Khas-Mahal is the **Diwan-i-Khas** (Hall of Private Audience), constructed entirely of white marble and replete with arches. Here, the emperor would make crucial political decisions, consult privately with advisers, and speak with select visitors. Seeking to rekindle the old spark, Bahadur Shah II, the last Mughal emperor, held court here during the Mutiny of 1857; in retaliation, the British tried him in the Diwan-i-Am, then exiled him to Burma. As Mughal power declined, so did the glory of the Hall of Private Audience. The precious stones once decorating its interior are gone, its silver ceiling was carted off by the Marathas (the current wooden ceiling was painted in 1911), and the **Peacock Throne** which sat atop the marble pedestal was plundered in 1739 by Nadir Shah, a Turkish raider whose ferocious troops defeated Persia and killed 30,000 Delhi residents. The throne was commissioned by Shah Jahan upon his becoming emperor; it was completed seven years later to meet the emperor's ostentatious specifications. The throne's feet were solid gold, its canopy inlaid with diamonds, gems, and pearls, and a parrot carved from a single emerald was nestled behind the emperor's head. It's not difficult to imagine what inspired the court poet Amir Khusrau to write the verses carved over the corner arches on the north and south walls: "If there be a paradise on earth, it is this, it is this, it is this." Just north is the **Hammam** (Bath), with marble floors decorated in floral patterns. The westmost apartment, used mainly for dressing, contained a rosewater fountain. The two chambers on either side of its entrance are thought to be where the emperor's children bathed. West of the Hammam is the **Moti-Masjid** (Pearl Mosque), a small, delicate mosque built in 1662 by Emperor Aurangzeb for his personal use. The black marble outlines on the floor facilitated placement of the *musallas* (prayer mats).

Inside the Red Fort complex are two **museums,** each open Sat.-Thurs. 10am-5pm. Housed in Mumtaz Mahal is the better of the two, displaying porcelains, textiles, astrolabes, calligraphy, *hookahs,* and weapons with informative explanations. A less spectacular museum covering the military developments of the last two centuries is in the Naubat Khana. Another interesting way to learn about the Red Fort, and Delhi's history, is to see the nightly sound and light show (see **Entertainment,** p. 146). Open daily from dawn to dusk; admission Rs.0.50.

Jama Masjid

Built between 1650 and 1656 by Emperor Shah Jahan, the imposing Jama Masjid, 1km west of the Red Fort, is the largest active mosque in India. Set on a high platform atop a low hill, Jama Masjid lords over the surrounding streets, its elegant combination of red sandstone and white marble demanding attention, its domed minarets soaring into the sky. The three large gateways to the Jama Masjid separate the secular and the sacred. The east gate was reserved for the Mughal emperor and his family; now it is open to all worshipers Fridays and holidays. Tourists should enter by the north gate. Leave your shoes, but first establish the price with the "shoe guard," as he tends to get carried away. The 900m-square courtyard packs in nearly 25,000 faithful worshipers during Friday prayers. As in most South Asian mosques, a *hauz* (waterfilled tank) is at the center of the courtyard for cleansing feet and hands before prayer. Each rectangle designates the space occupied by one praying Muslim. The lines along the east side of the *hauz* mark the prayer positions for those mourning the loss of loved ones. The symmetrical pattern used on all the mosque's arches, representing the lotus flower, is also common at the Red Fort. Click your feet on some of the stones towards the priest's platform—the hollow sound comes from a tunnel connecting the mosque to the Red Fort, built so that Shah Jahan could read prayers more efficiently. Prayers are sung out from the priest's platform, under the center arch at the westernmost point of the mosque; before the invention of amplification systems, the two small posts between this point and the east gate were used by other priests who repeated prayers so those sitting in the back could hear. Just to the west of the mosque is the priest's home; priests have lived here since the time of Shah Jahan, and it's still possible to spot them hanging out before prayers. (Open for tourists 30min. after dawn until 12:20pm (noon on Fri.), 1:45pm until 20min. before *azan,* the call for prayer, and again after prayers until 20min. before sunset. Admission Rs.5; camera fee Rs.10; *lungi* to wrap around bare legs Rs.5-10.) For an extra Rs.5 (Rs.10 with cameras), the more foolhardy can climb one of the minarets that rise from the courtyard. While those with a touch of vertigo will want to stay put, the

Old Delhi: Bazaar or Bizarre?

From Jama Masjid, it's easy to begin an exploration of the dynamic tangle of shops and street vendors that constitute the bazaars of Old Delhi. While the streets surrounding Jama Masjid are cluttered with overpriced tourist-trap crap, walk 200m north, south, or west and you'll be in a part of town rarely visited by tourists, where getting lost is half the fun. Area vendors peddle wholesale paper, high-quality tools, used car parts, and all sorts of other goodies. For **one of the stinkiest places in the universe,** head south from Jama Masjid on a sunny summer afternoon toward the poultry markets, where chickens stacked atop one another in painfully cramped cages are selected by customers and then slaughtered and butchered on the spot, much to the delight of the legions of flies who call the market home. Beware of pickpockets and don't be shy about bargaining.

Ducking into any of the narrow alleys between the shops on the south side of Chandni Chowk leads to another bazaar-o dream world; follow the labyrinthine "street" any which way and stumble upon the aromatic spice market, snag a deal on gems from the jewelers (if you know what you're doing), or float from shop to shop. Don't forget to peek into the mosques, schools, and friendly faces that line the way.

views of smoggy Delhi from up top are amazing. Women should keep an arm ready to fend off groping men in the stairwell.

Raj Ghat

On the west bank of the Yamuna River, 1km directly east of the Delhi Gate, and nearly 2km southeast of the Red Fort, a perpetually burning flame and a simple black slab set in a grassy courtyard, Raj Ghat offers somber memorial to Mahatma Gandhi, cremated at this spot after his 1948 assassination by a Hindu extremist. Gandhi's name is nowhere inscribed on the monument—the only inscription is of Gandhi's last words, "He Ram" ("Oh God"). Hundreds of visitors come each day to cast flower petals and contemplate. Just south of the monument is a park full of trees and flowers planted by numerous dignitaries: gladiolas from Eisenhower, a pine from Queen Elizabeth II, and a slanted tree planted by Nasser. North of Raj Ghat is **Shanti Vana,** an eerily reposeful park where recreational and "domestic" activities are forbidden. Jillions of squawking birds nest in the trees. Geologically significant rocks from throughout India are on display, alongside memorials to the men and women who have earned a place in India's pantheon of political heroes. The memorial to Rajiv Gandhi is enthusiastically admiring of the slain prime minister. The monument to Rajiv's older brother Sanjay was at one point taken down after critics reminded the government that this Gandhi never served in office or accomplished all that much. After the monument was removed, however, Sanjay's admirers still put flowers at the barren spot, until eventually the monument was reinstated. Meanwhile, the humble grassy mound that marks the life and death of Jawaharlal Nehru mentions only Nehru's wish to have his ashes thrown in the Ganga. (Open April-Sept. 5am-8pm, Oct-March 5:30am-7pm.)

Central New Delhi

Of the scores of buildings built by the British for the purposes of moving their capital from Calcutta to Delhi in 1911, **Rashtrapati Bhavan** (President's Residence) and **Sansad Bhavan** (Parliament House), are the most prominent and impressive. Both were designed by the renowned architect Edwin Lutyens, and their hulking grandeur—not-so-subtly hinting at the vast reserves of British wealth and power—was meant to communicate imperial intentions to keep India the jewel in the British Crown. The effort backfired—the aesthetic anomaly of European-style buildings in the heart of an Indian city only reminded Indian nationalists of the moral anomalies of imperial rule. The buildings became a lightning rod for criticism. In one memorable outburst, Gandhi described Sansad Bhavan and Rashtrapati Bhavan as "architectural piles." **Sansad Bhavan,** at the end of Sansad Marg, 1.5km southwest of Connaught Place, is a massive circular building that looks like an enormous flying saucer. Because India's Parliament, the Lok Sabha, meets in Sansad Bhavan (see **Government and Politics,** p. 94), getting near the building can be difficult. To look inside the gates, you'll need a letter of introduction from your embassy, which can take time. To reach **Rashtrapati Bhavan,** head left from the entrance to Parliament and bear right at the statue of Govind Ballabah Pant. Alternatively, walk due west from India Gate down Rajpath. Once the residence of the Viceroy, the pink Rashtrapati Bhavan is now the home of India's president. Though the residence and the *faux-charbagh* gardens are ensconced behind iron gates and are strictly off-limits to tourists, it's worth climbing the **Raisina Hill** for a closer look. Note the sturdy pillars, massive copper dome, and Mughal-style kiosks (*chhattris*). The 145-m pillar between the gate and the residence was donated by the Maharaja of Jaipur and is called, reasonably enough, the **Jaipur Column.** The pillar is capped with a bronze lotus and a six-pointed star, which was then the shape of the Star of India. (Today's Star has five points.)

Flanking Raisina Hill on its north and south sides are the symmetrical **Secretariats,** which now house important government ministries. The buildings are adorned with a variety of imperialism-justifying slogans—the doozy over door number three reads: "Liberty will not descend to a people: a people must raise themselves to liberty. It is a blessing which must be earned before it can be enjoyed." For some shade, pass under the slogan and into the Great Hall, an airy room adorned with decorative medallions and crowned with a soaring baroque dome. Try to visit Raisina Hill on a Saturday, when troops parade with precision in front of Rashtrapati Bhavan (9:30-10am).

Looking east from the Secretariats, the arch in the distance is **India Gate,** a memorial to Indian soldiers killed during World War I and the Afghan War of 1919. Another memorial underneath the arch commemorates the men and women who were killed in the 1971 war with Pakistan. The wide thoroughfare connecting India Gate with Raisina Hill is **Rajpath,** which gets quite crowded on Sundays, when children frolic in the fountains, and on Republic Day, when it is the scene of a massive martial parade.

Jantar Mantar, on Sansad Marg, 750m southwest of Connaught Place, feels like an M.C. Escher lithograph rendered as a red-and-white stone diorama, its railless stairs lilting around tight bends and soaring upward towards the heavens, a hallucinogenic dream sprung to life. The name of the game at Jantar Mantar is not madness, however, but precision. Charged by the Mughal emperor Muhammad Shah with the task of revising the Indian calendar to accord with the knowledge of modern astronomy, Maharaja Jai Singh of Jaipur built Jantar Mantar in 1725 after studying both European and Asian science and spending years observing the skies above Delhi. The resulting creation is as scientifically impressive as it is visually striking: Jantar Mantar's massive sundials and instruments accurately tell time (in Delhi, London, and elsewhere), predict eclipses, and chart the movement of the stars. The **Bharion Mandir,** just to the south, is a lush yard with giant wooden elephants in it. This is where astronomical observers came to pray before digging their noses in the stars. (Open daily sunrise-sunset; admission Rs.0.50.)

Built in 1753-54 for the prime minister to the Mughal emperor Muhammad Shah, **Safdarjang's Tomb,** located at the end of Lodi Rd., is the last great piece of Mughal architecture in Delhi. With the decline of Mughal fortunes in the 18th century came the decline of Mughal architecture. Built at the center of expansive *charbagh* gardens, the domed, lanky edifice was constructed of marble and red sandstone snatched from another local tomb. (Open dawn-dusk; admission Rs.0.50.)

While the sign at the entrance is a bit worrisome—"shooting," it turns out, "is forbidden in the park"—the leafy glories of the **Lodi Gardens** are expertly maintained, and there are comfy stone benches. A wide variety of trees and birds make their home here—spread around a handful of crushed "Magic Masala" potato chips and you're likely to attract hordes of fluorescent green, hyper-aggressive urban parrots. Along with splendid scenery, the gardens boast a jogging trail (crowded on weekends with middle-class masochists), and a steamy greenhouse. A few ruined buildings, scattered throughout the garden, rise from the closely cropped grass. Towards the garden's center is the late 15th-century **Bara-Gumbad,** a square tomb made of gray, red, and black stones, topped with a massive dome. Scholars have been unable to determine who is buried here. Attached to the tomb is a mosque, built in 1494, whose interior is notable for its dense floral patterns and Qur'anic inscriptions. The square tomb just north of Bara-Gumbad is the early 16th-century **Shish-Gumbad** (Glazed Dome), decorated with the remnants of blue tiles that once completely covered it. Because the *mihrab* (arch) in its western wall was used as a mosque, Shish-Gumbad was built without an attached prayer hall. Nearly 200m north of Shish-Gumbad is the badly weathered **Sikandar Lodi's Tomb** (1517-18). For views of the park, climb atop the walls that enclose the tomb. Also in the Lodi Gardens, 200m southwest of Bara-Gumbad, is **Muhammad Shah's Tomb,** a high-domed octagonal building constructed in the mid-15th century, and 75m east of Sikandar Lodi's Tomb is a 16th-century bridge with seven arches.

At the Central Bureau of Investigation, in Block 4 of the massive CGO complex, Lodi Rd. (tel. 436 0334), is the **National Police Museum.** Everyone knows that some pretty gruesome stuff goes down in India, but rarely do visitors get to see the gore up close and personal. At this simple, one-room exhibition, crime-solving techniques and bloody crime pictures are presented in their full gory glory. Learn of murderers who sought shelter in Paharganj. See smugglers' and counterfeiters' tools, bad-ass weapons such as the steel-claw, and try not to stare too long at photos of "putrefied dead bodies with stab wounds." You won't learn all that much about the Indian police, but it's bloody fun. (Open Mon.-Fri. 10am-5:50pm; free.)

From underneath the India Gate, walk east to the edge of the grass, bearing slightly to the right. The tan-and-red building enclosed by a gate is Jaipur House, in which the **National Gallery of Modern Art** is located. Buses #621 and #622 stop at Jaipur House. Once the Delhi home of the Maharaja of Jaipur, the National Gallery (tel. 338 2835) is now home to a culturally enlightening collection of art produced in India over the last 150 years. The highlights of the collection are the paintings produced by artists associated with the turn-of-the-century Bengal School, which was inspired by South Asian folk art and East Asian high art. For excellent examples, see Abanindranath Tagore's searching water colors, Nandalal Bose's small, sensitive paintings, and landscapes by the poet Rabindranath Tagore. Other highlights include Kunhi Raman's cubist-influenced concrete sculpture "Standing Figure" and two 1986 masterpieces by Kapor Wasim that sardonically depict a society withering into bleakness. (Open Tues.-Sun. 10am-5pm; free.)

On Janpath, just south of Rajpath, is the **National Museum** (tel. 301 9538). The museum's mission to provide an overview of Indian life and culture from prehistoric times to the present, is ambitious, and the museum by and large accomplishes its aim. Ground-floor galleries showcase some of the museum's most crowd-pleasing items. The decorative arts gallery displays small and graceful copper vessels as well as several wondrous wooden pieces, including a massive 18th-century South Indian ornamented door. Displays elsewhere on the ground floor trace the international development of Indian scripts, iconography, and coins over the past 16 centuries. (To see the actual coins, head up to the second floor.) An air-conditioned, room-sized vault is the setting for the museum's jewelry collection. Highlights include gaudy gilded earrings, necklaces, and bracelets dating from the first century AD, a 19th-century Rajasthani pen stand in the shape of a boat, and a chariot pieced together in the 20th century. A gallery focusing on bronze sculptures features a wealth of pieces from South India's Chola period. Another first-rate ground-floor gallery hosts beautiful South Asian paintings, the most striking of which are from Tibet, Nepal, and Rajasthan. Also on display on the ground floor is a good-sized collection of Neolithic stone tools (3000-1500 BC), which resemble plain old stones more than anything else. The first floor offers a small but enjoyable gallery of India's "maritime heritage" with a decidedly modern flavor. Also on the first floor is a collection of Mughal and Rajasthani miniature paintings, and an array of folios and manuscripts. On the second floor, the weapons and armor exhibit includes a colorful, brass-reinforced Rajasthani vest, an 18th-century bejeweled rhino-hide shield of Maharana Sangram Singh II, and the torturously curved and serrated weapons of the Pahari. More pacific pleasures can be found among the galleries of colorful masks and clothing associated with the tribal peoples of the northeastern states. The top-notch collection of musical instruments in the Sharan Rani Gallery, donated in 1980 by the renowned sarod player Sharan Rani, has unusual breadth, displaying handcrafted Indian instruments such as sarangis and sitars, as well as clarinets and trombones made in London in the 19th century. (Open Tues.-Sun. 10am-5pm. Film shows: Tues.-Fri. 11:30am, 2:30 and 4pm, Sat.-Sun. 10:30, 11:30am, 12:30, 2:30, and 4pm. Guided tours begin at enquiry counter: 10:30, 11:30am, noon, 2, and 3:30pm. Admission Rs.0.50, students free; camera fee Rs.2.)

On Mandir Marg, 2km west of Connaught Place, is the **Lakshmi Narayan Temple (Birla Mandir).** Built in honor of Lakshmi, the goddess of material well-being, in the middle decades of this century, and funded by the wealthy Birla family, Birla Mandir is a marvel of neo-Orissan temple architecture. A Chinese Buddhist Brethren Bell and Japanese Drum were donated to the temple as measures of goodwill. The room of mirrors at the back of the temple allows you to see yourself together with the infinite reflections of the Krishna statue in the middle. The surrounding gardens delight children (and the young at heart) with ping-pong tables, a brightly colored fountain in the shape of cobras, slick-slides, gaily painted stone sculptures of tigers and elephants that welcome "riders," a plaster cave entered through a gaping lion's mouth, and a sweaty gym where burly boys build bodies by Birla. In sobering contrast, the men in khaki shirts labeled "L.N. Temple" make their living keeping out the dusty children who beg on the sidewalk outside the temple.

You can obtain a pass to the **National Philatelic Museum** (tel. 303 2481) at the reception office in the ground-level parking garage at the oversized post office on Sansad Marg. Only confirmed philatelic phanatics will find much of interest in this tiny museum. Highlights include India's first machine-made multi-color stamps, and stamps issued in 1947 to commemorate Indian Independence. Of the recent series on display, yoga (1991) and vintage locomotives (1993) are particularly striking; also see the older series on South Asian dance (1975). (Open Mon.-Fri. 9am-4pm; free.)

In Chanakyapuri, near Nyaya Marg and Shantipath, is the **National Rail Museum** (tel. 601816). Portions of the museum function as an outdoor retirement home for locomotives and sleeper cars. The first-class passenger compartments in the older trains are swish-city, especially when compared to their counterparts in modern trains. The *Fairy Queen,* the "oldest preserved steam locomotion in India," is here on display. The indoor museum has some basic interactive models, a history of the railways, and even a multi-media computer display (Rs.5 per 10-min. turn). Even if you're less than locomotive about trains, come take a ride on the "Joy Train," a miniature kiddie-train with a psychedelic locomotor and wild orange Mirinda cars chugging along behind. (Adults Rs.5, but there must be 10 people to go. Buy 10 tickets to ride alone!). There's also a semi-functional monorail and a whistle section. (Open Tues.-Sun. 9:30am-7:30pm; last joy ride 6:05pm; admission Rs.5; camera fee Rs.10.)

On Teen Murti Rd., north of Chanakyapuri near the intersection with Murti Marg, is **Teen Murti Bhavan,** containing the **Nehru Memorial Museum and Library.** Built inside the home of Jawaharlal Nehru, India's first prime minister, the museum reveals as much about the Independence movement as a whole as it does about Nehru. Between voyeuristic peeks into Nehru's study, office, and bathroom, check out the pictures of Nehru as dour youth (with equally somber-looking relatives), as ambitious student at Harrow and Cambridge, and as humble, generous leader of India. Newspaper clippings and photographs lead through the turmoil of India's long struggle for self-rule. (Open Tues.-Sun. 9:30am-4:45pm.)

Adjacent to the Teen Murti Bhavan is the **Nehru Planetarium** with showings of "Our Cosmic Heritage" or current shows, Tues.-Sun. at 11:30am and 3pm (Rs.5). There is a small exhibition hall inside the planetarium (Rs.1), and whoever can figure out the "human sundial" out front wins the big, big prize.

The **Crafts Museum** is at Pragati Bhawan, Mathura Rd. (tel. 337 1641, 337 1887), 700m north of Purana Qila. Enter near the India Trade Promotion Organization sign. Built in 1991, the mid-sized Crafts Museum is one of the finest in South Asia, and not everything here is stuck in glass cases. The museum is divided into three sections.

Entering the museum, you'll pass through an open-air demonstration area where craftspeople wield their art, casting metal for sculptures, stringing jewelry, and making baskets from straw. Also outdoors is a village housing complex, filled with life-sized reproductions of rural huts and houses, built by craftspeople brought to Delhi from their native regions. Especially interesting is the vibrantly painted Orissan Gadaha Hut, and a spare construction associated with Nagaland's Konyak tribe, where boys are schooled in preparation for life in the community. Inside, displays spotlight the mind-bending diversity of traditional Indian crafts, including 18th-century wood carvings from Karnataka, dazzling storytellers' paintings, and a brightly decorated model of a Bihari wedding chamber. (Open daily 9:30am-5pm.)

Just off Mathura Rd., 1km east of India Gate, the **Purana Qila (Old Fort)** is a giant "X" for archeologists, marking a spot continuously inhabited since the Mauryan period (324-184 BC). Treasure troves of artifacts have been unearthed here, including a gold-plated coin adorned with an archer dating from the Gupta period, and a piece of 15th-century porcelain with a "made in the great Ming Dynasty" inscribed in Chinese. But none of these early finds were as important as the discovery of shards of Painted Gray Ware, which were dated to c. 1000 BC. This type of shard had been discovered at locations associated with the great Hindu epic the *Mahabharata*—their discovery at Purana Qila seems to have vindicated bearers of local tradition, who have long contended that the fort was built atop the site of Indraprastha, the capital city of the heroes of the *Mahabharata*, the Pandavas. There's never been much doubt as to the 16th-century role of Purana Qila—the massive walls, finely preserved mosque, and ruined library that formed the centerpiece of Humayun's (and later Sher Shah's) Delhi are still standing for all to see. Built in 1541 by Sher Shah, **Qila-i-Kuhna Masjid** (Mosque of the Old Fort) is a wonderfully ornate tangle of calligraphic inscriptions and red sandstone. Less impressive (and less intact) is the **Sher Mandal**, which Humayun used as a library and observatory after snatching Purana Qila from Sher Shah. Aside from sightseeing, there's not much to do at Purana Qila but stroll about the expansive grounds, trying to avoid eye contact with the frolicsome couples attempting inconspicuous business or pleasure on the grass. A small, free, museum on the premises showcases some of the artifacts discovered in and around Purana Qila. The Shunga period (184-72 BC) plaques are particularly good. To get a good sense of the incredible height of the fort's walls, walk the **exercise trail,** which begins just left of the entrance to Purana Qila. The trail winds pleasantly around a small **lake** (dry during the summer) well-stocked with boats for rent. As you stroll, stop for a bit of fitness—the ominous blue pole labeled "spinal exercise" should provide hours of family fun. (Open daily dawn-dusk; admission Rs.0.50.)

Next to Purana Qila is the wheelchair-accessible **National Zoologic Park.** On sunny summer Sundays, the expansive zoo teems with dozens of delighted Delhi denizens (most of them children), though the animals have less frolicsome fun than the kids. While in the park, be sure to check out the three much-raved-about white tigers; there are only 105 such tigers in captivity in the world's zoos. The zoo's carefully labeled trees offer little shade, so bring extra sunblock. (Open Sat.-Thurs. 9:30am-4:30pm; admission Rs.3.)

South Delhi

At the intersection of Aurobindo Marg and Mehrauli Badarpur Rd., 14km southwest of Connaught Place (take bus #505 from Ajmeri Gate), is the **Qutb Minar Complex.** Though located in a part of Delhi speckled with crumbling mosques and decaying ramparts, the ruins of the Qutb Minar complex know no rivals. The construction of the complex began in 1199 after the Turkish ex-slave Qutb-ud-din Aibak swept into North India and defeated the Rajputs. Qutb-ud-din Aibak installed himself at Lal Kot, the site of an old Rajput city, and when his boss, Muhammad Ghuri, was murdered in 1206, he founded the Delhi Sultanate, India's first Muslim kingdom. The events that led to the building of the complex were epoch-making, and the Qutb Minar serves as a 72.5-m-high exclamation point.

Qutb-ud-din Aibak began constructing the stunning red sandstone **Qutb Minar** as a celebration of his triumphs in North India and as a milestone marking the eastern frontier of the Muslim world. As one of the tower's inscriptions notes, "the tower was erected to cast the shadow of God over both East and West." Modeled on the brick victory towers of Central Asia, the Qutb Minar also served as the minaret for the Quwwat-ul-Islam Masjid (see below). Before dying, Qutb-ud-din Aibak was able to complete only the first three stories of the tower. His son-in-law Iltutmish added a fourth story, and Firoz Shah Tughluq tacked on a fifth after repairing damage caused by a 1368 lightning strike. The fifth-story cupola erected by Firoz was felled by an 1803 earthquake and was replaced by a British Major, Robert Smith; Smith's Mughal-style cupola now sits in the gardens, having been removed from the Qutb Minar because it seemed so awkward. Visitors have been forbidden from climbing the minaret since 1981, when more than 30 panicked schoolchildren were trampled to death during a power outage. While most of the calligraphy carved on the minaret is of passages from the Qur'an rendered in Arabic, a few Devanagari inscriptions prove that at least some Indian craftsmen had a role in the building's construction.

Just north of Qutb Minar is the **Quwwat-ul-Islam Masjid** (Might of Islam Mosque), which is the oldest extant mosque in India aside from those in western Gujarat. Begun in 1192 and completed in 1198 (extensions were added over the next two centuries), the mosque was built from the remains of 21 Hindu and Jain temples destroyed by the fanatically iconoclastic Qutb-ud-din Aibak (according to the inscription over the main entrance). The pillars from the razed temples support the east end of the mosque; note the carvings of bells, lotuses, and other Hindu and Jain remnants. At the center of the courtyard is the 98% pure iron **Gupta Pillar.** According to the Sanskrit inscription, the pillar was erected in honor of Vishnu and in memory of Chandra, believed to be the Gupta emperor Chandragupta II (r. 375-415 AD). Tradition holds that Anangpal, the founder of Lal Kot, brought the pillar to the area. It is said that anyone who can wrap their hands around the pillar behind their back will be blessed with good luck.

Just south of Qutb Minar is the domed red sandstone **Ala'i Darwaza,** built in 1311, to serve as the southern entrance to the mosque. Praised for its well-proportioned balance, the building also boasts India's first true arches. Just east of Ala'i Darwaza, the domed octagonal tomb with the *jali* decorative screens holds **Imam Zamin,** a Sufi saint who came to India from Central Asia early in the 16th century.

North of the Quwwat-ul-Islam Masjid is a massive, unfinished minaret, **Ala'i Minar.** Expansion had doubled the size of the mosque, and Ala'i Minar was to be twice as tall as Qutb Minar in order to be proportional. After its first 24.5-m-high story was completed, construction was stopped and the wildly ambitious minaret was abandoned. Just south of Ala'i Minar is the **Tomb of Iltutmish,** which the sultan erected himself in 1235, four years after building a tomb 8km from Qutb Minar for his son. While Iltutmish's red sandstone tomb isn't particularly interesting from the outside, have a look at the artfully decorated interior, with its mingling of Hindu and Jain themes (wheels, lotuses, and bells) and Muslim motifs (calligraphic inscriptions, geometric patterns, and the Mecca-facing alcoves built into the west wall). Directly south of Iltutmish's tomb are the ruins of a *madrasa,* an institution of Islamic learning. In keeping with Seljuk Turkish traditions, the tomb of the madrasa's founder, Ala-ud-din Khalji, has been placed within it; look for the L-shaped mound of earth and rubble. (Open daily dawn-dusk; admission Rs.5.)

Atop a lonely, rocky outcrop on the Mehrauli Badarpur Rd., 9km due east of the Qutb Minar Complex and 16km southeast of Connaught Place, is **Tughluqabad,** built as a fortified city by Ghiyas-ud-din Tughluq, who ruled the Delhi Sultanate between 1321 and 1325. These days, the abandoned fort has been invaded and conquered by weeds, aggressive monkeys, and a palpable sense of desolation. If you come, have a close look at the absolutely massive 10-15m-high rubble walls that run along the 6.5-km circumference of the fort. Thirteen separate gates lead through the walls, which are topped with husky stone battlements. The **Tomb of Ghiyas-ud-din Tughluq,** a red sandstone and white marble affair, employs the first set of sloping walls to grace a Muslim-made building in India. Shortly after Ghiyas-ud-din Tughluq was murdered in 1325, Tughluqabad was abandoned, having been occupied for a grand total of five years.

Just east of the Lodi-Mathura intersection, 2km south of Purana Qila, **Humayun's Tomb** is a husky structure of red sandstone and white-and-black marble. Set amid carefully laid-out gardens and rows of palm trees, the domed tomb possesses both a blunt beauty and a serene grandeur. A bellicose drug addict, Humayun was the second Mughal emperor, ruling from 1530 until he was vanquished by Sher Shah in 1540, and again from 1555 until his death in 1556. Humayun's death had all the unimpeachable trappings of piety and scholarship: walking down the stairs of his library, Humayun heard the *azan* and quickly sat himself down on the nearest step; upon rising, the emperor tripped and slid down the stairs. The injuries incurred in his fall proved fatal, and in 1565, nine years after his death, Humayun's eldest widow, Bega Begam (Haji Begam), began directing the construction of his tomb. In later years, many prominent Mughals were buried at Humayun's Tomb, including Bega Begam herself and Bahadur Shah II, the last of the Mughal emperors, who was captured here by the British during the Mutiny of 1857. Humayun's Tomb is located at the center of a squarish, quartered garden laced with channels and paths *(charbagh),* a type of garden whose development reached its apex with the building of the Taj Mahal. A pioneering work of Mughal architecture, the tomb itself is built in the shape of an octagon and is situated atop a massive pedestal; the tomb's double dome rises to a height of nearly 40m and is home to hordes of squealing bats, birds, and swarms of summertime bees. The high arches, porches, and stone screens would all become important features of Mughal tombs. Southeast of Humayun's tomb stands a square, double-domed tomb commonly called **Barber's Tomb.** While the inside of the tomb has offered a few clues—Qur'anic inscriptions, two graves, and the number 999 (which may be an Islamic date, equivalent to 1590-91 AD)—no one knows who is buried here. Outside the walls that surround Humayun's Tomb and Barber's Tomb is **Nila-Gumbad** (Blue Dome), an octagonal tomb whose dome is covered in blue tiles. While some archeologists contend that it was built in 1625 by a Mughal nobleman for a devoted servant, others have pointed to Nila-Gumbad's lack of a double dome and its slender, elongated neck as evidence that this tomb was built even before Humayun's. (Open dawn-dusk; admission Rs.0.50; video camera fee Rs.25.)

Four kilometers north of Tughluqabad is the **Baha'i Temple.** Over the past three decades, members of the Baha'i faith have donated millions of dollars toward the construction of seven Baha'i Temples in international locations such as Uganda, Samoa, and the midwestern United States. The latest addition to this series of temples was built between 1980 and 1986 and is situated in South Delhi on a 26-acre expanse of closely cropped grass and elegant pools. The temple, which inevitably draws comparisons to the Sydney Opera House, is built from shimmering white marble in the dome-like shape of an opening lotus flower. Silence is requested of visitors; there's little to do but settle comfortably onto one of the wood-backed benches, listen to the dull thudding of bare feet, and gaze up at the clean lines of the temple's splendid dome, which soars overhead to a height of 34m. The view from above is even more stunning. (Open April-Sept. Tues.-Sun. 9am-7pm; Oct.-March 9:30am-5:30pm; free.)

ENTERTAINMENT

As one might expect in a city with so many politicians and diplomats, there's not much nightlife in Delhi. A traveler's best bet for a break from the nightly rooftop rounds at Paharganj is to check out the weekend edition of a daily paper (p. 2 or 3), *The Delhi Times,* or the weekly *Delhi Diary* (Rs.7.50), with all sorts of tourist tips, including up-to-date listings of discos and upcoming cultural events. **Dances of India** is a nightly performance of Indian dance and music, including Kathak and Manipuri (nightly at 7pm, in Parsi, Anjuman Hall, opposite Ambedkar Football Stadium, Delhi Gate; tel. 331 7831, 332 0968). For **disco dancing** Delhi-style, moneyed Delhi-ites head to the five-star hotels, to Xcess in Vasant Vihar's C-block, or to the Village Bistro in Hauz Khas village (see **Food,** p. 134). Discos far enough out of the city to be in Haryana are subject to prohibition. There are several **movie theaters** in Delhi, which show Hindi movies, racier A-rated movies (which count as porn, but which have as much sex as something like *Basic Instinct*), and some English movie theaters, especially out in suburban South Delhi (admission Rs.40; looks like a multiplex in the United States, only walls of potato chips). Check daily papers for movie listings.

The Red Fort's nightly **Sound and Light Show** is unexpectedly entertaining. The fort is surreal at night, the silhouetted sitting halls and mosques invoking the voices of past rulers. The Sound and Light Show conveniently provides those voices for you, along with sound bites of court music, psychedelic, quadrophonic laughter effects, and some charming dialogue to convey the fort's history. And the lights? Well, a Pink Floyd concert it's not, but the buildings are, in fact, lit up in turn, even with colors, and it's as good a history lesson as you're likely to get anywhere else in Delhi. (English shows Feb.-April 8:30-9:30pm, May-Aug. 9-10pm, Sept.-Oct. 8:30-9:30pm, Nov.-Jan. 7:30-8:30pm. Admission Rs.10/20. Go for the cheap seats—they're just as good, despite what the ticket guy says.)

SHOPPING

Connaught Place is divided into blocks labeled A-N by seven **radial roads,** each of which is home to booths peddling small curio items, souvenirs, and cold drinks. While prices are better at the Palika Bazaar (located beneath the grassy knoll nestled between Radial Rd. 1 and 8), the bazaars of Old Delhi, or even the markets of South Delhi, the radial roads' stores offer good variety. If you're ready for some bargaining, they offer fairly good value as well. Follow the hordes of Western tourists south along **Radial Road 8,** which becomes **Janpath,** and leads toward the cheapest souvenir shops, government tourist offices, and the **Central Cottage Industries Emporium** (Jawahar Vyapar Bhavan, Janpath (tel. 331 2373)). The Emporium has pricey furniture, clothes, and high-quality knick-knacks from all over India—a good place to stop for gifts en route to the airport. (Open Mon.-Sat. 10am-7pm.) Across the way is a good **Tibetan Market,** priced for tourists but with a wide variety of Kashmiri crafts, *chillums,* jewelry, etc., as well as light-weight travel clothes. **Old Delhi** carries it all, starting on **Chandni Chowk** (where sari salesmen pull you into various shops "just for looking") and winding into the maze of alleys off to the sides. **Bina Musical Stores,** 781 Nai Sarak (tel. 326 3595), has several tablas and sitars, as does A. Godin and Co. on Sansad Marg, though the latter is a bit overpriced. **Hauz Khas** has several boutiques and shops with exotically un-Indian names like "Passion Wagon," "Vibrations," and "Allure Lingerie."

Uttar Pradesh

Uttar Pradesh, the "Northern State," is India's true heartland, filled with the landscapes that form many people's image of India: parched plains of wheat and rice, springing to life at the coming of the monsoon, it is the country where the mother-river Ganga descends from the mountains to join her sister the Yamuna in cutting across the earth. Uttar Pradesh, which has been called "U.P." for short ever since the British carved it out as the United Provinces, is India's most populous state, with 138 million residents in all. U.P. has been the cradle of Indian civilization from the time of the Aryan chieftains to the reigns of the great Mughal emperors, giving India the *Ramayana,* the Hindi language, and since Independence, eight of its 12 prime ministers. But many of India's most terrible conflicts have grown out of U.P. as well. In 1992 the state's BJP government encouraged the destruction of the Babri Masjid in Ayodhya, leading to thousands of deaths in communal riots across India. The state remains a flashpoint for Hindu-Muslim tensions. Radical affirmative action politics for Dalits (former untouchables) also have a strong base in U.P. The eastern half of U.P. is

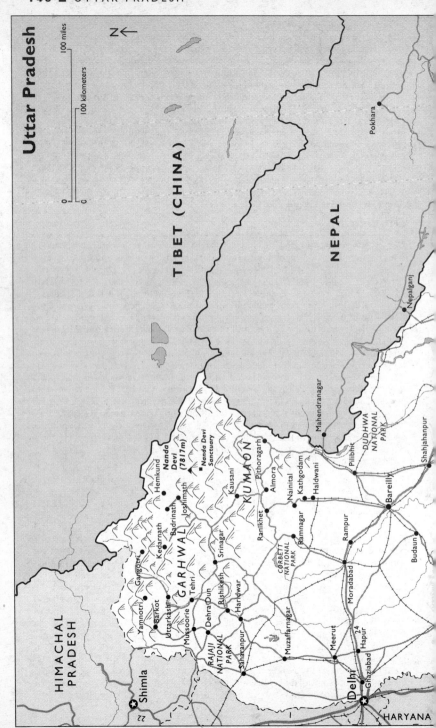

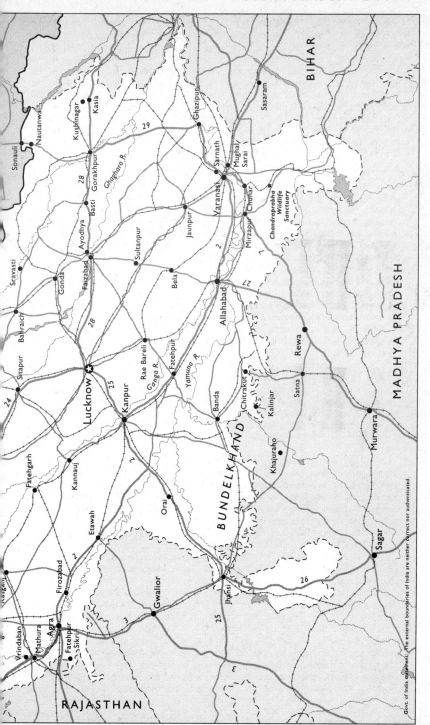

one of India's most economically depressed areas, while western U.P. has shared in the prosperity of neighboring Delhi. U.P. has a wealth of tourist attractions, from the Hindu holy city of Varanasi to the hill stations and pilgrimage centers of the Himalaya, and, of course, the Mughal capital of Agra with its Taj Mahal. Few people visit India without going to U.P., and yet the state could comfortably accommodate more visitors. The path to many of its interesting places, such as the old Muslim city of Lucknow, or the sacred cities of Ayodhya and Mathura, has yet to be beaten hard, and many visitors remain unaware of U.P.'s present condition while steeping themselves in its glorious past.

GARHWAL AND KUMAON

The neighboring northern regions of Garhwal and Kumaon, filled with 7000m peaks and towering *deodar* forests, have little in common with the lowland regions of Uttar Pradesh. The best way to see Garhwal and Kumaon is probably to trek—starting from just about any road, one can hike up through dense forests to small villages and then follow a cattle trail to the *bugyals* (meadows above the treeline). This land of numerous lakes and rivers (the sources of both the Ganga and the Yamuna are in Garhwal) also has a rich cultural history. The mountains have kept these areas relatively inaccessible for thousands of years, enabling many local customs to survive; they have also fascinated Hindu thinkers for millennia, and many Hindu myths are supposed to have taken place here. In the 9th century AD the South Indian saint Shankara came to Garhwal, bringing the local population into the Hindu fold and establishing several important temples. Now the mountains are also the sacred destination of thousands of Hindu pilgrims every year who come from across India to places such as Badrinath. The most amazing thing about this region is the curious mixture of faith and fitness it seems to demand.

In the early 19th century, Garhwal and Kumaon were overrun by the Nepali commander Amar Singh Thapa. In 1816 these areas (apart from Tehri, which remained a princely state) passed under British control, and were later made part of the United Provinces. Recently, many Garhwalis and Kumaonis have agitated for a separate state within India to be called Uttarakhand ("Land of the North"). In 1994 several protesters in the hill station of Mussoorie were shot by police. In 1996 the region appeared to be calm, as its demands for statehood began to be recognized by the central government.

Travel in the mountainous parts of Garhwal and Kumaon is difficult. Some areas, including the major pilgrimage sites, are only open between May and November. Travelers must be flexible and stoic. Buses must pass along winding roads that drive even locals to vomiting, roads get blocked by landslides, and vehicles frequently break down. Little English is spoken. On the other hand, these are some of the gentlest regions of India for women travelers—people care far less about what women wear—although standard precautions should still be followed. The hill stations of Garhwal and Kumaon, such as Mussoorie and Nainital, are also cool oases of laid-back attitude—the only problem travelers might anticipate here is a tourist season that peaks out of sync with that of the plains. There are crowds and clouds in the summer, discounts and chills in the winter

The temple towns of Yamnotri, Gangotri, Kedarnath, and Badrinath form an important quartet of pilgrimage sites. Until the 1960s, these could only be reached by foot from the plains, but the building of roads has now made them accessible to package-tour pilgrims on buses from Rishikesh. Due to the religious importance of many towns, visitors should note that no meat is available, and sometimes eggs and even onions are not allowed. Accommodations are provided at *dharamshalas* as well as the hotels of the Garhwal Mandal Vikas Nigam (GMVN), a hilly subsidiary of U.P. Tourism. GMVN hotels are reliable and clean but expensive, and they must be booked about a month in advance. The towns themselves, packed full of pilgrims, are primarily of interest to those serious about Hinduism, but many of them are also good bases for exploring the natural wonders around.

■ Dehra Dun

That Dehra Dun has two bus stands—one for Delhi, one for Mussoorie—reveals much about the town's polarized character. On the one hand, the city clearly strives for the capital's modernity, with fuming auto-rickshaws racing past rows of shops filled with English books, saris, and car parts. Dehra Dun is the training ground for much of India's elite, who come to learn at the Indian Military Academy, at the ultra-prestigious Doon School, or as students of nature at the megalithic Indian Forest Research Institute. As the terminus of the Northern Railway, Dehra Dun has one eye oriented toward its older brother to the southwest.

But there is also a gentler side to Dehra Dun, with its heart in the laid-back, life-loving ways of the nearby mountains. For as much as the buses race and the auto-rickshaws clamor for room, their drivers do it with a smile. Most travelers to the city are less torn, as most use Dehra Dun as a one- or two-day stopover before going to the Siwaliks, the Himalayan foothills to the north, and the hill station of Mussoorie, whose lights are visible from Dehra Dun at night. There is enough to keep a visitor occupied here, including temples, parks, and sulphur springs, but in the end there's too much "city" and not enough "town" to hold Dehra Dun's denizens down.

ORIENTATION

Understanding the three main areas in Dehra Dun helps drastically with orientation. The first area, around the **railway station,** is to the south; the **Mussoorie Bus Stand** is right next to this station, while the **Delhi Bus Stand** (servicing most destinations *not* in the immediate hills, including, more often than not, Nainital) lies a 5-minute walk away north along **Gandhi Road** (a major thoroughfare), just past the hard-to-miss, peach-colored **Hotel Drona.** Following Gandhi Rd. north feeds you into the **central area,** which lies around the tall **clock tower.** Gandhi Park, north of the clock tower, is litter-strewn, but still pretty and peaceful. The City Bus Stand is just north of the clock tower along **Rajpur Road,** where many services, high-end hotels, and restaurants lie. This strip is referred to as **Astley Hall** or Dilaram Bazaar farther north. The vast web of market streets just south of the clock tower is known as **Paltan Bazaar;** the part of the bazaar nearest to the railway station is known as **Darshani Gate.**

PRACTICAL INFORMATION

Tourist Office: U.P. Tourist Office (tel. 653217), in Hotel Drona, next to the Delhi Bus Stand. This is the most helpful tourist office in town, providing a rough map of the city and tips about nearby sights in Dehra Dun and elsewhere in Uttar Pradesh. Open daily 8am-8pm in season; otherwise 10am-5pm. For trekking tips and other information about the Garhwal region, try the **GMVN Headquarters** (tel. 656817, 654408), out on Rajpur Rd. across from Hotel Madhuban. Open Mon.-Sat. 10am-5pm.

Trekking Agency: Various private agents, such as **Trek Himalaya** (tel. 653005) or **Garhwal Tours and Trekking,** in Rohini Plaza near Hotel Ambassador, can help with planning treks.

Currency Exchange: State Bank of India, (tel. 657425) with main office on Rajpur Rd. at Rohini Plaza in Hotel Ambassador, but there are a few branches throughout the town. Changes traveler's checks and foreign currency. **Bank of India** (tel. 657375), next door, does so less frequently. Both banks open Mon.-Fri. 10am-2pm, Sat. 10am-noon.

Telephones: STD/ISD booths are ubiquitous. All 5-digit numbers in Dehra Dun beginning with 2 have now become 6-digit numbers beginning with 65.

Trains: As terminus of the **Northern Railway,** Dehra Dun has frequent trains departing for all over India. Enquiry office is in main terminal; all-class booking office next door; Computerized Reservation Complex across the way (open Mon.-

Sat. 8am-1:50pm and 2-8pm, Sun. 8am-2pm). To: Haridwar (8 per day starting at 8am, 45min., Rs.20); Delhi (*Shatabdi Exp.* 2018, 4:30pm, 5½hr., Rs.315 for A/C chair only; *Mussoorie Exp.* 4042, 9:30pm, 9½hr., Rs.110/331 for 2nd/1st class; Bombay (*Dehradun-Bombay Exp.* 9020, 11:20am, 29½hr., Rs.243/1075 for 2nd/1st class); Varanasi (*Dehradun-Varanasi Exp.* 4266, 6:20pm, 23hr., Rs.205/336 for 1st/2nd class; *Doon Exp.* 3010, 8:30pm, 20hr., Rs.960 with A/C); Amritsar (7:05pm, 13hr., Rs.77/387 for 2nd/1st class); Lucknow (*Dehradun-Varanasi Exp.* 4266, 6:20pm, 19½hr., Rs.152/470 for 2nd/1st class)

Buses: U.P. Roadways (tel. 653797) and **Himachal Bus Lines** (tel. 623435) run buses from the **Delhi Bus Stand,** next to Hotel Drona. To: Delhi (every hr., 5:15am-10:30pm, 6½hr., Rs.72, 5:15am deluxe Rs.131); Haridwar (every 30min., 5am-8pm, 2hr., Rs.15); Rishikesh (6:30 and 8:30am, 1hr., Rs.13); Haldwani (7:25am, 5pm, deluxe 8pm, 9hr., Rs.105/145 for express/deluxe); Shimla (especially with Himachal Bus Lines: 7 per day, 10hr., Rs.96); Amritsar (5:30am, 14hr., Rs.166). U.P. Roadways also leaves from the **Mussoorie Bus Stand.** To: Mussoorie (daily every 30min., 6:30am-8pm, 1½hr., Rs.14); Nainital (daily 7:15 and 8:15am, 11hr., Rs.114); Almora (daily 6am, 12hr., Rs.125). Look for signs around town for speedy, deluxe **van** service to Delhi (Rs.150-200). **Taxis** parked across from either bus stand go pretty much anywhere, including Mussoorie (Rs.50).

Local Transportation: Local **buses** go to nearby destinations from the City Bus Stand, north of the clock tower. **Tempos** are unusually common in Dehra Dun and they're a better bet than **auto-rickshaws,** though they may only get you part of the way to your destination. By auto-rickshaw to Botanical Gardens, Rs.30-40.

English Bookstore: English Book Depot, next to Kumar Restaurant on Rajpur Rd., has many good titles. Open Mon.-Sat. 10am-1:30pm and 2:30-8pm. The **Grand Book Fair,** near the clock tower of Gandhi Rd., is inexpensive and has old issues of popular U.S. magazines. Open daily 10am-9pm.

Market: Paltan Bazaar, between the clock tower and railway station, has hundreds of shops, selling everything from sitars to saris, and panties to pineapples.

Pharmacy: Many all over town, such as **Fair Deal Chemists,** 14 Darshani Gate (tel. 625252). Open daily 8:30am-9pm.

Emergency: Police, Dhara Chowki (tel. 653648); **Fire Brigade,** tel. 657007.

Post Office: Head Post Office, by the clock tower, has *Poste Restante* (Mon.-Sat. 10am-6pm) and EMS speed post services (parcels Mon.-Fri. 10am-4pm, Sat. 10am-3pm; speed post Mon.-Sat. 10am-8pm). **Postal Code:** 248001.

Telephone Code: 0135.

ACCOMMODATIONS

Hotels closer to the bus stands or clock tower tend to be either bland high-end boxes or dingy budget dives, but the noise and stink are tolerable if you're only staying a night. Classier hotels line Rajpur, along Astley Hall and beyond.

Hotel White House (tel. 652765). One block east of Rajpur Rd. on Astley Hall. Just far enough out of downtown Dehra Dun, and with relatively presidential panache at a pittance, it's a sound choice for all but those making the briefest of stopovers. Colossal rooms (some with fireplace), bird-chirpy garden, and kind manager. Singles Rs.65, with bath Rs.135. Doubles Rs.130, with bath Rs.235.

Hotel Prince, Gandhi Rd. (tel. 627070). Two blocks south of the Delhi Bus Stand and 2 blocks east of the Mussoorie Bus Stand. A multi-story business hotel without the high-end price and pretense—basic, stone-wall rooms have good fans, comfortable mattresses, and occasional hot water. Try to get the top floor to enjoy the roof's view. Ajay, the eager lad who comes by each night to take dinner orders, is alone friendly enough to merit a stay. Singles Rs.100-115. Doubles Rs.220, deluxe (with color TV) Rs.400.

Meedo Hotel, 71 Gandhi Rd. (tel. 627088). One block from the railway station. Not to be confused with the expensive Meedo Grand out on Rajpur Rd., which also shares the Meedo's out-of-place neo-deco architecture. Your grandmother hits harder than these showers, but the toilets have seats, and the rooms are clean but not sterile. Restaurant attached. Singles Rs.150. Doubles Rs.230, deluxe (with TV and A/C) Rs.236 or Rs.275, depending on road side.

Oriental Hotel, 4 Darshani Gate (tel. 627059). A block into Paltan Bazaar from the railway. Look for their mascot, a Punjabi cartoon man, on the sign. A choice low-end spot. It isn't the Taj, but good fans and wood paneling create a thin aura of old-style sophistication. Eats are there, too. Central balconies overlook other rooms. Singles Rs.70, with bath Rs.80. Doubles, single occupancy Rs.100, double occupancy Rs.150.

Osho Resorts, 111 Rajpur Rd. (tel. 659544). About 1km beyond the GMVN Tourist Office. This "retreat with a waterfall" combines well-kept rooms with TVs and hot water with the ready worship of Bhagwan Shree Rajneesh-Osho himself! Read Osho books, watch Osho TV, or seek enlightenment in the lush meditation center. Rooms range from standard to posh-o "Osho Rajsi" rooms (with A/C, carpets, and all the fixings). Singles Rs.220. Doubles Rs.290.

Hotel Dai Chi, (tel. 658107). One-half block between Rajpur Rd. and the White House Hotel. An in-betweener. Rooms look like what the modern, pricey business hotels will all look like in 20 years. Seat toilets, hot water, and fans, but feels as if it has suited too many weary businessmen. Singles Rs.160, with A/C Rs.225.

FOOD

Restaurants near Astley Hall and out on Rajpur Rd. are bound to be better than those in the grime of the bus stand area. Hotel Prince has an unduly dim, but good restaurant, and **Heavenly Gardens,** at the Osho Resorts hotel, also has a good reputation. The Paltan Bazaar area has many good bakers and sweets vendors, plus a row of fruit stands toward the clock tower side. If you're just stopping over, the **Venus** and **Ahuja restaurants** (across from the explosives plant on Gandhi Rd., just east of the railway gate) are open all day and serve *dosas,* omelettes, and other dishes. And wherever you are, it's wise to try some of the local specialties, including coffee toffee and the sweet, creamy *gajar ka halwa.*

Kumar Foods Restaurant, Astley Hall (tel. 657060). Between the post office and Motel Himshri. This, together with the **Kumar Vegetarian Restaurant** (½ block to the north) and **Kumar Sweet Shop** (next to the clock tower), rule the food scene in Dehra Dun. Magically delicious portions of those Indian specialties you've been afraid to try—*rogan josh* (Rs.40), *alu mutter,* etc. Try it with their great *naan* and a *lassi* (Rs.15, request no ice). The service lives up to the food, and the ambience (except for the cheesy Zamfir pan-flute music) is appropriately subdued and classy. Open daily 11am-4pm and 7-10:30pm. Closed last Sun. of the month.

Motimahal Restaurant, Rajpur Rd. (tel. 657307). Across from the Hotel Ambassador. Quality non-veg. food from a large menu in a dim, beige dining room with humbling prints of Indian heroes—but dig the cheezy clock over the door to the kitchen! No fewer than 18 fans plus A/C make this the coolest duckaway spot in town. Try the omelette with chopped veggies and ketchup (Rs.14), the pineapple *raita* (Rs.24), or the mutton burger (Rs.18). Open daily 9am-10:30pm.

Daddy's, Rajpur Rd., next to the Hotel President. A wanna-be Western-style burger joint that comes through on all but interior design: where there should be neon and diner booths, floral wallpaper and green chairs have been installed. Mughlai, South Indian, and Chinese food accompany a menu of pizza, "thirst aids," and theme burgers—e.g., The Great Daddy's Twin (Rs.36). "Undisputably, these chicken burgers are the supreme of the Burger Family," boasts the menu. Daddy's hosts "kitty parties," too. Open daily 9:30am-10pm.

SIGHTS AND ENTERTAINMENT

Any attempts to sight-see in Dehra Dun require jaunts to the city's near and far peripheries. Buses and tempos leave for all destinations from the City Bus Stand; taxis and auto-rickshaws charge Rs.40-100 for individual trips to any of the sights. If you really want to take your time, pick a destination and milk it for a full day's excursion. But if seeing is more important than staying, then a good option is the GMVN day-long package bus trip, **Doon Darshan,** which covers the FRI, Tapkeshwar Temple,

Malsi Den Park, and Sahastra Dhara (Rs.50), with Robber's Cave occasionally thrown in for Rs.10. The bus stops for 45 to 90 minutes at each place (leaves daily at 10:30am, returns at 5pm). Contact Drona Travel (tel. 654371), next to the Hotel Drona at 45 Gandhi Rd. Book in advance.

Dehra Dun is the immensely and justly proud home of the Indian **Forest Research Institute (FRI).** Started under British auspices back in 1906, and residing in its current location since 1924, the FRI has led the country (and the world) toward a better understanding of the uses and abuses of various aspects of foresting, botany, and biodiversity conservation. With 13 divisions (ranging from chemistry and genetics to cellulose and mensuration), the FRI is simply huge and several esteemed visitors (including Indira Gandhi) have visited the institute's grand estate.

Visitors may be surprised by the immensity of the complex; the long building is beautifully and incorrigibly colonial, and the vast lawn is reminiscent of a European royal palace. Even if you're not into forestry, there's still quite a bit to do here; there are, in fact, six museums and a beautiful garden, and the lawn has infinite picnic potential. But most of the museums are esoteric—the best is that of the pathology division. If you can break through the barrier-like stench of mothballs, marvel at morbid collections of plant diseases like "heart rot," "root rot," and "unsoundness," while feeling up the blobby mushrooms. Other museums feature tools, well-crafted models of deforested areas (before and after), and some overly dramatic paintings of forest life. To see the **Botanical Gardens,** you need a permit from the entrance. The main gate for visitors is at Trevor Rd. Feasting in your own nook of the estate is allowed by permission of the director. There is a canteen for afternoon tea or snacks, and at the far corner of the institute is an **information desk** (tel. 627021, ext. 297) with pamphlets about the institute's many functions. (Open Mon.-Fri. 9am-5:30pm.)

The **Tapkeshwar Temple,** 6km northwest of town, isn't far from the FRI, and the two can easily be combined into one action-packed day. Dedicated to Shiva, the temple is the most sacred in the immediate area. Built into a mountainside beside a running stream, the inside is damp, cool, and filled with a curious combination of incense and mist. Note the central *linga* onto which water drips from above. There are actually several shrines around the temple's entrance. The nearby stream also serves as a popular swimming hole for locals and visitors alike. The temple is the site of a large Shivaratri celebration (March 7, 1997).

Another, more natural picnic spot near Dehra Dun is **Robber's Cave,** also called Buchu Pani, located about 8km north of town. Transport has to leave you about 100m from the entrance to the "cave," which is actually a 200-m-long, 15-m-high chasm. Visitors wade through the stream at the small canyon's bottom, where the water has smoothed the grey rock. At the other end is an opening with large boulders for climbing and even a few little pools for swimming. Wear sandals to Robber's Cave, as the rocks in the stream can be sharp. There's a "real" swimming pool about 100m on the other side from where tour buses stop.

An overwhelming favorite among the hordes of Indian visitors to the area is **Sahastra-Dhara,** a village with a series of cold sulphur pools about 14km northeast of Dehra Dun's center. It's by far the most touristy and kitschy of the local sights, but if you come in the early morning or during the off-season, it could also be the most rewarding. The stream has been dammed at several points, so swimming in the pools is easy. There are changing rooms, along with several food and junk stands, and even a **Tourist Rest House,** with rooms with common bath for Rs.90.

The **Survey of India** also has its headquarters in Dehra Dun, on New Cantonment Rd. Various city maps and trekking maps are available, although the most detailed maps are not sold to foreigners.

▓ Mussoorie

The mountain hill station of Mussoorie is chintzy, overpriced, and often overcrowded; it's also refreshingly cool, near tranquil forests, and because of (*not* in spite

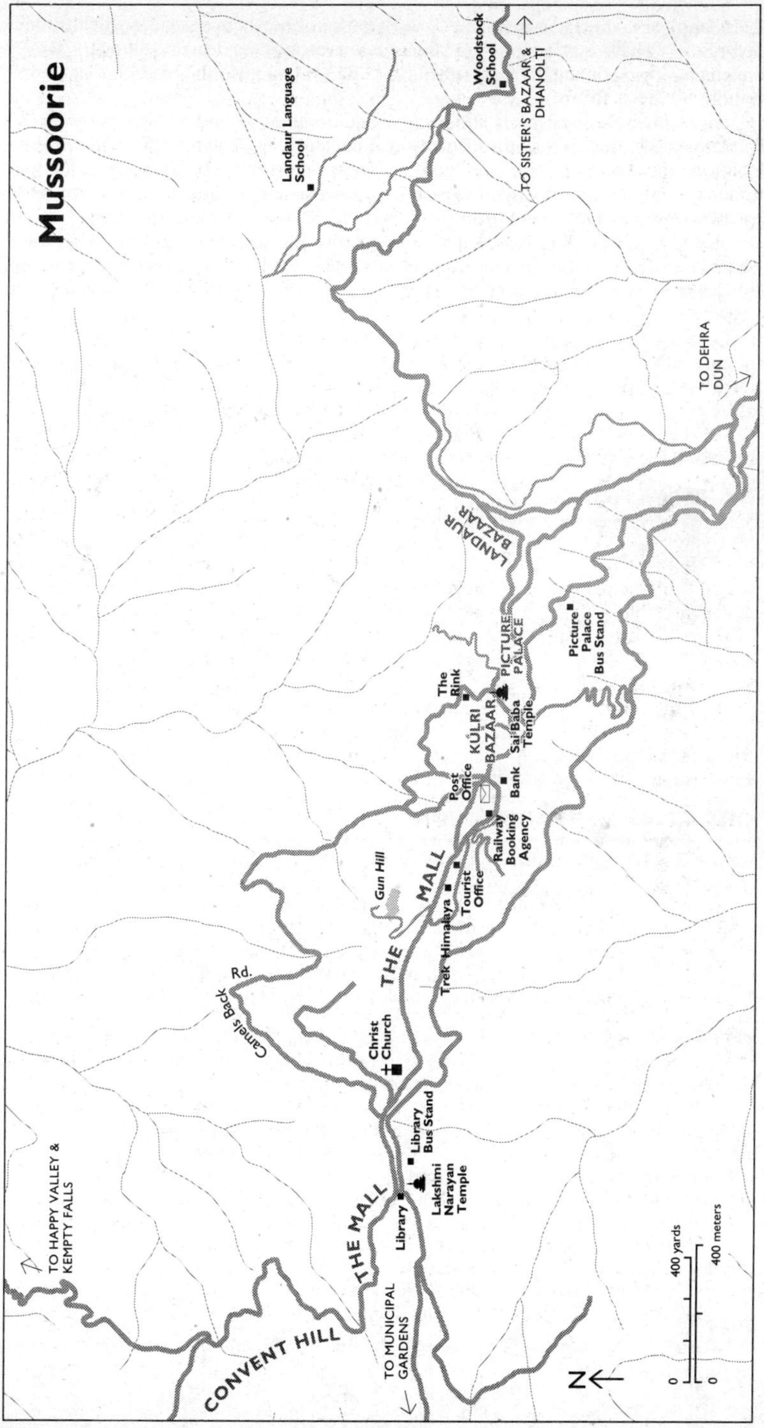

Mussoorie

Woodstock School

TO SISTER'S BAZAAR & DHANOLTI

Landaur Language School

LANDAUR BAZAAR

TO DEHRA DUN

The Rink

PICTURE PALACE

KULRI BAZAAR

Sai Baba Temple

Picture Palace Bus Stand

Post Office

Bank

Railway Booking Agency

Gun Hill

THE MALL

Tourist Office

Trek Himalaya

Camel's Back Rd.

Christ Church

Library Bus Stand

Lakshmi Narayan Temple

Library

THE MALL

CONVENT HILL

TO MUNICIPAL GARDENS

TO HAPPY VALLEY & KEMPTY FALLS

N

400 yards

400 meters

0

of) its touristy carnival atmosphere, a hell of a lot of fun. The town certainly isn't for everyone—travelers attempting to shun commercialism in favor of spirituality should stay in nearby Haridwar or Rishikesh, and those hoping for mountain tranquility may be better off in Kumaon. But anyone with an interest in the bizarre subculture of Indian tourists could find no better point of observation.

While today the focal destination for heat-fleeing tourists from Delhi (Mussoorie is the closest hill station to the capital), the town was first settled in 1827 by an Englishman, Captain Young. British officials later developed Mussoorie into a Victorian home-away-from-home-away-from-home, complete with an exclusive club, libraries, and an Anglican Church. The central promenade—the Mall—was made for afternoon strolls and crusty chit-chat while stopping to gape at the snow-peaked Himalaya to the northeast (including the Gangotri group) and across the Doon valley to the south with Nag Tibba.

Since then, stiff-upper-trippers have yielded to middle-class Indians, most of them coming in peak season between May and July. November through March is distinctly off-season, and you're more likely to find solitude then, with less of the Disneyland atmosphere. "Season" extends from July to October and March to May, and prices at this time are mid-range. Note that winter can be pretty chilly, and that during the monsoon fog enshrouds the mountainside, obstructing the view.

ORIENTATION

Mussoorie is about 15km long, stretching around the mountain overlooking Dehra Dun, though the town proper is much more compact. There are two hearts of the town, the **Library** and **Kulri Bazaar** areas, connected by about a 15-minute walk along **the Mall,** which is lined with murals. Most buses from the valley stop near the Library Bazaar, so called because the numerous hotels and restaurants are built around the old Mussoorie Library. The plaza in front of the Library, with a statue of the Mahatma, is called **Gandhi Chowk;** the gate by the Library is Gandhi Gate. There is also a bus stand in the other main part of town, at Kulri Bazaar. **Camel's Back Road** runs along the back side of the mountain and connects the two bazaars more circuitously. **Landaur Bazaar,** to the east, is less kitschy than the rest of town; the **clock tower** stands in the middle of this area.

PRACTICAL INFORMATION

Tourist Office: Near the Ropeway, halfway between Kulri and Library Bazaars (tel. 632063). Provides a handy photocopied sheet about Mussoorie and local sights, with map. Also has some brochures about nearby treks. Open Mon.-Sat. 10am-5pm.

Currency Exchange: There are several banks, with branches in both main bazaars. **State Bank of India,** in Kulri Bazaar (tel. 632533), cashes AmEx checks (U.S. dollars). **Thomas Cook,** in the heart of Kulri Bazaar, accepts U.S. dollars and pounds sterling efficiently and without commission. Open Mon.-Fri. 10am-2pm, Sat. 10am-noon.

Telephones: STD/ISD booths abound in Mussoorie. STD booth by the Rock Wood and Regal hotels charges Rs.5 per min. for incoming calls. **Telephone exchange/ telegraph service** in Kulri next to the post office.

Trains: No rails come up to Mussoorie, but reservations to and from other Indian destinations can be made at the **Northern Railways Out Agency,** on the Mall below the post office. Open Mon.-Sat. 10am-4pm, Sun. 8am-2pm.

Buses: U.P. Roadways, leaving from the **Kulri** or **Library Bus Stands** (both below the Mall) and servicing only Dehra Dun. From the Library Bus Stand (tel. 632259): every hr. on the hr., 7am-6pm, 1½hr., Rs.14. From the Kulri Bus Stand: (tel. 632258): every 30min., 6am-7pm, 1½hr., Rs.14. Several signs around town advertise daily direct Dehra Dun-Delhi deluxe service with pick-ups in Mussoorie. One service has booking opposite Hotel Regal, on the lower side of the Mall (call 632056 for info.). Daily at 11:30am and 10pm from Dehra Dun (lux. Rs.125, with A/C Rs.180).

Taxis: Booking stands next to both bus stands (tel. 632361). To Dehra Dun (Rs.50 per seat, Rs.250 per car) and Haridwar (Rs.70-80 per seat, Rs.600 per car).

Market: Tibetan Market, along and below the Mall near the Library, and many stores around town specialize in curios (walking sticks, etc.), woolens, and tourist crap. Try bargaining.

Library: The attractive **Mussorie Library,** for which its neighborhood of Library Bazaar is named, squats over several food stores. It has a good collection of fiction, but the librarians don't let visitors in without Rs.250 security deposit and Rs.25 monthly subscription fee. Open Mon.-Sat. 10am-1pm and 3-6pm. The **Tilak Memorial Library,** off the Mall in Kulri, is open 9am-noon and 4-8pm.

English Bookstore: Several good bookstores along the Mall in Kulri, usually open 8am-8pm, with magazines, comics, fiction, and nonfiction. The **Grand Book Fair,** below the Tilak Library, has good prices but a limited selection.

Pharmacies: These, too, are ubiquitous along the Mall. **P.B. Hamers & Co.,** up from the Rialto Cinema by President's Restaurant, has a whole lot of everything. Open daily 10am-10pm. **Pioneer Medical Store** (tel. 632302), in Kulri across from Hotel Victoria, is well-stocked. Open daily 9:30am-9:30pm.

Hospital/Medical Services: The **Community Hospital** is in Landaur near the clock tower. For more private treatment, try the **clinic** of Dr. Ranar and Dr. Nautiyal (tel. 632594), on the road above the Kulri Mall between the post office and Hotel Hill Queen. Near the Library, try Dr. Sethi at the Library Gate.

Police: (tel. 632005). Above the Mall near Hotel Western and Hakman's Grand Hotel. Station open 24hr. There is also a "police outpost" close to the Palace Cinema, and a small police stand in the plaza in front of the Library.

Post Office: (tel. 632806). Near State Bank of India, above the Mall in Kulri. Has registered and speed post (via EMS), and *Poste Restante* open until 4pm. Most services available Mon.-Fri. 9am-1pm and 1:30-5pm, Sat. 9am-noon. **Postal Code:** 248179.

Telephone Code: 0135.

ACCOMMODATIONS

Mussoorie has so many hotels that one wonders where the locals live. Both bazaar areas suit a variety of budgets, though Kulri and Landaur have fewer posh hotels and more densely packed low-end places. The list below is just a beginning, and in most cases you'd be better off wandering around and asking rates for yourself—a hotel's lobby is usually a reasonable indicator of the rates it charges. In the peak season (May-June), amazingly enough, the hotels fill to near capacity. Expect boosted rates at this time, with discounts during "season" (March-May and July-Oct.), and slashed prices from Nov.-March.

Kulri and Landaur

Hotel Broadway, Camel's Back Rd. (tel. 632243). Near the rink on Camel's Back Rd., near Kulri Bazaar. A converted English guest house, the Broadway retains charm in a peaceful setting, away from all clamor but that of the roller rink and the nearby mosque. Mr. Malik, the owner, is generous to foreigners, and supplements his good rates with a gentle demeanor. Ask for the corner single upstairs, replete with fashion pin-ups. In season: singles Rs.200. Doubles Rs.400. Triples Rs.500. Off-season: singles Rs.75. Doubles Rs.150.

Hotel Nishima, Landaur Bazaar (tel. 632227). Not far from the clock tower. Popular among language school students. Hot water in big buckets, thickish mattresses, hearty metal doors, and a view of the nearby electrical plant's roof—plus the mountains. Clean, bright, and the lobby has a TV. In season: doubles Rs.250. Off-season: singles Rs.60. Doubles Rs.100.

Hotel Hillview (tel. 632764). Upper side of the Mall on the road near the more visible Rock Wood and Regal hotels. Large, clean rooms with embroidered pillows and slightly scummy attached bath. Views, as the name suggests, often face into the hillside, and not onto the plains. Still, tea is served. Check-out 10am. In season: rooms Rs.250-300. Off-season: rooms Rs.75-200.

Hotel Everest, Camel's Back Rd. (tel. 632954). Near the rink at the beginning of the road. Massive "lobby," off of which rooms (bright to dim) mimic the slightly pricier

Hotel Roxy upstairs. Black-and-white or color TV. In season: doubles Rs.400, with color TV and hot water Rs.500. Off-season: doubles Rs.150. Extra bed Rs.25.

Hotel Saraswati (tel. 631005). Up the ramp from the more visible Hotel Amar, upper side of the Mall. A hidden location—they're likely to have rooms when all else is full. Tidy floors, beds, and attached baths. Beds have spiffy headlamps. In season: doubles Rs.400. Off-season: doubles Rs.100-250.

Hotel Deep, Camel's Back Rd. (tel. 632470). Next to Hotel Broadway, it offers similar views of the back valley and distant Himalaya. Laundry service, restaurant, good terrace. A high-end place with low-end options. In season: doubles Rs.490. Quads Rs.700. Off-season: doubles Rs.250. Quads Rs.350.

Hotel Clark's (tel. 632393). A massive wooden landmark on the Mall. Grand, old-fashioned lobby with 2 billiard tables, reminiscent of the Raj. Not modern, and overpriced during peak season. Off-season: doubles Rs.300-500.

Library Area

Hotel India (tel. 632359). Off the Mall, up the ramp from the horse stand—look for the alley access 100m toward Kulri from the Library. Wall-to-wall carpeting and TV in deluxe room, and the basics well-done in the not-so-deluxe. All rooms have bathrooms—don't be deceived by the rickety servants' quarters near the entrance. As a bonus, the name reminds you where the hell you are. In season: doubles Rs.300-500. Off-season: doubles Rs.100.

Hotel Snowview (tel. 632123—call after 8pm). Near Hotel India, up from the Mall. Stone bathrooms, checkered floors, and green shutters go with the excellent view. Prices are hefty; try bargaining with the old man at the desk. In season: rooms Rs.400 and up. Off-season: singles Rs.150. Doubles Rs.200.

Hotel Prince. Not far from Hotel India and Hotel Snowview. A bit more stodgy, with a ping-pong table in the wood-paneled lobby and a no drugs or alcohol policy. Meals served. Rooms have TV and bath. Spacious for a high-end hotel. In season: doubles Rs.400-630; quads Rs.800-1000. Off-season: doubles Rs.200-315. Quads Rs.400-500.

Hotel Garhwal Terrace (tel. 632682). Halfway down the Mall. A fancy GMVN place. Most rooms bust your wallet, but 20 dorm beds (in 4-bed or 8-bed dorms) are a last resort. In season: dorm beds Rs.75-100. Off-season: dorm beds Rs.50.

Hotel Jeet (tel. 631131). Directly next to the Library. Unextraordinary rooms with good mattresses, running hot water, and even carpets. Good views in some rooms, while in others guests can only stare at the walls. A bargain off-season; otherwise don't bother. Off-season: doubles Rs.100-250.

FOOD

Mussoorie's residents do their best to make sure the throngs of tourists don't starve; there are fast-food joints, large family restaurants, and restaurant-bars almost everywhere in town. Most hotels have some sort of tourist-trough attached. Corn-on-the-cob is sold along the Mall, sweets are scooped up at **Krishna's** in Kulri, and eggy treats are assembled at the **"Omelette Specialist,"** not far from Picture Palace Cinema (also in Kulri). Food prices, like hotel prices, are seasonal.

Sicoh Bar and Restaurant, Kulri Bazaar (tel. 632955). Near Rialto Cinema and President Restaurant. Exudes exclusivity—most guests are smooth-lookin' males. Meals here pack a punch: tasty chicken *korma*, delicate hot and sour soup, and good-to-guzzle Eagle Lager (not that the Sicoh can take credit, but at least they serve it!). Open daily 9am-10pm.

The Green, Kulri Bazaar (tel. 632226). Fills up around meal time; the masses come for great veg. fare, from breakfast (with the Green Special *paratha*, Rs.14) to dinner (with the Green Special *dal*) and with sweet treats (mango milkshake, Rs.16) to pack a full menu. Lewdly buttered *naan* shouldn't be missed. Open daily 8am-3:30pm and 7-10pm.

Rice Bowl, Kulri Bazaar (tel. 631684). Across from President Restaurant, upstairs. Dining cube with view onto the street, serves Chinese and Tibetan food—a rarity in Mussoorie. Try the special garlic chicken (Rs.40), veg. fried rice (Rs.20), or steamed mutton *momos*. Beware of sneaky monkeys reaching through the windows! Open daily 11am-11:30pm.

Jeet Restaurant, right on Gandhi Chowk, next to the Library and Jeet Hotel. The ideal place to plan your trek or your next move, since the tables have regional maps built into them. Nothing fancy-schmancy; cogitate over hot chocolate (Rs.18). Open 8am-11pm.

Le Chef, near the State Bank of India in Kulri. Tries really hard to be western—with chocolate doughnuts, "All-American Breakfasts" (Rs.55), take-out pizza, hot dogs (Rs.25), and even "gravy items." Popular teen hang-out, especially for the after-roller-skating crowd. Open 10am-11pm.

The President Restaurant, Kulri Bazaar (tel. 632042). A Mussoorian landmark. Sit at their outdoor tables next to a strange mobile window of scrawny chickens. Love ballads blare to ease your tongue's way through spicy chow mein (Rs.42), veg. *pakoras* (Rs.20), or tandoori chicken (full chicken Rs.85). Open daily 9:30am-11:30pm.

Howard Revolving Restaurant, Hotel Howard (tel. 632113). A prime spot for a hilarious afternoon snack or soda, though a full meal may be too expensive (entrees Rs.50-65). The small, cylindrical restaurant makes one noisy, kerklunkety rotation every 9 min.—you may not notice that you're rotating, but you'll wonder why the earth is shaking violently. Good cucumber and tomato salad (Rs.25).

SIGHTS AND ENTERTAINMENT

There are more things to do than there are to see in Mussoorie, but that doesn't mean the town lacks sights; the local tourist office has plenty of suggestions. Keep in mind, however, that any well-known sight is bound to be congested during the high season. Looming directly over the town is **Gun Hill;** the peak earned its moniker because of a pre-Independence ritual of firing guns from the top at midday—the townspeople would adjust their watches accordingly. It's possible to walk or ride rented horses to get to the top, but the best way is via Mussoorie's **Ropeway,** a gondola system which zips up the 500-m mountainside past hotel windows and with great view (open 8:30am-10:30pm, off-season 9am-7pm; Rs.25 up and down, under 5 free). The top of Gun Hill has several lookout points, small food vendors, a surreal and amusing "Laugh House," with loud laugh soundtrack and bent mirrors to distort your soul (Rs.5), and several photo stands, which will dress you up in glittery local costume and take a snapshot or a "trick photo," where they have you jump off a rock and try to make it look like you're levitating or flying. Since the picture quality is sometimes shoddy, a better bet is to have them take the shot with your camera.

There are several good spots for walking around Mussoorie, passing through cool, fragrant pine and *deodar* forests. **Camel's Back Road,** which winds behind the town, offers keen views of the Himalaya; points of interest include the **cemetery** (sometimes closed, but worth trying), with old stones sponsored by the British Association for Cemeteries in South Asia; **"Quiet Corner,"** a supposedly quiet lookout point, where kids charge Rs.5 for the use of their telescopes; and near the public school, **Camel's Back Rock** itself, which is shaped like you-know-what. The entire walk takes about 40 minutes.

To the west of town lie **"Happy Valley"** and the nearby **Municipal Garden,** which has a tiny pool for paddle-boats and much of the carnival-stuff you find on Gun Hill or in town, but there remain a few peaceful spots; along a different road is the house of **Sir George Everest,** Surveyor General of India, whose name lives on 8848m above Nepal. A more distant destination to the northwest of town is **Kempty Falls,** a popular "retreat," which has sadly gone from pristine, rushing falls and peaceful pools to the same old junk there's so much of in Mussoorie.

Follow the road to the east of Mussoorie through Landaur Bazaar and a few kilometers beyond to the **Woodstock School,** a Christian-based primary and high school with boarders from all over the world. At the top of the mountain above the school is **Sister's Bazaar,** site of a language school, a few shops, and even a Hotel Dev Dar Woods (tel. 632644; often full, so call ahead. Rs.300-500 per night). **Childer's Lodge,** the highest point in Mussoorie, is near Sister's Bazaar.

Have no fear of boredom if you feel bound to either of the two bazaar areas in town, however. There are an exceptional number of **video games** (some dating back to the pre-Pac-Man era) in the several parlors clustered in Kulri (Rs.2). The **Picture Palace,** in Kulri, and the **Rialto Cinema,** also in Kulri, across from the President's Restaurant, frequently show Hindi movies and the Rialto shows dated English-language movies Sat. and Sun. at 11am and 4:30pm. First-class seats are Rs.10, special class seats Rs.15, and "box" seats Rs.20-25. There are also recorded Hindi fortune-teller boxes and test-your-grip-stations (Rs.1-2) along the Mall, and countless stands for shooting pellet guns at walls of balloons.

All these minor amusements are a mere warm-up for the true good-time place in Mussoorie—**The Rink,** in Kulri, India's largest roller skating rink (though seeing it, one wonders what the smallest is like). Guys should don their tightest blue jeans (and women should *not* wear skirts) to be seen at this strut-your-ball-bearings hangout for the local and vacationing teen crowd. There's a ramp in the middle for hotshots; watch out for the Nepalese kids—they're speed demons. The rink itself dates back 100 years to when British couples likely experimented with what was all the rage back home—note the old-style observation balconies at the ends. Rent full-shoe "special" skates (Rs.20), or those that attach to your own shoes. Shops across the way rent skates, too. Five skating sessions thump to Indian and Western pop music daily (beginners: 8:30-10am; open skating 11am-1pm, 3-5pm, 6-7:30pm, and 8-9:30pm; admission with rental Rs.35, with special skates Rs.50; "spectators" pay Rs.5).

■ Haridwar

Haridwar is not known for its architecture or its natural beauty, but it is considered by Hindus to be a holy city. Marking the spot where the sacred River Ganga emerges from the mountains before its tortuous route across India, its name means "Gate of Hari"—Hari is another name for Vishnu. Followers of Shiva drop the "i," calling the city "Hardwar," or "Gate of Hara," using an alternative name for Shiva. Haridwar is a temple town; people come here to follow in the footprints of Vishnu, to bathe in the Ganga, to send off a flower-boat during the *arati* ceremony, and to worship at one of the many temples.

In some spots Haridwar is as noisy and crowded as any other town, but the high number of ashrams, *sadhus,* and temples seem to mellow the people out; in places, there really is something holy in the air. Not many foreign tourists come here, but a steady stream of pilgrims arrives year-round, especially Punjabi Hindus, who consider Haridwar the holiest place in India. Haridwar particularly becomes a holy hot-bed every 12 years at the Kumbh Mela (see p. 219). To bathe then is particularly auspicious, so millions rush the *ghat* at Har-ki-Pairi at once, creating dangerous stampedes that have resulted in death. The next Kumbh Mela in Haridwar will occur on the big day of April 13, 1998.

ORIENTATION

Haridwar runs parallel to and along the River Ganga, which flows from northeast to southwest. Buses and trains arrive at stations near the southwest end of **Railway Road,** the town's main thoroughfare, along which most services lie. Walking northeast on Railway Rd., you'll cross **Laltarao Bridge** (over a small stream, not the Ganga) before reaching the post office. The main bazaar in town is **Moti Bazaar,** which runs along the streets below Railway Rd., parallel to the river near **Har-ki-Pairi.** The main *ghat* in town, Har-ki-Pairi is at the northeast end of Railway Rd., attached to it by a little bridge. Beyond that is Broken Bridge, a broken bridge. A strip of land across the river hosts accommodations and the taxi stand. Temples lie to the north and south.

PRACTICAL INFORMATION

Tourist Office: GMVN, Railway Rd. (tel. 424240, 427370). At Laltarao Bridge. Provides good maps of Haridwar and Rishikesh. Staff knows about nearby treks and has information on pilgrimages. Open daily 10am-5pm. **U.P. Tourism** (tel. 427370). Next to Rahi Motel across from railway station. More regional information. Open daily 10am-5pm, closed Sun. off-season.

Budget Travel: Several private agents have information on treks and pilgrimages. Try **Ashwani Travels,** Railway Rd. (tel. 427125), near the sparkly white Rama Krishna Hotel. Open daily 8am-10pm.

Immigration Office: Foreigners Registration Office, Railway Rd., near post office, north of Laltarao Bridge. Register for long-term stays in Haridwar district (which doesn't include Rishikesh—Dehra Dun's the place to do that). Open Mon.-Fri. 10am-5pm.

Currency Exchange: Bank of Baroda, Railway Rd. (tel. 427535). North of Laltarao Bridge. Changes traveler's checks, and occasionally gives cash advances on Visa. Call ahead before making a special trip. Open Mon.-Fri. 10am-2pm, Sat. 10am-noon. The State Bank of India here doesn't change traveler's checks.

Telephones: STD/ISD booths in every nook and cranny.

Airlines: Indian Airlines, (tel. 427266). Across Railway Rd. from post office. Open daily 9:30am-1:30pm and 3-7pm.

Trains: Northern Railway Station is by the bus stand on Railway Rd.—enquiry on right-hand side, computer reservation counter on the other. Or buy general tickets at **Northern Railway Booking Office,** Railway Rd. (tel. 427724), north of Laltarao Bridge. Open daily 5am-10pm. To: Dehra Dun (8 per day, 5:22am-5:05pm, 2hr., Rs.18/125 for 1st class/1st class with A/C); Delhi (*Dehradun-Bombay Exp.* 9020, 1:25pm, 9hr., Rs.98/404; *Mussoorie Exp.* 4042, 11pm, 8hr., Rs.98/404; *Shatabdi Exp.* 2018, 5:50pm, 6hr., Rs.295 for A/C chair car only); Lucknow (*Doon Exp.* 3010, 9:55pm, 10½hr., Rs.145/442 for 2nd/1st class); Varanasi (*Doon Exp.* 3010, 9:55pm, 19hr., Rs.150/609 for 2nd/1st class); Bombay (*Dehradun-Bombay Exp.* 9020, 1:25pm, 2-day min., Rs.234/1144 for 2nd/1st class).

Buses: Leave from the stand across from the railway station, at the southwest end of Railway Rd. **Himachal Roadways** services distant Shimla, Badrinath, and other destinations to the north. To: Badrinath (4, 4:30, 6, 9am, and noon, 14hr., Rs.127; buses leaving after 6pm stop for the night along the way). Nainital, Agra, and Kedarnath also served. **U.P. Roadways** (tel. 427037). To: Dehra Dun (every 30min., 5am-6:30pm, 2hr., Rs.15); Rishikesh (every 30min. "round the clock," 45min., Rs.7.50); Delhi (every 30min., 4am-11pm, 6hr., Rs.60); Lucknow (7:30am, 14hr., Rs.140).

Local Transportation: Tempos cluster on the east bank of the Shatabdi Bridge; from Railway to Har-ki-Pairi Rs.2-3; by **auto-rickshaw,** Rs.5.

Market: Moti Bazaar, 1 block north along Railway Rd. from Laltarao Bridge, then down 2 blocks. Copious shops selling clothing, wooden crafts, walking sticks, brass pots, and *pan.*

English Bookstore: Most of the small bookshops in Moti Bazaar specialize in religious literature, though some have a small selection of fiction and books about Garhwal. **Arjun Singh Bookseller,** Bara Bazaar (tel. 421449), has books on trekking and yoga.

Pharmacy: Milap Medical Hall, Railway Rd. (tel. 427193), south of and opposite the post office. Has drugs, sunscreen, and sanitary napkins. Open daily 8:30am-10pm. **Dr. B.C. Hasaram & Sons,** on Railway Rd., across from and near the post office, specializes in ayurvedic medicines.

Hospital/Medical Services: Several private clinics along Railway Rd., such as **Dr. Kailash Pande** (tel. 427302), north of Laltarao bridge. **Harmilap District Hospital** (tel. 426060), south of the post office, and **Chain Rai Female Hospital** (tel. 427490) next door.

Police: Har-ki-Pairi (tel. 425160).

Post Office: On Railway Rd. north of Laltarao bridge (tel. 427025). *Poste Restante,* speed post services. Open Mon.-Sat. 10am-4pm. **Postal Code:** 249401.

Telephone Code: 249401.

ACCOMMODATIONS

Travelers coming to Haridwar for only a short time may want to consider staying in one of the budget hotels near the railway station and the bus stand. The railway station has retiring rooms, and there are nicer places in this area as well. Those thinking of sticking around longer might want to get a room closer to the river and Har-ki-Pairi. As a holy city, Haridwar has plenty of ashrams and low-cost trusts, or *dharamshalas,* which may have rooms in low season. Jai Ram Ashram in Bhimgoda (tel. 427335) is grandiose, or try Narasingh Bhawan, on Upper Rd. (tel. 424219). There are also a few ashrams in Bhimgoda and Jairam. Pilgrimage seasons in Haridwar means that from November to March prices are 25-50% lower. Unless noted, the prices listed below are for high season.

Hotel Madras (tel. 426356). Off Railway Rd. 2 blocks north of the railway. Turn right after the Kailash Hotel, down one-half block. A low-end old-timer conveniently close to transport. Rooms built in 1950s have common bath, but they're renovating (and hoping to add attached baths, which may raise rates). Good restaurant attached. In season: singles Rs.50. Doubles Rs.80. Off-season: singles Rs.30. Doubles Rs.60.

Nirmal Divine Mission, on left-hand side of the same street as Madras, 2 blocks down (almost to the end). Look for the large Hindi and small English signs. Humble, pleasant place with gracious owner. Big rooms, good fans, erratic water and plumbing, western toilets. Front-side rooms have balcony. Singles a rather arbitrary Rs.75. Doubles Rs.100—it's a mission, so don't argue!

Hotel Brij Lodge (tel. 426872). Just north of Har-ki-Pairi near the broken bridge ("brij"). With its own access to the Ganga, and best of all, a balcony with a decent view of Har-ki-Pairi, for watching the evening *arati* ritual. Languid owner, common bath. In season: doubles Rs.250-300. Quads Rs.600. Off-season: 80% discount.

Tourist Bungalow (tel. 426379). Across the river from town, toward the railway end; buses pass it on the way in, so keep an eye out and ask the driver to stop. Run by U.P. Tourism, it's pricey, but it's the best place for peace and pristine enjoyment of the area, with its own little lawn, garden, and strip of riverbank. A hike from most sights, but well-kept and worth it for many. Check-out noon. In season: beds in 20-bed dorm with storage cabinet Rs.50. Singles Rs.375, with A/C Rs.600. Doubles Rs.400, with A/C Rs.700. Quads Rs.350. Off-season: 25% discount.

Hotel Shivoy, Upper Rd. (tel. 422524). Not far from the bend down to Har-ki-Pairi. Uninspired, mid-range rooms with enough perks to make it worthwhile: hot water in attached bath, shower, brain-sucking fans, TV in lobby. Deluxe rooms (with A/C) available. Check-out noon. In season: doubles Rs.300. Off-season: doubles Rs.200-250.

Hotel Bhaskara (tel. 425473). Heading north on railway, it's on the right about halfway from railway station. Deluxe rooms are dirty with noisy A/C. Ordinary rooms are immaculate, have great mattresses, attached bath and shower—you make the call. Trippy painting in the stairwell. In season: ordinary singles Rs.300. Off-season: singles Rs.200. Prices may be negotiable.

FOOD

Purity of diet follows purity of spirit in Haridwar, so alcohol and meat are not available. Most major restaurants are on Railway Rd., midway between the bus stand and Har-ki-Pairi, though some of the little places tucked into the bazaar near Har-ki-Pairi make mean and clean breakfast *puris.* In any case, there are *pan-wallahs* to help with digestion.

Chotiwala. The main branch of this place is on "Asli" Railway Rd. near Laltarao Bridge, across from Hotel Vishul, but the imitation version just off the bridge at Har-ki-Pairi has an air-fresh outdoor dining area and keeps long hours. Both are delicious and affordable. The Har-ki-Pairi Chotiwala serves *dosas* (Rs.12), *dal makhani* (Rs.12), and *shahi paneer* (Rs.25), but the real Chotiwala is better. Har-ki-Pairi branch open 7am-midnight.

Ahaar Restaurant, Railway Rd. (tel. 427601). Next to main Chotiwala. The Sikh boss lords over guests from his desk as they enjoy exceptional South Indian, Chinese, and Punjabi dishes in a dark, tranquil chamber below street level. The hefty

Punjabi thali (Rs.36) is delicious and not as spicy as many other dishes. Other *thalis* as low as Rs.25; Ahar's special *kofta* Rs.35. Open daily 10am-4pm and 6-11pm.

New Mysore, Railway Rd. (tel. 426684). On west side of Railway Rd., two-thirds of the way to Har-ki-Pairi. "The only South Indian-run restaurant in town" has an unassuming atmosphere, cool air, and great prices. *Tomato utthapam* Rs.12, full *thali* Rs.20. Open 7am-10pm.

Swagat Restaurant, in Hotel Mansarovar on Railway Rd. (tel. 426501). Extensive menu includes *Amritsari chana* (Rs.25), vegetable sizzlers (Rs.40), and daily specials. Every table has its own little artificial floral arrangement. Open 6am-11pm.

Hari Darbar, Railway Rd. (tel. 426542). Closer to the railway itself than the other restaurants. Unusual selections include *matar* "massroom" (Rs.30), *meetha gulab jamun* (Rs.10), and veg. tandoori dishes. Open 9am-11pm.

SIGHTS

The most important spot in Haridwar is the sacred *ghat* of **Har-ki-Pairi,** the supposed site of Vishnu's footprint, where the sacred Ganga enters the plains. The most spectacular time to come is for the evening *arati* ceremony, but visiting Har-ki-Pairi at other times of the day is rewarding too. Many people bathe at sunrise, and throughout the day—it's a good spot because there are chains to keep bathers from getting swept off to Varanasi by the deceptively fast current. The area is packed with beggars, lepers, and several uniformed men who wander the area asking for donations for various "trusts." Enough of these guys are shysters or "volunteers" who pocket their earnings. It's much better to donate via the charity boxes around the area, or to the office of Ganga Sabha, above the temple at the *ghat;* money given here is more likely to work good, and they'll give you a box of rice to offer to the gods.

In the summer of 1996, 26 people were killed in a stampede at Har-ki-Pairi. This was hardly the first time that tragedy has struck the *ghat.* In 1991, five people were killed at the Mansa Devi Temple, and in 1986, 50 were killed during the Kumbh Mela (see p. 219). Hindus take holy Haridwar very seriously. As a tourist, it's not as easy to be so earnest. For within Haridwar's blessed boundaries, Hindus have erected a number of temples, some of them way over the top—it has an amusement-park feel to it. Just above the city is the **Mansa Devi Temple,** for example. To honor the goddess, stand in line for one of the exciting ropeway trolleys (roundtrip Rs.13) to whisk you up and over a garden to the hilltop, where views, food vendors, and the temple await (open daily 7:30am-7:30pm). The fervor of Hindus offering their coconuts to the shrine can be pretty extreme here, so stand back to observe.

A few kilometers north of town is a small cluster of unusual temples. Some would call them opulent and justly grand; others might say they're chintzy and overdone. The **Pawan Dham Temple,** first along the road from Haridwar, is most representative of the local houses of worship. Its many shrines are made almost entirely of mirrors

---

Arati

The most beautiful of Haridwar's tourist attractions is not as much a sight as it is an experience: the *arati* ceremony, every evening at Har-ki-Pairi, is not to be missed. At sundown, thousands gather at Vishnu's footprint to pay tribute to the gods. Oncoming darkness is broken only by the hundreds of glowing *diyas,* colorful boats made out of cupped leaves filled with flower petals and a lit candle. Sending a *diya* down the river is thought to fulfill one's wish—it's possible to see the magnitude of the wish (or of the wisher's bank account) by the size of the *diya*—most cost a few rupees each, but others, veritable yachts of flowers, cost hundreds of rupees. Accompanying the luminescence of the *diya*-filled Ganga is the ceremony itself—gongs ring along the shore, people sing out chants, and at the main *ghat,* priests elevate huge plates of fire to the sky, and then bring them to the water, a process they repeat for several minutes. Arrive early in the high season—the best place to watch is from the bridge on the south end of Har-ki-Pairi or from the strip by the clock tower.

and stained glass. Shiva and Arjuna ride atop mirror-covered horses; Krishna sees his 100 lovers in 100 different directions. The small Jain statue is duly underdone. Venture off to the **Sapta Rishi Ashram,** at the north end of the cluster, to pay homage to the seven saints in seven temples.

The **Bharat Mata Mandir,** the six-story shrine to Mother India and its leaders at the north end of the temple cluster, resembles a modern apartment building with temple domes on top. The top story (reached by elevator for Rs.1) houses the Hindu gods, while the floor below hosts the goddesses, including the goddess Ganga and Saraswati, goddess of knowledge. Descending floors honor the saints of India's various religions (from Guru Nanak of the Sikhs to the Buddha and Vivekenanda), sisters (including Gandhi's devotees Annie Besant and Sister Nivedita), and other fighters for freedom and independence. The second floor has paintings highlighting characteristic features of India's states, and the ground floor has a giant relief model of the country. It's an interesting blend of history and religion. Indians pay tribute to Shrinathji and Vyankatesh, not only the names of saints, but also of well-known cricket bowlers.

Next on the tour of trippy temples is nearby **Maa Vaishnodevi Mandir,** which attempts to simulate the experience of visiting a cave in Kashmir—complete with artificial mango trees (bearing fruit), a giant Ganga Mata with a crocodile, and even a tunnel with knee-deep water, through which visitors duck and wade. **Bhuma Niketan,** south of Maa Vaishnodevi Mandir, has the added bonus of "modern" technology—pay one rupee to enter a room with mechanized robotic mannequins of various Hindu heroes doing their stuff; their movements are only occasionally discernible. In the middle of the room is a giant dinosaur. A tempo driver will charge about Rs.150 for a three-hour tour of these temples, but it's smarter to let the tempo go once you're at the temples; all are within easy walking distance of each other.

Another nearby temple is the **Daksha Mahadev Temple,** southeast of town. Myth holds that the father of Shiva's wife Sati declined to invite his daughter's mate to a sacrifice here (see **Divine Dismemberment,** p. 404). **The Bhimgoda Tank,** reachable by walking the road by Har-ki-Pairi north for 10 minutes, is unexceptional. It is a stone pool, thought to have been formed by knee of Bhima, Hanuman's brother.

■ Rishikesh

Most travelers come to Rishikesh to *find* something—a cure to some deep-rooted ailment, a spiritual leader, or, most often, themselves. And indeed, something about Rishikesh suggests a power to transform—sages first came here to find a splash of holiness along the crashing Ganga before wandering north toward the accessible pilgrimage sites. Every year, thousands turn up in early February for International Yoga Week. Even the Beatles sought (and found) a new path here, as a few weeks of study with the Maharishi Mahesh Yogi sent their tried-and-true pop style down a sinister road of sitar-laden psychedelia.

In the end, what travelers find is almost invariably to their liking. Few manage to crack themselves (though there are a few who think they come close), but most at least settle in for some quality yoga and meditation instruction, cherish the company of fellow soul-searchers, and most importantly, reap Rishikesh's major reward—an aura of peace for a good, laid-back time. Summer is yoga off-season; winter has fewer Indian tourists. There are fewer temples in Rishikesh than in Haridwar, but more Westerners, more ashrams, and more *sadhus.*

ORIENTATION

There are three, or five, main parts to Rishikesh, depending on how you look at it. The main city of **Rishikesh** is farthest south, closest to Haridwar. Buses arrive at the southern end of this city center. **Agarwal Road** runs north-south near here, and **Railway Road,** which reaches west to the train station and east to near the river, is also not far off. **Dehradun Road** runs at the northern end of town along the Chandhabhaga River, and at the east end, intersects with **Virbhadra Road** (also called **Laxman-**

jhula Road), the main thoroughfare heading across the Chandhabhaga and along the Ganga toward the first bridge, known as **Ramjhula.** In addition to the rickshaw stop, there are a few services here and more across the bridge, in an area also known as Ramjhula. Farther north is **Laxmanjhula,** the second major bridge. This, too, has services on both sides. Most travelers head toward the bridges for accommodations.

It's a sizeable hike into Rishikesh if you're staying in Laxmanjhula, so this may not be the place to stay if you've got yoga classes in town. From the Laxmanjhula Bridge to the road and taxi stand is itself a surprisingly arduous trek. But both of the bridges are slightly wobbly, adding a dash of playground-fun in the crossing.

PRACTICAL INFORMATION

Tourist Office: U.P. Tourism, 1st fl. office on Railway Rd. (tel. 430209). West of the State Bank of India, near Agarwal Rd., a 5-min. walk from Laxmanjhula Rd. Provides Haridwar/Rishikesh map and the general assortment of brochures about regional treks, but the staff's English is limited.

Budget Travel: Several agents are clustered on Virbhadra Rd., north of the dry river bed, on the way to Ramjhula. **Step Himalayan Adventures,** Virbhadra Rd., (tel. 432851), on the right-hand side on the way out of town, provides information and sets up treks and rafting trips. Open daily 10am-5pm. Closed Sun. and holidays during the off season (Nov.-March).

Immigration Office: Foreigners Registration Office, Railway Rd., in the police office complex. Register for long-term stays. Open Mon.-Fri. 10am-1pm and 2-5pm. There is also a branch in Ramjhula.

Currency Exchange: The **State Bank of India** has offices at Ramjhula and Laxmanjhula, but only changes foreign currency at its main Rishikesh office, on the north side of Railway Rd., a 5-min. walk from Laxmanjhula Rd. (tel. 430114). The bank changes U.S. dollars, pounds sterling, Deutschmarks, and yen traveler's checks from AmEx, Citicorp, and Thomas Cook. Open Mon.-Fri. 10am-2pm, Sat. 10am-noon. The smaller branches change only rupee traveler's checks. The **Bank of Baroda** changes currency, too, but does not advance cash on credit cards.

Telephones: STD/ISD booths are taking over your soul, beginning with Rishikesh. Telegraph/fax services are available near the railway station, on the east end of Railway Rd. and in the main post office.

Trains: Railway Station, at west end of Rishikesh on (surprise!) Railway Rd. Make reservations 10am-1:30pm and 2-4pm. Many connections to major destinations in Haridwar. To Haridwar (6:30, 9:15am, 2:15, 3:15, and 6:40pm, 45min., Rs.4) and Delhi (6:30am, 5, 6:40, and 11pm, 6½hr., Rs.102; *Shatabdi Express,* 5:45 and 10pm, 5hr., Rs.299).

Buses: To confuse travelers, Rishikesh has 2 bus stands. Smog-snorters heading for the plains leave from the **U.P. Roadways** bus stand, on Agarwal and Bengali Rd. (tel. 430066), on the south side of central Rishikesh. To: Delhi (every hr., 4am-10:30pm, 6-7hr., Rs.72); Haridwar (every 30min., 4am-10:30pm, 1hr., Rs.7.50); Dehra Dun (every hr., 6am-6pm, 1hr.45min., Rs.12); Lucknow (6am, 14hr., Rs.148, express on alternating days Rs.160); Nainital (8:15am, 10½hr., Rs.96); and Chandigarh (5:40 and 9:40am, 6hr.). For buses to the hills, go to the **Yatra Bus Stand,** on the northwest end of Rishikesh on Dehra Dun Rd., to get buses to the northern pilgrimage areas. A rickshaw from the U.P. stand costs Rs.5-10. To: Uttarkashi (every hr., 4am-8am, 8hr., Rs.70); Gangotri (5:30am, 12hr., Rs.112); Tehri (every 30min., 4:30am-4pm., 3½hr., Rs.32); Srinagar (U.P.) (every 30min., 3:30am-4pm, 4hr., Rs.42); Badrinath (3am and 5am direct, 12hr., Rs.180); Badrinath via Chamolhi (7hr., Rs.79), Joshimath (10hr., Rs.100), and to Kedarnath (3:45 and 6:30am). Tehri and Uttarkashi serve as launching/halfway points for Yamnotri and Gangotri; Srinigar for Kedarnath and Badrinath. **Shared taxis** to Uttarkashi (4hr., Rs.125) congregate outside the bus stand. If you are going to Uttarkashi and can't find a cab and can't face the bus, ask an auto-rickshaw to take you to Sharma News Agency. Taxis carrying newspapers depart for Uttarkarshi at 5:30am. Be prepared to be squeezed in.

Local Transportation: Getting to and from Ramjhula and Laxmanjhula from Rishikesh is best done with one of the **tempos** that run along Laxmanjhula Rd. (Rs.2-5).

Both bridges must be negotiated by foot—no cross-river traffic, though there are taxis and jeeps in and between the 2 eastern bridge towns. A seat in a taxi to Haridwar from the Ramjhula Bridge costs Rs.20.

Market: The **Main Bazaar** in Rishikesh, toward the river from the post office, has various knick-knacks. There's a didgeridoo shop near the main State Bank of India branch. Laxmanjhula is the place for video and audio Hare Krishna audiotapes and small ceramic *linga*-ashtrays, while Ramjhula is the place for books on yoga and religion, and for ayurvedic medicine.

Pharmacy: Dehradun Rd., west of the police office, has many chemists and "medical stores." Some, such as **Asha Medical Agencies** (tel. 432696), profess to be open 24hr. There are pharmacies at Ramjhula and Laxmanjhula as well.

Hospital/Medical Services: Government General Hospital and **Ladies' Hospital** are on Dehradun Rd. There are several **specialist clinics** along this road, and the **Dashmesh Hospital** (tel. 431444), between the police station and Yatra Bus Stand, has consultations 10am-2pm.

Police: Main Rishikesh Office, Dehradun Rd. (tel. 430100). There's a branch on the south end of Laxmanjhula (tel. 430228). Both are open 24hr.

Post Office: Main office in **Rishikesh,** in the center of town east of Laxmanjhula Rd., next to the big Hotel Basera, has EMS and speed post. Open Mon.-Sat. 9:30am-5:30am. **Ramjhula,** Swargashram. Open Mon.-Sat. 9am-5pm. **Laxmanjhula,** a 5-min. walk south from the bridge. Open Mon.-Sat. 9am-5pm. All branches have *Poste Restante.* **Postal Codes: Laxmanjhula,** 249302; **Rishikesh,** 249201; **Ramjhula,** 249304.

Telephone Code: 0135.

ACCOMMODATIONS

Where you stay in Rishikesh depends on what you want to do. Students of yoga may want to stay in an ashram, students of nature can stay in one of the guest houses west of Laxmanjhula, scholars of mellow and quiet punctuated with revelry should cross the Laxmanjhula Bridge, and learners of the laws of layovers might as well stay near the bus stands in Rishikesh.

Hotels and Guest Houses

Bombay Kshetra, a.k.a. Bombay Guest House (tel. 403648). In Laxmanjhula, turn left after crossing the bridge, head down 50m, and it will be on the right. Feels like an abandoned ruin of an Arabian palace taken over by backpackers. Guests get large, echoing rooms with fans, a serene central courtyard, excellent roof-space (try crashing out on the top level under the stars!), and a super-cool owner. Functional toilets and shower in the back. Cows guard the front gate; bring your own padlock. Singles Rs.40, with 2 beds Rs.50. Doubles Rs.60.

Cozy Guest House, right next door to the Bombay, it is part of the Shree Satyanarayan Trust. Similar feel, with the option of paying a bit more for a room with attached bath close to the Ganga. Other rooms are behind the temple; all are reasonably clean, spacious, and away from street noise. Singles behind temple Rs.40, on Ganga Rs.60. Doubles behind temple Rs.50, on Ganga Rs.90.

Hotel Rajdeep, behind Swargashram in Ramjhula (tel. 432826). A new kid in town (since June 1996); still rough around the edges, but promising with clean, new rooms. Convenient to Ramjhula Ashram. In season: singles Rs.200. Off-season: singles Rs.150.

Green Hotel, behind Gita Bhavan in Ramjhula (east bank). Walk away from the bridge along main walkway; after 200m turn left and walk up 50m. Established, well-run place really is green, with green walls (of every shade) and green beds. Immaculate rooms; good attached restaurant. Prices listed are for foreigners. In season: singles Rs.150. Doubles Rs.200, with air-cooling Rs.300. Off-season: singles Rs.125, with air-cooling Rs.250.

Ramu Hotel, just east of the Green Hotel. Not as clean, but more down-to-earth and rustic than its neighbor. Semi-squalid common bathrooms. Check out the closet-like "massage centre." Loud, mind-blowing fans. Singles and doubles Rs.70.

Bhandari Swiss Cottage (tel. 432676). Up the road branching up to the left near Laxmanjhula (west side). Follow the trail 200m up. A few rooms in their own little natural setting, with garden and good views. Bedrooms are clean, but bathrooms are dirty. Neat balconies. Singles Rs.50, with bath Rs.100. Fixed rates.

High Bank Peasant's Cottage (tel. 431167). Before the Bhandari, on the same trail, on the left side. Same virtues as Bhandari (beautiful garden and views), plus a few bonuses: cleaner, bigger rooms, a garrulous owner, and attached tourist services, including car/scooter use and trekking arrangements. Attached bath with hot water, shower. Prices are higher, although they may be negotiable. Singles Rs.200. Doubles Rs.300.

Hotel Menka (tel. 430285). In Rishikesh, directly opposite Roadways Bus Stand. A safe bet if you're overnighting. Unsullied chambers with attached bath off a stone courtyard with potted plants. In season: singles Rs.100; doubles Rs.125. Off-season: singles Rs.80. Doubles Rs.100.

Hotel Shivlok (tel. 431055). In Rishikesh, near Chander Bhaga Bridge, Laxmanjhula Rd., one-quarter of the way to Ramjhula. An affordable choice among the several business hotels sputtering around. Western toilets, cool staff, shower heads and hot water in attached baths, and some rooms have balconies. Singles Rs.200, with A/C Rs.400. Doubles Rs.350, with A/C Rs.550.

Ashrams and Yoga

No matter what peculiar yoga position you have managed to twist and bend yourself into, an ashram is never out of sight in Rishikesh. Most westerners head to Ramjhula for ashram stays, which are occasionally combined with yoga and meditation classes. Also remember that staying in an ashram isn't like bunking up in a hotel—the meditative atmosphere demands that certain rules be followed. These include total avoidance of meat, eggs, and smelly food (including onions and garlic), abstention from alcohol, tobacco, or drugs of any kind (including *pan*), and adherence to total quiet (no music or late-night talking). Most also demand daily bathing, and request that menstruating women stay out of the ashram centers. Many ashrams have curfews, times when they simply lock the doors. Some of the ashrams (i.e. Swargashram and Parmath Niketan) are more set up for pilgrims and Hindu worshipers, less for yoga and meditation.

Yoga Study Centre, far south end of Laxmanjhula Rd. (tel. 431196). Nearly outside of town, on the river side of the road. Despite its distance from the bridges, a good place to learn *ayangar yoga* if you don't want to stay in an ashram. General, special, and curative classes (for those with proven physical disorders). Three classes per day on alternating days. Hard-cores go here for advanced classes. Three-week winter season course (Feb. 8-28, 1997); summer course (April 4-25, 1997); and intensive course (Sept. 2-24, 1997). Lodging can be arranged. Rudra, the main instructor, has a good reputation. Pay on donation basis only: Rs.200 per week is adequate.

Ved Niketan, south end of Ramjhula's east bank (tel. 430279). Caged deities line the entrance to this large ashram along the rocky beach of the Ganga. The main guru here is around a lot; he's very much got an aura, though pictures of him look nerdy. Popular with foreigners. Day-long yoga fee of Rs.50 includes 6:30-7:30am meditation, 9-10:30am lecture, and 5-7pm yoga. Rs.50 to stay the night. Rooms Rs.100-150.

Omkarananda Ganga Sadan, west side of Ramjhula (tel. 431473, 430763). Big, sterile building just south of the taxi/rickshaw stand. An ashram that feels more like a hospital—clean, dazzling white rooms. Try for a river view. Some rooms have attached bath. Rooms Rs.50 per day; 3-day min. stay (if you bail early, lose a Rs.90 deposit). Open 6am-9:30pm; check-out noon. Yoga instruction: Rs.100 per week, one lecture/class each evening Mon.-Fri. Another branch in Laxmanjhula is more rustic and less sterile.

Bhakta Samaj, at Kailash Gate (tel. 431297). New *madhuban* ashram on the river side between Ramjhula and Rishikesh. Hare Krishna ashram has no yoga program, but they'll bring in a teacher. Upscale, very clean, sparse rooms (no bedframes!). Hot water, shower. Rs.300 per night, Rs.200 for room in basement.

Baba Kali Kamli Wala Panchayet Kshetra, in Ramjhula, south of the Green Hotel (tel. 430811). 135 rooms with attached kitchen/bathroom. Canteen with meals (Rs.15). Big, big place. Popular with Indians. Rooms Rs.50 per night.

Yoga Niketan (tel. 430227). Set in tranquil hills over Ramjhula. Hard-core yoga boot camp. 15-day min. stay includes 3 meals, 2 yoga classes, and 2 meditation classes each day. Strict rules to keep the peace; guests help with cleaning each week. Lockout 9:30pm. Office open 9am-12:30pm and 1:30-6:30pm. Rs.125 per day. Lock your own valuables.

FOOD

There are restaurants in every part of Rishikesh, although none of them serve alcohol or meat. The **Ganga View Restaurant,** in Laxmanjhula (east side) across the road from Bombay Kshetra, has an excellent reputation, though they were renovating when this book was researched. Once it reopens, it will again become *the* place in Laxmanjhula, with slightly different, delicious *thalis* every day.

Amrita, 50m from the Ramjhula rickshaw stand, toward the bridge (west side). This hole-in-the-wall looks like every other place, but Shankar, the owner, is something else—he's traveled in Japan and Europe and knows backpackers' needs. There's a little library of western books (Rs.100 deposit, Rs.5 per day charge). Offers outstanding fresh baked raisin bread, jars of pure honey, cheddar cheese, pizza (Rs.50, order in advance), and banana pancakes (Rs.20). Also look for the newly opened second branch near the taxi stand in east Ramjhula.

Chotiwala, in east Ramjhula near the bridge (tel. 430070). Impossible to miss—as much a landmark here as in Haridwar. The 2 parts, side by side, were supposedly divided by 2 brothers. The right has a better reputation, though the one on the left has a dark den upstairs with wicked A/C. Very popular among Indians. Chotiwala special *thali* with four *chapatis* and nine different dishes, Rs.32. Good *lassis,* too. Open daily 8am-10pm.

Ganga Darshan Restaurant, across from Bombay Kshetra in Laxmanjhula. Closer to the bridge than the Ganga View, and not as good. Still, inexpensive *thalis* are filling (Rs.15-20), and some special dishes (like "cheese chow mein") aren't as heavily spiced as much Indian food. The tables on the balcony are awesome. Open daily 6am-9:30pm.

New Vishal Vaishnav Restaurant, Laxmanjhula Rd. in Rishikesh, 1 block north of Hotel Basera. Very popular, simple restaurant with tasty, tummy-packing *thalis* and various cheap dishes: *khorya paneer* (Rs.8), *fry dal* (Rs.5), *thali* (Rs.36). Open daily 8am-4pm and 7-11pm.

Madras Cafe, in Ramjhula rickshaw stand area (tel. 249192). It's closer to the rickshaws than Amrita. Cleaner than most, with many *dosas* (Rs.10-20) and *thalis* (Rs.25). Great place to sip tea (Rs.4-8) while contemplating rickshaws. Open daily 7am-9:30pm.

SIGHTS AND ENTERTAINMENT

With yoga classes, *chillum* smoking, and requisite chit-chat to keep them busy, most travelers to Rishikesh don't end up doing a lot of anything, but that's partly because the town doesn't offer a ton of distractions, either. There's a **cinema** next to the State Bank of India in Rishikesh, showing Hindi movies. Let your mind dance while buying kids' **spirograph** creations (available in Ramjhula, east side) and perpetuate the survival of a great old toy. **Boats** can be taken across the Ganga at Ramjhula below Sivananda Ashram (one way Rs.3, roundtrip Rs.5); more adventurous travelers can **shoot the rapids** of the holy river—outfitters on the north end of Rishikesh, such as Step Himalayan Adventures (tel. 432581), charge Rs.400-500 per person for transport and a 15-km, 3½-hr. rafting trip through four "good" and two small rapids. After it's all over, settle in for a **massage** at the well-advertised Baba Health and Massage Centre in Rishikesh 100m east of Hotel Shivlok. Enjoy an ayurvedic, Swedish, and/or shiatsu full-body massage (they even massage your ears) in a dark, cool room with freaky, space-age music. (Open daily 8am-5pm; Rs.100per session.)

The *arati* ceremony at **Triveni Ghat,** on the south end of Rishikesh, takes place at sundown. It's not as elaborate as the one in Haridwar. The ancient **Laxman Temple,** on the west bank, is easy to find—look for the engraved, "This is the Ancient Temple of Laxman Jhula," over the arch—although the inside of the temple is not thrilling. The two 12- and 13-story mega-temples on the other side of it are also disappointing, with more jewelry shops than shrines as you climb to the top. The view from above is good, however.

Those who are sticking around can enhance their stay by taking **music lessons,** learning to play the didgeridoo from the shop in Rishikesh (see p. 166) or the tabla from the music school in Rishikesh on the north end of Laxmanjhula Rd. **Hindi lessons** are offered between 11:30am and 12:30pm at Ramjhula, Swargashram, near the Ganga General Store.

■ Near Rishikesh

Try to wait for a clear day to head up to the temple of **Kunch Puri.** The temple sits atop a nearby mountain, and can command views of the whole region, including Haridwar and the snow-capped Himalaya. The temple itself is disappointingly modern and small, though the priest is friendly to visitors. To get there, take a bus headed for Tehri from the Yatra Bus Stand; tell the driver you want to get off at Hindolakhal (1hr., Rs.10). From there, it's a one- to two-hour walk up the mountain along a paved road and up a surreal, narrow stairwell at the very top.

Another destination for a day-hike is the temple at **Neel Kanth Mahadev,** a place to which so many pilgrims have brought milk, *ghee,* and Ganga water that the *linga* has eroded down to a few inches. The temple and nearby bazaar are too modern and hectic for that to be the sole point of the walk—it's the jungle trail along the way, inhabited by wild elephants, that makes the hike worthwhile. Go early, since it's a four- to five-hour climb with no stops, and the temple is more likely to be peaceful early in the day. Ask for the trailhead at the Ramjhula taxi stand, since it branches off from a road on the way there. Jeeps leave from the Ramjhula taxi stand, and there are great views along the way.

■ Yamnotri

The source of the Yamuna River and the first stop on the Garhwal pilgrimage circuit, Yamnotri is accessible only by a 14-km trek from the town of Hanuman Chatti. During the tourist season, 2000 pilgrims come to Yamnotri every day—in whatever way they can. Old women and men walk carrying bundles of clothes, rich businessmen are carried up in *palkis* and on horses, and kids are carried in baskets, all traveling to reach the temple at the top. Yamnotri consists of a temple surrounded by 10 to 15 concrete structures and numerous *dhabas.* The temple remains open from May to November, after which the image from the temple is carried to Kharsoli, a village opposite Janki Chatti. Heavy snows erode the temple so much that it has to be rebuilt every few years, so its architecture is nothing special—a slapdash construction with dressed-up concrete walls and a corrugated metal roof. Next to the temple is a hot-water *kund* where pilgrims bathe. Opposite the temple in the Hanuman Mandir is a *maharaji* who has stayed here year-round for the last 30 years.

The path to Yamnotri angles gently upwards from Hanuman Chatti (2134m) for 8km to Janki Chatti (2676m), and then turns steeply uphill until Yamnotri (3235m). Start early in the morning—there is no shade for the first 10km out of Hanuman Chatti, and by then the higher altitudes and steep path will drain any energy you have left. The path is lined with *chai* and cold drink stands, and sleeping arrangements are available at Janki Chatti. The closest **hospital, post office,** and **communications** system (wireless, only for emergencies) are at Janki Chatti. A seasonal **police** station is set up every year at Yamnotri. Hanuman Chatti is well-connected by buses from Dehra Dun (163km) and Rishikesh (209km). During the pilgrimage season, Hanuman

NORTH INDIA

Chatti is overcrowded, and it may be a better idea to stay overnight at Barkot, 40km south, and take an early morning bus or taxi to Hanuman Chatti.

The GMVN Lodge in Yamnotri is located just above the temple. Cross the bridge and take the uphill path to the left. With a restaurant, garden, electricity through a generator, and hot water (Rs.8 per bucket), this is probably the best place to stay in Yamnotri. The rooms are clean and spacious, and the bathrooms are well-scrubbed. The lodge has three dorms with eight beds each (two have attached bathrooms). In season: dorm beds Rs.80. Off-season: dorm beds Rs.50 (no bedding off-season). There is also a large tent with beds for Rs.8. Reservations must be made a few weeks in advance at any GMVN office. The **Yamuna Ashram** next to the temple is over-crowded, good only as a last resort. Dorm rooms Rs.250. More private rooms Rs.300. In Barkot, lodging is available at the **Raivat Hotel** near the bus stand. The toilets work here and the rooms are reasonably clean. Singles Rs.100. Doubles Rs.200. **Food** is available at any of the *dhabas* along the road, or at the canteen at the GMVN Lodge (veg. *thalis* Rs.25).

■ Uttarkashi

This busy town on the banks of the Bhagirathi River is the administrative center of Uttarkashi District, and the last place to fill a shopping list or catch a Hindi movie before you head out for a trek or climb. Uttarkashi is a typical "modern" hill town with a busy market, buses spewing black smoke, and numerous *chai* shops where travelers can sit and discuss their plans. This is a good place to break a long journey from the plains before heading to Yamnotri or Gangotri.

ORIENTATION

Uttarkashi occupies the space between the **Gangotri Rd.** and the **Bhagirathi River.** There are few specific addresses—most places are located "behind the bus stand" or "in the main market," both of which are impossible to miss, being on the main road.

PRACTICAL INFORMATION

Tourist Office: at the bus stand (tel. 2290). Helpful, English-speaking staff offers a colorful brochure about Uttarkashi District, but not much else. Open May-June and Sept. daily 9am-6pm; Oct.-April and July-Aug. Mon.-Fri. 10am-5pm.

Trekking Agency: Mt. Support, B.D. Nautial Bhawan, Bhatwari Rd. (tel. 2414). Walk along the Gangotri Rd. about 10min. past the bus stand; Mt. Support will be on your left. This trekking agency has a good reputation.

Currency Exchange: Mt. Support has a license to exchange currency but charges a heavy commission.

Telephones: STD/ISD booths all over town.

Buses: To: Gangotri (May-June and Sept., 7 per day, 5am-2pm; Oct.-April and July-Aug., 7, 11am, and 2pm, Rs.45); Rishikesh (May-June and Sept. every hr., 6am-noon; Oct.-April and July-Aug. 5, 7, 8, 10am, and noon, 8hr., Rs.65); Barkot (for Yamnotri, 7:30, 9am, and 2pm, Rs.45); Bhatwari (for treks to Sahasratal and Kedar-nath, 7, 9, 11am, 1, 2, and 3pm, Rs.12); Gaurikund (7:30am, Rs.100), Sangam Chatti (for Dodital trek, 8am, 12:30, and 3:30pm, Rs.14).

Market: Blending into the town, the market lines the Gangotri Rd. and fills the little alleys off to the right towards the river. Open Tues.-Sun.

Hospital: Midway between the Gangotri Rd. and the river, near the post office. X-ray and ambulance available. Open May-June and Sept. 7am-noon and 2-7pm; Oct.-April and July-Aug. 9am-5pm.

Police: Gangotri Rd., 15min. from the bus station on the right.

Post Office: Midway between the Gangotri Rd. and the river. Open daily 9am-5pm with a variable break for lunch.

Telephone Code: 01374.

ACCOMMODATIONS

Bhandari Hotel, bus stand (tel. 2203). Impossible to miss, Bhandari is a favorite with trekkers and climbers because of its restaurant and its proximity to the bus stand. Two beds and a table in a small room, with bathrooms added almost as an afterthought (most are functional). The buses and the lively crowd ensure that nights here are never too quiet. The owner is extremely friendly. Catch taxis to Rishikesh outside. In season: doubles Rs.225. Off-season: doubles Rs.60.

Meghdoot, main market (tel. 2278). Although the builder tried to squeeze as many rooms as possible into this small space, the Meghdoot still feels airy. English is spoken, and a kitchen and dining hall are open for the culinary efforts of guests. The windows only have views of concrete buildings, but tacky nature pictures on the walls inside remind you you're in the hills. Seat and squat toilets available. Hot water is available for Rs.5 per bucket. Check-out noon. May-June and Sept.: doubles Rs.250, with hot water and TV Rs.450. Oct.-April and July-Aug.: doubles Rs.100, deluxe Rs.220.

Garhwal Mandal Vikas Nigam (tel. 2271). Walk along the Gangotri Rd. for 5min. until you see a sign for GMVN on your right. Running hot and cold water, laundry, attached restaurant, a nice garden, and clean rooms make the GMVN ideal, albeit a little pricey. Dorms have 6 beds each. Dorm beds Rs.60. In season: doubles Rs.250, with TV and fancy furniture Rs.450. Off-season: doubles Rs.180, deluxe Rs.250. May-June and Sept., book at least a month in advance.

FOOD

The many *dhabas* that line the Gangotri Rd. serve standard vegetables, rice, and *dal.* No meat is available. Try the **Roopan** opposite the bus stand, or the **Preeti,** which serves South Indian food and is on the left. Lunch and dinner cost about Rs.25-30. For breakfast, nothing beats the butter toast and omelette or *alu paratha* and *achar* at the Bhandari Hotel.

SIGHTS

The **Vishwanath Temple,** located midway between the river and the Gangotri Rd., cements Uttarkashi's connection to the holy city of Varanasi in the plains (see **Varanasi,** p. 220). Uttarkashi means "northern Kashi," and Kashi, "the Luminous," is another name for Varanasi. But the Vishwanath Temple in Uttarkashi, built in 1857 by Maharaja Sudarshan Shah, is not nearly as significant to Hindus as its lowland namesake. A large ancient *trichul,* made of iron and brass, sits in front of the temple.

■ Gangotri

After Bhatwari, the road from Uttarkashi narrows, and the surrounding mountains become more severe, until the shimmering slopes of Mt. Sudarshan (6500m) are finally visible, towering above the small town of Gangotri. At an altitude of 3140m, 98km northeast of Uttarkashi, Gangotri is the source of the Ganga River (here known as the Bhagirathi), and a center for *sadhus* from all over India. According to Hindu mythology, the goddess Ganga, whose river once flowed through the heavens, was pulled down to earth by the ascetic meditations of the saintly King Bhagiratha. Bhagiratha's 60,000 blundering ancestors had been burnt to a crisp years earlier by the sage Kapila when they had interrupted his meditations. In order to revive the souls of his cousins, Bhagiratha meditated in the high peaks above Gangotri and enticed the Ganga to descend to earth. The force of the falling Ganga was tamed by Shiva, who spread out his matted hair and trapped the waters within his locks. The waters of the Ganga followed Bhagiratha in his divine chariot down to Mrityalok, the land of death, where they washed over Bhagiratha's ancestors and released them. The actual site of Gangotri is said to be the place where Bhagiratha rested and prayed to the Ganga for a day after the river's descent. Recent improvements in transportation mean that nearly 1500 pilgrims visit Gangotri every day during the June to September season, leaving their mark in the form of strewn rubbish and rapidly decreasing forests.

ORIENTATION AND PRACTICAL INFORMATION

Gangotri is accessible from late April to early November. To get to Gangotri, take a bus or a shared taxi from Uttarkashi (see **Uttarkashi,** p. 170). Buildings sit on both sides of the **Bhagirathi River.** The main bridge is just next to Dev Ghat, where the Bhagirathi and the **Kedar Ganga** meet. Two parallel paths run on either side of the Bhagirathi, along which all the *dhabas* and hotels are located. Practical affairs such as currency exchange should be taken care of before coming to Gangotri. There is a **post office** near the small bridge (open 8-10am and 3-5pm), but it sometimes runs out of stamps. The **hospital** near the post office has two beds and two oxygen cylinders but emergency care is all it really provides. Prayer accessories, Dickens novels, and other sundry items can be purchased at the **market,** which is basically a line of small shops leading to the temple. Except with regard to prayer accessories, all prices are negotiable. Emergency communiques can be sent via **wireless** from the GMVN office down the road from the hospital. **Telephone** service is slated to begin sometime this year.

ACCOMMODATIONS

Tons of small, dingy places line the area between the bus stand and the temple. In most places, rooms are unpainted, plaster is crumbling, and beds are dirty—bring a sleeping bag. Accommodations across the river from the temple are quieter and more secluded. The best place to stay in Gangotri *if* you have the right connections is the Forest Rest House—permission is given only to VIPs, usually ministers and high-ranking civil servants. If you want to try, contact the District Magistrate at Uttarkashi for permission to stay in the New Log Cabin, or the District Forest Officer in Uttarkashi for permission to stay in the Old Log Cabin. Most ashrams in Gangotri do not accept foreign guests. May and June are high season in Gangotri.

Manisha Cottage, near the bus stand, has 6 plain rooms with a common bathroom, although deluxe rooms with attached bathrooms are coming soon. Rooms are small and have 2 beds. Balcony with river view, power generator, room service, and assistance finding a guide are all provided. Buckets of hot water Rs.10. At the time of this research, the hotel was undergoing major renovations. In season: suites with common bath Rs.200, deluxe Rs.450. Off-season: suites Rs.125, deluxe Rs.300. Discounts for longer stays. Hot water Rs.10 per bucket.

GMVN Guest House (tourist lodge), ideally located next to Gaurikund and away from the bus stand and its teeming crowds. Rooms are spacious and clean, and all have electricity until 11pm. A beautiful garden and a tasty restaurant are both attached. Deluxe rooms have carpeting, double bed, and attached bath. The normal option consists of 2 small rooms and a common bathroom. Often booked-up during season. The 2 dormitories have 6 beds each (with attached bath); there are 2 dorms. In season: dorm beds Rs.75. Normal rooms Rs.350, deluxe rooms Rs.480. Hot water Rs.8 per bucket. Reservations can be made through GMVN offices in Delhi, Bombay, and Calcutta, but the main booking office is at Rishikesh (Yatra office, Muni-Ki-Reti; tourist office open May-Nov.). Book early.

Ganga Lodge, next to the main bridge, across the river from the temple. Eighteen rooms each with 3-5 beds. All rooms have common bathrooms. This place is a bit garish—lots of light, loud music blaring from the stereo, and crowds of people. Rooms are small with beds jammed together. Rates fluctuate. In season: 3-bed rooms about Rs.250. Off-season: rooms as low as Rs.75. Negotiate for longer stays.

Yoga Niketan. This is a place to meditate and study yoga, but non-yoga minded tourists are welcome when there's extra space. Cottages have 2 beds, some cottages have attached baths. Guests often stay for 6 months at a time. Two 1-hr. yoga and two 1-hr. meditation sessions daily. Open May-Oct. Cottages Rs.100-125, including yoga lessons and food.

> ### Snake-Eating Sadhus of Gangotri
>
> Hashish and tobacco, smoked through a *chillum,* are a big part of the daily intake of most *sadhus,* but really dread-inspiring holy men try something else: a krait (an extremely poisonous snake) is rolled up between two unbaked *rotis* with its tail sticking out. This deadly sandwich is then shoved into the fire. When the *rotis* are fully baked, the *sadhu* removes the preparation from the fire and pulls off the snake's tail, bringing the skin and bones with it. Then, preparing himself, he puts a jug of water by his side. He takes two to three bites of the snake and immediately goes into a coma. Every eight to ten hours the *sadhu* wakes up to drink some water and take another bite, sending himself back into a poisoned stupor. The whole process lasts three to four days. **Warning: requires 30 years of practice—do not attempt!**

FOOD

Small *dhabas* flock to the edge of the bus stand. Since meat, eggs, and onions are prohibited, the standard fare is rice, *dal,* vegetables, and *chai.* Prices are the same everywhere, and they remain the same throughout the year: *dal* Rs.15, vegetables Rs.24, *rotis* Rs.2, and rice Rs.10. The food at Ganga Lodge and Manisha Cottage is not bad. The GMVN has recently opened a new restaurant which is a bit more expensive than other places in town, but has a beautiful setting.

SIGHTS

The present **temple** at Gangotri was built by the Gorkha commander Amar Singh Thapa in the early 19th century as a replacement for an older structure. Next to the temple is the **Bhagiratha Shila,** the spot where Bhagiratha prayed. Steps here lead down to the *ghat* where pilgrims bathe. A small bridge from the bus stand arches over to Gaurikund, where the Ganga (also called the Bhagirathi) gushes out of the rock into a beautiful pool.

■ Near Gangotri: Gaumukh

Gaumukh ("Cow's Mouth"), a 17-km trek from Gangotri, is the spot where the Bhagirathi-Ganga emerges from the Gangotri glacier. There are excellent views of the Bhagirathi peaks along the way. The trail passes through the town of Bhojabasa, which has a GMVN rest house, but it's still best to bring your own sleeping bag and tent. The 24-km-long Gangotri glacier, which looks like a giant white ramp to the sky, dumps water from a snout-like cavern. Lal Baba's Ashram is near the glacier, providing accommodations fit for a *sadhu.*

■ Treks Around Uttarkashi and Gangotri

Uttarkashi's marketplace can fulfill most trekking requirements, other than high-altitude food. A number of trekking and mountaineering agencies have opened in Uttarkashi, but the guides they provide are not always reliable for some of the lesser-known treks. Mt. Support in Uttarkashi (tel. (01374) 2419) is generally reliable. The Nehru Institute of Mountaineering in Uttarkashi, located across the river, is also useful. One of the best independent guides for high altitude treks or climbs in the region is Pyar Singh, Village Salang, P.O. Bhatwari, Uttarkashi District—he has guided expeditions to 12 peaks above 6000m. Write well in advance.

From Gangotri

The **Gangotri-Bhojabasa-Tapovan-Nandarvan-Gaumukh-Gangotri trek** takes seven to 10 days. Starting from Gangotri, walk along the path to Gaumukh, stopping at Bhojabasa for the night. From Gaumukh, follow the steep glacial moraine to the fluttering hay in the huge high-altitude meadows of Tapovan, with Shivling and the magnificent Bhagirathi trio in the background. Cross the glacier to Nandarvan on the other side, and then return to Gangotri. Acclimatize in Gangotri for one day before setting out.

The trek from **Gangotri to Kedar Tal** via Bhoj Karak and Kedar Kharak and back is a beautiful and not-too-difficult week-long excursion that approaches an altitude of 5000m. Kedar Tal is the base camp for Brighupant.

The route from **Gangotri to Kedarnath** is a serious high-altitude trek that will take 15 to 20 days, reaching altitudes of over 5600m. This is not a trek for beginners.

From the Uttarkashi-Gangotri Road

The **Saharasratal (Vintage Garhwal)** trek starts at Malla, 27km north of Uttarkashi (near Bhatwari). Trek up the steep path to Sila, where visitors can stay at the Forest Rest House. Trek on the Papur (4hr.), or Ghotu if you are fit (8hr.). Ghotu is a huge meadow above the treeline, and from here the trek follows a ridge all the way to the lakes of Sahasratal, Lama Tal, Parital, Gaumukhi Tal, and Parshan Tal. Located at heights of 4600-5200m, the lakes are the focus of local pilgrimages in October. They are best visited after the monsoon, when the snow and ice have melted. From Darshan (Gaumukhi Tal), descend on the other side of the Khatling Trail and from there on to Ghuttu. Catch a bus from Ghuttu to Rishikesh. This trek will take about 15 days. Very few people descend on the Khatling side, so a reliable guide is essential.

One of the most beautiful but least known treks in the region stretches from **Salang to Khera Tal to Bukki.** Five kilometers beyond Bhatwari, a bridge leads to a path which will take you to Salang village. From here, climb to the high pasture of Chipliya and Bhu Top (3600m). Walk along the ridge, enjoying the clear views of Gangotri range, and descend to Khera Tal, a massive meadow and beautiful lake. Descend from there to a midway camp, and then on to the Gangotri Rd. via Bukki. This trek takes eight to 10 days. Most villagers from Salang know the route.

■ Kedarnath

Kedarnath is an ancient Hindu holy site, one of the 12 *jyotirlingas* of Shiva in India, and hence one of Shiva's main residences. According one myth, the Kedarnath temple was constructed thousands of years ago, when the Pandavas, the heroic brothers of the *Mahabharata,* came here to look for Shiva and pray for his forgiveness. Shiva, who regarded the Pandavas as sinners for having killed their own kin in battle, didn't want the Pandavas to find him, so he transformed himself into a bull, grazing on the *bugyal.* When the Pandavas saw through this disguise Shiva turned to stone and tried to escape into the ground. But as soon as his front half vanished, one of the Pandavas, Bhima, managed to catch Shiva's rocky rear end. Pleased with the Pandavas' diligence, Shiva appeared in his true form and forgave them. The back half of the stone form is now worshiped at Kedarnath. Shiva's front half is said to have disappeared into the ground, broken off, and reemerged in Nepal, where it is venerated at the Pashupatinath temple (see p. 700). The other parts of Shiva turned up at Tungnath (arm), Rudrandath (face), Madhyamaheshwar (navel), and Kalpleshwar (locks), where together with Kedarnath, they form the "Panch Kedar" ("Five Fields") pilgrimage circuit. Kedarnath remains open from May until late October.

Since the construction of a metalled road to Gaurikund, the temple site of Kedarnath has gradually been expanding and developing. Today it is a crowded town with loud music, hundreds of pilgrims, and ugly concrete hotels concentrated around the temple. Nothing, however, can ruin the splendor of Kedar's surroundings: the clean granite and ice sweeps of the Kedarnath range and the meadows all around, coupled with numerous possible excursions make this *dham* a must on the Garhwal circuit. Kedarnath ("Lord of the Field") is the only major pilgrimage site above the treeline in Garhwal, and is a good place to experience what Garhwalis go through as they take their cattle to high pastures during the summer months.

Kedarnath is accessible by way of a 14-km trek from the trailhead town of Gaurikund, which can be reached by bus from Rishikesh (216km) via the ancient capital of Garhwal, Srinagar (not to be confused with its namesake, the capital of

Jammu and Kashmir). The trek up to Kedarnath takes four to six hours and is steep for the first 12km. The overpowering stench of horses (about 1000 pass each day) is an added difficulty—you need nose filters or extreme self-control to deal with it. It's best to start early in the morning or late in the afternoon to avoid the midday sun.

PRACTICAL INFORMATION

The **State Bank of India** is just behind the temple, and there is a **hospital** next to the road on the temple above the main bridge. STD **telephone** facilities exist, but the link is extremely frail and the connection keeps breaking down. There is a **market** near the temple, and a **post office** just north of the temple.

ACCOMMODATIONS AND FOOD

The minute you hit town, touts will accost you to rent a room from their "brilliant" hotels. A lot of small, private "hotels" have emerged in Kedarnath, and if you have not booked in advance, one of these much-touted places might be your best bet. Expect a bed, water, and electricity from 7 to 10pm. Prices are completely discretionary so bargain hard, especially if you turn up after 7pm. Rates are generally Rs.100 for a single and Rs.200 for a double in season.

The **GMVN** has two guest houses in Kedarnath, one immediately on your left as you approach the town (tel. 6210), and a second across the river and below the hillside (tel. 6228). The one across the river has an excellent lounge, clean and spacious rooms, and a friendly staff. The rooms are clean and comfortable if a bit cramped. Two beds, a table, a bathroom, and electricity from 7 to 10pm make this seem like heaven on earth. The hotel is usually fully booked in season, and from September to October. In season: dorm beds Rs.100. Doubles Rs.450. Off-season: 25% discount. Hot water Rs.12 per bucket.

Many **ashrams** will not accept foreigners, but if the GMVN is booked and you don't want to resort to private hotels yet, try either the **Bharat Seva Ashram** or the **Temple Committee**—both reluctantly accept foreigners on occasion. The Bharat Seva has both big, crowded dorm rooms and small private rooms. There is a canteen where one can cook and eat. No alcohol or smoking. Dorm beds free. Rooms for 4-5 people Rs.150-200. The **Temple Committee** has several cottages and rooms and altogether houses about 50 people. Some cottages have attached bath and kitchen. If a VIP shows up, expect to get bumped. Rooms or smaller cottages about Rs.100. Deluxe cottages Rs.300. Book early; reservations can be made at Okhimat off-season and at Kedarnath in season.

As usual, most of the *dhabas* are clustered along the temple road. Food is standard and prices are high. Try the **Tiwari Restaurant** ("Your satisfaction is our motto") or the temple committee *dhaba* behind the temple. If you are sick of *dal bhat*, vary your diet with Maggi noodles at the exorbitant price of Rs.20 per plate. Breakfast is the standard *alu-paratha* with *achar* and *drai*.

SIGHTS

Looking at the magnificently constructed **temple,** with its huge, evenly cut gray blocks and intricate carving, it is hard to imagine how it could have been constructed without the help of the mighty Pandavas, especially since the temple is believed to date from the time of Shankara, about 800 AD. The large stone *mandapa* contains a huge statue of Nandi, while inside the sanctum a rock is worshiped as Shiva's rear end.

The **Gandhi Sarovar,** a one- to two-hour walk from Kedarnath, is more exciting than the temple, and provides a breather from the crowds. Most likely, your only company at this emerald green lake will be the majestic Kedarnath mountain range. To get to the lake, cross the log bridge (or the main bridge) and scramble up to a well-marked trail, clearly visible behind the temple on the left. Although the river starts from beyond the lake, it's quite a trek to get to the source. Allow one to two hours for the walk each way.

Follow the zig-zagging trail to the right of the temple for 20 minutes until you see fluttering flags on top of a rock—these mark the **Bhairava Mandir,** just across from which is the *goota* of **Phalari Baba.** Phalari Baba has rows of books, comfortable sofas, and a telephone. A great person to talk to, he speaks English and frequently bursts into heartening laughter. A visit to Phalari Baba is a great way to get away from the bustle of the main town.

Nine very steep kilometers beyond Kedarnath is **Vasuki Tal** (4150m). Few people go here and many "guides" will claim falsely that there's too much snow along the way to get there. Vasuki Tal is part of a series of lakes passed by serious trekkers going from Khetling Glacier to Kedarnath. Further from Kedarnath are **Maser Tal,** where pilgrims bathe in the freezing water, and **Pain Tal,** where it is often extremely cold. These trails are treacherous; only accomplished and accompanied trekkers should try the whole trek.

■ Badrinath

The temple town of Badrinath is probably the most famous of Garhwal's Hindu pilgrimage sites, attracting pilgrims from all across India during its summer season (May-Nov.). Badrinath is the northern *dham* established by the southern saint Shankara in the 9th century. Along with Puri in Orissa, Rameswaram in Tamil Nadu, and Dwarka in Gujarat, it forms a compass-point for India's sacred geography. Badrinath is located on the Alaknanda River 297km from Rishikesh, not far from the overpowering Nilkanth peak as well as the Tibetan border. Because Badrinath is accessible by road, it now attracts growing numbers of pilgrims and secular tourists every year—coming by bus, they forego the austerity of walking that the pilgrimage once required. Badrinath can be reached by bus from Rishikesh via Srinagar, Rudraprayag, and Joshimath. Buses also frequently come here directly from Kedarnath.

The Badrinath **temple** is colorful, with a long main entrance gate (the Singh Dwara) through which worshipers must pass for *darshan* of the meter-high Badrivishal image inside. The temple's architecture is an unusual mixture of Buddhist and Hindu styles, and there is a large debate over whether it was in ancient times a Buddhist or Hindu temple. The priests in charge of the temple are to still to this day recruited from Shankara's home village in Kerala. Before visiting the temple, worshipers must bathe in the **Tapt Kund** hot spring, where the temperature of the water is often about 45°C. This balmy bath is usually juxtaposed with a dip into the icy waters of the Alaknanda.

Accommodations available from numerous *dharamshalas,* or at the hotel run by the GVMN, are very basic. There are numerous *dhabas* around the temple site, but no fancier forms of food.

■ Corbett National Park

A painted rock on the way into Corbett National Park reads, "Study Wild Creatures—it will help us learn about ourselves." There may be no better place in India than Corbett to explore this method of self-discovery. Founded in 1936, Corbett was India's first national park. Originally called Hailey National Park, after the governor of the province, Sir Malcolm Hailey, the park was later renamed to honor Jim Corbett (1875-1955), a British gentleman who was renowned as a hunter of tigers and other large felines. Corbett quit killing tigers for sport in the 1920s, but he was still called upon to shoot tigers and leopards when they threatened human lives. Corbett became famous for his photographs of tigers and for the books he wrote, including *The Man-Eaters of Kumaon.*

The park itself is magnificent, particularly the area around the Dhikala station; distant mountains envelop the vast, peaceful swath of plain and jungle. Nestled within this splendor hide Corbett's true treasures: the abundant wild animals which include countless birds, spotted deer, crocodiles, langur monkeys, rhesus macaques, porcupines, pythons, and elephants, turtles, and boars. Of course, there are also tigers—

about 80 of them. Visitors to Corbett are sure to see a few, if not many, of these species, and a lucky handful even see the striped Bengali beast itself.

PRACTICAL INFORMATION

Corbett is open from November 15 to June 15. The wildlife viewing is best late in the season, although anytime is great for soaking in the park's beauty.

All visitors to Corbett must first obtain a **permit** in the nearby town of **Ramnagar,** 16km from the main gate entrance. The **Office and Reception** (tel. (05945) 85489) of the park's field director is the place to do this. The office is across from the bus depot toward the large bridge; look for the large sign on the left on the way in. The office will also book lodgings at Dhikala, inside the park. (Open daily 8am-1pm and 3-5pm.) Some travelers have had to wait a few days in Ramnagar for a room to be available in Dhikala. (See **Accommodations and Food,** below.) Ramnagar offers most basic services: for last-second **currency exchange,** the State Bank of India (tel. (05945) 85337) has a branch a few blocks down and a few blocks left of the bus depot. They change traveler's checks (Open Mon.-Fri. 10am-2pm, Sat. 10am-noon.) A direct **bus** leaves daily for Dhikala, inside the park, from the bus stand in Ramnagar near all the hotels (4pm, 3hr., Rs.22). Buses leave Ramnagar more frequently for Ranikhet (where you may want to go if you are faced with a few days' wait for accommodations in Dhikala), passing Dhangarhi Gate on the way—make sure the driver knows you want to stop. At Dhangarhi Gate, you'll have to wait for transport into Dhikala. Day visitors cannot enter at Dhangarhi or go to Dhikala—they must go in at **Bijrani,** and a permit is still required. A **taxi** from Ramnagar to Dhangarhi Gate will take one hour, and it's another one and a half hours to Dhikala. The trip will cost about Rs.500 plus the car and driver's entrance fees.

The **Office at Dhangarhi Gate** is open 6am-6pm; no one may enter after dark. Here, you'll pay the fees you didn't pay at Ramnagar. Entrance fees are Rs.100 for foreigners, Rs.15 for Indians. The car fee is Rs.50, camera fee Rs.50, video camera fee Rs.500. There is a small **museum** at the gate (Rs.10 for foreigners), which consists of one room filled with bizarre and morbid exhibits. Beyond the scale model of the park, there are stuffed specimens of several mammal species, with signs reporting how the animals died: "This tiger was crushed to death when wild elephants broke a tree branch." There are also panther and tiger embryos kept in jars, and a spotted deer fetus crammed into a glass cube.

Before **leaving** Dhikala, all visitors must obtain a **clearance certificate** and fill out a questionnaire, both of which should be turned in at Dhangarhi upon leaving. The **bus** from Dhikala to Ramnagar leaves at 9am (9:30am in winter) and takes 2½ hours (Rs.22). If you want to go through Ranikhet instead (since the route is shorter than through Nainital), get out at Dhangarhi (Rs.13) and wait by the side of the road for buses headed north. (Last bus is at 2:30pm, 4hr., Rs.33.)

ACCOMMODATIONS AND FOOD

The options for **lodging** at the village of Dhikala inside the park may be decided for you at the Office and Reception in Ramnagar—foreigners often get thrown into the bunk houses, especially if many Indian families are around. The bunks are stacked four-high, and the "mattresses" aren't the most comfortable, but they are good enough for a night's sleep. The bathrooms, in a separate hut from the bunks, have low water pressure and are a haven for mosquitoes. Guard your belongings; this place could feel more secure. Check-out 11am. Cabin lodging Rs.450 per suite. Tourist Hutment (triple suite) Rs.240. Bunk in the log hut Rs.50. Bedding Rs.25. (These prices are for foreigners; Indian nationals pay approximately two-thirds less.)

There is a small **"café"** at Dhangarhi Gate, where bottled water and other munchies are sold. These are more expensive inside the park, so you may want to stock up. Though many travelers report drinking the water from the faucets near the station office without problems, this water is not filtered. There are two restaurants at Dhikala, both serving Indian, Chinese, and Continental food for breakfast, lunch, and dinner. The **KMVN Restaurant** serves large portions of food so over-spiced as to be completely devoid of taste. Vegetable *korma* Rs.32, spicy but filling vegetable fried rice Rs.22. At the other end of the camp the **Canteen** serves similar fare for less money but without the comfort (omelette Rs.10). Both restaurants are open 5am-2pm and 4-10pm. Inquire at the office about boarding meal packages.

If lodgings are not immediately available inside the park, the **Tourist Rest House** (tel. (05945) 85225), next door to the park office in Ramnagar, is more than adequate; the four-bed dormitory rooms and super-deluxe suites are well-kept, have hot water showers and squat toilets, as well as high powered ceiling fans. Dorm beds Rs.30. Deluxe Rs.300. Super-deluxe with A/C Rs.400. Extra bed Rs.60. Extra person Rs.30. For food, the dim, rough and tumble **Corbett Outpost Bar and Restaurant,** near the rest home, serves non-veg. fare. (Open daily 10am-11pm.)

SIGHTS

However you decide to enjoy Corbett, adhere to all the park's rules and regulations about treating nature right. Don't throw burning cigarettes around, feed the animals, or act noisy or raucous. One of the best things about the park is its serenity—cars are even forbidden to use their horns! For your own safety (as attacks by tigers are not unheard of), don't ever walk outside the camp perimeter, and be careful at night. Driving after dark is forbidden.

There are ways to get down and dirty in Corbett without breaking the rules. By far the best is taking an **elephant ride.** For Rs.50, visitors get a two-hour tour across the prairie and through the jungle, all from a pachyderm's perspective. This is the best way to try to see a tiger, or to come close to wild elephants and other animals. Sign up for a ride at the station office; during the high season, expect to wait up to a few days—there are eight elephants, each of which can carry six people. Tours go at 5:15am or 4:30pm. Both tours have their benefits (either sleep or cool weather) and sightings are equally likely at either time. From atop your elephant (and elsewhere, even on the camp), marvel at what seems to delight tourists most: yes, those are, indeed, 3m-tall cannabis plants, acres and acres of them.

You can hire a **jeep** at the same time—up to eight may ride with one or two guides around the Dhikala Station area. You cover more ground than on the elephants and can get all the way out to the reservoir where the crocodiles play.

The only excursion on **foot** permitted outside the camp (and then only before 4:30pm) is to the nearby **Gularghati Watchtower,** which offers a good view of the landscape. There are free guided **bird tours** Sat. and Sun. from 6-8am or 7-9am. Inquire at the office. At night, **films** about nature and the park are shown behind the restaurant. Check the office for schedules. To pack your brain with info about what you've encountered, there's a small **library** adjacent to the office, with numerous

---

Project Tiger

Faced by a shocking drop in the tiger population due to hunting and industrialization, Indira Gandhi inaugurated a drastic initiative to save tigers in 1973. Named Project Tiger, it set aside nine areas of tiger territory as national parks and hired a staff of armed guards to patrol the areas and thwart poachers. The initiative was initially successful, and the tiger population grew from several hundred to several thousand. Ten more national parks were set aside. Lately, however, poaching has been on the increase (tiger products fetch incredibly high prices) and the armed guards are less formidable than in the beginning. The tiger remains an endangered species and some fear it could face extinction by the end of this century. The best places in India to try to catch a glimpse of the beasts are Corbett National Park in Uttar Pradesh (home of the administrative offices of Project Tiger) and Kahna National Park in Madhya Pradesh.

books about nature. (Open summers daily 9am-12:30pm and 5:30-8pm; winter daily 9am-noon and 5-7pm.)

■ Nainital

When the body of Shiva's consort Sati was chopped into various pieces (see **Divine Dismemberment,** p. 404), one of her eyes, it is said, fell into the hills and so the stunning emerald lake of Nainital was formed. British colonialists, never ones to pass up a good fallen eyeball, were the first to reap (and rape) the lake area's beauty. A Mr. P. Barron of Shahjahanpur was the first Brit to come here. He brought a yacht and built a "pilgrim cottage," setting in gear what would eventually become a popular British hill station and the summer capital of the United Provinces (the British name for Uttar Pradesh). In 1880, a disastrous landslide killed 151 people, but the flattened part of the town was merely incorporated into its design; today it is used for field hockey games. Modern Nainital still serves its "original" purpose as an escape for Indian and foreign tourists fleeing the searing summer sun of the plains. But even with an annual high-season (May-June and October) that brings the town's capacity way beyond its limits (exacerbating the lake's pollution), the lake still radiates some aura of divine resilience into the cool mountain air.

ORIENTATION

The town of Nainital is split into two major parts—**Tallital** and **Mallital**—which are connected by **the Mall,** a road running along the east side of the lake. Tallital, which hugs the southern tip of the lake, is where buses arrive. From there, it's a 15-20-minute walk along either the Mall or the road on the west side of the lake to Mallital. Most hotels are found along the Mall, while most services are in one of the two town parts. The **Flats,** a large, common area used for field hockey, sprawls between Mallital and the water.

PRACTICAL INFORMATION

Tourist Office: (tel. 35227), about three-quarters of the way to Mallital along the Mall. Provides basic information about the town and region, and can help with transport to nearby sites. Open daily 10am-5pm.

Budget Travel: Several tour agents line the Mall, such as that at the base of Hotel Elphinstone, Shivam Tour and Travel (tel 35269); "evening branch" on the Mall near Tallital open Mon.-Fri. noon-4pm, Sat. noon-2pm. Runs trips to local sites such as Cheena Peak and Hanumangarhi, and often offer advanced bookings for night buses to Haridwar and Delhi. Avoid day trips to Corbett as these allow you hardly any time off the bus.

Currency Exchange: A surprising number of shops take Visa and MasterCard. **State Bank of India** has a branch in Mallital just beyond the Flats (tel. 35645). Exchanges traveler's checks. Open Mon.-Fri. 10am-2pm, Sat. 10am-noon.

Telephones: STD/ISD booths are everywhere in Mallital and Tallital. The guy on the left side of the main bazaar in Tallital, near the bus stand, lets you receive calls for Rs.3 per minute. Note that recent changes have turned the first "2" of four-digit numbers into a "35" or a "36."

Buses: Arrive at and depart from the lake front, Tallital. Haldwani is the nearest major hub, and nearly every bus goes there first. Before giving up hope on direct routes from Nainital, ask about service from Haldwani. To: Haldwani (every 15min., 5:10am-6pm, 2hr., Rs.16); Kathgodam (90min., Rs.15); Bareilly (7am, 1:30, and 5:30pm, 5hr., Rs.22); Ramnagar (5, 7am, and 3pm, 3½hr., Rs.23); Almora (7am and noon, 3hr., Rs.28); Ranikhet direct (6am, 12:30, and 2:30pm, 3hr., Rs.27); Dehra Dun (5:30, 6:30, 7am, 4:30, and 8pm, 10hr., Rs.136); via Haridwar (8hr., Rs.106); Delhi (8 per day, 6:30-8:30am, 8-9hr., Rs.95/118/170 for semi-direct/express/super-direct). Note that tickets on buses to Dehra Dun and Delhi are often sold to the travel agents that line the Mall. Book ahead, although it's sometimes possible to wait for no-shows and grab a seat at the last second.

Local Transportation: Rickshaws charge Rs.3-5 to drive the length of the Mall. During May, June, and Oct., traffic is closed to heavy and light vehicles and cycle rickshaws in the morning and afternoon.

English Bookstore: Modern Bookstore, on the upside of the Mall near the Flats, has a good selection. Open Mon.-Sat. 10am-9pm.

Library: Durga Suh Library, lakefront along the Mall, allows readers to check out one English book at a time. Rs.10 admission, Rs.30 deposit. April-Sept.: open Mon.-Sat. 7:30-10:30am and 5:30-8:30pm. Oct.-March: open Mon.-Sat. 8:30-10:30am and 4-7pm.

Market: The area west of the Flats in Mallital hosts a largeish market with food and various wares. Scrunched into the west part of this area is a **Tibetan Market.**

Pharmacy: Indra Pharmacy, by the bus stand in Tallital (tel. 35139), is well-stocked and keeps long hours (Mon.-Sat. 6:50am-10pm, Sun. 6:50am-5pm).

Hospital/Medical Services: Dr. D.P. Gangola (tel. 35039) is a consulting physician at Indra pharmacy (daily 9am-2pm); he also keeps hours in Mallital. Dr. G. P. Shah operates a clinic (tel. 35778) near the entrance to the Flats on the Mall. **B. D. Pandey Hospital** is near the State Bank of India in Mallital.

Police: A small stand is in front of the Hotel Mansarovar on the Tallital end of the Mall. Tallital (tel. 36470), Mallital (tel. 35445). There are also **state police** (SSP, tel. 35586).

Post Office: The GPO has its main branch on the north side of Mallital, a few blocks up from the Mall's extension. *Poste Restante* open Mon.-Sat. 9am-5pm. There's also a branch in Tallital. **Postal Code:** 263002.

Telephone Code: 05942.

ACCOMMODATIONS

More than anywhere else in Kumaon, prices for lodging in Nainital are subject to change by season. Listed prices are high-season rates, except where noted; expect a 25-75% drop outside of May, June, and October. November to March is the cheapest time to come. There are dozens of hotels in Nainital; shop around if you can. Those places set higher on the hill have better views and less street noise, though most places along the Mall (where most hotels are) are still pretty sedate. Almost every place follows the government-mandated 10am check-out.

KMVN Tourist Rest House (tel. 35570). About 200m in the opposite direction from the Tallital bus stand and from the Mall; follow signs from the ramp. Set above the road, away from the noise, with rooms offering grand views of the lake and distant hills. Very popular. 8-bed dorms are often full. Hot water, shower, western toilet. Super-deluxe rooms have TV, telephone and balcony. 30 rooms, 120 beds, restaurant serves all meals. Dorm beds Rs.40. Two-bed suites Rs.800. Extra bed 20% of room rate. Extra person 10%.

Hotel Evelyn (tel. 35457). One-third of the way from Tallital on the Mall. Relatively posh rooms and suites with telephone, speakers with piped-in Hindi pop music, and posters of the Himalaya to remind guests where they are. Some rooms have baths, showers, hot water, TV, and sitting rooms. Doubles Rs.200-600, depending on view.

Hotel Gauri (tel. 36617). On the road parallel to the Mall, behind the Hotel Mansarovar, near Tallital. Dim halls lead to cheery rooms with 2 chairs, TV, and sometimes even hot showers. Quaint balcony with views. In season: doubles Rs.450. Off-season: doubles Rs.100, Rs.150 with shower.

Hotel Samrat (tel. 35768). One-half block away from the lake in Tallital, across the gully. Rooms with attached bath have comfy beds but are noisy when the buses leave, starting at 5am. The owner's helpers are friendly. Singles Rs.100. Doubles Rs.150-200.

Ashok Hotel (tel. 35721). Near Samrat in Tallital, a little farther from the bus stand. A budget beast—small beds in blue rooms off halls with blue slanted ceilings. Rooms are cell-like; the sink is down the hall and the toilet is communal. Singles Rs.150. Doubles Rs.300. Prices subject to *much* change.

Hotel Punjab (a.k.a. "Nirmal Palace"), behind Hotel Mansarovar. Three hundred rooms with good views, kind owners, cold showers, working toilets, and maddeningly mauve walls. Off-season fares are a steal: singles Rs.45, with bath Rs.50. In season: prices increase 100-300%.

Fairhavens Holiday Home (tel. 36057). Adjacent to the Head Post Office, Mallital. Nainital's place to kick back and enjoy life whatever the cost. Instead of the normal, sterile modernity of other high-end hotels, Fairhavens offers retirement-home-style relaxation and pure, old-style colonial class. Other guests are stuffy and old, but ignore them and enjoy the view from the verandah. Piped music, TV, hot and cold water, and attached restaurant. Singles Rs.300. Doubles Rs.900.

FOOD

Whereas most of Nainital's budget hotels are at the Tallital end of the Mall, the Mallital end is grounds for gathering grub. Corn-on-the-cob and similar delectables can be bought along the Mall, and the market west of the Flats has several cheap vendors selling tasty food of questionable quality. Eat at your own risk. In Tallital, the main bazaar is lined with little restaurants such as Neeru's (6am-11pm) selling *chola bhatura* for Rs.8. The one with the Brooke Shields poster, across from Anupam, makes a scrumptious bun omelette for Rs.6. Many of the hotel restaurants serve decent fare. Restaurant prices are seasonal.

Tandoor Restaurant (tel. 35557) next to Hotel Menino, halfway down the Mall. Enjoy black-and-white Hindi TV with a delectable veg. *thali* (Rs.30), mutton curry (Rs.35), or *seekh kabab* (Rs.30). Open daily 9am-10pm.

Ahar Vihar Restaurant (tel. 35446), upstairs from the well-lit variety stores on the Mall near Mallital. Popular, low-end restaurant. Well-lit and cheery, feels like Mom's kitchen with various scrawlings on the wall. Gregarious owner assures "every bite a delight." Green peas *masala* Rs.15, pizza Rs.20, and Rajasthani *thali* Rs.30. Open daily 9:30am-9:30pm.

Nanak's Restaurant (tel. 35336), between the library and Mallital on the Mall. A would-be Western restaurant serving fast-food veg. burgers (Rs.20), "Jughead's trip in life" (a.k.a. pizza), milkshakes, and mango sundaes (Rs.25-50) in a loud, neon setting. Popular among Indian tourists' children. Open daily 8:30am-11pm.

Green Restaurant, in Bara Bazaar in the heart of Mallital. A bit more elegant than the nearby Shivas and Paradise. Green has "misri roti stuff" (Rs.10) and a wide range of Chinese dishes. Open daily 7am-1pm.

SIGHTS AND ENTERTAINMENT

The thousands of Indian tourists who migrate annually to Nainital do so primarily to escape the heat, but locals and Mother Nature have made sure they won't be bored once they're here. The first joy is the **lake** itself. To really get out in the middle of Sati's emerald eyeball, there are places that rent **boats.** Do the work yourself in a paddle boat (Rs.25 per hour for a 2-seater, Rs.35 for a four-seater), or sit on the colorful throne as a boatsman gracefully hauls you around (Rs.45 for full round of the lake, Rs.30 for one trip across). You can rent yachts from the Nainital Boat Club, though they might insist you become a member (Rs.50 per hr.). There are occasional yacht regattas throughout the year. While cruising around, buy drinks from one of the prudent kids who set up shop under the brush along the water, where only the boat-bound can find them.

Just walking around the lake yields its own delights. Snake charmers and musicians sometimes strut their stuff near the Flats, and there's a small fairground near the Tibetan Market west of Mallital (with rickety rides that look like an accident waiting to happen). Most underappreciated is the placid, cool walk along the side opposite the Mall, where there are two small temples and a few ledges near the water.

Away from the water, the mountains around Nainital are alluring and accessible. The easiest way to get to the top of **Snowview** is with the **ropeway** (gondola-style chairlift) which leaves from a clearly marked building about 20m up from the Mall in Mallital. Everyone wants to get their binoculars to the viewpoint at the top, so opening time (8:45am) is the best bet for sure tickets and clear views. Roundtrip Rs.35, with an hour stop at the top. One way Rs.20; it's a 2.5-km walk down.

Other popular destinations for day hikes around Nainital include **Cheena (China) Peak** (2611m), 6km away or a 2½-hr. walk, where the views are best since the peak is the highest around. Start in Mallital or have a taxi take you to Tonneleay on Kilbury Rd. to shorten the trip. Land's End, on the back side of Tiffin Peak (the one immediately west of the lake) offers a humongous view of the sprawling valley to the west. Farther up Tiffin Peak is **Dorothy's Seat,** a flat, green area near the top, named after a woman who was killed in a crash. At the very top is the aptly named **Tiffin Top,** where binoculars can be used for about Rs.5. The views from Tiffin Top are good, and there are snack shops.

The best way to get to Tiffin Top (or past Land's End and to views of Cheena Peak) is by **horse.** There is a stall in Mallital just beyond the Flats and they'll charge Rs.50 straight to Tiffin Top and back (30min.) or Rs.100 with four "sites" along the way, although the only thing that's really thrown in is a stop at Land's End. If you want a guide who can keep up and occasionally bring you to a gallop, you'll have to pay for his horse as well. Otherwise, they'll lope along in front. They'll go to other spots on request, though they push the Tiffin Top package heavily.

Wandering up the road heading west of Tallital leads to the remarkably British-looking **Governor's House** (dating back to 1899), the adjacent **Golf Course** (which isn't supposed to be open to the public, although it's worth pushing the issue), and, farther along, to **Hanumangarh** (a small temple) and the **Observatory** (about 3.5km from Tallital), both of which are mostly renowned for their sunset vistas. The observatory (with "satellite tracking cameras," i.e., a big telescope) can be visited independently with prior approval.

For evening entertainment, a **stroll along the Mall** becomes less hectic as darkness magically enshrouds the piles of chintz in the stores. If it's cool, that's a good time to snag a shawl, quality specimens of which are produced here and in Almora. **Capital Cinema,** near the Flats, runs Hindi movies regularly, and, as a last resort in this resort town, there are various **video game arcades** in both Mallital and Tallital. The ones on Mallital are better, with Super Mario Brothers in color for Rs.1.

■ Ranikhet

Ranikhet is the most alpine of Kumaon's hill stations; from the town center, it's only a short walk up to forests of pine and deodar trees inhabited by *kakar* (barking deer). Vertiginous travelers will also note that looking down from town, the land feels steep—although the soaring, snowcapped Nanda Devi (7817m) and other mountains show the true meaning of steepness. The name Ranikhet comes from a legend that an ancient queen played here, though the majority of the town's history reflects a more kingly sport—the British used it as a hill station, and as a headquarters for the Kumaon Regiment. The army presence is still discernible along the road behind the town. With less traffic noise than the other hill stations, and markedly less to do, Ranikhet is a prime spot for hikes and relaxation; fewer travelers come here. But as a local tourist brochure points out, "how long Ranikhet can maintain its virginity is a million dollar question."

ORIENTATION

Travelers need to be concerned with two parts of Ranikhet: the **bazaar** in the town center, along which most services and numerous hotels and restaurants are found, and **the Mall,** a road extending up the mountain and away from the chaos. Some more expensive hotels are situated along the Mall. Buses arrive at either end of the bazaar; U.P. Roadways buses stop at the east (downhill) end, and KMOU buses arrive and depart on the west end. The town is located on the northern slope of a mountain.

PRACTICAL INFORMATION

Tourist Office: (tel. 2227). At the east end of the bazaar, just up from the U.P. Roadways bus stand. Friendly, knowledgeable staff can provide a booklet about Ranikhet with phone listings not in *Let's Go*. Open daily 9am-6pm.

Currency Exchange: The **State Bank of India** (tel. 2262) and **Nainital Bank** (tel. 2637), both of which are on the road above and parallel to the bazaar. Several other banks in town also exchange money.

Telephone: Several STD/ISD stands line the bazaar; one is beneath the Alka Hotel toward the west end of the bazaar.

Trains: The closest stations are in Kathgodam and Ramnagar.

Buses: U.P. Roadways (tel. 2645) and **KMOU** (tel. 2609) share service to and from Ranikhet. Roadways tends to take the longer routes, but you'll have to ask to find out which company is running a particular route at any given time. To: Almora (8 per day, 5:30am-5:15pm, 2hr., Rs.22); Nainital (8, 8:30, 10:30am, and 2:30pm, 3hr., Rs.23); Ramnagar (7, 8:30, 10am, 1:30, and 3pm, 4hr., Rs.37); Haldwani (11 per day, 5:30am-4pm, 4hr., Rs.33); Dehra Dun (8:30am and 3:30pm, 13hr., Rs.110); Delhi (3, 4, and 4:30pm, 12hr., Rs.106).

Pharmacies: Many line and surround the bazaar.

Medical Assistance: The **clinic** of Dr. Prakash Srivastava (tel. 2101) is towards the east end of the bazaar, upstairs.

Emergency: tel. 100.

Police: tel. 2232.

Post Office: The main branch is along the mall, about 2km from town center, but there's a smaller branch near the tourist office. Open Mon.-Fri. 9am-2pm, Sat. 9am-noon.

Telephone Code: 05966.

ACCOMMODATIONS

Hotels along the bazaar are noisier and less well-kept, but less expensive, than those tucked among the hills along the Mall.

KMVN Kalika Tourist Bungalows (tel. 2893). Look for the signs along the Mall, beyond the main post office. Has cheap dormitory beds that offer serenity but little privacy. The whole establishment is well-organized, simple, and nestled in its own chunk of forest. Bathrooms are clean and have hot water but no showers. Super-deluxe rooms have carpeting and color TV. Dorm beds Rs.40 year-round. In season: Deluxe rooms with black and white TV Rs.550. Super-deluxe Rs.800. Off-season: deluxe rooms Rs.275. Super-deluxe Rs.800. Extra bed 20% of room rent. Extra person 10%.

Hotel Rajdeep (tel. 2247), near Midway closer to the west end of the bazaar. Popular among Indian and foreign travelers alike. Rooms are very basic but cleaner than the rooms downstairs at the Natraj. Singles Rs.150.

Natraj Hotel (tel. 2378), downstairs from Rajdeep. The beds are flea-ridden, the rooms musty, and the water non-functional, but it's cheap. Singles Rs.75.

Hotel Everest (tel. 2402). A good bargain. Watch the bizarre bazaar from the spiffy balcony, but note that no liquor is allowed. Rooms have mirrors, and common bathrooms are tidy. Off-season: Singles Rs.35, with bath Rs.75. Doubles Rs.75, with bath Rs.120.

Tribhuwan Hotel (tel. 2524), on the west end of town. A mighty beast composed of three buildings. Its 2-sided balconies can't be beat, and there's a restaurant for the exclusive use of guests! Deluxe rooms are huge, fresh, and carpeted with TVs and buckets of hot water. In season: basic rooms Rs.250. Deluxe rooms Rs.350. Off-season: prices drop 25%.

Parwati Inn (tel. 2325), down the road by the Roadways station, touts its three-star rating. "Economy" rooms have no view, but pricier rooms do, and all have carpet, telephone, shower, and, best of all, access to a billiard room. Economy rooms Rs.350. Semi-deluxe Rs.550.

FOOD

Good budget restaurants are fewer and farther between than cheap sleeps, although there are numerous fruit vendors and small restaurants along the bazaar.

Moon Hotel, across from Hotel Rajdeep, has the best restaurant in town. The long, airy halls are so elegant they seem out of place along the bazaar. There are several "Moon specialities" but the chicken (particularly the pulled chicken) is outstanding for Rs.50. Butter *naan* (Rs.10) goes well with anything. Open for lunch and dinner.

Tourist Bungalows has a restaurant that doesn't merit a visit from town, but it's good if you happen to be along the Mall. Munch down "fingar chips" (Rs.18), or vegetable *pakoras* (eight for Rs.18) while sipping tea (Rs.5) in front of the TV (free). Open summer daily 7-10:30am, 1-3pm, and 8-10pm; open winter daily 7-10am, 12:30-2:30pm, and 7:30-9:30pm.

SIGHTS AND ENTERTAINMENT

Most of the kicks to be found in Ranikhet come from the area behind the town along the Mall. Farthest away is the most renowned attraction in the area, the **Chaubatia Garden.** Originally developed as a "Fruit Research Centre," Chaubatia has several orchards and charming gardens. Sneaky travelers sometimes do their own "fruit research" while following one of the trails along the mountainside through the forests of fruit trees. Indian tourists swarm the garden in the high season, attending "garden parties." It's free, refreshing, and plum juice is sold near the entrance (Rs.6). Open daily 6am-9pm. Buses leave regularly for Chaubatia from the Roadways stand, stopping for pick-ups along the Mall. A taxi all to yourself will cost Rs.60, shared Rs.5. Closer to Ranikhet along the Mall sits the Hindu temple of **Jhula Devi.** It's small, but the gates around it are covered with bells of all shapes and sizes.

It's possible to walk back toward the Mall from town—and not to have to follow the road. First, visit the impressive new (1994) **Mankameshwar Temple** up from the telephone exchange and Nainital Bank and across from it. Pay a visit to the Shawl and Tweed Factory, a dilapidated church converted into a source of loom-spun herringbone and houndstooth tweed. (Open Mon.-Fri. 10am-5pm.) Just down from the factory is the Nar Singh Stadium. Cut through and follow the trail back over the mountains. It's more up-and-down than the road, but shorter (and prettier) in the long run. There are also other hiking trails off the Mall.

By far the most extraordinary of Rahikhet's offerings is its nine-hole **golf course,** Upat Kalika. The clubhouse is 6km from town on the way to Almora. It's relatively pricey but golfers worldwide would fork out a fortune for a chance to see the course's unbeatable mountain views. Foreigners pay Rs.400 for nine holes, Rs.100 to rent clubs, Rs.90 for a ball and Rs.25 for a caddy (plus tip, if he's helpful). Rs.615 total for a chance at a Himalayan hole-in-one. (Open Tues.-Sun. 7am-6pm.)

■ Almora

Almora is known as the town of temples for good reason. This hill-station is surrounded by modern and ancient Hindu temples and, off in the distance, by the magnificent natural shrines of the cloud-piercing Himalayan peaks. While still an important agricultural market for the area, Almora remains the most mystical of Kumaon's hill stations, having drawn peace-seekers as varied as Gandhi and Nehru (who used to meet here to talk) to Swami Vivekananda and Timothy Leary.

As tranquil as Almora is, it's only fitting that (unlike nearly Nainital or Ranikhet) the British weren't the first to develop it. From 1560 to the end of the 18th century, Almora served as seat of the Chanda dynasty before it was captured by the Gorkhas and then the British. A stroll through the old bazaar evokes those bygone days—the buildings are fading, but colorful façades and cobbled streets could well come from centuries past. What truly defines Almora, though, and what draws travelers here, has not changed in 400 years. The mountains, which offer opportunity for day hikes and exploration, remain oblivious to passing decades and dynasties.

ORIENTATION

Almora wraps around its mountain on only four parallel streets. The **Mall,** the major thoroughfare for traffic and the site of most hotels and services, is where buses stop; walking northeast (toward the visible Hotel Shikhar) leads to some restaurants and to the road to Kasar Devi; southwest along the Mall lie most other services. The **Bazaar** is the first major parallel street up from the Mall. It can be steep walking anywhere in Almora, but the Mall is flatter than the Bazaar. **Town center** is where the buses stop.

PRACTICAL INFORMATION

Tourist Office: The **U.P. Tourist Office** (tel. 22180) is about 800m southwest of the bus stands on the road veering off the Mall by the post office. They carry information about Almora and Kumaon, but hold loose hours—try Mon.-Fri. 10am-5pm. A better bet for information on small or large sojourns out of Almora is one of the local **trekking companies,** including **Discover Himalaya** (tel. 23507), across from the post office; **High Adventure** (tel. 23445), on the Mall a bit closer to town center (open daily 8am-8pm); **Ridge and Trek** (tel. 22492) is on the balcony, first floor, still farther down the Mall. Mr. Shah at the Kailas Hotel is also very knowledgeable about the local sights.

Currency Exchange: The **State Bank of India** branch on the Mall (tel. 22084), near town center. Readily changes AmEx checks and grudgingly changes other checks or currencies—be persistent. Mon.-Fri. 10am-5pm, Sat.10am-2pm.

Telephones: STD/ISD booths dot the Mall.

Trains: The nearest station is in Kathgodam.

Buses: U.P. Roadways and KMOU buses leave within 50m of each other on the Mall at town center. KMOU serves Ranikhet (every hr., 7am-2pm, 2hr., Rs.22) and Nainital (6:30 and 9:30am, 3 hr., Rs.28). U.P. Roadways covers most longer routes: Delhi (5, 7am, and 5pm, 11hr., Rs.120/151 for regular/semi-deluxe) and Dehra Dun with connections to Mussoorie, Rishikesh, and Haridwar (5, 8am, and 4pm, 12hr., Rs.120-144). Haldwani serves as a major hub; buses leave Almora several times a day between 5am and 5pm, 4hr., Rs.39. Roadways also goes to Nainital (8am, 3hr., Rs.33) and Ranikhet (6am, 2hr., Rs.23).

Taxis: congregate near the Hotel Shikhar.

English Bookstore: The store next to High Adventure trekking carries English paperbacks and guides to the region. Open daily 9:30am-9pm.

Pharmacy: There are several along the Mall and bazaar, including the basic **Himalayan Medical Store,** across from Hotel Trishul (open daily 8:30am-9pm).

Hospital: Civil Hospital (tel. 22322).

Post Office: (tel. 22230/22019). On the downside of the Mall about 600m southwest of the bus stand. Offers *Poste Restante* and telegram services. Open daily 7am-6pm for enquiries; Mon.-Fri. 10am-4pm, Sat. 10am-3pm for other services.

Telephone Code: 05962.

ACCOMMODATIONS

Most of the hotels in town lie along the Mall, with dingier but often cheaper places clustered around the center. For a splurge or respite after a trek, **Hotel Shikhar** (tel. 22253) comes with its own little mall, awesome views, an elevator and luxuriant rooms ranging from Rs.200-800. More relaxed, isolated accommodations, including the Holiday Home and the unbeatable Tranquillity Retreat, dot the surrounding hills (see **Near Almora,** p. 187).

Kailas Hotel (tel. 22624), across from the post office, about 10m above the Mall. This place is the unrivalled sweet spot for foreign budget travelers in Almora. The Kailas is (and seemingly always has been) run by the incomparably charming Mr. Shah, a kind, aging man who is a marvelous source for all sorts of tales and wisdom. Established in 1885, Mr. Shah reminds guests, the house is "as old as the Indian

National Congress." The rooms are fairly rustic, with no fans and erratic running water, but there's a common shower and a funky atmosphere to the whole place, which signs say is "run by housewives." Mr. Shah is a rich fount of information about nearby attractions and about India's history in general—ask him to show you his write-up in the 1947 *Who's Who in India*. Prices range from Rs.50 for a single without bath to Rs.240 for a quint. No bargaining, and he'll bill you at the end.

Trishul Hotel (tel. 22243), not far down the mall on the opposite side as the Kailas. The Trishul's owner, Mr. Shah, is not to be confused with Mr. Shah of the Kailas Hotel, but the Trishul's rooms are nice in their own right. Three-room doubles have double beds, sofas, fireplaces, and small sitting rooms with a nostalgic charm. Lower-floor singles Rs.100, upper-floor Rs.150. Lower-floor doubles Rs.150, upper-floor Rs.200. Triples Rs.250.

Hotel Pawan (tel. 22252), across from Trishul, closer to town center. Uninspired, but well-kept and sufficient, with bright rooms, large mirrors, and clean bathrooms. Sadly, the dining room is reserved for "special occasions." Singles Rs.100-110. Doubles Rs.190.

Hotel Vikas (tel. 23455), closer to the bus stand, has a pleasant balcony with views of the gas-belching vehicles below. A colorful, labyrinthine corridor leads to habitable but stuffy rooms. Singles Rs.90. Doubles Rs.110.

Tourist Cottage, near the Glory Restaurant on the northeast side of Hotel Shikhar, gets the honor of "town cheapie." The dim, musty cells share a common bath. The owner speaks no English, but is nonetheless a personality. Singles and doubles Rs.50. Triples with bath Rs.100.

FOOD

Almora is no paradise for foodies. If you're staying at **Kailas Hotel**, Mrs. Shah makes a tasty *thali*, though you never know just what you'll get or how much you'll pay for it.

Mount View Restaurant, inside Hotel Shikhar, is probably the prime place. They've got good breakfasts, great views, and an attentive waitstaff. *Korma* Curry costs Rs.30, while tandoori chicken goes for Rs.40. Open daily 6am-11pm.

Glory Restaurant (tel. 22279) across from Mount View, down the road to the northeast. Two cute little floors for vegetarian diners' delight. Cheese butter *masala* is Rs.38. They and the **Madras Restaurant** across the road do *dosas*. Open daily 7am-10:30pm.

Swagat Restaurant, on the side of the Hotel Shikhar, down some steps. An airy, homey place with a commanding view. All-veg. fare includes South Indian and Chinese dishes, such as ginger fried rice (Rs.20), and mango shakes (Rs.15-40). Open daily 6am-9:30pm.

SIGHTS

Almora proper doesn't offer much in the way of sights. There's the small, government-run **G.B. Pant museum** right in the center of town, across from the bus stand. Pant's museum features not Levi's but tools and other artifacts from the Katyuri and Chanda dynasties. It's a good way to kill time while waiting for the bus to leave. (Open Tues.-Sun., 10:30am-4:30pm; closed "Sunday next to second Saturday." Free.) Walk past the post office out of town about 750m and head up past the holiday homes to the production center of **Himalaya Woolens,** which makes quality tweeds and shawls (Rs.300-2500; Rs.850 for a jacket). The manager can explain the production process—how the yarn is brought from Australia, how it's set on the looms, etc. The real fun here is to marvel at the coordination of the guys churning out the products—they've got both feet flying between pedals and both hands performing different tasks. They work Mon.-Sat. 10am-5pm.

Wander through the **Bazaar** (especially the lower region) and you'll note a lot of pots. Almora is the center of production of *tamta*, a silver-plated copper. Anokhe Lal is a good shop for checking these pots out, though they'd be pretty heavy to carry in a backpack.

It's a morning's walk to the **Nanda Devi Temple** at the top of town, which pays homage to the goddess of the distant mountain. The **Nanda Devi Fair** is held here in September. The **Bright End Corner** at the south end of town is a popular spot from which to watch the sunsets. Aspiring musicians looking to hang around Almora for a while can seek tutelage at the Bhadkande College of Music, which has a branch in town.

■ Near Almora

The mountains around Almora are packed with other spots for good day or overnight trips. Popular destinations include the **Deer Park** (3km out of town), which also houses some leopards; the locally important **Chitai Temple** (where locals go to seek justice if they feel they've been wronged); and the 800-year-old **Sun Temple** at Katarmal (17km from Almora). More distant destinations commonly include Jageswar, featuring 165 ancient temples (34km), and Baijnath (71km) and Bageswar (90km away)—starting points for treks along the Pindari Glacier. Ask Mr. Shah at Kailas Hotel, or check with High Adventure, Discover, or one of the other local trekking agents for more information on any of these sights.

The **Kasar Devi Temple,** near the "town" of Kasar Devi, about 7km from Almora, can be reached by a long hike or by taxi (Rs.10-15 per person there, Rs.5 each return). The temple emits an aura of mysticism, but the visitor's urge to meditate comes mainly from the temple's spectacular setting, on a giant, sloping rock atop a mountain with sweeping panoramas of the whole area. The temple is known as a center of spiritual energy. Swami Vivekananda came here to meditate, as did many soul-searching Americans and Europeans, some of whom still hang around the nearby tea stands today. Follow the trail past the temple through "town" for the best views of the distant Nanda Devi mountain range.

Tucked between two hills, and far from everything but its own splendor and the jaw-drop views, the **Tranquillity Retreat** is a tiny utopia for the short- or long-term visitor. Run by Armelle, a French woman who first came 15 years ago, the retreat is small and simple, with only three stark and comfortable rooms, plus two in the house if they're available. The guest house provides worship at the shrine of nature—it has a balcony that faces the distant mountains and its own organic garden and orchard. Rooms are only Rs.30 per night, or Rs.800 per month. Once you've arrived, a long-term stay may be inevitable, especially given Armelle's cooking; the number of delicious dishes Armelle prepares is amazing considering her limited access to supplies. Plates of baked eggplant in tomato gravy (Rs.25), salad with French dressing (Rs.10), or pancakes (Rs.12) will be served to you on the roof top of the guest house as you contemplate the cosmos. With all its seclusion, the Tranquillity Retreat is not easy to find. About a 10-minute walk on the road up to Kasar Devi, look for a small blue sign with the retreat's name. Follow the trails over the ridge and keep veering until you see a beige building, with two adjacent buildings below. There's no telephone access; the best way to contact Armelle is to leave a message at Tara's Tea Stand, near Kasar Devi.

THE U.P. PLAINS

▓ Mathura

The city of Mathura teems with temples due to its significance as the suspected birthplace of Lord Krishna. Hordes of Vaishnava pilgrims come each year, particularly in August and September, around Krishna's birthday, paying homage to the blue-skinned hero of Hindu lore. The city of nearly 300,000 bustles with a spirited zeal, even between sessions of worship, and though a bit bland and grimy in places, the town is a convenient stop on the way into (or out of) Agra.

ORIENTATION

At the heart of Mathura is the bazaar, stretching north from the **Holi Gate,** on the east part of town near the river. The **Old Bus Stand** is 500m south of the Holi Gate, while the more frequently used **New Bus Stand** is 1km west and 500m south of the old one. The **railway station** is 2km south of the New Bus Stand. The other major landmark in town is the temple **Shri Krishna Janmasthan (Janmbhoomi),** dedicated to the spot of Krishna's birth and 2km to the northwest of the New Bus Stand.

PRACTICAL INFORMATION

Tourist Office: U.P. Tourism, north end of Old Bus Stand (tel. 405351). Provides cheesy brochures and no maps, but staff is knowledgeable about temples.

Currency Exchange: State Bank of India, main branch (tel. 407647). One kilometer east of the new bust stand, not far north of the railway. Foreign exchange and traveler's checks on 2nd fl. The branch near Shri Krishna Janmasthan doesn't change currency.

Telephones: STD/ISD booths (some with fax) are everywhere, especially near the Holi Gate.

Trains: Railway station, 1-2km south of bank. Mathura is connected by several trains to Delhi, Agra, Varanasi, Patna, Jaipur, and other popular destinations.

Buses: Buses from the **New Bus Stand** go to: Delhi (every hr., 6am-9pm, 4hr., Rs.43); Jaipur (every 30min., 7am-10:30pm, 6hr., Rs.75); Bharatpur (every 30min., 6am-10pm, 1hr., Rs.13); and Agra (every 30min., 7am-10pm, 2hr., Rs.16). **Old Bus Stand** (tel. 406468). U.P. Roadways buses go to: Vrindaban (6:30, 8, 9am, 7pm, 30min., Rs.4); Haridwar (10pm, 8hr., Rs.120); Dehra Dun (5am, 9hr., Rs.125); Jhansi (4:30am, 12hr., Rs.150); Varanasi (2:30pm, 16hr., Rs.225).

Local Transportation: Unusually long **tempos** cruise regularly to Vrindaban (Rs.5) and around town. **Rickshaws** (Shri Krishna Temple to New Bus Stand Rs.10) and **auto-rickshaws** (same trip Rs.15) whizz by **tongas** (same trip Rs.10).

Market: The **main bazaar** area extends just south of and a long way north of Holi Gate and carries everything from spices and chutneys to drums. **Fruit market** next to Jama Masjid.

Pharmacy: Many along the street north and south running under Holi Gate.

Hospital: District Hospital, near Old Bus Stand (tel. 403006, 406315). **Methodist Hospital,** Jaising Pura, Vrindaban Rd. (tel. 406032).

Post Office: Small branch in complex next to Shri Krishna Temple. **Postal Code:** 281001.

Telephone Code: 0565.

ACCOMMODATIONS

Location is probably the most essential consideration when choosing a place to stay in Mathura, since the bus stands, Shri Krishna Temple, and the old city are not within easy walking distance of each other. The area near the Holi Gate is liveliest and noisiest part of town, though Shri Krishna has Hindi pop blaring all day. Mathura has a few ashrams, including the Keshvjee Gaudig, across and up from the Old Bus Stand (Rs.30 per room).

International Rest House (tel. 405888). In the complex just east of the entrance to Shri Krishna Janmasthan temple. Inexpensive rooms for pilgrims, and a garden to kick up your feet. Singles Rs.25. Doubles Rs.45, with bath Rs.100.

Hotel Brij Raj, across the street and a bit down the street from Shri Krishna Janmasthan. Large lavender rooms set around a plant-filled courtyard have huge beds and clean attached bath. Balcony is unfortunately accessible to the public. They have a generator. Doubles with bath Rs.120.

Hotel Nepal (tel. 404308). Across from and just west of New Bus Stand. Simultaneously away from the street and near the bus stand. Basic rooms, many with air-cooling. Singles Rs.100. Doubles Rs.150.

Hotel Modern (tel. 404747). Across the street from the Old Bus Stand. Stuffy rooms need paint, but wall posters remind you that more serene places exist. Dark, ominous bar next door. Singles Rs.100. Doubles Rs.150.

Gaurav Guest House (tel. 406192). Walk 100m south of Government Museum. Simple rooms have squishy, soft beds, table, and mirror. Owner is funny and speaks English well. Common bathroom is kept fairly clean. Check-out noon. Singles Rs.75, with air-cooling Rs.100. Doubles Rs.150, with bath Rs.200, with TV Rs.225.

FOOD

The fruit market is next to Jama Masjid, and the bazaar near there has inexpensive snacks. Across from the Shri Krishna Janmasthan, are a strip of cheap *dhabas* selling good South Indian food—these include the Prateek and the Madras Cafe (on the corner, not the imposter farther along), as well as those listed below.

Hotel Brij Raj Cafe, across from Shri Krishna Janmasthan, below and to the side of Hotel Brij Raj. Superb *thalis* (Rs.20) and a variety of Gaylord's ice cream treats—a butterscotch cup goes especially well with the fresh espresso pressed from the antique machine. Open daily 7:30am-10:30pm.

Deepak Hotel, across from the bus stand, next to Hotel Nepal. Not a hotel but an understated restaurant, with crisp *chapatis* made fresh, creamy *Malai kofta* Rs.20, and many veg. and non-veg. entrees Rs.15-30. Open daily 9am-11pm.

Brijwasi, across from Shri Krishna Janmasthan with another branch near Holi Gate. *Samosas* and excellent milky sweets such as *burfis.* Open daily 7am-11pm.

Brij-Bhoj Restaurant, inside Hotel Mansarovar Palace, across from State Bank main branch. Chilled, elegant chamber with both meals and snacks—only the non-veg. items have out-of-control prices. *Pakoras* as they're supposed to taste, *paneer mutter* (Rs.28), cucumber salads (Rs.18). Open daily 7am-11pm.

Kwality Restaurant, just north of the Old Bus Stand. Not the usual air-conditioned, sterile chain restaurant, but a stark room with few tables and inexpensive food (Rs.15-25). Stuffed tomato Rs.25, omelette Rs.15. Open daily 7am-11pm.

SIGHTS

Most of the sights in Mathura revolve around Krishna, the playful boy whose birth put this town on the map. Pay a visit to the Shri Krishna Janmasthan temple to see the actual spot of "Krishna's appearance"—the original temple, Kesava Deo, was destroyed by Aurangzeb and replaced with a mosque. The similarities between the scenario here and that at Ayodhya, at Rama's birthplace, have made the military and police particularly cautious—visitors must leave all belongings (bags, cameras, etc.) in the cloakroom off to the left (Rs.2), then pass through a metal detector and over-zealous frisking. Along with the souvenir shops, the complex includes several small shrines (open daily 5-11am and 4-9pm). The main shrine, located in the back of the complex to the right as you come in, is a cavernous, dim room marking the site of the birth and representing the prison cell Krishna was born into while the nefarious King Kamsa held his parents captive. To the back of the shrine, the heavy-duty barbed wire between the temple and mosque is sharp enough to cut the tension in the air. Nearby **Potara-Kund** is also related to the Hindu god's birth.

Mathura's other attractions are back on the east side of town. Continuing north from the bazaar, the **Dwarkadheesh Temple** is on the left. Built in 1814 by local pious merchants, this temple is the main point of worship for local Hindus, and its interior colors are accentuated when the afternoon sun performs shadow dances on the wire-mesh roof. A bit south on the bazaar, the street forks off to the right toward the river and the sacred **Vishram Ghat,** where Krishna came to rest after slaying the menacing King Kamsa, and where many pseudo-priests, would-be guides, and not-so-needy beggars now congregate. Brush off unwanted attention or simply offer a kind "Lord Krishna" greeting and walk away. At the *ghats,* **boats** take visitors on an hour-long tour of the city's shore (Rs.40-50), with a prime view of the dilapidated **Sati Bur,** built in 1570 and dedicated to the *sati* of Behari Mal. Sunset boat trips offer a front-row view of the nightly *arati* ceremony, when priests lift fire and bring it to the sacred water amid the sound of gongs.

Back towards the bazaar and farther north is the **Jama Masjid,** the main mosque in town, built by Abo-in Nabir Khan in 1661. The mosque is unusually colorful, its teal domes brightening up the already striking bazaar and fruit market. Set one floor above street level, voyeurs are able to observe the goings-on below.

Mathura's only sight, aside from the mosques, that is not related to Krishna is the **Government Museum** (tel. 408191), Dampier Nagar, 1km northeast of the New Bus Stand, 1km west of the Old Bus Stand. Home to one of the largest collections of ancient Indian sculpture, the pieces here shed light on Mathura's religious importance even before the days of Krishna. For 1200 years, Mathura served as the artistic center for early Indian, Indo-Scythian, and visiting Hellenistic cultures. Today, the museum (founded in 1874, but moved to the current building in 1930) has thousands of stone sculptures, terra-cottas, and coins. Many depict the Buddha in various moods and improbable contortions; others highlight the hairstyles of the contemporary women. The museum's true treasures are two Buddha statues from the 4th and 5th centuries that are in pristine condition. Sculptures are planted among the flora outside in the courtyard as well. (Museum open Tues.-Sun. 10:30am-4:30pm; free, camera fee Rs.20.)

■ Vrindaban

While the birthplace of Krishna understandably draws a fair number of devotees, the main religious center of this area is the nearby town of Vrindaban, where a young and frisky Krishna is said to have performed the deeds for which he was later deified: lifting up a hill (actually at nearby **Govardhan**), jamming on his flute, and cavorting with all the *gopis* (milkmaids) he could find. Legend has it that in order to dance with several maidens at the same time, Krishna would multiply himself, a feat few disco studs have managed to emulate. Ever since the Bengali teacher Chaitanya discovered the site's importance in Hindu legend, it has been a huge draw for Vaishnava, including the International Society for Krishna Consciousness (Hare Krishnas).

As medieval and as rustic as the town feels in places, there are a fair number of con-men and would-be guides (pay no more than Rs.30-50 for a tour of all the temples). **Buses, trains,** and **tempos** from Mathura arrive south of the heart of town, a labyrinthine and often confusing tangle of narrow streets. There are small restaurants, a few basic hotels, and tea stalls near the major temples for mid-worship munchies. It's also possible to stay at ISKCON (see below).

The **Govind Dev Temple** is a squat, sprawling edifice in the shape of a Greek cross. It lacks the characteristic tower of most temples and the top three stories of the upper level were destroyed by Aurangzeb and never replaced. Rhesus monkeys hang out on the meticulously handcarved overhangs outside, while bats crowd the temple on the inside. Raja Man Singh, who built the temple in 1590, clearly meant for this sturdy structure to stick around awhile.

One hundred meters to the northeast of the Govind Dev is the **Rangaj's Temple,** India's longest. Seth Govind Das combined Rajput and South Indian designs when he built the temple in 1851. The 15-m **Dhwaja Stambha,** the central column, is said to be plated in gold. Non-Hindus are not permitted inside, but can catch a glimpse of the shimmer through either entrance. In two small galleries next to the entrance gate, twitching robotic puppets dramatize episodes from Lord Krishna's life, including his mellow interaction with the ecstatic *gopis* (admission Rs.1).

Of the other, more notable temples around Vrindaban, **Madan Mohan Temple,** along the river near Kali Ghat, has a small shrine in the base of its tall, sandstone tower, today sprouting a good amount of flora. Other popular sights include the dilapidated **Radha Ballabh Temple,** dating from 1626, the more modern **glass temple,** east of the Rangaji Temple, and **Bankey Bihari,** literally "crooked Krishna," named for Krishna's traditionally bent body.

Amid all holy places in Vrindaban, none draws more foreigners than the **Krishna Balram Temple** (tel. (0565) 442478), the dazzling marble house of worship of **ISKCON,** the International Society for Krishna Consciousness. The founder of the society, Srila Prabhupada, lived and worked here before embarking at the advanced age of 69 on a world tour to spread the word of Krishna consciousness. Next to three shrines and several murals of Krishna's exploits is a life-like mannequin of Prabhupada over the place he is buried. This part of the temple echoes with the chants, drums, and donation requests. Still, the whole place is soul-soothingly placid. In the back is a clean **restaurant** serving some of the best Indian breakfasts in the country (Rs.16) with good ginger, tea, and *chiku* milkshakes (Rs.8-12). There is also a **guest house** (tel. (0565) 442478), with 45 clean doubles with attached bath for Rs.175. Hare Krishnas, who come here from all over the world, are delighted to talk to newcomers. The temple is likely to be full during August, September, and March. An enlightening **museum** dedicated to Prabhupada (whose would-be 100th birthday in 1996 was celebrated around the world), shows the swami's rooms as he kept them, and books, clothes, jars of vaseline, and other toiletries he used while here (open daily 9am-4:30pm).

■ Agra

Over the last decade, the average tourist's stay in Agra has declined from 1.7 days to barely 12 hours. As you travel in North India you'll understand why. For at the edges of all the roads and rail lines leading to Agra, the conventional wisdom has left behind a kind of verbal underbrush, and everyone seems to be mumbling the same thing: Agra is a dump. But this is not true. Sure, the main budget hotel center, Taj Ganj, is full of aggressive rickshaw-*wallahs* and inlaid marble and rug vendors. But give the city a chance. In the Cantonment area, for example, there are wide, clean streets, upscale stores, and a string of pocket parks maintained by the local Sheraton, which has a multi-million dollar stake in seeing Agra put its best foot forward. But of course, Agra's real draw is the incomparably grand Taj Mahal.

Agra's amazing monuments were all built under the Mughals, who swept into India from Central Asia early in the 16th century. At the Battle of Panipat (1526), the Mughal warrior Babur crushed the ruling Lodi dynasty; as a direct result, the Mughals won a great South Asian empire, which included Agra, the Lodi dynasty capital. For the next 150 or so years, the location of the Mughal capital flitted back and forth between Delhi and Agra, leaving both cities with a gaggle of timelessly beautiful landmarks. With the slow decline of Mughal power in North India, Agra fell on hard times, and the new kids on the block—the British—made Calcutta (and later Delhi) their capital, and encouraged Allahabad to surpass Agra as a local political powerhouse.

Lately, Agra has worked hard to re-invent itself, recycling the foreign exchange it earns from tourists into industrial development and smoggy economic progress, growing into a city of over 1 million. Even if you're not particularly interested in Agra's modern side, plan to spend some time in and around the city—there's almost a sexual delight to be taken in lingering for a day in Agra before seeing the Taj Mahal, in catching fleeting glimpses of its sensuous beauty so as to enhance and intensify your eventual pleasure. Of course, if that doesn't turn you on, you can always be in and out in under 12 hours—you wouldn't be the first.

ORIENTATION

Agra is a large and diffuse city, most of which sprawls west from the banks of the **Yamuna River,** where lie the Taj Mahal and Agra Fort separated by 1.5km and the **Shah Jahan Park. Yamuna Kinara Road** runs along the Yamuna River's western banks from the Taj Mahal to **Belan Ganj,** a bustling neighborhood 1km north of **Agra Fort Railway Station,** where trains from east Rajasthan pull in. Tourist facilities cluster south of the Taj Mahal and Agra Fort. Bargain-basement accommodations are ubiq-

> **Warning:** Agra, like all major tourist hubs in India, has a number of swindlers who'd love a piece of those dollars you're stashing. First, be aware that rickshaw charges are excessive and the commissions-incentive means that they take you to the hotel of their (and not your) choice. Insist at the least on going to a specific area of town. Ask other drivers and non-driver locals if the price you're quoted seems too high. Also watch out for crafty salesmen who persuade tourists with "parties," tea, and sweet talk to buy rugs and resell them in salesmen's homes. Numerous cheats (credit card fraud, false identities, etc.) can stem from this, so don't get lured in. If it seems too good to be true, it is.

uitous in **Taj Ganj,** a neighborhood just south of the Taj Mahal, while upscale hotels show up along **Fatehabad Road,** even farther (1km) south of the Taj. **Mahatma Gandhi Road, Gwalior Road,** and **General Cariappa Road** are three major thoroughfares that cross both **the Mall** and **Taj Road,** which are south Agra's longest east-west avenues. From the upscale **Sadar Bazaar,** which is nestled between Mahatma Gandhi and Gwalior Rd., it's 2km due west to **Agra Cantonment Railway Station** and its long-distance trains; its 2km northwest along Fatehpur Sikri Rd. to the **Idgah Bus Stand.**

PRACTICAL INFORMATION

Tourist Office: Foreigner mecca that it is, Agra boasts 3 different tourist offices. **Government of India Tourist Office,** 191 the Mall (tel. 363959, 363377). Across from the post office. The most convenient and informative tourist office, providing a good guide map, brochures on Agra and all parts of India, and general guidance. Open Mon.-Fri. 9am-5:30pm, Sat. 9am-1pm. **U.P. Government Tourist Office,** 64 Taj Rd. (tel. 360517). Near the Clarks-Shiraz. This friendlier but less well-stocked office has brochures on Kumaon, Garhwal, and Varanasi. Their **branch** for the just-arrived at Agra Cantt. Railway Station is across from the inquiry booth (tel. 364439).

Immigration Office: Foreigners Registration Office, 16 Idgah Colony (tel. 269563). Near the bus stand. Register for long-term stays.

Currency Exchange: Central Bank of India (tel. 331357), in the southeast part of Taj Ganj, changes major currencies and traveler's checks and gives small (up to US$100) cash advances on Visa and MasterCard. Open Mon.-Fri. 10am-2pm, Sat. 10am-noon. Some of Agra's other banks, including **Andhra Bank,** change money. **LKP Merchant Financing Ltd.,** Fatehabad Rd., tourist complex area (tel. 330480; fax 331191). Buys and sells traveler's checks. Open daily (sometimes closed Sun.) 9:30am-8pm. Outside of these hours, many hotel proprietors in the Taj Ganj change money on the black market; those who attempt to change money illegally should do so discreetly.

Telephones: STD/ISD booths at all touristed areas, including Taj Ganj and Sadar Bazaar. **Global Enterprises,** Chowk Thana, Taj Ganj (tel. 330932). Foreigner-friendly enterprise charges Rs.1 for call-back service. Open daily 8am-midnight.

Airport: Agra's **Kheria Airport** is 9km southwest of the city (enquiry: tel. 263982, 361185). Flights on Tues., Thurs., and Sat.-Sun. To: Delhi (3:55pm, 40min., US$35); Khajuraho (7:35am, 45min., US$35) en route to Varanasi (2hr., US$76). Book flights at the Indian Airlines office (tel. 360948, 360153; open daily 10am-4:30pm), adjacent to Hotel Clarks Shiraz, or from Sita World Travel (tel. 363013), north side of main shopping bazaar, Sadar Bazaar.

Trains: Agra has several railway stations: **Agra Cantonment, Idgah, Agra Fort, Yamuna Bridge** (across the river), **Agra City** (north of town), and **Raja Ki Mandi** (northwest of Old Agra). Be sure you know in advance where your train arrives or departs. Agra Cantt. Railway Station is the main terminal, southwest of the city and at the west end of the Mall Rd. running toward Taj Ganj. Enquiry: tel. 131, 133, 134. A special window at the computer reservation complex on the south side makes bookings for foreign tourists (as well as for VIPs and freedom fighters—which are you?). To: New Delhi (*Shatabdi Exp.*2001, 8:18pm, 2½hr., Rs.250 for A/C chair); Bhopal (*Shatabdi Exp.* 2002, 8:15am, 6hr., Rs.405 for A/C chair; *Punjabi*

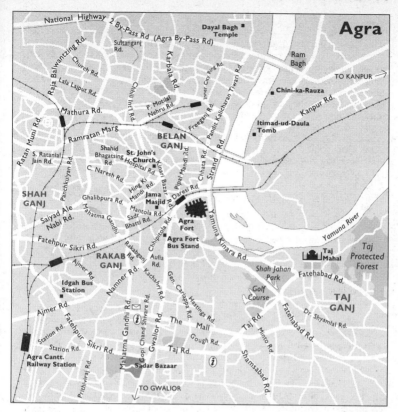

Mail 1037, 4:45pm, 3½hr., Rs.49/202 for 2nd/1st class); Bombay (*Punjabi Mail* 1038, 9:19am, 23hr., Rs.200/877 for 2nd/1st class); Howrah (*Udyan Abha Toofan Exp.* 3008, 12:40pm, 6½hr., Rs.191/833 for 2nd/1st class); Lucknow (*Ahmedabad-Gorakhpur Exp.* 5045, 6:50am, 6hr. 45min.).

Buses: Most leave from **Idgah Bus Terminal,** a short distance to the northeast of Agra Cantt. Railway Station. To: Jaipur (every 30min., 6am-10pm, 7hr., Rs.67) via Bharatpur (1½hr., Rs.16); Delhi (every 30min., 4am-9:30pm, 5hr., Rs.67); Jhansi (5am, 10hr., Rs.70); Udaipur (6pm, 14hr., Rs.175); Ajmer (9am and 5 per day, 5-10pm, 9hr., Rs.100); Bikaner (11am, 12hr., Rs.153); Mathura (every hr., 6am-8:30pm, 1½hr., Rs.14). Buses to Varanasi (5pm, 18hr., Rs.199) start at the Agra Fort Bus Stand, to the southwest of the fort. Deluxe buses to Jaipur, Delhi, and elsewhere leave frequently from other places—contact a travel agent in Taj Ganj for daily bookings.

Local Transportation: Despite all the rip-offs, **cycle-rickshaws** are still a good way to get around. Pay no more than Rs.15-20 for a cycle-rickshaw and no more than Rs.20 for an auto-rickshaw going between railway or bus stations and Taj Ganj or Agra Fort. Rickshaws can be hired for a day for Rs.100. Agra is easy to zip around in on your own **bicycle;** there are rental shops all around town, including **Shah Jahan Lodge** in Taj Ganj (Rs.15-20 per day). And if you have some money to spare, hire **car and driver** from one of the numerous places around the tourist centers: **R.R. Travels,** Fatehabad Rd. in Taj Ganj, charges Rs.600 (Rs.900 with A/C) for a one-day tour that includes Fatehpur Sikri.

Luggage Storage: Available at Agra Cantt. Railway Station and on a short-term basis at many hotels.

Market: Cottage Industries Exposition Ltd., 39 Fatehabad Rd. This white bohemoth building has marble, rugs, silk ties, and other local specialties—high quality for high prices. Open daily 8:30am-8pm. For simpler shopping needs, **Taj Ganj** has a surprising number of shops off the main strip and a lot of inlaid marble. **Old Agra** is one big bazaar for buying belts, shoes, car parts or whatever; **Kinari Bazaar,** extending northwest from the fort, is especially loaded. Specialty markets abound, so ask a local to point the way. Resist handicrafts salesmen pulling you into their shops. Shop around and always try to bargain (unless a sign claims fixed prices).

English Bookstore: The Modern Book Depot (tel. 363133) has an extensive selection of books in addition to language dictionaries and magazines. Open Wed.-Mon. 10am-9pm.

Pharmacy: Chemists abound near the major tourist areas. **Shalya Medical Centre,** Fatehabad Rd. (tel. 331106). Well-marked and well-stocked. Open daily 8am-10:30pm.

Hospital: District Hospital (tel. 364738). **Sarojini Naidu Hospital** (tel. 361318), west of Old Agra near Bageshwarnath Temple and Kali Masjid.

Emergency: Police, tel. 100, 361120. **Ambulance,** tel. 102.

Post Office: GPO, on the Mall (tel. 363588). Opposite the tourist office. Massive and intimidating, and also notoriously inefficient. Speed post and *Poste Restante* available Mon.-Sat. 10am-6pm; stamps sold Mon.-Sat. 7am-3pm. Other offices are around the city, including one southwest of the fort. **Postal Code:** 282001.

Telephone Code: 0562.

ACCOMMODATIONS

> **Warning:** Shortly before this book went to press, the government announced plans to bulldoze all buildings within 200m of the Taj Mahal. Some of the hotels listed may have already met a grisly demise.

Unlike the seedy budget hotel centers of some other major cities (like Paharganj in Delhi), Taj Ganj, the area immediately to the south of the Taj Mahal, testifies to how competition keeps prices in check. Rooms here are surprisingly cheap—there's absolutely no need to pay more than Rs.100 for a double. While hectic, dirty, and at times aggravating, this area is closest to the Taj itself. Mid-range and hit-the-roof expensive hotels are mostly to the south of Taj Ganj—from their rooms with a view, the tomb is but a wee thing. The other major centers, near the bus stand, Sadar Bazaar, and Cantonment areas, pay off for their convenience, spaciousness, and overall interest in running a tight ship. Prices may vary by season; around Christmas, accommodations providers may hike their prices above the off-season rates that are listed below.

Taj Ganj Area

For orientation's sake, start with the central hub, the rickshaw-cluttered area in front of Joney's Place; Taj Ganj forks to the north (toward the Taj), east, and west. Roads also run along the sides of the Taj Mahal toward the gates.

India Guest House (tel. 330909). On the left side of the street between the hub and the Taj. Welcoming stone courtyard with grapevines and pomegranate tree, and welcoming family—share in bliss and strife, and squat on the toilet as grandma nurtures her *linga* in the adjacent shrine. Simple, spacious rooms have 2 beds per room, a fan, and ceramic walls. Singles Rs.25-30. Doubles Rs.40-50.

Shahjahan Hotel (tel. 360842). Just west of the hub. Owner loves to do all sorts of business, so he lowers prices to entice guests to eat in his restaurant and buy his marble goods. Adequately comfortable rooms. Singles Rs.20, with bath Rs.30. Doubles Rs.40, with bath Rs.60.

Hotel Siddhartha, West Gate (tel. 331238). Resting a bit too comfortably on its popularity, the prices are relatively high. Still, rooms around spacious courtyard are hard to pass up. Rooftop has seats; rooms have dank stone bathrooms and fans. Singles Rs.80. Double Rs.115.

Hotel Sheela, East Gate (tel. 331194). Garden and patio, rooftop Taj view, many facilities, and generally clean to the extreme. The management has integrity—no commissions or scams here. Singles Rs.75. Doubles with fan Rs.100. High season: doubles Rs.150-250.

Hotel Taj Khema (tel. 360140). A short walk east of East Gate, on the left. Run by U.P. Tourism, this place is clean and good for mid-range travelers. Guests get access to the grassy hill (they have the gall to charge non-guests up to Rs.25), where there's a nice shot of the Taj. Luggage storage. Singles Rs.125, with bath Rs.200. Doubles Rs.150, with bath Rs.250, with A/C Rs.450.

Hotel Pink, East Gate (tel. 330115). More of an orangish mauve, actually, Hotel Pink has rugs, squat toilets, and nice mattresses in rooms around a classy, florid courtyard. Singles Rs.50. Doubles Rs.70. Deluxe Rs.120.

Hotel White House (tel. 330907). Near Honey's Restaurant way east of the hub. The one room to the right of the entrance wins a gold medal for Rs.50; the others are average, with squat toilets and air-coolers. Singles Rs.40. Doubles Rs.60.

Shanti Lodge (tel. 361644). On the left side walking east from the hub. The tallest hotel in Taj Ganj, its rooftop restaurant has an unspoiled view of the Taj. Still, the prices are too high and the hotel is more geared toward Taj-touring businessmen than backpackers. Singles Rs.80. Doubles Rs.100. Rooms with a view Rs.150.

Rahiv Guest House (tel. 330112). Just past Shanti Lodge, tucked back to the left. Basic, cheap rooms, where the toilet is under the showerhead, and you may have to make naked dashes through the lobby to the shower. A must for exhibitionists. Singles Rs.30, with bath Rs.40. Doubles Rs.40, with bath Rs.50.

Hotel Kamal (tel. 330126). Good rooftop, but relatively pricey rooms are stuffy and dim. Rooms with fan Rs.120, with air-cooling Rs.150.

Beyond Taj Ganj

Tourists Rest House, Kachahari Rd. (tel. 363961). Off Gwalior Rd., northeast of the GPO. Don't confuse it with imposters that go by similar names. Two levels of rooms around a lush courtyard, many foreigner-friendly facilities, and an honest owner. Singles Rs.60. Doubles Rs.120.

Major Bakshi Tourist Home (tel. 363829). Charming and quaint, this old-school family guest house is adorned with pictures of the major in his military glory days. Today, grandma rules the place. Home-cooked food available. Singles Rs.150. Doubles Rs.300. Quad Rs.500.

Hotel Akbar Inn, 21 the Mall (tel. 363212). Halfway between Taj Ganj and the railway station. On a peaceful, albeit litter-cluttered strip of the Mall's garden, this place oozes tranquility. Simple, stuffy, dim rooms with common bath (and urinal!) Rs.40, with bath with spigot shower Rs.80, with more amenities Rs.120.

Agra Hotel, F.M. Cariappa Rd. (tel. 363331). Not far south of Agra Fort, but well outside the city's chaos. Pleasant garden area with rooftop. Spacious, airy rooms. Singles Rs.150. Doubles Rs.200. Triples Rs.350. Quads Rs.375. Extra bed Rs.50. Credit cards accepted.

Hotel Akbar (tel. 363312). Just south of Agra Hotel, with similar garden and rooftop languor, but slightly simpler and cheaper rooms. Various types of toilets and floor surfaces and varying degrees of hygiene. Singles Rs.45. Doubles Rs.60-150.

Pawan/Jaiwal Hotel, 3 Taj Rd., Sadar Bazaar (tel. 363716). The only hotel in the main Sadar strip, with surprisingly quiet, bright, and cheery rooms, but worn around the edges. Singles Rs.150. Doubles Rs.200, with TV Rs.300.

Hotel Rose, 21 Old Idgah Colony (tel. 369786). North of Idgah Bus Stand. Unusual generosity to foreigners (for whom rooms cost 50% of the price Indians pay!) and sanitary crimson or olive-green rooms. Some squat toilets. Doubles Rs.125, deluxe Rs.175, with A/C Rs.400.

Hotel Ritz (tel. 269501). On the road running west of the Idgah Bus Stand. Best of the cheaper places for late-night or early-morning arrivals and departures. Reasonably new and clean. Singles and doubles Rs.125. Triples Rs.250.

Hotel Kant, Fatehabad Rd. (tel. 331332). Across from Mughal Sheraton. By far the best bet for high-end accommodations—standard rooms have disinfected toilet, bathtub, and color TV. Singles Rs.500. Doubles Rs.700. Taj-facing deluxe single occupancy Rs.1050, double occupancy Rs.1250.

FOOD

Most of Agra's restaurants—or at least those that are marginally kind to tourists' bellies—are clustered in **Taj Ganj,** in **Sadar Bazaar,** and in other tourist centers south of the old heart of town. There are a few cheapies near Jama Masjid, and numerous **snacks stalls** around the Red Fort, but most travelers stick to places close to (or inside) their hotels. Many of the more expensive hotels south of Taj Ganj have fancy-schmancy dining rooms and mid-range coffee shops; the Sheraton has a scrumptious breakfast buffet for Rs.150 and most (the Clarks-Shiraz included) have elaborate lunch and dinner buffets for Rs.300-400—bring an inflated, eager appetite, or languish in waste.

Taj Ganj Area

The restaurants near the Taj Mahal are disappointingly similar, offering under-spiced Indian food, and a good range of Western dishes. The area is notorious for poor hygiene; most who stay more than a few days get something akin to the "Delhi Belly" frequently acquired in the capital. To avoid such nasty nonsense, stick to a place that treats you right and avoid dubious meat and dairy dishes. Many of the rooftop places are better for a coffee at sunset than for a full-blown meal. The ubiquitous Rs.15 breakfasts are among North India's best.

Evergreen Restaurant, on the road running along west side of Taj, next to Hotel Siddhartha. Newly conceived, soon to have 3 levels, the economist owner strives for hygiene and deliciousness. Delectable mutton curry Rs.35, burning banana crepe Rs.20, cheeseburger Rs.15. Open daily 8am-10pm.

Shankara Vegis (tel. 331384). Just east of the hub. Generally known to be the best of the rooftop places. Bland but filling *thali* (Rs.35), decent curry dishes, yummy *pakoras*, and many other Continental and Indian dishes. Bob Marley plays in the background. Brimming beers for Rs.40 (and sometimes Rs.30) beam at Happy Hour, from 9-10pm, but if you beg enough any hour can be Happy Hour. Open daily 7am-midnight.

Joney's Place, at the main hub of Taj Ganj. Small quaint restaurant that predates its imitation neighbors (many with homonym names like Johnny's, Join-Us, etc.). Renowned for their banana *lassis;* their Rs.15 breakfasts are also good, while their Indian dishes (Rs.10-30) are variable. Receptive waitstaff. Open daily 5am-11pm.

King's Krown, on lowered 2nd story, just east of Shankara Vegis. The Krown is crowned with the comfiest chairs and coziest ambience around. Play chess or read under colored bulbs, while eating their hearty breakfast (Rs.25) or *thali* (Rs.35), which lack flavor but include dessert. Open daily 7am-11pm.

Treat Restaurant, at the Taj Ganj hub, south side, kitty-corner from Joney's Place. Cute rooftop patch, where customers perched in wicker chairs watch rickshaw-*wallahs* lure in foreigners. Typical Rs.15 breakfast is tasty and filling, but the Rs.10 mini-breakfast is the best breakfast buy around. Also serves *thalis* (Rs.20) and the usual grub. Open daily 6am-10:30pm.

Lucky Restaurant, west of the hub, but east of the road running along west Taj. Longtime favorite has a stereo and air-cooler for an unassuming ambience. The "Panish Farmoon," with coconut, chocolate, banana, and curd is a delight. Israeli food, spaghetti, and mega *thalis* (Rs.50). Stereo and air-cooler for atmosphere. Open daily 7am-10pm.

Join-Us, across from Shankara Vegis, rooftop of Full of Joy. Eager, grinning owner baits all passers-by for decent special *thalis* (Rs.35), big salads (Rs.20), curries, chow mein, and other menu choices. Open daily 6am-midnight.

Relax Restaurant (tel. 330902). Off the main strip, near the east gate of Taj Mahal. Long revered early-comer to the rooftop scene, with *thalis* (Rs.30-40), crepes (Rs.30), and Indian dishes (Rs.10-30). Open daily 7:30am-10pm.

Stuff-Makers, in Hotel Kamal. Ambiguous name reflects the restaurant's reputation: fans of the place say the "stuff" is as good as gold, while detractors are not so sure. Tasty *alu matar*, doughy *chapatis,* and weak hot chocolate. Most items Rs.10-30. Open daily 7am-10pm.

Saeed Restaurant, near Taj Ganj hub. The food is tasty and clean. With fans and TV, it's ideal for an afternoon lemon soda. Egg curry Rs.15. Open daily 6am-10pm.

Taj Restaurant (tel. 313344). Immaculate, mid-range bar and restaurant west of the Taj's west gate. Highest quality food in the area. Mausoleum-like ambience and sterility for veg. *thalis* (Rs.65), *masala* peanuts (Rs.18), and 30-ml premium whisky (Rs.40). Nice garden out back. Open daily 10am-6pm.

Beyond the Taj Ganj

Sadar Bazaar is the hub of food outside Taj Ganj, though other restaurants dot the Cantonment landscape. In addition to the budget eateries listed here, the Park and Prakash restaurants at the east end of the bazaar are well-sealed and have good reputations among locals. Many travelers also like the Only Restaurant, southwest of Taj Ganj at the roundabout, for mid-range Mughlai cuisine.

Sonar's, 25 the Mall, Phool Sayed Crossing (tel. 360295). Heavily air-conditioned, isolated building amid gardens. Exquisite Mughlai and Continental cuisine, but not out-of-control prices. *Murg Mughlai* Rs.66, sliced lamb with mushroom and garlic sauce Rs.95, mega-*thali* Rs.150, and South Indian *thali*. Spice and price are determined by looking at you. Open daily 7am-10pm.

Lakshmi Vilas Restaurant, 50/A Taj Rd. (tel. 262750). East end of Sadar Bazaar. Excellent and bountiful *dosas*. Special *rawa sada dosa* with cashews and raisins, light and flaky (Rs.20), *paneer masala dosa* (Rs.25), hearty *thali* (Rs.25). Open daily 7am-10pm.

Priya Restaurant. There are 2 restaurants by this name, one next to Tourist Rest House north of the Sadar area and the other behind Hotel Ratan Deep, off Fatehabad Rd. The former is popular and not too expensive. The latter has Mughal ambience, a large menu with tasty Indian and Mughlai dishes (Rs.35-95), and a *Shah Jahan thali* that will pop your trouser buttons (Rs.200). Open daily 7am-midnight.

Zorba the Buddha, Gopi Chand Shivare Rd. (tel. 367767). In the shopping strip stretching north of the main part of Sadar Bazaar. Dreamy new age Oshoism taken to food and ambience—all pure-veg. food combines (as Osho intended with the restaurant's title) sensuality and zest with spirituality. Float your way through *koftas, paneer,* or a dish called "Alice in Wonderland" (Rs.50); most dishes Rs.50. Open daily noon-3pm and 6-9pm; closed May 16-July 5.

R. Gaylord Bar and Restaurant, 1 Sadar Bazaar (tel. 363458). East end of strip. Lounge about in plush red booths while sipping gin and juice and counting down your rupees. Roast of grilled chicken, chips, and vegetable Rs.88, *malai kofta* Rs.35, beer Rs.45. Heavy duty A/C. Open daily 11am-11pm.

Garden Restaurant (tel. 361865). In the same eastern bit of Sadar as Lakshmi Vilas, a bit farther down. Inexpensive *dosas,* simple *thalis* (Rs.24), more elaborate thalis (Rs.45), and veg. snacks and sandwiches. Open daily 7am-11pm.

Kwality Restaurant, next to R. Gaylord's in Sadar Bazaar. Pricey but hygienic Indian, Chinese, and Continental food, just as you'll find in other links in this mighty restaurant chain. Attached bakery offers eclairs, black forest pastry (Rs.8), and other goodies to go with Poulet a la Kwality (Rs.70) and other specialties. Open daily noon-3:30pm and 7-11:30pm.

Hot Bite (tel. 264615). Across the street from Kwality et al. Overpriced (you pay for the frigid A/C), but sound Continental and Indian offerings. Tomato and cheese pizza (Rs.65), *chole bhatura* (Rs.40). Open daily 10:30am-11:30pm.

SIGHTS

In Agra, more so than in other tourist hubs, sight-seers seem to share the same set of priorities. First on their list is the Taj Mahal—preferably experienced at dawn or dusk—followed by its next-door neighbor, the Agra Fort. Time permitting, tourists often squeeze in a trip to nearby Fatehpur Sikri and the Itimad-ud-Daulah.

Taj Mahal

Even if they've never actually stood before its bulbous white marble domes, many travelers assume that a first visit to the Taj Mahal will provoke feelings of *déja vu.*

After all, pictures of the Taj adorn a great many Indian restaurants, postcards, and tourist trinketry. So why read the book when you've seen the film? Because the Taj's sensuous beauty is so imposing that no amount of overexposure can diminish it. Indeed, for all the interminable hype and silly hoopla, the Taj Mahal is heart-achingly splendid, and even the most jaded of globe-trotters often find themselves smiling in joy and wonderment as they stand before it. One of only a handful of constructions with the audacity to deem themselves "the most beautiful building in the world," the Taj Mahal is India's ultimate must-see.

The tale of the Taj is a sad, sweet love story. When he became Mughal emperor in 1628, Shah Jahan brought with him a great many things—intellect, political acumen, and, not least, a love for buildings that were delicate and sensuous. Three years after becoming emperor, Shah Jahan received news that rent his heart asunder—after 18 years of marriage, his favorite wife, Arjumand Bann Begum, had died while giving birth to the couple's 14th child. In his grief, Shah Jahan decided that his beloved should be buried in a tomb of timeless beauty—as the Bengali poet Rabindranath Tagore said, the Taj Mahal was designed as a "tear [that] would hang on the cheek of time."

Work on the Taj began in 1632, one year after the death of Arjumand Bann Begum. Marble was quarried in Makrana, Rajasthan, and precious stones were brought to Agra from Yemen, Russia, China, and Central Asia. Architects were brought from Persia, and French and Italian master craftsmen had a hand in decorating the building; in all, nearly 20,000 people worked continuously on the construction of the Taj. By the time the Taj Mahal was completed in 1653, a great many things had changed—the Mughal capital had been moved from Agra to Delhi, Arjumand Bann Begum had become popularly known as "Mumtaz Mahal" ("Elect of the Palace"), and one of Shah Jahan's sons, Aurangzeb, had grown to manhood. In 1658, the severe, reclusive Aurangzeb staged a coup, violently surmounting the opposition of his three brothers and imprisoning Shah Jahan in Agra Fort, where he lived out his days under house arrest, staring out across the Yamuna River to the Taj Mahal. The walk from the fort to the Taj is hardly 2km, but Shah Jahan was never allowed to traverse the distance so long as he lived. Only in death would Shah Jahan and Mumtaz Mahal be reunited. When the deposed emperor passed away in the winter of 1666, his body was interred next to his wife's.

Enter the Taj through the south, east, or west gate. The enclosed Taj Mahal complex is approached through the **Chowk-i-Jilo-Khana,** a small red sandstone area laced with walkways and cluttered with kiosks selling overpriced souvenirs and handicrafts. The original entrance to the complex now serves as its exit—as you head out, pause to check out the **Qur'anic inscriptions** that adorn the sizeable gateway. The large silver doors that once outfitted the original entrance were hauled off by brash plunderers during the middle decades of the 18th century.

Through the entrance, you'll be just over 100m from the Taj Mahal. From this point, the **gardens,** which may be the best-maintained in all of South Asia, and the identical red sandstone buildings that flank the Taj are visible. The Taj itself is perched atop a large square pedestal made of white marble. Slender, purely ornamental minarets punctuate each corner. Be sure to get a close-up look at the meticulous craftsmanship that went into building the Taj. Precious stones were painstakingly inlaid in the white marble to create the meandering floral patterns. Also have a look at the Arabic script that adorns the Taj Mahal's soaring arches; from the white marble pedestal, each letter appears to be exactly the same size, an effect achieved by ever so slightly varying the height and width of the letters depending on precisely how far above the pedestal they are.

While much of the building's interior is off-limits, visitors can enter the octagonal room that contains the **cenotaphs** of Shah Jahan and Mumtaz Mahal. The cenotaphs are adorned with detailed **inlay work;** Mumtaz Mahal's is inlaid with the 99 names of Allah. In keeping with the principles of Mughal tomb design, the cenotaphs merely point the way: the real tombs of Shah Jahan and Mumtaz Mahal lie directly below in a musty, unspectacular chamber. If you're not Taj-ed out, go to the small **Taj Museum**

Mughal Mausolea

The Mughal emperors left a trail of exquisite palaces, impregnable forts, and enormous mosques across India. But the most glorious physical testimony to India's Islamic golden age must be their gorgeous garden tombs. The Taj Mahal, which has set the global standard for architectural elegance since its construction, is only the most celebrated example of a highly developed tradition.

The Taj's "cross-in-a-square" floor plan derives from the Persian pleasure pavilion where the first Mughal emperor, Babur, spent the few idle moments of his youth in Afghanistan and Central Asia. He introduced the design to India when he ordered the construction of four boats shaped like bisected right angles, or short arrows. He had the peculiar vessels lashed together in the middle of the Yamuna River near Delhi to form a floating cross-in-a-square pleasure pavilion.

Babur's son Humayun spent his years of exile in the Persian capital, Isfahan. Perhaps the monumental cityscape there inspired him to employ the hitherto purely sybaritic, secular scheme in his own tomb in Delhi. Like all subsequent rulers, he placed the mausoleum on a platform in the middle of formally-quartered *charbagh* gardens—an allusion to Qur'anic images of paradise. The Taj too soars from *charbagh* gardens, which were popular in 17th-century Central Asia. At the center of a *charbagh* garden is a water tank, symbolizing the Qur'anic pool of plenty, *al-kawthar*. The four waterways that emanate from the central tank symbolize the four rivers of paradise, which flowed with milk, water, wine, and refined honey. To some, the gardens were more precious than the building they enclosed; the inscription on the Taj Mahal's central arch proclaims, "O soul thou art at rest, return to the Lord, at peace with Him, and He at peace with you. So enter as one of his servants; enter his garden."

Humayun's successors also made their own modifications to the model. Akbar mixed Islamic arches and domes with Hindu posts and lintels in his tomb at Sikandra, in a reflection of his tolerant, syncretic ethos. Aurangzeb's architects had to reduce the scale and cost of his wife's tomb at Aurangabad, while maintaining the basic plan as a sign of imperial dignity.

(open Sat.-Thurs. 10am-5pm) to see the face of the woman all the fuss is about; the museum showcases paintings of Shah Jahan and Mumtaz Mahal and architectural renderings of the Taj complex.

The best time to visit the Taj Mahal depends on what you want to see. The monument is open from dawn to dusk. Admission is Rs.100 between 6 and 8am and 5 and 7pm, Rs.10.50 at any other time, and free on Fridays. If you like the thought of a mausoleum crammed with jillions of live visitors, show up on Fridays when admission is free. If you'd prefer a more serene, private audience, show up at dawn, preferably between Monday and Thursday—you'll have the place to yourself, but you'll have to pay extra for the privilege. The first arrivals at 6am on Friday get in free, but the crowds start moving in after only a half-hour. Showing up in the early morning also insures that one of the flashlight-equipped attendants will have time to illuminate the interior of the Taj for your viewing pleasure; expect to fork over a bit of *baksheesh*. Changing light patterns affect the aesthetic experience of seeing the Taj. On a cloudless day, the Taj exudes a piercingly bright, almost angular white light; in the early morning and toward twilight, the Taj looks softer and grayer, different but no less beautiful.

Agra Fort

While the Taj Mahal is surely the most magnificent monument raised by the Mughals in Agra, the sprawling, stolid Agra Fort finishes a respectable second, even though much of it—including the impressive Moti Masjid—is off-limits to visitors. Wedged between Yamuna Kinara Rd. to the east, Powerhouse Bus Stand to the west, and Agra Fort Railway Station to the north, Agra Fort is 1.5km northwest of the Taj Mahal and 2.5km southwest of Itimad-ud-Daulah. Emperor Akbar initiated construction of the massive fort in 1565. The stronghold was made stronger over the years, and during his rule (1658-1707), the pious Mughal emperor Aurangzeb completed the fort's 2.5-km-long bulky, red sandstone walls. Of the three outer gates that lead through the walls and into the fort, only the **Amar Singh Gate,** decorated with colorful glazed tiles, is accessible to the public. The gate is said to be named for a Rajasthani maharaja who killed the royal treasurer before the emperor's eyes and jumped the wall here in 1644 while escaping guards.

Due north of the Amar Singh Gate is the breezy **Diwan-i-Am** (Hall of Public Audience), a low three-sided structure that served as Shah Jahan's court while Agra was the Mughal capital. In Agra's Mughal heyday, the Diwan-i-Am was cluttered with the privileged few, in this case nobles and courtiers, and with plenty of regal furnishings, including heavy drapes and lustrous carpets. Sitting in his throne, which was perched atop the graceful platform at the east side of the hall, the emperor was gazed upon by all members of the court, as a god would be gazed upon by worshipers in a Hindu temple. The low marble platform just in front of the throne was reserved for the emperor's chief minister. The tomb at the center of the courtyard belongs to a British official who was killed here during the Mutiny of 1857.

In the **royal chambers,** which are wedged between the eastern ends of Diwan-i-Am and Agra Fort's ramparts, the emperor slept, prayed, and entertained himself in privacy. From Diwan-i-Am, the first chamber is the expansive **Macchi Bhavan** (Fish Palace), which gets its name from the fish that were dumped into its water channels so that the emperor could amuse himself with rod and reel. The chamber as it now stands is not as elegant as it once was—blocks of mosaic work and huge chunks of the royal bath have been hauled off over the centuries. In the northwest corner (left with your back to Diwan-i-Am) of the Macchi Bhavan is the pleasantly petite **Nagina Masjid** (Gem Mosque) built by Shah Jahan for the women of his *zenana* (harem).

Southeast of Macchi Bhavan is the fabulous **Diwan-i-Khas** (Hall of Private Audience), where the emperor received VIPs after its completion in 1637. Although its interior is off-limits, the **terrace** just east of Diwan-i-Khas offers views of the Yamuna River and Taj Mahal. Just south of the terrace is the sturdy, two-storied **Musamman Burj** (Octagonal Tower) with dense inlay work. Legend has it that Shah Jahan lived out his last hours here, as an imprisoned man staring out wistfully at his Taj Mahal (mirrors on each wall had a reflection of the Taj). On a more gruesome note, the emperor peered with pleasure at some combination of man, tiger, and elephant, pitted against each other in the cramped area between inner and outer walls. Heading south from the tower, it's a hop, skip, and a jump to **Sheesh Mahal** (Palace of Mirrors), where royal women took their royal baths. South of Sheesh Mahal is a breezy enclosure that includes the 80-m square **Anguri Bagh** (Vine Garden). On the east side of the garden are three buildings; the **Khas Mahal** (Private Palace) is at the center, flanked by the **Golden Pavilions.** Rendered in cooling marble, the Khas Mahal is reportedly where the emperor slept. The pavilions seem to have been women's bedrooms, with walls that had been discretely packed hidden jewelry. Note the pavilions' roofs, which were built to look like the roofs of Bengali thatched huts. The **Jahangiri Mahal,** the large sandstone palace to the south, was designed for the Hindu queen Jodhi Bai. The minute etchings and detail in the stone make it look like timber. Once bright gold and blue, the palace's now faded color is still marvelous. And out in front of this palace is a large tub, thought to be where Queen Nur Jahan took her rose-scented baths. (Fort complex open daily sunrise-sunset; admission Rs.10.50.)

Jama Masjid

Made mostly of sandstone spliced with ornamental marble, **Jama Masjid,** Agra's main mosque, is 100m west of Agra Fort Railway Station. Built by Shah Jahan in 1648, the mosque complex was damaged during the Mutiny of 1857, when British forces deemed the main gate a threat to the strategically important Red Fort; the gate was promptly leveled along with some of the front cloisters of the mosque. For a while, all of Jama Masjid was even held as a sort of hostage-at-gunpoint—the mosque was wired with explosives, and the British authorities loudly proclaimed that if the Mutiny

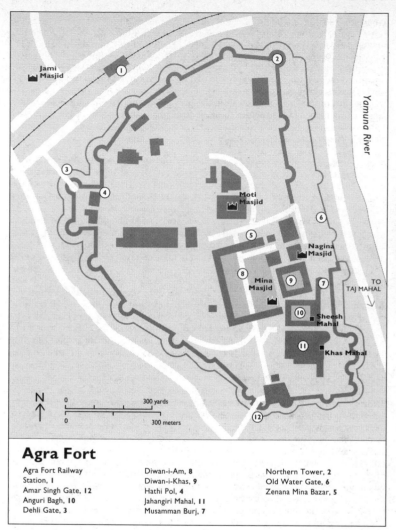

Agra Fort

Agra Fort Railway Station, **1**	Diwan-i-Am, **8**	Northern Tower, **2**
Amar Singh Gate, **12**	Diwan-i-Khas, **9**	Old Water Gate, **6**
Anguri Bagh, **10**	Hathi Pol, **4**	Zenana Mina Bazar, **5**
Dehli Gate, **3**	Jahangiri Mahal, **11**	
	Musamman Burj, **7**	

gained a large enough following in Agra, the Jama Masjid would suffer the consequences. The Jama Masjid remained standing, though it has become a bit disheveled, frequently needing repair, and the ever-present scaffolding and smaller size make it less impressive than the one in Delhi.

Across the River

Across one the four bridges from Agra over the Yamuna are a few other remnants of Mughal days of yore. A small, squat, and entirely exquisite tomb, **Itimad-ud-Daulah** is much less crowded than its cross-river rivals. The tomb was built between 1622 and 1628 for Ghiyas Beg, a Persian diplomat who served as Emperor Jahangir's chief minister and was dubbed Itimad-ud-Daulah (Pillar of Government) for his loyal and exemplary service. Situated in an intimate garden designed by Ghiyas Beg, the tomb itself was built by his daughter Nur Jahan, whom Jahangir married in 1611. The semiprecious stones inlaid throughout the tomb's white marble give it a dense, dazzling beauty. Several of Nur Jahan's relatives were subsequently buried in the central tomb.

A walk of 1km north of Itimad-ud-Daulah brings you to **Chini-ka-Rauza** (China Tomb), the decayed burial chamber of Shah Jahan's chief minister, Afzal Khan. Glazed tiles once covered the entire construction—the few are left are severely weathered. Continuing north from Chini-ka-Rauza, it's 2km to **Ram Bagh,** a garden said to have been designed by Babur. Though there is talk of restoring it, the garden now stands scruffy with weeds. The ruins host peacocks and wild flora—but few foreigners come here, and women shouldn't come alone.

■ Near Agra: Sikandra

A small town just outside Agra, Sikandra is famous as the home of **Akbar's Tomb.** Akbar, who ruled as the Mughal emperor between 1556 and 1605, was a great patron of the visual arts and a respectful admirer of Hinduism. The most impressive of the constructions at the tomb complex is the outlandishly outsized **Buland Darwaza** (Gateway of Magnificence). Adorned with geometric patterns and Qur'anic inscriptions, the gate is a bulky, blocky beauty. The expansive tomb complex is divided into quadrants by unusually wide pathways. Akbar's central mausoleum is sparsely adorned with colonnaded alcoves and marble domes. A ramp on the south side of the mausoleum leads to Akbar's humid, relatively humble crypt. Mornings and evening are pleasantly less crowded while on Fridays the joint jumps with the usual mix of hawkers, hustlers, and picnickers. The untended grassy area between the north wall of the mausoleum and the wall that encloses the entire complex, which is crowded with animals, is an entertaining place—the monkeys and cavorting deer accentuate the grandeur of Akbar's tomb. Despite being 15km northwest of Agra Fort, Sikandra is quite accessible: rickshaw-*wallahs* typically charge about Rs.75 for a round trip journey and Mathura-bound buses, which can be boarded at the station or along Mathura Rd., all pass Akbar's tomb. (Open dawn-dusk; admission Rs.11, free Fri.)

■ Fatehpur Sikri

Despite having the Mughal universe in the palm of his hand, Emperor Akbar, who ruled from 1556 to 1605, lacked what he most desired: a son to take over. Despite covering all his bases by keeping three wives—one Hindu, one Muslim, one Christian—Akbar's quest for a successor became so desperate that he ventured out of Agra. Wandering through the village of Sikri, Akbar came across a Sufi mystic called Salim, who consoled the ruler, promising him no fewer than three sons. When, a year later, the foretold son arrived, Akbar repaid the saint not only by naming the son Salim, but by moving the entire court nearer to the saint's village of Sikri. And so, to the disbelief of the whole population of Agra, the palace of Fatehpur Sikri became the new capital of the Mughal empire.

Following a hurried construction of the exquisite and original palace, Fatehpur Sikri served as the Mughal center for 15 years before the court was shifted back to Agra. Some say drought forced the Mughals out, others say the death of Salim prompted the move. In any case, the abrupt decision left a ghost-palace in immaculate condition. Not until the 19th century was it rediscovered, still ringing with the barbed decrees of Akbar and the tunes of Miyan Tansen and other court musicians. The pristine Fatehpur Sikri casts a haunting spell on visitors, especially at dawn and dusk, when the sun performs colorful dances in the palace courtyards.

ORIENTATION AND PRACTICAL INFORMATION

Vehicles drive into Fatehpur Sikri from an access to the east of the palace complex—a fee of Rs.4.50 per passenger is assessed at the entry gate. The deserted city sits atop a hill overlooking the not-so-modern town to the south. If arriving by bus or train, it's a 5-min. walk up the hill to the ancient city complex. To the north of Fatehpur Sikri is a tranquil artificial lake.

Most services, including the **bank,** are near the bus stand, though it's difficult to change money or traveler's checks. In desperate cases, ask around at the hotels at the base of the **Buland Darwaza,** the huge gate on the south entrance of **Jama Masjid.** Buses to: Agra (every 30min., 6am-7pm, 1hr., Rs.12); Bharatpur (9, 11am, 1, 3, and 5pm, 1hr., Rs.8); Mathura; and infrequently to Jaipur. An auto-rickshaw to Bharatpur takes about 30min. (Rs.50). **Trains** to Agra leave daily at 5:30, 11am, and 4pm. **Postal Code:** 283110. **Telephone Code:** 05619.

ACCOMMODATIONS AND FOOD

All hotels in Fatehpur Sikri are within walking distance of the palace. In peak season (Oct.-Mar.), hotels fill up and prices may rise. The best place to stay is in one of the six rooms at the **Archaeological Survey Rest House,** just east of Diwan-i-Am in the ruins. For only Rs.9 per night, you're within sight of the palace and have access to an inexpensive, old-style dining hall. But rooms must be booked ahead of time at the survey's office at 22 the Mall in Agra. The **Maurya Rest House** (tel. 2348), down the steps from the base of Buland Darwaza, has spacious, almost tidy rooms off a lovely, tucked away garden patio. Some are dark, others gorgeous, but all come with the friendly vibe of the owner and his sons. Singles Rs.60-80. Doubles with toilet and shower Rs.120, with A/C Rs.200. Down the path to the bus stand right next to the Whiskey Shop, the **Shree Tourist Guest House** has roomy rooms (some with attached bath), a pleasant roof area, tiny kitchen, and a common bath off the front balcony. Singles Rs.60-80, with bath Rs.100. Doubles Rs.120. Just at the base of the big gate is the **Rang Mahal Guest House,** a fallback option if you can't get a room on the courtyard. Singles Rs.70. Doubles Rs.150. At the **Prince Tourist Lodge,** on the road below the palace, the owner offers cramped, suffocating rooms. Singles Rs.100. Doubles Rs.150. East of the Prince about 1km from the monument, U.P. Tourism's **Gulistan Tourist Complex** (tel. 2490) feels like a Mughal palace—though here they have swing sets, cows, and nice, meticulously kept singles and doubles for Rs.300-350. Doubles with A/C Rs.525. Beds in 12-bed dorm Rs.60.

Come chow time, indulge in a Rs.25 *thali* at Haji Abdul Gani Urf's **Kallu Restaurant,** now managed by the *haji's* ultra-mellow son. The food is tasty, but hygiene doesn't quite match up (open daily 7am-11pm). The same owner runs the **Nainital Restaurant,** on the path toward the Whiskey Shop. Along this strip you'll also see bakers toiling in sordid shops to make *khataie,* slightly sweet cookies (for sale all around the bazaar). For a real feast and classier food, the **Gulistan Tourist Complex** offers lunch and dinner buffets (Rs.200), and Indian dishes (Rs.30-70), as well as soups, snacks, and desserts.

SIGHTS

Wherever tourists and their buses congregate, so do **"guides"** eager offer tours of the deserted palace. Many guides falsely claim to be licensed; others insist they are students whose "duty" it is to show you around, only afterwards hinting for a bit of *baksheesh,* or leading you right into their handicrafts shops. Even so, it may be helpful to have someone show you around—just pick someone with good English and don't pay more than Rs.40-50.

The base of the **Buland Darwaza** is 13m above street level and its gate 40m above that, making it the tallest in Asia. The gate was only added to the complex in 1595 following Akbar's triumph in Gujarat. As you pass through the gate and take off your shoes (either depositing them for Rs.2 or carrying them). The head of the sprawling **Jama Masjid** is off to the left, facing Mecca. In the middle is the **mausoleum of Saint Salim,** the sage who prophesied the birth of Akbar's sons. The core of the tomb is mother of pearl, and visitors can hang a thread from the marble latticework walls. The story of Salim's "summoning" of Akbar's sons brings many sonless women here to pray. Pungent incense burning on the inside and *qawwali* singers on the outside complete the sensory stimuli—you can almost taste the tomb's holiness. It's customary to leave a small donation at the tomb itself. Coming out of the mosque, head left through the other main gate, **Badshani Darwaza,** ignoring the vendors, and cross through the parking lot across the palace complex to the east.

Head along the path toward the palace; coming from the east, you'll pass the **Naubat Khana** (Drum House), which was used to signal the emperor's arrival and the ticket office (admission Rs.0.50). Both paths lead into the **Diwan-i-Am,** the court where from a throne perched between two sandstone slates, the emperor heard the pleas and petitions of common men. The stone ring in the grass to the northeast is thought to have held down either *shamianas* (huge festival tents) or as a more sinister version has it, the leash of the Elephant of Justice, who determined guilt or innocence by either trampling or sparing the accused men. To the west toward the throne is the main courtyard of the palace (don't forget your ticket).

For orientation's sake, look for the stone plaques in front of each structure. Starting off to the right is **Diwan-i-Khas** (Hall of Private Audience). Here Akbar is thought to have spoken with VIPs and relatives. The illusion of a two-story structure is revealed when you peek inside and see one massive story supported in the middle by an overwhelmingly ornate **column,** meant to represent an opening flower. Out to the left is a meticulously carved gazebo, thought to be the sitting chamber of either the treasurer or royal astrologer.

Looming over the courtyard on the west side is **Panch Mahal,** a five-story tower with columns—the ground floor has 84, the top only four. You can walk up this through the stairs on the west side; stop on the second floor to note the seemingly tangible details columns' designs. Access to the top is sometimes closed, but even the lower levels offer excellent views. On the south side of the courtyard is a grid tank called **Anup Talao,** perhaps the favorite performing spot of the legendary Mughal crooner Miyan Tansen. More finely carved columns and walls may be seen at the nearby **Turkish Sultana's Palace.** To the north of Anup Talao stands what served as the royal **banquet hall.**

The path from Panch Mahal leads west to **Birbal's Palace,** which probably housed either the daughters of the minister or one of Akbar's queens. Head back toward Panch Mahal, stopping at the small **garden,** more accurately described as a lawn, off to the left. Legend holds that the bratty young prince Salim, later to be called Jahangir, fell in love here with his future wife Nur Jahan.

Before Panch Mahal in the middle of the courtyard is the small **Mariam's Palace** with fading, but eerie wall paintings, left over from the palace's more colorful glory days. From here, proceed to the south and cut right to the entrance of **Jodh Bai's Palace,** which reverberates with Persian voices of days gone by. In the large courtyard, symmetrical patterns and sandstone flowers surround a central fountain (thought to hold *tulsi,* a medicinal plant). The pigeons and green parrots who nest in the dark, urine-stinky chambers add color to the courtyard. Most likely, this complex was used for the harem—apparently a great necessity for a man with only three or four wives. Note the azure-glazed tiles on the roof along the second story. The path out of the palace leads off to the right, and brings you back in the parking lot leading toward Jama Masjid. But first, stop in at the marble shop. "One elephant two rupees—looking no buying!"

■ Lucknow

Uttar Pradesh's capital looks on the surface much like any big city, but for an excess of officialdom: political posters are glued everywhere, and government institutes lurk behind many of the city's walls. This façade serves to cover up an older, much more cherished Lucknow—a city that for over a century before 1947 was the center of Indian Muslim culture. Lucknow's refined citizens are said to have spoken the most poetic Urdu and kept their great Muharram festival going for two months and eight days.

The city's name is thought to derive from Lakshmana, who is said to have received Lucknow as a fief from his brother, the Hindu god (and king) Rama. Modern Lucknow, however, grew up around a 13th-century fort, and its glory days began after

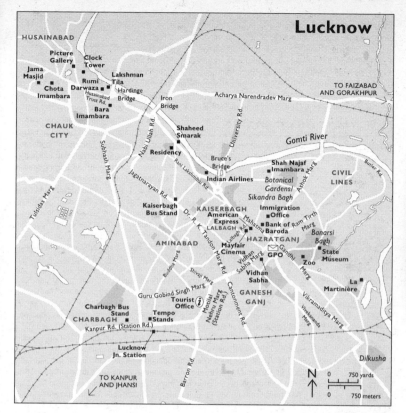

1775, when it became capital of Avadh ("Oudh"), one of the small kingdoms born out of the collapsing Mughal Empire. Asaf-ud-Daula and subsequent *nawabs* of Avadh made Lucknow a cultural center, but they were terrible rulers, more interested in their *hookahs* than their subjects. Nawab Wajid Ali Shah, who took power in 1847, was so incompetent and "slothful" (though an excellent dancer) that the English East India Company could not restrain its grabby fingers—it marched in and annexed Avadh without a fight in 1856. The annexation of Avadh was one of the events that led to the Indian Mutiny the following year.

A pair of fish, the emblem of the *nawabs,* can still be seen all over Lucknow, notably on the U.P. state legislature where it holds up the Indian flag. Lucknawi traditions such as *chikan* embroidery endure, and Urdu is still spoken with pride. But much has changed since the Partition of India in 1947, when most of the city's elegant Muslim upper classes went to Pakistan, leaving a city that had to steer itself into a new ethos. Now the old fine Lucknawi brickwork competes with the concrete chaos of a modern Indian city of 1.8 million people.

The Shi'a Muslim festival of Muharram (also known as Ashoora) is the most exciting time to be in Lucknow. In 1997, the festival falls on May 17.

ORIENTATION

Lucknow occupies the south bank of the **Gomti River** and extends quite far inland. **Hazratganj** is the center of the city. The main road in this area is **Mahatma Gandhi (M.G.) Marg,** a wide street that has the spiffiest shops and plenty of hotels and restaurants, running through the city from northwest to southeast before sweeping south and out of the city. To the northwest is **Husainabad,** where many of Lucknow's monuments are located on **Husainabad Trust Road.**

The main railway station (and one of the bus stations) is at **Charbagh** in the south, which is why so many hotels are in the area. The way from Charbagh to Hazratganj is a major route, going along **Motilal Nehru Marg** and then **Vidhan Sabha Marg** past the state legislature (Vidhan Sabha). **Subhash Road** will take you almost directly from Charbagh to Husainabad, so there's a kind of Hazratganj-Husainabad-Charbagh triangle. In the middle of them all is **Aminabad,** an old bazaar area.

PRACTICAL INFORMATION

Tourist Office: U.P. Government Tourist Reception Centre, Lucknow Railway Station, Charbagh (tel. 52533). Inside the railway station, near the entrance. Helpful English-speaking staff. Sponsors a 5-hr. (9am-2pm) group tour of the Nawabi Monuments (Rs.50). Open daily (including holidays) 7am-8pm. **U.P. Tourist Office,** 10/4 Stadium Rd. (tel. 246205). From Charbagh Station, walk straight 100m to Station Rd. and take a right. At the first major intersection, turn left and hop in a tempo (follows a fixed route; Rs.1) in the left lane (going away from the station). The well-marked tourist office will appear on your right, next to the City Montessori School. Open Mon.-Sat.10am-5pm.

Immigration Office: Jawaharlal Bhavan Marg (tel. 280635). Take a rickshaw several blocks from M.G. Rd. (Rs.5). Will only extend 3-month visas to 6 months. Open Mon.-Sat. 10am-5pm.

Currency Exchange: Main branch of the **State Bank of India,** Motimahal Marg (tel. 213074). Near Clarks Avadh Hotel. Open Mon.-Fri. 10am-2:30pm, Sat. 10:30am-12:30pm. Foreign exchange branch of the **Bank of Baroda,** M.G. Rd. (tel. 215462). Several doors down from the main branch, opposite the British library. Open Mon.-Fri 10:30am-2:30pm, Sat. 10:30am-12:30pm.

American Express: M.G. Rd. (tel. 226534), next to Mayfair Cinema. Cash advances for a 2% fee. Open Mon.-Fri. 9:30am-7:30pm.

Telephones: 24-hr. **STD/ISD,** 39/55 Ram Tirth Marg (tel. 220038, 210910), on the left in the large well-lit office after the Hotel Naresh. Incoming international calls cost Rs.3.50 for 3min.; international collect calling through AT&T.

Airport: Amousi Airport (tel. 256327), 11km from Charbagh. Hire a taxi or autorickshaw in front of the main railway station. To: Bombay (1-2 per day, 2-3½hr., US$190); Calcutta (Mon., Wed., and Fri. 1 per day, 2½hr., US$119); Delhi (3-5 per day, 1hr., US$102); Patna (Mon., Wed., and Fri. 1 per day, 1hr., US$69).

Trains: Lucknow has 1 main railway station called **Lucknow Station,** Charbagh, 3km from Hazratganj. Tempos follow fixed routes between Station Rd. (100m in front of the station) and Chowk, Aminabad, Kaiserbagh, and Lalbagh/Hazratganj. To: Delhi (*Shatabdi Exp.* 2003, 3:25pm, 6½hr., Rs.408/415 for executive class/chair car); Agra (*Avadh Exp.* 5063, 8:55pm, 8hr.); Kanpur (*Barauni-Amritsar Exp.* 5207, 6:55pm, 1½hr.; *Avadh Exp.* 5063, 8:55pm, 2hr.; *Chhapra Gwalior Mail* 1144, 7am, 1½hr.); Faizabad (*Farakka Exp.* 3484, Tues., Thurs.-Fri., and Sun., 8:15am, 2½hr.; *Saryu-Yamuna Exp.* 4650, Mon., Wed., and Sat., 6:30am, 2½hr.); Gorakhpur (*Avadh-Assam Exp.* 5610, 6:05pm, 5½hr.; *Avadh Exp.* 5064, 8am, 6hr.); Varanasi (*Kashi Vishwanath Exp.* 4058, 11:20pm, 6½hr.; *Varuna Exp.* 4228, 6pm, 5½hr.); Allahabad (*Nauchandi Exp.* 4012, 6:05am, 5hr.; *Ganga-Gomti Exp.* 4216, 6:30pm, 4hr.).

Buses: The main bus station, with buses to Delhi, Agra, Varanasi, and Allahabad, among others, is located on Station Rd. From the railway station, walk straight 100m to the first main road. Take a left; the station is 100m down on the right. Buses are cheap but very inconvenient. All timetables are in Hindi. Timetables in English are supposed to be available, but this is irrelevant because the buses never run on time. Another bus station is located in Kaiserbagh; take a tempo from Station Rd. This station has buses to Kathmandu.

Local Transportation: Hire **auto-rickshaws** and **tempos** outside Lucknow Station. These are unmetered so be prepared for heavy bargaining. Hire **rickshaws** anywhere in the city. The ride from the station to Hazratganj costs Rs.10, but only after a lot of bargaining; a 1-hr. ride should never cost more than Rs.30. Tempos follow fixed routes from Station Rd. to all major points in the city. Hop in a tempo at Hazratganj (M.G. Rd. or Lalbagh) to get to Chowk or the railway station (Rs.2). Ride a tempo from Chowk (in front of the Bara Imambara) to Hazratganj or the train station (Rs.2). There are no direct tempos to Aminabad from Chowk or Hazratganj; you will need to return to Station Rd. and switch tempos. There are no official tempo stops. Just go to a main road, flag one down, and tell the driver where you're going.

Library: British Council Library, M.G. Rd., Hazratganj, near Mayfair Cinema. Members only. Open Tues.-Sat. 10:30am-6:30pm.

English Bookstore: Universal Bookseller, 82 M.G. Rd., Hazratganj (tel. 225894). Take a left onto M.G. Rd. from Vidhan Sabha Marg (the main road from the railway station). The bookstore is on the left about 1 block up. English fiction and philosophy at English prices. Open Mon.-Sat. 9:30am-8pm.

Market: Main bazaars at **Aminabad** and **Chowk.** Tempos from Station Rd. go to both locations; those from Hazratganj go only to Chowk. Open daily dawn-dusk. At the main fruit market on **Ram Tirth Marg** (rickshaw from M.G. Rd., Rs.5), pick up the delicious mangos for which Lucknow is known. Open daily dawn to around midnight.

Pharmacy: There are several pharmacies in the Hazratganj area; most are open daily 8am-11pm.

Hospital: The main civil hospital is **Balrampur,** located near Kaisarbagh (tel. 224040, emergency tel. 102). The staff does not speak much English. A smaller private hospital is **Nishrat** on 3 J.C. Bose Marg, Kaisarbagh. Friendly staff speaks little English; quite clean. 24-hr. emergency services.

Police: Hazratganj Police Station, M.G. Rd. (tel. 222555). Big yellow building, sitting slightly back from the road, opposite Mayfair Cinema.

Post Office: GPO, Vidhan Sabha Marg (tel. 222410). Take a right from M.G. Rd. to Vidhan Sabha. The GPO is a yellow building across the street. Open Mon.-Sat. 7am-7pm.

Telephone Code: 0522.

ACCOMMODATIONS

Unfortunately, most of the hotels in Lucknow are located along major thoroughfares. A number of comfortable, mid-range hotels cluster around the noisy Lalbagh traffic circle near M.G. Rd. And only a few quiet, clean bargains can be found on the side streets of the Hazratganj area.

Chowdhury Lodge, 3 Vidhan Sabha Marg (tel. 221911, 273135). From the railway station, take a tempo- or cycle-rickshaw along Vidhan Sabha Marg to the Hazratganj area. Nestled in its own alleyway about 20m before Vidhan Sabha Marg intersects with M.G. Rd., the Chowdhury Lodge is a quiet oasis in the heart of the city. In the morning, go out for an earful of the din and bustle of M.G. Rd. and Lalbagh, then return to your room for a thoroughly satisfying siesta. Beds and bathrooms are clean, and the staff is generally friendly and accommodating (although they never seem to be able to make change). Bring mosquito repellent during the summer and monsoon. Singles Rs.65, with bath Rs.100, with bath and air-cooling Rs.160. Doubles Rs.130, with bath Rs.150, with bath and air-cooling Rs.200.

Hotel Naresh, Ram Tirth Marg (tel. 228160). Walk 2 blocks past the intersection of Vidhan Sabha Marg and M.G. Rd. to the fork; veer right, and the hotel is 400m on the left. The cheapest place in the vicinity, with rooms available off the street and away from the noisy bazaar area. Despite its proximity to the main fruit market, it isn't too buggy. All rooms air-cooled. Singles Rs.90, with TV Rs.110. Doubles Rs.130, with TV Rs.150.

Avadh Lodge, 1 Ram Mohan Raj Marg (tel. 282861). A 10-min. rickshaw ride from M.G. Rd. Slightly more expensive than the lodges near M.G. Rd., the Avadh Lodge is probably the most pleasant hotel in town. Located in a very quiet neighborhood, nights at Avadh are restful (even without an air-cooler). The rooms are spacious and clean, with attached baths and fans. Thoughtful aesthetic touches (like decorative bedspreads) make the rooms even more inviting. This hotel has character, from the portraits in each room depicting episodes from the *Ramayana* to the green divans with the red-and-gold-banded legs in the lobby. Check-out noon. Singles Rs.180, with air-cooling Rs.260. Doubles Rs.280, with air-cooling Rs.360.

Hotel Ramkrishna, 17/2 Ashok Marg (tel. 280380). From M.G. Rd., take a left on Vidhan Sabha Marg. At the fork, go left; the hotel is 600m up, on the left. Not a great bargain, but located near the main road without being on top of it. Rooms are of variable quality: some have stained sheets, and less direct air-cooling (the air-cooler is hidden in a nook nowhere near the bed). The restaurant downstairs has slow service—it can take 10min. to get a coke. Attached baths. Check-out 24hr. Singles Rs.150. Doubles Rs.195.

FOOD

Most good, cheap restaurants are located in the area around M.G. Rd., though *dhabas* and small cafés dot the entire city. Avadhi cuisine (*kababs* and such cooked with distinctive spices) is hard to find, but some places offer one or two dishes.

Aahar Restaurant, Lalbagh. Turn left onto Lalbagh after the AmEx office on M.G. Rd. and head to the traffic circle; it will be on the left. Walk down from street level into a clean, A/C bistro. The food is tasty, especially the Kashmiri dishes, *pulao* (Rs.20) and *kofta* (Rs.30). Waiters are curiously inattentive. An empty Mirinda can rests at the bottom of an otherwise pristine fish tank. Open daily 10am-11pm. *Tandoori* (*naan*, etc.) starts at 7:30pm.

Ranjana, M.G. Rd., on the right past the police station. Attracts a large and diverse clientele, including businessmen, office workers, college students, and families. Inexpensive North Indian (including *kababs* for Rs.8), South Indian, and Chinese cuisines served in a cool, spacious hall well-decked-out in low plush couches. The staff is friendly but speaks little English. Open daily 10am-10pm.

Sharma Chat House, Lalbagh. From M.G. Rd., take a left onto Lalbagh; it will be on your right before the first traffic circle. Famous for cheap *chat*. Bring your own cold drinks. Open daily 10am-10pm.

Sham-e-Avadh, 52 Hazratganj (tel. 223458), in Cooper's Hotel on M.G. Rd. Clean, cool place, with Hindi jazz muzak in the background. Lucknawi chicken (Rs.45) is quite spicy. Waiters are aloof yet attentive: if you order a fresh lime soda, they bring you a forest of straws and a bouquet of napkins. Open daily 8am-11pm.

Falaknuma Restaurant, 9th fl., Clark's Avadh Hotel. From M.G. Rd., take a 10-min. rickshaw ride (Rs.10). Serves a full range of lamb and chicken *kababs* (starting at Rs.180) in a posh, A/C dining room. Beer and cocktails at exorbitant prices; live classical Indian music starting at 8:30pm. The waiters return friendliness in kind. Lunch served noon-3pm, dinner 8-11pm.

SIGHTS

Foremost among Lucknow's buildings are the monuments raised by its decadent *nawabs*. Indian Muslim architecture of the 18th and 19th centuries is considered flamboyant and excessive, and less perfected than the Mughal style, yet in Lucknow it's the most visible sign of the wealth and power of days gone by. Grandiose decorated archways are great to drive through in tacky plastic-frilled rickshaws. The biggest cluster of old buildings is on the northwest side of the city in the **Husainabad** area.

In 1784 a great famine inspired Nawab Asaf-ud-Daula to cook up the Great or **Bara Imambara** as a food-for-work scheme. An *imambara* is a replica of the tomb of one of the *imams*, descendants of the Prophet Muhammad who are revered by Shi'a Muslims. The Bara Imambara is noted for its sheer size—domes and arches are in a great blue hall, 50m long, 15m high, and 15m wide, built without a single structural beam. Running through its attic is the Bhulbhulaiya, a labyrinth on several levels. It might help to hire a guide for the Bhulbhulaiya—they claim to have undergone six months of training. Couples *must* be accompanied by a guide; this rule is an invitation for extortion. (The Rs.10 ticket to the Bhulbhulaiya also gets you into four other sights: the *bauli*, the Rumi Darwaza, the Picture Gallery, and the Shahihammam.) To the right of the Bara Imambara is Asaf-ud-Daula's mosque, more imposing than the *imam-bara*, but closed to non-Muslims (and there's not much to see inside anyway). Opposite the mosque is the *bauli*, an old step-well with a five-story tower around it. According to legend the well is connected to underground tunnels and a buried treasure (use the ticket from the Bhulbhulaiya to enter).

Back out on the street—actually straddling Husainabad Trust Rd.—is the **Rumi Darwaza,** another work of Asaf-ud-Daula's. This gate is intended as a copy of the Sublime Porte in Istanbul and it is covered by a spine of trumpets. Your ticket from the Bara Imambara lets you climb it (or you can sneak in by walking along the wall from the Bara Imambara). There are good views of the River Gomti from the top.

Keep going, through the Rumi Darwaza, toward the Husainabad clock tower, which holds the odd distinction of being the tallest clock tower in India (67m). Just past it, behind a tank of swans, the **Picture Gallery** is located inside an office building. It has a sorry collection of portraits of the *nawabs*—the succulent Wajid Ali Shah is painted here with his left nipple showing. (Open Mon.-Sat. 7am-7pm; use the same ticket from the Bara Imambara.)

Not too far down the same Husainabad Trust Rd. on the left is the Small or **Chota Imambara.** This *imambara* was built by Nawab Muhammad Ali Shah in 1837, again as a famine relief project, although Muhammad Ali Shah had himself buried here as well. Overall, things get tacky once through the gate: there's a big gold dome on the *imambara* and a pond full of weeds in front of it. On the right side is an ugly little copy of the Taj Mahal. Inside the *imambara* a cloud of glass chandeliers hangs over your head; the silver throne was used for Koran readings. The Chota Imambara is lit up each year for the Muharram festival.

Around the corner (down the road to the left after the Chota Imambara) is the **Jama Masjid,** whose construction was also initiated by Muhammad Ali Shah although it was completed after his death in the 1840s. This is the biggest mosque in Lucknow. It is, unfortunately, closed to non-Muslims, though anyone can approach it and see its painted ceiling of leaf patterns and fruit bowls. Nearby on the River Gomti close to the Hardinge Bridge is **Lakshman Tila,** the site of the fort around which Lucknow grew up. Now the spot is marked by Aurangzeb's Mosque, a rather plain mosque built by the emperor Aurangzeb.

If the British Raj still governed India, the ruins of Lucknow's **Residency** would be one of its proudest monuments. This complex of scaly brick buildings in a shady park near the center of Lucknow stands much as it was left by the turmoil of 1857: blasted by cannonballs into some sort of ancient ruin. One of the most stretched-out struggles of the great Indian Mutiny took place when mutinying sepoys (Indians enlisted in the East India Company's army) besieged Lucknow's British community (along with many loyal Indians) from June to November of 1857. The Residency, a mansion for the East India Company's agent in Avadh, was turned into a fortress for the 3000 people who were trapped there. After three months Sir Henry Havelock arrived to relieve the Residency, only to end up shutting himself and his troops inside. It was another month and a half before Sir Colin Campbell was able to break the siege. Only a third of the original 3000 defenders survived, but it was a miracle that they had kept fighting at all, after four and a half months of hunger, disease, and skillful enemies taking pot-shots through their windows. The Defence of the Residency was made into a legend of British bravery. As you enter the complex now through the Baillie Gate there are several buildings on the right and left that were used during the siege as hospitals and armories. The Residency building itself is beyond a wide lawn containing a monument to Sir Henry Lawrence, the man who gathered the British together and organized the Residency's defenses, only to be killed after four days of the siege. One tall tower still stands on the Residency building (though it no longer flies the Union Jack). A British cemetery is located down toward the river. There is a miniature version of the complex in the **Model Gallery,** but the model here seems to have endured some worse disaster than the actual buildings. Other exhibits in the gallery, including weapons, old prints, and a rather awkward poem by Tennyson, are more revealing. (Open daily 9am-4:30pm; admission Rs.1, Fridays free.) Below the Model Gallery is a basement where many of the British women and children hid. Be careful when walking around the Residency; many shady characters frequent this decaying monument and harass single women (or anyone else they find).

Just visible over the treetops from the Residency is the white marble flame of the **Shaheed Smarak.** This pillar, down by the Gomti River, is independent India's monument to the sepoys who died attacking the Residency, but it's really no match for the evocative power of the Residency's ruins.

Moving southeast toward Lucknow's center you'll reach the Kaiserbagh area; **Kaiserbagh Palace** here was built for Wajid Ali Shah, the last *nawab* of Avadh, though most of it was blown up during the 1857 Mutiny. What is left is now the home of the Raja of Mahmoodabad. On the grounds are the big sandy-brown **tombs** of Nawab Saadat Ali Khan (r. 1798-1814) and his wife Khursheed, which stand out boldly over Rani Lakshmi Bai Marg.

North of the Hazratganj area of downtown Lucknow is another *imambara*, the **Shah Najaf Imambara,** which holds the tomb of Nawab Ghazi-ud-din Haidar (r. 1814-27). It consists mainly of one large dome whose inside is painted with leafy patterns and decked with chandeliers. The lush and dense **Botanical Gardens** in Sikandra Bagh, very close to the *imambara,* draw many early-morning walkers. The plot once included Nawab Wajid Ali Shah's pleasure garden, where the final battle of 1857 for the relief of the Residency took place. Now it is home to the National Botanical Research Institute; you can buy plants from their nursery from 2 to 4:30pm. (Open April-Oct. daily 5-8am; Nov.-March 6-9am; free.)

Lucknow's **zoo,** like so many Indian zoos, makes you wonder why you should have such a nice park to walk around in while the animals are trapped in cages. Stare at them from a miniature train (donated by Sahara Airlines), which chugs around the zoo. (Open Tues.-Sun. 7:30am-5:30pm; admission Rs.5.) The **State Museum** is located on the premises (unfortunately there's no way to avoid paying both admission fees). The museum is quite good as far as Indian state museums go, taking visitors on a "journey of Indian sculpture" with a major stop in Mathura. The collection of *nawab*-era relics is disappointing, but the museum also contains (for some unknown reason) an Egyptian mummy. An unhappy bunch of statues of Queen Victoria and other imperial figures is imprisoned out back near the Indian Air Force jet. (Open Tues.-Sun. 10:30am-4pm; admission Rs.1.)

Last of all, to the southeast of Lucknow by the side of the Gomti, is **La Martinière,** a private boys' school and one of Lucknow's most unique sights. The French adventurer Major-General Claude Martin (1735-1800) amassed a fortune in India as an indigo trader and as a soldier for both the East India Company and the *nawabs* of Avadh. He decided to settle in Lucknow and designed his palatial home, Constantia, but died before it was completed. In his will, he asked that the house become a school, and left money to found schools in Calcutta and in Lyon, France. Lucknow's La Martinière became one of British India's most prestigious schools and is still going strong today. The building itself is fabulously eclectic, with curved ramps swooping up to frightened-looking lions and a ballet of classical figures making the roof their stage. At the top, bridges lead up to the sky, repeating a motif familiar in Lucknow. "Silence" signs are posted in the hall; if you want to look around, remember that this is still a school and be careful not to disturb lessons. It's best to check in at the principal's office. You might be assigned a servant to show you the chapel (with interesting memorials) and Claude Martin's tomb in the basement.

ENTERTAINMENT AND SHOPPING

Lucknow isn't known for fun, but if you need a drink to take the edge off a nerve-racking day, there are budget **bars** along Station Rd. and ritzy, pricey bars at Hotel Clark's Avadh.

Novelty Cinema, on Lalbagh opposite Aahar's Restaurant, shows English-language movies. For a real treat, try **Mayfair Cinema** on M.G. Rd., which shows Hollywood movies dubbed into Hindi.

Aminabad, to the south from here, is one of Lucknow's old bazaar areas and the best place to shop for Lucknawi crafts. Clothing with *chikan* embroidery flowering around the collar is the big deal here. There are plenty of stores, so shop around if you're thinking of buying. Tiny bottles of *attar,* perfumes worn by Indian Muslims, are also sold here, including one made from clay to give off the scent of monsoon-soaked earth.

■ Faizabad

Faizabad was the capital of the kingdom of Avadh until Nawab Asaf-ud-Daula moved to more luxurious Lucknow in 1775. Some monuments of Faizabad's historical splendor remain, including two famous mausolea (Shuja-ud-daula and Bahu Begur), which date from an earlier time than the Avadhi monuments of Lucknow and exhibit a slightly different style. But Faizabad serves primarily as the administrative center for the Faizabad district, which includes the holy city of Ayodhya (from which the name "Avadh" was derived in the first place). Travelers headed for Ayodhya should take a train to Faizabad and hop in a tempo in the Chowk region for a 10-minute ride to Ayodhya. Ayodhya has some cheap and comfortable accommodations, but Faizabad has a greater number of proper hotels with more amenities.

ORIENTATION AND PRACTICAL INFORMATION

There are two main roads in Faizabad: **Station Road,** which starts at the railway station, turns into **Civil Line,** and eventually leads to the **Chowk** area where hotels and sights are located; and **National Highway 28,** on the opposite side of town with buses going to Ayodhya and Gorakhpur. Distances are great in Faizabad, but easily traversed by rickshaws, which are readily available at the bus and train stations.

The **Regional Tourist Office** is located on Civil Line (tel. 813214). From the railway station, take a right on Station Rd. and take the middle road at the traffic circle. The road swings right and then left and after about 600m, there is a large sign on the left which reads "Tiny Tots School." Underneath is a sign that says "Regional Tourist Office." Although difficult to find (most rickshaw-*wallahs* don't know the way), it has great maps of Ayodhya. (Open Mon.-Sat. 10am-5pm). **State Bank of India,** on Civil Line (tel. 812210), changes money. From the railway station, take Station Rd. 300m past the traffic circle. The bank is on the left. (Open Mon.-Fri. 10am-2pm, Sat. 10am-noon). **Telephones** (including a 24-hr. STD/ISD booth) are located across the street from the train station. **Buses** to Gorakhpur leave regularly from the bus station on the national highway. Tempos to Ayodhya leave regularly from Gurdi Bazaar, Chowk, near National Highway 28 (Rs.3). Take a rickshaw from the railway station (Rs.15-20) or Chowk (Rs.5). **Trains** go to Lucknow (*Sealdah-Jammu Tawi Exp.* 3151, 6:15am, 2½hr.; *Doon Exp.* 3009, 4:10pm, 2½hr.; *Dhanbad-Ludhiana Ganga Satlej Exp.* 3307, 11:25am, 3hr.; *Saryu-Yamuna Exp.* 4649, 10:05pm, 2½hr.); Varanasi (*Doon Exp.* 3010, 11:30am, 4½hr.; *Ludhiana-Dhanbad Ganga Satlej Exp.* 3308, 3:05pm, 5½hr.). The **police** are at Kotwali, Riedganj, Chowk (tel. 812202, 812558). **Post office** (tel. 814227). **Telephone Code:** 0527.

ACCOMMODATIONS AND FOOD

There are several cheap, clean hotels in the Chowk area. A few of these have their own restaurants. Otherwise, roadside *dhabas* of uniform quality are the only choice for grub. **Hotel Abha** (tel. 812550), located in an alley off Bajaja Rd. in Motibagh (the rickshaw drivers are familiar with it), is probably the best of the small hotels in this area, and just five minutes from the bus and tempo stops. The sheets are clean, and telephones, fans, air-cooling, attached bath, TVs, and room service are all available. The air-conditioned restaurant downstairs is open daily from 7am to 11pm. The manager does not speak much English. The doubles are better, so it's best to get one even if you're alone. Singles with bath Rs.70. Doubles with bath and air-cooling Rs.100.

■ Ayodhya

The hometown of Rama in the *Ramayana* and one of India's holiest cities, Ayodhya is a popular pilgrimage site for Hindus in U.P. and all over India. It has many beautiful Hindu temples (as well as mosques and Jain temples) whose religious character is unsullied by a booming tourist trade—*bhang*, a lure for western tourists in Varanasi, is reserved strictly for *sadhus* in Ayodhya. The rare western tourist is gawked at but nevertheless respected and accepted for more than his or her moneybelt.

On December 6, 1992, religious fervor turned to violence when 200,000 militant Hindus descended on Ayodhya, smashing through police barricades to destroy Ayodhya's Babri Masjid and erect a makeshift temple in its place. The 16th-century Babri Masjid, which was built by the Mughal Emperor Babur on a site that many Hindus hold to be the birthplace of their god Rama, had become a symbol for the resentment and prejudice many Indian Hindus felt against Muslims. Thousands were killed in the riots that followed the destruction of the mosque, and Ayodhya remains a flashpoint for communal violence. A final decision about the holy site has been held in abeyance by the government; whenever the final decision is handed down, mass rioting is predicted. Festivals (especially Ramnaumi in April) are particularly heady and unpredictable events when travelers should be especially cautious. Under normal conditions, Ayodhya is quiet, peaceful, secluded, and rich in culture—an adventure to Ayodhya is an entirely different experience than a visit to Varanasi.

ORIENTATION AND PRACTICAL INFORMATION

National Highway 28 runs through Ayodhya on its way from Faizabad to Gorakhpur. The railway station, tourist bungalow, and some of the major sights (including Hanuman Gardhi and Kanak Bhavan) are all located within walking distance of the bus station and tempo stop. Several important temples and *ghats* along the **River Saryu** on the opposite side of town can be reached by rickshaw.

To reach the **tourist office** from the bus station walk right along National Highway. Take the first left after the Birla Dharamsala. Walk straight 600m to the railway station and take a left; the Tourist Bungalow is on the left, on Pathik Niwas Saket (tel. 52435). The small office offers excellent accommodations. (Open Mon.-Sat. 10am-5pm.) For currency exchange, go to the **State Bank of India,** at Shrinagar Hat (tel. 2053; open Mon.-Fri. 10am-2pm, Sat. 10am-noon.) The **post office** is at Shrinagar Hat (tel. 2025). (Open Mon.-Sat. 10am-5pm.) STD/ISD **telephone** booths are easy to find in the vicinity of the bus station, although none are open 24hr. There is sporadic **train** service in Ayodhya (some stop for 1min. on the way to or from Faizabad), but it's best to catch trains in Faizabad. Regular **buses** running to and from Gorakhpur stop briefly; catch them at the bus station on National Highway 28. Near the bus station is **Sri Ram Hospital** (tel. 2100). **Telephone Code:** 05276.

ACCOMMODATIONS AND FOOD

Accommodations are abundant in Ayodhya; after all, thousands of pilgrims flock here every year. *Ashrams* are popular among pilgrims, but do not serve Hindus exclusively. The nicer ashrams with single rooms (with attached bath and fan) are concentrated near the bus station. Better bargains might be located near the outskirts of town. Ayodhya's only proper hotel—the Tourist Bungalow—houses the town's only restaurant.

   Tourist Bungalow, Pathik Nikas Saket (tel. 52435). From the railway station take a right and walk 300m to the upscale building on the left. Undoubtedly the cleanest and most comfortable accommodation in Ayodhya or Faizabad, it rivals some of the more upscale ashrams in terms of price. Each room comes with a desk and 2 chairs, closet space, and a hot water heater in an attached bathroom. Some even have balconies although the view isn't spectacular. Tourist information office, restaurant, and day rooms on the ground floor. Check-out noon. Doubles Rs.100, with air-cooling Rs.150. Two-room suites with air-cooling Rs.300.

Birla Dharamsala, National Highway, right across from the bus station. Centrally located in a beautiful compound near the main road, this ashram offers basic doubles with fan and attached bath. Fairly clean, but bring your own sheets and a mosquito coil to make yourself a cozier bed. Doubles Rs.150.

SIGHTS

Every other building in Ayodhya is a house of worship of some sort (Jain, Buddhist, Hindu, Muslim), attesting to a rich and varied cultural history. Some of the most important temples are located within walking distance of the bus station and tourist bungalow/railway station. Not all of the temples are interesting in their own right, but the sheer agglomeration of temples in Ayodhya makes the town impressive.

The **Babri Masjid** is the contested holy site which led to Hindu-Muslim clashes in 1992 and brought international attention to Ayodhya. It is primarily of interest to the history buff or the student of contemporary Indian politics. The mosque, built by the Mughal emperor Babur in the 15th century, was believed by some Hindus to occupy the very birthplace of Lord Rama *(Ramjanambhoomi)*. On December 7, 1992, militants led by the Vishwa Hindu Parishad (VHP) and abetted by Uttar Pradesh's BJP government tore down the mosque in order to build a temple to Rama. The mosque is now a pile of rubble and the makeshift Hindu temple erected in its place is neither large nor especially beautiful. The compound is surrounded by high fences and many armed guards. The temple is a five-minute rickshaw ride from the bus station to the river. The **Ghats,** only a couple of blocks from the Babri Masjid/Ramjanambhoomi, are as impressive as the *ghats* in Varanasi, lacking only the aggressive boat-*wallahs*.

The **Birla Mandir** is a small (house-sized) but incredibly beautiful marble temple next to the Birla Dharamsala, across the road from the bus station. The triptych of Lakshmana-Rama-Sita, found in most Hindu temples in Ayodhya, is especially moving and haunting here. To reach the **Jain Temple** at Hanuman Rd., take a right from the railway station, walk 800m, take another right, and the temple will be on the right. Huge, well-maintained grounds with places to sit and relax surround an impressive Jain temple, containing a 9.5-m statue of Lord Rishabhadev. It's especially exciting at night, when legions of monkeys and indirect lighting lend the temple a spooky aura. **Hanuman Gardhi** is in a white fort to the left of the bus station. The closest thing to nightlife in Ayodhya, this is the place to come if you long for late-night crowds and noise. You are kindly requested to leave your shoes and socks at a roadside *dhaba*— meaning you must climb the 76 steps to the temple through mud and filth in your bare feet. One of the most important temples in Ayodhya, Hanuman Gardhi honors Hanuman, the monkey god, who is said to have lived here in a cave and protected the birthplace of Rama. **Kanak Bhawan** means "gold house" but there isn't that much gold to be found in this temple. There is, however, some wonderful marble work and a giant courtyard with benches. The Kanak Bhawan is much less crowded than Ayodhya's other big temples and a great place for staid contemplation on cool nights.

■ Gorakhpur

Because of its location in northeast Uttar Pradesh, the city of Gorakhpur is the major transportation hub between India and Nepal. Buses leave regularly for the border, and the main railway station has trains to major cities in India (Gorakhpur is the headquarters of the North Eastern Railway). The city itself is miserable, and the few hotels along Station Rd. are uncomfortable and expensive. Few travelers choose to spend time here.

Founded about 1400 and named after the Hindu saint Gorakhnath, Gorakhpur became an army town under the Mughals and again under the British, who also used it as a base for recruiting Gurkha soldiers from Nepal.

ORIENTATION

The cheapest hotels and the railway station are all located on **Station Road,** which turns into **Civil Line** farther down in both directions. The bus station is on a smaller street perpendicular to Station Rd. across from the railway station.

PRACTICAL INFORMATION

Tourist Office: Regional Tourist Office, 7 Park Rd., Civil Line (tel. 335450). A short rickshaw ride from the railway station (Rs.10-20), across from a major eye hospital. Not especially informative. Open Mon.-Sat. 10am-5pm.

Immigration Office: Chhote Kazipu (tel. 341931). Open Mon.-Sat. 10am-5pm.

Currency Exchange: State Bank of India, Bank Rd., Vijay Choraha. Short rickshaw ride from the railway station. Open Mon.-Fri. 10am-2pm, Sat. 10am-noon.

Telephones: 24-hr. STD/ISD booth in a small shop between the bus station and the railway station.

Trains: Railway station, Station Rd. To: Lucknow (*Cochin Exp.* 5011, 5am, 6hr.; *Amripali Exp.* 5207, 12:45pm, 6hr.; *Avadhi Exp.* 5063, 1:30pm, 6hr.; *Vaishali Super Fast Exp.,* 5:40pm, 4½hr.; *Goraknath Exp.* 5007, 11pm, 6hr.; *Gwalior-Chhapra Mail* 1144, 12:40am, 6hr.); Varanasi (*Gorakhpur-Varanasi Exp.* 5103, 4:50pm, 5hr.; *Chauri-Chaura Exp.* 5004, 10pm, 6½hr.; *Kashi Exp.* 1028, 4:30am, 5½hr.); Hajipur (*Amritsar-Barauni Exp.* 5208, 5:20am, 5½hr.; *New Delhi-Barauni Vaishali Exp.* 2554, 8:45am, 6hr.; *Kathgodam-Howrah Exp.* 3020, 12:40pm, 7hr.; *Lucknow-Barauni Exp.* 5204, 10:10pm, 5½hr.; *Delhi-Guwahati Avadh Assam Exp.* 5610, 11:30pm, 6hr.). To get to Patna, take a train to Hajipur, then catch a bus for the last 20km of the trip. Trains to Sonauli leave from the smaller **Nautanwa Station,** 4km from the main station at 1, 6am, 1, 5pm (3hr.).

Buses: From the railway station, walk 275m straight to the **bus station. Government buses** to Sunauli (Rs.25) do not follow a strict schedule, but they leave frequently starting at 5am. Ask someone at the station to point out the next departing bus. Make sure you are getting on a government bus. There are many **private buses** to Sonauli operating from the same area, but they are uneconomical. There are also buses that claim to go straight to Kathmandu or Pokhara in Nepal, but they do not actually go direct; you will still have to spend a couple of hours at the border arranging your visa, and then switch buses once in Nepal. For more information on transport to and from Nepal, see **Sunauli** (p. 741).

Post Office: Inside the railway station, all the way to the left of the tracks.

Telephone Code: 0551.

ACCOMMODATIONS

Most of the budget hotels are located across from the railway station, with the cheapest (and dirtiest) to the left. Mid-range hotels are located in the center of the city (Rs.15 rickshaw ride), and slightly more expensive hotels are located 4km from the railway station, down Station Rd. to the right.

Hotel Elora, L-block, Station Rd. (tel. 330647). Located across from the railway station, to the right of Hotel Standard. Fairly clean, although the fluorescent lighting makes everything look like it's crawling. Nevertheless, you'll get a restful night's sleep: the mattresses are thin (like everywhere), but the rooms deep inside the building are quiet, despite the hotel's proximity to the railway station. You can wake up to a hot shower and the sound of military exercises in the backyard. (Most of these exercises, especially in the summer, seem to consist of "standing at ease.") Rooms have attached baths. Check-out 24hr. Singles Rs.100. Doubles Rs.150. A/C rooms Rs.300.

Hotel Siddhartha, Station Rd. (tel. 334976). From the railway station, go right on Station Rd., past Hotel Standard and Hotel Elora. Room quality varies considerably, and some attached bathrooms are dirty, but thankfully the friendly staff will let you survey your options before you commit. There are some larger rooms that can squeeze in 3 or 4 people. Check-out 24hr. Singles Rs.75, with air-cooling Rs.125, with A/C Rs.250. Doubles Rs.110, with air-cooling Rs.160, with A/C Rs.300.

Hotel Raj, Station Rd. (tel. 336759). Across from the railway station on the left. The Raj is popular among Indian travelers. The staff speaks virtually no English, but is friendlier than some of the slick hoteliers around. The rooms are spacious, and the patterned faux-marble floors are less alienating than the bare cement found in most budget hotels. Because of its Indian clientele, there are fewer touts here waiting to prey on western tourists. Attached baths. No A/C available. Singles Rs.80. Doubles Rs.120.

Hotel Marina, Golghar (tel. 337630). Rs.10 rickshaw ride to the center of town. A more upscale hotel with some inexpensive, clean single rooms with common bath. Popular among Indian families. Inconveniently located, but quieter (except for the occasional squeal of a child) than the hotels near the bus station. Check-out noon. Singles Rs.75.

FOOD

Small *dhabas* serving *dal bhat* abound along Station Rd. and the road leading to the bus station. There are a few places that serve more elaborate dishes, Indian snacks, and Western breakfasts.

Vardan Restaurant, Station Rd. (tel. 338085), between Hotel Standard and Hotel Elora. Flee here for a cool, quiet atmosphere. The food is standard—omelettes, tomato toast, milkshakes (without ice cream)—and the service is slow. But the air-conditioning is super-cold, and the tinted windows shield you from the touts, and them from your sunburned wrath.

Hotel Ganges Deluxe Restaurant, Cinema Rd., Golghar (tel. 336330). Rs.10 rickshaw ride to the center of town. Offers a cool respite from the nervous bustle of Station Rd. The Indian food is basic and cheap (Rs.25 for *pulao*), although there are some more expensive tandoori items. There's a bar downstairs and the A/C blasts away until midnight.

■ Allahabad

Allahabad (pronounced EE-la-ha-bad) is the sacred city on the Sangam, the meeting point of the Ganga and Yamuna rivers, as well as the mythical stream of Saraswati, the river of wisdom. For thousands of years, the city reaching back from the river bank was called Prayag ("Confluence"). While this name is still sometimes used, more common is Allahabad, the Persian-Arabic name meaning "Place of God" given to it by the Mughal emperors who shaped the modern city around their fort overlooking the confluence. The British would later make good use of Allahabad, turning it into an important government center, the capital of the United Provinces (Uttar Pradesh's predecessor) after 1901. The Indian Independence movement was strongly rooted here, especially due to the work of the Nehrus, the Allahabad family that would forge a dynasty in India's democracy. Now Allahabad is a rather quiet city of 1 million people, with wide avenues and a fair number of British buildings set back from them. Every 12 years, attention is all on Allahabad when it hosts the Maha Kumbh Mela, the greatest festival in Hinduism, and millions of pilgrims charge for the Sangam, dwarfing the city.

ORIENTATION

Allahabad is divided both in body and spirit by the **railway.** North of the tracks is the shady British-built **Civil Lines** area, with all of its roads in a grid; south is the congested and gritty **Chauk** area. Both of these stretch east-west along the tracks. Not only do Chauk and Civil Lines look different, it is actually hard to get from one side to the other since only a few roads go over or under the tracks. At the center of town the two sides are completely divided.

In Civil Lines, **Mahatma Gandhi (M.G.) Road,** with a proud lineup of hotels, restaurants, and ice cream stands, is the road to stick to for orientation; its tall statues make memorable landmarks. **Kamla Nehru Rd.** turns up from Mahatma Gandhi Rd. toward

Allahabad University. **Leader Rd.** runs alongside the tracks on the Chauk side, while the **Grand Trunk Rd.** takes you through the heart of Chauk. Turning onto Triveni Rd. from the Grand Trunk Rd. you can reach the Sangam. Many cheap hotels dot **Dr. Katiu Rd.,** close to the train station between Leader Rd. and the Grand Trunk Rd. On the south side of Allahabad is the **Yamuna River,** and on the east side is the Ganga, but apart from the spiritual importance of the Sangam, the city is not very river-oriented. One bridge crosses each river, in the east toward Varanasi and in the south toward Madhya Pradesh.

PRACTICAL INFORMATION

Tourist Office: Tourist Bungalow, M.G. Rd. (tel. 601873). Just around the corner from the Civil Lines Bus Stand. A Rs.10 rickshaw ride from Allahabad Junction. Has a cluttered map of the city. Open Mon.-Sat. 10am-5pm.

Immigration Office: Local Intelligence Unit (LIU), 171 Colonel Ganj (tel. 608197). Near Anand Bhawan, 2 blocks from Kamla Nehru Rd. Open daily 10am-5pm.

Currency Exchange: State Bank of India, 4 Kacheri Rd., near District Court. Take a rickshaw up Kamla Nehru Rd.; take the 4th left after Allahabad Museum. Open Mon.-Fri. 10am-2pm, Sat. 10am-noon.

Telephone: Lots of **STD/ISD** booths are sprinkled along Leader Rd. and M.G. Rd.

Airport: Bamrauli Airport, 15km from M.G. Rd. (tel. 633930). **Indian Airlines** (tel. 624105). Currently no flights available.

Trains: Allahabad Junction Railway Station, Leader Rd. A 30-min. walk from the Civil Lines Bus Stand on M.G. Rd. With your back to the bus stand, walk left 6 blocks west until you hit the All Saints' Cathedral, take a left turn and walk 3 blocks to the train station. To: Agra (*Toofan Udyan Abha Exp.* 3007, 4:30am, 10½hr.; *Chambal Exp.* 1181, Thurs., 6:40am, 14hr.; *Chambal Exp.* 1159, Fri.-Sun., 6:40am, 14hr., Rs.94/338 for 2nd/1st class); Tundla (*Link Exp./Mahananda Exp.* 4083A/4083, 6:40am, 7½hr.; *Howrah-Kalka Mail* 2311, 9:15am, 7hr.; *Tata/Hatia-Pathankot Exp.* 8101, 9:40am, 6½hr., Rs.91/382 for 2nd/1st class; *Guwahati-New Delhi Poorva Exp.* 2381/2303, 10:55pm, 5½hr., Rs.114 for sleeper class); Delhi (*Rajdhani Exp.* 2301/2305, 2:27am, 7-7½hr., Rs.595/885 for A/C 3-tier/2-tier sleepers; *Puri-New Delhi Exp.* 2815, 7:25am, 9½hr., Rs.124/511 for 2nd/1st class; *Allahabad-New Delhi Prayag Raj Exp.* 2417, 9:30pm, 9½hr., Rs.155 for sleeper; *Howrah-New Delhi Poorva Exp.* 2311/2381, 10:55pm, 9hr., Rs.124/690 for sleeper/2-tier A/C sleeper); Kanpur (*Howrah-Kalka Mail* 2311, 9:15am, 3hr.; *Howrah-Jodhpur Exp.* 2307, 12:25pm, 2½hr., Rs.48/197 for 2nd/1st class); Lucknow (*Ganga Gomti Exp.* 4215, 6am, 3½hr., Rs.56/226 for 2nd/1st class; *Nanchandi Exp.* 4011, 5:30pm, 5hr., Rs.37/159 for 2nd/1st class; *Sarnath Exp.* 4259, 1:05pm, 3hr.; *Chauri-Chaura Exp.* 5003, 8:30pm, Rs.37/159 for 2nd/1st class); Satna (*Bhayalpur-Kurla Exp./Muzaffarpur-Kurla Exp.* 3417/5414, 8:20am, 3½hr.; *Howrah-Bombay Mail* 3003, 11:10am, 3hr., Rs.47/185 for 2nd/1st class; 4-hr. bus trip from Satna to Khajuraho); Kervi (*Bundelkhand Exp.* 1006, 6:25pm, 4hr.; *Chambal Exp.* 1159/1181, Thurs.-Sun., 6:05am, 4hr., Rs.29/135 for 2nd/1st class; 8-km bus trip to Chitrakut).

Buses: There are 3 main bus stations: **Civil Lines Bus Stand,** around the corner from the Tourist Bungalow on M.G. Rd., **Leader Road Bus Stand,** behind the main Allahabad Junction Railway Station, and the **Zero Road Bus Stand,** north of Chauk. Regular buses leave for Delhi and Agra from the Leader Road Bus Stand, and for Kausambi (every hr., 6am-8pm, 2hr., Rs.15). Regular buses leave for Varanasi, Lucknow, Gorakhpur, and Ayodhya from the Civil Lines Bus Stand. There are direct buses to Chitrakut from Zero Road Bus Stand (4hr., Rs.35) and buses from Zero Rd. to Kervi, 8km from Chitrakut.

Local Transportation: Rickshaws are the most common mode of transportation (Rs.10 from the Allahabad Junction Railway Station to the Tourist Bungalow on M.G. Rd.). Drivers are less cut-throat than those in big tourist cities. There are no auto-rickshaws, but you can hop in a **tempo** at any of the bus or railway stations. To reach the Sangam, take a tempo to Daraganj Railway Station and walk south from the tracks.

NORTH INDIA

Allahabad

N←

TO LUCKNOW

TO KANPUR

TO VARANASI

TO VARANASI

SANGAM

Ganga River

Yamuna River

Bandh Road

Prayag Railway Station

Prayaghat R.S.

Daraganj R.S.

Beni Bandh Road

Hanuman Temple

Fort

Triveni Road

Fort Road

Saraswati Ghat

Yamuna Bank Road

Minto Park

Grand Trunk Road (NH2)

Immigration Office

Anand Bhawan

Jawaharlal Nehru Marg

Motilal Nehru Road

Pannalal Marg

Mahatma Gandhi Marg

Lala Siram Road

Lajpat Rai Road

City Railroad Station

University and Archaeological Museum

State Bank of India

St. Joseph's Cathedral

Nehru Road

Allahabad Museum

Kamla

Nazareth Hospital

Kasturba Gandhi Marg

Yamuna Road

Yamuna Bridge

Laudar Road

Swami Vivekanand Marg

Zero Road

A.P. Banerji Road

N.S.C. Road

Zero Rd. Bus Station

Tilak Road

CHAUK

Shaukat Ali Marg

Tejbahadur Sapru Road

CIVIL LINES

Sardar Patel Marg

Tourist Office

Civil Lines Bus Stand

Smith Road

Muir Road

Clive Road

Maharshi Dayanand Marg

Naidu Marg

Indian Airlines

Sarojini

Tashkent Marg

Lal Bahadur Shastri Marg

Purshottamdas Tandon Marg

GPO

Colvin Rd.

Nawab Yusuf Road

All Saints Cathedral

Allahabad Junction

Leader Road

Dr. Katiu Rd.

Clock Tower

Khuldabad Mandi Bazaar

Nirula Road

Leader Rd. Bus Stand

Khusrau Bagh

Grand Trunk Road (NH2)

Carlappa Road

TO KANPUR

Luggage Storage: Luggage storage is available at the **Allahabad Junction Railway Station.**

Public Market: There's a large fruit market a **Khuldabad Mandi Bazaar** near the clock tower and at the intersection of Dr. Katiu and Grand Trunk Rd. (just northwest of Chauk).

English Bookstore: Bookstores abound in Allahabad. **M/S A. H. Wheeler Book Shop,** 19 M.G. Rd. (tel. 624106). Facing away from the Tourist Bungalow, walk 5 blocks to the left. It's on the left side, to the right of the Palace Cinema. Has new Penguin titles, as well as some gay and lesbian literature. Open Mon.-Sat. 10am-7pm. **Vohra Book Shop,** 36 M.G. Rd., behind Plaza Cinema, with a 2nd entrance around the corner on Sardar Patel Marg. Two blocks from the Tourist Bungalow, on the right. Incredibly cheap, used, high-brow books.

Pharmacy/Hospital: Nazareth Hospital, 13/A Kamla Nehru Rd. (tel. 600430). From the intersection of M.G. and Kamla Nehru Rd., it's 1km to the northeast, on the left side, marked by a red cross and the name of the hospital in Hindi. The best private hospital in town, with a fully stocked pharmacy.

Emergency: tel. 100.

Post Office: GPO, Queen's Rd. Go left from the Tourist Bungalow until you hit All Saints' Cathedral. Go right for 1 block. Open Mon.-Sat. 9am-5pm. **Postal Code:** 211011.

Telephone Code: 0532.

ACCOMMODATIONS

Civil Lines lends luxury to the hotel scene. Quiet, but not too pricey hotels are located along M.G. Rd. The cheapies are concentrated around noisy Leader Rd., especially near the bus stand.

Tourist Bungalow, M.G. Rd., near Civil Lines Bus Stand (tel. 601440). From the bus stand, walk left—it will be on the left. Rs.10 rickshaw ride from Allahabad Junction. The interior decorator of the new wing could have used an engineer's helping hand—the locks are on the outside of the windows (so you can't open them!) and the chairs seem to be too tall for the desks. But tasteful bedspreads complement the room and fancy mirrors glorify your image. Extremely clean with hard foam rubber mattresses. The restaurant downstairs serves up great mixed-vegetable omelettes. Check-out noon. Dorm beds Rs.30. Singles with bath Rs.150, with air-cooling Rs.225, with A/C Rs.400. Doubles with bath Rs.200, with air-cooling Rs.275, with A/C Rs.450.

Hotel Continental, Dr. Katiu Rd., near Allahabad Junction Railway Station (tel. 652098). From Allahabad Junction, walk toward Leader Rd., take a right turn onto Leader, then an immediate left onto Dr. Katiu Rd. Similar in quality to the Tourist Bungalow, it's in a somewhat noisier, more congested area. Clean, soft beds. Restaurant and 24-hr. STD/ISD service. During winter there's 24-hr. hot water. Check-out noon. Singles with bath Rs.100, with air-cooling Rs.120, with A/C Rs.300. Doubles with bath Rs.160, with air-cooling Rs.180, with A/C Rs.350.

Hotel Prayag, 73 Nirula Rd. (tel. 604430). From Allahabad Junction, take a right onto Leader Rd. and a left onto Nirula; the hotel is on the left. Slightly less clean and comfortable than the Continental, it has a greater range of available rooms and some cheaper deals on doubles. Singles Rs.60, with bath and air-cooling Rs.125. Doubles with bath Rs.135, with bath and air-cooling Rs.150.

FOOD

Dining *al fresco* is *de rigueur* along M.G. Rd. Crowded benches surround fast food stalls serving Indian snacks, cold drinks, and rip-offs of American junk food products. More typically Indian vegetarian and non-vegetarian restaurants carry clout in Chauk, especially along Dr. Katiu Rd. and Nirula Rd., while some gloomy bars border Leader Rd.

El Chico Restaurant, M.G. Rd. (tel. 604294). Several blocks from the Tourist Bungalow, near Sardar Patel Marg. A classy but unpretentious restaurant, it is, indeed, *el* *chico*. The presence of a Westerner doesn't cause the slightest ripple: the *maître d'* doesn't smile uneasily, the waiters don't kow-tow—in fact, they hardly take notice. The entrees, both Continental and Indian, are tasty but expensive. The prices are better for the salads, which are washed with filtered water, although you might want to insist on this when giving your order. Open 9am-10:30pm.

Hot Stuff, Sardar Patel Marg. Allahabad's coolest fast food joint ("fast food" Indian style—12min.). The selection of ice cream, pizzas, and lamburgers draws crowds of hip, English-speaking college students.

SIGHTS

Allahabad's chief attraction for millions of Hindu pilgrims is the **Triveni Sangam,** the confluence of the rivers Ganga, Yamuna, and Saraswati, and the site of the 12-yearly Kumbh Mela. The Yamuna skirts the south side of Allahabad, and the Ganga rushes along the east. The mythical Saraswati, the river of wisdom which completes the trio, is said to flow underground. At the meeting place of the rivers, boats linger in single file, flags flying high; for a negotiable fee they'll take visitors here from the riverbed by the fort. Sharing a boat with pilgrims costs much less and is much more interesting. The water is warm and shallow in summer; sometimes it's possible to walk out to the Sangam, over the floodplains that wrinkle out from the city. Millions of pilgrims make this their camping ground during the Kumbh Melas.

Alongside the road approaching the Sangam is the **fort** built by Emperor Akbar in 1583. The Indian army still finds the confluence strategically important, so the fort is full of soldiers, and visitors are not allowed entrance, except to a small courtyard in the east side of the fort. Beneath the dirt here is the **Patalpuri Underground Temple** and its weird toybox of gods and goddesses lit through grates in the ceiling. A tree from the underground temple once grew through an opening high enough for pilgrims to climb in and fling themselves to death and certain *moksha*. An Ashokan column from Kausambi, which Akbar liked so much he had it moved here, is inside the fort and off-limits.

In the shadow of the fort's outer wall facing the Sangam side is the **Hanuman Temple,** dedicated to the Hanuman monkey god. What looks like an orange King Kong lies buried in flowers in the basement; it is rare to see Hanuman lying down like this. The temple itself is only a shed, but a very popular one (not to be confused with the multi-storied affair grinning out over the trees—that's the Shankar Viman Manda-

---

The Kumbh Mela

The Maha ("Great") Kumbh Mela at Allahabad in 1989 set the world record for the largest gathering of humans. Thirteen million people are estimated to have come for this auspicious Hindu festival, the holiest time to bathe in the Sangam. At one precisely calculated moment, all of the pilgrims to the Kumbh Mela splash into the water, an act which is believed to undo lifetimes of sin. Columns of charging *sadhus,* often naked and smeared with ash, are among the most zealous bathers.

The story behind the Kumbh Mela has to do with a *kumbh* (pot) that contained an immortality-bestowing nectar. The demons battled the gods for this pot in a struggle that lasted 12 days, during which time four drops were spilled. One landed at Haridwar (U.P.), one at Nasik (Maharashtra), one at Ujjain (M.P.), and one at Allahabad. The mythical 12-day fight translates to 12 human years, the length of the festival's rotation between cities. Every three years a Kumbh Mela is held in one of the four cities. The Maha Kumbh Mela, held at Allahabad every 12th year, is the greatest of all. Smaller *melas,* known as Magh Melas, are held in Allahabad in off-years during the month of Magh (Jan.-Feb.). In the sixth year, midway between Maha Kumbh Melas, an Ardh (Half) Kumbh Mela is held. The next Kumbh Mela is scheduled to occur in Haridwar on April 13, 1998; the big one returns to Allahabad in 2001.

pam). The floodwaters are said to pour over Hanuman's feet each year before they recede.

To reach the other side of the fort, it is necessary to take either a boat ride or detour through the fenced-off military installation behind the fort—one can see there's no shortage of security for the Kumbh Mela. On the Yamuna bank beyond the fort is **Saraswati Ghat,** where boats dock and evening *arati* ceremony lamps are floated down to the confluence. Follow Yamuna Bank Rd. away from the fort to reach **Minto Park** on the right, where in 1858 Lord Canning proclaimed that India would be ruled by the Queen of England. Independent India has reclaimed the historic site by renaming the park for Madan Mohan Malaviya and erecting a part-Mauryan part-Italian monument. Allahabad teenagers have had the last word, however, with their graffiti.

At the northeast corner of the city, close to the Civil Lines, is **Anand Bhawan,** once the mansion of the Nehru family, now a museum devoted to their memory. Independence leader Motilal Nehru, his son Prime Minister Jawaharlal Nehru, and Jawaharlal's daughter Indira Gandhi all lived and worked here, and hosted meetings of the Independence movement. Their bedrooms and bookshelves can be peered at through glass panels. The house is immaculately dusted. True Nehruvians must make a pilgrimage here. (Open Tues.-Sun. 9:30am-5pm; admission Rs.2.) There's also a good bookstore at Anand Bhawan, and a planetarium (shows daily at 11am, noon, 2, 3, and 4pm; admission Rs.5).

The **Allahabad Museum** is on Kamla Nehru Marg. It houses numerous sculptures including many terra-cotta figures from Kausambi, the ancient city and Buddhist center unearthed 60km from Allahabad. There's also a room with good old photographs and a few mementos of Jawaharlal Nehru. (Open Tues.-Sun. 10am-5pm; Rs.2.) The once-renowned **Allahabad University,** north of the museum, was one of the first opened by the British in India. Many of its buildings are in the full 19th-century Gothic style.

The boldest reminder of the British in Allahabad is in Civil Lines, at the intersection of Mahatma Gandhi Rd. and Sarojini Naidu Marg. **All Saints' Cathedral** waits in the middle of the traffic circle here as if it were on a coaster. This smooth Gothic edifice with its stained-glass windows was designed by Sir William Emerson, the same architect who drew up the Victoria Memorial in Calcutta (services Sun. 8am).

Just as All Saints' is the most British thing in Allahabad, **Khusrau Bagh,** in the Chauk area across the railway lines, is the most Mughal. These gardens hold the stippled stone tomb of Khusrau, son of the emperor Jahangir. In typical Mughal family style, Khusrau plotted against his father and was subsequently murdered by his brother, the future emperor Shah Jahan, in 1615. The garden also has a smaller (unoccupied) tomb built for Khusrau's sister and one for his suicide mother. Fruit is grown in the gardens, where would-be civil servants sit and study for examinations.

■ Varanasi

To Hindus Varanasi (also known as Benares or Banaras) is the holiest place on earth, the chosen residence of Shiva, who abides in every nook and cranny, not only those populated by the seemingly omnipresent *linga*. Hindus claim the whole city to be a sacred zone, welling up with blessings—its power is reputedly so great that it shines out from the earth over the Ganga, hence its other name, Kashi ("the Luminous"). Everyone who dies in Varanasi is guaranteed *moksha,* or liberation from the cycle of death and rebirth—and everyone here knows it. This otherworldly confidence (and a growing population of 1.2 million) has shaped Varanasi into one of the world's most tangled and grimy cities. Its houses are pressed up to the waterfront, almost leaning over it for a splash of the sacred river. The Old City is a maze of tortuous lanes, smeared with cow dung and congested with men and beasts. Small boys make fortunes guiding foreigners to the Golden Temple through little-used alleys—mere troughs for urinating. Befuddled pallbearers, on their way to Manikarnika, the place of ritual burning, stop mid-chant to ask for hazy directions. Modernization, indeed, has arrived in Varanasi, but only in imperfect bursts. Sometimes a dead body,

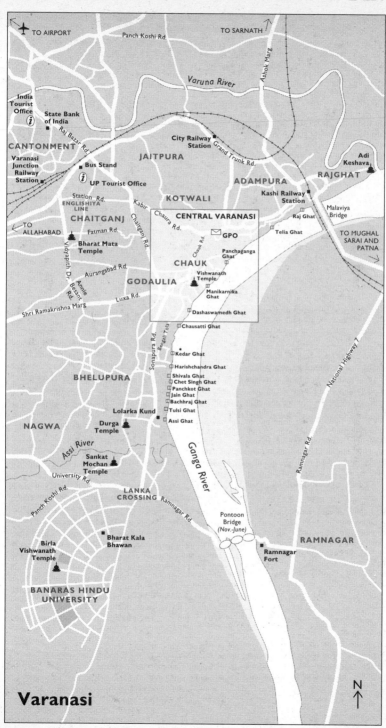

TO AIRPORT

Panch Koshi Rd.

TO SARNATH

Ashok Marg

Varuna River

India Tourist Office

State Bank of India

Raj Bazar Rd.

CANTONMENT

City Railway Station

Grand Trunk Rd.

JAITPURA

Adi Keshava

RAJGHAT

Varanasi Junction Railway Station

Bus Stand

UP Tourist Office

ADAMPURA

Kashi Railway Station

Malaviya Bridge

Station Rd.
ENGLISHIYA LINE

CHAITGANJ

Kabir

KOTWALI

CENTRAL VARANASI

Raj Ghat

TO MUGHAL SARAI AND PATNA

TO ALLAHABAD

Fatman Rd.

Chaura Rd.

GPO

Telia Ghat

Bharat Mata Temple

Chaitganj Rd.

Chaura Rd.

Panchaganga Ghat

Aurangabad Rd.

Vidyapith Dr.

GODAULIA

CHAUK

Vishwanath Temple

Annie Besant Rd.

Luxa Rd.

Manikarnika Ghat

Shri Ramakrishna Marg

Dashaswamedh Ghat

Chausatti Ghat

Sonapura Rd.

Bazari Tola

BHELUPURA

Kedar Ghat

Harishchandra Ghat

Shivala Ghat
Chet Singh Ghat
Panchkot Ghat
Jain Ghat
Bachhraj Ghat
Tulsi Ghat
Assi Ghat

Lolarka Kund

Durga Temple

NAGWA

Assi River

Sankat Mochan Temple

University Rd.

Ganga River

National Highway 7

Ramnagar Rd.

LANKA CROSSING

Ramnagar Rd.

Panch Koshi Rd.

Bharat Kala Bhawan

Pontoon Bridge (Nov.-June)

RAMNAGAR

Birla Vishwanath Temple

Ramnagar Fort

BANARAS HINDU UNIVERSITY

N

Varanasi

What Makes Varanasi Holy?

Holy cities in Western religions usually owe their sanctity to specific people and events, often recorded by secular histories as well as religious scriptures. Varanasi's qualifications as a holy city are not so obvious. Several myths establish it as the city of Shiva, but none of them seem to give Shiva credit for the city's greatness. In the principal story, Shiva chooses to settle in Kashi with his new bride Parvati after their marriage in the Himalaya. Shiva is so awestruck by the city when he discovers it that he vows never to leave. A myth that is sometimes connected to this one tells of a great King Divodasa, who ruled Kashi with perfect efficiency but banished all the gods from the city. Even without the gods Divodasa's Kashi was still the most auspicious place on earth, and Shiva had to trick Divodasa into leaving so he could take over with his retinue of gods. Neither of these stories proves that Shiva is what makes Varanasi holy.

There are countless temples, tanks, shrines, and street corners in Varanasi that claim some sort of divine origin. Many of them look to gods other than Shiva, and their stories and histories seem to conflict with each other or with the claims made for Shiva's power in the city. There are other pilgrimage sites all over India that claim all the holiness Varanasi claims, and Varanasi in return has its claim! The sacred geography of India is riddled with *tirthas*, crossings where the heavens are said to be easily accessible.

It becomes quite clear that Varanasi is but one stunning example of how divinity can manifest itself in geography: how any and every place can be a *tirtha*. Varanasi's long and brilliant history has attracted religious attention, made it the goal of pilgrimages, even made it the city of Shiva. But Varanasi's holiness really could be anywhere, and actually continues to be everywhere.

stretched between two bicycles, is wheeled to the pyre amid the traditional chant, "Ram Nam Sata Hai" ("Ram is Truth"). On the main street, buses slop exhaust over strings of shaven-headed pilgrims, honking madly at any stragglers. The electricity fails almost every night; until the ugly fluorescent lights stutter back to life, the unprepared visitor must navigate the slippery lanes by the teasing flicker of a candle flame.

Amid this cacophony and confusion, it's difficult to discern Varanasi's inspired side. Its glory takes time and timing to fully appreciate. At sunrise a quiet band of thousands descends to the riverside *ghats,* flashed head-on by a godlike sun (since Varanasi is on the west bank of the Ganga at a point where the river meanders to the north). The water oozes with disease; refuse and even human corpses can be seen bobbing by. But this has no apparent effect on Varanasi's efficacy as a place to bathe, nor on the taste of its liberating waters.

The physical condition of the city of Varanasi is due in part to five centuries of Muslim levelings, from 1200 to 1700. No building in the city is more than 300 years old. But the attacks never really succeeded—they wiped out the city's temples and images, but not the traditions that have kept Varanasi going from at least as far back as the 6th century BC. Varanasi is among the world's oldest continuously inhabited cities. It sat at the great ford where traders traversing North India would cross the Ganga back in the early days of Aryan settlement in India. It gained fame as a glorious bazaar town, but also as a center for spiritual life. Teachers and ascetics came to mingle their beliefs with the local deities in the ponds and rivers of the Anandavana ("Forest of Bliss") that grew here before the city. The Buddha came here, to Sarnath on the outskirts of Kashi, to preach his first sermon. Varanasi's Hindu priests were active in developing their religion through all of its millennia. The city itself was soon an object of worship.

Usually humble in political power, Varanasi became a sanctuary for Indian culture, renowned for its silk brocades, its refined Sanskrit and Hindi, as well as its music. Today Varanasi, especially since the foundation of Benares Hindu University, continues to support a thriving culture. It stays a shining city in the midst of all the muck. But the piety and devotion are the main attraction for the millions who come for brief visions of the city, and also for the many who come to settle and die in Varanasi. The living here can frolic knowing this life is their last, and, whatever the city looks like to them, it is just a dusty trace of its divinity.

ORIENTATION

Varanasi is pressed up against the west bank of the Ganga at a point where the river flows north. There is nothing on the east bank; it's believed that those who die there will return as donkeys. Varanasi is laid out with such ideas in mind, so it can be a mess to move through as an outsider. But since the geography has so much religious significance locals tend to know it intimately. Banarsis (natives of Varanasi) are great givers of directions. And you'll need them to find your way through the city's cranky lanes, which are often just one cow wide.

Sticking to the river is the best way to navigate through Varanasi, and most points of interest are along the waterfront anyway. **Assi Ghat** marks the south end of the riverbank; **Raj Ghat** is farthest north. Trains from the east cross the **Malaviya Bridge**, next to Raj Ghat, to enter Varanasi, and the railway stations are inland from this north part of the city. **Dashaswamedh Ghat** is the city's main *ghat*, easily reached on **Dashaswamedh Road** from **Godaulia Crossing,** a central traffic circle. The surrounding area, known as Godaulia, hoards many of the budget hotels, near the **Vishwanath Temple.** Godaulia is connected to the northern parts of Varanasi by **Chauk Road,** one of the few roads here wide enough for cars.

Varanasi's city limits are marked by the **Varuna River** in the north and the **Assi River** in the south; hence the hybrid name of Varanasi. The **Panch Koshi Road,** which circles around the city at a 16-km radius, marks the boundary of the sacred zone of Kashi.

PRACTICAL INFORMATION

Tourist Office: Uma Shankar, the branch manager of the **U.P. Regional Tourist Office** in the main railway station, is your best friend in Varanasi. If you have the time, he'll give you a frank (though long-winded) pep-talk for surviving and thriving in the Old City. Open 6am-8pm. The staff at the main office in the **Tourist Bungalow** (tel. 335450) have more brochures, including a complete up-to-date list of paying guest accommodations. Open Mon.-Sat. 10am-5pm.

Immigration Office: Siddh Giri Bagh (tel. 53968). From Godaulia Crossing, facing away from Dashaswamedh Ghat, walk to the third traffic circle (including Godaulia Crossing). Turn right. Open Mon.-Sat. 10am-5pm.

Currency Exchange: State Bank of India, Cantonment (tel. 43445). Between the Hotel Saryu and Hotel Ideal Tops. Open Mon.-Fri. 10am-5pm, Sat. 10am-2pm. **Bank of Baroda,** Godaulia (tel. 32 14 71). Between Godaulia Crossing and Dashaswamedh Ghat, on the left. Credit cards only. Open Mon.-Fri. 11am-3pm, Sat. 11am-1pm.

Telephones: A 24-hr. STD booth, with no call-back facility, is located on the left side of the railway station. STD/ISD booths with shorter hours are everywhere.

Airport: Babatpur Airport (tel. 43742), 22km from Varanasi. Minibuses go to and from the **Indian Airlines office,** Cantonment (tel. 43746, 45959). To: Agra (1 per day, 2hr., US$76); Bhubaneswar (1 per day, 1hr.15min., US$90); Bombay (1-2 per day, 3-5hr., US$179); Calcutta (Wed. and Fri. 2hr., US$100); Delhi (3-5 per day, 1hr., US$143); Khajuraho (Tues., Thurs., Sat.-Sun., 45min., US$54); Kathmandu (Tues., Thurs., Sat.-Sun., 1 per day, 1¼hr., US$71); Lucknow (1-2 per day, 45min., US$46).

Trains: Varanasi Junction Railway Station is located at the intersection of the Grand Trunk, Cantonment Station, and Vidyapith Rd. (Rs.10 by rickshaw or Rs.20 by auto-rickshaw from Godaulia Crossing). To: New Delhi (*Neelachal Exp.* 8475, Tues., Fri., and Sun., 7:35am, 14hr.; *Samastipur-Delhi Exp.* 4007A, Mon. and Wed., 12:40pm, 14hr.; *Muzzafarpur-Delhi Exp.* 4007, Thurs. and Sat., 12:40pm, 14hr.; *Kashi Vishwanath Exp.* 4057, 2pm, 14½hr., Rs.177/583 for 2nd/1st class); Kanpur (*Neelachal Exp.* 847, Tues., Fri., and Sun., 7:35am, 14hr.; *Farakka Exp.* 3483 or 3413, 12:35pm, 10hr., Rs.83/341 for 2nd/1st class); Lucknow (*Neelachal Exp.*

8475, Tues., Fri., and Sun., 7:35am, 5½hr.; *Kashi Vishwanath Exp.* 4057, 2pm, 5½hr.; *Shramjeevi Exp.* 2401, 3:20pm, 5hr., Rs.68/281 for 2nd/1st class); Allahabad (*Mahanagri Exp.* 1094, 11:30am, 3hr.; *Varanasi-Madras Ganga Kaveri Exp.* 6040, Mon.-Tues. and Fri., 5:45pm, 2½hr., Rs.46/184 for 2nd/1st class); Gorakhpur (*Varanasi-Gorakhpur Exp.* 5104, 5:50am, 5hr.; *Kashi Exp.* 1027, 1:20pm, 6hr.; *Krishak Exp.* 5002, 4:30pm, 5½hr., Rs.56/226 for 2nd/1st class; *Chauri-Chaura Exp.* 5003, 11:40pm, 6hr., sleeper class Rs.70, A/C 2-tier sleeper Rs.338); Patna (*Bhiwani-Malda Town Farakka Exp.* 3484/3414, 3:20pm, 5hr., Rs.56/226 for 2nd/1st class); Gaya (*New Delhi-Howrah Poorva Exp.* 2382, 5:10am, 3½hr.; *Doon Exp.* 3010, 4:15pm, 5hr., Rs.56/219 for 2nd/1st class); Calcutta (*Amritsar-Howrah Exp.* 3006, 4:45pm, 13hr.; *Jammu Tawi-Howrah Himgiri Exp.* 3074, Mon., Thurs., and Sun., 9:05pm, 14½hr., sleeper class Rs.143, A/C 2-tier sleeper Rs.647); Agra (*Farakka Exp.* 4383/3413, 12:35pm, 17hr., Rs.169 for 2nd class) or, indirectly, to Tundla (*Poorva Exp.* 2381, Wed., Thurs., and Sun., 8pm, 8hr., Rs.160) and then a 24-km bus ride to Agra; Satna (for Khajuraho, *Kashidadar Exp.* 1028, 10:50am, 6hr.; *Mahanagar Exp.* 1094, 11:30am, 6hr., *Sarnath Exp.* 4260, 11:50am, 6hr.; *Tirupati Exp.* 7492/90, Thurs.-Fri. and Sun., 9:45pm, 6hr., *Pawan Exp.* 4248, 11:30pm, 6hr., Rs.110/350 for 2nd/1st class) and then a 4-hr. bus trip from Satna to Khajuraho.

Buses: Cantonment Bus Station, 200m to the left on Station Rd. coming from Varanasi Junction Station. To: Delhi (7pm, 20hr., Rs.180); Agra (5pm, 17hr., Rs.160); Kanpur (5pm, 10hr., Rs.90); Lucknow (5pm, 7hr., Rs.90); Allahabad (every 30min., 6am-8pm, 3hr., Rs.40); Gorakhpur (every hr., 6am-8pm, 6hr., Rs.80); Gaya (6am, 7hr., Rs.80); Sonauli (3, 5, and 6pm, 8hr., Rs.110). Buses to Chunar leave from a smaller station at **Pilikothi,** near Varanasi City Railway Station, east of the main Junction Station. To Chunar (every 30min., 6am-8pm, Rs.10).

Local Transportation: Auto-rickshaws from Varanasi Junction Station to Godaulia or Cantonment area cost Rs.20, or Rs.5 in a shared auto-rickshaw (but you may end up sharing a corner of the driver's seat—goats and luggage not allowed). Rickshaws, whose drivers are notoriously deceptive and belligerent, run between all major points in the city; it helps to know where you are going and to be assertive. Tempos run between less touristy spots, like Lanka and Ramnagar Fort (Rs.5), and the Civil Court and Sarnath.

Luggage Storage: There's a luggage storage at the main Junction Station. Open 24hr.

Market: Large fruit markets are located at **Vishersarganj** near the GPO and in **Chauk.** Hop in a rickshaw at Godaulia Crossing for a short ride north.

Bookstore: Universal Booksellers, Jangambali (tel. 323042). From Godaulia Crossing, facing Dashaswamedh Ghat, turn right—it will be on the right, 750m up. Sells new English and American books, as well as books specific to Varanasi.

Pharmacy: Heritage Hospital, Lanka (tel. 313977). From Godaulia Crossing, take an auto-rickshaw toward Lanka and Benares Hindu University in South Varanasi. Right before Lanka Crossing, Heritage Hospital will appear on the left. It has a 24-hr. pharmacy.

Hospital/Medical Services: The best private hospital in Varanasi is the **Heritage Hospital,** Lanka (tel. 313977, 313978). From Godaulia Crossing, a Rs.20 rickshaw ride to Lanka Crossing in South Varanasi. The hospital is right before the crossing on the left. You can usually see an English-speaking doctor right away. Also has an ambulance service.

Emergency: tel. 197.

Police: The Dashaswamedh Police Station (tel. 352650) has jurisdiction over the Old City.

Post Office: Kotwali (tel. 332090). Rs.10 rickshaw ride from Godaulia Crossing through Chauk. *Poste Restante.* Open Mon.-Sat. 10am-6pm. **Postal Code:** 221001. **Telephone Code:** 0542.

ACCOMMODATIONS

Dozens of budget hotels are packed into the winding maze of the Old City, near Godaulia Crossing. A few waterside lodges are cooled by air wafting up from the Ganga. Mid-range hotels can be found throughout the city, especially along Vidyapith

Rd. (leading away from the railway station) and on the main streets in Godaulia. More expensive hotels tower over the Cantonment area north of the railway station.

As in other major North Indian tourist destinations, the rickshaw-*wallahs* in Varanasi often collect commissions from hoteliers for delivering guests. Beware of the promises made by rickshaw-*wallahs* at the train or bus station. It is best to be firm about where you want to go, or to find a mellow (perhaps non-English-speaking) rickshaw-*wallah* who won't harass you. Don't believe your rickshaw-*wallah* if he tells you that the hotel you asked for is "full" or "closed"—this usually just means it isn't paying commissions.

Ganga Fuji Home, D. 7/21 Sakarkand Gali, Old City (tel. 327333). Near Golden Temple, Main Ghat, and Dashaswamedh Rd. From Godaulia Crossing, walk toward Dashaswamedh Ghat; after the Bank of Baroda, take the first left (there will be signs for Yogi Lodge, Golden Lodge, and Fagin's Restaurant). Take the 3rd right through an archway and down some steps; take the next right, following the winding path—the hotel will appear on your right. If the gate is closed, ring the doorbell. The Ganga Fuji Home is certainly true to its name. The owner, an educated globetrotter, is more like a host than a hotelier. He has a doctorate from BHU in Ayurvedic medicine (he'll tell you his somewhat thin mattresses are better for your back) and palmistry (a full reading costs Rs.500, which goes to a children's charity). There's a comfortable couch in the quiet lobby where you can eat and socialize (until the rooftop restaurant is finished), and with some advance notice the owner's mother will cook a homemade Indian meal. The bedsheets and bathrooms are extremely clean; the gates are locked most of the day to keep out unsavory visitors; the kitchen is spotless, and the water is filtered (so the *lassis* and lime water are safe). There are no attached baths (although these are planned). Singles Rs.60, with air-cooling Rs.80. Doubles Rs.100, with air-cooling Rs.120.

Shanti Guest House, Old City, near Manikarnika Ghat. From Godaulia Crossing, facing toward Dashaswamedh Ghat, take a left turn onto the road leading to Chauk. Several hundred meters up, take a right turn into a small alley, when you see a sign for Shanti Lodge. Follow the signs through winding streets, or alternately follow the procession of pallbearers toward the burning *ghat,* whose route passes directly in front of the lodge. Gorged by its popularity among Western tourists (especially Israelis), the Shanti is constantly expanding. In the past 2 years, they've added 2 new levels, including an observation deck (*sans* telescope) which overlooks the Ganga. Some new modern bathrooms have been added, but prices remain relatively low. The bedsheets are clean, and the mattresses are soft. The 24-hr. rooftop restaurant is party central in the Old City; guests and chipper young waiters chatter away late into the night. Singles Rs.60, with bath Rs.100, with air-cooling Rs.125. Doubles with bath Rs.150, with air-cooling Rs.175.

Trimurti Guest House, CK. 35/12, Saraswati Phatak, Old City (tel. 323554). From Godaulia Crossing, follow Dashaswamedh Rd. toward Dashaswamedh Ghat. Take the last left before the *ghat* (there will be signs for Trimurti and for Kashi Vishwanath Temple, i.e. the Golden Temple). Follow this small road straight for 4km; the guest house is on the right. One of the largest hotels in the Old City, the Trimurti has basic rooms with plenty of space for drying laundry, but no attached baths. Excellent rooftop view of the Golden Temple (just about the best you'll get if you're not a Hindu). Rates go up in the winter (to offset the cost of hot water). In season: singles Rs.60. Doubles Rs.80. Off-season: singles Rs.45. Doubles Rs.60. Fourth floor double with a balcony and a great view Rs.80.

Om Lodge, Bansphatak area, Old City (tel. 322728). From Godaulia Crossing, facing toward Dashaswamedh Ghat, take a left turn onto the road leading to Chauk. Take a right turn at the signs for Shanti Lodge; eventually you'll spot signs for the Om Lodge. Follow these down increasingly narrow and desolate alleys. The Om Lodge is the best bargain in the Old City. The owner is a jolly, yet sagacious fellow—a Santa Claus turned *sadhu.* Bearded, with a heavy paunch overhanging his loosely-tied *lungi,* he reclines in the lobby in self-satisfied ease, chuckling and handing out choice words like precious little gifts. There's a TV and VCR in the cramped, but cozy lobby; guests often rent (pirated) movies from local shops. The rooms are, of course, extremely basic, although A/C is available. Dorm beds Rs.15. Singles Rs.25, with air-cooling Rs.35, with A/C Rs.55. Doubles Rs.55, with air-cooling Rs.75, with A/C and bath, Rs.100.

Hotel India, 59 Patel Nagar, Cantonment (tel. 342912). From the railway station, take a Rs.10 rickshaw ride along Patel Nagar. The pink turrets of Hotel India will appear on your right. In this up-and-coming mid-range hotel in the posh and quiet district north of the railway station, the staff is eager and friendly, without being fawning. The rooms are smaller than those of deluxe hotels, but come with the same amenities and are more tastefully arranged, with inviting earth colors. The hotel contains several excellent restaurants including the Palm Springs which serves imaginative Continental dishes, like *A La Betty Lue,* fish served on a bed of corn with sautéed almonds, bananas, cherries, parsley, and butter (Rs.90). Singles Rs.225, with A/C Rs.400. Doubles Rs.300, with A/C Rs.500.

Yogi Lodge, D 8/29, Kalika Gali, Old City (tel. 322588). From Godaulia Crossing, facing toward the Dashaswamedh Ghat, take a left turn onto the road leading to Chauk. Take a right turn at the sign for Yogi Lodge (and Shanti and Golden Lodges). Follow the signs straight, to the right, and then left down a short flight of steps. The Yogi Lodge has an inspired atmosphere. Swarms of small boys—hired help and children of the Burmese owner—bustle to and fro in perfect sync carrying trays heaped high with club sandwiches from the in-house restaurant. The owner's wife greets guests at the kitchen door with an infectious grin. Her eldest daughter, educated at an English-medium convent school, engages guests in fluent conversation. The restaurant consists of two large tables, creating an intimate familial atmosphere among the guests. The rooms themselves are spare—the beds don't even have mattresses. Dorm beds Rs.25. Singles Rs.50.

Tourist Bungalow, Pared Kothi, Cantonment (tel. 43413). From the railway station, walk left, take first right—it's set back on the right. Conveniently, yet quietly, located between the railway station and Godaulia, the Tourist Bungalow offers a range of clean, comfortable rooms (from dorm beds to full-fledged suites). Even the cheapest single rooms have satellite TV, and the more expensive rooms have big, beautiful bathrooms. There's a stark but air-conditioned restaurant that's open until 2am; and the tourist office has an exceedingly friendly, if not particularly informative staff.

Hotel Ideal Tops, the Mall, Cantonment (tel. 348091). From the railway station, Rs.10 by rickshaw, Rs.20 by auto-rickshaw. The Hotel Ideal Tops (or "Ideal" for short) is India's platonic response to the Best Western—at least in name. In fact, it is very much like its American counterpart, only slightly more pluralistic: there are copies of both the Bible and the Gita on the bedside table. The rooms have all the amenities of the slightly more pricey hotels along this strip (i.e. refrigerators, bathtubs, A/C, Star TV, soft beds), and the service is much quicker. There are a couple of good restaurants and a bar with a tense atomsphere. Singles Rs.995. Doubles Rs.1195.

Scindia Guest House, above Scindia Ghat, up the beach from Manikarnika Ghat . From Godaulia Crossing facing toward Dashaswamedh Ghat, turn left onto the road to Chauk; turn right at the sign for Shanti Guest House; follow the signs until you pass in front of the Shanti Guest House; take the first left, there will be signs for the Scindia Guest House. Hear Hindi devotional prayers and see Hindu ritual ablutions without leaving your bed. Rooms are simple, without attached bath, but you pay for the prime location. The path to the guest house can get rather slippery, especially in the monsoon. Singles Rs.100. Doubles Rs.120.

FOOD

Keshari Restaurant, on a side street between Godaulia and Dashaswamedh Ghat (tel. 321472). From Godaulia Crossing, walk toward Dashaswamedh Ghat. Take the first left. This open-front restaurant will appear immediately on your right. Popular among upper-middle-class Indians, this cool dark veg. restaurant serves some of the best *thalis* around, including a special house *thali* with cheese, cauliflower, potato, brown *dal, raita,* and fruit salad (Rs.50, feeds 2 easily). The staff is friendly but not intrusive. The street in front is certainly calmer than Dashaswamedh, but nevertheless full of life: friends of the staff and owner are constantly visiting, joshing one another, getting into mock fights, and ribbing small children. Open 9:30am-10:30pm.

Palm Springs, in Hotel India, 59 Patel Nagar, Cantonment (tel. 342912). From the railway station, a Rs.10 rickshaw ride; from Godaulia, a Rs.20 rickshaw ride. The subtly spiced veg. and non-veg. dishes rival even those of five-star restaurants. The dishes are somewhat pricey: veg. starts at Rs.60 and non-veg. at Rs.90, but it's well worth the cost. There are 2 dishes *raan e sikandari* (whole roast leg of lamb) and *shan e murgh* (chicken kababs) which each cost Rs.250 and require 3hr. advance notice. Open 7am-11pm.

Shanti Guest House Rooftop Restaurant, Shanti Guest House, near Manikarnika Ghat. From Godaulia Crossing, facing toward Dashaswamedh Ghat, take a left turn onto the road leading to Chauk. Take a right turn at the sign for the Shanti Guest House—follow the signs at regular intervals. The 24-hr. rooftop restaurant offers the only nightlife in the Old City, unless sacred-cow-tipping's your thing. Guests exchange uproarious stories of the day's adventures late into the night. Diminutive waiters flit back and forth, chirruping "Sugar, madame" and "Fresh lime, sir." Things quiet down around 2am, when you can sit and enjoy the fine view of the Ganga. The food itself (omelettes, tomato toast, some Indian snacks) is tasty and substantial, but unimaginative. And the service is slow, especially when the place is packed. The gate of the Shanti Guest House closes at midnight, but you can knock loudly for entry.

Restaurant at Trimurti Guest House, CK. 35/12, Saraswati Phatak (tel. 323554). From Godaulia Crossing, walk toward Dashaswamedh Ghat, take the last left before the *ghat*, go straight for 2.5km. Popular among tourists, the Trimurti Restaurant offers the same fare as the Shanti Guest House, but is quieter and more laidback. well-lit, with a small library, it's a great place to chat or read. Open 7:30am-10:30pm.

Yelchico Bar and Restaurant, Near Godaulia Crossing (tel. 323248). From Godaulia Crossing, with your back to Dashaswamedh Ghat, it's 1 block up on your left, inside a mall and down a flight of stairs. It's difficult to believe that such a casually cool and quiet bar like the Yelchico exists just a few steps away from the noisiest and most irksome part of Varanasi. A dark, spacious, subterranean restaurant, where you can sit without being gawked and yelled at, the Yelchico has drinks at standard prices (Rs.50 for beer) and some excellent snacks (e.g. *masala* peanuts), although the measly chicken sandwich is overpriced. Open 11:30am-10:30pm.

Ganga Fuji Restaurant, Sakarkand Gali, near Trimurti Guest House (tel. 327333). From Godaulia Crossing, walk toward Dashaswamedh Ghat, take the last left before the *ghat*, and walk straight 2.5km; the restaurant is on the left. The Japanese food is admittedly mediocre, though there are good Indian dishes at reasonable prices. The live Indian music is genuine and discreet, unlike the muzak at some 5-star hotels. Open 8am-11pm. Show starts at 7:30pm in season (mid-July through April).

SIGHTS

Varanasi can be quite a place for sight-seeing. Pilgrims come here for the sights: they make the circuit to experience *darshan,* the sacred seeing of gods through images. Those to whom this practice is foreign can still roam the city and look, but they might not see what pilgrims see. Some religious imagination is needed to bring Varanasi—its temples, its tanks, and especially its *ghats*—to life. The *ghats,* the staircases down to the sacred Ganga, stand out in Varanasi partly because the Delhi Sultans and the Mughals spent 500 years destroying all the temples (as a result, all the existing architecture is a product of the past three centuries).

The holy Ganga is the chief attraction of life in Varanasi. Thousands come at dawn to bathe in and make offerings to the heavenly water. But the *ghats* are not reserved for sacred activities. While matted-haired *sadhus* wander, teenagers in swimming clubs dive bravely from the steps, and others wash their clothes and tend to their goats and cows. The Ganga tempts all sorts of life, and death as well, for in Varanasi Hindu pollution beliefs are reversed so that cremation grounds are wholly auspicious. Cremations take place right on the *ghats,* rather than out of town on cursed soil as in most cities. The bodies of those who can't afford cremation, as well as holy men, babies, and certain others, are consigned to the river, and can sometimes be seen bobbing along. *Let's Go* does not recommend bathing, except for those with exceptionally good *karma*.

The steps themselves are huge, usually numbering over 100 from top to bottom, though some are hidden when the water is high. Each *ghat* has its name painted in Hindi, in large black-and-yellow letters. Many *ghats* are named after princely states, whose rulers donated money to pave them.

The Riverfront and Back Lanes from Assi Ghat to Adi Keshava

The south end of Varanasi's riverfront begins with **Assi Ghat.** This first of the *ghats* is a broad clay bank at the confluence of the Ganga and Assi River. The Assi has recently shifted south into a *nala*, or stream, but Assi Ghat is still considered the south edge of Varanasi and is a busy religious center. Along with *Shivalingams* it has an array of shops and cold drink stands.

Inland from Assi Ghat are some of Varanasi's more important temples. The **Sankat Mochan** temple, dedicated to Hanuman, has orange *sindar* smears that attest to its popularity. Up the road is the **Tulsi Manas Temple,** a modern Vishnu temple erected in honor of Tulsi Das, the premier poet of the Hindi language, who wrote the Hindi version of the epic *Ramayana*. Built of white marble and flanked by palm trees, the Tulsi Manas Temple looks like a five-star hotel from the front. The walls inside are inscribed with Tulsi Das's verses, and on the second floor at the back, Hindu religious images have entered the fourth dimension: a spinning factory of figures acts out Lord Rama's life with cuckoo-clock precision. It's extremely popular with pilgrims (admission Rs.1). Very close to the Tulsi Manas Temple is the ornate, red-and-white **Durga Temple,** which is the focal point of fairs in July and August, as well as a tank where the embattled goddess Durga is said to have rested after she defeated her demon.

Tulsi Ghat is the next significant *ghat* after Assi; it was here that Tulsi Das lived in the 17th century. His house is at the top of the *ghat*, and you may be able to find your way in. Back from the water above Tulsi Ghat is one of Varanasi's most ancient sacred spots, the **Lolarka Kund.** Sunk precariously in the ground, this tank was at one time the site where early Hindus worshiped Surya, the sun god; now the tank is cherished only once a year, in August or September, when couples come to pray for their sons.

Tulsi Ghat is followed by the city water intake, but the *ghats* resume up north. **Chet Singh Ghat** is topped by the palace of Maharaja Chet Singh, who rebelled against the British in 1781. Stacks of firewood and groups of solemn people distinguish the next major *ghat* from the others—**Harishchandra Ghat** is Varanasi's second most important cremation ground. It's an old and sacred site, though less renowned than Manikarnika up north. Photography is strictly prohibited at both.

The *ghat* with the red-and-white painted circus stripes is **Kedar Ghat.** The Kedar Temple is one of Varanasi's oldest and most important Shiva temples. Kedar means "field," and this is the field where liberation is said to grow. **Chauki Ghat** has a fierce collection of *nagas*, early aquatic snake-gods, around a central tree. From this point on a long stretch of *ghats* is used for laundry, with a collage of colorful saris and pants stretched out to dry.

Dashaswamedh Ghat, the next major bathing spot, is the most crowded *ghat* in Varanasi, the place boatmen call the "main *ghat*." The wide approaching road lures buses filled with pilgrims. Bamboo parasols heighten Dashaswamedh's beach-like atmosphere, and kids clamber up and down the steps selling flowers for offerings. Dashaswamedh Ghat is where the creator god Brahma is said to have performed 10 royal horse-sacrifices for the mythical King Divodasa, making the waters auspicious. The area up Dashaswamedh Rd. is known as Godaulia, after a stream that once flowed into the Ganga here. Just south of Dashaswamedh Ghat the "cold" goddess of smallpox and other diseases, Shitala, is still loved and appeased, as seen in the colorful paint and tinsel that adorns the square white **Shitala Temple,** and heard in the music which blares in stereo. This maverick goddess' temple is more popular than any of

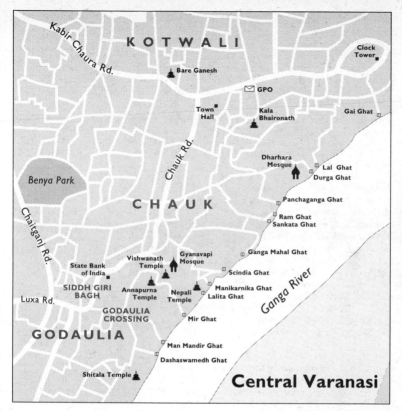

Central Varanasi

the *lingas* of Dashaswamedh. Also on the *ghat* is Brahmeshwar, the *linga* that Brahma is supposed to have established.

Go up Dashaswamedh Rd. and turn right through a funny temple-like archway (braving the drug pushers), and signs will lead you to the center of Varanasi's religious geography: the temple of Shiva as **Vishwanath** ("Lord of All"). Nicknamed the "Golden Temple," the Vishweshwar *linga* it contains is claimed to have been the first one on earth; it is one of India's 12 *jyotirlingas,* which are said to have shot from the ground as shafts of light. All of Varanasi is measured in circles around Vishwanath, and it is the most important place for pilgrims. The temple is closed to non-Hindus, but shopkeepers across the road are glad to charge visitors for the view from their rooftops. One can gaze at the gilded spire of this "Golden Temple" and listen to the bells inside. The present temple is relatively recent, dating from 1777, but many versions stood here before.

The carpeted corridor to the right of the temple leads to the **Gyanavapi** ("Well of Wisdom"), which is protected under columns and a roof. The well's opening is thoroughly sealed off, but its sacred waters of wisdom, said to have been tapped from the earth by Shiva, are ladled out daily under police supervision. The police are nervous about the Gyanavapi because it sits between the Vishwanath Temple and the **Gyanavapi Mosque,** which the Mughal emperor Aurangzeb built in 1669 from the rubble of an earlier Vishwanath Temple he destroyed. The mosque is now ringed with barbed wire and only open at prayer times, a precaution against Hindu communalist threats to knock it down.

The most important goddess temple in Varanasi is dedicated to Shiva's consort in the form of **Annapurna.** It is across from Vishwanath, just down the lane, and it too is closed to non-Hindus. Annapurna is a true mother figure and a provider of food, armed with spoons and saucepans. A "Mountain of Food" festival occurs here in late October or early November.

The next *ghat* on the river from Dashaswamedh is **Man Mandir Ghat,** topped by one of the observatories built by Maharaja Jai Singh of Jaipur in the 18th century. Climb up on the right side of the building to see an arsenal of astronomical scales made of stone. Above **Mir Ghat** and **Lalita Ghat** are a few important temples. The **Vishalakshi Temple** belongs to a "Wide-Eyed" local goddess, but it is also a *Shakti pith*—the eye of the goddess Sati (or by some accounts her earring) is said to have landed here when she was chopped apart in the heavens (see **Divine Dismemberment,** p. 404). Nearby, a deep well, the **Dharma Kup,** marks the site where Yama, the god of death, paid homage to Shiva. Lalita Ghat also has above it a brick and wood **Nepali Temple,** which looks like it's straight out of the Kathmandu Valley.

An axis of holiness runs between the Vishwanath Temple and the next *ghat,* **Manikarnika Ghat.** This is the most sacred of the *ghats* and the last stop pilgrims make on the river. Manikarnika's holiness is such that the area just south of it has become the city's prime cremation ground. Boats full of wood are moored here and the pyres emit a campfire-like smoke, consuming the corpses of those liberated by Kashi. There is ritual: bodies are carried down on stretchers and dipped in the Ganga, then burned for three hours on fires lit from an eternal flame that stays going on the *ghat.* Members of the formerly untouchable Dom caste manage the ceremony. When the burning is complete the eldest son of the deceased throws a pot of Ganga water onto the fire and the ashes are sprinkled in the river. Local commentators will tell you that the shoulder bones of men (because of their strong hearts) and the pelvic bones of women (because of their strong wombs) are unable to burn, and that these are thrown in the river along with the ashes. Above the *ghat* are many hospices where the dying come to wait their turn.

Visitors can watch the cremations from boats or from buildings above the *ghat,* but mourners and workers get annoyed (or feign annoyance) with anyone who lingers on the *ghat.* **Photographing the cremations is not tolerated.**

Manikarnika Ghat takes its name from **Manikarnika Kund,** the small white-painted tank just past the cremation grounds, which Vishnu is said to have dug out at the beginning of time and filled with his sweat. This first pool of water so delighted Shiva that he dropped his "jeweled earring" *(manikarnika)* in it. Vishnu's footprints have been installed nearby under a circular shelter. Destruction and creation are both present at Manikarnika; bathing here and worshiping at Vishwanath is a daily pattern for many Banarsis, and the essential part of any pilgrimage.

Off the north end of Manikarnika Ghat there is a tilting temple that collapsed into the water sometime in the 19th century, testimony to shaky construction on the riverbank. This is at the edge of **Scindia Ghat,** a tall, multicolored affair.

One next approaches **Sankata Ghat,** above which is the baby-blue temple of **Sankata Devi,** a powerful mother-goddess. But the next important *ghat* at which to bathe is **Panchganga Ghat.** Here five rivers are said to converge: the Ganga, Yamuna, and Saraswati, which flow together from Allahabad upstream, and two old rivulets, the Dhutapapa and Kirana, which have now disappeared. Vishnu chose this place as the greatest spot in Kashi, and his creaky painted temple of **Bindu Madhava** sits above the *ghat.* During the month of Karttika (Oct.-Nov.) the temple and the *ghat* are decked with lamps at night. The rest of the year the most prominent feature of Panchaganga Ghat is the tall and bony **Dharhara Mosque** perched at the top. Emperor Aurangzeb built this on the ruins of an earlier Bindu Madhava temple, and now it dominates a section of the riverbank skyline (with *baksheesh* you can get to the roof for great views).

A statue of a sacred cow at **Gai Ghat** watches over an array of *Shivalingas.* Close to this is **Trilochan Ghat,** with the popular temple of the "Three-Eyed" Shiva. Varanasi Devi, the city-goddess of Varanasi, also inhabits this temple.

North from this point along the riverboat the *ghats* begin to thin out, both in construction and population. This is the oldest part of the city, but it was also the part

Muslims overran and settled in. Many ancient Hindu spots now lie forgotten. The next *ghat* of visible importance is **Raj Ghat,** the last before the Malaviya Bridge. This is the crossing-point where traders since ancient times have forded the Ganga or ferried across it (now people tend to use the bridge).

The temple of **Adi Keshava** ("Original Vishnu") sits on a high, lonely bank to the north of the bridge. Vishnu supposedly washed his feet here, at the confluence of the Ganga and Varuna rivers, but the confluence is also sacred as the northern city limit of Varanasi. Vishnu's tall temple here is at a very ancient sacred place, predating the city of Varanasi.

Inside the City

In general, the farther one is from the water in Varanasi the less there is to see. There are always exceptions, however, and up Chauk Rd. from Godaulia, near its intersection with Kabir Chaura Rd., is the temple of **Kala Bhaironath,** the mustachioed police chief of the holy city. Once an angry and sinful form of Shiva, Kala Bhaironath (also known as Bhairava) chopped off one of the heads of the god Brahma. As a punishment, the rotting head stuck to his hand, and for years Bhairava had to wander in fits of remorse. It was not until he got to Varanasi that the head (which was just a skull by this point) miraculously dropped off his hand. After this he became responsible for watching that the citizens of Varanasi live righteously. Not too far away, on the other side of the Chauk-Kabir Chaura Rd. crossing, is the temple of **Bare Ganesh,** the central Ganesh shrine in Varanasi. Fifty-six others radiate out from it in seven concentric circles.

A spirit of urbane and modernized Hinduism can be seen in the **Bharat Mata Temple,** on the city's western outskirts south of the Cantonment. Mahatma Gandhi inaugurated this temple, which has a swimming-pool-sized marble relief map of India in place of a deity. There's a good view from the upper balconies.

Varanasi's other sights are outside the city proper. Across Panch Koshi Rd. at the south end is **Benares Hindu University (BHU).** Founded in 1916 by the reformer Madan Mohan Malaviya, it was designed to merge modern ideas with the best traditions of Hindu learning. For those not stopping to study Indian languages or philosophy here, there are two places suited to shorter visits. One is the **Birla Vishwanath Temple,** the most enormous temple in the city, with its tasteful white spire meant to copy the one knocked down by Aurangzeb in 1669. The second sight on campus is the **Bharat Kala Bhawan,** the BHU museum. Hauled together by some true believers in Indian culture, its collections of paintings, artifacts, and sculptures are extensive and come from a great range of styles, even if they do appear a bit neglected now. There is plenty here from Varanasi too, from 19th-century etchings of *ghats* to a great statue of Krishna lifting Mt. Govardhana. (Open May-June Mon.-Sat. 7:30am-12:30pm, July-April Mon.-Sat. 11am-4:30pm; admission Rs.5.)

The barren expanse of the east shore of the Ganga holds one point of interest, the **Ramnagar Fort.** This is the castle of Varanasi's maharaja, located in the village of Ramnagar, approximately opposite BHU at the south end of the city. The river can be crossed on a pontoon bridge in winter or a ferry in summer. The fort contains a royal museum with plenty of sedan chairs and swords from the royal family's past, though all of the exhibits are quite dilapidated. Ramnagar is probably not worth the detour unless it's for the **Ram Lila,** the festive pageant of the *Ramayana* staged by the maharaja in September and October.

SHOPPING

Varanasi is famous for its silk, and the touts will never let your forget it. Like a mutating strain of bacteria, the touts are constantly finding new ways to assail their potential victims. It is best not even to open your ear to them. There are seven silk shops in Varanasi which have fixed prices and where the government exercises quality control. Three of these are located on Vishwanath Gali in the Old City, on the same road as the Golden Temple: **Mohan Silk Stores,** 5/54 Vishwanath Gali (tel. 322354); **Bhagwan Stores,** D 10/32 Vishwanath Gali (tel. 322365); **J.R. Ivory Arts and Curios,** D 20

Vishwanath Gali (tel. 321772). Two others are at Sindhu Nagar, a small colony off Aurangabad Rd. near the intersection of Aurangabad and Vidyapith: **M/S Bhagwanlila Exports,** 41 Sindhu Nagar Colony, Sigra (tel. 356607); **Mahalakshmi Saree House,** 16 Sindhu Nagar, Sigra (tel. 356607). And in two other spots in the city: **Choudary Brothers,** Thatheri Bazaar (tel. 320469), opposite the Chowk police station; **Mehrotra Silk Factory,** S.C. 21/22 Englishia Line, Cantonment (tel. 45289), off Cantonment Station Rd. right before it intersects with Vidyapith. It's a good idea to visit these shops, and to get a sense of the prices of top-quality silk, before trying to bargain in the Chauk or Old City (where, if you are careful, you might get a great deal).

MUSIC

Varanasi is well-known as a bastion of Indian classical music. Many Westerners come to Varanasi to learn how to play the sitar or tabla. The best resource in this respect is the music school at Benares Hindu University (BHU), located near Lanka Gate, south of Godaulia (tel. 310290, ext. 241). Though the school itself only offers degree courses (which require one year's attendance and cost Rs.6000 per year, including mandatory dorm rent), the faculty offer private lessons and can refer the student to other teachers. Another good place to learn sitar or tabla is the **Triveni Music Centre,** on Keval Gali in Godaulia, not far from Baba Restaurant (tel. 328074). Instructor Nandu and his father are particularly recommended. The **International Music Centre,** near Dashaswamedh Ghat, offers private sitar and tabla lessons for Rs.60 per hour. From Godaulia Crossing, walk toward Dashaswamedh Ghat. When the road splits, go right, and at the sign for the Kali Temple, go right again. The path swings to the left. Take the first right turn, the next left and walk straight and the school will be on your left.

Buying musical instruments can be a tricky business. Sitar and tabla stores abound in the Old City area. There is one sitar store recommended by the faculty at BHU, located near the Jangambali Post Office. From Godaulia Crossing, facing Daswamedh, turn right, go straight, turn into the third lane on your left (1km from Godaulia Crossing); the Jangambali (or Beagalitola) Post Office will appear immediately on your left, and the unmarked sitar store is several doors down on the left. *Sitars* range from Rs.2000 to Rs.5000. One tabla shop comes highly recommended by the old guy who runs the sitar shop: **Imtiyaz Ali,** Siddh Giri Bagh, near a mosque and the palatial residence of former M.P. Kumala Pathi Tripathi. From Godaulia Crossing: facing away from Dashaswamedh Ghat, walk or take a rickshaw to the third big intersection (including Godaulia Crossing), take a right turn, and after 1km this small shop appears on the left. A pair of tablas with copper drums costs Rs.2000. A pair of tablas with brass drums costs Rs.1500.

■ Sarnath

In the wooded suburbs north of Varanasi lies Sarnath, the site of Gautama Buddha's first sermon and, some say, his last (since subsequent teachings were in the form of dialogues, like those of Socrates). After the Buddha attained enlightenment in Bodh Gaya, the Awakened One walked 200km to Sarnath, lotuses blooming where his feet touched the ground. He gathered his former companions, and here, among the deer and peacocks, revealed the Eight-Fold Noble Path. In later years, during the rainy season, he occasionally returned to this quiet grove to meditate amid the lush vegetation.

In the 3rd century BC, under the rule of the Mauryas, *stupas* were built to commemorate the visits of the Buddha. This construction continued in force until the 4th century AD, when the Hindu Guptas rose to power and Buddhist influence began to wane. It was at this point, however, that Sarnath became famous for its sandstone images of Buddha. Sarnath's prestige as a center of Buddhism came to an abrupt end in the 12th century when it was demolished by Qutb-ud-din Aibak. Although Sarnath's Deer Park is dotted with the foundations of many small and large *stupas,* only one monument, the Dhamekh Stupa, remains intact. Nevertheless, simply by walking around the sites, it is possible to get some sense of the breadth, if not the depth, of Sarnath's devotion to Buddhism. Reaching back further still, it is possible to imagine the Buddha himself walking these same paths, feeding cucumbers to the deer.

ORIENTATION AND PRACTICAL INFORMATION

Ashok Marg, which runs north from Varanasi, turns into **Dharmapal Road.** On the left side is the official entrance to the sites; on the right side is the Archaeological Museum. The **bus stand** is 500m away at a small intersection. Most people, consequently, start their tour at **Mulgandha Kuti Vihar.**

The **post office** (tel. 385013; open Mon.-Sat. 10am-5pm) and **Tourist Bungalow** are located on a side road near the bus stand. From the bus stand, facing toward the sites, turn left onto a small road, and it's 200m down on the left. There's a small information counter in the bungalow, open Mon.-Sat. 10am-5pm. STD/ISD **telephone** booths are located nearby on Dharmapal Rd. A small **train station** lies 1km from the bus stand on Dharmapal Rd., but few trains stop here. Try local **buses** instead, which go to Lanka/BHU and the Varanasi Railway Station. **Tempos** go to the Civil Court, Cantonment, Varanasi. **Auto-rickshaws** go "wherever you want, baby." There's a small **government hospital** in a yellow building across from the Tourist Bungalow. The **Mahabodhi Society,** Dharmapal Rd., between the bus stand and the Archaeological Museum, is currently equipping a small hospital.

ACCOMMODATIONS AND FOOD

Most tourists don't spend the night, but it's possible to stay in some of the monasteries for a small donation. The **Tourist Bungalow** has doubles, each with bath, air-cooling, and soft mattress. Single occupancy Rs.150, double Rs.175. There's one restaurant worth mentioning: the **Rangoli Garden Restaurant,** 1km after the Tourist Bungalow on the left (tel. 385025). A friendly Bhutanese family prepares great Chinese food in exactly the right amount of time. Fried rice starts at Rs.25; garlic chicken costs Rs.50.

SIGHTS

Sightseeing in Sarnath is more like *site*-seeing. Most points of interest are piles of rubble, only recently excavated. The first stop, however, is completely intact. From the bus stand, walk 100m along shop-lined Dharmapal Rd., turn right under the arch, and walk 200m toward the sandstone spires of the modern Buddhist temple **Mulgandha Kuti Vihar.** The interior is decorated with wall paintings (by the Japanese artist Kosetsu Nosi) inspired by the *Buddhacarita (The Acts of the Buddha).* The *pipal* tree growing in the shrine is, purportedly, a close relative of the tree under which Buddha achieved *sambodhi.* A book stall sells Buddhist pamphlets and a bilingual edition of the *Buddhacarita.* The architecture of the temple itself is uninspiring. Oddly, the outside is adorned with many small *dharma*-wheels with their bottoms cut off. The Buddha is said to have "turned the *dharma*-wheel" when he gave his first sermon at Sarnath.

Leaving the temple, walk right along a clay path to **Dhamekh Stupa,** the only ancient structure left intact by Qutb-ud-din's armies. It commemorates the spot where the Buddha delivered his first sermon. Built in either the 5th or 6th century AD, in the twilight of Buddhist predominance in North India, it remains unfinished. The bottom is made of elaborately decorated stone, with eight window-like depressions, presumably made to shelter small statues of the Buddha. The top is composed of small bricks, made from the clay abundant in the area.

Walk straight ahead to the foundational bricks of the **Dharmarajika Stupa.** The breadth of the foundation indicates a massive structure. It was built by the Mauryan emperor Ashoka in the 3rd century BC to house the relics of Buddha which, these days, are displayed at the Buddha Purnima festival in May. Unlike other structures at this site, the Dharmarajika Stupa was destroyed only recently (1794) by greedy treasure-hounds.

To the rear of this are the remains of the **Main Shrine,** also built by Ashoka, to commemorate the place where Buddha meditated. To the left down a shallow well is the bottom portion of **Ashoka's column.** The column is engraved with Buddhist edicts in Brahmi script. When Ashoka had been converted from a warlord's life to the path of *dharma,* he advertised his new beliefs in edicts on many such columns. The capital has also been preserved, and can be viewed in the Archaeological Museum.

Walking back from the **Main Shrine,** or taking a roundabout clay path which starts to the left of Ashoka's column, you arrive at the high fence which girds the deer sanctuary, known today as "Deer Park," although, historically, this name belongs to all of Sarnath. Peacocks cavort with long-horn stags, as they are said to have done in the Anandavana ("Forest of Bliss"), the ancient forest which covered southern Varanasi. Only now the animals' unself-conscious play is broken by the bewildering "deer calls" of young touts jockeying for *baksheesh*.

Exiting the site through the official entrance in front of the Dharmarajika Stupa, cross the street to the **Archaeological Museum.** Inside the museum, the splendidly engraved capital from Ashoka's column, with four roaring lions seated back to back, is one of the great masterpieces of early Indian art. It was adopted by Jawaharlal Nehru as the emblem of the Indian republic and appears on all Indian currency. The museum displays at its entrance a first-century AD standing Buddha from Mathura. With his broad shoulders and strong arms, this Buddha looks more like a god than a wandering ascetic. Other pieces of note include a perfectly wrought teaching Buddha from the Gupta period. The Buddha sits, serenely contemplative, holding forth on some *topos* of the Eight-Fold Path. Gathered below, in miniature, are six disciples, Buddha's companions from Uruvela and, perhaps, Yasha, the son of a wealthy Varanasi merchant who renounced his patrimony to follow in the Buddha's steps. (Open Sat.-Thurs. 10am-5pm; admission Rs.50.)

Madhya Pradesh

Madhya Pradesh means "Middle State" in Hindi. True to its name, it sprawls smack dab across the middle of the country, the bedrock of North India's Hindi-speaking Saffron Belt. Although Madhya Pradesh covers a larger area than any other state, its population numbers less than 80 million, thanks to an often arid and inhospitable climate. The Narmada River valley provides heavily populated fertile farmland, but scrubby hills and steep ravines cover much of the rest of the state, furnishing a refuge for dacoits (bandits) and tigers, a home for Gond and Bhil tribal peoples, and an impediment for tourists.

This difficult terrain has sheltered many natural and historical treasures which might otherwise have disappeared. Madhya Pradesh has India's largest tiger population—and Kanha National Park, of *Jungle Book* fame, is the best place to see them. The forests also conceal the two ruined cities of Mandu and Orchha, where palaces and creepers fight it out under the tourists' gaze and the infamous temples of Khajuraho, where carved sexual contortionism keeps visitors riveted. The three largest cities, Indore, Bhopal, and Jabalpur, revolve mainly around business and administration, but the fourth, Gwalior, huddles at the feet of one of India's oldest and most impressive forts. Historical remains in Madhya Pradesh date back to the 3rd century BC, when the Emperor Ashoka founded Sanchi as a religious center. A succession of Buddhist and Hindu dynasties gave way to Muslim marauders from the north. The Mughal emperors eventually lost control of the region to the Marathas, whose leading families, the Scindias and the Holkars, ruled right up until Independence and beyond. The present and the past are so hopelessly muddled in Madhya Pradesh that one wing

Madhya Pradesh

UTTAR PRADESH

BIHAR

ORISSA

Varanasi

Allahabad

Kanpur

Bilaspur

Mahanadi R.

Raipur

43

Son R.

Rewa

Khajuraho

Panna

Satna

Bandhavgarh
National Park

Mandla

Kanha
National Park

Kawardha

Murwara

Jabalpur

Nagpur

(See inset map at upper left)

Sunar R.

Orchha
Chhatarpur

BUNDELKHAND

Datia

Jhansi

Gwalior

Chambal R.

Shivpuri
N.P.

Chanderi

Sagar

Udayagiri

26

12

Chhindwara

Piparia

Pachmarhi

Betel

MAHARASHTRA

N

Kota

Udaypur

Vidisha

Sanchi

Raisen

Bhojpur

Bhopal

Bhimbetka

Namoda R.

Ujjain

Dewas

Indore

Mhow

Omkareshwar

Khandwa

Burhanpur

Jalgaon

6

Ratlam

Dhar

Mandu

Maheshwar

Bagh

RAJASTHAN

Chittorgarh

60 miles

60 kilometers

0

Ahmadabad

GUJARAT

Vadodara

Surat

BASTAR

Jagdalpur

43

6

of the Jai Vilas Palace in Gwalior is open to tourists, while in the next, Maharaja and Congress M.P. Madhavrao Scindia feuds with his mother, a BJP M.P.

■ Bhopal

Mention Bhopal, and many people pale. To this day, foreigners know the city, if at all, as the site of the world's worst industrial accident. In the middle of the night of December 2, 1984, a cloud of lethal methyl isocyanate gas leaked from the Union Carbide fertilizer factory in the north of the city. By morning, 2000 people had died and many thousands more had been crippled for life.

But as a state capital with 1.2 million inhabitants, a slew of museums, and a lively Muslim bazaar quarter, Bhopal has more to offer tourists than memories of tragedy. The sequence of enlightened women rulers who embarked on a program of civic improvements during the 19th century have bequeathed a city interspersed with lakes and parks, and studded with the minarets of massive mosques. The Taj-ul-Masjid is no Taj Mahal, but Bhopal remains a good staging point for the nearby Buddhist ruins at Sanchi and other sights in the state and a pleasant city in its own right.

ORIENTATION

The huge **Upper Lake** and smaller **Lower Lake** separate Old Bhopal in the northwest from the new city to the southeast. **Hamidia Road** runs from near the Taj-ul-Masjid (the city's largest mosque) on the western fringes of the old town, past the bus stand to the railway station in the east. There, amid many cheap hotels and restaurants, it turns right and runs south toward the new town. Among the many neighborhoods in the diffuse colonial area is **T.T. Nagar,** the home of the MPTDC, Indian Airlines, and one of the rare State Banks with foreign exchange facilities.

PRACTICAL INFORMATION

Tourist Office: MPTDC, 4th fl., Gangotri Building, T.T. Nagar, New Town (tel. 554340), just past the Rang Mahal movie theater. In addition to bombarding visitors with glossy pamphlets, the staff will book afternoon city tours (departing from MPTDC Hotel Palace, daily 2pm, 5hr., Rs.30) and reserve rooms at all MPTDC hotels in the state. Open Mon.-Sat. 10am-5pm.

Currency Exchange: State Bank of Indore, Parcharad Building, New Market Rd., T.T. Nagar (tel. 551804 or 550131). Open Mon.-Fri. 10:30am-2:30pm.

Airport: Agra Rd., 12km from city center (tel. 521277). Indian Airlines, next door to the Gangotri Building in T.T. Nagar about 100m on the left past the Rang Mahal cinema (tel. 550480). Open Mon.-Sat. 10am-1:30pm and 2-5pm. To: Bombay (1 per day, US$74) via Indore (30min., US$35); and Delhi (Mon.-Sat. 1-2 per day, US$65) via Gwalior (Mon., Tues., and Thurs. 1 per day, 45min., US$54).

Trains: The station is on Hamidia Rd. (tel. 536827). Reservation office outside platform 1, on the far right as you face the station. Open Mon.-Sat. 8am-2pm and 2:15-8pm, Sun. 8am-2pm. The best trains are: Delhi, Agra, Gwalior, and Jhansi (*Shatabdi Exp.* 2001, 2:40pm); Jabalpur (*Narmada Exp.* 8233, 11pm); Indore (*Narmada Exp.* 8234, 6:20am); Bombay and Jalgaon (*Pushpak Exp.* 1034, 6:40am; or *Punjab Mail* 1038, 5:25pm); and Hyderabad (*Dakshin Exp.* 7022, 9:20am).

Buses: The station is on Hamidia Rd. (tel. 540841). Frequent departures for Sanchi (10 per day, 1½hr., Rs.12); Indore (20 per day, 5hr., Rs.45); and other cities around the state. For long distance travel, one of the many private operators nearby might offer more luxurious vehicles.

Local Transportation: Auto-rickshaws and **taxis,** most useful for getting to the airport (Rs.60). In addition, an efficient **minibus** system connects the bus stand on Hamidia Rd. with most parts of town (Rs.2 per ride).

Market: The fruit and vegetable market, which stretches to the left off Hamidia Rd. into the bazaars as you go from train to bus station, is one of the best in India.

Pharmacy: Hamidia Hospital houses a 24-hr. pharmacy.

Hospital: Hamidia Hospital, Sultania Rd., near Taj-ul-Masjid (tel. 540222).

Police: SPO, Sultania Rd. Jehangirabad (tel. 100).

Post Office: GPO, Sultania Rd., near Taj-ul-Masjid. For *Poste Restante* ask at the inquiry counter (number 1). Open Mon.-Fri. 10am-6pm, Sat. 10am-noon.
Telephone Code: 0755.

ACCOMMODATIONS

Lodging in Bhopal caters mainly to business travelers, leaving little in the cheapest range. To add injury to insult, all hotels levy taxes and service charges of up to 20% extra. On the other hand, this does mean that most rooms include conveniences like TVs, telephones, and attached bathrooms.

Hotel Ranjit, 3 Hamidia Rd. (tel. 533511). Between the bus and train stations, on the right, about 200m before the road turns. The shoebox rooms share a building with Bhopal's busiest restaurant and bar. But high turnover allows the management to keep the room prices down. Singles Rs.100. Doubles Rs.130.

Hotel Taj, 52 Hamidia Rd. (tel. 533162, 536379, 536261), opposite the Ranjit. Although their rates run as high as Rs.800, even those in the cheapest rooms enjoy the attentions of the bellboys, bearers, and cleaners. The atrium design, set back from the road, insulates guests from the Hamidia brouhaha. Check-out noon. Standard singles Rs.100. Doubles Rs.250.

Hotel Alishan, near Alpara Talkies, Hamidia Rd. (tel. 535778), opposite the Ranjit. The bright blue carpeting distracts attention from the cramped cubic rooms. The receptionist has been known to balk at backpackers, but can be persuaded. Singles Rs.120. Doubles Rs.200.

Hotel Sonali, near Radha Talkies Rd., 3 Hamidia Rd. (tel. 533880, 533990). Down the small alley to the right of Hotel Raijit and around to the right. This busy, sparkling new spot promotes its mainly air-conditioned rooms with the slogan, "vibrates in the memory." The mural of tulips interrupted by electrical circuitry might not seem so exciting—but the good-value rooms do strike a chord. Singles Rs.135, with air-cooling Rs.160. Doubles Rs.195, with air-cooling Rs.220.

Hotel Meghdoot, Hamidia Rd. (tel. 511375). On the leg of the street south of the train station, on the right about 200m before the turn. One of the cheapest deals in Bhopal, it has all the standard facilities, but in a noisy, all-male, betel-stained atmosphere. Singles Rs.121. Doubles Rs.132, including tax.

FOOD

Ranjit, inside Hotel Ranjit, 3 Hamidia Rd. Bhopal's most popular dinner joint features many levels of bar and restaurant lit by uniformly low lighting. Big portions of Indian chicken or mutton dishes go for Rs.36, while veggie fare ranges up to Rs.45 for *kaju* curry. Subcontinental Chinese costs Rs.24-45. Open daily 11am-11pm.

Riviera Bar and Restaurant, Hotel Red Sea Plaza, Hamidia Rd. (tel. 536979). On the 4th fl. of the building in the crook of the road, near the lane to the train station. Bhopal's closest thing to nightlife consists of all-male clientele swilling beers from the vinyl banquettes, while a local pop band with 1 female (shock! horror!) vocalist churns out covers of filmi music (daily 7-11pm). The big menu features snacks and sandwiches (Rs.10-30), *biryanis* (Rs.35), *paneer makhani* (Rs.32), and something called "fish special" (Rs.48). As you await your order, meditate on their motto, "Because we count the moments, not the hours." Open daily 8am-11pm.

Hotel Surya, Hamidia Rd. (tel. 536925 or 536926). On the southern branch, on the right as you approach the station, about 200m before the turn. Following Bhopal's slogan mania, Surya states itself "for those who value class." While the classy dim lighting turns the trip to the table into a spelunking expedition, the restaurant shows distinction in their *paneer parathas* (Rs.10), chicken dishes (Rs.30), and *paneer butter masala* (Rs.30). Beer Rs.48-52. Open daily 8am-11:30pm.

Indian Coffee House, next to Sangam Cinema off Hamidia Rd. and on New Market Rd. opposite the State Bank of India. The unruffled waiters in their ruffled headgear serve delightful South Indian snacks to their delighted guests. Special *dosa* or *utthapam* Rs.11. Delicious sugarless coffee Rs.3. Open daily 7am-9pm.

NORTH INDIA

SIGHTS

Bhopal's status as an independent Muslim-ruled princely state until 1952 has endowed the city with a strongly Muslim character and a wealth of impressive mosques. The old Muslim bazaar quarter, or **Chowk,** nestling in the crook of Hamidia Rd., has the strongest Islamic flavor. Although most of the area's old buildings have disappeared, the men with hennaed hair and beards and the women in full *chadors* peering out from shops piled high with picturesque, but prosperous, stacks of merchandise and the narrow, twisting streets full of goats browsing in the central gutters constitute spectacle enough.

The **Taj-ul-Masjid,** Bhopal's biggest mosque, is spectacular in a different sense. The plans of the Victorian Nawab Shajehar Begum were so grandiose that they have not been completed to this day. But the 18-story minarets, the vast, hot courtyard, and the three huge domes over the prayer hall seething with Qur'an students nonetheless create a grand impression. Despite the huge staircase on Sultania Rd., the mosque can only be approached from Royal Market Rd. (Open Sat.-Thurs. dawn-dusk; free.)

Other interesting mosques dot the old town. The **Jama Masjid,** built by Kudsia Begum in 1837, struts its stuff with gold-spiked minarets. The **Moti Mahal,** constructed in 1860 by Kudsia Begum's daughter Sikander Jehan, continues the Mughal tradition of small-scale, elegant, "personal" mosques. Although less opulent than its counterparts in Agra or Delhi, this mosque lifts many features (including striped domes) from the most magnificent Indian mosque of all, the Jama Masjid in Delhi.

On the shores of the Upper Lake in the new town stands Bhopal's newest sight, **Bharat Bhavan.** The local authorities advertise it as a "non-building," but the big lopsided domes decorated with folk art cry out for attention. Part subterranean museum, part garden-*cum*-auditorium, part weird, this complex of cultural centers provides an ideal spot to unwind after a hard morning's sight-seeing in the Chowk. A picnic in front of the lakeside view and a stroll through the collection of tribal and folk art and the modern art galleries will put all the horns and hassles of old Bhopal far behind. (Open Tues.-Sun. 2-8pm; admission Rs.1.)

The fabulously wealthy Birla family has slapped up yet another gaudy **temple** to the adulation of the masses. But this one comes complete with a first-rate religious sculpture collection. The views are also divine—the Birlas naturally selected some of Bhopal's most expensive real estate high on Arena Hill. (Open Tues.-Sun. 9am-noon and 2-6pm; admission Rs.2.)

■ Sanchi

In the 3rd century BC, the emperor Ashoka founded the Buddhist retreat at Sanchi as a haven for peaceful meditation. Twenty-two centuries have not succeeded in undermining his purpose. Although Buddhism as a living faith in India has long-since flowered and withered, the deserted complex of *stupas* and monasteries on the remote hilltop still preserve the same meditative quietude that first prompted the great Mauryan emperor to build on this site. The huge, white hemispherical *stupas,* and the subsequent encrustations of exquisite sculpture, lure tourists chiefly on day trips from Bhopal, about 50km away by bus or train.

ORIENTATION AND PRACTICAL INFORMATION

Sanchi only reemerged into history when one of those aimless British officers, roaming about India in search of a civilizing mission, stumbled across the ruins in 1818. It remains a tiny village sustained by a tourist trade. One road leads from the **railway station,** past the few budget hotels, up the hill to the **main gate** to the ruins. The road to Bhopal crosses this street at right angles, continuing on to Vidisha 10km north. The **small market** and **bus stand,** which boast an ill-equipped **pharmacy** and an STD/ISD **telephone** booth, occupy the quadrant on the station side of the main road and the Bhopal side of the cross road. Buses leave for Bhopal at least every hour from 6am-6pm (1½hr., Rs.12)—but some take the slow route through Raisen. Although Sanchi sits on the main line from Bhopal to Delhi, express **trains** only stop here for 1st class or A/C passengers who have traveled 161km, or 2nd-class journeyers in groups or 10 who have racked up 400km! The Bhopal station masters seem more officious in this matter than those at Sanchi so although you may have trouble getting here by train (trains from Bhopal: the *Punjab Mail* 1038, 4:27pm or 1458, 10:40am, 30min.), you should be able to snag a seat on the way back (*Punjab Mail* 1037, 9:15am, 1457 Down 2:25pm, Rs.16). If you're coming from Delhi (Rs.127), Agra (Rs.99), Gwalior (Rs.77), Tharsi (Rs.57) or Bombay (Rs.153), then you can invoke the 161km clause if you have the extra cash to pay for first class. Otherwise, find nine well-traveled friends.

ACCOMMODATIONS AND FOOD

Should you want to stay overnight (most visitors see the signs in 2hr. or so), the **Railway Retiring Rooms** come complete with a dressing room, a showerless bathroom, tatty mosquito nets, and high ceilings for Rs.60 (single or double; prices rise after 24hr.). The **Sri Lanka Mahabodhi Society Guest House** (tel. 81239) on the left just outside the station, has a range of rooms: the best deal is a bare cell with attached squat toilet and cold tap water for Rs.40. **The Tourist Cafeteria** (tel. 81243), just before the museum, has bright, airy spotless rooms for a hefty Rs.225 per single and Rs.275 per double, plus Rs.50 for use of the cooler. As its name suggests, it serves food in a pleasant, modern hall. Snacks and sandwiches range from Rs.12 to Rs.25, while *palak paneer* at Rs.50 and tandoori chicken for Rs.20 are also decent values. Open daily 7am-9pm. **Stalls** and **street vendors** sell cold drinks and snacks.

SIGHTS

The complex at Sanchi chronicles the whole history of Indian Buddhism, from its glorious ascent under Ashoka to its abrupt decline in the medieval period. Bypass the **museum** at first, but hold on to the ticket from the kiosk outside, which alone gains admission to the ruins atop the hill. The **lower kiosk** also sells an informative guidebook and map for Rs.12. At the end of the stiff climb up the hill, either by the road or by the stairs to the right, the massive **Great Stupa** (*stupa* number 1) greets the footsore tourist. At the opposite side, the **south gate** once constituted the main entrance, as evidenced by the stump of the pillar erected by Ashoka (a local zamindar broke off the rest to use in a sugarcane press) and the staircases leading to the raised balcony. The Shunga dynasty added these to the original brick mound of Ashoka. But it was the Satavahanas who, in the first century BC, tacked on Sanchi's richest addition: the four monumental **gateways** facing the points of the compass. So detailed is the sculpture that archeologists attribute it to ivory carvers accustomed to making maximum use of minimum surface—a theory borne out by a Pali inscription on the south gate. Since all the sculpture save the **four seated Buddhas** inside each gate dates from the Theravada period, no direct depictions of the Buddha appear in the *stupa;* he is referred to obliquely with symbols such as the lotus flowers (for his birth), the *pipal* tree (for his enlightenment) and the wheel (for his sermons). Figures commonly depicted include six *manushis*—Buddha's predecessors to Gautama who appear as *stupas* or trees, each of a different species. *Jatakas* (tales from the Buddha's previous lives) such as the **Chhadarta Jakata** in which the Buddha, as an elephant, helps a hunter to saw off his tusks, and stories from the subsequent history of Buddhism, particularly those detailing the distribution of the Buddha's relics are also illustrated here. The middle rung of the South Gate shows one of the latter: Ashoka's army has arrived (on the right) at the last of the eight original *stupas* containing the Buddha's relics at Ramagrama. But he is prevented from carting off the loot (as he had at the other seven) by the army of snake people to the left. On the inside, the middle rung depicts the Chhadarta Jataka, with the Buddha as the six-tusked elephant, while above this scene are the trees and *stupas* of the *manushi* buddhas. The bottom rung shows the siege of Kushinagar, where eight armies imminent clash over those sought-after relics was averted by equitable distribution. The front face of the **west gate** features (from top to bottom) more *manushis,* the Buddha's first sermon (note the wheel) and more scenes of Chhadarta. Inside the top two rungs show more wrangling over relics, while the bottom reveals the Buddha achieving enlightenment despite the distracting demons sent by Mara. On the south pillar of this gate, the **Mahakapi Jataka** shows the Buddha as a monkey turning himself into a bridge so that his brethren could escape to safety over a river. The **north gateway,** which has endured the ravages of time less scarred than its counterparts, shows around both sides of the bottom rung the **Vessarkara Jataka,** in which the Buddha gives away successively a magic elephant, his horse and chariot (on the front) and then his children and wife before being reinstated to his princedom (on the rear). While the upper registers of the east gate repeat earlier scenes, the south pillar below shows the Buddha walking on water on the outside, and facing a fearsome cobra unhurt on the inside. Below this scene, the villagers try to make a sacrificial fire in thanksgiving—but the wood won't burn without the Buddha's permission. Open daily dawn-dusk. Admission to the ruins costs Rs.50; Fri. free.

■ Indore

With a population of 1.2 million, Indore is the Mammon of Madhya Pradesh. More people pack its cityscape, more businesses clutter its buildings, more industry sears its escarpments, and more money flows through its coffers than any other city in the state. The whirlwind wheeling and dealing, by contrast to Bhopal's staid bureaucracy, surges through the streets in the form of discarded receipts, rapid handshakes, and the profit-tolling patter of calculator keypads. It was not always so—until the 18th century, Indore amounted to little more than a trading post and way station en route to more significant cities like Ujjain, Mandu, and Dhar. But when the leadership of the local Maratha clan, the Holkars, passed to Rani Ahilya Bhai, Indore vaulted to centerstage. The "let them eat public works" philosophy bombarded the capital with schools, hospitals, and charitable institutions while her industrial initiatives are echoed to this day in the nearby auto-city of Pithampur. All this amounts to a smoggy whistle-stop for the average visitor who might take in the Lal Bagh Palace on the way to Mandu.

ORIENTATION

Indore is shaped like your average garden-variety blob. In the middle, **Station Road** leads south from the railway station to the **Sarawate Bus Stand** about 500m away. Northeast of here stretches a neighborhood of not-cheap-enough hotels. Just beyond, **Tagore Road** runs northwest past the MPTDC to **M.G. Road,** the main drag, which connects the city's market and few sights to the center. Finally, the **My Hospital Road** leads southeast from the station area to the GPO, the State Bank of India, and the museum.

PRACTICAL INFORMATION

Tourist Office: MPTDC, behind Ravindra Natya Graha Hall, R.N. Tagore Rd. (tel. 430653, 541818). On the right next to the tourist bungalows as you walk away from the railway station. The affable staff members console mapless tourists with offerings of glossy brochures and 1-day tours of Mandu, Omkareshwar, and Maheshwar and Mandleshwar (8am, 12hr., Rs.100) that theoretically operate Mon.-Sat. but are really subject to demand. Open Mon.-Sat. 8am-8pm.

Currency Exchange: State Bank of India, Agra-Bombay Rd., just south of My Rd. on the left. Foreign exchange on the 1st fl. Open Mon.-Fri. 10:30am-2:30pm, Sat.10:30am-12:30pm.

Telephones: Telegraph Office, near M.G. Rd. Open 24hr. The area by Sarawate bus station has many STD/ISD booths.

Airport: 10km west of town center along M.G. Rd., about an Rs.40 auto-rickshaw ride. To: Bhopal (Mon.-Tues., Thurs., and Sat. 1 per day, 35min., US$35); Bombay (1-2 per day, 1hr., US$66-100); Delhi (Mon.-Sat. 1 per day, 1-3hr., US$100); Gwalior

(Mon.-Tues., and Thurs. 1 per day, 2hr., US$75); Pune (Tues., Thurs., and Sat. 1 per day, 1½hr., US$115). Several private airlines offer more expensive flights to various destinations.

Trains: the railway station is on Station Rd. Despite being a commercial hub, Indore sits astride one of the Western Railway's most antiquated and inefficient lines which demands time-consuming changes or recouplings when joining the main routes. Unlike the rest of India, bus travel to and from Indore tends to be faster and more efficient than taking the train. To: Bombay (*Bhagalpur-Bombay Exp.* 3417, 11:20pm, 10hr., Rs.143/772 for sleeper/1st class); Delhi via Ujjain, Bhopal, Jhansi, Gwalior, and Agra (*Malwa Exp.* 4068, 3:05pm, Rs.141/856 for sleeper/1st class); meter-gauge to Udaipur (4:30pm, 10hr., Rs.91/426 for sleeper/1st class).

Buses: Sarawate Bus Station at intersection of My and Station Rd. serves all destinations except Mandu and Dhar, which are served from the Gangawal **Bus Stand,** 3km west of the center. To Mandu (Rs.26) via Dhar (Rs.16), buses depart frequently from 6am-6pm. From Sarawate to: Bhopal (every 30min., 5am-midnight, 5hr., Rs.46/57 for ordinary/deluxe); Jalgaon (5am and 8:30pm, 8hr., Rs.86); Maheshwar (2, 3, and 4pm, 3hr., Rs.20); and Omkareshwar (frequent morning departures, 3hr., Rs.18).

Local Transportation: Walk, or foot the bill for the expensive, unmetered **auto-rickshaws** that abound.

Pharmacy: Suyhesh Hospital houses a 24-hr. pharmacy.

Hospital: Suyhesh Hospital, Agra-Bombay Rd. (tel. 493911).

Police: For personal contact, head to the stand in the Sarawate Bus Station. Control booth open 24hr. (tel. 533026, 533355).

Post Office: GPO, Agra-Bombay Rd., between the State Bank of India and the museum, on the left just south of My Rd. Open Mon.-Sat. 10am-8:30pm, Sun. 10am-4pm. **Postal Code:** 452001.

Telephone Code: 0731.

ACCOMMODATIONS

Hotels in Indore fill up fast with itinerant businessmen—especially in the first part of the month. The concentration of relatively cheap places behind the Sarawate Bus Station offers modest mod-cons to the middle class Indian entrepreneur—including 24-hr. checkout. Normally, grandiosely entitled, pricier rooms yield only extra knick-knacks and thin carpeting.

Hotel Payal, 38 Chhoti Gwaltoli, near bus stand (tel. 463202, 464967, 478460). In the row of hotels hidden behind the Patel flyover, just around the corner from Sarawate. The extravagantly stingy might want to consider the dirty rows of beds in the basement dorm before succumbing to the TVed and toileted rooms above ground. Dorm beds Rs.15. Singles Rs.100. Doubles Rs.140.

Hotel Ashoka, 14 Nasia Rd., opposite Sarawate Bus Station (tel. 477239), 100m to the right as you exit the station. All rooms feature the standard-issue TV, telephone, and bathroom in various states of repair. Upgrade yourself from the basic rooms to get a quieter room at the back away from bus stand noise. Basic singles Rs.90. Basic doubles Rs.140.

Hotel Sant Plaza, 9/1 Kibe Compound, Chhoti Gwaltoli Chouraha (tel. 463116, 467106). One block south of the circle with the statue of Nehru at the start of My Rd., on the corner. The cooling wall mural of a waterfall stands prelude to quiet, airy rooms with all the usual amenities. Singles Rs.125. Doubles Rs.160.

Hotel Dayal, attached to the Sant Plaza by an industrial-style bridge of sighs. This cheapie offers a bewildering variety of rooms featuring intimidatingly heavy-duty coolers. Singles Rs.75. Doubles Rs.95.

Hotel Neel Kamal, near Sarawate Bus Station (tel. 465951). Turn right down the alley 100m further from the bus stand along the overpass than the Hotel Dayal. The Neel Kamal can be recognized by its balcony loaded with potted ferns overlooking the first intersection with another back alley. Since both windows and doors open onto the open-air hallway, privacy suffers—but the back alley location guarantees relative quiet. Singles Rs.95. Doubles Rs.125.

FOOD

Siddharth Restaurant, opposite Sarawate Bus Station (tel. 460154), on the left as you emerge from the flyover. Sixties synthetic in the psychedelic rooms. The bar battles nature's purest form with a tree trunk enclosed within the dining room. The veg. menu features tasty yellow *dal* fry (Rs.10) and veg. *biryani* (Rs.16) as well as cold beers. Open daily 9am-11:30pm.

Indian Coffee House, M.G. Rd., on the left as you head away from the city center about 100m past the Central Hotel. Part of the India-wide chain, the trusty old ICH serves tasty *masala dosas* (Rs.10) and special *dosas* with cashews (Rs.12). The real highlight is, as always, the unsugared coffee (Rs.3). Open daily 7:30am-10pm.

Apsara Restaurant, Ravindra Natya Graha, R.N. Tagore Rd. (tel. 430640). Inside the same compound as the MPTDC, but no English sign—just a picture of an *apsara* (heavenly dancing girl). The entertaining menu with headings like "Cold Treasure" and "Gossiping Delights" and the dim interior with the rattling fan do nothing to prepare the visitor for some of India's best *bhindi masala* (Rs.17) and other veg. dishes (Rs.16-27). Open daily 9am-11pm.

Woodlands Restaurant, Hotel President, 163 R.N. Tagore Rd. (tel. 433156, 433211). Next to the Nehru statue at the start of R.N. Tagore Rd., this ritzy crystal dining room of an upmarket hotel lays on a buffet lunch of veg. dishes (Rs.62) daily 12:30-3:30pm.

SIGHTS

Little of the early history of Indore endures. Instead, the city detains the tourist with the Raj-era excess of the Holkars' **Lal Bagh Palace.** The later maharajas, blind to the logic of history and the tradition of Ahilya Bhai, began construction on this rather Renaissance, neo-Neoclassical, barely Baroque blow-out in the 1870s and continued building right until Independence. Along with the usual stuffed tigers and crystal chandeliers, they fitted out their folly with a state-of-the-art suspension system for the ballroom dance-floor and a subterranean tunnel connecting the main house with the kitchens on the opposite side of the nearby river. Huge gardens complete with a suitably severe statue of Queen Victoria and soft-drink stands surrounding the building. (Open Tues.-Sun. 10am-6pm; admission Rs.2. Florid and uninformative booklet costs Rs.5).

About 2km north of the palace, the **Jain Kanch Mandir** occupies a plot right in the middle of the bazaar district, near Jawahar Marg. The name means "mirror temple," clearly for want of a Hindi word for kaleidoscope. Hundreds of thousands of tiny pieces of glass, many of them colored, coat the interior of the temple and reflect the station in the central vitrine. Tiffany meets *tirthankara*. (Open daily 8am-5pm; free.) Next door to the GPO on Agra-Bombay Rd., Indore's uninspiring **Central Museum** presents religious sculpture from Madhya Pradesh and exhibits on the area's prehistory. Although several works are beautiful, the drab presentation and tatty infocards detract. (Open Tues.-Sun. 9am-5pm; free.)

■ Mandu

Hard to get to and harder to leave, Mandu rewards the few intrepid tourists who make it out here with postcard perfect ruins, a spectacular setting, and peace unimaginable in larger cities. Ruined cities are a dime a dozen in India—but not ones placed high on a serene, green plateau in the Vindhya range, commanding sweeping vistas of the frenetic Narmada Valley below. Mandu's golden age dates from the 14th century, when its Muslim sultans renamed it Shadiabad ("City of Joy"). Nearly 250 years of architectural extravagance, leisure, lust, and intrigue ensued, culminating in the Akbar-crossed love of Roopmati and Baz Bahadur. In 1561, the lecherous Mughal dispatched yet another army to bring back yet another beautiful dancing girl, ushering in Mandu's era of decline and abandonment.

ORIENTATION AND PRACTICAL INFORMATION

The small village is in the center of the ruins. A **main road** runs through the old city **gates,** past the Jama Masjid, the **market square,** the GPO, and the MPTDC hotels to the Dewa Kund group of ruins 5km away at the southern edge of the plateau.

Frequent **buses** from Dhar (Rs.10) pull into the market square. From Dhar, even more frequent connections depart for Indore (Rs.16) up until about 7pm and Dhammod (Rs.10) for Maheshwar up until 5pm. **Bicycles** can be rented at the Market Square for Rs.2 per hour. There is no tourist office, no bank to change money, no STD/ISD **telephone** service, and only a very sub-looking **post office** (open Mon.-Fri. 10am-5pm, Sat. 10am-2pm). Indore is practical; Mandu is peaceful. **Telephone Code:** 0729263.

ACCOMMODATIONS AND FOOD

The impractically persistent can worm their way into the **Forest Guest House,** near MPTDC Tourist Cottages on the main road, about 2km south of the town square. Call Dhar's Deputy Collector (tel. 22703), the deputy forest officer (tel. 22250), and any other official whose number you can get hold of. Your efforts will reward you with a spacious, slimy-sheeted, froggy bathroomed double with verandah for Rs.15 per night. **SADA** runs a tourist rest house at the corner of the main square opposite the Jama Masjid (tel. 234). Behind the blue wooden latticed porches lower dank-cement bunkers, complete with squat toilets, which go for Rs.50 per double. MPTDC has two excellent but pricey hotels in Mandu. Reserve either in advance at any MPTDC office. The **Travelers' Lodge,** on the main road, 1km north of the square (tel. 221) has lovely views over the eastern ravine from its comfortable, seat-toileted double rooms stretched along a motel-like block. Singles Rs.275. Doubles Rs.350. The **MPTDC Tourist Cottages,** on the main road 2km south of the square (tel. 235), has nicer rooms in small cottages, but no views. Singles Rs.275. Doubles Rs.350. Both have restaurants (cottages outdoor, lodge indoor) with the standard MPTDC menu of snacks (from Rs.10 for veggie sandwiches to Rs.35 for fish fingers several hundred kilometers from the sea), Continental dishes (Rs.32 for fish and chips), vegetarian (*paneer shahi korma* Rs.25), and non-veg. (chicken *masala* Rs.35). Open daily 7am-11pm. The only other game in town is the **Roopmati Restaurant** just north of the Travelers' Lodge on the main road (tel. 270), which stands out for its comprehensive bar featuring "beer" at Rs.50. Veggie dishes in this open-air pavilion, overlooking a worn lawn, range from Rs.15-25, while non-veg. dishes run as high as Rs.60 for butter chicken. Open daily 8am-11pm.

SIGHTS

The ruins fall into three main areas: the **Royal Enclave** in the north, the central "central group," and the Rewa Kund complex in the south. The **central group,** named for its location in the middle of both the plateau and the village, includes Mandu's beautiful **Jama Masjid.** Like the other monuments here, it showcases the austere Afghan style of architecture imported by its patron, Hoshang Shah. The regional (and relatively unrefined) style of the building is evident in the clumsy transition from walls to dome inside the entrance porch—but the sheer scale and simplicity of design still impress the visitor. The huge, flowery courtyard and bird-blown prayer hall retain an unassuming grandeur despite some structural damage.

Behind the Jama Masjid, Hoshang Shah's son built a white marble **mausoleum** for his father in the mid-15th century. The structure so inspired Shah Jahan that he sent his architects to study it before they began work on the Taj Mahal. Opposite the Jama Masjid, the over-ambitious and underachieving **Ashrafi Mahal** proves the patience and skill that went into Mandu's other monuments. In the 15th century Mahud Shah Khilji tried to slap together a huge tomb and seven-story victory tower so quickly and carelessly that most of it has subsequently collapsed, leaving only a *madrasa* (theological college) complete with students' cells.

The road next to Hoshang Shah's tomb continues to the Royal Enclave. Just inside the gateway, the Sybaritic Sultan Ghiyas Shah constructed the huge **Jahaz Mahal** to house his equally large harem. The long, narrow floorplan (120m by 10m) and the two artificial lakes to either side help the building live up to its nickname of "Ship Palace." The complex system of once-tinkling pools and conduits, the cool breezes, and the wide-open views would have provided the perfect backdrop for Ghiyas Shah's endless sexual shenanigans. Behind stands the **Hindola Mahal,** so named because its chunky sloping buttresses are supposed to look like they are swinging out at an angle. Ghiyas Shah also had the ramp built so that he could ride to the upper floor without going through all the hassle of getting off his elephant. Among the many other nearby ruins is the **Taveli Mahal,** with a dull **Archaeological Museum.** (Open daily 9:30am-5:30pm.)

At the southern end of the village, a fork leads right (west) from the main road to the **Nil Kanth Temple,** 3km away. The building was originally a Mughal pleasure pavilion, complete with water flowing over ribbed stones, and in front of candles to create visual effects. Today, the Shaivas have taken over. From this inspirational spot perched just below the clifftop on the valley slopes, they worship an incarnation of Shiva whose throat turned blue when he drank poison.

The main road ends at the **Rewa Kund** complex, named after the tank which used to supply the nearby palaces. The last independent ruler of Mandu, Baz Bahadur, built his eponymous **palace** in the 16th century as a quiet retreat with views of the surrounding greenery. But even this tranquil spot would not satisfy the stunning Roopmati, the sultan's favorite dancer. Life on the plateau made this plains-dweller homesick. Legend has it, she demanded that Baz Bahadur build her a pavilion on the crest of a hill, from where she could see her former village in the Narmada Valley far below. But no sooner had the dutiful Sultan completed **Roopmati's Pavilion** than the jealous Akbar marched on Mandu in order to seize the renowned dancer. Baz Bahadur fled, Roopmati took poison, and Akbar, after a brief stay, let his testosterone guide him to the next desirable dancing girl (see **Orchha,** p. 254), leaving Mandu desolate. The unparalleled view over the plains from the palace is sobering—villages, trees, and field recede in a patchwork haze to where the silver smudge of the Narmada shakes along the horizon.

■ Jabalpur

The Madhya Pradesh tourism office tries to promote protracted sojourns in this dusty town of just over 1 million people (it seems like 100,000) on the basis of some scenic white cliffs nearby. In other words, there is nothing to see in Jabalpur, and as far as most tourists are concerned, the city is nothing but a staging point for Kanha and Bandhavgarh National Parks.

ORIENTATION

Collectorate Road curves around from the rear of the railway station past the hospital and Gothic High Court to the **clock tower** marking the beginning of the **bazaar area** 1.5km away. **Station Road,** outside platform one, leads left toward **Residency Road** and right to the center of town. Two hundred meters before the Empire Cinema, the street to the right leads under the railroad tracks to **Russel Chowk,** the center of the city. A fork to the right just beyond the underpass passes the State Park of India on its way to Collectorate Rd. From Russel Chowk, the main drag heads north to the bazaars over the **Navdra Bridge,** while another leads West, past the museum, the temple stand for the Marble Rocks, and a bridge to the bus station.

PRACTICAL INFORMATION

Tourist Office: MPTDC, inside the railway station (tel. 322111). The extremely helpful Mr. Shukla makes reservations at MPTDC facilities at Kanha and Bardavgarh, books tours to the Marble Rocks, and fields general questions while his apathetic supervisor looks on superciliously. In theory, a tour leaves daily at 4pm for the Marble Rocks (Rs.50 including shacks but not the boat ride) but the requisite 6-person minimum often fails to materialize. In season, bookings for accommodations in parks should be made at least 72hr. in advance from this or any other MPTDC office; 100% payment required. Open daily 9am-6pm.

Telephones: No convenient telephone office but STD/ISD booths everywhere.

Currency Exchange: State Bank of India, opposite Hotel Rishi Regency, near the railway underpass (tel. 322259). The international banking division lives upstairs, past murals of peaceful alpine scenes. Open Mon.-Fri. 10:30am-2:30pm.

Trains: The railway station is a Rs.5 rickshaw ride to the east of Russel Chowk (tel. 320378, 131 1132). The A/C computerized reservation office, to the left of the main building is open Mon.-Sat. 8am-2pm and 2:15-8pm, Sun. 8am-2pm. Window number 3 serves tourists. To: Umaria (for Bandhavgarh National Park; *Narmada Exp.* 8233, 6:30am); Delhi (*Gondwana Exp.* 2411, 3pm, Rs.159/640 for 2nd/1st class); for Bhopal (*Narmada Exp.* 8234, 10:15pm, Rs.76/311 for 2nd/1st class); Varanasi (*Mehanagri Exp.* 1093, 4:35pm, Rs.104/4264); Satna (for Khajuraho; *Pawan Exp.* 4257, 4:10am, *Howrah Mail* 3004, 2:05pm, Rs.48/196); Patna (*Patna Exp.* 5213/3418, 3:45pm, Rs.135/558 for 2nd/1st class); Jalgaon (for Ajanta Caves; *Ajanta Exp.* 3417/5214, 5:30pm, *Mahangawi Exp.* 1094, 7:15am, Rs.687/1186 for 2nd/1st class); Calcutta (*Bombay-Howrah Mail* 3004, 2:05pm).

Buses: the chaotic bus stand (tel. 25147, but no one speaks English) has both public (MPSRTC) and private sections. For any but the short regional trips, shop around for the comfiest private service—or better yet, take the train. For Kanha National Park go to Kisli (7 or 11am, Rs.40) or Mukki (9am, Rs.50); for Bandhavgarh take a bus in the direction of Satna and change at Katui, or take the train to Umaria and bus on from there. (4 per day, 8am-7pm, 1hr., Rs.10). To Khajuraho (9am, 10hr., Rs.75).

Local Transportation: Unmetered **auto-rickshaws,** although **tempos** do run from the museum to the White Rocks for Rs.8. The town is manageable on **foot.**

Pharmacy: 24-hr. pharmacy at Medical College.

Hospital: Medical College, Nagpur Rd. (tel. 22117, emergency 321650), south of the bus stand.

Police: Collectorate Rd., Civil Lines (tel. 320400). Near the High Court.

Post Office: GPO, Residency Rd. Out of the station, turn left on Station Rd. and then right on the next main road. The GPO is about 500m down on the left. *Poste Restante* languishes in the cupboard behind counter 6. Open Mon.-Sat. 10am-6pm.

Postal Code: 482001.

Telephone Code: 0761.

ACCOMMODATIONS

Anywhere decent slaps on 15-20% tax—check to discover what the total price will be. Most places offer 24-hr. checkout.

Hotel Natraj, (tel. 310931) near Karamchand Chowk. Heading north (away from Russel Chowk), cross the Navdra bridge and take the first major right; it's on the left, just past the Indian Coffee House on the opposite side. Rooms with attached baths feature TVs and air-coolers, dirty curtains, and hand-held showers. Singles Rs.70, with bath Rs.95. Doubles Rs.95, with bath Rs.150.

Hotel Vikram, (tel. 323566, 324566), Station Rd. Exit the station from the rear, over the bridge past platform 4. It's on the right of the alley straight in front, about 200 meters down. The deluxe rooms are spacious digs with TVs, phones, and basins set in counters. Even the green carpets and floral curtains of the super deluxe rooms cannot compete with the mirrored ceiling and padded corduroy medallions of the faintly kinky-looking lobby. Singles Rs.138, super-deluxe Rs.180. Doubles Rs.161, super-deluxe Rs.210.

Hotel Utsav, Surya Commercial Complex, Russel Chowk (tel. 26038, 23538). Economy rooms have all amenities. Singles Rs.192. Doubles Rs.240.

Hotel Swayau, opposite Jyoti Talkies, Navdra Bridge (tel. 325377, 325659) In a noisy part of town, around a noisy atrium. Rooms have attached baths and TVs. Singles Rs.50. Doubles Rs.80.

FOOD

Indian Coffee House, Malaviya Marg, near Karamchand Chowk, opposite Hotel Natraj. The whole chain is headquartered in Jabalpur, but this place looks more like a club bar than a flagship fastfood joint—except for the pink trim. The usual *dosas* and *utthapams* (Rs.9.50) as well as other snacks and great, unsugared coffee (Rs.3). Open daily 7am-9:30pm.

Satyam Shivam Sundarum Restaurant, next to Jyoti Talkies, near Navdra Bridge. (tel. 21130) Up the blue stairs to the left of the building. The special *thali* makes a great, filling lunch (Rs.25), while the four huge oval paintings on the ceiling somewhere in the liminal zone between Raphael and the illustrations to an Enid Blyton book constitute a feast for the eyes. Open daily 9am-11pm.

Avfar Restaurant and Sidharth Bar, Dr. Barat Rd., near Russel Chowk, (tel. 32420). About 100m down the road immediately to the left of Hotel Utsav. Perhaps Jabalpur's fanciest restaurant, the prices factor in a heady surcharge for overhead expenses like A/C. Rs.40 buys an order of veg. hardi or *paneer makhani*, while mutton *sag wallah and* chicken Mughlai retail at Rs.50. The drinks menu features beers at Rs.60. Open daily 10am-12:30am.

SIGHTS

On the road from Russell Chowk to the bus stand sits the local museum (open Tues.-Sun. 10am-5pm) which houses temple sculpture from the region. About 20km from the city, the Narmada River passes through the white-cliffed gorge so beloved by the MPTDC. For Rs.5 per person, you can view the rocks from a rowboat. These White Rocks receive full illumination by night to maximize tourist viewing hours. On the way, tempos (Rs.8) pass the old grand fortress of Madan Mahal.

▓ Kanha National Park

Kanha has a counterintuitive history. The same Brits who cantered across the continent with their rifles driving game to the brink of extinction set aside Kanha as a hunting preserve. This doubtless saved it from the encroaches of local population until Kanha became a wildlife reserve in 1933 (hunting continued until 1955). The result is nearly 2000 square kilometers of bona fide *Jungle Book* jungle—the source of Rudyard Kipling's inspiration. Many tourists make the arduous 175-km trip from Jabalpur with visions of Mowgli and Baloo dancing in their heads. They are not far off—with over 100 tigers as well as leopards, deer, sambar, wild boar, bears, pythons, and porcupines, there are enough animals for everyone to run with. Although the tiger population is thought to be declining again due to poaching, your chances of seeing one here are better than anywhere else in India. For more information, see **Project Tiger,** p. 178.

Buses for Kanha National Park depart from Jabalpur to Kisli (7 or 11am, Rs.40) or Mukki (9am, Rs.50). For more information, see **Jabalpur: Practical Information,** p. 245. The park has two main **gates**—at **Kisli** in the northwest and **Mukki** in the center on the western side. Both have visitor centers run with the assistance of the U.S. National Park Service, as does Kanha village in the middle of the park's core area. In addition to their displays, they sell brochures and postcards and show films. (Open daily 7-10:30am and 4-6pm.) The park itself is open only for morning and evening excursions from November 1st to June 30th; it closes completely during the monsoon months. Each entry costs Rs.2 per person and Rs.10 per vehicle. Except for the **MPTDC hotels,** all accommodations are outside the park concentrated at Khatia near Kisli. The MPTDC operates Baghira Log Huts (Singles Rs.400. Doubles Rs.450) and a Tourist Hostel (dorm beds with full board Rs.160) near Kisli and the Kanha Safari Lodge (Singles Rs.300. Doubles Rs.450) near Mukki. For information or reservations for these hotels, contact one of the MPTDC offices in major Madhya Pradesh cities or Bombay, Calcutta, or Delhi. The head office is in Bhopal (tel. (0755) 554340). Book MPTDC hotel rooms in advance at high-season. The MPTDC hotels also function as a staging point for **jeep trips** into the park. Consult the managers for a seat in one of the six-man vehicles. The rate usually works out to about Rs.10 per kilometers, or about Rs.400 for a whole session between six. Book these berths as soon as you arrive, since they are understandably popular as the only means of visiting the park. Elephant safaris have been discontinued and pedestrian excursions to pet the tigers are not allowed.

▓ Khajuraho

The tiny village of Khajuraho in northern Madhya Pradesh contains some of India's most beautiful temples. Medieval craftsmen fit together these classic examples of North Indian medieval temple architecture, out of pink-and-yellow sandstone and draped them with inspired sculpture. Stately gods and goddesses, rolling dragons, elephants in tumultuous cavalcades, and flirtatious, idealized women have all found their places on these walls. Most of the fanfare here however has focused on one dubious aspect of the sculptures: erotica. Nowhere else in India are so many couples shown prominently copulating in every position and direction; each explicit detail is chipped into the sandstone leaving nothing to the imagination but the question of what might have inspired such a holy peep-show. Visitors come to this town as much for titillation as for art appreciation, and no one cares to hide it. The name "Khajuraho" has now become so linked to debauchery that it graces the labels of a cheap brand of Indian beer.

All of Khajuraho's temples come from a brief burst of creativity between 900 and 1100 AD. The Chandela dynasty, a Rajput clan that claimed to be descended from the moon god, reigned here and sponsored the construction. When Chandela power waned, however, the temples were forgotten. They lay hidden in jungly obscurity for 700 years before the outside world (in the form of the British officer T.S. Burt) stumbled across them in 1838. Of an original 85 temples 25 still stand today.

Tourism has totally transformed this once-normal Indian village, which takes its name from its date palm trees. There are no railways within 100km of Khajuraho, and yet the government has built an airport here. A "new village" consisting entirely of hotels, handicraft shops, and STD/ISD booths has sprung up around the temples. To the locals, tourists are the main attraction, and they're bound to get their share in this boomtown. The year's biggest event in Khajuraho is the Festival of Dance in March, for which the government flies in some of India's best classical dancers to perform in front of the temples.

ORIENTATION

Khajuraho has just one **main road,** running from the airport in the south, past several luxury hotels, to the **Western Group of Temples** in the new village and beyond. Just opposite the police stand, the tourist office, and many cheap hotels and restaurants. From here, **Jain Temple Road** leads east past more hotels to some Jain temples. A fork to the left at the Plaza Hotel leads to the Old Village and several temples in the **Eastern Group.** The bus stand stands on the grandiosely designated **Link Road Number Two,** about a ten-minute walk down the main road toward the airport, and then slightly left (east).

PRACTICAL INFORMATION

Tourist Office: Main Rd., opposite Western Group. (tel. 2047). Hands out photocopied maps and tourist information. Helps arrange sight-seeing with one of its 27 licensed guides (English, French, German, Italian, Japanese, or Spanish) for Rs.200 (up to 4 people) for a half-day, Rs.300 for a full day. Suggests various jeep excursions to nearby waterfalls and wildlife parks. Open Mon.-Fri. 9am-5:30pm and Sat. 9am-1pm. The **MPTDC** at the bus stand only really books its own pricey hotels. Their head office occupies the Chandela Cultural Centre, which is neither central, nor cultural, nor has it anything to do with the Chandelas.

Currency Exchange: State Bank of India, Main Rd., opposite Western Group, changes traveler's checks. Open Mon.-Fri. 10:45am-2:45pm, Sat. 10:45am-12:45pm.

Telephones: Lines are few, but STD/ISD booths are many. Try the one beneath Ristorante Mediterraneo, open daily 8am-10pm.

Airport: Khajuraho Civil Aerodrome, 6km south of the Western Group. Indian Airlines, Main Rd., next door to the Clarks Bundela Hotel (tel. 2035; airport 2036). Open daily 10am-1:15pm and 2-5pm. To: Varanasi (1 per day, 45min., US$54) and Delhi (1 per day, 2hr., US$71) via Agra (45min., US$58). The same flight leaves daily from Delhi (6:25am), Agra (7:25am) and Varanasi (1:25pm) on the way to Khajuraho. It's currently the only flight, and popular, so book in advance.

Buses: Apart from flying, the only way to get to Khajuraho. Frequent departures for the nearest railheads at Satna, Mahoba, and Jhansi. To: Satna (7:30, 8:30, 9:30am, 2:30, and 3:30pm, 14hr., Rs.30 for trains to Varanasi and Jabalpur); Mahoba (9 per day, 7am-7pm, 14hr., Rs.20 for trains to Varanasi); and Jhansi (5:30, 9am, 12:45, 3:15, and 4:45pm, 15hr., Rs.45 for trains to Gwalior, Agra, Delhi, and Bhopal). **MPTC** runs a "luxury" coach (that coordinates with the *Shatabdi Exp.*) leaving Khajuraho at 4pm (Rs.70) and continuing from Jhansi to Gwalior. The 9am Jhansi bus continues to Gwalior and Agra, while the 7:30am Satna bus roves as far as Jabalpur—but trains are preferable. On the way to Khajuraho, the last bus leaves Satna at 3:30pm, from Jhansi at 1:15pm and Mahoba at 5pm.

Local transportation: Bicycles can be rented at hotels or stands in the square for Rs.15 per day. The few **auto-rickshaws** are overpriced. Apart from the Chaturbhuj Temple, everything is manageable on **foot.**

Hospital: next to the police station and bus stand. Houses the 2 **pharmacies.** But it's not very high-tech (it has no telephone) so wait until you get to Jhansi or Satna to get sick.

Police: In the booth opposite the Western Group, or next door to the bus stand (tel. 2032).

Post Office: Opposite bus stand. Open Mon.-Sat. 10am-6pm. **Postal Code:** 471606. **Telephone Code:** 07686.

ACCOMMODATIONS

Prices vary enormously with the season. There is a mini-boom in July and August, but between April and June they should drop, and in December through January and in March (for the dance festival) they rise. At peak times, you should book in advance. Check-out time is noon.

Yogi Lodge, Main Square (tel. 2158). Down a narrow alley by the Terazza Restaurant, on the left side of the square with your back to the Western Group. Simple, clean rooms with bathrooms and air-cooling available. Singles Rs.40 and up. Doubles Rs.50-100. Triples Rs.100 and up. Discount 20% off-season.

Hotel Surya, Jain Temple Rd. (tel. 2145). On the right about 200m from the main road, opposite Ristorante Mediterraneo. This spotless, friendly place offers spartan rooms with squat toilets and brighter, air-cooled rooms with balcony. In season: singles Rs.150, deluxe Rs.250. Doubles Rs.200, deluxe Rs.300. Off-season: singles Rs.100. Deluxe Rs.150. Doubles Rs.125, deluxe Rs.200.

Hotel Jain, Jain Temple Rd. (tel. 2052). Next door to the Surya. This popular spot offers cramped but clean rooms around a central courtyard. Attached restaurant closes in the summer. In season: singles Rs.80, with air-cooling Rs.125. Doubles Rs.100, with air-cooling Rs.150. Discount 20% off-season.

Hotel Lakeside, Main Rd., opposite Shiv Sagar Park, next door to the museum (tel. 2120). Another simple, clean spot with a wide terrace facing the sunset. All showers hand-held. Off-season: dorm beds Rs.30. Singles Rs.80. Doubles with bath Rs.100, with air-cooling Rs.150. Prices increase 20-100% in season.

Hotel Plaza, Jain Temple Rd. (tel. 2373, 2186). Just after the Hanuman Shrine, on the left where the road forks. About a 10-min. walk from The Western Group in a peaceful spot halfway to the Old Village. Much better value than the places in the square, the Plaza offers singles with baths, grubby linen, and hard beds. Off-season: singles Rs.40. Doubles Rs.60. In season: singles Rs.60. Doubles Rs.80.

FOOD

Ristorante Mediterraneo, Jain Temple Rd. (tel. 2340, 4255, 2341). On the left, opposite Hotel Surya, 200m from Main Rd. About 1000km from the nearest source of mozzarella, the Mediterraneo beats the odds. The *fettucini alla malanzana* (Rs.55) tastes surprisingly like the real thing, not just because of the fork and spoon. Pizzas, pasta Rs.46 and up. Open daily 7:30am-10pm.

Lovely Restaurant, Main Rd., next to the Western Group. This clean, bare *dhaba* offers good-value *thalis* at Rs.10-20 for varying degrees of grandeur. Veg. dishes Rs.8-20. Snacks and sandwiches Rs.10-20. Open daily 7am-10pm.

Raja Café Swiss Restaurant, Main Rd. In a leafy courtyard directly opposite The Western Temple Group. The Swiss sisters who run the Raja not only proffer *rosti* (Rs.30) and pancakes with bechamel (Rs.40-65), but also will exchange temple ash-trays for anything imported! They also pack lunches (Rs.40-55) and arrange tours to treehouses. Open daily 8am-10pm.

Safari Restaurant, Jain Temple Rd. On the left 20m from the intersection with the Main Rd. By late June 1996, a picture of Netanyahu already jostled with the various flags and graffiti on the pink walls. But they mix no politics with their no-nonsense breakfasts of pancakes (Rs.25), banana porridge (Rs.15), cornflakes (Rs.15), or omelettes (Rs.10-18). Also standard Indian (Rs.20-40), Chinese (Rs.20-60), Italian (Rs.30-45) and Continental (Rs.35-40). Open daily 6am-10pm.

SIGHTS

The morning is the best time of day to make your tour of Khajuraho's temples. Not only is the morning the coolest and quietest time, but almost all of Khajuraho's temples face east. The morning light reveals sculptures that are hard to see later on. By convention there are three "groups" of temples at Khajuraho, some more cohesive than others.

Western Group of Temples

The western temples are the easiest to find since the new tourist-oriented village has grown up across the street from them. They contain the best of the bunch. The Archaeological Survey of India has mercifully built a fence to enclose most of the group and charges Rs.0.50 admission; above all this brings protection from unwanted guides. These magnificent temples can be enjoyed in peace.

According to the custom of *pradakshina* you should walk around the whole group clockwise, and circumambulate each temple the same way. The first stop on your *pradakshina* of the fenced-in temples is the least impressive: the Lakshmi Temple, a small shrine that 19th-century repairs left with a jagged cement roof. Next door, the open-air **Varaha Mandap,** built for Vishnu's boar incarnation, offers a more promising beginning. The huge sandstone boar is so well-polished that it shines like glazed porcelain, and it is blanketed with hundreds of tiny gods and goddesses. The shrine dates from the 10th century AD.

The **Lakshmana Temple,** across from the Lakshmi and Varaha temples, is also no disappointment. Dating from 941 AD, it is one of the largest of Khajuraho's temples and one of the most famous. A trip around the base of the temple reveals a stream of carvings of a military procession which flourishes here and there into bizarre erotica. Soldiers get into somewhat unprofessional relationships with their steeds, while lusty women leaven the martial monotony. The temple itself has four halls leading up to its *shikhara,* and subsidiary shrines at the four corners of its platform. A band of hulking elephants in the stonework supports the temple, and the higher carvings have plenty of sex and many scantily-clad women. High up on the west side one figure arches her back away from the viewer, her clothes dripping wet as she leaves her bath. Two-thirds of the way around clockwise, a winsome, limber maiden picks a thorn from her foot in a fine example of a common Khajuraho theme. The interior of the temple has columns as if an audience hall for the presiding Vishnu. There's a passage for circumambulation of the inner sanctum.

Straight ahead at the far end of the park, three temples stand together on the same plinth. The **Kandariya Mahadev Temple** on the left with its 31-meter *shikhara* is the tallest temple in Khajuraho and the most architecturally perfect. Rows of ornamental pots squiggle down over the perforated stone, while the lower walls are endlessly indented, projected, articulated, refracted, and retracted to create an intricate 3-D stage for sculpture. On the south side, one of Khajuraho's most contorted yet unstoppable sex scenes delights many gawkers. However, the complexity of these kinky calisthenics pales in comparison with the orchestration of the temple's overall design. Circular *amlakas* sit like spinning gears atop square mini-*shikharas,* and lower down, angular pieces form lids to set off the human figures. Staggered stories of sculptures appear to climb all the way to the top. The Kandariya Temple's beauty is heightened because it hasn't blackened with age as the other temples have. Over the doorway is a stone garland of flowers, and in the sanctum is a *linga.* This temple was built between 1025 and 1050, marking the zenith of Chandela patronage.

Next to the Kandariya Temple on the same platform is the **Mahadev Shrine,** with no sacred image, but only a statue of a lion grappling with a human figure of indeterminate gender. It has no religious significance, so it is thought to be a Chandela symbol. The same pair of figures can be found all over Khajuraho. On the other side of the Mahadev Shrine is the **Devi Jagadami Temple.** This temple is smaller than the Lakshmana and Kandariya temples, but it has good sculpture, notably its directional guardians, which are stationed between boldly flirting women and delicate erotic scenes. The image inside is of Kali, but this was once a Vishnu temple, as the sculptures of Vishnu all over the outside and inside attest.

The overall shape of the **Chitragupta Temple** is identical to that of Jagadami, but this is Khajuraho's only temple to Surya, the sun god. A small band of processions runs low around the temple, and higher up are many large amorous couples, but much of the wall and roof are broken and have been repaired with concrete. Most of the statues inside the temple have their heads bashed off, but the main image of Surya, driving his chariot across the sky, is missing only its arms.

Continuing around the circuit you should next hit the small and damaged Parvati Temple. It is overshadowed by the more spectacular **Vishvanath Temple** next to it, a large Shiva temple dated to 1002 by the inscription inside. Notice the elephant guardians as you approach the stairs to the temple: the *mahout* on the right side has fallen asleep. The erotic sculptures on the Vishvanath Temple are perhaps the best of all: whole dramatic scenes appear in which the couples' attendants also get caught up in the action. There are fascinating sculptures of posing women here—look for the one on the south side twisting her hair to dry, and the one on the ceiling inside holding a tiny baby. The Vishvanath Temple originally had a shrine at each corner of its plinth, like the Lakshmana Temple, but only two remain. This loss is amply compensated for by the **Nandi Mandap** in front of the temple, an open shrine where Shiva's bull Nandi sits and looks into the temple. The serene image of Nandi has been burnished and shines much like Varaha in the Varaha Mandap. The whitewashed temple on the way back to the enclosure gate is a recent construction and not of much interest.

The two members of the western group that stray outside the fence are older and noticeably different from the others. Just over the fence from the Lakshmana Temple is the **Matangeshvar Temple.** Built around 900-925 AD, it is still in use unlike Khajuraho's other temples. More people come here to worship than to look at the architecture. It is a rather plain temple, with only thin stripes of sculpture, but it has a 2.5 meter *linga* inside which sits on a huge *pitha* platform that you must circle before climbing on it.

Following the main road south from the square one comes to the Shiv Sagar tank, a small "lake" used for bathing and laundry, and fenced off apparently to keep out cows. Along the south side of it a tree-lined path leads off the main road and out to the temple of **Chausat Yoginis** (Sixty-Four Goddesses). The high building is made of crudely cut blocks of granite, piled together like sandbags. Around the top is a gallery of empty shrines—there were once 64 of these little windows, but now only 35 are left. The Chandelas used this temple for worship early in their reign; it is Khajuraho's oldest, dating from the 9th century.

Across the street from the western group enclosure, the **Archaeological Museum** houses sculptures separated from their temples. A large dancing Ganesh undulates at the entrance, but perhaps the most interesting piece is in the center of the "Miscellaneous Gallery" on the right. A stout king and queen sit together making an offering; this is possibly a portrait of the sculptor's Chandela patrons. Also note the unfinished amorous couple whose small noses have been left stuck together in a gooey thread. Open Sat.-Thurs. 10am-5pm. Admission with same ticket—same day only—from western group of temples.

Eastern Group of Temples

The eastern group is scattered in and around Khajuraho village. On the way there you will come across a **Hanuman Shrine** on the left of Jain Temple Rd. The large monkey image is gooped with orange *sindur,* and is one of Khajuraho's oldest sculptures, dating from the 9th century.

Crossing the bypass road and entering Khajuraho village, the path veers to the left along the side of a seasonal pond called the Khajur Sagar. Not far along it on the left is the small **Brahma Temple,** misnamed by 19th century art historians. A four-faced Shiva *linga* sits in the sanctuary and Vishnu is carved on the lintel above the door. The **Vamana Temple** is at the end of this lakeside path. It is as large as some of the western temples, but distinguished by its single, non-multiplying *shikhara.* By the time this temple was built, between 1050 and 1075, Khajuraho's sculptors seem to have toned down their erotic fantasies. The outer porch has collapsed, giving the temple an appearance that often gets described as "stunted," which seems only fitting since Vamana was Vishnu's incarnation as a dwarf.

The **Javari Temple** stands in the nearby fields of Khajuraho village. This small and slim temple has had some repairs done to it, but it still has good sculpture. A stone flower garland spans the entrance just as in the Kandariya Temple. Continuing through the center of the village you'll reach the Ghantai Temple. Some round columns and a roof are all that's left. The temple is named for the bell shapes cut into the columns.

A section of the eastern group consists of Jain temples, walled into a Jain monastery complex on the far side of Khajuraho village. The old temples here are mixed in with new ones, and this variety is embodied in the **Shantinath Temple,** which is recent but has heavy pillars and doorways taken from old temples. The inside has a collection of photographs and posters of Jain pilgrimage sites.

Over to the left of the Shantinath Temple is the best of the Jain temples, the **Parsvanath Temple.** Architecturally it's noted for its simple plan (there are no balconies) and the small shrine at the back. The sculptures on the outside include just about every Hindu deity, in addition to Jain *tirthankaras,* so it's thought this was once a Hindu temple. Some of the most famous posing women in Khajuraho are here, including one putting on ankle-bells and another using eye make-up. On the other side of a big mango tree is the **Adinath Temple,** whose porch has been reconstructed with concrete. The temple has flexible female figures. Both temples have shiny black images of their respective *tirthankaras.*

Outside the Jain temple complex is the small and uninteresting **Jain Museum,** which has more Hindu and Jain sculptures including all 24 *tirthankaras.* (Open daily 7am-6pm; admission Sat.-Thurs. Rs.1., free on Fri.)

Southern Group of Temples

The southern group isn't really a group at all, just two temples further from one another than from the other groups. A paved road off to the right from the Jain Temple Rd. marked "Dhulade" leads to the **Duladeo Temple.** This temple's *mahamandapa* room has an elaborate star shape, and is wide with a great rotunda ceiling. The top of the *shikhara* has been broken and the blocks used to repair it give an idea of

NORTH INDIA

Sex in Khajuraho

I found in the ruins of Khajrao seven large Diwallas, or Hindoo temples, most beautifully and exquisitely carved as to workmanship, but the sculptor had at times allowed his subject to grow rather warmer than there was any absolute necessity for his doing; indeed, some of the sculptures here were extremely indecent and offensive...

—T. S. Burt, 1838.

Ever since a Victorian officer was guided to Khajuraho, art historians and religious scholars have wracked their brains to figure out why so much sex would be carved onto the walls of temples. Some have suggested that the sculptures were used for sex education or for a study of the art of lovemaking, just like the small copies of the *Kama Sutra* sold by temple touts in the streets of Khajuraho today. Or perhaps they were offerings to voyeuristic gods, especially Indra, the lord of lightning, who had to be entertained lest he destroy the temples.

A more recent theory gives a deeper significance to the sculptures and seems a bit more plausible. In the new explanation, sexual intercourse is symbolic here of male and female elements in the universe uniting to make the world go round. Such a view of the cosmos was certainly held by Tantric cults that may have used the temples for ritualized sex. More mainstream Hinduism has a popular story that is built on the same theme, however: the marriage of Shiva and Parvati. Much of the sculpture in Khajuraho can be read as part of this wedding myth. The posing women, who seem to have been caught unawares looking in the mirror or pulling up their pants, have stopped whatever they were doing in order to watch the wedding procession pass through the street. All the other gods are here as guests. And of course, finally, the wedding is consummated—in a great lovemaking session that lasts 1000 god years.

Of course not all the sculptures fit into the story, and not even all the erotic scenes are depictions of Shiva and Parvati. The main theme has clearly spun many interpretations and side stories. Ultimately, the sculptures are the work of the sculptors themselves, craftsmen who had instructions to follow, surely, but who also found room for a few private jokes. Some of the more bizarre carvings can only be attributed to this. Dwelling on the explicit sexual depictions misses the wood for the trees. The sculptures and architecture at Khajuraho are exuberant, vital, and expressive enough to project a near-sexual energy regardless of the specific scenes shown.

its underlying shape. By 1100 AD, the time this temple was built, sculptors were getting carried away with ornaments and jewelry on their human figures and the sculptures themselves are not very good. The *linga* inside the Duladeo Temple looks scaly because it is carved with innumerable replicas of itself.

Chaturbhuj Temple is a few kilometers' rickshaw or bike ride into the countryside south of Khajuraho. It's a trip best made in the late afternoon, for Chaturbhuj is the only big temple in Khajuraho that faces west. The light shines warmly on its 2.7-meter *dakshinamurti* statue: one stone, but three deities. This huge image is thought to be a combination of Shiva, Vishnu, and Krishna. Archaeologists have been unsure what to make of the symbolism here, so the temple's name means only "four hands." The sculptures around the outside include another interesting hybrid: on the south side, an image of Ardhanarishvara (half-Shiva, half-Parvati), split down the middle.

■ Jhansi

Jhansi exemplifies strip development Indian style. Endless greasy single-story garages fight for frontage along dusty, jarring streets, punctuated by intermittent cinemas and permit rooms. Trucks roar, crowds mill, rickshaws riot, urbanism sprawls, and tempers fray. As enticing as all this sounds, Jhansi draws tourists due to its proximity to Orchha and its status as a railhead for Khajuraho. Although Jhansi is actually located in a strange peninsula of Uttar Pradesh, it is placed here in the Madhya Pradesh chapter for convenience. Schedules may conspire to detain you here, in which case you can while away the hours in rapt contemplation of Maharani Lakshmi Bai's last stare at the city's otherwise uninspiring fort. A celebrated revolutionary, Lakshmi Bai joined the anti-British sepoys in the Mutiny of 1857. As the British recaptured the region, Jhansi was one of the last rebel holdouts. Dressed as a man, her guns blazing, the maharani rode out into battle to meet her final demise.

ORIENTATION AND PRACTICAL INFORMATION

Downtown Jhansi and most tourists who pass through it cover a 5-km span from the station in the west to the bus stand in the east. From about 1km north of the station, **Shivpuri Road** runs straightish all the way across town. **Tempos** for most destinations and rapacious **rickshaws** abound on the main streets while tempos for Orchha (Rs.5) leave directly from the bus stand. **U.P. Tourism's** useless main office (open daily 10am-5pm) lurks in the Veeranganga Hotel—but they have no maps, no phone, and direct all inquiries to their rivals at the MPTDC. The **MPTDC** booth on platform 1 of the railway station (tel. 442622, open daily 6am-11pm) makes reservations on the 11am deluxe bus to Khajuraho (Rs.72). The regular 6am and 7am **buses** (Rs.48) also leave from the railway station, while the 11:45am and 1:15pm services depart from the bus stand. The best train to Delhi (4hr.), Agra (2hr.), and Gwalior (1hr.) is the superfast, all air-conditioned *Shatabdi Express* 2001 at 5:55pm. Take the *Shatabdi* in the other direction to Bhopal (10:47am), and the *Gondwana Express* to Jabalpur (2412, 8:12pm). The **Reservations Office** (on the left as you face the station) opens Mon.-Sat. 8am-2pm, 2:15-8pm and Sun. 8am-2pm. The **State Bank of India** (tel. 440534), Jhokar Bagh Rd. near the Elite Crossing at the center of town changes traveler's checks (open Mon.-Fri. 10am-2pm, Sat. 10am-noon). The **telegraph office** sits opposite Hotel Pujan on the Gwalior Rd. (open Mon.-Sat. 10am-5pm). Mani Chowk houses the district **hospital** (tel. 440521), while the police station is located on the Main Rd. (tel. 440538). **Postal Code:** 284001. **Telephone Code:** 0517.

ACCOMMODATION AND FOOD

Travelers coming to see Orchha are better off staying in Orchha itself—Jhansi doesn't offer many amenities that can't be found in Orchha. **The Prakash Guest House,** Sardarilal Market, Civil Lines (tel. 443133, 441904), just south of the fort, has pleasant mid-range rooms. The air-cooled rooms also feature wall-to-wall carpets and elliptical blue bath tubs. Singles with bath and air-cooling Rs.175, with A/C Rs.275. Doubles Rs.175, with A/C Rs.325. The nearby **Hotel Pujan** (Gwalior Rd., opposite telephone office, tel. 443037) exacts a plunge in comfort for a modest reduction in prices. *Pan*-stained singles Rs.125. Doubles with headless showers Rs.150.

The Prakash Guest House features a restaurant and bar called **Sagar.** Businessmen tuck in to rich chicken dishes (Rs.40) or butter *masala* (Rs.35) in the *de rigeur* dim mirrored interior typical of any classy Indian eatery. Brave souls might sample the *paneer pasendida,* "stuffed with sultans," for Rs.28. Open daily 6:30am-11pm.

SIGHTS

Jhansi Fort has little to offer but a sequence of curiously proportioned equestrian statues and lackluster views. The silver lining is a life-sized model of a battle from the Indian Mutiny in site below the Southern Wall. Local mailmen proved their resemblance to other dashing uniformed types by converting old letterboxes into literally barrel-chested redcoats and rebels. Mailbox cannons appear to have inflicted garishly bleeding mortal wounds on several mailbox Brits, much to the satisfaction of Indian onlookers. If this stirring scene quickens the pulse, the nearby museum will undoubtedly induce catatonia. (Open July-April 15 Tues.-Sun. 10:30am-4:30pm; April 16th-June Tues.-Sun. 7:30am-12:30pm.)

■ Orchha

Dotted through the small town of Orchha, on a loop in the Betwa river 16km from Jhansi, is one of India's most wistful sets of ruins. An abandoned 17th-century city shoots up out of the hills and trees, its tumbledown towers still grasping the rocky terrain assertively amid today's agrarian tranquility. Orchha was capital of the small Bundela kingdom during its heyday in the 16th and 17th centuries, but had to be abandoned in 1783 after too many attacks from Mughals and Marathas. The Bundelas left a landscape filled with palaces and temples, and nothing has interfered with them for 200 years but the forces of nature. But this seems fitting in Orchha—the name means "hidden," and when human rulers gave up the attempt to conceal the city from invaders, nature took up the challenge. Vines hang over cracked walls, and cow dung is strewn over palace floors.

Raja Rudra Pratap Bundela chose Orchha as the site for his capital in 1531 and the Bundelas' fortunes grew as they kept the Mughal Empire at bay. Raja Bir Singh Deo (r. 1605-27), the greatest Bundela king, managed to befriend the emperor Jahangir and even had him visit Orchha. Under Bir Singh Deo the Bundelas expanded to control the whole region of Bundelkhand, which still uses their name. Later Bundela rulers succeeded in annoying the Mughals, however, and the emperor Shah Jahan attacked Orchha, initiating a long, slow decline.

ORIENTATION AND PRACTICAL INFORMATION

Tempos sputter to Orchha from Jhansi (Rs.5) and from the intersection of the **Orchha Road** with the highway running from Jhansi to Khajuraho. They deposit their passengers just to the south of the village's only **crossroads.** South beyond the bus and tempo stand lie the pricey MPTDC Betwa Cottages and the royal cenotaphs along the banks of the **Betwa River.** The right-hand (eastern) crossroad leads past the **Post Office** and some fruit and *chai* stalls to the bridge to the main palace complex. Within lurk the best-preserved sights, the MPTDC's Sheesh Mahal Hotel and its Marsarovar Hotel, more stalls, the Chaturbhuj and Ram Raja temples, and the Palki Mahal Hotel on the way to the Lakshminarayan Temple at the western edge. **Police:** tel. 622 (works only within the village). There are no STD/ISD **telephone** services in Orchha, no telephone numbers that work from out of the village, no long-distance transport, no alcohol, no hospital or pharmacy, no tourist office, and no need to worry, since all these omissions provide a justification for Jhansi's existence.

ACCOMMODATIONS AND FOOD

The MPTDC has converted an 18th-century palace in the middle of Orchha's ruins into the moderately priced **Sheesh Mahal Hotel.** Although the rush-matting carpets and the insect and rodent activity hardly justify the price, the gorgeous peaceful setting and former palace cachet certainly do. Their restaurant, open to guests and non-guests, features the standard MPTDC menu of Indian dishes (Rs.15-20), mutton curry (Rs.30), and Continental staples like fish and chips (Rs.32), as well as breakfast and snacks. (Open daily 7am-10pm.) Singles with bath Rs.100. Doubles with bath Rs.250. Try to book at an MPTDC office up to a month in advance.

The local SADA runs the two budget hotels: the **Palki Mahal** inside the Phool Bagh Palace (next door to the Ram Raja temple) combines dorm beds (Rs.25) with history; while the **Mansarovar** by the crossroads mixes threadbare sheets with banal modernity. Singles Rs.50. Doubles Rs.75.

SIGHTS

The ruins of Orchha are scattered just about everywhere around this bend in the Betwa, and they spill across from the main "island" to the modern town and beyond. Nothing has happened in the last 200 years to clear them away, so many old buildings still linger all over the landscape, poked by trees and unsure of their purpose. There are many more slumping towers and gateways—unnamed landmarks. Orchha really is a whole deserted city.

Hotel Sheesh Mahal offers a **walkman tour** for Rs.25 with Rs.500 deposit that takes up to two hours (depending on your propensity to fast-forward) and covers the three main palaces. Although the voiceovers frequently descend into hackneyed "picture-the-scene" sequences, complete with cheap sound effects, it's quite informative about Orchha's history.

The two biggest palaces face each other across a quadrangle which has for a third side the whitewashed palace of the Sheesh Mahal Hotel. The **Raj Mahal,** on the left side as you face the hotel, is the same building that looks like a perforated concrete curtain from the town across the river. It's one of the earlier buildings in Orchha, begun by Rudra Pratap, the first Bundela here. This was the king's usual residence and has a room for his private audiences as well as several chambers for his harem. The building is quite blocky but some of the ceilings inside are painted with botanical patterns and mythical scenes. The top windows offer a good view of the town.

The steps to the right of the Raj Mahal take you down to the public audience hall, after which the path veers down and to the right through numerous ruins. You'll pass an old tree with roots oozing from its branches and a few misplaced leaning walls. The next complete palace is the **Rai Praveen Mahal,** which was built for Raja Indramani's favorite dancing concubine. This palace was intended to be level with the treetops in the Anand Mahal gardens behind it, which can be viewed from the second floor, each shrub sticking out of its octagonal berth in the concrete.

Continuing along the same path that brought you to the Rai Praveen Mahal will take you to a Royal Gate. Walk through the arch and head up the hill to the right (you'll pass the camel stables) and you should be able to enter the main door of the **Jahangir Mahal** palace. (If the door is locked try scrambling around the stone apron to the left of the building to the entrance opposite the Raj Mahal; the less game will have to retrace their steps all the way.) Two happy concrete elephants ring bells at the outer entrance to welcome Emperor Jahangir on his visit to Orchha in 1606. The Bundelas built a better palace for their imperial guest than they ever did for themselves. The Jahangir Mahal is light and airy, filled with balconies, walkways, and railings. Traces of Islamic style are visible in the stone screens and decorated domes; the Bundelas evidently aimed to please. The view to the east from the third-floor balconies are Orchha's best: the Betwa river can be seen curling past all the little palaces, and it is easy to get an overall sense of the area.

The north end of Orchha's island is reached by turning left after passing through the Royal Gate, and passing through another archway in a wall. This is a good place to fight back the thornbushes and explore—it's dotted with old temples that have been largely neglected and are now besieged by small wheat farms. People dip into the ancient wells for their drinking water here and in some cases the temples have become toolsheds and kitchens.

An arching granite bridge over a small stream takes you back to the town of Orchha. The best Bundela temples are in the town, and the two most prominent ones have an interconnected history: the devout Raja Madhukar Shah carried an image of Lord Rama all the way to Orchha from Rama's hometown, Ayodhya. He meant to install it in the **Chhaturbhuj Temple,** but first he put it down in his own palace, where it refused to move. The palace had to become the **Ram Raja Temple,** where, in keeping with the setting, Rama is worshiped in his role as a king. Ram Raja is now a popular temple, and it is painted pink and yellow and overlooks a cobbled square. The Chhaturbhuj Temple however is defunct, and is left with a great arching assembly hall and several large spires. Spiral staircases at each corner of the cross-shaped floorplan lead to high lookout points.

The **Lakshminarayan Temple** is a short walk west of the town atop a hill. Its location seems like the place for a fort, and the temple is built like a fort too, with four high walls and turrets at the corners. The best painted ceilings in Orchha are inside the temple—some of them date from the 19th century, including one fabulous scene of uniformed British soldiers swarming around an Indian fort.

The boxlike Bundela **royal chhattris** (cenotaphs) cluster on the bank of the Betwa south of town. Even though the Bundelas burned their dead, they borrowed the Mughal custom of mausoleum-building. The *chhattris'* river-bank location is peaceful. The other side of the river is covered with forest, and from there you can see the *chhattris* reflected in the water.

■ Gwalior

The largest city in northern Madhya Pradesh with a population of 800,000, Gwalior has been known for centuries for its fort, a floating hilltop bastion which the first Mughal emperor, Babur, called "the pearl amongst the fortresses of Hind." Whole genealogies of conquerors brought their business here, from Rajputs and Marathas through the Mughals and the British to the Scindia family. During the Raj, the Maharaja of Gwalior earned one of the five 21-gun salutes accorded to Indian potentates by the British thanks to his loyal behavior during the Mutiny, a stark contrast with nearby Jhansi's Maharani Lakshmi Bai. The Scindia royal family is still the focus of civic pride in the city of Gwalior: their nineteenth-century temple to tastelessness the Jai Vilas Palace, preserves a glimpse into history almost as fascinating as the fort, while helping to explain why Scindias still dominate local politics. Gwalior's business holiday is Tuesday.

ORIENTATION

Gwalior wraps itself in a "U" shape around the feet of the **fort** in its center. This stronghold, a hill with a wall crinkling around its top, is Gwalior's most obvious landmark. The **Old Town** is to the east of the fort, the **Morar** area is to the southeast, and the **Lashkar** area is in the southwest. Lashkar is the heart of the modern city of Gwalior, including its fearsome bazaar area and its rather pleasant **Bada (Jiyaji) Chowk** where the GPO and Bank of India are located. Gwalior is quite spread out and it can take a while to get around. **Maharani Lakshmi Bai (MLB) Road** is a sure bet to get you across town, however; it squiggles from northeast, near the station, to Lashkar in the southwest.

PRACTICAL INFORMATION

Tourist Office: MPTDC, Hotel Tansen, Gandhi Rd., near bus stand (tel. 340370, 342606). No real office, but the hotel receptionists will offer to book city tours which take in the fort, museum, sun temple, and tombs of Tansen and Mohammed Gaus (daily 9am, 5hr., Rs.40) or the fort's sound and light show (Sept. 15th-July 1st, daily 7:30pm, Rs.35) as a consolation prize for the lack of maps. Open Mon.-Sat. 10am-5pm.

Currency Exchange: State Bank of India, Bada Chowk. 1st fl., main building. Open Mon.-Fri. 10:30am-2:30pm, Sat. 10:30am-12:30pm.

Airport: Located about 10km from the city on the Bhind Rd., past the station (tel. 368272). **Indian Airlines** (tel. 326872), MLB Rd. before the station flyover. Open Mon.-Sat.10am-5pm. Flights on Mon., Tues., and Thurs. to: Delhi (1 per day, 1hr., US$47); Bhopal (1 per day, 1hr., US$54); Indore (1 per day, 2hr., US$75); and Bombay (1 per day, 3½hr., US$121).

Trains: Railway Station, MLB Rd., Morar (tel. 131, 341344, 340306). The reservation office is at the far left as you face the building (Open Mon.-Sat. 8am-8pm, Sun. 8am-2pm). To: Delhi (*Shatabdi Exp.* 2001, 7pm, 3½hr., Rs.366 for A/C chair car); Agra (*Shatabdi Exp.* 2001, 7pm, 1hr.); Bhopal (*Shatabdi Exp.* 2002, 9:33am, 4hr., Rs.419 for A/C chair car); Jhansi (*Shatabdi Exp.* 2002, 9:33am, 1hr.) ; Bombay (*Punjab Mail* 1038, 11:10am, 10hr., Rs.235/929 for 2nd/1st class).

Buses: The State bus stand is near the railway station off MLB Rd. (tel. 340192), while the private bus stand inhabits the wilds of Lashkar, not too far from Bada Chowk. From the state bus stand to: Jhansi (5 per day, 3hr.); Agra (5 per day, 3hr.); Delhi, Khajuraho (1 per day, 9hr.); and Bhopal.

Local Transportation: Tempos cruise down MLB Rd. from one side of town to the other. Hail them, and always check before you climb in, because destinations and rates vary slightly (Rs.2). There are also **auto-rickshaws** and **taxis.**
Pharmacy: Kasturba Medical Stores, at J.A. Hospital. Open 24hr.
Hospital: J.A. Hospital, Lakshar (tel. 323950). Open 24hr.
Police: Jayendra Ganj (tel. 26268).
Post Office: GPO, Bada Chowk. Ask the postmaster for *Poste Restante*—he's generally around late on weekday mornings. Otherwise open Mon.-Sat. 8am-8pm, Sun. 10am-6pm. **Postal Code:** 474001.
Telephone Code: 0751.

ACCOMMODATIONS

Hotel India, Station Rd., Morar (tel. 341983). From the station, turn right, then head left at the traffic circle. Since the place is run by the Indian Coffee House chain downstairs, breakfast (or any other meal) is never a problem. Far from the city and sights, however. Beds in 4-bed dorms Rs.60. Huge range of prices for rooms. Doubles with TV and seat toilet Rs.130-170.

Ranjeet Hotel, Nair Sarak (tel. 327138), near Savala Bazaar. Dim, deserted-looking place has central shared bathrooms and a restaurant so dark you can barely read the menu. Unwashed linen in the rooms. Singles Rs.50. Doubles Rs.90.

Hotel Fort View, MLB Rd. (tel. 331586). Views not only of the fort's fearsome walls, but also of the local populace climbing up the fort slopes for their morning *toilette*. In general, the rooms in this mid-range, midtown hotel improve in value as their descriptions (executive, deluxe, etc.) get less grandiose. Regular rooms are losing plaster fast, and sporting the occasional divot in the concrete floor, but are clean and liveable. Regular rooms Rs.170-200.

Regal Hotel, Shinde Ki Arhawari, MLB Rd. (tel. 22599, 331469, 331642). A whole range of rooms, with the best value at the bottom end. The standard doubles, off the pleasant rooftop terrace, have clean shared bathrooms and are one of Gwalior's few good deals. Noisy on busy bar nights. Standard doubles Rs.100.

FOOD

Indian Coffee House, Station Rd., underneath the India Hotel, 2 low-ceilinged pokey rooms attract the same middle-class clientele as always. *Dosas* and *utthapams* (Rs.11) and Rs.3 coffee. Open daily 7am-8pm.

Kwality Restaurant, Deendayal Market, MLB Rd. (tel. 423243, 310907). Chalk up another for the dim, non-descript, air-conditioned chain with a spelling problem. A standard range of north Indian veg. dishes (Rs.18-35), chicken (Rs.30), and mutton (Rs.28). Open daily 11:30am-11pm.

Volge Restaurant, inside Hotel Surya, Tayendra Ganj (tel. 321092). The *dahi-de-la-dahi* of Gwalior society frequent this chandeliered and air-conditioned bastion of the bourgeoisie. Rich, delicious chicken *tikka masala* (Rs.50). The *dal makhari* (Rs.18) swims in *ghee*. Open daily 11am-11pm.

SIGHTS

The Fort

Gwalior's amazing fort, almost 3km long and 1km wide at points, has collected palaces and temples through the ages, and more recently a prestigious boys' school, a TV relay station, and two post offices. Long roads swirl all around the fort, empty save for the occasional cycling young men careening past. The fort is Gwalior at its best, and it yet is so removed from the city, up there on its high plateau, that it doesn't seem like Gwalior at all.

The fort is a delight to behold, not to besiege. It sits 90m above the city on an artificially steepened hill, with 10-meter walls and its own water tanks. Gwalior Fort has been the center of control for this region for longer than history has recorded. According to legend it was built in the first century AD by a king named Suraj, who was cured of leprosy here by a saint named Gwalipa. Out of gratitude Suraj named the fort Gwalior. Later the fort came to be ruled by all of the succeeding dynasties in the region: Rajputs, Delhi Sultans, Mughals, Marathas, and British. The reign of the Tomars, a Rajput clan that resisted the Delhi Sultans for the entire 15th century, is looked upon as a glorious time for the fort. Most recently, since 1886, the fort has belonged to the Scindias, Gwalior's present royal family.

There are two entrances to the fort, the **Gwalior Gate** on the northeast side, adjacent to the Old Town, and the **Urwahi Gate** on the southwest, which is approached through a long gorge. Both have long, steep ramps which must be climbed on foot, although cars and taxis (not auto-rickshaws) can enter through the Urwahi Gate.

It's worth entering at the Gwalior Gate for the view of the Man Mandir Palace's picture-postcard towers above you as you climb. At the base of the hill just inside the Gwalior Gate is the Gujari Mahal Palace, built by Man Singh Tomar for his favorite queen. The sunny courtyard now has an **Archaeological Museum** with a mixed bag of sculptures and paintings from the region. (Open Tues.-Sun. 10am-5pm; admission Rs.2.) There is one priceless piece of Indian art history here in the Salabhanjika miniature, a sculpture of a tree-goddess from Gyraspur. It is usually kept locked up but the curator brings it out for those with a good reason to see it.

The northeastern ramp continues up through a series of archways past Jain and Hindu shrines. Looming overhead are the blue-splotched towers of the **Man Mandir Palace.** As you pass through the Elephant Gate (there was once a big stone elephant here) into the fort itself, Raja Man Singh Tomar's creation on your right becomes livelier, with blue, green, and yellow tiles forming pictures of plants and ducks. Inside the Man Mandir Palace are many small rooms split by lattices carved in the shape of animals and dancers. A flashlight can lead the way down to the dungeon complex, where in the 17th century, the Mughal emperor Aurangzeb had his brother Murad chained up and slowly killed through starvation and intoxication, feeding him nothing but boiled and mashed-up poppies.

Near the Man Mandir Palace is another **museum,** this one run by the Archaeological Survey of India. It's not as impressive as the one at the bottom of the hill, but it is free, and the staff sells cold drinks. (Open Sat.-Thurs. 10am-5pm.) On the other side of the Elephant Gate from the Man Mandir palace are seats where a **sound and light show** is held (English shows daily 7:30pm; admission Rs.10).

To reach the north end of the fort pass through the gate that is to your right as you exit the Man Mandir palace. This area is a barren landscape where ruined palaces and dried-out tanks cling to the edge of the hill. There are four palaces here, two built by the Tomar Rajputs and two by the Mughals. The huge **Jauhar Tank** next to them is remembered for the *jauhar* (mass suicide) of Rajput queens that took place here in 1232 when Sultan Iltutmish of Delhi was about to capture the fort.

Other points of interest in the fort lie down at the south end. About midway along the eastern edge is the **Sas Bahu** pair of temples, whose name means "mother-in-law and daughter-in-law." The Kachhapaghata kings built these Vishnu temples in 1093. The mother-in-law temple's spire has fallen, but its assembly hall, still standing, has a beautiful stack of skewed false stories. The edge of the fort here offers a drab view of the city, although the big brown dome of Muhammad Gaus' tomb is visible. The west side of the fort has better views of the craggy landscape.

Close to the Sas Bahu temples is the tall, white **Bandi Chhor Gurudwara.** It marks the spot where the sixth of the ten Sikh gurus, Hargobind, was imprisoned for two years under Emperor Jahangir. Cloths are provided for you to cover your head before entering the *gurudwara,* where young men sit and chant out Sikh scriptures. This is a well-known Sikh pilgrimage site and there are often Sikhs wandering around the fort.

The **Teli-ka Mandir** (Oilman's Temple) is a tall building, though it doesn't rival the nearby TV mast. Its roof rolls up into a cylinder shape, commonly but incorrectly said to be a South Indian design. In fact this is a very early northern style. The Teli-ka Mandir dates from the 9th century. It was once a Vishnu temple, but when the British occupied the fort in the 19th century they turned it into a soda-water factory. The sculpture on the outside is excellent but eroded. Close to the Teli-ka Mandir is the more-than-Olympic-size **Suraj Tank,** whose drafts, administered by Gwalipa, cured the legendary King Suraj of leprosy.

The southwestern entrance passes through the long Urwahi Gorge, a natural split in the side of the hill. Its walls have been adorned with rows of **Jain sculptures** from the 7th to the 15th centuries. These figures of *tirthankaras* still stand impassively above the road despite the efforts of the Mughal conqueror Babur, who smashed many of their faces and genitals. One statue, an image of Adhinath, is 19m tall. There are more of these carvings on the southeast side of the fort, including one still used as a Jain shrine.

The City

Second only to the fort is the home of the Maharaja Scindia, the **Jai Vilas Palace.** Maharaja Jiyaji Rao Scindia had a British architect put together this great white whale of a complex to impress the Prince of Wales (later Edward VII) on his state visit in 1875. Generations of Scindias filled it with the most outrageous *objets d'art* and kitsch, and now part of it is open as a museum (the rest is still a house). Furniture from Versailles, silly old prints, toys: the decadence goes on, roomful after roomful like reflections in mirrors placed opposite each other, and of course there are plenty of mirrors too. A ceremonial swing used each year to cradle the baby Krishna is made of cut glass from Italy; stuffed tigers fill up the "Natural History Gallery" accompanied by black-and-white photographs of the royal hunting parties that shot them. From the gilded ceiling of the Durbar Hall hang two enormous Belgian chandeliers, each weighing 3.5 tons, and below them is the largest handmade carpet in Asia. Downstairs (down a crystal staircase, that is) the dining table has tracks for a silver toy train that would wheel around brandy and cigars after dinner. A Rolls-Royce waits outside. (Open Tues.-Sun. 10am-5pm; admission Rs.50 for foreigners; be sure to keep your ticket stub for entry to both wings.)

To the east of the fort in the Old Town is the **Mausoleum of Muhammad Gaus,** a Muslim saint who helped the emperor Babur capture Gwalior Fort. The walls of this fine early-Mughal monument are composed of cut-stone screens with entrancingly rhythmic geometric patterns. The **Tomb of Tansen** in the same graveyard evokes a different kind of rhythm: the 16th-century Tansen was one of the greatest musicians in Indian history. A prestigious classical music festival takes place here each November or December. Chewing the leaves of the tamarind tree near the tomb is supposed to make your voice as sweet as Tansen's (although it certainly won't sweeten your palette).

In the Lashkar area, **Bada Square** is one of the most scenic parts of Gwalior. Palm trees and benches are ringed around the Henry VIII-like figure of Maharaja Jiyaji Rao Scindia. The architecture in this busy circle features frilly arches and a clock tower.

Gwalior's newest big thing is its **Sun Temple,** located to the east in the Morar area. Built by the philanthropic Birla family, it is a shabby scaled-down knock-off of the great Sun Temple in Konark, Orissa. Those who've seen the real thing probably won't be impressed with Gwalior's version, which is made of red stone and is sparse in sculpture, though unlike the temple at Konark this one has an intact *shikhara.* Gwalior's Sun Temple has a theme-park atmosphere, and oddly enough, crowds come here to worship Surya, the sun god, who is otherwise just about obsolete. All of the gods on the outside of the temple are labeled in Hindi.

Rajasthan

The exotic state of Rajasthan, southwest of Delhi, is a cornucopia of romantic geography, chivalrous history, and colorful culture. Known as the Land of Kings, Rajasthan was home to the medieval warrior Rajputs, known for their knightly codes of honor, which demanded fights to the death and *jauhar,* or mass suicide (by immolation) of

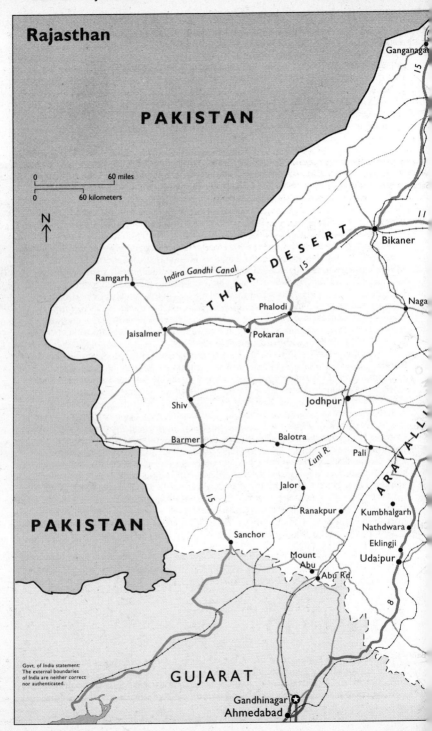

Rajasthan

PAKISTAN

0 _____ 60 miles
0 _____ 60 kilometers

N

PAKISTAN

GUJARAT

THAR DESERT

ARAVALLI

Ganganagar

Bikaner

Naga

Ramgarh

Indira Gandhi Canal

Phalodi

Jaisalmer

Pokaran

Shiv

Jodhpur

Barmer

Balotra

Luni R.

Pali

Jalor

Ranakpur

Kumbhalgarh

Nathdwara

Sanchor

Eklingji

Udaipur

Mount
Abu

Abu Rd.

Govt. of India statement:
The external boundaries
of India are neither correct
nor authenticated.

Gandhinagar
Ahmedabad

15

11

15

15

8

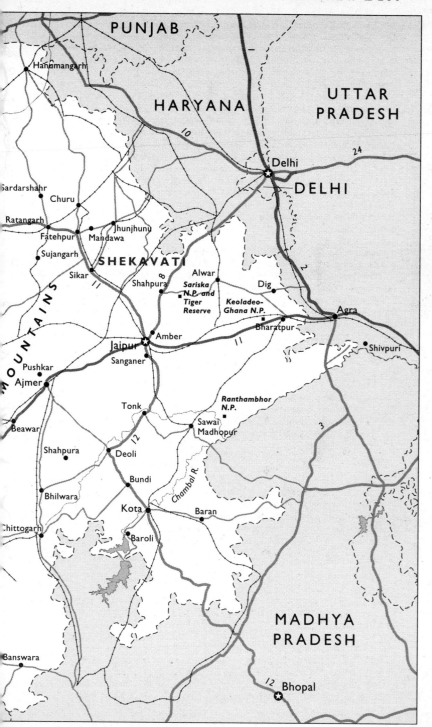

women and children in the face of insurmountable odds. Although these regimens are no longer in practice, the characteristic nobility of the Rajputs is still visible throughout Rajasthan, from the unequivocal pride of traditional village textile artisans to the opulent reserve of the remaining maharaja lines. These qualities proved troublesome to the ruling Rajputs of old, who were incessantly concerned with their own independence and honor to such an extent that Rajasthan devolved into a mess of uncooperative kingdoms that were quickly overthrown by the Mughal Empire. Over the centuries, the Rajputs were resistant to Mughal subjugation, and the Mughals soon discovered that granting them some power in their ruling hierarchy was more effective than punishing battles with such stubbornly honorable foes. As the Mughal Empire declined in the late 1600s, so did the Rajputs' position. They quickly joined in with the new forces in power, the British Raj, and proceeded to enjoy a life of rich indulgence that depleted the wealth of the state while arresting its social and economic development. With Independence, the newly named Rajasthan had to face the real struggles of a developing state. Now, as the state rapidly advances with new technical businesses popping up by the day and public education on the rise, the remnants of those fairytale Rajputs are still to be seen, in the forts, palaces, and temples that fill the state and the turban- and veil-clad townsfolk whose pride and independence are still in force.

Rajasthan can be geographically divided into three regions. In the northeastern and eastern part of the state, rolling plains underlie a combination of rich national parks and cosmopolitan centers such as the famed Jaipur, the state's capital and part of the Delhi-Agra-Jaipur "Golden Triangle" of tourism. To the west, the plains gradually yield to the arid lands of the Thar Desert, whose Saharan dunes and imposing forts place it in the heart of the classic Rajputana of old. To the south, the majestic Aravali Mountains decorate the landscape with verdant valleys and numerous mountain lakes, creating a romantic atmosphere that integrates remarkably with the harsher desert nearby.

■ Jaipur

Rajasthan's prosperous capital, Jaipur, is a city to be lingered over and savored. Although the sights can be hit in three days, don't be surprised if you stay three weeks, trying a bit of the city each day, sampling its easy-going cosmopolitan spirit, enjoying its effortlessly elegant architecture, and being lulled into sweaty afternoon naps by its deliciously dry heat.

To an unusual extent, the story of Jaipur is the story of one man, maharaja Sawai Jai Singh II. By all accounts, Jai Singh possessed rare erudition and ferocious curiosity for the sciences. He had little time for scholarship during the early years of his reign, when his kingdom was threatened by both the Marathas and the Mughals. However, time was on the Maharaja's side—his intelligence won him the Mughal emperor Aurangzeb as an ally, and the might of his Rajput forces dealt crushing blows to the Marathas. By the mid-1720s, Jai Singh was ready to settle down, and he set about designing a city for himself in collaboration with the renowned Vidyadhar Bhatcharya, a Bengali Brahmin. The result of their efforts is the architecturally magnificent walled city of Jaipur.

Jaipur's original layout was based on a 3-by-3 grid of squares and was intended as an earthly microcosm of the Hindu universe. (Speculations in the German press that Jaipur's design is copied from drawings of European cities are groundless.) In laying out Jaipur, Jai Singh and Vidyadhar Bhatcharya made the city not only beautiful, but also functional. The city's walls provided solid defense, and Jaipur's wide sidewalks and streets were designed to allow easy movement of pedestrian traffic. Underground aqueducts were set up to distribute ample drinking water, and the entrances to stores and homes were placed on side streets so the Maharaja's massive royal processions could pass without disturbing the daily habits of Jaipur's residents.

Over the years, inevitable changes to the city occurred. The most striking change came in 1853, when the city painted itself pink in honor of a visit by Prince Albert;

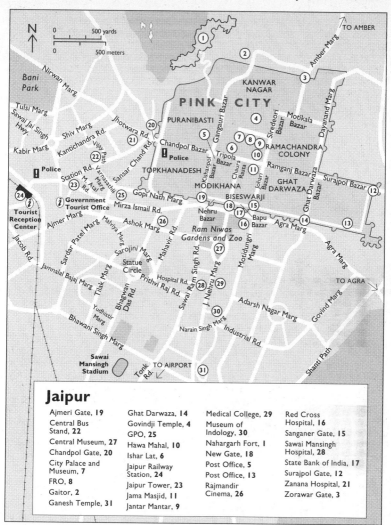

Jaipur

Ajmeri Gate, 19	Ghat Darwaza, 14	Medical College, 29	Red Cross
Central Bus	Govindji Temple, 4	Museum of	Hospital, 16
Stand, 22	GPO, 25	Indology, 30	Sanganer Gate, 15
Central Museum, 27	Hawa Mahal, 10	Nahargarh Fort, 1	Sawai Mansingh
Chandpol Gate, 20	Ishar Lat, 6	New Gate, 18	Hospital, 28
City Palace and	Jaipur Railway	Post Office, 5	State Bank of India, 17
Museum, 7	Station, 24	Post Office, 13	Surajpol Gate, 12
FRO, 8	Jaipur Tower, 23	Rajmandir	Zanana Hospital, 21
Gaitor, 2	Jama Masjid, 11	Cinema, 26	Zorawar Gate, 3
Ganesh Temple, 31	Jantar Mantar, 9		

newsman Stanley Reed dubbed Jaipur the "Pink City," and the name stuck. While modern Jaipur with its population of 1.7 million has sprawled outside the walls of Reed's Pink City, Jaipur's heart and soul remains within this wonderful enclave, replete with extraordinary museums, forts, temples and palaces, dreamt up more than 200 years ago by the visionary Jai Singh.

ORIENTATION

Though Jaipur is a good-sized city, getting around isn't particularly difficult—provided you can keep track of street name changes. The Pink City's wide, straight streets are especially easy to navigate. The west gate of the walled Pink City is **Chand-pol Gate.** The road that runs under it is called **Nirwan Marg** outside the Pink City, but changes names four times before it leaves the city at its easternmost gate, **Surajpol Gate.** From the **railway station,** the center of town is best reached by walking 500m

Warning: Spending even 10 minutes in Jaipur's old city bazaars, visitors are almost inevitably accosted by oh-so-friendly people interested in talking to them about tourism, education, the city, life abroad, and various other subjects. Having thus established themselves as "friends," they offer travelers their hospitality: "You're a guest in my country. The least I can do is invite you to my place for dinner [or drinks, snacks, or lunch]." Nine times out of ten, their "place" is a **jewelry** or **gems** shop. Eventually, travelers are offered the opportunity to carry anywhere from US$500 to US$10,000 worth of jewelry abroad to be handed over to their "overseas partner" (who, despite "evidence" to the contrary, is usually a fictional character). In return, these dealers offer a 100% commission. The rationale is straightforward. Export laws impose a 250% tariff on gems and jewelry. Foreigners with tourist visas are allowed to carry a certain amount of gems and jewelry out of the country. So, by having tourists do their exporting for them at 100% commission, gem dealers save a lot of money. The gem dealers call it "carriering," and insist it's done all the time. The Indian government calls it smuggling, and punishes it with long prison terms. Stay away from these offers. If you're interested in buying gems and jewelry for yourself, try to go with a local so such issues won't come up in the bargaining process.

north along **Railway Station Marg** and making a right onto **Mirza Ismail (M.I.) Marg,** which is Jaipur's main east-west thoroughfare and which becomes **Agra Marg** as it passes the three gates that lead into the heart of the Pink City: **Ajmeri Gate, New Gate,** and **Sanganer Gate.** From Ajmeri Gate, **Kishanpol Bazar** (which becomes **Gangauri Bazar**) leads north towards the edge of the Pink City. From Sanganer Gate, **Johari Bazar** (which becomes **Siredeori Bazar**) runs north for nearly 2km. Just south of New Gate and beyond the **Ram Niwas Gardens, Jawaharlal Nehru Marg** runs south for nearly 2km before changing names. The **Central Bus Station** is on Railway Station Marg to the northeast (left with your back to the station), and Chandpol Gate is 1km away; **Mirza Ismail Road** is a bit more difficult to reach—with your back to the station, make a right and then a quick left. After about 5-10 minutes of walking, make a right onto Sansar Chandra Marg; walk 4-7 minutes and make a left onto Mirza Ismail Marg. Ajmeri Gate is nearly 2km east along Mirza Ismail Marg from where you're standing.

PRACTICAL INFORMATION

Tourist Office: RTDC Tourist Information Bureau, on platform 1 of the railway station (tel. 315714). Provides maps, brochures, books—all the information you'll ever need. Extremely friendly, helpful, English-speaking staff. Open daily 6am-8pm. **Other RTDC Offices** are located on platform 2 of the Sindhi Camp Bus Stand (open Mon.-Sat. 10am-5pm), and in the RTDC-run tourist hotels: Hotel Gangaur, Sansar Chandra Rd. (tel. 371641); Hotel Swagatam, across from the railway station (tel. 310595); Hotel Teej, Bani Park Circle, off station Rd. (tel.374373); Tourist Hotel, off M.I. Rd. near the GPO (tel. 360238). **Government of India Tourist Office,** in Hotel Khasi Kothi (tel. 372200), near M.I. Rd. and Station Rd. intersection. Limited information available. Open Mon.-Fri. 9am-5pm, Sat. 9am-1pm. The monthly **publication** *Jaipur Vision,* available at most bookstores for Rs.20, has useful tourist information.

Tours: RTDC offers a range of **city tours.** These depart from the Tourist Information Bureau at the railway station, and also pick-up at RTDC-run Hotel Gangaur, Hotel Teej, and Tourist Hotel. **Half-day tours** visit the Hawa Mahal, Amber Palace, the Jai Mahal, Gaitor, City Palace and Museum, Jantar Mantar, and assorted craft shops (8am, 11:30am, and 1:30pm, 5hr., Rs.60 plus entrance fees). **Full-day tours** include, in addition to the half-day sights, lunch at Nahargarh Fort, Jaigarh Fort, and the Dolls Museum (9am-6pm, Rs.90 plus entrance fees). **Evening tours** (6-10pm, including veg. dinner) visit Nahargarh Fort (Rs.85) and Chowki Dhani (Rs.160). Arrange all tours through the Tourist Information Bureau at the railway station. Both the RTDC Tourist Information Bureau and the Government of India Tourist

Office can arrange for **private approved guides**: Rs.200 per 1-4 persons, Rs.300 per 5-15 persons, 4hr.; Rs.300 per 1-4 persons, Rs.400 per 5-15 persons, 8hr.; Rs.100 extra for French, German, Italian, Japanese, or Spanish guides.

Budget Travel: Rajasthan Tours, in Rambagh Palace Hotel (tel. 381041). Open daily 9am-6pm. **Tourist Guide Service,** M.I. Rd. (tel. 378377). Open Mon.-Sat. 10am-4:30pm. **Travel Corporation of India,** Jamnal Bajaj Marg (tel. 380050). Open Mon.-Sat. 9am-6pm. **A-1 Tours and Travels,** F-34 Azad Marg, C-Scheme (tel. 383757). Open Mon.-Sat. 9am-6pm, Sun. 9am-noon. **Sita World Travels,** Station Rd. (tel.364104), near Polovictory Cinema. Open daily 9am-5:30pm.

Immigration Office: Rajasthan Police Headquarters, behind Hawa Mahal, through the gates to the City Palace and Museum, on the left. Contact at least 1 week before visa expiration date. Open Mon.-Sat. 10am-5pm. Closed 2nd Sat. of each month.

Currency Exchange: State Bank of India, M.I. Rd. (tel. 380421) near Sanganeri Gate. Currency exchange, traveler's checks. Open Mon.-Fri. 10am-2pm, Sat. 10am-noon. **Bank of Baroda,** Johari Bazar (tel. 563900). Currency exchange, traveler's checks. Open Mon.-Fri. 10am-2pm, Sat. 10am-noon. **State Bank of Bikaner and Jaipur,** opposite the GPO (tel. 372912). Currency exchange, traveler's checks. Open Mon.-Fri. noon-4pm, Sat. noon-2pm.

Thomas Cook: M.I. Rd. in Jaipur Tower, near Station Rd. intersection (tel. 360940). Open Mon.-Sat. 9am-6pm.

Telephones: Central Telegraph Office, in GPO. Open 24hr. Private STD/ISD booths are everywhere. Some offer fax service. Most open daily 6am-11pm. Many hotels have 24-hr. STD/ISD facilities. The railway station has a **fax** booth.

Airport: Sanganer Airport, 15km south of the city (tel. 550222). An airport bus leaves Sindhi Camp Bus Stand every 15 min., Rs.20. A taxi ride costs close to Rs.150. To: Bombay (3-5 per day, 1½-4hr., US$123)); Delhi (3-5 per day, 1hr., US$46); Jodhpur (Mon.-Tues., Thurs., and Sat., 45min., US$54); Udaipur (2-3 per day, 1-2hr., US$54); Ahmedabad (Thurs.-Tues. 1 per day, 50min., US$54). **Air India,** opposite All India Radio on Station Rd. (tel. 368569). Open daily 9am-6pm. **Indian Airlines,** Nehru Place, Tonk Rd. (tel. 514500). **Modiluft,** Ahinsa Circle (tel. 363373), north of Statue Circle. Open daily 10am-6pm.

Trains: Jaipur Railway Station (tel. 131). To: Delhi (*Shatabdi Exp.* 2016, 6pm, 5½hr., Rs.315/630; *Intercity Exp.,* 6:05am, 5½hr., Rs.82/198; *Jammu Taljai,* 4:30pm, 5½hr., Rs.109/409; *Mandor Exp.,* 11:50pm, 5½hr., Rs.109/369; *Shekhavati Exp.* 9734, 6:05pm, 5½hr., Rs.133/421); Bombay (*Superfast Exp.,* 1:50pm, 18hr., Rs.253/750/1095); Jodhpur (*Mandor Exp.* 2461, 2:25am, 5hr., Rs.100/350; *Marwar Exp.,* Wed., Fri., Sun., 5am, 5hr., Rs.70/251; *Intercity Exp.,* 5:30pm, 5hr., Rs.89/214); Udaipur (*Chetak Exp.* 9515, 10:10pm, 11½hr., Rs.114/528; *Garib Nawaz Exp.* 2915, 12:20pm, 11½hr., Rs.120/386); Bikaner (*Bikaner Exp.* 4737, 9:05pm, 9hr., Rs.119/492; *Intercity Exp.* 2468, 2pm, 9hr., Rs.89/243); Agra (*Jodhpur-Howrah Exp.* 2308, 11:15pm, 6½hr., Rs.54/206/465); Ahmedabad (*Delhi Exp.* 9903, 5:20pm, 14hr., Rs.117/433/986); Kota (passenger, 5:15pm, 6hr., Rs.55; fast passenger, 11:25pm, 5½hr., Rs.54/206; *Superfast Exp.,* 1:50pm, 5½hr., Rs.50/79). **Advance Reservation Office,** left of Jaipur Railway Station (tel. 135). Has a tourist quota line and English-speaking staff. Open Mon.-Sat. 8am-8pm, Sun. 8am-2pm.

Buses: Sindhi Camp Central Bus Stand, Station Rd. (tel. 375834). To: Delhi (A/C: 8:30am, noon, 4, 10, and 11:30pm, 5hr., Rs.215; deluxe: 14 per day, 5am-1am, 5hr., Rs.125); Agra (A/C: 7:45am, 5hr., Rs.125; deluxe: 10 per day, 6:30am-midnight, 5hr., Rs.75); Jodhpur (deluxe: 12 per day, 5am-11pm, 7hr., Rs.101); Udaipur (A/C: 10pm, 10hr., Rs.152; deluxe: 10am, 8:30, 9, 10:30pm, and midnight, 10hr., Rs.120); Jaisalmer (deluxe: 10pm, 13hr., Rs.187); Kota (deluxe: 6 per day, 7am-11:30pm, 7hr., Rs.77); Chittorgarh (deluxe: 6 per day, 10am-midnight, 8hr., Rs.91); Abu Road (deluxe: 8pm., 10hr., Rs.157); Mt. Abu (deluxe: 8pm, 10½hr., Rs.157). Private buses depart from the same station. Private bus companies line Station Rd. and Motilal Atal Rd., off M.I. Rd.; private bus arrangements can also be made through most hotels. Private and government bus services combined, there are approximately hourly departures to everywhere.

Local Transportation: Unmetered **auto-rickshaws** and **rickshaws** are the best ways to get around the city. They can be found in especially high concentrations around the bus and railway stations and around major sights. Getting around anywhere within the old city should cost Rs.10 by auto-rickshaw, Rs.5 by rickshaw. Traverse the entire city for Rs.30 by auto-rickshaw, Rs.15 by rickshaw. Expect to be charged at least quadruple these fares at first. You'll have to bargain hard. It helps to have a local assist you, and it may be worthwhile to have a local rent one for you for a full day (Rs.100-300). Dangerous **tempos** also can be found just about anywhere. The ride is hair-raising but cheap at Rs.2. **Local buses** depart from the Central Bus Stand, from all the sights, and at most major intersections every 5min. They go everywhere for Rs.2. A/C Ambassador **taxis** can be picked up at the railway station. The ride is comfortable, but steep (Rs.10 per km), with variable minimum rates. **Bicycles,** convenient for exploration, can be rented from several places in the city. Near Ajmeri gate in Kishanpol Bazaar, you can rent bicycles for Rs.10 per day. Open daily 8am-10pm. Many Budget hotels will arrange bicycle rentals. **Car-and-drivers** can be rented from the RTDC at the Tourist Hotel on M.I. Rd. for between Rs.120 for 1hr. and Rs.600 for 12hr., and from some private holds as well. Personal **car rental** is not recommended, but can be arranged through Hertz in Holiday Inn, Amber Rd.

Luggage Storage: Jaipur Railway Station. Rs.3 for first 24hr., Rs.5 for second 24hr., Rs.6 for additional 24hr. **Sindhi Camp Bus Station.** Rs.3 per day, Rs.2 per day with advance reservations.

English Bookstore: Books Corner, M.I. Rd. (tel. 366323). Good collection of English books, also international newspapers and magazines. *Jaipur Vision* available (Rs.20). **The Book Shop,** in Rambagh Palace Hotel, off Bhawani Singh Marg (tel. 381430), **Usha Book Company,** Chaura Rasta (tel. 312034), and **Dirya Drishti,** in Hotel Bissan Palace, north of Chandpol Gate outside the old city (tel. 320191), all have smaller collections of English books.

Market: Fresh food and vegetable stalls are everywhere in the old city, most notably along the Chandpol-Ramganj-Surajpol bazaar stretch, outside Chandpol gate, and also along M.I. Rd. Most bazaars open 8am-9:30pm, closed Sun.; some also closed Tues.

Pharmacy: Pharmacies can be found everywhere, but tend to cluster around hospitals. Prices for most common medicines are surprisingly bargainable. Most open daily 8am-10pm.

Hospital/Medical Services: Sawai Mansingh Hospital, Sawai Ram Singh Rd. (tel.56029). Government-run, large, efficient, organized, English-speaking. A bevy of **private hospitals** can be found around the city. The best (English-speaking, clean, large, open 24hr.) include **Zanana Hospital,** Chandpol Gate (tel. 378721), **Getwell Polyclinic,** Jawaharlal Nehru Marg (tel. 563743); and **Santokba Durlabhji Hospital,** Bhwani Singh Marg (tel. 566251). The **J.K. Mother and Child Health Institute** specializes in child care. The **Red Cross Hospital** is near Sanganeri Gate (tel. 48677).

Police: Main Police Station, in King Edward Memorial Bldg., near Ajmeri Gate (tel. 100). Many branches are scattered around—look for the red-and-blue diagonal pattern. A major, conveniently located branch is across from the railway station (tel. 311677). Most branches have English-speaking staff.

Emergency: Police, tel. 100; **Fire,** tel. 101; **Ambulance,** tel. 102.

Post Office: GPO, M.I. Rd. (tel. 368740). Packaging, philately museum, *Poste Restante.* Open Mon.-Sat. 10am-6pm. Major **branch offices,** located in Tripolia Bazaar and past Bapu Bazaar. **Postal Code:** 302001.

Telephone Code: 0141.

ACCOMMODATIONS

The budget hotel situation in Jaipur is frustratingly competitive: exit the bus or railway station and prepare to be mobbed by rickshaw drivers flashing business cards and urging you to pick a particular hotel. It's a win-win-win situation for them—if you choose their hotel, they'll get a 50% commission, which translates into your hotel bills being higher; if you insist on another budget hotel, they'll simply charge you triple fare (or refuse to take you); and if you opt for a higher-end hotel, they'll quadruple their fare since you're "rich." Unlike some other cities, letting rickshaw drivers battle it out for your patronage won't work in Jaipur—they know the tourist scene too well. Your best bet is to shell out the triple fare and go where you want. It'll be cheaper in the end. Or just walk down a block (or three) and find less ruthless local transportation.

As in most cities, hotels are peppered around the bus and railway stations. A fair number occupy M.I. Rd. and vicinity. Unfortunately, few hotels can claim the Pink City proper as turf. It may be worth looking into home-stay accommodations, arranged through the tourist office at the Railway Station, generally for less than Rs.300 per night.

Aangan Guest House, 4 Park House Scheme (tel. 373449). Off Moti Lal Atal Rd. A homely, familial, friendly, all-around great place to stay, featuring really hot water! A relaxing garden completes the scene. STD/ISD and fax, 24-hr. room service, telephones and TVs in all rooms, car rental facilities. Check-out noon. All rooms with attached bath. Singles Rs.175. Doubles Rs.250. Triples Rs.350. One A/C double at Rs.500.

Atithi Guest House, 1 Park House Scheme (tel. 378679). Off Moti Lal Atal Rd. A true home-away-from-home nestled in a pleasantly quiet corner near all the action. Family-run with great veg. food and spotless rooms, all with attached baths. Check-out noon, limited room service. Singles Rs.250, with larger room Rs.400. Doubles Rs.300, with larger room Rs.450. Extra bed Rs.100.

Madhuban, D-237 Behari Marg (tel.319033; fax 322344). Off Sawai Jai Singh Highway before Bani park, on the right. Serene, tastefully decorated rooms with antique furniture set around picturesque garden. Amenities include a travel desk, STD/ISD and fax, 24-hr. room service, laundry facilities. Check-out noon. All rooms with attached bath. Standard singles Rs.250, larger with more antiques Rs.500, with A/C Rs.600. Doubles Rs.300/550/650. Extra bed Rs.100. Rs.50 discount off-season.

Jaipur Inn, Shiv Marg (tel. 316821). From Sawai Jai Singh Highway, right onto Shiv Marg, 5min. down the circle, in the large, unoffendingly pink building. Clean, well-illuminated, plant-filled rooms and corridors. Incredible roof-top restaurant. Cooking area for guests. Facilities include a ping-pong table, luggage storage, laundry, and a store. No room service. More expensive rooms offer attached baths, air-cooling, and great views. Check-out 10am. Dorm beds Rs.50-60. Camping Rs.25. Singles Rs.100, deluxe Rs.300. Doubles Rs.150, deluxe Rs.400. Reservations recommended.

Chandra Vilas Hotel, Station Rd. (tel. 376181). Opposite the bus stand. Good bang for your buck rooms, all with TVs, telephones, and attached baths. Esoteric wall paper that changes every 50 ft. Decent veg. restaurant, 24-hr. room service. 24-hr. check-out. Singles Rs.150, with air-cooling Rs.200, with A/C Rs.350. Doubles Rs.200, with air-cooling Rs.250, with A/C 450. Extra bed Rs.50.

Hotel Arya Niwas, Sansar Chandra Rd. (tel. 372156; fax 364376). A large, simple, spacious hotel built in a renovated *baveli*. Lots of natural lighting and cross-ventilation keep the place bright and cool. Travel counter, laundry, car rental, shop, STD/ISD, currency exchange, dining hall, and full handicapped access. Check-out noon. All rooms have attached bath. Singles Rs.200-400, depending on size and location. Doubles Rs.300-500. Reservations highly recommended.

Swagatam Tourist Bungalow, across Railway Station Rd. (tel. 310595). A solid place, conveniently located with a small garden. Rooms well-maintained and modestly decorated (a painting here and there). Check-out noon. Tourist information, a good open-air restaurant and bar, limited room service. Dorm beds Rs.50. Singles with bath Rs.125, larger with air-cooling Rs.250. Doubles with bath Rs.175, with air-cooling Rs.350.

Hotel Kailash, Johari Bazaar (tel. 565372). One of the lucky few located in the heart of the Pink City proper. Sure, it's noisy, but in the middle of the action with a great view of the Hawa Mahal. Adequate simple rooms, all with attached baths, TVs, and central air-cooling. Backside singles Rs.90, with great views and more noise Rs.245. Backside doubles Rs.100, louder, scenic doubles Rs.295. Extra bed Rs.35. Reservations required in season.

Evergreen Guest House, off M.I. Rd. (tel. 363446; fax 371934). Walk down M.I. Rd. past the GPO on the left, and take the next right. Here's where to mingle with countless other tourists all day and night. Abundantly populated with trees, shrubs, and foliage. By contrast, the rooms are rather bare. Swimming pool, restaurant, STD/ISD service, laundry, luggage storage. All rooms with attached bath. Hot water buckets Rs.5 after the first. Check-out 10am. Dorm beds Rs.50. Singles Rs.100, with air-cooling Rs.175, with A/C Rs.400. Doubles Rs.120, with air-cooling Rs.200, with A/C Rs.450. Reservations highly recommended in season.

Karni Niwas Guest House, Moti Lal Atal Rd. (tel 365433). An interesting blend of quasi-*haveli*-style decor and modern amenities, all under congenial management. Beautiful rooftop view of the distant fort. Limited room service, good restaurant, telephones in all rooms. Check-out 10am. Singles with bath and air-cooling Rs.250, with A/C Rs.550. Doubles with bath and air-cooling Rs.300, with A/C Rs.650.

Hotel Diggi Palace, Sawai Ram Singh Marg (tel. 373091). About 1km south of Ajmeri Gate. Spacious 200-yr. old converted palace with a quiet location and mellow staff. Terrace restaurant. Check-out noon. Singles with bath start at Rs.175. Doubles start at Rs.225. Reservations recommended.

Tourist Hotel, M.I. Rd. (tel. 360238). In the palatial-looking old Secretariat building off M.I. Rd. Rooms lean towards the threadbare, but are well-managed and clean. Tourist information is readily available, as the name suggests. Check-out noon. All rooms with attached bath. Dorm beds Rs.50. Singles Rs.125, with air-cooling Rs.200. Doubles Rs.175, with air-cooling Rs.275.

Bombay Hotel, outside Chandpol Gate (tel. 304412; fax 304181). A morals-conscious place for the family: family-sized rooms, no alcohol permitted, and prominent "please save water" signs everywhere. Strictly veg. restaurant, 24-hr. room service, telephones, TVs, attached baths, and air-coolers in all rooms. Check-out 24hr. Singles start at Rs.150. Doubles Rs.200. Extra beds Rs.40. Family-sized rooms for 4 start at Rs.400.

Youth Hostel, intersection of Bhagwandas and Bhawani Singh Rd. (tel. 375455). Pretty much your standard youth hostel. Curfew 10pm. Duties required. Maximum 4-day stay. Clean common baths. Dorm beds for members Rs.10, nonmembers Rs.20. A pair of doubles at Rs.50 each.

Kaiser-I-Hind Hotel, (tel. 310195). Off Station Rd., follow signs for Welcomgroup Rajputana Sheraton. An old, run-down palace filled exclusively with unrenovated antiques—from the doormats and fans to the toilets and desks. Mark Twain, Mahatma Gandhi, Rockefeller, and Mussolini's bro' all supposedly stayed here. Family-run and quite an adventure. 24hr. room service, restaurant, laundry. Check-out noon. Singles with bath Rs.120. Doubles Rs.300. Suites Rs.550.

Hotel Sweet Dream, Nehru Bazar (tel. 314409). Another rarity in the Pink City proper. Noisy, but the location is prime, and the rooftop restaurant Ariana is quite good. Car rental, travel desk, STD/ISD, 24-hr. room service. Check-out 24hr. All rooms with attached bath. Singles Rs.170, with TV and air-cooling Rs.250, with A/C Rs.400. Doubles Rs.225, with TV and air-cooling Rs.300, with A/C Rs.450.

Hotel Sangam, Motilal Atal Rd. (tel. 377241). Simple rooms decorated with random but tasteful paintings. Travel counter, veg. dining hall, laundry, car rental, 24-hr. room service. All rooms with attached bath. Singles Rs.150, with b/w TV Rs.250, with color TV Rs.250, with A/C Rs.500. Doubles Rs.250, with b/w TV Rs.300, with color TV Rs.350, with A/C Rs.600.

FOOD

A city of Jaipur's size cannot fail to disappoint—all types of food for all types of budgets are readily available. Jaipur doesn't have its own renowned specialties, but you'll find a range of Rajasthani classics in most places. For cheap quickies, the *bhojnalyas* on Station Rd. and on M.I. Rd. around the GPO are where the locals go, and if the sweet tooth calls, know that the *mishri, mawas,* and *ghevars* of Jaipur are considered the best in the state.

Niro's, M.I. Rd. (tel. 374493). Past the GPO, on the right. Their card claims "quiet grandeur, warm hearted courtesy, personalized service." Add cool A/C to get the best non-veg. food in town. Expect a crowd. Indian, Chinese, Continental entrees at a hefty-but-worth-it Rs.80-100. Open daily 9:30am-11pm.

LMB, Johari Bazar (tel. 565844). Incredible veg. food in an air-conditioned, eccentrically decorated environment. Featuring a range of specialties from all over the Subcontinent, for Rs.30-50. Live classical music after 7pm. Open daily 9am-11pm.

Bismallah, Chandpol Gate. A non-veg. place that doesn't serve the common Continental-Chinese-Indian melange—definite Islamic cuisine. Most items around Rs.20. Open daily 8am-10pm.

Milky Way, off Bhagwandas Marg (tel. 366234). Roughly halfway between M.I. Rd. and Statue Circle, on a side street to the left. The most popular ice cream joint in town—Italian ice creams, thick shakes, fountain sodas. Unique "herbonic shake" Rs.20. Open daily until people leave (around 1am).

Hanuman Dhaba, near where Govind Marg turns into Industrial Rd. This is where locals go to get Niro's/LMB-quality veg. food at normal prices. Outdoor street-side seating with full views of the busy kitchen. Most food around Rs.20. Open daily 9:30am-11pm.

Surya Mahal, M.I. Rd., next to Niro's and Books Corner. Popular among locals and tourists alike, with veg. pizzas and *dosas*. Expect a wait. Entrees around Rs.30. Open daily 10am-10:30pm.

Garden Cafe, A-6 Mahaveer Marg, near Statue Circle. The closest you'll get to fast-food pizzas, burgers, fries, shakes—and their South Indian equivalents. Cheap dishes around Rs.15-20. Open daily 9:30am-11pm.

Shri Shanker Bhojnalya, Station Rd. (tel. 78015). Near the main bus stand. Perhaps the most popular *bhojnalya* in town. Cheap, quality food—excellent *thalis* for only Rs.24. Open daily 8am-11pm.

Suvarna Mahal, in Rambagh Palace (tel. 381919). If you're gonna splurge, you might as well do it in style: beautiful, air-conditioned dining room, dim lights, mellow music, excellent service, and superb food of assorted cuisines. Expect to dish out around Rs.500 for the night. Open daily 7am-11pm.

SIGHTS

Pink City

Built between 1729 and 1732 by Jai Singh as a home for himself and his successors, the **City Palace,** at the very center of the Pink City, is a wonderful place to spend a couple of hours. Flanked by Gangauri Bazaar to the west and Siredeori Bazaar to the east, the palace is huge, encompassing nearly 15% of the Pink City's total area. The home of the current maharaja, Sawai Bhawani Singh, much of the palace is off-limits, but what you can see is delightful. Open daily 9:30am-4:45pm. Admission (palace and museum) Rs.30, students Rs.15; camera fee Rs.50, video fee Rs.100, no photography allowed in the galleries.

Architecturally, the palace has changed little since it was built, but its character and the culture it has accommodated has changed substantially over time. Until the decline of the Rajputs during the middle and late decades of the 19th century, the maharaja of Jaipur was the most important ruler in what is eastern Rajasthan today. Early maharajas filled the palace with scientific and artistic treasures. Others concentrated on public affairs. Those interested more in pleasure than business cultivated a lively palace harem, which, it is said, held over 1000 women into the 20th century. Lately, the palace has taken on a fresh aspect: it opened to tourists in the 1950s, and over 400 films—including *North by Northwest* and the Errol Flynn version of *Kim*—have had scenes shot within its walls. Over the last few decades the palace has also played host to many renowned guests, including Queen Elizabeth II, Jawaharlal Nehru, the Shah of Iran, and Jacqueline Kennedy Onassis. In the early 1990s, the king of Nepal and his son paid frequent visits to the palace— local rumor had it that the Nepalese prince and the maharaja's daughter (his only heir) would marry. Alas, the rumors remain unsubstantiated.

After paying your admission fee, you'll find yourself in a large courtyard enclosed by yellow-and-red mortar walls whose balconies and arches are rapidly decaying. At the center of the courtyard is an attractive though monotonous building, adorned with the usual carved patterns, marble pillars, and arched balconies. The building

Meeting the Maharaja

The current maharaja of Jaipur, Sawai Bhawani Singh, is a friendly and hard-working man of rare gentleness. Paying him a visit is about the coolest thing you can do in Jaipur. An old military man, the maharaja is an avid polo player who enjoys driving top-of-the-line cars, and who talks with real excitement about computers and ham radio. He is also India's High Commissioner to Brunei, and so knows a great deal about that country.

The maharaja typically grants **private audiences** to visitors on weekdays. Appointments are necessary. To make an appointment, ask at the main entrance of the City Palace for the ADC (Aide de Camp) Office. There you can speak with the PPS (Principal Private Secretary), who organizes the maharaja's schedule. It's best to give the PPS a couple of days' advance notice. Throughout the process—and especially when meeting the maharaja—modest, respectful clothing and behavior are appreciated and expected.

once served as a secretariat, containing the offices used by the maharaja for state business. These days, the ground floor houses the offices of the director of the palace, a museum complex, and a library—accessible only to serious scholars. The library holds nearly 90,000 items, including centuries-old manuscripts collected by the maharajas, photo albums, and recent periodicals. The second floor of the building holds a **Textile Museum,** with solid collections of cloth and costumes, including the massive *atamsuk* of the reputedly sexually ravenous "fat maharaja," Sawai Madno Singh I, who was 2.15m tall and is said to have weighed over 250kg. Also noteworthy are the 19th-century prints produced in the nearby village of Sanganer, made by a traditional wood-block process sill used there today. A few musical instruments and pieces of glasswork are also displayed.

In the northwest corner of the courtyard is the **Arms and Weapons Museum.** Of its excellent collection, best are the displays just to the right of the entrance, which showcase daggers whose large hilts contain secret chambers, and gunpowder holders made of seashells. Look up and admire the ceilings, too, expertly decorated with mirrors, paintings of women, and dense floral patterns. The museum also offers delightfully hokey pleasures—keep your eyes peeled as you enter and exit to spot a heady glimpse of WELCOME and GOODBY spelled out in daggers and pistols respectively.

Exiting the courtyard, you'll pass through an elaborate gate with massive brass doors flanked by two marble elephants. Centering the next courtyard is the **Hall of Private Audience,** where two *Gangajalis,* silver urns built to contain incredible quantities of Ganga River water, are on display. A sign notes that each urn holds 9000 liters of water, weighs 345kg, and has the Guinness-certified distinction of being the largest piece of silver in the world. In the corner of the courtyard is the **Hall of Public Audience,** housing the **Art Museum,** which displays a hodge-podge of terrific objects collected by the maharajas over the centuries. The walls are lined with massive, rolled-up carpets, most commissioned by the maharajas in styles popular in eastern Persia. A large collection of manuscripts demonstrates the maharajas' traditional patronage of learning, and provides excellent opportunity to see examples of old Tamil and 16th-century Assamese. The collection of works on astronomy boasts a 16th-century translated edition of Aristotle's scientific writings. A highlight of the museum is its outstanding collection of vibrantly rendered miniature paintings. Particularly interesting is the **Well of Mercury,** a painting of a beautiful woman in front of flowing water that has caused something of a controversy among scholars. While the painting can be understood strictly as an illustrated version of a Hindu myth, some argue that the painting is a coded instruction book, which explains how to extract mercury from the earth. Also on display is a series of black and white 19th-century photos taken by the then-maharaja.

Exit that courtyard and you'll find yourself in a smaller one, surrounded by four gates, each representing a different season. Lording over the courtyard is the **Chandra Mahal,** the maharaja's residence. Parts of the first floor are open to the public.

Hawa Mahal (Palace of the Winds) (tel. 48862), is a segment of the east wall that encloses the palace complex; have a look at it from Siredeori Bazar. The five-story pink sandstone *mahal,* with overhanging balconies, is the most eminently recognizable landmark in Jaipur. Built in 1799, the palace was the brainchild of Maharaja Sawai Pratap Singh, who wanted a comfortable place where he could compose his devotional songs to Krishna, some of which are still sung in the nearby Govindji Temple. The palace was designed to catch the breeze, and takes its name from the many brass wind vanes that adorned it (until the 1960s), each set at different levels to point in a variety of directions as they caught different inspirations. Spacious underground tunnels connected the palace to the harem. (Open daily 10am-4:30pm. Admission Rs.3 (Mon. free), camera fee Rs.50, video fee Rs.100.)

Next to the entrance to the palace is the inadequately maintained **Jantar Mantar,** one of the massive astronomical observatories built by Maharaja Jai Singh. Jaipur's Jantar Mantar looks a great deal like its cousins in Delhi, Ujjain, and Varanasi. Before building his observatories, Jai Singh sent emissaries to the East and West; they returned with cutting-edge technical manuals, including a copy of La Hire's "Tables," which the maharaja had coveted. After building Jantar Mantar, Jai Singh found that it produced readings 20 seconds more accurate than those reported by La Hire. The observatory features 18 large instruments—impressive, but confusing and inexplicable without a guide. The 30-m-high sundial is particularly grand. (Observatory open Sat.-Thurs. 9:30am-4:30pm. Admission Rs.10 (Mon. free), guides Rs.25, camera fee Rs.50, video fee Rs.100.)

Behind the city palace sits the **Govindji Temple,** perhaps the most popular Hindu temple in town, dedicated to Lord Krishna. It is ornately sculpted and positioned in a way that allows the maharaja to see it from his window in the Chandra Mahal. Visit during daily ceremonies, 8:15am or 6:30pm. Also in the city is **Ishar Lat,** the "heaven-piercing minaret," near Tripolia Gate. It provides a panoramic city-view.

South of the Pink City

As Chaura Rasta leaves the Pink City via **New Gate,** it becomes Jawaharlal Nehru Marg, a thoroughfare dotted with successive diversions. **Ram Niwas Gardens,** 50m south of New Gate, nests at its center Jaipur's **Central Museum,** often called **Albert Hall.** The museum complex is a breezy mixture of pillars, arches, and recessed courtyards adorned with murals. The ground floor of the museum offers informative displays of various facets of Rajasthani culture and history, including miniature paintings and ivory carvings, shields depicting scenes from Hindu epics, costumed mannequins, and recently excavated stone sculptures. An exceptionally good central hall exhibit showcases the splendid blue pottery long in production in the city. The second floor of the museum is a fascinating period piece. Small dolls dressed in East Asian costume—and a few outfitted as Alpine milkmaids for good measure—neighbor all-too-encyclopedic collections of Indian rocks and minerals, a handful of dead snakes coiled tightly in glass jars, and plaster models of the kind used to teach anatomy in medical school. The Indian painting and sculpture here is not particularly good, and it's altogether overshadowed by the plaster busts of Pericles and Marcus Aurelius. (Open Sat.-Thurs. 9:30am-4:30pm; admission Rs.3 (Mon. free); photography prohibited.)

The **Jaipur Zoo,** 30m south of the museum, is fairly clean and well-maintained by the standards of South Asian zoos. But the animals have little room to roam, and the zoo does not seem interested in educating visitors. If you visit, see both sides of the coin—have a look at the endangered greater adjutant stork, as well as the tiny, rat-infested iron cages where the lions spend their days sleeping and being harassed. (Open daily 9:30am-4:30pm; admission Rs.2. Hold on to your ticket stub.)

About 2km south of the zoo, just off Nehru Marg, is the eccentric, encyclopedic, privately funded **Museum of Indology,** featuring the troves of **"Vyakul"**—poet,

NORTH INDIA

painter, and super nice guy who has been collecting all sorts of stuff since he was 13 and can't bear to part with any of it—knick-knacks, curio pieces, and, yes, real treasures. The museum holds a massive collection of textiles, architectural drawings, and 20,000 buttons. In one room, the marriage contract of the last Mughal emperor vies for attention with a grain of rice on which a full-color map of India has been drawn and a single strand of hair onto which the text of the Bhagavad Gita has been crammed. (Open daily 9am-6pm. Admission, with guide, Rs.30.) Also about 2km south of the zoo is the **Dolls Museum,** located on Nehru Marg, with a collection of dolls made in India and throughout the world. (Open daily 10am-4pm; admission Rs.1.)

Five kilometers south of the zoo on Nehru Marg, the white marble **Lakshmi Narayan Mandir** is rapidly becoming one of Jaipur's most beloved buildings. Commonly called the **Birla Mandir,** the temple was built by the wealthy Birla family. Designed as an expression of the Birla's multi-denominational approach to religion, the temple has three domes, each styled according to a different type of architecture. Pressing the theme of pluralism at subtler levels, the artwork in the *parikarima* was done by a Muslim, and the pillars flanking the temple include carvings of Hindu deities as well as depictions of Moses, Jesus, Zarathustra, and many others, including Socrates. People of all castes and religions are welcome. Once inside, check out the striking stained-glass windows, and the lotus flowers that adorn the ceiling, each crafted from a single piece of marble. Turning around so that you're facing the temple entrance, note the shadow cast as sunlight slips through the translucent, polished, marble sculpture of Ganesh. The allegorical mural to the left of Ganesh's shadow shows an episode from the Gita: Krishna, with his steady control of the five horses, is implying that if you don't keep your five senses on a tight rein, they'll lord over you. (Open daily 8am-7:30pm. Free guide available 8-11:30am and 4:30-7:30pm. Prayers are said at 8am and 7pm.) On the hill overlooking the temple are the crumbling remains of **Motidungri Fort.** The property is owned by the Maharaja, but he doesn't maintain it. The fort complex encloses a **Shiva temple** and is open to the public only once a year, on Shivaratri.

A rarely visited cluster of sights is along the shadeless Agra Rd., 4.5km east of the zoo or New Gate. **Sisodia Rani-ka-Bagh** is a complex of palace and gardens built in 1710 by the maharaja of Amber for his wife. A recent repainting and refurbishing job has made the former grandeur of the palace more palpable, while simultaneously transforming the entire complex into a shiny, happy parody of itself. (Open daily 8am-6pm; admission Rs.3.) On the road back to Jaipur, about 400m east of Sisodia on Agra Rd., is **Vidyadharji-ka-Bagh,** a well-maintained but bland complex of gardens named for the Bengali Brahmin who helped design Jaipur. (Open daily 9am-6pm; admission Rs.2.)

Also off Agra Rd. is the pilgrimage destination of **Galta.** A series of temples and pavilions hidden in a gorge surround a natural spring considered holy. The nearby **Sun Temple** offers a great view of the city, and provides for a popular picnic spot.

North of the Pink City

Standing sentinel over the Pink City below, the three Garland Forts dominate the northern horizon. Foremost among these is **Amber,** also locally known as Amer. Amber today is a reflection of the quasi-legendary Kachhwaha dynasty, a Rajput clan that dominated the area from the 12th to 18th centuries. Constructed in 1592 by Raja Man Singh, Amber Fort is a blend of Indian and Islamic architecture. Solidly built, with defense as its top priority (witnessed by its hilltop location, winding roads, and multitudinous gates), the fort nonetheless smoothly integrates artwork and creature comforts. Amber is situated 11km north of Jaipur and is a common stop on tours. A bus leaves for Amber from in front of the Hawa Mahal every 4min., Rs.2.5. (Open daily 9am-4:30pm; admission Rs.4, camera fee Rs.50, video camera Rs.100.)

From the main road, half the fun is getting up to the fort itself. Walking up the steep, curvy road takes 15min., with beautiful views of the surrounding valleys. Other means include jeep rides (Rs.10), or a languid elephant ride (for a whopping Rs.250

for up to 4 people). Once in the fort complex, you can ride an elephant around the main courtyard for a more modest Rs.20. To the side of this courtyard is the **Shri Sila Devi Temple,** dedicated to the goddess of strength. Entry through the majestic silver doors leads to a black marble idol of the deity. From the main courtyard, a flight of stairs leads to **Diwan-i-Am** (Hall of Public Audience), a pillared, latticed meeting gallery. Opposite is the magnificently frescoed and mosaic-tiled **Ganesh Pol,** which marks the entrance to what used to be the maharaja's apartments. From here, it's fun just wandering around getting lost among numerous corridors, courtyards, balconies, terraces, and rooms—some empty and threadbare, others adorned with blinding mirrorwork and beautiful coloring, such as the famous **Jai Mandir** (Hall of Victory). Other attractions include the **Sheesh Mahal,** the original private chambers of the maharaja, whose walls and ceilings are completely covered with colored glass and mirrors, and the **Sukh Mahal** (Pleasure Palace), which features a remarkable air-cooling system that works by wind passing through water sheets which in turn pass through small perforations along the marble walls.

From the Amber Fort balconies, the stocky **Jaigarh Fort,** second of the Garland Forts, can be seen perching on a nearby hilltop. Its chambers and courtyards are nowhere near as elaborate as Amber's, but it does possess the gigantic **Jaivana,** the biggest cannon on wheels in the world, which could fire a shot 60km. Jaigarh's museum contains the expected armory and moderately interesting assorted relics. A noisy, badly performed puppet show takes place in one of the rooms. The view of Amber and Jaipur from the ramparts is breathtaking. The fort can be reached after a long climb from Amber, or by vehicle. No buses head out here, but rickshaws from Amber are available for Rs.20. (Open daily 9am-4:30pm; admission Rs.10, students Rs.5, camera fee Rs.20, video fee Rs.100.

Nahargarh Fort, the third Garland Fort, also known as the Tiger Fort, is a delightfully solitary, even romantic place, especially before 11:30am and after 2:30pm, the three-hour interval when the fort is pelted with tour buses. As a result of renovations, the fort's many chambers are painted in an amazingly wide variety of brightly hued floral patterns; getting lost as you stroll about is half the fun. The view of the valleys around is also stunning. A shady, open-air cafeteria next to the fort provides slightly overpriced food and drink. To reach the fort, enjoy a shadeless 20-minute walk uphill from the road leading to Jaigarh. (Open daily 9:30am-5pm; admission Rs.2., camera fee Rs.30, video fee Rs.70.)

Back towards Jaipur is **Gaitor.** Finding the way is difficult even with a map, so taking a rickshaw or asking lots of questions makes good sense. Gaitor is a complex of domed memorials built in memory of maharajas who have died. Each *chhattri* (cenotaph) is made of stone or white marble and is a riot of perforated screens, ornamented relief, and bas-relief sculptures, each built in accord with the particular predilections of the royal family member being commemorated. Though it has become a bit scruffy, infrequently touristed Gaitor merits a visit if you have some energy left over from the climb up to Nahargarh. Nearby is **Maharani-ka-chhattri,** cenotaphs for the female members of the royal family. The **Jal Mahal,** a small palace set in the middle of a small lake, is also in the vicinity.

ENTERTAINMENT

After a long day of emptying your pockets at the shopping bazaars, the nightlife of the city is welcoming. Jaipur's 16 **cinemas** are packed with people at every showing. Regardless of your interest in or comprehension of Hindi films, worth experiencing is the plush, luxurious, world-renowned **Raj Mandir Cinema,** off M.I. Rd. (tel. 379372). The four daily showings (12:30, 3:30, 6:30, and 9:30pm) are *always* sold out; arrive *at least* 1 hour in advance to get tickets—"diamond box seats" Rs.35! ("Emerald" suffices at Rs.26., and two other classes are offered.) A tourist/student queue conveniently exists. Other popular, but less elaborate movie theaters include **Gem Cinema,** off M.I. Rd. (tel. 561788), and **Moti Mahal,** off Station Rd. (tel. 317323). Check local newspapers for movie listings, and the Sunday paper for information about English movies—some are shown at these theaters on Sunday mornings.

Fairs and Festivals of Jaipur

Although any time's a good time to see Jaipur, it's especially fun to come for one of the annual festivals. The **Gangaur Festival,** dedicated to the goddess Gauri, celebrates women and lasts for the 18 days after Holi. The festival is accompanied by singing, dancing, and phenomenal parades with incredible costumes and decorations. For 1997, it begins on April 10-11. The **Elephant Festival** needs to be seen to be believed. An elephant parade gets things going, while fast-paced elephant polo and an elephant vs. humans tug-of-war complete the festivities. For 1997, the festival will be held March 23. The **Teej Fair** (Festival of Swings), celebrates the beginning of the monsoon season. Decorated swings are hung from trees, and the city goes wild. In 1997, it's August 6-7.

For authentic, traditional Rajasthani **dance and music,** both the **Welcomgroup Rajputana Palace Sheraton,** near the railway station (tel. 360011), and the **Panghat Theater,** in Rambagh Palace, off Bhawani Singh Rd. (tel. 381919), offer in-season nightly performances in high-class surroundings for high-class prices. Shows are generally 7-9pm. Call in advance. Ravindra Manch (tel. 49061), and Jawahar Kala Kendra (tel. 510501), also occasionally offer folk events. Call for details.

Due to a strange prohibition law that's been in effect for years, only hotels can legally serve alcohol stronger than beer. Of course, some restaurants take this restriction with a grain of salt, but in general, if you're looking for the **bar scene,** hotels are it. For air-conditioned, high-class boozing, the popular **Polo Bar** in Rambagh Palace, off Bhawani Singh Rd. (tel. 381919), **Rana Sanga Roof Top Bar** in Mansingh Palace, off Sansar Chandra Rd. (tel.378771), and the **Sheesh Mahal** in the Welcomgroup Rajputana Palace Sheraton, near the Railway Station (tel. 360011), are all open until 11pm, and all do nicely. On the other hand, imbibing at cheaper prices with locals and budget tourists is better accomplished at the **Sagui Bar,** in Gangaur Tourist Bungalow (tel. 371641), and the **Talab Bar,** in Swagatam Tourist Bungalow (tel. 310595).

For an authentic glimpse of inauthentic village life, **Chowki Dhani,** 20km south of the city, promises a night of wild entertainment. Camel and ox rides, parrot astrology, palmistry, snake charming, *mendhi* hand-art, puppet shows, acrobatics and tribal music, all in traditional style, are available in this replica of village living. The highlight of the evening is the over-spiced dinner, served on leaf plates in a large mud hut. Open daily after 8pm. Accessible by private transportation or by RTDC night tours.

SHOPPING

Jaipur's old city is essentially a series of interconnected bazaars, and in fact, so is the new city. Shopping in Jaipur means heavy bargaining and constant harassment—it can be draining, but the effort is well worth it. You'll find a huge assortment of handicrafts, clothing, textiles, jewelry, and perfumes. Local specialties unique to Jaipur include *meenakari* (enamel work on silver and gold) and blue pottery. The jewelry and gemwork of Jaipur is world-famous, and remarkably inexpensive, but unless you know your stuff you'll have to be on the lookout for scams galore. In the Pink City, **Johari Bazar** and two lanes off of it—**Gopalj ka Rasta** and **Haldiyon ka Rasta**—are where you'll find a barrage of jewelry and gem stones, and gold and silver smiths. You'll also find a standard range of textile and tie-dye shops. Parts of the bazaar are closed on Sunday and Tuesday. Connecting the Ajmeri, New, and Sanganer gates are **Nehru Bazaar** and **Bapu Bazaar.** These specialize in textiles, rather unique perfumes (desert scents), local camel-skin shoes, and *mojiris* (a type of sandal). These bazaars are closed on Tuesday and Sunday respectively. **Tripolia Bazaar** and **Charra Rasta,** closed Sundays, have a variety of stores selling lacework, ironwork, miscellaneous wooden and ivory relics, and local trinkets. Watch master carpet-makers at work in **Siredeori Bazaar,** while off of **Chandpol Bazaar** you may find exquisite marble sculptures and carvings. **M.I. Road** outside of the city is a tourist-trap potpourri shopping district. You'll find all of the above, plus souvenirs—and more, lining the busy street. Several Government Emporiums offer solace from the bazaars' commotion, but with higher fixed prices and minimal bargaining possibilities, you'll be missing out on the true Jaipur shopping experience. Finally, to watch the famous blue pottery being made, make your way to **Shiva Marg,** west of the city. In general, shoppers' savvy involves walking around, finding a store you like, and locating the inevitably similar shops next door and across the street. Go back and forth between the lot of them to get a good deal.

■ Near Jaipur

Forty-two kilometers northwest of Jaipur sits the small village of **Samode.** The fairytale **Samode Palace,** rising from its simple surroundings, is the main attraction in town. A renovated 18th century three-level palace, Samode harbors painting and mirrorwork even more spectacular than Amber's. It is now a high-end hotel, and most parts are only open to guests. Public transportation to Samode is hazardous and only available from the village of Chomu.

Sixteen kilometers south of Jaipur, **Sanganer** has established itself as the local center of traditional crafts, especially paper-making, blue pottery, and block-printing. The best bargains in Rajasthan are here, since you can deal with the artisans themselves. Jain temples and abandoned palaces complement a delightful town. Buses leave to Sanganer from the main bus stand for Rs.4.

▓ Sariska Tiger Reserve and National Park

Nestled in the dry, temple-studded Aravali Mountains, 120km northeast of Jaipur and 200km west of Delhi, the 800-square-kilometer **Sariska Tiger Reserve and National Park,** maintained by Project Tiger (see p. 178), features a rich population of wildlife, including *nilgai* (blue bulls), *sambar* (large deer), spotted deer, wild boar, common langur, rhesus monkeys, leopards, hyenas, wild dogs, peafowl, and of course, tigers—whose numbers sadly continue to decline because of poaching. In the evenings, head near the water holes, where hides have been set up for tiger-spotting. Bring food, drinks, a comfortable sleeping bag, and insect repellent if you plan to spend time hide-hopping. In the dry season, most wildlife congregates around these holes. Other attractions in Sariska include **Kankwadi Fort** and the **Neel Kantha Mahadev Temple.** Sariska is open Sept.-June, daily dawn-dusk. Admission Rs.25 per person, Rs.100 per jeep. Buses leave on the hour from Alwar (Rs.5, 1hr.). Buses from Jaipur are rare—contact a private company and try your luck.

Accommodations include the popular **Hotel Tiger Den,** next to the park entrance (tel. (0144) 41342). Dorm beds Rs.50. Singles Rs.375, with A/C Rs.600. doubles Rs.500, with A/C Rs.675. Extra person Rs.100. The converted hunting lodge **Hotel Sariska Palace** (tel. (0144) 41322) has more expensive rooms starting at Rs.900. Both hotels have a bar and restaurant, and arrange park **jeep tours** starting at Rs.300 per 3hr. **Please note: Do not support the poaching industry by buying tiger-skin products.**

▓ Bharatpur

As a convenient stop on the popular tourist route between Agra and Jaipur, Bharatpur merits attention for its spectacular Keoladeo-Ghana National Park, one of the premier bird sanctuaries in India and the world. Founded by Badan Singh in 1732 as a princely state, Bharatpur soon became known for its heavy-duty fort. But what draws thousands of migrating birds and foreign travelers each year, especially between October and March, is the splendidly rich ecology of the well-maintained park. Settle in one of the convenient nest-like hotels nearby, and you'll soon chirp out the praises of each passing sunset and know why flocks and bevies of guests stop here all the time.

ORIENTATION AND PRACTICAL INFORMATION

Both the bird sanctuary and the adjacent hotels are a few kilometers southeast of the center of town. **Buses** coming from Jaipur drop passengers on the west side, but **rickshaws** (Rs.15-20) are available to make the journey to the hotel areas. At the core of town lie the remnants of the old fort, but most travelers never see this, instead taking refuge near the birds. The area between **Jama Masjid** and the old **Laxman temple** functions as a sort of downtown and here you'll find the densest population of services. Nearer to the sanctuary, **Hotel Saras** serves as a good starting point when looking for rooms, as it's right at the center at the intersection of the road leading to Fatehpur Sikri.

The **tourist office** (tel. 22542) is adjacent to the Hotel Saras; it has basic booklets about the area and Keoladeo, and its staff offers wisdom about rooms (open Mon.-Sat. 10am-5pm). The **State Bank of Bikaner and Jaipur** (tel. 22441), near Binarayan Gate, northwest of birdland, exchanges most currencies and traveler's checks (open Mon.-Fri. 10am-2pm, Sat. 10am-noon). STD/ISD **telephone** booths also populate this area. **Trains** leave from the station a few kilometers north of town (railway enquiry, tel. 23535). To: Mathura (1, 6, 8am, and 3:30pm, 45min., Rs.15) en route to Delhi (3-4hr., Rs.50-55). **Buses** leave from the main bus stand on the southwest side of town, but most, particularly those heading toward Agra, can be waved down by the Hotel Saras. To: Fatehpur Sikri (every other hr., 8am-4pm, 1hr., Rs.8); Agra (every 20min., 6am-11pm, 1hr., Rs.20); Delhi (every hr., 5am-5pm, 5hr., Rs.55-60); and Mathura (every hr., 7am-9pm, 1hr., Rs.15). The bus stand also has government or private transport to Jaipur (every 20min., 4hr., Rs.45), and occasional direct buses to Ajmer, Bikaner, or Udaipur (bus enquiry: tel. 23434). **Bicycles** are for rent at several hotels near the sanctuary (Rs.10-30 per day). **Omson's Medical Agencies** (tel. 23261), near the government library and not far from Jama Masjid, stocks many drugs at wholesale prices. **General Hospital**, tel. 23633; **emergency**, tel. 22451; **police:** tel. 22526. The **post office** is across from Jama Masjid to the east. **Postal Code:** 321001. **Telephone Code:** 05644.

ACCOMMODATIONS AND FOOD

The road to the park has everything from simple camping plots and dorm beds to full-blown rooms with attached bath. Many hotels rent bicycles, binoculars, and birding books. Room prices go way up in the high bird season (Oct.-March), particularly around Christmas; unless noted, prices here are off-season tariffs. If you're looking to go low-end, try the popular **Tourist Lodge,** near Mathura Gate (tel. 23742), near the railway station. Singles Rs.70-150.

Prices are much higher inside the park itself. The **Ashok Forest Lodge** (tel. 22722) and **Forest Lodge** (tel. 22670) charge about Rs.2200 for a room. When they are not around park officials sometimes make their few boarding house rooms available for Rs.300 per person. For **camping,** try the Wilderness Camp, next to the Annexy Hotel; a plot between eucalyptus tree costs Rs.30-50.

The **Hotel Saras** (tel. 23700) is both visible and visibly expensive. Still, there is a great garden and a rave restaurant added to clean ordinary rooms with chairs, full-size sinks, and mirrors. Dorm beds Rs.50. Singles Rs.250, deluxe Rs.400. Doubles Rs.275, deluxe Rs.450. Just to the east, the **Spoonbill Hotel** (tel. 23571), is of another feather. The super-friendly ex-general and his kind, lovely daughters make you feel right at home in big, blue rooms with warped western toilets. The Rs.100 room is the best deal, though they range up to Rs.200. Luggage/valuables storage is available. Up the road toward the park, **Hotel Sunbird** (tel. 25147) has clean rooms and a small bookshop. Singles Rs.150. Doubles Rs.200. Prices can double around Christmas time. Closer to the sanctuary still, **Hotel Pelican** (tel. 24221) is efficiently run, and the owner (also owner of the Tourist Lodge in town) is a naturalist and eagerly shows what he knows. Quaint rooms with funky lampshades. Singles Rs.100. In season: singles Rs.200. Doubles Rs.300. Try bargaining off-season. And lastly, **Hotel Prajap Palace** (tel. 24245) has comfy pillows and beds, but rooms are otherwise stark. Singles Rs.150. Doubles Rs.250.

Most of the hotels have attached restaurants, some with rooftops for sunset, binocular-aided birding. The **Spoonbill** has vegetarian, non-vegetarian, Indian, South Indian, Chinese, and Continental dishes and lots of them (entrees Rs.25-40). The **Hotel Sunbird's** colorful chairs, crepes, and Chinese offerings complement an Indian menu (Rs.20-50). The **Pelican** offers ultra-rich *lassis* and many delicious dishes, and they'll pack you a lunch (with tea or coffee in a thermos) to take to the park for Rs.30. The **Krishna Restaurant,** in Prajap Palace has pricier (and presumably more carefully prepared) vegetarian and non-vegetarian dishes (Rs.30-80).

SIGHTS

The main reason foreigners come to Bharatpur is to go cuckoo for the hordes of birds at Keoladeo Ghana National Park (see below). Still, if you're in town, and have rings around your eyes from staring through binoculars for so long, check out the town's old **Lohagarh Fort,** near Nehru Park, north from the core of town. The fort was built by Maharaja Suraj Mal and has been notoriously resistant to attack—even heavy British armaments are said to have virtually bounced off the walls. The **museum** here features two large galleries of ancient Jain sculpture, a gallery of the fort's artifacts, including gaudy vases, photographs of stern maharajas, and stuffed miniature bears, and a gallery of arms, including maces, spears, and miniature cannons from the mid-18th century. (Open Sat.-Thurs. 10am-4:30pm; admission Rs.2.)

Keoladeo Ghana National Park

Bharatpur's 29 square kilometers of pride and joy, the Keoladeo Ghana National Park, annually plays host to one of the world's most impressive assemblages of feathered friends. The marshes, woodlands, and grassy pastures draw hundreds of bird species each year, including VIBs (very important birds) such as the rare Siberan Crane, the painted stork, shoveller, widgeon, and grey, purple, and night herons. Along with the birds, there are pythons, spotted deer, jackals, and several other reptiles and mammals. Ironically, the local maharaja set aside the land as an elaborate hunting ground—a sign inside the board relates how British Viceroy "won" the prize, having killed 4273 birds in a single day back in 1938; the bloodsport didn't stop until 1972.

Visitors must rent a **bicycle** or **rickshaw** to explore the grounds because motor vehicles are not allowed past Keoladeo's only entrance. The **main office** at the gate rents cycles for Rs.10 (depositing your passport or Rs.1000), and many local hotels do the same for Rs.10-30. Only rickshaws that wear a special "yellow plate" have paid their dues and are certified to enter. Inside the office, a small visitors' center features nests, eggs, and stuffed animal specimens, as well as a color map of the park. Several charges are also levied at the gate: admission for non-Indians costs Rs.25, plus additional charges to bring in a cycle (Rs.3), camera (Rs.10), or video camera (Rs.100). Tonga (Rs.50) and cycle-rickshaws (Rs.25 per hr.) leave from the gate on tours throughout the park. Some rickshaw drivers know enough to serve as guides, but while your wallet is open, it might be better to hire one of the certified **naturalist guides** from the office—they have keen eyes for spotting and identifying birds and bird calls.

Inside the park you can also hire a **boat** (1hr. minimum, Rs.60-120, available Oct.15-March) or follow one of the **walking tours** suggested in the guide (Rs.3), available at the office. To help with all the aviary name-knowing, a reference book with all the common English, Hindi, and scientific names of the various species is available for Rs.10. The park has strict rules against smoking, noise-making, and other pollutant activities in order to preserve the environment's immediate and long-term tranquility.

The park is open daily 6am-6pm during the monsoon, sunrise to sunset in the high season (with the extreme ends of the day being particularly beautiful and bountiful). For more information, contact the office at the gate at tel. 22277.

NORTH INDIA

■ Ajmer

The small town of Ajmer, 13km west of Jaipur in the heart of the Aravali Mountains, is more interesting from a tourist perspective for its proximity to Pushkar than for its own sights. Nonetheless, Ajmer is remembered as the final resting place of Khwaja Muin-ud-din Chishti, founder of India's premier Sufi order, and as a result thousands upon thousands of Muslims make a yearly pilgrimage to Ajmer during the Urs Mela (Nov.1-11 in 1997). During this time the town bursts at its seams with people and festivities. The annual Pushkar Camel Fair induces even wilder surcharges. Apart from these special occasions, Ajmer remains a relatively calm town—nearby Pushkar has a mellowing effect. Ajmer was founded in the 11th century, and after switching hands a few times became an important Mughal holding. Throughout its dynamic history, the one constant has been its perpetual tribute to its Sufi saint.

ORIENTATION

Ajmer is a small town, only about 3m long, and if you wander around for a bit its geography becomes clear. **Station Road** runs east-west in front of the **Railway Station.** From the station, points of interest are straight ahead in **Diggi Bazaar,** the main commercial area, and to the right on **Kutchery Road,** which darts southeast, dead-ending into **Jaipur Road.** Take a right on Jaipur Rd. to get to a circle near the **Main Bus Stand;** take a left on Jaipur Rd. for **Prithviraj Marg.** In one direction Prithviraj Marg brings you back to Station-Kutchery Rd. junction and the GPO; in the other direction it passes **Nasiyan Temple** and dead-ends in another road. There a left leads to **Agra Gate, Delhi Gate,** and nearby **Dargh Bazaar, Nalla Bazaar,** and **Naya Bazaar.** The right passes JLN Hospital, before circling Ara Sagar as **Circular Road.**

PRACTICAL INFORMATION

Tourist Office: Tourist Information Bureau, next to Hotel Khadin (tel. 52426). Extremely helpful staff provides maps, brochures, travel information, and Pushkar information. Open Mon.-Sat. 8am-noon and 3-6pm. A smaller Tourist Information Bureau is in the railway station.

Currency Exchange: State Bank of India, near the Tourist Information Bureau (tel. 20048). Open Mon.-Fri. 10am-2pm, Sun. 10am-noon. **State Bank of Bikaner and Jaipur,** Station Rd. (tel. 23080). Open Mon.-Fri. noon-4pm, Sat. noon-2pm. Both banks exchange foreign currency and traveler's checks.

Telephones: Private STD/ISD booths are all over the city. A few have fax capabilities. Railway Station has a 24-hr. STD/ISD and fax office. **C.T. Scan Centre** on Kutchery Rd. is a 24-hr. pharmacy with attached STD/ISD booth. **Central Telegraph Office,** in GPO. Open 24hr.

Trains: Ajmer Railway Station, Station Rd. (tel. 131). Reservation office open Mon.-Sat. 8am-8pm, Sun. 8am-2pm. To: Udaipur (*Chetak Exp.* 9615, 1:48am, 10hr., Rs.64/230; *Garib Nawaz Exp.* 2915, 3:50pm, 10hr., Rs.70); Jodhpur (4893, 5:45am, 6hr., Rs.62/130); Delhi (*Chetak Exp.* 9616, 2:35am, 9hr., Rs.59/202; *Ashram Exp.* 2906, 1:50am, 9hr., Rs.110; 9904 and 4894, 6:45am, and 8:25pm, 9hr., Rs.50; *Shatabdi Exp.* 2016, 3:10pm, 7hr., Rs.94/180). Several of the Delhi trains stop at Jaipur, but schedules are changing rapidly due to gauge conversion. Check in advance.

Buses: Main Bus Stand, Jaipur Rd. (tel. 20398). Luggage storage Rs.4 per day. To: Ahmedabad 6 per day, 12:30am-8:45pm, 12hr., Rs.139); Abu Road (8 per day, 5:45-11:15pm, 10hr., Rs.91); Bikaner (express, 10 per day, 5am-9:30pm, deluxe, 8 and 10pm, 7hr., Rs.71/85 for express/deluxe); Kota (express every hr., deluxe 1 and 4pm, 5hr., Rs.53/Rs.62 for express/deluxe); Chittorgarh (every 30min., 6am-midnight, 4hr., Rs.48); Jaipur (every 15min., 6am-midnight, 3hr., Rs.36); Jaisalmer (8am, 12hr., Rs.125); Jodhpur (every 30min., 7am-11pm, 4½hr., Rs.74); Udaipur (every 45min., 6am-10pm, 7hr., Rs.75). **Pushkar Bus Stand,** near Station-Kutchery Rd. junction, by the GPO. To: Pushkar (every 10min., 5am-midnight, 30min., Rs.5). **Private bus** companies line Kutchery Rd. and have deluxe buses to most destinations. Most will pick up in Pushkar if needed; check in advance. **Ekta Travels** and **Shrinath Travels Agency** are recommended.

Local Transportation: Ajmer can easily be traversed by foot. **Cycle-rickshaws** and **auto-rickshaws** abound—Rs.10 will get you anywhere. Crowded **tempos** charge Rs.2. Popular in Ajmer are **tongas,** which charge around Rs.5 to get between the bus stand and train station. **Ambassador taxis** line Station Rd. **Bicycles** can be rented from several places across from the railway station and near Delhi Gate for Rs.15 per day.

Luggage Storage: Ajmer Railway Station. Rs.3 for first 24hr., Rs.5 for second 24hr., Rs.6 for additional 24hr.

English Bookstore: Bookland, Kutchery Rd., has a small collection of paperbacks and magazines. Open daily 10am-7pm.

Market: Diggi Bazaar, opposite the railway station, and **Nalla, Naya,** and **Dargah Bazaars,** on the north end of town near Agra and Delhi Gate, are shopping areas. Food and vegetable stalls are mainly in Diggi, but can be found everywhere. Most open daily 7am-9:30pm. Some parts of the bazaars are closed Sun.-Tues.

Pharmacy: Pharmacies bunch around JLN Hospital and around Pratap Memorial Hospital on Kutchery Rd. Most open daily 9am-9pm. The **C.T. Scan Centre** on Kutchery Rd. is a pharmacy and STD booth. The standard range of anti-malarials, anti-diarrheals, and painkillers are available. Open 24hr.

Hospital: JLN Hospital (tel. 21420). English-speaking, government-run. Open 24hr. Dr. Yadava's **Pratap Memorial Hospital,** Kutchery Rd. (tel. 20402), is the best private hospital. English-speaking. Open 24hr.

Police: Main Police Office, opposite railway station (tel. 100). English-speaking.

Emergency Numbers: Police, tel. 100. **Fire,** tel. 101. **Ambulance,** tel. 102.

Post Office: GPO, Prithviraj Marg. *Poste Restante.* Open Mon.-Sat. 10am-7pm, Sun. 10am-6pm. **Postal Code:** 305001.

Telephone Code: 0145.

ACCOMMODATIONS

Hotels in Ajmer aren't bad, but few offer anything special. Most tourists head to Pushkar for a better selection of accommodations, visiting Ajmer as a daytrip. Across from the railway station is a noisy bunch of no-frills, dirt-cheap hotels. Prithviraj Marg hosts a similar congregation of hotels. Expect prices to skyrocket during Urs Mela and the Pushkar Camel Fair.

Hotel Samrat, Kutchery Rd. (tel. 31805). Good-sized, clean, well-maintained rooms with minimal decor. Friendly staff. All rooms come with 24-hr. room service, satellite TVs, phones, and attached bathrooms. Laundry, travel services, car rentals, STD/ISD. Check-out 24hr. Service charge 10%. Singles Rs.150, with air-cooling Rs.200, with A/C Rs.450. Doubles with air-cooling Rs.250, with A/C Rs.550.

Bhola Hotel, Agra Gate (tel. 23844). Best of the "cheapies," Bhola has simple, well-decorated rooms and a restaurant that's hard to beat. 24-hr. room service, laundry, attached baths. Check-out 24hr. Singles Rs.100. Doubles Rs.150. Extra bed Rs.40. Air-cooling Rs.50.

Hotel Nagpal, Station Rd. (tel. 21603). Surprisingly quiet given its central location, Nagpal features clean rooms with TVs, phones, and attached baths. Laundry, travel services, 24-hr. room service. Check-out 24hr. Singles Rs.100-150, with air-cooling Rs.225, with A/C Rs.450. Doubles Rs.200, with air-cooling Rs.350, with A/C Rs.550. Extra person Rs.75, in A/C rooms Rs.150.

Hotel Sobhraj, Delhi Gate (tel. 30222). A slightly higher-end hotel. A picturesque red-and-white façade encloses large, well-kept rooms with large attached baths, phones, and satellite TVs. Laundry, travel services, 24-hr. room service, and restaurant. Check-out 24hr. Singles Rs.250, with air-cooling Rs.300-400, with A/C Rs.450-600. Doubles Rs.300, with air-cooling Rs.350-450, with A/C Rs.500-650. The A/C Mughal-e-azam, the Mirror Room, costs Rs.750.

Hotel Khadim, near Main Bus Stand (tel. 52490). Standard RTDC-tourist-bungalow-style with good-sized, but rather plain rooms. The staff is business-like. Restaurant, bar, 24-hr. room service. Check-out noon. Dorm beds Rs.50. Singles Rs.200, with air-cooling Rs.250, with A/C Rs.375. Doubles Rs.250, with air-cooling Rs.375, with A/C Rs.500.

FOOD

There aren't too many restaurants in Ajmer, but the few to be found are decent. For a quick bite, jet over to the snack, egg (Rs.10 for 5 hard-boiled), and juice stalls around Delhi Gate.

Honeydew Restaurant, Station Rd. (tel. 32498). Opposite the railway station, to the left. Considering the meager competition, Honeydew wins the prize for the best food in town for their high-quality veg. and non-veg., Continental, Chinese, and Indian cuisine. The outdoor seating is especially enjoyable. Entrees are around Rs.35. Open daily 8am-11pm.

Bhola Restaurant, Agra Gate (tel. 23844). Cooled, dim, pure-veg.-only Indian cuisine. Most entrees Rs.20-25; snacks under Rs.15. Open daily 8am-10:30pm.

Jodhpur Sweets, Prithviraj Marg (tel. 20916). The name says it all—sweets galore! Everything is also available in bulk for you to smuggle to Pushkar or to your friends at home (that is, if you don't devour them first). Open daily 7am-9:30pm.

Sabras, Prithviraj Marg (tel. 3095). Pure veg. underground dining. Popular among local families with decent food for Rs.20-25, and desserts for under Rs.15. Open daily 9am-11pm.

SIGHTS

When thousands of devotees flock to Ajmer during Urs Mela, **Dargah** is their destination. On the north side of town in the old city, the tomb of the Sufi saint **Khwaja Muin-ud-din Chishti** majestically erupts from the surrounding bazaars at the foot of a hill on the left side of Dargah Bazaar. Originally a simple brick cenotaph, Dargah has expanded to an elaborate marble complex as rich rulers have paid tribute. A tall, elaborate gateway leads to the first courtyard, where two massive cauldrons called *degs* are filled with rice that is then sold to devotees as *tabarukh,* a sanctified food. Akbar's mosque is to the right, and the exquisitely grand mosque of Shah Jahan farther inside. The tomb of the saint himself is in a central marble mosque, encircled by silver railings. Respectful behavior and a small donation is expected at Dargah.

Continuing on the road past Dargah about 500m takes you to the **Adhai-din-ka-jhonpra** (Mosque of 2½ Days) named for the time the legendary Muhammad of Ghur took to build it in 1193. Persian calligraphy climbs the seven arches of the façade, behind which giant pillars boast their individual forms. A 3-km hike along the road will elevate you to **Taragarh Fort,** or Star Fort, but your tiring effort will be rewarded with no more than a striking view.

Back in town, not too far from the GPO, is the **Daulat Khana Palace,** once the residence of the Mughal emperor Akbar. It now has been converted to the **government museum,** with usual collection of statues and assorted relics. (Open Sat.-Thurs. 10am-4:30pm; admission Rs.1. Photography prohibited.)

In the northeast side of town is the often-dried artificial lake **Ana Sagar.** It's a nice spot for a stroll or picnic when there's water (winter months), and the **Dault Bagh** gardens along the banks provide for a relaxing interlude. If you parade the busy bazaars of town, the magnificent rich red of the **Nasiyan Temple** may lure you in for a visit, and the **Jubilee Clock Tower** and **Edward Memorial Hall** near the railway station deserve an extended glance if you're in the area.

■ Pushkar

Legend holds that at the beginning of time Lord Brahma dropped a *pushkara,* or lotus flower, into the desert. Where the flower fell, a holy lake sprung—with its purifying waters pilgrims could be cleansed of all their sins. The lake is now the central attraction of the calm town of Pushkar, the site of the only Brahma temple in all of India. Some Hindu pilgrims consider Pushkar the final stop on their pilgrimages—a

> **Warning:** Given its religious and cultural roots, Pushkar is a purely vegetarian town, with strict prohibition of alcohol and drug use (the drug and alcohol scene in this quasi-hippie town is entirely underground). Although Pushkar's policies may clash with many Western conceptions of a good time, be respectful of the heritage and traditions of the town.

dip in the waters completes the circuit of redemption. Visitors come for a variety of reasons—if not for spiritual enlightenment, merely for some respite from the hassles and hustles of the bigger cities. The noisy auto-rickshaws that plague the cities are delightfully absent in Pushkar; a stroll around the 1-km-long city is peaceful and relaxed. This serenity is transformed into a beehive of activity in November for the annual Pushkar Fair, but otherwise the mellow mood prevails.

ORIENTATION

Pushkar runs less than 1km in each direction, so getting lost is hardly an issue. Most travelers arrive from Ajmer at the **Ajmer Bus Stand,** on **Ajmer Road** in the southeast side of town. Upon entering town, Ajmer Rd. becomes **Badi Basti** (Main Bazaar), the main thoroughfare, which follows the north "shore" of **Pushkar Lake.** Badi Basti terminates on the east side of town, near **Brahma Mandir.** A right-turn on one of the many meandering side streets off Badi Basti leads to a main road that marks the northern boundary of the town and hosts the GPO, the **Marwar Bus Stand,** and a few hospitals.

PRACTICAL INFORMATION

Tourist Office: At the time of publication, a tourist office was under construction. **Ajmer's Tourist Information Bureau** has the information about Pushkar. During the Pushkar Fair, the RTDC-run **Tourist Village** (tel. 72074) provides a wealth of information.

Currency Exchange: State Bank of Bikaner and Jaipur, Badi Basti, opposite Varah Ghat. Exchanges foreign currency and traveler's checks. Open Mon.-Fri. 11am-3pm.

Telephones: Private STD/ISD booths are virtually everywhere along Badi Basti. Many have fax services and call-back capability. A handful are open 24hr.

Buses: Ajmer Bus Stand, Ajmer Rd. To: Ajmer (every 10min., 6am-midnight, 30min., Rs.5). All other destinations can be reached through the **Main Bus Stand** in Ajmer. **Marwar Bus Stand,** on the north side of town, is where **private buses** depart from. Private bus companies line Badi Basti and the area around Marwar Bus Stand. For most destinations, they provide free jeep transportation to Ajmer, where their main offices are located and where most of their buses depart from. Some daily buses to Jaisalmer, Jodhpur, Udaipur, Bombay, and Delhi leave from Pushkar directly at the Marwar Bus Stand. **Ekta Travels** and **Srinath Travels Agency** are recommended agencies; they have offices throughout town. Most hotels make private and government bus and train arrangements for guests.

Local Transportation: The streets of Pushkar are quiet because rickshaws, taxis, jeeps, and large vehicles are prohibited. Most visitors travel everywhere on **foot. Bicycles** can be rented from several stops near the Ajmer Bus Stand (Rs.3 per hr. or Rs.20 per day on average).

English Bookstore: Laldon Bookshop, Badi Basti (tel. 72599), has a decent new and used paperback collection and some international magazines. Open daily 9am-11pm.

Market: Badi Basti is the main commercial area for all shopping, from foods to crafts. Most stalls open daily 8am-11pm, although some are closed Sun.

Pharmacy: Most pharmacies line the northern side of town, near the hospitals and Marwar Bus Stand. Most open daily 8am-11pm.

Hospital: Government Hospital, near Marwar Bus Stand (tel. 72029). English-speaking, reputable, open 24hr. Smaller private hospitals are located on the same road, but don't have the reputation of Government Hospital.

Police: Main Police Station, next to Government Hospital (tel. 72046). Tourist-friendly and English-speaking. Open 24hr.

Post Office: GPO, north side of town near Marwar Bus Stand. *Poste Restante,* packages. Open Mon.-Sat. 10am-6pm. A branch office is on Badi Basti for basic mail services only. **Postal Code:** 305022.

Telephone Code: 0145.

ACCOMMODATIONS

Pushkar's budget hotels number close to 100, with more being added by the week. Most are simply converted houses with clean cots and common baths. Lakeside views are rare, but rooftop sunsets generally don't disappoint. Hotels have different policies regarding drinking, smoking, and curfews—check in advance if you have preferences. Expect to get harassed at the Ajmer Bus Stand (and even in Ajmer) by assorted hoteliers. But remember that because Pushkar is so small, you can safely hit the hotels one by one with baggage in arms. The many *dharamshalas* around town are only available to Indian pilgrims. The prices of accommodations at least quadruple during the Pushkar Fair.

Peacock Holiday Resort, near Ajmer Bus Stand (tel. 72093; fax 422974). This resort has rooms of all types around a large lush garden and swimming pool. Attached baths, travel services, laundry, 24-hr. room service, restaurant. Check-out noon. Singles Rs.100-120, with air-cooling Rs.200. Doubles Rs.175, with air-cooling Rs.225. Extra bed Rs.50. Reservations highly recommended.

Sarovan Tourist Bungalow, off Ajmer Rd. (tel. 72040). This is not the ordinary RTDC tourist bungalow—in addition to good prices, it has sprawling gardens, a spacious lobby, a calm swimming pool, and immaculate rooms. Restaurant, STD/ISD booths, tourist information at hand. Six-day max. stay. Check-out noon. Dorm beds Rs.50. Singles Rs.100, with bath Rs.175, with air-cooling Rs.225, with lakeside view Rs.275. Doubles Rs.125, with bath Rs.225, with air-cooling Rs.275, with lakeside view Rs.350.

Hotel Pushkar Palace, off Ajmer Rd. (tel. 72001; fax 72226). A quality, high-end place with budget rooms. Situated around a lakeside garden and terrace, the rooms are clean with heritage decor. Limited room service, travel counter, laundry service, car rentals, luggage storage, STD/ISD, safaris, and excellent buffet restaurant. Check-out noon. Singles Rs.100, with bath and air-cooling Rs.250, with A/C Rs.750, with A/C and lakeside view Rs.950. Doubles Rs.150, with bath and air-cooling Rs.450, with A/C Rs.850, with A/C and lakeside view Rs.1050.

Krishna Guest House, Badi Basti (tel. 72091). A friendly, fun-loving family runs the house, with 30 basic rooms around a lush central garden. Laundry, travel services, safaris, rooftop restaurant. Check-out noon. Singles Rs.50, with bath Rs.60. Doubles Rs.100, with bath Rs.150. Triples with bath Rs.200.

Hotel Akash, near Brahma Temple (tel. 72498). Plain, baby-blue rooms are sparse, but the view of nearby temples is not. Travel services, laundry, room service. Check-out noon. Singles Rs.20-30, with bath and air-cooling Rs.50. Doubles with bath and air-cooling Rs.30-40.

Hotel White House, between Badi Basti and Marwar Bus Stand (tel. 72147; fax 72950). Although the name says white, the rooms are blue—and spotless, too. Gardens all around. Fresh milk and sweet and savory mango tea in rooftop restaurant. Run by an friendly family. 24-hr. room service, laundry service, safaris. Check-out 10am. Singles Rs.50, with bath and air-cooling Rs.80. Doubles Rs.100, with bath and air-cooling, Rs.150.

Hotel Brahma, across from Marwar Bus Stand (tel. 72361). Big, clean, simple rooms where you can "come and relax your mind, body, and soul." Garden restaurant, yoga, and meditation available. 24-hr. room service. Singles Rs.30, with bath Rs.60. Doubles Rs.40, with bath Rs.80. Air-cooling Rs.20. Extra bed Rs.10.

Hotel Oasis, Ajmer Bus Stand (tel. 72100). Delicate garden is an "oasis" amidst rather large, but bare rooms. Rooftop view of distant temples. 24-hr. room service, small swimming pool. Check-out noon. Singles with bath Rs.125, with air-cooling Rs.200. Doubles with bath Rs.150, with air-cooling Rs.300.

RTDC Tourist Village, northwest corner of town beyond Marwar Bus Stand (tel. 72074). Originally set up only for the Pushkar Fair, the Tourist Village is now available for year-round accommodations, even though many facilities such as currency exchange, tourist bureau, medical center, shops, and restaurants may be dormant. The Tourist Village is made up of hut accommodations. Singles Rs.125, with air-cooling Rs.175. Doubles Rs.150, with air-cooling Rs.225. Extra bed Rs.100. Tents available during the fair. Reservations required well in advance for the fair dates—contact the head RTDC office in Jaipur (tel. (0141) 60586).

FOOD

While Pushkar has its share of good Indian cuisine, Western food is what travelers come to savor here. Baked potatoes, pancakes, pizzas, pies, cereals, pastas, and sandwiches are everywhere, almost as common as the rather unpleasant, but trendy all-you-can-eat buffets with their reheated food. Pushkar is by law strictly vegetarian—no meat, no eggs. All alcohol and drugs are also banned. For quick snacks and sweets, a stroll down Badi Basti should satisfy a craving.

Raju Garden Restaurant, Ram Ghat (tel. 72356). On a side street off Badi Basti near Ram Ghat. A full range of excellent Indian, Continental, and Chinese dishes "all cooked with love by Raju." Outdoor seating in verdant setting. Indian dishes under Rs.25, others Rs.30-40. Open daily 8am-11pm.

Prince Restaurant, in Hotel Pushkar Palace, off Ajmer Rd. (tel. 72001). Outdoor seating with lakeside view. The best buffet in town—a bit pricey but the food is excellent. Expect to pay Rs.40 for most entrees. Open daily 6am-10:30pm.

Sarovar Garden Restaurant, near Ajmer Bus Stand. Good food, fast service, standard range of mixed cuisines, and, of course, all-you-can-eat buffets. Open daily 7am-10pm.

Venus Rooftop Restaurant, Badi Basti (tel. 72323). Another multi-cuisine restaurant, but with particularly tasty Indian dishes and a rooftop view of the lake and city. *Thalis* Rs.25. Open daily 7:30am-11pm.

Rainbow Rooftop Restaurant, near Brahma Temple (tel. 72044). Delightful, well-prepared Indian and Western dishes and a menu that is as extensive as the rooftop view. Prices lean markedly on the high side: pizzas (Rs.45-50), pastas (Rs.40-50). Open daily 8am-11pm.

Sun-n-Moon Garden Café, Badi Basti (tel. 72142). A good assortment of everything in a beautiful and bugless garden setting. Specializes in snacks and quick meals, most under Rs.25. Open daily 8am-10pm.

R.S., opposite Brahma Temple. Popular among locals. Good Indian dishes for under Rs.25. Garden and terrace seating. Open daily 7am-11pm.

SIGHTS

Most of Pushkar's 400 **temples** were rebuilt after assorted raids and pillages by the Mughal emperor Aurangzeb in the 17th century. A few of the temples are only open to Hindus. The most visited temple is the **Brahma Mandir,** which has the surprising distinction of being the only temple in India dedicated to Brahma, the Hindu creator god. The temple has a red minaret with a painted blue-and-green base and smaller shrines flanking the sides. Expect to be mobbed by eager guides; their services are hardly necessary to view the temple. There are two major hillside temples in Pushkar, offering superb panoramic vistas of the town and valley, especially at sunset and sunrise. Named after two of Brahma's wives, **Saivitri Mandir** and **Gayitri Mandir,** crown hills on the east and west side of town that demand an intense one-and-a-half-hour climb. Other temples of interest include the **Rangji Mandir** with its white stone facade, the **Hanuman Mandir,** a colorful tower depicting Hanuman's exploits, and the turquoise-green **Baba Ramdev Mandir.**

Encircling Pushkar Lake are broad **ghats,** connecting the temples and the holy waters. Of Pushkar's 52 *ghats,* the most important are the **Gau Ghat,** where an assortment of politicians, ministers, and VIPs have paid their respects, **Brahma Ghat,** which Brahma himself is said to have used, and the central **Varah Ghat,** where

> ### The Pushkar Fair
>
> The annual Pushkar Fair is an event of colossal numbers, crowding 200,000 people from all over the world into one square kilometer. Thousands of pilgrims bathe in the lake's holy waters seeking redemption for their sins. At the same time, an enormous camel fair brings in over 50,000 camels, who excite the masses in races, auctions, contests, parades, and, of course, safaris. Performers are at every corner while the streets are crammed with stalls selling handicrafts and unique items from all over India. And it wouldn't be a fair without food—you won't be able to keep away from the specialty cuisines. At night, the air echoes with the sound of bells and songs, and is thick with scented smoke from campfires around the edge of town. The dates vary each year as per the lunar calendar; in 1997, the fair is November 11-14. The RTDC's Tourist Village is filled to capacity to accommodate the rush; make reservations well in advance. Expect prices of everything to at least quadruple.

Vishnu is said to have made an appearance in the form of a boar. Signs in almost every hotel instruct visitors to remove their shoes 50m from the lake, and to refrain from smoking and photography while at the *ghats*. Respectful, modest behavior is expected. Pilgrims and tourists at the *ghats* request local Brahmins to perform a Pushkar *puja*, a ceremony of scripture-reading and rose-petal-scattering for a donation which generally goes to the temple, but occasionally to the Brahmin. Do not feel pressured into donating the exorbitant amounts that the priests insist are "standard." After the *puja*, your patronage is officially recognized with a red wrist-band—the "Pushkar Passport"—giving you the freedom to visit *ghats* and stroll around town without harassment from Brahmins.

ENTERTAINMENT AND SHOPPING

The **Pushkar Fair** is jam-packed with entertainment opportunities; otherwise, Pushkar caters to the mellow, relaxing side of things. Most visitors enjoy meandering the tiny streets, visiting the temples and *ghats,* and maybe making the hike up to a nearby hill for the view. **Camel safaris** into the desert are becoming increasingly popular in Pushkar, along with **camel treks** across the desert to Jaisalmer, Jodhpur, or Bikaner. Many hotels and most travel agents make these arrangements for you; Expect to pay around Rs.250 per day for a good camel safari. If you don't have enough time for a safari or trek but want to make friends with a hump-back, go for a **camel ride**—loop around the city Rs.50 per hour. To beat the heat, take a dip in the Peacock Holiday Resort's **swimming** pool for Rs.40.

The **shopping scene** is expansive but expensive, especially during the Pushkar Fair. Nonetheless, it's fun to stroll down Badi Basti, visiting clothing, music, and handicrafts shops, bargaining big-time along the way of course.

■ Kota

The city of Kota, situated 230km south of Jaipur, is fast on its way to becoming Rajasthan's most industrialized city, with its bevy of chemical industries, hydroelectric centers, thermal power stations, and its nuclear plant. Unfortunately, industrial development means pollution, noise, and the occasional accident. In 1992, radioactivity levels in the area were found to be "abnormally high." Nonetheless, Kota holds on to its medieval past with its stone fort and enclosed museum, which is perhaps the best in Rajasthan. Originally part of Bundi, Kota became a separate state in 1624 and remained sovereign into this century. Relatively untouristed, Kota is striving to take on an important role in the state, through booming industry and tourism promotion. The latter endeavor is most successful during the Dusshera Mela Festival (Oct. 9-11 in 1997), a celebration marked by theatrics and goat sacrifices.

ORIENTATION

Kota sprawls along the east bank of the cool and clean **River Chambal.** In the north end of town sits the **railway station,** with the busy **Railway Colony** around it. The road south into the city is **Civil Lines.** Three kilometers down Civil Lines is **Collectorate Circle.** A bit ahead is the GPO on the right and Maharao Bhim Singh Hospital on the left. Less than 1km farther ahead lies another circle—go right for the bus stand, straight ahead for the commercial **Nayapura** area and fort, and left followed by an immediate right (past green gardens) to reach the Tourist Reception Centre. From here you can continue straight ahead to **Kishor Sagar,** the artificial lake that marks the center of town. On the other side of the lake, **Jhalawar Road** runs southeast through **Gumanpura.** At the intersection near the State Bank of India, **Chhatrapuna** runs south 3km through the **airport, Talvandi Scheme,** and **Instrumentation Colony,** home of the big industries. The fort can also be entered from the south side of town—just follow the walls to an entrance. **Naya Darvaza** is the main entrance.

PRACTICAL INFORMATION

Tourist Office: Tourist Reception Centre, Nayapura (tel. 27695). Next to Chambal Tourist Bungalow. Provides maps, assorted brochures from all over Rajasthan, and transportation schedules. No tours available. Open Mon.-Sat. 8am-6pm.

Currency Exchange: State Bank of India, Jhalawar Rd. (tel. 25417). Slow currency and traveler's check exchanges. Open Mon.-Fri. 10am-2pm, Sat. 10am-noon. **State Bank of Bikaner and Jaipur,** Instrumentation Colony (tel. 421784). The only SBBJ branch in the city with foreign exchange services, including traveler's checks. Open Mon.-Sat. noon-4pm.

Telephones: Private STD/ISD booths dot the city street. Few have fax services. The railway station has a **telecom booth** with STD/ISD and fax services, open 24hr. **Central Telegraph Office,** in GPO, open 24hr.

Trains: Railway station (tel. 441162). A Rs.15 rickshaw ride or a Rs.2 minibus/tempo ride from the city. Both the telecom and reservation offices are Hindi-speaking only. To: Jaipur (191 and 193, 5:30am and 11:45pm, 5hr., Rs.30; *Bombay-Jaipur Exp.* 2995, 8:30am, 4hr., Rs.62/250); Chittorgarh (82, 7:10am, 5½hr., Rs.15).

Buses: Main Bus Stand (tel. 24154). To: Ajmer (every 30-45min., 4:30am-11pm, 5½hr., Rs.52); Bundi (every 15-20min., 4am-midnight, 50min., Rs.10); Jodhpur (express, 7 per day, 5:15am-9pm, deluxe 7 and 10pm, 10hr., Rs.68/Rs.100 for express/deluxe); Udaipur (9:15am, 2, 8:15, and 10pm, 8½hr., Rs.80); Mt. Abu (7pm, 12hr., Rs.115); Chittorgarh (8:30, 9:15am, 2, 8:15, and 10pm, 6hr., Rs.53); Jaipur (every hr., 8am-10pm, 6½hr., Rs.62/Rs.78 for express/deluxe). Some government buses leave from **Gumanpura Circle** as well. To Chittorgarh (noon and 3pm, 6hr., Rs.53). A few private bus companies with limited routes are around the bus stand and near the GPO.

Local Transportation: Auto-rickshaws are everywhere, and will generally try to charge foreigners double fare. From the railway station to the bus stand, pay no more than Rs.15. For **cycle-rickshaws,** equally ubiquitous, expect to pay around Rs.8. **Minibuses** and **tempos** go everywhere and make the journey from railway station to bus stand, packed full of people, for Rs.2.50. Ambassador **taxis** can be found near Collectorate Circle, before the GPO, and charge about Rs.8 per km.

English Bookstore: A few news agencies in the Railway Colony and in Gumanpura have magazines in English.

Market: Street bazaar areas are located in **Railway Colony,** around the railway station, **Gumanpura** and its associated **shopping center,** and inside the fort. High concentrations of fruit and vegetable stalls. Most open Mon.-Sat. 8am-10pm.

Pharmacy: A slew of pharmacies surround Maharao Bhim Singh Hospital on Civil Lines and Baheti Hospital on Talvandi Scheme. Most open 9am-9pm.

Hospital: Maharao Bhim Singh Hospital, Civil Lines (tel. 23261). English-speaking, big, and government-run. Open 24hr. The best private hospital is **Baheti Hospital and Research Centre,** Talvandi Scheme (tel. 427359), before Instrumentation Colony. Open 24hr.

Emergency: Police, tel. 100. **Fire,** tel. 101. **Ambulance,** tel. 23261 (MBS Hospital).
Police: Main Police Station, Civil Lines (tel. 100). Near GPO. English-speaking.
Open 24hr.
Post Office: GPO, Civil Lines (tel. 2759). One kilometer before the bus stand on the
right, from the railway station. *Poste Restante.* Open Mon.-Sat. 8am-10pm. **Postal
Code:** 324001.
Telephone Code: 0744.

ACCOMMODATIONS

Kota's budget hotel scene mirrors its tourist industry—scarce'and generally ill-main-
tained. Clusters of decent hotels can be found around the railway station, but these
are far from the action. Noisy and dingy places shadow the area around the bus stand
and Nayapura. It's worth digging a bit deeper in your pockets to get decent accommodations in Kota. Homestay accommodation is also available through the tourist
office for Rs.300-500 per night.

Phul Plaza, Civil Lines (tel. 22356; fax 22614). Before the GPO. A great value—
travel counter, taxi services, laundry service, good restaurant, color TV, attached
baths, 24-hr. room service. Well-kept rooms. Check-out noon. Singles Rs.200, with
A/C and larger room Rs.600. Doubles Rs.320, with A/C and larger room Rs.700.
Service charge 10%.
Hotel Brijraj Bhawan Palace, Civil Lines (tel. 450529; fax 450057). On a road to
the right before the GPO, coming from the railway station. Still the home of the
Maharaja of Kota, this hotel features luxurious peacock-filled gardens flanking the
Chambal River, and magnificently decorated rooms and lounges. The dining hall
(for guests only) has the best food and stuffed tiger heads in town. Travel counter,
car rentals, laundry service, satellite TV in lounge. Check-out noon. Service charge
10%. All rooms have A/C and attached grand bath. Singles Rs.800. Doubles
Rs.1050. Suites Rs.1300. Reservations necessary in season.
Shri Anand Hotel, Railway Colony (tel. 441157). The best of the distant railway sta-
tion bunch. Good-size rooms decorated in pastels. Decent veg. restaurant, STD/
ISD, 24-hr. room service, check-out 24hr. All private rooms have attached baths.
Dorms Rs.30. Singles Rs.150. Doubles Rs.250. Extra bed Rs.25.
Chambal Tourist Bungalow, Kishor Bagh (tel. 26527). Rooms are simple and
sparsely decorated. Relaxing gardens outside. Restaurant, 24-hr. room service,
tourist information, attached baths, air-cooling. Singles Rs.225, with A/C and TV
Rs.400. Doubles Rs.275, with A/C and TV Rs.450. Extra person Rs.100.
Hotel Marudhar, Jhalawar Rd. (tel. 26186; fax 24415). Near the State Bank of India.
A solid place with a wealth of services including STD/ISD, fax, laundry, travel
counter, 24-hr. room service, and photocopier. Check-out noon. Service charge
10%. Good-sized, clean, carpeted, rooms with TV and attached bath. Singles
Rs.115, with A/C Rs.300, larger with A/C Rs.400. Doubles Rs.165, with A/C Rs.350,
larger with A/C Rs.450. Reservations recommended.
Hotel Chaman, Nayapura at the end of Civil Lines (tel. 23377). Threadbare, rooms
are dirt-cheap. Check-out 24hr. Singles Rs.30, with bath Rs.55. Doubles with bath
Rs.80. Triples with bath Rs.140.

FOOD

Culinary creations are not quintessential Kota. There are few stand-alone restaurants
in Kota; most are attached to hotels and offer decent, but not delectable meals. A
number of cheapies are in Railway Colony, fewer in Nayapura and along Jhalawar Rd.
The best food in town is in the Hotel Brijraj Bhawan Palace—but you must be a guest
to enjoy the best.

Maheshwari Bhojnayal, Nayapura (tel. 27662). All veg., high-quality food under
Rs.25, in a cooled dining hall. Popular in the area. Open daily 9am-11pm.

Plaza, in Hotel Phul Plaza, Civil Lines (tel. 22356). Dimly lit in the basement of the hotel, this restaurant serves tasty veg. fare for around Rs.30 and a host of snacks for under Rs.20. Open daily 7am-11pm.

Ratan Sev Bhander, Nayapura. Jump up and down and wave a Rs.10 note (the locals wave Rs.5) to get through the mob to the most popular snack shop around. Open daily 10am-10:30pm.

SIGHTS

The **fort** and its enclosed **city palace,** among the largest in the state, proudly dominate Kota, jutting up from the bustling street below. The fort, originally built in 1264, didn't reach its current level of grandeur until 1625, with the completion of the city palace. Now, as the unmaintained fort becomes increasingly run-down, the palace retains its historical elegance. By far the most impressive part of the palace is the **Maharao Madro Singh Museum,** considered by most to be the premiere museum in all of Rajasthan. Enter the museum through **Hathian Pol,** a highly decorated and colorful gateway flanked by brass cannons and painted elephants. Inside to the right, the **Raj Mahal** dazzles with its intricately painted chamber and nearly blinds with its mirrored surfaces. To the left is a gallery of miscellanea, including statues, instruments, silver waterpipes, Chinese porcelain, clocks, scales, vases, chess sets, and Kota *kamba*—painted miniature figurines, a regional specialty. Around the corner is yet another weapons gallery featuring a vast assortment of rifles, swords, armor, guns, arrows, and polearms. In the basement, there is another collection—this time, it's assorted stuffed animals in a wildlife gallery. Finally, there is a not-so-interesting black-and-white photograph collection. (Open Sat.-Thurs. 11am-5pm; admission Rs.40, camera fee Rs.35, video fee Rs.75.)

Outside the fort walls lies the artificial lake **Kishor Sagar.** When it is filled (winter months), it provides for a picturesque view of the fanciful, multi-tiered **Jagmandir Palace** in the middle. Unfortunately, the palace is not open to the public. To see it, you need special permission from the Public Works Department behind Collectorate Circle. You can get a close view, however, in the RTDC paddle-boats that line the banks (Rs.30).

About 2km south of the fort sit the lush **Chambal Gardens,** a popular picnic and hangout spot. The garden's dwindling population of crocodiles and gharials is the main attraction. The **Chhattar Bilas Gardens** near the Tourist Bungalow are peaceful with its collection of *chhattris,* each guarded by a pair of simple stone elephants.

On the north side of Kishor Sagar is the government-run **Brij Vilas Palace Museum,** a moderately interesting collection of statues, weapons, clothing, paintings, and battle plans. (Open Sat.-Thurs.; admission Rs.5, camera fee Rs.35, video camera fee Rs.75.)

▓ Chittorgarh

What do you get when you mix chivalry with the sacrifice of legendary Rajputana? Chittorgarh. Its massive fort is perched on a prominent plateau 115km northeast of Udaipur; its prime location has made it a a point of contention for centuries. In Chittorgarh's battle-scarred history, three moments stand out that effectively summarize the Rajput ideal of "death before dishonor." In 1303, the Delhi Sultan Ala-ud-din Khilji besieged the city in an attempt to capture the beautiful Padmini, wife of Maharaja Ratan Singh. The odds were overwhelmingly against the starved Chittorgarhi people. In an act of sacrifice, 13,000 women declared *jauhar* (self-immolation), throwing themselves on a funeral pyre to save themselves from the conquerors, while 7000 warriors donned orange robes and went forth into battle certain of defeat and death. Then, in 1535, the Gujarati Sultan Bahadur Shah attacked by surprise, annihilating another generation of Rajput warriors. In 1568, Akbar of the Mughals laid siege to the city, killing over 30,000 inhabitants. In both cases, the women committed *jauhar* in their relentless loyalty to Rajput duty. Nevertheless, the Rajput Udai Singh founded a new capital in Udaipur, where the royal family remains to this day. The people of

Chittorgarh remember their turbulent history proudly, although thankfully the town has quieted. It's rather surprising that Chittorgarh and its impressive array of sights are so rarely visited.

ORIENTATION

Chittorgarh is fairly spaced out and unfortunately not very conducive to travel by foot. The **railway station** is on the east side of town. The major branch to the right of **Station Road,** which runs straight north out to Ajmer, is **City Road.** The GPO and General Hospital are near this junction. City Rd. passes the **Roadways Bus Stand** before proceeding to the base of the fort, where it turns into **Fort Road.** The main commercial area and the new city are here. Fort Rd. zig-zags steeply up to the fort, which sprawls 7km across the plateau. One main road loops around inside the fort and leads to all of Chittorgarh's major sights.

PRACTICAL INFORMATION

Tourist Office: Tourist Reception Centre, Station Rd. (tel. 41089). Provides maps, brochures, travel information. Open Mon.-Sat. 10am-1:30pm and 2-5pm.

Currency Exchange: State Bank of Bikaner and Jaipur, Station Rd. (tel. 41708). Open Mon.-Sat. 10am-2pm, Sun. 10am-noon. **State Bank of India,** near Roadways Bus Stand, City Rd. (tel. 40902). Open Mon.-Sat. 10am-5pm. Both banks exchange foreign currency and traveler's checks.

Telephones: Private STD/ISD booths can be found along Station Rd. and down City Rd. up to the base of the fort. A few have fax services. None open 24hr. Most open 8am-11pm.

Trains: Railway Station, Station Rd. (tel. 131). Reservation office open daily 10am-5pm. No luggage storage. To: Udaipur (*Chetak Exp.* 9615, 6:30am, 4hr., Rs.70/112; passenger, 1:30pm, 6hr., Rs.41); Ajmer (*Pink City Exp.,* 9:20am, 6hr., Rs.55/230; *Passenger,* 11:30am, 6hr., Rs.45); Kota (*Niraj Kota Exp.,* 2:10pm, 5hr., Rs.40/80); Jaipur (*Chetak Exp.* 9615, 10pm, 8hr., Rs.90/150; *Pink City Exp.,* 9:20am, 8hr., Rs.90/280).

Buses: Roadways Bus Stand (tel. 20398). To: Udaipur (every hr., 6am-11pm, 3hr., Rs.35); Jaipur (express, 7 per day, 6:15am-10:45pm; deluxe, 6 per day, 10:30am-10:30pm, 8hr., Rs.80/120 for express/deluxe); Ajmer (all buses to Jaipur stop at Ajmer, 5½hr., Rs.56); Kota (7:30am, 4, 9:15, and 10:30pm, 6½hr., Rs.50); Abu Road (7am, 12hr., Rs.90); Jodhpur (9:30am, 8½hr., Rs.100). A few private bus companies located on Station Rd. operate to most destinations.

Local Transportation: Unmetered **auto-rickshaws** and horse-pulled **tongas** are the most common modes of transport. An auto-rickshaw ride up to the fort costs Rs.20; tongas won't make the climb up. Many auto-rickshaws operate tempo-style—cramming people in and charging Rs.5 to get around the city, Rs.10 to get up to the fort. A roundtrip up to the fort, around all the sights, and back again should cost Rs.100, Rs.50 off-season. You can rent **bicycles** from places near Railway Station (Rs.15 per day). You'll have to walk the bike up to the fort, but the cruise down is thrilling.

Market: The main market area for food, provisions, and general crafts is around Fort Rd., at the base of the fort. Most stores open daily 9am-9pm.

Pharmacy: A collection of pharmacies exists around the General Hospital near the Station City Rd. intersection. Most open daily 9am-10:30pm.

Hospital: General Hospital, Station Rd. (tel. 102). English-speaking, large, efficient, open 24hr. There are a number of private hospitals around—the best are **Aditya Hospital,** Station Rd. (tel. 41544) and **Jainani Hospital,** City Rd. (tel. 40222). Both English-speaking and open 24hr.

Police: Main Police Station, opposite Roadways Bus Stand (tel. 41060).

Emergency: Police, tel. 41060. **Fire,** tel. 41101. **Ambulance,** tel. 41102.

Post Office: GPO, Station Rd. (tel. 41159). *Poste Restante,* packages; helpful staff. Open Mon.-Sat. 10am-1pm and 2-6pm. **Postal Code:** 312001.

Telephone Code: 01472.

ACCOMMODATIONS

There's little in the way of good accommodations in Chittorgarh. There is a cluster of basic, noisy places near the railway station—better lodging is further away. Rickshaw-*wallahs* operate on commission, so be wary of Rs.2 offers for rides to hotels.

Hotel Pratap Palace, opposite GPO (tel. 40099; fax 41042). Large, clean, modern singles with comfortable pillows. Attached baths, laundry, 24-hr. room service, guides, safaris (Rs.600 per day), car rentals, travel counter, excellent garden restaurant, bar. Check-out noon. In season: singles Rs.250, with air-cooling Rs.375, with A/C Rs.500. Doubles Rs.280, with air-cooling Rs.425, with A/C Rs.580. Off season: 20% discount.

Hotel Panna, off Station Rd. (tel. 41238). Standard RTDC tourist bungalow accommodations—well-maintained, but bare rooms. Dining hall, bar, guides. Check-out noon. Dorm beds Rs.50. Singles with bath Rs.100, with air-cooling Rs.200, with A/C Rs.400. Doubles with bath Rs.150, with air-cooling Rs.275, with A/C Rs.500. Extra bed Rs.100.

Hotel Chetak, opposite Railway Station (tel. 41588). Best of the Station Rd. cheapies, the Chetak is modern, but can be noisy at times. Limited room service, veg. restaurant, STD/ISD. Attached baths. Check-out 24hr. Singles Rs.150-200, larger with color TV Rs.250. Doubles Rs.225-275, larger with color TV Rs.350.

Shalimar Hotel, opposite Railway Station (tel. 40842). Threadbare, noisy rooms, but clean and well-maintained. 24-hr. room service, restaurant, check-out 24hr. Singles with bath Rs.80, with air-cooling Rs.150. Doubles with bath Rs.125, with air-cooling Rs.175. Extra bed Rs.25.

Natraj Tourist Hotel, near Roadways Bus Stand (tel. 41009). Conveniently located but on the loud side. Central garden is calm. No-frills rooms. Singles Rs.30, with bath Rs.60, with air-cooling Rs.100. Doubles Rs.45, with bath Rs.90, with air-cooling Rs.150. Hot water buckets Rs.2.

FOOD

There are some cheap eateries around the railway station, good for snacks and drinks, but otherwise restaurants are scarce and unspectacular. Hotel restaurants are your best bet.

Morcha Restaurant, in Hotel Pratap Palace (tel. 40099). Peaceful and comfortable garden dining, with a range of cuisines. Prices on the high side; most are Rs.30-40. Open daily 7am-10:30pm.

Melody Restaurant, near Railway Station (tel. 41415). Cheap veg. and non-veg. food. Continental, Chinese, Indian, snacks, and desserts. Most less than Rs.25. Open daily 8am-11:30pm.

SIGHTS

Jutting suddenly from the flat plateau below, Chittorgarh's **fort** is perhaps the most impressive structure in all of Rajasthan. **Padan Pol** is the first *pol* (gate), in a series of seven that meander 1km from the east side of town to the fort entrance. The climb to the top is grueling; even rickshaws tend to struggle. Near the second *pol* are the *chhattris* (cenotaphs) of the heroic martyrs **Kalla** and **Jaimal,** who died in the final sack of Chittorgarh in 1568. The final gate, **Rama Pol,** serves as the entrance to the fort proper. All the sights of interest in Chittorgarh are inside the fort, and the view from the ramparts on all sides is spectacular. Although rickshaw drivers will persist in their offers to take you around the fort, it's worth taking the time to walk the narrow tree-studded streets from sight to sight.

The 15th-century Jain temple **Shingara Chauri Mandir** is just inside the fort to the right. Its elaborate decoration points to Hindu influence. Just ahead is the quasi-ruined **Rana Kumbha Palace,** where the third *jauhar* of Chittorgarh supposedly took place in an underground cellar. But after the siege of the city, only stables and a temple to Shiva remain. The **Fateh Prakash Palace** is architecturally uninteresting, but houses a **government museum,** featuring a poorly illuminated collection of weapons and sculptures. (Open Sat.-Thurs., 10am-4:30pm; admission Rs.2, photography prohibited.) The towered **Kumbha Shyam Mandir** and the elegant **Meera Mandir,** which honors the Jodhpuri mystic poetess Mirabai, are also nearby.

Following the shady Fort Rd. south leads to the **Jaya Stambha** (Tower of Victory), which adorns every brochure and postcard of Chittorgarh and a good amount of RTDC literature. The sandstone tower boasts Chittorgarh's story and glory from an imposing 37m. Elaborate multi-denominational sculptures grace the exterior. The tower's construction began in 1458 to commemorate an important victory in 1440, and took 10 years to complete. You can climb its nine stories for Rs.0.50; if your breath is not taken away by bumping your head on the low ceilings, it will be by the awesome view. The ramparts around the tower are a popular relaxation spot as well. The **Sammidheshwar Mandir** is nearby on the hill, as is **Mahasati** with its frighteningly large collection of *sati* marks.

Off the main road a bit further south is the **Gaumukh Kund** (Cow's Mouth Tank), so named because of the carved cow's mouth from which a spring feeds a tank. Continue down the main road to **Padmini's Palace,** a dainty but run-down palace sitting in a shallow pool. According to legend, Ala-ud-din-Khilji saw beautiful Padmini's reflection in a palace mirror, and setting his sight on her (and his might on Chittorgarh), he staged the first siege of Chittorgarh that led to the horrendous acts of *jauhar.* The **Kalika Mata Mandir** is right across. It was originally dedicated to the sun god Surya back in the eighth century, but now pays tribute to the goddess Kali. The carvings on the outside depict divine figures and myths.

The road continues down south for a while, looping past the often-empty **Deer Park,** the quiet **Bhimlat Tank,** and a small crack-in-the wall where traitors and political prisoners were thrown to their deaths 200m below. The road then turns north again past **Suraj Pol,** the eastern gate of the fort, and Chittorgarh's number two tower—the **Kirti Stambha** (Tower of Fame) at 22m. Built by a wealthy Jain merchant, the tower wears decorative images of the Jain pantheon, particularly that of Adinath, the first Jain *tirthankara,* to whom the tower is dedicated.

■ Near Chittorgarh

Forty kilometers south of Chittorgarh rests **Bijaipur,** an unspectacular village with a spectacular 200-year-old palace. The palace is now **Hotel Castle Bijaipur** (tel. 40099). The hotel is related to Hotel Pratap Palace in Chittorgarh, but it maintains the antique furniture, and the original courtyards and alcoves. The palace offers fancy rooms and blissful solitude, along with village safaris (Rs.700 per day), and horse and camel safaris. Check-out noon. Singles Rs.725. Doubles Rs.800. Excellent dinners Rs.225. Ninety kilometers towards Bundi lies **Meral,** a series of 12th-century Shiva temples surrounded by rumbling waterfalls and foliage.

■ Udaipur

Udaipur ("City of Lakes"), is the romantic epitome of nature, chivalry, and artistry. Countless visitors plan to tour the sights in a few days, but end up staying for weeks. The enchanting old city overlooking the green Lake Pichola is postcard-perfect and delightfully removed from the industrialization and commercialization farther out. But even in Udaipur, the logging industry has taken its effect, replacing the once lusciously arboreal valleys with barrenness and higher temperatures.

After Chittorgarh's final siege in 1568, Maharaja Udai Singh II fled to Lake Pichola, where he founded Udaipur. Four years later, Udai's son, Pratap, led the troops that successfully defended Udaipur against invasion by Akbar's fierce forces. For the next 150 years peace was the norm. The city grew in opulence with support for the arts. Miniature painting became a specialty as architects had field days creating majestic palaces all around. In 1736 the city was crippled by the destructive Marathas, but bounced back with British aid while remaining firmly independent. Since then, the

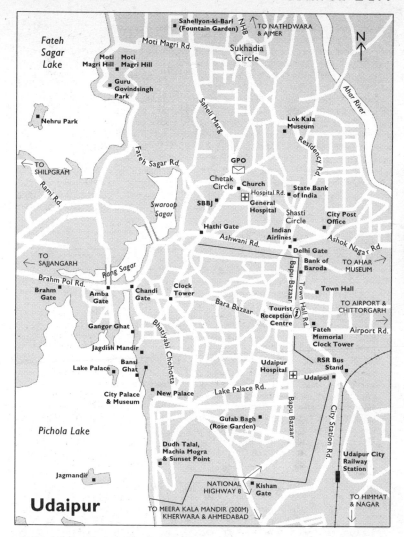

Udaipur

Map labels:

Fateh Sagar Lake
Sahellyon-ki-Bari (Fountain Garden)
NH8
TO NATHDWARA & AJMER
Moti Magri Rd.
Sukhadia Circle
Moti Magri Hill
Moti Magri Hill
Guru Govindsingh Park
Nehru Park
TO SHILPGRAM
Fateh Sagar Rd.
Saheli Marg
Lok Kala Museum
Residency Rd.
Ahar River
GPO
Chetak Circle
Church
Hospital Rd.
State Bank of India
Swaroop Sagar
SBBJ
General Hospital
Shasti Circle
City Post Office
Ashok Nagar Rd.
Hathi Gate
Ashwani Rd.
Indian Airlines
Rami Rd.
TO SAJJANGARH
Rang Sagar
Delhi Gate
Bank of Baroda
TO AHAR MUSEUM
Brahm Pol Rd.
Brahm Gate
Amba Gate
Chandi Gate
Clock Tower
Bara Bazaar
Bapu Bazaar
Town Hall Rd.
Town Hall
TO AIRPORT & CHITTORGARH
Gangor Ghat
Tourist Reception Centre
Fateh Memorial Clock Tower
Airport Rd.
Jagdish Mandir
Bhatiyabi Chohotta
RSR Bus Stand
Bansi Ghat
Lake Palace
Udaipur Hospital
Udaipol
City Palace & Museum
New Palace
Lake Palace Rd.
City Station Rd.
Pichola Lake
Gulab Bagh (Rose Garden)
Bapu Bazaar
Dudh Talai, Machia Mogra & Sunset Point
Udaipur City Railway Station
Jagmandir
NATIONAL HIGHWAY 8
Kishan Gate
TO HIMMAT & NAGAR
TO MEERA KALA MANDIR (200M) KHERWARA & AHMEDABAD

city's arts have continued to flourish along with its romanticism. More recently, the locals are still hyper over the James Bond movie *Octopussy*, which was filmed here. The Mewar Festival (April 10-11 in 1997), is particularly lively with dances, music, fireworks, and a brilliant lake parade.

ORIENTATION

Situated 113km southwest of Chittorgarh and 270km south of Ajmer, Udaipur rolls gently with the green hills of the surrounding Aravali mountains in the south of Rajasthan. Udaipur is composed of the **old city,** which straddles the northeast bank of the deep green of Lake Pichola and the **new city,** which expands to the north, east, and south. The city is laid out with little rhyme or reason.

The first area of practical interest is the **Udaipur City Railway Station,** which sits to the southeast of town along **City Station Road.** Taking a right out of the station and trekking about 2km north will land you at the city's bus stand, just opposite **Udai Gate,** one of the four main entrances to the old city. Following the same main road will lead to **Suraj Gate,** another city entrance, which also opens into two of the city's main shopping drags: **Bapu Bazaar** and **Bara Bazaar.** Bapu Bazaar leads off to the right (north) to **Delhi Gate** and runs parallel to **Town Hall Road,** home to many banks.

Another important area is **Shastri Circle** to the northeast. The RTDC tourist complex is located less than a block away. The street directly ahead houses the City Post Office. The road that forks to the left leads away from Shastri Circle to Delhi Gate and to **Chetak Circle** on the right or **Hathi Gate** on the left. Chetak Circle is a nearly 1-km walk from Shastri Circle. When approaching from this side, the GPO lies on the first street to the right.

Hathi Gate is on the north end of the old city and affords the easiest access to its focal points—the **City Palace** and **Jagdish Mandir** by way of the **clock tower.** At the clock tower, the right fork uphill leads toward the Jagdish Mandir as the left fork leads back toward Suraj Gate, which leads into the old city via **Lake Palace Road** and **Bhatiyani Chohotta (B.C.).**

PRACTICAL INFORMATION

Tourist Office: Tourist Reception Centre, Suraj Gate (tel. 411535). Moderately helpful staff has up-to-date maps and brochures. Open Mon.-Sat. 10am-5pm. **Tourist Information Bureau,** at the railway station, has a smaller collection of maps and brochures and basic information. Open Mon.-Sat. 7:30-11:30am and 4-7pm. A smaller tourist information counter is at Dabok Airport. **Tours** are offered from **Kajri Tourist Bungalow** (tel. 40501). Around: Udaipur (8am, 5hr., Rs.40); Haldighati, Nathdwara, and Eklingi (2pm, 5hr., Rs.70); Chittorgarh, Ranakpur, Kumbhalgarh, or Ghanerao (daylong, includes lunch, by demand only, 10-person min.; Rs.200).

Budget Travel: Dozens line City Station Rd. and the Jagdish Mandir area, and there are more around Delhi Gate and Chetak Circle. Most hotels are front-ends for these agencies as well. Travel agencies offer a combination of train, bus, and plane tickets, city tours (Rs.40-50), airport shuttles (Rs.150), private car rentals, and tours of Haldighati, Nathwara, Eklingi, and/or Ranakpur (Rs.200-1000). Tours to other sights around Udaipur are available on a demand-only basis. Prices between agencies are virtually equal due to competition. Reputable agencies include **Shrinath Travels Agency** (tel. 524333) and **Rajasthan Tours** (tel. 525777), which have agents all over the city, and **Comfort Travels** (tel. 411661), **Haveli Tours and Travels** (tel. 523500), and **Gangaur Tours and Travels** (tel. 527528), all on Lake Palace Rd.

Currency Exchange: State Bank of India, Hospital Rd. (tel. 528857). Open Mon.-Fri. 10am-2pm, Sat. 10am-noon. **Bank of Baroda,** Town Hall Rd. (tel. 411326). Open Mon.-Fri. 10am-2pm, Sat. 10am-noon. **State Bank of Bikaner and Jaipur,** Chetak Circle (tel. 525066). Open Mon.-Fri. noon-4pm, Sat. noon-2pm. All three exchange foreign cash and traveler's checks. Some travel agencies do so as well.

Telephones: Private STD/ISD booths are everywhere in the city. A good number are open 24hr., especially around the Lake Palace Rd./Jagdish Mandir area. Many offer fax and call-back facilities as well. There are no telecom centers at the bus and railway stations. **Central Telegraph Office,** in GPO. Open 24hr.

Airport: Dabok Airport, 25km east of Udaipur (tel. 410999). A taxi ride into the city costs around Rs.200. Private agencies (see **Budget Travel** above) offer shuttles to the airport for around Rs.150. **Indian Airlines,** Delhi Gate (tel. 410999). Open daily 10am-1:15pm and 2-5pm. **Air India,** Delhi Gate (tel. 411536). Open Mon.-Fri. 9:30am-5pm; Sat. 9:30am-2pm. **ModiLuft** only flies sporadically in season; flights and reservations can be arranged through independent travel agents. To: Bombay (2-3 per day, 1½hr., US$71); Delhi (2-3 per day, 3hr.; US$60); Jaipur (2-3 per day, 2hr., US$43).

Trains: Udaipur City Railway Station (tel. 131). Reservation office open Mon.-Sat. 8am-8pm, Sun. 8am-2pm. To: Delhi via Chittorgarh, Ajmer, and Jaipur (*Garib Nawaz,* 5:40am, 15hr., Rs.99/293; *Chetak Exp.,* 6:10pm, 15hr., Rs.110/303); Ajmer (passenger, Delhi train, 8:30am, 12hr., Rs.38); Chittorgarh (*Mewar Fast,* Delhi train, 7:05pm, 4hr., Rs.88); Ahmedabad (passenger, 9:30am, 11hr., Rs.60; express, 7pm, 7hr., Rs.130); Jodhpur (passenger, 6am, 12hr., Rs.61).

Buses: Main Bus Stand, (tel. 484191). To: Ahmedabad (every hr., 6am-10pm, 7hr., Rs.78); Delhi (4 and 7pm, 17hr., Rs.122); Jaipur (every hr., 6am-11pm, 10hr., Rs.107); Jodhpur (10 per day, 5:30am-11pm, 8hr., Rs.95); Mt. Abu (7, 9am, 6, and 9:30pm, 5hr., Rs.64); Kota via Chittorgarh (every 1½hr., 7am-10:30pm, 6½hr., Rs.70); Kota via Ranakpur (every 1½hr., 6am-11pm, 2½hr., Rs.25); Kota via Ajmer (every 45min., 6am-10pm, 8hr., Rs.100). For information about **private bus companies,** see **Budget Travel** above. Between the lot of them, there are hourly departures to all major cities. Private buses depart from all along City Station Rd.

Local Transportation: Auto-rickshaws are just about everywhere and are unmetered. Getting around the city costs Rs.15-20, Rs.5-10 to a hotel where the auto-rickshaw drivers get commission (sometimes they'll even use a meter if you ask nicely). **Taxis** can be rented from most travel agents and cost around Rs.8 per km. Often rates are fixed to given locations. By far the most convenient way to get around is by **bicycle,** which are available for rental at outlets along Lake Palace Rd. and around the clock tower (Rs.15-20 per day). There are no local buses.

English Bookstore: Mayur Book Paradise, 60 B.C. (tel. 410316). Wide multi-lingual paperback selection plus some international magazines. Open daily 10am-7:30pm. **Suresh Book Service,** Hospital Rd. Lots of English paperbacks, with a strong technical and scientific slant. Open daily 10am-8pm.

Market: In addition to Bara Bazaar and Bapu Bazaar, market areas are located around Jagdish Mandir, the clock tower, and Delhi Gate. Food stores and stalls are widespread, but concentrated to some extent in the latter three areas. Most open daily 7am-11pm.

Pharmacy: Hospital Rd. and Udaipol are filled with pharmacies. Most open daily 7am-9:30pm. Udaipur Hospital has a 24-hr. well-stocked pharmacy.

Hospital: Arenti General Hospital, Hospital Rd. (tel. 102). Government-run. Open 24hr. **Udaipur Hospital,** Udaipol (tel. 561222) is an excellent private ultra-modern hospital with pharmacy. Both English-speaking and open 24hr.

Police: A major police station is at every gate. The biggest are at **Delhi Gate** and **Udaipol.** There are also stations near the bus and railway stations. Police control room, tel. 100.

Emergency: Police, tel. 100. **Fire,** tel. 101. **Ambulance,** tel. 102.

Post Office: GPO, Chetak Circle (tel. 528622). Open Mon.-Sat. 10am-6pm, Sun. 10am-3pm. **City Post Office,** Shastri Circle (tel. 413905). *Poste Restante* is here, not at the GPO. Open Mon.-Fri. 10am-3pm, Sat. 10am-1pm. **Postal Code:** 313001. **Telephone Code:** 0294.

ACCOMMODATIONS

Most of Udaipur's 200-plus hotels pay commission to auto-rickshaw drivers who deliver accommodations-seekers to their doorstep—it's a fact of life in Udaipur, and it's futile to complain. But because most of the hotels are in one of three clusters, you can ask to be dropped at one hotel or area and easily check out the many others nearby. The hotels in the largest cluster, around Jagdish Mandir on the beautiful east bank of Lake Pichola, are by far preferable to any others in the city. Many are family-run with views onto the lake. The hotels along Lake Palace Rd. and B.C. are a good second choice, often with large gardens and view of the City Palace complex. The location of the third cluster—a continuum around the tourist bungalow, near Shastri Gate, and stretching along noisy and polluted City Station Rd.—is far from ideal. Hotels here lack pizzazz and should be avoided if at all possible. Home-stay accommodation, which has its origins in Udaipur, is an alternative. Currently over 200 families participate. The Tourist Reception Centre (tel. 411535) has details and makes arrangements; expect to pay Rs.150-400 per night.

Jagdish Mandir/Lake Pichola Area

Ratan Palace Paying Guest House, 21 Lal Ghat (tel. 561153). A family-run place with clean, well-decorated rooms. Rooftop view, 24-hr. room service, attached baths in all rooms, good restaurant. The guest book is filled with endless pages of rave reviews. Check-out 10am. Singles Rs.300. Doubles Rs.500.

Nukkad Guest House, 56 Ganeshi Ghat. Run by an upbeat, bubbly family, visitors call it "Hotel California" for its power to lure them back time and time again. Bare, but bright rooms. Attached baths, laundry service, 24-hr. room service, travel counter, rooftop restaurant, and a cooking area for guests. Check-out 10am. Rooftop tents Rs.50. Singles Rs.40-50. Doubles Rs.60-100. Extra bed Rs.100.

Jag Niwas Guest House, 21 Gangor Marg. Maharaja-owned, with stylish decor and a mellow atmosphere. Big rooms with attached baths and tubs. 24-hr. room service, laundry, travel services, STD/ISD, rooftop restaurant. Check-out 10am. Singles with air-cooling Rs.60-80. Doubles with air-cooling Rs.175. Extra bed Rs.25.

Hotel Natural, 56 Rang Sagar (tel. 527879). Located on the west bank of Rang Sagar between the 2 bridges, Hotel Natural offers a different lakeside view. Good-size rooms with way cool elephant paintings. Run by a friendly family, with excellent restaurant, attached baths, 24-hr. room service, laundry, travel services, and beauty parlor. Check-out 10am. Price varies according to decor, size, and balcony option. Singles Rs.60-120. Doubles Rs.120-200. Extra bed Rs.20.

Jheel Guest House and Paying Guest House, 56 Gangaur Ghat (tel. 28321; fax 520008). Right on the edge of the lake. Big, well-kept rooms display a range of simple to elaborate decorations, and some come with a balcony. Laundry, restaurant, limited room service, travel counter. Check-out 10am. Singles Rs.100. Doubles with attached bath Rs.200-600, depending on size and decor (for single occupancy Rs.150-550).

Evergreen Guest House, 32 Lal Ghat (tel. 26746). A popular choice with decent-sized undecorated rooms, good rooftop view, and restaurant, 24-hr. room service. Attached baths. Check-out 10am. Singles Rs.80. Doubles Rs.150.

Shiva Guest House, 74 Nav Ghat (tel. 23952). This lakeside hotel has simple, tastefully decorated rooms, with common baths. Laundry, travel services, 24-hr room service, restaurant for guests only. Common baths. Check-out 10am. Singles Rs.75. Doubles Rs.100. Extra bed Rs.25.

Lake Corner Soni Paying Guest House, 27 Nav Ghat. Accommodations are a good deal, even though the rooms, which surround a central courtyard, could use some character. OK rooftop restaurant. All rooms have attached baths. Check-out 10am. Singles Rs.80. Doubles Rs.100. Hot water buckets Rs.3.

Sai Niwas Hotel, 75 Nav Ghat (tel. 524909). Colorful walls and bright carpets electrify the rooms with a hint of psychedelia. All rooms have attached baths. Family-run with a phenomenal but pricey restaurant. Limited room service, laundry, lake view. Check-out 10am. Price varies depending on the view. Singles Rs.475-775. Doubles Rs.550-850.

Lake Palace Road/Bhatiyani Chohotta (B.C.) Area

Hotel Shakti Palace, 76 B.C. (tel. 29440). Clean, modern rooms and airy halls. Laundry, 24-hr. room service, full-fledged travel counter, excellent rooftop restaurant. Check-out noon. Singles with bath Rs.70-90, with air-cooling and TV Rs.125-150. Doubles with bath Rs.80-120, with air-cooling and TV Rs.175-300.

Hotel Kumbha Palace, 104 B.C. (tel. 27702). The central garden snuggles up against the city walls. Rooms are decorated in wares from the Jaisalmeri desert and have attached baths and air-coolers. Laundry, travel services, 24-hr. room service. Check-out 10am. Singles Rs.80. Doubles Rs.150.

Pushkar Palace, 93 B.C. This family-run "palace" offers well-maintained rooms with funky colorful bedspreads. Laundry, travel services, 24-hr. room service, rooftop view, attached baths. Check-out noon. Singles bath Rs.50. Doubles Rs.80.

Ashirwad Paying Guest House, 33 Lake Palace Rd. (tel. 27394). One of a few paying-guest houses in the area, this family-run place has a relaxing garden and a range of interestingly decorated rooms. 24-hr. room service; 24-hr. check-out. Singles with bath Rs.150. Doubles with bath Rs.150-250. Long stay discounts. Free hot water buckets.

Tourist Bungalow/City Station Road Area

Hotel Kajri Tourist Bungalow, near Shastri Circle (tel. 410501). Standard tourist bungalow. Good-size rooms with minimal decor and attached baths. Starting point for RTDC tours. Decent restaurant and bar, taxi service, shops. Check-out noon. Dorm beds Rs.50. Singles Rs.200, with air-cooling Rs.300, with A/C Rs.500. Doubles Rs.250, with air-cooling Rs.375, with A/C Rs.600.

Hotel Manidhar, City Station Rd., Suraj Gate (tel. 522887). If you're not a deep sleeper, don't try to stay at this noisy location. Rooms have attached baths, TVs, and telephones. Singles Rs.125. Doubles Rs.250. Triples Rs.325. Quads Rs.400.

FOOD

Udaipur has a fairly good range of restaurants to choose from. Most are hotel rooftop eateries, but quality stand-alones are growing in number. For snacks, sweets, or *bhojnalya*-style dining, any of the main bazaars should suffice. Kwality ice cream is in Chetak Circle. Many restaurants have a nightly showing of the James Bond flick *Octopussy*, which was filmed in Udaipur. If you spend any amount of time in the city, you'll end up seeing it over and over.

Hotel Natural Rooftop Restaurant, 55 Rang Sagar (tel. 527879). Peaceful location with an alternative lakeside view. More than just the standard Continental-Chinese-Indian menu—we're talking Tibetan, Italian, and Mexican, plus all-you-can-eat buffets. Entrees around Rs.30-35. But save room for a hefty slice of home-made cake (Rs.20). Open daily 7am-midnight.

Parkview Restaurant, opposite Town Hall (tel. 528098). Refreshingly cool with A/C. Fancy, and unusually dim. A full range of cuisines but Indian dishes are their specialty. Serves both veg. (Rs.30) and non-veg. (Rs.40) entrees. Open daily 8:30am-11pm.

Mayur Roof Cafe, Shakti Palace Hotel, 76 B.C. (tel. 29440). Admire the views of the City Palace and garden while trying to ignore the Hindi film song "muzak" that plays in the background. Good Indian selection, and some Continental and Chinese (generally less than Rs.30). Open daily 7am-11pm.

Sai Niwas, Hotel Sai Niwas, 75 Nav Ghat (tel. 524909). Deciding what to order could be more fun than you're used to, and you'll owe it all to the pictorial menu-with elaborate descriptions of the esoteric entrees. The food is family-cooked and lives up to the menu descriptions, but it's very pricey at Rs.70 and up. Open daily 7:30pm-midnight.

Mayur Café, Gangaur Ghat. Quality food and quick service win out over the dull setting, making the Mayur a local favorite. Especially popular are the Indian *thalis* and snacks, and Western favorites like pasta and pie. Dishes under Rs.25. Open daily 6am-11pm.

Gayitri Dosa Centre, Lake Palace Rd. A quasi-stall eatery with dozens of *dosa* permutations and Indian snacks. Everything under Rs.20. Open daily 7am-11pm.

4 Seasons Restaurant, near Jagdish Mandir (tel. 524546). A popular local joint featuring a decent range of all cuisines for Rs.25-30. A good place for a quick, tasty bite. Open daily 8am-10:30pm.

Hariyati Restaurant, Lake Palace Rd. (tel. 521888). Serves specialty pure veg. South Indian cuisine; Continental and Chinese are also available. Garden and terrace dining make for a pleasantly laid-back atmosphere. Open daily 8am-11pm.

SIGHTS

While the visual focal points of Udaipur are the elegant palaces rising from the deep green of Lake Pichola, the historical focal points are the **City Palace** and **Jagdish Mandir** to the west of the old city. Despite its rather worn beige exterior, the grand palace, begun in 1559 by **Udai Singh,** the proud Mewar migrant and founder of the city, today represents the combined architectural efforts of over 20 kings. Like a decorated wall balancing domed cupolas, the City Palace is currently part museum, part royal residence, and part luxury hotel. The palace is gender divisible by its ladies'

NORTH INDIA

(Janana Mahal) and mens' (Mardhana Mahal) palaces. The latter's proud face bears a brilliant gold moustached *surya-orsena,* whose worship was the inspiration for valor in battle as well as the blue-and-white "Surya Prakash" balconies, constructed to face its rising and setting brilliance. Before entering the museum, take a look around what used to be the sight of elephant fights (the two large paved stone indentions were once elephant beds!) The museum opens into the Raja Angan Chowk surrounded by rooms of Udaipuri miniature paintings, one of which appears in three dimensions when viewed at a distance. This vast courtyard was also a Holi playground.

The palace is also filled with tributes to Rana Pratap, Udai Singh's heroic progeny. Among them are an eerie white larger-than-life marble bust and 400 year old armor that once graced his equally valorous horse, Chetak. The palace is most well-known for its **Mor Chowk** with its blue and green inlay glass peacocks and convex mirrors. **Krishna-vilas,** a small room whose walls are completely covered by miniature paintings, is dedicated to a 16-year-old princess, Krishna Kumari, who was betrothed to two princes and chose self-sacrifice to avoid an almost sure war for her delicate hand. The **Mardhana Mahal** ends in a museum with armor and paintings depicting the story of Pannadhai, yet another in Mewar's history of inspiringly valorous women. The **Janana Mahal** is disappointingly less-maintained and houses little more than Maharaja Bhopal Singh's 1922 Rolls-Royce.

Tours run Rs.60 in English (or any language other than Hindi) and are good but a bit rushed. The palace is chock full of low doorways and narrow halls (all of which demand that visitors bow their heads entering and leaving safely in single file) opening into magnificent albeit sterile palace rooms. Open daily 9:30am-4:30pm. Admission Rs.15, camera fee Rs.30, video fee Rs.200.

Just down the steep hill from the palace is **Jagdish Mandir,** a 17th-century temple built by Maharaja Jagat Singh. Legend has it that Jagat Singh received the inspiration for the temple in a dream. He began construction on the site where he left four *kardas* into which rose the central black marble idol. Completed in 1652, the outer structure rises in a pyramid-like *shikhara* of worn stone decorated with sculpted rows of elephants and dancers, along with figures depicting episodes from Mewari mythology. The entrance is guarded by a large model of Garuda. The rather worn cornerstone at the left base of the stairs is said to bestow good luck on any who rubs it seven times. The central dome is alive with mythological figures while a huge silver bed meant for gods rests in front of the sanctuary entrance. This *mandir* is in the heart of the old city and is actively visited daily by worshipers.

Once the royal summer palace, **Jag Niwas** (Lake Palace) seems to float lightly on the gentle green waters of Lake Pichola along with the stolid red sandstone **Jag Mandir,** famous for the safety it provided the exiled Shah Jahan. The two splendid edifices can be seen blossoming from the depths of the lake from any of its banks and from the many levels of the City Palace. In the "sleep cheap and eat well" category, the Lake Palace (now a luxury hotel; tel. 527961) is well worth the dinner reservations required for short boat rides over from **Bansi Ghat.** The palace grounds and water-dotted, open-air courtyard cafés with white marble inlay and corner towers and turrets, are stunning. Dinner is a tasty buffet that runs Rs.500 and is well-attended by similar-minded tourists. The hotel also has a bar, shopping arcade, and coffee shop, all open to visitors to this island jewel. Jag Mandir can be visited by boat as well: hour-long cruises around the lake departing from Bansi Ghat cost Rs.125 (operate daily 2-6pm); 30-min. boat cruises are also available for Rs.40 (operate daily 10am-noon and 2-5pm).

The **Bharatiya Lok Kala Mandal Folk Museum** (enquiry tel. 529296) is a large complex of wooden-looking buildings intended as a center for the preservation and distribution of tribal folk arts. The museum collection consists of several rooms off one main hall, each containing a variety of items ranging from colorfully painted caricature masks used in dance dramas to clay figure dioramas depicting local festivals to a rather dusty collection of life-sized models of the peoples of local tribes. There is also a collection of photos for those interested in visualizing tribal life through a glass case. The museum's highlight is the collection of traditional Rajasthani puppets called *kathpurli*—wide-eyed wooden string puppets dressed brightly in traditional costumes. A minimalist puppet show is put on every 20 to 25 minutes in the puppet theater, complete with musical accompaniment and the wildly active hips of wooden dancing girls. The puppets are expertly manipulated and a joy to watch. The Lok Mandal has an attached school that puts on dance performances (6-7pm; admission Rs.20). Open daily 9am-6pm; admission Rs.7, camera fee Rs.5.

Shilpigram (tel. 560304), situated a few kilometers west of Udaipur off Lake Fateh Sagar, is a self-dubbed "rural arts and crafts complex." Set out along spacious cleared paths are the representative homes of specific rural and tribal communities of Rajasthan, Gujarat, Maharashtra, and Goa. From the circular, white stone, clay-roofed homes of the Meghwal Bahni to the thatched-roofed square home of a Kohlapuri shoe maker, each model is accompanied by a plaque offering sparing details about living in these communities. Aside from the home-arama, the village redeems itself with tents of rural crafts for sale and lively performances that provide the true sounds of folk culture—showcased by musicians and dancers, potters and cloth makers from various rural communities who live in the village for short periods of time. While the village forms a kind of cultural petting zoo, presenting a brief glimpse into the richness of folk culture, a visit can be fun and interesting if taken with a grain of salt. Shilpigram can be accessed only by private transportation. Rickshaws cost around Rs.50 each way, making bikes a more economical option. (Open daily 9am-8pm; no performances between 11am and 5pm. Admission Rs.2.)

Udaipur is known for its gardens as well as its palaces. Nehru Park, Saheliyon-ki-Bari, and Sajjan Niwas are the best maintained, but also the most tourist-traversed. **Nehru Park,** built in part as a public works project to create jobs in famine, sits prettily in Fateh Sagar (open 8am-6:30pm; admission Rs.3). Spread over the fairly open and fountain-dotted grounds, it appears as a flat bed of beige domed cupolas, swaying palm trees, and bright bushes of bougainvillea. Small, undoubtedly crowded, low-riding boats with their hand-cranked motors precariously leave the banks of Fateh Sagar every 20 minutes for the island. They offer a funny, if rather nerve-racking adventure and were more likely than not salvaged from the relics in the palace museum. It is also possible to take a 30-minute tour around the lake for Rs.40.

The 18th-century **Saheliyon-ki-Bari** (Garden of the Maids of Honor) lies 2km to the north of town and was built by Maharan Sangram Singh for the maharani and her corps of royal friends and servants. The lusciously green garden with its palm-lined walks and lotus pool is unfortunately much more of a tourist sight than the herbaceous refuge it was once meant to be. During the monsoon rains the lotus pool is quite spectacular.

Sajjan Niwas, set on Lake Palace Rd., and the nearby **Gulab Bagh** (Rose Garden), are sprawling, thickly vegetated dream gardens. The former's wide paths are lined with sporadically labeled, local flora including giant umbrella neem trees. There is a kiddie train that doesn't often run. The garden is popular with local cyclers and provides several smaller wooded paths for the die-hard garden-goer. The gardens around Moti Mayri Hill on the north side of town offer another opportunity to escape the city.

If you prefer not to spend your time relaxing by the lake, a few smaller sights in and around Udaipur can be visited. Two kilometers east of Udaipur (Rs.20-25 rickshaw) is the run-down site of the **royal cenotaphs.** Near these *chhattris* about 1km south is the **Ahar Museum** with its ancient archeological exhibits (open Sat.-Thurs., 10am-5pm; admission Rs.2). Back in town near Jaydish Temple is **Bagore-ki-hardi,** which now contains an art gallery (open daily 9:30am-6pm; admission Rs.25). For a mind-blowing view of the city and valley, head to **Sajjangarh (Monsoon) Palace,** perched on a steep hill 5km west of Udaipur. Good luck getting up by bike; even auto-rickshaws need their luck to get up (Rs.100 roundtrip—well, at least up to the port).

ENTERTAINMENT AND SHOPPING

Fortunately, in a city that entices many a traveler to sojourn much longer than planned, Udaipur has more than just boat rides and *Octopussy* in every other restaurant. Traditional Rajasthani folk dances and music performances involving a dazzling blend of earthy tribal trances and circus-like balancing feats are held Mon.-Sat. 7-8pm at **Meera Kala Mandir** (tel. 583176), near the Pars Theater in Sector 11 (tickets Rs.35). Tickets to the show cost Rs.35; a rickshaw ride from the old city costs Rs.25-30. For information about the puppet shows at the **Bharatiya Lok Kala Folk Museum** and the dances at **Shilpgram,** see **Sights,** above. **Shopping** is huge in Udaipur. Around Jagdish Mandir, Lake Palace Rd., Bara Bazaar, and Bapu Bazaar are countless clothing, jewelry, textile, and handicrafts shops featuring wares from all over Rajasthan at inflated but negotiable prices. Some government emporia are scattered around as well, but their prices are even higher, although there are no hassles. If there can be said to be an Udaipuri specialty, it would have to be miniature paintings. Lake Palace Rd. has a series of shops where skilled artists can be watched at work without any obligation (despite extortion) to buy. In general, it's best to explore shopping areas on your own. "Guides" will offer to take you to the best textile, handicrafts, and jewelry, stores, but they receive 20% commission, meaning you pay 20% more.

Other entertainment includes **swimming.** If you are tempted to stroke natural waters, remember that Lake Pichola is artificial and the *dhobi* ghats aren't for you; several places offer the swimming pools for public use for a price—Shilpi Restaurant in Shilpigram (tel. 522475) for Rs.80 and Laxmi Vilas Palace Hotel between the two lakes (tel. 529713) for Rs.150 are popular choices.

■ Near Udaipur

Twenty-two kilometers north of Udaipur in the heart of marble-producing territory is the inspiring village of **Eklingi,** home to a magnificent temple of Shiva. In an exquisite contrast, the temple itself is vanilla marble white and encloses a four-faced solid black idol of Shiva. Silver doors, silver lamps, silver parcels, and a solid silver bull adorn the interior as well. The stonework of the temple and surrounding shrines is also impressive. Temple open daily 4:30-6:30am, 10:30am-1:30pm, and 5:30-6:45pm. Photography is not permitted. Eklingi is a stop on many city tours, and is also accessible by bus from Udaipur (every hr., 6am-midnight, 30min., Rs.16).

Forty-eight kilometers north of Udaipur is the important pilgrimage destination of **Nathdwara,** built entirely around its incredible **Nathji Mandir,** dedicated to Krishna as Srinathji. Legend maintains that in the 17th century a chariot bearing Krishna's image from Mathura to Udaipur suddenly became trapped in the mud; the bearers interpreted the situation as a divine signal and built the temple at the spot. The Nathdwara Temple's image of Sri Nathji with blazing diamond-studded eyes and Mughal dress is commonly found on decorative items in households all over India. The stalls outside the temple have commercialized the image—the assortment of Krishna paraphernalia is immense, though prices are high. The temple's architecture is visually stunning, but the ceremonies attended by many and revolving around a prescribed schedule of feeding, bathing, and resting the image are fascinating, especially at 5pm. Photography is strictly prohibited in the temple. Guard all your belongings here—if at all possible, leave everything including your shoes in the bus. Nathdwara is a stop on many tours and is easily accessible by bus from Udaipur (every hr., 6am-midnight, Rs.21).

Eighty-four kilometers north of Udaipur atop a huge hill over 1km up sits the remote solid virtually impregnable **Fort Kumbhalgarh.** It was built in the 15th century by Maharana Kumbha and has only been besieged once, by a force of combined armies that had to resort to poisoning the water supply. The massive crenellated fort walls are imposing, and guard assorted temples, courtyards, palaces, gardens, and tombs. A **wildlife sanctuary** with a significant wolf population is nearby. Antelopes, leopards, flying squirrels, and bears are also around. Buses to Kumbhalgarh leave from Udaipur (8, 11am, 2, and 2:30pm, 3hr., Rs.26).

■ Ranakpur

Eighty kilometers north of Udaipur, roads zig-zag through the verdant Aravali mountain valleys to Ranakpur's complex of Jain temples. The main white marble **Chaumukha Temple,** built in 1439, was dedicated to the first *tirthankara* Adinath. The three-tiered entry facade is delicately crenellated and punctuated by sculpted squashed minarets along both sides. Inside, each of the 29 halls and 1444 pillars is intricately carved and sculpted—even the last bead on a dancer's earring is pronounced with meticulous detail. The most embellished carvings of this grandiose temple surround a four-faced image of Adinath in the innermost sanctum. Inside the complex are also smaller shrines to **Parshvanath** and **Neminath,** with similarly impressive architecture. A Hindu temple to Surya is also part of the complex, and though a bit weathered down, the sculpture and latticework shows through. Temple open daily to non-Jains noon-5pm; camera fee Rs.20, video camera fee Rs.100.

Ranakpur is well-connected to Udaipur and Mt.Abu. Most buses from Udaipur to Jodhpur stop at Ranakpur; check in advance (see **Udaipur,** p. 126). Private bus companies in Udaipur and Mt. Abu arrange frequent departures and tours to Ranakpur as well. From Ranakpur, private buses leave to Jodhpur, Jaipur, and Udaipur throughout the day, about every two hours. There is an STD/ISD **telephone** booth and a **post office** in Shilpi Tourist Bungalow (open Mon.-Sat. noon-5pm).

There are only two accommodation options in Ranakpur proper. The *dharamshala* offers simple lodgings and simple but plentiful vegetarian lunches and dinners, asking for a donation in return. Alcohol and smoking are prohibited; lights must be turned off at 10pm. The **Shilpi Tourist Bungalow** (tel. (02934) 3674) has reasonably clean but plain rooms and an expensive restaurant. All rooms with attached baths. Check-out noon. Singles Rs.150, with air-cooling Rs.225. Doubles Rs.175, with air-cooling Rs.275. Some luxury accommodations and heritage hotels are available several kilometers outside of Ranakpur. Food is limited to these accommodations and a small stand by the main entrance, offering drinks and a few snacks.

■ Mt. Abu

They say "it's lonely at the top," but this is surely not true of the top of Rajasthan. Situated 1220m above sea level on a temperate plateau, Mt. Abu is an ever-popular destination for honeymooners and families. Once a part of the kingdom of the Chauhan Rajputs, who ruled from nearby Sirohi, Mt. Abu is now a resort, boasting temperate weather year-round. While the town centers around the carnival atmosphere of Nakki Lake, it is not a destination for fun-seekers only. It is also an important pilgrimage site and the home of the architecturally breathtaking Delwara temples. Although some have complained that the hordes of honeymooners and tourists have ruined the romantic atmosphere of Rajasthan's only hill station, nothing can spoil the experience of watching the sun set over the granite rock-flanked lake and the ubiquitous palm trees. During the Summer Festival, held annually June 1-3, tourists anywhere nearby head to Mt. Abu to experience tribal dances, folk music, rest, and relaxation.

ORIENTATION

Mt. Abu is small enough to be easily and best traversed by foot. It consists of one nameless main drag that leads into town from the ride up from **Abu Road.** Moving northwest, the road passes the Railway Out Agency and the main bus stand, right across the street from the friendly Tourist Reception Centre and the Police Station.

A block down on the left is the taxi stand, which marks the start of the **Polo Grounds.** The left road here eventually reaches and circles **Nakki Lake,** as do all the roads to the left of the **Central Bazaar.** The road straight ahead leads to the Central Bazaar. The road to the right leads to the State Bank of India, the General Hospital, and the GPO, then on past the picturesque Our Saviour's Church to Delwara and Achalgarh.

PRACTICAL INFORMATION

Tourist Office: Tourist Reception Centre, opposite the bus stand (tel. 3151). Provides a wealth of maps, brochures, and travel information for all of Rajasthan. City tours available (8:30am and 1:30pm, 5hr., Rs.30). Open Mon.-Sat. 10am-1:30pm and 2-5pm.

Currency Exchange: State Bank of India, near GPO (tel. 3136), **State Bank of Bikaner and Jaipur,** near GPO (tel. 3224), and **Bank of Baroda,** near the taxi stand (tel. 3166), all exchange currency and traveler's checks. All open Mon.-Fri. 10am-2pm, Sat. 10am-noon.

Telephones: Private STD/ISD **telephone** booths are located along the main road. A handful are open 24hr. and offer fax services. The **Telecom Centre,** east of the GPO (tel. 3107), houses the Central Telegraph Office. Open 24hr.

Trains: All trains depart from the **Abu Road Railway Station** (tel. 22222), 27km away. Leave 1hr. to reach Abu Rd. from Mt. Abu (see **Local Transportation,** below). There is a **Railway Out Agency,** 300m south of the Tourist Reception Centre on the main road (tel. 3353), that handles reservations and inquiries. Open Mon.-Sat. 9am-1pm and 2-4pm. To: Ahmedabad (*Surya Nagri Exp.* 2907, 1:45am; *Ashram Exp.* 2905, 8:20am; *Ranakpur Exp.,* 1pm; *Delhi Exp.,* 5:20am; *Aravali Exp.,* 2pm, 5hr., Rs.55/192 for 2nd/1st class; *Agra Fast,* 8:18pm, 8hr., Rs.79); Jodhpur (*Surya Nagri Exp.* 2908, 1:15am; *Ranakpur Exp.* 4828, 2:50pm, 6hr., Rs.60/ 180 for 1st/2nd class).

Buses: Main Bus Stand (tel. 3434). To: Jaipur (6:30am, 11hr., Rs.159); Udaipur (8:45, 9:45am, and 4pm, 7hr., Rs.52; 7:30pm, 11hr., Rs.89); Ahmedabad (9 per day, 6am-9pm, 7hr., Rs.52). **Private bus** companies line the main road and offer service to most destinations in Rajasthan and Gujarat. **Shobha Travels** (tel. 3302) and **Baba Travels** (tel. 3300) are recommended. Private buses depart from the taxi stand. All bus transportation arranged in Mt. Abu departs from Mt. Abu. **Arrangements from other cities to Mt. Abu may only come as far as Abu Road. Check in advance.**

Local Transportation: Buses to Abu Road are frequent and depart from the Main Bus Stand (every 30min., 6am-9pm, 1hr., Rs.10).The only local transportation in Mt. Abu consists of jeeps and minivans serving as **taxis,** departing from the taxi stand. A crowded shared taxi to Abu Road costs Rs.10. A private taxi costs at least Rs.200. From the Taxi Stand to the Delwara Temples, a private taxi costs Rs.30. Shared taxis to the Delwara Temples leave from the Central Bazaar for Rs.2. Taxis can be rented for the day for Rs.400.

Market: The **Central Bazaar** is the main market for fresh foods and general shopping. The main road past the Central Bazaar towards Nakki Lake also has an assortment of stores. Most open Mon.-Sat. 8am-11pm.

Pharmacy: A handful of pharmacies surround the General Hospital. Open daily 9am-9pm.

Hospital: General Hospital, behind Central Bazaar, towards the lake (tel. 3535). A green chalet-like building. Open 24hr.

Police: Main Police Station, opposite Main Bus Stand (tel. 3333). English spoken. Open 24hr.

Post Office: GPO (tel. 3170). Packaging, *Poste Restante.* Open Mon.-Sat. 9am-noon and 3-5pm. **Postal Code:** 307501.

Telephone Code: 02974.

ACCOMMODATIONS

Most of the hotels in Mt. Abu cater to the honeymoon crowd so doubles are the norm. In quite a few places, singles are no cheaper than doubles. Some hotels offer romantic honeymoon suites, which are often booked weeks in advance. The high season in Mt. Abu is different from that in the plains. Visitors arrive in flocks from April to June and September to December, and especially around Diwali (Oct. 30-Nov. 3, 1997). Prices of accommodations at least triple during these peak times, and reservations are essential. As in most popular tourist locales, touts will accost you in force at the bus and taxi stands. The dozens of "youth hostels" around town are not conventional youth hostels but are intended for students at Mt. Abu private schools.

Hotel Panghat, Nakki Lake (tel. 3386). Unspectacular rooms, but a lovely view and low prices combine to make this place a good value. The rooms are good-sized with coordinated floral and dull pink furniture. The lakeside terrace is a relaxing place to hang out. Limited room service, laundry, travel arrangements, a small restaurant, and TVs in all rooms. Check-out 9am. Singles with bath Rs.60, by the lake Rs.70. Doubles with bath Rs.80, by the lake Rs.100.

Hotel Lakeview, Nakki Lake (tel. 38659). An odd, irregularly leveled, whitish building, with a step-garden in front that adds to the image. The rooms are big and well-lit, with reflections off the bright rainbow tie-dye bed spreads in each room. All rooms have satellite TVs and attached baths, and the lakeside ones have swings on the balconies. The view is excellent. Laundry, travel services, STD/ISD, snack-food restaurant. Check-out 9am. Singles Rs.150. Doubles Rs.200 in the back, Rs. 250-400 up front, depending on the view.

Shree Ganesh Hotel, near Nakki Lake on the road up to the Maharaja of Jaipur's summer palace (tel. 3591). This place is a popular choice due to its separation from the main clusters and is generally cheaper than elsewhere. The rooms are hardly decorated but they have TVs, and the owner will gladly keep talking and talking to entertain you or keep you occupied. Limited room service, travel services, laundry, luggage storage. Check-out 9am. Doubles with bath Rs.50-100, depending on size and TV type. Rs.10 discount for single occupancy.

Hotel Vrindavan, near Main Bus Stand (tel. 3147). A charming place to stay—the building is a brown-and-white, crenellated, Swiss-style cottage. The rooms aren't quite so classy and many are filled with mismatched velvety furniture. Clean and well-kept. Featuring a restaurant with good Gujarati *thalis,* travel service, laundry, limited room service, and a terrace-top garden. Check-out 9am. Singles and doubles Rs.150-250, with TVs and better furnishings Rs.300-400.

Hotel Rajdeep, opposite Bus Stand (tel. 3525). The arched building that houses this hotel looks like it has seen better days. Still, the rooms here are clean and large (though begging for decor). Limited room service, travel arrangements, laundry, and popular restaurant. Check-out 9am. Singles and doubles with attached bath (same price) start at Rs.100 and climb to Rs.200 as floral bedspreads and marble floors are added. Hot water buckets Rs.3 each. Extra bed Rs.20.

Hotel Sudhir, up the hill east of the taxi stand (tel. 3311). Neat, quasi-modern, curved-edge building surrounded by verdant vegetation. They know how to decorate—rooms have Persian rugs, carved bed-frames, unique lampshades, antique box TVs, clean attached baths. Limited room service, travel service, laundry. Check-out 9am. Singles and doubles Rs.300. Quads Rs.400-500.

Hotel Samrat International (Hotel Navjivan), on the main road opposite the Polo Field (tel. 3173; fax 3467). Prides itself on its honeymoon specials. The ordinary rooms are simply decorated, clean, and comfortable. The honeymoon and VIP suites, individually named (Geetanjali, Ghoomar, etc.) are well-equipped, with arched wood beds and swings and mild erotica on the bathroom tiles. The honeymoon suite fad could well have started here. Travel service, laundry, 24-hr. room service, restaurant. Check-out 9am. Ordinary singles with attached bath Rs.150. Doubles Rs.250. A TV and a bigger room adds Rs.100. Air-conditioned honeymoon and VIP suites start at Rs.930.

Hotel Surya Darshan, west side of Polo Field (tel. 3165; fax 3576). The best value of the west Polo Field group. One piece of furniture in each room is incongruous with the rest. Rooms are big and clean, and the management makes tries to keep everything in form. Travel and laundry service, veg. restaurant, limited room service. All rooms have attached baths. Check-out 9am. Singles Rs.100. Doubles Rs.150, bigger, with marble tiles and color TVs Rs.250. Extra bed Rs.75.

FOOD

A range of restaurants in Mt. Abu serve both Gujarati and Rajasthani cuisines. Between the Central Bazaar and the main bus stand, *dhabas* offer Gujarati, Punjabi, and Rajasthani food with roadside seating. Near the lake are a bevy of refreshing juice and ice cream shops.

M.K. Restaurant, head of the road to Nakki Lake (tel. 3531). A little corner-shop-type place with an extensive menu. Quietly detached from the standard roadside eating scene. Assorted South Indian entrees for Rs.30-40. Popular cream floats for Rs.22. Open daily 8:30am-11pm.

King's Food, head of the road to Nakki Lake (tel. 3328). This is as close to fast food as it gets in Mt. Abu. The grease is authentic. Burgers, pizzas, hot dogs, shakes all for under Rs.25. Indian and Chinese also available. Open daily 8:30am-11:30pm.

Dairy King, opposite King's food (tel. 3328). The best of the many ice cream joints around Mt. Abu. All items prepared "to go" but some indoor seating is available. The mango and pineapple shakes are stupendous and cost Rs.20. Floats, ice cream, and sundaes, all in many flavors, also available. Order, pay, then join the hordes (all clutching receipts) waiting to get their goodies. Open daily 8:30am-11:30pm.

Karak Dining Hall, near Main Bus Stand (tel. 38305). Come around lunchtime to see the stainless steel fly in this spacious, undecorated dining hall. Crowds swarm to the excellent Gujarati *thalis* for Rs.35. Assorted other Indian veg. snacks and food available—but you've come for the *thalis.* Open daily 7:30am-11pm.

Veera Restaurant, main road past Bus Stand (tel. 3448). A roadside eatery with a palm tree sprouting up through the concrete in the middle and the menu painted on the walls. The staff can get sarcastic at times but the food is good and the place is fun. Everything from *dosas, utthapams,* and *thalis* to burgers and soups, generally for under Rs.25. Open daily 8am-11:30pm.

Sarovar Restaurant, Nakki Lake. The RTDC finally gets creative—a fake plaster cruiser boat jutting into Nakki Lake houses this small restaurant. The view is beautiful—lakes up front and gardens to the rear. Occasionally, fishermen try their luck on the deck as well. Veg. buffet Rs.45, snacks less than Rs.15. Open daily 8am-10pm.

SIGHTS AND ENTERTAINMENT

The **Delwara Jain Temple** stands out in all its marble splendor. Situated about 3km from Mt. Abu on the northeast road out of town, this cluster of Jain temples houses within its worn grey simple stone exterior some of the country's most amazing examples of marble sculpture. The main temple, an 11th-century construction by minister Vimal Shah, is dedicated to the first *tirthankara*, Adinath. Devotees of Adinath and art alike flock to Delwara to view the immaculately carved pillars of dancing ladies and spiralling lotus domes that adorn the halls that house 57 smaller *tirthankara* statues. The ceiling depicts stories from mythology, one playfully illustrating Krishna and his Gopis playing *holi* with smooth bulls' horns. Other domes depict various goddesses soaring overhead, detailed even down to the fingernails.

The central dome is alive with dancing ladies and a triumphant marble elephant overhead, his smooth white trunk turned up in homage to Adinath. Sarnavasaian workers worked on this colossal achievement for 14 years, supposedly being paid in amounts corresponding to the weight of marble removed, inspiring them to create the finest, most intricate carvings. Notice the balconies to either side of the main sanctuary built by two brothers, with almost identical art save that the last figure on the left is bent in due respect to the work of the elder.

A step into the outer sanctuary and the pomp and design are left far behind. The dome and walls are uncarved so as to not disturb meditation. The statue of Adinath is modeled on a 3500-year-old granite statue housed in the back corner of the temple, which, according to legend, was discovered under a sweet-smelling *champa* tree on the very spot revealed in a dream to Vimal Shah.

Even more intricate are the curling arches of the second largest temple, dedicated to the 22nd *tirthankara*, Neminath, also the cousin of Krishna. Its breathtaking tiered lotus dome was carved from a single marble stone. Both temples also house marble memorials to the donors to the temple, seated atop models of the elephants who faithfully transported the building materials. There are three other temples in the complex, the first a 16th-century dedication to Mahavira and the fourth another tribute to Adinath Rishabdeo housing a 4000-kg statue composed of five different metals. Another is a memorial to the gifted workers, constructed of every type of stone used (no doubt those left-over) and dedicated to *tirthankara* Parshvanath. The center is beautifully adorned with Khajuraho-style sculptured ladies gracefully turned to see their dressing reflections. Tours are unofficially available in English from the stationed guards who appreciate a tip or a donation to the temple. (Open to non-Jains noon-6pm. Free. No photography.)

Visiting **Nakki Lake,** where most of Mt. Abu's activity is focused, is a bit like visiting a carnival—small shops crowd the short street to the lake, alongside popcorn sellers, fast-food restaurants, and the rather conspicuous photo stalls, and the square is crowded with brightly decorated ponies available for riding (Rs.20 per 30min.). There's always a crowd clamoring for the "boating," paddleboats or rowboats, available from the dock from competing agencies (Rs.45 per 30 minutes). A walk along the left bank, past decked-out posing visitors and racks of bright skirts, leads past the small **Ragunath Temple** to the opposite quiet bank lined with its huge estates and stately homes. Walks along the narrow winding road to the opposite bank offer pretty views of the town. Keep your eyes open for the many bizarre granite rock formations, such as "Toad Rock," which overlooks the lake. Others, such as "Camel Rock" and "Nandi Rock," were supposedly named by honeymooners who had too much to drink—a real stretch of the imagination is needed. Several roads off the town's main drag lead quickly away from the crowded town to tree-covered back roads and hills. Don't worry about getting lost—it's a small place.

Sunset Point lies along the left fork from the main road past the taxi stand. Although once it surely offered a beautiful cliff view of the setting sun soaking the valley below in warm colors, it is now much more of a people-watching spot. A constant flow of tourists mobs the place daily. A similar fate has befallen **Honeymoon Point,** off the road leading northwest behind Nakki Lake. The view from here is superb, but the name has drawn in honeymooners by the dozen and the romance has disappeared. Better viewpoints are **The Crags,** beyond Honeymoon Point, the remote **Shanti Shikar,** east of the Crags, and the surprising **Summer Palace** of the maharaja of Jaipur, sitting on the hill south of Nakki Lake. If you choose to avoid the crowds by exploring these more remote areas, it's best not to do so alone.

A left off the northeast road to Delwara leads to the base of what can easily prove to be a good 30-minute exercise. Three hundred and sixty steps make their way up the mountainside to the **Adhar Devi Temple,** dedicated to the patron goddess of Mt. Abu. The "temple" is actually a natural cleft in the rocky mountaintop that can only be entered by crawling, and offers a spectacular view of the green valleys below. The blue paint along all of the rock spoils the mystique, but not the climb or the view.

Back in town across from the GPO is the **Government Museum.** This place is bizarre. An orange sculpture on the outside walls lures you into a huge collection of stone chunks and slabs from assorted archeological hunts. The stuff dates from the eighth through 12th centuries and most of it comes from Jain temples. Some brass work and textiles are also on display. The back garden has 50 or so more slabs sitting there on the lawn. This is a good place to check out if you're around the GPO. (Open Sun.-Thurs. 10am-4:30pm. Free.)

■ Near Mt. Abu

Past Delwara another 8km along the same road and off to the right is **Achalgarh,** famous for a 9th-century temple to Achaleshwar Mahadev, an incarnation of Shiva. The temple is small and is filled with the heavy sweet scent of the plentiful *champa* trees. The temple marks a small crater that, legend has it, was created by the impact of Shiva's big toe and is said to have no bottom. Many a man has tried to fill its unquenchable depths. Outside the temple is a tank which, according to legend, was once filled with *ghee*. Demons dressed as buffalos came to steal it but were killed by the king. The three stone buffaloes flanking the tank are all that's left.

Another five minutes up this same road is **Guru Shikar,** the highest point in Rajasthan at 1721m above sea level. It is marked by a *nadar* and a small temple. The long climb up will make you appreciate the drink stand back at the bottom.

■ Jodhpur

Arriving in Jodhpur, on the eastern edge of the Thar Desert, is like stepping through a window in time. The cars, lights, and billboards of Rajasthan's second-largest city (with a population of 720,000) blend with scenes of traditional and resilient Rajasthan. Winding streets and centuries-old stone homes gather densely around the base of a sandstone cliff topped by the Meherangarh Fort. The white dome of the fort temple rests like a small beacon atop the jagged canopy of stone homes in the crowded heart of the Old City. Jodhpur is awash with color, from the reds and yellows of *bandhani* cloth to the bright fuschia of hanging bougainvillea, from the brilliant yellow of the scorching desert sun to the water-blue walls of old city houses (explained as a status symbol, a mosquito repellent, or a means of camouflaging the city from Pakistani jets). Set away from the central hustle-and-bustle, the Umaid Bhawan Palace and the Jaswant Thada complement the Fort, standing as solitary, seemingly remote restraints against rapidly growing commercialization.

Once the capital of the state of Marwar and home to the warrior clans of Rathore, Jodhpur's history is rife with royalty, battle, and classic romanticism. In an especially chivalrous display in the 18th century, Maharaja Ajit Singh, exiled as a child when the Mughals overran Jodhpur, returned 30 years later to reclaim his kingdom. Jodhpur cultivates such legends, and even the modern city is engulfed by their spirit.

ORIENTATION

Jodhpur's **sher,** or old city, is enclosed by a stone wall with seven entrance gates, of which **Jalori Gate** and **Sojati Gate,** on the south side of town, are the most commonly used. The busiest commercial centers surround these gates. The **new city** expands to the south and east of the *sher.* **Jodhpur Railway Station** lies to the southwest of Sojati Gate along the cleverly named **Station Road.** Outside of the station, three main roads fan out from a statue of a horseman. The road to the far left leads to the **GPO** and the **telegraph office.** The road directly ahead of the statue leads to Jalori Gate, the best way into the old city, while the road leading off to the right, toward Sojati Gate, is lined with cheap hotels and restaurants. **High Court Road** is the main east-west avenue, running from Sojati Gate past the **Umaid Gardens** and the **Ghoomar Tourist Bungalow** to the distant **Raika Bagh Railway Station,** just opposite the **bus stand.** It then bends north towards **Paota Circle.**

Nai Sarak, or New Road, leads through Sojati Gate to the old city's biggest shopping drag and then to the market area, **Sadar Bazaar,** at the base of the **clock tower** that marks the center of Jodhpur. From the base of the clock tower, you'll see the magnificent **Meherangarh Fort** to your left (way up there), and **Jaswant Thada** straight ahead. Both can be reached by a short auto-rickshaw ride up a winding mountain road. In the other direction, the **Umaid Bhawan Palace** sits alone in the distance. The airport is a 15-minute drive away in the same direction.

PRACTICAL INFORMATION

Tourist Office: Ghoomar Tourist Bungalow, High Court Rd. (tel. 45083). From the Railway Station, down Station Rd. to High Court Rd., past the Umaid Gardens, on the left. Helpful, English-speaking staff provides maps, brochures, train and bus schedules, and reservations. Tours of the sights operate daily in season (off-season: Mon.-Sat.) 9am-1pm and 2-6pm, Rs.50 per person, plus entry fees; 4-person minimum. Open Mon.-Sat. 8am-7pm, Sun. 8am-noon; closed Sun. off-season.

Currency Exchange: State Bank of India, High Court Rd. (tel. 45090). Near intersection of Banar Rd. Currency exchange and traveler's checks, with no service charge. **State Bank of Rajasthan,** High Court Rd. (tel. 20587). Along High Court Rd., before Sojati Gate. Smaller banks along High Court Rd. and Station Rd. will do

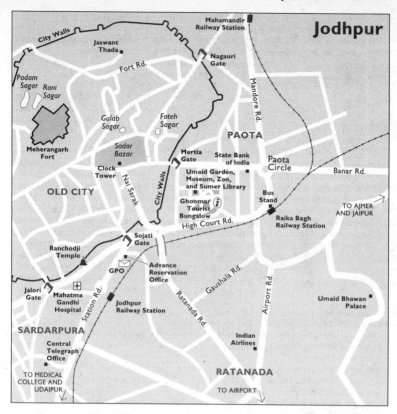

currency exchange, but not traveler's checks. All banks open Mon.-Fri. 10am-2:30pm, Sat. 10-11:30am.

Telephones: Private STD/ISD booths are found at virtually every block. Some near Sojati Gate and along Station Rd. have fax services. Near the Raika Bagh Railway Station over the bridge is a 24-hr. private booth. For a rather unique telephone experience, the **Hello Hut** (across from the main railway station) provides a circular arrangement of telephones in an arboreal setting. It also has fax services. Open daily 5am-5pm. **Central Telegraph Office,** Sardarpura (tel. 31303). A 10-min. walk from the Railway Station (away from Sojati Gate), on a side-street to the right. Open 24hr.

Airport: Jodhpur Airport, (enquiries, tel. 142). About 6km from the city center, down Airport Rd. A Rs.40 auto-rickshaw ride or a Rs.90 taxi ride from town will get you there in 15min. To: Bombay (Mon., Wed., Fri.-Sat. 1 per day, US$71); Udaipur (Mon., Wed., Fri.-Sat. 1 per day, US$25); Jaipur (Mon., Wed., Fri.-Sat. 1 per day, US$34); Delhi (Tue. and Thurs. 2 per day, US$64). **Indian Airlines,** Airport Rd., (tel. 36757). Open daily 10am-1:15pm and 2-4:30pm. **Jagson Airlines,** at the Airport (tel. 44010, ext. 360). Open Mon.-Sat. 10am-5pm.

Trains: Jodhpur Railway Station, Station Rd. (tel. 131132). To: Jaipur (*Intercity Express,* 6am, 4½hr., Rs.79/298/424/666); Delhi (*Mandor Express,* 6:30pm, 11hr., Rs.155/505/686/1151); Udaipur (10:15am and 10pm, 11hr., Rs.49/262); Ahmedabad (*Marwar Express,* 3:25 and 9:05pm, 8hr., Rs.122/396/532/898); Jaisalmer (11:15am, 9-10hr., Rs.75/170); Bikaner (4:45pm, 5½hr., Rs.87/264/383). Make reservations at the **Advance Reservation Office,** Station Rd. (tel. 36407). Located to the left of the GPO. A tourist quota line is available. Open Mon.-Fri. 8am-1:45pm and 2-8pm. **Raika Bagh Railway Station,** High Court Rd. Down High Court Rd.

under a bridge, near the bus station. East-bound trains stop at this station after departing from the main station.

Buses: Main Bus Station, High Court (tel. 44686). Features a retiring room and a badly organized ticket-purchasing system. To: Jaipur (10 deluxe per day, 5:30am-10:30pm, 7hr., Rs.100; express every hr., 6am-11pm, 8hr., Rs.85); Udaipur (deluxe at 5:30, 7am, 3, 9:30, and 10:30pm, 7hr., Rs.81; express at 7:30, 10am, noon, 1:30, and 9pm, 8-9hr, Rs.68); Jaisalmer (deluxe at 5:30am, 5hr., Rs.88; 7 express per day, 6am-11am, 6hr., Rs.60); Ahmedabad (deluxe at 6pm, 11 hr., Rs.130; express at 6:30, 9:45am, and 7:30pm, 12hr., Rs.102); Delhi (deluxe at 4pm, 12hr., Rs.224; express at 9am and 11:45am, 14hr., Rs.152); Bikaner (deluxe at 7am, 7pm, and 8pm, 5hr., Rs.78; 12 express per day, 5:30am-8:30pm, 6hr., Rs.66); Osian (9 express per day, 5:30am-5pm, 2hr., Rs.16). **Private bus companies** number in the dozens and most are located along High Court Rd. Their fares are generally lower than the government bus fares, but their departure times are less rigid. **Solanki Tours,** Station Rd., located opposite the railway station, is recommended.

Local Transportation: Local **buses** can be picked up at the railway stations, the bus stand, and along all major roads. Coming by every 2-5min., with fares at Rs.1-3, buses are a convenient way to get around. Air-conditioned **taxis** can be found at all the major sights and in front of the tourist bungalow. Fares are normally Rs.50-200. Some smaller side streets are inaccessible by taxi, particularly in the old city. **Taxis can be rented** for longer periods from Ghoomar Tourist Bungalow and Solanki Tours, Station Rd., opposite the railway station, for Rs.3-6 per km. **Auto-rickshaws,** the preferred way to navigate the small streets of the old city, tend to congregate around all the major sights and stations. You should be able to get anywhere around the city for Rs.10-30. Rates are unmetered and bargainable. **Tempos,** though less common than auto-rickshaws, can be found all over the city. **Bicycles** are a convenient but chaotic way to explore the city. They can be rented from the **Hanif Cycle Store,** across from the railway station, for Rs.20 per day. Personal **car rental** is not available in Jodhpur.

Luggage Storage: Jodhpur Railway Station. Rs.3 for first 24hr., Rs.6 per additional 24hr. period.

English Bookstore: Rathi's Media Centre, Sojati Gate (tel. 34580). The only English bookstore in Jodhpur. Has a large collection of assorted paperbacks, plus international magazines and newspapers.

Library: Sumer Public Library, High Court Rd., located in the middle of the Umaid Gardens, has a small collection of English books and newspapers. No check-out fee. Open Mon., Wed.-Sun. 7am-8pm.

Market: High Court Rd., Nai Sarak, and Sadar Bazaar are the main shopping areas. Fresh fruit and vegetable stalls and stores are found in high concentrations in Sadar Bazar and along Station Rd. For other shopping, see **Entertainment,** below. Most stores open daily 8am-10pm, closed on the 28th of each month. Parts of the Sojati Gate market are also closed on Mondays.

Pharmacy: Found in particularly high concentrations near hospitals, around Sojati and Jalori Gates, and along Nai Sarak. Most are open daily 8am-11pm. Surprisingly, prices *are* negotiable, especially if you look willing to walk to the pharmacy next door to try your luck. **Mehta Medical Hall,** Jalori Gate (tel. 35300) is open 24hr.

Hospital: Mahatma Gandhi Hospital, High Court Rd. (tel. 36437). Between Sojati and Jalori Gates, also accessible from the Station Rd. side. English-speaking staff available. Open 24hr. **Private hospitals** abound. The best are **Goyal Hospital,** Residency Rd. (tel. 32144), **Rathi Hospital** (tel. 33261), and **Jodhpur Hospital,** Shastri Nagar (tel. 33466), all near the **Medical College,** and **Sun City Hospital,** Paota Circle (tel. 45455).

Police: Ratanada Rd. (tel 33700). English-speaking, particularly helpful to tourists.

Emergency: Police, tel. 100. **Fire,** tel. 101. **Ambulance,** tel. 102.

Post Office: GPO, Station Rd. (tel. 36695). Large building on Station Rd., near the main Railway Station. *Poste Restante* is not available. Branch offices are located in Paota Circle and on Nai Sarak, but all mail is transferred to the GPO in 1-2 days, so it is much quicker to go directly to the GPO. No English-speaking staff. Open daily 10am-5pm. **Postal Code:** 342001.

Telephone Code: 0291.

ACCOMMODATIONS

Budget hotels tend to cluster in two main areas. Near the railway station hotels readily gobble up newly arrived tourists, while 16 hotels along Nai Sarak stand ready for whoever comes through. Some of these hotels are good, but it is worth looking at other accommodations options in the city. The Ghoomar Tourist Bungalow will set up tourists with local families for Rs.100-350 per night, and all travelers should at least visit the phenomenal Ajit Bhawan.

Ghoomar Hotel, High Court Rd. (tel. 44010). Adjacent to the tourist bungalow, this hotel is loaded with tourist goodies. Features a travel agency, local tours, instant reservations in other RTDC hotels, and all the information about Jodhpur you'll ever need (in several languages). Check-out noon. 3-day max. stay. 24-hr. room service, telephones in all rooms, and running hot and cold water. Large, simply-decorated rooms. Dorm beds Rs.50. Singles Rs.175, with air-cooling Rs.375, with A/C Rs.500. Doubles Rs.250, with air-cooling Rs.425, with A/C Rs.600.

Shanti Bhawan Lodge, Station Rd. (tel. 21689). Directly opposite the railway station. Small, basic rooms overlooking a noisy main road. But the staff is friendly and the rooms are clean and cheap. 24-hr. check-out, laundry service, room service, STD/ISD phone, beauty parlor, and travel arrangements available. The Midtown Restaurant is right underneath. Hot water Rs.3 per bucket. Singles Rs.50, with bath and air-cooling Rs.150. Triples with bath and air-cooling Rs.225. Reservations recommended.

Hotel Arun, Sojati Gate (tel. 20238; fax 43019). Opposite Sojati Gate. The best of the Sojati-cluster budget hotels. Moderately sized rooms with a good view of the crazy streets around. Surprisingly quiet, given its location. Room service 6am-10:30pm, dining hall, travel agency, laundry service, STD/ISD phone, fax, photocopier, currency exchange, massage. Dorm beds Rs.50. Singles Rs.140. Doubles Rs.200. Triples Rs.230. Quads Rs.280. Air-cooling Rs.30 extra. Reservations recommended.

Hotel Akshey, opposite Raika Bagh Railway Station (tel. 37327). Away from the bustle of the city in an area devoid of other hotels, this place is serene, laid-back, and a great value. 24-hr. room service, travel services (including 5hr. village safaris for Rs.350), currency exchange, laundry services, TVs and phones in all rooms, STD/ISD phone at reception, running hot and cold water. The dining hall is convenient, but meals in the central garden are especially enjoyable. Dorm beds Rs.40. Singles Rs.150, with air-cooling Rs.250, with A/C Rs.400. Doubles Rs.200, with air-cooling Rs.300, with A/C Rs.450. Extra beds Rs.40. The deluxe guest house nearby (which must be booked through Hotel Akshey) has rooms for Rs.200-500.

Hotel Marudhar, 12 Nai Sarak (tel. 27429). Centrally located, and good value. Moderate-size rooms with balconies overlook busy Nai Sarak. 24-hr. room service, running hot and cold water, travel agency, phones and TVs in all rooms, attached baths in all rooms, laundry services, friendly and helpful English-speaking staff. Singles with air-cooling Rs.175. Doubles Rs.400. Reservations recommended.

Hotel Priya, 181 Nai Sarak, Sojati Gate (tel. 47463). At intersection of Nai Sarak and High Court. Noisy, but clean and homey. Very friendly English-speaking staff. Running hot and cold water, 24-hr. room service. Popular snack food and ice cream joint below. 24-hr. check-out. Singles Rs.150, with air-cooling and bath Rs.220, with A/C Rs.400. Doubles Rs.200, with A/C and bath Rs.500.

Sun City International Youth Hostel, Airport Rd. (tel. 20150). Adjacent to the Indian Airlines office. Small and bare hostel rooms around a central courtyard. 3-night max. stay, 10pm curfew, no alcohol or smoking allowed. Check-in 7-10am, check-out 4-9pm. Large lockers provided—bring your own lock. Some chores required. Nature treks available. Dorm room Rs.20 for members, Rs.50 for non-members. Doubles Rs.70, with bath Rs.80.

Charli Bikaner Lodge, Railway Station (tel. 33949). Just opposite the station. You can't get more basic than this. 24-hr. check-out, hot and cold running water, laundry services, 24-hr. veg. room service. A bit noisy, but bearable. Singles Rs.55. Doubles Rs.100. Triples Rs.120. Quads Rs.130. Air-cooling Rs.40 extra.

Adarsh Niwas, Station Rd. (tel. 627338). Opposite the railway station. Plain-look-ing, decent-sized rooms. A convenient location coupled with numerous facilities make this a popular choice among tourists. The excellent Kalinga restaurant and an air-conditioned bar are attached. 24-hr. check-out, laundry services, running hot and cold water, 24-hr. currency exchange, fridges and TVs in all rooms. Singles Rs.400, with air-cooling Rs.500, with A/C Rs.800. Reservations recommended.

Ajit Bhawan, Airport Rd. (tel. 37410; fax 37774). Down Airport Rd. before the Indian Airlines office. A resort to gawk at if not to stay in. Peacefully located away from the commotion of the city, this hotel features individually decorated cottages around a beautiful garden and pools. Facilities include a travel agency, currency exchange, a shopping arcade, a health club, and a fantastic restaurant. Village safa-ris Rs.400 per person, 8am-1pm. Just for fun, look at several rooms before choos-ing. Singles Rs.1300. Doubles Rs.1550. Extra bed Rs.350.

FOOD

Although Jodhpur offers many cuisines, it is enriching to explore the Rajasthani and Marwari specialties that the townspeople eagerly recommend. Dishes such as *kab-uli*—a rice preparation—and *chakki-ka sagh*—a spongy wheat dish—should defi-nitely be savored, preferably over a refreshing *mousmi*—an orange drink—or a cold glass of famous saffron-flavored *makhania lassi*. Along Nai Sarak you will find a wide assortment of small **fast-food restaurants** and **stalls** selling assorted drinks, fresh fruits and vegetables, and snack foods. Many hotels have good, inexpensive restau-rants attached. A popular dining strategy is to skip lunch, and then hit several stalls along any road before ending up in a small restaurant for dinner.

Agra Sweets, Sojati Gate. Located directly opposite Sojati Gate. Perhaps the most popular refreshment spot in Jodhpur, where mobs descend on that oh-so-refresh-ing *makhania lassi* at Rs.8 a hit. Try *mava kachori*, a Jodhpuri specialty. A wide range of sweets and pastries is also available. Open daily 7am-10:30pm.

On the Rocks, Ajit Bhawan (tel. 611410). Adjacent to Ajit Bhawan Hotel, on Airport Rd. Enjoy an arboreal and aquatic interlude in the only outdoor restaurant in Jodh-pur proper. The bar (indoors) is well-stocked. Excellent food, Indian and Continen-tal—a bit of everything, with a separate veg. section. Entrees are Rs.80-100. Open daily 11am-midnight.

Kalinga Restaurant in the Adarsh Niwas Hotel, Station Rd. Located opposite the Railway Station. Indian, Continental, Chinese, Italian—a veritable potpourri. Be sure to try items from their "Marwari Food Festival" menu, featuring regional spe-cialties for Rs.40-70. Their package specialty deals—the *Marwari thali* and *shahi thali*, for Rs.50 and Rs.80, are particularly excellent. A local hang-out. Open daily 11am-3pm, 6-10pm.

Midtown Restaurant, in the Shanti Bhawan Lodge, opposite the Railway Station (tel. 27226). A veg. restaurant featuring a host of Rajasthani and Jodhpuri special-ties, including *kabuli* and *chakki-ka sagh* (Rs.40 each). Continental and Chinese food also available. The *Rajasthani maharaja thali*, for Rs.70, mixes together many of the local specialties. Quick service, but no alcohol. Open daily 7am-11pm.

Jodhpur Darbar BBQ, in the City Palace Hotel, 32 Nai Sarak (tel. 27130). Tasty dishes fresh off the grill or the *tandoor*, on a rooftop with a panoramic view of the city. Rs.70 entrees are well worth the price. Continental and Chinese food is also available. Alcohol is served. Open daily 6am-10:30pm. Reservations recommended.

Gossip Restaurant, in the City Palace Hotel, 32 Nai Sarak (tel. 27130). With veg. food as good as the tandoori above, Gossip has become a local favorite. Entrees Rs.40-50. Open daily 7am-10:30pm. Reservations recommended.

Delux, High Court Rd., at intersection of Station Rd. and High Court Rd. A popular drinks store where you can grab a variety of cold drinks, milk shakes, flavored waters, fruit juices, and *lassis*—including the famous *makhania lassi*. Just jump into the mobs of people and scream your order. Everything is Rs.5-15. Open daily 6am-11pm.

Punkhaj, Station Rd. An earthy, familial veg. restaurant. The mixed vegetable dishes are recommended. Entrees are under Rs.40. The tandoori *naan,* Rs.10, is considered the best in the area. Open daily 7am-10:30pm.

Risala, Umaid Bhawan Palace (tel. 22516). It's expensive, but it'll be an evening you won't forget. In an ornately decorated dining hall, a vast array of assorted cuisines are presented as a banquet, with live sitar, sarod, and tabla as accompaniment. Both veg. and non-veg. dishes are available. Non-guests of the hotel pay a Rs.330 cover charge, deductible from the final cost; expect to spend Rs.500-600, but it's worth it. Open daily 6am-11pm. Reservations required.

Gypsy, 9th C Rd., Sardarpura (tel. 33288). A crowded fast-food joint for twentysomething Jodhpuris. Eccentric veg. cuisine, including pizzas, *dosas,* veggie burgers, and Chinese food. Entrees Rs.20-30. Open daily 9am-11pm.

Ajit Bhawan Palace Hotel Restaurant, Airport Rd. (tel. 20409). Off Airport Rd., before the Indian Airlines office. In the beautiful main courtyard of the hotel, enjoy a buffet dinner with live Rajasthani folk music and dance, all for Rs.185. The food is superb and plentiful. Explore the wonderful hotel while you're here. Open daily 9am-11pm. Reservations generally required 2hr. in advance.

SIGHTS

The sights in Jodhpur are few, but fabulous. Many tourists spend only a day in Jodhpur before catching a night bus to Jaisalmer. Ghoomar Tourist Bungalow provides guided tours of the main city attractions and of Mandore Gardens (see p. 304).

Meherangarh Fort is what Jodhpur sightseeing is about. Crowning the city below, the fort is a blend of well-designed defense systems and amazing artistry. Seven *pols,* or gates, mark the entrances to various parts of the fort. The formidable **Jayapol** is the main entrance commemorating Maharaja Man Singh's war achievements, and the impressive **Fatehpol** (Victory Gate), created by Maharaja Ajit Singh after his fairytale return from exile, marks the original entrance into the fort. The **Lohapol** (Iron Gate), where 15 handprints mark the *sati* sacrifice of Maharaja Man Singh's widows, is particularly dramatic. Despite modern anti-*sati* sentiment, Jodhpuris pay tribute at this gate daily. The final gigantic **Surajpol** marks the entrance to the **Fort Museum,** located in the sculpted red sandstone palace. Features of the museum include extravagant *howdahs,* or elephant mounts, exquisite wood and ivory artifacts, including assorted boxes, pipes, toys, and carpet-holders, a weapons room, the royal dumbells of the maharani (!), a beautifully woven 250-year-old tent canopy, 150 types of cannons (so they say), fancy baby cradles, musical instruments, paintings, and a 300-piece turban collection. Of particular interest is the **Phool Mahal** (Flower Palace), an elaborately mirrored dining hall. Turn off the flash on your camera here or risk blinding everyone in the room. The **Moti Mahal** (Pearl Palace), a conference room with a glass and gold ceiling, is calm, mellow, and beautiful. The nearby **Chamunda Temple** is less interesting, but check out the view of the blue city from the fort before leaving. The fort (tel. 48790) is open daily 8:30am-5:30pm. Admission Rs.50, camera fee Rs.50, video camera fee Rs.100, lift fee Rs.10 (waived for disabled persons), government-guided tours (1-4hr.) Rs.100. When you exit, noisy "traditional" musicians will surround you, demanding *baksheesh.*

Ten minutes from the fort by foot down a windy road is the **Jaswant Thada,** a pillared marble memorial to the beloved Maharaja Jaswant Singh II, erected by his wife after his death. Locals compare it to a miniature Taj Mahal, as the structures are quite similar, and the reasons for construction are the same. Smaller marble cenotaphs are nearby. The view of the city from here is also quite a sight. (Open daily 9am-5:30pm; free.) Photography not allowed inside. Back in the center of the city, the **Clock Tower** stalwartly marks the center of the *sher* and the crazy and crowded Sadar Bazar, i.e. shopping central (see below).

Along High Court Rd. lie **Jalori Gate** and **Sojati Gate,** large, simply carved structures, more interesting for their adjoining commercial centers than as sights, and the **Umaid Gardens** near the Tourist Bungalow. The gardens are a pleasant place to stroll, and they contain the Sumer Library, a rudimentary "zoo," and a rather boring museum. The museum is open daily 10am-5:30pm; admission is Rs.2 and hardly worth it.

The **Umaid Bhawan Palace** is a magnificent marble-and-sandstone palace dominating the eastern part of the city. The palace offers well-kept picnicky gardens. A grandiose hotel and restaurant take up half the palace, while an eccentric museum containing traditional art, models, weapons, trophies, and miscellaneous relics—all belonging to the maharaja—occupies the rest. The museum is open daily 9am-5pm. Admission is Rs.40, and cameras are *strictly* prohibited.

ENTERTAINMENT

Nightlife in Jodhpur is surprisingly limited given the city's size. The **bar scene** is geared toward foreign tourists. On the Rocks Restaurant and City Palace Hotel both have popular, well-stocked bars. Two **Hindi cinemas** exist: Girdhar Cinema on Nai Sarak, and an unnamed establishment on High Court Rd. past Sojati Gate.

The annual **Marwar Festival** showcases local culture, history, dance, music, art, and most of all, food. All restaurants load their menus with high-priced regional specialties. Less theme-oriented than other Rajasthani festivals, the Marwar Festival is simply meant to be a good time. In 1997, the festival will take place October 15-16.

SHOPPING

The shopping scene in Jodhpur is large and intense. The **Sojati Gate** and **Nai Sarak** areas, including **Sadar Bazar** by the Clock Tower, are studded with stalls, markets, emporia, and department stores. Everything can be found here, from craft works to stereo equipment. Bargaining is possible everywhere. The embroidery and sari stores are particularly popular. Specialty antique stores line the road connecting the Umaid Bhawan Palace to Airport Rd. Prices are remarkably high due to the predominantly foreign clientele, however. Most stores are open daily 8am-8pm, closed the 28th of every month.

VILLAGE SAFARIS

Guided tours of the villages in the desert around Jodhpur allow visitors to witness and participate in carpet-making, weaving, spinning, foraging, indigenous medicine, and local cuisine. In particular, the villages of the **Bishnoi** leave visitors feeling enlightened and green: their religion is devoted to environmental protection and conservation, founded upon 29 principles originating in the 15th century. Maharaja Swaroop Singh personally leads tours, arranged through the Ajit Bhawan Hotel (tel. 37410), for Rs.400 per person, 5hr., 8am-1pm, including lunch. Mr. Parbat Singh arranges tours and cross-desert camel safaris (as far as Jaisalmer and Bikaner), for Rs.500-900 per person. Contact him at Meherangarh Fort (tel. 48790). The **Ghoomar Tourist Bungalow** has 5-hr. tours for Rs.700 per two people and day-long tours for Rs.485 per person. **Hotel Akshey** (tel. 37327) has 5-hr. tours for Rs.350 per person, 8am-1pm and 2-7pm.

■ Near Jodhpur

Once the capital of Marwar, the town of **Mandore**, 9km north of Jodhpur, still houses the cenotaphs of the Rathore maharajas, including that of Ajit Singh. Near the tidy garden where the cenotaphs stand is The Hall of Heroes, a series of 15 colorful, life-size statues of Hindu gods and Rajput warriors carved out of one large rock wall. Also nearby is the Shrine of the 330 Million Gods, a triumphal site for polytheism. Mandore is accessible from Jodhpur by local buses for Rs.2-3.

The ancient town of **Osian**, 65km north of Jodhpur, is surrounded by sand dunes and is home to 16 remarkably sculpted Jain and Hindu temples from the 8th-11th centuries. Osian is accessible by regular buses from Jodhpur (see **Practical Information,** p. 306).

■ Jaisalmer

In the heart of the Thar Desert, 285km west of Jodhpur and 100km from the Pakistan border, lies the "Golden City" of Jaisalmer. As other cities in Rajasthan are invaded by billboards and traffic, Jaisalmer is still proud to be dominated by its fort and its balconied sandstone houses, rising gracefully out of the arid, wind-blown landscape. Most of Jaisalmer's old city is still contained within the remains of its city walls, and its winding, sand-dusted streets are rarely frequented by vehicles. Exploring these streets can truly convey a feeling of the ancient fairytale Rajputana of temples, bazaars, and desert wanderings. Although Jaisalmer is flooded with tourists during the winter, the local people's traditional, conservative way of life preserves the city's identity and prevents it from feeling like a tourist town.

Jaisalmer's history is turbulent and majestic. Built originally as a strategic fort, Jaisalmer was twice sacked and conquered by Muslim invaders before becoming a prosperous trade center for camel caravans in the 17th century. But maritime trade under the British eclipsed the desert trade routes, and Partition in 1947 cut them off altogether, diminishing Jaisalmer's wealth and importance. With the Indo-Pakistan tensions of the 1960s, however, Jaisalmer became a military outpost, and the army presence is now a source of income second only to the booming tourism industry. Now Jaisalmer is primarily about camel safaris amidst Jain temples, desert craftwork and cuisine, and painted *havelis* that retain memories of the city's golden years. As the sun sets on Jaisalmer, turning the city golden-brown, one can envision a rich past.

ORIENTATION

The RTDC-run **Hotel Moomal** lies on the west end of town, just off **Sam Road,** and is a good place to get your bearings on the city. Sam Rd. leads east past the hospital to **Hanuman Circle,** just outside **Amar Sagar Pol,** the main entrance to the old city. Hanuman Circle is littered with jeeps, buses, and taxis for hire, and the adjacent market is easily identified by a bizarrely placed jet, a relic from a war with Pakistan. The **local bus stand** is in this circle. Walking straight along this same road will lead into the city, while taking a right will land you at the **GPO.** Just inside Amar Sagar Pol is **Gandhi Chauk,** the main market area. The entrance to **Badal Mahal,** the old royal palace, is just in the gate area on the right. This same road leads narrowly through the market to the **fort.** The road continues in front of the fort to the **Gopa Chauk** market before winding its way to **Gadi Sagar Pol,** the west gate of the city. From here the road becomes **Gadi Sagar Road,** and ends at Lake Gadisan, or Gadi Sagar. A left turn just outside of Gadi Sagar Pol leads to the remote **Main Bus Stand** and **Railway Station.** Turning right at Gadi Sagar Pol leads to the **Tourist Information Centre.**

PRACTICAL INFORMATION

Tourist Office: RTDC (tel. 52406). Exit Gadi Sagar Pol and turn right at the first intersection. The tourist bureau is on your right after a 3-min. walk. Provides bus, train, plane, and camel safari information, maps, and reservations at other RTDC hotels. Offers daily tours of local sights (9am-noon, Rs.40), and to Sam (4pm-7pm, Rs.70). Open daily 8am-6pm. This bureau used to be situated in the **Moomal Tourist Bungalow,** on the other side of town off of Sam Rd. (tel. 52392). The bungalow still provides basic information and map services.

Budget Travel: Safari Tours, near Amar Sagar Pol (tel. 41058) is an excellent source of information on everything in and around Jaisalmer. Open daily 8am-8pm. For more information, see **Camel Safaris** (p. 317).

Currency Exchange: State Bank of India, in Nachana Haveli, near Amar Sagar Pol. Currency exchange, traveler's checks. Open Mon.-Fri. 10am-2pm, Sat. 10am-noon. **Bank of Baroda,** Amar Sagar (tel. 52402). Just inside Amar Sagar Pol on the right. Currency exchange, traveler's checks, V/MC cash advance. Open Mon.-Fri. 10am-1pm, Sat. 10-11am.

Telephones: STD/ISD private booths are located everywhere in the city. A 24-hr. booth is located across Nachana Haveli near Amar Sagar Pol, and in the fort on the first side street to the right. Fax services are available in major hotels.

Airport: Army Airport, 4km west of the city. A Rs.30 rickshaw ride. Currently served only by **Jagson Airlines,** Moomal Tourist Bungalow (tel. 52392). Reservations and information available from all hotels and travel agents. To: Jodhpur (Tue., Thurs., Sat., 1:30pm, Rs.2275) then on to Delhi (Rs.5250).

Trains: Railway Station (tel. 52354). Out of Gadi Sagar Pol, bear left, 10min. away on your left. Has a tourist lounge with information, maps, and showers. Open daily 8-11am and 2-4pm. To Jodhpur (7:20am, 9-10hr., Rs.85/160).

Buses: Main Bus Stand (tel. 53141), near the Railway Station. To: Jodhpur (deluxe at 5pm, 5hr., Rs.88; express at 7am, noon, and 1pm, 5½hr., Rs.58); Bikaner (6 express per day, 6:30am-10pm, 7hr., Rs.89; passenger at 8:30am and 12:30pm, 8hr., Rs.72). All buses leave 30min. earlier from the more conveniently located **Local Bus Stand** in Hanuman Circle. **Private buses** leave frequently, but departure times are less strict. *All* hotels and *all* travel agents can arrange both government and private bus reservations.

Local Transportation: By **foot,** it takes 10-15min. to traverse the city. Winding, disorganized streets make this the best method. **Auto-rickshaws** are unmetered and can navigate the tiny streets easily. You can find them almost anywhere in town; auto-rickshaws are not permitted in the fort proper. Most charge Rs.10-15. **Bicycles** are a convenient means of touring Jaisalmer. They can be rented in season from inside Amar Sagar Pol, and from near the fort gate for Rs.20 per day. **Jeeps** are needed to get to places outside of the city. Expect to pay Rs.3 per km for custom routes. Travel agents and hotels have their own jeeps which can be rented at cheaper rates for fixed tours.

English Bookstore: Bhatia News Agency, Gandhi Chauk (tel. 52671). On the right past the State Bank, coming from Amar Sagar Pol. Features English, French, Italian, German, and Hindi books, magazines, and newspapers, new and used. Open daily 8am-10pm.

Market: Gandhi Chauk is the main commercial center. **Hanuman Circle** and the **Fort Gate area (Gopa Chauk)** are also shopping districts. Dry food stores are clustered along the main city throughway, between Gandhi Chauk and Gopa Chauk. Fresh fruit and vegetables are sold from stalls mainly in Gopa Chauk. Most stores open daily 8am-10pm.

Pharmacy: Located everywhere in the city especially around the hospitals. None are open 24hr.

Hospital: Sri Jawahar Government Hospital (tel. 52343). Large pillared building on the left of Sam Rd. before Amar Sagar Pol. English-speaking, clean, helpful. **Sri Maheswari Hospital** (tel. 40024). On the left of Sam Rd. before the government hospital, before Amar Sagar Pol. Private; English-speaking staff.

Police: Main Police Office (tel. 52332). Down Sam Rd. towards Amar Sagar Pol, right at Hanuman Circle, on the right side 3min. down. English-speaking. A **Tourist Protection Service** is based here as well.

Post Office: GPO (tel. 52407). Near the police station, 5min. from Amar Sagar Pol. The **telegraph office** is also located here. Open Mon.-Sat. 8am-8pm. **Branch Office,** near fort gate, on the right under a big tree. Open Mon.-Sat. 10am-6pm, Sun. 9am-4pm. **Postal Code:** 345001.

Telephone Code: 02992.

ACCOMMODATIONS

Jaisalmer is filled with budget hotels. New ones pop up by the month as tourism takes over more and more of the city and homes and *havelis* are converted to meet its demands. Large clusters of hotels are found in the fort area and outside the city walls along Sam Rd. All hotels *without exception* offer travel services, laundry service, and of course camel safaris. See **Camel Safaris** (p. 317) for more information on the insanely competitive safari situation. Additionally, expect all rates to *at least* double during the Desert Festival (see **Entertainment,** p. 316).

Jaisalmer

Railway Station

TO BIKANER AND JODHPUR →

Main Bus Stand

TO BARMER →

Barmer Rd.

City Walls

Kishanghat Pol

Gadi Sagar Pol

Gadi Sagar Rd.

Gadi Sagar

Tilon-ki-Pol and Jaisalmer Folklore Museum

Malka Pol

Chainpura St.

Jama Masjid

Patwon-ki-Haveli

Nathmalji-ki-Haveli

Salim Singh-ki-Haveli

GOPA CHAUK

Tourist Information

State Bank of India

GANDHI CHAUK

Badal Mahal/ Mandir Palace

FORT

Palace

Jain Temples

Jaisal Castle

City Walls

Amar Sagar Pol

Local Bus Stand

HANUMAN CIRCLE

Sam Rd.

Police Station

Post Office

Hospital

Ramgarh Rd.

Bara Bagh

TO AIRPORT, AMAR SAGAR, AND SAM →

Moomal Tourist Bungalow

Jawahar Niwas Palace

Government Museum

Hotel Renuka, Chainpura St. (tel. 52757). Enter Amar Sagar Pol, left on Chainpura, 5min. down. Very friendly, familial, and clean—a great value. 24-hr. room service from veg. restaurant. Check-out 10am. For camel safaris, only pay 50% up front, Rs.250/750 per day for 2½ day jeep/camel safari. Singles Rs.40, with bath Rs.70. Doubles Rs.60, with bath Rs.90-110. Reservations recommended. Folk dancing and music can be bought for Rs.500 per 3-4hr.

Hotel Rajdhani, Patwon-ki-Haveli (tel. 52746). Clean, modern rooms surrounding a sunny central courtyard. Beautiful rooftop view of the nearby havelis and of the fort and city. Check-out 9am. 24-hr. veg. room service. Camel Safaris Rs.650 for 1½days, Rs.750 for 2½days, Rs.850 for 3½days, Rs.300 for each additional day. All rooms have attached bath with running hot and cold water and have air-cooling. Singles Rs.125. Doubles Rs.150. Extra bed Rs.25.

Hotel Pleasure, Gandhi Chauk (tel. 52323). In Amar Sagar Pol to the left. An excellent value. The rooms are simple, tiled, and of decent size. Breakfast room service available. Free luggage storage. All rooms have air-cooling. Check-out noon. Camel safaris Rs.300 per day. Singles Rs.40. Doubles Rs.60, with bath Rs.80.

Hotel Paradise (tel. 52674). In the fort to the left. An amazing rooftop view of the city and environs, especially at sunset. Carpeted rooms around a central garden. Once a part of the royal palace. 24-hr. room service. Three hours of traditional music and dance in rooftop restaurant for Rs.400-500. Location allows for effective "natural" air-cooling. Camel safaris Rs.150 for day, Rs.550 for 2½days. Singles Rs.60-100. Doubles with bath Rs.250-350. Stellar double with balcony Rs.450.

Moomal Tourist Bungalow, Amar Sagar Rd. (tel. 52392). Spacious rooms, decent restaurant, and all the tourist information you'll ever need. RTDC-run. The outdoor cottages with air-cooling make for particularly enjoyable stays. All rooms with attached baths. Two-hour traditional dance and music program Rs.1500. Camel safaris Rs.250 per day, deluxe Rs.550 per day. Singles Rs.250, with air-cooling Rs.450, with A/C Rs.600. Dorm beds Rs.50. Doubles Rs.300, with air-cooling Rs.500, with A/C Rs.675. Single cottages Rs.250. Double cottages Rs.300.

Hotel Starmoon, in fort (tel. 40363; fax 40323). Enter the fort, walk 5min. to the right, and you'll find it. Extremely friendly and helpful staff. Good-size rooms with simple decor and excellent views of the city and sunset. Check-out 9am. Camel safaris Rs.150-350 per day. Dorm beds Rs.10. Singles Rs.80, with bath Rs.100. Doubles with bath Rs.100, with deluxe balcony Rs.250.

Hotel Jag Palace, Patwon-ki-Haveli (tel. 40438). Friendly, laid-back staff and comfortable, simple rooms. Solid modern facilities. Check-out 9am. Camel safaris 650 for 1½days, Rs.750 for 2½days. All rooms with attached bath and running hot and cold water. Singles Rs.150, with air-cooling Rs.250. Doubles Rs.200, with air-cooling Rs.250. Reservations recommended.

Hotel Swastika, Chainpura St. (tel. 52483). Well-run, well-decorated, decent size rooms, good value. Private library. Telephones in rooms. Check-out 9am. Camel safaris Rs.250 per day. Dorm beds Rs.30. Singles Rs.60, with bath Rs.120. Doubles Rs.80, with bath Rs.150. Reservations recommended.

Upscale Accommodations

Hotel Nachana Haveli, Gandhi Chauk (tel. 52110). Inside Amar Sagar Pol to the right. A renovated *haveli* with room decor that includes bear skins and spears. Large rooms with air-cooling attached bathrooms. Extremely familial staff. Central garden is relaxing. Attached Skyroom Restaurant is excellent. 24-hr. room service. Check-out noon. Camel safaris Rs.750 per day. Singles Rs.600. Doubles Rs.1000. Off-season 50% discount.

Narayan Villas, Malkaprol Rd. (tel. 52283). Near Patwon-ki-Haveli, next to the cinema hall. Run by Maharaja Govind Singh, this delightful *haveli* features traditionally-decorated rooms, a wonderful rooftop view, and a relaxed attitude. 24-hr. room service. Check-out noon. Camel safaris arranged through Sahara Tours. Singles Rs.475, with A/C Rs.650. Doubles Rs.650, with A/C Rs.850. Extra bed Rs.125. Reservations required.

FOOD

Food in Jaisalmer is as impressive as the sights and safaris. While every restaurant features Continental and Chinese food, Jaisalmer also has earthy desert cuisine that you won't find elsewhere. Local specialties are basic and savory. Be sure to the experience *ker sangri,* a mix of desert capers and beans (it looks like a bundle of gravied twigs), *gatte,* a gram flour preparation, and *kadi pakoras,* a yogurt-based appetizer.

Trio Restaurant, Amar Sagar Pol (tel. 52733). Next to the Badal Mahal, in Gandhi Chauk. Considered by many to be the best restaurant in Jaisalmer, Trio features first-class service, well-prepared local specialties, and traditional Rajasthani music for a very reasonable price. The view is great and a backup generator keeps the place lit during power outages. Entrees range from Rs.30-60; *ker sangri, gatte,* and *kadi pakoras* are all under Rs.35. Open daily 7am-10:30pm. Reservations recommended.

Kalpana Restaurant, Gandhi Chauk (tel. 52469). Located in the heart of Gandhi Chauk, Kalpana offers a rooftop view, specialty *tandoor* cuisine, and one of the best bars in the city. This place is very popular, and not just among tourists. Prices are reasonable at Rs.30-35 per entree. Open daily 7am-11pm.

Jain Restaurant. Enter Amar Sagar Pol and follow the right wall down 10min. This is perhaps the last restaurant in town that hasn't succumbed to the Continental/Chinese-trend—this is pure-veg.-Indian-only-don't-speak-English. Get away from the tourists and enjoy the popular *kaju* curry for Rs.35; most entrees are Rs.15-20. Open Mon.-Fri. 9am-11pm.

Natraj Restaurant, Salim-Singh-ki-Haveli (tel. 52667). An up-close-and-personal view of a *haveli* with good food for slightly higher than average prices. Standard range of dishes, all well-prepared. Beer bar. Entrees Rs.30-50. Open daily 8am-11pm.

Kanchan Shree Restaurant (tel. 40890). Follow prominent signs down left side streets from the fort gate. This is refreshment central, with juices, ice cream, homemade peanut butter, and 18 flavors of *lassi* for relief from the sun. Open daily 7am-10pm.

Midtown Restaurant, Gopa Chauk (tel. 40242). Solid Continental, Chinese, Punjabi, and Italian veg. food at reasonable prices, with a sunset rooftop view. A Rajasthani *thali* costs Rs.40. Open daily 7am-11pm.

Monica Restaurant, Gopa Chauk (tel. 53186). Left of the fort gate. A local favorite (not just a tourist hangout) with a range of cuisines. Their fruit preparations are especially recommended. Entrees are Rs.30-40. Open daily 8am-11pm. Reservations recommended.

SIGHTS

Jaisalmer should truly be appreciated as a whole experience and not just as a sum of its tourist spots. The narrow streets, rising on both sides into soft sandstone buildings, all glow golden in the desert sun. Camel safaris, rolling dunes, and the sand-dusted fort of the old city all contribute to the unique atmosphere of Jaisalmer, mysteriously held in medieval glory.

Jaisalmer's **fort,** founded in 1156 by Maharaja Jaisal, a king of the Bhatti clan of Rajputs, overlooks the city from the south. Its 99 circular bastions house within them a labyrinthine world of small homes and shops along narrow gullies winding around the old palace. Enter from Gopa Chauk, the commercial square outside the fort's main gate. The **city palace,** just inside the fort, is open to visitors and is composed of five smaller palaces, one of which has a dancing hall decorated with blue Chinese tiles and green screens from the Netherlands. The old stone rooms are half-preserved; some even remain closed by their original locks, while others store decaying elephant *howdahs.* A climb to the windy ramparts affords a great view of the fort and old city. It is said that the fort has not a single cemented joint in its foundation, but is constructed stone upon stone from its foundation up. (Open daily 9am-5:30pm. Admission Rs.5, camera fee Rs.15, guided tours Rs.25.)

A cluster of seven interconnected **Jain Temples** lies within the fort a short walk from the entrance to the palace along the second road off to the right. Built on a raised platform, the temples' low archways and tiny halls display amazing sculpture, with not a visible inch spared. A winding staircase leads up to a circular balcony with an open view of the sanctuary below, as well as the temples' dome. The temples are open daily from 7am to noon. Free, camera fee Rs.25, video fee Rs.50. Menstruating women are forbidden to enter lest they "violate the sanctity of the temple." A magnificent library with ancient relics is below, open daily from 10 to 11am by request. A small offering of Rs.5 in any donation box is customary.

Lake Gadisan, or Gadi Sagar, an artificial reservoir, was once Jaisalmer's only source of water, visited daily by town girls who would carry away their aqueous loads in large pots balanced on their heads and hips. Today, it is frequented by bathers, *dhobis,* and visitors who come to view the **Folklore Museum,** which contains quirky paintings and carvings (open Mon.-Sat. 9am-1pm; admission Rs.5, camera fee Rs.10) and the yellow sandstone gateway, the **Tilon-ki-Pol.** With its grand arched windows, this gate once held beautifully carved windowed rooms for monsoon visits by the royal family. Said to have been built by one of the king's dancing girls (or prostitutes, depending on the story), the gate was once a source of great controversy for the town's citizens, who refused to allow their womenfolk to walk beneath the "tainted" creation. As a compromise, a smaller entrance was built to the right side. The lake is now decorated with a few royal stone *chhattris.*

Any walk through the old city will inevitably bring you to one of the three large *havelis,* or mansions. The *havelis* are all open daily from 10:30am to 5pm. **Patwon-ki-Haveli,** the most impressive of the three, is composed of five joint *havelis* built in the early 1900s by a family of wealthy merchants. The single golden façade rises four dramatic stories, each fitted with stone balconies topped by arched stone umbrellas and exquisite lattice-work windows. While some of the *haveli* is now occupied by shops selling jewelry and embroidered cloth, two doors still open to reveal stairs up to the haveli's towering rooftop view of the surrounding sand-brick street. **Nathmalji-ki-Haveli** is another architectural monument built by two rather stubborn brothers, who each took one half of the building's face. The intricate carvings on the left and right sides of the main door, are evidence of their difference. This haveli can only be seen from outside, since lucky families currently live here. **Salim Singh-ki-Haveli,** with peacock buttresses adorning its exterior, was built by the infamous prime minister Salim Singh Mohta around 1800. Considered a tyrant for his crippling taxes, Salim Singh impoverished the people while building up his own immunity to royal edicts through bribery and clever legislation. In a remarkable episode, 84 nearby villages were vacated one night in response to one of his policies. He is said to have attempted to construct two additional levels on his own *haveli* in order to make his home taller than the maharaja's, but the maharaja had the additional levels torn down. Finally, Salim Singh's audacity drove the maharaja to have him covertly assassinated. The *haveli* is as beautiful as Salim Singh was cruel. The entrance fee is Rs.10.

ENTERTAINMENT

Jaisalmer has little nightlife, but plenty to keep you occupied: the best time to come to Jaisalmer is for the annual **Desert Festival.** All prices are at least doubled, and the place is mobbed with tourists, but you'll be able to enjoy traditional music and folk dance, camel races, camel polo, camel dances (indeed, everything camel), puppeteers, moustache contests, and more. RTDC sets up a special tented tourist village for accommodations. The affair is not traditional—a definite tourist trap—but enjoyable nonetheless. In 1997 the Desert Festival will take place Feb. 20-22.

Other miscellaneous entertainment includes **swimming**—Hotel Gorbandh Palace, 2km from town, allows use of their pool for Rs.200; **Hindi movie theaters**—at Ramesh Talkies, near Patwon-ki-Haveli (tel. 52242); traditional local **music shows** courtesy of Sarawar Khar, behind Patwon-ki-Haveli (tel. 41171); and a government-authorized *bhang* shop next to the Fort Gate.

SHOPPING

Jaisalmer is a haven for **crafts,** including embroidery, patchwork, and mirrorwork unique to the desert, as well as stonecarving, silverwork, and pottery. Bargain hard, and don't attempt to shop during the Desert Festival. Gandhi Chauk and all along the main road past the fort to Gadi Sagar Pol are the main commercial areas. In particular, the **Rajasthan Art Gallery** (tel. 52137), run by friendly Swaroop, has an extensive collection of embroidery, carpets, and clothes which you can peruse without hassle and purchase at uninflated prices, and then have shipped abroad.

CAMEL SAFARIS

Camel safaris are what Jaisalmer is all about these days, and the local establishments all realize this. As such, the camel safari business has become ruthlessly competitive. *Every* hotel offers camel safaris, and several independent agencies do as well. But few hotels actually have their own camels; most operate through the independent agencies. Hotels pay the agencies about Rs.100 per day just for the camels, with food and equipment costs added. For the hotels to make a profit, they must charge at least Rs.200 per day. Indeed, **the RTDC has established a minimum rate of Rs.250 per day.** Deluxe safaris with tents, quality food, portable bars, dancing, music, and other goodies can cost over Rs.1500 per day.

If you take the train or bus to Jaisalmer from Jodhpur, expect to be hassled by hotel agents en route. You will be offered incredible deals such as Rs.10 hotel rooms, provided you go on that hotel's safari. When you arrive in Jaisalmer, you will be mobbed by touts offering similar deals. All will offer free transportation to the hotel in question. If you express interest in another hotel, touts will pull out the business card of that hotel, saying they are authorized to transport patrons. **Most touts carry a full deck of Jaisalmer hotel business cards.** They will then give you a story about that hotel being closed or full, and take you to their hotel. However, some hotels do provide free transportation without hassle. **Look for hotel banners, not business cards.**

This might sound bad, but the real scams haven't even begun. At some hotels, **if you go on another hotel's or agency's safari, you will be kicked out. Hotel agents will follow you around town** making sure you don't visit other places. If you go on your own hotel's safari, **you may be kicked out the next day as more tourists arrive.**

Once you've chosen a safari, still be wary. Cheap safaris often have **hidden costs,** such as Rs.50 or more for bottles of mineral water in the desert heat. Cheap safaris also often skimp on basic amenities such as blankets (it gets very cold in the desert at night) and English-speaking guides. Furthermore, several scams exist to steal your possessions on the return trip. **Never accept offers to watch your luggage** while you explore a sight.

Of course, not all hotels run scams. Many hotels have honest, decent, and inexpensive safaris. The most reliable camel safaris are booked through independent agents. **Safari Tours,** just inside Amar Sagar Pol (tel. 41058) is excellent (for general tourist information as well). Basic safaris cost Rs.450 per day, and deluxe safaris start at Rs.750 per day. Safari tours is one of the few that genuinely tries to keep the desert clean. Other reputable agencies are **Royal Safari** in Nachana Haveli (tel. 52538), basic Rs.450 per day, deluxe Rs.1000 per day; **Golden Tours,** in Gandhi Chauk (tel. 53330), basic Rs.250 per day, deluxe Rs.2000 per day; and Mr. Desert's **Sahara Travels** near the Fort Gate (tel. 52609), basic Rs.250 per day, deluxe Rs.500 per day. Ask safari agents to specify all food and equipment, as "deluxe" and "basic" can mean many things.

Camel safaris generally head to the spectacular Sam sand dunes, stopping at nearby villages and sights along the way. A roundtrip takes 4½ days. All hotels and agents offer shorter jeep/camel combinations for assorted prices, but with these you might not get the chance to sleep under the stars in the Thar Desert. Longer cross-desert safaris to Bikaner or Jodhpur are also available.

■ Near Jaisalmer

The areas surrounding Jaisalmer are as interesting as the city proper. Camel and camel-jeep safaris stop at many of these locales on their way to the sand dunes, and are the best means of experiencing them. The area 45km west of Jaisalmer is restricted because of border disputes. To go there, special permission is required from the District Magistrate Office, located near the police station. Permission is rarely granted, and never for tourist reasons.

About 5km north of Jaisalmer is **Bada Bagh,** where a 500-year-old barrage of sculpted sandstone cenotaphs stands next to the 300-year-old mango trees of the royal garden. An old dam and plush foliage provide for a popular picnic spot and sunset watch. Another well-known picnic spot is **Amar Sagar,** 5km northwest of Jaisalmer. A beautifully carved Jain temple, similar to, although not as elaborate as, the ones in the fort, guards an often-dried lake and fertile gardens. The temple has been under renovations for the last 25 years.

Once the capital of the region, **Lodurva** now lies in ruins 15km north of Jaisalmer. Rebuilt Jain temples are the only remnant of the town's former splendor. As in Jaisalmer, the temple carvings are exquisite. A 1000-year old archway from the original temple still stands in the courtyard of the new one. A cobra occasionally emerges from a small side-hole in the temple, and those who catch a glimpse of it are deemed lucky. (Open daily 6am-8pm; free, camera fee Rs.25, video fee Rs.50.)

One way or another, all the camel safaris end up in **Sam,** an expanse of rippling, hot, soft desert 42km west of Jaisalmer. The dunes are beautiful at any time, but especially at sunrise and sunset. Most safaris spend the night on the dunes, sleeping under the stars or in a tent. The RTDC-run Hotel Sam Dhani is also available, as is the 2m-square Hotel-Al-Fathe. Camel rides are available here for Rs.30-50 per half hour. A daily bus comes to Sam from Jaisalmer.

■ Bikaner

The fourth largest city of Rajasthan, Bikaner has been trying to pull in tourists, but remotely located, and with more spectacular neighbors—Jaisalmer to the west and Jodhpur to the south—this desert city has had a tough going. Yet, for those who take the time to trek out here, Bikaner rewards with Jain temples with painted interiors, an enchanting fort, and all things camel. Moreover, for those tired of the tourist infestation in the rest of the state, Bikaner offers an untouristed (but still very commercial) feel.

Bikaner was founded in 1488 by Rao Bika, one of the sons of the founder of Jodhpur, and originally served as an important trade center and camel breeding grounds. During the present century, the city has been almost exclusively concerned with its own economic advancement, and as such has become increasingly industrialized, commercialized, and well-connected to the rest of India. Only recently has Bikaner looked to tourism as another possibility for expansion and economic development. The best time to come to Bikaner is during the annual Camel Festival, a celebration of food, music, and all things camel—races, contests, parades, trading, and more. Safaris are common at this time. Expect prices of everything to double (at least). For 1997 the Camel Festival is Jan. 22-23.

ORIENTATION

Bikaner lies in the center of the hot Thar Desert, 240km northeast of Jodhpur. The layout is pretty straightforward outside the old city. Noisy **Station Road** is the hotel strip and runs parallel to the tracks in front of the **railway station.** From the station, you can head right or left on Station Rd., or straight ahead towards Deshnok. Heading right intersects the main commercial throughway, **KEM Road,** and then continues to behind the **Junagarh Fort** and the **GPO.** Left on KEM Rd. leads to **Kote Gate,** the main entrance to the walled old city; right on KEM Rd. leads to the front side of the Fort, where you'll find the **State Bank of Bikaner & Jaipur** and the **Central Tele-**

graph Office. Back at the Railway station, a left on Station Rd. leads past the **Clock Tower** through two intersections. Left at the second leads to a big circle. From the circle, the right road is the **PBM Road,** on which **PBM Hospital** is situated, and which ends in **Major Pooran Singh Circle,** very near **Dhola Maru Tourist Bungalow** and the **Golden Jubilee Museum.** Left at the circle eventually takes you back to KEM Rd.

PRACTICAL INFORMATION

Tourist Office: Tourist Reception Centre, Hotel Dhola Maru Complex (tel. 27445). From the railway station, head down the left road parallel to the tracks, and turn left at the second intersection, towards the hospital. Pass a circle and bear right, past PBM Hospital, then turn right at Major Puran Singh Circle. Dhola Maru is on your left. Helpful English-speaking staff provides maps, transportation schedules, and food and accommodations information. Open daily 10am-5pm.

Budget Travel: Desert Tours, behind GPO (tel. 521967) provides a wealth of useful current tourist information. Organizes tours of the city and surrounding areas: Rs.55 per half day, Rs.75 per full day, Rs.150 per camel tour. Open daily 8am-9pm.

Tours: For more information, see **Entertainment,** p. 322.

Currency Exchange: State Bank of Bikaner and Jaipur, opposite fort entrance (tel. 27368). Currency exchange, traveler's checks. Open Mon.-Sat. 10am-2pm, Sun. 10am-noon. **Hotel Joshi,** on Station Rd. (tel. 26162) and **Hotel Lalgarth Palace** (tel. 61963), also have currency exchange centers.

Telephones: Private STD/ISD booths are everywhere. No 24hr. booths exist, except in a few hotels (Hotel Joshi is one). The **Central Telegraph Office,** near State Bank of Bikaner and Jaipur, is open 24hr.

Airport: 15km away and not operational.

Trains: Bikaner Railway Station, (tel. 2333). A Rs.15 auto-rickshaw ride from anywhere in the city. To: Jodhpur (393, 4am, 6½hr., Rs.35/264); Jaipur (391, 2:40pm, 10½hr., Rs.42; *Bikaner Exp.* 4738, 8:25pm, 10½hr., Rs.83/344/477; *Intercity Exp.* 2467, 5am, 6hr., Rs.104/208/498); Delhi (*Bikaner Exp.* 4790, 8:35am, 10½hr., Rs.99/404/542; *Bikaner-Delhi Link Exp.* 4710, 5:50pm, 11½hr., Rs.99/404). **Advance Reservation Office,** next to the railway station. Open Mon.-Sat. 8am-8pm, Sun. 8am-2pm.

Buses: Main Bus Stand, 3km north of the city across from Lalgarh Palace (tel. 26688). To: Delhi (express, 5:30, 7:30am, 7:30, and 9pm, 11hr., Rs.115); Jaipur (deluxe, 4:30 and 7:45am, 7hr., Rs.106; express, 9 per day, 5am-10:30pm, 7hr., Rs.90); Jaisalmer (express, 6 per day, 5am-10:30pm, 7½hr., Rs.88). Private buses can be arranged through hotels, excursion agents, and the bus agencies which congregate around Goga Gate, south of Kote Gate, and behind the Fort. Private buses leave frequently to all major cities from the Main Bus Stand and from smaller, more conveniently located stands near Goga Gate and behind the Fort.

Local Transportation: Auto-rickshaws are unmetered and will take you anywhere around the city for Rs.15-20. **Bicycles** can be rented from 2 stores on Station Rd. and are convenient for exploring the city (Rs.2 per hr. or Rs.15 per day). **Jeeps** serving as taxis can be found near the railway station and can be rented for Rs.3-5 per km. They are unable to traverse the streets of the old city. There are no **local buses** in Bikaner.

Luggage storage: Rs.6 per day at the railway station.

English Bookstore: Narayug Giranth Kuteer (tel. 520836) and **Goyal and Co.** (tel. 26113), both inside Kote Gate, have small collections of English books. English magazines and newspapers are not available. Both open daily 9am-9pm.

Market: Fresh fruit and vegetable stalls, found everywhere, are in especially high concentrations along KEM Rd. and in the old city, to the left of Kote Gate and straight ahead near the Jain Temples. A meat market is located to the right of Kote Gate outside the walls. Most stores and bazaars open daily 8am-9pm.

Pharmacy: Located throughout the city, especially around PBM Hospital and around Kote Gate. None are open 24hr.

Hospital: PBM Hospital, PBM Rd., near the tourist bungalow (tel. 61931). Government-run, English-speaking, efficient, and considered the best in town. Open 24hr.

Police: Main office next to railway station (tel. 61840). English speaking. Open 24hr.
Post Office: GPO, behind Junagarh Fort (tel. 524985). No *Poste Restante.* Open
Mon.-Sat. 10am-5:30pm, Sun. 10am-3pm. **Branches** located near PBM Hospital,
inside Kote Gate, and near State Bank of Bikaner and Jaipur. **Postal Code:** 334001.
Telephone Code: 0151.

ACCOMMODATIONS

There are a fair number of budget accommodations in Bikaner—unfortunately, most
are clustered on the extremely noisy Station Rd., and all are pretty much the same.
Other options are some distance away. Home-stays with local families can be
arranged through the tourist office (Rs.100-350 per night). Due to daily extended
power outages in Bikaner, a flashlight and/or candles are highly recommended.

Thar Hotel, PBM Hospital Rd. (tel. 27180). Facing PBM Hospital, a 2-min. walk to
the right, located in the circle. Good-size quiet rooms in a reasonable location.
Amenities include laundry service, travel counter, folk music, TVs and intercoms,
and an excellent restaurant. Camel safaris Rs.300 per day. Singles with air-cooling
and bath Rs.475. Doubles Rs.600.

Hotel Joshi, Station Rd. (tel. 527700; fax 521213). Located across from the police
station. Modern, centrally located, with business-like staff. Check-out 24hr. Comfortable air-conditioned lobby, good veg. restaurant, STD/ISD phone, currency
exchange, laundry services. Singles with bath Rs.255, with A/C Rs.425. Doubles
Rs.290, with A/C Rs.525. Bigger doubles Rs.675. Reservations recommended in
season.

Green Hotel, Station Rd. (tel. 23396). Near the railway station. Big green building
with green decor. Travel desk, laundry service, 24-hr. room service. 24-hr. check-
out. Singles Rs.60, with bath, air-cooling, and TV Rs.90 (great value!). Doubles
Rs.90, with bath, air-cooling, and TV Rs.125. Triples Rs.150.

Dhola Maru Tourist Bungalow, near Major Pooran Singh Circle (tel. 28621). Distant from city center, but quiet. Offers a full range of tourist services, plus laundry
services, room service, and a decent restaurant. Simple, rather threadbare, cheaply
carpeted balconied rooms, all with attached baths. Four day max. stay. Check-out
noon. Dorm beds Rs.50. Singles Rs.125, with air-cooling Rs.225, with A/C Rs.400.
Doubles Rs.175, with air-cooling Rs.275, with A/C Rs.450. Extra bed Rs.75, with
air-cooling Rs.100, with A/C Rs.125.

Hotel Amit, Station Rd. (tel. 28064). Near the railway station, behind Green Hotel.
Basic but clean slightly-larger-than-bed-sized rooms. Hot water buckets Rs.4 each.
Check-out 24hr. Singles Rs.75, with bath Rs.100. Doubles Rs.100, with bath
Rs.125.

Hotel Deluxe, Station Rd. (tel.23292). Small no-frills rooms. Some have balconies,
with less than spectacular views. Decent restaurant below (where the staff will
pressure you to eat). Singles Rs.90. Doubles Rs.125, with bath.

Hotel Heritage Bhairon Vilas, behind fort (tel. 28051; fax 523642). A beautiful
heritage hotel away from the noise and conveniently near the bus stand, old city,
fort, and GPO. Fanciful animal skins, old paintings, and weapons for decoration.
The owner is head of Desert Tours, so tourist information is readily available.
Check-out noon. Excellent restaurant, travel desk, 24-hr. room service, library, and
local music shows. Camel safaris Rs.500-1000 per day. Large singles with air-cooling Rs.1000. Doubles Rs.1200.

FOOD

Bikaner features a decent range of fast-food and snack restaurants. A number of small
joints along Station Rd. serve up tasty local specialties (excellent *rasgullas,* and "take-
with-1-liter-of-Bisleri" spicy *namkins).* Most restaurants in Bikaner are strictly vegetarian.

Moomal Restaurant, near Dhola Maru Tourist Bungalow. A quiet, unimaginatively
decorated veg. restaurant presenting standard Chinese, Continental, and Indian

cuisine. Fast service. Expect to pay Rs.70-100 for a hearty dinner. Open daily 8am-10:30pm.

Chhotu Motu Joshi Restaruant, Station Rd. (tel.527700). In Hotel Joshi. Very popular among locals of all ages, and bound to be packed solid. Pretty good veg. food, lots of snacks, *lassis,* sweets, and of course, hot spicy *namkin.* Most food less than Rs.20. Open daily 8am-11pm.

Kesariya Restaurant, Sagar Rd. About 5km down Sagar Rd. (towards Jaipur), across from the State Bank of Bikaner and Jaipur Training Centre. Softly lit, open-air, veg., resort-style restaurant. Prices a bit high—expect to pay Rs.150-200 for a meal. Open daily 11:30am-11pm; only for dinner off-season.

Amber Restaurant, Station Rd. All veg. with a definite Punjabi bent. Quite crowded in the evenings—a favorite among adult locals. Prices are moderate: Rs.30 for most entrees. Open daily 6am-10pm.

Annapurna Cafe, KEM Rd. (tel. 27674). On KEM Rd. near the back of the Fort. Good-value place with a mellow attitude featuring Continental, Chinese, and Indian cuisines. Soups are the specialty. No smoking. For any meat variation, call in advance. Entrees around Rs.25. Open loosely Mon.-Fri. 8am-10:30pm.

Delux, Station Rd. (tel. 23292). Beneath the hotel of the same name. Cheap snack-food type quickies for Rs.15. *Namkin, rasgullas,* and similar fare. Popular local hang-out. Open daily 6am-10pm.

SIGHTS

Bikaner's most prominent and famous attraction is the **Junagarh Fort.** Constructed in 1589 by Rai Singh, the fort is distinguished as one of the few in the country that has never been conquered. It stands as a solid, densely packed, ground-level structure with a 986-m-long wall capped with 37 bastions, surrounded by a 9-m-wide moat. It looks pretty damn impregnable. The fort can be entered from the east side through a succession of gates. Near the second gate, Daulat Pol, are 24 dramatic handmarks of women who performed a *sati* self-sacrifice after their husbands had perished in a successful attempt to prevent a siege. The fort's main entrance is the **Suraj Pol** (Sun Gate), a large iron-spiked door flanked by two rather badly painted stone elephants.

The fort is an intricate complex of palaces, courtyards, pavilions, and temples—37 in all—each added to the original structure by successive rulers. The complexes were built to harmoniously connect to the previous structures, so there appears to be one elaborate but continuous palace. The **Karan Mahal,** built after an important victory over the Mughal army of Emperor Aurangzeb, features fancy gold-leaf paintings and the regal silver throne of Lord Karen Singh. It served as a court for meetings with the most distinguished knights. The **Chandra Mahal** (Moon Palace), is a beautifully painted *puja* (prayer) room adorned with Hindu gods and goddesses. To the side is the **Sheesh Mahal** (Mirror Palace), a room studded with mirrors that provide a magnificent glitter. (Light a match or shine a flashlight and enjoy the dazzle.) The **Phool Mahal** (Flower Palace), features glamorous floral mirrorwork and masterpiece Muslim paintings known as *ustas.* The **Anup Mahal** is an elegant and richly decorated hall that served as a reception room for VIPs. Ornately sculpted lattices and precision mirror-work accompany mosaic ceiling tiles and an extravagantly large carpet made by inmates at the Bikaner Jail. Coronation ceremonies often took place in this palace. The **Rang Mahal** and **Bijai Mahal** also have noteworthy tilework and paintings. The fort's courtyards are impressive too. The **Durga Niwas** is adorned with fine paintwork and tiling, while the **Ganga Niwas'** latticework along its edges is spectacular. The fort temple is the **Har Mandir,** dedicated to Lord Shiva and beautifully designed. The **Ganga Singh Hall,** the last portion of the fort, houses the **museum,** with a weapons collection coming soon, assorted miscellaneous relics belonging to past rulers, and some random World War II aircraft parts. The fort is open Mon.-Thurs., and Sat.-Sun. 10am-4:30pm. Admission Rs.50; camera fee Rs.25, video fee Rs.100. Government authorized guides Rs.100.

Three kilometers north of the city, across from the Main Bus Stand, is **Lalgarh Palace,** a large multi-tiered red sandstone palace. It was designed for Maharaja Ganga Singh in 1902 as a combination of European opulence, Oriental majesty, and Rajasthani tradition, but lacks in each, and isn't as spectacular as other Rajasthani Palaces (despite some amazing exterior sculpture). The royal family of Bikaner lives in part of it, a luxury hotel takes up some more, while the **Sri Sadul Museum** occupies the entire ground floor. The museum has an especially interesting collection of miniature sandalwood items in nutshells, a huge collection of rather uninteresting photographs, coins, statues, personal items of the maharaja, and stuffed animals. Also in the palace is the **Anup Sanskrit Library,** a collection of original manuscripts and engravings. The palace and library are open daily 10am-5pm. Admission Rs.25; camera fee Rs.25, video fee Rs.50.

Following the main road through Kote Gate will eventually lead you to the base of the old city, where two extraordinary **Jain temples,** built by merchant brothers in the 16th century, can be found. The **Bhandeshwar Temple** is adorned with gilded leaf and floral motifs and artfully sculpted pillars. A marble stature of Lord Sumatinath graces the second floor. The **Sandeshwar Temple** also features intricate gold-leaf painting, and is decorated with sculpted marble rows of popular saints. **Laxminath Temple,** next door, is a masterfully carved stone temple with superb views of the desert and city.

The **Ganga Golden Jubilee Museum** contains a curious collection of artwork, glass and wooden relics, carpets made by prisoners in Bikaner Jail, weapons, instruments, costumes, and fascinating terra-cotta wares. It is located on National Highway 8, about 5 minutes from the Tourist Bungalow. It's worth stopping by if you're in the vicinity. (Open Mon.-Thurs., and Sat.-Sun. 10am-4:30pm; admission Rs.2; photography not permitted.)

ENTERTAINMENT

Although nowhere near Jaisalmeri proportions, **camel safaris** have recently become quite popular in Bikaner. Most camel safaris begin with a tour of the city and nearby sights, followed by a trek through the desert, with frequent stops at rarely touristed traditional villages, where you can witness local handicrafts and desert lifestyles. Also common are **intercity safaris** to Jaisalmer and Jodhpur. As in Jaisalmer, the safaris can be hybrid jeep/camel, horse/camel, jeep/horse, or just jeep, or just horse. Few hotels offer safaris, and the ones that do operate exclusively through independent agencies. **Desert Tours,** located behind the fort near the GPO (tel. 521967), offers a wide range of assorted safaris for Rs.300-500 per day. **Rajasthani Safaris & Treks** (tel. 28557), and **Victor Travels,** near the railway station, are other good agencies.

Nightlife in Bikaner is practically nonexistent. **Bars** are only found in top hotels and are only frequented by tourists. Two **movie theatres** showing Hindi films can be found in Kote Gate down the main road—Prakesh Chita Cinema and Vishra Jupti Cinema.

SHOPPING

Bikaner is a haven for desert **handicrafts.** The government-approved internationally funded shop, **Abhivyakti,** located just inside the fort, sells high-quality wares from 70 villages around the city. Shop hassle-free and rest assured that proceeds go directly to the local village artisans. The primary commercial areas are **KEM Road** and essentially all of the **old city.** KEM Rd. is a typical potpourri bazaar. The city is one huge melange of stores—walk around for just a while and you'll find anything you need—though several industries do tend to form clusters. Just inside Kote Gate on the left are cloth and textile stores, and a fruit market. Near the Jain temples, leather, and other craft stores congregate. Of course, bargain hard and shop around both in and out of the old city.

■ Near Bikaner

Devi Kund Sagar, 8km west of Bikaner, contains the marble and red sandstone royal *chhattris,* or **cenotaphs,** of Bikaner rulers. The marble cenotaph of Maharaja Surat

Singh is especially majestic. Buses to Deri Kund Sagar depart from Bikaner's main bus stand (every hr., Rs.5). City tours also usually visit.

The **Camel Breeding Farm,** located 10km south of the city is the biggest in Asia, breeding 50% of India's bred camels. In the early evening hundreds of camels of all ages return here from the desert—an overwhelming sight. During World War II, the British Imperial Army's Camel Corps was pulled from this farm. Of course, during the Camel Festival, this place goes ballistic. A stopping point on city tours, the farm can also be reached by auto-rickshaw (roundtrip Rs.55-60). Open daily 3-5pm. Photography permitted outside only.

At the **Karni Mata Temple** in Deshnok, thousands of holy rats, called *kabas,* run rampant at the feet of thronging admirers. Worshipers here consider it auspicious to have rats run over their feet. Those lucky enough to see a white rat can consider themselves blessed. Although entering the temple is not recommended for the faint of heart, it is worth visiting the temple for the magnificent solid silver gate donated by Maharaja Ganga Singh, and for its ornate stone carvings. According to regional legend, the Bikaner patron deity, Karni Mata, was once asked to resurrect her drowned beloved nephew. She called up the god of death, Yama, who told her the boy had already been reborn as a rat. After some heated discussion, he promised her that all her male descendents would first be born as rats in her temple at Deshnok, and then as humans in her Depavat family after the end of their rat lives. The best time to visit is during the Navratri festival in March, when the temple is swarmed with devotees. The *kabas* are fed *prasad* every morning—what's left is given to worshipers, who eat it without compunction, as the rat-saliva-covered *prasad* is also considered auspicious. The temple is accessible by taxi (expect to pay Rs.200 roundtrip), by hourly buses from Bikaner (Rs.15), and is a stop on the city tours. Camera fee Rs.10.

Gajner Wildlife Sanctuary, 32km west of Bikaner, was once the location of the royal hunting grounds. It then became a resort for important visiting dignitaries and now stands as sanctuary for antelopes, black bucks, gazelles, and assorted birds. Famous Siberian imperial sand grouse migrate here every winter. The elegant palace on the lake has been converted into the high-end Gajner Palace Hotel. Accessible from Bikaner by buses departing the main bus stand, from behind the Fort (every 30min., Rs.8 one way).

Punjab and Haryana

The name "Punjab," as it refers to the state in northwest India, is a misnomer; following the 1947 Partition only two of the five rivers to which the Sanskrit word "Punjab" refers still lay within India's borders. A similar identity crisis ensued 19 years later when what was left of the Indian Punjab was again divided, this time along primarily linguistic lines (between Punjabi and Hindi), forming the state of Haryana. These two states have in many respects gone their separate ways. For example, while Punjab boasts the largest per capital alcohol consumption in India, Haryana reimplemented prohibition in 1996. But although one state is "dry" and the other notoriously "wet," Haryana and Punjab share a fertile geography, a capital (the city of Chandigarh serves as the governmental center of both states), and the pride of overcoming a long and turbulent history to become one of India's most prosperous regions.

Punjab has long been a corridor through which foreign invaders have entered India. The Vedic texts and the *Mahabharata* were born in this area after the Aryans arrived here about 1500 BC. The Battle of Panipat in 1526 asserted Mughal rule in India; later battles in 1739 and 1761 set the course for British rule and Mughal decline. Despite the late 18th-century rise of Sikh power in Punjab, British rule dominated until the 1947 Partition rent the state asunder.

Despite the division of Haryana and Punjab in 1966 (following decades of demands for Haryana's separation by Lala Lajpat Rai and other non-Sikh leaders), both states

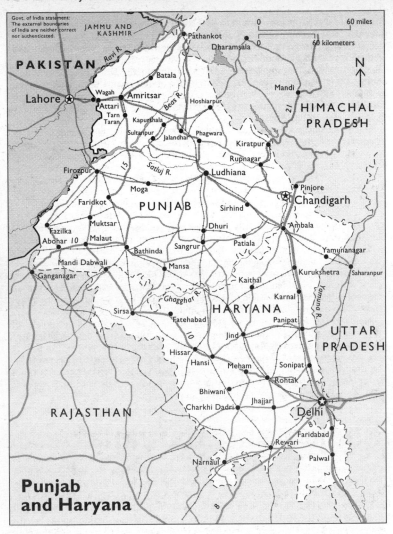

Govt. of India statement:
The external boundaries
of India are neither correct
nor authenticated.

**Punjab
and Haryana**

reap the rewards of the 1960s "Green Revolution" in agricultural technology. The two states account for a sizeable chunk of India's wheat and dairy supply. Meanwhile, industrial centers such as Jalandhar and Ludhiana are successful in their own right—for example, the area produces more bicycles than any other state.

But prosperity and peace have not gone hand in hand, and there has long been tension in Punjab between moderates and Sikh militants who would like to form an independent Sikh state, "Khalistan." Tensions escalated in 1983, when the Sikh militant leader Sant Bhindranwale, sequestered in Amritsar's Golden Temple, Sikhism's most sacred *gurudwara,* incited acts of violence against Hindus. Murder begat murder, the Punjab was convulsed with violence, and Indira Gandhi's government dismissed the state government and began to rule the Punjab directly. By the summer of 1984 over 350 people had been killed and the government decided that something had to be done. In June, the army stormed the Golden Temple, acting on a plan called "Operation Bluestar." What was supposed to have been a commando raid became a bloody three-day siege. More than 750 people were killed, including Bhindranwale and 83 soldiers. The attack on the Golden Temple was viewed by many Sikhs as disgraceful sacrilege, even though four of the six generals who had planned Bluestar were Sikhs. Thousands of Sikhs deserted the army in disgust, and hundreds of young Sikh soldiers mutinied, but by autumn things seemed to have quieted down. The calm was broken on the last day of October, when Indira Gandhi was murdered by two of her Sikh bodyguards. Hindus repaid the assassination with massive riots in Delhi, killing thousands of Sikhs. While Sikh resentment against the military occupation of Punjab mounted, the Khalistan movement gained adherents. In 1985, Rajiv Gandhi came to an agreement with the regionalist Akali Dal party, who won a majority in the subsequent parliamentary elections. But the party then split with the extremists, who made Khalistan their goal. Violence again escalated after 1988 with the reoccupation of the Golden Temple, and Sikhs boycotted elections in 1992. Since that time, however, the Punjab has cooled markedly. Although militant groups continue to demand independence, they lack popular support and do not pose a threat to travelers.

Many travelers merely pass through without stopping while heading from Delhi to Himachal Pradesh or Pakistan. Still, while the states pack little punch for visitors, the Sikh culture is extraordinarily welcoming, and the Golden Temple in Amritsar and the Rock Garden in Chandigarh are first-rate attractions.

■ Chandigarh

Although much of India manages to evoke in visitors a feeling of temporal and spatial displacement, the city of Chandigarh, capital of Punjab and Haryana, summons travelers to a very distinct period of western European history. A planned city, Chandigarh emerged from the 1960s craze of creating huge, geometrically quirky human environments considered symbolic of the future "order" of humanity. A European architect, Le Corbusier, was called in to design the city as a symbol of India's advancement towards a more democratic, modern, and in many respects "Westernized" future. Chandigarh's extravagantly wide roads, lined with gardens, were meant to be progressive and futuristic. But like everything Western and "modern" that finds its way to India, the Le Corbusian "ideal city of man" seems anomalously contrived. What "modern" means in Chandigarh, probably the cleanest city in India, is alarmingly clear: the casement of a place meant to be futuristic, but still waiting for the future to arrive. Chandigarh's inhabitants nicknamed their city "Sun, space, and silence." Government officials took it as a compliment, but "sun and space" were probably coined by the rickshaw-*wallahs* dripping with sweat after pedaling city block after city block in the scorching heat, and "silence" more likely refers to Chandigarh's uncanny un-Indianness—no horns blare at 5am, no generators roar at noon. It's easy to see why some feel uneasy in this dreamland, and it's not surprising that an inordinate number of film and videotape businesses have located here.

Chandigarh was born out of India's Independence. The Punjab had been split, and its capital, Lahore, was now in Pakistan. A new center of government was needed for the state of Punjab, which then included Punjab, Haryana, and parts of Himachal Pradesh. Ironically, Punjab was divided again in 1966, eliminating the need for a bright new capital city. Chandigarh is now a union territory, functioning simultaneously as a capital for both Punjab and Haryana. Chandigarh is without many of India's usual tourist excitements, but its museums, lake, and gardens are pleasant, and a stay in Chandigarh can actually feel like a vacation from average Indian cities.

ORIENTATION

No one can say that Chandigarh is confusing. The whole city is a massive grid, making disorientation impossible. Each block is a "sector," with **Sector I** to the north, where the main government buildings are situated. The rest are numbered in boustrophedonic order (from west to east, then east to west) in rows proceeding to the south.

Buses stop at the south end of **Sector 17,** where most services are located. Sector 17 is the primary "downtown" zone. **Sector 22,** immediately south, comes in a close second with its many hotels and restaurants.

PRACTICAL INFORMATION

Tourist Office: CITCO (tel. 704614), the Chandigarh Industrial and Tourism Development Corp., has an office upstairs in the bus stand, offering a confusing guide map, a 1993 brochure about the city, and reference material on other parts of India. Open Mon.-Fri. 9am-1pm and 1:30-5pm, Sat. 9am-1pm. The **Punjab Goverment Tourist Information Centre** is also in the bus stand (open Mon.-Fri. 9am-1:30pm and 2-5pm); the **U.P., Haryana,** and **Himachal Pradesh** offices are across the way in Sector 22.

Budget Travel: Aroma Tours and Travel (tel. 708686, 700045) in the Hotel Aroma Complex, Sector 22. Books flights to Kulu and Delhi. Open daily 8am-9pm. There are international flight agents at the north end of Sector 17.

Immigration Office: Foreigners Registration Office (tel. 44064, 44074, ext. 382), in SSP, Police Headquarters, across from the southwest corner of Sector 9 (northeast of the museum). Foreigners can register for long-term stays here. This office also infrequently extends visas. Open Mon.-Fri. 10am-noon and 3-4pm.

Currency Exchange: Many banks are clustered in Bank Square, the central and northern parts of Sector 17. **State Bank of India** (tel. 708359), with scary, pendulous fans, changes AmEx and Thomas Cook traveler's checks and major currencies. Open Mon.-Fri. 10am-2pm, Sat. 10am-noon. **Tradewings Ltd.,** 1068 Sector 22 (tel. 709666), across from the bus stand, also changes traveler's checks, and stays open longer. Open Mon.-Sat. 9:30am-6pm.

Telephones: Many of the STD/ISD booths in Sector 22 also offer fax services. Other ISD/STD booths are in Sector 17, and everywhere else in the city.

Airport: Chandigarh's airport is about 11km out of town, a Rs.50-100 auto-rickshaw ride. Indian Airlines (tel. 704539) accepts credit cards to book flights. To: Kulu (1 per day, 30min., US$44), and Delhi (1 per day, 40min., US$47). There is one weekly flight to Leh (Tues., US$45), but book far in advance.

Trains: Chandigarh's **railway station** is an annoying 8km to the southeast of town. Local buses #37 and #85 connect the railway station with bus stand (30min., Rs.4). On the 2nd floor of the bus stand there's a **Railway Reservation Office** (tel. 702260), open Mon.-Sat. 8am-1:45pm and 2:15-8pm, Sun. 8am-2pm. The *Shatabdi Express* (and several others) run to Delhi (*Shatabdi Exp.,* 6:50am and 12:40pm, 3hr., Rs.270 A/C chair only; ordinary: 5:30pm, 1am, 5-6hr., Rs.72/181 for 2nd class/A/C chair); Shimla (5:30, 7, 11:40am, 4-6hr., Rs.97 for A/C chair); and Jammu (10:15pm, 12hr., Rs.137). Amritsar and Rishikesh can be reached by catching a train first from Chandigarh to Ambala (several daily, 1hr., Rs.42).

Buses: Chandigarh's **Inter-State Bus Terminal** is better than most; timetables are laid out clearly in English, and it's central to the city, on the south side of Sector 17, across from the hotels in Sector 22. Buses depart for Delhi (every 20min., supposedly 24hr. service, 5½hr., Rs.69); Jaipur (3:45am, 12hr., Rs.137); Amritsar (every 30min., 4:15am-11pm, 5hr., Rs.62); Shimla (every 15min., 4am-11pm, 4½hr., Rs.49/59/250 for day/night/deluxe); Manali (several, 5:45-2:30am, 11-12hr., Rs.130/152 for day/night); Dehra Dun (5 daily, 4:30am-9pm, 6hr., Rs.66); Rishikesh (9pm, 8hr., Rs.85); Jammu (10:30pm, 11hr., Rs.120); Dharamsala (11:40am, 6:30, 7, and 8:30pm; deluxe at 11pm, 8hr., Rs.102). The bus to Jalandhar (every 20min., 4hr., Rs.41) goes most of the way to Amritsar.

Local Transportation: Chandigarh is so spread out that walking is rarely an option. Cycle-rickshaw-*wallahs* break a sweat after a block or two. Blue **auto-rickshaws** may charge Rs.10-20 for a 2-sector trip. Starting from the local bus stand (west of the interstate bus terminal), buses go to the **Rock Garden** (Sector 8, Bus #13, 30min., Rs.4), **railway station** (Buses #37 or #85, 30min., Rs.4), and the **airport** (Buses #7, #7a, #79, #26).

Luggage Storage: The cloak room at the bus terminal charges for locked luggage—Rs.2 per item per day for the first 2 days, Rs.3 per day for up to 3 months thereafter.

Library: Central State Library, Sector 17, has good selections of old and new books and periodicals. Rs.100 refundable deposit, Rs.10 temporary membership. Open Mon.-Sat. 11am-6pm. Closed the last Sat. of every month.

English Bookstore: There are plenty of these in affluent Chandigarh. **Capital Book Depot,** SCO 3, Sector 17E, has as good a selection of travelers' reads as anyone. Open daily 10am-1:30pm and 3:30-8pm. **Asia Book House,** farther south in Sector 17, has more trashy magazines and paperbacks among its offerings. Open Mon.-Sat. 10:30am-2:30pm and 4-8pm.

Pharmacy: Chemists abound around the medical center in Sector 17. In Sector 22, in the row across from the buses, are several later-night pharmacies, such as **Anil and Co.,** Bayshop #42 (tel. 706282). Open daily 8am-10:30pm.

Hospital/Medical Services: Chandigarh Medical and Research Centre or **CMC,** Sector 17 (tel. 703152, 702543). Provides a number of superb specialists and general physicians, and the atmosphere is not too hectic. Dr. Khurana is amicable and speaks English well. Open 24hr.

Emergency: tel. 100.

Post Office: GPO, at the northwest corner of Sector 17, has *Poste Restante* and EMS **speed post** services. Open Mon.-Fri. 9am-4pm, night post office until 7pm. There are also express couriers in Sector 17. **Postal Code:** 160000 (put sector number at end; 160001, 160017, etc.).

Telephone Code: 0172.

ACCOMMODATIONS

Chandigarh's hotel owners assume that because their city is affluent, the city's guests must be, too. As a result, there is nary a room for under Rs.100. In cases of total desperation, there are **retiring rooms** at the railway station, and one at the bus stand. Otherwise, merely step across the street and over the fence from the bus stand to get to Sector 22 and hotels galore.

Jullundur Hotel, Sector 22 (tel. 706777, 701121). Opposite the Interstate Bus Terminal, next to Sunbeam. The best bet for close-to-the-middle, spare-your-wallet rooms, ranging from air-cooled, attached-bath singles to doubles with TV. Courteous staff, early morning newspaper delivery. Singles Rs.180. Doubles (fancy-schmancy) Rs.275.

Hotel Divyadeep, Sector 22 (tel. 705191). On the northeast side of Sector 22, adjacent to Bhol Restaurant. Immaculate, spacious, old-style, wood-panelled rooms with seat toilets. Surprisingly classy for the price, though it ain't the Ritz. Singles Rs.140, with A/C Rs.250. Doubles Rs.170, with A/C Rs.300.

City Motel, Sector 22 (tel. 708992), on the street just behind Jullundur and Sunbeam Hotels. Tight little place, but some rooms (a few with attached baths) have tie-dyed sheets and plush red sofas. Purely unintentional funkiness. TV in every room. Singles Rs.150. Doubles Rs.200-400.

Peeush Motel, Bungalow #1233, Sector 22 (tel. 701090). Farther to the west on the same row of bungalows behind the strip on Sector 22. Peeush yourself through these doors for not-so-peeosh rooms, though many have A/C, TV, and attached bath where you can take a peeiss. Not as good a deal as City, but close. Singles Rs.150, with A/C Rs.400.

Chandigarh Yatri Niwas, Sector 24 (tel. 545904). Just across from Sector 15. Outside the heart of the hubbub, but an excellent, peaceful retreat for a few relaxing days. Double beds are huge, the toilets are big, stone, and have seats, and the whole place has a comfortingly airy, natural feel. Rasoi Restaurant attached. Singles Rs.200, semi-deluxe Rs.250, deluxe with A/C Rs.350.

Hotel Amar, SCO 805, Sector 22 (tel. 704638) Western end of north side of Sector 22. Similar to Jullundur in style and convenience, and not as pricey as its nearest neighbors. Singles Rs.250. Doubles Rs.300, with A/C Rs.450.

Hotel Shivalikview, Sector 17 (tel. 700001, 703521). In the southwest corner of Sector 17. If you must splurge in Chandigarh, might as well do it here, where the prices are under control. High-quality business hotel with Chandigarh quality excessive space, well-equipped rooms, and complimentary breakfast. Standard singles Rs.900. Deluxe doubles Rs.1400.

FOOD

You won't find any stomach-sticking Rs.15 *thalis* in Chandigarh, but there's no dearth of restaurants. Fast-food joints abound in Sector 17, as do classier "special night out" places, many of which have attached banquet halls. In fact, there's food wherever you go in Chandigarh—a café at the lake, a café in the Rock Garden, and a Kwality Branch out by the university (a.k.a. Ginza & Tandoor, open daily 8am-11pm). Along with Pub 22, there are several reasonably clean and cheap places along the strip across from the bus stand, including 3-Aces.

Pub 22, Sector 22 (tel. 701345). Downstairs from Nirankari Restaurant in the strip across from the bus stand. An fun place to grab a bite in an absurd cocktail context (dim blue lighting and blonde cardboard cut-out). TV, draft beer (Rs.20), and edible food (Indian dishes Rs.10-60). Open daily 8am-midnight.

Hot Millions, Sector 17. Several branches in Sector 17, including one across from the CMC. Hot Millions 2, farther southeast, has more ambience. The city is proud of this little food chain, which was started here as an ice cream joint in 1979 by Col. Anat Singh and his family. The menu lists 186 items, most of them ice cream, burgers, or similar Indian fast-food variants—and they're dying to blow away any incoming multinational chains! Filling, if not always tasty food. Jumbo Burger Rs.44, pizza Rs.30-45. Open daily noon-10:30pm.

The Eating House, Hotel Aroma Complex, Sector 22. Western dishes in wanna-be-cool place—western-style pastries (puffs, cakes, toffee) and real food to go along with wall-hung caricatures of Bruce Springsteen, Sting, various Sikhs, and Mother Teresa. Busy bunny with figs and honey Rs.20. Open 24hr.

Ghazal Restaurant and Pub, SCO 189, Sector 17-C (tel. 548473). Elegant, doorman-type place specializing in Mughlai and tandoori cuisine, at not-necessarily-ball-busting prices. Draft beer Rs.16 "regular," Rs.18 "strong." Meaty menu. *Methi* chicken with world's finest fenugreek Rs.90, mushroom *mattar* Rs.54. Open daily 11am-11pm.

Khana-e-khaas Restaurant, Sector 17 (tel. 703061). Across from the Ghazal. Similar to the Ghazal—and nearby Mehfil—but not quite as stuffy, although the waiters wear bowties. *Rogan josh* Rs.55, mutton *korma* Rs.75. Comfy, cool, relaxing booths. Open daily 10:30am-11:30pm.

Vatika/Tingo's Fast Food and Restaurant, Sector 9. Just north of Sector 17 in the strip on the south side of Sector 9. Downstairs dining area is popular at lunchtime. Filling plates of mushroom *korma* Rs.38, spring rolls Rs.32, veggie mini-meal Rs.20. Open daily 10am-11pm.

SIGHTS

All the governmental influence in Chandigarh has led to the development of an impressive number of museums, gardens, and attractions. But the one sight that will really knock your socks off stems not from the government but from the genius of a single humble man. Nek Chand's **Rock Garden,** in the north part of town in Sector 1, is not to be missed. A road construction worker by trade—now an internationally acclaimed artist, Mr. Chand started his rock garden as a hobby, but it eventually developed into an escapist fantasy world, in which a path through stone walls leads through hanging gardens, waterfalls, blobby curvaceous sculptures made from bathtub porcelain and scrapped bracelets, and through small communities of bewildering, abstract, miniature people fashioned from stone or scrap materials. It's hard to resist the urge to lose oneself forever. Highlights of the journey include the waterfall, giant rope swings, miniature kiddie-boats (Rs.10), the small hut where the garden had its humble start, and rows of anthropomorphic figurines looking as perplexed to see us as we are to see them. (Open April-Sept. daily 9am-1pm and 3-7pm, Oct.-March daily 9am-1pm and 2-6pm; admission Rs.1.) Sometimes there is a camel out front for quick rides (Rs.20, negotiable). Purchase your ticket at the tiny window at the end of the stone wall closest to the road—enter through the gate at the other end. The artist frequently stops by the garden when he's in town. To meet him, ask at the ticket window, and they'll give you a time to wait at the cafeteria until Mr. Chand is ready. The soft-spoken artist warmly receives guests inside his small hut—when asked, he confides that "the whole thing" is his favorite part.

Along with the Rock Garden, Sector 1 plays host to a few notable attractions. The **Capital Complex,** with its huge, monumental, concrete buildings, was Le Corbusier's way of staging the functions of government in symbolic and geometric relation to one another and to the rest of the city (as "head" to "body"). Visit the **High Court** and **Open Hand Monument** if you come here—they are more accessible than the **Legislative Assembly** and heavily-guarded **Secretariat.**

Also in the north is **Sukhna Lake,** a small reservoir which CITCO has neatly turned into a tourist sight with cafeteria, mini-amusement park, and paddle boats (2-seater Rs.25 per 30min., 4-seater Rs.50 per 30min.). Come at sunset, hop in one of the swan boats if possible, and float over to the mangrove alcoves across the lake.

Leisure Valley is the term Le Corbusier used for the long parkland stretching through the heart of Chandigarh. It is meant to provide "care for the body and spirit." The highlight of this park is the Dr. Zakir Hussain **Rose Garden,** supposedly the largest in Asia. There are spritzy fountains to the north, species of roses (try to visit in spring when they are in bloom), and a giant Rose Festival usually held at the end of February. It's free, but hard to find.

▨ Amritsar

Perhaps it is because Guru Nanak, the founder of Sikhism, had traveled so widely through India and even the Middle East before his death in 1539 that the city of Amritsar, founded later in the century by subsequent Sikh gurus, is particularly hospitable to modern backpackers. Amritsar, named after the sacred tank or "pool of nectar" that formed the city's heart, is the largest city in Punjab and the focal point of Sikhism. An awe-inspiring monument to the faith, Amritsar's Golden Temple is a must-see both for Sikhs and for travelers and tourists alike.

Guru Ram Das initiated the construction of the temple in 1579, but the city did not begin to form around it until the 5th guru, Arjun, enshrined the Sikh holy book, the Granth Sahib, here. Centuries of Mughal invasions led to a continuous cycle of destruction and reconstruction of the Golden Temple, but had minimal impact on the growth of the population, which now numbers 800,000. Despite this history of warfare, Partition riots, and recent violence between the Indian government and Sikh fundamentalist groups, the city opens its arms to the visitor without the usual follow-up offer of dubious business.

ORIENTATION

Amritsar's **railroad tracks** divide the city into north and south sections. The major vehicle crossing in the very center of town is the **Bhandari Bridge,** which runs over the tracks and over a hill, and which irks cycle-rickshaws to no end. The older, more lively part of the city is through the gates to the south of the railway; several bazaars (52 markets total in Amritsar!) and the Golden Temple draw in locals and visitors alike. Northeast of the temple across the tracks is the **bus stand,** and west of that is the newer part of town, sprawling around the **railway station** to the north. Here, gardens and posher hotels spread themselves along **Mall Road** and **Lawrence Road,** the two major thoroughfares.

PRACTICAL INFORMATION

Tourist Office: Punjab Government Tourist Office (tel. 231452) is sadly out of the way, 1km east of the bus stand on Railway Rd.; ask for the youth hostel and look for the building (with a guide map plastered on its façade) set back 20m from the road. Ultra-amiable staff knows a lot about Sikh gurus and nearby towns. The office has only a feeble city map, but is otherwise well-stocked. Open Mon.-Sat. 9am-5pm. **Information Centre** at Golden Temple.

Currency Exchange: Most major banks have branches in both the north and south parts of the city. **Bank of Punjab** (tel. 554895) has a branch at the Golden Temple's north side. Open Mon.-Fri. 10am-5pm, Sat. 10am-2pm. **R.K. Traders,** base of Mehra Hotel, right across from the railway station (tel. 212701). They legally change traveler's checks after hours. The railway area also has several offices that change Pakistani currency. Money changing office is next to the **State Bank of India,** nearer to the Golden Temple.

Telephones: STD/ISD booths near Golden Temple, railway station, and one block east of Tourists' Guest House. The phone office at the GPO charges official (i.e. not boosted) rates.

Airport: Raja Sanhsi Airport, 12km northwest of town, has a small tourist office and other basic services. Flights go only to Delhi (Mon.-Tues., Thurs., and Sat., 55min., US$69) and Srinagar (Mon., 50min., US$60). Book from the travel agent in Mohan International Hotel, or from Indian Airlines in the Ritz Hotel on Mall Rd. (tel. 226606). Open daily 8am-7pm.

Trains: The **computer reservation** complex is on the back side of the railway station; walk over the platforms on the bridge (enquiry: tel. 62811, 62812, 62813). Open Mon.-Sat. 8am-1:30pm and 2-8pm, Sun. 8am-1:45pm. To: Delhi (*Shatabdi Exp.*, 5:10am, Rs.123-160); Bombay (*Frontier Mail,* 36hr., Rs.317); Haridwar (9pm, 12hr., Rs.73); Lahore (Mon. and Thurs., 9:30am, 3hr.); and Chandigarh (2hr.). Trains leave for other destinations, including Bhopal, Agra, Patna, and Lucknow.

Buses: Enquiry office (tel. 51734). To: Delhi (several daily, 5:40am-6:50pm, 10hr., Rs.121); Chandigarh (several daily, 4:40am-8:30pm, 5hr., Rs.62; 5:20am luxury bus Rs.124); Dharmasala (noon, 7hr., Rs.64; frequent connections from Pathankot (4hr.); Manali (3pm, 14hr., Rs.170); Shimla (5:50, 7:20am, 10hr., Rs.115); Kulu (2:30pm, 12hr., Rs.145); Rishikesh (7:45am, 11hr., Rs.123); Dehra Dun (7am; 10hr., Rs.119); and the Pakistan border at Wagah (several daily, 7:10am-6pm, 1hr., Rs.9).

Local Transportation: Bicycle rental available at a couple of the bike shops across the street north of the bus stand. **Sigma Cycles,** for example, charges Rs.15 per day, with a hefty Rs.1000 deposit. Open Mon.-Sat. 9am-8pm. **Rickshaws** of all shapes and sizes populate Amritsar. Cycle-rickshaws from the railway area go to the bus stand (Rs.5-10) and to Golden Temple (Rs.10-15), but can be frustrating, especially if you're toting luggage, since they make you get out and walk over the Bhandari Bridge.

Luggage Storage: The cloakroom at the railway station charges Rs.3 per day for luggage storage. Some hotels, such as Tourists' Guest House, office this service only begrudgingly.

Market: The **bazaar** immediately in front of the main entrance to the Golden Temple carries a wide selection of goods from Rajasthani shoes to Sikh daggers and swords. **Mementos India** (tel. 549886) carries antiques and handicrafts, while **Baba Kishan Singh & Co.** (tel. 49271), near Jallianwala Bagh, specializes in musical instruments. The steel bracelets *(kara)* worn by all Sikhs and symbolizing strength of will and determination are available here. The strength of *kara* that are not made of stainless steel will certainly erode after a few months of wear.

Library: Sri Guru Ram Das Library, next to the Sri Guru Ram Das Niwas Gurudwara at the Golden Temple, has a collection of books in the back corner about Sikhism and the temple, as well as daily periodicals. Open summer Mon.-Sat. 7:30am-5:30pm, winter 8am-5pm (sometimes slow to open).

English Bookstore: A few of the tourist shops in front of the Golden Temple have good souvenir literature, though much of their material is in Hindi. Newsstands at the railway station (platform 1) have English magazines and sleazy paperbacks.

Pharmacy: Although they can be found all over town, several chemists are clustered on Cooper Rd., around the corner from Crystal Restaurant and northeast of the railway station by several blocks. Among these, **Amritsar Medicare** (tel. 212320) carries tampons and is otherwise well-stocked. Open daily 8am-11pm.

Hospital: Kakkar Hospital, Green Ave. (tel. 210964; emergency tel. 62018). Near Mall Rd., northwest of the railway. The most reputable hospital in town, enough people know the name to point the way.

Post Office: On Court Rd. (tel. 66032). Northwest of the railway station. Offers *Poste Restante* (c/o Post Marshall), but no EMS speed post. Open Mon.-Sat. 9am-5pm. There is a **Golden Temple post office** for stamp sales (open Mon.-Sat. 9am-6:30pm). **Postal Code:** 143001 for main GPO, 143006 for Golden Temple area. **Telephone Code:** 0183.

ACCOMMODATIONS

Amritsar has a bevy of hotels to suit nearly every price range, though the depths of low end accommodations haven't found a niche here yet. There are, however, a number of cheap hotels across from the bus stand on the east side, near the Sangam Cinema. The Hotel Taj Mahal (tel. 549174) here, for example, has singles for Rs.75, and the Capital, Standard, and other hotels promise to be similarly cheap.

Some travelers end up staying in the north end, near the railway station, and visiting the Golden Temple from there. Admittedly, hotels near the temple are more scarce, but the southern part of the city is more vibrant and alive (not to mention hectic). The best place to stay, of course, is in the temple itself, though this may be taxing after a few days.

Railway Area (North of Bhandari Bridge)

Tourists Guest House, G.T. Rd., Hide Market (tel. 553830). On the road from the bus stand to the railway, closer to the bus stand. Foreigners funnel in here for a peaceful, homey rooms with wafer-thin mattresses, but good fans. Food is known to be pricey, but heeding demand, they now offer *thalis* (Rs.25) as well as corn flakes, toast, and tea. Back rooms are more removed from the indoor activity, but less so from the noisy railroad outside. Singles Rs.110. Doubles Rs.120, with bath Rs.140, with TV, air-cooling, and hot water Rs.150-220.

Chinar Hotel, one-half block up Railway Links Rd. (tel. 64655). A distance of 300m from railway station. Spotlessly clean and newly painted, with huge front-side rooms. Room service 6am-midnight. Check-out noon. Doubles with TV, cupboard, and mirror Rs.150, with bath Rs.250.

Hotel National (tel. 65075). Opposite railway station to the west; look for the Deepak Orchestra sign. Spacious, spartan rooms with chairs to enjoy swell views of the railway rickshaws. Basic rooms, but big beds. Singles with bath Rs.100. Doubles Rs.150. Rates negotiable.

Hotel Palace/Pegasus (tel. 64778). Just west of Hotel National, opposite railway station. Massive front-side doubles, semi-massive enclosed doubles, and singles all have TVs, air-coolers, and attached baths. Rooms Rs.125-175.

Mrs. Bhandari's Guest House, 10 Cantonment (tel. 22290). About 2km west of town along Mall Rd. Pleasant retreat spot rooms decorated grandma-style, with fans in the bathroom and quaintness *ad nauseum.* Popular among tour groups; their no-Indians policy is as dated as the rest of the place, but not at all charming. Current manager, Kumaria, is very cool. Swimming pool use Rs.50. Playground and lovely garden with bungalows. Expensive restaurant with personal servants. Doubles Rs.300. Triples Rs.450. Deluxe rooms Rs.600-900.

Golden Temple Area

Sharma Guest House, one block northeast of Golden Temple. Rooms over the Sharma Dhaba, Jallianwala Bagh, come with TV, good beds, and attached bath. Tasty food downstairs. Rooms Rs.150.

Shri Gujrati Lodge and Guest House (tel. 557870). Entrance tucked into alley between Jallianwala Bagh and music stores, 1 block in front of main Golden Temple gate. Popular among Indians. Quasi-clean rooms have telephone, stereo, and seat toilet. Avoid the 6-bed dorm. TV and food in the lobby. Dorm beds Rs.35. Doubles Rs.80, with air-cooling Rs.125, with bath Rs.150.

Sindhi Hotel (tel. 553790). Southeast of Golden Temple, near giant gray mushroom tower. Bare-bones rooms, most with attached bath. More privacy and tobacco-tolerance than the temple can offer. Low ceilings, bizarre stairwell, and a common balcony to go with the grime. Singles Rs.70. Doubles Rs.120.

Hotel Sita Niwas, Sarai Guru Ram Das (tel. 543092). Southeast of temple; look for signs along the bazaar in front of the temple. This enterprising hotel offers services galore, but rooms are cramped and lack privacy, mattresses are thin, and one must cross the courtyard and parking lot to get to the common bathroom. Bedding costs extra, but bedspreads are colorful. Taxi, car hire, car parking, STD/ISD, and attached veg. restaurant. Check-out 24hr. Singles Rs.120, with bath Rs.150. Doubles Rs.150, with bath Rs.200.

Hotel City Heart (tel. 545186). Big, well-marked hotel one block north of Golden Temple main gate across from Jallianwala Bagh. Upscale option near the temple—clean rooms with blinding carpets and shining color TV. Singles Rs.350, with A/C Rs.450. Doubles Rs.550, with A/C Rs.650. Extra bed Rs.150.

Inside the Golden Temple

Sri Guru Ram Das Niwas Gurudwara, outside the east gate of the temple past the community kitchen. As the main Golden Temple housing complex the set-up is basic. All guests are entitled to use the washing spouts and showers as well as the dank line of toilets. Foreign guests, shunned of the privilege of sleeping in real rooms, make beds out of floor mats in a small, corner section of the courtyard, behind a closed, guarded door. No smoking, no drinking rules certainly make it a mellow place. Despite the nighttime heat and the periodic wails of crying babies in the courtyard, the overall experience is fun. It's free, though donations at the charity box out front are appreciated. Be sure to keep a close eye on your belongings—the glowering expressions in convicted robbers' mug shots at the *gurudwara*'s entrance explain why.

Sri Guru Hargobind Nawas, 100m south of Ram Das Niwas Gurudwara. If the free accommodations are a bit *too* free for your tastes, this is a sparkling new, marble-covered, spotlessly sterile residence for pilgrims willing to pay a token tariff for a double with attached bath. The same prohibitive policies apply here. The temple manager can be reached at 553953; the extension of the Hargobind Nawas is 323. Doubles with bath Rs.50.

FOOD

Eat at least one meal in the Golden Temple itself—the *dal* may surprise you and bring you back longing for more. If not, ask a local about a favorite *dhaba* and everyone generally knows which are clean enough for Western stomachs. Bubby Vaishno Dhaba, directly across from the main access to the Golden Temple, has clean *channa puri* for pre-temple-tour breakfast. For air-conditioning, head to one of the ominous tinted-windowed places on Lawrence Rd., or hit the reputable 24-hr. coffee shop in the Mohan International.

Bharawan Dhaba (Dahotel), Town Hall (tel. 552275). Near Punjab National Bank, south of the train tracks, not far from Golden Temple. Well-known, well-endowed, well-lit *dhaba* with superb *thalis* (Rs.26)—save room for their thick *kheer.* Speedy service and foreigner friendly. Open daily 8am-11pm.

Vaishno Kundan Dhaba (tel. 44493). Opposite railway station, next to Hotel National. Tasty, cheap *thalis* (Rs.30), piping hot *chapatis,* all cooked in pure *desi ghee.* Low on ambience, high on budget value. Open daily 7am-11pm.

Sharma Dhaba, below Sharma Guest House on Jallian Bagh Wala. One block north and ½ block east of Golden Temple. Another simple-simon, no-frills joint, but this one makes a menacing *malai kofta* (Rs.18), and whips out good, stuffed *paratha.* Open daily 7am-11pm.

Neelam's (tel. 556353). Near music stores in bazaar in front of Golden Temple, not far from Jallianwala Bagh. One of the few restaurants in this area with a fully closing door, plus A/C, tinted windows, and a meanish, creamy *malai kafta* of their own. Veg. soup is bland but kind to the bowels. Open daily 10am-11pm.

Meesaal Beer Bar and Restaurant, Court Rd. (tel. 228494). One block north of the railway station; take Links Rd. Four types of beer, *paranthas* (Rs.8) to soak up the brew, and veg. and non-veg. entrees (Rs.20-80). Wall posters of glowering Indian starlets add to the somewhat seedy atmosphere. Open daily 10am-11pm.

Burger King, 1-A Lawrence Rd. (tel. 225053). Opposite Corporation Bank. No Whoppers, but otherwise Western to the T, with videos, foot-long pizza-type thingies, Chinese, fried chicken, mini-meals, actual pizzas, burgers, and the local youth. Surprisingly good grub, though. Open daily 10am-11pm.

Mrs. Bhandari's Guest House, 10 Cantonment (tel. 22290). Expensive but satisfying "English-style" meals with multiple courses. The dinner served outside in the garden is a feast to say the least—steamy soup, several scrumptious veg. dishes, heaps of rice and bread, and fruit or pudding for dessert. Veg. dishes (Rs.150), non-veg. (Rs.200). Make advance reservations if not staying in the guest house.

Sindhi Coffee House, Lawrence Rd. (tel. 66039). Across from Ram Bagh Gardens. Deep-freezed, damn dark diner with overpriced mineral water, but good ice cream, and Indian/Chinese dishes. *Paneer* cock roll Rs.24, chicken cock roll Rs.39, mutton cock roll Rs.34. Open daily 9am-10pm.

SIGHTS

The Golden Temple

No matter what you choose to call it—the Golden Temple, Hari Mandir, or Darbar Sahib (as its known in Punjabi)—Amritsar's focal monument is awesomely serene and beautiful. The Golden Temple's tranquility is especially impressive given the tumultuous history of the Sikhs and that of the temple itself. The nearly 400 years of the temple's existence has been marked by incessant destruction and desecration from outsiders. But an indelible, almost haunting feeling of peace and humility is impressed upon all who pass through the temple's gates. This is especially true for Sikhs, all of whom try to make a pilgrimage here at least once in their lifetime. But other religious groups have also sought serenity of the *amritsar* ("pool of nectar") tucked into the Punjabi woods. Lord Buddha suggested that Buddhist monks head here to attain *nirvana,* and unbeknownst to most, Tibetans believe the pool to be the birthplace of Padmasambhava, founder of Tibetan Vajrayana. But while Buddhists eventually deserted the spot, and the number of Tibetan pilgrims at the temple dwindled, the Sikhs took responsibility for transformed the pool of nectar into the holiest of places.

Though Guru Nanak, the founder of Sikhism, once lived near the modern tank, it was Guru Ram Das who sparked the growth of a religious center when he cleared the pool in 1574, a task which was completed under Guru Arjun 15 years later, when the area was officially named Amritsar. Guru Arjun constructed the Hari Mandir in the tank's center and placed the Guru Granth Sahib, the Sikhs holy book, inside the temple.

A series of destructive Mughal invasions followed the 1601 completion of the temple. In response to Mughal control of the temple starting in 1740, two Sikhs snuck into the temple and cunningly killed the Mughal leader, Massa Ranghar. Also in 1757, following a brief period of Sikh sovereignty in the area, Ahmad Shah Abdali plundered the temple. The back and forth continued, and in the battle of Ghallughara, Ahmad Shah Abdali again took the temple, and this time taking no chances, blew it to smithereens. Finally, under British rule, the Sikhs reclaimed the temple. The Punjabi ruler Maharaja Ranjit Singh rebuilt the complex, beautified parts with marble and copper, and the Hari Mandir with gold leaf. Several years thereafter the British assumed management of the temple and disregarded the most basic tenets of Sikhism; it took a veritable renaissance during the 1920s to restore the practice of pure Sikhism within the temple's walls.

In the mid-1980s, Sikh extremists under the leadership of Jarnail Singh Bhindranwale led Sikh extremists to occupy the temple, creating a base for his movement for a separate Sikh state. Having transformed the temple into a war-ready headquarters, poised with machine guns, Bhindranwale and his troops put up a three-day fight when Indira Gandhi sent troops into the temple in a maneuver code-named "Operation Bluestar." Tanks entered the east gate and shot cannons at the Sikh parliament, or Akal Takht, on the other side. Bhindranwale was killed. Indira Gandhi was assassinated by her Sikh bodyguards five months later. In 1988, a smaller militant group emerged and again occupied the temple, only to be thwarted by local police. Tension still sits hot and heavy between Hindus and Sikhs. Tour guides and locally published tourist literature are hush-hush about this latter-day violence.

As much as visitors are welcomed to the Golden Temple, the welcome is contingent upon adherence to certain rules. **No tobacco, alcohol, or narcotics** of any kind are to be carried into the temple complex. Visitors must deposit cigarettes a block away from the temple's entrance; this restriction has made it impossible to buy smokes without hiking a good five minutes north of the temple. In addition, all visitors must leave their **shoes, socks,** and **umbrellas** behind; there are free depositories at each of the main entrances and at the tourist information center. Any scarf, baseball cap, or towel can serve the purpose of covering your head, which is required before entering the temple and at all times while inside. The tourist information center provides free **headcovers,** while nearby tourist trinket and shawl vendors sell them for Rs.5-7. Finally, visitors must **wash their feet** in the tanks in front of the entrances. Photography is allowed inside the temple complex, but not inside the temple itself. Colorfully clad Sikh guards with spears will promptly jab anyone who fails to comply with any or all of these rules.

The main entrance to the Golden Temple is on the north side, beneath the **clock tower.** This side also has the main shoe depository, several tourist stands, and the **tourist information centre** (tel. 553954; open daily 8am-1pm and 2:30-8pm). Among innumerable services, the staff provides informative brochures about the temple and Sikh gurus and runs mumbled hourly tours of the temple (in English), in which guides tend to skirt around the subject of temple's recent, violent past.

The clock tower leads to the **Parikrama,** the 12-m-wide marble promenade encircling the tank. Guru Arjun intentionally lowered the tank below ground level so that even the humblest visitors would have to step down to enter it. The four entrances to the temple and to the complex signify an openness to visitors from all sides—both geographically and metaphorically, in terms of caste and creed.

At the immediate entrance blocks of marble are inscribed with the names of the temple's generous financial contributors, including the Europeans whose patronage was motivated simply by a liking for the tenets of Sikhism. These minor memorials may go unnoticed, however, as you inhale the vision of the blindingly white temple, the steely water of the tank, and the glimmering radiance of the Golden Temple in the middle of it all. The eerie tranquility of the temple visit is enhanced by speakers piping the perpetual performance sounds of *kirtans* (devotional songs) and *gurbani* from inside the temple throughout the complex.

Traffic moves clockwise around the Parikrama. Here, the **68 Holy Places** are deemed symbolic of the 68 holiest Hindu sites in India—merely walk along this northern edge, Guru Arjun declared, and one has attained the holiness a Hindu takes a lifetime to acquire. The small tree at the northeast corner of the tank is said to have been the site of a miracle healing of a cripple; healthy, wealthy, crippled, and destitute alike indulge in the tank's mysterious powers at the consequent **bathing ghats.** Just next to the *ghats* along the tank is one of four booths in which priests read from the Guru Granth Sahib, the religious book of the Sikhs. Ongoing readings are meant to ensure the perpetuation of Sikh beliefs; with each priest reciting for three hours, a complete reading takes about 50 hours.

On the other side of the Parikrama are the **Ramgarhia Minars,** two brick towers which were damaged when tanks rolled through this entrance in 1984. This access leads to the Guru-ka-Langar, the communal kitchen, and the *gurudwaras,* the housing for temple pilgrims (see below).

The south side of the tank has a shrine to Baba Deep Singh, whose headless exploits made him a Sikh hero (see **Headless Heroism,** p. 337). The west end of the tank has several notable structures. First on a clockwise rotation is the window where devotees collect *prasad,* the sweet lumps of cornmeal used as an offering inside the temple. Farther on, across from the entrance to the Hari Mandir, is the **Akal**

Takhat, which is the second-most sacred place here. Guru Hargobind, the sixth Sikh guru, built the Akal Takhat in 1609 as a decision-making center. Many weapons, fine pieces of jewelry, and other Sikh artifacts are stored here, but access is limited because of structural damage that occurred during Operation Bluestar (though reconstruction is nearly complete).

The two towering **flagstaffs** next to the Akal Takhat represent the religious and political facets of Sikhism; that the two are joined by the **double swords of Hargobind** reflects how intertwined these sides of Sikhism are. Lit up at the very top, the poles are intended as a beacons for pilgrims heading into Amritsar, though they aren't glaringly visible from afar. The covers on the flagstaffs are changed once a day. Near the flagstaffs is the shrine to last and most militant guru, Gobind Singh.

The last noteworthy spot along the Parikrama, other than the Hari Mandir itself, is the feeble, wizened 450-year old *jujubi* tree. Baba Buddhaja, the temple's first priest, is thought to have hung around here, though at that time there was likely not the umbrella of braces which support the tree's haggard limbs today. Still, even in its old age, the tree is thought to be a source of great fertility for those who touch it.

Seemingly floating in the middle of the tank, the actual Golden Temple is the holiest part of the complex. Photography is not allowed past the gate to the temple walkway. The architecture of the Golden Temple incorporates Hindu and Muslim styles into its own artistic style. The three stories, topped by an inverted lotus shaped dome, are made of marble at the base, copper, and some 100kg of pure gold leaf, respectively. The temple is over 12 square meters, its platform 20 square meters, and its entry gate at the west end of the ivory-etched **causeway** 3.5 meters tall. Inside the temple on the ground floor, the chief priest and his musicians perform the *gurbani,* or hymns, from the Guru Granth Sahib. Devotees sit around the center and toss flowers and money toward the jewel-studded canopy, where lies the silk-enshrouded Guru Granth Sahib.

The book is brought to the temple from the Akal Takhat each day and returned at night. The morning ceremony takes place at 4am in the summer, 5am in the winter. At the nighttime ceremony (10pm in winter, 11pm in summer) the temple complex gains (remarkably) even more serenity. The lights that reflect off the blackened tank and the lanterns that illuminate the causeway enhance the temple's vivid colors. Arrive about one hour early to observe the ceremony. Hymns echo through the building before the book is finally revealed and the priest takes over the prayers and chants, folds the book in gold leaf and more silk, and finally places it on the golden *palanquin.* Head downstairs at this point, and you may end up in the line of devotees waiting to shoulder the book as it is carried out of the temple. Non-Sikhs are allowed this privilege, though often decline, leaving it to the more fervent visitors. Finally, a blaring serpentine horn and communal drum beating signal a final prayer that puts the book to bed, literally, near the flagstaff. The entire ceremony lasts about an hour and a half.

Step outside to the left (north) side, onto the *pradakhina,* the marble path leading around the temple. On this north side is a stairwell leading to the second floor, where flowers, animals, and hymns ornament the walls and where you can catch a good look at the procession and Adi Grantha below. On the east side of this floor is a small *shish mahal,* or hall of mirrors. Once occupied by the *gurus,* the chamber is now filled with the voices of modern-day priests engaged in the *akhand path,* the ongoing reading of the holy book. On the ground floor on the east (back) side of the temple is the **Har-ki-Pari** (Steps of God), which allow visitors easy access to the holy water at this most sacred section of the tank.

No visit to the Golden Temple is complete without a meal at the **Guru-ka-Langar,** the enormous **community kitchen** which is characteristic of all Sikh temples. Sikh founder Guru Nanak instituted the custom of *pangat* (dining together) to reinforce the idea of equality. This custom continues in the dining hall here, where basic meals are dished out daily to some 20,000 people who sit in a single unifying row, regardless of wealth or caste. As one group eats, the next gathering waits by the door out front in an ongoing cycle. The meal itself begins only after all have been seated along

---

Gataka

The Sikhs' success in resisting 400 hundred years of oppression is in part attributable to their skill as warriors. Through centuries of battles, the group developed an esoteric martial art known as *gataka*. Today, young would-be warriors practice *gataka* on the roof of the Guru-ka-Langar, the community kitchen, between 8:30 and 11pm. They enjoy having visitors watch as they deftly wield the *neja* (spears), swords, bamboo stocks, and other ancient weapons and practice *talwar baji* (fencing), or as it's more bluntly known, *kripan* (the art of stabbing). The coolest weapon is the *chakkar*, a wooden ring with stone spheres dangling off it by 4-foot strings. The warrior stands in the middle and spins the ring, the whirling balls forming a barrier around him, then tosses it up into the air (still spinning) for someone nearby to catch. Watching the nightly spectacle is exciting, but participating in it is even better—they'll let you try the weapons out. To really indulge in *gataka*, they recommend heading out to Raia, 50km outside of Amritsar, where Baba Bakala, the training center for the most hardcore students, is located on G.T. Rd.

---

one of the mats and a prayer has been sung—tempting as it is to dive into that *dal*, wait until those around you have started. After that, it's all-you-can-eat *dal-chapatis;* simply hold out cupped hands as the *chapati* chap walks by and he'll toss you more. Afterwards, as they're cleaning out the spillage, kindly leave a donation in one of the charity boxes, since this ongoing charity is largely funded by such contributions. A glimpse of the kitchen will reveal the heaps of *chapatis* that are nimbly tossed over flaming woodstoves, and a gigantic cauldron of simmering *dal*. The kitchen is a particularly mystifying at night, when the fire's glow and smoke envelop the toiling workers.

The **Central Sikh Museum,** or Gallery of Martyrs, is housed in the northern part of the temple complex; the entrance is on the right of the main gate. There are portraits of renowned Sikhs, including Baba Deep Singh and Sevapanthi Bhai Mansha Singh, who swam across the tank amid gunfire to keep the temple's light lit. The display of heavy duty arms includes everything from spears to blunderbuses. Paintings of martyred bodies that were boiled or sawed at Chandni Chowk in Old Delhi and photographs of slain Sikh martyrs with pop-eyed, bloody faces spare no detail. Less gruesome is the verse of Sheikh Farid Ji, a poet and painter who predates the Sikhs. (Open daily 8:30am-5pm.)

Just past the more modern Hargobind *gurudwara* to the south is the nine-story **Tower of Baba Atal Rai.** Supposedly, the tower is named after the son of Guru Hargobind, who perturbed his father with his precociousness in performing a miracle at age nine. In shame, the young *baba* came to this spot and died. On the first floor are some detailed miniatures depicting episodes from Guru Nanak's life and a *nagarah* (drum) for your beating pleasure. The other floors are empty, but you can climb past them to the top for the unsurpassed view of Amritsar, the Golden Temple, and the tank of Kamalsar to the south.

Other Sights

Although the Golden Temple manages to tap most of Amritsar's touristic energies, the city does have other interesting sights. About two blocks north of the temple's main entrance is **Jallianwala Bagh,** the site of one of the most disturbing and horrific moments in Indian and British history. In 1919, the notoriously iron-fisted Lt. Governor of the Punjab became annoyed by a series of Indian protests against the Rowlatt Acts, which entitled the British to imprison Indians without a trial. He declared martial law and brought in troops under Brigadier-General Reginald Dyer. However, no one suspected that a peaceful meeting at the Jallianwala Bagh on April 13, 1919 would end in violence. Standing behind 150 troops in front of the main alley, the only exit to the lot, Dyer ordered his men to open fire, without warning, on the 20,000 unarmed people who had gathered there. The shooting continued for an estimated 6 to 15 minutes. Men were shot as they perched to jump over walls; others drowned after diving into wells. In all, the death toll is thought to include 337 men, 41 boys, and one baby, while 1500 were wounded. The massacre backfired, as it sparked a rallying cry for Indian insurgence. Dyer was reprimanded and relieved of his duties but never charged. Jallianwala Bagh is now a calm garden, a memorial to the incident and its victims. The stone well is a monument to the drowned Indians who jumped in attempting to flee and **Martyr's Gallery** features portraits of heroes related to the event. (Open summer daily 9am-5pm, winter daily 10am-4pm) The densely-planted area outside is too alive and organic to summon the deepest feelings about the massacre. (Open summer daily 6am-7pm, winter daily 7am-6pm; smoking prohibited.)

Two blocks west of the Jallianwala Bagh is the one room **Spiritual Museum,** dedicated to the teachings of the Brahma Kumaris' Spiritual University. Quirky murals and paintings depict the importance of character development by showing how sins like litigation, lust, and child-spoiling lead to "next birth in vicious atmosphere." (Open daily 8:30am-7:30pm.)

The high profile of the Golden Temple overshadows the existence of the tiny Hindu shrines tucked into alleyways in the immediate vicinity, and more impressively, the **Durgiana Mandir.** This temple, set back from the busy street four blocks northwest of the Golden Temple, honors the Goddess Durga. The exterior is surprisingly like the Hari Mandir, set on a platform on a medium-sized tank, although its chintzy interior bears no resemblance to that of the Golden Temple.

In the northern part of Amritsar, **Ram Bagh** is a park between Mall and Queens Rd., northeast of the railway station. On the northwest corner of the park is a menacing statue of Maharaja Ranjit Singh, the Sikh responsible for the early 19th-century restoration of the Golden Temple. Ram Bagh served as his summer residence between 1818 and 1837, and the central building (central to three houses where his queens resided) now houses a museum in his name, containing oil paintings, weapons, manuscripts and miniatures from the maharaja's era. The tourist office's pamphlet *Amritsar: Spiritual Centre of Punjab* is a good guide to the museum. (Open Tues.-Sun. 10am-4:45pm; admission Rs.5.) Ram Bagh also contains a miserable little **zoo** (admission Rs.1), where a pair of beautiful bears are tragically caged, and where guinea pigs, guinea hens, and other fowl live in foul conditions. The Lion's Club **Children's Park** has quirky rides and several signs laden with Coca-Cola ads and public service propaganda. Across the street from this park on Lawrence Rd., east of the Sindhi Coffee House, the **art gallery** in the Indian Academy of Fine Arts has a small but interesting collection, featuring Sobha Singh's *Bapu,* a portrait of Gandhi, and Wadanagekar's watercolor portrait *Life.* (Open winter daily 10am-1pm and 3-7pm, summer daily 8-11am and 4-8pm; admission Rs.1.)

■ Near Amritsar: Tarn Taran

Once the Hari Mandir has whet your appetite for shiny, golden Sikh temples, head 25km south to the town of Tarn Taran. Buses stop on the main road, and it's a 5-minute walk through the narrow alley of the bazaar up to the local *gurudwara.* Its founder, Guru Arjun Dev, built the 1768 temple to commemorate Guru Ram Das.

Headless Heroism

Baba Deep Singh, a Sikh leader, began an attack on the Golden Temple from 10km outside Amritsar. Baba Deep had sworn to reach the temple, but halfway in, had his head nearly cut off by a Muslim soldier. Legend has it that, disembodied head in hand, the Sikh leader trudged on, eventually passing the temple's gates and plopping his skull in the water before finally buying the farm. On the road to Tarn Taran is a large shrine to Baba Deep Singh. All passing vehicles stop here to offer a prayer of appreciation for the man's spectacular, acerebral exploits. The shrine is built on the spot where Baba Deep is thought to have started his valiant tirade.

Border Ballet

Many people go to Wagah for border crossing; many also go for border closing. A half-hour before sunset (approx. 7pm in the summer) an elaborate nightly ritual accompanies the border's closing and the lowering of the neighbor nations' flags. Tourists crowd around the gate on either side and vie for the best views. Right on schedule, with a silly, natural dose of military overseriousness, the ceremony proceeds. As one officer barks an order and another follows with frenzied saluting and wild high-stepping, the crowds on both sides applaud the performance. After some machismo-packed face-offs and lengthy, siren-like yells, the respective flags are lowered, the lights go bright, the bugles blare, and the visitors crowd the gates for a glimpse of faces on the other side—or for a chance to take a quick step over the white line.

Guru Ram Das is known, in an act of selflessness, to have slept side by side with a leper, and though local clinicians don't provide any evidence for the common belief that the water here cures leprosy, they do attest to its curative effects on several minor skin conditions. The architectural style here resembles that of the Amritsar complex. With the long marble *panikrama* and still water reflecting the blazing sun above, it gains its own type of a serenity. The *gurudwara* in Tarn Taran has free accommodations and a community kitchen that dishes out an Amritsar-like *dal.*

■ Near Amritsar: Pakistan Border

On Attari Rd., on the way out of town, keep an eye out on the right side for the impressive edifices of Khalsa College. Amritsar is the first or last stop in India for travelers heading to or from Pakistan; the *only* border crossing between the two countries is at **Wagah,** 32km from Amritsar, though trains cross at the town of **Attari,** 25km away. Attari Road is the main route to Wagah.

The border is open daily 9am-4pm. There is a **Punjab Tourism** information center, a **State Bank of India** branch for foreign currency exchange, and a post office for last second send-offs. Those leaving India have to declare currency and go through customs, though tourists do not need to obtain an export certificate. Also at the border are several eager and friendly cold drink and food vendors. If you're looking for a basic restaurant or a place to crash, head to the **Neem Chameli Tourist Complex,** which has gargantuan, fresh rooms with showers, great beds and chairs, and a garden. The fans, however, are too high to be at all effective. Singles with fan Rs.150. Doubles Rs.200.

Himachal Pradesh

Himachal ("Lap of Snow") separated from Punjab in 1966, and is today a land of orchards, mountains, deserts, and amazing people. Different worlds are side by side in Himachal—the high mountain passes seem like warps in space and time. Cross the Rohtang Pass and the rain-drenched forests of Manali become suddenly the rock, ice, blue skies, and harsh winds of Spiti; travel from Shimla to Kaza, and Hindu temples and beliefs are replaced by Buddhist prayer flags and *gompas*. The vast emptiness and harsh heat of Lahul, Spiti, and Kinnaur is a counterpoint to the crowded hill towns of Shimla and Manali and their heavy monsoon showers.

There are three main tourist towns in H.P., and each acts as a gateway to the worlds beyond. Dharamsala in the east has a Tibetan population and is the starting point for treks into the Dhauladhars and the Pir Panjal. In the center, Manali and Shimla are favorites with both Indian and foreign travelers. The rainshadow areas—Lahul, Spiti, and Upper Kinnaur—can be approached from Manali via the Rohtang

Pass or Shimla via Kalpa and Kaza. Road maintenance is difficult in these places, and routes that are theoretically open from June to September can shut at any time.

Although the tourist season in most of Himachal Pradesh is from May to June and September to October, the winter (Dec.-Feb.) is also an ideal time to visit H.P. Prices are lower, and the snow adds to the peaceful atmosphere. The roads to Shimla, Manali, Dharamsala, and from Shimla to Chango remain open in winter.

▓ Shimla

Though encumbered by the usual tourist trappings—inflated prices and an abundance of banks and camera stores—Shimla, at an altitude of 2206m, still manages to soar. Set amid the magnificent forests of the Himalayan foothills, Shimla is India's most famous hill station and one of the prettiest towns in Himachal Pradesh. In the winter, Shimla is blanketed with snow and largely empty; in the summer, it is crowded but retains a spacious charm that makes it a pleasant stopover on the way to Kinnaur or Manali.

The modern period of Shimla's history began at the start of the 19th century, when Gorkha raiders ravaged the small village with fearful persistence and efficiency. Local rulers appealed to the British for military aid; the British, seeing an opportunity to extend their power into the Sutlej River area, were eager to provide it. In 1815, British-led forces defeated the Gorkhas. Over the next half-century, injured British soldiers and well-to-do British officers began to flock to Shimla each summer in search of rest, relaxation, and cool breezes. In 1864, imperial authorities made the summer haul to Shimla official, declaring the town the hot-season hot-seat from which the Subcontinent would be governed. During the summer months—and especially during the World Wars—Shimla was a busy, bustling place, filled with Raj officials and their incredible numbers of servants (who were not allowed in the Mall), and in 1946 leaders of the Indian nationalist movement came to Shimla for a crucial conference that paved the way for Independence.

British control has left Shimla an aesthetic anomaly: an Indian town—a state capital, no less—that has the look and feel of a village in northern England. Keep your eyes peeled in the Mall and you might catch a glimpse of some of the aging, tweedy Brits who "stayed on," and still make their homes in Shimla, nearly 50 years after Independence. Down any of the steps from the Mall lies a maze of alleys and crushed houses where, as Kipling said, you can stay hidden from the police for months on end. The European-Asian divide is obvious in the contrast between the ordered graciousness of the Mall and the crowded confusion of the lower bazaars. In the winter, Shimla's 110,000 residents are buried under heavy snow, and walking around town becomes difficult, even dangerous.

ORIENTATION

Shimla stretches from west of **Himachal Pradesh University** to an area east of **Lakkar Bazaar,** the street off which many of the town's 5000 Tibetan refugees live. The small, easily navigable center of town is off-limits to all motorized vehicles and contains not just hotels, restaurants, and banks, but also the ambitions of most tourists. Major streets run from east to west, each at a different level of elevation. Trains arrive on **Cart Road,** as do many buses. Above Cart Rd. is the crowded jumble of the bazaar, and above the bazaar is Shimla's main drag, **the Mall.** At **Scandal Corner,** named for the elopement of a British soldier with an Indian princess, directly above the main bus stand, the Mall divides into a wide, upper section called **the Ridge,** which becomes Lakkar Bazaar as it curves beyond the yellow **Christ Church,** and a lower section, which is still called the Mall.

Himachal Pradesh

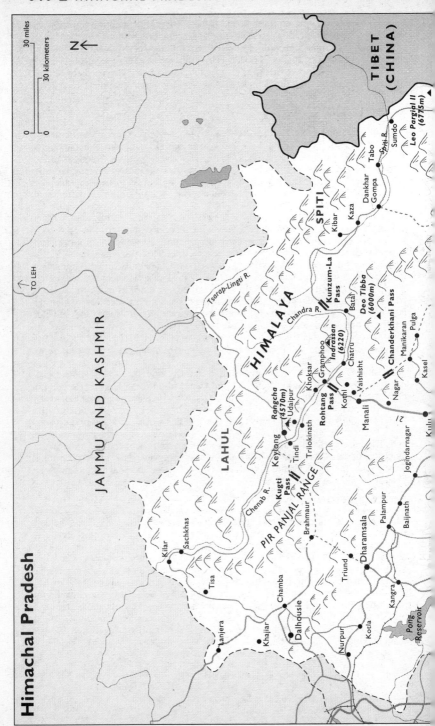

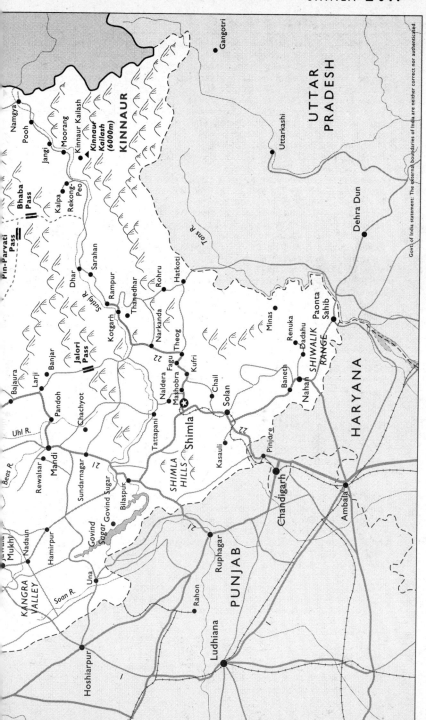

PRACTICAL INFORMATION

Tourist Office: Himachal Tourism Marketing Office (tel. 212591), next to Scandal Corner, on the left. Friendly staff can help out with information on H.P. Brochures about, hotel bookings in, and buses to major tourist destinations.

Budget Travel: There are travel offices on every corner, all offering transport and trekking. **Span Tours 'n' Travels,** the Mall (tel. 201360; fax 201300) and **Ambassador Travels,** the Mall (tel. 780014; fax 211139) are reliable.

Currency Exchange: Punjab National Bank, ANZ Grindlays, and the **State Bank of India,** all on the Mall. All open Mon.-Fri. 9am-2pm. Many travel agents are also authorized to exchange money.

Telephones: STD/ISD booths line the Mall.

Airport: Jubbarhatti, 20km from town. Flights to Delhi (Fri.-Wed., 1hr., US$96) and Kulu (Tues. and Sat., 30min., US$57).

Trains: Shimla is connected by a narrow gauge track to Kalka (5 per day, 4hr., Rs.26/116 for 2nd/1st class). The journey has over 100 tunnels. Kalka has connections to Chandigarh, Bikaner, Jodhpur, and Delhi.

Buses: There are 2 main bus stands in Shimla: one is next to Victory Tunnel which deals with buses going towards Kalka and around Shimla and one next to the Rivoli Cinema with buses going towards Rampur and Kinnaur. Buses towards Kinnaur leave frequently, 5am-noon. Buses to Chandigarh and Delhi leave from Victory Tunnel in the afternoon and evening.

Police: Main station, past the Mall (tel. 72123) handles regular complaints. The Control Room, the Mall, handles immediate problems (tel. 212322).

Hospital/Medical Services: Himachal Pradesh Civil Hospital, Lakkar Bazaar. Private doctors are much more helpful. Ask your hotel manager to get you one.

Pharmacy: There are a number along the Mall.

Post Office: GPO, just above Scandal Corner. Speed post counter for express deliveries. Open Mon.-Sat. 10am-7pm. **Postal Code:** 171001.

Telephone Code: 0177.

ACCOMMODATIONS

The prices at the over 500 hotels in Shimla skyrocket during the high season (May-June and Sept.-Oct.) when millions ascend from the steaming plains. Decent rooms run about Rs.400 in season. Reservations aren't generally necessary. The really cheap places near Victory Tunnel and the bus station are congested dumps with common baths and spartan rooms that charge about Rs.100-150 during the season. The cheapest of the cheap are Brothers Hotel (tel. 78364), Himachal Hotel (tel. 5466), and Hotel Metro (tel. 72638). Nicer hotels are located up the Mall. All prices are for in season. Expect discounts of up to 50% off-season.

Hotel Ridgeview (tel. 201240, 240859, 203916). In the Mall, just above Mayur Hotel. Doubles with attached bathrooms are Rs.200-450. The more expensive rooms come with a TV and hot water geyser. Room and laundry services available. Attached baths. Doubles Rs.200-450.

YMCA (tel. 204085; fax 211016), on the path between the Mayur Hotel and the Ritz Cinema south of the Mall. Clean rooms in an old red brick building with a lovely terrace. Breakfast included. Doubles Rs.200, with bath Rs.280. Membership fee Rs.40. Reservations essential 3 months in advance in season.

YWCA (tel. 203081), opposite the Main Telegraph Office. The rooms are in the third-oldest building in town and they retain a colonial ambience. The garden lends a sense of space rare in most Shimla hotels. Rooms Rs.150-250. Membership fee Rs.10. Hot water and quilt Rs.3.

Diplomat Hotel, Lakkar Bazaar (tel. 72001, 77754), in the middle of the bazaar and impossible to miss. Rooms are clean, carpeted, and have attached baths. Rs.400, with a view Rs.500.

Mayur Hotel, the Mall (tel. 72392, 72393). The sign is visible from as far as Prospect Hill. Rooms are a bit cramped, but come with a clean, attached baths, cable TVs, and friendly service. Rooms Rs.450-850.

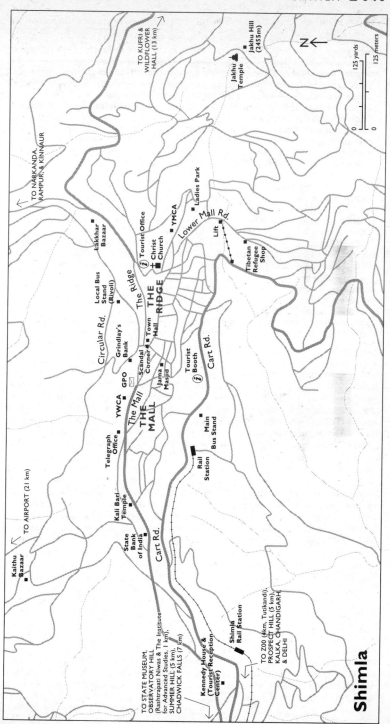

Shimla

TO KUFRI &
WILDFLOWER
HALL (13 km)

TO NARKANDA,
RAMPUR, & KINNAUR

Jakhu Hill
(2455m)

Jakhu
Temple

125 yards

125 meters

0
0

Ladies Park

Lower Mall Rd.

Tourist Office

YMCA

Christ
Church

Lift

Lakkhar
Bazaar

The Ridge

Local Bus
Stand
(Rivoli)

THE
RIDGE

Tibetan
Refugee
Shop

Circular Rd.

Grindlay's
Bank

Town
Hall

Scandal
Corner

Cart Rd.

GPO

Jama
Masjid

Tourist
Booth

YWCA

The Mall

THE
MALL

Telegraph
Office

Main
Bus Stand

Kali Bari
Temple

Cart Rd.

Rail
Station

State
Bank
of India

TO AIRPORT (21 km)

Kaithu
Bazaar

TO STATE MUSEUM,
OBSERVATORY HILL
(Rashtrapati Niwas & The Institute
for Advanced Studies, 1 km),
SUMMER HILL (5 km),
CHADWICK FALLS (7 km)

Kennedy House &
(Tourist Reception
Center)

Shimla
Rail Station

TO ZOO (4km, Tutikandi),
PROSPECT HILL (5 km),
KALKA, CHANDIGARH
& DELHI

Hotel Mehman, Daisy Bank Estate (tel. 213692). Beyond the Ritz Cinema on the left. Rooms are almost identical to those at the Mayur Hotel. Rooms Rs.550-1100.

FOOD

Goofa, Aashiana and **Quick-Bite,** the Mall. The HPTDC owns this complex of three restaurants. The fancy Aashiana has fancy prices—expect to pay Rs.150 for a decent meal. The outdoor terrace may compensate in nice weather. Service is slow, leaving plenty of time to listen to the loud Hindi music. Quick-Bite serves cheap South indian food.

Aunty's, down some steps to the right after Scandal Corner. A group of small Chinese restaurants with dim lights, courting couples, and Michael Bolton on the stereo. Standard Indian versions of Chinese cuisine, including the hybrid "American Chop Suey," for which neither the Chinese nor the Americans will claim responsibility. Dinner Rs.40-60.

India Coffee House, on the right coming from the railway station—impossible to miss. A thin pall of cigarette smoke hangs over this crowded café and a sari-clad woman beckons from a poster with the "nothing but delicious coffee" sign. A favorite hang-out with locals and tourists alike, ICH is always packed and finding a table during lunch hours is a pain. South Indian food (Rs.20-30) and snacks.

Baljees/Fascination, Scandal Corner. Following a curious Shimla tradition, these 2 restaurants have the same kitchen and menu but different names. The Shimla hip crowd hangs here during dinner hours. Continental, Chinese, and Indian food. Main dishes Rs.60-80.

Embassy. The site for the collegiate crowd, this place is justly famous for its softies—ice cream swirled in cones available until 11pm. Also serves Chinese, Indian, and Continental cuisine.

Sher-e-Punjab, just below Christ Church. Unassailable dishes for the meat fanatic. Everything from mutton curry to tandoori. Meals Rs.60-100.

SIGHTS

Shimla's most popular sights all require some pleasant—though often strenuous—walking from the center of town. To reach the **Himachal Pradesh State Museum**—walk west along the Mall until you reach a concrete ramp labeled "Museum;" the museum is atop the ramp, while the ramp is directly next to the Ambedkar Chowk sub-post office and a 40-minute walk from Scandal Corner. Although the walk is long, the two-story museum has a wide-ranging collection and informative placards explaining the sights. The ground floor exhibits small collections of jewelry, wood-carvings, musical instruments, wall paintings from Chamba, and masks from the Dattatreya Temple. A gallery labeled Archaeology displays a collection of stone pieces from throughout India, including remarkably well-preserved terra-cottas from the Shunga period (2nd-first century BC) and Chola period sculptures of Annapurna and Sri Devi. Across the hall, a collection of sculpture produced in Himachal Pradesh showcases the diverse subjects and styles that have fired the imagination of local artists over the past 14 centuries. A collection of about 45 vibrantly colored **Pahari miniature paintings** is the cream of the museum's crop. While some of the paintings have about them the frenetic, cluttered quality of Mughal miniature painting, many other pieces are tranquil and spare, with single-hued color fields occupying much of the composition. See especially "Woman Writing Letter," an 18th-century work produced in the Kulu Valley. If you plan to hike up to the Jakhu Temple (see below), the precisely rendered "Hanuman Adoring Rama" is worth a special look. More miniature paintings are on view on the second floor, as are bushels of paintings by contemporary H.P. artists. The second floor also boasts a small collection of stamps, photos of H.P. temples, and an assemblage of weapons emphasizing muskets and daggers. A collection of coins discovered in H.P. includes some well-preserved examples of 2nd-century BC Indo-Greek coins, while a collection of dressed-up mannequins and dolls showcases India's splendid (and colorful) sartorial diversity. The *de rigeur* collection of Gandhi memorabilia—mostly photos and photocopies of letters—occupies a few second-story galleries. (Open Tues.-Sun. 10am-1:30pm and 2-5pm; free.)

To reach the magnificent **Viceregal Lodge (Rashtrapati Nivas),** pass the entrance to the state museum and walk west along the Mall for 10 minutes. The Lodge, which now houses the fellows of the **Indian Institute of Advanced Study,** is beyond a marked gate. Built between 1884 and 1888, the mock-Tudor lodge is an unabashedly grand building nestled amid well-manicured formal gardens. The summer headquarters of the Raj, the lodge was designed to impress—it was the first government building in British India to be equipped with electricity, and its gray limestone was quarried a full 8km away. Over 800 men and women—including 40 gardeners—were employed at the lodge. A guided tour features the splendid ground floor of the lodge, which is furnished with floral-patterned period chairs and couches. The breezy entrance hall has Burmese teak paneling. (Open daily 10am-1pm and 2-4:30pm. Guided tours Rs.3.)

Just next to the entrance to the Indian Institute of Advanced Study is the **Himalayan Aviary,** opened in August 1994. The small, chain-link enclosed aviary showcases red jungle fowl, perky pheasants, and some magnificent peacocks. With white feathers filling the air, the aviary can feel like the inside of a fluffy pillow. (Open Tues.-Sun. 10am-5pm; admission Rs.5.)

The gated asphalt road just to the left of the main entrance of the Indian Institute of Advanced Studies leads to the much-ballyhooed **Prospect Hill** (2176m). Follow the asphalt out the Institute's back entrance to a small market and bus stand; behind it, a steep road leads to the top of the hill. Atop the hill is an entirely unspectacular shrine to **Kamana Devi** and a ratty, lonesome picnic area that affords nice views of Shimla on clear days.

At the east end of Shimla, the **Jakhu Temple** sits atop a 2455-m hill. The 20-minute walk up to the top of the hill is a steep huffer and puffer, and if you've been smoking too many *bidis* you'll feel it. The trail begins just left of the pale yellow Christ Church and is marked by a sign put up by the local Lions' Club. The red-and-yellow temple atop the hill is architecturally uninspiring, but inside are what some believe to be the footprints of Hanuman, the commander of the monkey army that came to Rama's aid. Hordes of pesky, aggressive monkeys crowd the area around the temple, which also boasts a canteen, a swing, and, on clear early mornings, mountain views. Two networks of paths lead back toward town. While both sets of paths cut through magnificent, lush forests, the sinuous paths directly to the right of the temple afford better opportunities for seeing pristine forests and taking pleasant detours. Neither set of paths is marked, but all paths eventually lead down. Allow 45 minutes to an hour to reach town on the way down Jakhu; expect to emerge from the forest near Lakkar Bazaar, 25 minutes or so from Scandal Corner.

ENTERTAINMENT

To keep themselves amused, most visitors are content to simply stroll along the Mall or the Ridge, where the breezes are cool, the architecture is pretty, and the company is friendly. Diverting pit-stops abound. The Mall boasts a high number of book shops, and stores selling ice cream, nuts, and candy, making the street a snacker's paradise. In addition, the Mall is home to a second-story **billiard hall** and numerous small **video arcades** for those craving a Super Mario Bros. fix. For sudsy diversions, the Mall offers a few **pubs.** Himani's serves drinks at inflated prices until 9 or 10pm. The small bar next to Whiteway Dry Cleaners (it doesn't have a name, just a Chilled Beer sign) caters to locals. Other options for booze are the bar at **Rendezvous,** just next to the statue of Lalalajpatrai, and **The English Wine Shop,** which sells of bottled alcohol from a spot on the Mall located below Christ Church.

For **movies** in English, head to **Rivoli** or **Ritz.** Rivoli usually shows its English-language flicks at 5pm (buy tickets by 4:30pm); it's down the ramp nestled between ANZ Grindlays Bank and Rendezvous. Ritz usually screens its (often quite sexy) English-language films at 5:30pm; it's just east of Christ Church, on the ramp leading up to the YMCA Guesthouse. Just below Rivoli is an **ice-skating rink,** which rents skates, and typically opens for the season in January. A minuscule **roller-skating rink,** on Lakkar Bazaar just east of Christ Church, has skating in 45-minute sessions to the accompaniment of blaring Indian music. (Skating Rs.10, skate rental Rs.10.)

SHOPPING

For **Shimla shawls** and other examples of the area's justly famous handicrafts, check out any of the many stores that crowd the Mall. Prices are lower in the tame **bazaar** below the Mall; be prepared to bargain.

While it was the British who bequeathed to Shimla the delightful habit of mingling business with pleasure, it is Rajiv Sud who has perfected the practice. Sud is the soft-spoken and affable owner of **Maria Brothers,** an antiquities store that specializes in old books and which Sud hopes to turn into a museum. Maria Brothers was founded just after Independence by Sud's father, a geographer by training who penned a few books on Shimla and southern Himachal Pradesh. Over the years, the Maria Brothers collection has swelled and swelled. The shelves are packed with antique maps, wood carvings, Tibetan *thankas,* and lithographs. And then there are the books—a *Who's Who of India* from the 1940s, bound editions of *The Shimla Times* from the early 20th century, and all sorts of swashbuckling books printed in the 19th century on the Central Asian imperial struggles that Rudyard Kipling called "the great game." Prices aren't cheap, but Sud is as nice to browsers as he is to buyers. The shop is on the Mall, at number 78, just below the church. Open daily 10:30am-1pm and 3-8pm.

■ Dharamsala

The headquarters of the Kangra district, Dharamsala is divided into two sections, with a 500-m difference in altitude between the two. Upper Dharamsala, or McLeod Ganj (named after a governor of Punjab, David McLeod), is where most tourists head unless they have an early morning bus to catch. The unusual geography was the result of a massive earthquake on April 4, 1905, which destroyed all buildings and killed 900 people in the Kangra Valley. Alarmed at the debacle, the British shifted the administrative headquarters down, and established the Kotwali Bazaar and District Courts. Dharamsala underwent a second major change when the 14th Dalai Lama was given political asylum in McLeod Ganj in 1959. Since then, there has been a steady influx of Tibetan refugees, and today McLeod Ganj is a peaceful mix of Tibetan shops and establishments, Indian businesses, and a colonial hangover which manifests itself every now and then. Devotees and students of Tibetan Buddhism flock here. McLeod Ganj is beautifully located in the midst of pine and *deodar* forests, and several easy hikes take you into the Dhauladhars within a few hours. The off-season, though, is wet—Dharamsala's reputation for heavy, continuous rain is well-deserved.

ORIENTATION

Divided into **Lower Dharamsala** and **Upper Dharamsala (McLeod Ganj),** the town runs north to south along curvy mountain roads. The Museum of Kangra Art, the State Bank of India, and the tourist office are all on the main road in Dharamsala. The GPO is a steep 1km south of town.

In McLeod Ganj, two parallel roads run north-south, **Temple Road** to the west and **Jogibara Road** to the east. A *chorten* and prayer wheels mark the center of town. The bus stand is to the north at the intersection of the two main roads.

PRACTICAL INFORMATION

Tourist Office: Himachal Tourism Marketing Office (tel. 24498), in Lower Dharamsala next to the Bazaar. Helps out with local sightseeing, treks, and accommodations.

Budget Travel: Most agencies organize treks in the Pir Panjal and Dhauladhar ranges (Rs.600 per day, per person; all inclusive), but will be happy to provide a group with a guides or porters if you have your own equipment or food. Check out **Summit Adventures** (tel. 24519).

Currency Exchange: State Bank of India, between Jogibara and Temple Rd., McLeod Ganj and on the main road in Lower Dharamsala. Open Mon.-Fri. 10am-2pm. **Punjab National Bank,** Lower Dharamsala. Open Mon.-Fri. 10am-2pm.
Telephones: Tons of STD/ISD booths all over.
Airport: Domestic flights operate to Gayal Airport, 20km from Dharamsala.
Trains: There is a broad gauge train to Pathankot, and a narrow gauge one to Kangra (18km from Dharamsala).
Buses: The bus stand in Lower Dharamsala in on the main road, while the McLeod Ganj bus stand is north of town, at the main intersection. To: Delhi (4:15am and 5pm (deluxe), 8:30pm (semi-deluxe); Pathankot (5:30, 7, 10:10, 11:50am, 3, and 4:30pm); Dehra Dun (8pm). To get to Dharamsala, most buses go to Pathankot from where buses leave every hr. for Dharamsala (3hr.).
Local Transportation: The best way to get around is to walk. Buses run between Lower Dharamsala and McLeod Ganj and auto-rickshaws are available.
Hospital: Himachal Government Hospital, McLeod Ganj (tel. 22189, 22133); **Tibetan Administration Hospital,** McLeod Ganj (tel. 22053). Ambulance Service: tel. 23118.
English Bookstore: A lot of bookshops in McLeod Ganj sell second-hand stuff. Check out the **Occidental Book Shop** next to the bus stand, **Book Worm,** or the Tibetan Review (c/o Tibetan SOS Hostel, Sector 14 Ext., Rohini, Delhi 110085). A monthly publication of Tibetan news and articles, you can get an annual subscription (US$20) by writing to the address above.
Police: The station in Forsyth Ganj, west of McLeod Ganj, is the closest (tel. 22183).
Post Office: GPO, Lower Dharamsala, 1km south of town. **Post Office,** along the Jogibara Rd., 5min. from the center, McLeod Ganj. Both have *Poste Restante.* Letters not addressed specifically to McLeod Ganj end up at the GPO. Both open Mon.-Fri. 9am-2pm and 3-5pm. **Postal Code:** 176215.
Telephone Code: 01892.

ACCOMMODATIONS

A 10-minute walking radius from the bus stand covers most of the accommodations in McLeod Ganj, although those who are staying for a long time might prefer to head out to Dharamkot where there are rooms in houses with extremely basic facilities. If you are in McLeod Ganj for only a week or so, it's advisable to book in advance. If you are hanging out in Lower Dharamsala, try **Hotel Dhauladhar** (tel. 01892, 22889, with doubles around Rs.175 (off-season) the **Basera Lodge** (tel. 22234, 24257) or **Rising Moon** in the Kotwali Bazaar for rooms in the lower reaches. There are numerous *dhabas* in the Bazaar.

Ekant Lodge, 10 minutes from the post office along the Jogibara Rd., McLeod Ganj. The lodge has 6-8 clean double-bed rooms. The bathrooms (incredibly enough) have 24-hr. hot running water. Doubles Rs.150.
Seven Hills Lodge, McLeod Ganj (tel. 22887). A quiet, small guest house and a relaxing garden. Dogs and chickens will keep you company along with the Colonel downstairs. Pleasant, clean rooms Rs.90-150.
Kalsang-Tsomo International Guest House, McLeod Ganj (tel. 22609). Go up the dark stairs with Tibetan prayer paraphernalia looming out until you see the light at the reception. Rooms along the corridor are clean and prices range from Rs.90-300.
Paljor Chakyil Guest House, McLeod Ganj. A nice, open courtyard and decent rooms. Dorm beds Rs.35. Rooms Rs.150-250.
Hotel Tibet, McLeod Ganj (tel. 22587, 24327). Probably the best value for money hotel in the mid-range, with clean, spacious rooms (cable TV, laundry service) and spotless bathrooms. Rooms Rs.440-660 (no discounts).
Bhagsu Hotel, McLeod Ganj. The Himachal Tourism-run hotel at the end of the mall road has standard carpeted rooms with cable TV, room service, a restaurant, and a bar. In season: rooms Rs.500-1200. Discount 20-30% off-season.
Blue Heaven, Dharamkot. A steep 20-minute walk from the bus stand in McLeod Ganj takes you to the small village of Dharamkot. The Blue Heaven is extremely popular with both trekkers as well as those staying for a long time. Clean bed-

---

Recycling in McLeod Ganj

The only hill town with a comprehensive recycling policy, Dharamsala is now getting rid of the bottles and plastics that littered the slopes of McLeod Ganj. Started two years ago by the Tibetan Welfare Officer Dawa Tsering, along with Dutch coordinator Jen Willem Den Besten and five green workers, the program picks up all plastic, bottles, and paper from McLeod Ganj for recycling at Pathankot and Kanagra, and also maintains a green shop (Bhagsu Nath Rd.), which sells boiled water (Rs.5 per liter) and environment-friendly products. Volunteers are always welcome—write to the Tibetan Welfare Office, Upper Dharamsala 176215, H.P. (tel. 01892-22059; e-mail: tcrc@dsala.tibetnet.ernet.in).

---

rooms, made-to-order meals, and an ultra-helpful staff. In season: doubles Rs.150. Off-season: doubles Rs.100.

Hotel Meghavan, Bhagsu-Nag (tel. 23277). Just above Bhagsu, with a clean view that sweeps over McLeod Ganj and Dharamsala, Meghavan has all the facilities without the charm and the rooms are not very clean. Off-season: rooms Rs.150-300.

FOOD

Dharamsala cuisine is based on Tibetan and Indian food, with a bit of European and American stuff thrown in. Most restaurants are in McLeod Ganj, with a few *dhabas* churning out Tibetan standards in Lower Dharamsala. Tibetan and Chinese food is served by a dozen restaurants just behind the temple—the stuff is good and cheap, but can take a long time (30min.) arriving, since most of these places are family-run.

Friends Corner Restaurant, Bus Stand, McLeod Ganj. A friendly and clean place, and more spacious than it looks from the outside. Excellent place for breakfast—the variety here boggles the mind—with everything from *tsampa* with banana (a kind of Tibetan porridge) to seven different kinds of pancakes. Prices are reasonable—about Rs.30 for breakfast, Rs.50-70 for lunch or dinner.

McLLo's Restaurant, Bus Stand, McLeod Ganj. The huge 2-story complex that can't be missed, McLLo's is a busy place, thanks to the variety of lagers (Rs.55 per bottle) available. The menu also covers a wide range of cuisine, from South Indian to Tibetan. A bit expensive (Rs.60-70 for main dishes).

Snowland Restaurant, Jogibara Rd., McLeod Ganj. Typical of the Tibetan restaurants along this road, the Snowland has 6 tables, a sparse atmosphere, and excellent food. Eric Clapton, mint tea, and chow mein are an excellent combination (Rs.25), although dishes take around 30min. to prepare.

Take Out, next to Tibet Hotel, McLeod Ganj. Extensive menu includes croissants, burgers, spring rolls, and chocolate cakes for Rs.10-20.

Ashoka Restaurant, Jogibara Rd., McLeod Ganj. This posh restaurant in the middle of town (wooden ceilings, mirrors) has the best North Indian menu, coupled with the highest prices (Rs.70-90 for a main dish), and an almost exclusively foreign clientele.

Tsong Kha Restaurant, McLeod Ganj. Vegetarian version of Snowland on the 2nd floor of the building opposite. Mushrooms fried with noodles is a tasty entree.

Chocolate Log, Jogibara Rd. and opposite the bus stand. Confectioners with a variety of cakes and pastries. You can sit at the Jogibara Rd. branch, but the bus stand location is take-out only.

TIBETAN AND BUDDHIST CENTERS

The Library of Tibetan Works and Archives (Gangchen Kyishong), halfway between McLeod Ganj and Dharamsala along the Jogibara Rd. (tel. 2467). houses all the administrative offices of the **Tibetan government** in exile, including the **library.** The library has a valuable collection of archival material and also offers courses in Tibetan and Buddhist philosophy. The **museum** upstairs has beautiful *thankas* and Tibetan coins. (Advanced and beginner Tibetan language courses; 3 terms of 3 months each, Rs.200 per month. Open 9am-1pm and 2-5pm). The **Dalai Lama** also holds public audiences. To find out when the next one is scheduled, write to The Office of His Holiness the Dalai Lama, Thekchen Choeling, McLeod Ganj, Dharamsala, 176219. It is difficult to get a private audience.

The **Buddhist Temple,** opposite the abode of the Dalai Lama, has images of Lord Buddha, Padmasambhava and Avalokitesvara. Built by Songsten Gompo, a Tibetan monk, the image of Avalokitesvara, the *bodhisattva* of compassion, was rescued from the Tokhang Temple in Lhasa and brought here during the Cultural Revolution. Open daily sunrise-sunset.

The **Tushita Retreat Centre** (tel. 22266) is a mediation center 20min. from McLeod Ganj along the Dharamkot Rd. Founded in 1969 by Lama Thubten Yesho, the center runs meditation courses and retreat programs, and has accommodations for trainees.

SIGHTS AND ENTERTAINMENT

St. John's in the Wilderness, a 15-minute walk from McLeod Ganj and curiously in the wilderness despite being five minutes from the road, is a functioning relic of a bygone era. The tin church's roofing sounds an incongruous note, but the way it looms in the dusk fog and the crosses marking the English graves combine to present a feeling of timelessness. Check out the stained glass windows, donated by Countess Elgin. Lord Elgin, viceroy of India, is buried here. Open daily 8am-6pm for regular services.

The **Bhagsu-Nag Temple** is 2km from town in Bhagsu-Nag. According to legend, 9035 years ago, there was a drought in the kingdom of Ajmer. In order to save his realm, King Bhagsu headed out to a peak 5400m high, where he discovered two lakes and trapped the waters in his bowl. Unfortunately, as the king lay down to sleep, Nag, the cobra who owned the lakes, challenged him to a fight. Although the heroic king was mortally wounded, he made a a dying wish that the people of Ajmer be rid of the drought. Pleased with Bhagsu's devotion to his people, Nag granted him his wish. The ancient temple at Bhagsu-Nag marks the event and the god's respect for the king (the king's name comes first). A lesser-known result of that fateful battle is today known as the Indira Gandhi Canal, which irrigates most of Rajasthan. The *kund* (pool) is a major bathing site for devout Hindus.

The **Museum of Kangra Art,** Lower Dharamsala, which was established in 1900, houses miniature paintings and local artifacts. (Open Tues.-Sun; free.)

Video parlors keep opening and closing in McLeod Ganj. Surprisingly recent (one year-old) American movies are shown for Rs.10, three or four times a day.

■ Trekking Around Dharamsala

Treks starting from Dharamsala either cross to Manali, or traverse the Dhauladhars to Bhahmaur and Chamba. From Bharmaur, three high passes—the Kugti (5060m), the Chhobia (5200m), and the Kalicho (5600m) cross the Pir Panjal and descend into Lahul.

Tibetan SOS Children's Village and Handicraft Centre

The Children's villages at Leh and Dharamsala are part of a unique initiative started in 1976 under the patronage of the Dalai Lama. Unlike most schools in India, the institute at Choglamsar also has a center where students are carefully taught the intricacies of Tibetan *thanka* painting and carpet weaving, along with other handicraft activities. While those continuing their education move on to Dharamsala, the options presented by an alternative training system means that students interested in pursuing a career in the crafts are well-equipped to earn a livelihood. Take a look at their showroom on the airport road—the prices are reasonable and the manager Tsering Dorje is a helpful guide for a shopping expedition.

Indrahar Pass

This trek starts in Dharamsala, goes on to Triund, Lahesh Cave, Illaqa Gat, and Kuarsi, before ending at Bharmaur. A classic in this region, it is busy during the tourist season. This trek crosses the Indrahur Pass (4425m) on the fourth day. Amazing views of the Dhauladhars, and a strenuous hike.

Minkiani Pass

The less crowded option, goes along a parallel pass after crossing Kareri village and the lake of the same name. A trek worth doing for the lake and the views along the steep trail to the top. The funny bit about these two passes is that although the side facing Dharamsala has no snow by June, the other side will have snow almost until September. This pass also leads into the Chamba district. From Brahmaur: you can either take a bus back to civilized lands, or trek along the *gaddi* routes into Lahul. The *gaddis* are the shepherd of this region, who cross into the green Lahul pastures during the summer months, and return in the winters. The most popular pass is the Kugti, which is approached from Brahmaur via Kugti village. The less-traveled passes—the Chhobia and the Kalicho—are more challenging but just as enjoyable.

■ Dalhousie

Built around five small hills along the edge of the Dhauladhars, this town is named after Lord James Ramsey, Marquis of Dalhousie, who became the Governor General of India in 1848. Today, Dalhousie manages to remain off the tourist trail, and receives far fewer visitors than Dharamsala or Manali. The best way to get here is from Pathankot (a 3½-hr. bus ride). Dalhousie is a long way from other hill towns, 8 hours from Dharamsala and 18 hours by bus from Shimla. Getting oriented can be slightly confusing—it's best to start from Gandhi Chowk from where roads lead to Pathankot, Subhash Chowk, Panch Pulla, and Bakvota. Most of Dalhousie is along these routes.

The **Tourist Information Bureau** (tel. 2136) is opposite the bus stand. There are a number of STD/ISD **telephone** booths. Overpriced **taxis** are the only option for local transportation. **Telephone Code:** 018982.

There are few genuine budget hotels in Dalhousie, and the prices generally double during the season. The best low-range places are the **Moonlight Hotel** (tel. 2439) and **Hotel Glory** (tel. 2533). The **Youth Hostel** offers dorm beds for Rs.35 each, although cleanliness is not a priority here. In the mid-high range, **Hotel Chaanakya** (tel. 2670, 2671) and the **Aroma-n-Claire** (tel. 2199) are lovely, and an excellent value when the prices plummet off-season. Aroma-n-Claire still has 1930s burners reminiscent of the British occupancy. There are a number of *dhabas* near Subhash Chowk and Gandhi Chowk. The **Punjabi** near Subhas Chowk and the **Moti Mahal** near Gandhi Chowk are the pride of an uninspiring bunch.

Panjpulla, 2km from Gandhi Chowk, the site of Five Bridges, is the spot where Ajit Singh, son of the legendary martyr Bhagat Singh, died on the day of Independence. Dainkunt Peak, a beautiful 9km uphill from Gandhi Chowk, is the town from which all the major rivers of the area—the Chenab, the Beas, and the Ravi—can be seen on a clear day. The plains above Khajair, 22km from Dalhousie, aren't that stunning but the **Kalatope Sanctuary,** home to a great variety of wildlife, sits on the ridge above.

■ Manali

Manali is one of those places which just grew out of itself—there is nothing around Manali to explain the thousands who come here during summer, except the presence of others like themselves. Beginning in the 1970s, Manali swelled slowly and then exploded after fighting began in Kashmir. Today, the longest one can walk without passing a hotel is about 80 seconds (between John Banon's and Holiday Home) and during May and June there are more tourists in Manali than coal ovens in Calcutta. Manali is a lot of things for a lot of people—a big market for traders, a hang-out joint for hashish-seeking hippies, *the* destination for honeymooning couples, and the starting point for treks and climbs in this region.

ORIENTATION

Warning: Manali has been touted as the cool place to hang out and smoke hashish; cannabis grows wild around here, but stories of local use have been blown out of proportion. It's used only at times of extreme hard work or in cold weather. Recently, hard drugs like LSD and cocaine have hit Manali and many predict that drug-related crimes and arrests will soon become a problem here as they are in Goa.

From the main bus stand, **the Mall** goes left to **Old Manali** and Hachamba temple, and right across the river, and on to Vashisht and Rohtang. Opposite the bus stand is the maze of alleys and concrete structures called **Model Town.** The **Beas River** cuts through town, roughly parallel to the Mall. The river forks in the **Deodar Forest Reserve,** north of town near Vashisht, and the western fork is called the **Manalsu River.** Across the Beas to the east is **New Manali.**

PRACTICAL INFORMATION

Tourist Office: HPTDC (tel. 52175), on the Mall, 5min. from the bus stand. The helpful staff provides information about hotel accommodation and treks.

Budget Travel: Zillions of them, offering treks and rafting. Treks are around US$30 per day, per person, all inclusive, and rafting is Rs.850 and up per day. The reliable companies are: **Dragon Tours** (tel. 52290, 52790; fax 52669), opposite the bus stand, and **Himalayan Journeys** (tel. 52365, 53355; fax 53065), just after the bus stand, along the old Manali Rd. **Himalayan Adventures,** the Mall (tel. 53050, 52750, 52182), offers standard trekking/rafting fare.

Currency Exchange: State Bank of India, near the Municipal Gardens on the Mall. past the Forest Reserve. Accepts Thomas Cook and AmEx, but not Visa. Open Mon.-Fri. 9am-1:30pm.

Telephones: Plenty of STD booths with call-back facilities (Rs.3 per min.).

Airport: The nearest airport is in Bhuntar, 52km from Manali.

Buses: The main bus stand in Manali has tons of buses going all over Himachal. The buses over Rohtang Ave. depart in the morning, while those to Delhi (16hr.) leave in the mid-afternoon and evening. There are also private deluxe buses to Shimla, Dharamsala, and Delhi, tickets for which you can be booked tickets through any travel agent.

Local Transportation: Expensive **auto-rickshaws** abound in Manali, Old Manali, and Vashisht. There is a **taxi** stand near the tourist office, 5min. up the road from the bus stand.

Hospital: Mission Hospital, Model Town (tel. 52379). **Civil Hospital** next to the deluxe bus stand.

Police: Station is next to the deluxe bus stand (tel. 52326).

Post Office: Head Post Office, right off the Mall past the Mountview Restaurant. *Poste Restante.* Open Mon.-Sat. 9am-5pm.

Telephone Code: 01901.

ACCOMMODATIONS

Accommodations are concentrated in two areas—across the Indian-foreigner divide in Old Manali, and opposite the bus stand in Model Town. Old Manali is about 20 minutes away from the bus stand by foot. Expect prices to drop off-season.

Old Manali

The upmarket hotels are on the right from the bridge, while the quieter guest houses are further up on the road on the left.

Hotel Bridge View. A small place, before the Moondance Café, with extremely basic rooms (2 beds and 4 walls), a common bathroom, and an excellent terrace for the good weather days. In season: singles Rs.75. Doubles Rs.150.

Dragon Guest House (tel. 52290, 52790, 52796; fax 52669). Ideal place, below Hotel Diplomat, set in the middle of an apple orchard with balconies and a terrace overlooking the river below. The rooms are spacious, carpeted, and spotless, with 24-hr. hot running water in the bathroom. In season: rooms Rs.250 and up. Off-season: rooms Rs.175 and up.

Hotel Splendour (tel. 52709). Run by a friendly Delhi couple, Splendour is a quiet small hotel 5min. away from the road, just below Dragon. The hotel is located on a rise, and on a good day, the whole valley from Deo Tibba to Vashisht opens up outside your window. Rooms are carpeted and clean with superb mattresses and a kitchen to feed the hungry. You can also pitch your own tent or rent one on the premises. In season: tent site Rs.50, with tent Rs.100. Rooms Rs.225. Off-season: rooms Rs.150.

Nature Paying Guest House (tel. 52383), Old Manali. Clean rooms a bit on the spartan side. Attached bathrooms with hot water in buckets. In season: rooms Rs.200. Off-season: rooms Rs.150.

Hotel Krishna (tel. 53071). Further up the road from Diplomat, the Krishna has slightly musty doubles. Good value, but breathing space is a problem, since the road is on one side, and the Rockland Hotel blocks air from coming in on the other. Doubles Rs.75.

John Banon's Guest House, Old Manali Rd. (tel. 52335; fax 52392). One of the oldest hotels in Manali, John Banon's was opened in 1960 on the edge of town. A mere 5-min. walk from the Mall, it remains curiously isolated. Spacious rooms with huge windows and a working fireplace. Doubles Rs.500. Reservations recommended a month in advance in season.

Model Town

Mass-produced concrete structures filled with rooms with attached bathrooms proliferate. Prices gyrate wildly here, with up to 70% discounts off-season (bargain hard). There is a wide range: try **Hotel Pushpak** (tel. 53338) or **Hotel Monalisa** (tel. 52447) in the mid-range, and the **Central** or **Ambika** in the lower range.

FOOD

Just after the bus stand on the right is a small maze of alleys with tons of Tibetan "restaurants" which serve *thukpa* and *momos*. Horribly located next to meat shops and dirty paths, their food is authentic and excellent, as well as cheap (Rs.30-40 for a meal).

Sher-e-Punjab. There are at least three Sher-e-Punjabs ("The Lion of Punjab") in Manali—the genuine one has a toilet. Authentic greasy Punjabi food for those of us seeking relief from momos and subtly flavored dishes. *Makki-ki-voti* and *sarson-da-sang* with tons of butter and screw the calories. Decently priced (main dishes Rs.30-50) and a favorite with Indians and enlightened foreigners.

Mountview (tel. 53379), opposite the bus stand. Centrally located, Mountview is a favorite with tourists because of its varied menu and tasteful decor. Main dishes Rs.50-70. A good place to leave notices if you are looking for travel companions.

Moondance Café, Old Manali. A favorite hang-out for hippies addled by hashish, this open-air restaurant offers a decent fare of Chinese and Indian and luncheon food at reasonable prices.

Peter's Café. A small, dingy lane behind the State Bank leads to the psychedelic color and the "Please No Chillums" signs of Pete's Café. An excellent place for breakfast and snacks with Muesli, cheddar cheese toasts, and a variety of eggs—the whole lot costs around Rs.40. The soul behind it all is an institution by himself—the one and only Pete.

Mona Lisa Restaurant (tel. 52448). Next to the bus stand, the congested surroundings are made up for by the excellent food (Rs.45-50 for a main dish). The TV can distract, but the music is good. Crowded in season.

German Bakery, next to the State Bank in Old Manali. Freshly baked bread (Rs.25-30) and pastries (Rs.20-25) go well with coffee.

Madras Hotel, Mission Rd. Authentic South Indian food. Cheap at Rs.30. for a *thali*. The *dosas* are excellent.

SIGHTS

To get to the **Hadimba Temple,** walk along the Old Manali Rd. and take a left after five minutes. Follow the signs. The four-tiered temple with a pagoda-shaped roof is dedicated to the demoness-turned-goddess Hadimba, wife of Bhima. The king rewarded the temple's builder by cutting off his right hand to prevent duplication. Undaunted by the amputation, the builder trained his left hand and constructed a more elaborate temple at Tritoknath. This time, he lost his head.

Arjun Gufa, the site of Arjuna's meditations, the cave is a good 90 minutes from the mall. Cross the bridge, and keep walking (away from Vashisht) until you pass the Holiday Inn. A little further is a small stream and a path leading up. A steep walk takes you to the *gufa*.

Rohtang Pass (3998m), the pass of "dead bodies," is open only from June to September (erratic dates), and is the only motorable way into the Lahul-Spiti area from Manali. Nowadays, it's best described as a rubbish dump—the place is a complete *mela* of tea shops and sled rides, with debris scattered all around. Numerous buses as well as HPTT Tourism tours will take you here.

The **Manu Temple,** in Old Manali is claimed to be the spot where Manu stepped on earth after the great deluge, and the birthplace of the human race. "Manu-Alaya," the "home of Manu," became Manali, although Hashish-Alaya probably suits it better today.

NORTH INDIA

■ Near Manali

Three kilometers from Manali, on a detour from the Rohtang highway, **Vashisht** offers great views of the Pir Panjal range, a relaxed atmosphere, and excellent budget accommodations. The **Hot Bath Complex** run by HPTC is a great relaxant after a tiring trek, although over-indulgence in the sulphurous waters can cause headaches. (Open 7am-1pm and 2-8pm. Rs.25-60.) The stone temple is dedicated to Vashisht Muni, owner of the cow whose milk cannot be exhausted, Kamadhenu. Budget accommodations are plentiful, although in the busy season things get so crowded that floor space is rented out. Rooms are standard, with 2 beds (not too clean) and common bathrooms. Try the **Kalpatru Guest House** (tel. 53443); **Dharma Guest House;** the **Sonam;** or the **Negi Guest House.** All are within a 5-min. radius from the temple, and charge Rs.100-125 for doubles. Food is catered to by a group of glorified *dhabas*—try Dreamland or Freedom—and Superbake for cakes and breads.

The **Mountaineering Institute** is 2km from the center of town, towards Aleo. Various courses in mountaineering, skiing, and water sports are offered throughout the year, with fees ranging from US$170 (skiing) to US$230 (mountaineering, a 4-week course). The institute can also organize trips for larger groups—for more information, write to Mountaineering Institute, H.P. 175131.

■ Treks Around Manali

The classic **Chandratal Lake** trek from Manali, over the Hamta Pass, is amazing for the variation in terrain and the lake at the end of it all. The **Manali-Chhika-Chhatru** trek goes over the Hamta at 4300m. From Chattru, take a bus to Batal, or walk for 2 days. The trek from **Batal to Chandratal** is a long 18-km hike. Return the same way. You can take a bus back from Batal over the Rohtang if available. Another option is to continue onwards from Chandratal to Baralacha La in three days. Again, from Baralacha you can take a bus back, if available.

■ The Kinnaur-Spiti Road

One of the most incredible routes in the world, the road from Shimla traverses all of Kinnaur and Spiti, eventually crossing the Rohtang Pass and descending into Manali.

For much of the route, the only accommodations options are PWD or Irrigation and Public Health (IPH) resthouses. Permits for these are extremely hard to get, and even with a permit you may not get a room if an official turns up. The best thing is to bring a tent and sleeping bag—there are plenty of spots to camp along the way.

The Shimla-Kaza road is open virtually year round, although there are often blockages on the Shimla-Peo stretch. The Kaza-Manali road is theoretically open from mid-June to mid-September, but weather makes Kunzum-La unreliable. You need to get a permit (available in Peo, Shimla, and at the home office in Delhi to groups of four or more accompanied by a travel guide) but won't need to show it until Sumdo.

From Shimla, the road climbs to rainy **Narkanda** (60km), and then descends steeply to **Rampur** (120km), the first major town on the route. A dirty old town, with plenty of waste from all around, Rampur has no decent hotels or restaurants and entry into the spectacular Padam Palace is prohibited. Twenty-three kilometers further is **Jeuri**. Buses depart from Jeuri for the 17-km ride to **Sarahan** (buses at noon, 4:30, and 10:30pm, Rs.200), the site of the architecturally amazing **Bhima-kali Temple.** The temple was the site of human sacrifice until this practice was banned by the British. The road continues along the banks of the wild **Sutlej River** to Rekong-Peo, 70km from Jeuri, the district headquarters of Kinnaur. (see p. 355).

From Peo, elements of Buddhism start creeping in, and by **Pooh,** the town 50km down, most people are Buddhists. The change in beliefs seems to mirror the transformation from greenery to rainshadow; from Pooh onwards, the land is dry and sand, stone, ice, and burning sun seem to dominate everything else in the land Kipling thought was "uninhabitable." Mud houses are bleached by the sun, prayer flags are strung up across hills, and on high ridges protecting the village from evil spirits, a splash of color in the *gompas* marks the beginning of Buddhist country.

Three hours from Peo, at **Khab** (or Khabo), the meeting place of the Spiti and Sutlej Rivers, the road turns left and starts climbing to the plateau at the top. In the middle of this brown plain is a splash of green—Village **Kah.** Further down, in **Yangthang,** you can branch off to see the beautiful lake in **Nako** (14km from Yangthang). **Chango,** 100km from Peo, is one of the most prosperous villages in the region. Check out the Chinese shop in the center, and the ancient temple (13th century) hewn out of a single stone, said to have been made in a day. From Chango the bus proceeds in fits and starts, stopping at **Shalkar,** at the checkpost at **Sumdo** (the Spiti boundary) and then at **Tabo,** made ultra-famous by its millennium celebrations in 1996, when the *kalachakra* ceremony was performed here by the Dalai Lama. Tabo monastery lies in a hot plain 47km from Kaza. Tabo has a PWD rest house. There are also rooms in the *gompa* and some village houses offer one or two rooms.

After Sumdo, the responsibility for road maintenance passes from an army organization to the Public Works Department and the transfer in authority shows. Beyond Tabo, road quality declines sharply—the ride is incredibly bumpy. On the way to Kaza (66km from Tabo) a detour from Shichling (38km) takes you to Dankar *gompa*. The sheer power of the *gompa's* location—precariously perched on towers of shale and mud—is worth the drive. If you walked up, or want to stay the night, the small *gompa* next to the road has accommodations—it's advisable to get your own food.

Strong Stuff

There are two kinds of alcoholic drinks—*chang* and *ghanti*—that abound in the towns along the road to Manali. *Chang* is peaceful. *Ghanti* comes in three varieties, depending on the number of times the barley is brewed. The product of the first brewing, called *moori,* is ultra-strong (70% alcohol) while the third is very light—try to gauge the strength from your first cup.

Donations are expected and appreciated (Rs.50-100). The last big town on the way to Manali is **Kaza** (see p. 356).

From Kaza, the bus goes to **Losar** (50km), winds its way up Kunzum-La (4500m), then drops to Batal. The next checkpost is at **Gramphoo**. The road to Manali climbs to the Rohtang pass and then descends.

■ Rekong-Peo

A small town halfway between Shimla and Tabo, Peo is also the district headquarters of Kinnaur. Just off the main road, the town is a small collection of concrete structures and donkeys which bray deep into the night. A bus to Kalpa offers escape the from cloud of bureaucracy that hangs over Peo. The views of the Kinnaur Kailash are beautiful on the journey up, but bus services are infrequent, and if you are only halting overnight, it's best to stay on at Peo.

ORIENTATION AND PRACTICAL INFORMATION

There is one main road along the **market**. Mandala Tours and Fairlyland Hotel are just above it to the left. A small footpath leads beyond the *dhabas* to the bus stand and the Shivling View Guest House. **Mandala Tours and Travels,** Gongma House (tel. 2504) offers Jeep safaris (Rs.1000 per day) and a trekking guides (Rs.300 per day). The owner, Sher Singh Negi, is friendly, and goes out of his way to help out travelers. Write well in advance, either to the Peo address or to S.S. Negi, c/o Amar Singh Negi, VPO POOH, Pooh Tensil, Kinnaur District, H.P. (tel. 017853-2208). There is one STD/ISD **telephone** booth in Peo market, and it gets crowded. Open daily 6am-9pm. The **bus** stand is just above the town (a 10-min. walk). The **buses** which come from Rampur or Tapri are quite crowded by the time they reach Peo so try and take a bus which originates at Kalpa or Peo for your onward journey. To: Kalpa (8, 9am, 2, and 5:30pm), Shimla (4:30, 7, 4, and 6:15pm), Delhi (11am, 22hr.), Hamirpur (4:30am), Mandi (4:45am), Chandigarh (5:30am), Nako (5:30am), Chitkul (9:15am), Kaza (6:30am with a change at Yangthang and 7:30am), and Rampur (2:30pm). The **police station** is near the market. For **medical assistance,** there is a health center above the town. The **post office** is just next to the bus stand, above the main town (open Mon.-Fri. 9am-1pm and 2-5pm). **Postal Code:** 172107. **Telephone Code:** 017852.

ACCOMMODATIONS AND FOOD

Some hotels have attached restaurants and there are *dhabas* serving Tibetan food along the road between the bus stand and the market. Try A liquor store sells "English" wine and beer in the market.

Shivling View Guest House (tel. 2421), near main bus stand. Conveniently located, this newly developed hotel has only 5 rooms. Hot and cold running water, an in-house restaurant, and clean rooms come as a welcome respite after 14hr. in a smoke-spewing bus. Beautiful view of the Kinnaur Kailash from the terrace. Doubles are Rs.200.

Fairlyland Hotel (tel. 2477), just above the market. Attached restaurant and daily bus service to Kaza and Shimla. Clean rooms, but water is only available for 2hr. in the morning and 2hr. in the evening. Bring a sleeping bag. Doubles Rs.250.

■ Near Rekong-Peo: Kalpa

Kalpa, or Chini-Gaon (Chinese-Village), is 14km north of Peo. Located on a verdant plateau, Kalpa offers breathtaking views of the Kailash range and numerous long walks for the hiker. It is the first predominantly Buddhist village on the way up through the mountains.

Kalpa shares all its facilities with Peo—even the telephone code is the same. There are no separate services here. Three **buses** a day come here from Peo, and buses head

Gompas, Mani Walls, and Chortens

No village in Tibet or adjacent regions of India is complete without the most visual impressions of Buddhism: its own *gompa* where monks pray in an expanse of silence, *chortens* which are built as memorials to dead *lamas*, and *Mani* Walls. Architecturally, *gompas* differ widely across regions, from the cramped and precariously constructed Dankar or Kyi monasteries in Spiti to the spacious and elegant lines of Hemis or Thikse in Ladakh. But once you enter, the familiar smell of salt tea drifts up and you hear the incessant chanting of *lamas*. Most *gompas* are colorful affairs: red and yellow outside, decorated with brightly colored murals depicting various deities and devils on the walls inside, while around the deity exquisite *thankha* hang from rafters. All *gompas* are built high above the village as a symbol of the supremacy of the spiritual leader over the material world. Constructed with mud bricks and sloping walls, monasteries are also the training schools for young monks. When walking around a *gompa* (or *chorten*) always keep the structure to your right, and before entering a monastery be sure to remove any footwear. If turning prayer wheels, rotate them clockwise.

Chortens, white circular structures with a spire on top, are memorials to dead *lamas* and are found in all Buddhist villages of the high mountains. After cremation, a part of the *lama*'s ashes are mixed with clay and molded into a small image of Buddha which is placed, with sacred texts, inside the *chorten.* Remember to keep them to your right as you walk around.

Inscribed with the prayer "Om-Mani-Padme-Hum" ("Hail, Jewel in the Lotus"), the stone *Mani* Walls are believed to shelter the spirits of the departed. Approaching Leh you will see a double line of *manis,* put up by Deldun Namgyal in 1645. The two mani walls are 500 and 360 paces long.

from here to Shimla and Chandigarh. It is also possible to take a **taxi** from Peo (Rs.150) or walk 14km through the forests.

The **Private Guest House** (tel. 6019), 15min. down the road above the PWD rest house, has spacious but dreary rooms, buckets of hot water, and food cooked on order. Doubles Rs.150. The **Timberline Trekking Camps** are next to the village. Ask for the tent colony. The camp is open in April and May. Pleasant but overpriced tents have two beds, chairs, and a table for Rs.950. Reservations possible at 206/207 Allied House, 1 Local Shopping Centre, Madangir, Delhi, 110062 (tel. (011) 643 2903, 643 1746, 621 4037; fax 632 1746). **Food** is available at hotels or at the Tibetan *dhabas* in the center of town.

The *gompa* with the massive statue of Buddha is 20 minutes out of Peo. The site of a *kalachakra* ceremony performed by the Dalai Lama in 1992, the *gompa* is a good place to visit on the way to Kalpa. There are also many short (4-5hr.) hikes around Peo and Kalpa. **It is easy to get lost, especially if clouds come in. Be cautious on the trail or take along someone who knows the route.**

■ Kaza

From Tabo, the road winds up the Sutlej valley, and the ride becomes even bumpier and bumpier. The dust floats through the windows until everybody starts looking like a worker in a cement factory. When you think you've just about had it, the valley broadens out and the vast *matar* (pea) fields and sandy plains of Kaza appear in the distance. Traditionally an important trade center, today Kaza is an important government post, and the first big town on the Manali-Shimla route. Close to the Kyi Monastery, Kaza has a link road to Kibar and great chillout potential.

ORIENTATION AND PRACTICAL INFORMATION

The whole town, both **Old Kaza** and **New Kaza,** lies between the **road** and the **river.** A small **stream** (often dry) separates the new (shining tin roofs) from the old (mud houses and thatched roofs). The **bazaar** and eateries are all in Old Kaza while the hospital, police station and government administrative buildings have come up in the newer part of town. There is a **hospital** (tel. 2218) in a big shed in New Kaza which runs an ambulance service. The **police** station is in New Kaza. The **post office** in Old Kaza, two minutes from the road, sells stamps. Open Mon.-Fri. 9:30am-5:30pm. **Postal Code:** 172114.

ACCOMMODATIONS AND FOOD

Accommodations in Kaza are available from April to November. In addition to the standard options of hotel dining and Tibetan *dhabas* (Rs.15-20 for spicy *thukpa*), Kaza does not offer a great deal of variety for the gourmet. The **Karma Bakery,** next to the bus stand, makes tasty biscuits and breads.

Sakya's Abode (tel. 2213, 2254, 2256). Probably the best place to stay in Kaza, this place is often full. Doubles are clean and have attached bathrooms with running water. The garden, views, cooking, and dining room make this place a favorite. The staff is helpful with general information. Doubles Rs.200.

Zumbala Hotel (tel. 2250), in Old Kaza 5min. from the road. A hulking yellow building, with basic rooms with 2 beds, a dining hall, and a kitchen. Dorm beds Rs.35. Doubles Rs.150.

Milarepa (tel. 2234). Named after the 11th-century Great Sorcerer who repented and, after enduring incredible austerities, attained Buddhahood in one lifetime, this place inflicts few hardships. A mud-brick hotel, Milarepa has doubles with attached baths (a small room with a hole in the ground), but no running water. Rooms and common bathrooms are clean. In-house kitchen and a small dining room help fill empty stomachs. Doubles Rs.100.

■ Near Kaza

The **Kyi Monastery,** 18km from Kaza, is one of the most impressive monasteries in Spiti. Small mud houses containing *lamas* cling to the mountainside, which rises high above the sand plains near Kaza but is dwarfed by the mountainside opposite. The monastery houses 1000 *lamas,* and is an important center for Buddhists around the world. The monastery also houses an exquisite collection at *thankas* which is now kept locked up after reports of theft or purchase by wealthy tourists in other places. The *gompas* in Spiti and upper Kinnaur are smaller than those in Ladakh—the tiny mud rooms have a musty, heavy atmosphere that conjures up images of incessant chanting and ceremonial trumpets. Kyi is connected to Kaza by two morning buses but it is also possible to stop off on the way back from Kibber or take a taxi from Kaza.

A small path from Kaza leads to Village **Kaumik** high above. It takes two to three hours to walk here but the views are stunning, especially at sunset.

A link road from Kaza leads to **Kibber,** which at 4250m is reputed to be the highest village in the world reachable by motor vehicle. The bus from Kaza leaves early in the morning (7am) for the 28-km ride to Kibber, and returns after only 15 minutes. If 15 minutes isn't enough here, it is possible to walk back to Kaza, although the four-hour

Stiff Demons

After banging their heads repeatedly on small doors, many travelers begin to wonder (provided they can still think at all) why many entrances and exits seem to be boobie-trapped. It's to hinder the progress of evil spirits. The deal is that the spirits are as tall as humans but cannot bend, and therefore small doors bar their way (and the way of flexible but absent-minded travelers).

hike is hot and dusty. Apart from the altitude, Kibber is like many other Himachal villages, with white mudbrick houses, thatched roofs, a *dhaba* (with great *alu paratha*) and a couple of family-run guesthouses. Kibber is at the start of a trail through the high Parang La pass that used to be used by people carrying goods to the Leh bazaar on ponies and yaks.

Jammu and Kashmir

The northernmost state in India, Jammu and Kashmir rolls over 222,000 square kilometers of mountains, valleys, and plateaus, only two-thirds of which are in fact controlled by India. The rest of the state, in portions to the northwest and northeast, are ruled by Pakistan and China respectively. Kashmir is India's most volatile region, and travelers are advised not to visit the western part of the state, which is currently the site of an armed insurgency. The beautiful capital, Srinagar, in the west, whose balmy lake was once a major attraction, is now dangerous to visit. However, the violence has so far been confined to the western half of the state, which includes the verdant Kashmir Valley, which is predominantly Muslim, and the region of Jammu, populated by Dogra Hindus. The eastern part of the state, comprising the Tibetan Buddhist regions of Ladakh and Zanskar, remains free from violence. Leh in Ladakh has to some extent replaced Srinagar as a major tourist destination.

Kashmir's troubles began when India was partitioned along religious lines in 1947. Although the population of Kashmir was predominantly Muslim, the Hindu raja did not want to let his kingdom become part of Pakistan—and Kashmiri Muslim leaders agreed with him. But in late 1947, thousands of Pathan tribesmen, supplied with arms by Pakistan, rushed across the border in an attempt to force Kashmir into Pakistan. Desperate, the maharaja turned his state over to India in exchange for military help. The Indian government accepted the offer, promising that a plebiscite would be held to determine whether the Kashmiri people, and not just the maharaja, wanted to join India. When the shooting stopped, however, Pakistan had snatched a large chunk of Kashmir. In 1962 China annexed the area of the state now known as Aksai Chin. India and Pakistan went to war over Kashmir again in 1965, although no territory changed hands. The 1948 cease-fire line remains the de facto India-Pakistan border.

Kashmir is politically important to both India and Pakistan. As a Muslim-majority area, Kashmir is an important part of Pakistan's theory that all of South Asia's Muslims belong in a separate homeland. But India sees Kashmir's apparent choice to remain part of India as vindication of its tolerant secularism. (Both claims seem to fall apart when force is needed to control the state.) Competing with the two claims is a Kashmiri nationalist movement seeking total independence.

Since the 1947 conflict, both India and Pakistan have worked to integrate their respective slices of Kashmir into their nations. During the 1950s and 60s, the Indian portion of Kashmir remained somewhat autonomous, with a special status in India's constitution. But in the 1970s and 80s, the prominent Kashmiri leader Sheikh Abdullah, who had at times leaned toward independence, and his son Farooq Abdullah, who succeeded him, moved closer to Delhi. Kashmiri fears of absorption into India led to an outbreak of violence in 1989. Since that time, the western half of Indian-held Kashmir has been battered by the Jammu and Kashmir Liberation Front (JKLF), fighting for total independence; by various Islamic groups fighting for a merger with Pakistan; and by the Indian army, whose troops now occupy the state. While India accuses Pakistan of supplying arms to the rebels, human rights groups accuse the Indian army of torturing and summarily executing its opponents. Meanwhile, fruit exports and tourism, Kashmir's main sources of income, are smothered by civil war. In 1995 five foreign tourists were taken hostage in Kashmir; one of them was executed. But with Kashmir shakily under control, India held elections in the state in

May and September 1996, with decent voter participation. Many see this as a sign that the government has regained control, and that the insurrection is slowly dying.

> **Warning:** Travelers are advised not to visit the western half of Jammu and Kashmir, including the Kashmir Valley and the Jammu region. Foreign tourists have been targeted in recent acts of violence.

■ The Manali-Leh Road

Two roads connect Leh to the rest of the world. Both are two-day hauls, and involve crossing passes well over 5000m. These roads are supposed to be open from early June-September, but in the last few years weather conditions have been atrocious and the road condition is totally unreliable (If you are on a tight schedule, fly down). The **Srinagar-Leh** route is not safe for foreign travelers. The **Manali-Leh Road,** the world's second-highest motorable road, is crowded with buses, cars, and motorcycles during the summer. The road was opened to foreign travelers in 1989. It is a two-day journey that crosses the Rohtang pass (3980m) to get into the rainshadow and then the Baralacha La (4892m) and Tanglang La (5325m) before descending to Upshi and following the Indus River to Leh. The trip costs Rs.700 in a private bus, Rs.1600 in a public bus, and Rs.10,000 in a taxi. Although the route is amazing, the thrill begins to wear off after 20 hours on a crowded bus, and most travelers are delighted to see the signs that they've finally arrived—the crumbling palace, the prayer flags high above the town, and an old man turning a giant prayer wheel.

■ Leh

> **Warning: When arriving by road, carry your passport with you at all times** since this is a border region in an unstable state. The routes to Leh come close to areas under Pakistani control, and there are checkpoints along both roads.
>   **When arriving by plane,** remember that Leh is 3505m above sea level. **Rest for a day** before undertaking anything strenuous, and **watch for any signs of acute mountain sickness (AMS).** The symptoms—headaches, breathlessness and nausea—normally develop during the first 36 hours and not immediately upon arrival (see p. 58). Leh has an emergency facility for dealing with AMS (tel. 212, 213, 214 daily 10am-4pm, tel. 520 24hr.).

Leh, the capital of Ladakh, is remarkably different from other towns in the region. Located at the corner of a desert plateau, Leh has developed to cater to the tremendous influx of tourists it receives every summer. Open-air bars, travel agents, bakeries, and guest houses abound, and most visitors spend five or six days soaking it all in and revelling in this curious East-West cauldron. While the town itself has a lot to offer—the palace, Sankar Gompa, Shanti Stupa, numerous *chang* bars—Leh is also an ideal starting point for treks in Ladakh or for visiting the famous monasteries of Thikse, Hemis, Alchi, and Lamayuru. In older days, traders used to come from all over, via the Karchovam Pass (5600m), the Chang-La (5574m) or the Khardung-La to this important center.

ORIENTATION

The huge **palace** towers over the north-east part of town, called **Old Town,** and is a landmark that is almost always visible. The **bazaar** is south of the palace and marks the center of town. **Old Fort Road** heads west out of the bazaar towards the neighborhood of Suku. **Library Road,** which runs north to south, intersects Fort Rd. about five minutes west of the bazaar. Most restaurants and hotels are concentrated in this area and north along **Chamspar Lane,** which heads west off Library Rd. The **bus stand** is five minutes south of the bazaar, off **Airport Road.**

PRACTICAL INFORMATION

Tourist Office: Tourist Information Centre (tel. 2497, 2295). Inconveniently located 2km from town on Airport Rd., but worth a visit. Offers brochures on Ladakh and staff helps with trips around Leh. Also hires out trekking equipment.

Budget Travel: There is a travel agent every 2m in Leh, and all kinds of excursions are offered, from river-rafting to mountaineering. Although all travel agents are registered, not all are qualified to handle high-risk activities. Ask around to find out who to trust. **Snow Leopard,** P.O. Box 46 (tel. 52074; fax 52355) and **Ibex Tours and Travels** (tel. 52661) are well-reputed agencies that handle trekking and rafting. **Explorer TransHimalayan Agency,** Old Fort Rd., P. O. Box 14 (tel. 52048; fax 52735). Walk down Old Fort Rd. for 5min. beyond Dreamland. A good place to go if you want to trek on a tight budget. The travelers' shop (owned by the same person) hires out equipment (tents Rs.50-90, sleeping bags Rs.50 per day). Guides are Rs.300-350, and the manager will arrange routes without taking a commission. Yak Hotel and the tourist office also hire out trekking equipment.

Currency Exchange: State Bank of India (Old Fort Rd., next to the Taxi stand), **Hotel Khangla Chan,** and **Hotel Singye Palace** on Airport Rd.

Telephones: STD/ISD booths abound and connections are good, although rates are very high.

Airport: (tel. 53388), 4km from Leh. **ModiLuft** and **Indian Airlines** both operate out of Leh. Flights are often delayed and/or canceled depending on the weather. During summer, flights to Leh are booked up well in advance—plan your trip several months ahead. The Modiluft office is next to the taxi stand, while the Indian Airlines office is beyond Hotel Rafica. To: Delhi (Mon.-Tues., Thurs., and Sat. 1-2 per day, 1-3hr., US$86); Jammu (Mon.-Tues., Thurs., and Sat. 1-2 per day, 1hr.,

US$50); Chandigarh (Tues., 1hr., US$56); and Srinagar (Sat., 1hr., US$43). **Batteries and lighters are not allowed in carry-on luggage flown out of Leh. Bags are opened and checked at least twice.**

Buses: (tel. 3982 for the private bus office). Turn right from the filling station on the airport road. Both state and private buses have routes here. Depending on weather and road conditions, schedules change frequently. It's best to check the day before for information on routes and times.

Local Transportation: The **taxi** union is in the center of town. There are fixed rates for all destinations during the season (July-Aug.). Bargain with the driver off-season. Tourist season rates are about Rs.10 per km for a roundtrip fare, Rs.15 per km for one way. The best way around town is on **foot.**

English Bookstore: Book Worm and **Prakash,** just off Fort Rd. towards the castle, sell second-hand books. Prices are exorbitant—try and point out to the seller that the new book price is lower than his second-hand one. **Artou's** (Zangsty Rd.) has a decent collection of books on Ladakh while **Syed Ali's** postcard shop in the old town puts up photographic exhibitions.

Library: The best library is in the **Ecology Development Centre,** next to Mona Lisa. Open 10am-5pm.

Cultural Center: Mahabodi Society, left on the Zangsty T, then right and follow signs. Meditation meetings Mon.-Sat. at 5:30pm. The center has a library and information counter. Open Mon.-Sat. 11am-8pm.

Laundry: Leh does not have a water refining plant, so all dirty water feeds into the river. All the runoff from laundry, done individually or by hotels, eventually finds its way into the river, and can be extremely polluting because of the use of non-bio-degradable detergents. An eco-friendly women's organization runs **DZOMSA,** a laundry service with 2 pickup points in Leh. It protects the river by using a desert pit away from Leh. The service is highly recommended.

Hospital: SNM Hospital (tel. 52014), just before the bus station. Well-maintained, with 2 ambulances.

Police: Station (tel. 52018) is just left of the Zangsty Rd. T-junction.

Post Office: GPO, 2km from town next to the tourist office. Open Mon.-Fri. 9:30am-5:30pm. There are **post boxes** all around Leh and stamps can be bought at Syed Ali's. **Postal Code:** 194101.

Telephone Code: 01982.

ACCOMMODATIONS

Accommodations in Leh are concentrated in three sections: the center of town, where the most expensive hotels are; Karzoo and Chamspar, which is quiet and pleasant; and Old Town, where cheap prices compensate for the crowded alleys. Most places are clean, but check on the water situation before taking a room. Hotels in Leh are classified into classes A, B, and C and guest houses into upper-class and economy. In season, rates for doubles range from Rs.1800 in an A-class hotel with all meals included to Rs.250 at an economy guest house, and the rates vary depending on the tourist traffic. A-class hotels are worth checking out off-season since rates plummet. It's always advisable to carry a sleeping bag.

Old Ladakh

Namgyal Guest House, near Polo Ground. Cut across the polo ground and start drifting aimlessly around—the Namgyal is hidden behind a number of large *chortens,* just behind the large auditorium. A family-run mud-brick house. The Namgyal is popular with those on tight budgets. Common baths. In season: doubles Rs.60-80.

Old Ladakh Guest House, near Royal Palace. The oldest guest house in Leh (established in 1975). Small alleys lead up to this mud and wood guest home, with traditional Ladakhi rooms, complete with Tibetan carpets hanging from the walls. Five rooms are kept open throughout the year. Movie hall next door is slightly noisy. In season: doubles Rs.150-300. Write ahead for reservations in season.

Palace View Guest House, near Polo Ground. Extremely standard and a bit cramped. Hot water in buckets. In season: doubles Rs.100.

Karzoo and Chamspar

Two Star (tel. 52250). The 2 stars are the owner's kids. This place's rating would be more like five stars. The mudbrick house is set in the middle of a vegetable garden with a water channel running through. Ideal place to have a cold beer at the end of the day. Further attractions are the Ladakhi dining hall and the extremely friendly owner (G.O. Giri). Attached baths. In season: doubles Rs.200.

Rainbow Guest House, around 15min. from the center of town. From the Zangsty road crossing turn left, and then right (follow the signs). Although the Rainbow is a bit cramped, the rooms are clean with windows looking out on green fields. Kitchen serves breakfast and snacks. In season: doubles Rs.150.

Center of Town

Hotel Skalzang, Old Rd. (tel. 52304). Along the road from the airport just before the bus station. The rooms are clean and basic and hot water is provided in buckets. A good place to stay if you are in Leh for a short while and have a lot of luggage. In season: doubles Rs.250.

Indus Guest House, Pharka. Further down the alley from Bimla is this all-time tourist favorite. A Ladakhi-style sitting room (carpets on the floor with exquisite hand-carved tables), a wide variety of rooms catering to different budgets, and views of the palace make the Indus a crowded place. One of the oldest guest houses (founded in 1977). The Indus also comes out tops during winter, when *bukharis* (wood-heated stoves) are used in every room. Doubles Rs.150-400.

Behind Palace

Antelope Guest House, Sankar Rd. (tel. 52086). Central, but just about far enough to be quiet. The shortcut to the Antelope is straight down from Syed Ali's; the normal way is to continue along the road from Mona Lisa. Beyond the glaring stuffed yak in the garden await clean rooms with attached baths, a restaurant, and travel services. Doubles Rs.100, with bath Rs.250.

FOOD

Food in Leh is a curious combination of Chinese and Tibetan cuisine, although if you are sick of the *thukpa-momo*-chow mein combo, several restaurants serve various versions of Italian and Kashmiri dishes.

> **Warning: Do not drink the water in Leh.** There is no sewage system and no clean water except in bottles. **Meat is unsafe to eat.** It has usually been transported in unrefrigerated trucks for at least two days.

Tibetan Kitchen, further down Old Fort Rd. and impossible to miss. Elegant decor and a variety of daily specials. Good soups (Rs.25) and kitchen specials such as noodles with mushroom and cheese. Main dishes Rs.30-50.

Wok Restaurant, just before the mosque, on the 2nd floor. A favorite with locals serving Tibetan-Chinese standards at reasonable prices.

Mona Lisa Restaurant, to the right from Zangsty Rd. T-junction. Open air bar and restaurant with high chill-out potential. Beer Rs.55 per bottle, meat dishes Rs.60-70. A good place to leave notices if you need partners for a trek.

Pumpernickel German Bakery, Old Fort Rd. and Market. Indulge your sweet tooth. Besides serving an amazing variety of desserts (Rs.25-30) the German Bakery does an excellent Yak cheese-tomato sandwich (Rs.28). One of the few places in Ladakh that plays Jethro Tull. A great place for light lunch or dinner.

Summer Harvest, Old Fort Rd., next to Dreamland. A central location, a decent breakfast, and a menu which includes North Indian stuff, apart from the routine *thukpa–momo*-chow mein combo. One of the few places in Leh where one can find standard Delhi *dhaba* food such as mixed vegetables (Rs.30), *raita* (Rs.20), and rice.

Mentokhling Restaurant, Zangsty Rd. just left of the Zangsty Rd. T-junction. Open-air bar and restaurant.

The Ecological Development Centre

The Ecological Development Centre, left from the Zangsty-T in Leh is a brave attempt to re-examine conventional notions of "development" and to re-think policy prescriptions for Ladakh. Helena Norberg Hodge, one of the driving forces of the project (and its founder), has been working in Ladakh for the last 15 years, and is the author of numerous books, including *Ancient Futures.* The center screens a video on Ladakh at 4:30pm on Monday, Wednesday, and Friday off-season and everyday in season, and distributes a pamphlet on dos and don'ts for tourists in Ladakh. The complex has a small library on mountain regions. The center has ongoing projects which need volunteers from time to time.

SIGHTS

Sengge Namgyal's nine-story **Palace,** in the Old Town, was started in 1553 and was said to have inspired the Potala in Lhasa. Follow signs for the palace from next to the mosque; it is clearly visible from every house in Leh. The palace contains 1000-year old *thankas,* gold statues, and swords. In its prime, a lion guided by a rope would enter and leave a cage roaring every time the East Gate was opened. The palace was badly damaged during the war with General Zorawar Singh and today only a small temple on the first floor is accessible to visitors. (Open daily 7am-5pm; admission Rs.51). High above the palace, the Khang-La (House of God) in the red **Tsemo Gompa** contains the amazing two-story statue of Chamba in meditation. Ask a monk to open the door. (Open daily 7am-9pm; admission Rs.5).

A long line of prayer flags flutter in the wind, connecting the granite tops above the **Old Leh Castle and Gompa.** Toil up from the Chamba statue for another 10 minutes, and you will reach a blue sign which announces your arrival to the "Castle." In a broken-down and dilapidated condition, the main reason to go up here is for the excellent views of Leh and the Stok-Kangri range.

Referred to by the locals as the "Japan Stupa," the **Shanti Stupa,** Chamspar village, 3km west of the bazaar (walk to Chamspar and the follow a direct line to the *stupa*) is up 560 steps (excellent for acclimatization) that lead you panting and puffing to the legacy of Fujii Guraji, a Japanese Buddhist who moved to India in 1931. One of several monuments erected in India by Japanese Buddhists, the white *stupa* was built in 1983, and features gilt panels showing episodes from Buddha's life. (Open daily 5am-7pm.)

The **Zorawar Fort** was built by General Zorawar in 1836 and was the site of the successful stand by the Dogras against repeated Chinese attacks from 1847 onwards. It is under reconstruction at the moment, and will open to visitors around 1998.

The reading of the *namaz* can be heard throughout Leh five times each day from the large **Leh Mosque** at one end of the main market. The mosque, like many monasteries in the area, was built by Singge Namgyal as a gift for his mother, Avgyal Khatoon, Princess of Skawdu. Built in 1555, the large and imposing mosque displays Turkish and Iranian architecture at its best.

Walk along the footpath across the fields from the Ecological Centre to get to the **Sankar Gompa,** the official residence of the reformist Gelug-pa (Yellow hat) sect. The main deity is the hundred-headed, thousand-armed Avalokitesvara. (Open daily 7-10am and 5-7pm; admission Rs.10.)

SHOPPING

There are plenty of opportunities to shop (and get ripped off) in Leh. Masks, carpets, jewelry, clothing and so-called "antiques" abound in the shops around the main market, but prices are often significantly higher than Delhi, Shimla or Dharamsala, and most of the traders are Kashmiris who come to Leh only during the tourist season. The two places worth a visit are the **TCV Handicrafts Centre** (see p. 349) next to the filling station and the **Co-operative stores** in the Galdan hotel complex just off the Old Fort Rd. Both sell a variety of objects made by Ladakhi craftsmen, at reasonable, fixed prices. Shopping elsewhere closely resembles a sophisticated mugging.

■ Near Leh

Sixteen kilometers from Leh is **Shey,** the summer palace built by Deldun Namgyal, son of the famous Singge Namgyal. Walk up to the *gompa* (entry Rs.5) and see the three-story-high Buddha, built in 1633. Just to the left of the *gompa* is a victory *stupa,* topped with pure gold.

Built by the intrepid constructor Singge Namgyal, the expansive *gompa* **Thikse** is accentuated by an open courtyard decorated with murals and a giant prayer flag. The Du-Khang, up a steep flight of stairs, houses the ancient image and scriptures. Once a year, at the time of the Thikse Gustor festival (Nov. 17-18, 1997), giant *thankas* are unraveled and displayed. Climb up to the roof of the old Kali temple and library. The incredible views of the Indus valley plains around Leh and the Stok-Kaupri range beckon from across the river. *Gompa* admission Rs.15. Buses leave every hour from the stand in Leh.

Forty-two kilometers from Leh is the Ladakh's largest and richest monastery, **Hemis.** The ideal time to go here is during the festival held in June or July when people from all over Ladakh trek down for a few days of rituals and festivities. Old, old villagers wearing *lams* (shoes made of yak skin and wool) and twirling prayer wheels mingle with foreigners to watch the unraveling of the immense *thanka*—said to be the largest in the world—which is hung for two hours from the side of the palace. (The main competition for this *thanka* also comes from Hemis—there is yet another one which is shown only once every 12 years (next time is 2004). This *lamasey* is a wide and sprawling mud-brick building with several chambers built by Singge Namgyal in 1620. The presiding deity is a Buddha inlaid with precious stones. You can get here either by bus (one in the morning—not too reliable) or taxi (Rs.825 roundtrip to Leh).

■ Trekking Around Leh

Leh-Kaza via Parang-La

This beautiful trek goes by the 23-km-long Tsomoriri Lake at 4480m. The pastures surrounding Tsomoriri are used by *changpas* (nomads) to graze yaks and goats. The trek crosses the Parang-La at 5490m. and then descends down to Kibber and Kaza. It is an extremely demanding trek. On the fourth day of the trek, one crosses the Phirsta Phu, a river which originates in the swamps of Tibet. The river usually flows from Tibet to Tso Morivi, but seasonally, when the water levels change, it reverses its flow.

Nubra Valley Trek

Opened recently to tourists, the Nubra valley is reached by crossing the highest motorable pass in the world—the Khardung-La at 5414m. The Nubra valley is famous for the double-humped camels which were used in earlier days for transport along the ancient silk route. The trek goes through Khaphang meditation center and finishes at Khalsen (9 days).

Stok-Hemis via Markha Valley

This is a classic trek with well-defined trails and bridges across rivers. It can be cut short after crossing the Stok-La by coming down to Runbak (3 days). The visits to *gompas* are separated by enough trekking days to avoid cultural overload. Cross the Stok-La (4900m) to Yurutse, and then onto Maukha village and Hemis (8 days, with plenty of acclimatization required before crossing the Stok-La).

EAST INDIA

West Bengal

The river Ganga starts its sweeping turn toward the sea in West Bengal, creating the world's largest delta, criss-crossed by brown rivers and inlaid with rice paddies. West Bengal is India's most cultivated state, with 65% of its land used for farming, and as a result it is also India's most densely populated state, with 766 people per square kilometer. It is a land where nature is uncertain: the silty soil is devoid of rocks, substitutes for which are baked in the coal-powered brick kilns whose smokestacks dot the landscape. Bengali roofs are curved as a precaution against cyclones.

Growing on India's eastern frontier, Bengal has been far enough from the center of North Indian civilization to develop its own language, Bengali, and its own religious traditions. Until the present millennium, most Bengalis worshiped indigenous goddesses, and while West Bengal was brought into the Hindu tradition, East Bengal converted to Islam. Bengal's position at the mouth of the Ganga made it a rich agricultural and commercial region, attracting European plunderers in the 17th and 18th centuries. After the Battle of Plassey in 1757, when Robert Clive defeated Nawab Siraj-ud-Daula and claimed Bengal for Britain, Bengal became preeminent in British India. Exposed to British rule for so long, Bengalis initiated the 19th-century revival of Indian culture. Among the leaders of the Bengal Renaissance was Rabindranath Tagore, India's greatest modern poet, whose songs still permeate the land. Massive protests and terrorism foiled a British attempt to partition Bengal along religious lines in 1905. But when India was partitioned in 1947 the eastern half of Bengal became East Pakistan, eventually becoming independent Bangladesh in 1971.

West Bengal's capital, Calcutta, is the hub of eastern India. Most visitors only stay in West Bengal long enough to see Calcutta and Darjeeling, the northern hill station that is more like a lost fragment of Nepal. To the south of Calcutta, however, are the Sunderbans, the world's largest mangrove forest. In the central portion of the state is Santiniketan, home of the university founded by Tagore, and numerous historic cities such as Bishnupur, Murshidabad, Maldah, Gaur, and Pandua, their buildings now elegantly decaying.

■ Calcutta

Eastern India's great urban center, Calcutta draws passionate reactions from almost every visitor, even those who've heard of Calcutta's legendary poverty and suffering. The sidewalks are jigsawed apart and populated by bookstands, beggars, and men selling squeaky toys—one can't just walk down the street in Calcutta, one must step into it, over and around it, breathing in layers of snot-blackening soot. Humans trot through the traffic by day, hauling the world's last fleet of hand-pulled rickshaws; families by the thousands roll up to sleep on the pavement at night. Calcutta can sometimes seem like a human version of one of the terrible cyclones that ravage the Bengal coast. Yet the same Calcuttans who lament their city's traffic jams, power cuts, and crowded suburbs and slums (in a city of 12 million people), also sing of their hometown as a warm and compassionate metropolis, a "City of Joy." Calcutta churns out poets and painters and saints, becoming India's cultural capital. From the rain on moldy pavement around its parks and palaces, Calcutta musters an exuberance no other Indian city can match.

Calcutta is a British-built city, founded by the East India Company agent Job Charnock, who bought three villages on the bank of the Hooghly River to set up a trading post in 1690. Bengal, rich in rice and textiles and far from the Mughal emperor, made an ideal base for early European merchants. By 1750 the British "factory" at Calcutta had swollen into a city of over 100,000, complete with a fort. This upstart success irked the nawab of Bengal, Siraj-ud-Daula, who attacked Calcutta in 1756, while his underlings stuffed the surrendering British into the infamous "Black Hole" prison. The following year the British retaliated, sending Robert Clive to defeat Siraj at the Battle of Plassey. Bengal became the first large chunk of India to be ruled directly by the East India Company. In 1773 Calcutta became capital of all British lands in India.

As the British plundered Bengal, they transformed Calcutta into India's main commercial center, filling its ships with opium and indigo and fanning railroads out from it to the rest of eastern India. The first British governor-general, Warren Hastings (r. 1774-1785), attempting to impress Indians with pomp and ceremony, crammed Calcutta with gardens and mansions, making it into a place for *sahibs* to dine and duel. For its power and majesty Calcutta soon became known as the "second city of the British Empire." Meanwhile, the "natives" of the capital got more than their share of the blessings and betrayals of British rule—some were granted an English education. An elite group of Calcuttans asserted themselves in the 19th-century Bengal Renaissance. Ram Mohan Roy (1774-1833) started the trend, pushing for social and religious reform. Calcutta's upper-class mansions hosted a revolution in literature, music, dance, and painting, culminating with the work of Rabindranath Tagore. Calcutta also became a center for virulent anti-British politics. When the British tried to partition Bengal in 1905, they were met with bombs and boycotts. The city that grew from a British trading post was becoming fervently Indian.

Even at the end of the 19th century, however, Calcutta had its critics. Rudyard Kipling, judging the city filthy and crowded, called Calcutta a "Chance-erected, chance-directed, city of Dreadful Night." A series of blows in the 20th century would give Calcutta the squalid reputation it has today. After abandoning plans to partition Bengal, the British moved their capital to Delhi in 1911. Meanwhile, the Suez Canal route to Europe gave Bombay a commercial advantage over Calcutta. Most devastating, however, was the 1947 Partition, in which East Bengal became part of Pakistan, while Calcutta and West Bengal remained in India. Calcutta was smashed by riots and swamped with refugees, and its industries were cut off from their agricultural base in the east. Urban problems have mounted since Independence, with millions of migrants arriving from various parts of India. West Bengal's communist government, in power since 1977, has done little to alleviate Calcutta's problems. Mutterings about Calcutta being a "dead city" abound. But with flashing neon billboards and roadside electronics shacks, Calcutta is now gaining the trappings of a regular Asian metropolis. In 1984 Calcutta inaugurated its Metro, the first such system in India, and the government is currently developing Salt Lake to the east as a "second Calcutta." Ambivalent about its traditions, Calcutta squelches along, tracking the past behind it with heavy steps.

ORIENTATION

Calcutta is among the world's largest cities, and most maps (including the ones in this book), brush off its details without giving a sense of the distances involved. Street names, too, are unhelpful. Often there's a choice to be made between the government's proud new name for a street and the familiar colonial name that everyone uses (if they use one at all). This guide sticks to whichever is more useful, case-by-case, but watch out for alternatives. Mercifully, Calcutta's layout is straightforward. The city sits on the east bank of the Hooghly River and hugs the **Maidan,** a huge and conspicuously spacious central park near the river. Most of Calcutta's main thoroughfares run north-south, east of or north of the Maidan.

The most important road is **Chowringhee Lane (Jawaharlal Nehru Road),** which forms the Maidan's east edge. Most of Calcutta's hotels, shops, and restaurants for tourists are in the Chowringhee area. The real tourist ghetto is **Sudder Street,** near the north end of Chowringhee, where the budget hotels are piled. **Park Street,** coming off Chowringhee at an angle farther south, has many good shops and restaurants.

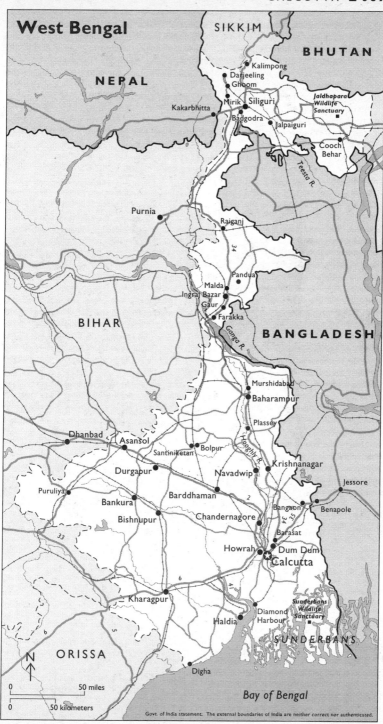

West Bengal

SIKKIM

BHUTAN

NEPAL

Kalimpong
Darjeeling
Ghoom
Mirik   Siliguri
Kakarbhitta   Bagdogra
Jalpaiguri

*Jaldhapara
Wildlife
Sanctuary*

Cooch
Behar

Teesta R.

Purnia

Raiganj

34

Pandua

Malda
Ingraj Bazar
Gaur
Farakka

BIHAR

BANGLADESH

Ganga R.

Murshidabad
Baharampur

Plassey

Dhanbad   Asansol
Santiniketan   Bolpur
Durgapur

Hooghly R.

Krishnanagar

Navadwip

Jessore

Puruliya

Barddhaman

Bankura

2

Bishnupur

Chandernagore

Bangaon
Benapole

34
35

Barasat

33

Howrah   Dum Dum
Calcutta

Kharagpur

6

4

Diamond
Harbour

*Sunderbans
Wildlife
Sanctuary*

Haldia

SUNDERBANS

5

N

ORISSA

6

Digha

0   50 miles
0   50 kilometers

Bay of Bengal

Govt. of India statement. The external boundaries of India are neither correct nor authenticated.

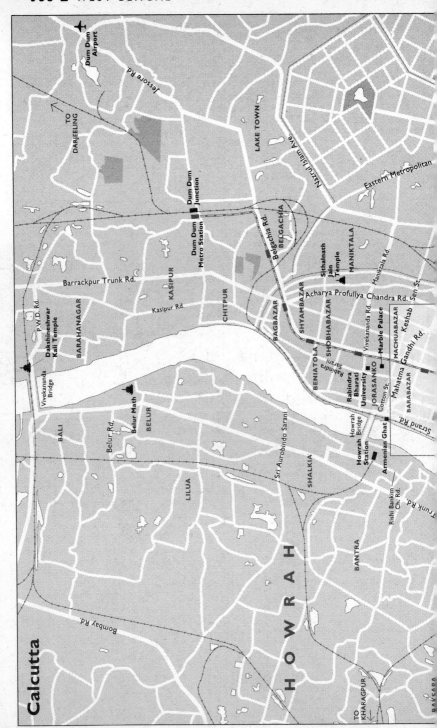

Calcutta

TO DARJEELING

Dum Dum Airport

Jessore Rd.

LAKE TOWN

Nazrul Islam Ave.

Eastern Metropolitan

Dum Dum Junction

Dum Dum Metro Station

Belgachia Rd.

BELGACHIA

Barrackpur Trunk Rd.

KASIPUR

Kasipur Rd.

CHITPUR

BAGBAZAR

SHYAMBAZAR

Sithalnath Jain Temple

MANIKTALA

Maniktala Rd.

Sen St.

Acharya Profullya Chandra Rd.

Gandhi Rd.

Keshab

SHOBHABAZAR

Vivekananda Rd.

Marble Palace

MACHUABAZAR

P.W.D. Rd.

Dakshineshwar Kali Temple

BARAHANAGAR

BENIATOLA

Rabindra Sarani

Rabindra Bharati University

JORASANKO

Cotton St.

BARABAZAR

Mahatma Gandhi Rd.

Strand Rd.

Vivekananda Bridge

BALI

Belur Rd.

Belur Math

BELUR

Sri Aurobindo Sarani

Howrah Bridge

Howrah Station

Armenian Ghat

LILUA

SHALKIA

Rishi Bankim Ch. Rd.

BANTRA

H O W R A H

Trunk Rd.

Bombay Rd.

TO KHARAGPUR

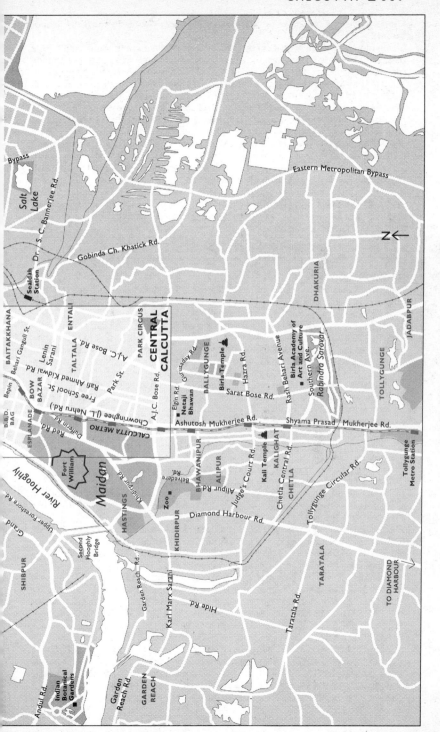

Connecting the two, parallel to Chowringhee, is **Mirza Ghalib Street (Free School Street).**

Downtown Calcutta is north of the Maidan, centered around the square known as **BBD Bag** (formerly Dalhousie Sq.). The main bus depot is close by, at the **Esplanade** (rhymes with "hand grenade"), at the north end of Chowringhee on the corner of the Maidan. **Chittaranjan Avenue** and **Government Place West** (which becomes **Netaji Subhas Road**) are two of the large north-south streets leading through central Calcutta into North Calcutta. **Strand Road** runs all along the riverside, from the Maidan to North Calcutta. **Mahatma Gandhi Road** (M.G. Rd. or Harrison Rd.) is the main east-west route in North Calcutta.

South Calcutta is the area past **Acharya Jagadish Chandra (AJC) Bose Road (Lower Circular Rd.),** the south edge of the Maidan (AJC Bose Rd. also turns north and runs east of Chowringhee—this was once a ring road for the city.) **Ashutosh Mukherjee Road,** the extension of Chowringhee in the south, heads straight down through South Calcutta. Two bridges cross the Hooghly to **Howrah.** The beams and girders of the **Howrah Bridge** attach Strand Rd. in North Calcutta to Howrah Station. South at the end of the Maidan is the more modern and sprightly **Second Hooghly Bridge.** The **Grand Trunk Road** is the main road through Howrah.

GETTING THERE AND AWAY

By Air

Dum Dum Airport, officially called Netaji Subhas Chandra Bose Airport (tel. 511 8070, -9), is 2km northeast of the city. The prepaid taxi stand in the domestic terminal is the best bet for a reasonably priced ride into downtown Calcutta (1hr., Rs.87). City buses #303, #46, and #510 (Rs.2) and the less direct E3 (Rs.5) all run between the Esplanade and the airport. Minibus #151 (Rs.10) goes from BBD Bag to the airport. The airport has a money exchange counter (to the left in the international terminal), a post office (domestic terminal), West Bengal and India tourist offices, and the carriers Indian Airlines, East-West Airlines, Modiluft, Jet Airlines, Sahara India Airlines, and Skyline NEPC. The train ticket counter has tickets to Delhi, Bombay, and Madras only. With proof of a layover of under 24 hours, the airport manager in the Domestic Terminal can arrange beds for tired, transitory travelers.

All carriers also have offices at the airport. **Domestic Airlines:** Indian Airlines, 39 Chittaranjan Ave. (tel. 266869, 262548, 264433; fax 262415). Open 24hr.; tourist window (number 12) open daily 9am-7pm. Hotel Hindustan branch, 235/1 AJC Bose Rd. (tel. 247 6606). Open Mon.-Sat. 10am-1:15pm and 2-6:30pm. Great Eastern Hotel branch, 1-3 Old Court House St., 2nd fl. (tel. 248 0073, 248 8009). Open Mon.-Sat. 10am-1:30pm and 2-5pm. East West Airlines, 2A Sarat Bose Rd., 1st fl. Naragane Bldg. (tel. 745179, -80, airport branch tel. 511 8782, -87, ext. 2416, 2417). Open Mon.-Fri. 9:30am-1pm and 2-5:30pm. Jet Airways, 230 AJC Bose Rd. (tel. 240 8646). Open Mon.-Fri. 9am-1pm and 2-5pm. ModiLuft, 2 Russell St. (tel. 297301, 297006, 298437, 298438, 294236). Open Mon.-Fri. 9:30am-8pm. Skyline NEPC, 25 Sarat Bose Rd. (tel. 745226, -9). Open Mon.-Fri. 9:30am-1:30pm and 2-5:30pm. Sahara, 2A Shakespeare Sarani (tel. 242 8969, 242 7686, 242 9067, 242 9075). Open Mon.-Sat. 9am-5pm. **International Airlines:** AeroFlot, 58 Chowringhee Lane (tel. 242 9831, 242 3765). Open Mon.-Fri. 9:30am-1pm and 2-5:30pm, Sat. 9:30am-1pm. Air France, 46 Chowringhee Lane (tel. 296161). Open Mon.-Fri. 9am-5:30pm. Air India, 50 Chowringhee Lane (tel. 242 2356, 242 1187). Open daily 9:30am-5pm. Alitalia, 228A AJC Bose Rd. (tel. 247 1777, 247 5794). Open Mon.-Fri. 9am-1pm and 1:30-5:30pm, Sat. 9am-1:30pm. American, 2-7 Sarat Bose Rd. (tel. 745 091, -3). Open Mon.-Fri. 9am-1pm and 1:30-5:30pm, Sat. 9am-1:30pm. Air Canada, Gulf Air, and TWA, 230A AJC Bose Rd. (tel. 247 2526, 247 5576). Open Mon.-Fri. 9am-1pm and 1:30-5:30pm, Sat. 9am-1:30pm. Bangladesh Biman, 30A AJC Bose Rd. (tel. 292844, 293709). Open Mon.-Fri. 9am-1:30pm and 2-5:50pm. British Airways, 41 Chowringhee Lane (tel. 299162, 293450, 293453, -4). Open Mon.-Sat. 9:30am-1pm and 2-5:30pm. Canadian, SAS, South African, and United, 2-7 Sarat Bose Rd. (tel. 747622, -3, 745370). Open Mon.-Fri. 9am-1pm and 2-5:30pm, Sat. 9:30am-1pm. Cathay

Pacific, 1 Middleton St. (tel. 403 2112). Open Mon.-Fri. 9:30am-1pm and 2-5:30pm, Sat. 9:30am-1:30pm. Delta, 13D Russell St. (tel. 293873, 293826). Open Mon.-Fri. 9:30am-5pm, Sat. 9:30am-1pm. Japan Airlines, 35A Chowringhee Lane (tel. 298370). Open Mon.-Fri. 9:30am-1:30pm and 2-5:30pm, Sat. 9:30am-1pm. KLM, 1 Middleton St., Jeevan Deep (tel. 240 4452, airport branch tel. 511 8329). Open Mon.-Fri. 9am-5pm, Sat. 9am-1pm. Lufthansa, 30A/B Chowringhee Lane (tel. 299365; fax 294010). Open Mon.-Fri. 9am-1pm and 1:30-5:30pm. RNAC, 41 Chowringhee Lane (tel. 293949, 298534). Open Mon.-Fri. 9am-1pm and 1:30-5:30pm, Sat. 9am-1pm. Thai, 18G Park St. (tel. 299 8464). Open daily 24hr; tourist window (number 12) open Mon.-Fri. 9am-1pm and 2-5pm.

To: Bagdogra (1-2 per day, 1hr., US$65); Bangalore (2 per day, 3½hr., US$203); Bhubaneswar (Tues.-Sun. 1-2 per day, 1hr., US$62); Bombay (5-6 per day, 2hr. 40min., US$175); Delhi (5-7 per day, 2hr., US$151); Guwahati (4-5 per day, 1hr. 10min., US$58); Hyderabad (1-2 per day, 2hr., US$163); Lucknow (Mon., Wed., and Fri., 2½hr., US$119); Madras (3-4 per day, 2hr., US$172); Patna (Fri.-Wed., 1½hr., US$70); Port Blair (Mon., Wed., and Fri., 2hr., US$166); Dhaka (2-4 per day, 70min., US$57); Kathmandu (Thurs.-Tues., 1½hr., US$96).

By Rail

Calcutta has two stations, **Sealdah Station,** northeast on AJC Bose Rd., with trains to the north, and **Howrah Station,** across the Hooghly River from Calcutta, with trains to the south and the rest of India. The best way to get to or from Howrah Station is by ferry at Fairlie Place (Rs.1.50). There is a prepaid taxi stand at the station (Rs.24 to downtown Calcutta), but the Howrah Bridge is notoriously congested. There is a West Bengal Tourist Office here. Open Mon.-Sat. 7am-1am, Sun. 7am-12:30pm. Tickets can be purchased at the **Railway Booking Office,** 6 Fairlie Place (tel. 220 3496), near BBD Bag. The Foreign Tourist Office is on the first floor. Stairs are on your right as you enter. Helpful staff and air-conditioned, but expect long lines. There are other train offices scattered around the city but this is the only one that sells from the tourist quota. Pay in foreign currency or rupees with encashment certificate.

From Sealdah Station, trains depart to: New Jalpaiguri (for Darjeeling; *Darjeeling Mail* 3143, 7:15pm, 13hr.; *Kanchenjunga Exp.* 5657, 6:25am, 12hr., Rs.126/523 for 2nd/1st class); Patna (*Sealdah-Delhi Exp.* 3111, 8:15pm, 11hr., Rs.111/457 for 2nd/1st class). From Howrah Station, trains depart to: Bhubaneswar (*Rajdhani Exp.* 2422, 7½hr., Rs.94/388 for 2nd/1st class); Bombay (*Howrah-Bombay Mail* 8002, 7:20pm, 12hr.; *Howrah-Bombay Mail* 3003, 8pm, 15½hr.; *Geetanjali Exp.* 2860, 12:30pm, 9hr., Rs.235/1144 for 2nd/1st class); Delhi (*Rajdhani Exp.* 2305, 1:45pm, 20hr.; *Rajdhani Exp.* 2301, 4:30pm, 17hr.; *Poorva Exp.* 2381 and 2303, 9:15am, 23hr., Rs.207/921 for 2nd/1st class); Madras (*Coromandal Exp.* 2841, 2:05pm, 27½hr.; *Madras Mail* 6003, 8:30pm, 33hr., Rs.218/1014 for 2nd/1st class); Patna (*Rajdhani Exp.* 2305, 1:45pm, 7hr., Rs.111/457 for 2nd/1st class); Puri (*Howrah-Puri Exp.* 8007, 10:15pm, 10hr.; *Sri Jagannath Exp.* 8409, 7pm, 11hr., Rs.102/421 for 2nd/1st class); Varanasi (*Howrah-Amritsar Mail* 3005, 7:20pm, 15hr., Rs.127/536 for 2nd/1st class).

By Bus

Buses are not an ideal way of getting to or from Calcutta. **Private buses** go to Siliguri (12hr.), a departure point for Darjeeling and Jalpaiguri. The most direct bus is run by West Bengal Tourism, departing Calcutta at 6pm, reaching Siliguri at 6am and Jalpaiguri at 11am (Rs.152). Tickets must be purchased in advance at the booth at the Esplanade; turn left off of Chowringhee Lane on S.N. Banerjee Rd. and the booth is on the right just before the tram tracks. Other private bus company booths are located to the left (follow the tracks). The bus to the Bangladesh border leaves at 6:45am. Make other bus enquiries at the bus ticket building to the right of these tracks (open daily 7am-6pm). No schedules are printed. Ask—it's all in their heads.

By Boat

Ships to Port Blair are erratic. Enquire at the Shipping Corporation Office, Strand Rd. (tel. 248 2354). Two blocks south of the Railway Booking Office, enter through the main entrance, go through the back door and up one floor. Ship fare is Rs.330/1200/1620 for bunk/2nd/1st class. Expect long lines; ships fill up weeks before departure. The **Silver Jet,** located just opposite the Shipping Corporation Office on the river bank, is a new catamaran service between Calcutta and Haldia. Boats leave Calcutta at 7:45am and 4pm and return at 9:50am and 6pm (2hr., Rs.400-1000).

GETTING AROUND

By Ferry

Ferries run on the Hooghly River from Howrah Station to Fairlie Place (train reservation office) to Babu (Chandral) Ghat every 10min. (Rs.1.50). They are the best and most enjoyable way to cross the Hooghly River.

By Taxi

The most convenient way to cover long distances in Calcutta is by taking one of the cabs that fill the streets. Name your destination and only get into the cab if the driver recognizes it. Don't ask about the price. If the driver states a charge and refuses to use the meter, get out of the cab; it's an argument you can't win. The meter begins at Rs.4, and there is a conversion chart to take into account the rising cost of gas. The fare should be a little less than double the meter—that is, while it is still light out. After dark, you're at the driver's mercy as far as the fare is concerned; you're always at the driver's mercy in terms of road safety. The prepaid taxi counters at the airport and Howrah Station may have long lines, but are worth waiting for. Fares are Rs.87 and Rs.24, respectively, to the center of the city.

By Bus

Calcutta's sluggish bus system is plagued by never-ending crowds and confusion. The buses are difficult to figure out; the best recourse is to ask a local what bus you need and hope that they know. Destinations are posted on the front of every bus (Rs.2—if you can get on). Published routes are available at most bookstands. Private mini-buses are also available (Rs.7) and ply similar routes, with similar crowds and confusion. Their routes are listed with those of the city buses.

By Rickshaw

Calcutta is one of the few cities in the world that still have **hand-pulled rickshaws** vying for space on the road. Understandably, rickshaw-*wallahs* have a short life-expectancy. In most cases, you can walk faster than they can pull. **Auto-rickshaws** can be quite efficient, but leave you open to breathe all the exhaust fumes.

By Tram

Trams are the major cause of traffic jams in the city, and there has been talk about removing them for 10 years now. Trams depart from the central Esplanade for their routes; they are slow and sporadically crowded. A list of routes can be purchased at any bookstand.

By Metro

India's first metro opened in 1984, extends in a virtually straight line from Tollygunge, up Chowringhee Lane to Dum Dum Station. From this station, a taxi or auto-rickshaw to the airport takes 45min. with traffic (Rs.40-50). The metro is relatively uncrowded and rapid (Rs.1-3). The metro line, of course, is limited to certain destinations; extensions to this line are planned before a new line will be built. Open Mon.-Sat. 8am-8:30pm, Sun. 3-8:30pm.

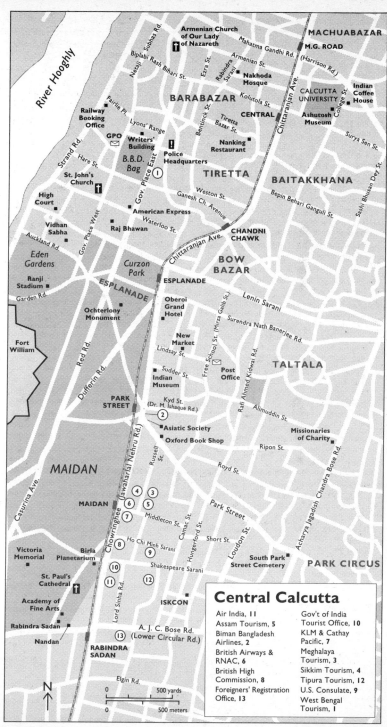

River Hooghly

MACHUABAZAR

Armenian Church of Our Lady of Nazareth

M.G. ROAD (Harrison Rd.)

Mahatma Gandhi Rd.

Biplabi Rash Bihari St.

Netaji Subhas Rd.

Armenian St.

Rabindra Sarani

Ezra St.

Nakhoda Mosque

BARABAZAR

Kolutola St.

CALCUTTA UNIVERSITY

College St.

Indian Coffee House

Railway Booking Office

Fairlie Pl.

Lyons' Range

Bentinck St.

Tiretta Bazar St.

CENTRAL

Ashutosh Museum

Surya Sen St.

GPO

Strand Rd.

Hare St.

Writers' Building

B.B.D. Bag

Police Headquarters

Nanking Restaurant

TIRETTA

BAITAKKHANA

St. John's Church

①

Gov. Place East

Weston St.

Ganesh Ch. Avenue

Bepin Behari Ganguli St.

Sashi Bhusan Dey St.

High Court

American Express

Waterloo St.

CHANDNI CHAWK

Vidhan Sabha

Auckland Rd.

Raj Bhawan

Gov. Place West

Chittaranjan Ave.

BOW BAZAR

Eden Gardens

Curzon Park

ESPLANADE

Ranji Stadium

Garden Rd.

ESPLANADE

Red Rd.

Oberoi Grand Hotel

Lenin Sarani

Mirza Galib St.

Surendra Nath Banerjee Rd.

Ochterlony Monument

New Market

Lindsay St.

Free School St.

Post Office

Rafi Ahmed Kidwai Rd.

TALTALA

Fort William

Dufferin Rd.

Sudder St.

Indian Museum

PARK STREET

Kyd St. (Dr. M. Ishaque Rd.)

②

Alimuddin St.

Missionaries of Charity

Asiatic Society

Oxford Book Shop

Ripon St.

Acharya Jagadish Chandra Bose Rd.

Russell St.

Royd St.

MAIDAN

Chowringhee (Jawaharlal Nehru Rd.)

④ ③

MAIDAN

⑥ ⑤

⑦

Middleton St.

Camac St.

Hungerford St.

Park Street

Victoria Memorial

Birla Planetarium

⑧

Ho Chi Minh Sarani

⑨

Short St.

Loudon St.

PARK CIRCUS

⑩

Shakespeare Sarani

South Park Street Cemetery

St. Paul's Cathedral

⑪

⑫

Academy of Fine Arts

Lord Sinha Rd.

ISKCON

Rabindra Sadan

Nandan

⑬

A. J. C. Bose Rd. (Lower Circular Rd.)

RABINDRA SADAN

Casuarina Ave.

N

Elgin Rd.

0   500 yards
0   500 meters

Central Calcutta

Air India, 11
Assam Tourism, 5
Biman Bangladesh Airlines, 2
British Airways & RNAC, 6
British High Commission, 8
Foreigners' Registration Office, 13

Gov't of India Tourist Office, 10
KLM & Cathay Pacific, 7
Meghalaya Tourism, 3
Sikkim Tourism, 4
Tipura Tourism, 12
U.S. Consulate, 9
West Bengal Tourism, 1

PRACTICAL INFORMATION

Tourist Office: Government of India Tourist Office, 4 Shakespeare Sarani (tel. 242 1402, 242 5318; fax 242 3521). The best source of information, this office provides customized computer printouts for desired locations in India. Ask for the map of Calcutta and the pamphlet of cultural events, *Calcutta This Fortnight.* Open Mon.-Fri 9am-6pm, Sat. 9am-1pm. Branch in the domestic terminal of Dum Dum Airport. **West Bengal Tourist Bureau,** 3/2 BBD Bag E. (tel. 248 8271). Open Mon.-Sat. 7am-1:30pm and 2:15-5:30pm, Sun. and holidays 7am-noon. Publishes *Calcutta This Fortnight* and provides tours of the city (full day, Rs.75). Information and tours for all of West Bengal. Passes available for wildlife parks and the Marble Palace. Information counters at airport and Howrah Station (tel. 660 2518). Open daily 7am-1pm. **State Tourist Offices: Andaman and Nicobar Islands,** 3A Auckland Pl. (tel. 247 5084). Open Mon.-Fri. 10am-6pm. In the CMDA Bldg. **Arunachal Pradesh,** 4B Chowringhee Pl. (tel. 248 6500). **Assam,** 8 Russell St. (tel. 298331). Open Mon.-Fri. 10am-4:30pm. **Manipur,** 25 Ashutosh Shastri Rd. (tel. 747937). **Mizoram,** 24 Old Ballygunge Rd. (tel. 475 7034). Open Mon.-Fri. 9am-5pm. **Nagaland,** 13 Shakespeare Sarani. **Sikkim,** 5/2 Russell St. Poonam Bldg., 4th fl. (tel. 29716, 244 6717). Open Mon.-Fri. 10am-5pm. **Tripura,** 1 Pretoria St. **Orissa,** 55 Lenin Sarani (tel. 244 3653). Open Mon.-Fri. 10:30am-4pm. **Bihar,** 26B Camac St. (tel. 247 0821), upstairs. Open Mon.-Fri. 9am-4pm.

Budget Travel: Every street corner seems to have a travel agent. Thomas Cook and AmEx also provide full service to members.

Diplomatic Missions: Bangladesh, 9 Circus Ave. (tel. 247 5208). **Bhutan,** 48 Tivoli Court (tel. 241301). **Denmark,** McLeod House, 3 Netaji Subhas Rd. (tel. 248 7478). Open Mon.-Fri. 9am-1pm. **France,** 26 Park Mansions, off inner courtyard (tel. 290978, 292793). Open Mon.-Fri. 10am-1pm. **Germany,** 1 Hastings Park Rd. (tel. 479-1141). Open, Mon.-Fri. 9am-4pm, Sat. 9am-noon. **Italy,** 3 Raja Santosh Rd., Alipur (tel. 479 2426). Open Mon.-Fri. 9am-4pm. **Japan,** 12 Pretoria St. (tel. 242 2241, -45). Open Mon.-Fri. 9am-1pm and 2-5pm. **Nepal,** 19 National Library Ave. (tel. 479 1003). One photo needed for visa (visas also available at the border). Open Mon.-Fri. 9:30am-12:30pm and 1:30-4:30pm. **Netherlands,** 18A Brabourne Rd. (tel. 220 8515). Open Mon.-Fri. 10-11:30am. **Thailand,** 18B Mandville Gardens (tel. 407836, 760836). Open Mon.-Fri. 9am-noon. **U.S.,** 5/1 Ho Chi Minh Sarani (tel. 242 3611). Open Mon.-Fri. 8:30am-12:30pm and 2-4pm. **U.K.,** 1 Ho Chi Minh Sarani (tel. 242 5171). Open Mon.-Fri. 9am-noon. **Sri Lanka,** Nicco House, 2 Hare St. (tel. 285102). Open Mon.-Fri. 10am-5:30pm.

Immigration Office: Foreigners Registration Office, 237 AJC Bose Rd. (tel. 247 3301). Provides long term visa extensions and work visas only. Open Mon.-Fri. 9am-1pm and 2-4pm.

Currency Exchange: Banque National de Paris, 4A BBD Bag E. (tel. 248 2166, 248 0197). Open Mon.-Fri. 10am-5pm, Sat. 10am-2pm. **Citibank,** 43 Chowringhee Lane (tel. 249 2484). Open Mon.-Fri. 10am-2pm, Sat. 10am-noon. **ANZ Grindlays,** 19 Netaji Subhas Rd. (tel. 220 1959). Window 3. Open Mon.-Sat. 10am-1:30pm. **State Bank of India,** Dum Dum Airport, international terminal. Open 24hr. **Hong Kong and Shanghai,** 8 Netaji Subhas Rd. (tel. 248 6363, -9). Holds mail. Open Mon.-Fri. 9am-4pm.

American Express: 21 Old Court House St. (tel. 248 2133, 248 9555; fax 248 8096). Travel services, currency exchange. Open Mon.-Sat. 9:30am-6:30pm.

Thomas Cook: 230A AJC Bose Rd., Chitrakut Bldg., 2nd fl., side entrance (tel. 247 4560; fax 247 5854). Travel office, currency exchange. Open Mon.-Sat. 9:30am-1pm and 1:45-6pm.

Telephones: STD/ISD booths are located throughout the city, and most have fax services. **Central Telegraph Office,** 8 Red Cross Pl. Open 24hr.

Luggage Storage: Howrah Station cloak room, track 12. Rs.3-6 per 24hr. Luggage must be locked. Note the "Beware of Rats" sign. Many of the nicer **hotels** also offer luggage storage.

English Bookstore: Oxford Book Store, Park St. (tel. 297662). Carries everything from Clive Cussler to James Joyce. Open Mon.-Fri. 10am-8pm, Sat. 10am-1pm. **The Modern Book Depot,** 15A Chowringhee Lane (tel. 249 3102). Just west of New

Market across the street from Light House cinemas at the entrance to Shreeran Arcade. Open Mon.-Fri. 10am-7:30pm, Sat. 10am-4:30pm. **Maps: Survey of India Map Sales Office,** 13 Wood St. Sign in; the guard will point the way. Many maps are restricted, but there is a good selection of trekking maps.

Library: National Library, Alipur Rd. near the zoo. India's largest library with 2 million books in all of the official languages. Ask for access as a casual visitor. Open Mon.-Sat. 9am-8pm, Sun. 10am-6pm. **Asiatic Society of Bengal,** 1 Park St. A Calcutta institution dating back to 1784. The best place to go to study Persian manuscripts and 19th-century academic tomes. Adjacent museum contains paintings by Rubens and Reynolds. Open Mon.-Fri. 10am-6pm. **U.S. Consulate,** 5/1 Ho Chi Minh Sarani (tel. 242 3611). Open Mon.-Fri. 10am-1pm and 2-4pm. **British Council,** 5 Shakespeare Sarani (tel. 242 5378, -80, 242 9108, 242 9144; fax 242 4804). Membership Rs.400. Open Tues.-Sat. 10:30am-6:30pm. **USIS,** 38A Chowringhee Lane (tel. 242 1211, -8). Open Mon.-Fri. 10am-6pm.

English Media: *The Statesman* (daily), *The Telegraph* (weekly); both newspapers focus on Calcutta. Nationwide English publications can be found in newsstands. *Calcutta This Fortnight,* published by West Bengal Tourism, provides entertainment schedules; copies available at the tourism office. *The Asian Age* (daily), a new newspaper, has an informative entertainment section.

Cultural Centers: Alliance Française, 24 Park Mansions, Park St., next to French Consulate, off inner courtyard (tel. 298793; fax 242 2863). **British Council,** 5 Shakespeare Sarani (tel. 242 5378, -80; fax 242 4804). Open Tues.-Sat. 10:30am-6:30pm. **USIS,** 38A Chowringhee Lane (tel. 245 1211, -8). Open Mon.-Fri. 10am-6pm. **Academy of Fine Arts,** Cathedral Rd. (tel. 248 4302). **Rabindra Sadan,** corner of Cathedral Rd. and AJC Bose Rd. **Birla Academy of Art and Culture,** Southern Rd.

Hospital: Kothari Medical Centre, 8/3 Alipur Rd. (tel. 479 2557). Highly recommended English-speaking doctors.

Pharmacy: Common throughout the city. **Dey's Medical Store, Ltd.,** 6A Nell Sengupta Sarani (tel. 249 9810, -1), on the left where Madge St. intersects New Market. Particularly large and well-stocked. Open Mon.-Fri. 8:30am-9pm, Sat. 8:30am-5pm.

Police: Police Headquarters, Lal Bazaar (tel. 255900, -15).

Emergency: Police: tel. 100.

Post Office: GPO, BBD Bag (tel. 248 2574). *Poste Restante.* Let the people outside help you avoid lines. Open Mon.-Sat. 7am-8:30pm. **Branch post offices:** Airport, Russell St., Park St., Mirza Ghalib St. **New Market Post Office** is just opposite Sudder St. on Free School St. **Postal Code:** 700001.

Telephone Code: 033.

ACCOMMODATIONS

There is a shortage of budget accommodations in Calcutta. Those that do exist are concentrated in the area around Sudder St. and New Market. A few others are located off Chittaranjan Rd., south of the Indian Airlines office, and also to the northeast of New Market. Calcutta's hotels are generally open 24 hours, but rooms often fill up before noon.

Salvation Army Red Shield Guest House, 2 Sudder St. (tel. 245 0599). Cheapest place to stay in Calcutta. Many of the people that stay here work for Mother Teresa. It's a clean hostel-like environment. Luggage storage Rs.5. Dorm beds Rs.40. Doubles with bath Rs.150-200.

Hotel Maria, 5/1 Sudder St. (tel. 245 0860). A spartan but congenial hotel. Often very crowded, with guests spilling out into the entry-way. Mattresses on roof Rs.40. Dorm beds Rs.50. Singles with bath Rs.150. Doubles Rs.120, with bath Rs.200. Triples Rs.300.

Modern Lodge, 1 Stuart Lane (tel. 244 4960). From east end of Sudder St., across from Astoria Hotel and down a small street on the left, upstairs. Run by an affable, who loves budget travelers. Breezy rooms, especially on the roof. Tables on the roof where drinks can be ordered in the evenings. Singles Rs.50. Doubles Rs.70-90, with bath Rs.120-200.

Hotel Paragon, 2 Stuart Lane (tel. 244 2445). Located behind the Maria Guest House on Sudder St. and across the street from the Modern Lodge. The first-floor rooms are cheerier than the somewhat-dingy ground-floor rooms. Dorm beds Rs.45-50. Singles Rs.90-100. Doubles Rs.110-150, with bath Rs.160.

Gujrah Guest House, Lindsay St. (tel. 244 0392, 245 6066; fax 5109). Circle around the right side of Lindsay Hotel and turn left on an alley behind the hotel. Rooms are upstairs on the left past the guard shack, 3rd floor. Clean and well-maintained facilities. No air-conditioning. Singles Rs.170. Doubles Rs.210, with bath Rs.390-520.

Centerpoint Guest House, 20 Mirza Ghalib St. (tel. 244 3928). Rather claustrophobic, but clean. Doubles Rs.175, with A/C Rs.350. Triples Rs.250.

Deeba Guest House, 18 Mirza Ghalib St. (tel. 244 9415). Next door to the Centerpoint. Often full, it is similar to but cleaner than its neighbor, with a patriarchal host. Singles Rs.110. Doubles Rs.250.

Times Guest House, 3 Sudder St. (tel. 245 1796). Upstairs near the Blue Sky Café, not far from the Tourist Inn. Sikh-run and friendly. Higher prices, but not upscale. Open daily 5am-1am. Dorm beds Rs.100. Doubles Rs.150.

Continental Guest House, 30A Mirza Ghalib St. (tel. 245 0663). Enter through courtyard from Sudder St. to 1st and 2nd floors. Not costly, but also not too cozy. Singles Rs.90. Doubles with bath Rs.130-150.

Tourist Inn, midway down Sudder St. Across the street from the Diplomat. Small and clean rooms. Common area is good for socializing. Free drinking water. Singles Rs.85. Doubles Rs.150, with A/C Rs.500.

Hotel Delux, B/33/H/4 Mirza Ghalib St. (tel. 292703). Hidden in a back alley. Follow signs for Hotel Paramount, opposite the How Hua Restaurant on Mirza Ghalib St., just south of Sudder St. Walk down alley, past Hotel Paramount and Ruby Hotel, and turn right. At the end of this narrow passage, behind Hotel Shab-nam, hides Hotel Delux on the 2nd floor. Good ventilation in clean, small rooms, but air-conditioning entails an extra charge. Singles Rs.150-200. Doubles Rs.200.

Palace Hotel, 13 Chowringhee Lane (tel. 244 6214). Next to Blue Sky Café on Sudder St., midway down on the south side. Enter through the courtyard in the back. Only 2 singles, but they're nice. Singles Rs.150. Doubles Rs.200.

East End Hotel, Kyd St. (tel. 298921). Right off Mirza Ghalib, 2 blocks off Sudder St. Expensive relative to the quality of the rooms. Singles Rs.200-250. Doubles Rs.350, with A/C Rs.450.

Hotel Neelam, 11 Kyd St. (tel. 299198). Across the street from East End Hotel in the orange house. More spacious rooms. Singles Rs.150. Doubles Rs.250-300, with A/C Rs.350.

Classic Hotel, 6/1A Kyd St. (tel. 290256). Just off Mirza Ghalib St., next to Mehfil restaurant and Dunlop House. Cramped and strangely aromatic. Singles Rs.115. Doubles Rs.205, with A/C Rs.450.

Broadway Hotel, 27A Ganesh Chandra Ave. (tel. 263930, -2; fax 264151). One block west on Chittaranjan Ave. from Indian Airlines office (towards Chittaranjan Ave.). One block down on Ganesh Chandra Ave., directly across the street from Mission Café. Rough around the edges, but clean, large rooms with ceiling fans. Authentic and popular. Open 6am-11pm. Singles with bath and TV Rs.220. Doubles Rs.320.

YWCA, 1 Middleton Rd. (tel. 297033). Right near intersection with Park St. All meals are included, as is access to badminton, lawn tennis, and table tennis. Open to both men and women. Doubles Rs.255, with bath Rs.410.

YMCA, 25 Chowringhee Lane (tel. 249 2192; fax 249 2234). From Sudder St., right on Chowringhee Lane and YMCA is on the right immediately. Large rooms, breakfast and dinner included. Dorm beds Rs.110, with dinner Rs.220. Singles Rs.325, with A/C Rs.565. Doubles Rs.460, with A/C Rs.730.

FOOD

Good food is not difficult to find in Calcutta. In addition to the Chinese and standard Indian fare that most restaurants serve, Bengali cuisine is also hot on the scene. Bengali cuisine consists largely or rice and fish, with mustard seasoning, but for the newly arrived, the difference might be difficult to distinguish. *Kati* rolls are readily available on the street along with a variety of Indian sweets—those whose stomachs that are strong enough for street food may want to peruse the stands that dot the city, particularly on Park St. The highest concentration of restaurants are here, many dating back to the jazz scene of the 1960s and 70s. Most restaurants close around 10 or 11pm, and reopen 12 hours later or even sooner if they serve breakfast.

Abdul Khalique and Sons Restaurant, 32 Marique Amir Rd. One block south of Sudder St. near the Jamuna Movie Theatre. Plate of rice Rs.1.50, eggrolls Rs.5, meat entrees Rs.5-10.

Khalsa Restaurant, Madge Lane, just north of Salvation Army Guest House on the left. Serves the best economy meals around Sudder St. Thick *dal* Rs.8. Open late.

The Friend's House and **Sarang House,** across the street from the Lighthouse and New Empire Movie Theaters, between New Market and Chowringhee Lane, 1 street north of Lindsay St. Excellent places for lunch or a snack (Rs.12-30). Wide selection of *dosas* (Rs.15), chum chum (Rs.3).

Blue Sky Café and **Zurich's,** 3 Sudder St., midway down Sudder St. at the corner of Chowringhee Lane. Both budget traveler hangouts, they even serve breakfast. The Blue Sky Café tends to be more popular and has a real budget traveler feel, while Zurich's has larger chairs, a quieter atmosphere, and arguably better food.

Nizam's, 22/25 New Market (tel. 245 2663). Northeast of New Market. Ask for directions—everyone knows where it is. Good *kabobs* in nest-like private booths. Delivery available.

La Bucheto Pizzeria/Snack Bar, 5 Old Court House St. (tel. 220 1225). Just north of the Great Eastern Hotel and American Express (across the street). Join the businessmen as they lunch here in air-conditioned comfort. Black-and-white decor for the fashion conscious. Margherita pizza Rs.35.

Mehfil Restaurant, 54 Mirza Ghalib St. (tel. 292059). Two blocks south of Sudder St. on the right. A sunken room at the corner. Excellent eggrolls Rs.7 and mutton dishes Rs.16.

Café 48, Mirza Ghalib St., 2 blocks south of Sudder St. next to Rambo Beer Pub on the right. Delicious veggie options. Entrees Rs.15-30.

How Hua, Mazha Ghalib St. (tel. 297819). Across from Hotel Paramount, south of Sudder St. Good Chinese food in clean dining room. Entrees Rs.40-80.

Badshah, Lindsay St., left off Madge Lane at New Market on the left. An old, ornate bar and restaurant, its glory days can only be reminisced about now. Good selection of fish; fish fry Rs.26. Thunderbolt beer Rs.45. Open 11am-10pm.

Mission Café, Ganesh Chandra Ave. Across the street from the Broadway Hotel. One block west of Indian Airlines office off Chittaranjan Ave. Yummy *masala dosa* (Rs.5-20).

Jharokha Rooftop Restaurant, 8A Lindsay St. Enter through Lindsay Hotel. Take elevator to 10th floor. Keep going until you see the patio. Decent Chinese food, but the real reason to come here is the spectacular view of Calcutta's skyline and the soaring 'Chil.' Entrees Rs.35-45. *Paneer butter masala* Rs.30.

Tulika's Ice Cream Parlor, Russell St., next to the post office across the street from the Royal Calcutta Turf Club. Possibly the best ice cream in Calcutta. Dutch chocolate Rs.14, black currant Rs.17. Take Tulika's ecstasy home with cakes and pastries. Open 8am-11pm.

India's Hobby Ctr., 1A Russell St., just on right from Park St. Houses Ice Cream Counter of Hobby Shop, Tulika's only competition, and, in back, Big Max—Indian fast food. Hot dogs Rs.31, veggie burgers Rs.27, and meat burgers Rs.40. Open daily 11am-11:30pm.

Flurys, 18 Park St. Large white building on the corner. A Calcutta tradition and a great place to relax. The café has a large pastry and sweets shop. Ask for a pastry assortment (Rs.8.50) with your tea while you decide what to take home. Open daily 6:30am-8pm.

Nahoum's and Sons, New Market. Northeast of the center in New Market. This bakery is worth the search. Open Mon.-Fri. 9am-8pm, Sat. 9am-3pm.

Hare Krishna Bakery, at the corner of Russell and Middleton St., 2 blocks west of the U.S. consulate. Excellent bread and other pastries. Open 10:30am-8:30pm.

Haldiram Bhujiawala, AJC Bose Rd. at the corner of Chowringhee Lane next to the AeroFlot office. One of the most popular sweet shops in the area and with good reason: the *kulfi* (Rs.12) is excellent.

Radhika's, 53 Syed Amir Ali Ave. (tel. 247 2602). About 10min. on foot north of the Birla Temple, on the right. A popular after-school hangout, with a large selection of pizza (Rs.15-30), *dosas* (Rs.15-30), and juices. Ice cream and sundaes served in air-conditioned comfort.

Indian Coffee House, 15 Bankim Chatterjee St., just of College St. near Calcutta University. Let the din of voices pummel you into your seat in this great green wind tunnel, a popular haunt of the Calcutta intelligentsia. A portrait of Rabindranath Tagore presides over the scene.

Anand Vegetarian Restaurant, 19 Chittaranjan Ave. A typical restaurant located between Indian Airlines office and Chowringhee Lane. Excellent *dosas* and coconut *naan*. Entrees Rs.12-32.

Bar B-Q, 43/47 Park St. (tel. 299916, 298885). An open, airy restaurant with red tables and the standard Indian and Chinese cuisine. Entrees Rs.40-60. Popular among locals. Open Fri.-Wed.

Silver Grill, 18E Park St. (tel. 299086, 294549). Good Chinese food. Take-out available, but many customers stick around for the air-conditioning. Entrees Rs.40-50.

Kwality, 17 Park St., next to Park Hotel. If you feel the need to be pampered, this is the place to go. It prides it self on its well-deserved reputation for attentive, courteous service. Entrees Rs.40-80.

SIGHTS

From Raj-era administrative buildings to delicate palaces, from crowded museums to secluded parks, Calcutta's sights are plentiful. This is city sight-seeing at its best. But take the time to look beyond the obvious monuments too: Calcutta's neo-Gothic and Palladian decorations give it the most consistently eye-pleasing architecture in India, a refreshing change from the ultra-modern and ultra-ugly square blocks of other cities. And below it, scenes of urban life unfold hour by hour on the sidewalk, as clothed men scrub themselves under gushing hand pumps, schoolboys fly kites on short strings, and naked *sadhus* ford the streams of Marutis.

The Maidan and Chowringhee

At the center of Calcutta is the **Maidan,** a vast space that is actually one of the world's largest urban parks. In this perpetually public place, aging ISKCON devotees do their morning meditations, young courting couples have intimate talks, kids kick around soccer balls and herdsmen parade their skinny cattle. In British times the Maidan was a dressy whites-only year-round garden party, and though it's public property now it retains some of its festiveness. The race course and the polo grounds are here, and parades take place on Red Road, which runs through the middle of the Maidan. The park is subdivided by large roads that cross through it. At the north end are the **Eden Gardens** with a small pond and a crumbling Burmese pagoda. The gardens dwell in the shadow of **Ranji Stadium,** where test cricket matches are played. **Curzon Park,** on the Chowringhee side, has colonies of communist statues, street performers, and rats. The tram lines all stop here, splitting Curzon Park into pieces. Nearby is the tall, cylindrical **Ochterlony Monument,** also called the **Shahid Minar,** which the British built for David Ochterlony and his war with Nepal in 1814-16. With police permission you can climb the 224 creepy steps. A "monument pass" must first be obtained at the police headquarters at Lal Bazar (close to BBD Bag). This takes a separate trip and passes are not always available. From atop the tower you can watch the Maidan up with the hawks, a relief from Calcutta's sidewalk claustrophobia.

Fort William, built by the British when they recaptured Calcutta in 1757, is submerged like an iceberg on the west of the Maidan, occupying a large spiky swath of land. The fort is now an Indian army base and tightly closed. The original purpose of the Maidan was to give Fort William's soldiers a clear shot. The south end of the Maidan is the domain of the **Victoria Memorial,** Calcutta's greatest flower of imperialism. The British spent 15 years (1906-21) building this, their Taj Mahal for their beloved queen. Four minarets surround a central dome of white marble. But unlike Agra's great white monument, the "V.M." is shaped in the angles and spheres of the Italian Renaissance, with a bronze winged statue of Victory on top. An aging Queen Victoria waits at the entrance to the complex, greeting the crowds who come to wander through her gardens and pools. A much younger lady stands inside the building, which has become a museum chock full of British war memorabilia and state portraits (open Tues.-Sun. 10am-5pm; admission Rs.2). One small air-conditioned section, the **Calcutta Gallery**, has one of the most comprehensive exhibits in all of India's museums; it gives a sleek and fact-packed history of Calcutta in paintings, maps, and dioramas. As with other Indian historic buildings, there's also a patriotic **sound and light show** that takes place at night outside (in English, Tues.-Sun. 8:15pm; admission Rs.10).

The **Chowringhee** area, east of the Maidan, also has its share of sights. The **Indian Museum,** at the corner of Sudder St. and Chowringhee, is India's largest and oldest museum, and its collections are comprehensive. Some parts, especially the geology and natural history sections, seem to be sequestered in endless glass cases, but artists bow down with sketchpads at the great sculpture collection. Many of the greatest works of Indian art have been transported here, including several Mauryan and Shunga capitals and a large section of railing from the *stupa* at Bharhut in Madhya Pradesh. The anthropology gallery has wonderfully stereotyped life-sized models of people from all over India. Ask to go upstairs and see the painting collection, which is usually closed off. (Museum open March-Nov. Tues.-Sat. 10am-5pm, Dec.-Feb. Tues.-Sat. 10am-4:30pm. Admission Rs.2.)

Near the southeast end of Park St., at the corner of AJC Bose Rd., is the **South Park Street Cemetery.** Wander through the weeds and the obelisks, cups, and pyramids: this is where the British buried and praised their dead from 1767 until about 1830. The inscriptions tell a fascinating story of life and death for the British in East India Company times. It's a cool, quiet place and the guidebook (Rs.25) is excellent. (Open daily 7am-4pm; free.)

At the south end of Chowringhee, on Cathedral Rd. opposite the Victoria Memorial, is **St. Paul's Cathedral,** the cavernous and friendly center of Anglican metropolitan Calcutta. The British moved their center of worship to this white Gothic building in 1847 (open Mon.-Sat. 9am-noon and 3-6pm. Services Sun. 7:30, 8:30, 11am, and 6pm). The **Academy of Fine Arts** next door, part of Calcutta's ongoing cultural buzz, holds exhibitions of local artists' work. (Open daily 3-8pm. Free.) The permanent collection here features many works by Rabindranath Tagore and the Bengal School painters. (Open Tues.-Sat. noon-6:45pm; admission Rs.2.)

BBD Bag and Central Calcutta

Most of Calcutta's historic buildings are located near its center, north of the Maidan. **BBD Bag,** the hub of this area, previously known as Dalhousie Sq., was renamed for Benoy, Badal, and Dinesh, three freedom fighters hung by the British during the protests following the 1905 partition of Bengal. A big square of water, the misty Lal Digha (Red Tank) sits in the center. Spanning the north side is the prickly red-brick caterpillar of the **Writers' Building.** No great literary figures toiled here other than the clerks of the East India Company, for whom it was built in 1780. It's now the lair of the West Bengal government, containing Kafkaesque tunnels of bureaucracy. Up Netaji Subhas Rd. to the left side of the Writers' Building is Calcutta's financial district. On **Lyons Range** *bakda-wallahs* sell stocks in the street. Only Indians can buy. A block farther is the **Exchange Building** and the candycane **Standard Chartered Bank** building.

On the west side of BBD Bag is the silver-domed **GPO,** which rises over the site of the 1756 Black Hole of Calcutta. Down Government Place W. (to the left if you're facing the GPO) is **St. John's Church,** the oldest British church in Calcutta, with its clumsy-looking spire. The octagonal mausoleum of Job Charnock, founder of Calcutta, is tucked away in St. John's grumpy churchyard. Through the trees you'll also find the British Indians' monument to their martyrs in the Black Hole incident, which previously stood out on BBD Bag. Some personal belongings of Warren Hastings, the first governor-general of India, are kept inside the church (open Mon.-Fri. 9am-noon and 5-6pm. Services with pipe organ Sun. 8am).

Diagonally opposite St. John's is one tip of the vast grounds of **Raj Bhawan** (Government House), the West Bengal governor's residence, formerly home to governors-general and viceroys. The furnishings inside are suitably palatial, but it's not open to the public, so enjoy the walk in the shade of the barbed wire. Nearby, on the other side of Government Place W., are the State Legislature and the cheerful tricolor Gothic **High Court.**

North Calcutta

Calcutta's busiest commercial areas and oldest Bengali neighborhoods are north of BBD Bag. **Barabazar** is a riverside market dating from before Calcutta's founding in 1690. Commerce rages here under five- and six-story apartment buildings. Nearby is the **Howrah Bridge,** a rugged steel frame that waves above the Hooghly with the rush of traffic. Built for weapons going to Burma in 1943, it is the world's longest single-span cantilevered bridge (450m from one pillar to the other), not to mention its busiest. The government's languor in building a Second Hooghly Bridge downstream suggests that congestion on the bridge had become a matter of civic pride in Calcutta. On the riverbank south of the bridge is **Armenian Ghat,** the liveliest of Calcutta's many bathing *ghats.* Until the 16th century, the Ganga flowed to the sea where the Hooghly flows now, and the Hooghly's water still comes from the Ganga in the north, so bathing here is sacred for Hindus. A flower market and jingling bells surround the early-morning bathers who come to scurry down the steps here. This bird-spattered sunrise can also be surveyed from the Howrah Bridge. Calcutta's *ghats* are used to immerse deities up and down the river during Bengali festivals, especially

Rabindranath Tagore

The Bengali poet Rabindranath Tagore (1861-1941) towers over modern Indian literature and Bengali life. The youngest son in the large family of the prominent *zamindar* and Brahmo Samaj leader Debendranath Tagore, Rabindranath dropped out of school at an early age to educate himself in English and Sanskrit. He found no lack of stimulation in his family's Calcutta mansion, where almost everyone was involved in some form of the arts. Rabindranath began writing poetry while still a boy, and before long his poems broke new ground, introducing English forms previously unknown in Bengali. He traveled around Bengal looking after his family's estates and acquiring a love for the countryside. Many of Tagore's poems and stories concern the lives of villagers in Bengal, and his songs draw from the melodies of Bengali folk music.

Tagore translated many of his verses into rhythmic English prose, catching the attention of Western readers. In 1913 he received the Nobel prize for *Gitanjali* ("Song Offerings"), a collection of poems expressing his wish to merge with God. Tagore was knighted by the British in 1915, but returned his title following the 1919 Jallianwala Bagh massacre. In his later years Tagore experimented with novels, plays, and elaborate songs, and near the end of his life he took up painting as well. Tagore spent much of his time at Santiniketan, north of Calcutta, developing a school he had founded in 1901 in an effort to revive ancient ways of learning. Gandhi and other political leaders considered Tagore an inspiration and frequently visited him at Santiniketan. Verses by Tagore now constitute the national anthems of both India and Bangladesh, and Bengalis concur that "in every situation of life there are words from Tagore." Tagore's plays are widely produced, his songs, known as *Rabindrasangit,* have become a genre of their own, and the filmmaker Satyajit Ray has produced interpretations of several of Tagore's novels such as *Charulata.* Opinions vary on how well Tagore stands up in translation. *Gitanjali,* his Nobel Prize-winning work, is representative and makes a good introduction.

at Durga Puja (Oct. 11-21, 1997), when thousands of 10-armed goddesses float down the river.

Many hard-to-find but fascinating spots are on or near Rabindra Sarani, one of the main north-south avenues of North Calcutta. **Rabindra Bharati University** is on Dwarakanath Tagore Lane. The old mansion of the prolific Tagore family has been expanded and turned into an arts college, and the house itself has been preserved as the **Rabindra Bharati Museum.** Beginning with the room where Rabindranath Tagore died, the museum traces the story of the Tagores and the Bengal Renaissance with a large collection of art and memorabilia. (Museum open Mon.-Fri. 10am-5pm, Sat. 10am-1:30pm; free.) The **Marble Palace,** a step back from the road on little Muktaram Babu St., was the splashiest mansion in Calcutta when it was built by Raja Rajendro Mullick Bahadur in 1835. "Please do not touch the *objets d'art,*" reads the sign inside, where you can weave your way among pianos, birdcages, and blue china vases. The patterned marble floor is fit for a Mughal monument, and the painting collection includes works by Rubens, Titian, and Gainsborough. The Mullick family still lives here but they hide while you see their stuff. A pass from the West Bengal tourist office on BBD Bag is necessary to visit the Marble Palace, but *baksheesh* works just as well, and you're as likely to feel watched by the garden statuary as by the guards. (Open 10am-4pm. Closed Mon. and Thurs.; free.)

Farther down on Rabindra Sarani, crumpled into height by the streets around it, is the red sandstone of the **Nakhoda Mosque,** Calcutta's largest mosque, with a marble goldfish pool inside (open daily, 6am-8pm). West of Rabindra Sarani on the small lane of Armenian St. is the **Armenian Church of Our Lady of Nazareth,** the oldest extant church in Calcutta. A tiny remnant of the Armenian merchant community that built the church in 1707 still comes at 9am on Sundays to celebrate amid much chanting. Tombstones, inscribed in curly Armenian script, are scattered like cards around the outside of the church.

Calcutta's **Chinatown** is located at the south end of Rabindra Sarani where it becomes Bentinck St. Calcutta's 200,000-strong community trickled out in the 1960s when India went to war with China. There are still many Chinese-owned shops here, and a few landmarks, including the once-roaring Nanking Restaurant on Sun Yat-Sen St.

Fluttering papers pad your passage on College St., whose bookstalls cater mainly to the students of **Calcutta University,** the first university opened by the British in India in 1857. The university's **Ashutosh Museum** has a good collection of Bengali art including temple terra-cottas and Kalighat *pats*.

The **Sithalnath Jain Temple,** built by a jeweler in 1867, is located to the northeast of the downtown area, but worth the cab fare. The temple has a garden of European statues and lacy railings, and the building chimes with mirrors and colored glass. Information on Jainism is available. (Open daily 6am-noon and 3-7pm.)

The **Dakshineshwar Kali Temple** lies quite far north of the city, but can be reached on bus #32 from the Esplanade. Hindu families file through a wide square to enter the white, rippled temple (open daily 6am-9pm). The Hindu spiritual teacher Sri Ramakrishna was a priest here when the temple was first opened in the 19th century. Here Ramakrishna had his vision of the unity of all religions. Needless to say, non-Hindus are allowed into this temple. Ramakrishna's bedroom is a shrine inside the temple complex. The headquarters of the Ramakrishna Mission are in Howrah.

South Calcutta

The area south of AJC Bose Rd. contains Calcutta's post-Independence residential neighborhoods, but the main attraction here is an ancient sacred site. The Kali Temple at **Kalighat,** probably gave Calcutta its name. According to Hindu myth this is where the goddess Sati's toe fell to earth when she was cut apart by Vishnu. Pilgrims come here to make offerings to the goddess Kali (see **Divine Dismemberment,** p. 404). The present temple was built in 1809. Chains of flower and image shops surround the temple complex, and priests happily lead visitors around, in front of, and behind worshipers at the shrines to various Hindu deities inside. The main temple, devoted to Kali, has a thatch-like Bengali curved roof. Inside you can gaze into the goddess's wise red eyes, which are reproduced on dashboards and refrigerators all over West Bengal.

Around the corner to the right of the temple is Nirmal Hriday, the first of the homes of the Missionaries of Charity (this one for the dying), opened by Mother Teresa in 1952. Mother Teresa favored a location next to a pilgrimage site because she knew it would attract dying people, not tourists—it is not a tourist spot. The Missionaries of Charity welcome volunteers though; for information ask at their office at 54A AJC Bose Rd. on weekdays between 5 and 6pm.

The **Calcutta Zoo** on Alipur Rd. is a popular place for family excursions. Leaves and trees fill the compound, but it's hard not to pity the animals in their cages. The chief attractions are the Asian lions, Bengal tigers, and a series of zoo-bred progeny: "tigons," "litigons"—the possibilities are endless. (Zoo open daily 6am-5pm; admission Rs.2.) Down Alipur Rd. to the left of the zoo, the **National Library** is stacked away in what was once the estate of the lieutenant-governor of Bengal.

The **Rabindra Sarovar,** a green and crusty lake in South Calcutta, is home to the city's rowing clubs, while the park around it is commonly used for sports. Beside the lake on Southern Ave. is the **Birla Academy of Art and Culture,** a large private gallery sponsoring international exhibitions. The academy's permanent collection is meant as a microcosm of Indian art, each floor housing a different period. The most recent acquisition is a 14-m monolith of Krishna, which stands out back. (Museum open Tues.-Sun. 4-7pm, exhibitions open Tues.-Sun. 4-8pm. Admission Rs.0.50.)

On Ashutosh Chowdhury Rd. in the suburb of Ballygunge, is the **Birla Temple** which mocks the concrete-block architecture around it. The Birlas, India's famous family of Marwari industrial barons, are orthodox Hindus and have poured their money into copies of India's great medieval temples. This Calcutta *avatar* is a sanded white Orissan-style job with three *shikharas*. (Open 5:30-11am and 4:30-9pm; no cameras or bags.) **Netaji Bhawan,** the home of Subhas Chandra Bose, Calcutta's gift to the independence movement, is on Elgin Rd. not far from Chowringhee. Bose led the volunteer Indian National Army against the British in the second World War, allying his troops with Japan. There is a small museum at his house, and his birthday is celebrated here on January 23. (Open Tues.-Sat. 1:30-4:30pm; admission Rs.2.)

Howrah

Calcutta's shadow across the river is best known for its crazy train station and its slums, including Anand Nagar, Dominique Lapierre's "City of Joy," but there are some peaceful places at both ends of Howrah. At the north is **Belur Math,** the headquarters of the Ramakrishna Mission, the movement founded in 1897 by Swami Vivekananda, disciple of the Hindu saint Ramakrishna. The Vivekananda Bridge links it to the Dakshineshwar Kali Temple across the river. Belur Math has a monastery with a riverside park for meditation, a museum with personal effects of Vivekananda's (admission Rs.1), and a soaring sandcastle-like temple of all religions. Open April-Sept. 6:30-11:30am and 4-7pm; Oct.-March 6:30-11:30am and 3:30-6pm.

Far on the south side of Howrah in Shibpur are the **Indian Botanical Gardens.** The Great Banyan Tree here is one of several in India claiming to be the world's largest. Although its main trunk has died, its standing roots survive, like a giant explosion of toothpicks. The gardens have a section for plants from every continent and every region of India. The wind floats off the Hooghly and the docks on the other side to the 100 hectares of foliage. (Open daily from dawn-dusk; free.)

ENTERTAINMENT

Calcutta supports a thriving tradition of **performing arts.** Bengali music, dance and drama are staged at several venues throughout the city. The Drama Theater at the back of the **Academy of Fine Arts** (tel. 248 4302) has shows daily at 6:30pm and Sat. at 10am and 3pm; admission Rs.10-25. On the corner of Cathedral Rd. and AJC Bose Rd. sits **Rabindra Sadan,** an important concert hall dedicated to Tagore and mobbed by well-to-do Calcuttans in the evenings.

Although Calcutta is supposed to be home to India's artsiest **film** industry, its cinemas, such as Globe Theater on the corner of Madge and Lindsay St., typically show Indian smut. The gigantic New Empire and Light House Cinema movie theaters, located side by side just west of New Market, both favor recent Western hits. For less carnal and more celestial viewing, the **Birla Planetarium,** a *stupa*-like edifice next to St. Paul's Cathedral (English shows at 1:30 and 4:30pm; Hindi and Bengali shows at 12:30, 2:30, 3:30, 5:30, and 6:30pm; admission Rs.10). For popular current film, the **Nandan Theater,** just south of the Academy of Fine Arts, has both English and Bengali productions. Films are typically shown at 2, 4, and 6pm; admission Rs.5-12. Check newspapers for listings and go early for tickets. The **Calcutta Information Centre** (tel. 248 1451) is located in the same complex as the Nandan and provides information on the various theater and film showings and other cultural events (open Mon.-Fri. 1-8pm).

Although Calcutta has numerous bars, most of the city's **nightlife** is not particularly welcoming to foreigners, especially women. For fun without the tension, the Oberoi Grand Hotel on Chowringhee has the **Pink Elephant** disco—"It's a jungle in the Pink." (open Wed.-Sat.; couples Rs.250, singles Rs.150). The "Pink" is one of the few discos where neither an invitation nor a membership is required. The theme changes monthly. Jungle boogie until 2am.

SHOPPING

The greatest treasure at the **Treasure Island** complex north of Sudder St. is the air-conditioning (open Mon. 1-8pm, Tues.-Sat. 10am-8pm). Other not-so-valuable discoveries at this mall include an overpriced food store in the basement. For real shopping, step into the enclosed, labyrinthine **New Market,** north of Lindsay St. (open dawn-dusk). There is a little of everything—Kashmiri carvings, film cassettes, food, clothes, animals—and a lot of chaos. Runners attempt to entice passersby to their shops, which are often nowhere in the vicinity. Don't bother trying to shrug off the clingy porters—they're an inevitable part of the New Market experience.

■ Siliguri and New Jalpaiguri

The last major stops before Darjeeling, Sikkim, Nepal, and most of the eastern Himalaya, Siliguri and New Jalpaiguri are transportation hubs. New Jalpaiguri is the last major rail stop before the mountains, and 8km to the north, Siliguri has the major bus terminus for mountain routes. In between the two, rickshaws zip by transporting wares. Hidden away in this strange gap of a town are some of India's most talented table tennis players. The game is taken seriously, and if you're lucky, there might be a tournament in town.

ORIENTATION

New Jalpaiguri (NJP) Station is the last major train station before the hills. The **Tenzing Norgay Bus Terminal** is located at the other end of Siliguri, 6km to the north (30min. on a cycle-rickshaw, Rs.15). The road between the two, **Hill Cart Road** (Tenzing Norgay Rd.), is an unglorified strip. **Siliguri Town Station** is useful as a landmark because it is situated halfway between NJP Station and the main bus station in Siliguri; **Siliguri Junction Station** is behind the main bus station. The Toy Train to Darjeeling stops at all three stations. The regional airport at **Bagdogra** is located 12km to the west.

PRACTICAL INFORMATION

Tourist Office: Sikkim Tourist Office, located at the Sikkim Nation Transportation (SNT) center across Hill Cart Rd. from the bus station 2min. south. It has the most up-to-date information on Sikkim. Permits for Sikkim available at no charge with 1 photo (takes 10min.). State buses run from here to Gangtok, Rs.50. **West Bengal Tourism** (tel. 431974/-79), just beyond the 2nd police box at the major intersection north of Siliguri Town Station, on the right. First floor, enter down alley on right. Information on the Jaldapara Wildlife Sanctuary, 124km east of Siliguri (open Sept. 15-June 15). Open Mon.-Fri. 11am-4pm. A less comprehensive branch is located at the NJP Station, track 4.

Immigration Office: Foreigners Registration Office, NJP Station, track 4, next to West Bengal Tourism booth. Open 7am-7pm.

Currency Exchange: Hotel Mainak, 5-min. walk north of bus station on Hill Cart Rd., on right. Traveler's checks not accepted. **Sinclair's Hotel,** another 10-min. walk north of Hotel Mainak, to the right over the raised overpass, on left. Traveler's checks accepted.

Telephones: STD/ISD booths common throughout the city.

Airport: Bagdogra Airport, 12km west of Siliguri. Take Hill Cart Rd. bus, which starts at NJP Station, stops in front Tenzing Norgay Bus Terminal, before arriving in Bagdogra (Rs.5), then a rickshaw to airport (Rs.10). The trip takes a total of 1hr. Rickshaws also go from Siliguri. The rumor is that this will be turned into an international airport, but for the moment it is a small station-sized airport surrounded by an air force base. To: Delhi (1-2 per day, 3hr., US$156); Calcutta (1-2 per day, 1hr., US$65); Guwahati (Mon., Wed., and Fri., 50min., US$41). **Indian Airlines,** Hill Cart Rd., 5-min. walk north of bus station on right in the Mainak Hotel Complex, on left side, 2nd fl. (tel. 431495). Open Mon.-Fri. 10am-4:30pm.

Trains: All trains to this area stop at **New Jalpaiguri (NJP) Station,** 7km south of bus station on Hill Cart Rd. The **Central Rail Booking Office** (enquiry tel. 423333, 436222; reservations 431493) is near the police traffic booth north of the defunct Siliguri Town Station, immediately on the right. Open 8am-8pm. To: Delhi (*Braamaputra Mail,* 12:30am; *Assam-Avadh Exp.,* 7:15pm; *Mahananda Exp.,* 11:45am, 30hr., Rs.300); Calcutta (*Darjeeling Mail,* 6:45pm; *Kamrup Exp.,* 5:20pm; *Kanchenjunga Exp.,* 9:15am, 11hr., Rs.177 for 2nd class).

Buses: The **Tenzing Norgay Bus Terminal** is located next to the dilapidated Siliguri Junction Station at the north end of Siliguri. Private buses congregate on Hill Cart Rd. next to the main bus station. To: Calcutta (12hr. (overnight), Rs. 135-140); Darjeeling (every hr., 7am-5pm, 3½hr., Rs.45); Kalimpong (3hr., Rs.30). **Sikkim Nation Transportation (SNT) Centre** is located across Hill Cart Rd. From bus station, it's a 2-min. walk south. Buses to Gangtok (every hr., 7am-3pm, 5hr., Rs.50). Buses for Kathmandu leave from Kakarbhitta, across the Nepali border. Take a city bus north along Hill Cart Rd. to the Nepali border town of Panitanki (1hr., Rs.6). From here, cycle-rickshaws cross the border to Kakarbhitta (Rs.10). Buses go from Kakarbhitta to Kathmandu.

Luggage Storage: Tenzing Norgay Bus Terminal, on right as you enter (Rs.3 for 24hr.); **NJP Station,** on track 4 (Rs.3 for 24hr.)

Pharmacy: Medical booths dot the city. The one most convenient to the bus station is across Hill Cart Rd. inside the passage next to Bank of India sign.

Emergency: Police: tel. 20101. **Ambulance:** tel. 20336.

Post Office: GPO, a sharp right at first police traffic booth north of Siliguri Town Station, up road on right.

Telephone Code: 0353.

ACCOMMODATIONS

Siliguri is packed with places to rent a room all along Hill Cart Rd., and your rickshaw driver will have a few ideas about places off the main street.

Rajasthan Guest House, 50m north of Siliguri Town Station on for left off of Hill Cart Rd. Away from the noise of the main drag, this is a popular guest house. The restaurant in the basement is dark, but serves decent food. Beer Rs.40. Singles Rs.60, with bath Rs.80. Doubles Rs.100, with bath Rs.120.

Siliguri Lodge, across the main street from the bus station and set back to the right. A quiet and quaint bungalow style lodge with garden in front. "Come as a guest, go as a friend" they claim. Doubles Rs.160-180. Quads Rs.250.

Hotel Mount View, Hill Cart Rd. (tel. 425919). Across the main street from bus terminal, a few minutes north. Back far enough from road to escape much of the noise. Friendly staff keeps this place impeccably clean. Singles Rs.150-250. Doubles Rs.250-350.

Hotel Nataraj (tel. 434179). A 5-min. walk north of Siliguri Town Station, up the road on the left. Reasonably priced but noisy (with the sound of street traffic outside). Singles Rs.75. Doubles Rs.120-140.

Holydon Hotel, an 8-min. walk north of NJP Station (tel. 423558). A relatively new hotel with clean rooms. Singles Rs.88. Doubles Rs.150-220.

FOOD

There are **fruit markets** at each of the train stations, and assorted **food stands** at the Tenzing Norgay Bus Terminal. The hotels and lodges listed above each have a decent restaurant. The best dining room in town is the Pink at **Hotel Sinclair,** a 15-minute walk north of the bus station on Hill Cart Rd., right over the overpass, and on the left. Open noon-3pm and 6:30-10:30pm. Entrees Rs.50-80. If you're stuck at the NJP Station, the **Restaurant Miami,** next door to the Holydon Hotel 8 minutes away, serves decent food (open until 10pm). Other supplies and goods are available all along Hill Cart Rd. Prices only get higher further on in the mountains, so this is a good place to stock up and outfit for hiking.

■ Darjeeling

To the world outside of India the name "Darjeeling" is virtually synonymous with "tea"—a well-deserved association, since some of the world's finest hot brews are plucked from shrubs in the area. But for those close enough to visit Darjeeling, it has long been known as a cool retreat with majestic mountain views. When the British chanced upon this wooded ridge in 1828, they were so enraptured with the location that they cornered the king of Sikkim into letting them use it as a health resort. Darjeeling's popularity with heatstruck *sahibs* and *memsahibs* grew and grew, and by 1861 Sikkim was forced to cede Darjeeling to Britain. As its bandstands and lookout towers attest, Darjeeling was one of the great playgrounds of colonial India, and it continues to be a favorite spot for holiday-makers from the plains.

As a getaway from India, Darjeeling is certainly a success—narrow roads tangling around hillsides keep out motor vehicles and welcome leaping children, the air is cool and windy, and in the monsoon the town is invaded by clouds. But Darjeeling also seems un-Indian because of a huge Nepali influence. Most of the population of this region was recruited from Nepal in the 19th century to work on British-owned tea estates. The ethnic Nepalis, or "Gorkhas" as they call themselves, brought with them the Nepali language as well as Nepali ideas about dress (much more "Westernized" than the Indian style) and the Nepali mixture of Hinduism and Buddhism. Darjeeling still has a distinctly Nepali feel. In the 1980s, the Gorkha National Liberation Front waged a violent battle to leave West Bengal and form a separate Indian state, "Gorkhaland." Thanks to a 1988 compromise the violence has ended, the Darjeeling Gorkha Hill Council has been allowed to run a Nepali-speaking enclave within West Bengal, and foreigners no longer need permits to head for the hills.

ORIENTATION

Darjeeling's roads follow the bumps and turns of the landscape according to a plan imposed by nature. Few Darjeeling streets are within range of cars, and staircases are often just as important as streets. The whole ridge Darjeeling hangs from is crescent-shaped, with its tips pointed north and south and its back to the east. The belly of the town is **Hill Cart Road** on the west side, near the bottom. This is where the train and bus stations are and where motor vehicles enter the town. It's a steep climb from here to **Chowrasta,** the town center near the top of the ridge. The Chowrasta intersection has a bandstand at one end and a fountain and the tourist office at the other. To the right of the fountain is **Nehru Road,** one of the town's main avenues for shops and restaurants (formerly called the Mall), along with **Laden La Road,** which runs right below it. The road to the left of the fountain (past the ponies) takes you to the TV tower area where many of the cheap hotels are. A useful landmark on the north side of town (on Mall Rd. W., to the left of the bandstand) is **St. Andrew's Church**— this old yellow Gothic construction sits where the road to Chowrasta meets the series of roads down to the bus stand.

PRACTICAL INFORMATION

Tourist Office: West Bengal Tourist Office, Chowrasta (tel. 54050). Just above the Indian Airlines office; enter around to the right, up ramp. Provides a vaguely useful hiking map and luggage storage. Runs a bus to Bagdogra Airport (4hr., Rs.55) if there are enough passengers—ask at the office for information. Open Mon.-Fri. 10am-4:30pm.

Immigration Office: The process of securing a **Sikkim permit** is simple, but will take an hour due to the bureaucratic mess. First go to the **Deputy Commissioner's Office,** 7min. down Hill Cart Rd., to the north from the bus stands; look for the "Sikkim Pass" sign. Office on 1st fl. of central building. Open Mon.-Fri. 11am-1pm and 2:30-4pm. With the stamped form, go to the **Foreigners' Registration Office,** Laden La Rd. next to ANZ Grindlays Bank, for a police signature (or stamp). Then return to the District Commissioner's Office for the official permit. Free and valid for 15 days. No photo necessary.

Trekking Information: The best source of information are reports from fellow travelers written in tourist logs (kept at Youth Hostel, Aliment Hotel, and Tower View Lodge). For more guidance, try **Trek-Mate,** Nehru Rd. across from tourist center (tel. 54074). Open 9am-5pm, but the woman in charge can be found until 6pm in the back room; ask at the desk.

Currency Exchange: Bank of India, Laden La Rd. The bank is plagued by long lines, though they try to hurry foreigners through. Open Mon.-Fri. 10am-2pm, Sat. 9am-noon. **ANZ Grindlays Bank,** Laden La Rd. (tel. 54551), just down from intersection with Nehru Rd. Accepts traveler's checks, cash, and Visa. Open Mon.-Fri. 10am-2pm, Sat. 10am-noon.

Telephones: STD/ISD booths common throughout town. Telephone exchange located above Nehru Rd. Open Mon.-Sat. 7am-9:30pm, Sun. 8:30am-6pm.

Airline Offices: Indian Airlines, Chowrasta (tel. 54230, 54231). Open Mon.-Fri. 10am-4pm, Sat. 10am-2pm. **Jet Airways** (tel. 55123), just below GPO, on alley across from the Forest Department. Follow the signs. Open daily 9am-5pm.

Trains: Reservation Booth, at train station (tel. 2555). Quota tickets available for major trains leaving NJP (Siliguri) Station. Open 10am-4pm. The train station services the Toy Train.

Buses and Jeeps: Virtually all rides out of Darjeeling leave from the main bus stand at the Bazaar, Hill Cart Rd. There are a lot of private companies, and it is not difficult to find a competitive price if you ask around. Jeeps tend to be slightly more expensive than buses. Buses to Siliguri (countless buses starting at 6am, 3½hr., Rs.40) for connections to major destinations; and Gangtok (5hr., Rs.70-80). Jeeps to Kalimpong (2½hr., Rs.30-50) and western Sikkim (1½hr., Rs.40) where service is available to all points north.

Luggage Storage: Available free of charge at the tourist office, Chowrasta, the Youth Hostel, and at most hotels and trek companies.

English Bookstore: Oxford Bookshop, Chowrasta, overlooking town. An excellent collection of fiction and nonfiction with emphasis on regional topics. Open Mon.-Fri. 9:30am-1:30pm and 3:30-7pm, Sat. 9:30am-2:30pm.

Pharmacy: The Economic Pharmacy, Laden La Rd. across the street from the GPO, at the bend. Open daily 10am-11pm.

Hospital: tel. 3210 or 2218.

Post Office: GPO, Laden La Rd., halfway down, just after sharp bend. Open Mon.-Fri. 9am-5pm, Sat. 9am-noon.

Telephone Code: 0354.

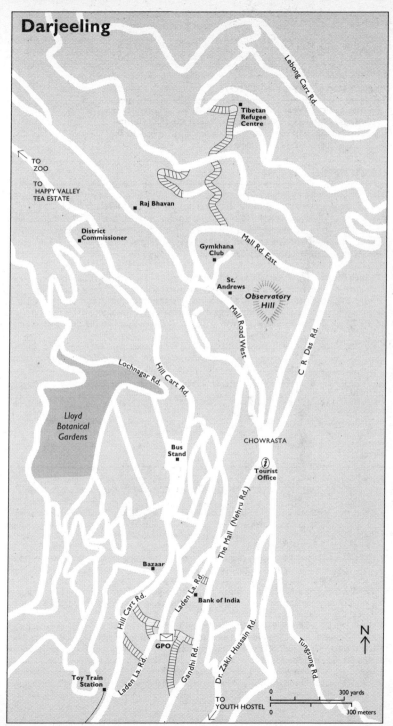

Darjeeling

TO
ZOO

TO
HAPPY VALLEY
TEA ESTATE

Lebong Cart Rd.

Tibetan
Refugee
Centre

Raj Bhavan

District
Commissioner

Gymkhana
Club

Mall Rd. East

St.
Andrews

Observatory
Hill

Mall Road West

C R Das Rd.

Lochnagar Rd.

Hill Cart Rd.

Lloyd
Botanical
Gardens

CHOWRASTA

Bus
Stand

Tourist
Office

The Mall (Nehru Rd.)

Bazaar

Laden La Rd.

Hill Cart Rd.

Bank of India

GPO

Gandhi Rd.

Dr. Zakir Hussain Rd.

Tungsung Rd.

Laden La Rd.

Toy Train
Station

TO
YOUTH HOSTEL

0   300 yards

0   300 meters

N

EAST INDIA

The Toy Train

The Toy Train traverses the route from Siliguri to Darjeeling, following the main road and crossing it at every switchback (close to 100 times). There's approximately 90km of track, and the route takes the Toy Train nine hours. The track, 60cm in width, was inaugurated in 1889, when specially built steam engines pulled four cars over the track. The Toy Train's tired steam engines now pull only three cars but continue to attract the attention of many tourists. The time-conscious alternative to the full nine-hour circuit is to ride the Toy Train for the one-hour leg from Darjeeling to Ghoom. Operation is sporadic—train generally leaves Darjeeling 8:25am (arriving at 2:30pm) and leaves Siliguri 9:30am (arriving at 5:30pm). Call ahead (tel. 52555).

ACCOMMODATIONS

Though hotels are springing up everywhere in Darjeeling, most are geared toward Indian tourists, who spend more than the typical foreign budget traveler. The least expensive of these are on the stairs directly up the hill from the GPO, between Gandhi and Laden La Rd. There are a few places that have adopted the budget traveler culture (including the prices) into their scheme. Off-season bargains are often available; in season, bargaining for a spot on the floor might be the only option.

Youth Hostel, Dr. Zakir Hussain Rd. From Chowrasta take the road to the left of the Indian Airlines office, and bear right at the intersection; at the next intersection, by the TV tower, turn left. Ask to see the tourist log for information on trekking around Darjeeling and Sikkim. Free luggage storage. Hiking gear for rent: packs Rs.20-30, jackets Rs.25-30. Curfew 9:30pm. Dorm beds Rs.40, Rs.20 for cardholders.

Tower View, Dr. Zakir Hussain Rd. (tel. 54452; fax 54330). Near TV tower; follow the signs. Outgoing owner caters to foreign travelers, sharing his knowledge about the area. The tourist log has good information about trekking. Rooms look out over Kanchenjunga. Dorm beds Rs.25. Singles Rs.40, with bath Rs.80. Doubles Rs.60, with bath Rs.120.

Aliment, 40 Dr. Zakir Hussain Rd. (tel. 55068). On the road to the Youth Hostel, on the left. An unassuming, expertly run hotel with an excellent restaurant. The owner and tourist log are helpful in planning treks. Hot water. Singles Rs.40. Doubles Rs.60.

FOOD

Restaurants abound in Darjeeling. Aliment is the best of the hotel restaurants. Numerous quasi-fast food joints are located on the Chowrasta and along Nehru Rd.

Shalimar Restaurant, Old Super Market Stand (tel. 2129), 1st fl. overlooking bus stand at south end. Relatively fast service and a good dwelling place if you're waiting for a bus. Quiet, with a pleasantly removed view of the chaos. Fish Rs.20-30, chow mein Rs.18-25, tea Rs.3.

Golghar, Hill Cart Rd. farther up to the south, in the middle of the first intersection, 1st fl. Just about as cheap and authentic as they come in Darjeeling. Food items Rs.2-20. Open 8am-7:30pm.

Wali's Bakery and Confectionery, Hill Cart Rd. just up from Golghar. A large selection of breads and cakes with a rapid turnover. Best place to stock up for any trek. Open 7am-7pm.

New Dish Restaurant and Bar, Hill Cart Rd. Take a left at Golghar, bear right at intersection. A new restaurant with decent food, though slightly overpriced. The real treat is the glimpse into the Indian tourist scene. *Thukpa* Rs.24-27, chow mein Rs.30-32, omelette Rs.22.

Stardust, Chowrasta, (tel. 54136). Extremely crowded, but great spot for people-watching and view-spotting. Soak up the heart of Darjeeling's tourist industry. Indian and Chinese entrees Rs.15-30.

Keventer's Snack Bar (Kev's), Nehru Rd. (tel. 54026) just down from Chowrasta. Kev's views from 1st floor to go along with Kev's cheeseburger (Rs.16) and cheese omelette (Rs.20).

Dekevas, Nehru Rd., across the street from Kev's farther south. Excellent food, but slow service. Entrees Rs.20-30.

Dafey Munal Rest, Laden La Rd. at intersection with Nehru Rd. A family restaurant, better atmosphere than most. Entrees Rs.15-30, curries Rs.15-25.

SIGHTS

From hotel rooftops to Tiger Hill, Darjeeling's most popular sight is **Kanchenjunga,** the world's third-highest mountain. Located on the border between Nepal and Sikkim, some 70km from Darjeeling, its 8586m cone is nevertheless visible on a clear day. Some of the chief places of interest in Darjeeling owe their fame to Kanchenjunga. **Observatory Hill** has a sacred shrine to Shiva as Mahakali in addition to mountain views. Multicolored tissue-like paper flags (a Buddhist decoration) are strung up around the temple complex. The wind on the hill is good for blowing prayers around, and monkeys like to hang on the strings as well—beware of their bite.

Below the Gymkhana Club is the **Bengal Natural History Museum,** which has an extensive bunch of stuffed animals, particularly birds. Dodge the hordes of the Indian tourists going berserk with cameras here; it's a small museum. (Open Fri.-Wed. 10am-4pm; admission Rs.1.)

Continuing down, below the bus stand, are the **Lloyd Botanical Gardens,** which specialize in alpine foliage, shooting up from a slope. Farther north on Hill Cart Rd., past the district magistrate's office, a rocky road drops down to the **Happy Valley Tea Estate,** the easiest place to see the famous Darjeeling tea growing. Pickers work through the shrubs on the hills around you, and the "factory" is open to visitors (open Mon.-Sat. 8am-4pm). A worker will take you through four days in the life of a tea leaf as it is processed by various machines.

At the north end of Darjeeling's ridge (about a 20-min. walk from Chowrasta, straight along the road to the left of the bandstand) is Darjeeling's zoo, the **Padmaja Naidu Himalayan Zoological Park** (open Fri.-Wed. 8am-4pm; admission Rs.3.) Though small, this zoo gives its animals much leafier spaces than most Indian zoos, and it has species rarely seen elsewhere: Siberian tigers and red pandas (much more of the raccoon than the bear persuasion). A few restless snow leopards are being coaxed into breeding in a separate section on the other side of the hill, where visitors are equally welcome. Above the Siberian tigers is the cenotaph of Tenzing Norgay, the Darjeelingite who co-conquered Everest with Sir Edmund Hillary in 1953. Tenzing was for a long time the director of the Himalayan Mountaineering Institute (HMI) adjacent to the zoo. HMI offers climbing courses only to Indians; its main function is to instruct the lowlanders of the Indian Army. Darjeeling has had a long connection with mountaineering, because until the 1970s Nepal had no roads to speak of. The earliest Everest trips took off from Darjeeling, and this is reflected in HMI's **Everest Museum,** which is full of relics (open daily 9am-1pm and 2pm-4:30pm; admission free). The displays in the **Mountaineering Museum** connected to it range from butterflies to icepicks to relief models of the Himalayas. Around the corner a telescope is set up to catch views of Kanchenjunga; it happens to have been a gift to one of the Rana prime ministers of Nepal from Adolf Hitler.

Clockwise around the ridge from the HMI is the starting point for the **Rangeet Valley Passenger Ropeway.** Due to technical breakdowns this cablecar no longer makes its full trip to Singla Bazaar north of Darjeeling, but it does go for a scenic half-hour dip over the tea shrubs. The round-trip costs Rs.30, and at least four passengers must be there for it to run (Mon.-Fri. 8am-noon and 12:30pm-3:30pm).

The **Ghoom Monastery** in Ghoom, 8km south of Darjeeling, makes an easy excursion; the Toy Train runs here twice a day. Don't be confused by the Samten Choling Ghoom Monastery, a new and not terribly interesting Buddhist monastery below the road to Ghoom. The original, Yiga Choling Ghoom Monastery, the most famous in the region, is above the road, close to the Ghoom railway station. Founded in 1850, its large shrine contains a 5-m golden statue of the Maitreya Buddha (the Buddha to come). The murals inside have just undergone rebirth.

For Kanchenjunga views, there's nothing better than sunrise on **Tiger Hill.** Land rovers leave Darjeeling at 4am on clear days, making for this hill 11km away. An observation tower on top of the 2590-m rise offers a view from the floodplains of the Ganga delta to the snows of the Himalaya, each peak lighting up in turn as the sunlight inches west. Everest and its neighbors are often visible. Breakfast on the tower comes with the price of admission (Rs.10) but there's nowhere to stay on the hill unless you camp, and most sunrise spectators come right back down once it gets bright.

ENTERTAINMENT

Below Observatory Hill on the town side, close to St. Andrew's Church, is the **Gymkhana Club,** a Raj-era recreation center that's still dustily kicking. A day-member charge Rs.30 (7am-8pm) allows visitors to tour the cane furniture and tiled fireplaces of the era. Rollerskating (10-1pm), table tennis (3-5pm), squash (6-9am), billiards (10am-1pm and 3-8pm), and tennis (7am-noon) come with an additional charge of Rs.10 each. Meals must be ordered a day in advance. One-week membership Rs.150.

SHOPPING

Chowrasta, Nehru Rd., and Laden La Rd. provide a nice, if pricey, line of shops. Of particular note is **Hayden Hall,** Laden La Rd. across from the Bank of India. This women's cooperative sells locally made handmade wares and gives the proceeds to needy women in Darjeeling. A larger and slightly more exotic collection of handmade goods is housed in the **Tibetan Refugee Self-Help Centre,** located beyond and below Observatory Hill. Follow Mall Rd. (to the left of the bandstand) around to the other side of the hill and follow the path and steps down, looking for its name painted on the roof; ask for directions. The Self-Help Centre was established by Tibetans who fled here in 1959, and its workshops, which produce carpets, sweaters, woodcarvings and other crafts, are open to visitors.

Darjeeling is surrounded by **tea estates,** like the Happy Valley Tea Plantation (see Sights), and tea shops. Darjeeling can't offer any special deals on its tea because of there is a set market price, but does offer pure and authentic Darjeeling tea rather than the blends commonly found elsewhere. However, some of the tea stands (especially along Hill Cart Rd.) sell lower priced tea—this "tea dust" is not the real thing. The best place to shop is along Laden La Rd. Prices also vary according to whether the tea plant is originally from China, or simply a clone. The tea from Darjeeling is called Orange-Pekoe, though it has nothing to do with oranges. There are two different variations—the inner (smaller) leaves are more aromatic, while the outer (larger) leaves make a darker brew used in milk tea.

■ Trekking Around Darjeeling

Trekking is the ideal way to get around the Darjeeling region and Western Sikkim from October to early December and from March to early June. Trekking in this area consists of day hikes of six or seven hours between villages, where small hotels (Rs.25 usually) and simple food is available. Water and trail snacks are usually unavailable on the trail and should be packed, along with a sleeping bag, warm clothes, and rain gear. The routes are often old jeep roads with trails bypassing large sections of the winding road. For the most recent, detailed, and opinionated information on the more common trails, consult the tourist logs at the Youth Hostel, Tower View, and Aliment Hotel. A good map of the trails simply does not exist; the only recourse is to ask everyone you encounter for directions.

Rimbik is the most common starting and finishing point for treks and has the most to offer in terms of good accommodations, food, and transportation. **Buses** run from Darjeeling (7am), and from Rimbik to Darjeeling (5:30am and 12:30pm, 5hr.). A popular loop is from Rimbik to Gorkhey, Phalut, Sandakphu, and back to Rimbik—each leg taking a day. For a longer trek, it is best to start in Manabhanjan (bus from Darjeeling, 7am, 1½hr., Rs.15), and hike north up the Singalila Ridge, pass through Sandakphu and Phalut, and end in Rimbik. North of Phalut, the ridge forms the border between Nepal and Sikkim and leads up to the peak of Kanchenjunga.

■ Kalimpong

Though less famous than its big brother Darjeeling, Kalimpong is important as a way-station to Sikkim. The town suffered when Sikkim was shut down as a trading route and is only now recovering. At the outset, Kalimpong seems nothing more than its central square consumed by buses and jeeps. Yet Kalimpong is also defined by the military presence that supports it, a diverse population (as it is on the corner of Nepal, Tibet, Sikkim, Bhutan, and Bengal), and missionary work dating from British times.

ORIENTATION

The **bus stand** gave birth to the **central square** that it consumes, and is the center of the town. On the east of central square is Hotel Cozy Nook, on the west is a corrugated roofed building. **Sikkim Nation Transport (SNT)** is located just to the left of the corrugated building and the Himilashee Lodge to the right. Just south of the central square is the **football stadium. Ongen Road** crosses the square at the west end. Parallel to Ongen Rd. is **Main Road,** extending from **Gompu's Restaurant** and the central bank to the post office, telephone exchange, police station, and Foreigners Registration Office (all just beyond the south end of the football field).

PRACTICAL INFORMATION

Tourist Information: The best information is found at the hotels. The **Deki Lodge** has maps and information on the area.

Budget Travel: Skyline Travels, Main Rd. (tel. 55741, 55697) contains the offices of **Indian Airlines** and **Jet Airways.** Open Mon.-Fri. 10:30am-7pm. **Kalimtrek Tours and Travels,** Main Rd. (tel. 55448; fax 55290), south of Skyline Travels. Offers expensive tours and occasionally has mountain bikes available for Rs.150 per day.

Currency Exchange: Central Bank of India, Main Rd. (tel. 55715). Enter on side next to Gompu's Restaurant, upstairs. Changes traveler's checks only. Open Mon.-Fri. 10am-2pm, Sat. 10am-noon.

Immigration Office: Foreigners Registration Office, next to post office, marked by a prominent sign.

Telephones: The main telephone exchange is located behind the post office.

Trains: Closest train station is NJP (Siliguri), but there is a **booking office,** 2nd street (alley) on right as you exit the central square toward Gompu's, about 5m from Rishi Rd. Quota seats available on major trains out of NJP station, but reservations must be made days in advance. Open daily 10am-1pm and 4-5pm.

Buses: Buses depart from the central square. Booking offices are along the perimeter, particularly bordering football field. To: Gangtok (3hr., Rs.40); Darjeeling (2hr., Rs35); Siliguri (2hr., Rs.27). **Sikkim Nation Transport (SNT),** central square, located just left of the corrugated building. Open daily 7:30am-2pm. Bus to Gangtok (8:30am and 1:15pm, 3½hr., Rs.30) is often crowded and 1 day's advance booking is wise.

Pharmacy: Misra Brothers Drugstore, Main Rd., next to Skyline Travels. Open Mon.-Sat. 9am-5pm.

Post Office: GPO, located 4min. south down Main Rd. at opposite end of football field, on right. Open Mon.-Fri. 9am-4pm, Sat. 9am-noon. **Postal Code:** 734301.

Telephone Code: 03552.

ACCOMMODATIONS

Himilashee Lodge (tel. 55070), central square, just to the right of the corrugated building, 1st fl. Only 5 rooms and often full. The place is cozy, but the noise starts early—you'll be in tune with Kalimpong life. Singles Rs.50. Doubles Rs.100. Doors locked at 9pm. Owner lives upstairs and is always on call.

Deki Lodge, Tripai Rd. (tel. 55095). Right at Gompu's Restaurant and up the hill to Richi Rd. Left branch off of Richi Rd. and uphill 10min. from central square; lodge is on the left. Popular with travelers interested in savoring life in Kalimpong for a while. Run by a friendly Tibetan family that provides a wealth of knowledge about the area along with a wide range of services.

Bethlehem Lodge, Rishi Rd. (tel. 55185). Just beyond the movie theater on the right. Immaculate rooms. Singles Rs.100. Doubles Rs.200.

Gompu's Hotel (tel. 55818), just west of central square. A good location if central Kalimpong interests you. Singles Rs.100. Doubles Rs.200.

Cozy Nook (tel. 55541), in central square. Offers little more than the basic necessities. Popular among Indian travelers. Singles Rs.100. Doubles Rs.200.

FOOD

Kalimpong has its charms, but food isn't one of them. Guest at the Deki Lodge luck out with good Tibetan food, and there are a few other less notable restaurants in town.

Kelsang Restaurant, down from the central square alongside the football stadium. Follow the path toward field, down steps into a cozy, if foreign, environment. No menus, but good, cheap Tibetan food—all you have to do is ask, even if the staff can't respond in English. Open 10am-8pm.

Mandarin Restaurant, in central square across from the football stadium. Weave your way through the SNT buses. The noise miraculously disappears once you're inside. Entrees Rs.20-50. Open lunch hour to 8pm.

Gompu's Restaurant, Main Rd., west of central square. Dim lighting, but good food. Entrees Rs.10-40. Order ahead for particularly large and well-prepared *momos*—must order at least 4 portions. Fast service.

SIGHTS AND ENTERTAINMENT

Kalimpong specializes in **flowers** and has a number of nurseries. The collections of orchids, amaryllises, roses, gladiolas, and dahlias are most impressive in the season from March to June.

On a small path off of Tripai Rd. is **Tharpa Choling Gompa Monastery,** a 40-min. walk uphill east of town beyond the Deki Lodge. The monastery was founded in 1892, though the existing structure is much more recent. Farther up Deolo Hill is the complex of **Dr. Graham's Home,** dating from 1900 when a Scottish minister set up a home for six orphan students. The school, which eventually acquired the whole hilltop and became largely self-sufficient, now has over 900 students. At the bottom of the hill is the brilliantly yellow **Bhutanese Monastery,** originally established in 1692. Ringkingpong Hill, 5km southwest of town, is dominated by an extensive army base, but also home to the **Zong Dog Palri Fobrang Monastery,** which was consecrated in 1976 by the Dalai Lama.

A **movie theater** is located in a large building on Rishi Rd. between Tripai Rd. and the central square. The evening shows (5:30pm) are often contemporary American movies. Showings at 11am, 2pm, and 5:30pm; admission Rs.3-9. An **Arts and Crafts showroom** just west of the central square. Follow the dirt path across the street from Gompu's Restaurant straight back (follow the best views) to the clearly labeled building on the right. Open Mon.-Fri. 8:30am-3:30pm, Sat. 8:30am-noon. The **Rambhi-Samthan Ropeway** west of Kalimpong at mile 27 used to be popular among daredevil travelers, but sadly it snapped June 19, 1996, killing six people.

Sikkim

TIBET (CHINA)

Kanchenjunga 8586m

NEPAL

Yumthang

Teesta River

Rangit River

Mangan

Yuksam

Phensang

Phodong

Pemyangtse
Pelling
Tashiding
Rumtek
Tsangu
Lake

Geyzing

Teesta River

Gangtok

Legship

Singta
31A

Namchi

Dhanbad

Jorethang

Rangpo

BHUTAN

Melli
Bazaar
31A

WEST BENGAL

Kalimpong

EAST INDIA

N

0   10 miles
0   10 kilometers

Govt. of India statement:
The external boundaries
of India are neither correct
nor authenticated.

Sikkim

Sikkim rises from 300m above the Indian plains to the edge of the Tibetan Plateau on its northern border, to the third highest point on earth, Kanchenjunga (8586m), on its border with Nepal. The earliest known inhabitants of Sikkim are the Lepchas, who arrived in the 13th century, followed later in the century by a group of Tibetan Buddhists led by Guru Tashi. The first *chogyal* (king) of Sikkim was appointed in the 17th century. Tibetans moved off the plateau because of strife between two Buddhist sects, the Nyingma-pa ("Red Hats") and the Gelug-pa ("Yellow Hats"). The Nyingma-pa remain predominant in Sikkim (as well as Nepal) while the Gelug-pa took over in North India. Under the British protectorate, which began in 1861, Nepalese were brought to Sikkim to work on tea plantations, soon outnumbering the Lepchas and Tibetans.

When India became independent in 1947, Sikkim was made a semi-independent Indian protectorate. But in the 1970s the Nepali population agitated for union with India, and the chogyal finally relented to a vote—97% of the electorate voted to join India, and Sikkim became the 22nd Indian state in 1975.

In Sikkim, people from the flatlands to the south are "Indian" while those who grew up in the mountains identify themselves according to their ancestry: Nepali, Bhutanese, Tibetan, or Lepcha. Recently there has been a resurgence of ancestral languages in response to the promulgation of English. In addition to these competing forces, Sikkim must also contend with a religious mix—the Hindu Nepalese currently represent 75% of the population, although Sikkim is historically a Buddhist kingdom, with over 250 monasteries of the Nyingma-pa sect. And now Sikkim is being forced into the late twentieth century and the era of TV, AIDS, rapid transit, and mass tourism; it is caught between being a stronghold for subsistence living and being the playground for the urban rich.

The best times to visit Sikkim are from late March to May when the flowers are in bloom and October through November when clear views are guaranteed. Visitors to Sikkim must first get permits. For more information, see **Special Permits,** p. 5.

■ Gangtok

The industrial town of Gangtok and its heavily subsidized trickle-down government channel most of their energies toward tourism. In order to extend Sikkim permits or obtain the appropriate documentation for trekking north of Yuksam or Phodong, travelers must deal with red tape and a Delhi-like bureaucracy—in Gangtok, it's hard to differentiate the government from the tourist industry. Gangtok also cultivates a type of Indian tourism where hard-working families spend less than a week in the mountains, spend enormous amounts of money, and go home with the pictures to prove it. As such, and as the capital of Sikkim, Gangtok is an expensive city—all the more reason to avoid it.

ORIENTATION

Gangtok spreads itself out along the **National Highway,** which cuts up the hill slope diagonally. Roads branch off horizontally above and below the highway. The **SNT Bus Terminal** is below the highway at the north and upper end of town, down an offshoot. **Mahatma Gandhi (M.G.) Road** splays horizontally above the highway 30m south of the intersection that leads down to the SNT Terminal. The tourist center dominates the intersection. M.G. Rd. becomes **Naya Bazaar** farther south, above the private bus and jeep stands.

PRACTICAL INFORMATION

Tourist Office: National Tourist Centre, corner of M.G. Rd. and the National Highway (tel. 23425). Ask for a map, though it is only of use as an amulet. There is little here but a wealth of statistics. Open Mon.-Fri. 10am-4pm.

Tours: Tour companies arrange permits, and provide guides and equipment. Expect to pay US$30-50 per day. For budget travelers, the best prices is the Modern Central Lodge, Tibet Rd. (tel. 24670), where lodging is not necessary.

Currency Exchange: State Bank of India, National Highway behind the tourist center (tel. 23326). Located on 1st fl., enter on the right through the side entrance. Traveler's checks accepted. Open Mon.-Fri. 10am-2pm, Sat. 10am-noon.

Telephones: The **telephone office** (tel. 22065), located in the same building as post office. Open Mon.-Sat. 7am-9:30pm, Sun. 8:30am-6:30pm. STD/ISD booths are located in tourist offices along this road. Usually open until 10pm.

Airline Office: Indian Airlines (tel. 23099), Tibet Rd., just above the private jeep stand on right. Open daily 10am-1pm and 2-4:30pm. The nearest airport is Bagdogra.

Trains: The **Railway Reservation Window,** at the far end of the SNT Bus Terminal, has quota tickets on the major trains that leave New Jalpaiguri Station. Open daily 9:30-11:30am and 1:30-3pm.

Buses: Sikkim Nation Transportation (SNT) Bus Terminal is a modern and open building located down from the National Highway at the north end of town. The buses are heavily subsidized and often very crowded, and hence the cheapest and slowest mode of transport. Book tickets early at left-most window (open 6:30am-3pm). To: Siliguri (every 30min. beginning at 6am, Rs.38); Bagdogra Airport (1 per day, 9am, Rs.45); Kalimpong (8:30am and 1:15pm, Rs.30); Darjeeling (every hr. beginning at 7am, Rs.34); Jorethang (7am and 2pm); Namchi (7:30am and 2pm); Rumtek (4pm, Rs.9); Yangan (2:30pm); Geyzing (7am and 1pm, 5hr.,

Rs.40). **Private buses** are available along the National Highway below and just above Naya Bazaar.

Jeeps: Available below Naya Bazaar just below the National Highway, jeeps are a more expensive but faster mode of transport. Prices are usually around Rs.55, and tend to exceed SNT bus prices by Rs.10-20. Make sure you are sharing a jeep (occupying only 1 seat) and not paying for the whole jeep (upwards of Rs.800). Front seat is more expensive than the back.

Local Transportation: Taxis ply the National Highway and shouldn't cost more than Rs.10 for the length of the city.

Pharmacy: Numerous pharmacies are located along M.G. Rd. and the Naya Bazaar. Most open 9am-6:30pm.

Hospital: tel. 22059. Located above the National Highway above the tourist center.

Police: tel. 100, 22033, and 22042.

Post Office: Halfway up street from SNT Terminal and National Highway. On left as you descend. Open Mon.-Sat. 9-11am and 2-5pm.

Telephone Code: 03592.

ACCOMMODATIONS

During peak season, when Gangtok is most expensive, consider staying near the Rumtek Monastery 24km across the river valley (taxi 1hr., Rs.50). In Gangtok itself, there are few options for the budget traveler—the city is exploding with new hotels, but most are oriented toward wealthier Indian tourists. The few places that have kept their prices low are always very crowded.

Green Hotel, M.G. Rd. (tel. 23354). On right just beyond the tourist center. The clean rooms in this popular and established hotel are usually filled to capacity. Restaurant on main floor. Singles Rs.80. Doubles Rs.150.

Modern Central Hotel, Tibet Rd. (tel. 24670). Up the hill from M.G. Rd. at the tourist center. Left on Tibet Rd. and on right around bend. Owner caters especially to foreign budget travelers and he provides a map of Gangtok along with other information. Dorm beds Rs.40. Singles Rs.60-100. Doubles Rs.120-200.

FOOD

Food, too, is expensive in Gangtok. Bulk foods for hiking are available along the Naya Bazaar, which offers the best selection in Sikkim. The restaurant in Modern Central Lodge is expensive, but not by Gangtok standards, and the quality justifies the price, while that in the Green Hotel is popular among locals.

Sagar, Daigha, and Laxmi Sweets, M.G. Rd. Located across from the Green Hotel and to the south. These three snack shops are located side by side and are extremely popular. They are good places to cool the heels.

Hungry Jack Restaurant, National Highway, south of the lower taxi/private bus stand, just beyond the gas pumps. Clean, open, and modern restaurant with a bar. Entrees Rs.25-45. Sikkim-brewed Dansberg beer Rs.28. Open 7am-9pm.

Tripti's Bakery Confectionery, National Highway (tel. 23464). Located below Hungry Jack; enter from highway side. Good stock of bread and sweets. Open Mon.-Sat. 6:30am-6:30pm.

SIGHTS

A 40-minute hike from Gangtok, the **Enchey Monastery** is perched on the landing spot of Lama Druptob Karpo, who is said to have flown from Maenam Hill over 200 years ago. The building itself dates from 1909. Farther south and closer to town is the **King's Palace** and the **Tsuglakhang,** or Royal Chapel. Both are closed to tourists, but early morning peeks of the Royal Chapel are sometimes possible.

The **Research Institute of Tibetology** (tel. 22525, 24822), located 1km south and downhill from the Naya Bazaar along a large road, was founded by the Dalai Lama in 1957 and now holds approximately 30,000 volumes of old Tibetan documents (mostly wooden boards called xylographs). The collection of *thankas* is impressive.

Though it is billed as the world's foremost center for Tibetology, there are now only a small number of researchers here. Open daily 10am-4pm, but the staff is gone on Sunday; admission Rs.2.

The **Government Institute of Cottage Industries** is 20 minutes north of the tourist center on the National Highway, on the left. It serves as a "factory" for handicrafts and furniture, and a display center where colorful, and occasionally artisanal-quality crafts are sold. Open Mon.-Fri. 9:30am-4pm, Sat. 10am-2pm, Sun. 9:30am-2pm. For additional shopping, the **Kunphenling Tibetan Co-operative Society Handicraft Emporium** is located just below the National Highway on the way to the SNT Terminal. Open Mon.-Sat. 9am-6pm.

■ Near Gangtok: Rumtek

Only 24km from Gangtok, accommodations in Rumtek are a high-season alternative to the crowds and high prices of Gangtok. The **Sangay Hotel** is located just up the hill beyond the checkpoint for the monastery. A friendly family runs the hotel and serves good, cheap food. Singles Rs.40. Doubles Rs.75-100. Farther up the hill are three houses that put up travelers. Follow signs for the **Kunga Delek.** If that one is full, the manager will put you in one of the others. The restaurant here has decent food. Singles Rs.75. Doubles Rs.150.

Rumtek is the head of the Kargyu order of Tibetan Buddhism. The **Rumtek Monastery,** built in the 1960s, is modeled on the main Kargyu monastery in Chhofuk, Tibet. Located in a back room is an impressive collection of golden statues of the 16th Gwalpa who fled Tibet when China invaded. Enter through the rear of the monastery. A 45-minute walk downhill is the impressive **Old Monastery,** which is visible from behind the Kunga Delek; ask a young monk to show you the path.

Two days before the Tibetan New Year and the 10th day of the 5th month of the Tibetan calender, Rumtek is the site of celebratory dances called *chaams.*

WESTERN SIKKIM

Western Sikkim is as far off the beaten track as foreigners are allowed to go with a Sikkim permit. The hills here are more rugged, the monasteries are more important, and a greater number of people are Sikkimese. The first Sikkimese capital was at Yuksam, in the north of Western Sikkim, and the ruins of second palace of Sikkim's *chogyals* (kings) lie near Pemyangtse Monastery. Western Sikkim not only holds the ancient heart and soul of Sikkim, it is where, barring the north (and it is barred), the foreigner is most likely to discover modern Sikkim.

The ideal way to enter Western Sikkim is by making the one or two day foot journey from Gorkhey to Dentam, where there is an Alpine Hut. Ask in Dentam or Gorkhey for explicit directions; you'll need a passport and permit. Once in Western Sikkim, all towns are a convenient five- to six-hour hike from one another. Always schedule a few extra days in case of cloudy weather—the views are too spectacular to pass up.

Western Sikkim is also accessible from Gangtok (5hr.) and from the south through Jorethang, the second largest town in Sikkim. Although there's little to attract tourists in this unpretentious working town, those who do end up spending the night are met with good food and friendly people. From Jorethang there are jeeps to Darjeeling (starting at 7am, Rs.55) on a regular basis and buses and jeeps to Siliguri (Rs.50).

■ Geyzing

Geyzing is the central transportation hub for Western Sikkim—and not much else. The SNT Terminal is down the main road from the central square at the bend in the road. The jeep stand is between the two, next to the large field and marked by a small gazebo. The town has the only STD/ISD **telephone** booth (for international calls), located next to the No Name Hotel in the central square. **Currency exchange** is available at the bank, located across the central square from the main road and down the small street on the right, second floor (open Mon.-Fri. 10am-2pm, Sat. 10am-noon).

Jeeps run frequently to Pelling (Rs.10). SNT **buses** go to: Pelling (Mon.-Sat., 7:30, 8:30am, 1, 2, and 4pm, Rs.4; 2pm bus continues on to Khechepalri); Siliguri (7am, 5hr., Rs.40); Gangtok (9am and 1pm, 5hr., Rs.35); Tashiding (1pm, Rs.12); Yuksam (1pm, Rs.20); Jorethang (8, 10, 11am, and 4pm, Rs.20). Jeeps are widely available in season, but more difficult to find off-season. Given the inevitable irregularities in the transportation schedule, walking from town to town is often more convenient than taking buses or jeeps.

The hotel scene in Geyzing is limited and Pelling, the small village one hour from Geyzing by jeep, is much more accommodating. The central square location of hotels in Geyzing makes them convenient for catching early buses. **Hotel and Restaurant Bamboo Grove** has three rooms. In season: singles Rs.20. Off-season: singles Rs.40. The **No Name Hotel and Restaurant** (tel. 50722, 50768) has dorm beds for Rs.25 and one triple for Rs.75. Both hotels function as little more than a place to sleep.

■ Pelling

Pelling is not much more than a hamlet above Geyzing (1hr. by jeep), but it serves as a good waypoint for travelers. Accommodations provide information on hiking and are otherwise geared to foreign travelers. Pelling's location is convenient to the short-cut paths to Yuksam, Tashiding, and Khechopalri Lake. Furthermore it is within easy walking distance of Pemyangtse Monastery (40min.) and numerous other sacred spots (enquire at any of the hotels). The **post office** is located on the side of the **Sikkim Tourist Centre** building (open Mon.-Fri. 9am-5pm, Sat. 9am-2pm). The service window and sign are all that is visible. **Telephone Code:** 03593.

Pelling is budding with new accommodations, many of which were not yet open at the time of publication. The majority cater to Indian tourists and are expensive. A few places, however, maintain low prices and are adequate for the traveler. **Hotel Garuda** (tel. 50614), right in front of the jeep stand (look for the sign), stocks a lot of information on the area. Ask to look through the tourist log which has extensive first-hand information on area hiking. Dorm beds Rs.30. Singles Rs.50. **Hotel Kabur,** just uphill of the Sikkim Tourist Centre, has similar offerings but was closed for renovation at the time of publication. Both of these places serve meals. The cheapest option for travelers is the **Denjong Padma Choeling Academy,** a 30-minute walk from Pelling toward the Pemyangtse Monastery and Geyzing. Take the stairs on the right, opposite a small badminton field. The head monk at Pemyangtse Monastery runs the school, which has volunteered to have foreign tourists stay for a small fee (Rs.20-40 per person). The children are all from Sikkimese families, and some are orphans. Donations and volunteer services are welcome.

■ Near Pelling and Geyzing

Founded during the reign of Chadov Namgyal, the third king of Sikkim, in 1705, the *gompa* of **Pemyangtse** ("The Sublime Perfect Lotus") is currently the principal monastery of the Nyingma-pa order in Sikkim with 100 monks. In the top room at the monastery is the **Sang Thog Palri,** a massive wooden representation of Maha Guru's Paradise. Working from a textbook drawing of Gualwa Lholsen Chenpo's vision, it took Dungzin Rempoche five years to complete the project. You may have to wait for a young monk to retreive a key before showing the way. Behind the white Buddhist *stupa* at the first bend in the road up to the monastery is the **Cheshay Gang**—an old seat for the three-trunked tree. The female buddhist Tantric practitioner who made the seat was the daughter of Terdaglingpa, the guru of Minduling Monastery who escaped to Sikkim through western Tibet during Dzongar Mongol Persecution. At Pemyangtse she first established and taught the four vehicles of Mindoling and gave *dharma* teachings to the monks of Pemyangtse (1718). The tree's branches make a shady spot to avoid the sun.

The **Rangdentse Palace ruins** are located past the entrance to Pemyangtse towards Geyzing. From the main road, take a left onto a small path just before the three mile marker. The path crosses a small meadow before it climbs to the main ruins. Sikkim's second king, Tensung Namgyal, built the palace in 1670, shifting the capital from Yuksam. On the right as you climb through the ruins are the remnants of the stable and military headquarters; on the left is the site of the main throne. The walls and the platform where the drums were played are still intact. The view from here captures the holiest areas of Western Sikkim, including Yuksam and Tashiding.

■ Khechopalri Lake

Located 30km from Pelling, Khechopalri is the holiest lake in Sikkim (make your wish wisely), and legend has it that a sacred bird removes the leaves from the lake as soon as they land in the water. No swimming is allowed. There is a festival here on the 15th and 16th of the first month of the lunar calendar.

There is a trekkers' hut (Rs.25-40) and pilgrims' hut (Rs. 40; the only toilet is the public one outside) at the monastery here. Food is available from the lady at the tea stall nearest to the monastery. Rice and noodle soup and *sabji dal bhat.* If you hike there, pack a lunch, as there is no food along the way. There is a 7am bus from Geyzing to Khechopalri.

■ Yuksam

This historic town is a three-hour bus ride or six-hour walk (via shortcut) from Pelling, and slightly shorter from Khechopalri Lake. According to one account, Yuksam became the first capital of Sikkim when in 1641 its king was consecrated by three Tibetan Lamas—hence the name Yuksam, which means "three Lamas" in the Lepcha language. The white stone throne in front of the monastery is called Norbugang Chorten. The **Dubdi Monastery,** which means "the hermit's cell," is a one-hour walk up the hill and is the oldest monastery in Sikkim. Founded by Gyalwa Lhabchen Chenpo in 1701, it currently has about 60 monks.

There are accommodations in the village, which is composed mostly of Bhutanese farmers. The Lepchas live downhill in the village of Ramgay Thang. Treks to Dzongri leave from here, but the tour companies here are of little use to foreigners, who must process their paperwork in Gangtok.

■ Tashiding

An unreliable two-hour bus ride or a five-hour walk (via shortcut) from Yuksam, the Tashiding Monastery is located on a *stupa*-dotted hill between the Rangeet and Ralhong Rivers up from the main town. The monastery dates from 1716 and now houses about 50 monks. Its main attraction is the Bhumchu (sacred water vase). There is a festival on the 15th of the first month of the Tibetan Calendar. Accommodations include a trekkers' hut and small hotels.

■ Trekking in Western Sikkim

Walking your way through Western Sikkim is easy, so long as you've prepared by bringing everything you need—Gangtok and Darjeeling are the last places with substantial shopping services. Starting in Gorkhey, the trekking loop goes to Dentam, Pelling, Khechopalri Lake, Yuksam, Tashiding, and then back to Pelling, Dentam, and Gorkhey. Each leg of the loop takes a day. Though trekkers can always find a place to eat dinner and a place to sleep, lunch isn't always available. The trek from Khechopalri to Yuksam to Tashiding is simple—just follow the road. There's also a shortcut to Yuksam from Pelling which takes five to six hours.

Northeast India

Northeast India consists of seven states connected to the rest of the country by only a narrow isthmus of land and an even narrower thread of cultural similarity. The state of Assam forms the center of the region, in the valley of the Brahmaputra River, while the surrounding states of Arunachal Pradesh, Nagaland, Manipur, Mizoram, Tripura, and Meghalaya occupy the hills near the borders of China, Burma, and Bangladesh. The hilly areas are largely inhabited by *adivasis* (tribal peoples) whose culture has little in common with that of the North Indian Sanskrit-based civilization. Until 1963, these seven states were one political entity—Assam—but the diverse tribes' struggles for autonomy led to the creation of six new states between 1963 and 1972. These changes happened only with great difficulty. The capital of Assam (which was situated at Shillong, in present-day Meghalaya) was officially moved to Guwahati in 1974, two years after Meghalaya became a separate state. And until 1981, Assam, Nagaland, Manipur, Tripura, and Meghalaya were administered by one governor. Like the movement of tectonic plates, these slow transitions have brought earth-shaking consequences. The statehood movements in Nagaland and Mizoram were fought by armed insurrectionists, and recently Assam has been wracked by political violence. These troubles, coupled with Indian fears of a Chinese invasion (China still claims Arunachal Pradesh), kept the entire northeastern region effectively closed to foreigners until 1995. Assam, Meghalaya, and Tripura are now open to unrestricted tourism. Arunachal Pradesh, Nagaland, Manipur, and Mizoram are still difficult to visit, although these restrictions will likely be abolished in the near future. For more information, see **Special Permits,** p. 5.

ASSAM

Stretching 800km through the low-lying Brahmaputra Valley, Assam is the largest state in Northeast India. Assam did not enter recorded history until the 13th century, when the Ahoms, a Buddhist tribe from Thailand, conquered the area's indigenous peoples and established a capital at Sibsagar. The cultural victory, however, belonged to the Hindus, who quickly converted their conquerors. Today Assamese-speaking and East-Asian-looking pilgrims perform *puja* alongside Hindi-speaking Aryan Indians. Hindered by a weak central government, Assam shifted in the 19th century from the Ahoms to the Burmese to the British, each trying unsuccessfully to amalgamate the dissolute tribes, and, in the last case, to assimilate Assam to Bengal. The British built huge tea plantations (Assam now grows over half of India's tea) and Asia's first oil refinery at Digboi. But Assam's resource-rich economy has languished since the British left.

Until recently, the Brahmaputra Valley was one of the few places in South Asia with a surplus of agricultural land. An influx of migrants from West Bengal and illegal immigrants from Bangladesh has added a substantial Muslim, Bengali-speaking population to Assam and led to tension between the new arrivals and the indigenous tribes. Anti-Bengali sentiment brought the now-entrenched Ahom Gana Parishad (AGP) party to power in the early 1980s. Bengali-Assamese tensions, which have never taken on the dimensions of a religious war, have supposedly improved in recent years. Yet frustration over the poor economy and the central government's neglect have led to the formation of Assamese separatist organizations like the United Liberation Front of Assam (ULFA), little more than a disgruntled urban gang that occasionally engages in acts of

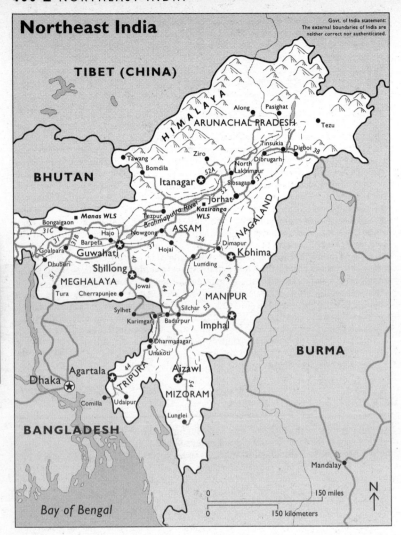

Northeast India

Govt. of India statement:
The external boundaries of India are
neither correct nor authenticated.

TIBET (CHINA)

HIMALAYA

BHUTAN

ARUNACHAL PRADESH

Along Pasighat

Tezu

Tawang Ziro Tinsukia Digboi 38

Bomdila North Dibrugarh

Itanagar 52A Lakhimpur 37

Sibsagar

52

Manas WLS Tezpur Jorhat

Bongaigaon Brahmaputra River Kaziranga WLS

31C Hajo ASSAM

31 Nowgong 36

Barpeta Hojai Dimapur

Goalpara Guwahati 31 Kohima

Dhubri 40 Lumding

Shillong NAGALAND

MEGHALAYA 44 39

Tura Jowai

Cherrapunjee MANIPUR

Sylhet Silchar 53

Karimganj Badarpur Imphal

Dharmanagar

Unakoti

Dhaka Agartala 44 Aizawl

TRIPURA 54

Comilla Udaipur MIZORAM

Lunglei

BANGLADESH

BURMA

Mandalay

N

0 150 miles

0 150 kilometers

Bay of Bengal

EAST INDIA

terror in Guwahati. Aside from blaring headlines in the morning paper, violence is
almost entirely hidden from foreigners. **But travelers are advised to keep abreast of
news and to avoid travel at night.**

Fed by rains from the Bay of Bengal, Assam is heavily forested and boasts two major
wildlife preserves, one of which is closed indefinitely due to political violence.
Bumpy rides on rickety buses lead from Guwahati to outlying towns rich in tribal culture. Because it is accessible to railway traffic, Assam is the gateway to the six hill
states that surround it on the north, south, and east.

■ Guwahati

Known in its sporadic appearances in ancient Indian texts as Pragjyotishpur ("City of
Astrology"), Guwahati became the capital of Assam in 1974. A few interesting sights,

including the Kamakhya Temple, have been pushed out to the edges of the modern city. In the east, Nilachal Hill foreshadows the mountainous regions to the north and south of Assam and casts its shadow over the Brahmaputra River, whose nourishing but destructive waters sometimes flood the city. With a population of 632,000, Guwahati does not seem remarkably different from many other North Indian cities, except that it is less congested and dirty. Good bars and restaurants have sprung up to accommodate the growing middle class; Guwahati also boasts several good universities and a strong student movement. But unlike other cities, Guwahati comes largely unprepackaged. A stray tourist won't feel pushed or prodded here.

ORIENTATION

The center of the city is small. The bazaars, railway stations, and important public offices are located within walking distance of one another. **Paltan Bazaar,** with many budget hotels, is immediately behind the railway station. **Pan Bazaar** (with more expensive places) and **Fancy Bazaar** are a 15-minute walk to the northwest. **Mahatma Gandhi (M.G.) Road** runs behind Pan Bazaar along the river's edge; government buses ply this route to the Kamakhya Temple, 8km to the west, and the Navagraha Temple, 1km to the east. Roads radiate from the center southwards, passing first through prosperous middle-class neighborhoods (with good restaurants) and then, on the outskirts of the city, through lower-middle-class colonies.

PRACTICAL INFORMATION

Tourist Office: Government of India Tourist Office, Dr. B.K. Kakoti Rd., Ulubari (tel. 547407). Southwest of Pan Bazaar at the one part of Ulubari that is not accessible to slow traffic such as rickshaws; go on the small lane across the road and take it around until you emerge on B.K. Kakoti Rd.; go right and the tourist office will be on your right. Open Mon.-Fri. 9:30am-5pm, Sat. 10am-1:30pm. **Assam State Tourist Office,** located on the left side of the road leading to the front of Guwahati Junction. Has a small library. Open Mon.-Fri. 10am-5pm, but the officer is not very punctual.

Immigration Office: Superintendent of Police, near District Court (tel. 540118). Open Mon.-Sat. 10am-4:30pm.

Currency Exchange: State Bank of India, M.G. Rd., near District Court (tel. 544264). Open Mon.-Fri. 10am-2pm, Sat. 10am-noon.

Telephones: Central Telegraph Office (CTO), Pan Bazaar (tel. 540209, 523435). Allows call-backs. Open 24hr.

Airport: Located 24km from town (tel. 84223). Buses go from Judge Field, adjacent to Nehru Park, every 2hr. To get to Judge Field from the front of the railway station, take a rickshaw (Rs.5) or walk straight through 2 major traffic circles. Frequent buses go from Judge Field to VIP Point, 2km from the airport, where you can get an auto-rickshaw for Rs.10-20. To: Calcutta (5-6 per day, 1hr. 15min., US$58); Delhi (1-3 per day, 2½hr., US$182); Bagdogra (1 per day, 45min., US$41); Agartala (Thurs. and Sun., 40min., US$36); Imphal (1-2 per day, 1hr., US$42-50); Dibrugarh (Wed.-Mon., 1hr., US$46); Dimapur (Sun., Tues.-Wed., and Fri., 1hr. 45min., US$45); Jorhat (Sun., Tues.-Wed., and Fri., 50min., US$45); Lilabari (Mon., Thurs., and Sat., 1hr., US$45); Silchar (Mon., Thurs., and Sat., 2hr.); Tezpur (Wed., Fri., and Sun., 45min., US$30).

Trains: The main railway station, **Guwahati Junction,** is centrally located between Pan Bazaar and Paltan Bazaar. Take advantage of the tourist quota by going to the main office at the **North-Eastern Railways Reservation Building,** 200m in front of the train station on the right. There is no train service to most of the other northeastern states, although it is possible to take trains to outlying cities in Assam, from which buses go to the capital cities of other states. To: Dimapur (for buses to Kohima and Imphal; *Delhi-Dimapur Brahmaputra Mail* 4056, 11:45am, 7hr., Rs.57/241 for 2nd/1st class); Silchar (for buses to Tripura and Mizoram; take *Delhi-Dimapur Brahmaputra Mail* 4056 to Lamding, 11:45am, 4hr., Rs.47/185 for 2nd/1st class; from Lamding take *Cachar Exp.* 5801 to Silchar, 5:30pm, 11hr., Rs.62/257 for 2nd/1st class); Harmoti (for buses to Itanagar; *Arunachal Exp.* 5813,

8:45pm, 12hr., Rs.74/334 for 2nd/1st class); Calcutta (*Kamrup Exp.* 5660, 7am, 24hr., Rs.208 for sleeper; *Guwahati-Howrah Exp.* 3046, Thurs., 6pm, 18½hr., Rs.208 for sleeper); Delhi (*Rajdhani Exp.* 2423, Mon., Wed., and Fri., 6am, 28hr., Rs.1135/1900 for A/C 3-tier/A/C 2-tier; *Northeast Exp.* 5621, 8:30am, 36hr., Rs.294 for sleeper.

Buses: The **ASTC bus stand** is located behind Guwahati Junction Station. Government buses go to Shillong (every 2hr., 4am-6pm, 4hr., Rs.30). Departures for each of the major cities in the northeast between 6 and 8am. To: Itanagar (12hr., Rs.175); Dimapur (10-12hr., Rs.140); Silchar (14-15hr., Rs.160); Imphal (21hr., Rs.200); Aizawl (20hr., Rs.180); Agartala (18-20hr., Rs.160); and Tura (8hr., Rs.80). Private buses leave from **Paltan Bazaar;** tickets can be booked at Blue Hills Travels or Network Travels in Paltan Bazaar. Private buses go to Shillong every hr., and to other major northeastern cities (every 30min., 6-8pm). Fares are 10% more than government fares. A Blue Hills bus goes to Calcutta via Siliguri (8am, 24hr., Rs.200).

Local Transportation: Rickshaws and **auto-rickshaws** whizz about. The main city **bus** station is at Nehru Park near Pan Bazaar. Catch a bus going west along M.G. Rd. to the base of Nilachal Hill and the Kamakhya Temple. **Ferries** to Umananda cost Rs.5 per person or Rs.100 per boat.

Luggage Storage: At bus and railway stations.

Library: District Central Library, Dighali Pukhri, near State Museum (tel. 543369). Open Mon.-Fri. 10am-5pm.

Hospital: Guwahati Medical College (GMC), G.S. Rd., Bhangagarh (tel. 569161, 562521), is good for trauma and common gastro-intestinal complaints. **Downtown Hospital,** Dispur, near Capitol Complex (tel. 560824, 562741), is good for extended stays, with fluent English speakers on staff.

Police: Pan Bazaar (tel. 540106). Paltan Bazaar (tel. 540126).

Post Office: GPO, Meghdoot Bhawan, near Pan Bazaar (tel. 541294). Open Mon.-Sat. 10am-5pm.

Telephone Code: 0361.

ACCOMMODATIONS

Some of the most inexpensive hotels in the Paltan Bazaar area have all the accoutrements of mid-range hotels: elevators, room service, STD/ISD booths. However, many of them are not authorized to receive foreigners. Other budget hotels are located in Pan Bazaar and Fancy Bazaar, and there are two excellent places on the riverside. Guwahati's hotels fill up quickly, so it's a good idea to book in advance; if you arrive late, you may have to spend a night in one of the more expensive hotels in Pan Bazaar or Paltan Bazaar.

Samrat Hotel, A.T. Rd., Santipur, Riverside (tel. 541657). A 30-min. rickshaw ride from the railway station (Rs.15). An upscale hotel with good budget options. The only hotel in Guwahati with a female manager; women can feel relatively comfortable here. The hotel is caressed by calming breezes from the Brahmaputra River. Economy rooms are spacious enough for 1 or 2 extra beds (Rs.25 each). Check-out noon. Economy singles with bath Rs.105. Economy doubles Rs.129. More expensive A/C rooms are neither cooler nor more comfortable. Reservations accepted.

Ambassador Hotel, K.C. Sen Rd., Paltan Bazaar (tel. 544886). Near Paltan Bazaar Police Station; a 10-min. walk along G.S. Rd. before making a left onto K.C. Sen Rd. The best budget option in Paltan Bazaar. Large rooms have desks, chairs and beds with straw-filled mattresses and mosquito nets. Intelligent English-speaking manager. Singles with bath Rs.90, with A/C Rs.193. Doubles with bath Rs.138, with A/C Rs.275. Advanced booking possible.

Broadway, M.G. Rd., Machkhowa, Riverside (tel. 548604). From the railway station, a Rs.15 rickshaw ride to the river. Broadway has a fine view of the treeline that obscures the Brahmaputra River in some places. Nevertheless, proximity to the water makes it cool. Rooms are clean and have working showers. Unfortunately, it's a bit of a boys' club: day and night a dozen or so men lounge around the lobby watching mythological dramas on the tube. Singles with bath Rs.60. Doubles with 1 bed and bath Rs.90, with 2 beds and bath Rs.100.

©1996 AT&T.

Someone back home *really* misses you.
Please call.

With **AT&T Direct**℠ Service it's easy to call back to the States from virtually anywhere your travels take you. Just dial the **AT&T Direct** Access Number for the country *you are in* from the chart below. You'll have English-language voice prompts or an AT&T Operator to guide your call. And our clearest,* fastest connections** will help you reach whoever it is that misses you most back home.

AUSTRIA●◇ 022-903-011	GREECE● 00-800-1311	NETHERLANDS● ...06-022-9111
BELGIUM● 0-800-100-10	INDIA✖ 000-117	RUSSIA●▲♪ (Moscow).755-5042
CZECH REP▲ 00-42-000-101	IRELAND 1-800-550-000	SPAIN◇ 900-99-00-11
DENMARK.................8001-0010	ISRAEL...................177-100-2727	SWEDEN................020-795-611
FRANCE...............0 800 99 0011	ITALY● 172-1011	SWITZERLAND● ..0-800-550011
GERMANY.................0130-0010	MEXICO▽ 95-800-462-4240	U.K.▲ 0800-89-0011

*Non-operator assisted calls to the U.S. only. **Based on customer preference testing. ●Public phones require coin or card deposit. ○Public phones require local coin payment through call duration. ◇From this country, AT&T Direct calls terminate to designated countries only. ▲May not be available from every phone/pay phone. ✖Not available from public phones. ▽When calling from public phones, use phones marked "Ladatel." ♪Additional charges apply when calling outside of Moscow.

Can't find the Access Number for the country you're calling from? Just ask any operator for AT&T Direct Service.

Photo: R. Olken

Greetings from LET'S GO

With pen and notebook in hand, a change of clothes in our backpack, and the tightest of budgets, we've spent our summer roaming the globe in search of travel bargains.

We've put the best of our research into the book that you're now holding. Our intrepid researcher-writers went on the road for months of exploration, from Anchorage to Angkor, Estonia to Ecuador, Iceland to India. Editors worked from spring to fall, massaging copy into witty and informative prose. A brand-new edition of each guide hits the shelves every fall, just months after it is researched, so you know you're getting the most reliable, up-to-date, and comprehensive information available.

We try to make this book an indispensable companion, but sometimes the best discoveries are the ones you make on your own. If you've got something to share, please drop us a line. We're Let's Go Publications, 67 Mount Auburn Street, Cambridge, MA 02138 USA (e-mail: fanmail@letsgo.com). Good luck and happy travels!

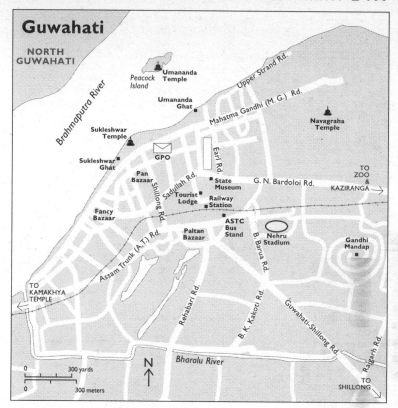

Guwahati

NORTH
GUWAHATI

Brahmaputra River

Peacock
Island

Umananda
Temple

Umananda
Ghat

Upper Strand Rd.

Mahatma Gandhi (M. G.) Rd.

Navagraha
Temple

Sukleshwar
Temple

Sukleshwar
Ghat

GPO

Earl Rd.

Pan
Bazaar

Sadullah Rd.

Shillong Rd.

State
Museum

G. N. Bardoloi Rd.

TO
ZOO
&
KAZIRANGA

Tourist
Lodge

Railway
Station

Fancy
Bazaar

Assam Trunk (A.T.) Rd.

Paltan
Bazaar

ASTC
Bus
Stand

B. Barua Rd.

Nehru
Stadium

Gandhi
Mandap

TO
KAMAKHYA
TEMPLE

Rehabari Rd.

B. K. Kakoti Rd.

Guwahati-Shillong Rd.

Rajgarh Rd.

0   300 yards
0   300 meters

N

Bharalu River

TO
SHILLONG

Hotel Vandana, G.S. Rd., Paltan Bazaar (tel. 543475). From the railway station walk along G.S. Rd. toward Paltan Bazaar. Vandana is on the right, near the Mayur Hotel, before the main part of the bazaar. This big, busy hotel has a large lobby-lounge area and an STD/ISD booth operating until midnight. The rooms are large, and the foam rubber mattresses are surprisingly pliant. Unfortunately, the bathrooms are a bit cavelike and not all the showers work. No alcohol allowed. Singles Rs.60, with bath Rs.80. Doubles Rs.80, with bath Rs.110.

Hotel Suradevi, Motilal Nehru Rd., Pan Bazaar. A Rs.10 rickshaw ride from the station; it's well-known. Male-dominated, but Indian couples are sometimes seen, and the staff is friendly. The beds are soft and the bathrooms clean. Motilal Nehru Rd. is quiet in the evening and less busy than the Paltan Bazaar during the day. Singles Rs.70, with bath Rs.80. Doubles Rs.90, with bath Rs.120. Often full; no reservations are accepted.

Hotel Kuber International, Ham Baruah Rd., Fancy Bazaar (tel. 520807). A 3-star hotel with some less expensive rooms, located in a relatively quiet area of Fancy Bazaar. Something of a landmark, though it's looking a bit run-down these days. Revolving rooftop restaurant and tattered carpets in the bedrooms are wistfully incongruous. Singles with bath Rs.200. Doubles Rs.300.

Kaziranga Hotel, G.S. Rd., Paltan Bazaar (tel. 542476). When G.S. Rd. swings right into the heart of the Paltan Bazaar, the Kaziranga Hotel is on the left. The only other budget hotel in Paltan Bazaar that currently receives foreigners. Green walls cower under stark fluorescent lighting. Staff is young and friendly but speaks little English. Singles Rs.75, with bath Rs.110. Doubles Rs.80, with bath Rs.120. Often full; no reservations are accepted.

Divine Dismemberment

Hindu mythology tells of a shady figure named Daksha, who held a sacrifice and invited all of the gods—all except his own son-in-law, Shiva. Daksha disapproved of Shiva's uncouthness, believing this deformed ascetic who covered himself in ash and carried a skull was an unworthy husband for his daughter, the goddess Sati. Shiva was indifferent to Daksha's snub, but Sati was mortally insulted, so she assembled a huge procession to make a scene at the sacrifice. But when she arrived, Daksha disowned her as well. Furious, Sati set herself on fire. When Shiva learned of Sati's death, he sent great demons with thousands of heads to kill Daksha, interrupt his sacrifice, and scatter his cosmic guests. Picking up Sati's body and holding it in his arms, Shiva began to weep in violent dance-like convulsions that shook the entire universe. In order to assuage Shiva and save the world from destruction, Vishnu stepped in, and, following Shiva around the skies, chopped off bits of Sati's charred body with his *chakra* (discus). These pieces fell to earth, and the places where they landed became *Shakti pithas*. Various scriptures put the number of these places anywhere between 4 and 108, but the number of temples that locally claim a chunk of Sati is even greater. The *Shakti pithas* began as independent centers of goddess-worship, but the myth of Sati's dismemberment provides a way for all these local traditions to consider themselves parts of a single Mahadevi (Great Goddess). This myth is one of the ways goddess-worship is embedded in the geography of South Asia. The most important *Shakti pithas* are those that came from the most magically potent parts of Sati's body—which is why the Kamakhya Temple in Guwahati is the greatest of all.

FOOD

Only one restaurant in all of Guwahati serves genuine Assamese cuisine, which consists of fish, rice, and heavy mustard seasoning. There are many fine places to have Chinese food. Some of the restaurants along Rajgarh Rd. ("Chinatown") far to the east near the Gandhi memorial are run by Chinese immigrants.

Paradise, Moniram Dewan Rd., Silpukuri (tel. 546904). Near Pan Bazaar. An unpretentious place—the men's and women's "bathrooms" consist of 2 adjacent stalls and a shared sink. Wonderful Assamese dishes. Non-veg. *thali* with 9 different samples (including fried fish, chilli chicken, and potato spiced with mustard), Rs.35. Beer served. Open 10am-9:30pm.

SIGHTS

The mighty **Brahmaputra** ("Son of Brahma"), the only male river in Hindu mythology, surges past the city in the north, often overrunning its banks in the rainy season and drowning the riverside settlements. From its banks or from any of the adjacent hills, the river looks sluggish or serene, but its undercurrents are swift, and it is said that if the motor on your ferry boat should suddenly cut out, you won't stop until you reach Bangladesh. The river's vast hydroelectric potential has not yet been exploited—the building of dams in an earthquake-prone area is extremely costly—but engineers have claimed that the Brahmaputra could satisfy 30% of India's energy needs. Ferries run regularly from Umananda Ghat, near the Brahmaputra Ashok, to the **Umananda Temple,** which sits on a small island in the middle of the river. The temple itself is unimpressive, but it offers the best possible view of the river.

From M.G. Rd. it's a 5-km bus ride west to the **Kamakhya Temple** on Nilachal Hill. Devout pilgrims approach the temple from the footpaths leading up from the road. The Kamakhya Temple is one of the most sacred *Shakti pithas* in Hinduism—it is said that the goddess Sati's vagina fell on this spot when she was cut into pieces by Vishnu. The temple, with its beehive-shaped spire, was built in 1665 by King Naranarayana, who is said to have inaugurated the temple by offering the goddess Kamakhya

140 human heads. On the right side, an orange image of Vishwakarma, the patron god of engineers, blesses the structure, which has stood for so many years without the aid of a single support beam. The shrine inside the temple is open to non-Hindus, but hour-long queues are normal. Inside, the Mother-Goddess is worshiped in the form of a crevice in a rock, rather than a sculpted image. The ancient stone bleachers that rise up from the base of the temple seat spectators eager to see animal sacrifices—male goats tied to the posts at the main gate of the temple each morning are decapitated by evening.

Navagraha ("Nine Planets"), a small temple located on a hill in east Guwahati, is a reminder that Guwahati was once a great center of astronomy and astrology. An echo chamber houses nine *lingas* dedicated to the nine heavenly bodies which ancient Indians identified without the aid of astronomical equipment—the sun, the moon, the ascending and descending nodes of the moon, Mercury, Venus, Mars, Jupiter, and Saturn. The dark, dank temple now seems more abandoned than mysterious.

■ Kaziranga Wildlife Sanctuary

Since its inception in 1908, the Kaziranga Wildlife Sanctuary, located in tea country 217km from Guwahati, has been wildly successful in its conservation project. The rhinoceros population, the park's main concern, has increased threefold since 1966. A visit to the park practically guarantees sightings of docile one-horned rhinos munching on marsh grass. The 430-square-kilometer sanctuary, only a small part of which is accessible to human traffic, is a hodge-podge of habitats. Swampland gives way to jungle, which rises up to deciduous forests and finally to the evergreen slopes of the Karbi Anglong Hills. This small space is inhabited by a wide array of animals, from vicious buffalo to delicate swamp deer to elusive tigers. But most visitors come for one-horned rhinoceroses, which is all many of them see. The sanctuary is open from late October to late April. During the monsoon, animals flee the flooded marshland for the muddy roads, making passage through the park dangerous or impossible.

ORIENTATION AND PRACTICAL INFORMATION

Kaziranga is 215km from Guwahati and 96km from Jorhat, the closest airport. Government buses depart from the main bus station next to Guwahati Junction Station between 6 and 10am (5hr., Rs.60). The most common way to visit the park is on the ATDC's **package tour,** a two-day trip including transportation in a luxury coach, one night's accommodation, and a one-hour elephant ride on the morning of the second day. The bus departs from the Assam Tourist Office, located just down the road from the railway station in Guwahati, and the whole package costs Rs.420. Unfortunately, this two-day tour involves a lot of waiting around and a very short amount of time in the park itself. It is possible to arrange a more economical, more exciting, and more personally inspired trip on your own or with a small group, but on the other hand, eastern Assam is unstable and a guided tour brings some peace of mind. During the monsoon, the Wild Grass Hotel sponsors excursions to choice vantage points on the edge of the preserve, but these are expensive and less satisfying.

Local buses and the tourist bus roll up at **Kohora,** a small collection of tea stalls and government lodges at the edge of the sanctuary. It is necessary to register at the **Directorate of Tourism** in the mid-range priced **Bonani Lodge.** A one-hour tour on a lumbering elephant provides only a glimpse of the park, while a noisy jeep, which penetrates much deeper into the sanctuary, scares away many animals. The road into the park diverges into three main routes: Kaziranga Range, Western Range, and Eastern Range. Details and maps of each can be obtained at the Directorate of Tourism; the Eastern Range passes near an observation tower from which it is possible to get a bird's eye view of wallowing rhinos. Five kilometers from Kohora is a small village called Bokakhad, and National Highway 37 continues on to Jorhat and Sibsagar, the ancient Ahom capital.

Exchange all currency in Guwahati. **Buses** to Guwahati pass through in the morning from 6 to 8am. **Jeeps** go to Guwahati for Rs.800. A one-hour jeep ride in the park, booked at the Directorate of Tourism, costs Rs.300. **Elephants** can be rented at the Directorate of Tourism (Rs.50 per person per hr.; each pachyderm seats four). Rides leave at 5, 6:30am, and 3:30pm.

ACCOMMODATIONS AND FOOD

Most travelers eat where they sleep, although anyone can mix and match. The **Aranya Tourist Lodge** has expensive air-conditioned rooms (Rs.400 for a double) and a Continental restaurant-bar. **Bonani** has similarly priced A/C rooms and a restaurant. **Bonoshree** has basic doubles with attached bath, overpriced at Rs.185. The best bargain is the dormitory in **Kunjuban,** with beds going for Rs.25.

SIGHTS

Your chances of seeing a tiger are close to nil, although wild buffalo, equipped with mammoth horns, abound. For the more peaceful at heart, placid rhinos are omnipresent. Their horns may look lethal, but they use them primarily to root around in the mud. Various kinds of deer, and occasional wild elephants, are also seen. For bird lovers, the treetops call out with the cries of fishing eagles and grey-headed pelicans. Most people come for the fauna, but the flora is nothing to sneeze at. A jeep ride passes through several environments, and a view from an observation deck at Sohola or Foliumare (located along the major road routes through the sanctuary) takes in a great swath of Kaziranga in all its vegetative splendor and variety.

MEGHALAYA

Similarities of culture, dress, and diet led to the creation of Meghalaya from the hilly southern region of Assam in 1972. But Meghalaya's people are by no means homogenous. Although the British converted many of Meghalaya's people to Christianity (and universally abolished the practice of human sacrifice), nearly 25% of the population still worships indigenous gods. Two distinct ethnic groups inhabit Meghalaya; the Proto-Australoid Hynniewtrep people, including the Jaintias and the Khasis, in the east, and the Tibeto-Burmese Achiks, also called Garos, in the Garo Hills in the west. But even though they don't worship the same deities or speak the same language, each group is drenched by the same torrents of monsoon rain and battered by the same chill winds that sweep across the hilltops in the winter. Meghalaya is a Sanskrit word meaning "Abode of Clouds," and its seven ranges of hills are swaddled by cumulonimbi which disgorge water from the Bay of Bengal, drown the valleys, cover the hills with vegetation, feed the Brahmaputra River, and make Mawsyn, south of Shillong, the wettest place on earth. The British found Meghalaya reminiscent of Scotland, so they built an 18-hole golf course in Shillong and made it the capital of Assam. Now Shillong and neighboring spots in the Khasi Hills are favorite retreats for heat-struck Assamese. Several wildlife sanctuaries in West Meghalaya are approached by bad roads from Shillong and better ones from Guwahati. Meghalaya has seen very few foreign tourists. Politically sensitive, it was only opened up to unrestricted tourism only in 1995.

■ Shillong

Although the name "Shillong" derives from that of a Khasi deity, the city's older aspects are hidden behind a British façade. Shillong was capital of British Assam as well as a *pukkah* hill station during the colonial period. Members of the exclusive Shillong Club emulate English English, black-and-yellow cabs swarm through the nest of streets, and cycle-rickshaws have not yet pedaled to Shillong's exalted heights. The locals keep pace with current Western fashion: hip young women wear combat boots and short skirts, and long-haired Khasi men thrash to the sounds of Pantera. An excursion to Bara Bazaar, a vast raucous market where villagers gather to sell fruits and vegetables, is the only way to get a glimpse of the agrarian societies that surround the city.

ORIENTATION

A map of Shillong resembles varicose veins. Many tiny nameless roads snake out from the MTC bus stand in **Police Bazaar. Guwahati-Shillong (G.S.) Road,** containing many budget hotels, twists westward, eventually leading to **Bara Bazaar** ("Big Bazaar"), the biggest bazaar in the Khasi Hills, a web of narrow lanes littered with pineapple tops and animal fat. **IGP Point** is what government officials (but no one else) call the road that twists away from Police Bazaar to the southeast, with many government offices. Along this wide, tree-lined boulevard you'll find the GPO, State Bank of India, and at its southern tip, the State Museum. Aside from **Ward Lake,** adjacent to one curve of IGP Point, most of Shillong's natural wonders—waterfalls and parks—are located on the outskirts of the city or even kilometers outside. The only way to reach them is by taxi from Bara Bazaar or Police Bazaar.

PRACTICAL INFORMATION

Tourist Office: Government of India Tourist Office, G.S. Rd. near Police Bazaar (tel. 225632). The tourist officer is a misplaced Bihari whose field of expertise is Buddhism. Open Mon.-Fri. 9:30am-5:30pm. Also try **Meghalaya Tourist Information,** bus stop, Police Bazaar, right across from the MTC building (tel. 226054). Conducts a good half-day tour of Cherrapunjee; bus departs from in front of the office at 8am; tickets available 7:30am. Open for tourist information Mon.-Sat. 10am-5pm.

Budget Travel: Travel agents around the bus stand in Police Bazaar book seats on private buses going to the other northeastern states.

Immigration Office: Foreigners Registration Office, IGP Point (tel. 224137). Across from the main office of the YMCA, near the Secretariat and State Museum. Open Mon.-Fri. 10am-5pm. Visa extension applications (rarely granted) can be filed at the **Secretariat,** a big white sore thumb (with a clock tower) 2 doors down to the right.

Currency Exchange: State Bank of India, Kachari Rd., near Shillong Club (tel. 223520). From the bus stand at Police Bazaar, with the Meghalaya tourist office on your left and the MTC building on your right, walk straight bearing left; after 500m, turn right onto Kachari Rd. Alternatively, share a cab going in the same direction for Rs.5. Open Mon.-Fri. 10am-2pm, Sat. 10am-noon.

Telephones: Central Telegraph Office, Bivar Rd., European Ward (tel. 226288). From IGP Point, with State Bank of India on your right, walk 500m, passing the Foreigners' Registration Office; at the next major intersection take a sharp left (but not the sharpest one) and walk 250m. Free call-backs. Open 6am-midnight.

Trains: Shillong has no train service, but reservations for trains elsewhere can be made on the 1st fl. of the MTC building near Police Bazaar. Tickets for trains leaving Guwahati are difficult to obtain; try to plan a week in advance. For specific trains see **Guwahati,** p. 401.

Buses: Government buses depart from the MTC bus stand in Police Bazaar; tickets can be purchased and reserved in the MTC building. To: Guwahati (every 30min., 6am-5pm, 4hr., Rs.40); Siliguri (8am and 3pm, Rs.150); Tura and Williamnagar Wildlife Preserve (7am, 10hr., Rs.150). Government buses leave for Ranikor; you can jump off en route and then walk 2km on a side road to Mawsyn. A government bus goes from Bara Bazaar in western Shillong to Cherrapunjee (7am, 2½hr., Rs.10), but this service is unpredictable and the return bus is very uncertain; given that there is no accommodation or local transportation in Cherrapunjee, the MTDC tour is much safer (see **Sights,** p. 409). Private buses to cities in other northeastern states leave from the **Polo Ground,** a Rs.10 cab ride from Police Bazaar. Tickets can be booked at any of the travel agents near the MTC bus stand in Police Bazaar. Many buses go to Silchar (7pm-midnight, 10hr., Rs.125); from there, buses go to

Agartala, Aizawl, and Imphal. For all three cities, buses leave throughout the morning (10hr., Rs.125).

Local Transportation: Shared taxis, at Rs.5 per kilometer, barrel through the city streets, not even coming to a complete stop to pick up passengers. Try to flag down a taxi that already has passengers, or the driver might think you want it all to yourself. Watch how much the other passengers pay. For about twice the normal rate, whole taxis can be hired for trips to more remote tourist spots in and around Shillong.

Market: Bara Bazaar in west Shillong carries everything from pineapples and star fruit to cow hooves and electronic equipment.

Library: State Library, M.G. Rd., next to the State Museum. From Police Bazaar, follow IGP Rd. 1km south to the big southward-facing fork; the State Museum and Library is on the right. Lots of big picture books. Open Mon.-Sat. 11am-5pm.

Hospital: Woodlands Nursing Home, Dhanketi, south Shillong (tel. 225240, 224885). Private hospital. Most up-to-date equipment.

Emergency: tel. 100.

Post Office: GPO, IGP Rd., (tel. 222768), around the corner from the State Bank of India. From the bus stand at Police Bazaar, walk 500m down IGP Rd., then turn left onto a small road perpendicular to the main IGP Rd., also called IGP Rd. (Rs.5 by taxi). Open Mon.-Sat. 10am-6pm. **Postal Code:** 793001.

Telephone Code: 0634.

ACCOMMODATIONS

Most of the old British hotels are now in disrepair, and the legendary Peak Hotel has been converted into a customs house. Budget hotels and family hotels are popping up like toadstools along the dank, dark lanes in Police Bazaar, with slightly better places on G. S. Rd. and Thana or Quinton Rd. (on the way to Cherrapunjee).

KJP Synod Guest House, IGP Rd. Located at the southern tip of IGP Rd., right across from the State Museum and Library (on M.G. Rd.), down the street from the YMCA. From Police Bazaar and MTC bus stand, follow IGP Rd. to the end. Run by a tiny little Khasi woman called "Madame" who bustles around squinting at her guests through thick glasses, chiding them kind-heartedly if they don't keep their space clean or if they don't eat their complimentary breakfast. Comfortable dorm beds in spacious rooms with fireplaces. Common kitchen. It's a Christian place: weekly services are held in a central chapel, and most of the guests are Christian tribals from Mizoram and Manipur. Check-out noon. Dorm beds Rs.60.

Monsoon Hotel, G.S. Rd., across from Government of India Tourist Office. The least claustrophobic of the G.S. Rd. hotels, both spatially and socially. Broad halls lead to vast rooms, and the clientele consists of both men and women; in fact, one of the managers is a woman. The mattresses are somewhat hard and the bathrooms rundown. Singles with bath Rs.95. Doubles Rs.150.

Delhi Hotel, A.C. Lane, Police Bazaar (tel. 223562). From G.S. Rd., walk past Broadway Hotel on your right; turn right onto A.C. Lane, and the hotel is on the left. The Delhi Hotel stands to compete with Mawsyn and Cherrapunjee for the title of wettest place on earth. In its public areas the floor is tracked with mud. Yet it is homey, even "earthy." Wisps of incense smoke obscure Hindu images at the front desk. The manager rushes from restaurant to kitchen to bedroom to common bath, trying to keep out the water. But unlike the lobby and bathrooms, the rooms are clean and dry. Check-out noon. Cramped singles Rs.40. Spacious doubles Rs.90.

Highway Hotel, G.S. Rd. (tel. 223681). One kilometer past the Broadway Hotel, on the right. The wood of the furniture and paneling in the lobby give off a pleasant smell in the humid Shillong climate, as the predominantly male clientele sits around watching Hindi flicks. Singles Rs. 60.

Shillong Club, Kacheri Rd., across from State Bank of India (tel. 226938). From the bus stand, with your back to the MTC building and the Tourist Information Office on your left, walk straight bearing left 500m; turn right onto Kacheri Rd. The club has suffered a bit since the British pulled out: the manager slips in and out of a Brit-

> ### Khasi Cuisine
>
> Pork is the most popular meat among the Khasis; anything with *"doh"* in the name is a pork product. *Dohjem* is pork intestine, and *dohsniang* is made from pork body, spiced with a mild black spice called *neiong. Tungrymbai* is a sharp bean chutney and *tungtap* is fish chutney. *Jadoh* is a kind of *pulao* made with special Meghalayan rice unavailable elsewhere.

ish accent, and the tennis courts are more like mudflats. Nevertheless, it's still pretty classy. The rooms are huge and "temporary membership" includes access to the club's billiard tables and 18-hole golf course. Singles Rs.235. Doubles Rs.425. Rooms must be booked in advance. Call or write to Shillong Club Ltd., Residential, P.O. Box 45, Shillong 793001.

FOOD

Decent Chinese food can be found in Police Bazaar, and Khasi food at many small shops in Bara Bazaar, though one glance at the meat market might dissuade you.

Abha Restaurant, Lower Lachaumiere, south Shillong. A taxi ride from G.S. Rd. or Police Bazaar costs Rs.10. A smaller, less inviting branch is located on G.S. Rd. Chinese food made by real Chinese people. Veg. chow mein Rs.35. Open 10am-8:30pm.

Trattoria, Police Bazaar (tel. 225345). With your back to the bus stand and the MTDC office on your right, walk straight for 100m, take the first sharp right, and the restaurant is on the right. A small, hygienic stall serving Khasi food in the center of Shillong's posh shopping district. Open 9am-7:30pm.

SIGHTS

The cheapest and most convenient way to see the city's major tourist attractions is to join the MTDC's half-day tour, which includes **Shillong Peak, Elephant Falls** and **Bishop Beadon Falls.** The tour leaves at 8:30am and costs Rs.75. Other less frequented and hence more peaceful spots include **Sweet Falls,** 8km from Police Bazaar. The falls themselves are unspectacular, but there are plenty of paths to explore and plenty of room for picnickers. **Crinoline Falls,** near Lady Hydari Park within the city limits, has a pool for swimming, although Shillong's cool, rainy climate doesn't encourage this.

Beetle fans will love the **Museum of Entomology.** The museum is hard to find. On G.S. Rd., walk past the Grand Hotel (on your right); take the first right (but not a sharp right) onto Umsohsun Rd. When this forks, go left and follow the curving residential street 500m. The museum is on the right and the sign is difficult to see, so ask locals, who know it as the "Butterfly Museum." This vast collection of butterflies and exotic bugs includes 30-cm-long poisonous stick bugs and what is claimed to be the world's heaviest beetle. Started by a Mr. Wankhar in the 1930s, the collection was passed down to his son in the 1960s, and now *his* son is being groomed for the job of caretaker.

The **Polo Ground,** a weed-infested patch 3km northeast of Police Bazaar, is the site of a daily **archery contest.** Opposing archery teams shoot a volley of arrows into a wooden target. The match, held at 4pm, is over within seconds, but the results reverberate through the city for the rest of the evening. Betting booths at the Polo Ground and in Bara Bazaar take bets on the last two digits of the total number of arrows that stick. This gambling has recently become legal, and the payoff is 8 to 1.

■ Near Shillong: Cherrapunjee

Until recently, the town of Cherrapunjee, 56km south of Shillong, held the record for the greatest rainfall within a 24-hour period. Unbelievably, 104cm of rain fell here on June 16, 1876; even more unbelievably, the record has recently been broken by the nearby village of Mawsyn. The only realistic way to see Cherrapunjee is by guided tour. One rickety bus goes to Cherrapunjee from Shillong in the morning. The sights are spread out over several kilometers on the outskirts of this small depressed town, which has no local transportation and no accommodations. But the MTDC tour is decent and covers all the major spots, stopping first at the Nohkalikai Falls, India's second-highest waterfall, which plummets into a lush valley. On a clear day, the deserted floodplains of Bangladesh are visible. The next stop is **Mawsmai Caves,** which are flooded during the monsoon; more adventurous guides will let you strip down and wade through to the jungle on the other side. At around 1pm, the bus pulls up to the cusp of a deep valley and stops at the Tourist Bungalow for lunch and a view of the Seven Sisters Falls. En route, the guide points out seasonal waterfalls and valleys set against a backdrop of Bangladesh.

OTHER STATES

With the exception of Tripura, the other states of the Northeast are difficult for foreigners to enter. For more information, see **Special Permits,** p. 5.

At the tail end of the Himalayas, **Arunachal Pradesh** ("Dawn-Lit Mountain State") has a thriving tribal culture, wildlife preserves, national parks, and the largest Buddhist monastery in India at Tawang. China still claims Arunachal Pradesh, making the political situation here unstable. There are airports at Along, Daparizo, Passi Ghat, Tezu, and Ziro. Itanagar, the capital, is accessible by bus from Harmoti in Assam, which is connected by rail to Guwahati.

Nagaland is very Christian, but still supports a thriving tribal culture (16 tribes in all). The insurgency of the fiercely independent Nagas was ended by the carving out of Nagaland in 1963. Dimapur has impressive monoliths, built before the invasion of the Ahoms in the 13th century. Outside the capital city of Kohima (74km from Dimapur) is a large old-fashioned Naga village. There is good trekking in the Dzukou Valley, 30km from Kohima, and around Mt. Saramati, 269km from Kohima. Nagaland's one airport is in Dimapur. Dimapur is connected by rail to Guwahati, and by bus to other towns in the northeast.

Polo in its modern form is said to have originated in **Manipur,** and Manipuri martial arts and dances, including the Jagoi form of dance, are known throughout India. Manipur was formerly a princely state, and its capital is at Imphal, 145km from Kohima in Nagaland and 215km from the nearest railhead at Dimapur. From here buses go to outlying villages.

Mizoram is rich in tribal culture. It has many hill stations and beautiful valleys. A Mizo insurgency during the 1980s led to the creation of the state in 1986. Aizawl, the capital city, is connected by air to major cities in India and by road to Silchar, which is accessible by rail from Guwahati.

The small state of **Tripura,** surrounded on three sides by Bangladesh, was formerly a princely state. The capital, Agartala, has a temple of Lord Jagannath from the 19th century and the Indo-Saracenic-style Ujjayant Palace, built by Maharaja Bikram Singh. Agartala is surrounded by hill stations, and 53km from Agartala is the Neermahal Palace, located in the center of a lake. Tripuran Bengalis and recent immigrants from Bangladesh now outnumber the state's tribal population, a fact which provoked an ethnic insurgency during the 1980s. An agreement with the central government brought peace in 1988. Agartala can be reached by bus from Silchar in Assam.

Orissa

Stuck out on India's east coast, the state of Orissa rests in contradiction. Orissa's 482-km Bay of Bengal coastline and its two major rivers have historically provided a channel for communication between North and South India and between Orissa and the

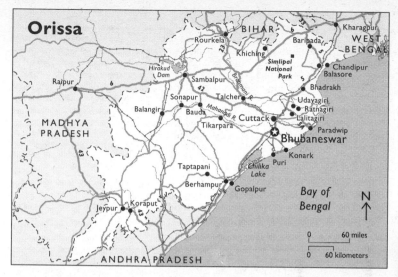

Orissa

Kharagpur
BIHAR
WEST
BENGAL
Rourkela
Baripada
Khiching
Chandipur
Balasore
Hirakud
Dam
Simlipal
National
Park
Raipur
6
Sambalpur
Bhadrakh
Sonapur
Talcher
Udayagiri
Balangir
Bauda
Rathagiri
Cuttack
Lalitagiri
Tikarpara
Paradwip
MADHYA
PRADESH
★ Bhubaneswar
43
Konark
Taptapani
Chilika
Lake
Puri
Berhampur
Gopalpur
*Bay of
Bengal*
Jeypur
Koraput
N
43
0   60 miles
0   60 kilometers
ANDHRA PRADESH

world. But in the western part of the state, the Eastern Ghats and various plateaus have tended to protect Orissans from invasion, thus allowing numerous indigenous populations to thrive. The capital city of Bhubaneswar and its neighbor Cuttack sit in a drippy coastal plain at the mouth of the Mahanadi River. Orissa's elevated back-country has historically been covered with thick, difficult forests and settled by *adivasis* (tribal peoples), while the people of the coast, as if overcompensating for their separation from the rest of India, cling to a fierce regional pride and seem to be more quintessentially Indian than other Orissans. The ancient Orissans, known as Kalingas, held out against the expanding Mauryan Empire in the 3rd century BC, capitulating only after a battle so infamously bloody that it convinced the emperor Ashoka to convert to Buddhism. Orissa also fought off Muslim rule until 1568, almost 400 years after surrounding regions were captured. This extra time allowed Orissa to develop one of India's finest styles of Hindu temple architecture, and the Odissi form of dance to go with it. Today Orissa is one of India's most uniformly Hindu states, with over 95% professing the religion (and worshiping first and foremost Lord Jagannath, a local version of Krishna).

■ Bhubaneswar

Bhubaneswar has been Orissa's capital since 1948, when Cuttack, the former Orissan capital 30km to the north, was diagnosed with overcrowding and self-destructive urban frenzy. Sleepy Bhubaneswar has not suffered the same fate: this is a planned city, where pleasant white lines painted down the middle of long, straight avenues and an abundance of public elbow-room provide for a small-town feel. This is not purely a government-built lagoon, however; an ancient Bhubaneswar, 2000-year-old capital of the powerful Kalinga kingdoms that ruled Orissa from the 5th to the 10th centuries, rumbles underneath the modern facelift. In the Old Town one can still feel its dominion: roads are winding, and neighborhoods crunched between lakes, canals, and old stone temples attest to ancient loyalties. Modern city planners may have looked to these past glories for inspiration, although they obviously built the New Town with more practical, utilitarian ideals.

ORIENTATION

Urban planning in Bhubaneswar's **New Town** has produced a spaced-out city. Large roads such as the north-south **Jan Path** and **Sachivalaya Marg** and the east-west **Raj Path** cut Bhubaneswar's New Town into neat squares called **"units"** or **"nagars."** As units these squares have numbers; as nagars they have names. There is no clear city center, but the closest approximation is **Station Square** near the railway station, with a huge horse statue in its roundabout in front of the railway station. To the north and west of Station Square are Ashok Nagar (Unit 3) and Kharavela Nagar, containing many shops and services. Many hotels are located around Station Sq., but the cheaper ones are at **Kalpana Square,** located at the junction of Cuttack Rd. and Raj Path, to the south. The railroad runs along the east edge of town, and **Cuttack Road** runs north-south just east of it. **National Highway 5** curves around the city to the west and north.

Bhubaneswar's **Old Town,** to the south of the main planned city, is haphazardly laid out and has no main roads. There are conspicuous landmarks, however: the lake known as **Bindu Sagar** sits in the center of the Old Town, and the tall **Lingaraja Temple,** just south of it, is visible from afar.

PRACTICAL INFORMATION

Tourist Office: Government of Orissa Tourist Office, 5 Jayadev Nagar (tel. 431299). Head south down Puri Rd. and turn right on Jayadev Nagar. Tourist office is 50m down the street on the left. Maps of Orissa (Rs.5) and an abundance of pamphlets listing everything from the districts of Orissa to the 42 best budget hotels in Bhubaneswar. Be sure to ask for a brochure listing the Buddhist relics of Orissa. Extremely helpful and patient. Open Mon.-Sat. 10am-5pm. Counters at the **Airport** (tel. 404006) and **Railway Station** (tel. 404715) are open 24hr. **OTDC,** on the corner of Puri Rd. and Jayadev Nagar (tel. 50099), near the Panthanivas Tourist Bungalow, can arrange cheap but rushed tours of Bhubaneswar, Puri, and Konark. Make enquiries by calling the Transport Unit Panthanivas (tel. 431515). All tours leave from in front of the Panthanivas. Expect to be rushed through the sights (just over 25min. at Lingaraj Temple) and to spend 10hr. on a bus, but you will see all of the temples for only Rs.85 (A/C bus Rs.130). Tours run Mon.-Sat. 8:30am-6pm. If you wish to focus exclusively on the major attractions of and near Bhubaneswar—the Temple complex, the caves at Udaigiri and Khandagiri, Dhauli hill, and the Nandankanan Zoological Park—plan on spending an equal amount of time but slightly less money (Rs.80, A/C bus Rs.100). Tours operate Tues.-Sun. 9am-5pm. Open Mon.-Sat. 10am-5pm. **ITDC,** B-21 Kalpana Area (tel. 54203). Follow Puri Rd. south past the State Museum, take the first left and follow the road directly to the office. Hyperfriendly, providing a plethora of information on other parts of the country. Open Mon.-Fri. 10am-5pm.

Budget Travel: Centre Point Travel & Tours, 79 Budha Nagar (tel. 417530, 417467; fax 409056). A 3-min. walk from Kalpana Sq., 2 doors to the left of Hotel Gajapati, this enthusiastic agency is prepared to meet your every travel need. Domestic airline tickets. Expensive private tours of Bhubaneswar and the surrounding areas get less pricey with a big enough group. Inquire as to potential discounts. Open daily 9am-9pm. **Swosti Travels,** 103 Jan Path (tel. 408738, 408526; fax 407524; e-mail swosti.swosti@axcessnet.in). From Station Sq., walk north on Jan Path past the Hare Krishna Restaurant. Breeze past the 3-star Hotel Swosti and into the travel agency. Upscale package tours of Orissa's textiles, wildlife, or tribes offered. Reputable and professional. Open daily 9am-8pm. More general budget tours of the Bhubaneswar, Puri, and Konark are best and most cheaply experienced with OTDC (see **Tourist Offices,** above).

Immigration Office: Foreigners, Registration Office, District Intelligence Bureau, Sahid Nagar (tel. 405555). From Station Sq. either cycle- or auto-rickshaw 3km north on Jan Path to the Jan Path-NH5 intersection. On the left is the FRO, located inside the building of the Superintendent of Police. Open Mon.-Sat. 10am-5pm. **Passport Office:** Unit 6 (tel. 404005). From Raj Mahal Sq., walk northwest up Raj Path past the old bus stand (on your right) and cross the Raj Path-Sachivalaya

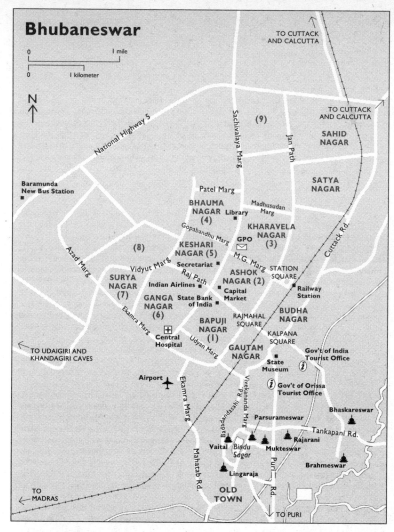

Bhubaneswar

0   I mile

0   I kilometer

N

TO CUTTACK
AND CALCUTTA

National Highway 5

Sachivalaya Marg

Jan Path

TO CUTTACK
AND CALCUTTA

SAHID
NAGAR

SATYA
NAGAR

Baramunda
New Bus Station

Patel Marg

BHAUMA
NAGAR
(4)

Library

Madhusudan
Marg

Gopabandhu Marg

KHARAVELA
NAGAR
(3)

GPO

M.G. Marg

Azad Marg

(8)

KESHARI
NAGAR (5)

Vidyut Marg

Secretariat

Raj Path

SURYA
NAGAR
(7)

Indian Airlines

ASHOK
NAGAR (2)

STATION
SQUARE

Railway
Station

GANGA
NAGAR
(6)

State Bank
of India

Capital
Market

BUDHA
NAGAR

Ekamra Marg

BAPUJI
NAGAR
(1)

RAJMAHAL
SQUARE

KALPANA
SQUARE

Central
Hospital

Udyan Marg

GAUTAM
NAGAR

TO UDAIGIRI AND
KHANDAGIRI CAVES

Gov't of India
Tourist Office

Airport

Ekamra Marg

State
Museum

Gov't of Orissa
Tourist Office

Vivekananda Marg

Badadandasahi Rd.

Parsurameswar

Bhaskareswar

Tankapani Rd.

Rajarani

Vaital

Bindu
Sagar

Mukteswar

Brahmeswar

Mahatab Rd.

Lingaraja

Puri Rd.

TO
MADRAS

OLD
TOWN

TO PURI

EAST INDIA

Marg intersection to the office situated on the left side of the street. Indians, foreigners, and everyone else are welcome here. Packed, slow, and prone to gluttonous bureaucracy. Open Mon.-Fri. 10am-5pm.

Currency Exchange: State Bank of India, Main Branch, Raj Path (foreign exchange dept. tel. 403810). A short walk from Raj Mahal Sq., on Raj Path across the street from Capital Market. No commission. Open Mon.-Fri. 10am-2pm, Sat. 10am-noon. Two other State Bank of India branches are located around the corner from the GPO on Sachivalaya Marg, and north on Jan Path near Raj Mahal Sq.

Telephones: STD/ISD vendors are as pervasive as rickshaw-*wallahs*. **Central Telegraph Office,** PMG Sq., on the corner of Mahatma Gandhi Marg and Sachivalaya Marg (tel. 409516). Crossing Jan Path from Station Sq., follow along Mahatma Gandhi Marg to the corner. Enter into the GPO complex; the GPO's next of kin is the telegraph office. Telephone calls can be made and telegrams sent nationally and internationally. Send a "good luck in your next life" telegram to someone you love. Open daily 8am-8pm.

Airport: Northwest of the temples in the Old Town (tel. 406472, 401084). No buses go to the airport, but rickshaws and auto-rickshaws can be hired for Rs.20-30. To: Calcutta (Tues.-Sun. 1-2 per day, 1hr., US$62); Delhi (1 per day, 2hr., US$164); Hyderabad (Tues., Thurs., and Sat., 3hr., US$123); Madras (Wed.-Thurs. and Sat.-Sun., 2hr., US$150); Nagpur (Tues., Thurs., and Sat., 1½hr., US$96); Visakhapatnam (Thurs. and Sat., 1hr., US$70).

Trains: Bhubaneswar Railway Station, Station Sq. (computerized reservation office tel. 402042). The South Eastern Railway timetable can be purchased for Rs.15 at the bookstand located to the right of the exit gate. All enquiries made at 2nd class railway booking and enquiry counter (tel. 402233). An unhelpful tourist information counter pushes expensive lodgings and offers maps of Orissa (Rs.5). To: Calcutta (several daily trains: *Dhauli Exp.* 2822, 2:10pm, 8hr., Rs.135 for 2nd class, *Puri-Howrah Exp.* 8008, 8:45pm, 9hr., *Sri Jagannath Exp.* 8410, 11pm, 9½hr.); Delhi (*Purushottam Exp.* 2801, 9:45pm, 31½hr., Rs.191/833 for 2nd/1st class); Hyderabad (*East Coast Exp.* 8045, 7:40pm, 20hr., *Falaknuma Exp.* 7003, Tues., Fri., Sun., 3:40pm, 19½hr., Rs.245/790 for 2nd/1st class); Madras (*Coromandal Exp.* 2841, 9:30pm, 20hr., *Madras Mail,* 6003, 4:30am, 25hr., Rs.250/830 for 2nd/1st class). Before purchasing a ticket or in case of travel emergencies, inquire about foreigners' quotas at the computerized reservation office.

Buses: Baramunda New Bus Station, National Highway 5 (tel. 470695, 470939). Nine kilometers from Raj Mahal Sq. All buses leave from this new station; the old bus stand on Raj Path is out of service. To: Balasore (every hr., 4hr.); Berhampur (every hr, 4-5hr.); Calcutta (4 per night, 8-10hr.); Cuttack (every 15min., 45min.); Konark (1 per day, 1½hr.); Puri (every 15 min., 1½hr., Rs.10). In theory, the sojourn from Bhubaneswar to Puri should take slightly over 1hr.; count on 2½. To avoid a nervous breakdown, board the bus at Baramunda to ensure a window seat, and do not travel at the end of a workday. Adventurous and reckless types catch the Puri bus at its second stop, the petrol station across the street from the Kalinga Ashok Hotel. Breathe deep and practice *ahimsa,* for this journey challenges even enlightened ones. If you are a *bodhisattva,* forget the rest of us and leave your body now.

Local Transportation: The New Town is easily walkable. To reach the temples in the Old Town, the airport, or Baramunda New Bus Station, **auto-rickshaws** are easy, cheap, ubiquitous, and exhausting. The going rate is approximately Rs.5 per kilometer but rarely does this hold. Haggle, haggle, and haggle more. Don't pay more than Rs.35 anywhere within the city. Positioned at every major square, **taxis** are best avoided, charging exorbitant fees—Rs.50 for a cross-town trip.

English Bookstore: Modern Book Depot, A/4 Surya Nagar, (tel. 402373). At the top of Station Sq., on the right. Offers a bit of everything for the intellectually inclined. A wide variety of maps and an extensive section on Orissan history and art. Open Mon.-Sat. 9am-2pm and 4-9pm.

Library: Harekrushna Mahtab State Library and **Bhubaneswar Public Library,** Sachivalaya Marg. From Station Sq., proceed northwest on Mahatma Gandhi Marg until you reach Sachivalaya Marg. Turn right and the library complex is a 7-min. walk on the left, across from the Reserve Bank of India (both libraries are in the same complex). In order to utilize the research facilities and reading room (i.e., to even enter the premises), written permission must be obtained from the librarian, who is located in a scantily decorated office, replete with half the library's books. Open Mon.-Sat. 8am-8pm.

Market: Capital Market, Unit 2, on Raj Path next door to Utkalika Handicrafts and across the street from the Indian Airlines office. High-quality market selling handicrafts, clothing, and fresh fruit and vegetables at more than reasonable prices. Open Tues.-Sun. 9am-8pm.

Pharmacy: Allopathic: **Rabindra Medical Store,** Bapuji Nagar, off Jan Path near Raj Mahal Sq. and **Balaji Medical Store,** Bapuji Nagar nearby. Both open 24hr. Homeopathic: **Janata Homeo Pharmacy,** Kharavela Nagar, Jan Path, north of Station Sq. Open 24hr. Behind the Railway Station, south on Cuttack Rd., near the

Bhubaneswar Hotel, is a **Skin and STD Clinic**, run by Dr. S.C. Mallik. Consulting times Mon.-Sat. 8:30am-12:30pm and 5-9pm, Sun. 8:30am-12:30pm.

Hospital: Capital Hospital, Unit 6 (tel. 400688). From Raj Mahal Sq., proceed south on Jan Path. After 1 long block, turn right and head west on Udyan Marg, cross the intersection of Udyan Marg and Sachivalaya Marg. A wee bit to the left is the 24-hr. English-speaking hospital and attached pharmacy. **Ayurvedic Hospital,** Malisha Sq. (tel. 432347). Near the Orissa Administrative Tribunal, a short distance to the east of Vivekananda Marg. From the east side of the train station, go south on Bhubaneswar Marg (also known as Cuttack Rd.) past Kalpana Sq. and the Kalinga Ashok Hotel. At the fork in the road, veer to the right and head south on Vivekananda Marg. Directly across from Rameshwar Temple is the Tribunal, behind which you'll find the Ayurvedic Hospital. Somewhat difficult to find. **Ambulance:** tel. 50389.

Post Office: GPO, PMG Sq., on the corner of Mahatma Gandhi Marg and Sachivalaya Marg (tel. 406340). From the big horse in Station Sq., cross Jan Path and walk to the end corner of Mahatma Gandhi Marg. Inquire about *Poste Restante* at window 6. An emergency mail counter is open all night. Stamps and Postal Stationery sold at window 1; parcels packaged and sent from the 2 multi-purpose counters. Open daily 8am-8pm. **Postal Code:** 751001.

Telephone Code: 0674.

ACCOMMODATIONS

If you're interested in variations of sameness or have a particular taste for mediocrity *par excellence,* trek south on Jan Path and inquire about the limitless rooms for unspeakably low prices. If you prefer less dingy surroundings, challenge yourself to the bustle of Kalpana Sq. This is Bhubaneswar's busiest neighborhood, and though most shops close before 11pm, a cacophony of inexplicable noises prohibit any REM sleep. The least exciting, least scenic, but most peaceful part of Bhubaneswar can be found on the east side of the railway station along Cuttack Rd.

Hotel Swagat, Cuttack Rd. (tel. 416686, 413212). Exit the east side of the railway station (not the main exit facing Station Sq.) and walk 5min. This small hotel offers clean rooms at affordable prices. Relaxed conversations with inquisitive management reverberate through the reception area, and the rest of the hotel is peacefully quiet. Sanity restored by comfortable beds. Restaurant service offers breakfast 8-10am, lunch noon-2pm, and dinner 8-10pm. Though the hotel is open 24hr., visitors are not allowed after 10pm. Dorm beds Rs.50. Singles with bath Rs.100. Doubles with bath Rs.125, with TV Rs.175, with A/C Rs.350.

Hotel Pushpak, Kalpana Sq. (tel. 415545, 415943). From Station Sq., turn left onto Jan Path. Head south and make a second left on Raj Path which leads directly to Kalpana Sq. Images of Krishna bless travelers from every wall. The aqua-green walls are cooling in the summer and inviting in the winter, and the professionalism of the management soothes your mind year-round. There's a restaurant (10am-10pm), room service (6am-midnight), and full bar replete with color TV screaming Hindi hits (11am-11pm). Singles with bath, Rs.70. Doubles with bath, Rs.100, with A/C and TV Rs.300. Quad with bath Rs.180.

Hotel Kanishk, 134 Ashok Nagar (tel. 402961). From Station Sq., turn left and travel south on Jan Path. Located 1 block north of Raj Mahal Sq. A tiny, crowded room that passes as a reception office greets every traveler with a Thums Up and a smile. A lobby poster reading "Like a spring, the beginnings of all things are small," exemplifies the casual atmosphere. Here, you're less a tourist and more a member of the owner's extended family. Rooms with windows are cooler—if you can't get a room with a window, be baptized by Star TV. Clean bathrooms. Train and bus schedules posted on the reception counter. Room service 6am-1pm and 4-10pm. Singles with bath, Rs.100. Doubles with bath Rs.150. Extra person Rs.20.

Hotel Apsara, 18 Jan Path, Bapuji Nagar (tel. 404724). From the railway station, turn left at Station Sq., heading south on Jan Path. Cross Raj Path and continue south. Approximately 5 blocks from Raj Mahal Sq., the Apsara is a small, friendly, family-run hotel. Enthusiastic reception of all foreigners. Manager willing to provide any and every service unavailable at the hotel. Room "boy" will fetch food from one of the numerous nearby eateries 24hr. Laundry service Rs.4 per garment. Tie-dyed sheets welcome sleep. The place gets cleaner the higher up you go, and the balcony offers a more than decent view of a huge century-old medicinal *muskunda* tree. No smoking. Singles with bath Rs.80. Doubles with bath Rs.115. Triples with bath Rs.150. Extra person Rs.20. Discounts of 15% are offered off-season. Prices negotiable.

Bhubaneswar Hotel, Cuttack Rd. (tel. 416977). Exit east from the railway station and walk 10min. south on Cuttack Rd. This 4-floored, newly painted, white hotel rises above everything in the vicinity both in height and value. Shrouded by trees and a tall Victorian-style gate, it truly is an ideal residential hotel in the city, the most Westernized and respectable budget option in Bhubaneswar. Every room has bath, balcony, channel music, and telephone. The restaurant is open for breakfast 8-10am, lunch noon-2pm, dinner 8-10pm. Rail and air ticket booking. Singles with bath Rs.90, with bath and TV Rs.110. Doubles with bath Rs.135, with bath and TV Rs.150. Triples with bath Rs.190. Advance reservations accepted.

Hotel Gajapati, 77 Budha Nagar (tel. 417893, 417271). Just off Kalpana Sq., directly off Raj Path. Good air circulation, with incense always burning. Little English spoken. Bar with beer and all kinds of whisky available, and restaurant serving Indian and Chinese both open daily 10am-10pm. Room service 7-10am. No smoking. Open 24hr. Singles with bath Rs.50. Doubles Rs.65, with bath Rs.80, deluxe Rs.100.

FOOD

English biscuit-filled snack stalls, vendors selling bananas and green coconuts, street-side South Indian eateries, and unpretentious Indian and Chinese restaurants seem to multiply from corner to corner. Traditional Orissan cuisine, served in small *ginas* arranged on a large *thali*, is prepared and spiced lightly. This is a perfect opportunity to try the toned down Orissan rendition of South Indian food. The entirety of Jan Path and Raj Path, culminating in the Kalpana Sq. area, offer a wide and complete culinary variety of Bhubaneswar's most delectable vegetarian and non-vegetarian choices for under Rs.50.

Cook's Kitchen/Restaurant, 260 Bapuji Nagar (tel. 400025, 400035). From the Station Sq., turn left and travel south on Jan Path for several short blocks past Raj Mahal Sq. An unnamed street to the left marked by an enthusiastic "Cook's" advertisement announces your arrival. Take advantage of the street-side "take away service" kitchen offering well-endowed curry dishes for under Rs.15, or be initiated into Cook's air-conditioned restaurant, located on the first floor of Blue Heaven Hotel. Push on either side of the exaggerated entrance and step into a no-smoking world where well-dressed, bow-tied servers entreat you with tandoori and Chinese cuisine. Dare a daily special and be seduced by the restaurant's mural of the Goan beach. A local favorite. Open daily 10:30am-10:30pm.

Hotel Suruchi, Raj Path. Several blocks northwest of Raj Mahal Sq., near Capital Market and across from the State Bank of India. Devoid of decoration, color, and pretense, Suruchi sells itself solely on its South Indian culinary skill. Steep your senses in its spacious atmosphere and stuff your stomach with the suggested Rs.20 Suruchi special, consisting of a scoop of rice with *puri* and *ginas* swimming in spicy, strictly vegetarian South Indian sauces. Speedy service. Swarming with local families. Open daily 9am-10pm.

Bay Bali Restaurant, 150/c Ashok Nagar, Raj Mahal Sq. (tel. 409104). A glitzy new outdoor marquee lures you into a dimly lit environment. But don't feel misled by the red arrow—the lack of local customers is not the fault of the alacritous management. Obsessively attentive, they have recently established a "Happy Hour Menu" (it's always Happy Hour) with Continental foods such as pizza, burgers, and sizzlers. Specials include the Bay Bali pizza for Rs.20 and a more traditional Bay Bali *biryani* for Rs.35. Take out upon request. Coming soon: a fully stocked bar. Open daily 10am-10pm.

Hare Krishna Restaurant, Lalch and Market Complex, Master Canteen (tel. 403188; fax 407186). From the train station, walk up to Station Sq. and turn right onto Master Canteen. Directly across from the flashing Hotel Jajati. Richly decorated with plush red carpets and burgundy velvet tablecloths. This air-conditioned, exclusively veg. restaurant is truly a home of the gods. A 1.5-m Ganesh greets your entrance, and a larger-than-life statue of Krishna blesses the small, expensive portions of food, ensuring safe and smooth digestion. *Paneer* capsicum Rs.47. While a *roti* is Rs.1.50 elsewhere, it is Rs.6 where Lord Krishna abides. Owned and run by a Hare Krishna devotee. No alcohol on the premises. Open everyday for lunch 11am-3pm, dinner 7-11pm.

SIGHTS

It is said that there are more ancient temples in Orissa than in the rest of North India put together. Although Puri and Konark have more famous individual temples, Bhubaneswar has Orissa's best collection. Three hundred are said to be standing from an earlier approximate total of 1000, igniting a temple-viewing frenzy in even the most apathetic, religion-weary traveler.

The story of the resurgence of Hinduism in the first millennium AD is told in the sculptures on Bhubaneswar's temples, which were carved under several Hindu dynasties between the 7th and 12th centuries AD. The figure of a lion pouncing on an elephant is said to represent Hinduism's triumph over Buddhism. Lakulisa, a 5th-century AD Shaiva saint who converted many Orissans, is also frequently seen. Most of Bhubaneswar's temples are dedicated to Shiva.

At each temple you'll inevitably find yourself guided by temple **"priests."** These are sometimes real *pujaris* with hidden commercial talents; at other times they're local teenagers who'll earnestly show off the sacred thread under their polo shirt. Regardless of their spiritual attainment, many of them are badly informed, and they tend to rush through all the symbolism without allowing time to enjoy the art.

A green tank at the center of the Old Town has a central religious role: this is the **Bindu Sagar** ("Ocean-Drop Tank"), whose waters are supposed to contain drops from all the holy pools and streams of India. Early-morning bathers take advantage of the blessing they bestow, as does the image of Lord Tribhubaneswar, which is dipped in the tank during the local cart festival in March or April. The roads next to the Bindu Sagar's green expanse bustle with *pan* shops, wandering cows, and card-playing Brahmins.

The oldest and best preserved of the early group of Orissan temples can be reached by turning down the road to the left just before the tank as one approaches from the new town. Not far on the left is the boxy **Parsurameswar Temple.** Built in the 7th century, it has many of the common features of early temples, including the small, squat *shikhara* and the uncarved roof over the porch. The window-like shapes that frame many of its sculptures derive from an earlier tradition found in Buddhist temples; the beads and checkerboard patterns give this temple a quaint feel. To the left of the rear entrance is a *linga* with 1000 tiny *lingas* carved on it.

The **Mukteswar Temple,** just a short walk from the Parsurameswar Temple on the same road, was built 300 years later. Here, instead of the Parsurameswar's one building, there is a whole laid-out landscape of small monuments. Notable points include the bold, U-shaped archway in front, and the lotus carved into the ceiling inside the porch. The Mukteswar is considered to be one of the finest Orissan temples, both for its carvings and its state of preservation. A plainer temple, the **Siddheswar Temple,** is just a few steps beyond the Mukteswar, dating from the 11th century. Leaving the Mukteswar Temple, turn left past the souvenir stands and cold drink shops to reach the whitewashed **Kedareswar Temple,** which is very active. The small **Gouri Temple** in the same compound is more ancient, although it has a recent coat of red paint. Outside of the Mukteswar temple is a quiet, simple restaurant called Hotel Aahar, serving up decent vegetarian *thalis* on banana leaves.

The **Rajarani Temple** (11th century) is less typically Orissan. To reach it, go up the road behind the Mukteswar Temple, then turn right on the large Tankapani Rd. After

Orissan Temple Architecture

Until 1568, the Kalinga kings were able to stave off temple-breaking Muslim invasions, leaving Orissa with more beautiful examples of old stone Hindu temples than any other region of northern India. The style of building that emerged in Orissa between the 7th and 13th centuries was North Indian temple architecture *par excellence,* yet distinctively Orissan. Throughout their architectural history, Orissan temples went through a range of styles, but all temples had some common features which skilled architects strove to represent in a shared ideal of the perfect temple.

The most important part of a temple was the *deul* (inner sanctum), which housed an image of the deity. This room was usually small, dark, and square, but on top of it rose a huge, elaborately carved *shikhara* (spire). Orissan *shikharas* resembled tall, curved pyramids. The *shikhara* was built with vertical ridges; early desings had three on each side, but later ones had five, seven, or even nine bands up each side. Atop the *shikhara,* like a flying saucer, hovered a lotus-shaped stone called an *amlaka.* Above that was a small pot, and finally the deity's weapon: a trident on Shiva temples, or a wheel for Vishnu.

The sanctum was joined by a rectangular room, the *jagamohana* (assembly hall). These "porches" always had simpler roofs than the *shikharas* of sanctums, signaling lesser importance. Yet in time they too gained spires, made of flat stones that arched into a step pyramid. Bigger temples added still more rooms in single file behind the *jagamohana:* first a *nata mandir* (dance hall), then a *bhoga mandir* (offering hall).

As complex as the architecture was the sculpture that covered it. The designs and figures served various functions: aside from the consecrated images in the sanctum, there were symbols relevant to the temple itself (such as guardian figures) and illustrations of legends and secular scenes. Early temples had only their outsides carved with lavish ornamentation; later the temple interiors were worked on too. Orissan sculptures tend to be rounder and deeper than those in other parts of India. Since so much sculpture had to be produced to cover the walls of huge temples, much of it appears churned-out and amateurish, but the authentic wonders, such as the Jagannath Temple in Puri and the Sun Temple in Konark, were obviously the result of inspired chiseling.

a five-minute walk the temple will be on the right, at the end of a long tree-lined driveway through a field. The Rajarani Temple no longer houses any god (as the lack of flags on top of it indicates) so to all concerned it's an architectural curiosity. The *shikhara* is multiplied in the *shekhari* style, with miniature *shikharas* projecting from it on all sides. Though common in other parts of India, this type of tower is rare for Orissa. The carvings of the *dikpalas,* the guardians of the eight points of the compass, are the best around. These ancient Vedic gods stand stiffly with flags, thunderbolts, and nooses. The porch room is uncarved, but two jangly sea-serpents and a padlock guard its door.

The chunky and cement-splotched **Bhaskareswar Temple,** a short rickshaw-ride further down Tankapani Rd., past the sewage canal, is certainly no artistic triumph, but it contains a 3-m Shiva *linga* thought to be an Ashokan column from the 3rd century BC.

Wander down a cow-trampled lane to the right after the Bhaskareswar Temple to the **Brahmeswar Temple,** from whose silhouette lion figures fly on all sides. This well-carved temple dates from the 9th century and has a smaller Shiva shrine at each of the four corners of its compound. Some of the carvings illustrate temple dancers who once worked here. Unfortunately, the inside of the temple is closed to non-Hindus.

Bhubaneswar's biggest bouquet of flags flies atop the **Lingaraja Temple,** to the south of the Bindu Sagar. The Lingaraja's 45-m spire dominates the surrounding landscape. The entire temple compound is unfortunately closed to non-Hindus, but the

British smugly built a viewing platform right next to the wall, which still stands to gives tourists their token look. The compound contains a jungle of ornate stone— over 50 smaller temples are strewn around the main one. The Lingaraja is one of Orissa's great temples, notable especially for the balanced placement of sculpture on its spire. Built around 1100 AD, it has the full four-roomed structure: a sanctum (under the spire), a porch, a dance hall, and an offering hall. Shiva is worshipped at the Lingaraja Temple in the form of Tribhubaneswar, "Lord of Three Worlds," from whom Bhubaneswar takes its name. The temple is known as Lingaraja, however, derived from an earlier name for Shiva. The second-largest temple in the compound, in front of the main temple to the right, is devoted to Shiva's consort Parvati.

The **Vaital Temple,** sunk in the ground at a crossroads on the western side of Bindu Sagar, differs from the other temples with its oblong, rounded *shikhara*. This very old style, developed from Buddhist temple design, had vanished by the time most of Bhubaneswar's temples were built. Take a flashlight with you to illuminate the gory carvings inside the temple, depicting scenes of human sacrifices and the skull-clad goddess Chamunda with her attendant owl and jackal. Chamunda is a popular form of the Goddess nowadays, but in the 8th century when the Vaital Temple was built she was praised by Tantric cults with outlandish rituals. Beside it is the **Sisireswar Temple.**

The **State Museum,** a short walk from Kalpana Sq., contains the usual dusty and dilapidated exhibits. The museum's strengths are in sculpture and Orissan tribal peoples' personal things. (Open Tues.-Sun.10am-5pm. Admission Rs.1). The **Tribal Research Institute,** located in northwestern Bhubaneswar near Baramunda Bus Station, offers a unique gaze into the tribal cultures of Orissa. The garden display of reconstructed tribal huts was patterned and built by *adivasi* experts. (Open Mon.-Sat. 10am-5pm. Free.)

■ Near Bhubaneswar: Dhauli

The hill of Dhauli, 8km south of Bhubaneswar on the road to Puri, marks Orissa's claim to a place in world history. The Mauryan emperor Ashoka defeated the Kalingas in a horrific battle here in 261 BC, and was so appalled by the killing that he converted to nonviolent Buddhism. Ashoka the Terrible became Ashoka the Righteous and he proceeded to spread Buddhism through all of India and to the rest of Asia. A long-winded **rock edict** in Brahmi script at the foot of Dhauli Hill explains Ashoka's theory of government by *dharma*. (An English translation is posted near these inscriptions.) Coming out of the rock above is a gentle and elegantly sculpted head and forepart of an **elephant,** one of the earliest stone carvings in the embryonic stage of Buddhist India. In the 1970s a Japanese order of monks, known as the Japan Buddha Sanga, wanted to do something for the site, so they built the **Shanti Stupa** (also known as the **"Peace Pagoda"**) at the top of Dhauli Hill. This white, nuclear-age *stupa* is visible from all around, and the hilltop affords fantastic views of Bhubaneswar and the sandy River Daya. The inscription and elephant sculpture are now often overlooked by visitors who head directly for the *stupa*. To get to Dhauli Hill, head south on Puri Rd. (also known as Lewis Rd.). It is cheaper to take an auto-rickshaw there and leave with the same one. Expect to pay Rs.70-80 for this route; auto-rickshaws go directly to the site. Buses, though only Rs.5, drop passengers 3km short of the hill. At the bottom of the hill, snacks and bottled mineral water flow as freely as the River Daya. The sites of Dhauli are open daily from 5am to 8pm. Free.

■ Near Bhubaneswar: Udaigiri and Khandagiri Caves

More vestiges of antiquity can be found at the Udaigiri and Khandagiri Caves, 6km west of Bhubaneswar, less than 1km off National Highway 5, past Baramunda Bus Station. These twin hills contain 33 small niches that were cut into the rock in the 2nd and first centuries BC as sacred retreat spaces for Jain ascetics. Now the road divides the Udaigiri caves (on the right) from the Khandagiri caves (on the left). Many of the caves have sculpture, but in a style entirely different from the sculpture on Bhubaneswar's temples: it's romantically pudgy, and less stylized, the whole surface flowing in wrinkles and folds—obviously the work of a different era. The best sculpture is in and around Cave 1 of Udaigiri, the two-storied **Rani Gumpha (Queen's Cave),** with its faceless guardians. Cave 12 is carved as the gaping mouth of a tiger. Cave 14, the **Hathi Gumpha (Elephant Cave),** has an inscription on its ceiling from King Kharavela of the Chedi Dynasty, perhaps the greatest of Kalinga kings and certainly the patron of the caves. Jain legends, mythology, and iconography can be seen in **Rani Nur and Ganesh Gumpha** (Cave 10). The top of the hill, directly above this cave, has the foundation of an old building that was probably a Jain hall of worship.

The caves of Khandagiri are not as well-carved as those of Udaigiri, though here an active **Jain temple** sits at the top of the hill. From it, there's a great view of Bhubaneswar, including the Lingaraja Temple and Dhauli Hill in the distance. Close to the temple is a clearing where recent visitors have built bizarre stacks of stones. The best carvings at Khandagiri are in **Cave 3.**

The caves can be reached from Bhubaneswar by auto-rickshaw for about Rs.25. Cold drink stands are directly opposite the Udaigiri cave entrance, and a beaten-down grayish building on the Udaigiri side houses a pre-modern but user-friendly post office and local telephone facilities. Buy peanuts and feed the precocious monkeys who frolic all around the entrances to the caves. (Open daily 6am-6pm. Free.)

■ Puri

To travel to Puri is to experience a holy, healing retreat of one kind or another. Puri has been described as a resting point on India's long eastern coastline, a seaside resort whose cleansing Bay of Bengal waters soothe the weariness of traveling souls. Puri is also a sacred Hindu pilgrimage site, dominated since the 12th century by the powerful temple of Lord Jagannath.

Along with Puri's locals, three distinct populations of visitors are to be found here—international travelers, tourists from other parts of India, and pilgrims from various aspects of Hindudom. These delegations infuse Puri with its two primary identities of resort and religious center. Hippie-hoppy Western and Japanese travelers most typically escape into the eastern edges of town into the relative calm and simplicity of day-to-day beach life, while groups of extroverted middle-class Bengalis travel in jam-packed, frenetic tourist buses for a harried and often hurried (but thorough) vacation of resort rest, *dharma* duty, and temple touring. The third contingent consists of the thousands of focused Jagannath worshipers who fill the eight *dharamshalas* that line the busy Grand Avenue, leading directly to the temple.

Puri is a good place to relax from the travails of Indian travel, to tour beaches and temples, or practice your religious duties and devotions. It is not a town that many just pass through; most come to Puri very deliberately and, in one way or another, find themselves moved by its healing intensity.

ORIENTATION

Puri's busiest areas are along **Grand Avenue,** which runs east-west through the northern (inland) part of town, arching southwest near the **Jagannath Temple** to become **Swargardwar Road.** On its southern side, Puri is washed by the Bay of Bengal, and along the eastern shore runs **Chakratirtha (C.T.) Road,** with a concentration of budget hotels and resources. As it progresses west, C.T. Rd. becomes **VIP Road** and then **Marine Parade Road.**

PRACTICAL INFORMATION

Tourist Office: Government of Orissa Tourist Office, Station Rd. (tel. 22664). From the railway station, follow Station Rd. west 500m. Tourist office is on the right just before Station Rd. meets VIP Rd. Mediocre maps and reading materials. Open Mon.-Sat. 10am-5pm.

Budget Travel: Om Travels, C.T. Rd. (tel. 24174; fax 24474). This ashram-travel agency-religious bookshop offers some of the best deals in town. Tour number 1, to Puri, Konark, and Bhubaneswar, the caves at Udaigiri/Khandagiri, and a lion and tiger safari at Nandankanan departs at 6:30am and arrives back in Puri 12hr. later (Tues.-Sun. Rs.65). Tour number 2, to Chilika Lake and Kalijai Temple, departs and arrives at the same times but operates only on Mon. and Fri. (Rs.70.) Spiritual books, *malas,* and varied incense scents can be purchased. STD/ISD phone. Open daily 6am-10:30pm. MC/V.

Immigration Office: Foreigners' Registration Office, VIP Rd. (tel. 23940). Walk west on C.T. Rd., pass the Subhash Chandra Bose statue and continue west for approximately 5min. Also known as the DIB (District Intelligence Bureau), this run-down building on the right side of the street is the place to go for visa extensions and passport registration. Open daily 9am-10pm.

Currency Exchange: State Bank of India, VIP Rd. (tel. 22505, 23682). From the railway station, head west on Station Rd., turn left onto VIP Rd. and follow it south past the Chandra Bose statue and the Foreigner's Registration Office. No commission. Open Mon.-Fri. 10am-2pm, Sat. 10am-noon. **Andhra Bank,** Kutchery Rd. (tel. 23374). From the western part of VIP Rd., pass the State Bank of India and take an immediate right. Directly across from the GPO is Andhra, the only bank in Puri where Visa and MasterCard cash advances are authorized. Foreign transactions at no commission. Open Mon.-Fri. 10am-2pm, Sat. 10am-noon.

Telephones: Aside from the numerous STD/ISD booths, the **Telegraph Office** on Chandan Hazuri Lane (tel. 22806), across from the Ramakrishna Mission, offers STD, ISD, and trunk calls. Open Mon.-Sat. 7am-10pm, Sun. 8am-3:30pm.

Trains: Puri Railway Station, Station Rd. At the junction of Hospital Rd. and Station Rd., across from the Sri Sri Niva Khatanaka Temple. Regular trains run from Puri to Bhubaneswar, though the bus is more convenient. To: Calcutta (*Puri-Howrah Exp.* 8008, 6:45pm, 11hr., *Jagannath Exp.* 8410, 9:10pm, 11½hr., Rs.90/372 for 2nd/1st class); Delhi (*Purushottam Exp.* 2801, 8:15pm, 33hr., Rs.191/833 for 2nd/1st class). In case of an emergency, speak to the superintendent at the computerized reservation counter and ask about the 2nd class foreigners' quota. Computerized reservations open Mon.-Sat. 8am-noon, Sun. 8am-1pm. All foreign 2nd class tickets sold at window 7. The 2nd class booking office is open 24hr. A tourist information counter (tel. 23536) both inside and outside the station supplies brochures on Orissa and outdated maps of Puri. Open 24hr.

Buses: Bus stand, Grand Rd. At the eastern corner of Grand Rd., past Canara Bank. Buses to Konark leave from the New Bus Stand (every 2hr. starting at 6:30am, 30min., Rs.10). Numerous private companies (arranged from tour agencies or hotel desks) operate interstate buses. To: Calcutta (2pm, 12hr.), Cuttack (4:30pm, 2hr.), and Bhubaneswar (every 15min., 1½hr., Rs.10).

Local Transportation: The easiest mode of transport is by **rickshaw** or **auto-rickshaw.** A ride from one corner of Puri to another should not cost more than Rs.20. Responsible hotel owners say that the going-Indian-price is Rs.5 per kilometer; foreigners are charged more. No need to bother with **taxis;** they're overpriced and overrated. Stumpy **local buses** rarely run properly, if at all; though they tend to be cheap (fares are under Rs.5) they do not operate according to any fixed schedule. For those who wish to take their transport into their own hands, there are a plethora of **bicycle, scooter,** and **motorcycle** rentals: **Aju's,** east on C.T. Rd. across from the Holiday Home. Bicycles (Rs.15 per day), Sunys (Rs.150 per day), medium-sized motorcycles (Rs.215 per day), and attractive bullets for the motorcycle-experienced (Rs.350 per day). Open daily 7am-7pm. Many hotels and travel agencies, including **Tanuja Tribe Tour** on C.T. Rd. near the beginning of hotel land, and **Om Travels,** 5min. west of Aju's on C.T. Rd. (tel. 24174; fax 24474), also rent these handy but dangerous vehicles. Om Travels offers cheaper prices for Sunys (Rs.125 per day). Open daily 6am-10:30pm. Passports are generally required as collateral.

Bookstore: Loknath Bookshop and Library, C.T. Rd. Walk east on C.T. Rd. towards the fisherman's village. Next door to Raju's Restaurant is the famed

Loknath, opened with 50 books in 1993 with the help of a British tourist. In 3½ years it has accumulated an astounding total of 800. The entire 3-year history is chronicled on a small laminated paper inside. Three walls of Dutch, Swedish, French, German, and English books can either be rented (Rs.7 per day, with a Rs.300 deposit), purchased (Rs.200), or exchanged. From travel guides to William Burroughs, from V. S. Naipaul to Kurt Vonnegut. Audio books available. Passport photos are taken and stamps are fetched and sold as a "favor" to each voracious reader. In season: open daily 8am-10pm. Off-season: daily 8am-noon and 3-8pm.

Library: Puri Library, Temple Rd., above the Government of Orissa Tourist Office. Books in English, Hindi, and Oriya. Extensive selection on religion. Contact tourist office for more information. Open Tues.-Sun. 11am-8pm. **Raghunandan Library,** Grand Rd. (tel. 22252) straight across from Jagannath Temple with the infamous roof platform view. Historically a monastery and library, the 1st floor houses books and palmleaf manuscripts. Open daily 8am-noon and 4-7pm. **Ramakrishna Mission Ashrama** (tel. 22207), an internationally funded ashram in the western part of town, housing students from around the world, and humbly boasting one of the nicest guest houses in the area. Preference is given to members, but all are welcome. Living out of the ideal of freedom of self and service to humankind, these devotees offer religious lectures on Thurs. and a quiet library adjoined by a reading room. April-Sept.: library open daily 4-7:30pm. Oct.-March: daily 3:30-7pm. Office open daily 8:30am-noon and 4-7:30pm.

Market: Laxmi Market, west on Grand Rd. This wholesale, better-quality, and most expensive of the markets sells fresh fruits and vegetables, fish, and other grocery items, as well as clothing. A bit further east on Grand Rd. is the smaller **Municipality Market.** Near the railway station is another market called **Badasankha Station.** All are open daily 6:30am-10:30pm.

Pharmacy: Government Headquarters Hospital, Grand Rd. Open 24hr.

Hospital: Government Headquarters Hospital, Grand Rd. (tel. 22062). From Jagannath Temple, proceed 1.5km east on Grand Rd., past the town police station, Om Services, and the Hotel Shreeram. To the left is the GHH, an old and dilapidated government-run facility that is not so much a hospital as a hospice for the dying. Hope and pray you do not have to go here. Though a 24-hr. privately owned **pharmacy** provides constant drug access, English is barely spoken and the best aspect about this place is its large and decently run ambulance service (**emergency tel.** 23237).

Police: Town Police Station, Grand Rd. (tel. 22039). From Jagannath Temple, walk slightly northeast on Grand Rd. Police station is 5min. to the left near the old bus stand. The control room is open 24hr. **If a beach emergency occurs, contact City Beach Police** (tel. 22025, emergency tel. 100).

Post Office: GPO, Kutchery Rd. (tel. 22051) From C.T. Rd. walk west, past the Chandra Bose Statue and turn right just after the State Bank of India. Proceed north on Kutchery Rd. GPO is straight ahead at the end of the road. *Poste Restante* available. Stamps can be purchased Mon.-Sat. 8am-8pm, Sun. noon-5pm. All other enquiries must be made Mon.-Sat. 10am-6pm, Sun. noon-5pm. From the railway station, there is a smaller post office selling the basics, more accessible to the newly arrived traveler. Walk southwest on Station Rd., take the first immediate left and head straight south for 5min. Open Mon.-Sat. 10am-4pm. **Postal Code:** 752001.

Telephone Code: 06752.

ACCOMMODATIONS

Budget accommodations abound in the mellowed bustle of Puri's traveler scene, located on the crusty, dusty edges of the eastern beaches. According to recent tourist office calculations, Puri has 2322 budget beds, many of which are to be found in the area of Chakratirtha Rd., better known simply as C.T. Rd., a small international traveler-dominated stretch of beach which offers the least expensive hotels and lodgings, moped and bike rentals on every corner, and a number of relaxed, intestine-friendly restaurants. This hotspot is accessed most conveniently by the rickshaw-*wallahs* who scamper to attract every weary soul who wanders off the bus from Bhubaneswar. When approached, simply announce with confidence that you would like to go to C.T. Rd.

Hotel Gandhara, C.T. Rd. (tel. 24117; fax 22154). From the bus drop on Grand Ave., head directly south on Hospital Rd. following the winding road past the railway station and post office until you hit C.T. Rd. Turn left and walk for 10min. or so; Gandhara is on the left. This semi-modern hotel has a definite foreign feel about it. Catering primarily to international travelers, Gandhara entices many Japanese by a 7-tiered bookshelf brimming with Japanese books (the Indian owner is married to a Japanese woman) and tempts other foreigners by providing the best maps of Puri to date, a self-service bar stocked full of sodas, beer (Rs.45), and free filtered water, a comfy open-windowed TV common lounge, and a breathtaking 5th-floor outside view of the coastline. Two rather large and friendly dogs greet you upon arrival. Gandhara International Travel Agency is part of the hotel and the family. A professional and proficient staff organizes discounted air tickets, railway tickets, and tours in excess. No restaurant, but breakfast served 8-10am (Rs.15). Open 24hr. Check-out 9am. Dorm beds Rs.30. Singles with bath Rs.80. Doubles with bath Rs.80-150, with bath and A/C Rs.450-650. V/MC.

"Z" Hotel, C.T. Rd. (tel. 22554). Walk east of Hotel Gandhara, past Restaurant Peace. Directly beside Traveller's Inn, on the right, "Z" looks to be an open-aired and spacey white palace. Once home to a maharaja of Puri, the enormous old structure draws many a tourist, not necessarily by its increasing room tariffs, but by its seaview rooms, the serenity of its muticolored garden, and its direct beach access. The jazz-loving management is easygoing to the point of hypnosis. Rickshaw-*wallahs* are not given commissions; preceded by its reputation, "Z" has no need to play this game. A small thatch-covered restaurant is outside with continual room service and friendly, accommodating staff. Open 24hr., with 14 rooms available. Mosquito nets provided. Dorm beds (women only) Rs.40. Singles with bath Rs.100. Doubles Rs.200, with bath Rs.300.

Hotel Sea 'n' Sand, C.T. Rd. (tel. 23107). A 2-min. walk from "Z" Hotel, just barely off C.T. Rd., this brand new, unpretentious, 7-roomed hotel welcomes travelers and Indian families alike. A fresh work in progress. Earnest, humble, and honest young owner desperately wants to establish its reputation. A brightly colored reception desk sells everything from music tapes (Rs.24) to band-aids, and provides local and international telephone service. No restaurant or TV, but a more peaceful environment than other hotels. Open 6:30am-11pm. Check-out 9am. Nov.-Feb.: Doubles Rs.150-200, with bath Rs.250-300. Mar.-Oct.: Doubles Rs.70, with bath Rs.90. "Family" quad Rs.90 year-round.

Hotel Pink House, C.T. Rd. (tel. 22253). Located 5min. south of C.T. Rd. Sitting on the beach in dull pinkish splendor. A bit run down from constant sea winds, this ultra-budget cottage of sorts offers the open Bay of Bengal for next to nothing. If you wish to enwrap yourself in the water-thick winds and don't mind wet clothes, ask to throw a sleeping bag up on the pink roof. In season, bonfires light the party months aflame with beach cheer. Open 24hr. Pink House offers daily tours of Konark (Rs.80), and road-beat Suny cycles lounge around awaiting rental at Rs.150. The straw-roofed restaurant is open daily 8am-10pm. Enough flavors of milkshakes to keep you slurping all day. Mosquito nets, coils, and bug spray available. Singles Rs.40. Doubles with bath Rs.80, with bath and seaside view Rs.100.

Sri Balajee Lodge, C.T. Rd. (tel. 23388). Pushing the eastern edges of Puri about 500m before reaching the fisherman's village, past everything of interest on C.T. Rd., the maroon building of Sri Balajee stands to the left. The owner is friendly and, if you don't mind being asked every 30min. or so if he can be of assistance, this welcoming, family-infested lodge can provide "homely comfort." When you're not experiencing the joys of Indian families or listening to the young room cleaners sing Oriya tunes, you can always sit out on your own little verandah. Obsessively clean toilets. No restaurant, but an active kitchen bent on room service. International calling available and call-backs are welcome. A locker keeps valuables safe.

Air and train tickets arranged with commission. Open 24hr. Singles Rs.50-70. Doubles Rs.150-170.

Hotel Tanuja, C.T. Rd. (tel. 24823 or 24974). Across from Harry's Cafe and the Mickey Mouse Restaurant. This 24-hr. no-restrictions hotel is a haven for nocturnal spirits who wish to come and go as freely as the beach winds. Alcohol, smoking, and visitors are allowed in the rooms. A common TV room, laundry service (Rs.3 per garment), and in-house postal service complete the offerings of Tanuja. Also, the attendant Tanuja Tribe Tour agency provides extensive and affordable trips and more costly wild adventure tours in the great outback of western Orissa. Book in advance for Chilika Lake (Rs.80). Mosquito nets drape over drab-looking beds with fairly comfortable pillows. Singles Rs.50. Doubles Rs.60, with bath Rs.80-100. Special VIP doubles with bath and decoration Rs.120-150.

Hotel Grand, Swargadwari (tel. 23962). Off Marine Parade Rd. Economical, brand new, with an anxious and talkative manager and a crowd of older men who hang around the marble-floored lobby. Twenty-five rooms, housing many festival-going Indians and a few foreigners. No religious restrictions. English and French spoken. Luggage storage. Freshly painted and clean, but a distance from C.T. Rd. and right in the midst of a loud Indian tourist scene. Apanjan, the attached restaurant, serves heaps of Indian and Chinese cuisine. Tea 6-7am (Rs.2). Open daily dawn-11pm. Check-out 7am. Doubles Rs.150-350.

FOOD

Feeble attempts at Western food dominate the C.T. Rd. scene, though there are several street restaurants serving excellent Indian food as well as fresh banana custard.

Raju's, C.T. Rd. Next to the Loknath Bookshop. It is claimed that the 25-year veteran cook Raju is the best in the entire area. Dine in the windowless room, or join others outside at the picnic tables, where laughing, conversation, and even occasional guitar music combine to complete the experience. When the chatter dies down and the tabla joins with the Krishna chants from the temple across the street, sip a lemon tea (Rs.2) or attempt a fresh, warm banana custard (Rs.12). Foreigners and Indians mingle with ease here. Open daily 7am-10:30pm, a little later in high season.

Restaurant Peace, C.T. Rd. East on C.T. Rd. past the Holiday Inn and Xanadu, directly across the street from Harry's Cafe. The culinary talk around Puri is that the cooks at Restaurant Peace buy fresh fruits and vegetables daily, allowing groaning, disrupted stomachs an evening's peace. This is a place full of activity, inhabited by Puri natives, Bengali tourists, and travelers of every shape, color, and religious persuasion. A poster of Lord Krishna blesses your greedy eating. Dirty white walls are tempered by sparkling clean tables. Although you can trust all of the food here, the Western food imitations leave something to be desired (except for the melt-in-your-mouth banana pancakes, Rs.15). Open daily 7am-10:30pm.

Chung Wah, VIP Rd. (tel. 23397, 23647). Walk west on C.T. Rd. and take a right on VIP Rd. Less than 1km further, on the left side of the street, stands one of the coolest A/C spots in Puri. Hanging Chinese lanterns and a Kwan Yin calendar greet you at the entrance. Sink into big, squishy chairs and choose from a veg. and nonveg. menu. With some of India's best Chinese food, the Chung Wah increases one's sanity fourfold. Veg. dishes (Rs.20-25). On special request, rice noodles (Rs.12) and garlic fish (Rs.42) can be prepared. Soups Rs.15-28. Open daily for breakfast 7-10am, lunch 11:30am-3pm, snacks 4:30-6pm, and dinner 6:30-10:30pm.

Mickey Mouse Restaurant, C.T. Rd. (tel. 24146) past Harry's Café and Restaurant Peace, diagonally across the street from the "Z" Hotel. Before you have time to breeze through the menu, most likely you will be asked to choose a song from the young management's repertoire of Hindi pop tunes, Marley, Joplin, Dionne Warwick, and Public Enemy. Try one of 20 different *lassis* (Rs.12), one of 18 custard varieties (Rs.12) or one of 30 forms of pancakes. The coffee and honey combo (Rs.12) is a must. Omelettes (Rs.5), veg. curry (Rs.4), plain rice (Rs.3), while a complete *thali* runs a steady Rs.9.50. Alcohol is not sold here but can be brought in. Open daily 6am-11pm.

Harry's Café, C.T. Rd. (tel. 24907). Across from Restaurant Peace. Six huge green picnic tables sit coolly amidst swirls of incense, as earnest young boys serve coconut milkshakes (Rs.11), Om rice (Rs.14), and peanut butter chocolate pancakes (Rs.14). The menu is as big or small as your appetite. Fax and STD services available within the bamboo thatched café. No alcohol served. Open daily 7am-10pm.

Sea Pearl Restaurant, Marine Rd. (tel. 22753). Across from the Puri Hotel. Good for snacks, and its location could not be better; it is on the sandy beach side of the beach, close to the water but rather busy and noisy, with water-loving Indian tourists from everywhere. Flies tend to either blend in with the food or fly into your mouth while you eat. *Masala dosa* Rs.8, plain *dosa* Rs.6. Good ice cream—butterscotch (Rs.13), rainbow (Rs.15), and vanilla (Rs.11). Open daily 7am-2pm, rain or shine.

SIGHTS

Every pilgrim's entrance into Puri is initiated by a short devotional stop in front of the main *simhadwara* (lion gate), the eastern and most important entrance to the **Jagannath Temple.** Rising to an overwhelming height of 65m, it is not difficult to realize that this pilgrimage town is ruled by the "Lord of the Universe," the charcoal-black-faced Jagannath. One of the most sacred *dhams* in all of Hinduism, the magnificent temple of Lord Jagannath was constructed early in the 12th century by the Ganga king Anantavaram Chodaganga, and illustrates the integrity of Orissan temple architecture.

The three divine inhabitants of the temple have been roughly hewn into abstraction: dense, rectangular wooden blocks represent the bodies of Jagannath, his brother Balabhadra, and his sister Subhadra. Tiny arms extend from stumpy legless forms and enormous, unblinking eyes glare strangely out from disproportionately-sized circular heads. It is said that Lord Jagannath doesn't have eyelids because he wishes to continually look after the well-being of the world. Some say he never sleeps. His small arms project outwards in a gesture of unconditional love for all his devotees. *Yatripandas* (pilgrimage priests) and other temple priests cite ancient myths to explain the peculiarly shaped forms while many academics suggest that the deities' forms have indigenous, tribal origins.

The temple is closed to non-Hindus; unless you are an ardent and committed follower of the traditions and restrictions of the Vedas, expect a firm denial to any of the interior of the temple grounds. Don't take offense—Prime Minister Indira Gandhi herself was denied access because of her marriage to a Parsi. However, a comprehensive view of the eastern gate, the Jagannath Temple and the surrounding subsidiary smaller temples can be found atop the roof of the **Raghunandan Library,** located directly across the streets, where travelers are ushered by a palm-leaf manuscript expert and a gregarious and capricious congregation of temple monkeys.

Patterned on the same architectural principles as the older Lingaraja Temple in Bhubaneswar, the abode of Jagannath is structurally aligned from east to west. The *bhoga mandir* (offering hall) and *nata mandir* (dance hall) lie nearest to the entrance and were 15th- and 16th century additions to the original *jagamohana* (assembly hall). The *deul* (inner sanctuary), crowned by a 65-m pyramidal roof, signifies the presence of the divine familial trio.

Surrounded by a 6-m wall, the massive temple compound hosts action-packed days of *darshan* and treats worshippers to devotionals and sacred dances at night. The complex employs approximately 6000 temple servants—specially trained temple priests who care to the daily needs of the deity (waking, cleaning, feeding, and dressing), artist communities who produce ritual materials, and thousands who work throughout the days to prepare *prasad* for Jagannath himself. The kitchen to the left of the temple serves meals to 10,000 people daily and up to 25,000 during festival times, such as the Rath Yatra.

Rath Yatra

Sweating. Singing. Shouting. Praying. Loud, excited crowds move en masse, as an effervescent and colorful humanity swells to enact an event of cosmic proportion. The **Rath Yatra** ("Cart Festival") of Puri is celebrated two days after the new moon in the month of Ashadh (June-July). The word *ratha* (chariot) is often associated with the word "temple," understood as both the mansion and the vehicle of the deity. The moveable *rathas* are actually shaped like ancient Hindu temples.

The festival day begins with the Gajapati (the King of Puri) making a gesture of *chhera paharna*, ritually "sweeping" the *rathas* to symbolize humanity purifying itself in preparation for the mercy and goodwill of Jagannath. As the mesmerizing chants of the *sadhus* and the ecstatic shouts of "Jai Jagannath" fill the frenzied air, Jagannath arrives on the scene to take the yellow-and-red draped seat of pomp in his 13-meter, 18-wheeled, gold-domed chariot, otherwise known as *Nandigosha*. Once Balabhadra and Subhadra, the other members of the divine family, are placed in their respective chariots, movement can begin.

On the day of the festival, each of the three deities are pulled by approximately 4000 devotees from the main gate of the temple east on Grand Avenue. As if propelled by divine force, the *ratha* carriers proceed forward on a 3-km journey in the newly constructed chariots for a nine-day summer outing at **Gundicha Ghar** ("Garden House"). During this nine-day respite, the gods take rest, eat specially prepared sweet rice cakes, and dress anew each day. Their symbolic tour of the universe, equally as erratic and intensely delirious with the trip to the Gundicha Ghar, is completed when a repeat processional performance is made in the direction of the temple. Both journeys are extremely slow-going, taking anywhere from 8 to 24 hours. Nineteenth-century British observers reported that ecstatic devotees would sometimes throw themselves under the wheels of the carts to obtain death and instant *moksha*. The word "juggernaut" comes from the English corruption of the god's name.

An ancient Hindu calendar dictates that the wooden images must be replaced once every 12 or 19 years, when the renewed deities assume a new body in an event known as Nava Kalebara ("New Embodiment"). The temple priests are responsible for the tangible incarnation of the deities: with honed, skillful practicality, they carefully select the wood, carving and painting with meticulous detail; each priest knows only his specific function in this complex series of rituals. The embodiment process is fully completed when, at midnight, the senior priest, blindfolded with covered hands, transfers an unknown divine substance from the chest of the old frame to the chest of the new one.

ENTERTAINMENT

The **beaches** are all the entertainment most travelers need. Since much of the water is now being filtered with chemical protectants, the beaches are becoming even more populated, and unfortunately, are often ravaged by tourists. If you go to **Lonely Beach,** the eastern beach past the fisherman's village, take only lotions and plenty of drinking water. Leave all valuables in your hotel if it seems trustworthy. If you rent a bicycle or Suny scooter, take your mode of transportation with you to the water, or you may be hitching a ride back and paying big bucks later.

In a pilgrim city like Puri, there are an abundance of festivals during the year. Many of the local people do not tell interested foreign visitors because they see no profit in it; thus, numerous tourists have no clue about most fascinating cultural events. **Dance and theatrical programs** can be best arranged through the Government of Orissa Tourist Office. Check their bulletin board daily for up-to-date events. For more diversions, take an evening stroll along Marine Parade through the Swargadwar area and the **night market** in western Puri. Saris color the market landscape, and the bright lights from Puri's burning *ghats* can be seen in the distance.

■ Konark

The village of Konark, 35km east of Puri along the coast, is the site of the Sun Temple, one of India's greatest architectural marvels. Little is known about the ancient history of Konark; its name is derived from the god Konarka, meaning "the sun of the corner." Konark's Sun Temple was built in the 13th century by King Narasingh either to celebrate a victory over Muslim attackers or to cure some skin ailment—Surya, the sun god, is also the god of leprosy, and is said to have freed Krishna's son Samba from a 12-year affliction. After the 16th century, the Sun Temple fell into neglect and was left to the mercy of seaside winds and monsoons. The temple became a landmark for European sailors on the way to Calcutta, who nicknamed it the "Black Pagoda" in contrast to Puri's whitewashed Jagannath temple, the "White Pagoda." By the 19th century, the Sun Temple's spire had completely crumbled and other parts of the porous stone structure were buried in sand. But even in ruins, the Sun Temple is magnificent, and since the temple's excavation and restoration in the early 20th century, Konark has become a much-frequented tourist spot. Small hotels have sprung up by the temple, and con men and pushy salesmen abound.

ORIENTATION AND PRACTICAL INFORMATION

The streets of Konark resemble a "Z." The vertical stroke is the main street with the temple entrance and a bevy of small shops and eateries; the top stroke is the road to Bhubaneswar; the bottom stroke is the road to Puri, passing beautiful deserted beaches along the way. **Buses** stop on a big patch of dirt at the intersection of the main road and the road to Bhubaneswar. Buses and minibuses go to Bhubaneswar (every hr., 5am-6pm, 2hr., Rs.12) and to Puri (every 15min., 5am-8pm, 1hr., Rs.7-10). If you catch the air-conditioned OTDC tourist bus on the Bhubaneswar-Puri road, you will have to pay the full cost of the day tour (Rs.80). A small road leads east from the bus stand 22km to Kakatpur, the site of a Goddess Mangala temple which has an important role in Jagannath festivities. Konark has no hospital or legal currency exchange. There is one STD/ISD **telephone** booth near the bus stand. The unhelpful **Orissa State Tourist Office** (tel. 8820, 8821) is located in the Yatri Niwas tourist lodge on the road to Bhubaneswar. Next door is the **post office** and farther down are the **archaeolgical museum** and an open-air theater, where the OTDC sponsors an annual four-day dance festival (mid-Feb.). **Telephone Code:** 06758.

ACCOMMODATIONS AND FOOD

Traditionally, travelers have made daytrips to Konark from more accommodating Puri, but a handful of hotels are now located around Konark. The **Labanya Lodge,** located on the right side of the road to Puri, 10 minutes from the bus stand, caters exclusively to Western tourists. There is a 24-hour STD/ISD phone; the owner lends his moped for nocturnal trips to the drugstore or rents it for the day. An evergreen, towering over the lush garden, is decorated as a Christmas tree in December, and there's a big bash on December 25 (which, of course, doesn't rival week-long Hindu fetes). Singles Rs.60. Doubles with bath Rs.80-100. Extra person Rs.10. If you can't get a room at Labanya, or you are looking for something more peaceful, both tourist lodges have clean, spacious rooms. **Yatri Niwas,** on the road to Bhubaneswar, has bare rooms and a beautiful courtyard with a manicured lawn. Doubles Rs.100. Quads Rs.120. **Pantha Niwas,** on the main road, has more decorated rooms and the Geetanjali Restaurant. Doubles Rs.150, with A/C Rs.350. Other hotels along the main road are shabbier, and some employ annoying commission agents. The **Konark Lodge,** across from Labanya on the road to Puri, is cheaper than Labanya, but it lacks Labanya's charm. The owner also works as an unlicensed guide at the temple.

The restaurant scene is bleak. Most places along the main road offer bland knock-offs of Chinese food and a limited Indian menu. The **Sunset Temple** restaurant has the widest selection, including soups and different kinds of tea, but the service is ach-

EAST INDIA

ingly slow. The more expensive **Geetanjali Restaurant** attached to Pantha Niwas has mediocre fried rice, but quick service.

SIGHTS

Considered the apex of Orissan architecture, the **Sun Temple** in Konark once stood 69m over the surrounding area. Tourists are often advised to visit Puri and Bhubaneswar before coming to Konark, to best appreciate the style of work that developed in those places and culminated here. Despite a long history of neglect, the now well-maintained ruins are impressive, especially at night, when huge spotlights spray enough wattage on this temple to astonish a sun god. The unusually well-written and well-spelled brochure from the Archaeological Survey of India further illuminates the Sun Temple's architecture; it's available at the Archaeological Museum for Rs.13 and at the temple for Rs.90. The licensed guides, some of whom speak decent English, tell wonderful, though largely apocryphal, stories, and can point out some of the more hidden sculptures.

The most prominent feature of the ruined temple is the *jagamohana* (porch, or audience hall), a step pyramid rising up in the middle of the compound. Before the temple was ruined, the eastward-facing door would catch the light of the morning sun and transmit it to the sanctuary, which stood behind the porch and contained a giant statue of Surya, the Hindu sun god. But the sanctuary is now completely in ruins, and the doorway and the interior of the porch have been filled in to support the crumbling structure.

Both the sanctuary and the porch are mounted on an ornate **platform** carved with 24 giant wheels and, at the front, seven horses. The temple is supposed to look like the sun god Surya's chariot riding across the sky. Other images on the platform represent scenes from daily life: elephant caravans, warfare, and amorous rendezvous. Some of these images, separated into compartments by small columns, tell a story, but in most cases they depict distinct episodes. Together they give the impression of a rich world. The spokes of the chariot wheels are said to represent the hours of the day, like a clock, and in some cases, the images carved on them follow this logic. On one wheel toward the front of the porch on the south side, the first six spokes are decorated with images of a woman bathing and performing housework, while the last six spokes—the nighttime hours—show her making love to her husband.

The **porch** itself is carved all about with **erotic images.** On the right side of the door are the positions outlined in the *Kama Sutra*. On the north side of the porch, high up on the left side of a small alcove, is a larger-than-life sculpture of an extremely devout *sadhu* being seduced by a dancing girl sent by jealous gods. Behind the porch, steps lead up to three **images of Surya** in chlorite stone on the south, north, and west sides.

Two modern staircases lead from the three statues to the remains of the sanctuary itself. Before the temple was ruined, the sanctuary could only be reached through the porch. But since the porch was filled in, engineers have created this alternate route. The sanctuary itself is nothing special. The statue that once presided is no more, and archeologists can only speculate about its design. Some tour guides claim that the statue floated in the air, suspended by powerful magnets lodged in each corner of the sanctuary. It is more likely that it rested on the highly ornate **pedestal** still extant. The frieze on the east side of the pedestal shows King Narasingh, the financier of the temple, and his queen. The north and south faces depict the retinues of the queen and king, respectively.

Behind the sanctuary to the southwest are the remains of a temple popularly known as the **Mayadevi Temple.** Formerly thought to be dedicated to one of Surya's wives, it is now believed to be an older Surya temple. The temple is decorated with erotic images.

In front of the porch and main sanctuary is a huge platform with four thick columns rising up in the corners. Some say it was a dancing hall, but it was more likely used for ritual banquets in honor of the deity. The platform and columns are decorated with carnival scenes of dancers and musicians.

Various sculptures from the temple have been scattered about the site by plunderers and collectors. The two elephant figures on the north side and the war horses on the south originally faced outward. The column which once stood in front of the banquet hall was moved to the Jagannath Temple in Puri years ago. Some of the finest fragments from the temple, cleaned and polished, now reside in the **Archaeological Museum,** on the road to Bhubaneswar, down the road from Yatri Niwas (open Sat.-Thurs. 10am-5pm). Still others are in the Indian Museum in Calcutta and the Victoria and Albert Museum in London.

Bihar

This eastern segment of the Ganga Valley gets its name from the word *vihara* (monastery) recalling the secluded centers of learning that flourished here during the first millennium AD. Bihar has reason to be proud of its past: some of India's great formative events took place here in its one-time thick forests. In the 6th century BC the Buddha gained enlightenment under a tree at Bodh Gaya, and the Mauryan and Gupta empires both grew up from the city of Pataliputra (modern-day Patna). It's impossible to take two steps in Bihar without tripping over the Buddha's footprints. No fewer than eight townships are associated with the Buddha's life, and the so-called Lotus Circuit (Bodh Gaya-Rajgir-Nalanda-Vaishali-Patna) is frequented by Buddhist pilgrims.

But few tangible traces are left of Bihar's past glories. Bihar is now an overwhelmingly agricultural state, the least urbanized and poorest state in India. In addition, Bihari politics have seen an unending roll of dishonor and periodic outbreaks of communal and caste-based violence. Much of the Bihari countryside is effectively ruled by *goondas* with under-the-table connections to politicians. Partly as a result, Bihar draws few tourists. Most travelers just pass through Bihar on their way between India and Nepal.

A quick excursion to the south leads to the Chota-Nagpur plateau, comprising the mineral-rich town of Ranchi, hill stations, and a couple of wildlife sanctuaries (including Betla National Park). Other Bihari attractions include the world's largest cattle fair, held annually at Sonepur, 40km northwest of Patna, in November..

> **Warning:** Due to the lack of law and order in Bihar, women are advised not to travel alone, and all are advised not to travel by night.

■ Patna

Patna, the capital of Bihar, sees few travelers. Despite the city's few strange attractions and its old-fashioned feel (with pink-and-blue buildings and crowded lanes), many find Patna's essence captured in the name of one of its major streets—Boring Road. All this is quite in spite of Patna's illustrious past. Patna was, in a way, the first capital city of India. The Mauryan Empire was seated here in the 4th and 3rd centuries BC, when the city was called Pataliputra, and the Guptas, too, made it their capital in the 4th and 5th centuries AD. But Pataliputra was abandoned after the decline of the Guptas, to be refounded as Patna in 1541 by Sher Shah Suri, rival of the Mughals. Patna became a regional center for the Mughals and the British, under whose rule it grew into the big Ganga city it is today.

ORIENTATION

Patna is painfully stretched along the south bank of the Ganga and getting from east to west is a road trip in itself. **Ashok Raj Path** is the main thoroughfare, sticking close to the river the whole way, while **Kankar Bagh Road** (Old Bypass Rd.) covers the same distance on the southern side of the city, just south of the railroad tracks. The east end of town is Old Patna, with many small, creaky lanes. Most trains stop at the

Bihar

NEPAL

SIKKIM

0   60 miles

0   60 kilometers

N

Gorakhpur

Birganj

Raxaul

28A

28

Motihari

Gandak R.

Sitamarhi

Jaynagar

Madhubani

Kishanganj

34

Muzaffarpur

UTTAR
PRADESH

Vaishali

28

Purnia

31

Sonepur

67

Maner

★ Patna

Ganga R.

Arrah

Buxar

Munger

Bihar
Sharif

Bhagalpur

Nalanda

Rajmahal

30

Jahanabad

Pawapuri

Rajgir

Son R.

Sasaram

Gaya

31

Simaltala

Bodh
Gaya

2

Kodarma

Deoghar

Madhupur

Dumka

Tilaiya

Masanjor

Parasnath

Dhanbad

Hazaribag

Damodar R.

Sindri

2

Betla (Palamau)
National Park

Netarhat

23

Ranchi

WEST
BENGAL

MADHYA
PRADESH

Gumia

Jamshedpur

6

6

Govt. of India statement:
The external boundaries
of India are neither correct
nor authenticated.

ORISSA

EAST INDIA

west end, at **Patna Junction Station,** and run straight north from the station on
Fraser Road, where Patna's hotels, restaurants, and conveniences are concentrated.
The **Gandhi Maidan,** north of Fraser Rd. (touching Ashok Raj Path) is a major landmark. Next to the train station, **Station Rd.** leads west to the state secretariat and
other government buildings.

PRACTICAL INFORMATION

Tourist Office: Government of India Tourist Office, Sudama Palace Complex,
5th fl., Kankarbagh Rd. (tel. 345776). From the railway station, take a tempo or
rickshaw to Kankarbagh Rd., which runs behind the railway station. Located in a 6-
story building on the right side near the Jaisarmil Hotel; there is no sign on the
street, only on the balcony of the 5th fl. office. Extremely modern, A/C facility with

computer and laser printer. Open Mon.-Fri. 9am-6pm, Sat. 9am-1pm. **State Government Tourist Office,** Fraser Rd. (tel. 225295). Open Mon.-Sat. 10am-5pm.

Currency Exchange: State Bank of India, Gandhi Maidan (tel. 226134). From the railway station, take a tempo (Rs.3) to Gandhi Maidan, a big circular park near the river. The bank will be on your left, at the very beginning of the circle. Open Mon.-Fri. 10:30am-5:30pm, Sat. 10:30am-2:30pm. Five-star hotels, such as the Maurya Patna near Gandhi Maidan, will exchange currency for non-guests.

Telephones: STD/ISD booths are common, including one at the GPO that is open 24hr.

Airport: Patna Airport, 6km from the railway station. The ride from one to the other costs Rs.100 by taxi, Rs.60 by auto-rickshaw, and Rs.25 by cycle-rickshaw. To: Calcutta (Fri.-Wed. 1-2 per day, 1-3hr., US$70); Delhi (1-3 per day, 2-3hr., US$107); Ranchi (1 per day, 45min., US$47); Lucknow (Mon., Wed., and Fri., 1hr., US$69); Varanasi (winter only, Wed. and Fri., 30min., US$30). There are occasional flights to Kathmandu (1½hr., US$140) in winter.

Trains: Patna Junction Station is easily accessible by tempo. To: Varanasi (*Howrah-Amritsar Mail* 3005, 5:02am, 5hr.; *Howrah-Jammu Tawi Himgiri Exp.* 3073, Tues. and Fri.-Sat., 10:25am, 4hr.; *Howrah-Gorakhpur Exp.* 5049, Thurs., 10:25am, 4hr.; *Patna-New Delhi Shramjeevi Exp.* 2401, 11:20am, 3hr., Rs.35/152 for 2nd/1st class); Calcutta (*Gorakhpur-Howrah Exp.* 5050, Thurs., 1:40am, 10hr., Rs.118 for sleeper; *Jammu Tawi-Howrah Himgiri Exp.,* Tues. and Fri.-Sat., 1:40am, 10hr., Rs.118 for sleeper; *Rajdhani Exp.* 2306, 5:30am, 7½hr., Rs.560 for 3-tier A/C sleeper; *Delhi-Howrah Poorva Exp.* 2304, 7:45am, 8½hr., Rs.94/388 for 2nd/1st class); Gaya (*Palamau Exp.* 3348, 8:45pm, 2hr., Rs.25/116 for 2nd/1st class; numerous passenger trains starting at 6am); Lucknow (*Howrah-Amritsar Mail* 3005, 5:02am, 11hr.; *Howrah-Jammu Tawi Himgiri Exp.* 3073, Tues., and Fri.-Sat., 10:25am, 9hr., Rs.108/444 for 2nd/1st class); Ranchi (*Patna-Hatia Exp.* 8625, 10:25am, 10½hr., Rs.82/334 for 2nd/1st class; *Patna-Hatia Pataliputra Exp.* 8621, 3:50pm, 13½hr., Rs.103 for sleeper; *Patna-Hatia Exp.* 8623, 9:45pm, 11hr., Rs.103 for sleeper); Dhanbad (*Patna-Hatia Pataliputra Exp.* 8621, 3:50pm, 8hr., Rs.85/359 for 2nd/1st class; *Ganga-Damodar Exp.* 3330, 11:20pm, 6hr., Rs.107 for sleeper); New Jalpaiguri (*Mahananda Exp./A Link Exp.* 4084, 1:10am, 14hr., Rs.132 for sleeper; *Rajdhani Exp.* 2424, 5:17am, 8½hr.; *NE Exp.* 5622, 10pm, 12hr., Rs.132 for sleeper); Varanasi (*Varanasi-Gorakhpur Exp.* 5104, 5:50am, 5hr.; *Kashi Exp.* 1027, 1:20pm, 6hr.; *Krishak Exp.* 5002, 4:30pm, 5½hr., Rs.56/226 for 2nd/1st class; *Chauri-Chaura Exp.* 5003, 11:50pm, 6hr., Rs.70 for sleeper; connect for trains to Gorakhpur at Varanasi).

Buses: The **bus stand** is west of Patna Junction on Kankarbagh Rd. To: Calcutta (7pm, 12hr., Rs.125); Gaya (12:30 and 1:30pm, 6hr., Rs.25); Raxaul (noon, 1pm, and every 30min., 7pm-midnight, 6hr., Rs.65); Ranchi (every hr., 7-10pm, 12hr., Rs.100); Jamshedpur (every hr., 7-10pm, 15hr., Rs.125); Siliguri (every hr., 7-10pm, 12hr., Rs.150); Hajipur (continuously, 6am-6pm, Rs.8; connect for buses to Vaishali and Sonepur at Hajipur).

Local Transportation: Rickshaws and **tempos.** The major hub for tempos is Patna Junction; from there you can get tempos to many other places in the city.

Luggage Storage: At the railway station.

Market: Maurya Lok, Dak Bungalow Rd., is a major shopping center, with clothing stores, hair salons, and fast-food joints. There are several fruit markets including **New Patna Market,** in front of the railway station, and **Patna** and **Hatwa Markets,** on Ashok Raj Path near Gandhi Maidan and the Ganga.

Library: British Library, Bank Rd., near Gandhi Maidan and the State Bank of India. Air-conditioned. Open Tues.-Sat. 10:30am-6:30pm.

English Bookstore: Several bookshops located along Ashok Raj Path near Gandhi Maidan.

Pharmacy: Popular Pharmacy, near railway station. Open 24hr.

Hospital: Raj Lakshmi Nursing Home, Kankarbagh Rd. (tel. 352225 or 354320). They have specialists from the Patna Medical College on call 24hr. and an operating room.

Emergency: tel. 100.

Post Office: GPO, Station Rd., R-block (tel. 221620). From the railway station, take a rickshaw down Kankarbagh Rd. to the left (Rs.5). The post office is on the right. Open Mon.-Sat. 10am-6pm. **Postal Code:** 800001.
Telephone Code: 0612.

ACCOMMODATIONS

When it comes to hotels, everything in Patna conspires against the budget traveler. Many of Patna's cheaper hotels don't have the paperwork necessary to register foreigners, and turn away anyone who doesn't look Indian. The mid-range hotels along Fraser Rd. and Exhibition Rd. are often fully booked. And the international hotels are internationally priced. Nevertheless it is still possible to find a few decent bargains in the Fraser Rd. area. A cluster of budget lodgings on Hotel Lane, a creepy, dirty alley that slinks away from Fraser Rd. opposite the State Bank of India, must contend with the continuous daytime racket of the alley's Honda generators. And don't plan to sleep late in Patna either—*chai-wallahs* and newspaper sellers often circle through the hotels, banging on doors as early as 6:30am. The budget traveler may have more luck in the future as Patna's hotel scene is rapidly expanding west to Beer Chand Patel Marg and Boring Rd.

Ruby Hotel, S.P. Verma Rd. From the railway station, take a rickshaw up S.P. Verma Rd. The hotel is on the left side before the 2nd big intersection. An extremely laid-back, quiet place: the owner spends his days in a state of repose, unpredictably bursting into a hearty salutations. Set your alarm, since neither *chai-wallahs* nor noisy machinery will wake you up here; the quiet is the hotel's greatest asset. The beds are comfortable, although the rooms get stuffy. The fluorescent lighting is a bit harsh. Check-out 24hr. All rooms have attached bath. Singles Rs.50. Doubles Rs.70.

Hotel Anand Lok, Station Rd. Next to the railway station (tel. 223960). From the railway station, turn right onto Station Rd; enter the first alley on your right. The hotel is at the end on the left side. Run by a gravel-voiced yet chummy manager, the Anand Lok has all the amenities of the luxury hotels at a third of the cost. An elevator whisks guest to the quieter rooms on the top floor where they enjoy round-the-clock room service. All rooms have attached bath. Singles Rs.170. Doubles Rs.200.

Hotel Parker, Fraser Rd. Far up on the road on the left, across from the Rajasthan Hotel. The luxurious backdrop of Fraser Rd. hotels makes this simple (and somewhat grungy) hotel seem like a fish out of water. The rooms are bare (no table, no chair), the common bathrooms smell bad, and the staff doesn't speak any English. Singles Rs.50, with bath Rs.60. Doubles Rs.65, with bath Rs.70. Triples with bath Rs.90.

Hotel Prakash, Hotel Lane, off Fraser Rd. The entrance to the alley is near Dilal and Sons, across from the Samrat International on Fraser Rd. There's not much to recommend this place except its proximity to the railway station, its price, and its availability to foreigners. The halls are not always kept clean, the cramped rooms are secluded and lonely, and the mattresses are made of foam. All rooms have attached bath. Singles Rs.80. Doubles Rs.100.

Hotel Mayur, Fraser Rd., near the Ashoka Restaurant (tel. 224142). From the railway station, walk 500m up Fraser Rd.; it's on the right side. Clean, spacious rooms with easy-chairs and desks. Big bathrooms attached to all rooms, although the showers are not very powerful. Singles Rs.170. Doubles Rs.220.

FOOD

Most of the good restaurants are concentrated on Fraser Rd., although new places are springing up to the west on Buddha Marg. Fast food places can be found at the hip shopping arcade at Maurya Lok.

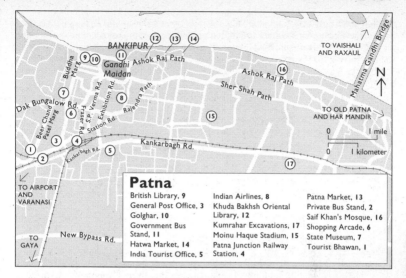

Patna

British Library, **9**
General Post Office, **3**
Golghar, **10**
Government Bus Stand, **11**
Hatwa Market, **14**
India Tourist Office, **5**

Indian Airlines, **8**
Khuda Bakhsh Oriental Library, **12**
Kumrahar Excavations, **17**
Moinu Haque Stadium, **15**
Patna Junction Railway Station, **4**

Patna Market, **13**
Private Bus Stand, **2**
Saif Khan's Mosque, **16**
Shopping Arcade, **6**
State Museum, **7**
Tourist Bhawan, **1**

Rajasthan Hotel Restaurant, Fraser Rd. North of the intersection of Fraser and Dak Bungalow Rd. If the consistent consumption of Indian food has waged war on your mouth, these subtly spiced veg. dishes, especially the soups, will gently revitalize your beleaguered tastebuds. The almond soup (Rs.30) and the Special *Naan* (stuffed with nuts and vegetables; Rs.12) are particularly pleasing. Open daily 8am-10pm.

Bansi Vihar, Fraser Rd. Near the intersection of Fraser and Dak Bungalow Rd. The air is thick with the intoxicating smell of South Indian food. The special *masala dosas* with cashews (Rs.27) are a revelation. Open daily 8am-10pm.

Mayfair Ice Cream Parlor and Restaurant, Fraser Rd., 5min. from the railway station. Every hour seems like Happy Hour at the Mayfair Restaurant. When the rest of the city is just waking up, the Mayfair is alive and kicking; in the evening it's packed with young people. The waiters, no doubt powered by the cold coffee, are efficient, so you never have to wait long for your ice cream (the house specialty) or your glass of hygienically prepared fresh juice. Open daily 8am-10pm

Hasty Tasty, Fraser Rd. Near the railway station. This popular open-air restaurant serves the only cheap Indian food along Fraser Rd. The service is fast and the drinks are very, very cold. Open daily 8am-10pm.

SIGHTS

Several big attractions scatter the length of Patna. In the twisting lanes of Old Patna is **Har Mandir,** a Sikh *gurudwara* marking the birthplace of the 10th and last Sikh guru, Gobind Singh (born 1666). The second-most important "throne" of the Sikh religion (after the Golden Temple in Amritsar), Har Mandir is set in an echoing blue enclave reached through a tunnel of shops. Visitors must have removed shoes and covered heads to enter the precinct (scarves are provided). The present building was constructed after a 1954 earthquake destroyed the original temple. Inside, young men drone the interminable verses of the Guru Granth Sahib, the Sikh holy book. Upstairs, a museum honoring Gobind Singh holds a few genuine relics and a lot of shoddy pictures. Har Mandir is a gathering place for Patna's substantial Sikh community.

The Ganga merges with several tributaries just west of Patna, so it's extremely wide here. At 7km, **Mahatma Gandhi Bridge,** built in 1983, is one of the longest bridges in the world. From the middle of the bridge, one can look out over the shivering river and the empty fields on the far shore.

What little remains of ancient Pataliputra is preserved on Old Bypass Rd. at the **Kumrahar Excavations,** where the fragmented wooden remains of a Mauryan assembly hall from the 4th century BC were discovered. A few pillar stumps are all that's visible—when the excavations aren't flooded, that is. The one-room museum has Mauryan terra-cotta figures and the foundations of a later Buddhist monastery can also be seen in the park that encloses the site. (Open daily 9am-5pm.)

One of Patna's most bizarre but popular landmarks is the **Golghar,** an egg-shaped grain storage bin near the Gandhi Maidan. Built by the British in 1786 to avert famine, it was never needed. Two staircases spiral up to 29m above the street—a quick climb. The blue corners of the city and the brown curls of the Ganga can be seen from the top.

The prized piece in the **Patna Museum,** located on Buddha Marg in a fortress-like building guarded by cannons, is a voluptuous stone Mauryan *yakshi* from the 3rd century BC, who stands in the middle of the first-floor halls, showing off the famous Maurya polish. The museum has labeled her simply "IDEAL WOMAN HOOD." Many less interesting sculptures surround the *yakshi*, but upstairs in glass cases there are good terra-cotta figures and heads, especially from the Mauryan era. There's also a substantial collection of *thankas* and other Tibetan artifacts. (Open Tues.-Sun. 10:30am-4:30pm. Free; Fri. admission Rs.0.25.)

The **Khuda Bakhsh Oriental Library,** located on Ashok Raj Path, houses a vast collection of Islamic literature and relics, mostly of esoteric interest. In the lobby display cases show off beautiful illuminated manuscripts hundreds of years old, weapons used by such illustrious figures as Aurangzeb, 19th-century astronomical and astrological equipment, and some very delicate wooden models of ships and mosques crafted by the library's assistant librarian. Mohammed Bakhsh, a lawyer from Bihar, started the collection. It was his resourceful and somewhat unscrupulous son, Khuda Bakhsh, however, who begged, borrowed, and stole as far west as Egypt to make the library what it is today. (Open Sat.-Thurs. 9:30am-5pm.)

ENTERTAINMENT

There is a burgeoning bar scene in Patna, along Fraser Rd. and Buddha Marg. The most impressive of the lot is the **Daawat Bar,** on the right side of Fraser Rd., near the railway station. The whole bar is designed according to a submarine theme: the bar itself is a large tank, filled with exotic tropical fish. Murky green light reflects off concrete walls depicting underwater scenes: bas-relief bass! It's a popular place among both men and women, and the drinks are reasonably priced (beer Rs.45).

■ Gaya

According to folklore, the name Gaya derives from the demon Gayasura, who purified himself through rigorous yoga and received as a reward this sacred tract of land along the River Phalgu. As a further reward, Gaya was imbued with the power to absolve ancestral sins—it is said that one *shraddha* (funeral rite) in Gaya is equivalent to 11 *shraddhas* at any other place. Hindu pilgrims would visit each of the 45 shrines in Gaya (including the Bodhi tree in Bodh Gaya), offering up prayers for the dead and rupees for the *gayaval* (attending priest). But today, most pilgrims, unable to afford the full circuit, restrict themselves to the Vishnupad Temple (housing the footprint of Vishnu) and the smaller shrines clustered around it.

The high season is in September when the Phalgu swells up with monsoon rains and thousands of pilgrims descend the *ghats* to perform their ritual ablution. Off-season, Gaya's religious character is harder to discern. Gaya's bustling commercial side seems far more impressive than the paltry and poorly attended shrines hidden in out-of-the-way crannies. Western tourists who wish to spend any time in Gaya are a complete mystery to the auto-rickshaw drivers lurking outside Gaya Junction, who can only repeat helplessly and hypnotically, "Bodh Gaya?," hoping to shuttle foreigners to the Buddhist center 13km south. Yet Gaya is as important to devout Hindus as its sister city is to Buddhists.

ORIENTATION

Gaya's boundaries are marked by the railway station in the south, the bank of the **River Phalgu** in the northeast, and the base of **Brahmyoni Hill** in the northwest. **Station Road** goes right from the railway station and then takes a sharp left turning into **Civil Lines,** the administrative center of the city where the post office, police station, bus stands, and banks are located. Continuing north, the broad lanes of Civil Lines dissolve into the cluttered streets of the **Kacheri Road Bazaar,** which approach the river and disperse east and west into narrow brick-laden paths, dotted with shrines and small shops. The spiritual center of the city is built around the **Vishnupad Temple** and the Phalgu *ghats.*

Gaya is 14km north of Bodh Gaya, the site of the Buddha's enlightenment, and 60km southwest of Nalanda and Rajgir, both important centers of Buddhist learning. Thirty-six kilometers to the north are the **Barabar Caves,** rock-hewn temples which figured prominently in E.M. Forster's *A Passage to India.* Gaya lies along major rail routes from U.P. to Calcutta.

PRACTICAL INFORMATION

Tourist Office: Inside the railway station. Carries wall map of Gaya. Open Mon.-Sat. 8am-8pm.

Telephones: 24-hr. **STD/ISD** booth located inside the railway station.

Trains: Trains leave from **Gaya Junction Station.** To: Patna (*Palamau Exp.* 3347, 4:22am, 2hr; *Hatia-Patna Exp.* 8626, 2:15pm, 2hr., Rs.26/116 for 2nd/1st class); Varanasi (*Neelachal Exp.* 8475, Tues., Fri., and Sun., 3:32am, 4hr.; *Doon Exp.,* 6:02am, 5hr.; *Howrah-New Delhi Poorva Exp.,* Wed.-Thurs., and Sun., 4hr., Rs.61/ 249 for 2nd/1st class); Mughal Sarai (*Howrah-Jodhpur Exp.* 2307, 6:32am, 3½hr.; *Purshottam Exp.* 2801, Tues.-Wed., and Fri.-Sun., 1:47pm, 3hr., Rs.57/241 for 2nd/ 1st class); Calcutta (*Rajdhani Exp.* 2302, 4:41am, 6hr., Rs.520/730 for 3-tier/2-tier sleeper; *New Delhi-Howrah Poorva Exp.* 2382, 8:56am, 7½hr., Rs.97/396 for 2nd/ 1st class: *Kalka-Howrah Mail* 2312, 11:20am, 7½hr., Rs.122 for sleeper); Ranchi (*Patna-Hatia Exp.* 8623, 11:50pm, 9hr., Rs.93 for sleeper; *Patna-Hatia Exp.* 8625, 12:45pm, 8hr., Rs.74/303 for 2nd/1st class); Bela (5:30, 7:10, 10am, 12:25pm, 1hr., Rs.10; from Bela to Barabar Caves, 12-km ride in tempo or tonga and 5-km walk to caves).

Buses: There are 5 major bus stands in Gaya. **Panchayati Akara Bus Stand,** 4km from Gaya Junction near Ram Shila Hill, has buses to Patna (6:30, 8am, 3:30, and 4:30pm, 4hr.). **Bihar State Road Transport** is located near Gandhi Maidan, a Rs.5 rickshaw ride from Gaya Junction. To: Ranchi (5:45, 6:30, 7, 9, 10, 11:10am, 3:15, 6:10, 7, 8, 9:30, and 10:30pm, 7hr., Rs.46-54); Jamshedpur (5:45, 7am, 6:10, 7, and 8pm, 11hr., Rs.76). The **Manpur Bus Stand** is across the Phalgu River near the bridge and has buses to Rajgir and Nalanda (every hr., 6am-6pm, 2hr., Rs.20). The **Zila School Bus Stand** is located near the Kachahari area and has buses to Bodh Gaya (every 30min., 5:30am-6:30pm, Rs.3). Buses to Varanasi leave from Bodh Gaya. One bus to Calcutta (7:30pm, 12hr.) leaves from **Gaya Junction,** in front of the train station.

Local Transportation: Rickshaws charge Rs.5 to go to the Zila School Bus Stand, where there are buses and tempos to Bodh Gaya; Rs.10 to the Vishnupad Temple or Shaktipith near the Phalgu River.

Luggage Storage: At Gaya Junction Railway Station.

Market: A large fruit market is located at **Purani Godam,** Tekari Rd., Chauk, between Gaya Junction and the Phalgu River.

Pharmacy: Many pharmacies located along Station Rd., but scattered among other locations as well. Most are open 8am-11pm.

Hospital: The **Lady Elgin Hospital,** Tower Chauk, near the Zila School Bus Stand, is a private medical facility.

Emergency: tel. 20999, 420059.
Post Office: GPO, Kachahari Rd. (tel. 20660). Rs.10 rickshaw ride from railway station, right along Station Rd. and then left through the main fruit market. Open Mon.-Sat. 10am-5pm. **Postal Code:** 823001.
Telephone Code: 0631.

ACCOMMODATIONS

Budget hotels have accumulated across from the railway station and to the right along Station Rd. These tend to be quite noisy. Other budget hotels, as well as pricier accommodations, are sprinkled throughout town. Room rent is negotiable in the off-season (May-Sept.)—some places, like the Hotel Classic directly across from the station, are willing to cut their prices in half.

Hotel Buddha, Laxman Sahay Lane (tel. 23428). Straight back from the railway station, at the end of a longish road perpendicular to Station Rd. The Hotel Buddha is much quieter than the hotels along Station Rd. The double rooms are clean, with comfortable mattresses (but hay-stuffed pillows) and good showers. The hotel, organized around a large atrium, is sunny and airy, and has a lot of space for drying laundry. Soft leather chairs and a television entice guests to gather in the spacious lobby downstairs. All rooms have attached bath. Singles Rs.85. Doubles Rs.135.

Station View Hotel, Station Rd. (tel. 20512). Several hundred meters to the right of the station, past the Ajatsatru Hotel, on the left side of the street. Don't be misled by the hotel's name: one of its main assets is its lack of a station view. The cheapest accommodation on Station Rd., it is consequently quite popular and often filled to capacity even off-season. Clean, spacious restaurant with some private booths (*dosas* Rs.8). The staff is friendly and laid-back, and they refrain from harassing foreigners with shouts of "come inside." All rooms have attached bath. Singles with bath Rs.35. Doubles with bath Rs.45

Ajatsatru Hotel, Station Rd. (tel. 21514 or 23714). Across from the railway station on the left side. The largest hotel along this strip (aside from the Siddharth International), it has a range of rooms, although the cheaper rooms are less carefully maintained. The air-cooled doubles are spacious and fairly clean with comfortable mattresses. Suites that include a kitchen should open Jan. 1997. There is a cool restaurant downstairs, shielded from the street by tapestries, and open relatively late (11:30pm). All rooms have attached bath. Singles Rs.107. Doubles Rs.134, with air-cooling Rs.161.

Hotel Satkar, Station Rd. (tel. 433035), on the left side, past the Station View Hotel and across from the Madras Hotel. From the railway station, walk right several hundred meters. Hotel Satkar has cramped but clean rooms with soft mattresses and decorative bedspreads. All rooms have attached bath, but most of the showers lack shower heads, so what might have been a weak spray is a mere dribble; the bath faucets have decent pressure. Singles Rs.50, with air-cooling Rs.75. Doubles Rs.80, with air-cooling Rs.105.

Hotel Surya, Dak Bungalow Rd. (tel. 24004). A 10-min. rickshaw ride from the railway station right along Station Rd. Located on a central thoroughfare, the traffic bickers noisily from 6am-9pm. The Hotel Surya nevertheless has the cleanest rooms around; they're spacious too. Sealed tight windows and powerful fans create a cool and virtually bug-free environment for a good night's sleep. The goofy friendliness of the manager and staff is infectious. Unfortunately, aside from the standard hotel restaurant, there are no restaurants or even cold drink stands within easy walking distance. All rooms have attached bath. Doubles Rs.125, with air-cooling and TV Rs.175.

FOOD

Most of the hotel restaurants along Station Rd. are narrow fly-infested holes. You may get eaten alive before you dig yourself out. There a few exceptions, including one good but expensive restaurant in the Siddharth International. Restaurants are rare in other parts of town, although *dal*-and-rice *dhabas* abound en route to the Vishnupad Temple.

Station View Hotel Restaurant, Station Rd. (tel. 20512), several hundred meters to the right of the railway station, on the left side. The best of the budget hotel restaurants, it has a spacious airy dining room and some small curtained booths for private dinners. Veg. cuisine (Rs.14 for good *masala dosa*). Open 7am-11pm.

Siddharth International Restaurant, Station Rd. (tel. 21480). From the railway station, walk right 500m; it's on the left. Air-conditioned restaurant serves Indian, Chinese, Continental veg. and non-veg. items. Veg. food starts at Rs.30; chicken starts at Rs.80. Continental soups and salads are cheaper, but still nourishing and delicious. Open 7am-11pm.

South Indian Restaurant, Station Rd. (tel. 420198), after the Siddharth International. From the railway station, walk right 750m; it's on the left, next to the Ajit Hotel. Cheap tasty South Indian food (*masala dosa* Rs.12). Standing room only, or rather, there's plenty of room but no seating. Fast service as in fast food. Open 8-11am and 3-8pm.

SIGHTS

The temples in Gaya are not nearly as spectacular as the temples in large pilgrimage centers such as Varanasi, and non-Hindus may not enter the main shrine, **Vishnupad.** Towering over the bank of the Phalgu River, this golden-spired temple is said to house Buddha's footprint, which is two yards long and enshrined in a silver basin. Non-Hindus can get a closer look at the sanctum (but not the print) by climbing the stairs at the back of the first shop to the left of the temple entrance. Continuing left along the row of shops and taking the first right, you can walk down to the bank of the river, where Hindus bathe and perform obsequial rites. Cremations are performed in a metal roofed shed along the beach to the right. Smaller temples cluster around Vishnupad, most of which are off-limits to non-Hindus.

One kilometer to the east is a rather mundane **Durga temple,** where non-Hindus can observe and even participate in the *shraddha*—funeral rites for dead ancestors. Pilgrims who wish to perform the *shraddha* at Gaya must first circle their own village five times. Once in Gaya, a *gayaval* (priest trained in this specific rite) guides them in performing a complicated ritual involving Sanskrit prayers and offerings of *pinda* (water and rice kneaded into a ball). The pilgrims usually repay the *gayaval* for his services with a hefty monetary donation. Two steps away lies **Shaktipith,** where Sati's breast is said to have fallen after she was destroyed (see **Divine Dismemberment,** p. 404). Images of the goddess are housed in a squat cave-like mausoleum, inscribed on the front with the epic verse of Sati's destruction. Open daily 6am-noon and 1pm-midnight—even for non-Hindus.

Two kilometers to the west is the entrance to the **Brahmyoni Hill.** Climb 1000 stone steps to Shiv Mandir, where cool winds whip across the top and views of Gaya (on the right) and Bodh Gaya (on the left) impress the impressionable. There is also a small goddess temple with an image of Shiva's foot at the door. The hill is sacred to Buddhists, as it is associated with Gayasirsan ("the Head of Gaya"), the mountain where Buddha is said to have delivered several important sermons. Young guides will try to tell you that Shiva's footprint is Buddha's, and even that the images of the goddess are statues of the Enlightened One.

■ Bodh Gaya

Strangely enough, the little village of Bodh Gaya, 13km south of Gaya, is the center of the Buddhist universe. It was here in the 6th century BC that Prince Siddhartha Gautama gained enlightenment under a *pipal* tree, launching his career as the Buddha. Buddhists consider the enlightenment the most important thing ever to have happened, and according to members of the Mahayana sect, the event will repeat itself in Bodh Gaya. So pilgrims from all over Asia make their way to this tiny green market town, whose population is primarily Hindu; although some locals worship the Buddha as one of Vishnu's incarnations, most are concerned with running restaurants and curio stalls. They make Buddhism seem like a stranger in its own home-town. The Buddhist presence in Bodh Gaya is in fact quite new. For although Buddhist monasteries thrived here centuries ago, they were left to sink into the mud after Buddhism faded out in India in the 12th century. Not until the 19th century, when Sri Lankan and Burmese monks led the campaign to restore the Mahabodhi Temple was Bodh Gaya revived as a religious center. Now each Buddhist country has a monastery in its own architectural style, serving its national cuisine to its pilgrims. Westerners are by no means excluded from the religious life here, and it can be an excellent place to study Buddhism. The Dalai Lama usually spends his winters here, bringing with him a large Tibetan contingent. During Bodh Gaya's season (Dec.-Feb.), the monasteries quietly fill up, visiting teachers offer meditation courses, and scads of tent-restaurants appear. The rest of the year Bodh Gaya can still be appropriately peaceful, dissolving back into the slippery Bihari countryside.

ORIENTATION

No one gets lost in Bodh Gaya, since there's only one noteworthy road meandering loosely from the northeast to the southwest. It is a direct continuation of the road from Gaya. All Bodh Gaya's activity is on this road, especially in the vicinity of the **Mahabodhi Temple,** a tall, thin pyramid whose compound takes up a large, fenced-in swath of the south side of the road.

PRACTICAL INFORMATION

Tourist Office: Market Complex, Bodh Gaya. Located across from the Mahabodhi Temple, in a small shopping center. Open 10am-5pm.

Currency Exchange: State Bank of India, Gaya Rd. (tel. 400737). As you enter Bodh Gaya, on the right side. **Bank of India,** on a small path leading to the International Meditation Centre (tel. 400750). From the Mahabodhi Temple, walk 10min. to the far side of town; turn right at the sign for the meditation center. Both banks open Mon.-Fri. 10:30am-2:30pm, Sat. 10:30am-12:30pm.

Telephones: Lots of **STD/ISD** booths as you enter town, at the market complex across from the Mahabodhi Temple, and near the Tibetan restaurants behind the Mahabodhi Society on the right side. Open 6am-11pm.

Buses: A bus to Varanasi stops in front of the Mahabodhi Society (on the right side, after the market complex) at 5:30am (Rs.54)

Local Transportation: Rickshaws charge Rs.10 from one side of town to the other. **Tongas** are also available.

Market: At the intersection of Gaya and Bodh Gaya Rd., there is a small lane to the left where you can buy fruit and handicrafts.

Library: Temple Management Committee of Bodh Gaya and Library (tel. 400735). Collection of current international magazines and Buddhist literature. Open 9am-5pm.

Pharmacy: Many pharmacies located throughout town are open 6am-10pm.

Emergency: tel. 400741.

Post Office: Gaya Rd. (tel. 400472). As you enter town, on the left. Open 10am-5pm. **Postal Code:** 824231.

Telephone Code: 0631.

ACCOMMODATIONS

There are few good-quality budget accommodations in Bodh Gaya, although some of the overpriced hotels lower their rates significantly in the off-season (March-Sept.). Some monasteries offer comfortable, inexpensive lodging, and if you're a *bona fide* pilgrim, your options are unlimited. Most of the monasteries cluster at the far end of town, although the Burmese Vihar (really a full-fledged hotel), is on Gaya Rd. at the entrance to Bodh Gaya. The monasteries provide rooms for a suggested donation (or, in some cases, a super-strenuously suggested donation).

Burmese Vihar Temple, Gaya Rd. (tel. 400721). As you enter Bodh Gaya, it's on the right side of the road, across from the seasonal Pole-Pole restaurant. During high season (Nov.-Jan.) 35 students from Antioch College in Ohio transform the usually serene Burmese Vihar Temple into a temporary American university dormitory, but there is plenty of room and transient tourists might be able to have their meals with the students. Flat mattresses, mosquito coils, and nets equip the rooms. Two peaceful ko deer—awkward, somewhat amorphous cousins of North American deer—roam the somewhat unkempt grounds. There's a large prayer hall, decorated by far-out Burmese portraits of the Buddha floating around in multi-colored balls of light. Dorm beds with common bath Rs.40. Double room with bath and water heater Rs.150 per person.

Bhutan Temple, Temple Rd. (tel. 8170). Near the statue of the Great Buddha. The temples along Temple Rd. are no longer accessible through their main entrances; enter through the rear. From Bodh Gaya Rd., turn left at the sign for the Shanti Buddha Hotel, across from the sign for the International Meditation Centre. The Bhutan is situated on peaceful, well-maintained grounds several hundred meters up on the right. Rooms are clean and spacious and have mosquito nets. Beds Rs.100, with attached bath Rs.150. Off-season: beds Rs.60.

Tamang Monastery (Nepalese), Bodh Gaya Rd. (tel. 400802). On the left side of the main road, after the Archaeological Museum, across from the International Meditation Centre. Clean but cramped rooms. The manager, a bent-over but sprightly old priest, is an amazing conversationalist, making up for the gaps in his English (and the gaps in your Hindi) with his inexhaustible patience and beaming smile. This place tends to fill up in the high season, so advanced booking is essential. Bed Rs.75, with bath Rs.150. Off-season: beds Rs.30, with bath Rs.100.

Mahabodhi Society and Sri Lanka Guest House (tel. 400742). On a dirt path, a right turn from Bodh Gaya Rd., across from the Mahabodhi Temple. Large dormitories with comfortable beds, but no mosquito nets or coils. The bathrooms are clean; the water pressure is positively explosive. The staff is friendly, but somewhat over-fastidious about energy conservation—it might take some convincing if you want extra light for reading. Check-out 24hr. Dorm bed Rs.40. Double with bath Rs.100 per person.

Root Institute for Wisdom Culture, at the very edge of town, down a long dirt path on the left (tel. 400714). A Rs.8 rickshaw ride from the bus/tempo stand. A licensed charitable trust currently overseen by 2 Europeans, the Root Institute offers clean, comfortable rooms with modern facilities. Perched about 500m from the Great Buddha's backside, the Root Institute is isolated and peaceful. It sponsors on-site winter season meditation courses and year-round social work. The restaurant is hygienic and filtered water is always on tap. Doubles Rs.100-300, depending on options—attached bath, meals (1,2, or 3), and meditation lessons.

FOOD

Restaurants are highly seasonal. In the winter months, pilgrims from Thailand, Tibet, Burma, Nepal, Bhutan, and Sri Lanka flock to Bodh Gaya in droves; temporary tent restaurants pop up to accommodate them. The gourmand can stray from the middle path and pick from a smorgasbord of international cuisine. Those restaurants that stay open in low season restrict their menus. The Pole-Pole Chinese restaurant, on Gaya Rd. near Shankaracharya Math, is quite renowned in the area. Tibetan restaurants line the dirt path behind the Mahabodhi Society and Tibet Temple.

Fujia Green Chinese Restaurant (tel. 400898). On the dirt path behind the Mahabodhi Society and Tibet Temple. You might get your socks giggled off by giddy first-year college students, but the food is amazing and the service is doubly amazing. Fujia Green offers a huge selection of Chinese dishes, including chicken *momos* (Rs.20) and vegetable *thukpa* (Rs.10) in both high and low seasons. Open daily 8am-10pm.

SIGHTS

Mahabodhi Temple

The main point of interest in Bodh Gaya is the Mahabodhi Temple, referred to as "the stupa" by most Buddhists. The tall, thin *shikhara* is covered with a jigsaw-puzzle-like pattern, and it towers over the many *chaityas* and other shrines in its courtyard. Monks can be seen strolling interminably around the marble sidewalk of the temple grounds snapping pictures with their automatic cameras. The temple is right next to the actual site of enlightenment, while some of the other shrines are linked to different stages in the Buddha's meditations. The emperor Ashoka built the first temple on this site in the 3rd century BC. The present temple dates from the 6th century AD and has been through layers and layers of restoration. Much of it is the work of the Burmese monks who came to the rescue of the temple in 1882, after they found it neglected and overrun by squatters. Many statues have been stolen from the temple's circular niches in the last 30 years. The oldest structure left on the site is the stone railing, which was built in the first century AD to keep out wild animals. But a quarter of it has been whisked away to museums in London and Calcutta.

At the back of the temple is the sacred **Bodhi Tree,** a grandchild of the tree under which the Buddha attained enlightenment. The emperor Ashoka is said to have killed the original tree prior to his conversion to Buddhism. Once he had converted, however, he sent his son Mahinda on a mission to Sri Lanka carrying an offshoot from the tree. This tree is still alive (just barely) in Anuradhapura, Sri Lanka, and it has sent Bodh Gaya back one of its pointy-leaved saplings. The Bodhi tree at Bodh Gaya is considered to be almost as good as the real thing, and it is surrounded by its own fence, which is only opened from 6 to 8am and 6 to 8pm. The platform between the tree and the temple is thought to be exactly where the Buddha sat. It is called the **Vajrasana** or "diamond throne," and some believe there is an enormous diamond buried beneath the earth here that fuels the site's spiritual power.

A large gold Buddha is kept behind glass in the temple, and another one, supposed to be remarkably true-to-life, is on the first floor, which is only open in the evenings for meditation. A part of the first floor is permanently closed off, due to one man's recent attempt to saw off a branch of the sacred tree as a souvenir. (Open daily 5am-9pm; admission free, camera charge Rs.5.)

Other Temples and Monasteries

The **Thai Temple** is Bodh Gaya's second-most prominent landmark, located just down the road from the Mahabodhi Temple. Opened in 1957, it is a large *wat* with the classic clawlike tips on its orange roof. The eclectic interior includes Thai tourism posters. Side-roads branch away from the main road on either side of the Thai Temple. To the left are the **Bhutan Monastery,** and the Japanese **Indosan Nipponji Temple,** the back wall of which has a mural showing a crushing landscape of people flocking to the Buddha. The Indosan Nipponji's peace bell rings with a swinging cadence throughout the morning. The lane on the right side of the Thai Temple leads to the **Kagyupa Tibetan Monastery,** which contains Disneyish larger-than-life murals depicting the life of the Buddha. Next door is the **Daijokyo Temple,** another Japanese construction with an oppressive modern concrete exterior. Just up the road from the Daijokyo Temple, the 25-meter tall **Giant Buddha Statue,** which was built by Japanese monks and inaugurated by the Dalai Lama in 1989, sits on a lotus, his robe rippling out of the red sandstone blocks.

The **Gelugpa Tibetan Monastery,** right next to the Mahabodhi Society near the center of town, is accustomed to sightseers. Its second-floor chapel has walls painted with *thanka*-style clouds, wheels, and *bodhisattvas.* Visitors are invited to turn the massive silo of a prayer wheel downstairs.

MEDITATION AND COMMUNITY SERVICE

Only two places in Bodh Gaya offer meditation courses. **The Root Institute for Wisdom Culture,** located on the outskirts of town, offers 10-day courses during the winter months with guest *lamas* in a quiet intimate setting. A fee of Rs.300 per day covers the cost of a double room with attached bath and a small prayer niche, as well as three meals per day. There may be the option of eating meals in town and retreating to the institute for meditation. **The International Meditation Centre** has one complex 5km outside of town, and a smaller complex across from the Thai monastery. Meditation courses in the Vipassana Method are offered year-round. The 10-day course costs Rs.100 per day, and includes a dorm bed and three meals.

There are a number of licensed charitable organizations in Bodh Gaya. The Root Institute is always looking for volunteers (and donations). They sponsor tree planting during the monsoon and in January toward the end of the tourist season, in addition to an all-year Leprosy Project and Destitute House. Many charitable organizations pop up during peak season—avoid anything that looks like a hit-and-run operation. Additional information is available at the Mahabodhi Society across from the Mahabodhi Temple.

■ Rajgir

Rajgir (also known as Rajagriha, "House of Kings"), nestled in a lush valley between the Ratnagiri mountains, is said to have magnetized the Buddha and lured him back for several return visits. The Buddha saw Rajgir in its heyday, when it was the first capital of the kingdom of Magadh, then the pre-eminent power in Bihar. Buddha's favorite spot was Gridhrakuta, a secluded mountain retreat overlooking the valley where he gathered his disciples to unfold the Four Noble Truths. Two caves in the Ratnagiri mountains identified with the Buddha's retreat are connected to the valley by a narrow stone path, which is said to have been built by King Bimbisara of Magadha so that he could visit the Buddha. There were hints of prosperity and organization in Rajgir: a monastery was constructed at Gridhrakuta and the first Buddhist Council to consolidate the teachings of Buddha was held on a small hill 3km away. However, in the end, Rajgir fell into neglect and was finally destroyed by Muhammad Bakhtiyar in the 13th century; only a few bricks remain from the great wall which once girded the entire city. But, like many Buddhist pilgrimage sites in India, Rajgir experienced a slight revival after Independence. The ancient university in nearby Nalanda has been excavated, an impressive new commemorative *stupa*, crowning the highest peak of Mt. Ratnagiri, is just barely visible from the caves at Gridhrakuta, and Japanese aid money has built a new power plant.

Jain influence in Rajgir is almost as strong as that of Buddhism. Jain temples dot the low hills around the city center, commemorating the 14 seasons which Mahavira is said to have spent in the tranquil valley. Hindus, of course, are omnipresent, and they celebrate the Magh Mas ("Excessive Month") every 33rd month. For 30 days, it is said, the entire Hindu pantheon of 330 million gods makes merry in the streets. But certainly they are not as rowdy as the flocks of peasants from outlying villages, who leave the place a wreck. The next festival will occur in March 1999.

ORIENTATION AND PRACTICAL INFORMATION

The modern city of Rajgir spreads itself out along the main road between Gaya and Patna, 15km from Nalanda. The **bus station, railway station,** and some cheap and noisy hotels are situated on the Patna side. Better hotels, shops, and restaurants are on the Gaya side. A series of secondary roads runs between the bus station and Gaya; in almost any other North Indian city this would be called the Civil Lines area, as it contains the **GPO, State Bank of India** (with foreign exchange), **police station,** and **market.** Most of the major sites are outside of town, along the road to Gaya.

ACCOMMODATIONS AND FOOD

The sights at Rajgir, spread out over 5km, require a two-day investment; and the buses to Gaya (every 30min., 5:30am-6pm) and Patna (6, 7am, and 1pm, Rs.25) each take four hours, so plan on spending the night. Most of the hotels in Rajgir are over-priced and underqualified, especially during the high season (Nov.-March). The best area is on the Gaya side of town near the hot springs. The brand-new **Calcutta Buddhist Society** rest house, located on the side road which leads to the civic area, offers the best accommodations around. As you enter your exquisitely clean, spacious room, drink in the smell of fresh wood emanating from your bedframe. Sink into the soft cotton mattress under the protective sheath of a mosquito net, while the fan—with power blades like a Huey Cobra attack helicopter—whips away. The suggested donation is somewhat steep, but you won't complain about an excellent sleep. Doubles bed with bath Rs.150. Off-season: Rs.100. Next door, the **Burmese Temple** with extremely cheap and relatively clean double rooms. The common baths don't have showers. Rooms Rs.30 per person. The **Hotel Gautam Vihar,** located on the main road near the bus stand, has some expensive air-conditioned rooms and decent dorms. Dorm beds Rs.45. Off-season Rs.25.

Good restaurants are equally hard to find. The **Green Restaurant** (tel. 5352), located in a small shopping center toward the Gaya side of town has a wide selection of cheap Continental, Chinese, and Indian fare. The owner is also the proprietor of the Siddharth Hotel and is much more knowledgeable than the tourist officer. Open 8am-10:30pm.

SIGHTS

Sights grace the base of the Ratnagiri mountains. After a short tonga ride (Rs.5 or Rs.25 to rent the whole tonga) to the base, take Bimbisara Rd. to **Gridhrakuta,** the Buddha's retreat. Two natural caves are recognized as sites of Buddha's sermons. Above the caves are the remains of a monastery from the Gupta period (early centuries AD). Backtracking a bit, there's a path that leads up to the new Japanese golden *stupa,* **Viswa Santi,** which sits atop a colossal sandstone dome. Around the dome are four images of the Buddha, representing his birth, enlightenment, teaching, and death. The teaching statue is a reinterpretation of the famous Teaching Buddha image from the first century AD now housed in the Sarnath Museum. Underneath the sitting Buddha are six figures; the long-haired one on the far left may represent Sujata, the peasant woman who brought Buddha rice as he was sitting under a banyan tree in Uruvela, or perhaps a young male convert from Varanasi. To avoid the climb, take a chairlift (open 9am-5pm, Rs.10) to the *stupa* and catch Gridhrakuta on the way down.

Just outside of town on the Vaibhora Hill is the **Saptapurni Cave,** where it is traditionally believed the first Buddhist Council was held. During the first rainy season after the Buddha's death, 500 monks gathered to compile and recite the Buddha's aphorisms and disciplinary rules. (Some modern scholars believe that this story is apocryphal.) Subsequent Buddhist councils, held at Vaishali and Pataliputra (247 BC), established fundamental differences between Theravada and Mahasanghika sects of Buddhism.

At the edge of town there are a number of **hot springs,** where Hindus perform ritual ablutions in the morning. The best time to go is in the early evening when it is still light and the springs are less crowded.

■ Near Rajgir: Nalanda

Nalanda is the site of one of the oldest universities in the world, built by the Guptas in the 5th century AD. Its reputation as a great place of learning dates back even further to the first millennium BC. It was here that the Buddha first came after he rejected his patrimony, to study the Lokayatas philosophy with local *gurus*. It was here also that he attracted his own disciples. Another famous Buddhist philosopher, Nagarjuna, is said to have begun his studies at Nalanda in the 3rd century, but the university itself wasn't inaugurated until two centuries later. Here scholars pursued studies in both Buddhist and Vedic philosophy, as well as in logic and medicine. In subsequent centuries, as Nalanda's fame increased exponentially, so did its size. New buildings soared to the height of nine stories, and with the aid of King Harsha of Kannauj, Nalanda amassed a library of over nine million manuscripts.

Excavations, beginning in the middle of the 19th century, have uncovered extensive ruins. It is now possible to walk among the remains of 11 monasteries, which housed 3000 students and teachers when Hsuan Tsang visited in the 7th century. Several impressive temples remain. The main temple is located at the south entrance of the site. Climbing to the top, the view extends to the north where the monasteries on the right face the temples on the left. A smaller temple to the right of the monasteries is sheathed in 6th-century wall-paintings of the Hindu pantheon. There is an on-site **museum** which houses excavated relics, including Buddha images. (Open Sat.-Thurs. 10am-5pm; admission Rs.10.) The Archaeological Survey's guidebook presents a more extensive account of the excavation and is available at the ticket counter (Rs.5).

There are no hotels or restaurants in Nalanda, although a few *dhabas* have sprung up around the bus stand. Minibuses leave for Nalanda every 10 minutes from the bus stand at Rajgir (Rs.3). From the bus stand in Nalanda, take a tonga (Rs.2 per seat or Rs.10 to rent the whole vehicle) to the site.

▓ Raxaul

With all the dirt but none of the charm you'll find elsewhere in India, Raxaul, 206km north of Patna, is used by travelers as a place to pass through, on the way from India to Nepal or vice-versa. Luckily, transportation is easy to come by, whether it's a rickshaw to the Nepalese border town of Birganj (less unpleasant than Raxaul) or a bus to Patna, with its train connections to Calcutta and Delhi.

ORIENTATION AND PRACTICAL INFORMATION

> **Warning:** Going from India to Nepal, you'll need US$15 or more to pay for your visa. **No other currencies are acceptable** and exact change is best. This would be just a slight inconvenience if there were any currency exchange facilities at the border but there aren't. The closest place to change Indian rupees into dollars is Patna, so plan ahead.
>
> Also, remember to get you passport stamped to say you left India, or you'll have trouble entering Nepal. The Indian **immigration office** is easy to miss, and most rickshaw-*wallahs* don't know where it is since Indians and Nepalis don't have to go there.

Raxaul's main street leads right over the Nepalese border, cutting through the market area, a tangle of alleyways to the east and west. Coming from Nepal, first you will have to stop at Indian **customs,** right after the bridge, then at the **immigration office** (open daily 4am-10pm), a little farther down the road on the right. Since Indians and Nepalis (the majority of people crossing the border) don't need to go through immigration, many rickshaw-*wallahs* don't know where it is. Be sure to stop there, or you'll run into trouble later on. There are no facilities for changing money in Raxaul—Birganj and Patna are the closest places to do so. STD/ISD **telephone** booths can be found along the main road. Between 7pm and 7am, **buses** leave from the bus park on the north side of town, just off the main road, near the railway tracks. During the day, buses leave from **Laxmipur,** 3km south of Raxaul (about Rs.6 by rickshaw). Buses to **Patna** leave approximately every hour, take 5 to 6 hours, and cost Rs.60. **Pharmacies** can be found along the main street. The **post office** is on the west side of the main street and is open Mon.-Sat. 10am-4pm. **Postal Code:** 845305. **Telephone Code:** 06255.

ACCOMMODATIONS AND FOOD

Raxaul is generally not a place most travelers want to linger. If you're stuck overnight, try the **Hotel Ajanta,** Ashram Rd. (tel. 22019, 62119), down a lane east of the main road, close to the border. The less-than-cheerful rooms all have fans, but only the rooms with attached bath (cold water only) have mosquito nets. The hotel boasts its own backup generator to keep the fan going when the electricity fails, and there's an attached **restaurant** with veg. (Rs.10-15) and non-veg. (Rs.15-40) dishes. Doubles Rs.90, with bath Rs.131, with bath and A/C Rs.183.

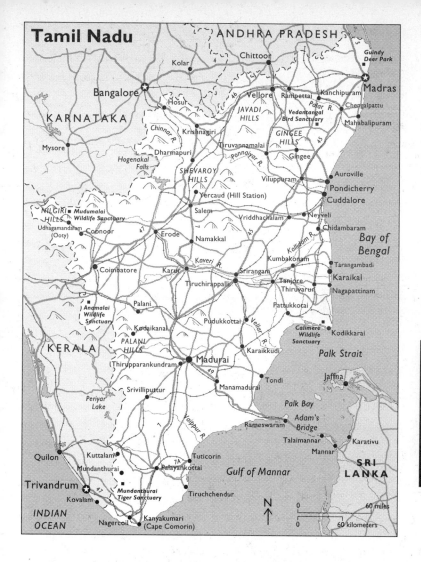

Tamil Nadu

ANDHRA PRADESH

Guindy Deer Park

Kolar
Chittoor

Bangalore
Hosur
Vellore
Ranipettai
Kanchipuram
Madras

KARNATAKA
JAVADI HILLS
Vedantangal Bird Sanctuary
Polar R.
Chengalpattu

Mysore
Chinnar R.
Krishnagiri
GINGEE HILLS
Mahabalipuram

Hogenakal Falls
Dharmapuri
Tiruvannamalai
Ponnaiyar R.
Gingee

Udhagamandalam (Ooty)
NILGIRI HILLS
Mudumalai Wildlife Sanctuary
SHEVAROY HILLS
Yercaud (Hill Station)
Salem
Viluppuram
Auroville
Pondicherry
Cuddalore

Coonoor
Erode
Vriddhachalam
Neyveli
Chidambaram

Bay of Bengal

Coimbatore
Karur
Kaveri R.
Namakkal
Kollidam R.
Kumbakonam
Tarangabadi

Anamalai Wildlife Sanctuary
Palani
Tiruchirappalli
Srirangam
Tanjore
Thiruvarur
Karaikal
Nagapattinam

KERALA
PALANI HILLS
Kodaikanal
Pudukkottai
Pattukkotai
Vellar R.
Calimere Wildlife Sanctuary
Kodikkarai

Thirupparankundram
Madurai
Karaikkudi
Palk Strait

Srivilliputtur
Manamadurai
Tondi
Jaffna

Periyar Lake
Vaipur R.
Palk Bay
Adam's Bridge

Quilon
Kuttalam
Rameswaram
Talaimannar
Mannar
Karativu

Mundanthurai
Palayankottai
Tuticorin
Gulf of Mannar
SRI LANKA

Trivandrum
Kovalam
Mundanthurai Tiger Sanctuary
Tiruchchendur

INDIAN OCEAN
Nagercoil
Kanyakumari (Cape Comorin)
N
0   60 miles
0   60 kilometers

SOUTH INDIA

Tamil Nadu

The southernmost state in mainland India, Tamil Nadu is considered the homeland of Dravidian culture. Some of the finest temple architecture in India is to be found here; *gopurams* (gateway towers) can be seen towering over huge temple-city complexes with streets spiraling around a central shrine. Tamil Nadu is also home to the sounds of Carnatic music and to *bharat natyam,* a classical dance form. Since at least the 1st century AD, Tamil Nadu has nurtured South India's oldest literary tradition, in its mother tongue, Tamil.

The Mauryan Empire, which controlled virtually all of India during the 3rd century BC, never made it this far south. During the last few centuries BC, Tamil Nadu was ruled by three rival dynasties, the Cholas, Pandyas, and Cheras. By the 4th century AD the Pallava kingdom gained ascendance, to be stopped in the 9th century by the Chola kingdom, which grew to rule all of South India. Not until the 14th-century growth of the Vijayanagar Empire was the present-day area of Tamil Nadu ruled by a kingdom based outside its borders. Under the British, Tamil Nadu was part of the Madras Presidency, which included parts of present-day Andhra Pradesh, Kerala, and Karnataka; this entity was divided according to language groups in the 1950s. Most people in Tamil Nadu speak at least a smattering of English, since fierce linguistic pride has caused them to resent the introduction of Hindi. Since Independence Tamil Nadu has also claimed a special place as the only Indian state apparently immune to outbreaks of Hindu-Muslim violence.

Tamil Nadu can be divided into the eastern plains along the Coromandel Coast and the northern and western hills, culminating in the Nilgiris, where the Eastern and Western Ghats meet. The hills were developed into tea and coffee plantations by the British. Tamil Nadu's only perennial river, the Kaveri, flows from the hills; it has been damned heavily and is now a mere trickle in places. The plains are home to paddy fields where the harvest festival of Pongal takes place every year in January. At Kanyakumari, the southern tip of the Indian peninsula is marked by sea-breeze, orange sunsets, and vast stretches of rocky beach.

■ Madras

India's fourth-largest city and South India's preeminent commercial center, Madras is pretty clean, pretty well-planned, and, in some places, plain old pretty. But in terms of tourist interest, Madras suffers by comparison with the magnificent temples and lush countryside which are so accessible from it. Many foreign travelers use Madras as little more than a well-equipped staging point, lingering in the city just long enough to change money, make an international call, and buy a bus ticket for a steamy southern destination. Still, those who linger in the city are usually rewarded with a good time, and Madras boasts plenty of excellent restaurants, shopping malls, beach-strolls, and top-quality cultural offerings.

Also known as Chennai, Madras was founded in 1639 as a "factory," or trading outpost, by Francis Day, an official of the English East India Company. Soon, Day's factory burgeoned—a fort and church were built, and the town became known as Madraspatnam ("White Town") on account of the British subjects who were arriving in droves. To accommodate the new arrivals, East India company agents purchased great swaths of land around the original Madraspatnam, creating an important metropolis in the process. Unfortunately for the British, what one empire built another coveted, and in 1746 French forces stormed the city, seizing and sacking it. Though a treaty returned Madras to British control two years later, the city's vulnerability had been demonstrated, and Calcutta began to supplant Madras as a center of imperial administration. While Madras ceased to be a place where crucial political decisions were made, it became a place where vital economic products were made, and the city's sprawling factories produced thousands of tons of export-grade cotton clothing throughout the late 19th and early 20th centuries. With the coming of Independence, Madras once again swelled (its population is now pushing 6 million) and began to assert power beyond its stretching city limits, this time as a center of Tamil culture and the capital of Tamil Nadu.

ORIENTATION

Extending more than 15km north to south along the western shores of the **Bay of Bengal,** Madras is a massive sprawl of a city. It is divided into three sections. The northernmost of these sections is **George Town,** an area of long, straight streets which run south to **Fort Saint George** and the **Central Railway Station.** George Town's major east-west thoroughfare is **NSC Bose Road,** which ends at its intersection with **Rajaji Road (North Beach Road),** a north–south thoroughfare which runs close to the shore and parallel with **Prakasam Road (Broadway).** The busy intersection of NSC Bose Rd. and Rajaji Rd. is called **Parry's Corner** and is full of buses and rickshaws. The southernmost of Madras's three sections is about 10km south of George Town and stretches from **Mylapore** in the north to the serene green areas south of the **Adyar River.**

Wedged between George Town and Mylapore is Madras's bustling center, which includes **Egmore** and **Mount Road (Anna Salai),** Madras's longest and busiest street. Egmore's northern boundary is **Egmore Railway Station,** which is just off the hotel-saturated **Gandhi Irwin Road.** Running roughly parallel to Gandhi Irwin Rd. is **Pantheon Road.** About 2km south of Egmore Railway Station is the Cooum River. Just south of the river is Mount Rd., which runs from northeast to southwest and traverses much of central Madras, passing tourist information centers and the offices of foreign banks as it goes.

GETTING THERE AND AWAY

By Air

Anna International Airport is slightly chaotic, but not as heavily used as Bombay's or Delhi's airports, making Madras a good port of entry and exit. A **minibus service** runs between the airport and the major hotels (Rs.100). This is a slow but sure and comfortable way of making it into the city. Local buses (#52, #52A, #52B, #52C, #55A) are too crowded to be useful. **Taxis** are available at the airport; a ride to downtown Madras should cost about Rs.150. The **pre-paid taxi booth** inside the international terminal operates at fixed rates. **International Airlines:** Air France: 7 Whites Sq., Whites Rd. (tel. 852 5377). Air Lanka: 758 Mount Rd. (tel. 852 5301). British Airways: Alsa Mall Khaleeli Centre, Montieth Rd. (tel. 827 4272). Delta Airlines: 42 Whites Rd. (tel. 852 5655). Gulf Air: 52 Montieth Rd. (tel. 826 7650). Lufthansa: 167 Mount Rd. (tel. 852 5195). Malaysia Airlines: 498 Mount Rd. (tel. 434-9574). Singapore Airlines: 167 Mount Rd. (tel. 852 2871). Swiss Air: 191 Mount Rd. (tel. 852 3453). **Domestic Airlines:** Air India: 19 Marshalls Rd. (tel. 827 4477). Indian Airlines: 19 Marshalls Rd. (tel. 827 7977). East West Airlines: Mootha Ctr., ground fl., 9 Kodambakkam High Rd. (tel. 828 108). To: Ahmedabad (Tues.-Sun. 1 per day, 3½hr., US$183); Bangalore (4-6 per day, 45min., US$49); Bombay (5-9 per day, 2hr., US$132); Calcutta (3-4 per day, 2hr., US$172); Cochin (1-2 per day, 2hr., US$84); Coimbatore (2-3 per day, 1½hr., US$67); Colombo, Sri Lanka (2-3 per day, 1½hr., Rs.2160); Delhi (3-4 per day, 2½hr., US$197); Goa (Tues., Thurs., and Sat., 2½hr., US$104); Hyderabad (2-3 per day, 1hr., US$80); Madurai (2 per day, 1½hr., US$70); Mangalore (Mon., Wed., and Fri., 2½hr., US$80); Tiruchirappalli (Mon.-Sat. 1 per day, 1hr., US$60); Trivandrum (1 per day, 1hr., US$86).

By Train

Egmore Railway Station forms the northern boundary of Egmore, about 2km north of the Cooum River, in the central section of Madras. The station is just north of Gandhi Irwin Rd., which is saturated with hotels. **Madras Central,** where most long distance trains arrive and depart, is in George Town near the Buckingham Canal, also fairly close to the hotels of Gandhi Irwin Rd. Madras is well connected to most Indian cities. From Madras Central to: Delhi (*Tamil Nadu Exp.* 2621, 9pm, *Grand Trunk Exp.* 2615, 10:15pm, 34hr., Rs.308/1235 for 2nd/1st class); Bombay (*Chennai Exp.* 1064, 7am, 24hr., *Madras-Bombay Exp.* 6012, 11:45am, 27½hr., *Madras-Bombay Mail* 6010, 10:20pm, 30½hr., Rs. 239/833 for 2nd/1st class); Calcutta (*Coromandel Exp.* 2842, 8:10am, 28hr., *Howrah Mail,* 10:30pm, 32½hr., Rs.273/995 for 2nd/1st class); Hyderabad (*Charminar Exp.* 7059, 6:10pm, 14hr., *Hyderabad Exp.* 7053, 4pm., 15hr., Rs. 179/596 for 2nd/1st class); Bangalore (*Brindavan Exp.* 2639,

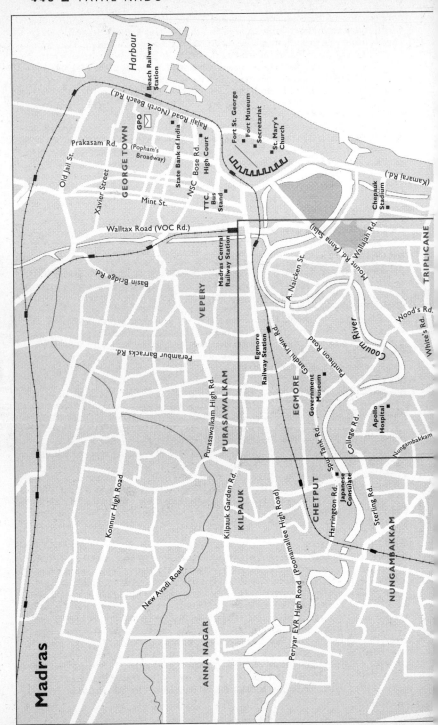

Madras

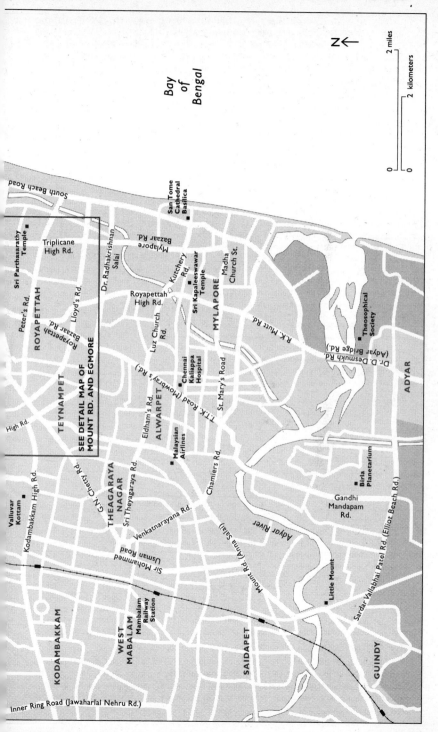

N

2 miles

2 kilometers

0

0

Bay
of
Bengal

South Beach Road

San Tome
Cathedral
Basilica

Triplicane
High Rd.

Sri Parthasarathy
Temple

Mylapore
Bazaar Rd.

Dr. Radhakrishnan
Salai

Peter's Rd.

ROYAPETTAH

Lloyd's Rd.

Royapettah
Bazaar Rd.

Kutchery
Rd.

Royapettah
High Rd.

Sri Kapaleeswarar
Temple

MYLAPORE

Madha
Church St.

SEE DETAIL MAP OF
MOUNT RD. AND EGMORE

TEYNAMPET

Luz Church
Rd.

R.K. Mutt Rd

Theosophical
Society

Dr. D. Desmukh Rd
(Adyar Bridge Rd.)

ADYAR

High Rd.

Eldham's Rd.

ALWARPET

Chennai
Kaliappa
Hospital

St. Mary's Road

T.T.K. Road (Mowbray's Rd.)

Chamiers Rd.

G.N. Chetty Rd.

THEAGARAYA
NAGAR

Sri Theyagaraya Rd.

Malaysian
Airlines

Vaiiuvar
Kottam

Kodambakkam High Rd.

Venkatnarayana Rd.

Birla
Planetarium

Gandhi
Mandapam
Rd.

Adyar River

Mount Rd. (Anna Salai)

Sardar Vallabhai Patel Rd. (Elliot Beach Rd.)

Sir Mohammed
Usman Road

KODAMBAKKAM

WEST
MABALAM

Mambalam
Railway
Station

SAIDAPET

Little Mount

GUINDY

Inner Ring Road (Jawaharlal Nehru Rd.)

7:15am, 6hr.; *Bangalore Exp.* 6023, 1:30pm, 7hr.; *Lalbagh Exp.* 2607, 4:15pm, 5½hr.; *Madras-Bangalore Mail* 6007, 10pm, 7hr., Rs.103/202 for 2nd/A/C car chair); Tirupati (*Sapthagiri Exp.* 6057, 6:25am, 3hr., *Tirupati Exp.* 6053, 1:50pm, 3hr., Rs.62/108 for 2nd/1st class); Ahmedabad (*Navjivan Exp.* 6046, Sat.-Thurs. 9:35am, 33hr., Rs.289/1102 for 2nd/1st class); Varanasi (*Varanasi Exp.* 6039, Mon. and Thurs. 5:30pm, 38½hr., Rs.315/1279 for 2nd/1st class); Mangalore (*Mangalore Mail* 6601, 7:05pm, 18hr., Rs.199/640 for 2nd/1st class); Coimbatore (5 per day, 6:15am-9:45pm, 7hr., Rs.128/250 for 2nd/A/C chair car); Trivandrum (*Trivandrum Mail* 6319, 6:55pm, 15hr., Rs.200/647 for 2nd/1st class). From Egmore Station to: Madurai (5 per day, 6:05am-10:30pm, 8hr., Rs.128/250 for 2nd/A/C chair car); Tiruchirappalli (5 per day, 6:05am-10:30pm, 6hr., Rs.95/187 for 2nd/A/C chair car); Tanjore (*Cholan Exp.* 6153, 9:45am, 9hr., *Thanjavur Passenger* 627, 9:40pm, 10½hr., Rs.99/326 for 2nd/1st class); Rameswaram (*Sethu Exp.* 6113, 6:05pm, 14½hr., *Rameswaram Exp.* 6101, 10:50pm, 14½hr., Rs.159/530 for 2nd/1st class).

By Bus

All buses leave from the TTC bus stand (tel. 534 1835) on the south side of George Town. RGTC buses to: Bangalore (17 per day, 5:30am-11pm; 8½hr., Rs.75); Mysore (5 and 8pm; 11hr., Rs.106); and Tirupati (15 per day, 5:20am-11:15pm, 4hr., Rs.41). TTC buses to: Ooty (5, 6, and 7pm, 14hr., Rs.125); Chidambaram (4:30, 5:30, 7, 8:45am, and 9:15pm, 5hr., Rs.37); Kanyakumari (6 per day, noon-9pm, 11hr., Rs.132); Kodaikanal (5:45am, 14hr., Rs.84); Madurai (every 30min., 5am-10pm, 10hr., Rs.72); Tanjore (every hr., 5am-9:45pm, 15hr., Rs.68). Take the KPN bus service to Tiruchirappalli. Catch the bus opposite the Egmore Railway Station (tel. 834433) at 1:30, 2:30, or 3pm (6½hr., Rs.95).

GETTING AROUND

By Taxi

Common but expensive, taxis are only necessary getting to and from the airport.

By Car

Wheels Rent-a-car, 281 Precision Plaza, Mount Rd. (tel. 455448). 24hr. service. Uniformed, trained drivers. Major credit cards accepted.

By Bus

Buses are the cheapest way to get around. Avoid rush hours, 7:30-10am and 5:30-7pm. The terminus is indicated. Ask the conductor or the people at the bus stop for information before hopping on. The buses are generally very crowded. Called "Pallavan," they can be identified by their green color.

Bus #	Route and Destination
18J, 70J	Airport-Mount Rd.
17A, 17G, 25E, 25B	Mount Rd.-Nungambakkan
4	Mount Rd.-Alwarpet-Besant Nagar
1A, 1C	Mount Rd.-Alwarpet-Royapettah-Tiruvanmiyur
21	Mount Rd.-Luz/Mylapore
12, 12A, 12B	Alwarpet-Theagaraya Nagar
10, 47A, 47G	Theagaraya Nagar-Nungambakkam
17D-E, 17T, 37, 37C, 37E	Kodambakkam-Nungambakkam

By Auto-rickshaw

Although the minimum charge is Rs.5.50, and Rs.0.20 is added per kilometer, most auto-rickshaw drivers tamper with the meters or ask for Rs.10-20 above normal charge. Especially if they know you're new, they'll take you on the most circuitous route possible. Look at a map and decide on the route before you hop in. Take the

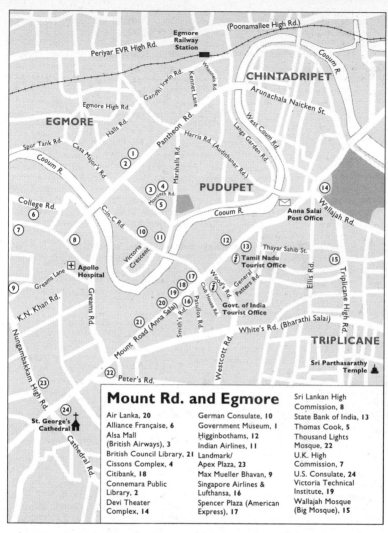

(Poonamallee High Rd.)
Egmore Railway Station
Periyar EVR High Rd.
Cooum R.
CHINTADRIPET
Gandhi Irwin Rd.
Kennet Lane
Whannels Rd.
Arunachala Naicken St.
Egmore High Rd.
EGMORE
Halls Rd.
Pantheon Rd.
Harris Rd. (Audithanar Rd.)
West Coum Rd.
Langs Garden Rd.
Spur Tank Rd.
Casa Major's Rd.
Cooum R.
Marshalls Rd.
PUDUPET
Monteith Rd.
College Rd.
Cooum R.
Anna Salai Post Office
Wallajah Rd.
Cin-C Rd.
Victoria Crescent
Thayar Sahib St.
Tamil Nadu Tourist Office
Apollo Hospital
Greams Lane
Woods Rd.
General Patters Rd.
Ellis Rd.
Triplicane High Rd.
Club House Rd.
K.N. Khan Rd.
Greams Rd.
Govt. of India Tourist Office
Smith's Rd.
Patullos Rd.
Mount Road (Anna Salai)
White's Rd. (Bharathi Salai)
TRIPLICANE
Nungambakkam High Rd.
Westcott Rd.
Sri Parthasarathy Temple
Peter's Rd.
St. George's Cathedral
Cathedral Rd.
Mount Rd. and Egmore
Air Lanka, 20
Alliance Française, 6
Alsa Mall (British Airways), 3
British Council Library, 21
Cissons Complex, 4
Citibank, 18
Connemara Public Library, 2
Devi Theater Complex, 14
German Consulate, 10
Government Museum, 1
Higginbothams, 12
Indian Airlines, 11
Landmark/ Apex Plaza, 23
Max Mueller Bhavan, 9
Singapore Airlines & Lufthansa, 16
Spencer Plaza (American Express), 17
Sri Lankan High Commission, 8
State Bank of India, 13
Thomas Cook, 5
Thousand Lights Mosque, 22
U.K. High Commission, 7
U.S. Consulate, 24
Victoria Technical Institute, 19
Wallajah Mosque (Big Mosque), 15

pre-paid rickshaws from Central Station. Note the number of any auto-rickshaw before you board, since you can complain to a policeman if you have a problem.

By Moped

In order to rent, you will need an international licence. **U-Rent Services Ltd.,** 36 II Main Rd., Gandhi Nagar (tel. 410544), Rs.100 per day. **Vee Rent,** 15/1 Raja Bather St. (tel. 828 1275), behind Pondy Bazaar police station. Kinetic Honda, Rs.80 per day.

PRACTICAL INFORMATION

Tourist Office: Government of India Tourist Office, 154 Mount Rd. (tel. 8524295; fax 8522139). This is the best place to start gleaning information. The staff is considerate and helpful. For further assistance, contact Mr. Narasimhan, the director. Open Mon.-Fri. 9:30am-5pm. **Tamil Nadu Tourist Office,** 143 Mount

Rd. (tel. 830498, 83090). Tours, tourist brochures, and hotel reservations for throughout Tamil Nadu. Open Mon.-Fri. 10:30am-5pm.

Budget Travel: Thomas Cook, Ceebros Centre, Montieth Rd., Egmore, (tel. 855 3276, 855 3263). **Sita Travels,** contact Judaline Bouvard, 26 CINC Rd., Egmore (tel. 827 8861).

Diplomatic Missions: Australia, 114-115, M.G. Rd. (tel. 827 6036). **Austria,** 115 Kothari Building, M.G. Rd. (tel. 827 6036). **Belgium,** 97 Mount Rd. (tel. 235 2336). **Denmark,** 8 Cathedral Rd. (tel. 827 3333). **France,** 202 Prestige Point Bldg., 16 Haddows Rd. (tel. 826 6561). **Finland,** 742 Mount Rd. (tel. 852 3622). **Germany,** 22 Ethiraj Salai (tel. 827 1767). **Hungary,** Tiam House, 28 Rajaji Salai (tel. 510 986). **Indonesia,** 5 North Leith Castle Rd., Santhome (tel. 234 1095). **Italy,** 19 Rajaji Salai (tel. 534 1110). **Japan,** 11 Rutland Gate, 4th St. (tel. 827 6694). **Korea,** 144 Nungambakkam High Rd. (tel. 825 2240). **Malaysia,** Asst. High Commissioner, 6 Sri Ram Nagar, North St. (tel. 434 3048). **Philippines,** Spic Centre, 4th fl., 97 Mount Rd. (tel. 434 665). **Russia,** 14 Santhome High Rd. (tel. 832 330). **Singapore,** Apex Plaza, 3rd fl., 3 Nungambakkam High Rd., (tel. 827 3795). **Spain,** 8 Nimmo Rd. (tel. 494 2008). **Sri Lanka,** 9D Nawag Mabibulla Ave. (tel. 827 2270). **Sweden,** 6 Cathedral Rd. (tel. 827 2040). **Switzerland,** 224 TTK Rd. (tel. 452301). **Turkey,** 202 Lingi Chetty St. (tel. 510214). **U.K.,** 24 Anderson Rd. (tel. 827 3136). **U.S.,** 220 Mount Rd. (tel. 827 3040).

Immigration Office: Foreigners Registration Office, 26 Haddows Rd. (tel. 827 8210). Visa extensions can be arranged here. These take about 2 working days and cost Rs.900. Take 3 passport-size photographs.

Currency Exchange: Bank of America, 748 Mount Rd. (tel. 852 5285). **Citibank,** 766 Mount Rd. (tel. 852 2151). **Thomas Cook,** El Dorado building, 112 Nungambakkam High Rd. (tel. 827 4941). They charge extra for non-Thomas Cook traveler's checks. Open Mon.-Fri. 9:30am-1pm and 2-4pm.

American Express: G-17 Spencer Plaza, Mount Rd. (tel. 852 3638). Open daily 10am-7pm.

Telephones: STD/ISD booths can be found in almost any part of the city. Mount Rd. has one every few yards. Luz has a bunch too. **Faxes** can be sent from **Ap-Xerox-Ap Fax,** 15 Gohul Arcade, 2 Sardar Patel Rd. (tel. 410013). **Worldwide Technologies Ltd.,** 704 Spencer Plaza, 769 Mount Rd. (tel. 852 4289).

Market: Mylapore Market, outside the Kapaleeswarar Temple. A crowded marketplace where you can buy fresh vegetables. It's noisy and the road is narrow. Wear your dirtiest pair of shoes and jeans before you battle the crowd. **Vitan,** 172-A Luz Church Rd., Mylapore (tel. 499 1484). A department store that sells fresh produce and groceries in orderly aisles. It's a little expensive but provides quality selection and a hassle-free environment.

Library: American Library, American Consulate Building. Good collection of American literature and history. Open Mon.-Fri. 9:30am-6pm. You can purchase a daily membership for Rs.30. **British Council,** 737 Mount Rd., part of the British consulate. Besides books on politics and history, they have a good collection of fiction. Temporary memberships available (Rs.100). **Connemera Public Library,** Pantheon Rd. (tel. 826 1151). The most extensive collection of books in Madras. Friendly staff; no membership required. Open Mon.-Fri. 9am-6pm.

Cultural Centers: Max Mueller Bhavan, 13 K.N. Khan Rd. (tel. 826 1341). Conducts German classes and screens movies. Also has a collection of German books. **Alliance Française,** 40 College Rd., Nungambakkam (tel. 827 9803). French classes, French movies, French books. No french fries. **Music Academy,** Mowbrays Rd. (tel. 827 5619). The place for an evening of Carnatic music. Check the local papers to find out what's going on in the biggest auditorium in Madras.

English Bookstore: Landmark Books, basement, Apex Plaza, 3 Nungambakkam High Rd. A lovely place to browse; the air-conditioning makes the shop an ideal refuge from the outside heat and mugginess. Books on any subject under the sun. Good collection of stationary and cards. **Fountainhead,** 27 Dr. Radhakrishnan Salai (tel. 826310). It's not just Ayn Rand. Fantastic collection of fiction. **Odyssey,** 15 1st Main Rd., Gandhi Nagar (tel. 412933). Very new, very cool, filled with a young college crowds and everything from Asterix to Jane Austen. Besides books, there's a selection of gifts, cards, and CDs. **Higginbothams,** 814 Mount Rd. One of the biggest bookstores, well-stocked with techie books for the geeks.

Pharmacy: Ideal Pharmacy, 107 G.N. Chetty Rd. (tel. 825 6177). **Janaki Pharmacy,** 4 Sardar Patel Rd. (tel. 413732). **Kala Pharmacy,** 421 Pantheon Rd. (tel. 825 0062). **Karuppiah Pharmacy,** 149 Luz Church Rd. (tel. 493 6417). Open 24hr.

Hospital: Apollo Hospital, 21 Greams Rd. (tel. 827 7447). **Chennai Kaliappa Hospital,** 43 2nd Main Rd., Roja Anna Malai Puram (tel. 493 6390). Open 24hr. Specialists in every field available to take care of you. **Malar Hospital,** 52 1st Main Rd., near Adyar Bridge (tel. 491 4023). Open 24hr. Accident care, orthopedic care, excellent lab facilities, and good specialists.

Police: Stations in Mylapore (tel. 852 0838), Adyar (tel. 491 5901), Guindy (tel. 234 1539), Kodambakkam (tel. 483 8428), Theagaraya Nagar (tel. 852 2581), Anna Salai (tel. 852 2581), Egmore (tel. 826 7575).

Emergency: Police: tel. 100. **Fire:** tel. 101. **Ambulance:** tel. 102.

Post Office: GPO, Rajaji Salai (tel. 514289). **Anna Road Head Post Office** (tel. 843700). **Nungambakkam** (tel. 827 0432). Open Mon.-Fri. 10am-4pm, Sat. 10am-2pm. **Postal Code:** 400001-400069.

Telephone Code: 44.

ACCOMMODATIONS

Accommodations in Madras are pricey compared to those in smaller cities. Many cheaper places are located in Egmore near the railway station, and are appropriate for a night's stay, but are inconveniently located. Any savings on hotel rooms here are offset by the cost of transportation to the Mount Rd. area.

Hotel Rohini International, 67 G.N. Chetty Rd., Theagaraya Nagar (tel. 828 0255). The best of the cheapies. You may have to perform histrionics to communicate with the Tamil-speaking reception. Singles have cots, attached baths, TVs, and phones. Singles Rs.200, with A/C Rs.500. Doubles Rs.320, with A/C Rs.650.

Hotel Maris, 9 Cathedral Rd. (tel. 827 0541; fax 825 4867). A comfortable, clean and relatively inexpensive place. Rooms are sunny, with cots, table, chairs, marbled bathrooms, small balconies, and good furniture. Singles Rs.260, with A/C Rs.325. Doubles Rs.365, with A/C Rs.450. Plus 20% tax.

Hotel Ganport, 103 N.H. Rd. (tel. 827 1889). Small rooms and you'll have to rough it out but it's centrally located. Singles Rs.350, with A/C Rs.550. Doubles Rs.400, with A/C Rs.600.

Hotel Guru, 69 Marshalls Rd. (tel. 855 4065). The rooms without A/C are a bargain. Furnishings a little moth-eaten. Doubles Rs.360, with A/C Rs.600.

Hotel Naveen International, 168/169 Arcot Rd. T. Nagar (tel. 825 6005). You can watch the interesting happenings of Pondy Bazaar from this green building. Receptionist is partial to those who attempt to speak a little Tamil. Rooms are small and basic. Bed and toilet are a little grubby. Singles Rs.300. Doubles Rs.350, with A/C Rs.450.

Hotel Dasaprakash, 100 Poonamallee High Rd. (tel. 825 5111). Quite a charming place and a definite bargain. Carpeted floors, neat beds, and clean toilets. Slightly inconvenient to hike to the commercial parts of the city. Singles Rs.250, with A/C Rs.350. Doubles Rs.350.

Hotel Ganga International, 47 Bazullah Rd., off North Usman Rd., Theagaraya Nagar (tel. 823 1340; fax 823 5193). Musty rooms, with cane furniture and lots of plants. Centrally located and comfortable. Singles Rs.750. Doubles Rs.850.

Dee Cee Manor, 87 G.N. Chetty Rd., T. Nagar (tel. 828 4411). The quiet, helpful reception will drive home that you've made a good choice. Decorated in shades of dark brown and wood with some Mahabalipuram-esque sculpture, the hotel is new, well-maintained, and neatly furnished. Singles Rs.975. Doubles Rs.1150. The attached veg. restaurant, Atithi, is cozy, quiet, and prices are reasonable. Open daily 6-11pm.

Nilgiri's Nest, 58 Radhakrishnan Salai (tel. 827 5111). A cozy hideaway right next to Nilgiris Supermarket. Complimentary breakfast everyday. Clean rooms, spongy beds, hygienic bathrooms. Singles Rs.500. Doubles Rs.675.

The Residency, 49 G.N. Chetty Rd. (tel. 825 3434). A comfortable, 5-year-old, 3-star hotel that's popular among Malaysian tourists. It has a pleasant, homey feel from the cane furniture to the soft beds. The employees are smartly turned out in brown pants and cream *kurtas.* Spacious bathrooms have showers, seat toilets, and toilet paper. Surja Kishore, the guest relations executive, is capable and efficient—she can fix anything and everything. **Chin Chin** is the attached Chinese restaurant. The weekend crowd is heavy, but the food is worth waiting for. Open daily 11am-2pm, 6:30-10:30pm. **The Right Place,** a 24hr. coffee shop, is attached. **Tinto,** the attached Mexican-style bar, is open daily 1-11pm. Singles Rs.1000. Doubles Rs.1150. Major credit cards and U.S. dollars, pounds sterling, and Deutschmarks accepted.

FOOD

Copper Chimney, 74 Cathedral Rd. (tel. 827 5770). The lights could be a little dimmer, but that would hinder your view of the art surrounding you—modern paintings which add a classy touch to the elegant decor. Try the cheese chicken *kabab*—a boneless chicken marinated in vinegar, cream cheese and Indian herbs. *Murg rahra* is another speciality—spicy tender chicken in Indian gravy. The Kashmiri *naan* is delicious. An unobtrusive waiter will guide you through the menu on request and coax your decision. A meal for 2 can cost between Rs.300 and Rs.400. Veg. menu available. Open daily 7:30-11:30pm.

Carnival, 68 C.P. Ramaswamy Rd., Abhiramapuram (tel. 499 6839). Deservedly popular with families and teenagers, this crowded, 4-year-old eatery serves North and South Indian food, as well as pizzas and burgers. Open daily 11am-11pm.

Cascade, Kakaine Towers, 15 K.N. Khan Rd. (tel. 825 3836). Elegant and pricey with an artificial stream that can't really be called a cascade without stretching the imagination. Pleasing profusion of plants. Good Chinese soups. Open daily 7am-10:30pm.

Kabul, opposite Sankara Hall, TTK Rd. (tel. 499 2435). This small restaurant specializes in North Indian food—spicy, hot, red, and yummy. Open daily noon-2pm and 5-11pm.

Woodlands, 72/75 Dr. Radhakrishnan Salai, Mylapore (tel. 827 3111). One of the oldest South Indian restaurants in Madras, frequented by middle-class families. *Idli, vadai, dosa* served promptly, if abruptly. The coffee is great. Open 7-10am and 3-11pm.

Tic Tac, 123 Nungambakkam High Rd. A cool, informal place to quench your thirst. Watch out for the huge coke can with its jazzy lighting. They specialize in *tandoor kababs.* Relaxed and unhurried. Enjoy the tandoor *tangri kabab* or the *kati* rolls. Open daily 6-11:30pm.

Cakes 'N' Bakes, 22 Nungambakkam High Rd. (tel. 827 7075). This famous pastry shop does a booming business with the college crowd. Try a piece of the black forest cake or the apple pie. Tasty milkshakes, too. Open daily 2-10:30pm.

Hot Breads, Alsa Mall, Montieth Rd., Egmore (tel. 826 6724). A mind-boggling selection of breads, pastries, pizzas, and soda for shoppers in the mood to consume goodies. Open daily 10am-10pm.

Freez Zone, 33 TTK Rd., Alwarpet (tel. 499 1394). One of the most popular ice cream joints in town. Look out for the huge ice cream cone on TTK Rd. to find the shop. The Freez Zone special is a combination of chocolate and vanilla ice cream with lots of chocolate sauce, fruits, and nuts. Open daily 6-11:30pm.

Snofield, Amaravati Complex, 1 Cathedral Rd. (tel. 827 0305). Opposite Music Academy. Popular among teenage daters, this place sees young romance blossom at its cozy tables nightly. Try the "Spanish Delight" or the "Honeymoon." Open daily 11am-11pm. Next door is **Nala's** where you can tuck in *bhel puri, pani puri,* and *aloo chat.*

Fruit Shop on Greams Road, 11 Greams Rd. (tel. 823 3548). Shakes to the left, shakes to the right. Fruit punch and fruit cocktails freshly made with mineral water. The "sheikh shake" is a yummy concoction made with dates and nuts. No syrups or artificial colors—it's all healthy and wholesome. Try the summer special, a mixture of apples and plums. Open daily 10am-8pm.

SIGHTS

For a city of 6 million, the sight-seeing pickings in Madras are surprisingly slim. The most absorbing of Madras's attractions is the **Government Museum** on Pantheon Rd. Established in 1857 by British imperial authorities, the museum's ambitions are decidedly Victorian, and its collection boldly seeks to cover all of the vast territory between nature and nurture. But the Government Museum's natural history holdings cannot compare to its other exhibits, whose highlight is the world's finest collection of South Asian bronze sculpture. Just beyond the museum's main entrance are the eclectic archeology galleries, which display examples of early Buddhist sculpture, many of which were discovered at the ruins of Amaravati. Also impressive are the early Jain sculptures recovered from Danavulapadu and the fragmentary remnants of the seminal Indus Valley civilization. The ethnology exhibits vary in quality, but the displays on local fishing techniques, South Indian costumes, and Tamil Nadu's puppet makers are especially good. The high point of the museum is the free-standing bronze gallery, just west of the ethnology galleries. The unparalleled collection of Chola bronzes includes a complete set of the key players in the *Ramayana* and some excellent 11th-century renderings of Shiva surrounded by a ring of fire, in the guise of Nataraja (King of Dance). Adjacent to the Bronze Galleries are the Children's Museum and the Art Galleries. (Open Sat.-Thurs. 9am-5pm. Admission Rs.3, Rs.10 with camera; free tours at 10am, noon, 2, and 4pm.)

Nearly 2.5km northeast of the museum is **Fort Saint George,** a massive complex 500m south of Parry's Corner, George Town. Supervised by Francis Day, construction of the fort began in 1640 and was completed later that year on Saint George's Day, April 23. While many of the Fort's original buildings were damaged or destroyed during mid-18th century French attacks, some original buildings remain. Highlights includes the houses of the adventurer Robert Clive and Elihu Yale, the founder of Yale University and governor of Madras. Saint Mary's, built in 1680, is South Asia's oldest Anglican church. These days, the fort complex is the churning center of Tamil Nadu's state government—most of the fort's buildings have been converted into government offices and the conversion has diminished the complex's appeal as a tourist attraction. To get some sense of what Fort Saint George used to be like, head for the **Fort Museum,** which is housed in the fort complex's Exchange Building. The museum displays an eccentric mix of items from British India, including paintings, weapons, uniforms, and a host of mementos left behind by Robert Clive. (Open Sat.-Thurs. 10am-5pm.)

Extending south from Fort Saint George is the second-longest urban beach in the world, a 12km-long flank of sand known as **Marina.** Both sunbathing and swimming are frowned upon here, but strolling along the shore front **South Beach Road (Kamaraj Road)** can be fun. Peddlers sell all sorts of tasty foods, while (especially on Sunday evening) thousands of Madras residents stroll away their worries. As you saunter along South Beach Rd., occasionally turn your attention from the beach to the buildings across the street—the dense concentration of colonial buildings is trippy. Look out for the Indo-Saracenic University of Madras buildings; the red-brick Presidency College is unusual because of its use of Italian design elements while the Senate House displays Byzantine influences. Also visible from South Beach Rd. are **Anna Park** and the antenna-like MGR Samadhi, memorials to former Tamil Nadu Chief Ministers C.N. Annadurai and M.G. Ramachandran respectively. Also along the Marina is a slimy aquarium and several decrepit swimming pools which are probably best avoided.

Nearly 500m west of South Beach Rd., in the neighborhood of Triplicane, is the **Sri Parthasarathy Temple,** which was originally raised by the Pallavas in the 8th century, and which has been renovated since then by the Cholas and the Vijayanagar Kings. The temple is dedicated to Krishna.

The **Sri Kapaleeswarar Temple,** in the Mylapore area off Kutchery Rd., is sacred to the Shaiva tradition. Built after an earlier temple on the same site was destroyed by the Portugese, this temple has a 40-m *gopuram*. The great saint Thirugnanasambandar is supposed to have sung the glory of the temple in his hymn and in the same temple, he is said to have brought back to life a girl who died of a snake bite. A shrine and statue commemorate this sacred event. Non-Hindus are only allowed to the outer courtyard which houses some statues. The field in which the girl's body was cremated now holds the P.S. High School, a government-run school for boys.

At the southern edge of the Marina, nearly 6km south of Fort Saint George, is the **San Tome Cathedral Basilica,** an important pilgrimage site built over the tomb of the apostle St. Thomas. Thomas is traditionally said to have arrived in India from Palestine in 52 AD; 26 years later he is believed to have been killed, his body buried near the beach. About 1000 years later, Thomas's remains were moved further inland and a new church was built, likely by Madras's Persian Christian community. In 1606, the church was refurbished and made into a cathedral; in 1896 it was rebuilt as a basilica. To celebrate the 90th anniversary of San Tome's basilica status, Pope John Paul II paid a visit, saying mass here in 1986. San Tome is more interesting historically than aesthetically, although the yellow church is pleasant and peaceful. (Open daily 7am-7pm.) A small **museum** on the premises contains a 16th-century map of South Asia. (Usually open Mon.-Fri. 9am-noon and 3-6pm.)

About 6km southwest of the Basilica and just south of the Adyar River is **Little Mount,** a complex of caves. According to local legend, the impressions in the rocky caves are Saint Thomas's handprints. Little Mount has two **churches,** both of which attract plenty of pilgrims. The older church was built in 1551 by the Portuguese while Our Lady of Health, behind which is a holy-water-spewing spring, was constructed in 1971. About 5km southwest of Little Mount is the 95-m-high **Saint Thomas Mount (Great Mount),** where Thomas is said to have been killed. The Portuguese-built church atop the Mount was raised in 1523 on the site of a church that had been constructed nearly 1,000 years before by Armenian traders. It is said that the current church's altar is built on the very spot where Thomas died, and that the paintings over the altar were done by St. Luke. The cross, which is claimed to have bled in 1558, is said to have been hand-carved by Thomas.

One kilometer south of Little Mount is **Guindy National Park,** a peaceful (though increasingly scruffy) expanse which is home to some deer and a decidedly mediocre **Snake Park.** (Open daily 9am-5pm.)

Five kilometers due north of Little Mount is **Valluvar Kottam,** a colorful, 33-m memorial to the poet Tiruvalluvar in the shape of a temple chariot. Inscribed on parts of the massive chariot are verse from Thirukkural, the Tamil classic which was Tiruvalluvar's masterwork. (Open daily 9am-7pm.)

ENTERTAINMENT

Marina Beach is a great spot to while the evenings away or to take a morning walk. Although swimsuits should be avoided, walking along the ocean's edge, then settling in to watch the sunset is not. There will be dozens of hawkers selling flowers, eats, balloons and kites.

A number of cinema houses screen English movies. Madras is home to India's second-largest film industry, so if you have time, take in a Tamil talkie too. Language barriers won't prevent you from understanding the story. The hero and heroine run around trees and sing love songs in which the heroine changes clothes at least ten times. The villain chases the heroine, the hero and the villain fight, the hero wins, marries the heroine and they live happily ever after. Keep an eye on the papers and plan to reach the theater about 20 minutes before the show begins. **Sathyam,** 8 Thurni Vika Rd., off Peters Rd., near New College (tel. 826 7813) has three screens. **Woodlands,** Royapettah High Rd. (tel. 823150), has two screens. **Devi**, Mount Rd. All have shows at 1, 4, 7, and 10pm.

There are music performances and dance dramas at Music Academy. The Carnatic Music and Dance Festival takes place annually, from Dec. 2 to Jan. 15. Narada Gana Sabha and Rani Seethai Hall also present various events. Scout the newspapers to find out what's going on at these places. In general, *The Hindu* is a good place to check to find out what's going on in any given week.

The best **disco** in which to jive through the night is **Gatsby 2000,** at the Park Sheraton. Cover Rs.400 per couple. Open 10:30pm onwards. **Socko,** Ambassador Pallava, is a popular disco playing Indian pop. **The Eclipse,** Quality Inn Aruna, 144 Sterling Rd. (tel. 825 9090) is a new disco with techno music and a yuppie crowd.

Kishkinta, Madras's number one **amusement park,** features rides like space-shuttle, wave pool, white water, and a flume ride. **B.M. Birla Planetarium** is located at Kotturpuram, with a computerized projector which depicts the night sky on a huge hemispherical dome. The planetarium offers audio-visual programs on various topics in astronomy—all you want to know about black holes, quasars, and pulsars. (English program 12:45am, 12:45, and 3:45pm; Tamil program noon and 2:30pm. Admission Rs.7, children 11 and under Rs.3.)

SHOPPING

Pavement shopping can be rewarding since hawkers are common and they often offer good deals. The best place for shirts is Pondy Bazaar, Theagaraya Nagar. Dozens of makeshift shops also line the streets in Luz, offering earrings, bracelets, shirts, hairbands—fashion was never so affordable.

Alsa Mall, Montieth Rd., is home to dozens of clothing stores, an ice cream parlor, and Hot Breads. The Golden Tulip has a limited selection of dresses and *salwars*. Art Arcade, B23 (tel. 855 4296) offers a selection of wooden carvings and ethnic semi-precious jewelry. Walnut boxes Rs.1500-2500, Rajasthani chairs Rs.900, necklaces Rs.60-500. **Spencer's Plaza,** 769 Mount Rd., is another mall where the beautiful and handsome do their shopping and have their fun. Aesthetica Creations, 2nd fl. (tel. 852 6475), carries *salwars* and evening wear. Yves St. Laurent and Gucci share the shelves with no-names at Prince perfumes, F-4E, 1st fl. (tel. 855 1515). **Cissons Complex,** next door to Alsa Malls, and **Fountain Plaza,** Pantheon Rd., offer more clothes, jewelry, music, books, and food.

Rex Fashions, 16 Luz Church Rd., Mylapore (tel. 499 5761), sells designer jeans made in Madras for Rs.500-800 per pair. **Radha Silk House,** or RASI, 1 Sannadhi St., Mylapore (tel. 494 0528), next to the Kapaleeswarar temple, is a hot favorite among foreign tourists: silk saris, silk material, silk ties—a profusion of colors. The basement boasts an excellent selection of gift items, wooden carved boxes inlaid with ivory, brassware, and paintings. An art collector's paradise, **Victoria Technical Institute (VTI)** 765 Mount Rd. (tel. 852 3141), is one of the best places to pick up paintings, woodwork, exquisite sculpture, brassware, and pottery.

▨ Kanchipuram

Dusty streets, *gopurams* towering above, small houses with Vishnu's mark painted on the walls, fruit vendors outshouting each other, devout Hindu women in their traditional nine-yard saris carrying flowers; Kanchi is the city of temples, "the Varanasi of the south." Counted among Hinduism's seven sacred cities (although of course there are many more than seven), Kanchi derives its name from the words "Ka," another name for Brahma, the creator, and "*anchi*," which means "worship." Brahma is said to have worshiped Vishnu and the goddess Kamakshi here, and the magnificent temples constructed by the Pallava kings (4th-8th centuries AD) in their capital city reinforce this myth. Kanchi was also the episcopal seat of the guru Shankara (780-820), and has been a center for philosophy and learning since that time.

Modern Kanchipuram is a place where the smells of *chakra pongal,* the sound of temple bells, and some of the most chaotic traffic in India combine to launch an assault on the senses. But look out here for the elegant saris worn by Tamil women as well—Kanchipuram silk saris are famous all over India, and the flourishing silk industry ensures the town's prosperity.

ORIENTATION

Kanchi is divided into two parts—**Little Kanchi** houses the important Vishnu temples and lies to the east of the bus stand, while **Big Kanchi,** or Shiva Kanchi, is located to the west of the bus stand. There are supposedly 1008 temples dedicated to Shiva and 108 to Vishnu in Big and Little Kanchi respectively. The bus stand is located on **Kamaraj Street** (also known as Kossa St.), which runs north-south through the center of town; most shops and eating places are here, and on **Nellukkara St.** (which runs east-west at the north end of Kamaraj St.) and **Gandhi Rd.**

PRACTICAL INFORMATION

Tourist Office: TTDC: Hotel Tamil Nadu, Kamatchi Amman Sannadhi St. (tel. 631502).

Currency Exchange: State Bank of India, 16 Gandhi Rd. (tel. 22987). Open Mon-Fri. 9am-4:30pm, Sat. 10am-noon. They accept traveler's checks only.

Telephones: STD/ISD booths located all over Kanchi, especially on Gandhi Rd., Kamaraj St., and Raja Veethi.

Trains: Railway Station (tel. 26444), on Station Rd., east of the Vaikuntha Perumal Temple. To Madras via Chingalpattu (1:55 and 7:50pm, 3hr., Rs.26/116 for 2nd/1st class).

Buses: Bus Stand at the intersection of Kamaraj St. and Nellukkara St. To: Madras (every 15min., 6:30am-10:30pm, 2hr., Rs.12); Tiruchirappalli (6:40, 9:20am, 7:15, 8:45 and 9:40pm, 9hr., Rs.15); Tanjore (6:55am, 5pm, and 10:30pm, 9hr., Rs.15).

Local Transportation: Buses (red and white) are frequent but the bus conductors don't speak English and don't announce the names of stops. **Taxis:** contact KGT Travels, 66D Salai St. (tel. 24179). **Auto rickshaws** can be flagged down on Kamaraj St. or Gandhi Rd., or picked up next to the bus stand. **Bicycles** can be rented from the cycle shop on Sannadhi St. (right outside the Varadaraja Perumal temple) for Rs.10 per day—the easiest way to navigate in Kanchi.

Market: Rajaji Market, at the intersection of Railway Rd. and Gandhi Rd.

Pharmacy: Tamil Nadu Medicals, 25 Nellukkara St.; **Karpagam Medicals** is next door.

Hospital: Government Hospital, Railway Rd. (tel. 22308).

Police: Police Office, Vandavasi Rd. (tel. 22728).

Post Office: Head Post Office, Railway Rd. (tel, 22080). Open Mon.-Fri. 9am-5pm. **Postal Code:**

Telephone Code: 04112.

ACCOMMODATIONS

Except for the TTDC Hotel, all other accommodations are fairly close to each other in the Nellukkara St.-Gandhi Rd. area.

Hotel Baboo Surya, 85 E. Raja Veethi (tel. 22555, 22556). Conveniently located near the Perumal temple about a 10-15-min. walk from the bus stand. The poshest hotel in the area, Baboo Surya flaunts an elevator with glass windows and a receptionist who speaks English. You'll love the light wooden furniture; the rooms are tasteful to the last detail. The small balcony doesn't afford much of a view, though. The most hygienic hotel in Kanchi. All rooms have Star TV. Singles Rs.225, 350 with A/C. Doubles Rs.275, 400 with A/C. MC/AmEx.

Hotel Jaibala International, 504 Gandhi Rd. (tel. 24453, 24348). The single rooms offer no-frills basics—a cot, 2 chairs, and a common bathroom. The doubles have creature comforts—dresser, mirror, mosaic floors, TV, and a cupboard. Its central location is convenient, but might make it noisy. A good bargain. Singles Rs.95. Doubles Rs.225, with A/C Rs.275.

TTDC Hotel, Kamatchi Amman Samadhi St. (tel. 23428, 23430). Conveniently located near the railway station, the Tamil Nadu Hotel offers spacious and clean rooms. Ignore the slightly musty smell when you arrive and leave the windows open. Doubles Rs.250, with A/C Rs.375, with TV Rs.400. Reservations must be made a day in advance.

Sri Krishna Lodge, opposite Sri Rama Lodge, Nellukkara Street. Smells of disinfectant; bright green, slightly dirty walls. Bring your own sheets. Singles Rs.49. Doubles Rs.80.

Sri Rama Lodge, 20 Nellukkara St. (tel. 22435, 22436). Surrounded by shops on a busy street, Sri Rama Lodge doesn't offer much privacy. Watch your step when you enter the rooms. Small TV, 2 beds. Bring your own sheets. Squat toilet. Walls are dirty, but if you're going to be out most of the day, this is the place. Singles Rs.60. Doubles Rs.100, with A/C Rs.330.

FOOD

Hotel Saravana Bhavan, within the premises of Jaibala International. The best place to try South Indian food. If the outside heat doesn't daunt you, go for that hot *masala dosa* (Rs.15). Or cool off with chocolate ice cream (Rs.20). Sweet, excellent *badam halwa* is also served.

Hotel Baboo Surya, 85 E. Raja Veethi. The restaurant here is the place to eat in Kanchi if you're paranoid about hygiene. Cereal and toast Rs.30-45. They also serve South and North Indian veg. food.

Srinivasa Vilas, 98 Kamaraj St. South Indian *thali,* unlimited rice for Rs.10.

Abirami, further down Kamaraj toward the bus stand. A small veg. hotel. Despite its somewhat run-down appearance, the food is good.

Sri Saravana, 546 Gandhi Rd. Another friendly South Indian neighborhood restaurant, with good, cheap food and quick service *Sambhar vadai,* (two per plate, Rs.6) and hot *idlis* (three per plate, Rs.7).

SIGHTS

A tour of Kanchi's temples takes about four or five hours by auto-rickshaw. If you'd rather walk, it's better to go in the evening and stay out of the morning sun.

The **Varadaraja Perumal Temple,** built by the Vijayanagar kings, marks the southeast corner of Kanchi. Check out the hundred-pillared *mandapa,* of which 96 pillars remain today. One pillar on the right side shows a circle of intertwined dancers, the knees of one dancer metamorphosing into the breasts of the next. The entrance to the *mandapa* is marked by Kama, the god of love, riding a horse. Open daily 8am-noon and 4-7pm. Camera fee Rs.2, video fee Rs.5.

Walking along Nellukkara Street, west from the bus stand to where it becomes Putheri Street, you'll reach the **Kailasnatha Temple,** marked by a tall *gopuram.* The temple was built by Rajasimha Pallava in the 8th century. Legend says that Lord Vishnu prayed to the *linga* in this temple to help him defeat the demon Tripurantaka. The special feature of this temple is that in order to circumambulate the image, worshipers must crawl on all fours through a hollow in a rock. Non-Hindus are not allowed inside the inner sanctum to attempt this, however. There are no lights outside, so plan to visit this temple before sunset. Open daily 8:30am-noon and 4-6pm.

The **Kamakshi Amman Temple,** which displays a golden *gopuram,* can be reached by turning right into Amman Koil St. from West Raja St. This temple is dedicated to Kamakshi, the resident deity of Kanchipuram, and it also contains a shrine dedicated to Shankara. Photography is not permitted within the temple. Open daily 5am-12:30pm and 4-8:30pm. Sannadhi St. will lead you to the **Ekambaranatha Temple.** *Yalis,* mythical beasts that are half-lion, half-elephant, stare from the pillars. There are a number of *lingas* outside the main shrine as well as statues of the 63 Alvar poet-saints. This temple is usually peaceful and quiet, unlike the other temples in Kanchi which are filled with noisy crowds. There is a famous statue of Vishnu as Nilakanta (the blue-throated one). Open daily, 6am-12:30pm, 4-8pm. Turning right from East Raja Street, you'll reach the **Vaikunta Perumal Temple.** This temple is deserted, and all of its sculptures have been repaired with plaster by the Archaeological Survey of India. The left corner at the back has a panel showing Hsuan Tsang, the Chinese Buddhist pilgrim who traveled all over India in the 7th century. The main image is that of Vishnu, reclining on the serpent Ananta.

SOUTH INDIA

SHOPPING

The biggest and most reputed of Kanchi's silk sari shops is **Nalli Silks,** 54 Nellukkara Street. You can also try **Srinivasan Silk House,** 17A T.K. Nambi Street. **Pavithra Silks,** No. 4 State Bank Colony (near Tollgate) has some unique prints, and the owner, Murugadass, can be persuaded to show you silk yarn and the process of making *zari* designs on saris. Weaving saris is done by hand in a fascinating process. Turn right onto the road perpendicular to Sannadhi St. (outside Varadaraja Perumal temple) and take a left at **Ammangar Street.** This street is full of silk weavers who will willingly demonstrate their craft in the morning hours. Each sari is a labor of love and takes fifteen days to complete.

■ Vellore

This once-important town on the southern bank of the Palar river has degenerated into a chaotic and slightly backward leather center. Vellore's fort, a well-preserved specimen of medieval military architecture and the site of several battles of the Carnatic Wars, is its only real attraction. More recently, Vellore's Christian Medical College, founded in 1900 by the American missionary Ira Scudder, has emerged as one of India's foremost medical institutes. More visitors come to Vellore for treatment than for tourism, so the town retains a slightly cosmopolitan feel.

ORIENTATION AND PRACTICAL INFORMATION

Vellore is not quite a grid, but its roads are straight and most of them meet at right angles. **Katpadi Road** is the central artery leading into town from the north; **Ida Scudder Road** runs perpendicular to Katpadi Rd. and is a bustling commercial center. Further south, parallel to Katpadi Rd., **Officers Line Road** lies along the eastern edge of the **fort. Trains** depart from the railway station on Katpadi Rd. (tel. 21150) to Bangalore (*Lal Bagh Exp.* 2608, 7:15, Rs.35/96) and Madras (*Brindavan Exp.* 6024, 5:50pm, Rs.35/96). The **bus station** (tel. 23080) on Officers Line has buses to Madras (PATC #220, #102, #83, #84, every 45min., 8am to 9pm, 5hr., Rs.26). Officers Line also forms the main route of **local buses.** Walking down Officers Line, you'll pass the **Police Station** (tel. 22777), the **State Bank of India** (tel. 21291) (currency exchange; open Mon.-Fri. 10am-2pm) and the **Head Post Office** (open Mon.-Fri. 9:30am-5pm). The **Christian Medical College Hospital** (tel. 22102) is also on Officers' Line. **Postal Code:** 632004.

ACCOMMODATIONS AND FOOD

All hotels in Vellore have a 24-hour check-out policy. A new addition to Vellore's small list of hotels, **Hotel Prince Manor,** Katpadi Rd. (tel. 22926, 27106, 27816, 27916) is modern, clean, and receives guests efficiently. Dark brown furniture and soft lights decorate its air-conditioned environment, but its main attraction is its proximity to the railway station. All rooms have Star TV. Doubles Rs.320, with A/C Rs.500. The **Hotel River View** on Katpadi Rd. (tel. 25568, 25672, 25723, 25218) encloses a winding circular staircase; it also has fountains, a garden, and a friendly reception desk. All rooms have Star TV. Singles Rs.250, with A/C Rs.390. Doubles Rs.300, with A/C Rs.470. The **Hotel Park Avenue,** 3 First Main Rd., Anna Nagar (tel. 20799, 20767), is comfortable and cheap, although it has no hot water and plaster peels off the walls. English is barely spoken at the reception desk. Singles Rs.95. Doubles Rs.199, with A/C Rs.325. Formerly known as Hotel Khanna, the **Hotel Ganga,** 16 Officers Line (tel. 23033, 23060, 23160, 23260) has clean white walls and sturdy furniture. Doubles Rs.300, with A/C Rs.350.

Inside Hotel Prince Manor, the hygienic **Kings** restaurant serves Indian and Chinese non-vegetarian dishes, heavy on the garlic (entrees Rs.50). Also in Hotel Prince Manor, **Princes** serves North and South Indian vegetarian food. A few flavors of ice cream are also available. **Ganga** is the vegetarian restaurant attached to Hotel River

View, serving both North and South Indian cuisine (*dosas* Rs.10). The lights are so dim you can barely see the food. The sweet corn soup (Rs.12) is hot and thick, and the mango juice is delicious (Rs.15). The **Simla Ice Cream Bar** at 88 Ida Scudder is misnamed—the only "cool" thing about this place is the hip clientele who come here to warm themselves with blazingly spicy North Indian food (*naan* Rs.10, entrees about Rs.35). The best place for Chinese food in Vellore is **Chinatown** on Gandhi Rd., with noodles, rice, and chicken Rs.20-30. Filling *thalis,* with unlimited rice and *chapatis,* are served at the **Palace Cafe** on Officers Line Rd. for Rs.15.

SIGHTS

The sheer size of Vellore's **fort** commands the attention of anyone walking down Officers Line Rd. Its huge gray stone walls, watchposts, and moat combine to make the fort seem like an impenetrable hideout as well as a place from which there is no escape. The fort was constructed by Bommi and Thimma Reddy during the reign of the Vijayanagar king Krishnadevaraya in the early 16th century. Legend has it that Bommi saw a hare in a dream; the next day, he chased a real hare, and the hare's path was fixed as the boundary of the fort—this accounts for the fort's irregular shape. The fort changed hands several times before coming under British control in 1760. After the fall of Tipu Sultan, the British imprisoned Tipu's sons and daughters inside the fort. Today, the fort houses courts, a police training center, a church, a mosque, and the grand **Jalakanteswara Temple,** a monument from the Vijayanagar era. Inside the temple is a *simhakulam* (well) which is rumored to be a secret escape channel leading to a similar well in neighboring Virinjipuram. Opposite the fort, the **CSI Church** holds the graves of some British officers and their wives who were killed in the final campaign against Tipu Sultan.

■ Mahabalipuram

Sixty kilometers south of Madras, on the shores of the Bay of Bengal, is the sleepy village of Mahabalipuram (officially and properly known as Mamallapuram). The village rises from its slumber into frenzied activity during the tourist season (Oct.-Jan.) and the Dance Festival in January. Mahabalipuram was the main sea-port of the Pallava kings, who ruled from Kanchipuram from the 4th to 8th centuries AD. The village is most famous for its architecture—sculptured panels, caves, temples, and monolithic *rathas* (temples shaped like chariots). But the miles of unspoiled beach also make Mahabalipuram, or "Mahabs," as it is called, an ideal beach resort. Mahabs is also a tourist town, and it proclaims that fact loudly. The streets are filled with artists carving stone, and every door on Kovalam Rd. is that of a hotel or restaurant.

ORIENTATION

Finding your way around in Mahabalipuram is a cinch. From the **inter-city bus stand,** it's a 500m walk due north along **East Raja Street** to the **tourist office,** which is next to the **post office** and a pungent outdoor fish market. At the tourist office, East Raja St. becomes **Kovalam Road,** a long, solitary thoroughfare which stretches out of town, passing a bunch of hotels as it goes. (If you're staying on Kovalam Rd. and don't feel like walking into town, there are plenty of bicycle and scooter rental shops in town. See **Practical Information.**) **West Raja Street** runs parallel to East Raja Street. To reach the **beach,** walk east from East Raja Street; the road which runs east to the Shore Temple is called **Beach Road.**

> **Warning:** The Bay of Bengal can be dangerous, and each year sees lives lost by drowning. Before venturing into the water, ask at the tourist office and at your hotel about the advisability of swimming. If you're not an experienced swimmer or if you've been drinking alcohol, stay away from the water.

PRACTICAL INFORMATION

Tourist Office: TTDC, E. Raja St., northern end, near Kovalam Rd. (tel. 42232).
Currency Exchange: Indian Overseas Bank, 130 T.K.M. Rd. (tel. 42222). Go down
E. Raja St. away from the bus stand and turn left on to T.K.M. Rd.
Telephones: STD/ISD booths are available on Kovalam Rd. The one opposite the
Indian Overseas Bank, 137 E. Raja St., is open 24hr.
Bus: Bus Stand, E. Raja St. To Madras (Every 30 min., 7am-10pm, 1½hr., Rs.10).
Local Transportation: Auto-rickshaws and tourist **taxis** are available outside the
bus stand. You can rent a **bicycle** or **motorcycle** in one of the many cycle shops.
Try **Nathan Cycle Works** opposite the Tourist Office (motorcycles Rs.200 per
day).
Pharmacy: Arafat Medical Store, TKM Rd., opposite Indian Overseas Bank. Open
Mon.-Fri. 9am-7pm.
Police Station: Vandavasi Police Station, Kovalam Rd. (tel. 42221).
Post Office: E. Raja St., near the tourist office (tel. 42223). **Postal Code:** 603104.
Telephone Code: 4113.

ACCOMMODATIONS

Most hotels are on E. Raja Street, Othavadai Road, and Kovalam Road. The pricier
ones are north of town (en route to Madras) and have their own stretches of beach.

Hotel Veeras, 106 E. Raja St. (tel. 42288). The friendly old man at the reception
desk is a good source of information about Mahabalipuram. Bring your own sheets.
Spic and span, tiny rooms. Bathrooms are equipped with handshowers. Singles
Rs.250, with A/C Rs.400.
Hotel Mamalla Bhavan, 105 E. Raja St. (tel. 42260). A good bargain. Clean marble-
tiled rooms with super-neatly made beds offer both quiet and comfort. Doubles
Rs.250, with A/C Rs.325.
Uma Lodge, 15 Othavadai St. (tel. 42322). A good place if you're on a tight budget.
The green hue of the walls is fearsome. Squat toilets. Singles Rs.50. Doubles Rs.60.
Hotel Tamil Nadu Camping Site, on the road right outside Shore Temple (tel.
42287). Don't be deceived by the name; there are no real tents in this camping site,
only cottages (Rs.200), and a large dormitory (Rs.30 per bed).
TTDC Beach Resort Complex, Mahabalipuram, en route to Madras on Kovalam
Rd. (tel. 42235; contact in Madras, (044) 830390). The reception is slow but
friendly. Rooms have water coolers, and outside each window there are potted
plants. The well-maintained garden is a pleasure to walk in, and all rooms open to
the beach at the back, affording a view of the sea and lots of sea breeze. Doubles
Rs.500, with A/C Rs.700.

FOOD

Mahabs is swarming with restaurants. Most of these are on Kovalam Rd. and East Raja
St. All the big hotels have comfortable, air-conditioned restaurants attached, but
smaller places are more friendly.

Curiosity Restaurant, 20 Othavadai St. A tiny restaurant (four tables in all), with
bright blue tablecloths, sea shells, and plants all over the place. Their grilled fish
masala and grilled prawns (Rs.30) are very popular with foreign tourists.
Sagar, 101 Kovalam Rd. (tel. 42472). Opposite the Government College of Architecture. This airy restaurant serves North Indian *thalis* for lunch and dinner.
Mamalla Bhavan (Golden Pallate), 105 East Raja St. (tel. 42260). This veg. restaurant serves some Continental fare for homesick foreign tourists, as well as South
and North Indian food. Don't miss out on the *Dosa Platter* (Rs.50) which comes
with a variety of *dosas*, including the unique *Banana Dosa*.
Mamalla Bhavan (another one), opposite the bus stand on East Raja St. Try the delicious South Indian *thali* (Rs.10) or the special *thali* (Rs.20). Their *masala dosas*
are mouth-watering.

Veeras, 106 E. Raja St. (tel. 42288), in the hotel of the same name. Except for the tacky artificial flowers on the tables, this restaurant is tastefully furnished. Good seafood, especially prawns.

Gazebo, E. Raja St. (tel. 42525), halfway between Othavadai St. and the bus stand. Although a map of Italy hangs on its wall, this friendly restaurant serves Chinese food. Try the lobster (Rs.45) or grilled fish (Rs.30).

Moonrakers, Othavadai St. (tel. 42566), opposite Curiosity Restaurant. Its popular among Western tourists is partly due to its collection of 1980s pop tapes—request that special Madonna song.

SIGHTS

While most of Mahabalipuram's magnificent rock carvings have been gently weathered by the combined effects of sun, sand, and surf, the town still boasts an incredible concentration of intact top-quality sculpture. Each stone breathes with life and sings the glory of the Pallavas. It is believed that these sculptures, seen in their rudimentary form at Mahabalipuram, later evolved into the fine figures seen at Kanchipuram. Little is known about what life was like in the area when local sculptors produced the work they did, but scholars agree that most of Mahabalipuram's masterpieces were produced under the patronage of the 7th-century Pallava leader Narasimhavarman I, who went by the fearsome moniker "Mamalla," or "Great Wrestler;" hence the name "Mamallapuram."

Mahabalipuram's most widely recognized landmark, the **Shore Temple,** juts into the Bay of Bengal 1km due east of the bus stand. Dedicated to both Shiva and Vishnu, the temple was built at the turn of the 8th century and is thought to have been the first South Indian temple built entirely of stone. The Pallavas' maritime commercial activities diffused Pallava ideas and styles, and echoes of the Shore Temple's lion carvings and stocky spires can be discerned in subsequent South Asian temple architecture. Though the area around the temple boasts a profusion of sacred Nandi (bull) images, there has been speculation that the Shore Temple once served a more secular purpose as a lighthouse.

Back in town, just behind West Raja Street, is the strikingly beautiful **"Arjuna's Penance,"** which is claimed to be the world's largest bas-relief sculpture. Particularly impressive is the elegant, witty depiction of animals and birds—look out for the delightfully out-sized renderings of an elephant family and the wry depiction of an ascetic meditating cat surrounded by jolly dancing rats. While it is easy enough to admire all the frenetic visual splendor, scholars have had a hard time figuring out exactly what is going on in the bas-relief. According to the "Arjuna's Penance" theory, the bas-relief depicts a well-loved story from the *Mahabharata*—the scrawny man standing on one leg is the archer Arjuna, who is gazing through a prism, doing penance, and imploring Lord Shiva for the *pashupatashastra,* a powerful magic arrow. According to another school of thought, the bas-relief represents Rama's ancestor, Bhagiratha, begging the gods to give the Ganga river to the people of the world (see **Gangotri,** p. 171). The gods have agreed to comply with Bhagiratha's request and the whole of creation—including the family of elephants—has turned out to watch the miracle of Ganga rushing down from the Himalaya. Those who interpret the bas-relief as depicting the descent of the Ganga find evidence for their views in the crack at the giant sculpture's center—the animals and demi-gods seem to be staring at the crack with rapt attention, while a tank above once collected water that poured down the face of the bas-relief, in imitation of the Ganga.

The area west of the bas-relief, from Koneri Rd. in the north to Dharmaraja Mandapa in the south, has an eerie, ashen ambiance. The hilly area is strewn with massive boulders and ten small **mandapas** (cave temples), which depict tales from Hindu mythology. Finding your way from *mandapa* to *mandapa* can be difficult, and making a systematic tour is tough. Still, getting a bit lost and stumbling upon *mandapas* can be lots of fun. North of the bas-relief the **Trimurti Temple,** next to a Pallavan water tank, boasts shrines to Shiva, Vishnu, and Brahma. The **Kotikal Mandapa,** which dates from the turn of the 7th century and is regarded as the area's oldest *man-*

dapa, is also here. Also north of the bas-relief are two massive, free-standing mono-liths, **Krishna's Butterball** and the **Ganesh Mandapa,** which was built during the 20th century. Heading south from the bas-relief, you first pass the 7th-century **Varaha Mandapa,** displaying four panels, the most impressive of which shows Vishnu with the goddess Bhudevi (Earth), seated in his lap. From the Vishnu Mandapa, walk 150m southeast to the exquisite **Krishna Mandapa,** a large mid-7th-century bas-relief which depicts Krishna raising up Mount Govardhana to protect his relatives from the god Indra. From the Krishna Mandapa, it's a short walk south past the decaying **Ramanuja Mandapa** to the **New Lighthouse.** Next to the New Lighthouse is the **Old Light-house**—a Shiva Temple perched at an especially high elevation, which was used as a lighthouse until the turn of the century. Near the lighthouse is the **Mahishasuramar-dini Mandapa,** adorned with a magnificent bas-relief of Durga destroying the buffalo demon Mahishasura.

About 2500m south of the tourist office is a collection of stunning monoliths, each of which was carved during the reign of Narasimhavarman I Pallava. Known as the **Pancha Pandava Rathas,** these are full-size monolithic models of different kinds of temples known to the Dravidian builders of the 7th century. The complex includes life-size depictions of animals as well as five temples influenced by Buddhist temple architecture and named for the five Pandava brothers, the heroes of the *Mahab-harata.* The largest of the temples is the Dharmaraja Ratha, adorned with various carvings of demi-gods and Narasimhavarman. The smallest temple is the Draupadi Ratha, which is named for the Pandava brothers' wife; this curious *ratha* is carved in imitation of a thatched-roof hut.

About 3km north of central Mahabalipuram along Kovalam Rd. is the **Government College of Sculpture and Architecture,** where hundreds of artisans learn their craft at a sprawling seaside complex. Though there are sculptors busying themselves with hammer and chisel throughout Mahabalipuram, the always-lively Government Col-lege can be a fun place; ask at the tourist office to make an appointment and have a look around. Two kilometers beyond the college is the supremely serene, shady **Tiger Cave,** with its expertly carved tiger heads.

■ Pondicherry

The onetime capital of French India, Pondicherry suffers from a great deal of hype. As a result, many visitors expect the coastal town to be something of a mini-Paris, a place of *liberté, egalité,* and *fraternité,* not to mention champagne, baguettes, and black berets. But the hype is hyperbole, and Pondicherry isn't Paris. Instead, it's a decidedly divided town, split both geographically and culturally by a narrow canal. To the west of the canal—on its left bank, if you will—Pondicherry is Pondy, your basic, bustling mid-sized South Indian city. To the east of the canal, Pondicherry is *Pondichéry.* The streets here are clean, the cops sport red *képis,* the restaurants serve up hefty help-ings of beefy French food, and much of the architecture is typically European, left over from Pondicherry's days as a center of imperial administration. Pondicherry is a promenader's paradise, its streets populated from early morning until late evening with magistrates in flowing robes, barefoot bourgeois joggers, and hip French dudes taking holidays in the sun. Of course things haven't always been like this, and 2000 years ago when the area was dominated by a Roman trading outpost, no one could have guessed that the Alliance Française would one day have an office in town. In the 9th century, the site of present-day Pondicherry was a center of Sanskrit learning, and at various times the Pallavas or the Cholas ruled the roost. Modern Pondicherry was established in 1673 by the Frenchman François Martin, who hoped to gain for his country a commercial advantage over the Dutch and the English, both then gaining a toehold in the area. Over the next centuries, the French ruled their smattering of South Asian colonial enclaves from Pondicherry. The French influence can be seen in the statues of Joan of Arc, the churches, and the grid-like lay-out of the roads. In 1954, the French handed over these scattered enclaves to India, which gave them the status of semi-autonomous territories and made Pondicherry their capital. Since achieving

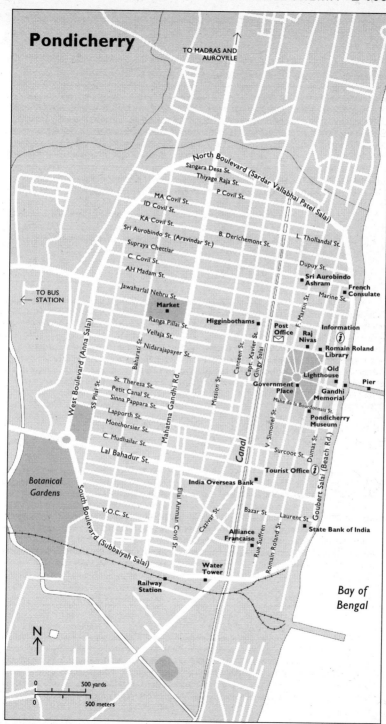

Pondicherry

TO MADRAS AND
AUROVILLE

North Boulevard (Sardar Vallabhai Patel Salai)

Sangara Dess St.
Thiyage Raja St.
P Covil St.

MA Covil St.
ID Covil St.
KA Covil St.
Sri Aurobindo St. (Aravindar St.)
Supraya Chettiar
C. Covil St.
AH Madam St.

B. Derichemont St.

L. Thollandal St.

Dupuy St.

**Sri Aurobindo
Ashram**

**French
Consulate**

Marine St.

Jawaharlal Nehru St.

TO BUS
STATION

Market

Ranga Pillai St.
Vellaja St.
Nidarajapayer St.

Bharati St.

Higginbothams

Canteen St.
Capt. Xavier St.
Gingy Salai

**Post
Office**

F. Martin St.

**Raj
Nivas**

Information

(i)

**Romain Roland
Library**

Mission St.

**Government
Place**

Mahe de la Bourdonnais St.

**Old
Lighthouse**

Pier

**Gandhi
Memorial**

West Boulevard (Anna Salai)

SS Pilai St.

St. Theresa St.
Petit Canal St.
Sinna Pappara St.

Lapporth St.
Monthorsier St.
C. Mudhailar St.

Lal Bahadur St.

Mahatma Gandhi Rd.

V. Simonei St.

Surcoot St.

Dumas St.

**Pondicherry
Museum**

Goubert Salai (Beach Rd.)

**Botanical
Gardens**

South Boulevard (Subbaiyah Salai)

V.O.C. St.

Canal

India Overseas Bank

Tourist Office (i)

Ellai Amman Covil St.

Ozivar St.

Bazar St.

**Alliance
Francaise**

Rue Suffren

Romain Roland St.

Laurent St.

State Bank of India

**Water
Tower**

**Railway
Station**

Bay of
Bengal

N

0 ___ 500 yards
0 ___ 500 meters

SOUTH INDIA

its new status, Pondy has worked hard to preserve its distinctive French heritage—and to attract Francophile tourists. Yet Pondicherry is also a city of India—The ashram of Sri Aurobindo is an all-pervading influence, and all roads seem to lead there.

ORIENTATION

Getting around Pondicherry could hardly be simpler. Bordered on the east by the **Bay of Bengal** and divided into eastern and western sections by a **canal,** Pondy's streets are laid out in a simple grid. Important east-west thoroughfares are the busy **Jawaharlal Nehru (J.N.) Street, Ranga Pillai Street,** and **Lal Bahadur Shastri Street.** East of the canal, the major north-south avenue is **Mahatma Gandhi Road.** West of the canal, the major north-south thoroughfares are **Rue Suffren** and **Romain Roland Street** (both of which end at the centrally located Government Place) and the long **Goubert Salai (Beach Road),** which runs along the western shores of the Bay of Bengal. As it heads south, Goubert Salai hooks west and becomes **South Boulevard (Subbaiyah Salai);** the rarely utilized **railway station** is off Subbaiyah Salai. As Subbaiyah Salai heads north, it passes the Botanical Gardens and becomes **West Boulevard (Anna Salai);** the **inter-city bus stands** are 600m due west of Anna Salai. To the north, **North Boulevard (Sardar Vallabhai Patel Salai)** completes Pondy's circumference, and links West Blvd. and Goubert Salai.

PRACTICAL INFORMATION

Tourist Office: Goubert Salai (tel. 37008). The office gives out maps and arranges tours of the town for Rs.25 per person. Open Mon.-Sat. 9:30am-6pm.

Diplomatic Missions: France: Compagnie St. (tel. 34174). Open Mon.-Fri. 10am-3pm.

Currency Exchange: The India Overseas Bank, Lal Bahadur Sastry St. (tel. 36761). Open Mon.-Fri. 9am-2pm, Sat. 10am-2pm. The State Bank of India, Goubert Salai (tel. 35528). Open Mon.-Fri. 9am-5pm, Sat. 10am-2pm.

Trains: The railway station (tel. 36684) is a sleepy, little used place on South Blvd. A train leaves daily for Vizhupuram (*Pondicherry-Vizhupuram Passenger 654*, 10:50am, 1hr., Rs.32/139).

Buses: Buses depart from the bus stand, on the road to Vizhupuram. To: Madras (every 30min., 5am-11pm, 3hr., Rs.25); Chidambaram (every hr., 6am-9pm, 1½hr., Rs.15); Tiruchirappalli (10, 11:15am, 3, and 5pm, 5½hr., Rs.40).

Local Transportation: There is a stand for **auto-rickshaws** on Capt. Xavier St. **Tempos** are cheaper but you'll get jostled pretty badly.

English Bookstore: Higginbothams, Capt. Xavier St., opposite rickshaw stand.

Cultural Centers: Alliance Français, 38 Rue Suffren (tel. 38146), conducts French classes and has a French library attached. Open daily 9am-noon and 4-7pm. **Romain Roland** (a French Public Library), Ranga Pillai St. Open Mon.-Fri. 11am-5pm.

Hospital/Medical Services: The best place to go for medical concerns is **Jawaharlal Institute of Medical and Educational Research** (JIPMER) (tel. 72380) outside the city. Take National Highway 45 straight.

Post Office: GPO, Ranga Pillai St. (tel. 33050). Open Mon.-Fri. 10am-5pm. **Postal Code:** 605001.

Telephone Code: 0413.

ACCOMMODATIONS

International Guest House, Gingy St. (tel. 36699). Like other ashram buildings, this cream-colored establishment has a well-maintained garden and lawn, as well as red terra-cotta pottery arranged aesthetically. They're wary of tourists and prefer to lodge ashram devotees, but unless they're full they won't turn you away. Wonderful prices, the gate closes at 10pm, and no smoking, alcohol, food, or drugs are allowed in the rooms. "Silence, discipline, and cleanliness to be maintained." Singles Rs.35. Doubles Rs.55.

Aristo Guest House, 50A Mission St. (tel. 26728), is a good, clean bargain. Rooms have attached baths (squat toilet). Singles Rs.90. Doubles Rs.120.

Park Guest House, Goubert Salai (tel. 34412). In the olive green and white building at the end of the street. This ashram guest house has clean rooms. The gardens and lawns keep the place cool despite the sweltering heat outside. Fishtanks near reception are pleasing. No TV, alcohol, or food inside the rooms. Curfew 10:35pm. Mainly caters to ashram devotees; tourists are unusual here. Doubles Rs.300. Family rooms (for 4) Rs.450.

Hotel Surguru, 104 North Blvd. (tel. 39022; fax 34377). A sprawling (by Pondy standards) garden, a brass Nataraja in the lounge, and a friendly reception. The rooms are quite spacious and have sturdy light brown furniture, Star TV, cute little stools next to the dressers, and large windows. Attached baths have seat toilets. Running hot water at 9:30am and 5pm, bucket hot water at all other times. Singles Rs.265, with A/C Rs.410. Doubles Rs.350, with A/C Rs.530. AmEx/MC/V.

Ajantha Guest House, 22 Goubert Salai (tel. 38898). Reasonably clean, with Rajput paintings adorning the walls. Rooms have attached bathrooms (seat toilets). "Seaview" rooms have windows that afford a view of the promenade, and all the rooms are breezy. Doubles Rs.200, with A/C Rs.300. Seaview rooms Rs.250.

Victoria Lodge, 79 Jawaharlal Nehru St. Fairly old but centrally located, with friendly staff and management. Singles Rs.80. Doubles Rs.120.

Hotel Mass, Maraimalai Adigal Salai (tel. 37221; fax 33654), next to the bus stand. The staff in this spacious but slightly run down (holes in the carpet) establishment wear black and purple uniforms. The deluxe room has a bathtub! Singles Rs.490. Doubles Rs.640. Deluxe room Rs.750.

FOOD

The commercial center of Pondy—the area by M.G. Rd. and J.N. St.—has long, narrow streets that are filled with shops and restaurants.

Hotel Surguru, 104 North Blvd., is a popular (read: crowded) veg. restaurant. Both North Indian (Rs.20-45) and South Indian (Rs.15-35) dishes available. Their Kashmiri *naan* is delicious. Open daily 9am-10pm.

Hotel Aristo, Jawaharlal Nehru St. This rooftop restaurant is a hot favorite among locals. Little potted plants everywhere, and small ledges with ceramic bowls. Everything is made to order, so be prepared to wait. Their menu has 200 items both veg. and non-veg. The Aristo chicken *masala* special (Rs.44) is heavenly, as is the walnut chicken with brown rice (Rs.49). Their cutlets are famous (Rs.12), and they also serve soups (Rs.12), seafood (Rs.40), noodles (Rs.30-50), tandoori (Rs.7-10), and vegetable dishes (Rs.25-30). Top it all off with the honeymoon special ice cream (Rs.20). Open daily 10am-10pm.

Surabhi, inside Anandha Inn on North Blvd. This veg. restaurant serves Continental and Indian food. Quiet and private, with dark brown tables, candles, and flowers. The bar downstairs is Ecstasy (cocktails Rs.75). Open daily 11:30am-10pm.

Sea Gulls, 19 Dumas St. More sea breeze and potted plants than variety in this small place with slow service. The cheap beer is its redemption. Open daily 9am-9pm.

Megala, attached to Hotel Mass, Maraimalai Adigal Salai, next to the bus stand. This small but comfortable restaurant offers soups (Rs.30), chicken (Rs.70), seafood (Rs.60-70), and North Indian veg. standards. The Rs.150 tandoori platter is a full meal for 2. Open daily 2-9pm.

Le Café, the only eatery on the Goubert Salai promenade. This small snack bar is good for a cup of coffee or something light, and Dollops ice cream parlor is just opposite. Open daily 3pm-1am.

Le Club, 33 Dumas St. This popular French restaurant is pricey because it caters mostly to tourists. Open Tues.-Sun. 8-10am, noon-2pm, and 7-10pm.

Bar Qualithe, in the unassuming white building next to Government Sq. The food isn't great but the beer is cheap even by Pondy standards. Open daily noon-11:30pm.

SIGHTS

Far and away Pondicherry's most popular attraction, the **Sri Aurobindo Ashram** on Marine St. teems with devotees from around the world. Sri Aurobindo Ghose was a Bengali mystic who evolved "internal yoga" as a way of mingling the principles of yoga with the findings of modern science. Sri Aurobindo's staunch opposition to British rule led to his imprisonment in 1908. It was in the confines of the prison cell that his spiritual evolution took place, and in 1910 he gave up political activities and headed for French-ruled Pondicherry. In Pondy, Sri Aurobindo met "the Mother," a French woman named Mirra Alfassa who would be his constant companion until his death in 1950. After Sri Aurobindo died, the Mother dominated the spiritual life of Pondicherry, lending her energy and charisma to "internal yoga" until her death in 1973. These days, the ashram, which was founded in 1926, houses an exquisite rock garden and the flower-strewn *samadhis* of Sri Aurobindo and the Mother. The ashram is open daily 8am-noon and 2-6pm. (No children under 8 permitted; photography allowed only with prior permission.)

Aside from the ashram, most of Pondicherry's attractions are clustered around **Goubert Salai,** the pleasant, mellow street where Pondicherriens go to see and be seen. The 1500m rocky beach is pretty to look at, but not safe for swimming. Along the beach is a 4m statue of a striding Mahatma Gandhi, as well as some splendid French architecture, including a monument built in memory of the Indians who died during World War I fighting on the French side.

About 1km north of the Alliance and just west of Goubert Salai is the grassy, pleasant **Government Place,** a complex which boasts the elegant French-built **Raj Nivas,** which is now the plush residence of Pondicherry's Lieutenant Governor. At the southern edge of Government Place is the **Pondicherry Museum,** which displays dusty 19th century French furniture and stone sculptures that have been dug up in the area. Open Tues.-Sun. 10am-5pm; free.

If shady pleasures and greener pastures are on your brain, follow Goubert Salai to South Boulevard off of which are the **Botanical Gardens,** which were planted by the French in 1826. (Open daily 9am-5:30pm.) On your way to the gardens, have a peek at Subbaiyah Salai's Gothic **Eglise de Sacre Coeur de Jésus,** whose altar is flanked by three stunning stained-glass panels depicting the life of Christ.

There's a **boating club** on the road to Auroville where you can rent boats or take a sea cruise and watch the dolphins play. This club is closed off-season; call the tourist office (tel. 37008) for more information.

SHOPPING

Pondicherry is a shopper's paradise, in part because there is a great variety of shops and in part because there's not much else to do. The commercial centers are accessed by walking along J.N. St. and M.G. Rd., where hundreds of hawkers sell export garment rejects for throwaway prices. The cheapest of these vendors is Abdul Rashid, opposite the Indian Coffee House on J.N. St. Stationery, marbled paper, marbled silk scarves, and semiprecious stone jewelry can be bought at **Ashram Cottage Industries** on Ranga Pillai St. For fashionable garments, assorted art objects, silk scarves, and shawls, try **La Tienda,** 28 J.N. St. or **Exotic India,** 79 J.N. St. **French Park,** 83 J.N. St., is a small shop that sells export garments for reasonable prices—mainly t-shirts, cotton shirts, and tank tops. For antiques and ceramic pottery, the best place is **Boutique D'Auroshri,** 18 J.N. St. (tel. 34823). Silk scarves (Rs.25), crushed cotton dresses (Rs.125), and paper lanterns (Rs.25) can be found in **Lahori Boutique,** 9 J.N. St. The girl at the counter will cheerfully help you choose.

■ Near Pondicherry: Auroville

Fourteen kilometers from Pondicherry, Auroville was an experiment in international living that arose from the vision of Sri Aurobindo and his disciple the Mother. Soil from 126 countries was placed in an urn at the community's opening in 1968, and the suburb is now made up of about 50 rural settlements composed of 800 people from all over the world, who live in self-fashioned and wildly original houses. According to Auroville's motto, "Auroville belongs to nobody in particular but to humanity as a whole...[it is a] place of unending education, of constant progress, and a youth that never ages." Those settled in Auroville strive to achieve those ideals. It feels like a cocoon where free growth is possible, unfettered by the evils of modern society. But ever since the Mother's death in 1973, which was followed by a bitter dispute over control of the community, there appears to be less of a driving force behind the project, and enthusiasm is running a little low.

The **Matri-mandir,** a domed structure that houses a crystal in a meditation room, epitomizes the spirit of Auroville. The banyan tree to the side has a story behind it—apparently, it was to be cut down during the construction of Matri-mandir but the tree's soul protested to the Mother, who then shifted the location of the temple.

If you intend to stay for more than a couple of days, rent a bike—walking all over can be a pain. The tourist office in Pondicherry conducts guided tours of the commune for Rs.25. Information is available at the **Visitor's Information Centre** (tel. 62239; fax 62274), open daily 9:30am-5:30pm. For information on arranging accommodations, contact Auroville Guest Programme, Visitors Centre, Auroville 605101, e-mail guests@auroville.org.in. Ashram Cottage Industries in Pondicherry also has information (tel. 27264).

■ Chidambaram

History has heaped affection on Chidambaram, entwining it in legend and lore and making it a sacred destination which draws pilgrims by the thousands. According to Tamil tradition, it is here that Shiva descended from the divine ferment, incarnated as Nataraja, and performed the Cosmic Dance. The forested clearing where Nataraja danced was tinged with holiness and the town which grew up around it was dubbed "Chit Ambaram," or "sky suffused with wisdom." Choosing Nataraja as their favored deity, the ascendent Cholas made Chidambaram their capital in 907 AD and from the time of Koluttanga (1070-1120 AD), the history of the Cholas merged with the history of Chidambaram, building the nucleus of a grand temple. Over the centuries, the temple, which is now called Sabhanayaha Nataraja Temple, was repeatedly enlarged and embellished. Today it dominates Chidambaram, occupying the center of town.

ORIENTATION AND PRACTICAL INFORMATION

A small town, Chidambaram is easy to navigate. The four bustling streets that form a rectangular border around the temple hold the GPO, a State Bank of India, and the police station. The thoroughfares are called **North Car Street, East Car Street, South Car Street,** and **West Car Street.** To reach the eastern part of town, follow South Car St. toward the small **Khansahib Canal.** Just east of the canal is the **tourist office** which gives out maps and a brochure detailing the interesting spots around here. The **bus stand** is just west of the canal. It sends buses to Pondicherry (every 30min., 5am-10pm, Rs.25) and Madras (9, 11am, 3, and 5pm, Rs.47). **Rickshaws** (auto and cycle) queue up just opposite the bus stand, near the **Government Hospital** (tel. 23099). **Pharmacy Palarriappa Medicals** (open daily 9am-9pm) is opposite the State Bank of India (no foreign exchange) on South Car Street. There is an STD/ISD **telephone** booth next door. The **post office** is on North Car St. (open Mon.-Fri. 10am-3pm). The rarely utilized **railway station** is 200m south of the tourist office on **Railway Feeder Road. Postal Code: 608001. Telephone Code:** 04144.

ACCOMMODATIONS AND FOOD

Chidambaram isn't very touristy or developed—that's good in terms of aura but bad in terms of finding places to eat and sleep. **Hotel Saradha Ran,** right opposite the bus stand, is the best in Chidambaram. Neat rooms with TV, telephones, and seat toilet attached. The batik prints on the walls add a touch of class. Two restaurants attached.

Singles Rs.200, with A/C Rs.325. Doubles Rs.225, with A/C Rs.350. AmEx/M/V and U.S. dollars accepted. **Pallavi,** their attached vegetarian restaurant, serves North and South Indian food, with delicious South Indian *tiffin* (Rs.30-50). The non-vegetarian restaurant is called **Anu Pallavi,** and serves decent food (including some Chinese) for Rs.30-60. **Hotel Tamil Nadu** is in the tourist office east of the canal. The rooms here could use some maintenance but they're fairly clean and have telephones and attached baths with seat toilets. They also offer dorm beds in their youth hostel, which are good for a one-day stay. The attached restaurant serves Chinese and Indian food (stick to the Indian) for Rs.20-45. Dorm beds Rs.45. Singles Rs.120. Doubles Rs.180, with A/C Rs.300, with A/C and TV Rs.350. **Star Lodge,** 101-102 S. Car St., is a cheap place for short stays. Hot water in buckets, and small rooms with no frills. Doubles Rs.60. **Shameer Lodge,** opposite the railway station, is another bargain hotel featuring small rooms with attached baths (squat toilets). Singles Rs.40. Doubles Rs.60. **Bhagyalakshmi,** S. Car St., offers good South Indian *thalis* (with unlimited rice) for Rs.25.

SIGHTS

The **Sabhanayka Nataraja Temple** dominates central Chidambaram and occupies an area of just over 45 acres. Though scholars believe that work on the temple began in the 10th century AD, local tradition holds that there has been a temple at the site for thousands of years. The modern Nataraja Temple, it is said, was built starting in the 6th century AD, when the Kashmiri monarch Simhavarman II (550-575 AD) made a pilgrimage to Chidambaram in the hope that bathing in the tank of the ancient Nataraja Temple would cure him of leprosy. Speedily recovering after his bath, the king (thereafter known as Hiranyavarman, or the golden-bodied one) was overwhelmed with feelings of joy and thankfulness and he ordered the temple enlarged and modernized. In addition, Hiranyavarman decreed that the holy entourage of 3000 Brahmin priests who had accompanied him from Kashmir should remain behind at Chidambaram, to serve the temple in perpetuity. (The priests, known as Dikhatars, can be recognized by the knot of hair at the front of their heads. It is their custom to intermarry.) Regardless of the legend's veracity, it is built around at least a kernel of truth—the Nataraja temple was not built all at once, but in stages; as such, its architecture mingles ancient and modern elements. Consider the temple's massive pyramidal *gopurams*. The eastern *gopuram,* profusely adorned with sculptures of deities, seems to date from the mid-13th century. Meanwhile, the western *gopuram,* embellished with the 108 dance poses associated with *bharat natyam,* is said to date from the 12th century, while the 42.4m northern *gopuram* bears an inscription claiming that it was erected by a 16th-century Vijayanagar king. Architectural mixing and matching is the rule at the Nataraja Temple.

A visual narrative of Shiva's cosmic dance carved (with remarkable detail) into hard stone greets visitors to the temple. After entering through the eastern gate, the good-sized **Shivaganga Tank** is in front of you; just right of the tank is the 103m long Raja

---

Sri Mambazha Vinayakar

The little image of Ganesh (also known as Vinayakar) on the east side of the Chidambaram temple comes from a story in which Lord Shiva held a contest between his two sons, Ganesh and Kartikkeya. A delicious *mambazha* (mango) was to be given to the son who could go around the universe and return first. Kartikkeya immediately mounted his peacock and set off, confident of victory. The short, plump Ganesh had only a little mouse for a mount. He thought for a while and then rode around his parents, Shiva and Parvati. When Shiva asked his son what he was up to, the clever Ganesh replied: "Going around the supreme Lord Shiva and Goddess Parvati who create and contain the universe is equivalent to going around the universe." Shiva smiled in satisfaction, and presented the mango to his slow-footed but clever son.

Sabha, the temple's "1000 pillared corridor" where the victory processions of the Pandyas, Cholas, and other local powers were held. Also near the tank is a temple dedicated to Shiva's wife Parvati, or Shivakumasundari; illustrations inside provide a sketchy map of the temple complex and depict Hirayna Varna Chakravarti being cured of his leprosy. Near the Shivakumasundari Temple are small shrines to the planets and to Shiva's son, Subrahmanya.

Having strolled around in the vicinity of the Shivaganga Tank, head for the inner chambers. The first of these inner chambers is a labyrinthine jumble of hallways. Look out for the Devasabha, where images of the deities are stored when not being used in processions and where temple administrators gather for meetings; also keep your eyes peeled for the **Nritta Sabha** ("Dance Hall"), which marks the spot where Shiva and Kali had their famous dance-duel, and which is adorned with 56 pillars representing various dance poses. The holy innermost chamber is off-limits to non-Hindus, though it's possible to get a glimpse of the gold-tiled **Chit Sabha** and **Kanaha Sabah** from the outside. The Kanaha Sabha houses a small image of Nataraja; the Chit Sabha houses the invisible "secret of Chidambaram," the **Akasa Linga,** which represents the elusive *akasa,* the invisible element. The temple is open daily 4:30am-noon and 4:30-9pm.

Annamalai University, a residential university founded by Raja Annamalai Chettair, is on the eastern outskirts of Chidambaram, about 2½km from the canal. It is a great center of Tamil learning and Carnatic music. The little village of **Pichavaran,** 16km from Chidambaram, attracts tourists and naturalists with its mangroves. Ten buses (7am-9:20pm) depart the Chidambaram bus stand headed for Pichavaran.

Tanjore (Thanjavur)

The small town of Tanjore, or Thanjavur, was the Chola capital between the 10th and 14th centuries AD. Those were Tanjore's days of grandeur, when the town was a center of learning and culture. The Chola bronzes, handicrafts, and the grand temple are some remnants of this golden era in the now dusty, unassuming, and agricultural town. Only an hour away from Tiruchirappalli, Tanjore remains laid-back and provincial. The lack of urbanization has its advantages—open space, fresh air to fill the lungs, cold fresh water and kind, hospitable people. Tanjore is an art enthusiast's delight, with paintings and Chola bronzes worth a mini-fortune abounding in the temple and in the museums.

ORIENTATION

Tanjore is divided into northern and southern sections by the **Anicut Canal.** South of the canal is the **railway station.** From the station, walk due north for 750m along Railway Station Rd. to reach the bridge which leads across the canal. Along the way you'll pass the tourist information office and then the intersection with **Kutchery Road,** the main east-west thoroughfare south of the canal. As it crosses the canal, Railway Station Rd. becomes **Gandhiji Road** and then **East Main Road.** The palace enclosure is just off East Main Rd. 1km north of the canal, while the **Brihadishwara Temple** is at the western end of **Hospital Road,** which is lined with bus stands; Hospital Rd. intersects Gandhiji Rd. a few hundred meters north of the canal.

PRACTICAL INFORMATION

Tourist Office: In the Hotel Tamil Nadu complex on Gandhiji Rd. (tel. 23017). Distributes free maps and lists of places to go in and around Tanjore. Open Mon.-Fri. 10am-2pm.

Currency Exchange: State Bank of India, Anna Salai (tel. 20082). Open Mon.-Fri. 9:30am-5pm.

Telephones: There are STD/ISD booths in the bus stand area and also right next to Hotel Tamil Nadu.

Trains: the railway station is on Gandhiji Rd. (tel. inquiries 131, station superintendent 21131). To: Madras Egmore (*Cholan Exp.* 6151, 8:45am, 8½hr.;

Rameswaram Exp. 6102, 8:40pm, 9hr.; *Thanjavur-Madras Passenger* 628, 7:50pm, 8½hr., Rs.99/326 for 2nd/1st class); Tiruchirappalli (*Cholan Exp.* 6153, 6pm, 1hr.; *Thanjavur-Tiruchi Fast Passenger* 621, 6:25am, 1½hr.; *Madras-Tiruchi Passenger* 109, 9:30am, 1½hr., Rs.17/83).

Buses: The bus stand is also on Gandhiji Rd. To: Tiruchirappalli (every 10min., 5am-11:30pm, 1½hr., Rs.12); Kumbakonam (every 15min., 6am-10pm, 1hr., Rs.9); Madras (10, 11:30am, 2:30, 5, and 7pm, 8hr., Rs.61); Pondicherry (10am and 4pm, 5hr., Rs.50).

Local Transportation: There is an **auto-rickshaw** stand right outside the railway station, and there are local **buses**.

Pharmacy: **Ganesh Medicals,** opposite bus stand. Open Mon.-Sat. 10am-10pm.

Hospital: Tanjore Medical College Hospital, Medical College Rd. (tel. 22459). About a 15-min. auto ride from the station.

Police: East Main Rd. (tel. 21450).

Post Office: Gandhiji Rd. (tel. 22022). Open daily 10am-3pm. **Postal Code:** 613001.

Telephone Code: 04362.

ACCOMMODATIONS

Hotel Karthik, 73 South Rampart St. (tel. 30116), opposite the bus stand. It's a bargain but it's a little grubby, with weird pink and white tiles. Bring your own sheets. Attached bathrooms have squat toilets. Small rooms. Singles Rs.75. Doubles Rs.150.

Hotel Tamil Nadu, Gandhiji Rd. (tel. 31421). Kashmiri wooden partitions, wall hangings, neatly made, comfy beds. Rooms have attached bathrooms with seat toilets that could be cleaner. Doubles Rs.300, with TV Rs.350, with A/C and TV Rs.500.

FOOD

There are many small vegetarian restaurants around the bus stand that cater to the local population. **Ananda Bhavan** is the most popular among these. Good old-fashioned South Indian food is served on banana leaves. There's lots of noise but you won't be lonely. Tiffin 7-10am, lunch noon-2pm, dinner 7-8:30pm. **Hotel New Anjalai,** Gandhiji Rd., serves non-vegetarian food (Rs.45-60) until 11pm. For a special meal and some privacy, splurge at **Les Repas,** the specialty restaurant at Hotel Parisutham. Continental or South Indian breakfast Rs.75, soup Rs.30. Their sizzlers are great (Rs.125). Also try their *thali* lunch, "Lunchtime at Thanjavur," Rs.60-70. Open daily 10am-2:30pm and 7-11pm.

SIGHTS

Far and away Tanjore's most impressive attraction is the **Brihadisvara Temple,** a serene example of Dravidian architecture. The temple was constructed by the Cholan King Raja Raja I (r. 985-1013AD). Unable to find a cure for his leprosy, Raja Raja turned to his religious tutor for guidance; the tutor promptly advised him to build a temple to Shiva using a *linga* from the Narmada River. Raja Raja rushed off to the river and pulled a *linga* from the water; as he pulled, the *linga* grew and grew and Raja Raja was left to build a massive temple to enclose it. The temple is massive—its *vimana* (tower) is over 60m tall and is capped by a 73,700-kg block of stone which was raised to the top by rolling it up a 7-km-long ramp. Proud of his achievement, Raja Raja inscribed the temple's main shrine with a tribute to the wealth he had acquired for the Cholas by plundering neighboring regions.

The entrance to the temple complex passes through two *gopurams,* each of which is carved with carefully wrought sculpted images. Note the *dvarpalakas,* the 10th century doormen who flank the entrance to the inner *gopurams.* Through the *gopurams* is a spacious courtyard; just in front of the courtyard entrance is a giant sculpture of Nandi, the bull who guards and carries Shiva. The inside of the courtyard is lined with pleasantly shady corridors; the corridors are colonnaded and boast some decaying sculptures and frescoes, which are being painstakingly restored.

Fourteen stories tall and densely adorned with carvings, the granite *vimana* soars over the *gopurams* in an inversion of the traditional South Indian architectural order (*gopurams* are usually taller than *vimanas*). The **temple** includes three concentric hallways. The outer hallway dates from the 16th century and is always accessible. The two innermost hallways, containing frescoes and the temples 4m-tall *linga,* are accessible only between 7am and noon or 4 and 8pm. Also in the temple compound is a small **museum** which has some interesting sculptures and copies of paintings, and marvelously blocky shrines and temples. Next to the temple is the Shivaganga tank and garden, ideal for an evening or early-morning stroll. *Banyan* trees abound— the roots of one tree have formed a natural archway.

Nearly 2km northeast of the temple, on East Main Rd., is the large **palace** built as a royal residence by the Nayaks in the 16th century and subsequently refurbished by the Marathas. These days, what you can see of the palace is substantially decrepit, and you'd have to squint to the point of blindness to get a sense of the royal residences' former grandeur. But housed inside the palace, are a few interesting museums, such as modest-sized art galleries displaying an excellent collection of Chola-era bronzes and stone sculpture. (Open daily 9am-1pm and 3-6pm.) Also inside the palace is the **Tamil University Museum** which displays antique musical instruments. Be sure to ask the curator to show you the wooden revolving chair—its maker would probably be shocked to see his design operational in modern office buildings. The curator will also show how the wood-and-ivory chessboard can be converted to a *pallanguzhi* board. The silver jewelry boxes are exquisitely carved. The palace also houses the **Saraswati Mahal Library,** which is famous for its collection of ancient palm leaf manuscripts. Open Thurs.-Tues. 9am-1pm and 2-5pm. Just near the palace is the **Schwartz Church,** which was built in 1779 by Raja Serfoji as a tribute to his tutor, the missionary F.C. Schwartz.

▓ Tiruchirappalli

For an industrial center that is home to over 700,000 people, Tiruchirappalli (commonly called "Trichy") is surprisingly spiffy—the city is reasonably clean and relatively tranquil. Present-day Tiruchirappalli has been continuously occupied for over 2000 years, and the city has been ruled at various times by the Cholas, Pandyas, Pallavas, and the Nayaks, who built Trichy's imposing Rock Fort. Since the late 19th century, when railroads brought the Industrial Revolution to South India, Trichy has been ruled by manufacturing, and today's Tiruchirappalli is a working-class population center where *bidis* and costume jewelry are produced in staggering abundance. Trichy's greatest attraction is the temple-city complex at Srirangam, 4km north of town across the Kaveri River.

ORIENTATION

Bordered to the north by the **Kaveri River,** Tiruchirappalli sprawls south, east, and west. While the **Trichy Town Railway Station** and the **Rock Fort** are within 1km of the river, the compact center of town is nearly 5km south of the river, in the neighborhood just north and west of the busy **Trichy Junction Railway Station.** The streets around the railway station offer hotels and bus stands as well as banks, the GPO, and the tourist office. From the station, **Madurai Road** runs north and **Junction Road** runs northwest; the two streets are connected by **Dindigul Road,** which, followed north, becomes **Big Bazaar Road** and leads to the **Rock Fort.** While it's still in the vicinity of Trichy Junction Railway Station, Dindigul Rd. intersects **McDonald Road;** McDonald Rd. runs east-west, intersecting **Williams Road** and then **Collector's Office Road,** each of which is parallel to Dindigul Rd.

PRACTICAL INFORMATION

Tourist Office: 1 Williams Rd., Cantonment (tel. 460136), opposite the central bus stand. Open Mon.-Fri. 10am-5:45pm. Seek out Mr. R. Dandapani.

Currency Exchange: State Bank of India, McDonald Rd. (tel. 460 125). Open Mon.-Fri. 10am-2pm.

Telephones: There are a number of STD/ISD booths in the bus stand area, on McDonald Rd.

Airport: The airport is 8km south of the city, 30min. by bus or taxi. To: Madras (Mon.-Sat. 1 per day, 1hr., US$60) and Colombo, Sri Lanka (Tues. and Sun., 1hr., Rs.1525).

Trains: To: Madras (*Pallavan Exp.* 2606, 6:15am, 5½hr., *Vaigai Exp.* 2636, 9am, 5½hr., Rs.187 A/C chair car, *Rockfort Exp.* 6178, 9pm, 8½hr., Rs.95/311 for 2nd/1st class; *Pandyan Exp.* 6718, 11pm, 7½hr., Rs.95/311 for 2nd/1st class); Madurai (*Madras-Madurai Exp.* 2637, 11:59am, 2½hr., Rs.128/421 for 2nd/1st class; *Vaigai Exp.* 2635, 5:52pm, 2hr., Rs.556 for 2nd A/C chair car); Bangalore (*Trichy-Bangalore Exp.* 6531, 9:10pm, 11hr., Rs.100/412).

Buses: Trichy is famous for its bus service. The central bus stand, McDonald Rd. in the middle of town, is like a maze but you'll be able to get a bus to almost anywhere from here. To: Madras (every hr., 6am-9pm, 8hr., Rs.65); Tanjore (every 5min., 5:30am-11pm, 1½hr., Rs.8.50); Pondicherry (11am and 2:30pm, 5½hr., Rs.55); Kodaikanal (6am, 5½hr., Rs.60); Kanyakumari (9pm and 1am, 11hr., Rs.65).

Local transportation: City **buses** leave from the main bus stand. **Auto-rickshaws** are available, too.

Pharmacy: Jambu Medicals, opposite central bus stand. Open Mon.-Sat. 10am-10pm.

Hospital: Government Hospital, Puthur High Rd. (tel. 24465). A good private hospital is **Sea Horse Hospital,** 6 Royal Rd. (tel. 462660).

Post Office: Head Post Office, Bharatiyal St. Open Mon.-Sat. 10am-5pm. **Postal Code:** 620001

Telephone Code: 0431.

ACCOMMODATIONS AND FOOD

Dingy meal joints serving decent South Indian food and road-side *dhabas* abound. The best and cleanliest restaurants are all in the hotels.

Hotel Femina, 14-c Williams Rd., Cantonment (tel. 461551; fax 460615). The rooms are dim but spacious. You can sink into the inviting cream beds and channel-surf or relax in the pink bathtub. The small balcony gets too sunny in the mornings. The attached veg. restaurant serves South Indian, North Indian, Continental, and Chinese food daily 11:30am-2pm and 5-10pm. The attached coffee shop, Golden Rock, is open 24hr. Singles Rs.250. Doubles Rs.350, with A/C Rs.600. Major credit cards, U.S. dollars, pounds sterling, and deutschmarks accepted. Reservations can be made in Madras (tel. (044) 826 9168).

Hotel Tamil Nadu, McDonald Rd., right next to the tourist office (tel. 460 383). The standard TTDC hotel, with cheap, comfortable rooms and friendly, eager staff. The dark bar looks better after a couple of drinks. (Open 11am-3pm and 6-11pm.) Singles with A/C Rs.300. Doubles Rs.200, with A/C Rs.400.

Hotel Gajapriya, 2 Royal Rd. (tel. 461144). Spacious rooms, some with mirrored walls. Attached bathrooms have seat toilets and smell of disinfectant. A laid-back place with an equally laid-back staff. Room service food 5am-11:30pm. The North and South Indian vegetarian restaurant tends to be crowded in the evening. Open 5am-11:30pm. The separate Chinese restaurant is reasonable but the food is oily. Open 11am-11:30pm. Singles Rs.160, with A/C Rs.400. Doubles Rs.300, with A/C Rs.500.

Ramyas Hotel, 13-d/2 Williams Rd. (tel. 461128). The name board is prominent but you'll have to climb up a dingy flight of stairs to the 1st floor reception. This new hotel caters to Indian middle class clientele; many families come here on vacation in summer and December. The mosaic floor has weird patterns. Attached restaurants are small and crowded. **Sri Ranga** serves vegetarian snacks, South Indian,

North Indian, and Chinese food. Reasonable prices. Noodles Rs.25-37, tandoori Rs.9-20. Open 6:30am-11:30pm. **Amaravathi,** the non-veg. restaurant serves good *kababs* and *tikkas* (Rs.45-75). Open 11am-3:30pm and 7-11pm. Major credit cards, pounds sterling, U.S. dollars, and deutschmarks accepted.

Jenney's Residency, 3/14 McDonald Rd. (tel. 461301). Sophisticated, with wine-colored chairs and a glass table in the reception lounge amid much lush greenery. Polished granite floors and white beds. Attached bath is ultra clean with toilet paper. They also boast a gym and a bar called Wild West. The South Indian restaurant is appropriately called **Suvia** ("Taste"). Breakfast (7-10am) is the usual *idli, dosa, vadai* deal. Lunch (1-3pm) *thali* is sumptuous for Rs.30. For a quick snack, try Jenney's tidbits (Rs.15). The **Peaks of Kunlun,** a Chinese and Continental restaurant, has Chinese dragons, streamers, and Chinese characters all over. Soup (Rs.20-35), rice and noodles (Rs.30). Open daily 2-11pm. Singles Rs.750. Doubles Rs. 900.

Hotel Sangam, Collector's Office Rd. (tel. 464700). Another pricey but classy place. The manager, G. Subramaniam (Subbu), can direct you to Trichy's attractions and also show you the hotel's goodies, including a health club, a sauna (Rs.75), a handicrafts shop, and a swimming pool. Air-conditioned rooms have floral curtains and blankets. Clean bathrooms have seat toilets and bathtubs. The bar, **Soma,** is relaxing. Open daily 11am-11pm. You can gaze at the artificial stream outside or admire the chandeliers. Friendly chatter drifts from the 24-hr. coffee chop, **Cascade.** The attached restaurant, **Chembian,** serves great *thalis* (Rs.30) on plantain leaves. The non-veg. *Chettinad* meal is delicious (Rs.46). Pizza and Chinese available. The *falooda* (Rs.30) is a good way to keep cool. Open daily 11am-10pm. Singles Rs.700. Doubles Rs.950.

SIGHTS

Trichy's most interesting sights cluster around the imposing **Rock Fort,** which lords over the northeastern corner of the city from its 85-m-high perch. The site was developed as a citadel by the Pallavas and later by the Nayaks. The way to the top of the fort is a breezy trek up more than 400 rock-cut steps; the work is hard at times, but the views from the top of the fort, of the Ranganathaswamy Temple to the west (left) and the Jambukeshwara Temple to the east (right), are splendid. The small Ganesh Temple at the Fort's summit is closed to non-Hindus. (Open daily 7am-8pm. Admission Rs.1, camera fee Rs.10.)

The neighborhoods at the foot of the Rock Fort offer plenty of opportunities for diverting strolls. The artificial cistern **Teppakulam** is surrounded by great sweets shops and mediocre book shops, while the streets around **China Bazaar** are crammed with stalls selling flowers and locally produced handicrafts. The huge church visible from China Bazaar is **Saint Joseph's,** a Catholic church modelled after France's Lourdes Basilica; 500m south of Saint Joseph's is the white domed **Nadir Shah Mosque.** Much further south, Trichy's **museum** is off Bharatiyar Rd., 800m northwest of the GPO; the museum displays an unspectacular collection of coins, stone sculptures, and items discovered locally by archeologists. (Open Sat.-Thurs. 9am-noon and 2-5pm. Free)

■ Near Tiruchirappalli: Srirangam

Board bus #1 at the central bus stand for a half-hour ride to the largest Vaishnava temple in South India. Three kilometers north of the city, the temple is located on an island in the Kaveri. The temple is surrounded by seven walls within which the town itself is located. Sri Ranganathaswamy, the presiding deity of the main temple, the **Sri Ranganathasvami Temple,** is a representation of Vishnu lying on his serpent Adisesha. This is by far the largest and most fully developed of all the temples in South India. It was built over many centuries, starting in the 12th century Pandya period and being expanded greatly during the Vijayanagar period. The sheer mass of the temple makes it unique; the outside walls of the complex contain nearly 700-square kilometers of land with an entire town inside. It is also unique in that it faces south. Legend has it that Rama intended to present the image to a temple in Sri Lanka, but it became fixed here and refused to move. The original destination was honored in the orientation of the temple.

The carvings date from many different eras, making it a destination for architectural historians as well as pilgrims and sight-seers. The temple has a 1000-pillared hall containing pillars carved in the shape of rearing horses and their clinging, heroic riders. The 21 *gopurams,* the magnificent collection of jewels, and the stone pillars of this masterpiece make the trek here rewarding. Non-Hindus cannot enter the inner sanctum, but can go into the fourth courtyard where the famous sculptures of the *gopis* in the Venugopala shrine are visible. For a small refreshment, try the fresh fruit juices at a stall called "Cool Sip" outside the temple. There is a small **museum** on the premises. The Vaikunta Ekadasi festival in December-January draws thousands of pilgrims.

■ Near Tiruchirappalli: Tiruvannaikaval

Buses from the central bus stand will drive to this *linga* submerged in water 6km east of Srirangam. The temple, one of the oldest and largest Shiva temples in Tamil Nadu, is named after a legendary elephant that worshipped the *linga*. The *linga* is called Jambukeswara, after the holy tree "Jambu" under which Shiva is present in the form of a *linga*. Try to make it to the temple at noon. Every day at this hour, a special ceremony takes place where one of the priests dressed in a sari and wearing a crown is supposed to represent the Goddess. After offering worship, the priest proceeds to the goddess' sanctuary in procession with an elephant.

■ Madurai

Since its founding more than 2500 years ago, Madurai has been a center of culture and learning, sheltering generations of artisans, craftsmen, merchants, poets, and scholars. Named the "sweet city," after a legend in which Shiva appeared with drops of sweet nectar falling from his locks, Madurai flourished as the capital of the ancient Pandya kingdom, which ruled central South India as far back as the 4th century BC. Madurai's prosperity is finely portrayed in the Tamil classics *Manimekalai* and *Shilappadigaram.* In the 14th century, Madurai was invaded by the armies of the Delhi Sultanate, and briefly became a sultanate of its own under Malik Kafur. But the Vijayanagar kingdom dominated throughout the 15th and early 16th centuries, during which time the temples and towers of Madurai's great Meenakshi Amman Temple were built. From 1559 onwards, Madurai was ruled by the Nayak dynasty. The best known of this series of able rulers, Tirumala Nayak (1623-59), displayed his taste in the showplaces of modern Madurai, the Teppakkulam and the Raya Gopuram. The rule of the Nayaks ended in 1736 when the East India Company bought Madurai. The British de-fortified Madurai, tearing down its city walls and filling in its moat, which flowed where the Veli streets run today, still marking the boundaries of the old city.

Madurai has survived the vicissitudes of political fortune to become an important commercial center with a population of 1.2 million. But the present-day growth of urban Madurai seems to have taken place in a haphazard manner. The huge English signboards, the large volume of traffic, and the overwhelming number of shops exist in a sort of chaotic balance, giving the town the feel of an ancient city trying to progress into the modern era but suffering from lack of direction. The city's textile industry is home to huge mills and garment shops, but it is still really temple *gopurams* that dominate the city's landscape. The city moves with the pulse of the temple's activities and the festival season sees the deities led around the town in processions followed by throngs of Madurai residents and visiting pilgrims.

ORIENTATION

Madurai sprawls to the north and south of the **Vaigai River.** South of the river, the city is bordered by railway tracks and dominated by the **Meenakshi Temple.** The **Central Bus Stand** and the busy **Madurai Junction Railway Station** are both off

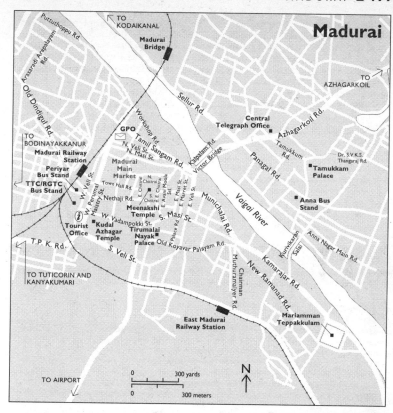

West Veli Street, 1km west of the temple. From the railway station, follow **Town Hall Road** east; from the bus station, follow **Dindigul Road.** In the vicinity of the temple, streets are arranged concentrically around the temple, forming an irregular grid. Closest to the temple are the North, East, South, and West **Chittrai Streets;** a bit further from the temple are North, East, South, and West **Avani Moola Streets;** next are North, East, South, and West **Masi Streets;** encircling the Masi streets are North, East, South and West **Veli Streets.** (These streets are named after the annual festival processions which take place there.) To cross the Vaigai River, head 1km northeast of the temple and across **Victor Bridge.** The road leading north from the bridge, **Algar Koil Road,** is intersected by the east-west **Tamukkam Road.**

PRACTICAL INFORMATION

Tourist Office: Tamil Nadu Tourist Office, 180 TB Complex, W. Veli St. (tel. 34757). Friendly staff answers questions about excursions from Madurai. Open Mon.-Fri. 10:30am-5pm. There are also offices at the airport and railway station.

Currency Exchange: State Bank of India, W. Veli St., opposite the railway station (tel. 33524; foreign exchange tel. 32650). Open Mon.-Fri. 10am-5pm, Sat. 10am-1pm.

Telephones: STD/ISD booths are found along Town Hall Rd. or Netaji Rd.

Airport: 15km south of central Madurai (tel. 25433, 37433). **Indian Airlines,** 7A W. Veli St. (tel. 541234). **NEPC,** Ram Nivas, 279, Goods Shed St. (tel. 540520). **East West Airlines,** 119 W. Perumal Maistry St. (tel. 542695). To: Madras (2-3 per day, 1½hr., US$50); Trivandrum (4 per week, US$30); Calicut (Mon.-Wed., Fri.-Sat., 45min., US$37); and Bombay (Tues., Fri-Sun., 2hr., US$110).

Trains: Madurai Junction Railway Station, W. Veli St. (enquiry tel. 543131). To: Madras (*Vaigai Exp.* 2636, 6:45am, 7½hr., Rs.117/285; *Pandian Exp.* 6718, 7:35pm, 11hr., Rs.143/441); Kanyakumari (*Kanyakumari Exp.* 6019, 4:10am, 6hr., Rs.374/787); Bangalore (*Bangalore Exp.* 6531A, 8pm, Rs.469/152); Rameswaram (*Rameswaram Exp.* 6115, 4:45am, 5hr., Rs.24/179); Coimbatore (*Coimbatore Exp.* 6116, 10am, 6hr., Rs.85/246).

Buses: Madurai has 4 inter-city bus stands. **TTC/RGTC Bus Stand** (tel. 25354). To: Madras (every hr., 4:45am-9:30pm, 10hr., Rs.88); Pondicherry (1:15 and 10pm, 8hr., Rs.51); Bangalore (6 per day, 8am-10:15pm, 9hr., Rs.98); Tirupati (5 and 6pm, 13hr., Rs.104). **Arapalayam Bus Stand** (tel. 603740). To: Coimbatore (every 30min., 7am-10pm, 10hr., Rs.29) and Kodaikanal (6:20, 7:40am, 1:20, 2:50, 4:55pm, 3½hr., Rs.18). **Anna Bus Stand** (tel. 533622). To: Tiruchirappalli (every hr., 5:30am-9pm, Rs.18); Rameswaram (8 per day, 1:15am-7pm, 3hr., Rs.24.20); Tanjore (12:30, 2:30, 11:45pm, Rs.22-30). **Palanganatham Bus Stand.** To: Kanyakumari (2, 8, 9:20am, noon, 7hr., Rs.47) and Trivandrum (every hr., 7am-8pm, 7hr., Rs.57).

Local Transportation: Local buses leave from the Periyar Bus Stand on W. Veli St., a 2-min. walk from the railway station (tel. 35293). **Auto-rickshaws** and **rickshaws** are easily available; the main auto-rickshaw stand is right outside the railway station.

English Bookstore: Higginbothams, W. Veli St. (tel. 24528). Head down W. Veli St. until the road turns. Take the second left.

Market: The chaotic **Central Market** on N. Avani Moola is filled with hawkers selling vegetables, fruits, and flowers. Bargaining is expected.

Pharmacy: Suresh Medical, 63 Town Hall Rd. (tel. 541625). Open Mon.-Sat. 7:30am-10:30pm. Sri Kartikeya Medicals, 59C Town Hall Rd. Open daily 8am-10:30pm.

Hospital: Government Hospital, Panagal Rd. (tel. 532535), across the Vaigai River. The private **Jawahar Hospital,** 14 Main Rd., K.K. Nagar (tel.42023, 42823), also on the northern bank of Vaigai, is better. **Aravind Eye Hospital** on Anna Nagar Main Rd. (tel. 532653; fax 530984) is quite famous.

Police: The main station (tel. 31396) is to the north bank, on the road to Natham.

Post Office: Head Post Office, on N. Veli St. (tel. 25756). Open Mon.-Sat. 11am-7pm, Sun. 10am-4pm. **Postal Code:** 625001-625020.

Telephone Code: 0452.

ACCOMMODATIONS

Most of the hotels, lodges, and restaurants are in the vicinity of the Meenakshi Temple, along Town Hall Rd. and Netaji Rd. A number of excellent hotels have just recently been opened on W. Perumal Maistry St.

Hotel Atavai, 86 W. Perumal Maistry St. (tel. 541446). The best of the cheapies on this crowded street, offering the basic bed, chair, and attached bathrooms with squat toilets. Singles Rs.49. Doubles Rs.88.

Hotel Sentosh, 7 Town Hall Rd. (tel. 542692). Long, dim corridors lead to small rooms. The attached bathrooms (squat toilet) is quite clean. Hotel Sentosh is a good deal if you plan to be out most of the day. Room service available. Singles Rs.45. Doubles Rs.80.

Hotel Aarathy, 9 Perumalkoil W. Mada St. (tel. 31571). The friendly, English-speaking reception will lead you to clean rooms with mosaic blue walls and brown tiles. The balcony offers a view of the frighteningly crowded street outside. Squat toilets. Check-out 24hr. unless otherwise stated. Piped-in music and Star TV. Singles Rs.150, with A/C Rs.250. Doubles Rs.250, with A/C Rs.350.

Hotel Laxmi, 36 Koodalagar Perumal Koil (tel. 33351). Small, clean rooms with no frills. Attached restaurant serves South Indian veg. food. Doubles Rs.120.

Hotel Ravi Towers, 9 Town Hall Rd. (tel.541961; fax 543405). Neat, tiled, cool rooms with clean sheets and bright red headrests on the bed. The mirror-lined elevators will take you up to your room. Room service is especially helpful. STD calls from room. Singles Rs.90, with A/C Rs.150. Doubles Rs.143, with TV Rs.172, with A/C Rs.270.

Hotel Times, 15-16 Town Hall Rd. (tel. 542651). This hotel is wired to capacity with TVs and telephones, and the comfortable rooms have hot water in their attached bathrooms. Singles Rs.90. Doubles Rs.180, with A/C Rs.280.

Hotel Empee, 253 Netaji Rd. (tel.541525). This 2-year-old hotel has modern, well-furnished rooms. Take the winding staircase and marble corridor (much more pleasant than the elevator) to your perfectly made bed. Enjoy the evening breeze on the balcony above the crowded street. A shopping complex is next door. Doubles Rs.180, with cable and Star TV Rs.220.

Hotel Sulochana Palace, 96 W. Perumal Maistry St. (tel. 541071; fax 540627). An elegant year-old hotel. The smart, gray-uniformed Rozario from room service can provide a wealth of information. Rooms have red carpets and chutney-green closets. Huge bathrooms. Elegant bar open daily 11am-11pm. Singles Rs.170. Doubles Rs.270.

Hotel Prem Nivas, 102 W. Perumal Maistry St. (tel. 542532, -9). Never mind the slightly dirty green walls; you'll get comfortable beds, Star TV, and an attached bathroom. Singles Rs.140. Doubles Rs.240, with A/C Rs.340.

Hotel Supreme, 110 W. Perumal Maistry St. (tel. 543151; fax 542639). Walk through corridors flanked by potted plants and wooden sculptures to rooms with dark brown furniture. Hypnotic curtains and paintings of Krishna add color to the rooms. The Duplex has a tub in addition to the usual attached bathroom. Rooftop restaurant, permit room, travel counter, and currency exchange. Doubles Rs.310, with A/C Rs.530. Duplex Rs.595. AmEx/MC/V.

Hotel Park Plaza, 114-115 W. Perumal Maistry St. (tel.542112; fax 542654). The newest hotel in the temple area, with every modern convenience. A huge brass lamp beckons guests into the lobby. The rooms are spacious, with marble floors and Rajasthani panels on the walls. They have TVs with Star and BBC, and the blue-tiled and black-enameled bathrooms have a bathtub and toilet paper. Dine at their restaurant (see **Food,** below), and keep up your spirits at Tropical Dowa, the air-conditioned bar (open daily 11am-11pm). AmEx/Diners/MC/V. Singles Rs.625. Doubles Rs.800.

FOOD

Hotel Arya Bhavan, 241-A W. Masi St. (tel. 540345). A hot favorite among Madurai residents. Try their *pakoras* (Rs.10) and butter roast *dosa* (Rs.12). The sweet shop has *jangri, laddoos,* and milk sweets, but *kalakand burfi* (Rs.120 per kg) is their specialty.

Hotel Vasantham, 11 TPK Rd. (tel. 540926). A noisy and crowded southie veg. restaurant. The grub (entrees Rs.10-15) and coffee inspire loud burps from the satisfied clientele.

Hotel Mahal, 13 Town Hall Rd. Right next to the Taj Restaurant. The cane lampshades filter the light into patterns, and fishtanks separate the tables. North Indian *thali* (Rs.30), tandoori (Rs.30), pasta (Rs.55), lamb (Rs.60).

Hotel Surya, 110 W. Perumal Maistry St. (tel. 543151). On the roof of Hotel Supreme, with a great view of Madurai and all 4 *gopurams* of the Meenakshi Temple. Service is efficient and beer can be discreetly arranged. Indian, Chinese, and Continental food. If you can't take the great outdoors, head to the inside tables, whose carved wooden partitions make them a good place for a secret rendez-vous.

Temple View, 114-115 W. Perumal Maistry St., on top of the Hotel Park Plaza. Obviously, a spectacular view of the temple. A good place to laze around and chatter away the evening over tasty South Indian fare.

The Park, 114-115 W. Perumal Maistry St., inside the Hotel Park Plaza. A private setting among crisp clean tables. Continental (Rs.30), South Indian (Rs.35). Their *Chettinad* food is spicy and lip-smacking.

Taj Garden Retreat, Pasumalai Hill. The place to go for a splurge. The weekend evening buffet on the lawns (Rs.150) is a good value for the money.

Hotel Ashok Bhavan, opposite the TTC bus stand. Generous helpings of South Indian food. Very spicy vegetable *biryani* (Rs.10-15).

Jam Jam Sweets, TPK Rd. Though the name sounds strange, this sweet and savory shop is lauded by Madurai residents. The *kara bundi* makes a hot, spicy snack.

SOUTH INDIA

SIGHTS

Meenakshi Amman Temple

Though everyone has a personal favorite, the Meenakshi Amman Temple, which draws over 10,000 tourists and devotees every day, is often described as the most dazzlingly wonderful of Tamil Nadu's temple-city complexes. Aside from the vibrant hues of the 30 million sculptures adorning the complex, the Meenakshi Amman Temple is impressive simply for its massive size: the complex covers an incredible 65,000 square meters and the tallest of the temple's *gopurams* spars to 49m. But the temple wasn't always this big. It was originally built by the Pandyas as a humble shrine. Peace and prosperity gave the Vijayanagar kings the opportunity to embellish the temple; when the Nayaks came to power in the 16th century, they continued this work, further expanding the complex and building the temple's out-sized *gopurams*. The temple is dedicated to both Meenakshi and Shiva. Meenakshi, the "fish-eyed" goddess (fishlike eyes being considered a mark of beauty), was born with three breasts and a huge amount of raw, angry, divine power. Meenakshi set out the conquer the world, which she did promptly by defeating other gods and demons. Only Shiva was left to defeat. But when Meenakshi confronted Shiva (known in Madurai as Sundareswar, the "good-looking lord") her heart turned to *ghee,* her third breast disappeared, and she was easily domesticated. Tradition holds that Meenakshi and Sundareswar were wed in Madurai where they jointly ruled the Pandya kingdom.

A visit to the Meenakshi Temple can be a bit overwhelming, as painted ceilings, rows of hawkers, and blaring music (at times) assault the senses at every turn. Systematic tours are difficult and not necessarily desirable. The best way to see the complex is to wander about, watching the bustling comings and goings and lingering at places that catch your eye.

Entrance to the temple complex is from East Chitrai St., just south of the eastern *gopuram*. After entering, you'll be in the brightly painted Shakti Mandapa, where hawkers peddle postcards, curios, and *puja* offerings. Continuing through the market, you'll pass on the left Pottamarai Kulai ("Golden Lotus Tank"), a tank accessible by *ghats* where Indra is said to have bathed. At the western end of the tank is the entrance to the Meenakshi shrine, which is closed to non-Hindus. The corridors outside the shrine are the Kilikootu Mandapa ("Parrot Cage Corridor"), where lucky green parrots were once kept in cages as offerings to Meenakshi, and the Oonjal Man-

---

Parrot Astrology

In ancient India, astrology was an important science, and many Indians still consult astrologers to foretell their future. A person's horoscope, or *jadhagam,* is determined at the time of her or her birth by the position of the various planets and stars. Thanks to computers, one can now have one's *jadhagam* plotted just by specifying the date of birth. One's future can also be told by *kili josyam,* or "parrot astrology." The "astrologer," in this case, has a number of cards with pictures of deities placed face down. To determine someone's fortune, he lets a trained parrot out from a cage, and the bird picks up one of the cards with its beak. Each deity corresponds to a particular chapter in the *Agastya Arudal,* an ancient treatise written by the sage Agastya. The astrologer then reads from this chapter and tells the person his or her future. The same astrologer is usually also a palmist and will coax you to show him your palm. He is often equipped with a number of small conch shells, which are scattered by the believer to help the astrologer to decide whether a particular time is auspicious or not. A number of such astrologers can be found outside the Meenakshi Amman Temple. One such astrologer is Balakrishnan, who has been making a living telling fortunes with his parrot for the last 25 years. The tradition, as in Balakrishnan's case, is handed down from father to son. In medieval India the art flourished; today some say it is becoming obsolete.

dapa (Swing Corridor), where on Fridays at about 5:30pm images of Meenakshi and Sundareswar are carried in, placed on a swing, and sung to. The temple complex is open daily from 5am to 12:30pm and 4:00 to 9:30pm. Camera fee Rs.25, no video cameras allowed.

North of the Meenakshi shrine is a shrine dedicated to Sundareswar, also closed to non-Hindus. The entrance to the shrine is via a brass-plated door donated by Shivaganga Zamindar. In the northeast corner of the shrine enclosure, and accessible to non-Hindus, is the Kambathadi Mandapa, adorned with elegant pillars, each of which bears a sculpture of Meenakshi or Shiva. A gaggle of sculptures of Shiva and Kali competitively dancing are pelted with small balls of *ghee* by devotees who hope to soothe the deities' competitiveness. Head east from Kambathdi Mandapa and you'll end up in the Ayirakkal Mandapa ("Thousand Pillar Hall") which boasts 985 carved pillars and has been converted into a small **museum** displaying sculpture (open daily 7am-7pm; admission Rs.1, camera fee Rs.5). The *mandapa* also has a set of pillars which sound the seven notes of a scale when tapped.

Tamukkam Palace and Museums

Nearly 2km north of the river on Tamukkam Rd. is the 17th-century palace of Rani Mangammal, which houses two museums. While nearly every mid-sized Indian city has its **Gandhi Museum,** Madurai's could well be the very best. Though small, the museum chronicles the events of Gandhi's life and intelligently discusses the social backdrop against which the Mahatma lived and worked. The museum begins with the arrival of Europeans in South Asia and carries the story through to Independence; unapologetically anti-imperialist, though occasionally a bit too local in scope, the museum makes for an enjoyable history lesson. The highlight of the collection, kept behind bulletproof glass in a black-painted room, is the faintly blood-stained *dhoti* Gandhi was wearing when he was murdered. (It's not clear why Madurai has been entrusted with this relic.) Open daily 10am-1pm and 2-5:30pm. Free.

The solid though not spectacular **Government Museum** boasts the usual mix of Indian government museum items: local geological specimens, stamps, 19th-century weapons, musical instruments, good bronze sculptures, and snakes in formaldehyde (open Sat.-Thurs. 9am-5pm; free). Just in front of the palace is a small garden complex dedicated to Gandhi, with a replica of the hut to which Gandhi retreated between 1936 and 1946, and a memorial pillar built atop the fraction of the Mahatma's cremated ashes that were placed here. Across the Gandhi complex is a small playground, but if you're looking for a fun place to take the kids, head 150m west along Tamukkam Rd. to **Rajaji Park,** a connoisseur's lavish playground where for a small fee kids can zip down colorful slides or mess around on electronically powered rides.

Other Sights

Nearly 2km southeast of the Meenakshi Temple are the uninspiring remains of the 17th-century **Tirumala Nayak Palace** (open daily 9am-1pm and 2-5pm; admission Rs.1). What's left of Tirumala's grand palace is the cavernous Swarvavilasam (Celestial Pavilion), an arcaded courtyard where the Nayak rulers held public audiences. Though heroic efforts are being made to renovate the courtyard, there will be no undoing the damage wrought by Tirumala's grandson, who hauled off much of the palace to inexpensively outfit a palace he was planning for himself at Tiruchirappalli. A **sound and light show** blares out the story of Tirumala and of the Tamil epic *Shilappadigaram* (in English, daily 8-9pm; admission Rs.2-5).

On Kamarajar Rd., 5km southeast of the train station, the **Mariamman Teppakulam** is a squarish water tank with a shrine in the center. In January, a colorful float festival is held here to celebrate the anniversary of Tirumala Nayak, who built the tank.

In the heart of the city, at the **Kudal Alagar Temple,** Lord Vishnu is depicted in three forms: Ninra Thirukolam (standing), Amarntha Thirukolam, and Kidantha Thirukolam (both resting). Each of the pierced granite windows lighting the passage around the shrine is different in design.

About 8km from central Madurai is the rock-cut temple of **Thiruparankundram,** dedicated to Subramanya—one of his six abodes. The #5 bus carries passengers from the Periyar bus stand to the temple for Rs.1.50.

Twenty-one kilometers northwest of Madurai on a wooded hill lies the temple of **Azhagarkovil.** Azhagar (also known as Vishnu) is said to have come to Madurai to attend the wedding of his sister, the goddess Meenakshi, to Sundareswar (an event celebrated every April or May during the Chittrai festival). But Azhagar arrived late and the marriage ceremony was concluded before he came to Madurai; here he is, caught on the outskirts.

ENTERTAINMENT AND SHOPPING

There are a few **cinemas** near the Periyar bus stand. Check with the tourist office for **cultural programs** in Lakshmi Sundaram Hall, Tallakulam (tel. 530858). Indoor **roller skating** is possible at Vandiyur Karmoy Tourist Complex (tel. 42918).

Madurai is filled with **textile shops** and sari showrooms. Parameswari Stores, 21 E. Chittrai St., just outside the southern *gopuram* of the Meenakshi Temple, is well-known for its silk-cotton mixtures. Cooptex Sales Emporium on W. Chittrai St. sells fabrics as well as saris. The Khadi Emporium on Town Hall Rd. is a good place to buy gifts and wooden carvings. Handicraft enthusiasts should visit the Madurai Gallery, Cottage Expo Crafts, 19 N. Chittrai St. (tel. 34064).

■ Rameswaram

A small island off the southeastern coast of India, sticking out toward Sri Lanka, Rameswaram is surrounded by the blue-green waters of the Bay of Bengal and the fragrance of stale fish. The train ride to Rameswaram from the mainland across the Indira Gandhi Bridge is one of the most spectacular in all of India. Yet Rameswaram is likely to be filled with Hindu pilgrims—not foreign tourists. A major pilgrimage site, Rameswaram is said to be the place where Lord Rama, the hero of the *Ramayana,* launched his attack on the armies of Lanka (see **The Ramayana,** p. 81). According to a later myth, Rama also made a *linga* of sand here after defeating the demon Ravana in their great comsic battle. The *linga* was meant to honor Shiva and expiate the sin of killing Ravana. Devotees of Shiva take this to mean that Shiva must be the greatest god of all, and the name Rameswaram, referring to Shiva, means "Lord *of* Rama." The *linga* at Rameswaram is also considered a *jyotirlinga,* a *linga* of light, one of 12 such *lingas* in India. Rameswaram also marks the southern holy "abode," one of four sacred places marking the cardinal directions. (The others are Dwarka in the west, Badrinath in the north, and Puri in the east.) The Ramanathaswamy Temple, the site of the *linga* Rama established, is frequented by thousands of pilgrims who come to bathe in the various *tirthas* within the temple and to build their own *lingas* of sand, which after worshiping they promptly toss into the sea.

ORIENTATION AND PRACTICAL INFORMATION

Navigating in Rameswaram is largely a matter of circling the four **Car Streets**—North, East, South, and West—which box in the **Ramanathaswamy Temple.** Most hotels, restaurants, and shops are located on these four streets. The **tourist office** on East Car St. is useful for their map of Rameswaram (which lacks street names). Traveler's checks are exchanged in the **Indian Bank,** W. Car St. (tel. 21234; open Mon.-Fri. 10am-4pm, Sat. 10am-noon). STD/ISD **telephone** booths can be found on Sannadhi St., off E. Car St. Head down Bazaar St., take the fifth left, then take the first right to reach **Rameswaram Station.** Trains to Madras (*Rameswaram-Madras Exp.* 6102, 12:40pm, 18hr., Rs.165/530; *Sethu Exp.* 6114, 3:50pm, 14½hr., Rs.165/530) and Madurai (*Rameswaram-Coimbatore Fast Passenger* 774, 7:15am, 5½hr., Rs.43/175; *Rameswaram-Coimbatore Exp.* 6116, 4:20pm, 5hr., Rs.43/175). The **bus stand** is on Bazaar Rd.; take an auto-rickshaw from the temple. Buses to Madras (4pm, 10hr., Rs.50); Kanyakumari via Madurai (every 30min., 6:30am-11:15pm, 11hr., Rs.70);

Madurai (every 45min., 7:30am-9pm, 4hr., Rs.20). Unmetered **auto-rickshaws** circulate though Rameswawam. **Pharmacies** including State Medical and Shekhar Medical can be found on Bazaar St. (open Mon.-Fri. 9:30am-9pm). The **Government Hospital** (tel. 21233) is near the railway station; going towards the temple, take a left off Bazaar St. before the Township Office. The **Police Station** (tel. 21227) is at the junction of East Car St. and North Car St. **Telephone Code:** 04573.

ACCOMMODATIONS

Except for the TTDC Rest House, most of hotels are located in the vicinity of the Ramanathaswamy Temple. Rameswaram's tapwater can be salty, and showers are extremely rare, so check the plumbing before checking in. Reservations are recommended during the pilgrimage season in July and August.

Lodge Santhya, W. Car St. (tel. 21329). Mosaic-floored rooms are above street level. Ask for rooms in their new building across the way. These rooms are brand new and the bathrooms even have showers—a luxury in Rameswaram. Great cross-ventilation as well. Singles Rs.30. Doubles Rs.47, with A/C Rs.99.

Temple Devasthana, North Car St. These small but clean rooms were built by the temple to house pilgrims; they're popular mainly among North Indians. No restaurant or room service. Singles Rs.25. Doubles Rs.40.

Santhana Lodge, South Car St. (tel. 21229). Right next to Hotel Venkatesh, this old lodge has slightly run-down rooms with attached bathrooms with squat toilets, but the rates are a bargain. Singles Rs.40. Doubles Rs.49.

Hotel Venkatesh, South Car St. (tel. 21296). One of the cleaner lodges near the temple. The reception will arrange for tea, coffee, and food, but the little boys who bring them expect tips. Attached bathrooms have squat toilets and baths (the water in the baths is so salty you won't need a ritual sea bath). Doubles Rs.99, with A/C Rs.250. Quads Rs.199.

Madhu Cottages, 18 Sannadhi St. (tel. 21280). Each cottage consists of 2 rooms and a kitchen, but no furniture beyond a pair of cots. An ideal place for stays of more than 2 weeks. Attached bathroom with squat toilet. Doubles Rs.125. Triples Rs.150.

Hotel Maharaja's, 7 Middle St. (tel. 21271). The newest and poshest hotel in Rameswaram. The squat toilets are clean and all rooms have Star TV. The brown-tiled floors are a welcome change from the dirty streets outside. Doubles Rs.172. Triples Rs.240.

Hotel Chola, North Car St. (tel. 21307). Airy rooms with clean sheets, ghastly green curtains, and small squat toilets. Doubles Rs.99. Triples Rs.149. Quads Rs.257.

Hotel Tamil Nadu (tel. 21227, 21064). Near the railway station. The Hotel Tamil Nadu has Rameswaram's only permit room—those who crave beer can sip it in a cane chair overlooking the sea. All rooms have a view of the sea. Dorm beds Rs.45. Doubles Rs.200, with A/C Rs.350. Make sure the power is on before booking a room with A/C.

Railway Station Retiring Rooms (tel. 21226). Ask the stationmaster about booking one of these spacious clean rooms right next to the railway station. A fairly long way from town, and the trains are noisy. Singles Rs.40.

FOOD

Most of the eating places are in the streets around the temple. There are many tea stalls which also sell some munchies. The roadside *bhajis* are very tasty.

Hotel Abirami, Sannadhi St. The best among the South Indian restaurants in the area, with clean beige tables and efficient service. Their tomato rice (Rs.7.50) and the paper roast *dosas* (Rs.20) are particularly delicious.

Hotel Ashok Bhavan, W. Car St. Their South Indian *thali* is a sumptuous way to spend Rs.15. *Idlis, vadai,* and *dosas* are served in the mornings (Rs.7-10).

SOUTH INDIA

Gujarati Bhojanalay, Sannadhi St. As the name suggests, this place caters mainly to Gujarati pilgrims. The food is simple and tasty but all the *sabjis* are a little sweet (Rs.5-7.50). Fresh *masala chai* (Rs.2).

Hotel Guru A small South Indian restaurant right next to the eastern entrance to the temple, with good *sambar vadai* (Rs.6.50).

SIGHTS

At the heart of Rameswaram, the **Ramanathaswamy Temple** is famous for its sculpted pillars, which form corridors measuring 264m from east to west and 200m from north to south. At the junction of the third corridor on the west and the path leading to the western *gopuram* is a chessboard-like structure called the **Chokkattan Mandapam.** The 1200 soft stone pillars in the outer corridor harmoniously unite structure and design. The temple was constructed in the 15th century by Udayan Sethupathi of Ramnad, whose statue (and those of his successors) can be found by the temple's southern entrance.

According to a later version of the *Ramayana* story, Rama sent his ally the monkey-god Hanuman to bring back a *linga* with which Rama could worship Shiva as penance for killing Ravana. But when Hanuman failed to return in time, Rama made a *jyotirlinga* of sand and installed it instead. This *jyotirlinga* is Ramanatha, the resident deity of the temple. Pilgrims come to Rameswaram to worship Rama worshiping Shiva. The *linga* that Hanuman finally brought now stands by the side of the main linga. Other important shrines in the temple honor Devi, Viswanatha, Ganesh, and Ashtalakshmi. A huge Nandi faces the main *linga.* Hindus consider the waters of Rameswaram to be holy, and there are twenty-two *tirthas* in the temple where devotees bathe—particular spots where buckets of water are dumped on them.

Northwest of the temple, up a steep hill, is the **Gandamadhana Parvatam (Ramar Padam).** Rama's footprints are enshrined at this site, where he is said to have stood and viewed Lanka across the channel. On clear nights the lights of Sri Lankan coastal towns can be seen from the hill. At other times it affords a good view of Rameswaram and some much-needed breezes.

The **Kothandaramar Temple,** also dedicated to Lord Rama, is said to mark the site where Ravana's brother Vibhishana was crowned king of Lanka after Ravana's death. The temple houses images of Rama, Lakshmana, Sita, and Hanuman with Vibhishana bowing to Rama, hands folded in reverence. This temple is open daily from 9am to 5pm; it has no electricity and hence no lighting after dark.

The southeastern end of Rameswaram's island forms a great finger of sand reaching out toward Sri Lanka. The railway line to **Dhanushkodi,** at the tip, was destroyed by a cyclone several years ago. Today one has to trudge about 6km in the sand or hire a jeep (Rs.500 from Ramanathaswamy Temple) to get here. There is no trace of human habitation on this stretch of sand, although until recently a small port town was situated here. Dhanushkodi is chilly early in the morning, and has stunning sunrises.

▓ Kanyakumari (Cape Comorin)

India ends at Kanyakumari. Here the bulky dust and brightness tapers to a southern point lapped by the Arabian Ocean to the west, the Indian Ocean to the south, and the Bay of Bengal to the east.

Hindu pilgrims (dredded *babus* in orange and red and laughing families holding hands) come in droves to sacred Kanyakumari. One legend says that virgin goddess Kanya Devi did heavy penance here in her desire to win the hand of Lord Shiva in marriage. Agreed, Shiva set off for the wedding ceremony, set auspiciously at midnight. The other gods, however, wanted Kanya Devi to remain a virgin, retaining her divine *Shakti,* and they schemed to make the wedding go awry. The sage Narada assumed the form of a cock, crowing to make Shiva think the dawn had come and he was too late. Shiva fell for it and went home. The heartbroken Kanya Devi remained a perpetual virgin.

ORIENTATION

Buses from Trivandrum and Madurai plow south down **Main Road** past the **railway station.** Hop off as the sparkling blue sea approaches, or wait for the bus to turn west, pass the square-towered **lighthouse,** and stop at the clean, organized **bus stand.** The Main Rd. continues south past this junction and the **tourist office,** petering out at the **Gandhi Memorial,** where Gandhi's ashes were briefly kept before being scattered to the seas. Dark hallways to the left lead past stalls stacked with shells painted "Kanyakumari" to the **Kumari Amman Temple** dedicated to the sad virgin Kanya Devi. Following the east shore north from the temple leads to a **hotel ghetto** and then to winding streets and narrow alleys paved only with drying fish innards and fishing nets, and with houses unbelievably yellow, green, and blue.

PRACTICAL INFORMATION

Tourist Office: Main Rd., north from the Gandhi Memorial, on the right. Capable of giving limited information. Open Mon.-Fri. 10am-5:45pm. The **TTDC** can be contacted at Hotel Tamil Nadu (tel. 71297). Ask at reception for more information.

Budget Travel: Many small offices sell private bus and train tickets; several are clustered in a road reached by emerging northward from the Kumari Amman Temple and turning right at the T-intersection.

Currency Exchange: Canara Bank, Main Rd., 5-10min. north of the intersection with the road to the bus stand, on the left. Accepts AmEx and Thomas Cook traveler's checks in U.S. dollars and pounds sterling. Open Mon.-Fri. 10am-2pm, Sat. 10am-noon.

Telephones: STD/ISD booths are common; some owners allow free call-backs (especially those in travel offices—try Kanya Travels).

Trains: The station is a 15-min. walk north from the sea on Main Rd., on the left. To: Bombay (*Kanniya Kumari-Bombay Exp.* 1082, 5am, 48hr., Rs.323/1485 for 2nd/ 1st class); Trivandrum (5, 7:20am, 12:50, and 5:40pm, 2½hr., Rs.14 for passenger, Rs.25 for express); Bangalore (express 6525, 7:20am, 17hr., Rs.217 for 2nd class); Nagercoil (7 per day, 5am-6:50pm, 20min., Rs.12); Ernakulam (5, 7:20am, and 12:50pm, 10hr., Rs.74/240 for 2nd/1st class); Madras (*Kanniya Kumari-Madras Exp.* 6020, 3:35pm); Jammu Tawi (*Himsagar Exp.* 6017, 12:50pm, 72hr., Rs.420/ 1922 for 2nd/1st class).

Buses: The neat and tidy bus stand has a posted schedule in English, computer reservations (Rs.2), and a helpful information desk. To: Madras (10 per day, 10:15am-8:30pm, 16hr., Rs.132); Madurai (20 per day, 24hr., 6hr., Rs.42); Rameswaram (8 per day, 6:30am-10pm; 10hr., Rs.68); Kodaikanal (8:45pm, 9hr., Rs.64); Ooty (6:30pm, 14½hr., Rs.91); Coimbatore (5:30pm and 6:30pm, 11hr., Rs.72); Kovalam (6:30, 7:05am, and 2pm, 2½hr., Rs.19); Ernakulam (7:15 and 9:15am, 9hr., Rs.89); Kottayam (7:15am, 8hr., Rs.89); Quilon (9:15, 8hr., Rs.84). **Private Buses:** Follow the steps north from the Kumari Amman Temple to the T-intersection; turn right to find many small travel offices. **Kanya Travels** (open daily 7am-10:30pm) runs daily buses to Bangalore, Madurai, Pondicherry, Tirupati, Coimbatore, Ooty, Kodaikanal, Rameswaram, and Madras.

Local Transportation: Kanyakumari is small enough to **walk** easily. Innumerable rickshaw-*wallahs* and taxi-*wallahs* will try to take you to Kovalam.

Post Office: GPO, Main Rd., just south of the Canara Bank. Sells stamps and will check the tiny stack of *Poste Restante* Mon.-Sat. 8am-noon and 1:30-4:40pm. **Postal Code:** 629702.

Telephone Code: 04653.

ACCOMMODATIONS

The flank of Kanyakumari close to the temples at the very last tip of India is tragically full of ugly hotels. In season (Aug.-Feb.) the prices fly upward to the realm of the gods, crashing back down to earth during the monsoon months.

Kerala House, from the bus stand, turn left and watch for the sign on the right. From the train station, turn right onto the main road, then right onto the road past the lighthouse, then left into the Kerala House driveway. Run by the KTDC, this is the southernmost hotel in India. The massive rooms have high ceilings, huge windows (some of which have a great view of the sea), dressing rooms, and bathrooms. Rs.240 per person, Rs.360 per 2 people, Rs.480 per 3, then Rs.120 per each additional bed until the room is filled with mattresses, if you so desire.

Shree Bhagavathi Lodge (tel. 71298). From the train station, turn right onto the Main Rd., then after about 10min., turn left down the hill and take the 3rd left. The rooms are clean and cheery and some have extras like mirrors or balconies with sea views. In season: doubles Rs.250. Triples Rs.400. Off-season: doubles Rs.100. Triples Rs.150. A deposit greater than the price of the room is sometimes required.

Lakshmi Tourist Home, across the street from Shree Bhagavathi Lodge. This place is a little more upscale and knows it. TV, hot water, classy furniture. Except for those rooms with a sea view (complete with sunrise), the place is a little gloomy. In season: doubles Rs.400-450. Triples Rs.500. Off-season: doubles Rs.300. Triples Rs.350.

Hotel Tamil Nadu (tel. 71257), off the road to the bus station and lighthouse, next to Kerala House. The TTDC organizes tours here; see reception desk. Rooms range from tiny mini-doubles (with high, sloping roofs) to dormitories to deluxe private cottages with air-conditioning and TVs. Many rooms have a sea view: Dorm beds Rs.45. Doubles with common bath Rs.75. Mini-doubles Rs.150. Doubles Rs.300. Twin cottages with A/C Rs.450.

NRS Lodge, from the train station, turn right onto the main road, then after about 10min. left down the hill, then take the 2nd left. The clean rooms are nasty green with nasty fluorescent lights. Clean white sheets and rubbery pillows also come with the room. In season: doubles Rs.80-450. Triples Rs.125. Off-season: doubles Rs.80-125. Triples Rs.125.

Train Station Retiring Rooms, upstairs in the train station. The high-ceilinged rooms are spacious and have mosquito nets. Singles Rs.40. Doubles Rs.80.

Bus Station Retiring Rooms, upstairs in the bus station. The rooms are big and feature hot water, crunchy beds, and dusty bathrooms with throne-like toilets. Some rooms have balconies with a view of the road, trees, and the sea. April-June and Oct.-Jan.: dorm beds ("gents only") Rs.41. Doubles and triples Rs.188. Off-season: dorm beds Rs.28. Doubles and triples Rs.138.

Hotel Sealand, next to Lakshmi Tourist Home, across the street from Shree Bhagavathi. Though the basic rooms are not spectacularly clean, bright paint and plaid sheets cheer things up. In season: doubles Rs.100. Triples Rs.125. Quads Rs.250. Off-season: doubles Rs.80. Triples Rs.80. Quads Rs.250.

FOOD

Famili Restaurant; from the temple, walk north up the steps and watch for this tiny blue crevice of a restaurant. It doesn't look good until you see the steam rising from a huge pot of fresh *idli,* or from the giant griddle where the *dosas* are cooked. South Indian food and meals served daily 10am-3pm.

Hotel Saravana has 2 shiny branches, both near the temple. The bigger branch is on the left heading up the hill from the temple. The snazzy restaurant offers air-conditioned dining and nice wooden chairs. South Indian breakfasts are available, as well as Gujarati, Rajasthani, Punjabi, and South Indian "meals" at lunch for Rs.15. North Indian food is also on the menu (try the gorgeous *palak paneer*). Open daily 6am-10pm.

SIGHTS AND ENTERTAINMENT

At the seaward end of Main Rd., an odd interpretation of an Orissan temple overlooks the last bit of India where she plunges under the turquoise waters of the mixed oceans. This building is the **Gandhi Mandapam.** The spot where the ashes of Mahatma Gandhi were stored briefly before being scattered in the sea is marked by a black marble box. The building is engineered so that every year on Gandhiji's birthday, October 2, a ray of sunlight falls here at noon. (Open daily 6:30am-12:30pm and 3-7:30pm.)

The seaside **Kumari Amman Temple** is a few hundred meters back from the last heaving tip of India, indelibly marked by the trademark red-and-white vertical temple stripes. Dedicated to the form of the goddess Parvati known as Kanya Devi, the temple celebrates the penance she did in hopes of winning the hand of Shiva. In the end, however, the engagement was broken and the goddess remained a virgin. Male visitors must be shirtless and clad in *dhotis* (although *lungis* may be OK). Non-Hindus may not enter the inner sanctum. (Open daily 4am-noon and 5-8pm.)

Accessible by ferry are two rocks, now swathed in concrete, to which the Hindu reformer Swami Vivekananda swam out and sat in meditation for several days in 1892. A glossy temple, the **Vivekananda Memorial,** commemorates the event. Also on the island is a temple built around a footprint left by the goddess Parvati. Curiously, the footprint is not indented but raised. After being herded through a cattle-run packed with parents and children onto the ferry (Rs.6), everyone whoops and laughs as the ferry rocks. Men with whistles on the island enthusiastically usher everyone to the ticket line (Rs.6) and arrows guide the walk around the island. (Ferries daily 7-11am and 2-5pm; catch the ferry from the east coast 100m up from the Kumari Amman Temple.)

Although the part of Kanyakumari near the temple and the cape is overflowing with charmless lacquered shells, "Ray Ban"-*wallahs,* and soulless hotels, the **village** on the east coast north of the hotel ghetto has bright lavender- and yellow-colored houses, small church-shrines, fish drying in tiny lanes, and fishermen repairing nets while their wives weave them. The hugely beautiful **St. Mary's** Church is on the south edge of the village.

■ Near Kanyakumari: Padmanabhapuram

On the way to Trivandrum, 45km from Kanyakumari, is **Padmanabhapuram,** capital of Travancore until 1798. Inside Padmanabhapuram's **fort** is a grand **palace** covering 2.5 hectares. Many tour buses from Trivandrum stop here on their way to Kanyakumari. (Open Tues.-Sun. 9am-5pm.)

■ Kodaikanal

Though Kodaikanal, 2133m above sea level in the southern crest of the gentle Palani Hills, is the most famous hill station in central Tamil Nadu, the town isn't haunted by the ghost of the Raj like so many other hill stations. There are few architectural or cultural reminders that the British dominated local life for the century between the 1840s (when Kodai was founded as an antidote to the sweltering, malaria-infested Tamil Nadu plains) and the 1940s (when India pushed for independence). Instead of the British empire, ambitious hotel developers have left their imprint on Kodaikanal, gumming up the works with places to stay and turning the town into a pleasant tribute to the leisure time tastes of India's burgeoning urban upper-middle class. Kodai boasts tranquil opportunities for strolling, boating, and, quite literally, smelling the roses. There are also a thousand and one chances to swell your midriff in Kodai—chocolate shops and pastry shops as well as restaurants serving up everything from Gujarati *thalis* to hearty Tibetan soups and *momos.* Of course the reason to visit Kodai is not to fill your tummy with food but to fill your lungs with crisp, fresh mountain air. Kodai can get a bit nippy, especially at night, and the daily high temperature is usually 10-20°C lower than the high in Madras.

ORIENTATION

Getting around in Kodai is a snap. Buses pull in on **Anna Salai (Bazaar Road),** the town's major east-west thoroughfare. North of Anna Salai, **Law's Ghat Road** runs roughly parallel to it; the two streets are connected by the 200m-long **Hospital Road.** South of Anna Salai is **Bryant's Park** and **Coaker's Walk,** while west of Anna Salai, Kodai's artificial **lake** sprawls in all directions. **Observatory Road** leads west past the lake and out of town.

PRACTICAL INFORMATION

Tourist Office: Anna Salai, a 2-min. walk from the bus stand. Not a good source of information, but runs good 1-day tours for Rs.125.

Currency Exchange: State Bank of India, next to the tourist office on Anna Salai. Open Mon.-Fri. 10am-2pm, Sat. 10am-noon.

Buses: Bus Stand, Anna Salai. To Madurai (6:50, 8:20, 9:40am, 1:30, 3:20, 6, and 6:30pm, 4hr., Rs.18) and Tiruchirappalli (3:30pm, 9hr., Rs.32).

Local Transportation: Taxis are available outside the bus stand but these are expensive. The best way to get around is to **walk.** You'll enjoy the fresh air, and Kodai is so small that nothing is more than 10min. away.

English Bookstore: CLS Bookstore, opposite the bus stand. Open Mon.-Fri. 10:30am-5pm.

Pharmacy: Many pharmacies line Anna Salai, including **Makuti Medicals** (open daily 9am-7:30pm), and **Balaji Medicals** (open daily 9am-6pm).

Hospital: Government Hospital, Seven Junction Rd. (tel. 41292). **Van Allen** (tel. 41273) is a private hospital near Coaker's Walk.

Police: Opposite the post office on Anna Salai (tel. 41290).

Post Office: A huge building on Anna Salai (tel. 32402). Open Mon.-Fri. 10am-4pm. **Postal Code:** 624101.

Telephone Code: 04542.

ACCOMMODATIONS

Lodge Everest, 8 20, Anna Salai (tel. 40100). One of the many small lodges on Anna Salai. The rooms are small but it's a good bargain. Dorm beds Rs.60. Singles Rs.125. Doubles Rs.250.

Hamidia Lodge, 7/192 Anna Salai (tel. 40108). Soft beds, bright curtains. Squat toilet attached. The red wall-to-wall carpeting is a bit moth-eaten. Hot water by the bucket. July-March: rooms Rs.100; April-June: rooms Rs.150.

Hotel Anjay, Anna Salai (tel. 41089). Friendly old man at the reception will show you to a room with warm blankets on the bed and a view of the mountains from the window. Attached bath with seat toilet. Hot water available. June-March: doubles Rs. 320. April-May: doubles Rs.370. Attached to Anjay is the nearly identical Hotel Jaya.

Hotel Sangeeth, opposite the bus stand (tel. 40456). Small doubles with blue, black, and green blankets. Squat toilet attached. Small balcony affords a not-so-romantic view of the bus stand. Room service is prompt. July-March: doubles Rs.170. April-June: doubles Rs.300.

Hotel Jewel, Seven Junction Rd. (tel. 41029). Maple-leaf patterned bedspreads and shiny brass lamps with straw lampshades make up for the grungy carpets. Attached bathrooms with hand showers. Doctor and beautician on call. Check-out 10am. July-March: doubles Rs.400; April-June: doubles Rs. 600.

Snooze Inn, Anna Salai (tel. 40837). Cozy beds surrounded by classy "ethnic" decor (Rajasthani wall panels and the terra-cotta animals). Ultra-clean, marble rooms with TV and attached bath with 24-hr. running hot water. June-March: doubles Rs.480; quads Rs.650. April-May: doubles Rs. 550; quads Rs.690. Heater Rs.30, extra blanket Rs.7. Major credit cards accepted with prior approval.

Hotel Tamil Nadu, Fern Hill Rd. (tel. 41336), a 5-minute walk from Anna Salai. Cushy blankets grace the beds in these slightly run-down rooms. Dorm beds (very popular with students) Rs.45 year-round. June 16-March 31: doubles Rs.400; quints Rs.450. April 1-June15: doubles Rs.500; quints Rs.850. TV Rs.50.

The Suhaag, opposite the bus stand (tel. 42312). Welcoming warm beds, grey-patterned curtains, piped-in South Indian instrumental music. Rooms have heaters and attached baths (squat toilets). July-March, check-out 24hr.; April-June check-out 9am. July-March: doubles Rs.300. April-June: Rs.625.

Greenland's Youth Hostel, Coaker's Walk (tel. 40899). The best place for backpackers and trekkers, with trippy views. You'll have to hike a bit for food, but one of Kodai's cheapest (and most scenic) places to crash. Dorm beds Rs.45. Doubles Rs.250.

Sterling Resorts, 44 Gymkhana Rd. (tel. 40313). About 5min. from the lake area. A posh 5-star holiday resort. Rooms equipped with oven, fridge, dining table, and 4 chairs. Bathrooms have shower curtains and seat toilets. The pictures of orchids on the walls add color; this is the ultimate place for comfort in Kodai. July-March: doubles Rs.1100; quads Rs.1500. April-June: doubles Rs. 1550; quads Rs.2050.

The Carlton, Lake Rd. (tel. 40056-71). Next to the lake, this 5-star hotel offers quiet, privacy, and comfort surrounded by trimmed lawns. The teak furniture, wooden floors, and telephones in the bathrooms whisper of a happy holiday. Restaurant and pool room attached. Check-out 9am. April 1-June 15 and Dec. 16-Jan. 15: singles Rs.1840; doubles Rs.3600. Jan. 16-March 31 and June 16- Dec. 15: singles Rs.1590; doubles Rs.2450. Season prices include breakfast, lunch and dinner, while off-season prices include breakfast and dinner. AmEx/Diner's Club/MC/V.

FOOD

Daily Bread, 3 Maratta Shopping Complex, Anna Salai (tel.40485). This new pastry shop run by a brother-sister duo enjoys booming business and deserves it, too. The glass shelves hold terra-cotta pots and plants for sale, and the reproductions of Rajasthani miniatures give the shop a homey Indian feel. Twenty varieties of bread and several kinds of cake are sold, and no chemical preservatives are used in any of their products. Either owner, Meenakshi Ghose or Prasanna Ghose, will coax your decision to stuff yourself with friendly smiles and chatter. Their coffee (Rs.3.50) is famous—you'll have to wait in line.

Honest Pav Bjaji (Bombay Masala), a tiny little tea stall right next to the lake. The enterprising owner speaks Hindi, Gujarati, Telugu, Kannada, Malayalam, Marathi, and Tamil, and will gladly rattle off sample phrases while you sip your *masala chai* (Rs.4).

Hotel Packia Deepam, next to Jaya Lodge on Anna Salai. Serves good South Indian tiffin, Rs.8-12. Try the tomato *utthapam.*

Hotel Astoria, opposite the bus stand. A posh, crowded restaurant. They have a unique Madras soup—hot and very spicy. If the spices are too much for your tear glands, try the boiled vegetables. Chicken dishes Rs.40-60, seafood Rs.30-60. For the finishing touch, soufflé Rs.20.

Wang's Kitchen, Seven Junction Rd. Horses sketched by the popular artist M.F. Hussein stare down from the wall as these chefs prepare steamboats at your table (Rs.165). Other Chinese dishes Rs.60-90. Their special desert is the ice *kachan,* Rs.50.

Hot Breads, Seven Junction Rd., past Wang's Kitchen. A pastry shop that serves pastries, pizza, hot dogs, and chips. Perfect for homesick Western tourists. Entrees Rs.12-15.

Eco-Nut, upstairs from Hot Breads on Seven Junction Rd., is a health food shop loaded with herbal concoctions, neem soap (Rs.7), henna (Rs.10), herbal cola (!), and natural perfumes (Rs.45).

Bombay Restaurant, Anna Salai. It's really tiny but the best place for take-out. The food is made fresh after the order has been placed; be prepared to wait 15min. for a sumptious meal. North Indian veg. dishes, Rs.25-30. Non-veg. Rs.25-40.

Punjabi Dhaba, Anna Salai, serves tasty North Indian veg. food (*thali,* Rs.35). A little crowded and noisy.

Little Silver Star, Anna Salai. Huge portions—a good value. North Indian tandoori (Rs.12-15), vegetables (Rs.30-45), chicken dishes (Rs.35-60).

Sterling Resorts, 44 Gymkhana Rd. A little out of the way, but private. Checkered chairs, pleated curtains, and a great view outside. Pizza, burgers (Rs.40), continental breakfast (Rs.45), Chinese (Rs.70), South Indian (Rs.45).

Sornam Restaurant, opposite the TTDC on Fern Hill Rd. South Indian veg. food; *pongal, vadai, idli,* but nothing compares to the *butter dosa.*

The Carlton, Lake Rd. Unquestionably good food is carted out for their buffet meals: (Rs.250; Rs.300 for Wednesday's barbecue). Dishes without eggs, onions, or garlic are also offered to please the pickiest of Jain ascetics.

SOUTH INDIA

SIGHTS AND ENTERTAINMENT

Though Kodai doesn't offer much in the way of wham-bam sight-seeing, there are a handful of diversions and more than enough mellow ambiance to go around. Kodai is a place where you can just keep walking and enjoy the mountain air. Tourist activity centers on the 24 hectare **lake**—the 5km path which circles it is dotted with bicycle rental stands, and the **Kodaikanal Boating Club** rents out paddle boats and rowboats for Rs.20-50 per half hour. Just south of the lake is **Bryant's Park** (open daily 8:30am-6:15pm; admission Rs.1, camera fee Rs.5) and a fragrant **botanical garden** founded in 1902. Expertly trimmed and clipped by a a staff of 45, the gardens contain numerous flowers and trees including a cactus-filled greenhouse and a rose garden. With your back toward the entrance, head left through the gardens (toward the painted tree stumps) and exit Bryant's Park; you'll end up at the entrance to **Coaker's Walk,** a 10-minute jaunt that traces an arc from Taj Lodge to Greenland's Youth Hostel. On clear mornings, the views from Coaker's are amazing, but most days the hillside is covered by mist and it's tough to see much of anything. While the walk has been popular since the late 19th century, the path was paved and lights and rails were added during the 1980s. During renovations a small "telescope house" was also built near Coaker's western end—for Rs.1 you can have a technologically enhanced peek at the surrounding countryside. (Open daily. Admission Rs.0.50, camera fee Rs.1, video fee Rs.5.)

For Kodai's best scenery, follow Observatory Rd. west and head out of town toward **Pillar Rocks,** an assemblage of boulders, one of which soars to 1222m. The walk is a mostly flat 8km from the bus stand area—Observatory Rd. is well-labeled and the way is not difficult to find. At the fork in the road, head right for the Astronomical Observatory (closed to visitors) and Trattoria Venice, an alluringly teeny-weeny Italian restaurant which serves up reasonably priced pizza and lasagna with 12 hours' notice (tel. 04542). If you head left at the fork, the road will take you past a toll-booth to the entrance to **Green Valley View,** which allows grand views of the surrounding countryside on only the clearest of days. Just beyond Green Valley View is the nonprofit **Kodaikanal Golf Club,** (tel 40323) which was founded in 1895. A round of the 18-hole course costs Rs.10 with temporary membership at the club (Rs.150 per day). Clubs can be rented for Rs.100-150. From the golf club it's a 25-minute walk to the **roadside promontory,** which offers superb views of the Pillar Rocks on clear mornings. About 40m beyond the promontory, a series of unmarked paths thread their way into the forest, which is usually crowded with loud vacationers scampering about. No matter though—the woods here are incredibly lush and there are many chances for seeing the hulking Pillar Rocks up close.

There are a couple of other interesting short excursions from Kodai. Three kilometers northeast of the bus-stand is **Chettiar Park,** a relatively secluded spot which renews its fame every twelve years when the chronically shy *kurinji* springs into colorful bloom; blossoms are next scheduled for 2006. Also in Chettiar park is the Kurinji Andavar Temple, dedicated to Muruga, which commands a panoramic view. Follow Law's Ghat Rd. southeast and out of town for about 3km to reach the **Flora and Fauna Museum** (open Mon.-Sat. 10-11:30am and 3:30-5pm), with one of South Asia's finest **orchid houses.** Abut 800m past the museum is the mid-sized **Silver Cascade,** a waterfall along the road to Madurai which is typically crowded with Indian tourists.

■ Ooty (Udhagamandalam)

Once the turf of pastoral tribal communities, Ooty (whose full name, Udhagamandalam, comes from the language of one of these tribes) was officially "established" in 1821 by an enterprising collector with the East India Company, John Sullivan. Sullivan conceived Ooty as a "hill station," a mellow place which would give Company officials harried by the heat and humidity (and Hindus) of the plains below a place to

Tribal Peoples of the Nilgiris

While different rulers came and went, the indigenous people of the Nilgiris stayed, forging distinct ways of life. Of these people, three tribal communities have been centrally important. Speaking a Dravidian-influenced language and living in immaculately kept oval-shaped bamboo and thatch huts, the **Todas** evolved a striking attire, wrapping their shoulders beneath red, white, and black striped shawls, women oiling their hair into long, coiling ringlets. Todas pay homage to the long-horned buffalo, giving it salt water and milking it for milk and curd—the key Toda deity is the buffalo's creator. The Todas believe they and their sacrificial buffaloes are to leap from nearby Mukerti Peak into the next world. More numerous than the Todas are the **Badagas,** whose language is closely related to Kannada and whose religious practice has been influenced by Hinduism. While the Badagas are primarily involved in working the soil, another major tribe, the **Kotas,** have traditionally made their living as artisans and musicians, working as blacksmiths or carpenters and playing the *buguri,* a six-holed recorder peculiar to the Nilgiris.

Since Independence, much has changed in the Nilgiris. New crops such as tea, eucalyptus, and the potato have made agriculture a highly lucrative business, and with the British gone, the mountains have rapidly filled with middle-class vacationers hoping to breathe a bit of cold, fresh air. While these changes have gilded the Blue Mountains with new wealth, they have also begun to undermine the traditions of the Nilgiris tribal communities, and the number of unassimilated Kotas, Todas, and Badagas is slowly declining.

chill out. Maharajas followed suit, transforming hill station into hunting station, and solidifying Ooty's reputation as an exclusive getaway.

You can still visit the tombs of John Sullivan's wife, daughter, and son in the cemetery of St. Stephen's Church in Ooty, but Sullivan himself is buried in his mother England, where he probably rolls in his grave, bemoaning the popularization of his virgin verdure. Since India's independence, Ooty has become a summer migratory spot for hordes of Indian tourists as well as the rich and famous—sullying Sullivan's sanctuary. Ooty is no longer the elite retreat Sullivan founded, and is often condemned as a tourist trap where bus exhaust fouls the crisp mountain air, rubbish defiles the once-pristine valley, and the over-booming hotel and restaurant industries undermine Ooty's quaint charms.

It may take a little scouring to escape the jungle of hypercommerciality, but such assiduity is well-rewarded: the people are still mellow, the tea, potato, and carrot plantations make for some lush scenery, and at 2638m, Mt. Doddabetta is the closest you can get to heaven in South India. Ooty's "season" runs from April 1 to June 15; temperatures hover around a dry 25°C during the day, and nights can be chilly. Monsoon season runs from July to August, and September sees the return of dry weather. Ooty's cold, relatively dry winter stretches from November to March.

ORIENTATION

Because its streets snake about the valley and surrounding mountainsides, getting around in Ooty can be somewhat disorienting. No worries though: the town is fairly small and locals are accustomed to directing tourists. Ooty's sprawling **lake** is in the southwestern portion of town, a 1-km walk from the **railway station** and the **bus stand.** From the railway station, walk northeast along **Hospital Road** for 1.5km and you'll reach **Charing Cross** in the town center. From the bus stand, you can reach Charing Cross by skirting the well-stocked fruit market via **Lower Bazaar Road,** which becomes **Commercial Road** 750m before hitting Charing Cross. From Charing Cross, follow **Garden Road** 1km north to reach the **Botanical Gardens.** Climb the hill 500m behind Charing Cross to reach **Town West Circle.**

PRACTICAL INFORMATION

Tourist Office: TTDC, Commercial Rd., Charing Cross (tel. 43977). Provides copious information and maps for the Nilgiri tourist. Books tours. Open Mon.-Fri. 10am-5:45pm. For reservations for Government Accommodations at Mudumalai Wildlife Sanctuary, contact the **Wildlife Warden** (tel. 44098), in the Mahalingam Building, a 5-min. walk up Conoor Rd. from Charing Cross (see **Mudumalai Wildlife Sanctuary,** p. 495), Open Mon.-Fri. 10am-5:30pm. Also contact the warden for permission to go trekking around the Nilgiris. He can provide trekking maps and may be able to contact a guide to assist you.

Budget Travel: Tour companies in Ooty are as numerous as *pan* stalls, and they all offer the same unimaginative tours of Ooty and the surrounding area. Almost all hotels, even the cheapest of the cheap, are affiliated with a travel agency. To book plane tickets, visit **M.B. and Company, Ltd.** on Commercial Rd., near Charing Cross. Open Mon.-Fri. 9am-1pm and 2pm-5pm, Sat. 9am-1pm (tel. 2604).

Currency Exchange: State Bank of India, Town West Circle (tel. 43940, 44099, 42813). Accepts only American Express and Thomas Cook Traveler's Checks in U.S. dollars and pounds sterling. Be prepared for a 15- to 20-min. wait. Open Mon.-Fri. 10am-2pm, Sat. noon-2pm.

Telephones: STD/ISD booths are located throughout Ooty. **Telephone Exchange Office:** Town West Circle.

Trains: Railway Station, North Lake Road. The Blue Mountain Railway (a.k.a. the "toy train") chugs along from Mettupalayam to Conoor to Ooty and back again. The 5-hr. trip through tea and potato plantations and rocky waterfalls is a favorite tourist attraction; population density on the cars is going up, but the journey provides ample opportunity to get to know your neighbor. The steam-powered mini-trains leave Mettupalayam at 7:50am to arrive in Ooty at noon, and leave Ooty at 2:50pm, to arrive at 6:30pm. April 1-June 15, an extra train departs from Mettupalayam at 9:30am. Fare Rs.9/75.

Buses: Bus Stand, next to the railway station. Most regional counters are open for reservations (which should be made 1 day in advance) 9am-5pm, or 9:30am-1pm and 1:30-5pm. To: Bangalore (11 per day, 6:30am-10:30pm (the 10:30pm is a superdeluxe)); Coimbatore (every 20min., 5:45am-8pm, 1hr.); Conoor (every 10min., 5:30am-10:45pm, 30min.); Madras (4 per day, 4:30pm-6:30pm); Mysore (5 per day, 8am-1:30pm, 5hr.); Mettupalayam (every 15min., 5:30am-8:30pm).

Local Transportation: Auto-rickshaws are not metered—plan on shelling out at least Rs.20 for a ride from the train station to Charing Cross. Taxis are more expensive. **Motorcycles** can be rented for Rs.50 per hr. or Rs.350 per day, from Kemp's on Etiennes Rd., 500m from Charing Cross. Rs.500 deposit required.

Market and Supermarket: K. Chellaram's, Commercial Rd. (tel. 42666). Offers amenities from cheddar cheese and toilet paper to eucalyptus oil and Nilgiri tea. Open daily 9:30am-1:30pm and 3:30-7:30pm.

Luggage Storage: Bus stand, Rs.5 per day. Open daily 6am-9pm.

Library: Nilgiri Library, Town West Circle. Open Mon.-Sat.

English Bookstore: Higginbothams, 2 locations: Supermarket Complex, Commercial Rd. (tel. 43736); Oriental Building, Town West Circle (tel. 42546). Well-stocked with cheap Wodehouse paperbacks, theses on economic development, and *Hobson-Jobsons.*

Pharmacy: Indu Medicals, Commercial Rd. (tel. 640001). Open daily 9:30am-9pm.

Hospital: Government Hospital on Jail Hill, Hospital Rd. **Vijaya Hospital** (private), Etiennes Rd. (tel. 42248). Behind Alankar Theatres. 24-hr. ambulance and emergency care.

Police: Town West Circle, near collector's office (tel. 43973, 42200; dial 100 or 2200 in an emergency).

Post/Telegraph Office: Town West Circle (tel 42776). Post Office open Mon.-Fri. 9am-5pm, Sat. 9am-2pm. Telegraph office open Mon.-Fri. 8am-10pm. **Postal Code:** 643001.

Telephone Code: 0423.

ACCOMMODATIONS

Lodging in Ooty reflects India's socioeconomic strata: lots of fly-infested overbooked hovels, a few overpriced luxury hotels, and not much in between. The luxury hotels dot the periphery of Ooty's city limits in the hills surrounding the town proper. These can only be reached by car. Especially during season (April-June) plan ahead and make reservations to avoid paying too much for too little.

The Reflections Guest House, North Lake Rd. (tel. 43034). 1.5km from the bus stand. Soft beds and woolly flannel bedcovers, wildflowers, and a view of the lake make this the budget traveler's favorite. Let Mrs. Dique, the grandmotherly owner, recount her memories of the Independence movement as the waitstaff serves you boiled veggies to soothe your stomach (the menu has waffles, mac and cheese, *bhel puri* and *papad*). Check-out noon. Seat toilets, luggage storage, and laundry service. Heat in the winter; hot water 6-11am. In season: rooms Rs.300 including breakfast and dinner. Off-season: rooms with meals Rs.150. The five rooms fill up fast—make reservations at least 2 weeks in advance during season.

The Hotel Little Paradise Guest House, North Lake Rd. (tel. 43538). Nearly 2km from the bus stand. A veritable steal among the verdant hills, containing clean bare-bones lodging. Their 8 rooms fill up fast in season. Check-out noon. Hot water 7-9am. No television, laundry, sheets, towels, but boy is it cheap. Off-season: singles Rs.40; doubles Rs.80; triples Rs.90. In season: rates go up 75%.

Tamil Nadu Youth Hostel, Carden Rd. (tel. 43665). Near Charing Cross. Clean, relatively safe hostel with soft beds, communal bathroom with seat toilet. Sunny restaurant, dank permit room. In season: dorm beds Rs.45; doubles and cottages Rs.350. Off-season: dorm beds Rs.30; quads and cottages Rs.200.

YWCA, Etiennes Rd., 500m from the racetrack. Slummier location than Tamil Nadu Youth Hostel but prettier garden and friendlier, more English-proficient staff. Comparable in price and amenities. In season: dorm beds Rs.60; cottages (private bath, hot water) Rs.275. Off-season: dorm beds Rs.45; cottages Rs.200; cottage suites, nestled among overgrown flower gardens, Rs.450.

Suryaa Holiday Inn, Upper Bazaar Area (tel. 42567). One of the few decent hotels in the Bazaar/Commercial Rd. area. Rooms are colorful, well-lit, and clean. Charming, obsequious staff. Common TV, centrally located running hot water from 7 to 9am. Squat toilet. Check-out noon. In season: singles Rs.150; doubles Rs.250. Off-season: singles Rs.85; doubles Rs.200.

Sabari Lodge, Upper Bazaar Area (tel. 2735). Simple but immaculate facility. Private baths (squat toilet), hot water in the morning; no towels or TV. Curfew 10pm unless prearranged. Check-out noon in season, 24hr. off-season. In season: singles Rs.100. Off-season: singles Rs.75.

FOOD

There's no better way for a budget traveler to fuel her day than with a Rs.6 foot-long *dosa*, or *gobi paratha*, or even a fluffy *masala* omelet. Tourists are eaters first, seers second, and eaters last, and Ooty consummately caters to their nutritional needs. Some highlights:

Archies, Charing Cross. Serves up fast food Indian-style: spicy "frankies" (chicken, mutton, or vegetable curries wrapped up in *parathas*), vegetable and mutton burgers, and shakes. A crowded, red-countered juke joint, patronized by western tourists and local high-schoolers from Hebron, the nearby international school. Open Fri.-Wed. 10am-7:45pm.

Shinkow's Chinese Restaurant, across from the State Bank of India, Town West Circle. Has been serving authentic stir fry to Ooty locals and tourists since the Raj. Meals cost about Rs.40. Open daily noon-9:30pm.

Tandoor Mahal, 69 Commercial Rd. Serves Indian (tandoori) and Chinese cuisine. This is the place to go if you're craving a *chapati* with that Manchurian chicken. Half-portions are available. Speedy service and excellent food. More expensive than other area restaurants, with food costing about Rs.70, but long hours. Open 9:30am-3:30pm and 6:30pm-midnight.

SIGHTS

Commercial sight-seeing in Ooty surmounts the pinnacle of Mt. Kitsch as well as Mt. Doddabetta—the jam-packed maxicab tours, though cheap at approximately Rs.100 for a whisk around the Nilgiris, are more likely to set you psychologically adrift in the half-desilted, half-sewage-filled Ooty Lake. You'll be happier if you go it alone. An 8-km hike up to **Mt. Doddabetta** (daily 8:30am to 5:30pm) takes about 1½-2 hours and offers technicolor detail you'll miss from an aisle seat.

Ooty's **Botanical Gardens** (open daily 8:30am to 6:30pm, Rs.5, children 5-10 Rs.2, camera fee Rs.25, video fee Rs.500), a cosmopolitan oasis of flora for landscaper and layperson alike, were designed in 1847, spruced up in 1995, and 150 years after their inception are green as ever. The vivids of the rose garden (India's largest) are comple-mented by the saris of Indian mothers basking in the sun with somersaulting young-sters and their fathers. Look for the map of India made out of plants (the Andaman and Nicobar Islands are a bit out of scale, but everything else seems to be in order), the expertly maintained rock garden, and the fossilized remains of a 20 million-year-old tree. At the Garden's head, to the east, is a Toda *mund* (village), with a few huts; next door is Raj Bhavan, the summer home of the governor of Tamil Nadu. A **flower show** during the third week of May is a veritable carnival of flowers.

One kilometer west of the gardens, just up the hill from Charing Cross, is the gothic-style **Saint Stephen's Church,** which was built in the 1820s atop the remains of a Toda temple with lumber from Tipu Sultan's palace. British colonialists are bur-ied in the spooky cemetery out back, under maudlin markers.

Three kilometers southwest of Charing Cross along Commercial Rd. is Ooty's **lake,** which was constructed in the 1820s by the ever-enterprising John Sullivan. Though packed with tourists and so polluted that parts can be called a swamp, the lake is undergoing desilting, which should clear it up within the next two years. Small crafts can be rented (rowboats Rs.15, pedal boats Rs.30 per 30min.), if that floats your boat. Equestrian types can rent horses from adolescent boys near the lake. They'll ask Rs.100 per hour but if you act indifferent they'll come down to Rs.50. Near the lake is a **children's playground** (Rs.2, camera fee Rs.5) with colorful jungle gyms and ant-eater- and elephant-shaped topiary.

ENTERTAINMENT AND SHOPPING

Climbing Doddabettas, rowing boats, and trekking all over the Botanical Gardens is bound to wear out the hardiest of tourists, no matter how many *idlis* he or she has consumed. Ooty's **"nightlife"** is thus explicably worn and dull. Most bars, if occu-pied, have but a few men in the corner. A somewhat cheerful watering hole is the bar at **Hotel Charing Cross** (tel. 45085), where you can drain a Kingfisher for Rs.40. (Open daily 10:45am-10:45pm.)

Survivors of the Atari era might resort to one of several **arcades** along Commercial Rd. Moodmaker's, near the Charing Cross Hotel, is open 10am-10pm. Denizens dish out Rs.1 for 10 minutes of Pac-Man, Super Mario Bros., or Tetris. About 750m up from Moodmaker's on Garden Rd. is **Assembly Halls Movie Theater** (2 shows daily, 2:30 and 6:30pm, Rs.2-15), which screens dated U.S. flicks. The **Race Course,** near the bus stand, is a 1¼-mile loop, where jodhpured jockeys test their horses to the delight of riotous but small-betting crowds. Races are run from April to June. **Wenlock Downs,** about 8km from the bus stand and rail station, has an 18-hole golf course spread over 100 square kilometers.

Shopping in Ooty is mediocre. **The Big Store,** equidistant between Charing Cross and the Lower Bazaar on Commercial Rd., sells Toda shawls (Rs.230), silver jewelry, and other handicrafts. They accept traveler's checks and major credit cards. A **Tibetan Refugees' Market,** along Garden Rd. near the Botanical Gardens, sells mohair sweaters and beefy, colorful wool blankets which you'll need to brave Ooty's freezing winter nights. (Open daily 6am-8:30pm.)

■ Near Ooty

Besides the Botanical Gardens, the best things about Ooty are outside of Ooty. Skip the tour bus companies, if possible, and hire private transport in order to best imbibe the incredible scenery of the Nilgiris. For the thriving tea industry nestled in its steep valley, "Ooh-tea" is aptly named. Arrange an appointment to tour a distillery and sip the freshest cup of *chai* you've ever tasted. Visit **Dhanalakshmi Tea Factory** (tel. 21122) or **National Tea Plantations** (tel. 20437), both in nearby Conoor (27km from Ooty). Twenty kilometers outside of town, the tranquil village of **Pykara** is a lush setting for those who crave sensory stimuli. A small boathouse on Pykara's **lake** rents out boats for Rs.30-40 per half hour and sells tasty *samosas* and omelettes, which you can munch on while overlooking the peaceful water. Near the lake is the **Pykara Dam;** 2.5km from the lake is an attractive series of rocky **waterfalls** which gush hardest in July and August.

■ Mudumulai Wildlife Sanctuary

Comprising 321 of 5000 square kilometers of government-protected land in the Nilgiri foothills, Mudumalai Wildlife Sanctuary is the ideal place to live out all of your Kiplingesque safari fantasies. (The only shooting you'll be doing, however, will be with your Canon 35mm; although the area was originally a popular hunting site, killing the animals has been entirely off-limits since 1966.) Covered in thick deciduous forest, Mudumalai is home to nearly 1000 gaur (Indian bison), 800 wild elephants, 25 tigers, some panthers and leopards, a few bears and hyenas, as well as parakeets and eagles, pythons, and cobras. Of course, whether or not you see any of these (often quite shy) animals and birds depends entirely on a combination of luck, keen eyes, and persistence. If you don't come to the sanctuary in a patient, forgiving mood, you are bound to be disappointed.

The two adjacent villages are almost as cut off from telecommunications, electricity, and other aspects of India's information age as the sanctuary itself. Cows in the middle of green fields, small-boned, cotton-saried women swinging their hips as they balance plastic water jugs on their heads, fuchsia- and violet-flowering trees against thirsty, saffron-bricked earth all combine to provide not only a respite from hyper-industrialized cities but also a rejuvenating adventure in itself.

Mudumalai is 60km from Ooty and 100km from Mysore. Private vehicles (including small tourist buses) generally take the torturous Sighur Ghat Road, which is barely wide enough for one vehicle, and has hairpin turns and swerves and bumps with sheer 300-meter drops on one side. The ride is gorgeous, and you're bound to enjoy it unless you have some digestive ailment. Less exciting and more perilous are the government buses which run to Mysore from Ooty and will arrive at Mudumalai about 2½ hours after they leave Ooty. The bus from Bangalore to Ooty via Mysore also stops at Mudumalai.

ORIENTATION AND PRACTICAL INFORMATION

Explorations of the sanctuary begin in the area around the reception in **Theppakadu.** Seven kilometers along Mysore-Ooty Rd. toward Ooty is the tiny village of **Masinagudi,** where the **Government Hospital, police station,** and the **telegraph and post office** are situated. Mudumalai's appeal lies, in part, in the absence of such technology like **telephones** (none can dial out of the country and most are capricious for local dialing) and **currency exchange,** so enjoy the inconvenience! Just make sure to take care of more worldly matters before you come. The nearest place for such amenities is **Ooty,** a 1½- to 2½-hr. bus ride up the mountain. **Bokkapuram,** home to a few upscale lodges, is 5km from Masinagudi.

Unless you have your own vehicle, you'll probably be depending on the ubiquitous **jeep-wallahs** to shuttle you to and from your inn to the sanctuary. From Chital Walk or Bokkapuram is about Rs.50. It's another Rs.50 from Masinagudi to Theppakadu. You can also try to flag down a Mysore-Ooty bus running to and from Theppakadu, which works only if you're patient and don't mind standing.

ACCOMMODATIONS AND FOOD

In Theppakadu, there are a few **Government Rest Houses** (Rs.40) and dormitories (Rs.5 per bed) which you can *only* book through the Wildlife Warden in Ooty (see p. 492). Even he is reluctant to rent them out, and not many people end up staying there. Everyone except the night watchman leaves after 7pm; electricity and hot water are fickle so it's probably not a good idea to stay there alone. Most hotels in and around Mudumalai are equipped with restaurants, and this is the customary place to find your sustenance.

Jungle Hut (tel. 56463, 56240) at the base of the Nilgiris, is probably one of the best places to stay and one of the furthest for Masinagudi. It is owned by a former tea CEO who, 10 years ago, gave up boardroom life to cultivate small scale luxury at his inn. Sunny cottages decorated with batik prints surround the pavilion area (3 meals, Rs.270) and an outdoor swimming pool. The family-run establishment organizes day treks up into the nearby Nilgiris. Prices are somewhat extravagant. Singles Rs.500. Doubles Rs.750. Additional 20% tax.

Belleview Resort (tel. 56351), 1km south of Masinagudi. A cheerful lodge with an attached restaurant. Rooms have hot water and seat toilets. Dorm beds (no sheets or towels) Rs.50. Singles Rs.250. Cottages Rs.750.

Hotel Tamil Nadu (tel. 56249), across the river from the reception office. The stuccoed cottages have hot water but the dorms do not. There is no smoking or drinking; the restaurant is open 6am-9pm. Check-out noon. Dorm beds Rs.40. Family cottages with 2 double beds Rs.350, plus 20% tax.

Jungle Trails (Chital Walk) (tel. 56256) is off the Ooty-Mysore Rd. about 15km from the sanctuary. Around 6pm most nights, you can watch wild elephants from the verandah. The soft-spoken owner has set up salt-licks and *machans* around his lodge for better viewing. Don't come here unless you're willing to keep your voice down—the owner reluctantly admits only 4-5 people into his lodge at a time so as not to disturb the beastly neighbors. All the rooms are decorated with wildlife paraphanalia. The dormitory is more of a bamboo-thatched loft, which can only be reached by ladder. Dorm beds Rs.125. Doubles Rs.400. Quads Rs.600. Meals provided at a charge.

SIGHTS

Excursions around the sanctuary begin at the reception office in Theppakadu. The area is criss-crossed by the crocodile-infested **Moyar River** and is home to a community of 250 Kurumbas, a tribal people whose language is related to Kannada. From the reception office you can book **elephant rides** (Rs.130 for 4 people) or a 45-minute **bus tour** (Rs.25 per person) of some of the sanctuary. Tours run from 6:30-9am and 4-6pm and there's generally a long waiting list that isn't as discouraging as it seems. Tours typically follow Circle Road, cutting through some lush forest and sometimes passing a herd of elephants before reaching the tour's climax, a promontory point which affords excellent views of the 150m Moyar River Waterfall.

Unfortunately, the only elephants you'll see around here are the domesticated ones doing the elephant *puja* and the elephant show. About 150m from the reception center is an **Elephant Camp,** where 17-20 elephants are kept at a time so that they may be studied and protected from nighttime poachers. At 6pm two elephants do *puja* at a small on-premises Ganesh (what did you expect?) temple built in the 1970s. After the elephants have circled the temple and knelt before the shrine, clanging the bells they cradle in their trunks, it's feeding time. You can stand next to the elephant-*wallahs* as they mash up the pachyderms' dinner—horse gram, salt, rice, coconut, and *ragi* flour—and feed it to them. You can even feed the elephants (Durga, John, and Santoshi, to name a few) sugar cane. After feeding, an English-language documentary film is usually shown. The camp also offers a small **museum** on local wildlife and an Elephant Show (Rs.20) on Saturdays and Sundays, which consists of your basic mix of elephants dancing, elephants racing through an obstacle course, elephants on a balance beam, and, of course, elephants playing soccer, Pele-style. It's more circus than wildlife reserve.

You probably won't see much wildlife at Mudumalai if you stick to the government-sanctioned tours—probably a peacock, some sambar, and hordes of chital (spotted deer). Until recently, the sanctuary was open to private vehicles, but the government banned them because cars would drive off the road in the dark. (Due to the threat of poaching, headlights are not allowed.) However, anyone at the Hotel Tamil Nadu or the tea stall adjacent can tell travelers how to hire a **jeep-wallah** for an illicit **"nighttime safari"** in the sanctuary. For Rs.350, one can embark on a completely illegal and sometimes dangerous ride into the heart of the park. For drivers with relatively good reputations, some travelers inquire at Hotel Tamil Nadu; otherwise Babu (tel. 56948) or K. Ramachandran (tel. 56306, 56351) can help safari-goers find drivers and jeeps (if the phones are working). Though it is illegal to go there by jeep, it is said that a morning ride to the **Segur Waterfalls** (also about Rs.350) is the best way to explore what is widely considered the sanctuary's most breathtakingly beautiful scenery. Those who have hired jeeps to take them to the falls report that it is easy to find drivers to make the trip. **Let's Go does not recommend illegal activities of any kind.**

> **Warning:** At no time are visitors to Mudumalai allowed to simply wander off into the sanctuary without a guide and permission from forest authorities. Rangers do not take kindly to such wanderings, and fines can be steep. To say the least, tigers can be a serious problem.

Kerala

Kerala, often called "the land of green magic," takes its name from the Chera kingdom, under whose ancient rule Kerala became India's foremost maritime trading center. By the 3rd century BC, Egyptians, Phoenicians, Chinese, and Babylonians had trade relations with Kerala. In 52 AD, St. Thomas the Apostle is believed to have arrived in Kerala; later Christian immigrants brought the still-practiced Syriac liturgy. Around or before this time, Jews arrived on the shores of Kerala, fleeing persecution in Palestine. Arab traders dominated Kerala's trade from the 8th century, when they brought Islam to Kerala, until the Portuguese landed at Calicut in 1498 and used their brutal style of diplomacy to gain exclusive trading rights. Meanwhile, rivalry between the port cities of Cochin and Calicut weakened both, and the Dutch and British ejected the Portuguese from their forts early in the 17th century. During the 18th century Kerala came under the control of the British. With Independence in 1947, the princely states of Cochin and Travancore were joined to form the state of Kerala.

> ### An Axe to Grind
> Legend roots the creation of the Malabar coast in the divine action of the sixth incarnation of Vishnu, Parasurama ("Rama with the Battle-Axe"). Born a Brahmin, Parasurama set out to regain the status of the priestly caste from the usurping *kshatriyas.* Parasurama disobeyed rules forbidding Brahmins to commit violence, wreaking bloody havoc until the sea god, Varuna, offered him a chance to create a land where Brahmins could live in peace. This land would emerge from the sea as far out as Parashurama could throw his mighty battle-axe. The Malabar coast rose from the waves up to the place where the axe fell.

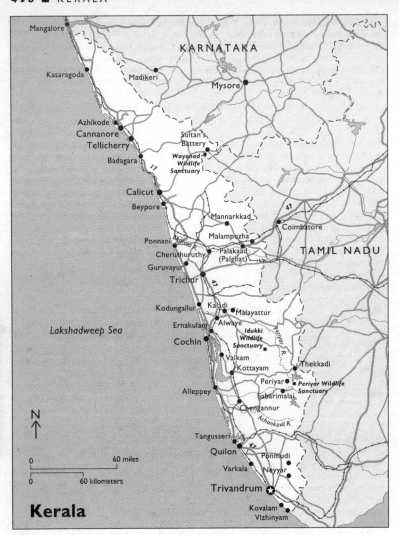

Kerala

In 1956, Kerala's boundaries were redrawn in an effort to include all Malayalam-speakers, tacking on land formerly in Madras state. In 1957, the people of Kerala became the first democratic population in the world to freely elect a communist government.

Kerala is one of India's most densely populated states, with 747 people per square kilometer. The majority (60%) are Hindu, 20% are Muslim, and 20% are Christian. Despite a low per capita income, reforms have brought Kerala the most equitable land distribution in India. Kerala's literacy rate, at around 90%, is the highest in India, around twice the national average. Keralan women's status is high, possibly due to vestiges of ancient matrilineal, polyandrous systems, such as that still practiced by the Nayar caste. Kerala has more women than men, probably attributable to low female infanticide and better health care for women, as well as the many Keralan men who go to work in the Gulf countries.

Tourism became an official industry of Kerala in 1986 (along with the export of coconut, spices, rubber, fish, and tea). Sun-worshippers are drawn to the palmy beaches, and then up into the misty hills of the Western Ghats and along the Keralan backwaters. Forty lazy rivers run from the Western Ghats to the sea, stymied in paddy fields and canals winding past islands where people, cows, goats, and chickens live a life intertwined with the magic green waters.

■ Trivandrum (Thiruvananthapuram)

The rolling city of Trivandrum is spread across seven coastal hills. This mellow capital of Kerala had a population of 825,000 in the 1991 census. The pilgrimage spot of Shree Padmanabha Swamy Temple, dedicated to the reclining Vishnu, the deity of the royal family of Travancore, attracts thousands of Hindus working on their *karma*. Speckled with parks, palaces, monuments, and museums, Trivandrum is spread over a wide area. The city was the capital of Travancore State for two centuries after Dharma Raja shifted administration here during the last days of his reign. Trivandrum became the capital of Kerala when the state was formed in 1956. The city's Malayalam name means "the city of Anantha," the serpent on which the reclining form of Lord Vishnu (Lord Padmanabha) lies.

ORIENTATION

The streets tangle over 74 square kilometers of coastal hills, but stick to the few main drags and navigation is easy. Like the easy pronunciation of its name, the skeleton of Tiruvananthapuram is laid out long and simple. **M.G. Road,** as main as a drag can be, runs widely through the length of the city center from north to south. At the northern end, M.G. Rd. dumps all its traffic into **Museum Road,** forming an intersection like a capital-T for Trivandrum.

Moving south from the T along M.G. Rd., passersby will encounter every sort of facility. Further south, M.G. Rd. cruises down a hill to a hectic intersection with the city's other main drag, **Central Station Road,** also known as Station or Subramaniam Rd. Left from M.G. Rd. onto Central Station Rd., then left at the Ambika Café is **Manjalikulam Road,** the home of the budget hotel ghetto. Further down Central Station Rd., the enigmatic **long-distance bus stand** awaits on the left with its herd of buses; a tiny bit further on the right is the **railway station,** a huge gray-and-yellow concrete and stone arched building on the right side.

M.G. Rd. continues south of the intersection with Central Station Rd., where footbridges cross the railroad tracks. This area is known as **East Fort,** the old part of the capital. A few blocks south, a large blank yellow gate marks the entrance to **Sree Padmanabha Swamy Temple.** Turning left off M.G. Rd. opposite the gate, the **local bus stand** features a herd of buses out to pasture and a line of covered stands. Buses to Kovalam frequently depart from a stand on the left side of M.G. Rd. south of the fruit-sellers. **Chelai Bazaar Road** here leads from behind the statue of Great Soul Gandhi through a bazaar area featuring everything from noserings to safety pins.

PRACTICAL INFORMATION

Tourist Office: The Department of Tourism's **Tourist Facilitation Centre** (tel. 61132; fax 62279) is on Museum Rd. across from the big red entrance gate to the zoo and museums (from M.G. Rd., turn right). The helpful staff may be disappointed if you want to chat for less than 30min. Equipped with maps, brochures, and a good knowledge of Kerala and India, as well as the Maldives, Sri Lanka, and Nepal, they will happily make an itinerary for any length of stay in India and its neighboring countries, including hotel reservations and train/bus times. Ask them about festivals occurring in Kerala. Open daily 10am-5pm. **KTDC Reception Centre** (tel. 330031) on Central Station Rd. between the intersection with M.G. Rd. and the long-distance bus station. The less energetic cousins of the Tourist Facilitation Centre, this office mainly promotes KTDC tours (see p. 505). Open Mon.-Sat. 6:30am-9:30pm. The **Kerala Department of Tourism** operates a small tourist counter in the long-distance bus stand womanned by a sweet, helpful person. Open Mon.-Sat. 10am-4:45pm.

Budget Travel: Airtravel Enterprises India, Limited (tel. 67183; fax 331704) is on M.G. Rd. just before the intersection with Museum Rd., on the right. The office sells tickets for destinations within India and abroad, dealing with many airlines. They can get visas, confirm tickets, and perform foreign exchange. Open Mon.-Sat. 9:30am-5:30pm. **Travel Destinations** (tel. 330702; fax 331346) is in the Chaitram Hotel lobby on Central Station Rd., between the intersection with M.G. Rd. and the long-distance bus station. The office can book international and domestic flights, confirm airline tickets for Rs.25, and make train bookings. Open Mon.-Sat. 9am-9:30pm.

Immigration Office: Foreigners Registration Office, Office of the Commissioner of Police (tel. 61399), Residency Rd. (take a rickshaw). Visa extensions not for tourist visas, but for student and entry visas "with proper documents." The process should take about a week; it's not necessary to leave your passport during that time. Open Mon.-Sat. 10am-1pm and 2-5pm; closed the 2nd Sat. of each month.

Currency Exchange: A branch of the **Central Bank of India** in the Chaitram Hotel (on Station Rd. between the intersection with M.G. Rd. and the long-distance bus station) can do currency exchange. Open Mon.-Fri. 10am-2pm, Sat. 10am-noon. The **State Bank of India,** on M.G. Rd. a little north of the Secretariat, changes currency and traveler's checks (U.S. dollars: AmEx, Barclay's, and Thomas Cook; pounds sterling: Thomas Cook) rather inefficiently. Open Mon.-Fri. 10am-2pm, Sat. 10am-noon. A block south of the Secretariat is **Andhra Bank** (look for a tiny sign against a Coir Handicrafts shop on the left side of the road, leading into a uphill alley)—pretty quick and efficient, they give credit card advances without sucking out any commission.

Telephones: STD/ISD booths line M.G. Rd., as well as many other parts of the city. Some cooperative booths allow **free call-backs!** Although the **Central Telegraph Office** gets even surlier at the mention of call-backs, collect calls are possible. Open 24hr.

Airport: Trivandrum's **international airport** is located a few kilometers outside town. Buses marked Shanumugham leave from the local bus stand (on M.G. Rd. a few minutes' walk south of the train tracks) every 15 minutes and stop at the airport. Trivandrum is a convenient and popular site for flights to and from Malé in the Maldives and Colombo, Sri Lanka, and several flights leave daily. **Indian Airlines Office** (tel. 62288) is 1 block left on Museum Rd. from the intersection with M.G. Rd. To: Colombo (1 per day, 1hr., US$42); Madras (1 per day, 1½hr., US$86); Cochin (Wed., Fri., and Sun. 7:45pm); Bangalore (Mon.-Tues., Thurs., and Sat., 1hr., US$82); Bombay (1-3 per day, 2hr., US$147); Delhi (1 per day, 5hr., US$274); Malé (1 per day, 40min., Rs.2045). Many international airlines have offices on M.G. Rd.

Trains: the **train station,** located on Station Rd. a few minutes' walk east of M.G. Rd., has a sleek Computerized Reservation Centre for long-distance trains. (Open Mon.-Sat. 8am-2pm, 2:15-8pm, Sun. 8am-2pm.) To: Alleppey (4:25pm, 3hr., Rs.43); Varkala (9 per day, 5am-8:35pm, 30min., Rs.16); Quilon (9 per day, 5am-8:35pm, 1½hr., Rs.21); Cochin (11 per day, 5am-8:35pm, 5hr., Rs.56); Kanyakumari (12:20 and 3:10pm, 2hr., Rs.25); Bombay (*Kanniya Kumari Exp.* 1082, 4:30am, *Trivandrum-Bombay Exp.* 6632, 7:30am, 46hr., sleeper Rs.317); Delhi (*Kerala Exp.* 2625, 9:45am, 55hr., sleeper Rs.402); Madras (1:10pm, 17½hr., sleeper Rs.214); Madurai (8:35pm, 9½hr., Rs.64).

Buses: the **long-distance KSRTC bus station** is on Station Rd., almost directly across from the train station. There's a **reservation counter,** but you'll be lucky to find anyone there. **Rajiv Gandhi Tours** also has an air-conditioned computerized reservation center here, and although they mostly run buses to Tamil Nadu, they have some long-distance buses to other destinations as well. Office hours daily 7am-9pm. To: Madras (7 per day, 12:30-7:30pm, A/C at 1:30, 2:30 and 3:30pm, 17hr. Rs.146, A/C Rs.242); Madurai (13 per day, 7am-10:30pm, A/C at 1:30, 2:30 and 3:30pm, 7hr., Rs.59, A/C Rs.69); Pondicherry (6pm, 15hr., Rs.127). KSRTC runs to: Alleppey (most of the buses leaving every 15-30min. for Cochin pass through Alleppey, 3½hr.); Bangalore (3 and 4pm, 15hr., Rs.225); Cochin (every 15-

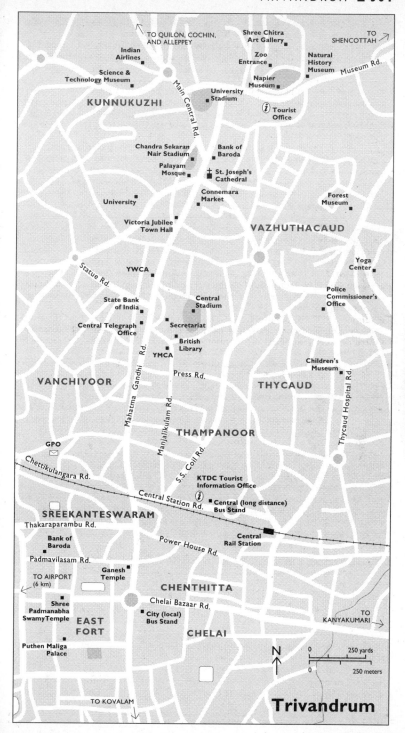

TO QUILON, COCHIN, AND ALLEPPEY

Shree Chitra Art Gallery

TO SHENCOTTAH

Indian Airlines

Zoo Entrance

Natural History Museum

Museum Rd.

Science & Technology Museum

Napier Museum

KUNNUKUZHI

Main Central Rd.

University Stadium

Tourist Office

Chandra Sekaran Nair Stadium

Bank of Baroda

Palayam Mosque

St. Joseph's Cathedral

Connemara Market

University

Forest Museum

VAZHUTHACAUD

Victoria Jubilee Town Hall

Statue Rd.

YWCA

Yoga Center

State Bank of India

Central Stadium

Police Commissioner's Office

Central Telegraph Office

Secretariat

Mahatma Gandhi Rd.

British Library

YMCA

Children's Museum

VANCHIYOOR

Press Rd.

THYCAUD

Manjalikulam Rd.

THAMPANOOR

Thycaud Hospital Rd.

GPO

S.S. Coil Rd.

Chettikulangara Rd.

KTDC Tourist Information Office

Central Station Rd.

Central (long distance) Bus Stand

SREEKANTESWARAM

Thakaraparambu Rd.

Central Rail Station

Bank of Baroda

Power House Rd.

Padmavilasam Rd.

Ganesh Temple

TO AIRPORT (6 km)

CHENTHITTA

Shree Padmanabha Swamy Temple

Chelai Bazaar Rd.

City (local) Bus Stand

EAST FORT

CHELAI

TO KANYAKUMARI

Puthen Maliga Palace

N

0   250 yards

0   250 meters

TO KOVALAM

Trivandrum

30min., 5hr.); Kanyakumari (9 per day, 3am-8:30pm, 2½hr., Rs.90); Mangalore (11:30am, 18hr., Rs.197); Quilon (frequent, 1½hr.); Varkala (11 per day, 7:50am-9:30pm, 1½hr., Rs.13). The **local bus station** is on M.G. Rd. a few minutes' walk south of the train tracks. Buses from here leave frequently both to Kovalam and the airport (marked Shanumugham).

Local Transportation: Auto-rickshaws are easily caught all over the city; they will usually set their meters without argument. They will go to Kovalam for about Rs.50. **Taxis** are also plentiful, especially outside fancy hotels, and will go to Kovalam for about Rs.150. It is easy to **walk** between most tourist facilities and sights.

English Bookstore: What a feast for the gentle soul of the bookworm! **Continental Books** is just off M.G. Rd. a bit north of Station Rd.; watch for East West Airlines sign, then hang a left. Their vast selection of fiction and non-fiction seems to completely neglect anything Indian except for cookbooks. Also for sale: stationery, cards, Barbie dolls, and good pens that work! Open daily 9:30am-8pm. **Higginbothams:** a rather large branch is located on M.G. Rd. 5min. north of Station Rd. on the right. A better selection of textbooks and Indian books is sold here. Open Mon.-Sat. 9:30am-1:30pm and 3:30-7:30pm. **Morning Star Books** has a small store in the Chaitram Hotel on Station Rd. with nightgowns, maps of South India, Kerala, Trivandrum, Cochin, etc., and books about India, Southeast Asia, as well as classics like the *Mahabharata.* Open daily 10am-1pm and 2-8pm, with a probable coffee break 4-4:40pm.

Library: The **British Library,** just off Manjalikulam Rd. where it swerves left, is officially open only to card-carrying members. If you nicely leave your bag at the front and say you're only in town for a few days, however, they will happily let you browse the several-days-old British newspapers and magazines, or sniff through the stacks. Open Tues.-Sat. 11am-7pm.

Market: Chelai Bazaar Road, which intersects with M.G. Rd. at the local bus station, is choked with fruit-and-vegetable-*wallahs,* bangle- and plastics-*wallahs,* and upper-crust jewelry stores. **Connemara Market,** on M.G. Rd. a few blocks north of the Secretariat on the right, has an even weirder assortment of plastics, palm-leaf baskets, fruits, vegetables, bangles, *salwar kameezes,* you name it. It also seems to be Beggar Central.

Pharmacy: although there is not a single 24-hour pharmacy, pharmacies near the hospitals on Thycaud Hospital Rd. trade the duty, so there is always one open.

Hospital: Several hospitals are located on Thycaud Hospital Rd. near the east terminus of Station Rd. Another good hospital is **Cosmopolitan Hospital** (tel. 448182), a little distance out from the center of town on the northwest side.

Police: The Office of the Commissioner of Police is on Residency Rd. It's best to take a rickshaw through the twisting streets.

Emergency: Police: tel. 100. **Fire:** tel. 101. **Ambulance:** tel. 102.

Post Office: the **GPO** does its best to elude detection. Follow Station Rd. west through the intersection with M.G. Rd.; at the next traffic circle make a hairpin turn to the right, and hope to see it on the left after a few blocks. Otherwise, ask for directions. *Poste Restante* is down some stairs, and can be claimed Mon.-Sat. 8am-4pm. **Poste Restante addressed to Kovalam tends to end up here.** Stamps may be purchased Mon.-Sat. 8am-8pm.

Telephone Code: 0471.

ACCOMMODATIONS

M.G. Rd. and Station Rd. offer plenty of large hotels, but Manjalikulam Rd. is the real budget hotel ghetto. It is a pleasant, quiet lane lined with hotels and is an easy walk from the long-distance bus station or the train station. Turn right from the bus station or left from the train station to walk 5min. west on Station Rd., take the first right after the bus station, bearing left at the V.) With the many options available here, it's almost ridiculous to list any. Here are a few dependable places—aside from these, happy hunting!

Manjalikulam Road

Pravin Tourist Home (tel. 330443), about a 5-min. walk north along Manjalikulam Rd., on the left. The super-friendly proprietor has a huge smile. The rooms are fairly good-sized and have big windows and clean bathrooms. TV in the lobby. Tax included. Singles Rs.76. Doubles Rs.136. Triples Rs.177. Quads Rs.210.

Hotel Regency (tel 330377), follow Manjalikulam Rd. to the first cross-street, turn right. Fancier than the standard fare, with big clean rooms with TVs with 24 channels (including MTV and BBC World) and running hot water. Gentle, fawning staff. Singles Rs.180. Doubles Rs.300. Extra person Rs.65. Extra charge for A/C.

Other Areas

Chaitram Hotel (tel. 330977) on Central Station Rd., a 5-min. walk west of the bus and train stations (turn right from the bus station or left from the train station onto Central Station Rd.). Along with a bookstore, foreign exchange counter, and travel office, the Chaitram Hotel features nice big rooms with TVs, beds with top sheets, and several restaurants. Singles Rs.300. Doubles Rs.350. Rooms with A/C available.

Nalanda Tourist Home, on M.G. Rd. on the south side of the tracks, on the right. Definitely not stunning, but fairly cheap and close to the temple and the local bus stand (i.e., buses to Kovalam). Rooms have attached baths. Singles Rs.60. Doubles Rs.90. Triples Rs.110.

Hotel Safari (tel. 77202; fax 450541), on M.G. Rd. a few minutes north of Central Station Rd. The huge rooms have bathtubs and hot water and a strange collection of cracking furniture. The pleasant restaurant has good views of Trivandrum. Singles Rs.100. Doubles Rs.150. Triples Rs.200. Rooms with A/C Rs.250. Extra person Rs.50, in A/C room Rs.75.

Omkara Lodge, on the left side of M.G. Rd., a few minutes' walk north from Station Rd. Its hallmarks are bright yellow walls, a strange musty smell, tiny rooms, and thin mattresses. Just repeat the universal *mantra* and your surroundings won't matter. Attached baths. Singles Rs.60. Doubles Rs.79.

FOOD

Trivandrum doesn't have any good Keralan restaurants, instead featuring small "hotels" with South Indian fast food and hotel restaurants with a mishmash of Continental, Indian, and Chinese cuisines. Many hotels including the Hotel Safari have rooftop restaurants with good views of the city.

Hotel Arroya, Station Rd., just before the junction with M.G. Rd.; watch carefully for the sign. This friendly hole-in-the-wall place offers smashingly great simple South Indian hotel fare. The *paratha* (Rs.8 for 2, with curry and onion *raita*) has been nominated the best in India by a panel of travellers.

Ananda Jyoti, on Manjalikulam Rd., a 2-min. walk north of Station Rd. in the budget hotel ghetto. Serves up mean, tasty Indian fast food at wicked cheap prices.

Snoozzer's Ice Cream, a tiny shop found by following Manjalikulam Rd. north until Residency Towers appears, then taking a right; Snoozzer's will be a little past Residency Towers on the right side. An extensive menu of ice creams, milkshakes, *falooda,* sundaes, "Special Delicacies Available Only At Snoozzer's," and "Mocktails," including Bloody Marys. Open Mon.-Sat. 9am-8pm, Sun. 9am-6pm.

Rangoli, on M.G. Rd. a minute or 2 south of the train tracks. The upstairs "family" restaurant is full of upper-middle-class families, not leering men. It's crisply red and white and serves moderately priced Chinese and Indian food to the tunes of Rod Stewart. Lunch is served 11am-3pm, snacks 3-6:30pm, dinner 6:30-10:30pm.

Sheetal Juice runs a clean, incredibly cheap juice stand in the midst of the local bus station.

The Promenade, in the Mascot Hotel (from M.G. Rd., turn left onto Museum Rd.). A café/snack bar catering to businessmen and people with post-*charas* munchies. Offers rather expensive snacks (*masala dosa* Rs.25), cheeseburgers (Rs.50), and sundaes (Rs.30-50). The immaculate interior is done in pink and lavender (even the menus). Open 24hr.

Ananda Bhavan, on M.G. Rd. just north of the Telegraph Office, is another South Indian fast food restaurant with an especially extensive sweet counter.

SIGHTS AND ENTERTAINMENT

The **Shree Padmanabha Swamy Temple,** visible from M.G. Rd. a few minutes' walk south of the train tracks are marked by a large yellow gate, was built on a temple site of uncertain but ancient age. The foundations of the present Gopuram were laid in 1566 and built up to the fifth story, the six and seventh lofty stories being added during the reign of the next Maharaja, Rama Varma. The current structure was completed in 1733. Although the temple itself, featuring a reclining Vishnu visible only by opening three doors (one at the sacred head, one at the divine midsection, and one at the holy feet), is open only to Hindus wearing *dhotis* or saris, non-Hindus may climb the steps and see the less-sacred images.

On the way back along the temple lane, through handicraft sellers persistently shouting "Elephant madam, tiny elephant sir sandalwood good smell, smell!," a vast green **tank** lurks peacefully on the left, used for bathing by pilgrims. A newly opened museum is on the right in the palace of Prince Swati Tirunal (also a famed musician and court composer). Every inch of the **Puthen Maliga Palace** or **"Horse Palace"** (so-called for the 122 galloping horse sculptures under its eaves) is intricately carved. Amazingly this beautiful work was reputedly completed in only four years, and the (ungrateful?) prince subsequently occupied it for only one year. It now houses life-size Kathakali figures in full regalia, paintings of the rajas and ranis of Travancore, weaponry, a Bohemian crystal throne, and many other gifts to the Maharajas from China, Italy, and other exotic locales. The **Sowdhy Musical Festival** (Feb. 26-March 4, 1997) presents evenings of classical music on the lawn in memory of Swati Tirunal's passion for music. (Open Tues.-Sun. 8:30am-12:30pm and 3-5:30pm. Admission

---

The Origin of the Shree Padmanabha Swamy Temple

According to a legend written in the palm-leaf records of the temple, the temple was founded on the 950th day of the kali age by a Tulu Brahmin hermit called Divakara Muni. This hermit, a great devotee of Vishnu, was doing penance when an exquisitely charming and loving two-year-old child came to him. Charmed, the sage requested the child stay with him, and the child accepted on the condition he should always be respected. Tolerating the child's, the sage gave him love and care.

One day, the child made such a nuisance of himself when the sage was in deep meditation that the sage became annoyed and punished him. The child immediately disappeared, saying only that if the sage wanted to see him he must come to Ananthankadu. The sage was immediately grief-stricken, realizing the divine child was Lord Vishnu himself. The sage began the journey, foregoing all food, sleep, or rest. In a forested area near the sea, he glimpsed the child disappearing into a massive *ilippa* tree (*Bassica longifolia*), which immediately crashed to the ground, assuming the shape of recumbent Vishnu (who in this form is called Padmanabha, meaning "lotus-navel," for in this form he is depicted with a lotus flower growing up from his sacred navel). The divine form was so huge as to have its head at Thiruvallam and its feet at Trippapur, with its holy midsection lying at Thiruvanathapuram. Overawed by the size and majesty of this divine form, the sage prayed that Vishnu would contract himself so that he might, with his limited sight, see the divine form all at once. Lord Vishnu complied, shrinking to a visible size.

Legend has it that the very *ilippa* tree which crashed to the ground was carved into the image of Lord Padmanabha, and a temple erected over it by the then-Maharaja of Travancore as the miracle came to his attention. The same *ilippa* statue is said to be the one in the temple even today. However, it is also said that Marthanda Varma replaced this statue with a new one during his reign.

Rs.5.) Tour guides who recruit on the street will expect a handsome donation to their pocketbooks but the information they give can be well worth the money.

Following this lane from the temple straight across M.G. Rd. leads past many **hand-loom stores** into the ancient **Chelai Bazaar,** hopping with fruit and vegetable sellers, upscale jewellers, plastics-*wallahs,* and people carrying various large objects in their heads.

Following M.G. Rd. north leads past the white colonial **Secretariat** whose road-side lanes are constantly "decorated" by crowds of protesters and strikers. M.G. Rd. leads next to the **Connemara Market** (filled with all sorts of plastics, palm-leaf baskets, fruits and vegetables, tacky clothing, and beggars), and then to the final intersection with Museum Rd. Bear right through the big red gate which is the entrance to the **zoo, public gardens, and museums.** Inside the zoo, set among woods and lakes, many animals probably have better habitats than animals elsewhere in India, but some inhabit small cages that strangely resemble Indian hotel rooms. And something seems to be eating the camel's nose, and the lions are groaning from the veterinary hospital... Open Tues.-Sat. 9am-5pm (tickets must be purchased before 4pm). Admission Rs.4, camera fee Rs.5.

Set in the lovely, 20-hectare public gardens dotted with moon-eyed couples, are the Napier Museum, the Shree Chitra Art Gallery, and the Natural History Museum. One might suspect one of Walt Disney's minions as the architect of the gabled red-, black-, and pink- tiled **Napier Museum,** fancifully striped on the inside in yellow, pink, red and turquoise. In reality, Robert Fellowes Chisholm designed the building as an experiment in the Indo-Saracenic style, attempting to incorporate the Keralan style into colonial architecture. The museum houses sculptures "all arranged in their proper order," a wooden temple car, an array of tacky gifts given to someone of importance, and Javanese shadow-play figures, among other things. Buy tickets (Rs.5 for admission to all three) at the Natural History Museum.

By contrast, the sophisticated **Shree Chitra Art Gallery** is fabulously decked with the Western-style portraits of the famed Raja Ravi Varma, Tibetan *thankas,* Japanese, Chinese, and Balinese paintings, 400-year-old Rajasthani miniatures, and modern Indian works.

The **Natural History Museum** houses all the dead animals from the zoo, stuffed or in skeletal form. One case features two leopards growling fiercely, one with flesh hanging from its mouth, fighting over a dead baby deer. The two black panthers above them stare, astonished, at what must be the Second Coming of Christ. Also featured: Sun Bear giving a lecture, a model of a traditional wealthy house in Travancore (mid-pageant it seems, with Kathakali dancers—check out the skin color of the Brahmin denizens), and a collection of dolls wearing traditional costumes from all over India. (Open Tues. and Thurs.-Sun. 10am-5pm, Wed. 1-5pm.)

The **Science and Technology Museum** (make a left turn from M.G. Rd. onto Museum Rd.) "exhibits items highlighting Science, Technollogy, and electronics." (Open Tues.-Sun. 10am-5pm. Admission Rs.1.)

The **Chachu Nehru Children's Museum,** in the east part of the city known as Thycaud, contains ritual masks, stamps, and a wacky assortment of over 2000 dolls. (Open Mon.-Fri. 10am-5pm.)

A school at West Fort called **MARGI** often gives free **Kathakali dance drama** and **Kutiyattum theater** (Keralan martial art) performances in the evenings. Contact them to find out when these will be offered, or to see if it is possible to watch a class in progress. The school can be found by following M.G. Rd. south over the train tracks, turning right at the bright corner temple, walking 10 minutes into West Fort until the street comes to a final T, and turning right; MARGI is behind Fort High School. Look for a big banyan tree.

Trivandrum boasts 18 **movie theaters.** Check a paper to see what's showing.

The **KTDC Tourist Reception Centre** on Station Rd. offers sightseeing tours. A **Trivandrum Tour** covers Sri Padmanabha Swamy Temple, the zoo, Science & Technology Museum, Veli Lagoon, Shanghumugham Beach, and Kovalam Beach, where the main attraction is gaping at fellow Westerners in bikinis. The museums are closed on Mondays. (Tour leaves 8am, returns 7pm, Rs.70.) A **Kanyakumari** Tour visits Kovalam Beach, Padmanabhapuram Palace (closed Monday), Suchindram Temple, and Kanyakumari. (Leaves 7:30am, returns 9pm, Rs.150.) A **Thekkady Tour** goes to **Periyar Wild Life Sanctuary** loaded with honeymooners. (Leaves Saturday at 6:30am, returns Sunday at 9am, Rs.300, not including accommodation.) Several other tours are offered; contact the KTDC Reception Centre if you're actually interested in being loaded onto a bus full of tourists and herded around.

■ Kovalam

Since the arrival of hippie sun- and soul-searchers in the 1960s, the pounding of hammers and pouring of concrete has gone on in Kovalam all day and through the night. Kovalam is by far Kerala's most popular beach resort, also one of the most popular in India. Lacking Goa's psychedelic paintings and raves, the beach-front restaurants play Pink Floyd, Santana, and the Pixies. The strip of land fronting the beach has been completely consumed by hotels of all prices and descriptions, persistent female fruit-sellers charging exorbitant prices and looking heartrendingly downcast, hordes of children and men selling "bedsheet-anklet-cigarette," restaurants built illegally close to the beach (paying *baksheesh* to the monsoon sea for their position as it crashes on their doorstep), and robbers and thieves in the guise of tailors and handicraft sellers. This tourist village is edging rapidly back into the peaceful rice paddies and the huts of the locals.Traversed by local fishing boats, the bays of Kovalam are made of black sand and turquoise waters.

> **Warning:** The Western beach party in Kovalam has its dangers. The **undertow and ripcurrents** here can be very strong, so follow the warnings of the signs, flags, and gesturing lifeguards with whistles.
>
> To avoid negative attention, **women should not wear bikinis.** Baring of womanly flesh in public simply does not exist in Hindu culture, so women in swimsuits inevitably attract negative attention from slobbering gawkers and, more quietly, Hindus who are offended by this immodest display. Women might consider swimming in a *lungi,* or light pants and t-shirts to get more respect and avoid the attention.

ORIENTATION

Kovalam Beach is composed of three coves divided by rocky promontories. A mystical lighthouse sweeps the southernmost **Lighthouse Beach.** Here, **Lighthouse Road** leads down to the water and the budget hotels. The beach is lined with restaurants proudly blocking the walkway with tables covered in dead sea creatures. North of the rocky promontory is the crescent called **Eve's Beach.** Here are more hotels (mostly expensive), restaurants and busloads of Indian tourists looking for bare flesh.

A road leads up from the north part of Eve's Beach past several travel offices and more handicrafts and tailors to the **bus stand.** Buses for Trivandrum leave here frequently and several go daily to Alleppey, Quilon, Cochin, and Kanyakumari. Taking a right turn leads to **Kovalam Junction,** where a left turn brings you to the **post office** and **Central Bank.** Between the two main roads up from the beach (Lighthouse Rd. and the road to the bus stand) twisting paths lead to quieter restaurants and hotels and through the rice paddies and past the houses of the locals.

PRACTICAL INFORMATION

Tourist Office: Tourist Facilitation Centre. From the bus stand, follow the road up to the Kovalam Hotel; the tourist office is on the left. Run by the KTDC, the office has maps of Kovalam, general information about Kerala, makes hotel bookings all over India, and arranges tickets for the Quilon-Alleppey backwater tour

(Rs.150). A larger tourist office next door is expected to open sometime this year. Open in season daily 10am-5pm; off-season Mon.-Sat. 10am-5pm.

Budget Travel: Smartly catering to the flocks of international beach-goers who carpet the sand here, several travel offices are located on the beach and along the road to the bus stand. **Western Travels,** right next to the bus stand, is energetic and competent. Staff can confirm plane reservations for the price of the phone charge, make plane reservations, and make bus and train reservations (Rs.50 service charge). A taxi is available for hire. STD/ISD with call-back facility (Rs.5 per minute), faxes received (Rs.15 per page) and sent (Europe Rs.120 per page, U.S. Rs.140 per page). In season they organize **sightseeing tours** from Kovalam: backwater trips (7:30am-9pm, 6hr., Rs.550), Kanyakumari trips (Wed. and Sun. 9:30am-9pm, Rs.300), Periyar Wildlife Sanctuary visits (Fri. 7:30am-Sat. 9pm, Rs.600), Ponmudi Hill Station trips (Thurs. 9am-7pm, Rs.300), Trivandrum City tours (Tues. 10am-7pm, Rs.150; visits the Sri Padmanabhaswamy Temple, the museums, Veli Lagoon, Shangumugham beach, a handicrafts shop). Prices do not include food. Open daily 7am-midnight. MC/V.

Currency Exchange: In season, some shops on the beach will exchange money. **Pournami** on the road to Kovalam Junction about a 10-min. walk from the bus stand gives a good rate. Open daily 9am-4pm in off season, 9am-7pm during season. There is also a **Central Bank of India** at Kovalam Junction.

Telephones: The STD/ISD booths in Western Travel and Elite Travel (on the road up to the bus stand) can do call-backs (both **Rs.5** per minute).

Buses: Bus stand, at the top of the road up from the north end of Eve's Beach. To: Trivandrum (every 20-30min. from early morning until about 10pm, 30min., Rs.3.50); Quilon-Alleppey-Cochin (7am, in time to make the backwater tour leaving Quilon); Alleppey-Quilon (10:40am); Kanyakumari (9:30am, 4:15, and 6pm, 2½hr.); Nagercoil (10pm).

Local Transportation: Rickshaws and **taxis** hover at the bottom of Lighthouse Rd., the bus stand, and Kovalam Junction. Often rickshaw-*wallahs* can be talked down to Rs.30 to Trivandrum. Local buses also go to Trivandrum from the bus stand (every 20-30min., 30min., Rs.3.50).

English Bookstore: United Arts and Books is on the road that starts at Hotel Sea Rock and runs up the hill to the left. They have a wide selection of Tin-Tin books, a narrower selection of India-related books, and a small section of literature.

Pharmacy: to the left of Kovalam Junction. Open 8am-10pm.

Hospital: Apsana Hospital, on the road to Kovalam Junction about a 10-min. walk up from the bus stand, but it's probably better to go to Trivandrum.

Police: the station is on the road to Kovalam Junction, about a 10min. walk up from the bus station on the left. During season, the hideous **Tourist Aid Post** on the beach might be of some help.

Post Office: GPO, can be reached by taking a left at Kovalam Junction. *Poste Restante.* Open Mon.-Sat. 9am-1pm, 1:20-5pm. **Poste restante sent to Kovalam sometimes ends up at the Trivandrum GPO. Postal Code:** 695527. **Telephone Code:** 04723.

ACCOMMODATIONS

Nothing in Kovalam is more plentiful than places to stay. Hotels begin to make an appearance just beach-side of Kovalam Junction, and the beach is choked with them—wherever there is an open piece of ground another hotel is going up, and wherever there is one story, another is being built on top. The accommodations range from the 5-star cottages of the **Hotel Ashok** to tiny concrete rooms with no bathroom. Prices vary accordingly. In Kovalam, prices are highly flexible; prices are affected by the high season with its great influx of travelers, proximity to the beach, and whether you are carrying your luggage. Prices peak around December and January. During the monsoon (June and July) it's possible to get gorgeous accommodations for Rs.40-75 (attached bath, balcony, sea view), but high season brings prices up to Rs.800 for the same room. Negotiate. Proprietors are willing to bring rates down for longer stays. The rooms behind the **Sea Fish Restaurant** on Lighthouse Beach are nicely equipped (lightswitches over the bed) and clean. Upstairs rooms share a common balcony with sea view. Just before the beach, **Paradise Rock** on Lighthouse Rd. has comfortable rooms with all the accoutrements (including such extras as locking cabinets). **Moonlight Tourist Home** on the road leading up from Hotel Sea Rock has the distinction of providing mosquito nets hung from its four-poster beds (Rs.200 for a double in off-season, about twice that in season). A path leads back from the beach at the tacky Tourist Aid Post: back here, many good accommodations hide away from the fray. Back in the rice paddies, **Green Valley** is constructed in a style reminiscent of a Keralan palace. Next door and up a dizzying flight of steps, **Silent Valley** has beautiful rooms, some with coir carpet, sliding glass doors, and balconies with paddy-view. The rooms here cost Rs.100 in off-season, increasing to Rs.400 and more in season.

FOOD

The restaurants here line the beach; some are falling into the sea. Starting at Lighthouse Rd., the beach-side tables spread in an almost uninterrupted sweep all the way to the road to the bus stand (the strategy is probably to trap customers like fish). Most offer the standard faves of the Western traveler in Asia: omelettes, milkshakes, fried rice, noodles, curries, fresh fish, pancakes. The service is slow (who cares with the waves rolling endlessly in), the menus similar and the prices high. Some have nightly movies.

The **German bakery** has fresh pasta, muesli, an assortment of bread, and pastries (sometimes not too fresh) among other things. **Milky Way** makes good curries. **Santana** cooks lovely curries and plays Santana. **Garzia** has fresh pasta. Some restaurants are also back from the beach hidden among the hotels. A few local places lurk behind Simi Cottages and the German bakery; they serve quick cheap breakfasts (*paratha*, curry, *chai* Rs.12) and "meals" at lunchtime. The *thali* at **Hotel Sunshine** on the road to Kovalam Junction is tasty (Rs.15).

SIGHTS AND ENTERTAINMENT

If you're tired of watching the waves, jumping in the waves, and hearing the waves, many places offer **ayurvedic massage**. In season there are **yoga classes.** Pirated **movies** with abysmal sound show nightly at several restaurants. During high season, "cultural nights," often Kathakali, take place at the Hotel Ashok on Saturdays and Sundays. Admission to the programs is generally Rs.100.

The small ramshackle village of **Vizhinjam** (pronounced veer-in-yam) is a 20-min. walk south of Kovalam along the coast road. Formerly the capital of the Ay Kings, only ruins of some small shrines remain. Fishing boats, many brightly painted, fill the harbor as tightly packed as cars in a mall parking lot on Christmas Eve. The catch is spread on the beach and trucked away for export. The north end of the harbor is crowned by a vast Disney-esque **mosque.**

■ Varkala

The mists at Varkala come in off the sea, rolling in on the waves and rising, then clinging to the cliffs and the coconut leaves. Sometimes sinister, sometimes lovely, sometimes both, the mists are like the waves that crash onto the coast. The beach at Varkala is now becoming a popular destination for foreigners, as it has been for years with Indian tourists, pilgrims, and *sadhus* building sandshrines on the beach and along the walkway to the Janardharna Temple. Huts and houses line the red cliffs which look as though they could give in to the Arabian sea's constant lashing at any moment and tumble. The beach runs under the cliffs, backed by a boulder seawall. In season, thousands of tourists descend on Varkala every day and participate in full moon parties atop the cliffs.

ORIENTATION

Trains come into the village 2km from the beach. At the beach, **Beach Road** runs perpendicular to the coast. At **Temple Junction,** about 500m back from the beach, there is an auto-rickshaw stand, a 2000-year-old temple complex at the top of a long stairway (non-Hindus welcome), and another temple next to the tank filled by mineral springs where locals do washing and swimming. At the beach, a path climbs the hill to the right, revealing the cliffside restaurants and hotels. About a five-minute walk along the **cliff** top, someone saw fit to build a **helipad.** Along the beach a few minutes to the right from the end of Beach Rd. hide two black pipes channeling fresh water from mineral springs.

PRACTICAL INFORMATION

Currency Exchange: Federal Bank, in town. Open Mon.-Fri. 10am-2pm, Sat. 10am-noon. Several other banks in town will also exchange currency.

Telephones: STD/ISD booths are located in town, some at Temple Junction in season. Some will allow call-backs but may charge up to Rs.7 per min. There's a government-run booth at the train station.

Trains: From the railway station in town. To: Quilon (11 per day, 5:47am-10:30pm, 30min., Rs.13); Mangalore (6:44am and 6:28pm, 13hr., Rs.117); Bombay (11:15am, 46hr., Rs.238); Bangalore (11:15am, 18hr., Rs.148); Kottayam (3:50pm, 2hr., Rs.31); Ernakulam (8 per day, 5:47am-10:30pm, 4hr., Rs.47); Kanyakumari (11:05am and 2pm, 3hr.); Trivandrum (8 per day, 1hr., Rs.18); Madurai (6:30pm, 8hr., Rs.41).

Buses: From Temple Junction, buses run to Trivandrum periodically throughout the day starting at 6am.

Local Transportation: Buses depart from Temple Junction for the town center every 30min. **Auto-rickshaws** lurk at Temple Junction and at the train station. They will probably refuse to set their meters. From Temple Junction to town should cost about Rs.10, from town to the helipad about Rs.20-25.

Laundry: Near the helipad, a 3-hr. laundry service charges Rs.5 per piece whether pieces are saris or underwear.

Post Office: In town. Open Mon.-Fri. 9am-5pm, Sat.10am-2pm.

ACCOMMODATIONS AND FOOD

Since Varkala is an infant resort, sleeping and eating are happily not yet institutionalized. In town, there is at least one hotel near the train station. At Temple Junction, there are a few mediocre restaurants, one overlooking the tank. Along Beach Rd. from Temple Junction toward the beach, there are several guest houses. Across the rice paddies looms the new Overlord, the Taj's 5-star resort, as well as a few guest houses. By taking a rickshaw from the train station to the helipad, you can save yourself a sort of tricky trek across rice paddies and up a hill path with backpack. Up here, families rent rooms and many small guest houses are being built right near the cliff looking down on the crashing waves. Inquire with restaurant owners and locals since many places do not have signs. In monsoon season (June-July), prices are gloriously low, foreigners few, guest houses empty, many restaurants closed, and the sea too rough for swimming. Peace and quiet reign (no honking). Big clean rooms with attached baths go for as little as Rs.50. The prices begin to go up in August and by the time the droves arrive for high season in December and January, the same rooms fetch Rs.300 to 500. In season, huts cost Rs.50 to 100, and rooms with no fan and a common toilet go for about Rs.75—if you can find one. Otherwise, locals rent roofspace (they will store your things) for Rs.10 and the beach is always free.

Coconut-leaf huts line the cliff-front and serve all sorts of food: Continental, pasta, Indian, Chinese, chocolate pancakes, juice...

■ Alleppey (Alappuzha)

Two canals running through the center of Alleppey were once the heart of a great shipping center, but now only luscious tangles of waterplants survive. Buses crank up and down Boat Jetty Rd. in great clouds of exhaust, and some modern buildings have sprouted along the main commercial road (which seems to remain nameless). The bustle of the town is due mainly to the amount of coir products being shipped through here to Cochin, often on small boats propelled by pole. Several snakeboat races, especially the Nehru Trophy Boat Race on the second Saturday of August, attract attention and international tourists. The international set also comes for the famous backwater tours, a chance to see the way many Keralans still live: fishing and washing in the great green canals, taking a living from rice paddies or coconut farming.

ORIENTATION

The village is sandwiched between two canals running from east to west: the **North Canal** and the **South Canal,** only about five to 10 minutes' apart. Between the two canals, the streets are fairly grid-like. The **KSRTC bus station** is at the east end of **Boat Jetty Road** (which runs along the southern bank of the north canal). A little to the west, on the southern bank of the north canal, is the **Tourist Information Centre.** Most public and private boats depart from the jetties near here.

The cross-street which has a bridge over the North Canal is **Mullakal Road.** To the north over the canal it leads to the fruit and vegetable **market.** Immediately after crossing the canal, take a right and then a left to reach the new office of the **Alleppey Tourism Development Cooperative (ATDC)** (formerly in the Karthika Tourist Home). The next cross-street to the west (nameless) features a footbridge over the north canal; to the south the street leads to several landmarks: the south canal and on the left corner the **Central Telegraph Office,** and, a few buildings down, the **Indian Overseas Bank** is on the first floor.

PRACTICAL INFORMATION

Tourist Office: Alleppey Tourism Development Cooperative (ATDC) (tel. 243462; fax 63572). Follow Mullakal Rd. north over the North Canal, turn right immediately, take the first left, the ATDC is on the left. A group of amiable, talkative guys offers services in cooperation with several private companies in Alleppey. **Tourist Information Centre** (tel. 62308), run by the District Tourism Promotion Council (DTPC) of Kerala, near the KSRTC bus stand, on Boat Jetty Rd., on the south bank of the North Canal. This state-government office offers nearly identical cruises. Open Mon.-Sat. 9:30am-7:30pm, closed 2nd Sat. each month. For more information, see **Backwater Cruises** (p. 512).

Currency Exchange: Indian Overseas Bank, from Boat Jetty Rd., follow the unnamed road with the footbridge south to the South Canal, turn left before crossing it, keep an eye out on the left for the signs of the bank. They accept only American Express and Thomas Cook traveler's checks in U.S. dollars and pounds sterling and seem to have some funny rules about which amounts they will change. If they are too unaccommodating, take a rickshaw to the main branch of the **State Bank of India,** a few kilometers away near the beach. Bank hours Mon.-Fri. 10am-2pm, Sat. 10am-noon.

Telephones: STD/ISD booths are located throughout the village. The **Telegraph Office** is on the corner of CCNB Rd. (which runs along the north bank of the South Canal) and Footbridge Rd.

Trains: the **Railway Station** is several kilometers outside the village near the beach. To: Quilon (*Guruvayar-Nagercoil Exp.* 6305, 12:50am, and *Ernakulam-Trivandrum Exp.* 6341, 7:40am, 2hr., Rs.30); Trivandrum (*Guruvayar-Nagercoil Exp.* 6305, 12:50am, *Ernakulam-Trivandrum Exp.* 6341, 7:40am, 3hr., Rs.38); Ernakulam (8 per day, 6 am-12:55am, 1-1½ hr., passenger Rs.9, express Rs.20).

Buses: KSRTC Bus Stand, east end of Boat Jetty Rd. To: Cochin (every 20min., 1½hr., Rs.15); Kottayam (10 per day, 7am-9pm, 1hr., Rs.12); Trivandrum (every

15min., 8am-8pm, also 2:15, 4:30, 6, 6:55, and 7:45am, 3½hr., Rs.39); Quilon (same as to Trivandrum, 2hr., Rs.21). Prices for Super Fast Green Express buses are "more costly." Tickets must be purchased on the bus, no coupons or reservations available. **Private buses** run for long-distance destinations: **Asha Travels** is on Boat Jetty Rd., in a shopping complex set back from the road between the footbridge and the traffic bridge. To: Coimbatore (11pm, 5½hr., Rs.90); Bangalore (6pm, 12hr., Rs.200); Bombay (6pm, 34hr., Rs.550); Mangalore (7 pm, 10hr., Rs.200).

Local Transportation: Most of Alleppey is traversed easily by foot. **Auto-rickshaws** are available from many stands.

Market: fruit and vegetable stands line busy Mullakal Rd. north of the North Canal.

Pharmacy: Inside the gates of **Medical College Hospital** (see below) there is a 24-hr. pharmacy.

Hospital: Medical College Hospital, from Boat Jetty Rd., south on Mullakal Rd. for 1km, turn left just past Palace Rd. It's on the left.

Post Office: A **branch post office** is located mysteriously at a dead end most easily reached by following Mullakal Rd. south from Boat Jetty Rd., taking the first right, and looking on the right for a small building behind a wall (ask for directions). Open Mon.-Sat. 9:30am-5:30pm. The **Head Post Office** has *Poste Restante* (although it may be hard to find someone who knows what it is). Follow Mullakal Rd. south from the North Canal, turn right on Collan Rd., walk until crossing over a canal, turn left, the HPO is huge on the right. Stamps available Mon.-Sat. 8am-5:30pm, parcels Mon.-Sat. 9:30am-2:30pm. **Postal Code:** 688007.

Telephone Code: 0477.

ACCOMMODATIONS

Alleppey isn't full of grandiose palace hotels, so grit your teeth and settle down. Most accommodations are centrally located between the canals or just north of them, within a 10-minute walk from the bus stand.

Komala Hotel (tel. 36131). Cross the North Canal to the north bank on the Mullakal Rd. traffic-footbridge, turn right, then left, and you will see the Komala Hotel on the right. A poster of Sai Baba blesses the downstairs hall with outstretched hands, and the first floor hall is filled with castoff furniture in various states of repair. Sweet lace curtains hang over the entrance to each big good-smelling (a miracle attributable to Sai Baba's blessing?) room, provided with topsheet and blanket and attached bath with glowing white tiles. The hotel also has a restaurant (open daily 7:30am-10pm) and bar. Lunch *thalis* Rs.20. Singles Rs.70. Doubles Rs.100. Triples Rs.140.

Karthika Tourist Home (tel. 245524). Follow Mullakal Rd. north over the North Canal traffic bridge, soon a sign for the hotel points off to the right. Freshly painted blue, the pretty building is set back from the road in a pleasant courtyard. By another miracle, the bathrooms smell good (although there may be cobwebs in the corners)—otherwise the rooms are quite immaculate). Attached baths available. Singles Rs.60. Doubles Rs.120.

Kuttanad Tourist Home (tel. 251354), conveniently near the KSRTC Bus Station. Walk down Boat Jetty Rd. parallel to the North Canal; it's almost immediately on the right. The massive building is institutional, but the rooms are big and the furniture is welcoming. Indian men seem to enjoy hanging out in the hallways. The Galilia is a pleasant rooftop restaurant and bar open 9am-11pm serving Chinese food (ginger chicken Rs.30) and Indian food (*alu mutter* Rs.16) and some Continental selections. Singles Rs.60. Doubles Rs.100. Triples Rs.150.

Alleppey Prince Hotel (tel. 243752) a few kilometers from the KSRTC Bus Station—the best way to get here is by rickshaw. Semi-luxury at a semi-affordable price. The lobby of the centrally air-conditioned Alleppey Prince Hotel is filled with antiques, lounging leopard statues, and a pricey giftshop (they will bargain). The swimming pool is almost big enough for laps. The rooms are large and air-conditioned, with table and chairs, cabinet and Star TV. The very good cheery poolside Vembanad Restaurant serves South Indian and continental breakfast, a gor-

Keralan Homebrews

The stark black-and-white roadside signs advertising "TODDY" point to toddy bars where sap from coconut trees is bottled, fermented overnight, and served. Those who tap the trees are "toddy-tappers" and often belong to powerful unions. A stronger form of the beverage, arrack, was banned midway through 1996 since even a small error in the brewing process can result in lethal wood alcohol.

geous lunchtime meal complete with Keralan sweets (Rs.40) and delicious Chinese and Indian dishes. Singles Rs.500. Doubles Rs.600.

FOOD

KTDC Restaurant, next to the Tourist Information Centre on Boat Jetty Rd. With the canal just below the windows, the restaurant seems almost like a floating boat. Serving Western and South Indian food and ice cream, the restaurant has a good "Kerala Meals Lunch." Veg. meal Rs.14, non-veg. meal Rs.20. Open 7-11am and noon-10pm.

Indian Coffee House has 2 branches in Alleppey: one on Mullakal Rd. a few blocks south of the North Canal on the west side of the street; another near the hospital on the north-south-running road, just south of the junction with Palace Rd. The waiters in immaculate whites and turbans bring a limited and cheap menu. *Masala dosa* Rs.6, meals Rs.10.

SIGHTS AND ENTERTAINMENT

The green backwaters which bring Alleppey a living as a passage for shipping coir rake in the international tourist dollars, too. The annual **Nehru Trophy Boat Race** is held on the second Saturday of August in the lake to the east of town. The Snake Boats, traditional battle vessels of Kerala, 60 to 65 meters long, are maneuvered by hundreds of oarsmen. Chants, beating drums, and cymbals accompany the end of the race. The first race was held "impromptu" in 1952, in the honor of Prime Minister Jawaharlal Nehru, who was so fascinated he donated a trophy to the winners. Tickets are available from the Tourist Information Centre and range from the crowded lawn at Rs.10 to the Rose Corner on an island at Rs.150 to the Tourist Pavilion at Rs.250.

Other snakeboat races are held during the year, among them the **Moolam Boat Race** a few kilometers away at Champakulam at the end of June. The ATDC arranges backwater boats there and back for Rs.100.

The **beach** is a few kilometers west of the town center, but it's not particularly stunning. A **lighthouse** is near the beach, by the south canal.

There is a **cinema** in town, reached by going south from Boat Jetty Rd. on the frustratingly nameless road with the footbridge over the North Canal. It's on the left.

BACKWATER CRUISES

For most of the year, daily backwater cruises run the green canals between **Alleppey and Quilon.** During off-season (the monsoon) in June and August, these trips are cancelled unless there happen to be four or five people interested on any particular day. The ATDC (private) and DTPC (government) both sponsor trips leaving Alleppey at 10:30am and arriving in Quilon at 6:30pm. Arrive at either office before 10am. Each trip makes several stops: the ATDC stops at an 11th-century statue of Buddha, a temple where a "great Malayalam poet met with a traggic death by drawning," a coir village, a swimming hole, an ashram, and a lunch break with a traditional Keralan meal on a banana leaf. Both the ATDC and DTPC offer one-way trips for Rs.150, although the DTPC says prices may go up. The ATDC arranges shorter trips on both motorized boats (Rs.150 per hour) and big paddle-powered country boats, as well as stays on traditional shipping boats converted into houseboats with tiny bedroom, bathroom, and dining area, and two guys to pole the boat around (Rs.3500 for 2 people for a day and night stay, food is extra). The DTPC also has houseboats at Rs.3000 including a cook, or the boats can be rented for Rs.600 per hour.

■ Periyar Wildlife Sanctuary

The legendary and much sought-after tiger and leopard reside in Periyar Wildlife Sanctuary, but after being hunted to the brink of extinction, they are not likely to emerge from their large habitats inside the 777-square-kilometer park for the gratification of human visitors. Periyar is a place to relax or start short treks, not a place to see tigers. Walking inside the park without an official guide is prohibited, for this is a wildlife sanctuary as well as home to beasts with massive fangs. Situated in lofty woodlands (750-1500m) interspersed with grasslands on the border of Tamil Nadu, the park is home to wild elephants, pigs, many species of birds, antelopes, sambar, monkeys, Malabar flying squirrels, and a 26-square-kilometer lake created by the British in 1895 to supply water to desiccated parts of Tamil Nadu. The sanctuary became a wildlife preserve in 1933 and was incorporated in Project Tiger (see p. 178) in 1979.

Necessary for a visit are a flashlight, some warm clothes for the chilly nights, and rain gear (it rains almost every afternoon). Right smack on the border with Tamil Nadu, the town of **Kumily** offers budget accommodation, loads of spice and handicraft shops, families with spare rooms to rent, and good cheap South Indian eats (J.J.'s has the best *parathas*). Four kilometers away, inside the park, the village of **Thekkady** is composed of more expensive hotels and restaurants (*chai* may cost as much as Rs.15). Right on the artificial lakeshore, Thekkady is the starting point for government and private cruises around the lake. If any animal shows its fuzzy head, everyone rises and shouts above the monstrous motor noise. The two-hour government trips cost Rs.25 for the lower deck, Rs.50 for the upper deck. The earliest (7am) and latest (4pm) trips are best: you don't roast and neither do the animals, who are more likely to come out to drink at these times.

Jungle walks are given by sanctuary guides. A three-hour walk departs from Thekkady at 7am every morning. Guides can also be hired at the **Wildlife Information Centre** near the boat jetty at Thekkady.

Probably the best way to glimpse the park's elusive beasties is to spend a night in one of the park's three **observation towers.** These vary in position from rather close to Thekkady to deep in the core area. They may be booked weeks in advance, and theoretically cost only Rs.50 per night, but the drop-off charges are upwards of Rs.150. Some guests wake to find leeches that have already had a lovely breakfast.

Buses stop at the edge of Kumily and in Thekkady. They come and go several times each day, connecting the park to Ernakulam (about a 6-hr. trip), the most popular point for traveling to the park. Many of these buses also stop in Kottayam. The beautiful bus ride through the Western Ghats is bumpy and winding enough to throw passengers to the floor. Buses also go to the hill stations of Munnar and Kodaikanal (each about 6hr. away) and daily to Trivandrum, Madurai, and Kovalam. **Local transportation** consists of the **buses** that run at least a few times a day between Kumily and Thekkady. **Auto-rickshaws** can be hailed to putt between the two. At several of the larger hotels, **bicycles** are available for hire.

■ Quilon (Kollam)

The appellation Quilon is giving way to the ancient name of the town, Kollam (Koy-LAM). Called Kaulam Mall by ancient Arabs, and Coilum by Marco Polo in the thirteenth century, the port once had great palaces and it was said that "he who has seen Kollam does not go back home." The 14th-century Moroccan traveler Ibn Battuta listed it as "one of the five chief ports seen in his twenty-four years of wanderlust." The Portuguese and the British used it as a commercial port. Quilon was "the centre of the heroic rebellion led by Veluthambi Dalava against the British rule." Little of this glory is visible in Quilon today. It is still an active industrial town and exporter of coconut, but a modern shopping mall and modern storefronts have obliterated both the ancient palaces and most of the village streets. People ask, "Where you are going? Alleppey? Varkala? Cochin?" since most foreigners stay only overnight, usually in conjunction with the infamous backwater tours to and from Alleppey.

ORIENTATION

The strange angles of the streets follow the bends of the canals. Navigation can be a little confusing, but some landmark will soon pop up. A main road crooks through town from the Railway Station northwest to the **Clock Tower** at the intersection with **Tourist Bungalow Road** (which leads northeast across the canal toward the famous Tourist Bungalow). The main road continues twistily (in an overwhelmingly northeast direction) past the **Post Office,** the sprawling **Bishop Jerome Nagar Shopping Centre,** then past the wild **Shrine of Our Lady of Velamkanni.** The next junction is with a road which leads to the right to the **KSRTC bus station** and the **ferry jetty.** To the left, this road goes past the **hospital** and then after about a 10-minute walk to the sprawling **fruit and vegetable market,** housed in small red-tile-roofed stores.

PRACTICAL INFORMATION

Tourist Office: Outposts of the **District Tourism Promotion Council (DTPC)** are located at the railway station and the bus station. They can book backwater tours, make hotel reservations, and perform all sorts of other feats for the weary tourist. Open Mon.-Sat. 8am-5:30pm.

Currency Exchange: PL Worldways (tel. 741096; fax 744823). From the gates of the post office, turn right onto the main road, take an immediate sharp right, it will be on the right. Accepts all brands of traveler's checks in all currencies, or such is their grand claim. Also books airline reservations as well as confirms airline tickets (for about Rs.25, or free if you are using any other service). AmEx cards accepted. Open Mon.-Sat. 9am-5:30pm, Sun. 9am-1:30pm.

Telephones: STD/ISD booths are a little difficult to find, and finding one with call-backs or collect call facilities is probably impossible. The **Telegraph Office** is on Tourist Bungalow Rd. (follow the main road southeast from the post office, take a sharp left at the massive intersection).

Trains: The **railway station** is on the main road southeast of the junction with Tourist Bungalow Rd.; take the flyover. To: Trivandrum (express 7:30 and 8:55am, 9 regular per day, 6:35am-8:30pm, 1½hr., Rs.21/90 for 2nd/1st class); Varkala (express 7:30am, 9 regular per day, 6:35am-8:30pm, 30min., Rs.13/65 for 2nd/1st class); Alleppey (5:50pm, 1½hr., Rs.25); Ernakulam (11 per day, 6:20am-11:15pm, 3½hr., Rs.42/168 for 2nd/1st class); Bombay (9am, 36hr., Rs.238/1152 for 2nd/1st class); Madras (2:30pm, 16hr., Rs.150/609 for 2nd/1st class); Bangalore (noon, Rs.144/608 for 2nd/1st class).

Buses: KRSTC bus station, follow the main road past the Shrine of Our Lady of Velamkanni, turn right at the big intersection, follow it down the hill toward the river and the boat jetty. To: Trivandrum (every 10-30min., 2hr., Rs.16); Varkala (9 per day, 5:30am-8pm, 1hr., Rs.7.50); Alleppey (every 20min., 2hr., Rs.21); Ernakulam (every 20 min., 3½hr., Rs.36).

Local Transportation: Local **ferries** depart from the **boat jetty,** crossing the canal every hour or so and running local routes. **Auto-rickshaws** are easy to find.

Market: a fruit and vegetable market district occupies a few blocks of the road that leads from the boat jetty into town (about a 15-min. walk from the boat jetty).

Hospital: On the road from the boat jetty into town, past the junction with the main road, on the left.

Post Office: Head Post Office, on the main road through town, northeast of the intersection with Tourist Bungalow Rd. on the left. *Poste Restante* is available from some mysterious corner.

ACCOMMODATIONS

The Tourist Bungalow, a few kilometers outside of town along Tourist Bungalow Rd., then left, then some confusing curving roads (take a rickshaw). In a beautiful old British mansion with a huge empty ballroom and enormous balconies occupied only by pigeons, the few rooms have 10m ceilings, antique furniture, and are large enough to hold waltzes. Almost always full (it even fills up during off-season) and reservations aren't possible. It's a steal. Singles Rs.50. Doubles Rs.60.

Yatri Nivas (tel. 78638), directly across the river from the boat jetty—if you phone from the boat jetty, they will come pick you up in the speedboat; or, take a rickshaw the long way around Tourist Bungalow Rd., then left. The large rooms are clean and have balconies which overlook the river and the village on the other side, with beautiful views of hunting wheeling birds. A restaurant and beer parlor operate in season, and loads of Indian men are likely to be attending a conference on tires in the meeting hall. All rooms have attached baths. Singles Rs.100. Doubles Rs.150. Extra person Rs.50.

Hotel Sea Bee (tel. 75371), on the main road near the intersection with the road to the boat jetty, across from the Shrine of Our Lady of Velamkanni. The marble lobby is classy, and so is everything else except the smudgy green paint in the rooms, which are big and have soft mattresses and clean sheets. The hotel has a restaurant, an "air-conditioned butterfly bar to send your spirits high," and an "eskimo shopee to satisfy your odds and ends." Singles Rs.130. Doubles Rs.180. Extra bed Rs.40.

Mahalekshmi Lodge (tel. 794440), across from the KSRTC bus station. This is definitely a bottom-of-the-line place with the right price. The walls are bright orange, the mattresses khaki and a little lumpy and thin, but everything is passably clean, even the common toilet and bath. Singles Rs.40. Doubles Rs.60.

FOOD

Jala Subhiksha, next to the boat jetty, is a floating restaurant in a lovely "traditional kettuvallam" (boat). A descriptive menu card of deliciously gorgeous Chinese and Indian dishes: saiwoo chicken Rs.55, Manchurian tofu Rs.45 (but don't be surprised if the tofu bears a resemblance to *paneer*). Open daily 6pm-10pm.

Indian Coffee House, from the post office, turn right onto the main road, then take the second right. It will be on the right set back a little from the street through a passageway. The service may be a bit slow, and the limited menu of South Indian and Western food dependably mediocre, but you can count on the waiters in white turbans. Ladies-and-families rooms provided.

Supreme Bakers, from the post office turn right onto the main road, then take an immediate right, it will be on the left. Fresh cakes and breads are available Mon.-Sat. 9am-8pm.

SIGHTS

The tall temple-esque **Shrine of Our Lady of Velamkanni** rises up above everything on the main road near the road that leads to the jetty.

The **market** area of town retains an old flavor and calm. Narrow streets pass between buildings roofed in red tile and fruits and vegetables stacked for perusal.

About 3km out of town in **Thankassery** is a lighthouse and the last skeletal ruins of a Portuguese fort and a British burial ground—the tombs have been absorbed into people's backyards and used as storage sheds. Brightly painted fishing boats are lined up all along the beach here, and loads of perfect shells lie on the sand.

BACKWATER CRUISES

The main attraction is, of course, the backwater tour to Alleppey. Run by the District Tourism Promotion Council (DTPC), tours leave at 10:30am from the DTPC office near the KSRTC bus stand and the boat jetty, arriving in Alleppey at 6:30pm. The reporting time is before 10am. The tour halts at an ashram for lunch, at the "death place of renowned Malayalam poet Kumaranasan," and at a statue of Buddha. The tour costs Rs.150. For more information, see **Alleppey: Backwater Cruises,** p. 512.

■ Cochin (Kochi) and Ernakulam

"Cochin" refers to an area encompassing the modern commercial city of Ernakulam, the peninsula of Fort Cochin and Mattancherry, VypeenIsland, and the smaller Willingdon, Vallarpadam, Gundy, and Bolghatty Islands, all arranged like petals around Vembanad Lake along the coast of Kerala. Cochin traces its history back to humble origins as a fishing village, but its identity was completely transformed in 1341 when torrential floods tore down from the Western Ghats and scoured out its perfect harbor—deep, safe, and internationally accommodating. Over the next centuries, the quiet fishing village became a wealthy port, attracting the attention of more rulers than Cochin's inhabitants might have liked. Chinese, Arab, Portuguese, Dutch, and British seafarers traded in Cochin. The first European settlement in India was established in Cochin in 1500 by the Portuguese, under the navigator Pedro Alavares Cabral. The first European fort in India followed in 1503. The raja of Cochin, in velvet garb stitched with silver thread, retained his status with the protection of the Portuguese, and continued to be borne through the streets in an ivory palanquin. The Dutch took control of Cochin in 1663, and renovated the raja's palace for him. Great prosperity came with Dutch influence, their export ships filled with fragrant spices, fragrant sailors, coconuts, and coir (coconut fiber). Cochin's Hindu majority, its Muslims and Syriac Christians, its Jewish community (which traces its roots in India back to the Diaspora), and its European newcomers all enjoyed its abundance. Britain got in on the action and began ruling Cochin in 1795. Accompanied by leaping dolphins, boats of all descriptions (from massive military ships and transport freighters to local, canoe-like double-bowed fishing boats) enter the harbor mouth of Lake Vembanad from the Arabian Sea to the west, passing between the peninsula tipped by Fort Cochin and Vypeen Island.

ORIENTATION

Set along the eastern shore of Lake Vembanad, **Ernakulam** is the modern commercial sector of Cochin. Since the central train and bus stations are in Ernakulam, the city functions as a gateway for travelers. Ernakulam's three main streets run north-south parallel to the shore. **Mahatma Gandhi (M.G.) Road** is the "middle" street and the city's main drag. The western (shoreside) parallel is **Park Ave.** (which splits at its northern end into **Shanmugham Road** and **Broadway**). The eastern (inland) parallel is **Chittoor Road.** M.G. Rd. is divided into three areas corresponding to its three main circles, called junctions, each with cross-streets leading to the lake shore. The northernmost, **Padma Junction,** is crossed by **Jews Street.** From the middle junction, **Shenoys Junction, Amman Kovil Road** leads east to the central bus station. About three long blocks south of Shenoys Junction, running east-west between M.G. Rd. and Park Ave. is **Hospital Road.** South of this is **Jos Junction,** crossed by **Durbar Hall (D.H.) Road** Taking Durbar Hall Rd. from Jos Junction towards the shore is the most efficient path to **Foreshore Road.**

Peaceful, romantically otherworldly, and chock full of historic sites, the Fort Cochin and Mattancherry **peninsula** offers a rest from Ernakulam. In **Fort Cochin,** at the tip of the peninsula, **Princess Street** is the main drag. Follow Princess St. northeast to the end of its first block and take a left to reach the **shore,** skirted by **Calvathy Road.** To reach **Mattancherry,** follow Princess St. southwest and take a left onto **Bastian St.,** continuing along this road until it terminates, then turning right. It's a 30- to 45-minute walk. This area is known as **Jew Town.** Following the street in a coiling U-turn, you'll reach the **synagogue** at the dead end.

By the early 20th century, Cochin harbor had grown noticeably shallow (filling with silt), and a monstrous dredging project created **Willingdon Island,** sandwiched between Ernakulam and the Fort Cochin/Mattancherry peninsula. Along with the airport, shipping warehouses have filled most of the available space on the island, and garishly painted trucks roar along with cargo, exclaiming DON'T KISS ME from their tailgates. Although a few luxury hotels have been set up, there are very few shops,

Cochin and Ernakulam

SOUTH INDIA

ERNAKULAM

Kaloor Bus Stand
Elamkulam Rd.
TO TRIVANDRUM
Single Lane Rd.
K.P. Vallon Rd.
KSRTC Bus Stand
Ernakulam Junction Railway Station
See India Foundation
Cochin Cultural Center
Parambhihara Rd.
Ernakulam Town Railway Station
Veekshanam Rd.
Amman Kovil Rd.
Chittoor Rd.
Ernakulam South Bus Stand
Jos. Junction
Buses to Fort Cochin
Manikath Rd.
Mahatma Gandhi Rd.
Gopalaprabhu Rd.
Banerji Rd.
T.D. Rd.
Market Rd.
Jews St.
GPO
Hospital Rd.
Durbar Hall Rd.
Post Office
Church Landing Rd.
Medical Trust Hospital
Broadway
Post Office
Park Ave.
Foreshore Rd.
Shanmugham Rd.
Police Commissioner's Office
Marine Dr. Walkway
Main Jetty
Tourist Desk
Indian Airlines
Mathai Manjooran Rd.
High Court Jetties
GCDA Shopping Centre
State Bank of India
KTDC Tourist Reception Center

Vembanad Lake

Bolghatty Island
Willingdon Island
TO AIRPORT
Cochin Harbour Railway Station
Brislow Rd.
Terminus Jetty
Embarkation Jetty
Milne Rd.
Malabar Hotel Jetty
Indira Gandhi Rd.
(i) TDC
Customs Jetty
Mattancherry Jetty

Arabian Sea

Gundu Island
Vypeen Island
Vypeen Island Jetty
Fort Cochin Bus Stand
Police
Calvathy Rd.
South Indian Bank
Bazaar Rd.
Fosse Rd.
Police
Dutch Palace
Synagogue
Moulana Azad Rd.

FORT COCHIN

Princess St.
Head Post Office
St. Francis Church
Dutch Cemetery
Santa Cruz Basilica
Napier St.
Calvathy St.
Padinara Mosque
Sri Gopalakrishna Temple Ave.
Jain Temple
Nehru Memorial Town Hall
Town Hall Rd.

MATTANCHERRY

Beach Rd.

restaurants, or activities here, and the island is without much character. The **Taj Malabar Hotel** sits at the northern tip of the island, with a 270° view of the harbor. The **airport** is also located on Willingdon Island, 2km south of the Cochin Harbour Railway Station.

PRACTICAL INFORMATION

Tourist Office: Tourist Desk (tel. 371761), in Ernakulam, in the dockside ticket office at the main jetty. Brimming with pamphlets, booklets, festival calendars, the staff will bend over backwards to answer questions. Outside the Tourist Desk during season is a news board for cultural events and dance performances. Open daily 9am-6pm. For information on their **Backwater Cruises,** see p. 526. **KTDC Tourist Reception Centre** (tel. 353234), Shanmugham Rd., Ernakulam, next to the State Bank of India. If challenged to a workout these guys would run out of energy long before their Tourist Desk competitors. But in addition to backwater tours (see p. 526), they offer waterfall tours to Atirappally/Vazachal (Rs.100), a Cochin museum tour (Rs.100), a ferry tour of various islands (Rs.50), and a sunset tour (Rs.30). **IDTC,** Willingdon Island, next to the Taj Malabar Hotel.

Immigration Office: Visa extensions are issued at the **Police Commissioner's Office,** in Ernakulam on Banerji Rd., east of the High Court Jetty, on the corner of Shanmugham Rd., on the left. Visa extensions may take up to 10 days; it may be necessary to leave your passport for the duration but a photocopy may suffice. Some visas cannot be extended. Open Mon.-Sat. 10:15am-1:15pm and 2-5:30pm. Closed holidays and second Sat. of each month.

Currency Exchange: In Ernakulam, the **State Bank of India,** Shanmugham Rd., 2 blocks north of the main jetty. Will only exchange Thomas Cook or AmEx traveler's checks and currency in U.S. dollars or pounds sterling. Open Mon.-Fri. 10am-2pm, Sat. 10am-noon. In Fort Cochin, **South Indian Bank** (tel. 226824), reached by going south on Princess St., then turning left at Elite Travels; after a few blocks the bank is on the right. Supposedly all brands of traveler's checks accepted. Ask for a receipt. Open Mon.-Fri. 10am-2pm, Sat. 10am-noon.

Airport: At the south end of Willingdon Island. Buses stop at the airport entrance (from Fort Cochin, take an Ernakulam-bound bus from the bus stand; from Ernakulam take a Fort Cochin-bound bus). A long line of taxis and rickshaws waits in the airport driveway. Remember when getting to the airport from Fort Cochin that taxis are extinct in the area (but can be arranged), and auto-rickshaws are scarce. **Indian Airlines** office is in Ernakulam, on Durbar Hall Rd. near the Park Ave. intersection. Open daily 10am-1pm and 1:45-5pm. To: Agatti (Mon. and Fri., 1½hr., US$150); Bangalore (Tues.-Sun., 1hr., US$57); Bombay (3 per day, 2hr., US$128); Delhi (1 per day, 4hr., US$256); Madras (1-2 per day, 1-2hr., US$84).

Trains: Cochin has 3 stations. **Ernakulam Junction Railway Station** is at the east end of D.H. Rd. (the cross-street at Jos Junction). Four kilometers north up the tracks, in the northeast corner of town, is the **Ernakulam Town Railway Station**—quite a distance from M.G. Rd. along Banerji Rd. There's little reason to use this station, as the other is very central to Ernakulam. **Cochin Harbour Railway Station** is on Willingdon Island. Few trains service the station. From Ernakulam Junction to: Trivandrum (8 per day, 12:50am-11:55pm, 4½hr., Rs.56/226 for 2nd/1st class); Alleppey (10 per day, 1:37am-11:35pm, 1hr.15min., Rs.90 for 1st class); Mangalore (11am, 10:55pm, 11hr., Rs.90/372 for 2nd/1st class); Bombay (*Kanyakumari Exp.* 1082, 12:55pm, 40hr., Rs.227/1081 for 2nd/1st class). From Ernakulam Town to: Calicut (*Parsuram Exp.* 6349, 11am, 4½hr., Rs. 48/197 for 2nd/1st class); Bangalore (*Bangalore Exp.* 6525, 3:47pm, 12hr.45min., Rs.124/511). When the Konkan Railway is completed, trains will run directly to Goa and Bombay.

Buses: The **KSRTC Bus Stand** is central to Ernakulam, east of M.G. Rd. at the end of Amman Kovil Rd. To: Calicut (every hr., 5hr., Rs.60); Trivandrum (over 50 per day, 4½hr., Rs.65); Alleppey (every 30min., 1½hr., Rs.20); Bangalore (8 per day, 5:30am-9:15pm, 13hr., Rs.154) via Mysore (10 hr., Rs.120); Coimbatore (15 per day, 2:30am-10:30pm, 4½hr., Rs.50); Madras (3:30pm, 17hr., Rs.159). **Private bus companies** also run long-distance buses from Cochin. Several agencies, including **Indira Travels** (tel. 360693), have offices near Jos Junction in Ernakulam. Many of these buses depart from the Ernakulam South Bus Stand. To: Madras (4:30 and

8:30pm, Rs.200); Bangalore (5:30, 6, 6:15, 6:30, and 7:30pm, 15hr., Rs.170); Coimbatore (8 per day, 7am-11:15pm, Rs.170). **Elite Travels,** on Princess St. in Fort Cochin, can arrange tickets for buses to Mangalore (8:30pm, Rs.200 for A/C); Bangalore (6pm, 15hr., Rs.170); Madras (8:30pm, 17hr., Rs.200); and Coimbatore (6:30pm, 4½hr., Rs.170). These depart from Jos Junction in Ernakulam.

Local Transportation: Ernakulam, the Fort Cochin-Mattancherry peninsula, and the islands are well-connected by bus and ferry, so getting around should never be a problem. All **ferry** commutes cost under Rs.2. There is a ferry lull around lunchtime, and you may have to wait up to 90min. From Ernakulam's **Main Jetty** (midtown) ferries course to Willingdon Island and to Fort Cochin (every 30min., 6am-9pm or 10pm). Buy tickets at the SWTD counter to avoid double charge. From Ernakulam's **High Court Jetty** they ply to Vypeen Island (every 20min., 5:30am-10pm), and to and from Bolghatty Island (every 10min., 5:30am-10pm). From Fort Cochin's **Customs Jetty** ferries are off to Willingdon Island's Terminus and Malabar Hotel Jetties (except Sun.), and on to Ernakulam (main jetty) (every 30min., 6:20am-6:30pm). From Fort Cochin's **Vypeen Island Jetty** (across from the local bus stand) ferries depart to Vypeen Island (every 20min., 6am-10pm). In Mattancherry, the jetty for ferries to Willingdon Island is across from the Dutch Palace. From Willingdon Island's **Embarkation Jetty** (northeast side) ferries depart for Vypeen Island (every 20min., 5:40am-10:40pm), and to Ernakulam (every 15min., 6:10am-9:20pm and 10:20pm). From Willingdon Island's **Terminus Jetty** (southwest side) ferries cast off for Fort Cochin and Mattancherry (every 30min., 6:20am-6:30pm; less frequently 11am-2pm). Ferries depart from Vypeen Island to Fort Cochin (every 20min., 6am-10pm), and also fend for Willingdon Island's Embarkation Jetty and Ernakulam's High Court Jetty. Red local **buses** honk and weave their routes in clouds of black exhaust—hop in for under Rs.2. In Kerala, some seats are reserved for women, a rule resented by the men, but enforced by the women. Around Ernakulam, local buses depart frequently from the KRSTC bus station or can easily be nabbed as they pass through town. The 3 major stops in Ernakulam are Pallymukku (pronounced "polly-muck") in the southern part of town, Jos Junction (central), and near High Court Jetty (northern). **Buses to Fort Cochin** depart from the east side of M.G. Rd. south of Jos Junction, to cross over on the bridges south of town. In Fort Cochin, local buses run from the bus stand across from the Vypeen Island ferry landing. Their usual route runs south, across the bridge onto Willingdon Island, past the airport, across the bridge to Ernakulam, and up M.G. Rd. (and vice versa on the return trip), stopping frequently to ringing and whistling. No buses connect Fort Cochin and Mattancherry, but the 30-min. walk through town is interesting, and there's little motorized traffic. In Ernakulam, **taxis** and **auto-rickshaws** are plentiful during the day but scarce at night. They lurk in flocks near jetties, bus, and train stations. In Fort Cochin, taxis do not operate and even cycle- and auto-rickshaws can be difficult to find. (Those that can be found are almost inevitably waiting for the school children they drive daily to and from school.) Try near the ferry landings or ask locals. Cycle-rickshaws are more expensive than auto-rickshaws. Fort Cochin and Mattancherry are navigable by **foot,** but a motorcycle would be really nice, and a **bicycle** useful (inquire at your guest house; about Rs.25 per day).

Telephones: STD/ISD booths abound in Ernakulam. In Fort Cochin, Elite Travels on Princess St. has an STD/ISD booth charging Rs.4 per min. for call-backs. Heading left past Santa Cruz Basilica, the main road is about a 10-min. walk. Here, some booths charge only Rs.2 per minute.

Market: In Fort Cochin, fishing boats beach on beaches south of the Chinese fishing nets and silvery fish are spread on tarps. Beach shacks sell the fresh catch.

English Bookstore: Bhavi Books, on Convent Rd., just west of M.G. Rd. in Ernakulam, has everything from Shakespeare to Larry McMurtry to Kahlil Gibran. Open Mon.-Sat. 9:30am-7:15pm. Also in Ernakulam, **Higginbothams,** on the corner of Chittoor and Hospital Rd., has a less highbrow selection, including such classics as *How to Play Guitar* and *How to Pick Up Girls.* Open Mon.-Sat. 9:30am-7pm.

Pharmacy: A 24-hr. pharmacy is located in Medical Trust Hospital.

Hospital: Medical Trust Hospital (tel. 371852), in Ernakulam on M.G. Rd., 3 blocks south of Jos Junction. The hospital is enlarging its facility with American medical equipment. Payment for foreigners is flexible: rupees preferred, but in emergencies credit cards are accepted and sometimes foreign currency. Doctor's visits Rs.50, private room with bath Rs.90. **Gautham Hospital** (tel. 223055, ambulance 227289), Fort Cochin. Complicated to find on your own; it's best to hop into a rickshaw or call an ambulance if need be. The chief medical officer is Dr. K. R. Jayachandran. For more advanced facilities, go to the hospital in Ernakulam.

Police: Police Commissioner of Cochin, in Ernakulam on Banerji Rd., east of the High Court Jetty, on the corner of Shanmugham Rd., on the left. The **police station** is north of the commissioner's office, on the left around the curve to the right. **Fort Cochin Police:** follow Rampart Rd. inland from the bus stand; the police office is on the left. **Tourist Police** booth: take Princess St. to the beach, turn right along Calvathy Rd.; it will be on the left.

Emergency: Police: tel. 100. **Fire:** tel. 101. **Ambulance:** tel. 102.

Post Office: The **Kochi Head Post Office** is located in **Fort Cochin.** All *Poste Restante* addressed to Cochin arrives here (Mon.-Sat. 9am-4pm). Telegrams accepted/ delivered, stamps sold Mon.-Sat. 9am-5pm; parcels accepted Mon.-Fri. 9am-3pm, Sat. 9am-2pm. Ernakulam's **GPO** is on Hospital Rd., midway between Park Ave. and M.G. Rd. **Branch offices** in Ernakulam can be found on Broadway just north of the split with Shanmugham Rd. on the right, and just south of Jos Junction on the right side of M.G. Rd. Another office is located on Willingdon Island, across from the Taj Malabar Hotel. **Postal Code:** 682001.

Telephone Code: 0484.

ACCOMMODATIONS

Ernakulam

Ernakulam offers plenty in the way of accommodation. Affordable lodging is easily found near the KRSTC Bus Stand.

Paulson Park Hotel (tel. 354002). From Jos Junction head east toward the Ernakulam Junction Railway Station, take the second left: the hotel is on the right. Mystical green light filters down from the atrium roof, bathing the courtyard. "A stone's throw away from the Railway Station" and very close to Jos Junction. Big, immaculate rooms with soft beds. Hot water 24hr. Rooftop and tandoori restaurants. Singles Rs. 150, deluxe with A/C Rs.280. Doubles Rs.240, with A/C Rs.400.

Hotel Luciya (tel. 354433). From the KRSTC bus station turn right, then take the first left. Hotel Luciya is immediately on the left. The doorman and the elevator give a touch of class, and the staff is very nice. Restaurant and bar provide room service 6am-10:30pm. All doubles have balconies. Singles Rs.80, with A/C Rs.175. Doubles Rs.160, with A/C Rs.250.

Hotel K.K. International (tel. 366010), opposite the Ernakulam Junction Railway Station. Uplifting halls and rooms filled with heavenly white light. Singles Rs.150, with A/C Rs.250. Doubles Rs.250, with A/C Rs.400. Triples Rs.320.

Sealord Hotel (tel. 352682), on Shanmugham Rd. across from the GCDA Shopping Centre. Classy marble lobby, plush blue carpets, central A/C, room service, (good) resident band at the Princess Restaurant, hot water in the bathtubs—the works. Many rooms have views of the harbor. Singles Rs.450, deluxe Rs.600. Doubles Rs.550, deluxe Rs.850.

Woodlands Hotel (tel. 351372), on M.G. Rd. 1 block north of Jos Junction. Though the hotel's grandeur and gold bedcovers are faded, diamond and jewelry shows still go on in the back exhibition hall. Carved wooden furniture graces rooms with color TVs, and the marble bathrooms have running hot and cold water. Singles Rs.200, with A/C Rs.250; extra person Rs.75. Doubles Rs.300, with A/C Rs.500; extra person Rs.100.

Hotel Sangeetha (tel. 368736). From Jos Junction head east along D.H. Rd. towards the train station, take the first left. Sangeetha is on the left. Friendly, smiling people behind the reception desk will escort you to a clean room with Star TV and soft beds with topsheets and blankets. Some rooms have balconies, sealed with unopenable windows. A funky sitting room in the hall features red furniture and skylights. Guests receive a "complimentary food coupon" for the hotel's veg. restaurant. Singles Rs.200. Doubles Rs.300. Extra person Rs.85.

Bharat Tourist Home, (tel. 353501), on D.H. Rd. near its intersection with Foreshore Rd. This place thinks it's cooler than *kulfi* with its guard, air-conditioned reception desk, sweets shop, and running hot water. Singles Rs.300, with A/C Rs.500. Doubles Rs.350, with A/C Rs.600.

Fort Cochin

Only a few guest houses are located in wondrous but inconvenient Fort Cochin. Entrepreneurs have caught scent of the money trail, however, and there are plans for new guest houses to open soon. Almost all accommodations are near Princess St.

Theravadu Tourist Home (tel. 226897), from the south end of Princess St. turn right, then left onto Quirose St. The atmospheric, well-maintained house has dimly-lit wooden stairs leading to gorgeously clean rooms. Some of the 8 rooms are bigger than others, and some share a common toilet and shower. Rooms Rs.105-155, based on size, shape, and availability of "Goofy" bedspread.

Hotel Seagull (tel. 228128), from St. Francis Church, follow Rose St. to the waterfront, turn right on Calvathy Rd., watch for the sign on the left after a 5- to 10-min. walk. Classier than run-of-mill guest houses, the spotless rooms are well-furnished. All have attached bath. Great views of the sea for those who are willing to pay; otherwise, catch the view from the restaurant. Doubles on the ground floor (no view) Rs.175, on the first floor with sea view Rs.250.

Elite Hotel, Princess St. (tel. and fax 225733). Pronounced "ee-light," this place is an institution among backpackers, and the management knows it. The Elite is more idiosyncratic and less clean than its competition. The spirits of dozens of brethren backpackers are present in the piles of candle wax left on the windowsills during power cuts. An Elite Annex has additional rooms. The downstairs restaurant is popular and unavoidable. Guests can receive faxes at Rs.25 per sheet. Singles with bath Rs.75. Doubles Rs.100, with balcony Rs.150.

Delight Tourist Resort, Rose St. From St. Francis Church, walk south (with the grassy playing field on your right). Delight is on the left before the end of the field. A blue balcony can be glimpsed behind a whitewashed wall and fluffy coconut trees. The hotel is reserved for foreigners only, and many families with children stay here (the courtyard is good for playing). The family who runs the new guest house can provide games, books, and food (in season), or arrange tickets for KSTDC tours or a picnic at Cherai Beach. All rooms have attached bath. Dorm beds Rs.50. Singles Rs.75. Doubles Rs.90, upstairs double Rs.125, upstairs double with balcony Rs.200.

PWD Guest House, turn left from the gates of St. Francis Church, then right onto Dutch Cemetery Rd. Maintained by the Indian government, the rooms are huge and palatial, with high, sloping tiled ceilings. Feel like a princess in the 4-poster bed. The garden in back fronts the beach by the Chinese fishing nets. Beware: several things must be broken before the government can approve a maintenance trip. Huge doubles Rs.100. Extra mattress Rs.20.

Grace Guest House. Follow Rose St. from the backside of St. Francis Church along the Parade grounds, turn left at the roundabout, turn right at the next circle onto Peter Celli St., and at the first junction Grace is on the left side (about a 10-min. walk). Bland, but with good mattresses, desks, and shelves in each room. Breakfast available 6-10am. All rooms with attached bath. Singles Rs.100. Doubles Rs.125, with A/C Rs.350.

FOOD

Ernakulam

Thriving off the comings and goings of the ships and fish, Ernakulam is a great place to find everything from South Indian fast food to Keralan cuisine and from pizza to gourmet Chinese food. However, most travelers avoid the big-city bustle of ernakulam and prefer to revel in the historic peace of Fort Cochin.

Bimbi's, Jos Junction. A landmark. The chaos is incredible, the method mysterious (at first), and the food good and cheap. Pay first at the register on the side, then claim it at the appropriate counter by showing the receipt (it make take 2 or 3 stops). Western and Indian selections. Excellent *masala dosa* Rs.9. Enormous selection of sweets at the front.

Khyber Restaurant, Jos Junction. Upstairs from Bimbi's. Air-conditioned and more expensive than its downstairs neighbor, with dim lights and marble floors, Khyber offers Chinese or Indian, veg. or non-veg. food. Luscious *kadai* ginger *paneer* (Rs.38), incredibly garlicky *naan* that no 1 member of a couple should eat alone (Rs.14), smooth, creamy *lassi* (Rs.12).

Hot Breads, Warriom Rd. Follow M.G. Rd. south from Jos Junction. Turning right onto Warriom Rd., Hot Breads is soon on the right. True to name, this is the only source of brown bread in Ernakulam (garlic and french varieties also available). Fresh baked goods line the shelves ready to satisfy cravings for croissants and doughnuts. Not limited to breads, the place sells pizza, burgers, and sandwiches. Open daily 9am-10pm.

Chinese Garden (tel. 363710). Follow M.G. Rd. south from Jos Junction, turn right at Warriom Rd. It is on the left just before Hot Breads. Crazy chinese lanterns and dragons welcome you to the air-conditioned restaurant with tinted windows. Pages and pages of delicacies on the menu. Sweet corn soup Rs.25, entrees Rs.35 up to Rs.100 for fresh prawn dishes. Open daily 11am-11pm.

Fruit Garden, at the corner of M.G. Rd. and Convent Rd. Careful arrangements of fruits upon zig-zaggy shelves advertise this as a great place for juice. Good places to sit as well. Fruity milkshakes Rs.10.

Caravan Ice Cream, where Park Ave. splits into Broadway and Shanmugham Rd., across from the State Bank of India and next to the church, a driveway leads back from the road. An array of ice creams, milkshakes, and sundaes (Rs.20-30).

Bharat Coffee House, Where Park Ave. Splits, follow Broadway; the coffee house will soon be on the left. Barefoot waiters in snappy white caps, shirts, and pants tool around offering limited selections of lip-smacking South Indian snacks and ice creams. Ladies' and family rooms offer refuge from mindless staring. Crispy *masala dosa* Rs.10.

Ancient Mariner, behind the mammoth GCDA Shopping Centre on Shanmugham Rd. Down a pier, this floating open-air restaurant serves Chinese and Continental food along with some Indian selections. Makes up in beer what it lacks in rhymes. The ambitious proprietor dresses like any good cowboy and plans Saturday night dance parties (Rs.250 per couple, dinner included) and speedboat service (Rs.500 per hr., Rs.200 to be picked up and dropped at Fort Cochin). Sept.-March a live band or solitary musician plays at night. Open daily 11am-11pm.

The Oven, Shanmugham Rd. Across Jews St. from the Sealord Hotel. Have Indian or Western baked goods in the air-conditioned parlor. The coffee and tea comes with frothed milk.

The Princess Room and **Sayanna,** both in the Sealord Hotel on Shanmugham Rd. across from the GCDA Shopping Centre. On the second floor, the Princess Room is "air-conditioned with a royal splendour" and boasts "the Resident Band to entertain you." Chinese, Indian, Keralan, and Continental cuisines. Keralan dishes Rs.45-90. The rooftop Sayanna "gives a splendid view of the Natural Harbor" and "offers Chinese cuisine but serves others as per your choices" (i.e. they bring it up from the Princess Room). Entrees Rs.45-90. The Golden Jug Bar has a "Mughal Splendour to warm up your spirits."

Fort Cochin

After (or before) you've exhausted the menus of Fort Cochin's few restaurants, try having fish just pulled from the water and grilled before your eyes in shacks down by the seafront. (Choose your own fish; often the more decrepit the shack, the better the fish.) *Dhabas* along the main road offer scaldingly spicy curries. Bakeries and vegetable stores can be found where Bastian St. intersects the main road.

Hotel Seagull Restaurant, Calvathy Rd. Good views of the harbor from the ground floor restaurant, but a gorgeous panorama spreads below the first-floor branch of the restaurant (follow the stairs to the left, disregarding the "FAMILIES ONLY" sign). Enjoy a large selection of seafood ("Nature's natural food") as the fishing boats and the dolphins cruise below. Crab fry Rs.40, mixed vegetable curry Rs.25. The lemon rice is tantalizingly titillating. Open 8am-10pm.

Elite Hotel, Princess St. Very popular restaurant on the ground floor. You may have to settle for whatever's in the cabinet: usually *paratha, appam,* and *channa* curry. *Dosas* appear after 6pm. Western breakfast treats and sandwiches available. Open 7am until the crowd trickles out, anytime from 9pm to midnight.

Chariot Fast Food, on the end of Princess St. toward the waterfront. Some Western food, some Keralan dishes (fish and curried rice), and lots of Chinese. Most dishes upwards of Rs.40; half-portions of some dishes can be had for half-price.

SIGHTS

Fort Cochin

The blessing of some goddess seems to hang over Fort Cochin, with its grassy fields, its massive churches, and the orange sun slipping into the sea behind the bony frame-works of its Chinese fishing nets. Hurry is against the nature of the place, and historic sites are more common than cows (but not as common as goats). Fort Cochin was the site of the first European settlement in India (1500), the first Portuguese factory, established by the explorer Vasco da Gama in 1502, and site of the first European fort in India, commissioned in 1503 by the Portuguese viceroy Afonso de Albuquerque. No trace of the fort itself remains, but the first European church in India, **St. Francis Church** (locally called the "Vasco da Gama Church"), constructed by Portuguese Franciscan friars in 1503, still stands among the houses built by British traders and Dutch farmers. When Vasco da Gama died in Cochin in 1524, his earthly remains were buried under the church floor. After 14 years, the remains of the remains were transferred to Lisbon. His tombstone remains embedded in the floor. The original wooden structure of the church was improved to stone during the mid-16th century. Cochin fell to the Dutch in 1663, and the church was Protestantized in 1779. Although the British occupied Cochin in 1795, the church remained a Dutch bastion, and the walls are lined with Dutch memorials. In 1864 the church finally became Anglican, and the Church of South India now fills the same stone walls with its faith-ful, who have dedicated the church to St. Francis. Open Mon.-Fri. 9:30am-1pm and 2:30-5:30pm. English Eucharist Sun. 8am; English matins every third Sun. 8am.

Turn left from the gates of St. Francis Church, then right onto Dutch Cemetery Rd., to reach the **Dutch Cemetery,** where crumbling tombs disintegrate beside the beach. A driveway next to PWD Guest House leads to the **beach,** where the faraway crowd at the water's edge consists of fishermen, fish sellers, fish buyers, and fish. The nearby skeletal cantilevered **Chinese fishing nets** were brought to Kerala by Chinese traders in the 13th century. A series of suspended rocks counterbalance the nets, which plunge into the sea at high tide. In a series of shacks, you can choose your own fish and have it grilled (try the one farthest left). As massive cargo ships pass into the harbor not so far away, fishermen return from the sea in long canoelike boats (pro-pelled by several buzzing Evinrudes) with the day's catch. Crowds clamor on the beach to purchase fish, prawns, and crabs directly from the boats.

The **Santa Cruz Basilica** can be reached by following Princess St. south until its end, turning left onto Bastian St.; the basilica is on the right. A church was built on this site first in 1505, replaced by a cathedral in 1558. This cathedral was consecrated in 1902. English mass Sun. 4:30pm.

Mattancherry

Following Bastian St. from the back of St. Francis Church until it ends, then turning right, a fast walker can reach the heart of Mattancherry in 30 minutes. (Mattancherry can also be reached by following Cavalthy Rd. directly from the Seagull Hotel.) Pass-ing shipping warehouses for many goods, the aroma of a whole warehouse of tea spills out onto the streets.

The **Mattancherry Palace** (a.k.a. the **"Dutch Palace"**) on the right hand side of the road houses the Mattancherry Palace Museum. The Portuguese built the palace in 1557 to compensate Raja Virakerala Varma for having plundered a temple in the vicinity. The Dutch renovated the palace in 1665 during their occupation, hence its name. Two **temples,** one dedicated to Krishna and one to Shiva, were also built on the palace grounds by the Portuguese, but today only Hindus may enter. The museum houses oil portraits of Cochin rajas and their palanquins, robes, weapons, and umbrellas. Detailed murals cover nearly 300 square meters of the palace walls. Every inch is loaded with the faces of gods and goddesses in scenes from the *Ramayana* and the Puranas. Downstairs in the queen's bedchamber, a number of less detailed paintings show scenes of a divinely sexual nature set in a beautiful forest (inspiration to produce a male heir?). In one, Krishna uses six hands and two feet to the pleasure of a herd of admiring *gopis,* and two more hands to play the flute. Open Sat.-Thurs. 10am-5pm.

Following Bazaar Rd. farther, the pedestrian enters an area known as **Jew Town,** where handicraft emporia and busily stitching tailors lines the road. Make a U-turn to the right and the **Pardesi Synagogue** (Pardesi refers to the "foreign," or "white" Jews) will be at the end of the street to the left. The history of Jews in Kerala goes back to trade between King Solomon's Israel (10th century BC) and the Malabar coast, which was known to the Jews by the name "Odhu." The destruction of the Second Temple in Jerusalem by the Romans in 70 AD led to diaspora of the Jewish people, some of whom landed in Shingly (30km north of Cochin, now know as Cranganore) in 72 AD. Around 500 AD, a large group of Jews immigrated to Shingly from Iraq and Iran. In the 16th century the Portuguese began a policy of intolerance, during which the Jews were expelled from Shingly. Legend has it that Joseph Azar, the last surviving Jewish prince, swam to Cochin with his wife on his shoulders. There the Jewish Keralans placed themselves under the protection of the raja of Cochin, who gave them a parcel of land next to his palace for a synagogue. The original building, constructed in 1568, was flattened by Portuguese shelling during a battle in 1662 and rebuilt two years later. Emigration to Bombay and Israel has dwindled Cochin's Jewish population down to about 20 members, but menorahs are still visible in some windows. For several years there has been no rabbi, so the elders of the synagogue make decisions and conduct ceremonies. The synagogue is lit by 19th-century oil-burning chandeliers in many colors of glass suspended over blue-and-white Cantonese tiles. The syangogue's Torah is inscribed on sheepskin scrolls and stored in ornate metal canisters, one of which was a gift from the raja of Cochin. Happy to discuss their future with visitors, the remaining Jews seem unworried about the survival of their community. Eighty or so Jews remain in Kerala, and 4000-5000 in India as a whole, mostly in Bombay. The synagogue is open to visitors Sun.-Fri. 10am-noon and 3-5pm. Requested donation Rs.1.

Vypeen Island

Miles of ignored beaches roll along the Arabian Sea on Vypeen Island, passing a **lighthouse** at Ochanthuruth (open daily 3-5pm) and the early 16th-century **Palliport Fort** (open Thurs.). The beaches are empty except for herds of sunbathing cows and a few fishing boats…until the foreigners arrive. Then men come running from the nearest village for the show. Women may feel more comfortable (and will be seen as more respectful) swimming in a t-shirt and shorts or pants. **Cherai Beach** is more frequented by foreigners and is probably safer than the others for women without an accompanying "husband." Toddy, tapped from coconut trees and fermented, can be sipped at a **toddy bar** on the right side of the main road about a five-minute walk from the Fort Cochin ferry landing. The bar closes around 9:30pm. Ferries run between Vypeen and the High Court Jetty in Ernakulam about every 20 minutes from 5:30am to 10pm. The same is true of ferries to and from Fort Cochin, which depart from the launch across from the bus stand.

Kathakali

Kathakali, which means "story play," is one of India's four schools of classical dance. A legend asserts that the ruler of Kottarakkara (in southern Kerala) asked the zamorin of Calicut send to his Krishnanattam (a Sanskrit temple art based on stories about Krishna) experts for a performance. The zamorin refused, mockingly replying that the southern ruler hadn't the knowledge to understand "the depth of Sanskrit" or "the nuances of Krishnanattam."

Deeply insulted, the ruler of Kottarakkara set out to help give shape to the art of Ramanattam, based on the exploits of Rama. Students of the art also took lessons in the martial art of Kalaripayatu. Ramanattam evolved into stories from traditional texts presented in the form of a dance drama, called Kathakali in the vernacular. Masks were originally used but have been replaced by face painting so that facial expressions can be seen. Some time during its history, Kathakali entered the temples of Kerala, where performances would begin in the early evening and last until 1 or 2am.

The modern art of Kathakali is most popular in a truncated form lasting only one hour and given in theaters filled with tourists who have come to "watch the Gods dance." Transformed into gods and demons by the application of wildly colored make-up, massive golden headdresses, and skirts bright and full enough to put any ballerina to shame, the performers are traditionally men who have studied scripture, Kalaripayatu, massage, and music for eight years beginning at the age of 10 or 12. The rigorous training lasts from 3am to 8pm every day, with morning studies concentrating on foot work, body movements, and exercises for the face and eyes, and evenings devoted to the study of texts and characters. Emphasis is given to proper lifestyle and the deep understanding of archetypes set out in the *Vedas*. The dancers communicate with the audience through the use of 24 basic *mudras,* hand gestures augmented by convulsive movements of the eyes and facial muscles and the pounding dancing of belled feet. By using combinations of these 24 *mudras* (signifying "love," "brave," "bee drinking from a lotus flower," etc.), stories from the *Ramayana* and *Mahabharata* can be told. Ear-piercing drums and classical vocals narrate the story.

ENTERTAINMENT

For those with the disco itch, **Ice's,** serves up Western and Hindi hits, and Pepsi and ice cream (but no alcohol). There's an outdoor patio and a disco-era dance floor. Between songs, try to explain to the owners about Pepsi in Burma. The resident band in the Princess Room at the **Sealord Hotel** cranks out a good "Mustang Sally," and here, unlike at Ice's, both ice cream and alcohol are available. The band stops around 10pm each night, but the club doesn't close until 1 or 2am.

The Sridar **movie theater** is near Vypeen Jetty across from GCDA Shopping Centre; the Deepa is near the Pollymukku bus stand; Kockers is in Fort Cochin.

The **Cochin Cultural Centre** offers teaching in dance, yoga, music, costume making, and more. The traditional Keralan martial art of Kalaripayatu, dating since Indian medieval times, is taught at the **ENS Kalari Centre** (tel. 809810). The school is about 9km from the city center; call for directions.

The Kerala Ayurveda Pharmacy (tel. 361202) on Warriom Rd. is one of many places offering **ayurvedic massage** in Cochin. An important part of Kathakali, several centers also offer massage, including the Cochin Cultural Centre (tel. 353732) and Kerala Kathakali Kendra (tel. 740030). Appointments are necessary.

For those who intend to stay a while, many **study and service opportunities** exist. If you are interested in being a "big brother" or "big sister" to a street boy, contact Rexy D'Cruz at Reflective Art Works, Panchalam (ask for "Sticker Boy").

Dance

Cochin offers several spectacular nightly performances of **Kathakali dance.** Geared for tourists, these performances are introduced by an explanation of the music, the hand symbols, the make-up, and a synopsis of the dramatic story being performed. Performances last from one hour to 90 minutes.

Cochin Cultural Centre (theater tel. 367866; office tel. 353732). From Jos Junction, follow M.G. Rd. south, turn left on South Overbridge Rd., right on Chittoor Rd., take the first left onto Manikath Rd. (a green Kathakali visage is painted in the wall at the corner), the center will be on the left until the new air-conditioned theater, on the right, is completed. Make-up begins each night at 5:30pm; show starts at 6:30pm. Admission Rs.50.

See India Foundation (tel. 369471). From M.G Rd. follow Warriom Rd. 2 blocks east; it will be on the right under the huge painted visage of a Kathakali dancer. Director Devan is the son of Guru Gopala Paniker ("who danced until he was 97" around the world), and has been putting on daily shows here for the last 26 years. Make-up begins at 6pm, followed by Devan's explanation of Kathakali and Hinduism, and then the dance itself, between 6:45-8pm. Admission Rs.50.

Kerala Kathakali Centre, housed in the Cochin Aquatic Club in Fort Cochin, also puts on nightly shows. Kathakali is performed here by a young, sincere troupe of artists nightly. Make-up starts around 5:30pm and the show begins at 6:30pm. Tickets for the small hall can be reserved at some Fort Cochin hotels.

Kerala Kathakali Kendra (theater tel. 355003; office tel. 740030). In the Bolghatty Palace on Bolghatty Island near the ferry jetty. The setting, Bolghatty Palace, was built by the Dutch in 1744. Make-up starts at 4pm, followed at 6pm by prayer, a demonstration narrated in English, and the play itself. Admission Rs.50.

Art Kerala (tel. 366238). From Jos Junction, follow Durbar Hall Rd. toward the railway station (east), take first right onto Chittoor Rd., then first left, right into Kannanthodath Lane, where it will be on the right. Before the show the elaborate make-up will be done, which gives an "ultra-terrestrial effect." The show itself begins daily at 6pm.

BACKWATER CRUISES

Beyond the city are magic green fields, bouffant palms, lazy backwaters—some of India's most remarkably green and beautiful landscapes. The privately run **Tourist Desk** offers backwater tours on non-motorized boats daily from 9am to 1:30pm and 2-6:30pm (Rs.250). These tours afford opportunities to see villages and to spot birds. The Tourist Desk also conducts special moonlight cruises on full moon nights. The **KTDC** provides backwater tours on country boats, leaving at 8:30am and 2:30pm (Rs.300). Two tours daily also go to the main historical sites (9am-12:30pm and 2-5:30pm, Rs.50). If you don't have much time in Cochin, this is an easy way to get around. A sunset tour runs daily (5:30-7pm, Rs.30). A Periyar Wildlife Sanctuary tour leaves at 7:30am on Saturdays, returning Sunday at 8pm (Rs.250, accommodation not provided). Several more tours are offered, and others can be arranged.

■ Near Cochin and Ernakulam

The hill station of **Munnar** is situated at an elevation of 1500-2500m, where three streams come together in a land of green tea plantations fading into misty blue. Popular with Indian tourists, especially Cochinites, the accommodations are often booked. A trek connects Munnar and Kodaikanal, and Ernakulam National Park is nearby (about 20km away).

Buses run between Munnar and Cochin (5 per day, 4½hr.); Kottayam (5 per day, 5hr.); Kumily (1 per day, 4½hr.); Madurai (1 per day, 5hr.); and Trivandrum (4 per day, 9hr.).

In the village of **Kadalikad,** 45km southeast of Cochin, the 2.5-hectare **Haritha Farms** was established in 1962 as a rubber and coconut plantation. In 1990, the farm converted to sustainable farming, discontinuing the use of all pesticides, and in 1993 eliminating unecological rubber trees and chemical fertilizers. Now planted with coconut, pineapple, banana, spices, and medicinal herbs, the farm seeks to be a model for "economically viable eco-farming," re-establishing an old Keralan farming system called *thodi*. Haritha Farms hosts a maximum of eight guests per day, offering traditional Keralan cooking (breakfast, lunch, and dinner), a tour of the spice garden with explanations of sustainable farming methods, and exploration of Kadalikad and the farm (by foot or by bicycle). KSRTC buses from Ernakulam, Trivandrum, Kottayam, and Calicut stop in nearby Muvattupuzha, where "every two minutes" a bus leaves from the private bus stand to Thodupuzha stopping in Kadalikad 150m from the farm. Reservations are necessary: contact the Tourist Desk in Ernakulam or call the farm (tel. (0485) 260216). Entry to the farm and food for the day Rs.300; entry, food and overnight stay Rs.450.

■ Calicut (Kozhikode)

Coveted Calicut, among India's best celebrated seaports, attracted Chinese traders at least as early as the 7th century, and prospered in the spice trade as the Indian port of choice among Middle Eastern traders. But Vasco da Gama, the first European to reach India by sea, tread his first subcontinental footsteps here (actually in Kappad, 16km north of Calicut) in 1498, starting a long spell of Portuguese interference in the spice trade. The Portuguese feuded with the local rulers, the zamorins, who had controlled the area for over seven centuries. For the next century and a half the zamorins fought a long series of naval wars with Portugal, finally breaking down and allowing the Portuguese to establish a factory. Dutch, French, and English traders all competed for Calicut throughout the 17th and 18th centuries, as did the king of Mysore, Haider Ali, and his son, Tipu Sultan. In 1792 Calicut was taken by the British, who lent its name to the fabric woven here, which they called "calico." But in spite of its history, there's not much to see in Calicut. Those who imagine a city filled with wharfside temples and cartloads of black pepper are disappointed to find boatloads of reeking fish and open sewers full of black ooze.

ORIENTATION

Calicut was laid out in the 14th century according to a Hindu grid formulated on a sacred diagram of Purusha, the cosmic man. The center of Purusha's body was the **Tali Shiva Temple,** but little else remains of the ancient master plan. **Ansari Park** (also called Mananchira Maidan) at the center of town, is flanked by the State Bank of India to the north, the CSI Church to the east, KTDC's Malabar Mansion Motel to the south, and a gleaming granite post office to the west. **S.M. Road** is a commercial center which runs south from the park. **Bank Road** runs north past the bank, and south along the park with a new name, **G.H. Road** Following Bank Rd. north, **Mavoor Road (Indira Gandhi Road)** runs off to the right. Many facilities, including Indian Airlines, PL Worldways, and the **KSRTC Bus Station,** are located near this intersection (as well as upscale shopping, banana-chips-fried-as-you-wait-stalls, and many fresh juice stands). Following G.H. Rd. south to its intersection with **M.M. Ali Road,** and then taking a left, leads to jewelry shops, temples, mosques, and a raging **fruit and vegetable market.** The **train station** can be reached by following **Town Hall Rd.** south from Ansari Park and the Post Office. The **beach,** 2km west of town center, is not safe for visitors walking alone.

PRACTICAL INFORMATION

Tourist Office: KTDC (tel. 721394, 721395), in the Malabar Mansion, on the south side of Ansari Park. City maps Rs.5, tourist brochures Rs.5, Kerala road guide Rs.30. If you ask a question the staff can't answer, they make a mysterious phone calls to a mysterious someone who knows all.

Budget Travel: PL Worldways (tel. 65121), 3rd fl., Lakhotia Computer Centre, at the intersection of Mavoor Rd. (Indira Gandhi Rd.) and Bank Rd. Books flights on domestic and international airlines, and obtains visas for foreign travel. Airline reservations can be confirmed for Rs.100 or free if they have an office in the city in question. Open Mon.-Fri. 9:30am-1pm, 2-5:30pm, Sat. 9:30am-1:30pm.

Currency Exchange: Banks exchange only cash. To exchange traveler's checks, inquire at hotels or go to **PL Worldways** (tel. 65121; see **Budget Travel,** above), where it's possible to exchange "all brands" of traveler's checks, and to purchase them with major credit cards. "Traveler's Hours" Mon.-Fri. 9:30am-1pm, 2-5:30pm, Sat. 9:30am-1:30pm.

Telephones: The **Telegraph Exchange** is across the street from the Seaqueen Hotel. They can be surly and refuse to allow collect calls, card calls, or call-backs. **Private operators** are more helpful, and some even allow free call-backs.

Airport: The airport is at Karippur, 23km from Calicut, accessible by taxi. **Air India** and **Indian Airlines** (tel. 766522) have an office, north of Mavoor Rd. on Bank Rd., on the right. Open Mon.-Fri. 9am-1pm and 2-6pm, and Sat. 9am-1pm. Many other travel agencies have offices between PL Worldways and Indian Airlines. Flights to: Bangalore (1 per day, 1hr., US$50); Bombay (3 per day, 1½hr., US$116); Coimbatore (1-2 per day, 30min., US$27); Goa (Thurs. and Sun., 1hr., US$27); Madras (1-2 per day, 2hr., US$67); Madurai (Tues., Thurs.-Sun., 45min., US$47).

Trains: The **railway station** is about 1km south of Ansari Park; follow Town Hall Rd. on the west side of the park south—it becomes Oyitti Rd. and then Railway Station Rd.; the station is on the right. Auto-rickshaws can easily take you to and from your hotel. To: Ernakulam (6:45, 9:10, 11:50am, and 7:10pm., 4½hr., Rs.48/196 for 2nd/1st class); trains go on to Trivandrum (10hr., Rs. 90/372 for 2nd/1st class); Mangalore (8 per day, 1:35am-5:35pm, 5hr., Rs.56/219 for 2nd/1st class); Bombay (indirectly) (11:50am and 6:05pm, 36hr.); Delhi (*Mangala Exp.* 2617, 3:40pm, 40hr., Rs. 305/1679 for 2nd/1st class).

Buses: Private buses run from the **new bus stand,** reached by following Mavoor Rd. (Indira Gandhi Rd.) east from the Bank Rd. side to where Stadium Rd. forms a T with Mavoor Rd. Take Stadium Rd. to the right; the bus station is on the left. Private buses are cheaper than state buses, and may even come with music or a movie. No buses run directly to Bombay, Trivandrum, or Bangalore. To: Mysore (express, 6 and 8:30am, 6hr., Rs.47); Mangalore (express, 5:45, 9:30am, 8:30 and 9:30pm, 6hr., Rs. 46); Cochin (16 per day, 6am-11:50pm, "ordinary" Rs.36, express Rs.45); Devala (near Ooty; 2:15pm, 10hr., Rs.40). Buy tickets ahead of time, since buses fill up. **KSRTC Bus Stand,** from Bank Rd. turn right onto Mavoor Rd.; the station is on the left. A little dirty and scary, but hey, so are you. To: Mangalore (12:40am, 8hr., Rs.77); Bangalore (14 per day, 12:30am-11pm., 8hr., Rs.94); Mysore (15 per day, 12:30am-11pm., 5½hr., Rs.47); Cochin (27 per day, 7:50am-2:30am, 5½hr., Rs.60); Trivandrum (13 per day, 5:30am-10:05pm, 10hr., Rs.135).

Local Transportation: Auto-rickshaws are easily available and cheap; they will use their meters (minimum Rs.4 for 1km). Rickshaws and taxis will take you to far-off attractions, too. **Local buses** run around town and to the beach: buses to Beypore run every 30min. from the New Bus Stand; green buses run from Malabar Mansion to West Hill, within walking distance of East Hill, where Pazhassiraja Museum, Krishna Menon Museum, and an Art Gallery are (ask the driver if the bus goes to West Hill—some green buses don't).

Library: Kozhikode Public Library and Research Centre, to the right of Malabar Mansion. The spacious library is air-conditioned and has a decent selection. Open Tues.-Sun. 2-8pm.

Market: An extensive fruit and vegetable market is on the left side of M.M. Ali Rd. Silver and gold jewelry-sellers are sequestered all along this road, too.

Pharmacy: The pharmacy attached to the **National Hospital,** on Mavoor Rd. is open 24hr. Additional pharmacies are scattered liberally around town.

Hospital: The best hospital in town is the **National Hospital** (tel. 66408) on Mavoor Rd., on the north side, near the KSRTC bus station. Next best is **Baby Memorial Hospital** (tel. 365162) on R.C. Rd.

Police Station: (tel. 300860) near the Railway Station.

Emergency: Police 100. **Fire** 101. **Ambulance** 102.

Post Office: On the west edge of Ansari Park. The impressive shiny marble-and-granite post office sells stamps Mon.-Sat. 8am-7:45pm, Sun. and holidays 2-4:45pm. Parcels may be mailed Mon.-Sat. 4-7:30pm, Sun. and holidays 2-4:30pm. **Postal Code:** 673001.

Telephone Code: 0495.

ACCOMMODATIONS

Near the Vegetable Market and the Silver and Gold Jewelers' Lane

Chamundeswari Tourist Home (tel. 60461). Coming along Palayam Rd. from the train station, take a right when you see the sign, then follow the narrow street to the left. Funkiest location in Calicut, this "stronghold of hospitality," is in an alley with an incense shop and a temple with a huge lotus. South Indian veg. restaurant. All rooms have attached baths. Check-out 24hr. Singles Rs.50. Doubles Rs.90. "Four-bed" Rs.150. Extra person Rs.25. Extra bed Rs.25.

Sasthapuri Tourist Home, further down Palayam Rd./M.M. Ali Rd., on the left. Makes you feel a bit like you're a part of the shopping mall it's in, but the most interesting part of town is just outside. Light-and-dark plywood paneling will take you right back to the 70s; some of the rooms are big enough to have a disco party. Singles with common bath Rs.50, with bath Rs.75. Doubles Rs.90-100. Triples (1 double bed, 1 single bed) Rs.135. Suite Rs.200, with A/C Rs.350.

Near City Center

Malabar Mansion (tel. 722391), on the south side of Ansari Park. KTDC-run with a tourist reception office, air-conditioned restaurant, air-conditioned beer parlor, snack bar, and room service. All rooms have TV, phone and attached bath. Air-conditioned rooms are huge, each outfitted with a divan, 2 chairs, a table, and hot water. Non-A/C rooms are smaller and smudgier. Singles Rs.150, with A/C Rs.315. Doubles Rs.200, with A/C Rs.350. Quads Rs.300. Extra person Rs.50, in A/C rooms Rs.100.

Kalpaka Tourist Home (tel. 720222), Town Hall Rd., just south of Ansari Park. The rooms open around an indoor courtyard. Some are a strange green, but they are big and beds have a top sheet and blanket. Good restaurant has limited selection. Hot water 24hr. Singles Rs.115, with A/C Rs.350. Doubles Rs.175, with A/C Rs.450.

Metro Tourist Home (tel. 673001), at the junction of Mavoor Rd. and Bank Rd. Set in the whizzing, grinding heart of town, and costs less than the others. Singles Rs.75. Doubles Rs.115, deluxe Rs.140, with A/C Rs.290, with A/C and TV Rs.315. Quads Rs.200.

Near the Railway Station

Heena Palace (tel. 673002), near the Sangam Theater on Railway Station Rd. Pastel blue rooms with matching flowered sheets. Balconies with chairs offer views of passing trains. All rooms have attached baths. Singles Rs.75. Doubles Rs.125, with cable TV Rs.200, with A/C Rs.350, with cable TV and A/C Rs.400. Triples Rs.150. Quads Rs.200.

Hotel Diplomat (tel. 302391), farther down Railway Station Rd. than Heena Palace, but still an easy walk from the train station. Rooms open around a covered courtyard, some done up in a red-and-dark wood. All rooms have attached baths. Deluxe rooms have hot water. Singles Rs.80. Doubles Rs.115, deluxe Rs.137, with A/C Rs.235. Triples with A/C and TV Rs.427.

Beach

Seaqueen Hotel (tel. 366904), about 2km west of city center. Follow R.C. Rd. west until it dead-ends at the sea, then left on Beach Rd. Seaqueen will be on the left. Or follow Court Rd. until it dead-ends at Convent Rd., zag right, then left, and Seaqueen will be on the left. Grand curlicue motifs adorn the curved plaster ceilings of the hallway, and the high-ceilinged rooms are big enough for 4 people to practice yoga, with ample space in the attached bathroom for another person to practice yoga while you laze in the bathtub. Linens changed daily, and the beds have top sheets, blankets, and bedspreads. The restaurant serves fairly good food, and fresh juice. Safe deposit boxes available. There's even a generator to fill in during power cuts. Singles Rs.235, with TV Rs.260, with A/C Rs. 385, with A/C and TV Rs.410. Doubles Rs.295, with TV Rs.320, with A/C Rs.445, with A/C and TV Rs.470, "deluxe" Rs.560. Suite Rs.660. Extra person Rs.60.

SOUTH INDIA

FOOD

Calicut is not culinary paradise. Among the city's best offerings are banana chips cooked fresh in a pan while you wait, and any of numerous fresh juices from vendors. You may as well stick to the restaurant in your hotel, or the nearest decent-looking *dhaba*.

In Paramount Towers, **Sana Rice Bowl** has a lunchtime buffet with fish and chicken curries for Rs.60. Good *dal* and *chapatis* cost around Rs.40. **"Sunset Point,"** on the tower's rooftop, serves up barbeque and great views. The restaurant at **Kalpaka Tourist Home** appears to be one of very few places open for breakfast, at which time they don't have a menu, but bring out smashingly good South Indian food from the tiny kitchen: soft, cup-shaped *appams (dosas* with "special Keralan stew") for Rs.12. The **Cochin Bakery,** across from the State Bank of India, has fresh goodies from 9:30am to 9pm—also mineral water and cold drinks, commodities hard to come by in Calicut. Try the cream-filled green cookies (Rs.3.50). Just a few doors down is the ritzy, air-conditioned **Regal Cakes.** The **Nest Restaurant** in the Seaqueen Hotel cooks good (if often scaldingly spicy) food, and several *dhabas* on Beach Rd. have views of the sea.

SIGHTS AND ENTERTAINMENT

Tourist pamphlets blithely suggest **shopping** is the premier entertainment in Calicut: fancy clothes stores line "Sweat Meat Street" (S.M. Street) and Mavoor Rd., jewelers pack into tiny shops on Palayam Rd., near the interesting gauntlets of the **fruit and vegetable market. Sangam Movie Theatre** near the railway station features Hindi flicks and B-grade Bruce Willis *pièces de resistance.* Every evening at Ansari Park, a little guy in a box madly flips switches to manipulate a **"Music Fountain"** choreographed to Hindi pop. Fascinated people come in droves (you'd think they'd never seen Star TV). The two-hour show starts at 6:30pm. Admission Rs.3.

Walks on the **beach,** just 2km from the city center, are not as nice as they sound. As a tourist handbook reads, "two sea piers almost 125 years old are a speciality." (Translation: two old rotting piers extend into the sea from a slightly muddy beach— and is that sewage running into the sea there?) **Warning:** some parts of the beach are known by locals to be "bad"—home to illegal drug trafficking and a dangerous drug culture. Heed local cautions and avoid these areas.

The **Tali Temple,** filled with murals depicting mythical scenes, dates from the 14th century and is still functioning. Only Hindus may enter. Follow R.S. Rd. until it dead-ends into Francis Rd.—take a left. The temple will be on the left.

Pazhassiraja Museum has copies of ancient mural paintings, bronzes, old coins, "dolmonoid cysts" (wouldn't want to have one on your foot), and "umbrella stones." Next door, the **Krishna Menon Museum** houses the personal belongings of the Indian president, and the **Art Gallery** has a collection of paintings by Raja Ravi Varma and Raja Raja Varma. Both museums are located at East Hill, 5km from Calicut. Arrange with a rickshaw or taxi, or take a green bus from in front of Malabar Mansion. (Ask the driver to make sure the bus is going to West Hill—the distance to East Hill is walkable from there.) All are open Tues.-Sun. 10am-5pm, but on Wed. the Krishna Menon Museum and Art Gallery don't open until noon.

Sixteen kilometers from Calicut at **Kappad,** a marker commemorates the landing of Vasco da Gama on May 27, 1498. Bring a picnic; the beach is said to be safe for swimming when the sea is not rough..

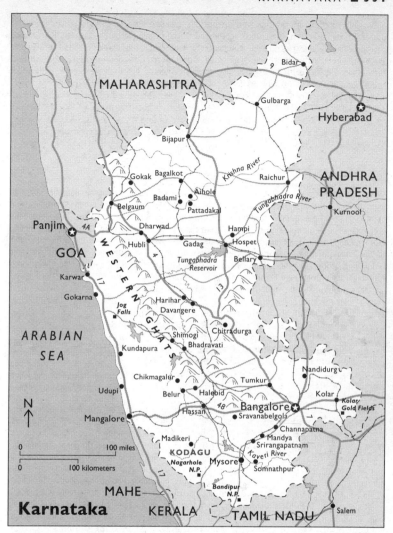

Karnataka

Karnataka's terrain is dominated by the Western Ghats, which jaggedly follow the course of the coastline and shield the Deccan Plateau from the torrential monsoons of the coast. On the plateau, rusty-saffron rocks give way to verdant fields, narrow rivers, and canals. The area upland of the Ghats is forested with teak and sandalwood, and the rivers produce enough hydroelectric power to export to neighboring states. The boulder-filled terrain around the Ghats provided material for some of India's ancient architectural masterpieces: in the north, Chalukyan temples and the Vijayanagar ruins at Hampi, and in the south, the florid temples at Belur, Halebid, and Somnathpur.

Despite its plethora of ancient monuments, and residents as mellow as the mild climate, the attitude here is neither overly traditional nor hopelessly stagnant. Karnataka is one of India's most progressive states. The British Raj had direct control of Mysore State for a relatively brief period, and the native maharajas who ruled the state under British protection until 1947 gave the state a cohesive vision—they were hailed for their modernization efforts. In 1956, Kannada-speaking regions in the north were added to the Mysore State, creating a Kannada-speaking state that would be renamed Karnataka in 1973. Bangalore, the state's capital, is today a mecca for information technology. Meanwhile, the state's literacy rate is one of the nation's highest, and whatever their political leanings, locals savor the fact that India recently elected a Karnatakan, H.D. Deve Gowda, as prime minister.

■ Bangalore

When Kempegowda, a petty chieftain under the Vijayanagar Empire, founded Bangalore in 1537, his son built four watchtowers and decreed that the city should never spread beyond them. Four and a half centuries later, the intended boundaries can still be seen—the remains of the towers are in Lalbagh Gardens, near the Bull Temple, off Ulsoor Lake, and near Sankey Tank—but modern Bangalore gushes far beyond these limits. Bangalore's rampant growth (the city now has a population of 4.5 million) has been accelerated by the influx of rural Karnatakans as well as Tamils, Keralites, and North Indians lured by Bangalore's mild climate and cosmopolitan feel. Bangalore seems to welcome its new diverse population, which includes a wealth of multinational corporations investing in the city. Bangalore's hospitality is part of its history. Legend has it that in the 12th century, a hunter lost his way at nightfall and came across a tattered hut. Disoriented and scared, he rapped at the door and a gnarled old woman appeared, offering him shelter and placing before him a plate of boiled beans. The hunter turned out to be the Hoysala king Veera Ballala II, and to show his gratitude he offered to grant her a wish. She simply requested enough food for herself and any other wayward traveler who might need her hospitality. The village acquired the name of "Bende Kala Uru," or "Town of Boiled Beans," which evolved into Bangalore.

Modern locals relish the story of their famed hospitality, but under their breath, Bangalorians grumble about the hysterical expansion of their town. Homes with double verandahs and lawns filled with mango, coconut, cherry, and *badam* trees are being razed almost daily to make way for high-rise apartment buildings. In return for the development of their land, the families who owned it generally get a few flats in the apartment building. Rapid development thus means an assault on joint family life. Old colonial bungalows, too, with their pillars or red-tiled roofs, are endangered by the city's growth, which many claim is unplanned and doesn't provide enough accompanying infrastructure to support the voracious metropolis. Landmarks are also in danger: in 1994, plans to demolish the Attara Kachar, a beautiful red Gothic building from 1868, were thwarted only by outraged architecture students.

Boiled Beans or Hot Potato?

After a confederacy of Deccan sultanates vanquished the Vijayanagar Empire in 1565, control of Bangalore shifted between rulers with more jolting abruptness than a rickshaw ride through Karnataka backcountry. Bangalore was offered and taken as a *jagir* too many times to count, proving that even though Bangalore is affluent now, money has always talked loudest. Some of the more noteworthy rulers included Shivaji's father (whose son, Bangalorians proudly relate, married a Bangalore girl); a Mughal governor, who sold the city for the equivalent of 300,000 rupees; Haider Ali and Tipu Sultan, who reigned from their capital at Srirangapatnam; puppet maharajas of Mysore, following Tipu's demise; the British for 50 years; and then the Mysore maharajas again until after India's independence.

Many fear that, without adequate planning, Bangalore is sure to end up like Bombay: overcrowded and saturated with larger-than-life attitude. Luckily, it's not there yet, but natives, immigrants, and travelers can still relish being at the apogee of cosmopolitan India. Hordes of multinational corporations, notably IBM, Apple, and Hewlett-Packard, have established themselves here in the "Silicon Valley of India." Because of the altitude, the weather is sublime, averaging 23°C and topping 34°C only in April. The atmosphere is wonderfully liberal if a little commercial, and locals are notoriously friendly and witty. Students and entrepreneurs from all over the country come to Bangalore to delve into its top-notch educational institutions and lucrative business opportunities—the pace of Bangalore's intellectual and cultural life is as quick as that of its vibrant nightlife.

ORIENTATION

In the days of the British Raj, Bangalore was politically and culturally divided between the Cantonment, encompassing the race course, high grounds, the M.G. Rd. area and everything north; and the rest of the city, which centered around the Old Fort area and City Market. Cautious elders in the city warned children not to venture past the Queen Victoria statue in Cubbon Park, and British officers avoided the rest of the city like the plague. The areas now form more of a continuum, with most hotels nestled along the historic boundary. The **Majestic** area, near the **City Railway Station** and **bus stand,** is fecund ground for budget hotels; five kilometers east is the **M.G. Road** area, the fashionable hub for hotels, restaurants, bars, and shops. To the south of the Majestic area is Bangalore's last stronghold against industry and technology, the **City Market** area, with unpaved narrow roads, bullock carts, temples, and mosques. Most of the museums are in **Cubbon Park,** which stretches along **Kasturba Rd.** from **Kempegowda Rd.** to M.G. Rd.

PRACTICAL INFORMATION

Tourist Offices: Government of India Tourist Office, 48 Church St. (tel. 558 5417). From St. Mark's Rd., walk 1 block and take a left, going past Berry's Hotel and U.S. Pizza. The office is 1 block further. The staff of ardent Bangalorians hands out decent city maps and tired brochures, and provides travel information for the rest of Karnataka. Open Mon.-Fri. 9:30am-6pm, Sat. 9am-1pm. **KSTDC,** 10/4 Kasturba Rd. (tel. 221 2901). Near the junction of Kasturba and M.G. Rd., opposite the Queen Victoria statue in Cubbon Park, 2 flights up in a big off-white building. Daily Bangalore bus tours (Rs.75) and tours of far-off Karnataka cities. This is also the place to book a night in 1 of KSTDC's myriad Mayura hotels. Open Mon.-Sat. 10am-5:30pm, closed the second Sat. of each month.

Budget Travel: Scads of travel agencies line the streets near the railway and bus stations, but they tend to focus on sight-seeing tours or private coaches to Bombay, Mysore, Ooty, and other locales. For car rentals and bus, rail, air, and tour bookings, go to **Trade Wings,** 48 Lavelle Rd. (tel. 221 4595), across the street from the Airlines Hotel. Their gray-carpeted office is air-conditioned. Open Mon.-Sat. 9:30am-1pm and 2-5:30pm.

Immigration Office: Office of the Commissioner of Police, 1 Infantry Rd. (tel. 225 6242, ext. 251). Walk north along Cubbon Park past the GPO onto Queen's Rd. Take a left 1 block later and walk to the middle of the block. The office is a yellow, red-tiled ex-bungalow. 6-month visa extensions issued free in 1-2 days. Open Mon.-Sat. 10am-5:30pm.

Currency Exchange: Thomas Cook, 55 M.G. Rd. (tel. 558 6742), just before the intersection of M.G. and Brigade Rd. This is the fastest place to buy your rupees. If you wish to deal with a 15-min. wait and the token system, enter any of M.G. Rd.'s numerous **banks**—they all do foreign exchange. (Banks are generally open Mon.-Fri.10:30am-2:30pm, Sat. 10:30am-12:30pm.) The 5-star **hotels** sell to their guests at a disadvantageous rate. There is a 24-hr. **ATM** which accepts cards with "Plus" or "Global Access" logos outside the Hong Kong Bank, Municipal Ctr., 47 Dickenson Rd. (tel. 558 5444). Walk east on M.G. Rd., 1 block past the parade grounds. Turn left on Dickenson Rd. at the East Parade Church.

SOUTH INDIA

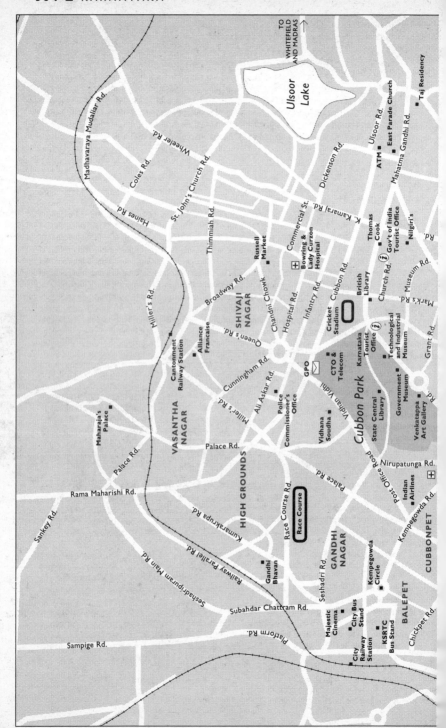

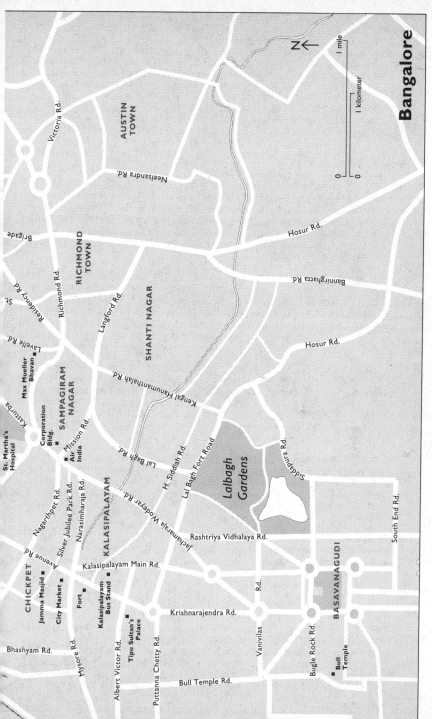

Bangalore

1 mile

1 kilometer

AUSTIN TOWN

Victoria Rd.

Neelsandra Rd.

Hosur Rd.

Brigade

RICHMOND TOWN

Richmond Rd.

St. Residency Rd.

Lavelle Rd.

Langford Rd.

SHANTI NAGAR

Banirghatta Rd.

Hosur Rd.

Kasturba

Max Mueller Bhavan

SAMPAGIRAM NAGAR

Kengal Hanumanthaiah Rd.

St. Martha's Hospital

Corporation Bldg.

Air India

Mission Rd.

Lalbagh Gardens

Siddapura Rd.

Nagarthpet Rd.

Silver Jubilee Park Rd.

Narasimharaja Rd.

Lal Bagh Rd.

H. Siddiah Rd.

Lal Bagh Fort Road

KALASIPALAYAM

Jachanaraja Wodeyar Rd.

Rashtriya Vidhalaya Rd.

South End Rd.

Avenue Rd.

Kalasipalayam Main Rd.

Rd.

CHICKPET

Jamma Masjid

City Market

Fort

Kalasipalayam Bus Stand

Krishnarajendra Rd.

BASAVANAGUDI

Mysore Rd.

Bhashyam Rd.

Albert Victor Rd.

Tipu Sultan's Palace

Puttanna Chetty Rd.

Bull Temple Rd.

Vanivilas

Bugle Rock Rd.

Bull Temple

Telephones: Central Telegraph (tel. 286 2325) and **Public Telecom** (tel. 286 4019) are located behind the GPO on Raj Bhavan Rd. STD/ISD, telex, and fax booths are everywhere; many are open 24hr.

Airport: in the southeast corner of the city, 8km from the M.G. Rd. area (tel. 526 6233, ext. 404, 140; city office tel. 221 1914, 221 1141). A Rs.20 auto-rickshaw ride from the center of the city. **Domestic Airlines:** Indian Airlines, Kempegowda Rd., Cauvery Bhavan, offers the most flights out of Bangalore. NEPC, 138A Brigade Gardens, Church St. (tel. 559 4860). Open Mon.-Fri. 9:30am-1pm and 2-5:30pm, Sat. 9:30am-1pm. Sahara, 1 Church St. (tel. 558 9848), on the corner of Church and Brigade St., opposite Hotel RRR. Open Mon.-Fri. 9:30am-1pm and 2-5:30pm, Sat. 9:30am-1pm. Jet Airways, 22 Ulsoor Rd. (tel. 559 9955), 1 block behind the Taj residency. Open Mon.-Fri. 9:30am-5:30pm, Sat. 9:30am-1pm and East West Airlines, 11A M.G. Rd. (tel. 5588282), near St. Mark's Rd. Open daily 9:30am-5:30pm. **International Airlines:** Air India, J.C. Rd., Unity Bldg. (tel. 227 7747), 1 block from Corporation Bldg. Open Mon.-Fri. 9:30am-1pm and 2-5pm, Sat. 9:30am-1pm. Air France (tel. 558 9397), Kuwait Airways (tel. 558 7709), and Gulf Air (tel. 558 4702) are all in Sunrise Chambers, 22 Ulsoor Rd., 1 block north of M.G. Rd., behind the Taj Residency, all open Mon.-Fri. 9:30am-1pm and 2-5pm, Sat. 9:30am-1pm). KLM, in the Taj West End Hotel, 3 Race Course Rd. (tel. 225 9281). Open Mon.-Fri. 9:30am-1pm and 2-5:30pm, Sat. 9:30am-1pm. Qantas, 13 Cunningham Rd. (tel. 226 4719), near Wockhardt Hospital. Open Mon.-Fri. 9:15-1pm and 2-5:30pm, Sat. 9:30am-12:30pm. Lufthansa, 42-2 Dickenson Rd. (tel. 558 8791), near Municipal Centre. Open Mon.-Fri. 9am-5:30pm, Sat. 9am-1pm. Swissair, 51 Richmond Rd. (tel. 221 1983), opposite BPL Plaza. Open Mon.-Fri., 9:30am-5:30pm, Sat. 9:30am-1:30pm. To: Calcutta (2 per day, 2½hr., US$203). Calicut (1 per day, 45min., US$50). Coimbatore (Mon.-Wed., Fri.-Sat., 40min., US$33). Delhi (3 per day, 2½hr., US$150). Hyderabad (2 per day, 1hr., US$59). Madras (2 per day, 1½hr., US$38). Bombay (5 per day, 1½hr., US$80).

Trains: City Railway Station (enquiry tel. 131, reservations tel. 132), at the end of Race Course Rd. and Bhashyam Rd. The reservation counter is in the building on your left as you face the station. Open Mon.-Sat. 8am-2pm and 2:15-10pm, Sun. 8am-2pm. Enquiries, with counters for women and foreigners, in the main building, open daily 7am-10:30pm. Trains from Bangalore are often booked weeks in advance. There's no tourist quota but the emergency quota is easy to get onto. To: Bombay (*Kurla Exp.* 1014, 12:10pm, 24hr.; *Udyan Exp.* 6530, 10:30pm, 24hr., Rs.188); Calcutta (*Howrah Exp.* 6512, Fri. 11:30pm, 38hr., Rs. 415/1304 for 2nd/1st class); Delhi (*Karnataka Exp.* 2627, 3:25pm, 42hr., Rs.263/1352 for 2nd/1st; *Rajdhani Exp.* 2429, Mon. 6:45, 34hr., Rs.800/1162 for 2nd/1st); Hubli (*Shatabdi Exp.* 2025, 2:30pm except Sun., 8hr., Rs.99/404 for 2nd/1st); Hospet (*Hampi Exp.* 6592, 9:55pm, 10hr., Rs.102/441 for 2nd/1st); Hyderabad (*Hyderabad Exp.* 7686, 5:05pm, 17hr., Rs.144/608 for 2nd/1st); Mangalore (*Bangalore Tiruchchi Exp.* 6532, 10:10pm, 26hr., Rs.88/363 for 2nd/1st); Mysore (*Kaveri Exp.* 6222, 8:25am, 3hr.; *Shatabdi Exp.* 2007, 10:55am except Tues., 2hr.; *Tippu Exp.* 6206, 2:25pm, 4hr., *Chamundi Exp.* 6216, 6:30pm, 3hr., Rs.55/125 for 2nd/1st); Madras (*Lalbagh Exp.* 2608, 6:30am, 5hr.; *Madras Exp.* 6024, 7:30am, 7hr.; *Brindavan Exp.* 2640, 4:30pm except Tues., 4½hr.; *Madras Mail* 6008, 10:15pm, 7½hr., Rs.82/334 for 2nd/1st).

Buses: KSRTC Bus Stand, Bhashyam Rd. (tel 287 3377). Enquiry and reservation counters in the building to the right as you approach from the rail station, open daily 6:30am-10:30pm. To: Arsikere (20 per day, 6am-11:30pm, 4hr., Rs.33/42/51); Bijapur (20 per day, 6am-11:30pm, 13hr., Rs.113/154); Bombay (8am, 2, and 4pm, 25hr., Rs.262); Hassan (25 per day, 6am-11:30pm, 4½hr., Rs.36/47/54); Hospet (10 per day, 7am-10pm, 8hr., Rs.70/101); Hyderabad (5:30, 6, 6:40, 7:15, and 8:30pm, 12hr., Rs.145/200); Mangalore (10 per day, 7:35am-11:40pm, 8hr., Rs.68/86/103); Madras (9 per day, 9:50am-10pm, 8hr., Rs.55/65/77); Mysore (30 per day, 5am-10pm, 3hr., Rs.27/34/41); Ooty (6:30, 10am, and 10pm, 8hr., Rs.65/97).

Local Transportation: From the city bus stand, **buses** to M.G. Rd. leave every 10-15 min. from platform 17. Best to use a tan **pushpack bus** if you're burdened with a backpack; pushpacks cost more (max. Rs.12) but no standing customers are allowed. Route #7 serves the corporation office and M.G. Rd. every 20min. from

7:20am. To Whitefield, take the #331e bus (Rs.7, 1hr.). Main **taxi** stands are located on Residency Rd. near the intersection with Brigade Rd.; Russell Market; and the City Railway Station. **Auto-rickshaws** are supposed to use their meters (Rs.5 per min.). If you arrive by bus or rail, go to the auto-rickshaw queue in the northeast corner of the rail station parking lot—there's a policeman there to ensure meter use. Otherwise, you'll probably get charged Rs.50 for a ride to M.G. Rd. From 9:30pm-5:30am, 50% is added to the meter charge. U-Rent Services, 19 RBDGT Bldg. (tel. 287 9760), rents **mopeds.** As you head out of the rail station, turn right and scan the "sidewalk" for their wooden sign. 24-hr. rental costs Rs.150 plus Rs.0.20 per km oil charge. Open daily 9am-6pm.

English Bookstore: Premier Bookshop, 46/1 Church St. (tel. 558 8570), around the corner from Berry's Hotel, is the type of bookstore that makes you aspire to own your own. The place is stuffed with paperbacks, floor to ceiling, and the shelves were either disposed of or obscured years ago. You'll find a wealth of established and up-and-coming South Asian writers, as well as Proust, Eco, Jung, and Ethan Canin. The closest thing to smut here is *Edwina and Nehru.* Open Mon.-Sat. 10am-1:30pm and 3-8pm. **Gangaram's Book Bureau,** 72 M.G. Rd. (tel. 558 6189). Horizontally and vertically immense with 3 well-stocked floors of literature, social sciences, stationery, clever postcards, and travel guidebooks for India and elsewhere (including a certain bright yellow budget guidebook). Open daily 10am-8pm. **Molital Banarsidass,** 16 St. Mark's Rd. (tel. 221 5389), has books on Indian religion, philosophy, yoga, ayurvedic medicine. The perfect place to select a translation of the Upanishads. Open Mon.-Sat. 10am-7pm.

Library: State Central Library, Cubbon Park (tel. 221 2128). Approach Cubbon Park from the Kasturba Rd. side; follow Lavelle Rd. into the park. The library is a red building with green sills. Thousands of dusty tomes, although most patrons seem to prefer newspapers. Sweet librarians. Open Tues.-Sun. 9am-7pm. **British Library,** 29 St. Mark's Rd. (tel. 224 0763), off M.G. Rd., near Koshy's Restaurant and Department Store. Technically they don't allow non-members, but in practice they're not that stuffy. It's air-conditioned. Overabundant Graham Greene section. Annual membership Rs.300 (no temporary memberships available) plus Rs.20 for each book borrowed. Open Tues.-Sat. 10:30am-6:30pm.

Cultural Centers: Max Mueller Bhavan, 3 Lavelle Rd. (tel. 221 4964). The end of Lavelle Rd. farthest from Kasturba Rd. Library and German language courses. Library open Mon., Thurs. 9am-1pm and 2-6pm, Tues. 2-6pm, Wed., Fri. 9am-1pm. **Alliance Française** (tel. 226 5390), Thimmiah Rd., near Cantonment Railway Station and opposite the United News of India Bldg. Membership Rs.300 (no temporary memberships). Library, French films, and cultural programs. Library open Mon.-Fri. 9am-1pm and 4-7pm, Sat. 9am-noon. **Bharatiya Vidya Bhavan** (tel. 226 7421), opposite the race course on Race Course Rd. The Bangalore branch of this all-India organization conducts cultural and literary activities. Library open Mon.-Fri. 10:30am-5:30pm, Sat. 10:30am-1:30pm. For **event listings,** check out The *Deccan Herald* (listings every day on p. 3; comprehensive listings Mon. and Fri.) or pick up a copy of *Bangalore This Fortnight* (free in hotels and restaurants). Prices and times are not always accurate, but the magazine does provide a good sense of Bangalore opportunities.

Market: Spencer's Superstore, 84 M.G. Rd. (tel. 558 7202) sells sodas (including Diet Coke for Rs.38!), corn flakes, whiskey, cosmetics, contact lens solution, and mosquito coils (Rs.42). Also stocks less portable items like computers and kitchen sinks. Open daily 10am-8pm. **Nilgiri's Supermarket,** 171 Brigade Rd. (tel. 558 7641), specializes in victuals. Pricey fruit stand outside. **Russell Market,** 2km north of M.G. Rd. off Cunningham St., is an indoor market selling fruit, flowers, veggies, and meat. The combined smells of raw fish and cilantro make for a unique olfactory experience. Generally open from dawn to dusk. **City Market,** 1½km southwest of the city rail station, near Jamma Masjid. also sells fruit, vegetables, meat, and flowers indoors. Make sure to wash your *chickoo* before biting into it. Open from dawn to dusk.

Pharmacy: Janata Bazaar (tel. 559 1362), on your left as you enter Bowring and Lady Curzon hospital premises off Hospital Rd. Open 24hr.

Hospitals: One of the government hospitals is **Bowring and Lady Curzon Hospital** (tel. 559 1362, ext. 244 for emergency), off Hospital Rd. 2km north of M.G. Rd. **St. Martha's Hospital** (tel. 227 5081), opposite the YMCA and the Reserve Bank of India on Nirupatunga Rd., is the second-oldest private hospital in India and is very modern.

Opticians: Opto, 66 M.G. Rd. (tel. 558 7503). New glasses take 2 days and cost Rs.400-6000. Contact lenses and solutions. Open Mon.-Sat. 9:30am-7:30pm.

Emergency: tel. 100.

Police: Commissioner's Office, 1 Infantry Rd. (tel. 225 4501). From the intersection of M.G. and Kasturba Rd., walk northwest so the Cubbon Park is on your left; follow Queen's Rd. to Infantry Rd. and take a left. There a branch in Cubbon Park (tel. 556 6242) next to the aquarium on Kasturba Rd. Headquarters (tel. 221 1803) are on Nirupatunga Rd., next to the YMCA.

Post Office: GPO, a stone colossus on the corner of Raj Bhavan and Ambedkar Rd. in Cubbon Park. Open Mon.-Sat. 10am-6:30pm. There are a few branches a mere 1-min. walk from M.G. Rd.: on Brigade Rd., halfway between KFC and Wimpy's across the street (open Mon.-Sat. 10am-6pm); on Museum Rd., at its intersection with St. Mark's Rd., there's a computerized post and telegraph office (open Mon.-Sat. 10am-6pm). **Postal Code:** 560001.

Telephone Code: 080.

ACCOMMODATIONS

Without a reservation or a convincing claim that you made one, it's difficult to find a decently priced room in the **Mahatma Gandhi Rd. (M.G. Rd.)** area. But hotels in this part of the are city are clean, modern, and have personality—this is the place to be in Bangalore. The area around the city bus stand and city rail stations, with its innumerable high-rise hotels of sixty or more rooms, has plenty of cheap places to stay, but they are impersonal and inconvenient compared to their M.G. Rd. counterparts. A string of hotels lines **Subahdar Chhatram Rd. (S.C. Rd.),** a five-minute walk from the City Railway Station. To get there, take the subway toward the bus station, and the pedestrian overpass to the street, continuing for one block in the same direction. Don't agonize about choosing a hotel in this area because they're all practically clones of each other: sleek lobbies, newly painted doors, ho-hum rooms, and cheap prices. But because of the location (5km from M.G. Rd.) you could end up paying more for auto-rickshaws than you'll save living on S.C. Rd. The two hotels near the Corporation Building are equidistant from M.G. Rd. and the rail station. The lodges in **City Market** are cheap, but they require residents to be adept at weaving through traffic, impervious to noise, and hooked on *faloodas*.

Airlines Hotel, 4 Madras Bank Rd. (tel. 227 3783). Off Lavelle Rd. Although it's a 10-min. walk from M.G. Rd. consumerism, this place is a mall in itself. The hotel complex houses a travel agency with 24-hr. car rental services, an STD/ISD booth with xerox and fax machines, a supermarket, a bargain sari shop, a real estate agency, and, for shadowing and protection services, the Asian Detective Agency (which specializes in infidelity investigations). The restaurant has outdoor dining around a banyan tree that seems unfazed by the proliferation of this strip mall. Rooms have telephones, towels, seat toilets, and running hot water until 10:30am. Laundry and room service. Check-out 24hr. Singles Rs.175. Doubles Rs.250, with TV Rs.350. Reserve 1 week in advance.

Nilgiri's Nest, 171 Brigade Rd. (tel. 558 8401). Although it's been around for a while, 20 years of sterilization have kept the Nest looking brand new. The staff possesses a mix of compassion, anxiety, and cleanliness that only your mother could match. All rooms have bathrooms with seat toilets and hot water 6-10am, Star TV, and vanity mirrors so you'll look your spiffiest at the pubs around the corner. Check-out 24hr. Nilgiri's is first and foremost a co-op dairy farm (est. 1905)—on the ground floor is a grocery store filled with tourists and Bangalore yuppies, on the first floor is Nilgiri's Café, and the second floor is the paperwork department. The Nest itself is perched at the top. Singles Rs.350. Doubles Rs.450. Credit cards and traveler's checks in U.S. dollars, pounds sterling, Deutschmarks, and yen accepted. Reserve a few days in advance.

Brindavan Hotel, 108 M.G. Rd. (tel. 558 4000). A budget hotel extravaganza, set in its own grounds with 112 rooms and attached restaurant (South Indian veg., down to the banana leaves), travel agency (daily coaches to Bombay and Madras), and annex store (with hairbrushes, soap, and candy). Quite possibly the largest budget doubles in Bangalore. Despite the hotel's megaplexiness, the rooms are homey, with tapestried chairs and paisley bedspreads. Telephones, color TVs, hot water 5-10am, and an astropalmist in Rm. 17. Check-out 24hr. All doubles have balconies. Singles Rs.195 plus tax. Doubles Rs.275 plus tax. Reserve at least a week in advance.

New Victoria Hotel, 47-48 Residency Rd. (tel. 558 4076). Several bungalows lost in rampant trees and wildflowers. The rooms are resplendent with Victorian relics: burgundy velvet burgundy chairs in the hallways, portraits on the wall, dark wood antiques, and a garden swing. This is the place to indulge your nostalgia for the 19th century—it was British military canteen and library until about 1935, and the British coat of arms still lurks in the stained glass above the reception. Expensive restaurant and bar, outdoor dining, room service, laundry. 24-hr. hot water and seat toilets. Check-out 24hr. Singles Rs.250. Doubles Rs.550-650. Credit cards and traveler's checks accepted. Reserve 1 week in advance.

Hotel Mahaveer, 8-1 Tankbund Rd. (tel. 287 3670). On the corner of Chickpet Rd. (on the right outside the rail station exit), a 5-min. walk from the rail station. Rock fountains (which trickle at best, depending on the Bangalore water supply), a friendly management accustomed to foreign tourists, and modern, clean, smallish rooms. All 66 rooms have attached baths with seat toilets, televisions, telephones, humidifiers, and fridges. Deluxe rooms have massive beds, wall-to-wall carpeting, and bathtubs. Running hot water 5:30-9:30am, same-day laundry service, travel counter, foreign exchange. Check-out 24hr. Singles Rs.160. Doubles Rs.230. Triples Rs.290. Deluxe rooms Rs.575.

Pai Vihar, OTC Rd. (tel. 221 5161), across from the Corporation Bldg. Cramped but spiffy rooms with tiny Mughal prints on red walls and ornate brass lamps suggest the touch of an interior decorator. Comfortable luxuries: seat toilets with toilet paper, soap and towels, 24-hr. hot water and room service, travel counter. The fare at the attached restaurant is reasonably priced (open daily 7am-9pm; *dosas* under Rs.10). Singles Rs.230. Doubles Rs.300, with A/C Rs.400. MC/V accepted.

Hotel Luciya International, 6 OTC Rd. (tel. 222 4148). Near Sri Rama Vilas temple and down the road from the Corporation Bldg. Six floors and 66 wallpapered and carpeted rooms, with phones, TVs, seat toilets and 24-hr. running hot water. The interior is a striking contrast with the dirt roads and BJP graffiti outside. A kiosk on the ground floor sells regional travel guides and soap, even though Luciya provides fresh soap along with towels. The attached North and South Indian restaurant has a live *ghazal* band until 11:30pm. Two pillows per person. Travel counter, room service, and laundry service. Check-out 24hr. Singles Rs.350, with A/C Rs. 450. Doubles Rs.450, with A/C Rs.550. Reserve 1 week in advance. Major credit cards accepted.

Blue Fox Lodging, 80 M.G. Rd. (tel. 558 3205). Two flights up from the neon-lit Blue Fox Restaurant and bar (next door to the "Indian-Jap Mannequin Co. The First One"). Slightly overpriced but the location is fantastic. Ten carpeted rooms fixed around a spiral staircase make for an escape from the typical cold-floored megaplexes. 24-hr hot water and room service. (You can shower at 2am and then regrease your fingers with a *dosa*.) TVs, telephones, laundry service. Check-out noon. Doubles Rs.460, with A/C Rs.575. Reserve a few days in advance.

Sri Ramakrishna Lodge, S.C. Rd. (tel. 226 3041). Next to Kapali Theater. Large, sun-flooded rooms with extra-cushiony beds. Two attached inexpensive restaurants (*thalis* Rs.17), travel counter, pharmacy, and face reader. Each floor has a verandah where you can chow your *bhel puri* and watch the bustle below. Squat toilets in immaculate bathrooms. Hot water 6:30-9:30am. Laundry and room service. Check-out 24hr. Singles Rs.95. Doubles Rs.200.

Hotel Imperial Lodge, 93-94 Residency Rd. (tel. 558 8391). Plain, entirely functional drab rooms. During the day, the place is quite cheery with large windows and the bustle of the street below, but at night it takes on an ominous character: narrow staircases and a garage off the reception where men smoke cigarettes and watch TV late into the night. Still, the reception is pleasant and all rooms are blessed with the TV, telephone, newspaper, and room service that are the norm in this neighborhood. Squat toilet, hot water in the morning. Attached restaurant and travel agency. Check-out 24hr. Singles Rs.95. Doubles Rs.175.

Sandhya Lodge, 70 S.C. Rd. (tel. 287 4065). Rooms are typically mediocre but at least the spiffy lobby, elevator boys, and sunny balconies on each floor give a feeling of extravagance. Fresh paint on the doors but stained walls in the rooms. Clean bathrooms with grimy windows, squat toilets with running hot water 6-9am. Telephones, clean bedding. Travel counter and kiosk store on the ground (subway) floor. Room and laundry service. Bulletin board with train and air timings and movie showings. Check-out 24hr. Singles Rs.149. Doubles Rs.180. Triples Rs.250. TV Rs.50-60 extra.

Hotel Shalimar, 127-128 N.R. Rd. (tel. 660 2227). Across from Jamma Masjid, opposite the bus stand. A oasis of Lysol in an area not known for its sanitation. Rooms are spotless if tiny, with airy hallways and large windows through which you can watch the raucous episodes of life in the City Market without being run over by rickshaws or hollered at. Squat toilets, running hot water in the mornings, laundry service, room service. Check-out 24hr. Singles Rs.105. Doubles Rs.185, deluxe Rs.225.

Chandra Vihar, MRR Lane, City Market, Avenue Rd. (tel. 222 4146). Opposite the City Market Bldg., 1 block from Jamma Masjid). So typical it's weird, with flaked pink paint, functional rooms, running hot water in the mornings, veg. room service, laundry service. Telephones in all 50 rooms. The only distinguishing features of the rooms are their toilets—Western sit-down style with Indian textured wings. Check-out 24hr. Singles Rs.105. Doubles Rs.180. Triples Rs.225. All prices plus 10% tax.

Royal Lodge, 251 S.C. Rd. (tel. 226 6951). Has a shabbier exterior than its newish neighbors but its rooms are just as functional, clean, and cheery, just a little lower to the ground. The beds are a bit leaner than some (which makes the rooms look larger) but they're cheaper too. Doubles have attached bathroom with squat toilets. No attached bathrooms for singles. Running hot water in the morning. There's a security guard on duty, which is reassuring when you're in the dim hallways. Check-out 24hr. Singles Rs.60. Doubles Rs.120.

FOOD

Inundated by Wimpy's, Baskin-Robbins, and, most recently, Pizza Hut, Bangalore seems to have no problem waging a culinary consumer war against these multinational corporations. The secret? Provide better food at cheaper prices, which isn't so tough. After all, who in her right mind would pass up tandoori chicken for KFC? Western cuisine in Bangalore is pricey compared to the Indian dishes served around the corner. But whether you're into burgers or *bhel puris,* eat up—Bangalore is the place to put back on that weight you've been losing.

Indian Coffee House, 78 M.G. Rd. (tel. 587088), possibly the cheapest and smartest sit-down place on M.G. Rd. to grab a cup of joe (Rs.3.50). Owned by the Indian Coffee Workers Co-op Society, its walls are coated with coffee propaganda: "Coffee—for gracious living" and "Indian coffee—the cup that XL's." The brew here does excel; besides, it's served by waiters in comedic old turbans, red and gold embroidered sashes, and canvas tennis shoes. The ideal place to peruse the morning's news over omelettes (Rs.7) and toast (Rs.4). Lots of cigarette smoking here—the only way it could be more bohemian would be if it stayed open later. Open daily 8:30am-8:30pm.

Shanbag Cafe, 92 Residency Rd., is the place for cheapish, pleasantly plump *dosas,* cumulo-nimbular *puris,* and *lassis* so viscous they get stuck in your straw. Lots of families sitting in the bright yellow booths. Service is mellow and conscientious—a rarity in Bangalore's meals restaurants. Open for *thalis* (Rs.17) daily 11am-3:30pm and 7-10:30pm, 4-10:30pm for *chats.*

Nilgiri's Cafe, 171 Brigade Rd. (tel. 558 8401), has a clientele so well-scrubbed that they look fresh from the dairy farm Nilgiri's founded in 1905. The average age on some days seems to be around 18. Into the mouths of babes goes fresh quiche (Rs.25), hefty, grilled sandwiches, flaky tuna croissants (Rs.30), and doughy cheese pizzas (Rs.30). Hazelnut milkshakes (Rs.25) are so good they bring customers to tears. Hip visual and aural decor: lime green walls with framed farm scenes, unvarnished wood furniture, and Lou Reed and the Cars crooning away. No smoking. Open daily 7am-11pm.

The Rice Bowl, 215 Brigade Rd. (tel. 558 7417). Just off M.G. Rd., this place is owned by the Dalai Lama's sister and niece (though you probably won't see them anywhere near Bangalore) and it represents the antithesis of everything His Holiness might recommend. The fried ravioli (Rs.70) is indulgent, the stir fry (Rs.50) over-abundant, and the date/banana pancake with ice cream blasphemously decadent. Indian tunes from the attached bar pound the walls. Open daily noon-3:30pm and 7-10:30pm.

Kamat, Unity Bldg. off J.C. Rd. (tel. 222480). One of Bangalore's best-value Indian restaurants. Overly generous *thalis* (served noon-3pm and 7-11pm) with your choice of *puri* or *chapati,* tomato soup, and 2 sweets for Rs.40. The A/C hall is packed at meal times, but service is impeccable. Shiny black tables and plush ruby booths convince you you're dining in a near-luxury establishment. Open daily 8am-11pm.

Coconut Grove, Church St. opposite the Gateway Hotel. Serves up the finest coastal cuisine this far from Kerala. Try the *appam* (Rs.9)—a *dosa*-like entity cooked with no oil, and crispy at the edges with a dense, soft center. Fish or vegetable stews complement the *appam* best, and the waiters are expert menu navigators. Pricey (count on Rs.200 for two) but worth it not only for the food but for the bamboo decor, candles, and soft tabla music. Try the tender coconut water with honey and mint. Open daily noon-3pm and 7-11pm.

Southern Comforts, in the Taj Residency, 41/3 M.G. Rd. (tel. 558 4444). A 24-hr. coffee shop with cappuccino, espresso (Rs.40), ice cream, and snacks. For Rs.50 you can get a huge bowl of soup with a basket of bread. After the pubs and discos close, this place fills up with teenagers scared to go home and college students grinding away at physiology tests. The service is obsequious; 5-star patrons demand nothing less.

The Only Place, 158 Nota Royal Arcade, Brigade Rd. (tel. 558 8678). This restaurant has been serving beef burgers (Rs.50), apple pies (Rs.25), pancakes (Rs.30), and lasagna (Rs.45) ever since the owner married an American co-ed studying in Bangalore. Perhaps the way to a man's stomach is through his heart, perhaps he married her for her recipes...whatever the case, The Only Place has become a Bangalore institution, outshouting its newer rivals, which are popping up in the vicinity with alarming regularity. Open daily 11am-3pm and 6:30-11pm.

Casa Picolla, Devatha Plaza, 131 Residency Rd. (tel. 221 2907), a 10-min. walk from the Brigade Rd. area, past Black Cadillac; half of it is underground. Frequented by young Indian couples imbibing the candlelight and fresh fruit juice (Rs.15). The food's not as ethereal as the decor, but it's cheap and filling—and where else in Bangalore can you get *Wiener Schnitzel* (Rs.58)? Pizzas, cheesy pastas come first, but be sure to save room for crepes, profiteroles, and cappuccino. Open daily 9am-10:30pm.

SIGHTS

Cubbon Park and Museums

Set aside in 1864 and named for the former chief commissioner Mark Cubbon, Cubbon Park consists of 132 hectares of lush greenery in the center of the city. The park extends from the corner of M.G. Rd. to the Corporation Building and provides much needed shade and escape from the buses, cars, and buildings that surround it. Cubbon houses the **K. Venkatappa Art Gallery** and **Government Museums** (tel. 286 4483). The former exhibits watercolor landscapes by K. Venkatappa, the Mysore court artist who painted much of the Maharaja's Palace in Mysore. You can catch a glimpse of Ooty before its commercialism in his ethereal "Dawn in Ooty," "Moonrise City," "Ooty at Midnight," etc. The second and third floors display works by contemporary Karnatakan artists. The **Government Museum**, celebrating its 111th year, is one of India's oldest museums. It houses Hoysalan sculptures and archeological finds such as arrowheads from Mohenjo-Daro, pottery, coins, and neolithic bones. (Both open Tues.- Sun. 10am-5pm. Admission Rs.5 to both.) Next door is the **Visveswaraya Industrial and Technological Museum** which celebrates Bangalore's industrial prowess, from 1905, when City Market lit India's first light bulb, to Bangalore's current "silicon valley" days. Use your brain and muscle power to learn about the inner workings of the pulley, the computer, and the nuclear bomb, and to teach yourself the binary system. (Open Tues.-Sun. 10am-5pm. Admission Rs.5.) Across the park lies the gothic **Attara Kachari** which housed the 18 departments of the secretariat until 1956 (*attara* means "eighteen" in Hindi). It's now the turf of the High Court, where you can mingle with black-robed barristers. Across the road is the **Vidhana Soudha,** which now houses the secretariat. In the early 1950s, members of a visiting Russian delegation quipped about the abundance of European architecture in Bangalore. Triggered by the Russians' remarks, the then-chief minister of Mysore decided to construct this spectacular neo-Dravidian structure. The Vidhana Soudha became not only an affirmation of Indian sovereignty but also an assertion of Bangalore's new-found legislative importance. It's built of pure Bangalore granite, and atop the main entrance sits Emperor Ashoka's four-headed lion (the symbol of the Indian nation which can be seen in all rupee notes when they're held to the light). Statues of Jawaharlal Nehru and B.R. Ambedkar stand in the front lawn, gesticulating at each other. The building is not open to the public, but the wonderful exterior is flooded with light every Sunday night. Nearby, across from Raj Bhavan on T. Chowdiak Rd., is the eight-year-old **Jawaharlal Nehru Planetarium** (tel. 220 3234), built to commemorate the 100th birthday of the freedom fighter and prime minister who called Bangalore "India's city of the future." (Open Tues.-Sun.; closed the second Tues. of each month. Kannada shows at 3pm, English at 4:30pm. Admission Rs.10, Rs.5 for children.) Across the Golf Course (High Grounds), down Kumara Krupa Rd. from the five-star Windsor, sits **Gandhi Bhavan** (tel. 226 1967). It's a beautifully organized journey through the Mahatma's life, with grainy blown-up photographs, quotations chock-full of Gandhian wisdom, and such artifacts as Gandhi's spartan wooden *chappals* and clay drinking bowls. Bring a rag to clear the half-centimeter of dust from the glass-encased letters to Franklin Roosevelt, Tolstoy, Gokhale, and Nehru. Few people visit this jewel; there's no permanent staff and you'll need to ask to have the door unlocked. Downstairs is a library selling cheap copies of Gandhi's writings. (Open Mon.-Sat. 10am-1:30pm and 3-5pm. Free.)

Lalbagh and Around

Haider Ali laid out Lalbagh Gardens in 1760; his son Tipu Sultan extended the 16-hectare gardens to 96 hectares and added the mango grove. After Tipu's demise in 1799, the British took over Lalbagh, and Prince Albert Victor of Wales built the Glass House as a homage to London's Crystal Palace in the late 1800s. The gardens are home to 150 different varieties of roses and 1000 kinds of tropical and subtropical flora and fauna, a giant floral clock, a lotus pond, and hundreds of walkers, joggers, and cyclists. One of the four watchtowers that Kempegowda built to mark Bangalore's city limits is here. (Open daily dawn to dusk.) The 18th-century Mysore maharaja Haider Ali also refurbished the **fort,** opposite Vanivilas Hospital on Krishnarajendra Rd. It was originally built in mud and brick by Chikkadevaraga Wodeyar in the late 1600s as an extension of the former fort built by Kempegowda in the area between the Corporation Offices and City Market. Though most of it was destroyed in the Anglo-Mysore War, the remains are beautifully preserved, with ornately carved Islamic-style arches and turrets, and the exquisite **Ganapati temple** inside. Five hundred meters south of the fort is **Tipu Sultan's Summer Palace,** which Tipu liked to call it Lask-e-Jannat, "The Envy of Heaven," although it is really a meaner replica of Daria Daulat in Srirangapatnam. The palace took 10 years to complete—not so much because it was an artistic feat, but because Haider Ali was killed during its construction and Tipu was busy avenging his death. Most of the original wall paintings have been obscured by shiny brown paint. South of the Palace on Bull Temple Rd. is the **Bull Temple,** with a massive Nandi over 500 years old. Legend has it that a raging bull used to torment local farmers by ravaging their fields at night. The frustrated farmers finally hired a night watchman who killed the bull with a crowbar. The next morning, they discovered that the carcass had transformed into a solid granite bull. You can still see the crowbar embedded in the poor beast's back. Open daily from 8am to 8pm.

Other Sights

To the north of the city is the **Maharaja's Palace,** dwarfed by its massive gardens. The palace is a monument to extravagance, a reminder of days when maharajas had nothing better to do with their money than outdo each other with ostentatious palaces. The Maharaja of Mysore wanted a palace on the lines of Windsor Castle in England, replete with parapets, battlement, and fortified towers. The palace is open to the public for only one week each November.

   Brindavan Ashram, 16km from Bangalore on Madras Rd. in Whitefield, is Sai Baba's Karnataka haunt. Much of the year, he's in Andhra Pradesh at his main ashram, Puttaparthi. Sai Baba runs free hospitals and schools, performs miracles, and has developed quite a following. When he's in Whitefield, devotees and interested travelers can stay there for about Rs.100 per night. For information regarding Sai Baba's presence and overnight stays, call the palace office (tel. 845 2233). City bus #331e runs to Whitefield, as do three trains (*Marikuppan* 256 and 254, 6:45am and 6:10pm, respectively, and the *Madras Passenger* 96, 10:30am, 1hr., Rs.4/65 for 2nd/1st class).

ENTERTAINMENT

Bars

Although Bangalore is plagued by water shortages, the city is never dry. Bangalore's burgeoning pub culture (second only to Bombay's) has earned the city the sobriquet "Bar Galore." But locals admit this is nothing new—a steady stream of liquor courses through Bangalore's history. Most pubs are clustered around Brigade Rd., and they're frequented by regulars who greet the pubs' godfather-esque owners with hearty hugs and call the bartenders by their first names. So no matter how newfangled they seem, most pubs already have distinctive characters. Due to a recent city ordinance, pubs must close at 11pm. The police come by around midnight, suggesting "Good people sleep early," and stragglers exit quietly through the back door. Unless noted, pubs are open daily from 11am to 2:30pm and from 5:30 to 11pm. A mug of draught beer typically costs Rs.20-25, pitchers about Rs.120, and mixed drinks and cocktails Rs.75. A word of caution to Western women: don't be lulled by the liberal tap into thinking you can throw decorum to the breezy Bangalore night. Deep-seated stereotypes about foreign women are exacerbated, rather than vanquished, by alcohol, and drunk men can be especially aggressive.

   The Cellar, 7 Curzon Ct., Brigade Rd. (tel. 558 2997). Opposite the intersection with Church St. Woody decor—no neon here—and booths that encourage sinking into over a good conversation. The mellow afternoon may have been invented here. Proportionate representation of the sexes. Open daily 11am-11pm; bottled beer only from 2-5pm.

   The New Night Watchman, 4611 Church St. (tel. 558 8372). Near Berry's Hotel. Caters to a largely North Indian crowd, which mean it's one of the only pubs around that plays *bhangra*. Regulars are so busy shaking their booties (an entertainment in itself) that it's pretty easy to find a seat, even on a Saturday night.

   Peco's Pub, 34 Rest House Rd. (tel. 558 6047). Off Brigade Rd. Hendrix, Marley, Joplin, and Zeppelin grace the walls as well as the stereo. Three floors packed with college-aged guzzlers imbibing mugfuls at Rs.19. Don't get too sloshed or that quaint spiral stairway won't lead to heaven.

The Pub World, 65 Residency St. (tel. 558 5206). Marginally more upscale than its neighbors, with oak banisters, lace curtains, and tapestried footstools. Bartendenders have honors degrees in chivalry. Open daily 11am-3pm and 5:30-11pm.

The Black Cadillac, 50 Residency Rd. (tel. 221 6148). A few blocks west of Brigade Rd., with a red neon sign that is obscured so that all you can see from the street is a giant cursive "C." This is where Bangalore's fashionable elite go to see and be seen, so dress appropriately. Model want-ads on the walls. Sublimate in the sublime garden area.

The Underground, 65 Blue Moon Complex, M.G. Rd. (tel. 558 9991). Near Brigade Rd. A little pricier (mugs of beer for Rs.25) but the bartenders make up for it in charm and cocktail expertise. Despite the neon sign outside and the ostentatious Kingfisher signpost, the interior is pretty tasteful. Not much room to kick back, but what did you expect in a bar named after a metro system?

Discos

A few of Bangalore's pubs used to have their own discos, where denizens would dance until dawn. Alas, a city ordinance has put an end to such scandalous shimmying. Much to the chagrin of local musicians, the city has also banned live music from any place liquor is served. Older locals support such restrictions, explaining that the government is responsible for its citizens' welfare, and many Bangalorians could not physically, mentally, or financially handle such debauchery. However, it seems that city ordinances are made to be evaded: after all, dancing is still OK outside the city limits. Ask around at the pubs for information about the discos that the five-star hotels occasionally stage.

The Club, 7th Mile, Mysore Rd. (tel. 860 0768). Ten kilometers out of the city; autorickshaw fare at night will be about Rs.40. The bastion of bacchanalia in the 'burbs, this place boogies 3 nights a week. Action starts around 10pm and the party usually rages on past 4am. The crowd is young, rich, and well (if scantily) dressed. The outdoor pool is put to good use despite a lack of swimwear. Open Wed. (no cover), Fri. (Rs.100 cover), and Sat. (Rs.200 cover, Rs.100 of which subsidizes drinks and snacks).

Other Diversions

Several **cinemas** in the M.G. Rd. area play English-language flicks. **The Plaza,** 74 M.G. Rd. (tel. 558 7682), and **The Rex,** 43 Residency Rd. (tel 558 7682), show not-too-old U.S. movies. Admission is Rs.10-30. One hour advance booking is recommended.

Nrityagram Dance Village, 30km from Bangalore on Bangalore-Pune Highway (tel. 846 6312), was established and is run by Protima Gauri, possibly the best Odissi dancer in India. Dancers from all over India come to train here and Gauri also conducts classes for children from neighboring villages. She changed her name from Protima Bedi upon coming to Karnataka because *bedi* means "loose motion" in Kannada. (She still uses her real name for an "agony aunt" column she writes in *Bangalore This Fortnight.*) The village is open from August to May, and it's possible to arrange an hour-long lecture-demonstration of Odissi and Kathak dance. Minimum four people, at Rs.500 each. Buses run regularly from Bangalore to Nrityagram, but the village is 5km from the bus stand and there aren't many auto-rickshaws around. It's recommended that you arrange for a private taxi (about Rs.500 roundtrip) or book through Cosmopole Travels (tel. 228 1591) or Cox and Kings Travels (tel. 223 9258). In the first week of February, the dance village conducts an all-night dance and music festival, free of charge, with performances by Gauri and her students as well as musical heartthrobs Zakar Hussain and Amjad Ali Khan. Buses run directly to the village during the program and the amphitheater is always packed with upwards of 25,000 people. Get there by 5:30pm if you don't want to stand all night.

The **Windsor Manor Sheraton,** 25 Sankey Rd. (tel. 226 9898), near the high grounds, will let you splash around in their outdoor swimming pool for Rs.300 (pool open 7am-7pm). The nearby **Holiday Inn,** 28 Sankey Rd. (tel. 226 2233), is marginally cheaper at Rs.250. If you're not into the bourgeois sports scene, and don't mind a much less luxurious atmosphere, go for a dip in the public **Kensington Swimming Pool** (tel. 563413), opposite Ulsoor Lake. Cost is Rs.100 membership fee, then Rs.3 per hour. Open daily 6am-5pm.

SHOPPING

Even if you spent all you money in Bangalore bars or are going through an austerity phase, you should still check out Bangalore's arts and crafts emporia: tables covered with handpainting or inlaid with precious gems, saris fit for a rani, sandalwood Krishnas taller than people. **Cauvery Arts Emporium,** 45 M.G. Rd. near Brigade Rd. (tel. 558 2656), run by the state government, has fair prices and a decent selection. Open Mon.-Sat. from 10am to 1:30pm and 3 to 7pm. You probably can't afford much at **Artefacts,** 56 Residency Rd. (tel. 559 6843) and it's more like an art gallery than an emporium. The paintings and giant statues provoke sharp intakes of breath—just hold it there, because exhaling might mar the works. Open Mon.-Sat. from 9:30am to 8:30pm. In general, the M.G. Rd. area is the emporiophile's paradise, with arts and handicrafts shops selling stuff from all over India. On **Commercial St.,** you'll find *salwar kameez* and saris in unthinkable permutations of style, color, and price.

■ Mysore

In pre-pre-pre-historic times, when gods and goddesses romped around their playground earth, the buffalo demon Mahishasura was having his own fun with the nascent human race, subjecting them to extortion, boils, murders, "disappearances"—the whole mean-spirited spectrum. The goddess Chamundi (in most versions of the story it's Durga, but this sort of thing is flexible) sensed a streak of genuine malice in Mahishasura's cruel antics and decided to knock him off, thus liberating the people of the Deccan. Their lives became one big celebration of the episode, from the city's name (which comes from a word meaning "Buffalo Town"), to October's 10-day-long Dasara festival, to the fact that Chamundi is the family deity of the Wodeyars, who ruled Mysore from around 1400 until Indian independence in 1947. With a population of over 700,000, Mysore is the second largest city in Karnataka, and the meters of hand-strung jasmine garlands lend Mysore the label "Jasmine City;" as the world's largest sandal oil producer, Mysore is also known as "Sandalwood City." It's no surprise that Mysore is one of the best-smelling cities in India. But Mysore's commitment to beauty is by no means limited to the olfactory—as the former capital of a princely state, Mysore is saturated with grand old palaces and other maharajas' ex-haunts, as well as monuments, statues, temples, gardens, and parks. Compound this with Mysore's silk industry, and what remains is an atmosphere of laid-back luxury.

ORIENTATION

Although Mysore is spotted with rotaries and streaked with unforgiving twisty-turny roads, the city is quite compact. A visit to the summit of **Chamundi Hill,** southeast of the city, provides a surprising perspective on Mysore's tidy boundaries. Running north-south, **Sayajit Rao Road** bisects Mysore proper into two equal halves, cutting through **K-R Circle,** the true center of the city. The city bus stand is off the southeast quarter of K-R Circle. If you head east from K-R Circle, you'll walk along the outskirts of the gigantic **Maharaja's Palace.** About 300m north of K-R Circle, Sayajit Rao Rd. meets the east-west **Old Bank Road (or Sardar Patel Road).** Old Bank Rd. leads east to a granite obelisk, a miniature rendition of Delhi's Gandhi Memorial: this is **Gandhi Square.** About 75m southeast is the Big-Ben-reminiscent **Clock Tower,** with a massive marble maharaja protected from the midday sun by a carnivalesque canopy. South of the clock tower, the road intersects Sri Harsha Rd., which leads east to a north-south thoroughfare, **Bangalore-Nilgiri (B-N) Rd.** North on B-N Rd., across from Wesley Cathedral, is the **Central Bus Stand,** and further north is **Irwin Road,** which leads west past the GPO, the State Bank of Mysore, and the tourist office. One block further west is the domed **railway station.**

PRACTICAL INFORMATION

Tourist Office: Karnataka Tourist Office: Old Exhibition Building, corner of Irwin and Diwan's Rd. (tel. 22096). One block (250m) east of the railway station. Slow service; lacking in brochures. Open Mon.-Sat. 10am-5:30pm. Closed the second Sat. of each month. **KSTDC:** Jhansi Laxmi Bai Rd. (tel. 423652). Adjacent to the KSTDC's Hotel Mayura. Will book you on exhausting, jam-packed day-long tours of Mysore or of Belur and Halebid for Rs.85. Open daily 6am-8:30pm.

Budget Travel: Many travel agencies are located in the Gandhi Sq. area. **Dasprakash Travel Agency,** in the hotel complex off Gandhi Square (tel. 24949). Books tours, air and rail tickets, and rents chauffeured cars and vans.

Currency Exchange: Many banks in the Gandhi Sq. area are authorized dealers in foreign currency. The **State Bank of Mysore** has a branch at the junction of Sayajit Rao Rd. and Old Bank Rd. **Syndicate Bank** in K-R Circle changes a number of currencies, as does the **State Bank of India** (annex building, 2nd fl.), at the intersection of Ashoka and Irwin Rd., across from the GPO. **Indian Overseas Bank,** across from Hotel Durbar (tel. 23573) changes only traveler's checks. Banks are open Mon.-Fri. 10:30am-2:30pm, Sat. 10:30am-12:30pm.

Telephones: Scores of private STD/ISD booths, some open 24hr., are concentrated in hotel-rich areas.

Telegraph Office: next to the State Bank of India on Sayajit Rao Rd., opposite the Maharaja's Palace. Open 24hr. for emergencies, daily 7am-5pm for regular wires.

Airlines: There are no direct flights to or from Mysore but there is an **Indian Airlines** office at the Hotel Mayura Complex, Jhansi Laxmi Bai Rd. (tel. 516948), 250m south of the railway station. Open Mon.-Sat. 10am-1:30pm and 2:15-5pm.

Trains: Railway Station: at the intersection of Irwin and Jhansi Laxmi Bai Rd. (tel. 131 for inquiry). The enquiry and reservation desks are open Mon.-Sat. 8am-2pm and 2:15-10pm, Sun. 8am-2pm. To: Bangalore (8 trains from 6am-11:30pm, 3½hr., Rs.22/36/140 for ordinary/2nd/1st); Hassan (8:10, 10:10am, 2:45, 6, and 7:45pm, 3hr., Rs.19/31/136 for ordinary/2nd/1st); Mangalore (10:10am and 7:45pm, 10hr., Rs.39/72/262 for ordinary/2nd/1st).

Buses: Long-distance buses leave from the **Central Bus Stand** on B-N Rd., near Wesley Cathedral (tel. 520853). Reservations (computerized!) can be made from 7:30am-10pm. To: Bangalore (every 15min. from 5:45am-9:30pm, 3hr., Rs.27/34/41 for ordinary/semi-deluxe/super-deluxe); Mangalore (19 buses from 5:15am-11:30pm, 7hr., Rs.50/64/76 for ordinary/semi-deluxe/super-deluxe); Ooty (13 buses from 7:15am-1:15am, 2½hr., Rs.33/44 for ordinary/deluxe); Coimbatore (20 buses from 7:15am-1:15am, 6hr., Rs.38); Madras (7pm, 11hr.); Hassan (22 buses from 7:15am-10pm, 3hr., Rs.24); Bannur (30min., Rs.5); Bijapur (1pm, 16hr., Rs.134). A few direct buses to Somnathpur leave from the street in front of Wesley Cathedral, but you may have to take a bus to Bannur (7km from Somnathpur) first, then catch a bus from there. Hordes of private bus companies clamber for space and customers around Wesley Cathedral. Most are open late into the night, but it is better to go early in the day (8-10am) to avoid the throngs.

Local Transportation: Buses: City Bus Stand off K-R Circle (tel. 25819). To: Chamundi Hill #101 (20min., Rs.2); Brindavan Gardens #150 (30min., Rs.3.50) Srirangapatnam #125 or #126 (30min., Rs.3). **Taxis** can be procured in Gandhi Sq. Fares must be decided beforehand; competition among drivers brings down prices. **Auto-rickshaws:** Fares *should* be metered (Rs.5. for 1st km., Rs.3 each subsequent km).

Luggage Storage: Railway Station, Rs.3 for the first day, Rs.5 for the second, and Rs.6 for each subsequent day. Open daily 6am-10pm.

English Bookstore: Ashok Book Centre, on Chanvantri Rd., near Sayajit Rao Rd. (tel. 435553). The latest Rushdie, Ishigaro, Gita Mehta—a post-post-colonial fiend's paradise. Open Mon.-Sat. 9:30am-2pm and 3:30-8:30pm. **Geetha Book House,** K-R Circle (tel. 33589). Open Mon.-Sat. 9am-1pm and 4-8pm.

Market: Devaraja Market, tucked behind the glitzy sari shops on Sayajit Rao Rd. and the sandalwood shops on Dhanvantri Rd. (open daily 7am-8pm—the times are

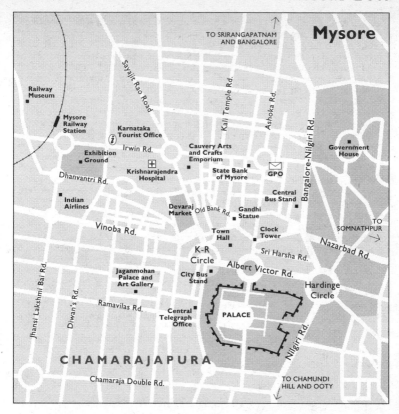

approximate, of course). Sells fresh vegetables and fruit, and color film so you can immortalize the visual orgasm. Wash down your snack with fresh coconut water or sugarcane juice. Hit the megaplexy **Pick 'n' Pack,** in the Hotel Luciya complex on Old Bank Rd. between Gandhi Sq. and Sayajit Rao Rd. (tel. 25445), for toilet paper, Ramen noodles, water bottles, maxi-pads and, of course, sandalwood soap. Open Mon.-Sat. 9am-9pm.

Pharmacy: Many are clustered near the hospital grounds, on Sayajit Rao and Dhanvantri Rd. **Sharada Medical and Optical Stores** (tel. 422472, 521650) fills medical and optical prescriptions, and has a giant stock of saline solution and contact lens cleaner. Open Mon.-Sat. 10am-9pm.

Hospital: K-R Hospital (tel. 20887, 23300), at the corner of Sayajit Rao and Irwin Rd., is the main government hospital in Mysore. **Holdsworth Memorial (Mission) Hospital** on Sawday Rd. (tel. 27716) is nicer, cleaner, and privately-run.

Police: Police Commissioner's Office (tel. 22200, 30908), 3km from Mysore center on Lalitha Mahal Rd. Grants 3-month visa extensions. Branch offices across from the GPO on Ashoka and Irwin Rd., and at the Central Bus Stand.

Post Office: GPO, intersection of Ashoka and Irwin Rd. (tel. 22165). About 750m east of the tourist office. Open Mon.-Sat. 9am-6pm. **Branch Post Office,** K-R Circle. Open Mon.-Sat. 9:30am-5:30pm. **Postal Code:** 570001.

Telephone Code: 0821

ACCOMMODATIONS

Hotel Indra Bhavan, on Dhanvantri Rd., on the SRRD side (tel. 23923). Manned by cordial and sometimes downright sweet old men who are inflexible about 3 things:

no alcohol, no meat, and the premises must be kept startlingly if not sparklingly clean. It's unclear whether their quest for cleanliness is, like the alcohol-meat ban, religion-related, but one thing is certain: in Indra Bhavan's corridors, the scents of lysol, jasmine, and sandalwood mix delightfully. Attached restaurants are two of the best in Mysore. Tourist bus information and arrangements, newspapers, and laundry available. Rooms are well-lit and ugly in a cheerful sort of way. Check-out noon. Singles Rs.90. Doubles Rs.100-115. Quads Rs.150-200.

The Ritz Hotel, 5 B-N Rd. (tel. 22688). 100m south of the Central Bus Stand (on your right as you exit). A former mansion-turned-restaurant/bar/hotel. Three generations of Mysore tourists have peacefully slumbered in these clean and sunny, wicker- and batik-decorated rooms, but you probably won't want to turn in too early, because the Ritz is first and foremost one of the most popular restaurant-bars in Mysore, offering patio dining amidst happily overgrown foliage, a common TV, and a stuffed tiger's head. For all its culinary prowess, however, the Ritz doesn't skimp on the quality of its accommodations, and the place is usually booked to the max. All 4 rooms have attached baths with seat toilets and 24-hr. running hot water. Check-out noon. Doubles Rs.200. Quad Rs.330.

Hotel Dasprakash, on the corner of Gandhi Sq. and Old Bank Rd. (tel. 24444, 24455). Multitudinous airy, clean rooms form the circumference of a large palm-treed courtyard. Houses an ice cream parlor for those mid-afternoon *kulfi* cravings, an astropalmist for those post-*kulfi* anxiety attacks, and a travel agency that'll whisk you off to Chamundi Hill to pray for a brighter future. Hot water 5am-noon; towels and jasmine soap provided; specify seat or squat toilet. The rooms are spacious and the location ideal. Veg. restaurant attached. Check-out 24hr. Singles Rs.100-175. Doubles Rs.205-275. Quads Rs.350-415.

KSTDC Hotel Mayura Yatrinivas, Jhansi Laxmi Bai Rd., opposite Hotel Metropole (tel. 423652). The clean but dingy rooms surround a pretty garden with funky-leaved plants. Some have views of the garden, but others face brick walls. Nevertheless, the KSTDC has decorated them with etchings of Srirangapatnam, Belur, and other Karnataka tourist hot-spots. All rooms have attached (grimy) bath with squat toilet and running hot water 6-9:30am. Check-out noon. Doubles Rs.200. Quads Rs.320. Six-bed rooms Rs.450. Eight-bed rooms Rs.500. Sixteen-bed dormitory (Rs.60 per bed) is open only to groups of 15 or more.

KSTDC Hotel Mayura Hoysala, Jhansi Laxmi Bai Rd., opposite Hotel Metropole. Next door to Hotel Mayura Yatrinivas is the KSTDC's ritzier attempt, with marble floors and oak-framed beds but no funky prints on the walls. Attached bathrooms have both seat and squat toilets, and running hot water 6-9:30am. Both hotels are next to the KSTDC travel agency and the Indian Airlines office. Attached to the Hoysala is the Indiana Garden Restaurant and the thatched-roof "Bamboo Grove" bar. Check-out noon. Doubles Rs.350.

Park Lane Hotel, 2720 Sri Harsha Rd. (tel. 30400). Noise might be a problem because all of their 8 rooms abut a popular, raucous bar, although the bar closes at 11:15pm on the dot, and proximity to liquor might be a good thing anyway. The doubles and singles are approximately the same small size, but they're clean and cheery with green and white decor and candles in the rooms. Extra (and extra fluffy) pillows and blankets in each room. Hot water 5-8am; squat toilet on the ground floor, seat toilet on the first floor. Check-out 24hr. Ground-floor singles Rs.99, first-floor singles Rs.124. Ground-floor doubles Rs.124, first-floor doubles Rs.149. Triples Rs.199. Quads Rs.240. AmEx/V/MC.

Hotel Palace Plaza, 2716 Sri Harsha Rd. (tel. 30875). Two doors down from the Hotel Maurya Palace. This 2-year-old hotel has a ruby-carpeted glass elevator with a view of the park across the street. Despite proximity to the local cinemas, the Palace Plaza screens its own flicks twice daily, on a rotating-regional language basis (English films are sometimes shown too). The carpeted A/C deluxe rooms have bathtubs, and all rooms get running hot water from 6-10am and 6-10pm. Doubles Rs.200-295. Triples Rs.400. Deluxe rooms Rs.525.

Hotel Maurya Palace, 2716,2-3-7, Sri Harsha Rd. (tel. 35912). A clone of the Hotel Palace Plaza, this place exudes class. The solemnly courteous staff take their job seriously; the waitstaff is perpetually sweeping the marble floors or dusting the wallpapered walls. Ask for a room facing the park, as those have humongous bay windows. Real locks on doors, seat toilets in all rooms, hot water 6-11am and 7-11:30pm. The triples have A/C and bathtubs. Check-out noon. Doubles Rs.185-235. Triples Rs.399.

Shree Krishna Continental, 73 Nazarbad Main Rd. (tel. 37042, 27044). A marble-floored lobby and staircase lead to 58 spacious, sparkly rooms overlooking a park. All have seat toilets and running hot water from 5-9am. Free laundry service, North and South Indian restaurant with "chat corner," travel counter, and 24-hr. check-out. Singles Rs.250. Doubles Rs.300-600. Triples Rs.800.

Sudarshan Lodge, opposite Jaganmohan Palace (tel. 26718). Despite the grungy location, Sudarshan exudes a homey atmosphere, where gingham bedspreads match the red-topped exterior. Rooms are clean but dim; try to get a window room. All singles have squat toilets; specify type of toilet for doubles. Running hot water in the mornings. Room service. Check-out noon. Singles Rs.75. Doubles Rs.150.

Hotel Durbar, in the heart of Gandhi Sq. (tel. 5200029, 33591). For the price, it's not too shabby. Singles have a common (squat) toilet and running hot water from 7-9am. There's a great view of the pleasant chaos below from the pink verandah or from the run-down roof garden bar, which serves drinks under the Mysore moonlight until 11:30pm. Check-out 24hr. or 6:30pm, whichever comes first. Singles Rs.60. Doubles Rs.80-100.

The Hotel Rajmahal Deluxe, Lakshmirilasa Rd. (tel.521195). To the right as you walk out of Jaganmohan Palace. The recently refurbished rooms have huge windows with side views of the Jaganmohan Palace; all have seat toilets attached with running hot water 6-8am. Room service. Check-out 24hr. Doubles Rs.150.

FOOD

Mysore's cheapest, most sumptuous, and most authentic food is to be ingested at one of the myriad "meals" or "tiffins" cafés, whose dingy multicolored signs proclaim, "Meals Ready!" in Kannada and English. And they are ready—one minute for 2 *idlis* at Rs.3 or a *thali* at Rs.12. These places are pretty much tourist-free—tourists tend to go for upscale "meals" joints (still a bargain at Rs.30) and menu restaurants.

Akshaya Vegetarian Restaurant, off Gandhi Sq. in the Hotel Dasprakash complex. Serves elaborate, though somehow bland, meals for Rs.20 or Rs.30, depending on the amplitude of your appetite. For dessert, they often supply a small bowl of *kheer*. Open daily noon-3pm and 7:45-10pm.

Swathi, across the street from the Aksyaya Vegetarian Restaurant off Gandhi Sq., is a tiny milk stall where *lassis* cost Rs.5 and, unlike more high-tech Osterized versions, are still manually frothed by a wooden stick rubbed at high speed for 1min. between the wet palms of the proprietor. Open daily 6:30am-8pm.

Bombay Indra Bhavan, Sayajit Rao Rd., near Old Bank Rd. Complete your feast at this sweets cafe where you'll find fudge-topped *burfis* and supple *gulab jamun*. Open daily 11am-10pm.

Samrat, on Dhanvantri Rd., next door to Hotel Indra Bhavan, A North Indian veg. restaurant guaranteed to satisfy your penchant for *paneer*. Meals cost about Rs.50, service is fast and attentive, and the waiters/DJs play a somehow classy mix of *bhangra* and Michael Jackson. Open daily 10am-3pm and 7-10:15pm.

The Ritz Hotel, 5 B-N Rd. May have the most attentively spiced and delicately crafted dishes in Mysore. Chinese, North Indian, South Indian, and Continental dishes, composed of the freshest fare, are so aesthetically pleasing that it's hard to start digging in. Service is delicate and winning, and the place is popular with mellow, affluent clientele. Indoor and outdoor candle-lit dining. Prices are high—about Rs.75 for a meal with drinks. Open daily 7am-11pm.

Jewel Rock Restaurant, 2716, 2-3-7 Sri Harsha Rd. (tel. 35847). Adjoining the Hotel Maurya Palace. Serves up Chinese and Indian food: delectable tandooris and *tikkas* and *ghee*-saturated *biryanis*. Flowered tables, dim lighting, red carpet, and cheesy soft jazz make Jewel Rock popular for classy clientele (or at least those who consider themselves classy). Possibly the only restaurant in Mysore Central that serves bubbly (Rs.700 for a bottle of Marquise de Pompadour). Open noon-3pm and 7-11:30pm.

SIGHTS

The home of the current Maharaja and the psychological center of Mysore, the **Maharaja's Palace** (a.k.a. Amber Vilas) is impressive in every way a monument should be: girth (it's more than 3.5 square kilometers, and 44m tall); worth (was completed at the cost of Rs.4.2 million, which was a lot of money 100 years ago); and birth (for the monument's history, even if not as concrete as the monument itself, is enough to pique any serious tourist's curiosity). In 1897, during the reign of Krishnaraja Wodeyar IV, who had been reinstated as ruler by the British 16 years earlier, the then wooden palace burnt to the ground. The cause of the fire is shrouded in myth and mystery, and we can only concoct conspiracy theories in an attempt to satisfy our quest for true knowledge of events past. Immediately afterwards, a bloke named Mr. Henry Irwin was commissioned to rebuild it, which took him and his Indian artisans 15 years and 4.2 million rupees. In Durbar Hall, there's a mural depicting scenes from the Dasara festival complete with scores of cavalry in various stages of uniform. There are gold chariots, Wodeyar family portraits (they all look the same—slightly plump and fair and androgynous), an ornate Burmese teakwood ceiling, a weapon room filled with scintillating scythes, Ganesh stained-glass windows, frescoes of Krishna and Radha, and a wax effigy of the maharaja with his piercing stare. Some rooms exude a gaudy carnival atmosphere, but others have soul-stirring potential. Built in the Indo-Saracenic style, this place is visited by viscous streams of tourists each day (open daily 10:30am-5:30pm; admission Rs.10; hold on to your entrance ticket because you'll need it when you leave). The **Maharaja's Residential Palace** (visible from the exit of the Palace proper) is an anti-climax after the grandeur of the real thing: cutlery and school uniforms, shabbily exhibited, just aren't impressive. But you don't have to go in to take a camel ride (Rs.10) or elephant ride (Rs.25) around the compound. On Sunday nights and government holidays, the palace is illuminated with 80,000 delightfully ostentatious light bulbs. To get to the palace, take a left as you exit the city bus stand along Sayajit Rao Rd. (or south from K-R Circle), following Albert Victor Rd. for 500m, passing the State Bank of Mysore and the Central Telegraph Office on your right. Turn left on Purandara Dasa Rd. (your first left). Or, from Hardinge Circle, walk 500m south (New Statue Circle will be on your right) and turn right on Purandara Dasa Rd. Open daily 10:30am-6:30pm, Rs.10.

The **Jaganmohan Palace,** containing the Jayachamarajendra Art Gallery (two blocks west of the Maharaja's Palace), is a mumble-jumble of ill-exhibited kitsch, as well as some fascinating watercolors, musical instruments, and ancient games, although little of it is explained beyond the title and artist's name. There are Gaganendranath Tagore watercolors, Raja Ravi Varna oil paintings, a collection of tablas, sitars, and veenas (displayed next to rusty clarinets), the life of Buddha carved on an elephant tusk (he's in the same meditating position the whole way down—he merely increases in size), ancient silk game boards (Chakuni's game in the *Mahabharata*), and dice. Open daily 8:30am-5pm; admission Rs.5.

The **Brindavan Gardens** and **Krishnarajendra Dam** are a popular picnicking spot for Mysorians and tourists alike. The dam was built across the Kaveri River at the turn of the century by Maharaja Krishnaraja Wodeyar Bahadur, and during monsoon season, the water level reaches nearly 37m. Abutting the dam are the Brindavan Gardens, with a plethora of fountains which let loose at night to the beat of Hindi and Kannada music, with "dancing" to the accompaniment of a multi-colored light show (Mon.-Fri. 7-7:55pm, Sat.-Sun. 8-8:55pm). To get there, take city bus #150. Open Mon.-Fri. approximately 7am-8:30pm, Sat.-Sun. 7am.-9:30pm, admission Rs.8-10.

Mysore Zoo has a pamphlet boasting, "See all the tigers you missed at Mudumalai!" Indeed, the tigers are here (including a white tiger), aimlessly and impotently prowling about their lush, enclosed grounds. Pure white peacocks, drag-queen-esque lemurs, ponderous pachyderms, and elegant emus eke out an existence here amidst expertly groomed topiary and gazing *Homo sapiens*. At a ripe 102 years, it's one of the oldest zoos in India, covering 250 acres of greenery. Efforts to couch the animals in their most natural habitat led to the 1994 escape of some vagrant crocodiles into rural Karnataka. The zoo is a hot-spot for breeding binturing and others: this seems to be Mysore's major make-out center! Open Sat.-Thurs. 8:30am-5:30pm. Admission Rs.8 for adults, Rs.2 for children aged 5-10.

Chamundi Hill

Even if you're not into the *devi* scene, the ride up Chamundi Hill, 4km south of the city center, is a religious experience. The view of the Deccan plain, with its squares of saffron and green, will at least provoke a sharp intake of breath, and roadside graffiti exhorting "Join RSS" adds an ecclesiastical element. Other angles afford terrific views of Mysore City—even at a distance, you can see the Maharaja's Palace in all its splendor. At the top of the hill a 16m Mahishasura, the buffalo demon who plagued Mysore (and from whom Mysore takes its name), greets you at the car park in all his gaudy statuesqueness. Chamundi, a.k.a. Durga, was the goddess who smote Mahishasura and the **Sri Chamundeswari Temple** at the hill's summit, with a 40m *gopuram*, is devoted to her. Near the Mahishasura statue is the tiny **Godly Museum** (in the same house as the temple), which is filled with dioramas depicting various stages of spiritual life. One exhibit delineates "Today's Problematic World: Man in Bondage, Poverty" (a picture of a family of seven on one bicycle), "wavering mind," and "over population" (with a prophetic picture of the bus you'll take down the hill: people standing almost on top of each other).

Pilgrims climb the 1000 steps up the 1062m hill, a journey taking at least two hours. Never fear; there's always city bus #101, which shuttles back and forth regularly and costs Rs.2. A taxi should cost about Rs.100. If you opt to foot it, however, don't miss the **Shiva Temple** one-third of the way up. The temple is protected by a corpulent granite statue of Nandi, Shiva's bull. Nandi has been protecting the temple for 300 years and it's whispered that each year he grows an itsy-bitsy bit. It is expected that in 300 more years, Nandi will be sitting atop Mysore—but that may just be a lot of bull. The temples are open daily 7am-1pm and 4-7:30pm.

ENTERTAINMENT

Cinemas proliferate in the Gandhi Square area, and on Sunday they're crammed with movie fiends. There are usually four showings daily, and the price of admission (about Rs.2-12) depends on where you'll sit. **Uma Talkies** in Gandhi Square screens English-language films, as does the further-off **Sterling Cinema** in Vidyaranyapuram (near the government silk and oil factories).

Bars

A bit of the Bangalore bar scene has now taken root in Mysore, with all of the excitement and a little more innocence. Some highlights include:

Royal Legacy, Nazarbad Main Rd. (tel. 34347). Next to the Shree Krishna Continental. A hip-hop happening club where you can get a mug of beer for Rs.20 or pay Rs.100 cover charge to go upstairs and boogy on down. The smooth DJ mixes happy dance tunes and honors requests. The "Swankiest Place" (as the neon blue in the blacklit sign calls it) makes for a fun and potentially exhausting evening. Open daily 11am-2pm and 5:30-11pm.

Ritz Hotel Bar, 5 B-N Rd. (tel.22688). The place to kick back if you're not one for dancing. Brown-uniformed waiters (complete with matching *chappals*) dote on you and cater to your every need. This is budget luxury at its best—pints of beer are Rs.35, and intricately spiced snacks cost around Rs.20. A meal for 2 with drinks costs about Rs.150. Open daily 11am-11pm.

Park Lane Hotel, Sri Harsha Rd. (tel.37370, 30400), near New Statue Circle. The Park Lane Hotel is a little more hyper than the Ritz, its menu solemnly notifying its customers in bold print that "Disposable vomit bags are available on request in case of need, as a consideration to fellow diners." The tables in the outdoor leaf-canopied section are lit by funky candle lamps, and sitting outside provides mouth watering wafts of barbecue. (The smell of burning animals is a rarity in India.) No dancing, which is unfortunate because the jivey Indian rap music sets everyone's ringed toes a-tapping. Pints of beer go for Rs.30, tantalizing tandoori grill items for Rs.70-90. Indian and Chinese entrees for about Rs.50. Open daily 10am-11:15pm.

SHOPPING

Mysore produces half of India's **sandal oil** as well as massive quantities of **silks, sandalwood,** and **jewelry.** The state government's **Cauvery Emporium** on Sayajit Rao Rd. (tel. 521258) is a giant warehouse of such exotica. They accept major credit cards and traveler's checks, and will arrange packing and export. Cauvery has an open-air annex near the Zoological Gardens. Open Mon.-Sat.10am-1:30pm and 3-7:30pm. Scores of private arts and crafts emporia are clustered near the annex. Though the sandalwood Lakshmi statuettes by the zoo are marginally more expensive than Cauvery's, the private emporia offer tremendous selection and solicitous service. Plus, they're open daily (generally 9am-7pm) and overseas shipping is free if you spend over Rs.5000. Cheaper mini-emporia with flexible prices crowd Dhanvantri Rd., near its intersection with Sayajit Rao Rd. Further down Sayajit Rao Rd., near K-R Circle, are silk stores which sell enough saris to wrap around Mother Earth. The **Government Silk Weaving Factory,** in Vidyaranyapuram, (tel. 521803) allows tours with prior permission. Here you can watch your silk being woven and later buy it at mill prices. Open Mon.-Sat. 8am-5pm. Next door is the **Government Sandal Oil Factory** (tel. 521889), where, again with permission, you can schedule a rather wafty tour. Open Mon.-Sat. 8am-5pm.

■ Near Mysore: Somnathpur

A tiny village 38km east of Mysore, Somnathpur is home to the famous **Keshava Temple,** built around 1268 AD. The village was established, and the temple commissioned, by Soma, a high officer under the Hoysala King Narasimha II, hence the name Somnathpur. Legend has it that when the temple was completed, it was so beautiful and grand (despite its minuscule height of 10m), that the gods thought it too good for this earth, and wanted to transport it to heaven. The temple quaked and began to levitate, and the chief sculptor in his horror began to mutilate some of the images on the outside wall to avert such a catastrophe. The slightly disfigured temple came crashing

The Tiger of Mysore

Few rulers of South India have made a mark so quickly as the two-generation dynasty of Haider Ali and Tipu Sultan, who ruled Mysore for 40 years during the 18th century. By 1761, Haider Ali had risen from his rank as army captain to topple his boss, the Hindu raja of Mysore. Haider Ali balanced threats from the French, British, and Marathas until his death in 1782, and was succeeded by an even more powerful figure, his son, Tipu Sultan. Known to the British as "The Tiger of Mysore," Tipu Sultan was fiercely opposed to European expansion, inflicting two stunning defeats on the British. But by 1792 the tides had turned, the French and the English were no longer adversaries, and Tipu was forced to surrender the Malabar coast to Britain. Tipu continued his father's balancing act until he was killed as the British captured his fort at Srirangapatnam in 1799. The young child of a deceased Wodeyar prince (the dynasty that had ruled Mysore before Haider Ali took over) was recognized by the British as the state's ruler. Both Haider Ali and Tipu Sultan were devout Muslims and their attitude toward Hinduism seems to have been one of politically motivated tolerance—Haider Ali understood that Hindu-Muslim unity would be necessary in order to repel the British. But near the end of his life, Tipu decreed Persian the official language of Mysore over Kannada and Hindi-Urdu, and began hiring only Muslim officials. Still, Tipu was generous to Hindu temples, and neither ruler allowed religious issues to distract them from their single-minded battle against European infidels.

back down to earth, which explains why the *Garudagamba* (stone pillar depicting the god Garuda) is not exactly opposite the entrance, as is usual, but slightly skewed to the northeast. The Keshava temple is saturated by carvings: six strata of friezes—elephants, scrolls, geese, scenes from the *Bhagavad Gita, Mahabharata*, and the Puranas, border the exterior—and scores of deity images fill the interior. Off the 144 large images, 114 are female. The temple was carved out of supple soapstone in order to give sculptors a chance to show off their artistic prowess, and the temple is one of the most exuberantly carved around. It's very dark inside, but Indra and company were thoroughly justified in their covetousness—the temple *is* too beautiful for this earth. Open daily 9am-5pm.

■ Near Mysore: Srirangapatnam

Sixteen kilometers from Mysore, this was the site of Tipu Sultan's island fort and the seat of his vast kingdom until the fourth Anglo-Mysore war in 1799. Tipu was killed during the British siege of his fort, barraged by British bullets until he tumbled off his horse into a pile of dead and dying. A British soldier is said to have caught a glimpse of Tipu's ostentatious gold belt buckle and tried to snatch it for himself but Tipu, still alive and reflexive, lanced him with his ever-ready sword. The soldier was merely injured and still sharp enough to lodge a bullet in Tipu's temple. Tipu had always said it was "better to die like a soldier than to live like a miserable dependent on the British," and his forces made South India a living hell for the British for some time. But his defeat here in 1799 put an end to his conquests and opened the path for the East India Company's expansion in South India.

Srirangapatnam is a history buff's heaven. You can still see **Daria Daulat,** Tipu's summer palace—his other palace was dismembered in 1807 by Colonel Wellesley, and its timbers went to build, among other things, the Maharaja's Palace in Mysore and St. Stephen's Church in Ooty. Daria Daulat houses some marvelous paintings—portraits of Tipu wearing his signature tiger stripes, and one of the Nizam of Hyderabad. The hospital which housed Colonel Wellesley and company is also on the premises, as is an obelisk commemorating British lives lost in the siege. The dungeons where Tipu held British soldiers are still intact, as are large rusty cannons and Tipu's racket court. (Open Sat.-Thurs. 9am-5pm; admission Rs.10) The **Jumma Masjid,** the mosque Tipu built on the grounds of an old Hindu temple, can also be seen, as well as **Gumbaz,** the haunting mausoleum where Tipu and his father, Haider Ali, lie. The **Sri Ranganatha Temple,** the town's namesake, is a temple from the Hoysala age—the Maharaja Krishnaraja Wodeyar II hid in its *gopuram* during the 1799 siege. (Open daily 8am-1pm. and 4-8pm.)

■ Near Mysore: Sravanabelagola

Sravanabelagola is renowned for its 17-m monolithic statue of Gommata, but the surrounding hills have been a Jain pilgrimage site since long before the statue was carved about 1000 years ago. Legend has it that Sravanabelagola ("Naked Ascetic of the White Pond") was first alighted upon in 300 BC by the Mauryan emperor Chandragupta, who abdicated his throne up north to retire here as an ascetic. His guru, Bhadrabahu, came with him, and attained a sacred state more rapidly than his pupil. Chandragupta (for whom the Chandragiri Hill is named) used to worship the footprints of his Bhadrabahu in a cave on Chandragiri Hill; the feet still attract pilgrims today. The *bastis* (Jain temples) dotting Chandragiri were built through the centuries and form a sort of architectural history book. Those built during the 1200s, for example, are typically Hoysalan in their soapstone star-shaped plan.

Of course, the main tourist attraction is the giant **Gommata (or Bahubali) statue** on Indragiri Hill, built around 980 AD by the Ganga king Chavundaraya. There are 500 steps leading to the statue; climb them, but if your soles are not ascetically hardened to the touch of by burning granite, wear a pair of thick socks. Bahubali's brother, Bharatesha, challenged his 100 younger brothers to claim the throne of their father Adinath, the first Jain *tirthankara*. Only Bahubali dared challenge Bharatesha—the other 99 brothers renounced the world and retired into the forest. Bahubali triumphed but he was so disillusioned by worldly victory and his brother's greed that he too retired to the forest, hoping to reach enlightenment. That didn't come until the two brothers forgave each other.

The statue of Bahubali wears the smile of enlightenment; vines creep up his legs and around his waist, and anthills sit at his feet to convey his ascetic's detachment from the world. Roughly every 12 years the Jain mega-festival Mahamastakabhisheka is held here. On the eve of the ceremony, scaffolding is erected behind the monument, and 1008 pots of sacred and colored water are placed in front of the statue. Priests (and wealthy devotees who have enough rupees to pay for a sacred anointing spot) cover Bahubali with the sacred water, chanting mantras; then they pour milk, curds, *ghee*, sugar, almonds, and gold and silver flowers over his head. The entire process is watched by thousands in absolute silence. The next Mahamastakabhisheka is scheduled for 2006-2008.

▨ Hassan

The busy, industrializing city of Hassan, filled with semi-trucks and plastics manufacturers, has little tourist appeal and no sights of its own—but Hassan and its complacent tourist industry are saved by their location. Hassan is situated about 40km from the temple villages of Halebid and Belur, and unlike the villages, Hassan has both train and bus stations and an array of hotels that would cause either Belur or Halebid to explode with commercialism. Though hardly engaging in and of itself, Hassan is a practical place to spend your nights and take care of business that demands more technological apparati than Belur or Halebid could provide.

ORIENTATION

It would take a supreme effort (or some spiked *pan*) to get lost in this tidbit city. Most hotels and lodges are within 500m of the **bus stand,** which is at the southwest corner of the aptly named **Bus Stand Road** (north-south) and **Church Road** (east-west). Running parallel to Bus Stand Rd. about 200m to the east is **Race Course Road.** It intersects the second east-west thoroughfare, **Bangalore-Mangalore (B-M) Road** about 300m to the south. The city's activity is largely centered around the bus stand and the intersection of Race Course Rd. and B-M Rd. Follow B-M Rd. 1km east to the railway station and about 275km further to Bangalore.

PRACTICAL INFORMATION

Tourist Office: Regional Tourist Office, Vartha Bhavan, B-M Rd. (tel. 68862). From the bus stand, walk 1 block south, turn left onto B-M Rd., walk 300m, and it will be on the left side of the road. A friendly joint where the head honcho will offer you some *chai* and brochures on Bangalore, hill stations in NW Karnataka, but zilch on Belur, Halebid, Sravanabelagola, or Hassan itself. Good source of advice on Hassan restaurants. Open Mon.-Sat. 10am-1:30pm and 2-5:30pm.

Budget Travel: Millions of **maxicab** services, all clustered on Church Rd. near the bus stand, offer A/C and comfy trips to Bangalore (about Rs.75). Strangely, none of the travel/tour agencies offer private tours of Halebid, Belur, or Sravanabelagola.

Immigration Office: Foreigners Registration Office, in the Police Station on B-M Rd., (tel. 68000), in the office marked "Women's Grievances." Open Mon.-Fri. 10am-5:30pm.

Currency Exchange: State Bank of Mysore, corner of Bus Stand Rd. and B-M Rd. Accepts US dollars and pounds sterling, and traveler's checks in US and CDN dollars, pounds sterling, Deutschmarks, and French and Swiss francs. Open Mon-Fri. 10:30am-2:30pm, Sat. 10:30am-12:30pm.

Telephones: STD/ISD booths clutter the pavement near the hotels and bus stand.

Trains: Train station: B-M Rd., a 2-km walk or Rs.7 auto-rickshaw ride from the bus stand. The ticket and inquiry offices are less subject to stringent hours of operation than those in larger cities. To: Bangalore (6 trains daily, 3hr., Rs.29/54/199 for ordi-

nary/2nd/1st class); Mangalore (872, 12:50pm, 874, 10:30pm, 3½hr., Rs.26/178 for
ordinary/1st class); Mysore (873, 3:25pm, 865, 5:35pm, 863, 9:45pm, Rs.19/126
for ordinary/1st class).

Buses: Bus Stand: Church Rd., across from the Maharaja's park. Hordes of private
bus companies offer Rs.50 service to Bangalore. Government buses: To: Bangalore
(every 15min. from 5:30am-7:45pm, 11:30pm, 4hr., Rs.36/46/55 for ordinary/semi-
deluxe/super-deluxe); Arsikere (every 30min. from 5:30am-10:30pm., 1hr., Rs.9);
Mangalore (every 30min. from 5:30am-11pm, 3½hr., Rs.24/30 for ordinary/
deluxe); Belur (every 30min. from 6am-8:45pm,1½hr., Rs.8/10 for ordinary/semi-
deluxe); Halebid (8 buses from 8:15am-7:15pm, Rs.6), Sravanabelagola (12:15pm.
1½hr., Rs.10). It is widely suggested (by tourists, tourism officials, and bus officials)
that you opt for an indirect route to Sravanabelagola through Channarayapatna,
because buses leave for Channarayapatna more often (every 30min. from 6:30am-
9pm, 1hr., Rs.10) and from there it's only a 5-min., Rs.2 bus ride to Sravanabelagola.

Local Transportation: You'll be able to walk almost anywhere within Hassan—
besides, you'll want to walk, considering the cool climate and luxury of fruit markets and streets not filled to capacity. The only place to which you might need a lift
is the railway station. Take an auto-rickshaw or taxi but be forewarned: neither is
metered and the rickshaw-*wallahs* here are notably swindle-savvy. A ride from the
bus stand to the rail station should cost about Rs.7.

Market: Along the west side of the bus stand and Maharaja's Park. Pyramids of tan-
gerines, grapes, apples, and luscious mangoes. The area is also swarming with *chat*
stands, tea stalls, and omelette fryers.

Pharmacy: Few of the many pharmacies on Bus Stand Rd. have staffers who speak
English. Gopal Medicines, across from Karnataka Bank, is open 9am-9:30pm.

Hospital: CSI Redfern Memorial Hospital, on Race Course Rd., 1 block north of
its intersection with Church Rd. (tel. 68288). **Government General Hospital,** on
Hospital Rd. (tel. 68444). From the bus stand, walk east 200m until you reach the
church, turn right; you'll be on Race Course Rd. Follow it until the massive Hotel
Amblee Palika is on your right, make a left and you'll be on Hospital Rd. Follow it
until you see a sprawling gray building on your left.

Emergency: tel. 100.

Police: On B-M Rd., opposite State Bank of Mysore (tel. 100).

Post Office: opposite Bus Stand on Bus Stand Rd. Open Mon-Fri. 10:30am-5:30pm,
Sat. 10am-1pm. **Postal Code:** 573201.

Phone Code: 08172

ACCOMMODATIONS

Hassan is accustomed to fleets of tourists who stay only one night. In spite of, or
because of this, there is no dearth of cheap and clean accommodation close to the
city center. Few hotels charge more than Rs.100 for a basic double.

Hotel Ashraya (tel. 67613). Walk out of the bus stand onto Bus Stand Rd., take your
very first right before the Satyaprakash Lodge, and walk to the end of that block.
Good views of the fruit market below, although the windows are criss-crossed
with iron bars. Firm-to-hard beds, but fluffy pillows, and funky neon green mosquito nets. Bucket hot water in the mornings. Check-out 24hr. Singles Rs.55. Doubles Rs.95.

Hotel New Abiruchi (tel. 67852). From the bus stand, walk 2 blocks south on Bus
Stand Rd. and take a right as soon as you pass the police station. All rooms are
equipped with telephones, and the singles have black-and-white TVs. The place is
clean and the beds comfy although the management can be a tad terse. A yummy
Indian-Chinese restaurant is attached. No hot water, not even in buckets. Check-
out 24hr. Singles Rs.60-100. Doubles Rs.100-150.

Hotel Harsha Mahal, Harsha Mahal Rd. (tel. 68533). Exit from the northeast corner
of the bus stand, walk east on Church Rd. one-half block, turn left on Harsha Mahal
Rd. It's the second hotel on your right. The Harsha Mahal has a solemn feel despite
canopied beds and colorful striped sheets. Spacious rooms overlook an inner courtyard. Running hot water in the mornings; room service from the spicy restaurant

below. Management speaks just enough English to supply *dosas* and coffee and take your rupees. Check-out 24hr. Singles Rs.65. Doubles Rs.100.

Vaishnavi Lodging, Harsha Mahal Rd. (tel. 67413). The place you'll pass en route to Harsha Mahal—see earlier directions. Vaishnavi Lodging has triple-duty overhead fans, humongous rooms, clean sheets, soft beds, fluffy pillows, and good lighting to show the dynasties of tiny ants tromping over the well-swept floor, onto the table, into the sink... Running hot water in the mornings, wide, sunlit hallways with funky circular windows, and room service. Check-out 24hr. A shameful bargain. Singles Rs.80. Doubles Rs.125.

Hotel Satyaprakash (tel. 68521). Across from the southeast corner of the bus stand. A tad run-down, but clean, with frayed mattresses and wall-stains almost obscured by the lack of light. That said, it's liveable, provided you live by the management's strict rules: no alcohol, no meat, no stays longer than 3 days, and, if you're out for a 24-hr. period, management reserves the right to enter your room and confiscate your stuff. (Yikes!) Plus: no visitors after 9:30pm. Room service 10am-2pm and 7-9pm; bucket hot water at 6am sharp. Check-out 24hr. Singles Rs.40. Doubles Rs.60.

Hotel Suvarna Regency, B-M Rd. (tel. 64006; fax 63822). From Bus Stand Rd. walk 1 block, turn right after the police station, follow B-M Rd. to where it turns south; you can't miss the Suvarna Regency's towers. The unspoiled elegance and beautiful amenities of this brand-new hotel—Star TV, telephones, seat or squat toilets, attached travel services, currency exchange, fluffy towels, soap, and daily newspapers—are stunning for Hassan. Potted saplings fill the marble hallways. Attached South and North Indian restaurant and bar. Check-out 24hr. Singles Rs.225. Doubles Rs.350, with A/C Rs.450. Quads Rs.600. MC/V.

FOOD

Granted, Hassan is not renowned for its culinary prowess; on the other hand, who could get sick of sub-Rs.15 *thalis* and locally grown tea and coffee? An added boon is Hassan's marketplace, around the periphery of the bus stand and Maharaja's Park, where fresh, ripe grapes, apples, and bananas, as well as *chats* and omelettes can be found cheaply.

Hotel Samman, B-M Rd. A favorite among locals and tourists for its scrumptious curries, spicy chutneys, and hot *rotis.* The *puris* here are consistently freshly made—three huge, steam-filled wonders practically reach eye-level when the plate is on the table. The *saga* is exquisite, flavored with a peanut sauce you'd call delectable if you weren't too busy sopping it up. The *chai,* too, is served in tall glasses, with a centimeter of cappucino-like foam on top. The service is efficient and jovial, and the clanging of plates and cups here is never annoyingly boisterous. Open daily 6am-9:45pm. Rs.12 *thalis* from 11:30am-4pm and 7-9:45pm.

Survana Sagar, B-M Rd. Attached to Hotel Survana. Dishes out competent if costly *thalis* (Rs.35) and tiffins in a tapestried-chaired, mega-friendly hall with lots of panache. They've scooped the competition when it comes to ice cream desserts: *lichi* splits, mango *kulfis, pista* milk shakes, and *lassis* in every fruity incarnation imaginable. Just limit your cool to desserts—sitting in the A/C section will land you a 15% surcharge. Open daily 7am-10:30pm.

Hotel GRR, Bus Stand Rd. Directly opposite the bus stand. Focuses all of its culinary energy on its *thalis* for Rs.13—no sweets, *lassis,* tea, or coffee. The *thalis* are served directly onto banana leaves. The *ghee* is gleefully abundant, as are the vegetable curries and spicy *sambar.* Ornate wooden chairs and stone kitchen make it an aesthetically pleasing place as well.

ENTERTAINMENT

Hassan's happening nightspot happens to be the bar at the **Malanika Restaurant,** atop Hotel Amblee Palika on Race Course and Hospital Rd. The place is characteristically dimly lit, with multicolored lightbulbs and blue-tinted windows providing hallucinatory effects to complement the beer (Rs.35 per pint). Meanwhile, there's an adjoining rooftop garden—if you plan to partake, smear on mosquito repellent first. The service is sweetly sycophantic.

The **Privthi Theater,** down B-M Rd. past the tourist office and before the railway station, screens three English flicks per day. Meanwhile, the more centrally located **Picture Palace,** across from the GPO on Bus Stand Rd., does Indian-language (mostly Kannada) films.

■ Belur

Belur, a tiny town set on the right bank of the Yagachi River, was the capital of the Hoysalan empire before it was moved to nearby Halebid. Seven hundred years and several dynasties later, Belur's two roads are lined with dank eateries, tea stalls, and a few meager stores that give no hint of the town's gilded history. Only the Chennakshava Temple stands at the end of Temple Rd., set off from the town by its tall *gopuram,* and steeped in an ancient aura of solitary might.

ORIENTATION

There are two roads in Belur. **Main Road** runs more or less perpendicular to **Temple Road,** which runs from the **bus stand** to the **Chennakeshava Temple.** Temple Rd. is dotted with restaurants and lodges.

PRACTICAL INFORMATION

Currency Exchange: State Bank of Mysore. Halfway between the bus stand and the temple on Temple Rd. Exchanges traveler's checks in U.S. dollars, pounds sterling, yen, and Deutschmarks. Open Mon.-Fri. 10:30am-2:30pm, Sat. 10:30am-12:30pm.

Telephones: STD/ISD booths line Temple Rd. across from the bus stand.

Buses: To: Halebid (23 buses from 6am-9pm, 40min., Rs.4); Hassan (26 buses from 5:40am-1am, 1hr., Rs.8); Arsikere (23 buses from 6am-9pm, 1½hr., Rs.10); Bangalore (15 buses from 6am-1am, 4hr., Rs.43/65 for ordinary/semi-deluxe); Mysore (18 buses from 5:40am-11pm, 3hr., Rs.31).

Local Transportation: The town is small, and if it's raining so hard, or your feet hurt so much, that you can't bear the ten-minute walk from the bus stand to the temple, an auto-rickshaw (unmetered) will shuttle you there for Rs.5.

Pharmacies: Several across from the hospital on Temple Rd. Try **Shri Chennakeshava Medicals,** open 8am-9pm.

Hospital: Government Hospital, on Temple Rd. (tel. 22333). It's not labeled in English, but it's the sprawling pink complex next to the sprawling saffron complex of Hotel Maurya Velapuri.

Police: Across from the bus stand on Main Rd. (tel. 22444).

Post and Telegraph Office: on Main Rd. Turn left from the bus stand and walk up the hill 250m (tel. 22230). Open Mon.-Sat. 8:30am-4:30pm. **Postal Code:** 573115. **Telephone Code:** 08177.

ACCOMMODATIONS

The limited lodging options in Belur run the gamut from cheap and functional to cheaper and less functional. No A/C or TVs here, but did you really come to Belur to watch Hindi movies in your 15°C hotel room?

Swagath Tourist Home, Temple Rd. (tel. 22159). Closer to the temple than Hotel Annapoorna. Cheaper, cheerier, and more personal than its neighbors, the Swagath Tourist Home is owned by the people running the market down below, and they're a mellow, smiling sort. Pretty pink painted balconies overlook a tiny green courtyard. Pillows and mattresses are tapestried or batiked in rich Indian designs; bathrooms (squat toilet) are assiduously sterilized throughout the day. The catch? No hot water, and no back-up generator to cover those frequent power outages. Singles Rs.40. Doubles Rs.50.

Hotel Mayura Velapuri, Temple Rd. (tel. 22209). A 2-min. walk from the bus stand. This KSTDC enterprise is the most expensive, and the most amenable hotel in Belur: red mat carpets, huge windows, and gleaming bathrooms (specify type of toilet) where hot water flows freely, unrestricted by the tyranny of the clock. Beds you can sink into after a long day on the temple circuit. Room service 7am-9pm, from the attached overpriced restaurant. Check-out 24hr. Dorm beds (less spiffy, only open to groups of 15 or more) Rs.30. Singles Rs.145. Doubles Rs.184.

Hotel Annapoorna, Temple Rd. (tel. 22423). Across from the Government Hospital). Uncovered pillows on top of hard mattresses. The walls are stained and the bathrooms (squat toilet) stale-smelling but clean. Running hot water from 5-8am; room service, laundry service. Ask the proprietor, Mr. Yoganarasimha, for one of his neon yellow bumper stickers advertising the joint. Check-out 24hr. Doubles Rs.100.

Vishnu Krupa Lodging (formerly Sri Vishnu Prasad), Main Rd. (tel. 22263). Walk 200m past the police station; it's a tall building for Belur, plastered with its name. Roughly the same quality as Annapoorna, but its rooms have large windows and softer beds. You have to hike up a steep, slippery staircase to get to them, though. Clean bathrooms with squat toilets, but no hot running water—it's delivered in a bucket outside your door at 6am sharp. Room service from the popular restaurant below. Check-out 24hr. Singles Rs.35. Doubles Rs.100. Quads Rs.175.

Sri Raghavendra Tourist Home (tel. 22372). To the immediate right of the temple grounds, with a close-up *gopuram* view. Bright hallways with yellow walls and orange doors. Accommodations that appeal to the ascetic in us all: doubles consist of 3 mats on the floor. Attached baths have squat toilets, and a steamy bucket of hot water arrives at 6:15am. No back-up generators here, either, and no room service. Check-out 24hr. Singles (two mats) Rs.75. Doubles Rs.100.

FOOD

All the restaurants in Belur serve standard vegetarian fare, so it's really a question of how much you'll pay for your *idli* or *thali.*

Hotel Mayura Velapuri Restaurant, Temple Rd. Actually does a few Continental dishes in addition to overpriced *thalis* (Rs.20): bread and jam, bread and butter, and wafer chips. At least the place is better lit than the other dungeon cafes. Open daily 7am-9pm.

Hotel Shankar, Temple Rd. Next door to the Hotel Annapoorna. Does remarkable *thalis*—fresh *papads*, medium-spicy veggies, and buttered *chapati*—for Rs.10. The waitstaff is solemnly conscientious and efficient, and the place is popular with locals and temple tourists alike. Open daily 6:30am-9pm.

SIGHTS

Facing the **Chennakeshava Temple** at Belur is a statue of Garuda, Vishnu's vehicle, with palms together, guarding the temple. Perhaps it was Garuda who protected Belur's Hoysala temple from the extreme ransacking to which the temple at Halebid was subjected. More likely, it was the fact that Belur was not, as was Halebid, the capital of the Hoysalan Empire at the time of the Delhi Sultanate's attack, and had hardly as much gold and jewels to plunder. Nevertheless, like the temple at Halebid, the Chennakeshava Temple was never finished because of the ruthless invaders. Work on it began in 1117 and, for 103 years, three generations of sculptors devoted their lives to it. The Hoysala king Vishnuvardhana built the temple to commemorate his conversion from Jainism to Vaishnavism. The temple is renowned for its bracket figures, or *apsaras*, which line the interior ceilings and exterior walls. Of the 42 bracket figures, only three are male. There are nine statues of Vishnu around the exterior. Like the temples at Halebid and Somnathpur, the temple base is covered with horizontal friezes alarming in their detail. To bear the weight of the temple, 644 elephants stand at the bottom; no two are alike. Outside is also the emblem of the Hoysalan empire: the boy Sala smiting a beast with the head of a tiger and the body of a lion.

When Sala was a boy, he and his classmates were sitting under a tree with their guru when this ferocious animal appeared. The other boys booked for home but Sala leveled his own fierce gaze with the tiger's, and uttered "Hoy-Sala," or "Kill-Sala;" thus the boy launched into greatness and founded the Hoysalan empire.

The detail of the bracket figures is awesome: voluptuous women carved out of a single stone, whose bangles and head pendants move; a lady, teeth bared, holding a letter to her lover while a lustful monkey tugs at the edge of her sari; and the famed *Thribhanghi Nritya*, a classical dancer contorting her body so perfectly that a drop of water from her right hand would gloss off the tip of her nose, her left breast, hit the thumb of her left hand, and land at the arch of her right foot. Supposedly, no real-life dancer has even been able to attain this pose. Inside the temple is a dancing platform and sitting area for the audience, as well as some fabulously lathed pillars. The pillars had to be turned by elephants while sculptors designed them. The Narasimha pillar at the center of the temple depicts, in miniature, all of the temple's carvings in the little squares. One square is left empty, either as a challenge to a future artist, or, by some more idealistic accounts, to affirm the place of art in life forever. The *gopuram* outside was originally constructed in 1397, but burned down and had to be rebuilt. On the bottom right-hand corner, as you exit the temple, are some particularly erotic engravings, and if you hire one of the ASI guides (Rs.50 for a very entertaining tour), he'll be sure to point them all out to you.

■ Halebid

It's difficult to imagine Halebid as "Dwarasamudra," the capital of the magnificent Hoysala Empire at its zenith in the 12th and 13th centuries. Halebid's current name means "Old Town," and the village is presently home to more cows than kings, more goats than ambitious sculptors. But the grandeur of Halebid's great temple fits well in this serene village of 3000—in the distance rise the Western Ghats, small children play games in the road, and old men gossip over *chai* in mud cottages. Halebid indulges all our romantic stereotypes of India's long-lost simplicity (or backwardness?), and no matter how politically incorrect the vision is, it's at least temporarily entrancing. That is, until one of the sweet children morphs into a vehement postcard tout, lurching you back to reality, a little relieved that the world is not as cut and dry as the soapstone engravings of the Hoysalesvara Temple.

ORIENTATION AND PRACTICAL INFORMATION

There are more twelfth-century shrines in Halebid than there are banks, police stations, hospitals, and telephone exchanges combined. The moral: bring rupees (you won't need many, anyway), watch your back (those Jain monks can be pretty dangerous), stay on the acidophilus, and you'll have to wait a bit to tell mummy about the fabulous temple. Across the street from the bus stand lies the **Hoysalesvara Temple;** because it's the only star-shaped soapstone edifice with exuberant engravings and figures in town, it's hard to miss. To the right as you exit the bus stand is the village's sole hotel, **Tourist Cottages,** manned by Department of Tourism employees. Five hundred meters down the road is the **Jain Mandir (Bagadi Hall).** If you take a left from the bus stand, you'll walk along Halebid's more commercial road, whose buildings include a Canara Bank (which doesn't do foreign exchange) and a **post office** (Open Mon.-Fri. 9:30am-5:30pm, Sat. 10am-1pm). **Postal Code:** 573121. **Telephone Code:** 08177.

Buses leave Halebid's bus stand for Belur (23 buses from 7:15am to 9:15pm, 30min., Rs.4); Hassan (15 buses from 5:45am-7pm, 1hr., Rs.6); Arsikere (10 buses from 6:30am-7:30pm, 1½hr., Rs.9); Bangalore (7 and 9:30am, 3hr., Rs.24); and Mysore (4:45pm, 4hr., Rs.29).

ACCOMMODATIONS AND FOOD

Halebid is an ideal place to stay if you don't mind the inconvenience, but its only hotel is the **Tourist Cottages** (tel. 3224). The rooms are carpeted and have pretty embroidered curtains on the unscreened windows. Seat toilet with 24-hr. running hot water. The seven dorm beds are not so nice—no carpet or wicker furniture and you'll need your own sheets and mosquito nets. Singles are Rs.60 and doubles are Rs.100. The compound is inspired by the monument grounds next door—a huge garden in the center of the hotel is full of brambles, flowering trees, funky lizards, and broken Hoysalan sculptures. The attached **restaurant** is open 6am-7pm, though room service continues until 9pm. The bus stand also has a **restaurant,** open 6am-7pm, with spartan *thalis*. Hordes of tea stalls and shacky restaurants surround the temple grounds.

SIGHTS

Set in vast lawns so immaculately groomed they seem out of place in a tiny farming village, the **Hoysalesvara Temple** is the largest of the Hoysalan temples. Work started on it in 1121, but before it could be completed town and temple were sacked by Malik Kafur and his Delhi Sultanate armies in 1311 and 1326. By India's independence only 14 of the original 84 large statues remained, and only one of the "bracket figures" (the mini-statues for which Belur's temple is famed) was left. But the Hoysalesvara Temple is still awe-inspiring and readily recognizable for the genius and assiduity that created it. In 1952 the Archaeological Survey of India got its digs on the temple to ensure its survival. The detail, humor, and accuracy of the temple's engravings is striking. Though the grounds it sits on seem incongruous with the village's landscape, the temple's majesty is somehow right at home here.

The temple is actually composed of two Shiva temples on one star-shaped platform. (The temple at Somnathpur had three temples on one platform; at Belur, only one. All three temples are typically Hoysalan in their star-shape.) The larger of the two was commissioned by the Hoysala king Vishnuvardhana, and the smaller by his senior wife, the famed dancer Shantaladevi. Over 20,000 elaborate figures remain in and around the temple, and ASI-sanctioned guides will explain the best and brightest for Rs.40. Get a guide, otherwise you won't know what you're looking at; besides, they're not of the stuffy sort you might have been trained to expect—they're hip, funny, and well-informed (probably underfed, too, as most are freelance post-grads searching for a job).

Six strata of frieze work border the base of the temple: elephants first, then lions, horsemen, scrolls, stories from the Puranas and epics, and geese. Meanwhile, larger (and more gory) engravings of gods and goddesses line the upper exterior walls: Shiva killing the elephant demon, somehow dismembering his trunk from his head, and dancing in the pachyderm's stomach to celebrate; various incarnations of Vishnu, in one of which he is peeling off the face of a demon like you would the peel off a plantain; Chamundi smiting the buffalo demon Mahishasura. Ganesha poses on his poor rat carrier—the rodent's eyes bulge to convey the immense weight of his load. Krishna is depicted lifting the mountain, and though the god takes up three-quarters of the carving, you can make out enormous detail on the mountain itself: banana trees, babbling brooks, monkeys. Inside the temple are two *lingas* and a dancing platform for devotional dances no longer performed. The temple has no *gopuram*, indicating that it's merely a monument and no longer a place of worship. Open daily 7:30am-7:30pm.

A (soap)stone's throw from the temple is the **Archaeological Museum.** Half of it is outdoors, and deity statues (fortunately, they're labeled) sit in a pretty, fountained garden as well as inside. It doesn't compare with the temple itself, but it's a turn-on to be able to get face-to-face with say, Arjuna, in good lighting. (Open Sat.-Thurs. 10am-3pm. Free.)

About 750m from the temple (turn left as you exit), is the 12th-century **Jain Bastis,** composed of three temples. One of them, the **Parswanathasmy Temple,** is held up by twelve lathe-turned columns, so remarkably plain that they convey the serenity and meditation of worship. You can see your own reflection in them, distorted differently in each pillar.

■ Mangalore

An important trading port for centuries, and a major shipbuilding center during the 18th century, Mangalore retains today the mercantile character but little of the glory of its former years. With its modern fame as the main export and processing center for India's coffee and cashews, and as a center for the production of *bidis,* the city harbors a-less-than-magnetic attraction for tourists. But as a transport node along the west coast between Goa and Kerala, Mangalore makes a serviceable stopover.

ORIENTATION

Defying logic or easy grasp, the streets of Mangalore cross and converge at kaleidoscopic angles more suited to snowflakes than city plans. It's not a bad idea to just hop in an auto-rickshaw and state your destination. The **Town Hall,** an auditorium for musical performances, ceremonies, and weddings, is flanked by **Maidan Road** to the north and **Dr. U.P. Mallya Road** to the southeast. Following Dr. U.P. Mallya Rd. northeast, there is a major intersection of six roads. **K.S. Rao Road,** lined with many hotels, goes north, past the **private buses** to the **KSRTC Bus Terminal,** about 3km north of city center. Running uphill to the **lighthouse,** in a northeasterly direction, is **Lighthouse Hill Road.** To the east is **Balmatta Road,** and to the southeast is **Falnir Road,** with the Hotel Moti Mahal, Indian Airlines, and Milagres Church. About 500m south of this crazy intersection is the railway station.

PRACTICAL INFORMATION

Tourist Office: KSTDC, Hotel Indraprastha lobby, Lighthouse Hill Rd. (tel. 421692). Books KSTDC trips and can help tourists get to Dharmasthala, nearby beaches, Sultan's Battery, etc. Open daily 10:30am-1:30pm and 2:30-5:30pm.
Currency Exchange: State Bank of India, K.S. Rao Rd., exchanges currency and traveler's checks. Open Mon.-Fri. 10am-2pm, Sat. 10am-noon.
Telephones: STD/ISD booths; the main **Telegraph Office** next to the post office on Dr. U.P. Maliya Rd. southwest of Shetty circle can perform collect calls, but don't try any fancy tricks.
Airport: Bajpe Airport, 22km from town, can be reached by local bus (#47A, #47b, #22) or taxi. **Indian Airlines** (tel. 424669) has an office in the Hotel Moti Mahal on Falnir Rd. near Milagres Church. Many other carriers are serviced from another office in the Hotel Moti Mahal. By the summer of '97, the airlines hope to offer common computer bookings, so by visiting any airline office, all flights will be available. To: Bombay (2 per day, 1hr. 15min., US$91); Bangalore (Mon., Wed., and Fri., 1hr., US$54); Madras (Mon., Wed., and Fri., 2hr., US$80).
Trains: The **railway station** can be reached by following the road that runs not immediately to the left of the Town Hall (when facing it) but the next one on the left. No advance tickets may be purchased. To: Bombay (indirectly) (*Netravati Exp.* 6636, 1:50pm, 36hr., Rs. 235/1144 for 2nd/1st class); Bangalore, by way of Mysore, (7:45am and 9:35pm, 10hr.); Calicut (7 per day, 7am-8pm, 5hr., Rs.53/238 for 1st/2nd class); Ernakulam (*Parsuram Exp.* 6350, 4:15am, 10hr.; *Malabar Exp.* 6030, 6pm, 10hr., Rs.88/363 for 2nd/1st class); Trivandrum (*Parsuram Exp.* 6350, 4:15am, 19hr.; *Malabar Exp.* 6030, 6pm, 19hr., Rs.124/511 for 2nd/1st class); Madras (*Mangalore-Madras Mail* 6602, 12:40pm, 18hr.; *West Coast Exp.* 6628, 8pm, 18hr.).
Bus: Private buses run from a stand in the alleyway near the intersection of Lighthouse Hill Rd. and K.S. Rao Rd. From the intersection, follow Lighthouse Hill Rd., then take a left at the rickshaws. Many companies have offices here, all offering slightly different services. **Ganesh Travels** appears to be the biggest. To: Goa (9:15pm, 9hr., Rs.110); Bombay (8am, 22hr., Rs.250); Mysore (10pm, 8hr., Rs.100); Bangalore (9:30pm, 8hr., Rs.115); Cochin (8:15pm and 8:45pm, 10 hr.,

Rs.160). **KSRTC Bus Stand,** 3km from city center via K.S. Rao Rd., proudly offers "computerised advance booking." To: Goa (semi-luxury at 8:30am, 10hr., Rs.99; super deluxe at 8:30pm, 10hr., Rs.140; luxury at 9:30pm, 10hr., Rs.118); Bombay (super deluxe at 10am, 24hr., Rs.325; semi-luxury at 3pm and 6pm, 24hr., Rs.263); Bangalore (ordinary at 6, 8, 11am, noon, and 2:30pm, 8hr.; semi-luxury at 6:30, 9:30am, 1, and 2:30pm, 8hr.; super-deluxe at 8:30, 10, 11:30am, and 1:30pm, 8hr., Rs.108); Calicut (5pm, midnight, 7hr.); Trivandrum (14hr.)

Local Transportation: Most local buses stop on Dr. U.P. Maliya Rd., near Town Hall. The KSTDC Tourist Office (tel. 421692) in the Indraprastha Hotel, can answer questions about buses in and around Mangalore. **Auto-rickshaws** are the easiest way to navigate. Most will use their meters.

English Bookstore: Higginbothams, on Lighthouse Hill Rd. near Hotel Indraprastha. Open Mon.-Sat. 9:30am-1:30pm and 3:30-7:30pm.

Hospital: Among many in Mangalore (there is a big medical college here, **Kasturba Medical College**), the government runs **Wenlick Hospital** (tel.425038), and **Lady Goshen Hospital** (tel. 423138).

Police: The main police station is across from the Railroad Station. Smaller stations are all over town.

Emergency: Police 100. **Fire** 101. **Ambulance** 102.

Post Office, Dr. U.P. Mallya Road. Southwest from Town Hall, past the park, Shetty Circle, and a mosque, next to the Telegraph Office. Open Mon.-Fri. 10am-6pm.

ACCOMMODATIONS

Hotel Cosmo, Shetty Circle (tel. 425554). With your back to the mosque, proceed up Telecom House Rd. Hotel Cosmo is on the right. The freshly painted hotel offers smallish rooms with soft beds. All rooms have attached baths, including showers/buckets, squat toilets. Singles Rs.45. Doubles Rs.75.

Hotel Naufal (tel. 428085). Facing Town Hall, follow Maidan Rd. (running past Town Hall on the right), and continue straight through Rao and Rao Circle onto Mission St. After about 10min. (from Town Hall), Hotel Naufal will be on the right. The smiley staff gathers around, asking "you are coming from?" before taking you to a room with attached bath and hot water from 6 to 9am. The waterfront is only a short walk away. The Jasmine Restaurant downstairs serves basic foodstuffs. Singles Rs.75. Doubles Rs.120. Triples Rs.160.

Hotel Indraprastha, Lighthouse Hill Rd. (tel. 425750). Follow Lighthouse Hill Rd. uphill; the hotel is on the left across from Kasturba Medical College. Lumpy crunchy mattresses and shredded curtains in massive rooms with marble floors, balconies, and a morning paper. Front rooms must endure the sound of rickshaws and trucks grinding tediously up the hill during the day. Check-out 24hr. Hot (5:30-9:30am) and cold running water in attached baths. Singles Rs.70. Double Rs. 135. Super deluxe double with A/C, Rs. 300. Extra Guest Rs.40.

Hotel Manorama (tel. 440306). Follow K.S. Rao Rd. from the intersection with Lighthouse Hill Rd.; the hotel will be on the right after about a 5-min. walk. "All rooms are equipped with telephone, channel music, and bath attached." Snazzy lobby. Check-out 24hr. Singles Rs.120, with TV Rs.205, with A/C Rs.250. Suite Rs.215, with A/C Rs.300. Extra bed Rs.40.

FOOD

Hotel Dhanraj, on K.S. Rao Rd., in the (under)ground floor of the Poonja International Arcade. The place is clean, the price is right, and the *dosas* are expansive. Good South Indian food is supplemented by Punjabi and tandoori offerings and fresh juice. All vegetarian. *Dosa* Rs.10, *paneer masala* Rs.20. Open 6am-10pm. (*Dosas* 8:30am-12pm and 3:15-8pm).

Tai Chien, in Hotel Moti Mahal, on Fahir Rd. near Milagres Church. An impeccable spread of silverware, porcelain, linens, sauces, and pickles becomes vaguely discernable in the gilded light of paper lanterns, but the food is so good you don't need to see it. Won-ton soup Rs.22, Szechwan pork ribs Rs.75, bean sprout mushroom with bamboo shoots Rs.35.

Palimar Restaurant (tel. 440139), in the Hotel Manorama, underground, on K.S. Rao Rd. Air-conditioned and with four TVs, the restaurant dishes out good Indian food. *Thalis* Rs.20-30, *palak paneer* Rs.20, *gulab jamun* Rs.10. Open 7:30am-10:30pm.

SIGHTS

The **Lighthouse** up on Lighthouse Hill Rd. is uniquely ugly (with an orange racing stripe), but surrounded by lovely gardens and serene hillside views. Further uphill is the Jesuit **St. Aloyisius College Chapel,** with painted ceilings dating from 1899. (Open 8:30-10am, 12:30-2pm, and 3:30-6:30pm, but ceiling oogling is not welcome during "divine service" Sat. and Sun. mornings.)

Five kilometers north of city center is **Sultan's Battery,** a fort on the headlands of the old port. Take the #16 bus, or a rickshaw (about Rs.40 roundtrip). The 10th-century **Manjunatha Temple** stands 5km north of city center at the bottom of Kadri Hill (reached by buses #19, #14, #14a, and #48). Once a center for the Shaiva and Tantric Natha-Pantha cult, the temple is noted for its many bronze figures, including a seated Lokeshvara considered among India's finest. The gabled, towered temple complex is surrounded by nine tanks. A path opposite the temple complex leads to several shrines, then to the **Shri Yogishwar Math,** whose Tantric *sadhus* involve themselves in contemplation of Kala Bhairawa (a terrifying aspect of Shiva), Agni (god of fire), and Durga.

■ Near Mangalore

The beach at **Ullal,** 13km south of Mangalore, has a moderately priced resort (reached by bus #44A). **Dharmasthala,** 75km east of Mangalore, site of the Manjunatha Temple, is an important pilgrimage destination for Jains. Another important site for pilgrims is **Udipi,** on the coast about 60km north of Mangalore, the birthplace of the 13th-century Hindu saint Madhva. A Krishna temple surrounded by eight monasteries founded by Madhva, is a site of almost constantly clanging *pujas* during daylight hours. Contact the Regional Resources Centre for the Performing Arts here (at MGM College) for information about local festivals, dance, music, and theatre—ask also about their film, video, and audio archives.

■ Hospet

The famed Vijayanagar king Krishnadevaraya built Hospet between 1509 and 1520 in honor of his favorite courtesan, Nagala Devi. He named the suburb "Nagalapur" and it became one of his favorite haunts. Today, all traces of the Vijayanagar Empire have been eradicated and Hospet is hum-drum Karnataka, treading the line between heavy industrialization (blaring, barreling trucks transporting the products of a burgeoning steel industry) and village life (pigs, roosters, and dogs sorting through the streetside trash, bicycles and tongas, shanties lining the roads). The only reminders of the Vijayanagar ruins here are the regular buses to and from Hampi (12km to the northeast) and the billboards plastered with hotel names. With a population of 150,000, Hospet is used by many travelers as a base for exploring Hampi, although accommodations and restaurants can also be found in Hampi Bazaar (see p. 567).

ORIENTATION

Hospet's main drag is **Station Road** (its new name is M.G. Rd., but no one calls it that); it runs more or less north to south from the railway station, past the bus station, and turns into **Main Bazaar Road** in Hospet's commercial area. It bridges two canals in the process, as well as the **Hampi Road** (which runs east) and the **Tungabhandra Dam Road,** which runs west and skirts the market area. Most hotels and eateries are on or around Station Rd. Most points in Hospet are within walking distance of each other.

PRACTICAL INFORMATION

Tourist Office: KSTDC (tel. 58537), at the corner of College and Old Bus Stand Rd. You can book a bus tour of Hampi and the Tungabhadra Dam here (daily 9:30am-5:30pm, Rs.60), and get a decent map of Hampi. Open Mon.-Sat. 10am-5:30pm; closed the second Sat. of the month.

Budget Travel: Monika Travels (tel. 58470), near the bus stand on Station Rd. across from the Children's Library, will book air, rail, and bus tickets. Will also rent cars at Rs.3 per km.

Currency Exchange: State Bank of India, Station Rd. (tel. 58470), just a few steps north of Hotel Priyadarshini. Changes cold hard cash in U.S. dollars and pounds sterling only. Open Mon.-Fri. 10:30am-2:30pm. **Monika Travels** (tel. 57446) on Station Rd., exchanges U.S. dollars, pounds sterling, Deutschmarks, and AmEx and Thomas Cook traveler's checks, but at slightly obnoxious rates. Open Mon.-Sat. 9am-9pm, Sun. 9am-7pm. **Malligi Tourist Home**, 6/143 Jambanatha Rd. (tel. 58101), will change traveler's checks in U.S. dollars, pounds sterling, and Deutschmarks; 1% commission. Open daily 8am-9:30pm.

Telephones: Numerous STD/ISD booths along Station Rd. **Telegraph Office** (tel. 58212), next door to the State Bank of India, on Station Rd., has a 24hr. STD/ISD phone.

Trains: Hospet Junction Station (tel. 58360) is 750m from the bus stand at the end of Station Rd. Enquiry and reservation counters open daily 9am-1pm and 3-5pm. To: Bangalore (*Hampi Exp.* 6951, 8:30pm, 10½hr., Rs.102/421); Hyderabad (go to Guntakal on the *Hampi Exp.*, change there for the *Rayalaseema Exp.* 7430, 10:15pm, 10½hr., Rs.102/421); Bijapur (change at Gadag—get there on the 6592 *Hampi Exp.*, 7:30am, the 7309 *Vijayanagar Exp.*, 1pm, or the 7301 *Passenger* to Miraj, Rs. 35/264).

Buses: The bus station (tel. 58802) is in the middle of town on Station Rd. across from Hotel Vishwa. Reservation counters open daily 8am-noon and 3-6pm. They only take reservations for trips to Bangalore, Mysore, and Hyderabad. Enquiry open 24hr. To: Badami (5 per day, 7am-7pm, 5hr., Rs.38); Bangalore (30 per day, 5:30am-1am, 8hr., Rs.67/101); Bijapur (15 per day, 5:30am-midnight, 6hr., Rs.48); Hassan (4 buses 5:30am-11:45pm, 10hr., Rs.75); Hubli (15 buses 7am-11:30pm, 4hr., Rs.31/47); Arsikere (buses at 1:15 and 1:30pm. 8hr., Rs.64); Hyderabad (5 per day, 9:15am-2am, 12hr., Rs.92/140); Mangalore (7 per day, 6:15am-11pm, 12hr., Rs.90/131); Mysore (4 per day, 5am-12:30am, 10hr., Rs.84/131).

Local Transportation: Auto-rickshaws are not metered. A ride from the bus stand to the railway station will cost Rs.10. Alternatively, ride with a **rickshaw** ("bicycle tonga"), as the rickshaw-*wallah* smokes a *bidi* to reduce the strain of pulling your weight. You really don't need anything but your feet in this two-bit town. **To get to Hampi** (12km), take a bus from platform 10 (every 30min., 6:30am-9:30pm, Rs.2.25), catch an auto-rickshaw (Rs.50-60), or rent a bike. **Bicycles** can be rented from Khizer Cycle Market, Station Rd. (tel. 55010, residence), across from the turn off the Malligi Tourist Home. Rs.2 per hr. or Rs.15 for 24hr. Open daily 7am-7pm.

Library: Hospet Public Library, across from the GPO. Open Tues.-Sun. 5-8pm.

Market: The bus stand area is a good place to stock up on munchies before leaving for Hampi. Iyenagar bakeries, which sell fresh breads, curry sandwiches, and cakes, aren't difficult to find. Fruit sellers cluster around the bus stand on Station Rd. There's also a fresh veggie market on Old Bus Stand Rd. near the bazaar branch of the State Bank of Mysore.

Pharmacy: Popular Medicines and General Stores (tel. 54806), on College Rd. off Station Rd. Fluent English spoken here. Open daily 7:30am-10:30pm.

Hospital: Government General Hospital (tel. 58199). Go west on College Rd. past the Evangelical Church and Vijayanagara College, and turn left immediately. Go over a canal and continue; the hospital will be on your right. Recently refurbished and very clean. The only hospital around for about 70km.

Police Station (tel. 41033). On the same block as the Tourist Office, 200m south.

Post Office: On Station Rd., a 5-min. walk south of the bus stand (tel. 58210). Open Mon.-Fri. 10am-4pm, Sat. 10am-3pm. **Postal Code:** 583201.

Telephone Code: 08394.

ACCOMMODATIONS

Hotel Priyadarshini, V/45 Station Rd. (tel. 58838), 500m south of the railway station. The 64 rooms are spacious and spotless, with telephones, gung-ho fans, room service, and super-duper same-day laundry. Each has a balcony which affords views of the parking lot or grassy field below. Amiable, professional staff. STD/ISD booth, bookshop, and KSTDC tour booking in the lobby. Hot showers in the mornings and seat toilets. Great restaurant attached. Check-out 24hr. Singles Rs.90. Doubles Rs.145. Quads Rs.195. A/C rooms Rs.380-425. TV Rs.100 extra.

Malligi Tourist Home, 6/143 J.N. Rd. (tel. 58101). From the bus stand, walk south 250m and turn left before the canal. Walk past the Saraswathi movie theater. Malligi is at the end of the block. Regular doubles are clean, with telephone and attached baths with squat toilets. More ritzy rooms have carpets, TVs, fridges, seat toilets, and fancy furniture. The luxury complex houses A/C suites with wicker chairs and white walls impervious to smudging; these rooms overlook a manicured garden with the mountains in the distance. Ebulliently cordial management will make sure you're comfortable every second of the day. They expect to open a swimming pool in 1997. KSTDC tour bookings, STD/ISD booth, handicrafts shop. Two attached restaurants and a bar. Check-out 24hr. Basic doubles Rs.145. Deluxe doubles Rs.550. Luxury suites Rs.1200-1500. Traveler's checks and major credit cards accepted. Reservations recommended.

Hotel Shalini (tel. 8901), 200m south of the railway station on Station Rd. "I know the rooms aren't much to look at but we treat the guests with love," is how the manager describes the set-up here. With flowering trees outside its tiny pink façade, the place makes up in character what it lacks in convenience. Not the most sterile of hotels, but more than liveable. You'll need your own sheets. Squat toilet and bucket hot water in the morning. Room service (tea and tiffin) and laundry service. The cheapest place in Hospet. Check-out 24hr. Singles Rs.40. Doubles Rs.75. Triples Rs.90. Quads Rs.150.

Hotel Vishwa, Station Rd. (tel. 57171), across from the bus stand. Clean, tiny singles with semi-clean squat toilets. Doubles and quads are more spacious. All rooms have telephones and fans. Sunny hallways, down to earth staff, room service, running hot water in the mornings. Check-out 24hr. Singles Rs.75. Doubles Rs.140. Quads Rs.240.

Sree Krishna Tourist Home (tel. 58835). From the Government Hospital, walk 50m toward the mountains and take a left at the brown Krishna Hotel sign. Sunny hallways, tiny beds with dingy sheets in small doubles. Seat toilets, running hot water in the morning. Deluxe doubles boast bigger beds, A/C, crackly black-and-white TVs, and telephones. Grimy windows filter the light. Room service, *dhobi*. Check-out 24hr. Doubles Rs.124, deluxe Rs.275.

FOOD

Naivedyam Restaurant, attached to Hotel Priyadarshini. Dishes out consistently fresh huge portions. *Thalis* (Rs.15/35), with a choice of *chapati* or *puri* and thick curries. *Alu* and *palak* prepared a million different ways. Best *lassis* around—ice cold and frothy-foamy. Open daily 7am-10:30pm, for *thalis* noon-3:15pm and 7-10:30pm.

Madhu Paradise, in the Malligi Complex (tel. 58101, ext. 121). Does American-style breakfasts—corn flakes, porridge, and toast—from 7-10:30am, *dosas* nearly all day, and *thalis* (Rs.15/35) 10:30am-3pm and 7-10:30pm. Macaroni served with tomato or garlic soup. Blessed with abundant variations on the *naan* theme—garlic, cheese, Peshwari, Kashmiri (Rs.10-15). Avoid the soupy ice cream.

Eagle Garden Restaurant and Bar, also in the Malligi Complex (tel. 5801, ext. 306). Indubitably delicious veg. and non-veg. fare in the garden or in a thatched bamboo cottage. Wear insect repellent—even though waiters gallantly battle the mosquitoes with coils, they can't seem to exorcise the blood-suckers. But once your food comes, you won't notice. *Kababs* (Rs.25-30) are excellent in any form, even if they're deep-fried like *pakoras* instead of skewered and grilled. The Rs.15 banana *lassi* is to die for. Lots of alcohol, too—bottled beer (Rs.35-45) and cocktails (Rs.40-60). Mellow Hindi tunes. Open daily 7am-11pm.

Iceland Restaurant, College Rd. (tel. 57347), scoops alarmingly massive sundaes (Rs.15), near-solid milkshakes (Rs.15), and stellar *kulfis* (Rs.17). Open daily 9:30am-11:30pm.

■ Hampi

Hampi and the surrounding areas have celebrated the past since ancient times, when pilgrims paid homage to the site where Rama slayed the monkey king Vali and hung out waiting for Hanuman to find Sita in Lanka (see **The Ramayana,** p. 81). The fabled hill of Kishkindha no longer exists, but locals and myth experts alike are certain that it was near Hampi—Hanuman is the most popular deity around here, and some *Ramayana* enthusiasts claim that the many monkeys in the hills are descendents of Vali, Sugriva, and Hanuman. Of more solid archeological importance are the ruins of the city of Vijayanagar. The Vijayanagar kings made the site their empire's bastion, protected by the torrential Tungabhadra River on one side and rugged hills on the other. Five dynasties ruled the resplendent kingdom from 1336 to 1565, building all manner of temples, pavilions, aqueducts, and palaces. In 1565, a confederacy of Muslim sultans from the north annihilated the empire, relegating it to the annals of the past.

Despite ongoing attempts by the Archaeological Survey of India to excavate and restore the Vijayanagar ruins to their 15th-century splendor, Hampi may never entirely dispense with the aura of decay that pervades all facets of life here: the desolate landscape strewn with empty palaces and temples, the languid pace of the locals' lives, and, perhaps most strikingly, the utterly decadent tourist culture that has popped up in the past few years. More than a few expats have turned a week's stay into years, eloping with Hampites and settling down on the other side of the Tungabhadra River to avoid the police. Isolated from time and urbanity, Hampi is an alluring and potentially permanent oasis for any traveler seeking to regress; the risk of going to admire Hampi's history is that you might get mired in the ruins.

ORIENTATION AND PRACTICAL INFORMATION

The ruins of Vijayanagar spread 26 square kilometers, and the bulk of them start at **Kamalapuram,** a village 4km southeast of **Hampi Bazaar.** The paved road from Kamalapuram to the Bazaar skirts the **Queen's Bath Royal Enclosure Area,** the **Krishna Temple,** and many other shrines, boulder formations, coconut groves, and sugarcane fields, before reaching the Hampi Bazaar. The **bus stand,** with plenty of unpredictable buses traveling to and from Kamalapuram (Rs.1.75) and Hospet (Rs.3.25), is at the junction of this road and the Main Bazaar. The **Virupakshi Temple** lies 300m west of the bus stand and has a 53-m *gopuram* you can't miss. The area between the bus stand and the temple teems with tiny restaurants, guest houses, and bauble shops. The only things set in stone around here are the ruins themselves; hours, prices, menus, and bus schedules all fluctuate manically. The **tourist office** (tel. 51339), 100m west of the bus stand, dishes out wise warnings against solo exploring (there have been a few narcotic-induced muggings here lately) and a detailed map of the ruins; private guides can also be hired here (Oct.-March Rs.500 per day, April-Sept. Rs.150). Open Mon.-Sat. 10am-5:30pm. Fifty meters behind the tourist office is a shack housing **Guru's Bicycle Shop** where you can rent a functional bike for Rs.20 per day or Rs.2 per hour. Open daily 7am-5pm. On the right side of the temple as you face the entrance is a path which leads to **Shambu Restaurant,** open only during the high season, which is an eatery-**currency exchange-travel** agency. Back on the Main Bazaar, halfway between the bus stand and the temple on the north side of the road, is **Aspiration Stores** (tel. 51254), which sells accounts of the Vijayanagar Empire, descriptions and maps of the ruins, books on Indian philosophy and religion, as well as an array of ayurvedic and herbal stuff. Open daily 9am-8:30pm. For toilet paper, soap, biscuits, and film, head to **Hampi Stores** (tel. 51374), open daily 6:45am-9:30pm. STD/ISD **telephone** booths are located at Hampi Bazaar on the left side of the Main Bazaar Rd. as you face the Virupakshi Temple; opposite the bus stand, and opposite the tourist office are 24-hour booths. Inside the temple, immediately to your right, is the Hampi Outpost **Police Station** (tel. 51241, ask the operator for the police station). Tourist office staff and tourist guides recommend that you register you and your belongings with the police before staying in Hampi. There's also a police station at Kamalapuram (tel. 51240) 200m east of the bus station there. Beside the *gopuram,* outside the temple, is the sleepy **post office** stall (tel. 51242), open Mon.-Sat. 8:30am-4:30pm. **Postal Code: 583239. Telephone Code:** 08394.

The **Vittala Temple** and other big-name sights are 2km northeast of the Bazaar. The dirt road that leads to them is fairly direct, though negotiable only on foot.

ACCOMMODATIONS

To 15th-century traveler Domingo Paes, the Hampi bazaar was "a broad and beautiful street, full of rows of fine houses and mantapas...there you will find all sorts of rubies, and diamonds, and emeralds, and pearls and seed pearls, and every other sort of thing there is on earth that you wish to buy." To the 20th century tourist, Hampi Bazaar, flanked by Virupaksha Temple's huge *gopuram* and the monolithic Nandi, is important not for its magnificent architecture, glimmering jewels, or vivid silks, but for its cheap rooms, pancakes and spaghetti, and stone(r)s of a slightly different variety than in Paes' day. Staying in the guest houses of the Bazaar, most of which are portions of homes, usually requires a lack of concern for cleanliness and sprawling space and a tolerance for buggies, doggies, and froggies.

Shanthi Guest House (tel. 51368). From the bus stand, walk left toward the Virupaksha Temple, turn right, walk around the Sri Rama Lodge. Enclosed garden area, cheerful exterior, and clean common toilets make it a wellspring of tourist camaraderie. Cold showers. Check-out 12:30pm. Singles Rs.50. Doubles Rs.70.

Vikki Guest House, 200m behind the tourist office. Huge beds, boulder-view, fans, and relatively clean common baths. Cold bucket showers. Check-out noon. Doubles Rs.40.

Sri Rama Lodge (tel. 51219). Hard, musty beds that occupy almost the entire room. Attached toilet with bath. Lighting is capricious at best. Check-out 24hr. Singles Rs.50. Doubles Rs.100.

Laxshmi Guest House has mattresses on the floor, common trough bath, and the loo is a 3-min. walk away. No padlocks provided. Check-out noon. Doubles Rs.30-40, depending on how far you can talk the manager down. Sleeping on the roof is free Oct.-March.

Hotel Mayura Bhuvaneswari, Kamalapuram (tel. 51374). Five hundred meters to the left (east) as you exit the Kamalapuram bus stand. There's a big blue sign on your right; hotel is at the end of a long, paved driveway. Spacious, spotless rooms with clean sheets, towels, and soap. Plants line the open-air hallways, and etchings of the ruins hang on the wall. Deserted in the off-season by all but the frogs and lizards, the doting waitstaff, and the way-cool Goan manager Mr. Murthy. Bicycle rental (Rs.30 per day) and good travel advice. 24-hr. hot water, seat toilets, laundry, and room service. Check-out noon. Singles Rs.180, with A/C 300. Doubles Rs.220, with A/C Rs.350.

FOOD

Open-air cafés line the main bazaar; most are extensions of people's houses, and usually there's a group of children watching TV near the kitchen. They cater to tourist palates: these are probably the only places in Karnataka that serve hummus and "falfel." Hybrid Indian-Western food means fruit *parathas,* chocolate *lassis,* and *masala* macaroni.

Shankar Restaurant, near the tourist office, is one of the better establisments. Great South Indian eats, as well as fluffy pancakes and stalwart sandwiches. Open daily 8am-8pm.

Ramsing Teashop, behind the tourist office, near Vikki Guest House. The owner cooks all the generous offerings himself, and offers 1 free meal per day to the financially defunct. His wife sells hand-embroidered hats and pouches. Open daily 7:30am-9pm.

Hotel Mayura Bhuvaneswari, Kamalapuram (tel. 51374). The only enclosed restaurant in the whole area. *Thalis* on Sundays (Rs.15) and toast, *dosas, chapatis,* and veg. and chicken curries all the time. Piles of veg. *pakoras* for Rs.10. Open daily 6:30am-10pm.

SIGHTS

The Viyajanagar ruins spread at least 26 square kilometers, and although it's impossible to see everything in one or two days, if you have stamina you can soak up the main sights in one foot-killing, back-aching, thigh-throbbing day. Renting a bicycle in Hospet, Kamalapuram, or Hampi Bazaar will help you see everything except the Vittala Temple area to the northeast (the path is narrow and rocky). Either lock your bike and leave it with the tourist office or approach Vittala from the southeast, along the tour bus route.

From the Kamalapuram bus stand, head right (east) for 100m; you'll reach Kannada signs with white arrows. For Hampi, make a left. Two hundred meters later, you'll hit the **Queen's Bath,** which from the outside looks like nothing more than a giant stone enclosure surrounded by a moat. The inside has a huge swimming pool where the queen supposedly kicked back after a hard day (although no one can prove whether she ever used it). Veer right off the main road after the bath, and you'll come upon the **Mahanavani Dibba,** crossed by ancient aqueducts and stone canals (all dry now), where the gala Dasara festival was held. *Dibba* means platform and this Dasara platform is one of the tallest and most ornate around. The Dasara throne, replete with gold and gems, was stored inside during the rest of the year. Because, like most other Vijayanagar monuments, it was carved out of granite, the frieze work and detail are not that fine, but what it lacks in embellishment it makes up for in stature. South of the *dibba* is the recently excavated (1986) **Pushkarini,** a deep sacred water tank with metronomically regular steps.

Get back on the dirt path and walk straight north, past the turn-off for the Hazara Rama Temple and past the pink Archaeological Camp House. This leads to the **Zenana Enclosure,** a stone wall within which sits the pink stucco **Lotus Mahal,** a sweet little example of Indo-Saracenic architecture. Nearby is a **watchtower,** used to survey the terrain for enemies, or, according to some accounts, to provide a vantage point for the King's wives to watch the goings-on without being spotted. Across from the Lotus Mahal are the **Guard's Quarters,** with high arches and polished floors. To the east and through the stone walls are the 11 domed **Elephant Stables,** where the royal beasts (more than 15,000 of them during the 15th century) slept, rested, and munched. Backtrack to the sign pointing to the **Hazara Rama Temple** and take that road east 500m. The enclosure walls are carved with relief work on both the inside (scenes from the *Ramayana*) and the outside (a parade of horses, elephants, dancing girls, and soldiers). Inside the sanctum are two rare images of Vishnu as Buddha—Buddha was supposedly Vishnu's ninth incarnation—luring the impious to destruction with his religion's blasphemies. A little to the west is the **Underground Temple.** Due to a collapsed roof, the former temple now fills up with rainwater and fish during monsoon season.

Turn right back on the main paved road from Kamalapuram to the Main Bazaar. You'll cross a rusty canal and lots of tender coconut groves before reaching the grassy path leading to the **Narasimha Lakshmi statue.** When the sultans sacked the city, they sliced open Narasimha's belly to see if the seven-meter high monolith had eaten any rubies or diamonds. They were disappointed, and Narasimha was disfigured, but he still cuts one of Hampi's most striking figures. Around the back you can see the feminine hand of his consort Lakshmi, who was probably depicted sitting on Narasimha's thigh. The ASI is trying to restore Narasimha to his original wholeness but this would mean sacrificing his monolithic nature to mortar. Next to the statue is the **Shiva Temple,** with a huge, flower dotted *linga* in a pool of water. Get back on the main road and you'll pass the **Krishna Temple** to your left. Further up the road to the left is the monolithic Ganesha, no longer worshiped since he was defiled by the Muslim invaders. Continue down the hill to reach the Main Bazaar.

To your left you'll see the 53-meter brick *gopuram* of the **Virupaksha Temple.** This was the king's personal temple; inside is a marriage hall and assembly hall. Toward the rear, you can enter a small room where a camera obscura of sorts throws an upside-down shadow of the *gopuram* on the wall. Walk back toward the *gopuram* and take a right before exiting. Hike up the stony hill, past the **Jain Temples** on your right (this is a great place to stop for a breather because of the beautiful views of Hampi), veer left and you'll approach some boulder-caves where armies used to chill in the shade. Go back through the Main Bazaar, past all the shops, to the 16th-century part where *mandapas* are being restored. On your left will be the **Photo Gallery** (tel. 51281) where you can look at Englishman Alexander John Greenlaw's 1856 photos of the ruins; next to each of his photos is a 1983 version by Australian John Collins. They're pretty eerie; nothing seems to have changed much—a permanent state of ruin. The gallery is open Tues.-Sun. 10am-5:30pm; free.

Continue on this path and it leads more or less directly to the famed **Vittala Temple.** On the way you'll pass some disused temples. Vittala looks unimpressive and small from the outside, but you'll know you're there from the cold-drink dealers and tourist buses. It sits on the south bank of the Tungabhadra River, and was never finished or consecrated. According to the 20-odd inscriptions in and around the temple, Vijayanagar King Krishnadevaraya began building it in 1513, and the work was probably halted by the city's destruction in 1565. Another bit of lore has it that Vittala, the incarnation of Vishnu to whom the temple is dedicated, came to look at the temple and found it too grand for him and hightailed it back to his humbler home in Maharashtra. The carvings here are the most ornate around the ruins. Fifty-six musical pillars inside the temple each sound a different note when tapped with the knuckles. The best way to hear the reverberations is to put your ear to one pillar and have a partner do the tapping. Outside the temple is the massive stone chariot for Garuda, Vishnu's mythical bird. It's not monolithic, but it's engineered so superbly that the stone wheels can move.

■ Near Hampi: Anegundi

The 5000-year-old cave temples at Anegundi are seldom visited by tourists. The Archaeological Survey of India isn't in charge here and getting to the caves is an adventure in itself. Because there are no signs, it may be best to solicit the assistance of a certified guide at Hampi's tourist office (Rs.400 in season, Rs.100 off-season). From the Vittala temple, continue on the main paved road along the Tungabhadra River. Eventually, the road deteriorates into a path leading to the river bank where two grass-basket boats shuttle people, bicycles, and (more perilously) motorcycles to and from Anegundi. Hop in and stay still—balance is key here. Once you reach the other side, walk straight up a small slope and you'll see the village. If not, just ask your boat-*wallah* ("Anegundi?"), and he'll point you in the right direction. A left turn at the first opportunity, and a subsequent left at the next fork in the road will lead you past the Andhra Bank and under a small gate. After the gate, turn left onto the paved road which cuts through rice paddies. A dirt path veers off the left; take it and you'll be at the base of a rocky hill you need to climb. At the midpoint is a **Durga Temple,** and the *swami* in charge will point you past his shrine and up the hill. The cave temples, which occasionally house wayward Hampites and tourists, are in a terrible condition. You can't see the ancient inscriptions on the roof because smoke from cooking fires has blackened them. There are still two rock slabs on either side which function as beds.

■ Badami

This jumping little town in the middle of nowhere was the capital of the mighty Chalukyan empire from 543 to 757 AD. Locals live beside or inside the ancient cave temples and edifices that dot the landscape, and though they are friendly, few speak English. The temples are situated high in the mountains surrounding an ancient Chalukyan tank, around which the thwacking and thumping of laundry reverberates. Nearby are Pattadakal (20km) where Chalukyan kings were crowned, and Aihole (47km) the first Chalukyan capital, on the Malaprabha River.

ORIENTATION AND PRACTICAL INFORMATION

Badami's main road is **Station Road,** probably the only straight path in the village. It runs from the **railway station** in the north to the **bus stand** (5km) and to the routes to Pattadakal and Aihole in the south. Most accommodations and cafes are around the bus stand. **College Rd. (Ramdurg Rd.)** is the other roadway in Badami—it runs east from Station Rd. and winds around to reach the KSTDC hotel 1km later. The Bhutanatha Temples are north of **Agastya Lake. Buses** from the bus stand (tel. 65055) make up with alacrity what they lack in punctuality. To: Aihole (9am, 1hr., Rs.8.50); Bijapur (7:30, 8, and 8:45am, 4hr., Rs.25); Hampi (2:30 and 3:15pm, 5½hr., Rs.40); Hubli (5, 6:45, 7:30, 11:45am, and 5:30pm, 3hr., Rs.14); Gadag (5:30, 7:30, 8am, 2, 4:50, and 6pm, 2hr., Rs.16); Mysore (4:40pm); Sholapur (6:45, 7:50am, and 5:45pm, 6hr., Rs.55). Badami Travels, to the right of the bus stand, operates daily private coaches to Bangalore. There are several STD **telephone** booths along Station Rd. The **police station** is opposite the bus stand. The **GPO** and **Telegraph Office** (tel. 65030) is just north of the bus stand. (GPO open Mon.-Sat. 7-11am and 2-5pm; telegraph office open 24hr.) **Postal Code:** 587201. **Telephone Code:** 08357.

ACCOMMODATIONS AND FOOD

The accommodations here are limited, but those at Pattadakal and Aihole are even fewer. **Mookimba Lodge,** across from the bus stand in Badami, is the cheeriest and cleanest of the hotels in the neighborhood. The rooms, whose attached bathrooms have running hot water in the mornings, are spotless. Screened windows look out upon the Chalukyan hills, and an in-house travel agency will help get you there. Check-out 24 hours. Singles Rs.85. Doubles Rs.125, although management says the rates are expected to change. To get to **Hotel Mayura Chalukya** on College Rd. (tel. 65046) from the bus stand, turn right, walk 500m and take the first right. Walk down this road 1km; the hotel is set back from the road on your right. This is monkey territory, but the rooms are huge, relatively clean, and look out on overgrown gardens. Mosquito nets are provided. This place exudes a familiar aura as only a tourist bungalow could. Check-out noon. Attached restaurant does average vegetarian and non-vegetarian cuisine, and toast, omelettes, and soup (open daily 6:30am-10:30pm). Singles Rs.145. Doubles Rs.185. Triples Rs.226. Room for five Rs.301. The **Hotel Badami Court** (tel. 65230) is on Station Rd., 2km northwest of the bus stand. Multi-colored flags out front flap their greeting to this three-star oasis of bathtubbed, carpeted life. Hot water runs 24 hours so you can wash off that grime you accumulated bellying through caves. Ultra-helpful management. The multi-cuisine restaurant (open daily 6am-11pm) is a bit pricey (Rs.100 for a meal) but well worth it. TVs and direct dial phones provided. Attached travel counter. Singles Rs.400, with A/C Rs.750. Doubles Rs.550, with A/C Rs.950. For cheaper **food,** try the stand-up, no-nonsense, clean **Geeta Darshini** (tel. 65234), where nothing on the menu costs more than Rs.5. Open Mon.-Sat. 6:30am-9pm.

SIGHTS

A visit to the cave temples near Badami is a great way to get filthy, and see some ancient beauty while you're at it. The **South Fort** cave temples, carved out of the red sandstone cliff and connected by steps, are some of the most important cave temples in India. To get from the bus stand to the cave temples, head right on Station Rd. and past College Rd. You'll see a statue of Dr. Ambedkar; turn left on the road he faces and head up the 40 giant steps to the first cave and the three younger caves. These temples are largely Hindu, but the influences of Jainism and Buddhism are apparent as well. **Cave 1,** the oldest, is a Shiva temple with sculptures of numerous deities. **Cave 2** is dedicated to Vishnu, as is **Cave 3,** the largest and best-sculpted of the group, dating from 578 AD. The 21-m-long façade of Cave 3 is delicately carved with figures of humans, gods, and dwarves, as are the pillars and the steps leading to the plinth. The path up to Cave 3 leads past a natural cave which was once used as a Buddhist temple; the Buddha image inside has been defaced. **Cave 4,** which was probably the only cave here used as a Jain temple, overlooks the lake and has sculptures of the *tirthankaras.*

To get to the **Bhutanatha Temples** (by the side of the Agastya Lake), the **North Fort** temples, and the **Archaeological Museum** (open Sat.-Thurs. 10am-5pm; free), head from the bus stand to your right and you'll find a sign proclaiming "Museum" which leads you through a tiny neighborhood on narrow stone paths. The **Upper Shivalaya Temple** is one of the oldest of the group at Badami. Carvings on it depict scenes from the life of Krishna, though they are damaged. The most spectacular of the North Fort temples is the **Malegetti Shivalaya,** which has a pillared hallway with Shiva on one side and Vishnu on the other. The **Jambulinga Temple,** from 699 AD, is on the side of the Agastya Tank near the rickshaw stand. The Bhutanatha Temples are on the opposite side of the Agastya Tank.

■ Near Badami: Pattadakal and Aihole

About 20km from Badami, Pattadakal was the Chalukyan capital during the 7th and 8th centuries AD and the site of all Chalukyan coronations. Today it's basically a temple town, with no real travel amenities—most travelers base themselves in Badami and make excursions here. Pattadakal can be reached from Badami on the same bus that takes travelers to Aihole.

Pattadakal's ancient temples are clustered at the base of a pink sandstone hill. The **Virupaksha (Lokeshwara) Temple** has a three-story spire with a large chlorite stone Nandi sitting in front of it. Passageways lead around the shrine to carvings depicting episodes from the *Ramayana* and *Mahabharata.* Next to it is the similar **Mallikarjuna Temple.** The 9th-century Jain **Meguti Temple,** about 1km south of the others, has an upper-story sanctuary accessible by a staircase. The trip from Badami to Pattadakal (on the Aihole bus) takes less than an hour. Call the Badami bus stand (tel. (08357) 65055) for information on fares and departure times.

Forty-seven kilometers northeast of Badami on the banks of the Malaprabha River, Aihole offers spectacular opportunities for temple viewing and not much else. Given the opportunities for lodging and eating here (there are virtually none) most travelers stay in Badami and visit Aihole only during the day.

There are over 100 temples in Aihole, including the **Durgigudi Temple,** whose round shape betrays its lineage among Buddhist *chaitya* halls. To its south is a rudimentary *gopuram.* In the northeast of the village is the Shaiva temple **Ravanaphadigudi.** The Jain **Meguti Temple** has a stone inscription dating it to 634 AD, making it one of the oldest dated temples in India. The **Ladh Khan Temple,** further south, is named after a Muslim who set up house in the sanctuary in the 19th century. Due to its similarity to megalithic caves, this temple was once thought to date from the 5th century, although now it is believed to have come from the early 8th century.

Buses to Aihole (Rs.8.50) depart from Badami at 9am, and the trip lasts just over an hour. Call the Badami bus stand (tel. (08357) 65055) for more information.

Andhra Pradesh

The state of Andhra Pradesh occupies a large section of southeastern India, from the dry lands of the Deccan Plateau to the Bay of Bengal coastline, where the Krishna and Godavari Rivers splash out in rich but cyclone-prone deltas. Inland, the higher part of Andhra Pradesh, known as Telangana, is poorer, but the Andhra people are linked by

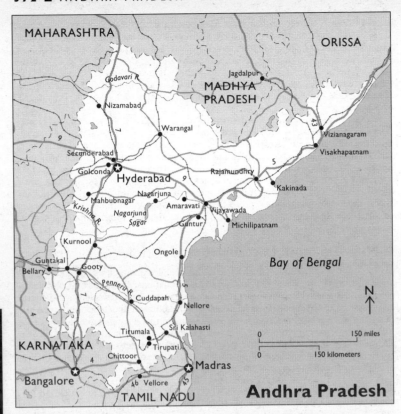

MAHARASHTRA

ORISSA

Jagdalpur

MADHYA
PRADESH

Godavari R

Nizamabad

Warangal

Vizianagaram

Secunderabad

Visakhapatnam

Golconda
Hyderabad

Rajamundhry

Kakinada

Nagarjuna

Mahbubnagar

Amaravati

Vijayawada

Nagarjuna
Sagar

Guntur

Michilipatnam

Krishna R.

Kurnool

Ongole

Bay of Bengal

Guntakal
Bellary
Gooty

Penneru R.

Cuddapah

Nellore

N

Tirumala

Sri Kalahasti

0   150 miles

KARNATAKA

Tirupati

0   150 kilometers

Chittoor

Madras

Bangalore

Vellore

Andhra Pradesh

TAMIL NADU

their language, Telugu. In 1953, Andhra Pradesh became the first state in India to
have its boundaries drawn along linguistic lines. The state was named for the kingdom of the Andhras, also known as the Satavahanas, who ruled most of the Deccan
from the 2nd century BC until the 3rd century AD. Beginning in the 16th century,
Andhra Pradesh was ruled by Muslims, first under the independent Golconda Sultanate, then briefly as part of the Mughal Empire, and last under the Nizams, who ruled
at Hyderabad under British protection from 1723 until 1948. When India became
Independent in 1947, Nizam Usman Ali refused to have his lands become part of
India. After a one-year standoff, India marched in and annexed the territory, which
was merged with other Telugu-speaking areas to form Andhra Pradesh. Hyderabad
remains one of India's great centers of Islamic culture, while remains of earlier ages
can be seen at Nagarjunakonda and Amaravati, southeast of Hyderabad, where *stupas*
and a 2nd-century AD Buddhist university attest to the region's stake in Buddhism. In
the state's southeastern corner, the richly carved thousand-pillared temple at Tirupati
evokes Hindu religious fervor unparalleled in South India.

■ Hyderabad

Andhra Pradesh's capital, Hyderabad, was founded in 1591 by Muhammad Quli Qutb
Shah, Sultan of Golconda. Though he was to ascend to the throne of one of the greatest kindgoms in India, the young Muhammad had fallen in love too hard and too fast
to heed religious and social barriers. His love Bhagmati was a simple but beautiful
Hindu dancer and singer. Muhammad risked his life and inheritance on monsoon

midnight horse back journeys from Golconda to a village north of the Musi River for his trysts with Bhagmati. Upon discovering Muhammad's smittenness, his father capitulated and allowed Muhammad to marry the common Hindu girl. Muhammad became king and founded a new city on the banks of the Musi, which he named Bhagnagar. Although the city was later renamed Hyderabad, and Golconda is now in shambles, its syncretic tendencies are still firmly rooted in legend. Founded as a testament to interreligious union, Hyderabad thrives. The metropolis (with a population of 4.7 million) has the highest proportion of Muslims of any city in the south, yet was one of the only places which did not erupt in riots following the 1992 destruction of the Babri Masjid in Ayodhya. The Muslim prince, or Nizam, ruled over a doting Hindu-majority state until his death in the 1950s. The city's architecture is striking not only for its grandeur (the last Nizam was reputedly the wealthiest man in the world, and liked to show it), but for its Indo-Saracenic character.

Perhaps the anomalous lack of religious strife here should be attributed to the city's languid-bordering-on-lethargic atmosphere. Cross the street in Abids, the city center, and for once you won't fear loss of limbs—cars slow down and auto-rickshaws and scooters politely weave (but watch out for the buses!). Rickshaw-*wallahs* here are more meter-vigilant than their customers. A visit to Hyderabad is likely to be pleasantly uneventful.

ORIENTATION

The **Musi River** divides the **Old City**—land of the Charminar, Mecca Masjid, and bazaars—from the **New City** of government offices, glitzy downtown shops, and glimmering Birla-commissioned landmarks to the north. The **Abids** area forms the heart of the New City: it's just south of the gargantuan Gautama-guarded **Hussain Sagar,** the artificial tank built during the Golconda empire, and houses **Nampally station,** one of the area's hubs. The other hub is in **Secunderabad,** to the northeast of Hussain Sagar, where the railway station handles many arrivals and departures. There's not much to see in Secunderabad, which was founded in 1806 and christened in the name of Nizam Sikander Jah, to serve as the British cantonment area.

PRACTICAL INFORMATION

Tourist Office: Government of India Tourist Office, Sandozi Building, Himayatnagar (tel. 763 0037). From Basheer Bagh, walk 750m down the road, on the left side. Two flights up. A fabulous source for information and advice regarding travel throughout India. Good (and free) Hyderabad city map. Open Mon.-Fri. 9:15am-5:45pm, Sat. 9:15am-1pm. **APTTDC,** Gagan Vihar, Mukarramjahi Rd. (tel. 473 2554). From the Hyderabad Railway Station, turn right. The office is a 500m walk, on the left side, 5th fl. Outdated maps and antiquated, though interesting, brochures of the city. They book APTTDC accommodations throughout A.P., as well as city tours and seats on the Golconda shuttle. Ask for a copy of the monthly "what's on" guide, *Channel 6* (Rs.10). Open Mon.-Sat. 10:30am-5pm, closed the 2nd Sat. of the month. There's an APTTDC counter at the Secunderabad Railway Station, but it probably won't help much. Also an office in Secunderabad, adjoining the APTTDC's Yatriniwas Hotel, Sardar Patel Rd. (tel. 843931).

Budget Travel: Sita World Travel, 3-9-4 Hyderguda Rd. (tel. 233628). Coming from Abids Circle to Basheer Bagh, take a right. **Sita** is opposite the Diagnostic Centre. Open Mon.-Fri. 9:30am-6pm, Sat. 9:30am-1:30pm.

Immigration Office: Foreigners Regional Registration Office, Commissioner of Police, Purana Haveli Rd. (tel. 809715), 500m southeast of the Salar Jung Museum. Special Branch open Mon.-Sat. 10am-5pm. Closed 2nd Sat. of the month. Registration fee Rs.125. Three-month tourist visas cannot be extended here. Fees range from US$5-100 for other extensions.

Currency Exchange: The main branches of banks usually have a foreign exchange department. **State Bank of Hyderabad,** M.G. Rd. (tel. 201978), 700m north of Abids Circle. Currency and traveler's checks in U.S. dollars, pounds sterling, yen, and Deutschmarks. Open for exchange Mon.-Fri. 10:30am-2:30pm. In Secunderabad, **Synergy Forexpress,** 62 Sarojini Devi Rd. (tel. 780 6552), near Gangaram's.

Open daily 9am-7:30pm. All currencies. No commission. **Thomas Cook,** 6-1-57, Saifebad (tel. 596524). Near the junction of Secretariat and Public Gardens Rd. Rs.20 encashment charge. Thirty currencies and traveler's checks changed here. Open Mon.-Sat. 9:30am-5:30pm.

Telephones: STD/ISD booths are all over Abids. **Telegraph Office,** Abids Circle (tel. 509929), adjoining the GPO on the right side as you exit. Open 24hr.

Airport: Begumpet Airport, on the north side of Husain Sagar, off Sardar Patel Rd. (tel. 141), 8km north of Abids. Auto-rickshaw-*wallahs* usually refuse to use the meter from Abids to the airport. **Airlines:** Air France (tel. 230946), open Mon.-Fri. 9:30am-5:30pm, Sat.10:30am-1:30pm; Air Canada, Royal Jordanian, TWA (tel. 230995); Kuwait Airways (tel. 234344); Gulf Air (tel. 230967); and Jet Airways (tel. 211899). All in the same building, 1 block (500m) north of Basheer Bagh, off the road, on the left side. Ethiopian Airlines (tel. 210100) is nearby, on Basheer Bagh Rd., across from Gandhi Medical College. Lufthansa, 3-5-823 Hyderguda Rd. (tel. 235537), to the right off Basheer Bagh Circle. Open Mon.-Fri. 9:30am-5:30pm, Sat. 9:30am-1:30pm. Air India, 5-10-193 HACA Bhavan (tel. 211804), opposite the Public Gardens. Open Mon.-Sat. 9:30am-1pm and 1:45-5:30pm. Indian Airlines, Secretariat Rd. (tel. 599333, 141) opposite Ravindra Bhavan. Open daily 10am-1pm and 2-5:15pm. Open Mon.-Fri. 9:30am-1pm, Sat. 9:30am-1:30pm, unless otherwise noted. To: Bangalore (3 per day, 1hr., US$75), Calcutta (1-2 per day, 2hr., US$163)), Delhi (3 per day, 2hr., US$154), Bombay (4-5 per day, 1hr. 15min, US$86), and Madras (2-3 per day, 1hr., US$80).

Trains: There are tourist quotas at each of the main stations: in Secunderabad, and at both Nampally (in Abids) and Kachegudi (east side of Sultan Bazaar) in Hyderabad (centralized inquiry tel. 135). Many trains stop at multiple stations a few minutes apart. Inquiry counters at the stations open 24hr. Reservations (tel. 131) open Mon.-Sat. 8am-2pm and 2:15pm-10pm, Sun. 8am-2pm. To: Bangalore (*Kachegudi-Bangalore Exp.* 7685, 5:35pm (Kachegudi), 6pm (Secunderabad), 17hr., Rs.180/608 for 2nd/1st class); Bombay (*Konark Exp.* 1020, 9:35am (Nampally), 19½hr.; *Bombay-Hyderabad Exp.* 7032, 10:20pm (Nampally), 17hr., Rs.179/596); Calcutta (*East Coast Exp.* 8046, 7:15am (Secunderabad), *Falaknuma Exp.* 7004 (Sun., Wed., and Fri.; Secunderabad), 30hr., Rs.264/965 for 2nd/1st class); Delhi (*Andhra Pradesh Exp.* 2723, 6am (Nampally), 6:30am (Secunderabad), 26hr.; *Hyderabad-Hazrat Nizamuddin Exp.* 7021, 10pm (Nampally), 36hr., Rs.295/1034 for 2nd/1st class); Madras (*Hyderabad-Madras Exp.* 7054, 3:45pm (Nampally), 4:15pm (Secunderabad; *Charminar Exp.* 7060, 6:40pm (Nampally), 7:10 (Secunderabad), 14hr., Rs.184/578 for 2nd/1st class); Tirupati (*Krishna Exp.* 7406, 5am (Nampally), 5:30am (Secunderabad); *Rayalaseema Exp.* 7429, 5pm (Nampally), 15 hr., Rs.172/574 for 2nd/1st class).

Buses: Hyderabad's main bus depot is **Gowliguda,** just across from the Musi River from the New City (tel. 513955). Open daily 8am-10pm. Enquiry (tel. 514406) open 24hr. Deluxe to: Bangalore (5 per day, 8am-7pm, 12hr., Rs.203); Bombay (7 per day, 10:30am-9:30pm, 16hr., Rs.265); Hospet (11am, 4, and 5:30pm, 8hr., Rs.100); Madras (4pm, 14hr., Rs.235); Tirupati (6 per day, 2:30-8pm, 14hr., Rs.203). Nampally Railway Station, Secunderabad Railway Station, and the Charminar teem with private coach companies vying for your enriching company on one of their daily trips to Bangalore (Rs.200), Bombay (Rs.250), Madras (Rs.250), and Tirupati (Rs.200). Fares quoted from Royal Travels, 5-8-230/c Public Garden Rd. (tel. 201983), across from Nampally Station, in the Royal Lodge complexes. Open Mon.-Sat. 9am-11pm.

Local Transportation: In Hyderabad, **buses** are the single greatest cause of road accidents. Furthermore, you'll probably need racing flats to catch one. Terminals at Nampally, Nurkhan Bazaar, near the Charminar, and Secunderabad Railway Station. Secunderabad Station to Nampally: #2 and #8A. Nampally to Golconda Fort: #119 and #142N. **Auto-rickshaw** drivers are sweet men who you don't need to hassle about the meter. Rs.4.80 for the 1st kilometer; Rs.2.40 for subsequent kilometers. **Taxis** are unmetered.

English Bookstore: A.A. Hussain & Co., 5-8-551 Arastu Trust Building, M.G. Rd., Abids (tel. 203742). Decent paperback collection. Open Mon.-Sat. 10am-8:30pm. **Walden's,** 6-3-871 Greenlands Rd., Begumpet (tel. 313434), en route from Abids

Hussain Sagar

TO BANJARA
HILLS

Raibhavan Rd.

TO SECUNDERABAD
AND AIRPORT

Tankbund Rd.

Indira
Park

Buddha
Purnima

British
Library

Secretariat Rd.

Thomas
Cook

Birla
Mandir

Birla Planetarium
and Science Centre

Himayatnagar Rd.

Alliance
Française

Naubat
Pahar

Indian
Airlines

Police Station

Basheer
Bagh
Circle

Government of India
Tourist Office ℹ

HIMAYATNAGAR

Legislative Assembly

Lal Bahadur
Stadium

Old MLA Quarters Rd.

University Rd.

Archaelogical
Museum

Public
Gardens

Public Gardens Rd.

NAMPALLY

Maharma Gandhi Rd.

King Kothi Rd.

Narayanguda Rd.

State
Bank of
Hyderabad

King Kothi
Palace

Nampally
Railway
Station

Doorshanchar
Bhavan

Station Rd.

Tilak Rd.

Mukarramjahi Rd.

ℹ APTTDC

ABIDS

SULTAN
BAZAR

✉
GPO

State Bank
of India

Mahipatram Rd.

Turrebazkhan Rd.

Bhagya Reddi Rd.

Darusalam Rd.

Jawaharlal Nehru Rd.

Maharani Jhansi Rd.

Maulvi Alauddin Rd.

GOSHAMAHAL

Gowliguda
Bus
Stand

TO VIJAYAWADA
AND MADRAS

City College Rd.

State
Library

Osmania
General ✚
Hospital

TO GOLCONDA

Musi River

Rajendranagar Rd.

Salar Jung
Museum

TO ZOO

Sardar Patel Rd.

Purana
Haveli
Palace

N

Charminar

0   500 yards

Mecca Masjid

0   500 meters

Hyderabad

SOUTH INDIA

Toddies for Tourists

Andhra Pradesh's temperance movement came to life in 1992, when village women participating in a literary campaign read a fiction story about wives who, to protest their husbands' boozing up, mobilized and refused to do household work. Fantasy became fact as the women ambushed liquor trucks, went on cooking strikes, and stormed the bars where their husbands drank away the household money. Politicians in the Telugu Desam party recognized their opportunity, and in 1994 ascended to power in A.P. on a prohibition platform. Prohibition laws apply only to Andhra residents; still, on your way into the state, you'll go through baggage checks. (Desperate Andhra residents have been known to smuggle vodka in their washer fluid tanks.) In Hyderabad, however, non-residents can get liquor at a reasonable cost, even outside the five-star hotels, although it's a bit of a bureaucratic hassle. First, go to Begumpet Airport (admission Rs.10), where near the exit terminal is the Prohibition and Excise Office (more like a desk), open Mon.-Sat. 7am-8pm. Show them your foreign passport, fill out a form requiring your promise that the liquor is for you, and pay Rs.110 for the permit. They allot two units per week, where a pint of lager equals one-eighth of a unit. Now highball—*whoops!*—hightail it to the Government Distillery in Narayanguda (tel. 240276), which is hard to find. Open Mon.-Sat. 10am-4pm. Bring a photocopy of your license. The distillery is actually a garage filled with boxes and boxes of the good stuff, and the bureaucracy is short, tolerable, and leavened by the evening's prospects.

---

to the airport. One of the best-stocked bookstores in South India. Open Wed.-Mon 9am-8:30pm.

Library: State Central Library, Turrebaz Khan Rd. (tel. 500107), near Osmania General Hospital. Open Mon.-Wed. and Fri.-Sun. 8am-8pm. **British Library,** 5-9-22 Sarovar Centre, Secretariat Rd. (tel. 230774). Members-only rule comes with a don't ask, don't tell policy. Open Tues.-Sun. 11am-7pm.

Cultural Centers: **Bharatiya Vidya Bhavan,** 5-9-1105 King Kothi Rd. (tel. 237825), off Basheer Bagh circle. **Alliance Française,** Adarshnagar (tel. 236646), next to the Birla Science Centre. Two movies per week, plus cultural events and short-term French courses. Office and library open Mon.-Fri. 9am-1pm and 3-6pm, Sat. 9am-1pm.

Pharmacy: Medwin Hospital Pharmacy, off Station Rd. in Chirag Ali Lane (tel. 202902), in a building so tall it's visible from the Nampally Railway Station. The pharmacy is inside the lobby to your left. Open 24hr.

Hospitals: Medwin Hospital (tel. 202902). **Osmania General Hospital** (tel. 500122; emergency tel. 119) is a government hospital, at the south end of Jawaharlal Nehru Rd. Emergency open 24hr.; outpatient visits Mon.-Fri. 8am-noon.

Emergency: Police: tel. 100. **Ambulance:** tel. 102.

Police: Abids Circle Police Station, to the right as you face the GPO (tel. 203531).

Post Office: GPO, Abids Circle (tel. 595978). *Poste Restante* is in the back left corner of the main room. Open Mon.-Fri. 10am-5pm, Sat. 10am-1pm. **Postal Code:** 500001.

Telephone Code: 040.

ACCOMMODATIONS

Budget dives are 10-paise-a-dozen in the Abids area, where mega-story hotels proliferated in the 70s. Around the Secunderabad Railway Station, too, there are a few decent lodges, but the surrounding area is much grungier than Abids. A third option is to check out the **guest houses** in Banjara Hills, a posh residential area 3km northeast of Abids. Originally established for film actors with bit parts, the guest houses offer cheap, ultra-comfortable home-style rooms, in an area of town close to good restaurants and as near to the sights as Abids.

Abids

Hotel Jaya International, 4-1-37/A&B Reddy Hostel Rd. (tel. 232929). Facing the GPO in Abids Circle, walk along Mahipatram Rd., to the left of the GPO, for 50m, then make a left. You should see Jaya in a narrow dirt road. Fastidious concern for details has made the potentially average lodge bloom into a budget hotel with personality. Clean, well-decorated rooms in good condition, with direct-dial phones, televisions, and large windows. From some balconies you can make out the Charminar. Seat toilets, showers, and 24hr. hot water. Even the waitstaff is proficient in English. The best part: the price includes a South Indian breakfast buffet the next morning. Check-out 24hr. Singles Rs.165, with A/C Rs.350. Doubles Rs.275, with A/C Rs.440.

Taj Mahal Hotel, 4-1-999 King Kothi Rd. (tel. 237988). Walk away from the GPO in Abids Circle and veer right after 200m. Although the idea of any likeness to its Agra (or Bombay) namesake is laughable, the Taj is one of Hyderabad's most popular hotels, and it's not hard to see why. Large, well-kept rooms with gleaming mirrors and polished (if not carpeted) floors. TVs, direct-dial phones, your choice of commode, 24-hr. hot water. Deluxe rooms come with couches, wall-to-wall putrid-colored carpeting, and iceboxes. Daily city tour leaves from lobby, Rs.75. Attached restaurant is a Hyderabad institution. Check-out 24hr. Singles Rs.250, with A/C Rs.350. Doubles Rs.350, with A/C Rs.500.

Hotel Saptagiri, 5-4-651 Nampally Station Rd. (tel. 503601). Turn left as you head out of the Abids Circle GPO and walk 200m before turning left down a narrow dirt road (i.e. alley). Saptagiri is just past an ice cream shop/bakery. Scrubbed and polished through and through, it's one of the few places in urban India that consistently passes the white glove test. The most for your money: balconies, telephones, 24-hr. hot water. Air-conditioned rooms have carpets, TVs, and seat toilets. Check-out 24hr. Singles Rs.115. Doubles Rs.170, with A/C Rs.300. Reservations recommended.

Hotel Annapurna, 5-4-730 Nampally Station Rd. (tel. 473 2612). One block past Hotel Saptagiri; across from the Collector's Office. With over 100 rooms, this place assures that you'll always have a place to stay in Abids. Even though it's unexciting, some rooms are funkily shaped, and all are clean, and furnished with TVs, direct-dial phones, and towels. Newspaper delivery. Deluxe rooms have seat toilets and a dank partitioned sitting room. Air-conditioned super-deluxe rooms have wall-to-wall carpeting, tapestries, iceboxes, and bathtubs. Room service but no restaurant. Travel assistance and rent-a-car in the lobby. Check-out 24hr. Singles Rs.145, deluxe Rs.175, with A/C Rs.250. Doubles Rs.220, deluxe Rs.250, with A/C Rs.350, super-deluxe Rs.500.

Hotel Rajmata, 5-8-230 Nampally Station Rd. (tel. 201000). Almost exactly across from the railway station. Lathed marble fixtures and Grecian statues in the halls. Doubles in newer wing are a good deal—TVs, telephones, seat toilets ("disinfected for your protection"), and 24-hr. hot water. Singles Rs.260. Doubles Rs.350. Rooms in the old wing (The Royal Hotel; tel. 201020) have cement floors, relatively non-grimy squat toilets, and clean sheets. All rooms have room service, *dhobi*, and attached restaurant and travel services. Singles Rs.50, Rs.59 with bath Rs.59. Doubles Rs.80, with bath Rs.100.

Hotel Sri Durga, Public Garden Rd. (tel. 202286). On the left corner of the street across from the rail station. Cramped but clean rooms with balconies that afford good views of the chaos down below. Squat toilets with hot water 6-9am. Check-out 24hr. Singles Rs.60. Doubles Rs.110.

The Residency, opposite the railway station on Public Garden Rd. (tel. 204060). Reasonably priced, brand new, 3-star hotel. From your spacious, air-conditioned room, you can coolly gaze at the hot, dusty outdoors through floor-to-ceiling windows. Best deal is the executive room, with carpet, bathtub, key tag lights. Thirty channels on the color TVs. Breakfast buffet included in the price. Check-out 24hr. Money exchange, 24-hr. room service, and travel counter. Singles Rs.700. Doubles Rs.900. Executive rooms Rs.1350. Executive suites Rs.1450.

Secunderabad

Hotel Sitara, 7-1-2, SPG Church Complex (tel. 770 0308). From the Secunderabad station, veer diagonally left (approximately northeast). By far the cleanest and friendliest of the hotels in the area. Broad, well-lit hallways, tiled bathrooms with flush squat toilets, balconies, and spacious rooms. Running hot water 5-9am. Singles Rs.130. Doubles Rs.175. Rooms with air-cooling Rs.215.

Sun Lodge, 8-3-4, St. Mary's Rd. (tel. 770 5670). Green building 500m north of the Secunderabad station. Clean and spacious if a tad dingy; pleasantly removed from the craziness of the station area. Clean, flush squat toilets. No hot water. Room service, laundry. Check-out 24hr. Singles Rs.60. Doubles Rs.90. Triples Rs.120. Quads Rs.150.

National Lodge, 9-4-48 Syed Abdulla St. (tel. 770 5572), opposite the Secunderabad station. As basic as they get: narrow beds, pale tube lighting, cold water only. But rooms and bathrooms are spotless, the management is ultra-friendly, and it's only 50m from your train to Bombay. Check-out 24hr. Singles Rs.55. Doubles with bath Rs.100.

Banjara Hills

Prashant Nilayam Guest House, 8-2-401/A Rd. No. 5, Banjara Hills (tel. 332 6892). Like living in a carpeted, slightly dusty, affluent Indian home. Huge rooms with telephones and TVs. Lush green gardens outside; terraces for dining (no canteen, but tiffin room service); mosquito screens in the large windows. Check-out 24hr. Doubles Rs.250, with A/C Rs.300. Reservations recommended.

FOOD

Traditional Andhra cuisine demands iron taste buds or stubborn stoicism. Either way, you'll never have clogged sinuses in Hyderabad. Pain is temporary, pride forever (diarrhea falls somewhere in between). To shorten your suffering, delve into one of the ubiquitous bakeries that have popped up in the past few years as a quasi-fast food option. Irani hotels serve Muslim-style delectables—*biryanis, kheemal* (ground mutton curry), mutton chops, along with pastries and *faloodas* for desert. You can easily get more benign South Indian cuisine too, but even the chutney here seems a little wicked. For gorging, try one of the ritzy hotels on the west side of Hussain Sagar—some of them do five buffets a day.

Taj Mahal, off M.G. Rd. on King Kothi Rd. (tel. 237988), is a Hyderabad institution for good reason: it's cheap, slightly upscale, and doles out large portions of South Indian favorites. *Masala dosas* cost Rs.10 in the regular section, Rs.15 in the air-conditioned section. North Indian dishes (all veg.) 11am-3:30pm and 7-10:30pm. Tiffins 7am-9:30pm. No smoking.

Grand Hotel, on the left side of the Abids Circle GPO (tel. 591364). Bushels of *biryani* (with chicken, Rs.32) served every day, and waiters serve almost as fast as customers eat their large portions. *Rotis* are hot, fluffy, and as big as record albums (Rs.2). Open daily 5am-11pm.

Paradise Heights, Triveni Complex, M.G. Rd. (tel. 232898). About 500m north of the GPO, 8th fl. Fabulous views of the city, especially the Abids area, through huge polished windows. Funky decor, especially the Mughlai chairs and Nizam portraits on the wall. Service is as deliberate as the decorations. Romantic at night. Multi-cuisine, but you'll be happiest if you stick to the Indian. The chicken *makhini* is sublime. Count on Rs.150 per person. Open daily noon-3pm and 7-11pm. Reservations recommended.

Chinese Garden, 6-3-349 Rd. No. 1, Banjara Hills (tel. 332 6978). Slightly mystical decor (deep blue carpets, pink tablecloths, red paper lanterns), but the food is excellent. One of the few Chinese restaurants around with more Chinese than Andhra influence. Fresh veg. dishes are yummy, and the steamed rice is fresh. But why not roll out with the not-too-greasy chicken fried rice and sliced Szechwan fish? Rs.60-80 per person. Open daily 12:30-3:30pm and 7-11pm.

Minerva Coffee Shop, 3-6-199/1 Himayat Nagar (tel. 230448). Slightly upscale veg. joint, *dosas* come in *avatars* like "Veg.-Cheese *Dosa*" (Rs.19); 1 *puri* (Rs.14) eclipses in size the head of the most ardent megalomaniac. The Minerva Special Ice Cream (Rs.38) is guaranteed to please. Open 7am-10pm; *thalis* (Rs.34/50, South/North Indian) 11am-2:30pm and 7-9:30pm.

SIGHTS

Golconda Fort, 8km west of the city, was the headquarters of the Qutb Shahi kingdom from 1512 to 1687 and is Hyderabad's most popular attraction. In its heyday, the Golconda empire stretched to the Bay of Bengal; now the circumference of the fort is a mere 6km. Crushed and annexed after two sieges by the Mughal emperor Aurangzeb, the kingdom was, during its apogee, a great center for arts and learning and a symbol of religious tolerance. At dusk, the crumbling ruins, shrieking bats, and sheer, unguardrailed drops on the path to **Durbar Hall** at the summit cause you to look over your shoulder, expecting to see specters of the Qutb Shahi Kings. Durbar Hall is supposedly a 1000-step climb, but it takes only 30min. That time is a good investment: from the top there is a panoramic view of not only the ramparts below, but also of Hyderabad landmarks—the Birla Mandir sparkles 9km away. Muhammad Quli Qutb Shah installed an 8-km-long underground tunnel leading from Golconda to the Charminar to facilitate his trysts with lady-love Bhagmati. Guides at the entrance will make sure you understand they're available (Rs.50 per hour), and if you enlist their services, they'll troop you around the fort, clapping at frequent intervals and suddenly demanding silence to demonstrate the fort's superb acoustics: Golconda was engineered so that a clap at the summit of Durbar Hall would reverberate at 5 places along the inside perimeter of the fortress wall. A clap at the Bala Hissar gate at the entrance to the fort can be heard at the summit, 11km away. (Open daily 7am-8pm. Free. Sound and light show every evening: March-Oct. 7pm, Nov.-Feb. 6:30pm, 1 hr., Rs.15 adults, Rs.10 children. English show on Wed. and Sun.)

About 500m from the fort are the **Qutb Shahi Tombs,** which house the remains of seven of the dynasty's patriarchs (each of whom supervised his tomb's construction). Each is built on a square base with an Islamic-style onion dome, but adorned with Hindu motifs like lotus friezes and leaves: a testament to the empire's religious tolerance and cultural syncretism. The sarcophagus in the center of the tomb overlies the real crypt below. (Open Sat.-Thurs. from 9:30am to 4:30pm.)

Golconda may be the prime tourist haunt, but the **Charminar** is Hyderabad's most enduring and ubiquitous symbol. The four-minareted edifice, built by Muhammed Quli Qutb Shah in 1591 to celebrate the end of an epidemic plaguing the city, adorns patches on school uniforms, is immortalized in miniature statuettes in kitsch shops throughout A.P., and most famously, graces every packet of Charminar cigarettes. (It's said that the last Nizam of Hyderabad refused to smoke any other brand.) There's not much to see in the building, since you're no longer allowed to climb the 149 steps to the small mosque on top, but a prime bazaar area surrounds it. There are enough pearl and bangle shops around here to bejewel the world several times over. **Mecca Masjid** is 100m south along Sardar Patel Rd. Like the Charminar, it was built during the sultanate of Muhammad Quli Qutb Shah, but after Golconda's fall completion of the mosque was left to Aurangzeb. Named as such for the few bricks from Mecca embedded in the walls, the *masjid* is the largest in Hyderabad, whose half-Muslim, half-Hindu population resides comfortably side by side. The mosque can accommodate 10,000 worshipers in prayer. Before entering the Mecca Masjid, take off your *chappals* at the podium on the left (Rs.5) and walk through a pavilion containing the tombs of the various Hyderabad Nizams.

The **Salar Jung Museum,** C.L. Badari Malakpet (tel. 523211), south of the Musi River, is touted as one of the world's largest one-man collections, but is actually the work of three generations of Salar Jungs, each of whom served as the Nizam's *wazir* (prime minister). The museum is huge, exhibiting an unbelievable range of genres. Everything from gorgeous Chola sculptures to mediocre European oil paintings can be found here. Check out Room 14, the Ivory Room, with a solid ivory chair given to Tipu Sultan by Louis XV. Room 17 has some marvelous modern Indian paintings (Ravi Varma, Abanindranath Tagore, K. Hebbar); in Room 18, next door, you can trace the chronological and regional evolution of Indian miniature paintings. Open Sat.-Thurs. 10am-5pm. Admission Rs.5 for adults, Rs.2 for children. Free guided tours depart from the office (which also has handy maps of the layout) on your right as you enter.

The **B.M. Birla Science Centre and Archaeological Museum,** atop Naubat Pahar hill (tel. 241067) is more like a precocious children's playground, with visitor-powered exhibits, optical illusions, and xylophones. The archaeological section downstairs is more interesting, with excavations from Vaddamanu dated 100 BC to 200 AD, wood and stone sculptures, and miniature paintings. It's air-conditioned and well-laid-out, although the security guard enjoys personally following visitors around. Open daily 10:30am-8:30pm, 3:30-8:30pm on the last Tues. of the month. Admission Rs.7.

Exit to the right and climb the stairs leading to the peace-domed **Birla Planetarium** (tel. 241067). The stardome is reportedly being developed into an astronomy-study center, but the didactic show on the existence of aliens is a little disappointing. English shows Mon.-Sat. 11:30am, 4, and 6pm; Sun. 11am, 3:45, and 6pm. Closed the last Tues. of the month. Admission Rs.10.

On the opposite hill from the Planetarium, Kala Pahar, stands the **Birla Mandir,** (tel. 43325). Commissioned by the industrial kings of India and built over a 10-year period, it affords awesome views of Hyderabad and Secunderabad. The elevation and the pure white marble of the temple set against the blue of Hussain Sagar combine to produce a heavenly impression. And the serenity is unmarred by shoe-touts or alms-driven priests. Open daily 7am-noon and 2-9pm. Illuminated at night.

Visitors to Hyderabad will spend much time within view of **Hussain Sagar,** the 6.5km by 800m artificial tank whose blue water decorates the city's vistas. Pragmatists say that the tank was constructed during the Golconda Empire, but some believe that the tank's origin is far less mundane. Legend has it that the tank was promised hundreds of years ago by a *sadhu* who collected large sums of money from the thirsty population. Weeks passed and no construction had begun, prompting the people to confront the *sadhu*, who promised to undertake the project or return their money. The next morning, the shimmering tank was in place, and the *sadhu* had disappeared. The magic continued in the 1980s, when a monolithic **Buddha statue** was hyped and then built near the other statues guarding the edge of the artificial lake. It promptly sank into the water, taking seven people with it. Several years ago, the statue was retrieved from the bottom and found to be intact, with no damage inflicted from the years under water or the crash from its original perch.

ENTERTAINMENT AND SHOPPING

The bazaar areas around the Charminar in the Old City are the best places to hone bargaining skills. If you're not into buying the outputs of Hyderabad's jewelry fetish (strands of imperfect pearls for Rs.100-500, armfuls of bangles, bridiware), then just stroll around and look into the stalls where thin Muslim men intently hand-pound sheets of silver foil. If you do plan to buy, dress like the locals—you'll get more good attention and more respect. Most of the shops in the Old City are open from 10am to 7pm; some observe Friday as a holiday. Emporia eagerly line the roads in the Abids area. **Kalanjali Arts and Crafts,** 5-10-194 Hill Fort Rd. (tel. 231147), across from the Air India office, is swanky and not eye-bulgingly expensive. The store has a wide selection of *kurta pajamas,* saris, furniture, and furnishings, but the jewelry section is a bit lean. Open daily 10am-8pm.

Hyderabad is justly proud of its myriad cultural events—dance programs, *ghazal* sessions, plays, etc. **Ravindra Bharati,** in the Public Gardens (tel. 233672), stages about four events per week at 6pm. Hyderabad unofficially claims more than 100 cinemas. The best English theatres are **Sangeet,** 23 Sardar Patel Rd., Secunderabad (tel. 330 3864), and **Skyline,** 3-6-64 Basheer Bagh Rd., Hyderabad (tel. 231633). There are generally three shows per day at 4, 7, and 10pm. Tickets cost Rs.25 for balcony seats. Tickets for sold-out shows can often be purchased from scalpers roving the parking lot, usually for 70% *baksheesh.* **Alliance Française,** Adarshnagar (tel. 236646), screens two flicks per week, one French, and the other German or English.

For a swim, try the **Ritz Hotel,** Hill Fort St., Basheer Bagh (tel. 233570), where you can swim the same routes of the Nizam's privileged guests. Open daily 3-7pm, Rs.40 per hr. If you can't handle the sultry mid-mornings, there is the **Taj Residency,** Rd. No.1, Banjara Hills (tel. 399999), open daily from 7am to 7pm. Time-efficient plea-sure-intake is key here: rates are Rs.150 per hr.

■ Tirupati and Tirumala

Hills of red rock covered by lush greenery form the setting for the temple of Sri Ven-kateswara at Tirumala, the most popular pilgrimage site in South India. Built in the 11th century by the founder of the Sri Vaishnava sect, Ramanuja, the place swarms with Hindu pilgrims at any time of the year. Battling the crowd for *darshan* of the image can be quite a nerve-racking experience. All economic activity centers around the temple—shops selling flowers and trinkets, lodges for pilgrims to stay in, and res-taurants. Only Devasthana buses are allowed to ply the 11-km roller-coaster ride from the town of Tirupati, at the base of the hill, to Tirumala at the top. Besides the temple, there's really nothing else to do or see in either town. If you're not a devout Hindu, make your trip on a weekday, preferably Tuesday, so you can avoid the weekend rush. Avoid the months of June and September and any public holidays. Non-Hindus are allowed all the way into the inner sanctum of the temple.

ORIENTATION

Tirumala is located at the top of a **hill,** 20km from the town of Tirupati where all trains and buses arrive and where hotels, restaurants, and other services center. The main **bus station** is 500m from the center of Tirupati. The **railway station** is at the center of town, near the **Govindaraja Temple.** The **Tirumala bus stand** is at the center of town about 250m from the railway station. **Alipiri Road** heads to Tirumala. Perpen-dicular to that is **Gandhi Road,** home to the post office, the Indian Bank, and the police station. The 20-km bus ride to Tirumala takes 45min. on curvy roads (featuring 57 hairpin turns) with crazy drivers.

PRACTICAL INFORMATION

Tourist Office: 139 T.P. Area (tel. 232208). Offers daily conducted tours (Rs.150, 9am-4pm). Since most of the places covered are temples, you'll have to shell out additional amounts to get tickets at each one.
Currency Exchange: Indian Bank, 214 Gandhi Rd. (tel. 22199). Open Mon.-Fri. 9am-5pm, Sat. 10am-2pm.
Telephones: STD/ISD booths abound in the railway station area.
Trains: Railway station inquiries tel. 20538, reservations 23500. To: Madras (*Tiru-pati-Madras Exp.* 6054, 10am, *Saptagiri Exp.* 6058, 5:30pm, 3hr., Rs.34/119 for 2nd/1st class); Madurai (*Tirupati-Madurai Exp.* 6799, 3:40pm, 18hr., Rs.126/521 for 2nd/1st class) via Tiruchirappalli (25hr., Rs.104/426 for 2nd/1st class).
Buses: To Hyderabad (2, 3:30, 6, and 8pm, 6hr., Rs.135); Vijayawada (8:30, 10:30, 11:15am, and 8pm, Rs.120); Bangalore (9 per day, 1:20am-6pm, Rs.150); Pondicherry (2:30pm, 7hr., Rs.125); Madras (every hr. 4am-noon and 2-8pm, 11pm, 3½hr., Rs.65).
Hospital: SVIMS (tel. 24777). Take an auto-rickshaw from the bus stand area.
Police: East Police Station, Gandhi Rd. (tel. 20301).
Post Office: Head Post Office Buildings, Gandhi Rd. (tel. 22103). Open Mon.-Fri. 10am-4pm. **Postal Code:** 517501.
Telephone Code: 08574.

ACCOMMODATIONS AND FOOD

Most of the good hotels and restaurants are in Tirupati. The only option in Tirumala are the Devasthanam dormitory rooms which offer the barest minimum and are usu-ally full. Aside from some grubby *dhabas*, the restaurants are all attached to hotels.

Hotel Vishnupriya, opposite APSRTC bus stand, Tirupati (tel. 25070). The best of the cheapies. Very basic—cot, table, chairs, TV, attached bathroom. Singles Rs.250, with A/C Rs.450. Doubles Rs.300, with A/C Rs.500.

Hotel Mayura, 209 T.P. Area, Tirupati (tel. 25925; fax 25911). One of the posher hotels. The cooperative reception can direct you to comfortable rooms that are oddly furnished. Dark brown sofas, orange artificial flowers, a Kashmiri screen, and huge beds, where you can relax and watch TV. The manager is a helpful, efficient, elderly man. Currency exchange. **Surya,** Hotel Mayura's veg. restaurant serves both North and South Indian food. South Indian fare comes with an assortment of 5 chutneys. Open daily 9am-10:30pm. Doubles Rs.395, with A/C Rs.645. Major credit cards accepted.

Hotel Guest Line, 14-37, Karakambadi Rd., P.O. Box No. 9, Tirupati (tel. 24868; fax 27774), 3.5km from the station. Away from the hustle and bustle, this is a luxury hotel filled with affluent pilgrims who want to complete their religious duties as comfortably as possible. The fragrant rooms are well-furnished and the attached bathrooms (seat toilets) are clean. Air-conditioned. Singles Rs.600. Double Rs.850. **Plantain Leaf** is their 24-hr. veg. restaurant. Breakfast (Rs.12-22), lunch (Rs.12-15), *thali* Rs.30.

Quality Inn Bliss, Renigunta Rd., Tirupati (tel. 25793; fax 21514). One more haunt of the wealthy Indian tourist. Sterile, white environment where everything's spick and span. The sheets, beds, and chairs are so spotless that you might ache for a little disorder. Air-conditioned. **Navrattan** is the veg. restaurant offering South and North Indian cuisine (open daily 7am-11pm). **Khazana** specializes in Andhra cuisine. Also serves veg. and non-veg. Indian, Chinese, and Continental cuisine. Singles Rs.650. Doubles Rs.795. Major credit cards accepted. Reservations from Madras (tel. (044) 825 9090).

SIGHTS

The **Sri Venkateswara Temple** at Tirumala is the star attraction and the only place of interest to the hundreds of pilgrims who flock to Tirupati. Buses are available to Tirumala from Tirupati every five minutes (Rs.12). Don't be surprised to find a number of pilgrims with shaved heads—pilgrims to Tirupati commonly make a sort of barter agreement with God—hair in exchange for some favor. Take the special *darshan* queue (Rs.30) to reduce the waiting time to about two hours. No *darshan* between 10am and noon. At 5pm, there's a ceremony outside with lamps that's a treat to watch. The *gopuram* is fully covered with gold and its dazzling brilliance is testimony to the wealth of the temple. The temple apparently made a collection of Rs.210,000 in one day on July 17, 1996. After all the waiting in line, *darshan* is very short and you get shoved by temple workers who yell at you in Telugu as they yank your arm to force your exit. The image is impressive—the mask of Vishnu drawn clearly on its forehead, wearing a gold crown and so covered with flowers that not much else is visible. The temple's wealth is used to run orphanages, schools, and colleges. All pilgrims are given free food. Opposite the temple is a small **museum.** (Open Mon.-Fri. 8am-8pm. Admission Rs.5.)

WEST INDIA

Maharashtra

Maharashtra straddles the Subcontinent, from the tropical coast to the arid Deccan Plateau, from the fringes of the hot and hectic Gangetic plain to the palmier, balmier, more easy-going south, and from isolated villages to Bombay's metropolitan modernity. While over half of India's foreign trade and roughly 50% of her tax revenue flows from the state, the majority of Maharashtra's population still survives by near-subsistence agriculture. The political scene shows similar schizophrenia: whereas the Congress controls Bombay's city council and keeps the state's powerful sugar barons in its pocket, the radical Maharashtrian Shiv Sena and the Hindu nationalist BJP run the state government. Only the Marathi language and the formidable tradition of martial independence embodied by the warrior-king and folk-hero Shivaji bind all this diversity together.

Shivaji's heritage endures in the typically Maharashtrian city of Pune and in the many forts which oversee the mountainous transition from the lush sugarcane plantations of the littoral to the parched grain fields of the plateau. But most tourists experience Maharashtra at its oldest and newest points: the ancient cave temples at Ajanta and Ellora and the ragged yet ritzy city of Bombay. In these two sights alone, the state subsumes the traditional, religious, meditative, and measured end of India's cultural and historical spectrum with the up-to-the-minute, godless, and careless cacophony of her commercial capital. Add to this diversity the red-robed acolytes of the Osho Commune in Pune, the white Mughal minarets piercing the skyline in Aurangabad, and the Bombayites in saris bathing at Janjira beach.

■ Bombay (Mumbai)

In attitude as well as population, Bombay is India's largest city, uniting all of the country's languages, religions, ethnicities, castes, and classes in one heaving, seething "sizzler" of an island. Bombay blends myriad traditions and innovations from each region, city, and village in India and beyond, offering everything from *bhel puri* to bell bottoms. The city alone accounts for 50% of India's imports and exports, its largest stock exchange and its densest concentration of industry. Rupee and dollar billionaires abound, while film stars, models, and politicians flock to frolic at the many opulent hotels, expensive discos, and ritzy restaurants. But Bombay is also India's poorest city: the endless shanties at Dharavi have expanded into Asia's (and perhaps the world's) largest slum. As many as half of Bombay's 15 million people live in shacks or on the street. Some sections of the city resemble a perpetual game of how-many-can-you-fit-in-a-telephone-booth, with densities approaching one million people per square kilometer. This unimaginable press of people, combined with arcane rent-control provisions, laws prohibiting the conversion of industrial to residential property, and the apathy or connivance of local politician-landsharks, has driven real-estate prices beyond those of New York or Tokyo in a country whose per capita income is just US$350. Right-wing and sectarian politicians stoked this pressure-cooker of economic disappointment, inconceivable crowding, wretched sanitation, hopeless congestion, choking pollution, and a volatile religious mix until it exploded into riots and bomb blasts in 1992-3. Yet hundreds of illiterate laborers from the countryside flood into Bombay daily to seek the fortunes in India's City of Dreams: the Big Mango.

Bombay blunders on irrepressibly. The slum-dwellers find jobs if not houses so they can blast the latest "Bollywood" blockbusters from their imported VCRs (Bombay is India's largest film production center). Cellular phone-toting "puppies" (Pun-

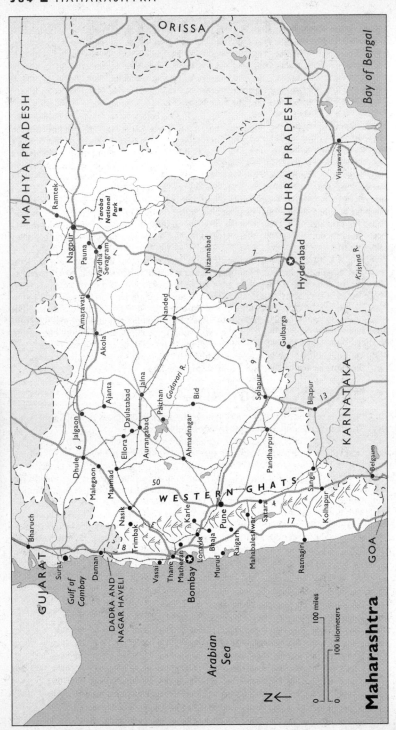

ORISSA

Bay of Bengal

MADHYA PRADESH

ANDHRA PRADESH

Vijayawada

Ramtek

Taroba National Park

Nagpur
Pauna
Wardha
Sevagram

Krishna R.

Nizamabad

Hyderabad

6

Amaravati

Nanded

7

Akola

Gulbarga

KARNATAKA

Ajanta

Jalna

Godavari R.

Bid

Bijapur

13

Daulatabad

Solapur

Jalgaon

Ellora
Aurangabad
Paithan

9

Dhule

6

Ahmadnagar

Pandharpur

Malegaon

50

Sangli

Belgaum

Mamad

WESTERN GHATS

Nasik

Karle

Pune

Satara

Kolhapur

Bharuch

Trimbak

Bhaja

Raigarh

4

17

Surat

18

Lonavla

Mahabaleshwar

Ratnagiri

GOA

GUJARAT

Daman

Vasai

Matheran

Murud

DADRA AND NAGAR HAVELI

Thane

Bombay

Gulf of Cambay

Arabian Sea

WEST INDIA

Maharashtra

100 miles

100 kilometers

N

0

0

jabi yuppies) jump off their mopeds to pay black money to sign-painters for their billboard blow-ups of Levi's or Colgate. Eve-teasers (cat-callers) whistle at miniskirted teens, while *dhaba-wallahs* (lunch delivery men) overload their bicycles with pickles and *papads* for double-breasted businessmen. Even the architecture expresses the city's exuberant schizophrenia, with Victorian-Gothic-Indo-Saracenic constructs of colonial condescension abutting frenetic Art Deco apartments crammed against the high-rises of international finance sandwiched between fire temples and *gaudi*, Hindu shrines hemmed in by bamboo lean-tos.

This urban extravaganza began modestly. Artifacts found in the suburb of Kandivli prove that the original seven islands which make up the city have been inhabited since the Stone Age. Although Ptolemy mentions the area in his second-century geography, successive ruling dynasties ignored Bombay's potential as a port for centuries. The Portuguese gained the islands in 1534, dubbing them Bom Bahia, or "Good Port"—but only the British made good this name after Catherine of Braganza handed over the islands in her dowry to Charles II of England. The fourth East India Company governor of Bombay, Gerald Aungier, set his pomegranate dreams in motions by ordering a construction spree in 1672. The Parsis built their first fire temple in 1675, initiating a continuous flow of affluent refugees. Bombay became the capital of the Bombay Presidency in 1687—and the rest is history.

The shortage of cotton in Britain occasioned by the American Civil War prompted a boom in Bombay, resulting in an impressive array of late Victorian public works, including the consolidation of the seven islands into one by reclaiming land from the Arabian Sea. At the same time, a fledgling organization called the Indian National Congress held its inaugural meeting in Bombay in 1885. At a Bombay session in 1942, the group voiced its first demand for full independence. After the nation realized that ambition in 1947, disputes between the Marathi- and Gujarati- speaking segments of the population ended in the partition of Bombay State into Maharashtra and Gujarat in 1960. Throughout the conflict, the economy boomed, and it continues to boom today.

Whatever affects it, Bombay somehow muddles through. The plague of tourists gawking at the city's insane extremes cause hardly a ripple. Although the array of conventional sights hardly overwhelms, the manic mix of London double-deckers and bullock carts, *sadhus* and stockbrokers, the din and crowds and constant kerfuffle will floor any first-time visitor. Bombay knocks expectations of an India filled with pot-bellied cows and ramshackle temples, although it has plenty of both. This Subcontinental super-combination forces travelers to confront a hitherto unimagined fusion of development and depredation. But whether it delights or disgusts, this unexpected, ebullient, eclectic city is the vanguard of the emerging modern India.

GETTING THERE AND AWAY

By Plane

Sahar International Airport, Ville Parle (tel. 836 6700; flight information 836 6767, 822-0404). This seedy, mosquito-ridden complex prepares arriving travelers for the continent beyond. For a laugh or a warning, read the Complaints Book. It's all one terminal, but has two arrivals halls. Most major European, Middle Eastern, and Asian airways serve Bombay, as do a couple of American ones. Departure tax Rs.300; Rs.150 to other South Asian countries. There are three different ways to get from the airport to downtown Bombay. The easiest, fastest, and most expensive is by taxi. If you are arriving, go to the 2nd pre-paid taxi counter you pass as you exit customs. They overcharge slightly (Rs.200 to Colaba as opposed to Rs.150 by meter), but if you go solo the airport taxi drivers will rip you off. From Bombay to the airport get the driver to set the meter. One step down in luxury is the Ex-Serviceman's Coach. It runs from Sahar to the Air-India Building downtown, at Nariman Point, via the Domestic Airport at Santa Cruz, for Rs.44 per head and Rs.7 per bag. Finally, the rock bottom method of getting into town is to take Bus 321 Ltd. to Vile Park Station (Rs.2) and then a commuter train to Churchgate (Rs.4), but this route is confusing, tiresome, and chest-

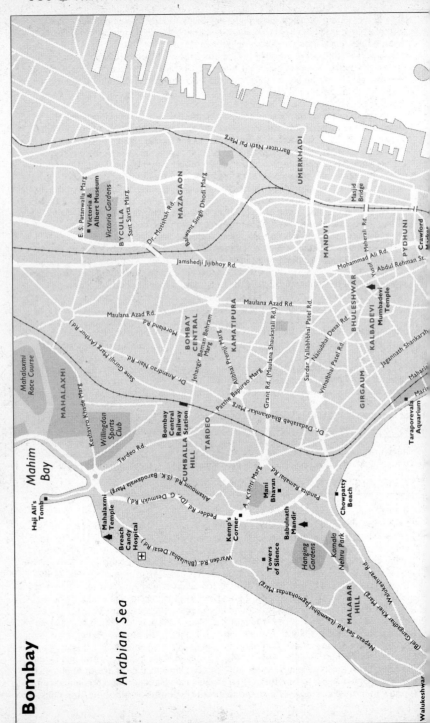

Bombay

Arabian Sea

Mahim Bay

Walukeshwar

Haji Ali's Tomb

Mahalaxmi Temple

Breach Candy Hospital

MAHALAXMI

Mahalaxmi Race Course

Keshavrao Khade Marg

Willingdon Sports Club

Bombay Central Railway Station

Tardeo Rd.

TARDEO

CUMBALLA HILL

Warden Rd. (Bhulabhai Desai Rd.)

Pedder Rd. (Dr. G. Deshmukh Rd.)

Altamount Rd. (S.K. Barodawala Marg)

Kemp's Corner

Towers of Silence

Hanging Gardens

MALABAR HILL

Kamala Nehru Park

Babulnath Mandir

Mani Bhavan

A. Kranti Marg

Pandita Ramabai Rd.

Chowpatty Beach

Nepean Sea Rd (Laxmibai Jagmohandas Marg)

Bel Gangadhar Kher Marg

Walkeshwar Rd

Sne Guruji Marg (Arthur Rd.)

Dr. Anandrao Nair Rd.

Moreland Rd.

Maulana Azad Rd.

BOMBAY CENTRAL

Jehangir Boman Behram Marg

KAMATIPURA

Patthe Bapurao Marg

Grant Rd. (Maulana Shaukatali Rd.)

Dr. Dadasaheb Bhadkamkar Marg

E. S. Patanwalla Marg

Victoria & Albert Museum

Victoria Gardens

BYCULLA

Sant Savta Marg

MAZAGAON

Dr. Mohilah Rd.

Balwant Singh Dhodi Marg

Jamshedji Jijibhoy Rd.

Maulana Azad Rd.

Maulana Azad Rd.

Albhai Premji Marg

Sardar Vallabhbhai Patel Rd.

Nanubhai Desai Rd.

Vithalbhai Patel Rd.

GIRGAUM

BHULESHWAR

KALBADEVI

Mumbadevi Temple

Jagannath Shankarsh

Taraporevala Aquarium

Mahari

Mari

Barrister Nath Pai Marg

UMERKHADI

MANDVI

Masjid Bridge

Mohammad Ali Rd.

Yusuf Meherali Rd.

Abdul Rehman St.

PYDHUNI

Crawford Market

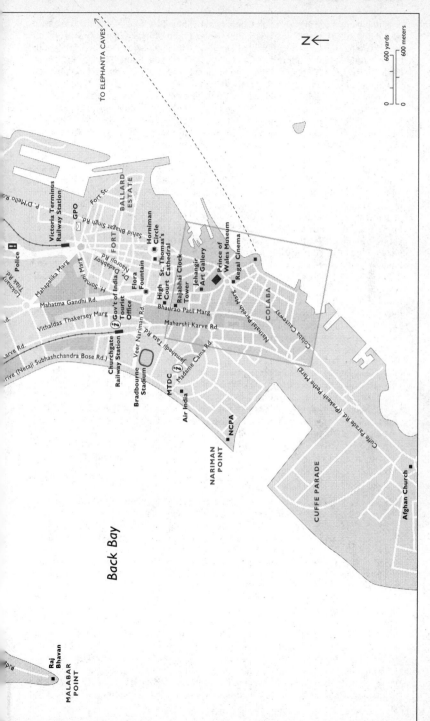

TO ELEPHANTA CAVES

N

600 yards
600 meters

P. D'Mello Rd.

Victoria Terminus Railway Station

GPO

Fort St.

BALLARD ESTATE

Sahid Bhagat Singh Rd.

FORT

Horniman Circle

St. Thomas's Cathedral

Police

Lokmanya Tilak Rd.

Mahapalika Marg

H. Somani Marg

Dr. Naoroji Rd.

Dadabhoy Naoroji Rd.

Flora Fountain

High Court

Rajabhai Clock Tower

Jehangir Art Gallery

Prince of Wales Museum

Regal Cinema

Mahatma Gandhi Rd.

Gov't of India Tourist Office

Vithaldas Thakersey Marg

Bhaurao Patil Marg

Maharshi Karve Rd.

Karve Rd.

Marine Drive (Netaji Subhashchandra Bose Rd.)

Churchgate Railway Station

Veer Nariman Rd.

Jamshedji Tata Rd.

Bradbourne Stadium

MTDC

Madame Cama Rd.

Air India

Natnatial Parekh Path Marg

COLABA

Colaba Causeway

NCPA

NARIMAN POINT

Cuffe Parade Rd. (Prakesh Pethe Marg)

CUFFE PARADE

Afghan Church

Back Bay

Raj Bhavan

MALABAR POINT

crushingly crowded at rush-hour. **Domestic Airlines:** East West, 1st floor, Lunat Mansion, Mint Rd., Fort (tel. 269 0646, 269 0648). Open Mon.-Sat. 9am-6pm; ModiLuft, Akash Ganga Building, 89 Bhulabhai Desai Rd., Breach Candy (tel. 363 5859, -60). Open Mon.-Fri. 9am-5:30pm; Skyline NEPC, Lyka Labs Building, 77 Nehru Rd., Ville Parle (E) (tel. 610 7356, 610 7171). Open Mon.-Sat. 10am-6pm; Jet Airways, Amarchand Mansion, Madame Cama Rd., (tel. 287 5086, -90). Open Mon.-Sat. 10am-5:30pm; Indian Airlines, Air India Building, 1st floor, Marine Drive, Nariman Point (tel. 202 3031 and 141). Open Mon.-Sat. 9am-6pm. International Airlines: Air India, Air India Building, Marine Drive, Nariman Point (tel. 202 4142, 287 4156). Open Mon.-Sat. 9am-6pm. **International Airlines:** Air Lanka, Mittal Tower, "C" Wing, Nariman Point (tel. 282 3288, 284 4156). Open Mon.-Fri. 9am-5:30pm, Sat. 9am-4pm; Bangladesh Biman, Airline Hotel Building, 199 J. Tata Rd., 32, Churchgate (tel. 282 4580, 282 4732). Open Mon.-Fri. 9am-5:30pm, Sat. 9am-4pm; British Airways, 202-B Vulcan Insurance Building, Veer Nariman Rd., Churchgate (tel. 285 2903, 282 0888). Open Mon.-Sat. 9:30am-1pm and 2-5:30pm; Cathay Pacific, Taj Mahal Hotel, Apollo Bunder, Colaba (tel. 202 9112, -3). Open Mon.-Sat. 9:30am-1pm and 1:45-5:30pm; Delta, Taj Mahal Hotel, Apollo Bunder, Colaba (tel. 283 7314, 283 1376). Open Mon.-Fri. 9am-5pm; Emirates, Mittal Chambers, 228 Nariman Point (tel. 287 1649, -52). Open Mon.-Sat. 9am-5:30pm; Lufthansa, Express Tower, Nariman Point (tel. 287 5264, 202 3430). Open Mon.-Fri. 9am-1pm and 1:45-5:45pm, Sat. 9am-1pm and 1:45-4:30pm; Pakistan International Airlines, 7 Stadium House, Veer Nariman Rd., Churchgate (tel. 202 1598, 202 1373, 202 1455). Open Mon.-Sat. 9am-5:30pm; Royal Jordanian, B1 Amarchand Mansion, Madame Cama Rd. (tel. 202 9050, 282 3080). Open Mon.-Fri. 9am-5:30pm; Royal Nepal, 222 Maker Chamber V, Nariman Point (tel. 283 6197, 283 5489). Open Mon.-Fri. 10am-6pm, Sat. 10am-2pm; Thai, Podar House, 10 Marine Drive, Churchgate (tel. 282 3085). Open Mon.-Fri. 9am-5:30pm, Sat. 9am-4pm; Singapore, Hotel Taj Mahal, Apollo Bunder, Colaba (tel. 202 2747). Open Mon.-Sat. 9:15am-5:30pm. To: Ahmedabad (6-8 per day, 1hr., US$62); Aurangabad (1-2 per day, 1hr., US$60); Bangalore (8-10 per day, 1½hr., US$103); Bhopal (Mon.-Tues., Thurs., Sat., 2hr., US$92); Calcutta (4-6 per day, 2½hr., US$175); Calicut (3 per day, 1½hr., US$116); Cochin (3 per day, 2hr., US$128); Coimbatore (1-2 per day, 2hr., US$113); Colombo (Mon., Wed., and Fri., 3½hr., Rs.5595); Delhi (20-25 per day, 2-4hr., US$139); Goa (5-6 per day, 1hr., US$76); Hyderabad (5 per day, 1½hr., US$86); Indore (1-2 per day, 1½hr., US$66-100); Jaipur (2-3 per day, 1½-3½hr., US$123); Kathmandu (Mon. and Fri., 3hr., US$257); Madras (6-9 per day, 2hr., US$132); Mangalore (2 per day, 1½hr., US$91); Pune (1-2 per day, 30min., US$65); Trivandrum (2-3 per day, 2hr., US$147); Udaipur (1-3 per day, 1-2hr., US$88); Varanasi (1-2 per day, 2-5hr., US$179).

By Train

The **Western Railways** connect the city to Gujarat, Rajasthan, and Delhi, while the Central Railways serve Delhi also, as well as other destinations. You must go to the right booking office to reserve a ticket. **Central Railways,** Reservation Office, Victoria Terminus (tel. 134, 265 9512 for inquiries; 265 6565 for automated arrivals and departures; arrivals from south 136; from north 137; from Pune 138). This air-conditioned office, adjacent to the long-haul platforms, becomes less confusing if you head straight for window 8, the Foreign Tourist Guide. They sell tickets for rupees if you have an encashment certificate, or for dollars or pounds sterling otherwise. They release the tourist quota the day before departure only, unless you hold an Indrail Pass (which they sell). To: Goa (*Mahalaxmi Exp.* 8:25pm, 10½hr.); Bhopal (*Punjab Mail* 1037, 7:10pm, 14hr.); Aurangabad (*Narded Tapovan Exp.* 7517, 6:10am, 7]hr.; *Narded Devagiri Exp.* 1003, 9:20pm, 8hr.); Pune (*Deccan Express* 1007, 6:40am, 4hr.; *Deccan Queen* 2123, 5:10pm, 3½hr.); Madras (*Madras Exp.* 6011, 2pm, 26½hr.; *Chennai Exp.* 1063, 7:50pm, 24hr.); Trivandrum (*Kanyakumari Exp.* 1081, 3:35pm, 48hr.); Ernakulam (*Netravati Exp.* 6635, 8:25pm, 35hr.); Agra (*Punjab Mail* 1037, 7:10pm, 22hr.); Hyderabad (*Hyderabad Exp.* 7031, 12:35pm, 18hr.; *Hussain Sagar Exp.* 7001, 9:55pm, 15½hr.); Calcutta (*Gitanjali Exp.* 2859, 6:05am, 35hr.;

Howrah Mail 8001, 8:15pm, 35hr.); Bangalore (*Udyar* 6529, 7:55am, 24]hr.; *Bangalore Exp.* 1013, 10:50pm, 22½hr.). All trains leave from V.T. unless otherwise indicated. Window 8 is open Mon.-Sat. 9am-1pm and 1:30-4pm. **Western Railways,** Churchgate Reservation Office, Maharishi Karve Rd., Churchgate (tel. 131 for inquiries, 132 for Delhi arrivals, 133 for Gujarat arrivals, 209 5959 for booking information). Opposite Churchgate Station, in the same building as the Government of India Tourist Office. To get to the Foreign Tourist Counter, ignore the first reservation office you see, walk past the entrance to the tourist office, and enter the next door on your left. Mr. Kamal Singh runs this facility with self-conscious aplomb. He will find you berths—and make you read endless glowing affidavits from middle-aged German women while he does so. Tourist quota tickets available only the day before. Dollars, pounds sterling, and rupees (with encashment certificate) accepted. To: Ahmedabad (*Shatabdi Exp.* 2009, 6:25am, 7hr.); Delhi (*Rajdhani Exp.* 2951, 16½hr.); Jaipur (*Jaipur Exp.* 2955, 7:05pm, 18½hr.). The Foreign Tourist Desk is open Mon.-Fri. 9:30am-1:30pm and 2-4:30pm, Sat. 9:30am-2:30pm. All these trains leave from Bombay Central, which can be reached from downtown Bombay. (For more information, see **Public Transportation,** below).

By Bus

State Transport Terminal, J.B. Behran Marg, Central (tel. 307 4272, 307 6622). Just opposite Central Railway Station, next door to the Maratha Mandir Cinema. **Maharashtra State Road Transport Corporation** runs relatively quiet, comfortable buses to the major tourist destinations in the state, although services are cut back during monsoon. To: Aurangabad (5:15pm, semi-luxury Rs.114; 8:15pm, luxury Rs.153, both 10hr.); Mahabaleshwar (6 and 7am, semi-luxury Rs.72; 8:30pm, luxury Rs.134, both 7hr., suspended during the monsoon). For other destinations in Maharashtra, travelers must book at the ASIAD office in Dadar, or on an MTDC luxury service at one of their offices, although trains are likely to be quicker and more convenient. Goa state transport (Kadamba) runs a daily luxury bus to Panjim (5pm, 15hr., Rs.228). Gujarat's Company lays on at least 3 services daily to Ahmedabad (6, 7, and 8pm, 12hr., Rs.114). Karnataka's company runs a service for the truly intrepid to Bangalore (10:30am, 2:30 and 7pm, 24hr., Rs.268). **MTDC,** CDO Hutments, Madame Cama Rd. (tel. 202 6713). Check with them to see what routes they offer, as their destinations keep changing. Currently to Mahabaleshwar (6:30am, 7hr., Rs.150) and Nasik (6am, 6hr., Rs.90).

GETTING AROUND

Just watching the local transport in Bombay evokes surges of pity and fear in the average bystander; riding it tends to deaden the senses, sap emotion, suck the pap out of space and time. Still, while the local trains and buses may shatter your worldview and your collarbone, they leave your finances largely intact.

By Bus

Buses are slightly easier to deal with than trains and, for most tourists, more useful. Try to learn the Hindi numbers so you can recognize the bus as it approaches. (The English number and destination is written only down on the side—often visible too late to secure footing before the bus roars off again.) Red numbers indicate "limited" services, which supposedly stop less frequently and certainly cost marginally less, but no fare in the city should exceed Rs.3, limited or otherwise. Climb in the rear door only (the front is for exiting), be ready to name a destination for the conductor, and keep hold of your ticket because there are frequent inspections. Buy your ticket on the bus as the conductor approaches with a click. All this sounds quite easy, but at rush hour, when a seething mass of commuters is tearing over one another, shirts off to fling themselves at the narrow metal door of a moving bus, you may feel more hesitant. Don't lose heart: outside the peak hours and on less traveled routes, buses are a convenience most tourists don't have the gumption to take advantage of.

Bus #	Route and Destination
1 ltd.	Colaba-Regal-Flora-V.T.-Crawford Market
3	Afghan Church-Colaba-Regal-Flora-V.T.
62	Flora-Metro-Marine Lines-Bombay Central-Dadar Station
61	Regal-Metro-Opera House-Bombay Central-Dadar Station
81 ltd.	V.T.-Kemp's Corner-Breach Candy and Haji Ali-Nehru Planetarium
106	Afghan Church-Colaga-Regal-Chowpatty-Kamala Nehru Park
108	V.T.-Regal-Chowpatty-Kamala Nehru Park
231	Santa Cruz (W)-Juhu Beach
321 ltd.	Airport-Ville Parle (E)
343	Goregaon (E)-Film City
132	Regal-Breach Candy and Haji Ali
188 ltd.	Borivli (E)-Sanjay Gandhi NP-Kanheri Caves
91	Bombay Central-Kural

By Train

Bombay's commuter rail system is more complicated than even its bifurcated long-haul cousin—and 10 times more crowded. Western Railways runs one line, from Churchgate through Bombay Central, Dadar, Bandra, Santa Cruz (for Juhu), and Ville Parle (for the airports) to Borivli (Sanjay Gandhi NP) and beyond. One-way tickets, sold in windows at each station, cost Rs.2-6 for 2nd class (depending on the distance traveled), and about 10 times as much in 1st class. First class has marginally more comfortable seats (but you're unlikely to get one), and is more civilized, although not less crowded, in rush hour. Outside rush hour, it doesn't make much difference. When boarding a train, make sure it's heading to the right destination by checking the digital display. It will read a letter code, then a time, and then F or S. The first code indicates the destination: B for Borivli, C for Churchgate, D for Dadar, B for Bandra, A for Andheri, etc. depending on which line you're on. The time is the scheduled departure (trains usually leave promptly every 10min. or so). Finally, F stands for fast and S for slow. Fast trains skip the stations whose names are illuminated on the board below. That's right, the names that are lit up brightly by the train are the places it does *not* go. There are special, less crowded, cars for women only (striped and stamped with a stencil of a damsel in a sari) on all trains. Keep hold of your ticket since there are periodic inspections, and be on the lookout for your stop since the platform side varies. If you can keep all of this in mind with one foot on the ground and the other out the open doorway, with hundreds of commuters pressed up against you, with the summer sun beating down on the little metal *tandoor* oven you're riding in, with your clothes torn by the crush and your bag ripped off your shoulder by the pressure of the mob, you should be fine. Otherwise, travel out of town in the morning, and return well after noon. The same rules apply to the Central Railways lines run out of V.T., which are of less use to the traveler. Byculla, for the Victoria and Albert Museum, and Kurla, for certain long-distance trains, are served by Central Railways.

By Taxi

Taxis rule Bombay, since rickshaws aren't allowed in the downtown area and since public transport is so crowded. Luckily, they are plentiful and the drivers only healthily argumentative. Set the meter and go—this shouldn't be the struggle it is elsewhere unless it's very late or the weather's very bad. You pay roughly 9 times what the meter shows—for the precise figure, consult the chart which the taxi driver should carry. He may deny it at first, but an imperious "chart de" usually conquers objections.

By Rickshaw

These only roam the suburbs, but the taxi fare rule applies. The conversion rate is just less than 6 times the amount shown.

ORIENTATION

Bombay is shaped like a vast lobster claw, reaching out into the Arabian Sea. The long pincer, **Colaba,** home to most of the budget hotels, faces the shorter, the recherché residential neighborhood of **Malabar Hill,** across the choppy waters of **Back Bay.** North of these two are piled successively the business and financial district, the bazaar district, the old mill areas, and then the suburbs—endless suburbs, stretching all the way to the end of Bombay Island, 50km north of the city center.

Most tourists only catch a fleeting, jet-lagged glimpse of these areas on their way to or from the international and domestic airports in the suburb of **Ville Parle,** about 25km from downtown. Instead, the Colaba district, centering on **Colaba Causeway (Shahid Bhagat Singh Marg)** claims most of their time. The Causeway ends at **Wellington Circle,** universally known as **Regal,** after the movie theater which presides over it. From Regal, **Madame Cama Road** runs west (left) to **Nariman Point,** Bombay's Wall Street, which houses the offices of many international banks and airlines, and even a few consulates. North of Regal runs **Mahatma Gandhi Marg (M.G. Rd.)** past the Prince of Wales Museum, the high court, and the University to **Flora Fountain (Hutatma Chowk).** From here, **V.N. (Veer Nariman) Road** leads left to Churchgate Station and **Marine Drive,** and right to the heart of **Fort,** Bombay's oldest neighborhood. **Dr. D.N. (Dr. Dadabhoy Naoroji) Road** proceeds north from Flora to **Victoria Terminus (V.T.),** the colossus of imperial delusion from which many of Bombay's long-distance trains depart. Beyond V.T., Dr. D.N. Rd. comes to a halt at **Crawford Market,** the beginning of the **bazaar district** and the location of the FRRO. Marine Drive follows the bay from Nariman Point all the way to Chowpatty Beach. A ten-minute ride north lies **Bombay Central,** another major railway station and the terminus for state-run buses.

Street Names in Bombay

Most tourists spin or stroll down Netaji Subhashchandra Bose Rd. in Bombay several times without even realizing. They, like all the city's residents, know it by its colonial name, Marine Drive. No matter how civic-minded or patriotic the new designations selected by the municipal corporation, latter-day Bombayites rebel against today's authorities by refusing to relinquish the monikers of past oppressors. No one calls Nepean Sea Rd. Laxmibhai Jagmohandas Marg; even the bus conductors say Ridge Rd. for Bal Gangadhar Kher Marg; Shahid Bhagat Singh Marg evinces blank stares from taxi drivers—but everyone recognizes Colaba Causeway. On the rare occasions when the populace accepts the new names, they inevitably abbreviate them beyond recognition: heedless city-dwellers compress Sir Pherozeshah Mehta Rd. into P.M. Rd.; Doctor Dadabhoy Naoroji barely escapes as Dr. D.N., and even the father of the nation gets unceremoniously squashed to M.G.

But Bombay's name game has developed from small-scale civil disobedience to big-time politics. The Hindu nationalist Shiv Sena party, senior partners in the state's coalition government, have decided that Bombay's streets by any other name would smell more sweet. In 1995 they blocked the opening of a critical new flyover because the municipal authorities had dedicated it to the recently deceased Bombay-born Prime Minister, Morarji Desai, who as chief minister of Maharashtra had ordered troops to fire on pro-Sena rioters. The now-open viaduct bears the name of Sena Supremo Bal Thackeray's father—a little-known cartoonist. A few months later, the Sena dropped their biggest bomb—literally. They renamed the whole city Mumbai, in line with its perceived "traditional" Marathi name. But the struggle continues: the underdog urbanites now wryly refer to the city as "Slumbai."

PRACTICAL INFORMATION

Tourist Office: Government of India Tourist Office, 123 Maharishi Karve Rd. (tel. 203 3144, 203 3145). About 100m along the road which runs down the right-hand side of Churchgate Station as you face it. The place looks a lot like a travel agency but those printers are churning out computerized tourist information for all of India. The friendly staff has a few non-electronic brochures and can answer questions about Bombay, but their map supply tends to dry up. Open Mon.-Fri. 8:30am-6pm, Sat. 8:30am-2pm. Also at Sahar International Airport (tel. 832 5331, open daily 24hr.) and at Santa Cruz Domestic Airport (tel. 614 9200, open at flight arrival times). **MTDC,** CDO Hutments, Madame Cama Rd. (tel. 202 6713). After Madame Cama Rd., enter the skyscrapers of Nariman Point, on the right-hand side as you face the sea, on the circle with the monstrous larger-than-life-size statue of Gandhi. The staff here will hand out maps when they have them, but are really glorified booking agents for the MTDC tours and hotels. Open Mon.-Fri. 9:30am-6pm, Sat. 9:30am-2pm. Also has branches at V.T., the Gateway of India, Santa Cruz, and Dadar (same hours).

Diplomatic Missions: U.S., Lincoln House, 78 Bhulabhai Desai Rd., Breach Candy (tel. 363 3611, -8). Registers U.S. citizens carrying their passports. issues travel advisories and lists of doctors and dentists. Replacement passport US$65. Open Mon.-Fri. 9am-12:30pm and 2-3:45pm. **Canada,** 41/42 Makers Chambers VI, Nariman Point (tel. 287 6027, -30). Replacement passport Rs.1500. Open Mon.-Fri. 9am-5:30pm. **U.K.,** Maker Chambers IV, 1st fl., 222 Jamhalal Bajaj Marg, Nariman Point (tel. 283 3602, 283 0517). Replacement passport Rs.1150. Mon.-Fri. 8am-12:30pm and 2-3pm. **Ireland,** Royal Bombay Yacht Club, Apollo Bunder, Colaba (tel. 287 2045, 495 1870). Open Mon.-Fri. 10am-noon. **Australia,** Maker Towers, 16th Floor, E. Block, Cuffe Parade (tel. 218 1071, -2). Replacement passport AUS$106. Open Mon.-Fri. 9am-5pm. **South Africa,** Gandhi Museum, Altamount Rd., near Kemp's Corner (tel. 389 3725, -7). Open Mon.-Thurs. 9am-5pm, Fri. 9am-2pm. **France,** Datta Prasad Bldg., N.G. Gross Rd., off Peddar Rd. (tel. 495 0918, 495 1870). Open Mon.-Fri. 9am-5pm. **Germany,** Hoeschst House, 10th fl., Nariman Point (tel. 283 2422). Open Mon.-Fri. 9am-4pm. **Netherlands,** International Bldg., Marine Lines Cross Rd. #1, Churchgate (tel. 201 6750). Replacement passport 55 guilders. Open Mon.-Fri. 9am-3:30pm. **Denmark,** L & T House, N. Morarjee Marg, Ballard Estate (tel. 261 8181). Open Mon.-Fri. 9am-1pm and 2-5pm. **Sri Lanka,** Sri Lanka House, 34 Homi Modi St. Fort (tel. 204 5861, 204 8303). Most visas obtainable on arrival in Sri Lanka. Open for visas Mon.-Fri. 9:30am-noon. **Thailand,** Krishna Bagh, 2nd fl., 43 Bhulabhai Desai Rd., Breach Candy (tel. 363 1404, 363 1426). Two-month visa Rs.400. Many nationalities can enter for under 2 months without a visa. Open Mon.-Fri. 9am-5pm.

Currency Exchange: Hong Kong Bank, 52160 M.G. Rd., Flora Fountain (tel. 267 4921). It's the huge building with the "Hong Kong" sign near on Flora Fountain. They give cash advances on Visa and MasterCard (up to Rs.6000). Their on-site **ATM** is connected to the Plus network. Open Mon.-Fri. 10am-2:30pm, Sat. 10:30am-12:30pm. ATM open daily 24hr. **Standard Chartered,** 81 Ismail Bldg., Dr. D.N. Rd., near Flora (tel. 204 5056, -7). The right hand side as you walk from Flora to V.T. Their 24-hr. ATM connects to both the Plus and Cirrus systems.

American Express, Regal Cinema Bldg., Shivaji Marg, Colaba (tel. 204 8291, 287 3856). Inside the Regal Cinema Bldg., on Wellington Circle. Inside this air-conditioned haven, AmEx card or traveler's check holders can collect their mail by showing their passport (mail held for 1 month), or have it forwarded. They change their own traveler's checks without commission, but charge 1% for most other brands. They also make travel arrangements, and will cash a cardholder's check for up to US$1000. Open Mon.-Sat. 9:30am-6:30pm.

Thomas Cook, Thomas Cook Bldg., Dr. D.N. Rd. Fort (tel. 204 8556, -8). On the left-hand side about 2 blocks up as you walk from Flora to V.T. They cash their own traveler's checks for free but charge Rs.20 per transaction for other brands. Open Mon.-Sat. 9:30am-6pm.

Telephones: ISD/STD booths, for local, long-distance, and international direct calling, occupy practically every street corner in Bombay, some working 24hr. A trip

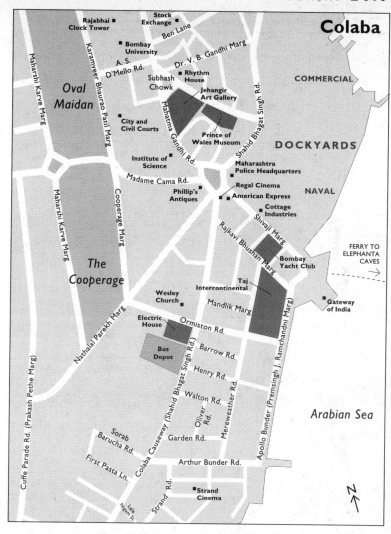

to the Government Telephone Office, Videsh Sanchar Bhavan (it's the huge building, covered with antennae, just north of Flora on M.G. Rd.), guarantees official
rates in plush air-conditioned surroundings. Offers telegraphs and telexes. Open
daily 8am-8pm.

Luggage Storage: Cloak Room at V.T. Inside the station building, near platform 13.
Bags must be locked closed (including the unlockable portion of backpacks).
Whatever you do, don't lose the receipt. The facility sometimes runs out of room,
at which point people sit around mournfully, waiting for collections to generate
space. For each bag, the charge for the first 24hr. (or portion thereof) is Rs.3, the
second Rs.8. The prices keep increasing: a 31-day deposit (the maximum) costs
Rs.182. Open daily 12:30am-7:30am, 8am-3:30pm, and 4pm-midnight.

English Bookstore: Crossword Bookstore, Mahalaxmi Chambers, 1st. fl., 22 Bhulabhai Desai Rd., Breach Candy (tel. 492 0253, 492 2458, 492 4882). The huge
crossword puzzle in the window gives it away. Inside, Bombay's best collection of

English-language fiction bursts from the bookshelves, along with a fairly good showing of Indian writers. Staff is happy to make suggestions. **Strand Book Stall,** 15 Dhannur, Sir P.M. Rd., Fort (tel. 266 1994, 266 1719). Take a right on P.M. Rd. from M.G. Rd., turn left after 2 blocks (at U.P. Handlooms); Strand is on the right. Almost as wide a range as Crossword cramped into a tiny store. Much more convenient to Colaba. Open Mon.-Sat. 10am-7pm, Sun. 10am-1pm. **Nalanda Bookstore,** Taj Mahal Hotel (tel. 202 2514). In the back of the modern wing. The best bookstore convenient to Colaba, it offers coffee table weights as well as paperback novels and Indian and Western music, all at distinctly non-Taj prices. Open daily 8am-midnight.

Library: American Center Library, 4 New Marine Lines, Churchgate (tel. 262 4590). The barricaded building on the right-hand side as you walk from Churchgate. The library caters to Ameriphile Bombayites more than expatriates, but for Rs.10 per day, nonmembers may sit in the air-conditioned calm and read dated U.S. papers or indulge in a reasonable American fiction collection in the library. Open Mon.-Tues. and Thurs.-Sat. 10am-6pm. **British Council,** A Wing, Mittal Towers, Nariman Point (tel. 282 3530). Although short-term visitors cannot join the library, they are suffered to glance through the British papers. Open Tues.-Fri. 10am-5:45pm, Sat. 9am-4:45pm. **Alliance Française,** Theosophy Hall, 40 New Marine Lines, Churchgate (tel. 201 6202, 203 6187). Directly opposite the American Center. Again, in theory, nonmembers have few rights, although they can *jeter un coup d'oeil* at the temporary exhibits and peruse the papers. Some even worm their way into a movie, depending on the pressure of numbers. Open Mon.-Fri. 9:30am-1pm and 2-5:30pm, Sat. 9:30am-1pm. **Max Mueller Bhavan,** Prince of Wales Annex, Kalaghoda (tel. 202 7542). At the back of the Prince of Wales Museum, next door to the Jehangir Art Gallery. German newspapers and books, and the occasional cultural event. Open Mon. 3-6pm, Tues.-Sat. 11am-6pm.

Market: M. Phule Market, Dr. D.N. Rd. Universally known as **Crawford Market,** despite the best efforts of several governments. This huge warren of fruit, vegetable, meat, and dry goods at the north end of D.N. Rd. furnishes flora and fauna you have never seen before, waking or sleeping. Open Mon.-Sat. 6am-6pm.

Pharmacy: Kemp & Co., Taj Market, Apollo Bunder, Colaba (tel. 202 3519). In the old hotel, at the beginning of the connecting corridor. Sells not only inexpensive pills, but also Barbie Dolls, chocolate, and cosmetics. Open daily 7am-11pm. **Bombay Chemists,** 39-40 Kakad Arcade, New Marine Lines, Churchgate (tel. 205 1173). Right next to Bombay Hospital. Open 24hr.

Hospital: Breach Candy Hospital, 60 Bhulabhai Desai Rd., Breach Candy (tel. 363 3651). On the sea-side of Warden Rd., just past the American Consulate and the Breach Candy Swimming Club. One of the most modern hospitals in Bombay. Open 24hr.

Emergency: Police: tel. 100. **Fire:** tel. 101. **Ambulance:** tel. 102.

Police: Police Commissioner's Office, D.N. Rd., Crawford Market (tel. 100). Opposite the market building behind an iron fence. At this head office you can report thefts but expect an endless bureaucratic nightmare. Try to find a smaller, local station.

Post Office: GPO, W. Hirachand Marg (tel. 262 0956). The huge stone building right next door to V.T. off Nagar Chowk. Tiny, individualized counter, with specialized functions detectable only by use of an out-dated wall chart, flourish in this cavernous tavern of communication. *Poste Restante* lives at counter 2 (on the left as you enter the main hall). Open Mon.-Sat. 9am-6pm, Sun. 10am-3pm. Counters 80-89 proffer stamps Mon.-Sat. 9am-8pm, Sun. 10am-5:30pm. EMS resides at counters 8-12, in the apse on the left of the main hall. Open Mon.-Sat. 9am-7pm, Sun. 9am-3pm. Parcels begin their journey from window 39, in Bicentennial Hall, up the stairs at the back of the mail hall. Open Mon.-Sat. 10am-4pm, Sun. 10am-2pm. The whole building is open Mon.-Sat. 9am-8pm, Sun. 10am-5:30pm. **Postal Code:** 400001.

Telephone Code: 022.

ACCOMMODATIONS

Colaba

Hotel Lawrence, 3rd fl., ITTS House, 33 Pope Walk Lake, off K Dubash Marg (tel. 284-3618). From Regal, follow the wall of the Prince of Wales Museum along M.G. Rd., past the Jehangir Art Gallery and Max Mueller Bhavan. Cross the road to the blue and white Trade Wings awning, and turn into the lane on the left. ITTS House is on the right. Ten reasonably sized rooms, with clean bathrooms, a friendly staff, and a few potted palms qualify the Lawrence as one of the few decent budget hotels in Bombay. Singles Rs.200. Doubles Rs.300. Triples Rs.400, breakfast included. Reservations recommended,

YWCA International Centre, 18 Madame Cama Rd., near Regal (tel. 202 5033, 202 0445, 202 9161). From Regal, follow Madame Cama Rd. towards Nariman Point. The third building on the left is the YWCA. The International Centre entrance lies on the right-hand side of the building. Although more expensive than most budget hotels, you get your money's worth at the Y. The price includes all-you-can-eat buffet breakfast and dinner, plus daily room cleaning, telephones, TV lounges, and other modern conveniences. The spotless, airy rooms, the breezy balconies, and the florid grey, pink, and blue curtains brighten the prospect of paying the price. All have bathrooms attached. Singles Rs.496. Doubles Rs.975. Triples Rs.1438. Reservations essential 3-4 weeks in advance, with a demand draft in rupees.

India Guest House, 1139 Kamal Mansion (3rd fl.), Arthur Bunder Rd., Colaba (tel. 283 3769). From Regal, follow Colaba Causeway to Arthur Bunder, 9 blocks down on the left. Just before Arthur Bunder meets the sea, an alley runs off to the right. Kamal Mansion's entrance stands in the alley, on the right. Faux pine plywood partitions mark off the windowless cubicles. Clean, and cheaper than most. Coffin-sized singles Rs.180. Doubles Rs.300.

Hotel Sea Lord, 1/29 Kamal Mansion (2nd fl.), Arthur Bunder Rd., Colaba (tel. 284 5392). In the same building as India Guest House. The whole hotel corridor is tiled—floors, walls, ceilings—like a shower, leading to a futuristic feel. But the cubicle-style doubles with attached shower bring the daydreamer firmly back to the present. Squat toilets. Doubles Rs.350.

Hotel Sea Grove, 1149 Kamal Mansion (4th fl.), Arthur Bunder Rd., Colaba (tel. 287 4237, -8). In the same building as the Hotel Sea Lord and India Guest House. A few rooms are sea views (meaning windows). All guests get to enjoy the pink stucco ceiling and head-height plastic potted plants. Serviceable but tiny singles Rs.250. Doubles Rs.350.

Salvation Army, 30 Mereweather Rd., Colaba (tel. 284 1824). Directly behind the Taj Mahal Hotel. From Regal, head down the Causeway, take a left on Rajkari Ghughar Rd. (by Mondegar's) and a right at the back of the Taj; it's on the right. High ceilings and dim lighting give the big complex an institutional feel. Passable dorms, and large, nondescript doubles. Curfew midnight. Check-out 9am. Dorm beds Rs.100 including breakfast, Rs.140 full board and dorm guests must rent lockers for Rs.3 per day (Rs.50 deposit). Doubles with bath and full board Rs.400, with A/C Rs.500. Rs.150 per head for 6-bed rooms.

Hotel Carlton, Florence House, 12 Mereweather Rd., Colaba (tel. 202 0642, 202 0259). One block before the Salvation Army, behind the Taj. Rambling, run-down old guest house, with broken furniture piled up in out of the way corridors. Small singles Rs.200. Doubles Rs.350, large doubles Rs.450.

Apollo Guest House, 1st fl., 43/44 Mathuradas Estate Building, Colaba Causeway, Colaba (tel. 204 5540, 288 3991). On the left-hand side of the road as you walk away from Regal, in the same block as Leopold's. Enter as signs instruct through what looks like a shoe shop. Tiny, low-ceilinged box-like rooms off a cramped, noisy warren. Single Rs.240. Double Rs.340.

Kishan Hotel, Shirin Manzil, Walton Rd., Colaba (tel. 202 1534, 283 3886, 284 1732, 284 2227). Walton is the 7th left off Colaba Causeway from Regal. Hotel Kishan is on the right. **Aga Beg Guest House,** which is run through Hotel Kishan, offers spacious, drab rooms with slightly tatty blanketed beds for Rs.260 per double. The air-conditioned rooms in the hotel proper, on the other hand, feature Arabic graffiti, stained tiles, and peeling paint for Rs.460 per double.

Hotel Prosser's, Curzon House, 2-4 Henry Rd., Apollo Rd., Colaba (tel. 284 1715, 283 4937). Where Henry Rd. (the 6th left off the Causeway from Regal) meets the sea. The high-ceilinged, relatively spacious rooms look like converted corridors, temporarily filled with old metal bedframes and dusty mattresses. Doubles Rs.300.

Oliver Guest House, Sorab Manor, 6 Walton Rd., Colaba (tel. 284 0291). Opposite Kishan Hotel. Probably your last resort: pock-marks and stains scar the wall, and there are no showers, only cisterns of water. Singles Rs.200. Doubles Rs.250. Triples Rs.300.

Whalley's, Jaiji Mansion, 41 Mereweather Rd., Apollo Bunder (tel. 282 1802, 283 4206). A big, breezy villa surrounded by greenery, where the birds make more noise than the traffic. Check-out noon. Singles Rs.350. Doubles Rs.450.

Bertley's Hotel, 17 Oliver Rd., Colaba (tel. 284 1474; fax 287 1846). A nice old house on a quiet, florid street offers decent-sized rooms, all with TVs and phones. Doubles Rs.550, with bathroom Rs.600.

Beyond Colaba

Fernandes Guest House, 3rd fl., Balmer Lawrie Bldg., 5 J.N. Heredia Rd., Ballard Estate (tel. 261 0554). The street on the left off Ballard Bunder after the monumental lamp post marks the turn for Sprott Rd. Huge, spartan rooms in the middle of a quiet business district. The manager, Pramod Nalawade, is chummy with Bombay's police bigwigs thanks to his work as an ombudsperson, so tourists enjoy special protection here. Lots of rules, including a laxly enforced 11pm curfew and an 8am (!) check-out. Singles Rs.200. Doubles Rs.400.

Hotel City Palace, 121 City Terrace, W. Hirachand Marg (tel. 261 5515, 261 4759, 265 0177, 266 6666). On Nagar Chowk, opposite V.T. Although most of their rooms cost more than they're worth, the tiny, box-like rooms on the ground floor offer cheap air-conditioning. Singles Rs.325. Doubles Rs.450.

Hotel Manama, 221-5 P. D'Mello Rd. (tel. 261 3412). Walk past the GPO on Hirachand Marg; take a left on D'Mello Rd.; Manama is on the right. This crowded, middle-class Indian hotel has uniformed bellhops and TVs in all the rooms, yet a reasonably sized double costs only Rs.300.

Hotel Victoria, 226 Shahid Bhagat Singh Rd. (tel. 261 1642, 261 2693). On the left just below W. Hirachand Marg, opposite the GPO. Rooms decorated like a circus sideshow with pink and blue vinyl seem all the gloomier for the forced cheer. No showers. Squat toilets. Singles Rs.100. Doubles Rs.220. Triples Rs.240.

Hotel Lord's, 301 Adi Marzban Path (Mangalore St.), off Shahid Bhagat Singh Rd., Fort (tel. 261 0077, 261 8310). At the intersection of Mangalore and SBS Rd., 4 blocks down from Hirachand Marg and the GPO. It's downhill all the way, from the grandiose reception desk, but the elaborate stucco ceilings in the rooms help distract attention from the cracked linoleum and the broken glass in the windows. Double Rs.225, with bath Rs.250, with A/C Rs.375.

Hotel Highway Inn Part One, Vishal Shopping Centre, Andheri-Kurla Rd., Andheri (E) (tel. 830 1494, -5). Just 3km from the airport. From Andheri Station, exit on the east side, turn left and then right at the intersection with Sir Mathurdas Vananji Rd. (the Andheri-Kurla Rd.). The Vishal Shopping Centre is about 500m on the left. One small, slightly grubby double available at Rs.275. Others are more expensive and offer TVs, bathrooms, and fridges.

Hotel Highway Inn Part Two, Vishal Shopping Centre, Andheri-Kurla Rd., Andheri (E) (tel. 832 0021, 832 0026, 832 5086). Next door to part one. Slightly less cramped, brighter atmosphere than it's neighbor. Small, simple doubles Rs.200 and up.

FOOD

Food in Bombay runs the gamut from gastronomy to gastroenteritis. The city's restaurants beckon with not only every type of Indian cuisine but also the best approximations of foreign food to be found in India. The street food ranges from stupefying to stomach-pumping. The big city prices constitute the only payoff.

Khyber Restaurant, 145 Mahatma Gandhi Rd. (tel. 267 3227, -9, 267 3584, 267 3973, 267 1605, 267 1942). On the far side of the parking lot behind the Prince of Wales Museum, right where the road begins to curve. The sumptuous antiques-and-mirrors decoration, the mural by India's most famous modern artist, M.F. Hussain, the intimate feel of the multi-storied nooks and crannies, and, above all, the excellent, rich, tender, Mughlai cuisine all conspire to make this Bombay's most popular restaurant. The chicken *makhanwala* swims in a thick, tangy tomato sauce (Rs.135). The *maa ki dal* undulates with unctuous, creamy intensity (Rs.90). The subtle flavoring of the chicken *bardami* sends a frisson through your taste buds (Rs.125). Open daily 12:30-3:45pm and 7:30-11:45pm. Reservations essential.

Madras Lunch and Coffee House, 56 Dr. V.B. Gandhi Marg. Down the street to the left hand side of Rhythm House, at the first intersection (Rope Walk Lane). The simple, clean office-workers breakfast and lunch joint offers authentic South Indian snacks. *Sada, rava, masala,* and *paper dosas* all for Rs.10-18. Also *upma, utthapams, idlis* and *vadais,* Rs.7-20. Open Mon.-Sat. 8am-8pm.

Trishna, 7 Rope Walk Lane (tel. 267 2176, 265 9644). One block left down Rope Walk Lane from the Madras Lunch and Coffee House. Bombay's finest seafood restaurant serves freakishly-sized shellfish at a fraction of their western price. Medium prawns (since the big ones are 2m long, these are pretty big) with butter, pepper, and garlic worth every paise of the Rs.140. A pomfret big enough for two costs Rs.200. Crisp calamari Rs.75. Ignore the Chinese and Indian selections—everyone has seafood here. Reservations recommended. Open daily noon-4pm and 6pm-midnight.

Edward VIII, 113/A Colaba Causeway (tel. 283 3975). Next to the gas station at the corner of Garden Rd., 1 block before Arthur Bunder. The 6 quiet booths provide a discreet spot for a *rendez-vous* with breakfast (Rs.25-60), burger (no beef), sandwiches (Rs.13-30), or a delicious fresh juice or shake (Rs.12-20). Gaze at the more-than-life-size portrait of Marilyn Monroe as you suck your mosambi juice. Open Mon.-Sat. 9am-9pm.

Delhi Darbar, Holland House, Colaba Causeway (tel. 202 0235, 202 5656). On the right hand side, about 3 blocks from Regal. Upmarket air-conditioned joint for businessmen and families offers good North Indian cuisine to the faint, encouraging tones of Flashdance, but without the taint of alcohol. Try the Parsi specialty *dhansak* here (Rs.55). Non-veg. entrees Rs.50-60; all veg. about Rs.40. Open daily 12:30-3:30pm and 6:30-11:30pm.

Kardeel Juice Stand, 95 M.G. Rd. Opposite AN2 Grindlay's bank, on the right side about 3 blocks from Regal. The best juices and shakes in Bombay—pre-prepared and dispensed over the obsessively wiped counter. Check the board to see what's in season. The peach shakes just slip down at Rs.16; the mango shake with bonafide alphonsoes in season Rs.18. Open Mon.-Sat. 9am-9pm, Sun. 5-9pm.

Mondegar's, Metro House, Colaba Causeway. The first corner on the left after Regal. The cartoon murals depicting dining hilarity (imagine getting bitten on the nose by a live lobster!) provide distraction while you eat an early breakfast (Rs.40-55) or a Continental or western meal (Rs.35-60). An extremely popular spot for beer (Rs.60 per bottle) and *chat* among tourists and locals alike, thanks in part to Bombay's only CD jukebox. Open daily 8am-11pm.

Leopold's, Colaba Causeway. On the left in the 3rd block down from Regal. The food here is slightly overpriced for the quality, but Leo's (both downstairs and up, see **Entertainment,** p. 599) remains Mondegar's rival in attracting a lively crowd of Indians and tourists to drink the day away under the slowly rotating fans. Beers Rs.60 per bottle. Decent *biryani* Rs.56. Omelette Rs.25. 10% tax extra. Open daily 8am-midnight.

Strand Coffee House, Strand House, Strand Rd. (tel. 283 3418). Turn right as you face the sea off Arthur Bunder at New Light of Asia Restaurant; Strand sits opposite the Strand Cinema. The elegant, faux alabaster sconces, tile floor, and wood-framed windows do not create quite the desired effect, thanks to the open counter and rubble outside—but the food is fine and reasonable. *Bhel puri* Rs.8. Sandwiches Rs.12-25. *Biryani* Rs.40. Roast chicken Rs.45. Open Mon.-Sat. 9am-3pm and 5-9pm, Sun. 9am-3pm.

WEST INDIA

Street Eats in Bombay

Life in the streets is tough in Bombay—you need a tough constitution just to eat there. But a streetwise stomach unlocks some of the city's greatest culinary pleasures. At every major intersection, several food stalls vie for the attention of passing pedestrians. One sidewalk staple, *pao bhaji*, consists of battered and fried balls of potato and chilies, served on a white roll. Other vendors proffer veggie sandwiches, spread with butter and green chutney, and stuffed beyond bursting with potatoes, cucumber, tomato, onion, and an optional slice of beetroot. But the most popular pavement peddling is the *puri*. This innocent-looking dried pastry shell appears in both flat, disk-like, and hollow, spherical *avatars*. The disk form serves to scoop up a sticky mixture of green chutney, tamarind sauce, chili paste, fried vermicelli, puffed rice, potato, tomato, onion, green mango, and coriander called *bhel puri*. As *sev puri*, the crunchy little frisbees act as platters for the same vegetable mix, without the rice or vermicelli. Other *Chat-wallahs*, as the snack merchants are known, fill the spherical *puris* with a thin sauce or a spiced curd to create *pani puri* and *dahi puri* respectively. Other salesmen vend roast peanuts, chickpeas, and "Bombay Mix" in Rs.1 servings. You can round off a full meal of these delicious tidbits with a plate of assorted fresh fruit, or, by request, with straight mango, papaya, or pineapple. Sugarcane juice, *nimbu pani* (lemonade), or coconut milk helps to wash it all down—but at no more than Rs.6 per portion, all these options slip down easily.

Majestic, Colaba Causeway. Opposite Mondegar's, up a few stairs. This huge hall of low tables under whirring fans furnishes only basic *thalis*—at an unbeatable Rs.16. Open daily 6:30am-10:30pm.

Beyond Colaba

Café Naaz, B.G. Kher Rd. (Ridge Rd.), Malabar Hill (tel. 367 2969). Opposite the Hanging Gardens (or Sir P.M. Gardens), just beyond Kamala Nehru Park. Perched on the tip of Malabar Hill, Café Naaz commands unparalleled views of all Bombay, from Chowpatty to Nariman Point and Colaba. The Irani meals (Rs.30-70) are tasty, but most come here for a beer (Rs.65 per bottle, Rs.30 per draft) or one of their many ice creams, juices, shakes, and sundaes (Rs.15-45) after a stroll in the nearby parks.

Under the Over, 36 Altamount Rd., Kemp's Corner (tel. 386 1393, 388 2979). Actually just beyond the flyover at Kemp's Corner. For tourists feeling homesick for European and American food, this place imitates it better than any other in Bombay. Barbecued chicken, complete with homefries and corncakes (Rs.145), fish 'n' chips (Rs.170), and chicken chimi changas (Rs.145) all taste remarkably like the real thing. Brownies (Rs.65) or cheesecake (Rs.75) to wind up. Open daily 12:30-3:30pm and 7:30-11:30pm.

Gaylord's, V.N. Rd., Churchgate (tel. 282 1259, 282 0985, 284 8031, 284 8076, 204 4693). On the left as you walk from Churchgate to Marine Drive. The sidewalk café, barricaded in by potted plants, offers a pleasant compromise between indoors and out. Their menu of drinks and snacks eclipses the indoor restaurant's overpriced fare. Concentrate on fresh baked goods from the bakery next door: doughnuts Rs.10, eclairs Rs.10, peach danish Rs.11. Open daily 9:30am-11pm.

Pizzeria, Soona Mahal, 143 Marine Dr., Churchgate (tel. 285 6115, 282 0883). Where V.N. Rd. meets Marine Dr. The cool wind off the bay and the red brick and straw blinds which help keep it out give this pizza joint an authentically mediterranean feel. The pizza itself is as close to authentic as Bombay can muster. Choices range from Margherita (Rs.80-135) to the stuffed-crust mixed seafood fisherman's wharf (Rs.160). Open daily noon-11:30pm.

Samrat, Prem Court, J. Tata Rd., Churchgate (282 0942, 282 0022). On the left-hand side of the road that leads to the right of Eros from Churchgate. This upscale pure veg. restaurant specializes in the slightly sweet *thalis* of Gujarat (Rs.70). Unlike more down-to-earth *thali* joints, you can wash down the plateloads of all-you-can-eat *chapatis, dal,* and vegetables with a bottle of beer (Rs.65). A pastel-painted frieze of Ashoka in triumphal procession downstairs, and the same sculpture in beaten metal upstairs stir stomachs to greater exploits. Open daily noon-10:30pm.

Rajdhani, opposite Mangaldas Market, near Crawford Market (tel. 342 6919, 344 9014). In the warren of bazaars near Crawford Market. Look down the crowded lanes on the opposite of D.N. Rd. from Crawford Market; Radjhani is on the right of the lane which reveals a many-turreted white building at the end. Offers the best, richest, most filling Gujarati *thali* in Bombay at lunch (Rs.75). At dinner, they switch to Maharashtrian, Kathiawadi, and Rajasthani *thalis*, but the quality is just as high. Open daily noon-3:30pm and 7-11pm.

Brittania and Co., Sprott Rd., Ballard Estate (tel. 261 5264). Opposite the F.P.O. on Sprott Rd., just half a block from the intersection with Ballard Bunder marked by an ornamental lamp post. A business-*wallahs'* lunch spot, teeming at midday with cuffs and collars. They come for the mutton and chicken *dhansak* (served Tues.-Wed. and Fri., Rs.48) and the Irani *Biryanis* and *pulaos*. Open Mon.-Sat. 10:30am-3:30pm.

National Hindu Restaurant, Sprott Rd., Ballard Estate. At the corner of Sprott Rd. and J.N. Heredia Rd., just half a block past Brittania and Co. Another office-*wallahs'* hang-out, simpler and cheaper than its famous neighbor. Upstairs serves *thalis* (Rs.15); downstairs offers South Indian snacks (Rs.5-15). Open daily 8:30am-7pm.

SIGHTS

A good starting point from which to lose yourself in the endless metropolis is the one which has welcomed visitors since the days of the Raj: the **Gateway of India.** Built to commemorate the visit of King George V and Queen Mary in 1911, this Indianized triumphal arch stands guard over the harbor next to the Taj Mahal Hotel. With a cosmopolitan nonchalance typical of Bombay, the gateway combines carved brackets derived from Gujarati temple architecture with Islamic motifs such as the minaret-like finials in a purely European building type. Especially in the evening, the schizophrenic sight now plays host to strolling couples, camera-happy tourists, peanut vendors, snake charmers, and touts pushing the perennially popular do-it-yourself embroidery kits with which to make your very own velour rendition of the celebrated archway.

In the small nearby park stands and imposing equestrian statue of the great 17th-century Maratha leader **Shivaji Bhonsle.** The reputation of this historical king and legendary hero has been hijacked by the right-wing Maharashtrian party, Shiv Sena, who deck out the unwitting image in marigold garlands and saffron flags.

The modern tower of the **Taj Mahal Hotel** just behind dwarfs the warrior, but the building's older wing really catches the tourist's attention. India's earliest industrialist, Jamshedji Tata, founded this luxurious Bombay landmark in 1899 in retaliation against the Europeans-only policies of Raj-era hotels. Like all the other Tata enterprises, which dominate the Indian economy even today, the Taj soared to success, monopolizing both the hotel industry and the city's early skyline. A self-assured expression wins even grubby backpackers access to the echoing air-conditioned corridors—but keep the budget guidebook hidden!

Colaba Causeway begins at Willingdon Circle, more popularly known as Regal after the grand old movie theater which faces it. Opposite the cinema stands the **Prince of Wales Museum** (tel. 284 4484). The intervening gardens provide a buffer between the newly restored domed gallery and the breakneck traffic outside. Within, cluttered displays feature everything from exquisite Mughal miniatures to stuffed animals and nth rate oil paintings. The first hall houses an amazing trove of archeological treasures dating back to the Indus Valley Civilization. They include exquisitely preserved stone tools and home burial urns from both Harappa and Mohenjo-Daro from 2500-1700 BC. Another highlight is the collection of 16th- to 18th-century metal deities, including one Shiva as Natraj, whose potent dancing both stirred the cosmos into existence and will eventually bring about its destruction. By far the most impressive exhibit, more than enough reason alone to visit the museum, is the collection of miniature paintings from the 16th- to 18th-centuries. These painstakingly detailed works showcase the various Rajasthani, Deccani, and Mughal schools in classic scenes of palace life, Krishna courting the *gopis,* royal portraits and naturalistic animal studies. (Open Tues.-Sun. 10:15am-6pm. Admission Rs.5.)

The **Jehangir Art Gallery** (tel. 204 8212), just behind the Prince of Wales Museum, hosts temporary art exhibits. The displays focus on contemporary Indian painting, providing a fascinating counterpoint to the miniatures next door. The quality of the art here is mixed, but it's free and air-conditioned. (Open daily 11am-7pm. Free.)

Down at the southernmost end of the Causeway stand the 19th-century **Afghan Church,** built to commemorate the soldiers who died to keep the Khyber Pass British, an old colonial cemetery, and the now defunct **Colaba lighthouse.** But the meat of Bombay's sight-seeing lies north of Regal. The buildings of **Bombay University** and the **High Court** line the left side of M.G. Rd. from the Prince of Wales Museum to Flora Fountain—but their finest façades face the Oval Maidan, one block to the west. These Victorian-Gothic extravaganzas, centering on the bebalachined, 85m-tall **Rajabhai Clock Tower** (open daily 11am-5pm), used to occupy the seafront until the vintage Art Deco neighborhood opposite was built on land reclaimed from the sea in the 20s and 30s. The pink-and-white wedding cake of **Eros Cinema** in the middle of this period-piece area, on the same square as the Victorian Churchgate station, exemplifies Bombay's unparalleled wealth of interwar architecture. Some of the surrounding buildings have been restored to their original waxy, zigzag glory—but most have suffered from damp, salty air and landlords constrained by rent control. Visitors strolling down the side of the maidan from Churchgate will find it hard to believe that these dilapidated apartments fetch millions of dollars on the rare occasions when they come up for sale. From the maidan, Maharishi Karve Rd. skirts Nariman Point. This is where India's wealthiest capitalists rub reluctant, resentful shoulders with the right-wing populist officials of the Shiv Sena government, headquartered at the adjacent Vidhan Sabha M.K. Rd. This road eventually merges with Cuffe Parade Rd., where an abrupt gap in the land reclamation schemes has left a small bay between the towers of Nariman Point and the Cuffe Parade Extension. A fishing village, still populated by the original inhabitants of Bombay, the Kolis, lines the shore here. The incongruous juxtaposition of the carved wooden boats and waterless, powerless shanties of the village with the high-rises of the multinationals next door strikes even the most hardened tourist.

In the opposite direction from Churchgate, **Marine Drive** stretches all the way from Nariman Point around Back Bay to Chowpatty Beach at the foot of Malabar Hill. Especially at sunset, Bombayites love to stroll, powerwalk, and jog along the seaface, chatting, buying snacks, and treating their children to rides on toy cars and makeshift merry-go-rounds. As the natural light fades, the neon ads and the string of streetlights seize the limelight and transform the seaside strip into what was once known as the **Queen's Necklace.** Just before Chowpatty on the left, the rather dismal **Taraporevala Aquarium** (tel. 208 2061, -2) specializes in fish with religious significance. (Open Tues.-Sun. 10am-7pm. Admission Rs.3.) Beyond the beach rises Malabar Hill, home to Bombay's wealthiest jet-setters.

The **Walukeshwar Temple** hides in one of the many old back streets lined with bright flower stalls and renegade chickens that wind through Malabar. In local legend, the area hosted the banished hero of the epic *Ramayana,* Rama, and his brother and companion, Lakshmana, as they traveled south to free Sita, Rama's wife, from captivity in the kingdom of the evil Ravana. In order for Rama to perform his daily worship, Lakshmana had to bring a *linga* from far off Varanasi. He was late one day, prompting Rama to create his own from the only material he had—*waluk* (sand), hence creating a *walukeshwar* (sand god). The temple's massive gray *shikhara* sits at the head of **Banganga Tank,** a huge rectangular pool of greenish water, surrounded by jagged lines of rundown settlements and as full of legend as it is of bathers and *dhobis.* What was once a celestial drinking fountain is now a glorified sink. The thirsty Rama created the tank by shooting his arrow into the ground, at which point water began to gush forth to relieve the parched deity. Just behind the temple, the maze of **dhobi ghats** along the shore is crowded with row upon row of half-dressed washermen crouched low on the rocks, rhythmically beating their washables (and those of everyone else in the city). While the city boasts even more impressive *dhobi ghats* near Mahalaxmi race course, these are less accessible to most tourists.

The seven massive **Parsi Towers of Silence,** upon which Zoroastrians set out their dead for vultures to eat, crown Malabar Hill. The whole complex is screened from sight by carefully landscaped trees, but the funeral customs of the Parsis nonetheless received close scrutiny a few years ago when the vultures threatened to contaminate the city's water supply by dropping leftover luncheon morsels in the nearby reservoirs.

The city's two most famous gardens are also located at the top of Malabar Hill. **Sir Pherozeshah Mehta Garden** (tel. 363 3561), locally known as the **Hanging Garden,** sits right at the terminus of buses #106 and #108. Along with the **Kamala Nehru Children's Park** across the street, it entices visitors with a topiary, penguin-shaped trash cans, a life-sized reproduction of the shoe in which the old lady lived, and stunning views of the city. In both parks, frolicking children and their parental chaperones face down the hordes of surreptitious smoochers, supposedly hidden from public eye by the single branch hanging over them. (Open daily 5am-9pm. Free.)

The entrance to **Babulnath Mandir** on Babulnath Mandir Rd. is an unassuming set of three connected small stone arches, seemingly held up by the throngs of flower sellers, holy men, and worshippers around their base. The gates open up to a world far removed from the jams of Marutis below, where a dense concert of blaring bells and voices reciting *arati* blankets the path up the stone stepped hill. The temple itself, with its small shrine, is loudly alive during worship times—the combination of sounds, crowd, and spirit fill you. As your ears ring with the memory on the way back down, don't be surprised to find lines of women squatting beside baskets of coiled cobras asking for money to feed their serpentine companions milk. Feeding them on certain days of the week is considered an auspicious tribute to Shiva.

As the site of the first meeting of Indian National Congress, it is only fitting that Bombay pay tribute to the Father of the Nation and onetime citizen of the city: Mahatma Gandhi. The Mahatma stayed at **Mani Bhavan,** 19 Laburnum Rd. (a quiet, leafy, lane in the streets behind the temple) during his frequent political visits to Bombay. The building now houses a museum to the great man with a huge research library on Indian history, Gandhi, and Independence. Along with a film archive, the museum includes a small collection of old photos and a "look-and-see" diorama version of the great moments in Gandhi's life and the struggle for Independence. (Open Tues.-Sun. 9:30am-6pm. Admission Rs.3.)

North past the flyovered shopping hub of Kemp's Corner lies **Mahalaxmi Temple,** near the sea on Warden Rd. (Bhulabhai Desai Rd.). The goddess (like Bombay) devotes herself to wealth and beauty—making this *mandir* the city's most popular. In addition to Lakshmi riding a tiger (normally Durga's vehicle), the temple contains images of Kali and Saraswati, the two other chief goddesses of the Hindu pantheon.

Just beyond Mahalaxmi, on an island in the middle of the Arabian Sea, the shrine of the Sufi saint **Haji Ali** battles the waves daily. The bright white building stands out against the pacific blue or stormy grey of the ocean like a beacon for all camera owners. The narrow causeway to the island disappears at high tide and during the monsoon storms, but at other times, even non-Muslims can stride past the expectant rows of beggars as far as the outer chambers. It's better from a distance.

On dry ground next to Haji Ali, the **Mahalaxmi racecourse** cuts a green gash through the grey cityscape. The races (and betting) run on weekends from December to May. On the way out of Mahalaxmi station, the bridge to the left affords a view of the main **dhobi ghats** of the city, where legions of diligent launderers relieve clothing of its dirt more through stern discipline verging on violence than use of soap products. These are more famous but less accessible that the *ghats* near Banganga Tank.

Further north still, on the edges of the upmarket neighborhood of Worli, the **Nehru Centre** showcases Indian history, culture, and scientific achievement. The theater offers both Indian and Western performing arts (see **Entertainment,** p. 596). The **Nehru Science Museum** (tel. 496 4676), the park leading up to it dotted with animal rides and old train cars, seems mostly geared to children, but contains an exhibit on Indian contributions to science, from ancient ayurvedic medicine and the dawn of mathematics to current genetic discoveries by H.G. Khorana. Open daily 11am-5pm. The **Nehru Planetarium** (tel. 492 0510) is open Tues.-Sun. 11am-1:45pm and 2:30-6pm. English shows (1hr.) at 3 and 6pm. Admission Rs.10.

Another area of attractions stretches north from **Flora Fountain,** now renamed Hutatma Chowk ("Martyrs' Square") in honor of the protesters who died agitating for a separate Marathi-speaking state in the 1960s. East of here lies the **Fort District,** named after the original British fortification which once occupied the site. Now foreign banks have seized control, separated by frequent ramparts of off-set printers and STD booths. In the midst of the commercial hubbub, Horniman Circle strikes a calm, dignified note. The elegant Neoclassical colonnade faces the early 19th-century **Asiatic Society Library** (originally the Town Hall) over a small park complete with fountain. The neighboring **Mint and Customs House** also date from the early 1800s. But Bombay's oldest English building is **St. Thomas's Cathedral,** on the south-west corner of the Circle. Although begun by East India Company Governor Gerald Aungier in 1672, when Surat was still the capital of the Bombay Presidency, St. Thomas languished incomplete until 1718. The architects must have hoped to intimidate the local populace into conversion with the gratuitous flying buttresses. The interior reveals a fascinating slice of colonial life with its *punkahs* (hand-operated cloth fans) and endless marble memorials to stiff-upper-lipped Englishmen lost in battle, from disease, or at sea, during the struggle to "civilize" the natives. (Open daily 6:30am-6pm.)

At the northern edge of the Fort area stand the grand colonial edifices of the GPO and **Victoria Terminus.** Opposite V.T., the **Bombay Municipal Corporation Building** comes as close to scraping the sky as any Victorian building. The 76m dome can be viewed from the interior during office hours. A quick stroll up D.N. Rd. from V.T., past the huge Times of India building and the Bombay School of Art, **Crawford Market** sends a lesser, if equally architecturally improbable spire into the sky. Lockwood Kipling, Rudyard's father, designed the rather condescending sculptures on the exterior—industrious peasants to suit the farmers' market within—during his tenure at the nearby art school. To the west of Crawford Market stretch endless neighborhoods of bazaars—first **Zaveri (Silversmiths') Bazaar,** then **Bhuleshwar Market** near the Mumbadevi Temple for produce and housewares, and finally **Chor (Thieves') Bazaar** northwards by Johar Chowk. Strolling and shopping in these areas provides a more traditionally Indian commercial foil to the faxes and stock-options of Nariman point.

North again from Johar Chowk along Sir J.J. Rd., in the neighborhood of Byculla, the **Victoria and Albert Museum** (now Veermata Jijabhai) (tel. 375 7943) receives relatively few foreign tourists. The exhibits on Bombay's history include the carved stone elephant which gave Elephanta Island its name. (Open Thurs.-Tues. 9:30am-5pm. Admission Rs.2.) For the real McCoy, head next door to **Bombay's Zoo** (tel. 372 5799), where mangy animals subsist in depressing surroundings. The adjacent Botanical Gardens provide a more salubrious setting for a stroll. (Open Thurs.-Tues. 9am-5:30pm. Free.)

Finally, the distant northern suburb of Borivli offers two diametrically opposed attractions. The same railway stop (Borivli) caters to both the **Sanjay Gandhi National Park,** with its rock-cut caves, and Esselworld, the larger of Bombay's two amusement parks. Kanheri features over 100 caves, although few of them amount to more than holes in the wall. Nonetheless, those planning to hit Ajanta, Ellora, or Karle and Bhaja can come here for a quick prep course, while others can visit as consolation. Cave 3, a colonnaded *chaitya* hall of the Theravada school of Buddhism guarded by two huge standing Buddhas added later, makes for the most interesting exploration. (Open daily 9am-5:30pm. Admission Rs.0.50.)

For **Esselworld** (tel. 492 0891, 492 5013, 807 7321, -2, 649 8727, 649 8737), head to Govai Creek (Borivli-W) where ferries whisk eager children and beleaguered parents to the 35-ride complex on Corao Island free of charge. The entrance charge is based on height (Rs.125 for those above 137cm) and entitles visitors to unlimited rides as well as access to the **Water Sports Complex.** Interesting for sociological as well as recreational purposes, Esselworld exhibits middle-class urbanite life at its most packaged and plastic for ruin-weary travelers. (Open daily 11am-7pm; ferries 10:30am-7:30pm.)

ENTERTAINMENT

Unlike most cities in India, Bombay has a nightlife—complete with bars, clubs and Western performing arts. Check the *Bombay Times* in the *Times of India* for the weekly bulletin of the latest concerts and plays at the **Tata Theater,** the **Nehru Centre,** and a host of smaller venues. Barbaric backpackers will be pleased to discover not a hint of culture at the city's many pubs and discos. But beware the pervasive (if sporadically enforced) "couples only" policies on busy nights and the occasional refusal of t-shirted or sandaled sybarites.

Bars

The Ghetto, 30 Bhulabhai Desai Rd., Breach Candy (tel. 492 1556), in an alley on the seaward side of the road, just before Mahalaxmi. Bombay's most happening bar seethes with yuppie kids every night. When the police close the front door, regulars slip in the side entrance. Beers Rs.40, spirits Rs.40 and up. (Open daily 6pm-until they get shut down—usually Sun.-Wed. about 2am, Thurs.-Sat. about 4am.)

Leopold Cafe, Colaba Causeway, Colaba (tel. 202 0131, 287 3362). About three blocks down from Regal, on the left-hand side. Tourists and Indians mix here, to eat, drink, and party. The dim air-conditioned section upstairs hosts the most serious drinkers amid a black and white check decor, punctuated by a psychedelic drawings. Beers Rs.35. Pitcher Rs. 170.Open daily 1pm-midnight. Downstairs open daily 8am-midnight.

The Other Room at Sundance Cafe, Eros Building, 42 Maharishi Karve Rd., Churchgate. (tel. 282 1286). In the same building as the pink and white wedding cake Eros Cinema, opposite Churchgate station. The entrance to The Other Room (not to be confused with the main Sundance Cafe) lies in an alley down the left-hand side of the building. This cool, secluded spot provides the perfect venue for a quiet day-time drink, disturbed only by the lilting cadences of the VJs perpetually grinning down from the idiot box. Draft beers Rs.30; tasty but pricey snacks around Rs.60. Open daily 11am-11pm.

Voodoo, Arthur Bunder Rd., Colaba. Four doors up on the left from the seafront. Bombay's only above-ground gay bar attracts an upmarket clientele of fashion designers and filmmakers, especially on Saturday nights. India's most famous gay rights activist, Ashok Rao Kavi, leads the regulars. Beers Rs.40. Open daily 6pm-11pm.

The Pub at Rasna, J.Tata Rd., Churchgate (tel. 283 6243, 282 0995). On the left on the road which leads to the right of Eros from Churchgate, just after the small traffic circle. Futuristic—if the future hinges on tall metal chairs, neon lights, streamlined design, and a confusing floor plan. Late on weekend nights, the children of Bombay's jet-set flood up against the aerodynamic bar, leaving breathing space only on the small dance floor. Beers Rs.35. Open daily 6pm-1am.

The Cellar, Oberoi Towers, Marine Drive, Nariman Point (tel. 202 4343, 202 5353). Inside India's most expensive hotel, the Rs.175 cover seems like a bargain. The faux stone arcaded booths and dance floor look more like a cheesy Italian restaurant than a disco—but the crowd boogies away unconcerned to the boppy dance tunes. Beers Rs.50. Open Sun.-Thurs. 10:30pm-12:30am, Fri.-Sat. 10:30pm-4am.

London Pub, 8 Dariya Vihar, 39B Chowpatty Seaface, Marine Drive (tel. 363 0274). Opposite Chowpatty Beach on Marine Drive. This tiny hole-in-the-wall herds them in on two stories, with the DJ suspended between the two. The Bombay chapter of the worldwide jogging club, the Hash House Harriers, makes this their off-track HQ. Lots of 40-something booties shaken to cheesy music here. Beers Rs.35. Open daily 5pm-1am.

Earthquake, 38 Sarvodaya Compound, Tardeo Main Rd. (tel. 495 2038). From Bombay Central, turn left, cross the railroad bridge, go straight through the intersection

WEST INDIA

and look for the blood-red sign on the left. The nephew of Bal Thackeray, the Hindu Nationalist leader, holds a stake in this bar. Think about where your Rs.40 are going each time you buy a beer. Open daily 5pm-1am.

Performance Centers

Nehru Centre, Dr. Annie Besant Rd., Worli (tel. 492 8192, 492 6042). In the same complex as the Nehru planetarium, on the right side just past Mahalaxmi race-course. Lots of Indian and Western Classical music as well as some theatre.

Tata Theatre, Marine Drive, Nariman Point (tel. 282 4567, 283 4678). At the very tip of Nariman Point, just beyond the Oberoi. The same compound includes the main theater, the experimental theatre and a third location scheduled to open in 1997. More European and American offerings than at Nehru, but good Indian music and theatre, too.

■ Near Bombay: Elephanta Island

About 10km off the coast from the Gateway of India, the quasi-tropical island of Elephanta in the Arabian Sea is a welcome respite from the congestion and commotion of downtown Bombay. The island has a small local fishing population, but is most renowned for its extraordinary cave temples dating to the 8th century. At the end of a 125-step climb up the mountainside, the cave itself covers over 5000 square meters many of which are filled with moss and bats in most areas. The main chamber has a cross-like arrangement of massive pillars with no functional purpose. The image of Shiva as the cosmic dancer Natraj is carved in detail near the entrance—the damage is due to the Portuguese who reportedly used it for target practice when they occupied the island in the 1800s. A weathered and beaten-up panel of Lakulisha, a Shaiva saint considered to be an incarnation of Shiva, is opposite. The main Linga Shrine in the center of the cave is accessed by entrances on all four sides, each flanked by a pair of **dwarapalas,** rather vicious-looking guardians. The other attractions in the cave are the elaborate wall panels depicting assorted scenes from Shiva mythology in remarkable detail. On the north side is a lively panel depicting Shiva as Bhairava killing the demon Andhaka, who was attempting to steal a divine tree. Opposite is a less gruesome scene, that of Shiva and Parvati's marriage but this panel is highly worn down. The three panels on the south side of the temple are the caves' central attraction. A massive and imposing 6-m-high bust of Shiva as the three-faced Trimurti, Lord of the Universe, is formidable. To the sides, the Descent of the Ganga and Shiva as Ardhanarishvara are shown, while near another entrance is a detailed panel showing Ravana's attempt to uproot Mount Kailasa.

The Elephanta Caves are accessible by boat from the Gateway of India. **Ordinary boats** make the one-hour trip for Rs.35. **Luxury boats** with tour guides do the same for Rs.50. Only ordinary boats run in the monsoon months, and then only when waters are navigable (Inquiries: tel. 202 6364). Both ordinary and luxury boats leave every hour from 9am to 2:15pm and return after four hours.

■ Lonavla

Lonavla has become a popular resort for no other reason than that it is a three-hour ride from Bombay along a major transportation route. The endless proliferation of weekend cottages and full-board hotels punctuated by stands selling the sticky nut brittle called *chikki* sits expectantly in the middle of nowhere, as if awaiting the arrival of some raison d'être. From the tourist's view, the only justification for an overnight is a visit to the Buddhist caves at Karla and Bhaja—and a cheek full of *chikki,* of course.

ORIENTATION AND PRACTICAL INFORMATION

The city rambles aimlessly over the rolling terrain. From the **pedestrian bridge** at the **train station,** the road to the right curves around an embankment before joining the main **Bombay-Pune Highway.** About 100m to the right is the police stand at the junction with **Shivaji Road** just behind sits the **bus station.** Both trains (local and long haul) and buses to Bombay (Rs.40-50, deluxe Rs.60) and Pune (Rs.21, deluxe Rs.30) leave practically around the clock. Buses to Karla leave at 6, 9, 10, 11am, 1:15, 3, and 6:30pm and return 35 minutes later. To see the caves at both Karla and Bhaja, you can hire a rickshaw for about Rs.150 including waiting time—bargain hard. **Telephone Code:** 02114.

ACCOMMODATIONS AND FOOD

Near the bus stand, about 100m further down Shivaji Rd. on the left is one of Lonavla's many overpriced hotels, **The Ardash** (tel. 72353). A clean but bare double with attached bathroom with squat toilet down a betel-stained corridor costs Rs.200. Opposite the bus stand, on the Bombay-Pune Rd., down a little lane labelled "Pitale," an old traditional Maharashtrian house revels in the grandiose title of **Madhu's Resort** (tel. 72657). The old villa has spartan wooden rooms with a color finish and even the closest thing to a girlie poster in respectable Indian society: a scantily saried woman trumpets the merits of Director's Whiskey from the walls. Rooms Rs.150 per person. Most hotels serve food, and *dhabas* abound.

SIGHTS

Try to put the grim lodging scene behind you as quickly as possible by distracting yourself with first-century BC cave architecture. On arrival at **Karla** (about 10km east of Lonavla), a steep staircase leads up from the drinks stalls to the outcrop high above the plain where the main cave is located. A later Hindu shrine and the pillar capped by four lions obscure the entrance to the *chaitya* hall. The *pipal*-shaped window, which signifies learning, illuminates the Buddhist *stupa*—the emblem of the Buddha. The capitals of the interior columns each depict two kneeling elephants carrying a couple—perhaps stylized donors in the construction of the cave. Although the cave, excavated entirely from solid rock, needs no structural support, wooden beams said to be original, stripe the ceiling in a hangover from earlier freestanding temples. (Open daily 8am-6pm; admission Rs.0.50.)

Unless you locate a rickshaw, a gentle 5-km walk beckons to would-be **Bhaja**-goers. Going back to the main road, straight across, and up the gentle incline over the railroad tracks at Malouvil Station leads to the tiny cold drinks stall at the edge of the minuscule Bhaja village. Another staircase leads up to the 18 caves which date from the 2nd century BC. The otherwise unremarkable *chaityas* and *viharas* feature some lovely sculpture, including a celebrated relief of a war elephant tearing up trees in its path. Behind the caves to the right stand 14 curious mini-*stupas;* further still a waterfall trickles over a sharp drop in the hillside. The caves are openly accessible (except for a couple covered by iron grilles) and free, although a wizened *chowkidar* who tries to make up for his abject lack of English by repeating his pearls of wisdom 10 times in Hindi expects a tip for his pains.

Looming in and out of the monsoon mists, or baking in the sunshine hundreds of meters above the caves, the **Lohagad and Visapur Forts,** from the Maratha era, cater to those with strong calves.

▨ Matheran

The hill station of Matheran, 170km east of Bombay, is a popular weekend getaway for big city dwellers. Renowned for its red clay pathways and absence of all motor vehicles, Matheran is spread out beneath a thick canopy of foliage. It exudes a relaxing peace and quiet that contrasts starkly with Bombay's downtown insanity. Founded in 1850, Matheran is packed with serenity-seekers from September to June and on all weekends, virtually shutting down in the monsoon months, when the heavy rains turn the quaint red pathways into streams of mud. There are several superb viewpoints of the valley and cities around, but few visitors even bother with them, preferring to spend their days relaxing.

ORIENTATION AND PRACTICAL INFORMATION

The access point for Matheran is the small town of **Neral,** at the base of the hill station. From Bombay V.T. Station, frequent local trains to **Karjat** stop at Neral (every hr., 6am-11pm, 3hr., Rs.14). Some of the Pune express trains stop at Neral (6:40 and 8:45am, 2½hr., Rs.25). Another option is to take a frequent local train from Karjat back to Neral. From Neral, Matheran is 6.5km up the hill, but the trip up is hardly as easy as the distance suggests. **Shared taxis** and **minivans** make the steep trip for Rs.40 per person, or Rs.200 for a solo trip. There's a **miniature train** (ultra-narrow gauge) that zig-zags through the scenic greenery from Neral up to Matheran as well (8:40, 11am, and 5pm; also 10:20am in April and May; 8:40am only in monsoon; 2hr., Rs.30/125 for 2nd/1st class). From Matheran back to Neral (5:45am, 1:10, and 2:35pm; also 4:20pm in April and May; 1:10pm only in monsoon; 2hr., Rs.30/125 for 2nd/1st class). Make advance reservations during the peak season.

Matheran is roughly lined along the north-south **Mahatma Gandhi Marg,** which becomes **Shivaji Marg** further south. The **Matheran Railway Station,** where the miniature train arrives, marks the center of town. If you enter Matheran by any means other than the miniature train, you'll be dropped off 2.5km north of the railway station at the **taxi stand,** the nearest to the center of the hill station that motor vehicles are allowed. From the taxi stand, the walk to town takes 30 minutes. A **horse ride** into town is rocky but fun (Rs.75). **Cycle-rickshaws** are also available for rides into town (Rs.100). There is a Rs.7 **entry fee** into Matheran.

The **tourist office** is opposite the railway station and has town maps (open daily 10am-6pm). Moving south down Mahatma Gandhi Marg, the **GPO** is on the left. STD/ISD **telephone** booths are in this area as well. Past the GPO, a fork to the right passes the **police station** before continuing on to **Charlotte Lake. Currency exchange** is only available in the top hotels, generally for guests only. **Telephone Code:** 021483.

ACCOMMODATIONS AND FOOD

There are few budget hotels in Matheran, most clustering near the railway station. Reservations are required in season at most places. In the off-season and monsoon months, many hotels close down or offer substantial discounts. Mid-week in Matheran, rates are generally negotiable. Since most hotels offer full- or half-board in Matheran, the outside dining scene is sparse. Some hotels allow non-guests to eat there, or will do so for the right price, but you're otherwise restricted to basic snacky eateries along M.G. Rd. The local specialty is *chikki,* a sweet peanut-brittle-like snack found everywhere, made with a range of nuts and sugary substances. **Nariman Chikki Mart** on M.G. Rd. (tel. 30221) has a wide selection.

Hope Hall Hotel, M.G. Rd. (tel. 253). A friendly family-run place with average-sized, simply decorated, spotlessly clean rooms and cheerful attached bathrooms. Limited room service. Check-out 10am. Doubles only, Rs.200 in high season.

Gujarat Bhavan Hotel, Maulana Azad Rd. (tel. 278, in Bombay (022) 388 1998). A resorty hotel with large, tastefully maintained rooms and clean attached baths. Staff is particularly friendly. Full veg. board and 24-hr. room service. Check-out 10am. Rs.350 per person in high season, Rs.425 with TV and better rooms. Cottages Rs.500 per person.

SIGHTS

The only sights in Matheran are the numerous viewpoints which mark the borders of the hill station. All offer views of the surrounding valleys from sheer cliff outcrops. The ones on the western side have views of Neral in the distance. The viewpoints at sunset and sunrise are particularly romantic, except when mobbed with lovey-dovey honeymooners. Women are advised not to explore the more remote viewpoints alone at night. **Panorama Point,** to the far north, has particularly breathtaking views. **Porcupine** and **Louisa Points,** west of town, **Monkey Point** to the north, and **Alexandra Point** to the south are also popular.

■ Pune

Bombay has become so cosmopolitan and disorienting in recent years that most Maharashtrians now look to nearby Pune as their cultural and spiritual capital. Birthplace of the Maratha hero, Shivaji, capital of his successors, the Peshwas, and almost purely Marathi-speaking, Pune lays a much more credible charm to son-of-the-soil status than its upstart cousin on the coast. Its position at the edge of the Deccan Plateau gives it a cooler and less muggy climate than Bombay, which sits at the bottom of the Western Ghats. But some of Bombay's urban sophistication has made the three-hour climb up to Pune, due to its many nationally and even internationally respected col-

---

Shivaji

By the time of Shivaji's birth in 1630, Muslims had dominated the subcontinent for 400 years. The last Hindu-ruled Kingdom of any significance, at Vijayanagar, had collapsed a century earlier. Many of the Muslim rulers of the time neglected or persecuted their Hindu subjects. Against this backdrop of oppression, the 16-year-old nobleman from the landowning Bhonsle family of the Maratha region of the Bijapur Sultanate declared his divine mission to restore religious tolerance to India.

In 1647, Shivaji began seizing some of the smaller outposts of Bijapur. By 1659, his daring attacks had so incensed the Sultan that he sent an army of 20,000 to squash the upstart. Shivaji lured the Muslim general, Afzal Khan, to a parley where he embraced him closely enough to rip out his innards with his *wagh nakh*, or metal "tiger claws." Meanwhile, his concealed troops ambushed and destroyed the Bijapuri army.

Shivaji's victory aroused the vigilance of the ardently Muslim Mughal emperor, Aurangzeb, initiating one of Indian history's great rivalries. Despite an overwhelming advantage in manpower and resources, Aurangzeb never overcame Shivaji's cunning and courage. In 1666, the Maratha gave himself up at Agra, only to smuggle himself out of house arrest in a basket of candy. On another occasion, he captured the sheer-walled fort of Simhagad (near Pune) by training lizards to carry ropes up the cliff face.

Shivaji's huge popularity among Hindus and Muslims alike helped fend off the Mughal colossus. He ruled with religious impartiality, recruiting officers from both faiths. His technological insight also contributed—he engineered a network of hilltop forts to maintain control of the countryside, while his navy could challenge even the European colonial fleets. Even after Shivaji died in 1680, the Maratha Confederacy he founded prospered, growing to encompass most of present-day Maharashtra and Madhya Pradesh and rapidly destroying the moribund Mughal Empire.

The British eventually subdued the Marathas, and Shivaji faded into a folk hero until the 1950s, when Balasahek Thackeray, a journalist-turned-politician, founded a political party in Maharashtra named Shiv Sena in Shivaji's honor. The Sena "supremo," however, does not share Shivaji's tolerance: his philosophy has evolved from anti-immigrant, pro-Marathi chauvinism to a more general Hindu nationalism hostile to Muslims. When the Sena gained power in the state in 1995, they changed the name of Aurangabad (Aurangzeb's eponymous capital) to Sambhajinagar (after Shivaji's son, Sambhaji), taking the epic rivalry into its fourth century.

---

leges and its strategic position on road and rail routes. The biggest dose of internationalism springs from Pune's infamous ashram, the Osho Commune International of the export guru Rajneesh (now deceased, and known as Osho). *Sannyasins*, as his devotees are known, journey from all over the world to undergo Osho's much-vaunted laughter therapy in red robes and wooden beads, while their antics provide unofficial laughter therapy for skeptical locals and tourists alike. Beyond this fascinating fusion of cultural idioms, Pune offers broad, leafy streets and relative calm after the crowds of Bombay, despite Pune's population of 3 million. But Pune's comparatively meager sights usually reduce it to a mere stopover on the way to Aurangabad to the north, Goa and Karnataka to the south, or Hyderabad to the east. Only hippy-dippy beandy-wiendies and Shivaji enthusiasts will find much to detain them.

ORIENTATION

Although Pune seems quiet by comparison to Bombay, its population numbers over three million spread out into three chief neighborhoods. The railway station and a major bus stand rub shoulders along **Sassoon Road** in Camp. Most budget hotels lurk in the leafy oasis of **Wilson Garden,** behind Sassoon Rd., or along **Connaught Road,** which crosses the latter at right angles a block east of the railroad station. Connaught Rd. leads south past the GPO and police station to **Moledina Road,** at the start of the modern commercial district. The busy parallel shopping streets of **M.G. Road** and **East Street** also house banks, airline offices, a telecom station and Thomas Cook.

A good 10-minute rickshaw ride west of here is the **Old Town,** where traditional *wadas,* or extended family houses surround the Swargate bus terminal, the **Raja Kelkar Museum, Phule Market,** and the ruined **Shaniwar Wada Palace.** Just across the Mutha River from here, the middle class neighborhood of Deccan Gymkhana stretches to Fergusson College Rd., where Pune's many students hobnob in an endless string of restaurants and cafes.

The **Osho Commune** occupies several blocks of the Koregaon Park suburb near Camp.

PRACTICAL INFORMATION

Tourist Office: MTDC, Central Building, I Block, Camp (tel. 668867, 669169). It's straight out of the main gate of the railway station, 10min. down on the left. Also at the **Railway Station** (tel. 625342), **Saras Hotel** (tel. 430499) and the **Airport.** The friendly staff members at these offices register genuine surprise when you ask for information: their job is to fob off copies of their colorful fire-starter-*cum*-map (Rs.5), book you in MTDC hotels, or slap you in one of their erratic tours of the city (theoretically daily at 8am or 2pm, Rs.40) or of Mahabaleshwar (daily in season, 7:30am-10pm, Rs.150). Open Mon.-Fri. 10am-6pm, Sat. 10am-2pm.

Budget Travel: For Airlines try **Apple Travels,** Amir Hotel, Connaught Rd., Camp (tel. 628185). Right where Sassoon and Connaught Rd. meet. Open Mon.-Sat. 9:30am-6:30pm. For buses, **Bright Travels** (tel. 629666), inside the gas station at 121A Connaught Rd., Camp, 1 block south of Sassoon on the left, offers private video coaches to Aurangabad (3 per day, 5hr., Rs.80), Hyderabad (2 per day, 10-12hr., Rs.250), Bangalore (3 per day, 18-20hr., Rs.250), Hubli (9:30pm, 10-12hr., Rs.180) and Goa (1 per day, 12hr., Rs.200). These prices may fall slightly in monsoon, but will rise during the peak season. Open daily 8am-midnight.

Currency Exchange: Central Bank of India, M.G. Rd., Camp (tel. 631413, -5). On the right-hand side, 5min. south of Moledina Rd. They advance up to US$500 on Visa or MasterCard. Open Mon.-Fri. 11am-1:30pm.

Thomas Cook: Ground floor, 13 Thacker House, 2418 General Thinimaya Rd., Camp (tel. 648188, 643026). About a 10-min. walk down M.G. Rd. from Moledina Rd., turn left down the sidewalk next to the villa labelled M. Nusserwanji. Cashes their own checks for free, and others for Rs.20 per transaction. Open Mon.-Sat. 10am-5pm for foreign exchange.

Telephones: STD/ISD booths are easy to come by on the main streets. There is a **Telephone Office** on East St., Camp, next door to Kayani Bakery, a 5-min. walk from Moledina Rd. Open Mon.-Fri. 10:15am-1:30pm and 2-5pm.

Airport: Pune Nagar Rd. (tel. 667538), 10km from the city center. An Ex-Servicemen's bus leaves every hr. from outside the GPO (Rs.20). **Indian Airlines,** Dr. Ambedkar Rd., near the Sangam Bridge, Camp (tel. 141, 142). **Skyline NEPC,** 17 M.C. Rd., Camp (tel. 637441, -2 or 633 125, -8). **Spar Aviation,** Vishnu Darshan 113213, Shivajinagar, Fergusson College Rd., Deccan Gymkhana (tel. 352478, 354481). To: Delhi (daily, 2hr., US$158); Bangalore (Mon.,Wed.,Fri., Sun., 2hr.,

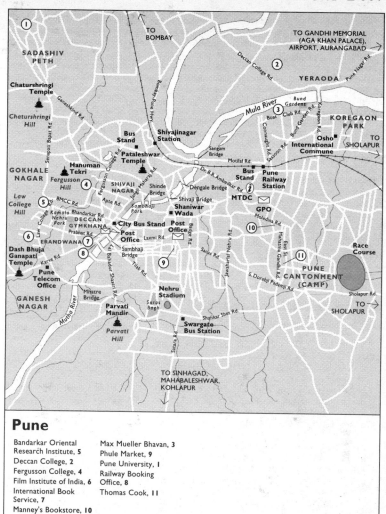

Pune

US$106); Bombay (daily, 30min., US$60); Goa (Tues., Thurs., Sat.-Sun off-season, daily in season, 1hr., US$85); Madras (daily, 3hr., US$132-140).

Trains: Railway Station, Sassoon Rd. The booking office lords it over the station complex. From the first floor of the sparkling new building on your left as you face the station. To: Bombay (Lonavla Station) (*Deccan Queen* 2124, 7:15am, 3hr., Rs.62 sleeper/159 chair car; *Indrayani Exp.* 1022, 6:30pm Rs.18/62); Miraj (for Goa) (*Sahyadri Exp.* 7303, 7:45pm, *Mahalaxmi Exp.* 1101, 1:20am, *Koyana Exp.* 7307, 1:50pm, Rs.82/383); Bangalore (*Udyar Exp.* 6259, 12:22pm, Rs.214/942); Hyderabad (*Hyderabad Exp.* 7031, 5:15pm, Rs.147/654); Aurangabad (passenger train 1321, 10hr.—the bus is a much better bet).

Buses: Pune has 3 main state stations as well as many private carriers. The most convenient station for tourists is the one right next to the railway station. Deluxe buses to Bombay depart from the counter around the corner to the right inside the building. To: Bombay (deluxe buses: every 30min., 5:30am-2am, 2hr. to Lonavla, 4hr. to

Dadar, Rs.50/80; ordinary buses: every hr., 5am-10pm, Rs.20); Mahabaleshwar (4 per day, 6-10am, 4hr., Rs.40); Panjim (Goa) (4:30am and 7pm, counter 4, 12hr., Rs.170). For Aurangabad, head to Shivajinagar Station in Deccan Gymkhana (10 per day, 6hr., Rs.100).

Local Transportation: The conversion rate for **auto-rickshaws** is roughly 3 times the meter reading; ask to see a chart. From the railway station, local **bus #4** goes to Deccan Gymkhana, while **#5, #6,** and **#31** go south towards Swargate bus station and the old town.

English Bookstore: Manney's Bookstore, 7 Moledina Rd., Clover Centre, Camp (tel. 631638). English books galore. Open Mon.-Sat. 9am-1pm and 4-8pm.

Pharmacy/Hospital: Pune Medical Foundation, Ruby Hall Clinic, Pound Garden Rd., Camp (tel. 623391). From Sassoon Rd., turn left on Connaught Rd., cross the railroad tracks and turn right—the clinic is on the left. The pharmacy here is open 24hr.

Police: Connaught Rd., Camp (tel. 100). Next door to the GPO. Open 24hr.

Post Office: Connaught Rd., Camp. A 5-min. walk away from the railroad lines (south) from the intersection with Sassoon Rd. On the right, in a Victorian domed stone building. *Poste Restante* at counter 2. Open Mon.-Sat. 10am-4pm. Stamps open Mon.-Sat. 10am-6pm.

Telephone Code: 0212.

ACCOMMODATIONS

National Hotel, 14 Sassoon Rd., Camp (tel. 625054). Just opposite the railway station. The friendly Baha'i management has kept up this old *wada* beautifully. The vast verandahs look out on small patches of well-tended garden; the din of the station somehow disappears. Basic singles are cramped and bathless, but deluxe singles (with high ceilings and attached bathrooms) are a better value. Check-out 24hr. Basic singles Rs.100. Deluxe singles Rs.200 in house, Rs.170 in cottage behind house. Doubles Rs.270, Rs.220 in cottage.

Green Hotel, 16 Wilson Garden, Camp (tel. 625229). To get to any of the Wilson Garden Hotels, take the small lane to the left of the National Hotel and turn right at the corner. This sensational Art Deco building, complete with stained glass, wood finish, wrought iron, and old furniture makes the Green Pune's most characterful budget dive. Singles Rs.125. Doubles Rs.175, with shower Rs.200, with full bath Rs.225. Triples and quads available.

Central Lodge, Wilson Garden, Camp. The mattresses here could be improved, but the common bathrooms (no showers, squat toilets) glisten—and it's cheap. Dorm beds Rs.40. Doubles Rs.100. Triples Rs.120. Quads Rs.160.

Ritz Hotel, 6 Connaught Rd., Camp (tel. 622995). Diagonally opposite the GPO. Resist the temptation to quip "By thy long grey beard and glistening eye, hast thou a room for me" to the gentleman at the first floor reception. But avail yourself of the spacious, spartan rooms (with bath and antechamber attached) in this run-down old villa. Check-out noon. Rs.95 per person.

Hotel Milan, 19 Wilson Garden, Camp (tel. 622024). One of the cheaper places to offer amenities like TVs and telephones—but those frills don't defuse some basic shortcomings like stained linen, dim rooms, and partitions between bedroom and bathroom that don't reach the ceiling. Still a good deal if you can't live without Wimbledon or the Simpsons. Singles Rs.250. Doubles Rs.275.

Hotel Alankar, 14 Wilson Circle, Camp (tel. 620484). A frieze of female musicians enlivens the otherwise simple, bright rooms. The shower nozzles are at war with the piping, resulting (in a Zen kind of way) in both more and less shower than you expected. Osho probably bathed here. Check-out 24hr. Singles Rs.200. Doubles Rs.250.

FOOD

Lieutenant Colonel Tarapore Marg, which crosses Connaught Rd. a block before Moledina Rd., serves as a huge open air café in the afternoons and evenings. Countless drink and *chat* stalls lure revelers into streetside seats to gossip and people-watch.

Coffee House, 2 Moledina Rd., Camp. A trendy, 2-tier, air-conditioned hang-out for Chinese and Indian dishes. Their mushroom fried rice packs a fungal punch—so many 'shrooms in one dish (Rs.24). Not to be confused with the Indian Coffee House chain, this place is one of a kind. Open daily 10am-10pm.

Touché the Sizzler: The Place, 7 Moledina Rd., Camp (tel. 634632). Another trendy, 2-tier (a Pune theme) air-conditioned hotspot, this place packs in Pune's yuppies nightly. While waiting for your order, you can muse on just what the restaurant's name means, and on just why anybody would want to eat a sizzler (an Rs.75-85 alarmingly flavored Mexican sausage concoction) when there are perfectly silent Mughlai and tandoori dishes around (Rs.70-100). The cold beer fizzes quietly (Rs.60). Open daily 11am-3:30pm and 7-11pm.

The German Bakery, North Koregaon Park Rd. (tel. 622994). From the ashram, walk north (to the right from the Gateless Gate) to the end of the road and turn left; it's on the right. Homesick Sannyasins spill crumbs from Gouda or Feta rolls (Rs.16), plum crumble (Rs.20), or cinnamon rolls (Rs.12) on their red robes. More upbeat devotees pick up their co-religionists with a cappuccino (Rs.14) and some fresh mango nut cake (Rs.18), secure in the knowledge that Osho has certified them HIV-free. Open daily 7am-11:30pm.

Shabree, Hotel Parichay, Fergusson College Rd. (tel. 321551, -4). At the corner of Shola Rd., opposite Deendayal Hospital. The majestically uniformed waiters serve up frabjous, unlimited Maharashtrian *thali.* As authentic as the soil on which the restaurant stands, the food is unrecognizable and unbelievable—and underpriced at Rs.40. Open daily 11am-3pm and 7-11pm.

Sagar Restaurant, Hotel Dreamland, Sassoon Rd. (tel. 626452). Near the corner of Connaught Rd. This place offers the staple of South Indian snacks (paper *masala dosa* Rs.14, *upma* Rs.7) as well as a few western breakfast items (omelette Rs.12, juices Rs.17-20). The huge room and family area also fills with office workers at lunch. Veg. dishes like *tikka masala* and vegetable *masala* Rs.27-30. Open daily 7:30am-11pm.

SIGHTS

Osho Commune International, 17 Koregaon Park, Camp (tel. 628561). From the station, cough up for a rickshaw or face a 30-minute walk down Sassoon Rd. to Koregaon Rd., then left over the railroad tracks. Double back on your right to the road the runs parallel to the tracks, and take the first left. The commune is the huge complex on the right. From the moment you pass through the Gateless Gate (marked by a huge wooden barricade—but it's all in the mind) you enter the wacky world of Osho, where things are not what they seem, unless they seem HIV-negative. *Sannyasins,* or followers of Osho, gather from all over the world to indulge in their deceased leader's penchant for puns and melodramatic clothing. They play "table tennis" at the "Club Med-itation," lend their energy to the buddhafield, and test themselves for HIV, amid black-painted pyramids and peacocks. Flowing red, white, and black robes and special courses in "multiversity" help the acolytes look deep within themselves before heading to the jacuzzi or the Zorba the Buddha community kitchen. Anyone can drink in all this wisdom during the two daily guided tours (10:30am and 2:30pm, 1hr., Rs.10), although it's a good idea to purchase tickets in advance. (Visitor's center open daily 9:30am-12:30pm and 1:30-4pm.) A longer stay requires an HIV test (Rs.125), two passport photographs, various colored robes and Rs.40 per day to use the facilities. Apart from six daily meditations, all courses, food, and other services cost extra. Consult the welcome center (open daily 9am-1pm and 2-3:30pm) for further details.

ENTERTAINMENT

One of the few disco/pubs around to cater to Bombay wanna-bes is the **Black Cadillac,** Grafikon Arcade, Bund Garden Rd., Camp (tel. 626500). In the shopping center, opposite the Ruby Hall clinic, round the back on the right side. Open daily 5pm-midnight. **Empire and West End Cinemas** in Camp often show pulpy English-language films. The **Film Institute of India,** on Law College Rd., offers more substantial movies, but in theory you have to be a member. The **Nehru Memorial Hall,** Camp, and the **Bal Gandharva Theater,** Jangli Maharaj Rd., stage performances of Indian drama, music and dance. For more detailed **listings** and schedules, see the "Pune Plus" in the *Times of India.*

■ Aurangabad (Sambhajinagar)

City life in Aurangabad, on the desiccated Deccan plateau, looks as dry as the climate. But in addition to the foreign tourists on their way to the caves at Ajanta and Ellora, tumultuous Hindu Nationalist politics are stirring the dusty streets. Far-right Shiv Sena city councilors, meeting in the shadow of the Deccan's only Mughal monuments, recently voted to rename the capital of the ardent Muslim emperor Aurangzeb in honor of a Hindu Maratha hero, Sambhaji. But the city's Muslim flavor endures amid the tourist boom and the economic development typical of Bombay's hinterland.

ORIENTATION

Tourist facilities tend to cling to **Station Road,** most of which runs north from the railway station. A splinter road claiming the same name, however, runs northwest to **Kranti Chowk,** home to the State Bank of India, past several hotels and restaurants. From Kranti Chowk, **Jalna Road** runs east to airline offices and the airport, while **Dr. Rajendra Prasad Marg** cuts back to Station Rd. W. North of this intersection, Station Rd. becomes **Dr. Ambedkar Marg** just before passing the bus stand, the turn off for Par Chikki on the left and the GPO on the right on its way to the north end of town near the Bibi-Ka-Maqbara and the Aurangabad Caves.

PRACTICAL INFORMATION

Tourist Office: Government of India Tourist Office, Krishna Vilas, Station Rd. (tel. 331217). On the right-hand side of the main (western) branch of Station Rd., about 250m from the eponymous station. Unusually helpful office has city maps, brochures, and general information. Offers daily tours of Ajanta, Ellora, Daulatabad, and Aurangabad. Open Mon.-Fri. 8:30am-6pm, Sat. 8:30am-1:30pm. **MTDC,** MTDC Holiday Resort, Station Rd. E. (tel. 331198). Only offers tours of Ajanta, Ellora, Daulatabad, and Aurangabad. Open daily 7am-9pm. **MSRTC** also offers daily tours to Ellora, Daulatabad, and Aurangabad (8am-5:30pm, Rs.55), and Ajanta (8am-6pm, Rs.105), including guide fees but not entrance tickets.

Budget Travel: Classic Travel, MTDC Holiday Resort, Station Rd. (tel. 335598, 337788). Inside the lobby near reception. Can arrange bus, train, and air travel. Open daily 7am-9pm.

Currency Exchange: State Bank of India, Dr. Rajendra Prasad Marg, Kranti Chowk. On the left, right on the square. Foreign exchange upstairs to the right. Open Mon.-Fri. 10:30am-2:30pm, Sat. 10:30am-12:30pm.

Airport: Located at Chikal Jhana, Jalna Rd. (P. Nehru Marg), 8km from city center. Buses run to and from the railway station (ask for Chikal Jhana, Rs.2). **Indian Airlines** (tel. 485421, 482421), next door to Rama International Hotel, Jalna Rd. Open daily 10am-1:15pm and 2-5pm. To: Bombay (1-2 per day, 1hr., US$51); Delhi (Mon., Tues., Thurs., Sat. 1 per day, 3½hr., US$127); Udaipur (Mon., Tues., Thurs., Sat. 1 per day, 1hr., US$84); and Jaipur (Mon., Tues., Thurs., Sat., 2½hr., US$103).

Trains: Train station, Station Rd. (tel. 331015). Daily service to Bombay (express 7618, 3:10pm, express 1004, 9:05pm, 10hr., Rs.497-119) and Pune (passenger 1322, 7:45am, 9hr.). Currently on Monday, but perhaps more frequently in the future, express 7612 serves Bhopal, Agra, and Delhi without a change (12:50pm, Bhopal Rs.163/435, Agra Rs.230/1032, Delhi Rs.250/1126 for 2nd/1st class).

Buses: Bus station, Dr. Ambedkar Marg. (tel. 331217). About 2km north of the railway station along the continuation of Station Rd. W. Daily service to Bombay (8am, Rs.156), Pune (5:30am, 11:45pm, Rs.74), Jalgaon (10 per day, 7am-9pm, Rs.44). Frequent local buses ply to Daulatabad (Rs.4), Ellora (Rs.8), and Ajanta (Rs.48).

Hospital: Kamalnayar Bajaj Hospital, near Kranti Chowk (tel. 331448, 334447), has a **24-hr. Pharmacy.**
Police: Kranti Chowk (tel. 331771).
Post Office: GPO, Juna Bazaar Chowk, Bazaar District. *Poste Restante* at counter #1. Open Mon.-Sat. 10am-5pm. **Postal Code:** 431001.
Telephone Code: 0240

ACCOMMODATIONS

Hotel Great Punjab, Station Rd. E. (tel. 336482-3). On the left, 100m from the station gates. Stained walls and a susceptibility to mosquito swarms, but good-value rooms include satellite TV, balconies, squat toilets, and even soap, towels, and a daily paper. Singles Rs.200, with A/C Rs.325. Doubles Rs.225, with A/C Rs.375.

Hotel Natraj, Station Rd. W, 100m north of the station on the right. The two Sharma brothers from Gujarat have run this place since 1938. The responsibility has bent their frames double over the years, but left their spirits, their tea-making skills, and their quiet, lime-green, single-story hotel intact. In season: singles Rs.90. Doubles Rs.100. Triples Rs.120. Off-season: singles Rs.70. Doubles Rs.80. Triples Rs.100.

Youth Hostel, Station Rd. W., 1km from the station, just before the intersection with Dr. Rajendra Prasad Marg, on the right (tel. 334892). This spotless, gender-segregated student hostel entices tourists with its cheap, mosquito-netted dorm beds, its bargain cafeteria (breakfast Rs.9, lunch and dinner Rs.15), and its rubbish bin in the shape of a penguin. Check-out 9am. Curfew 10pm. Dorm beds Rs.22, nonmembers Rs.42.

Hotel Panchavati, Station Rd., Padampura (tel. 28755, 25469), 50m down a lane to the right off Station Rd., 1km north of the station, just before the intersection with Dr. Rajendra Prasad Rd. The 70s ceiling in the lobby contributes to the seedy atmosphere near the bar and restaurant downstairs. Rooms make up in value what they lake in ambience. Hot water 6-9am. Balconied singles with bath Rs.75. Doubles Rs.115. Triples Rs.150.

Hotel Tourist's Home, Station Rd. W (tel. 337212). On the right, 150m north of the railway station. Spartan rooms set around a sun-baked courtyard, with a new building added at the back. Set-back from the road and peaceful. Singles 70. Doubles 120.

Hotel Ashiyana, Bansilal Nagar, Station Rd. W (tel. 29322). Down a lane to the right off Station Rd., 250m north of the station. This sparkling new, modern building includes rooms with hot pink seat toilets, TVs, and charming little conversation nooks. Doubles Rs.150.

FOOD

A company called Foodwala's has a lock on the restaurants in Aurangabad, outside the hotels. To escape their monopoly, try one of the ever-popular garden restaurants or buy snacks from the shops and street vendors along Station Rd. E.

Foodwala's Bhoj, Dr. Ambedkar Rd., (tel. 332672). In a big building 200m south of the bus stand, 1 floor up. Classy touches like painted fan blades, a small rock fountain centerpiece and lime cordial to sweeten your fresh lime soda mark this pure vegetarian joint as a haven for Aurangabad's elite. *Thalis* Rs.35, *dosas,* and *utthapams* Rs.9-14. Open daily 11am-3pm and 7-11pm.

Tandoor Restaurant, Shyam Chambers, Barsilal Nagar, Station Rd. E. (tel. 28482). The curious kitsch Egyptian theme decor does not detract from the quality of classic Mughlai (Rs.45) or butter chicken (Rs.88). Also Chinese (Rs.44-55). Part of the Foodwala's Empire. Open daily 11am-4pm and 6:30-11:30pm.

Foodlovers Restaurant, Station Rd. E. On the right, 250m from the station. This cavernous, dirt-floored, open-air thatched hall forms the most central proof of Aurangabad's garden restaurant fetish. The mammoth menu (353 items) features a table of contents to help the bleary-eyed eater navigate among chicken dishes (Rs.65 for a half), Chinese (Rs.35-50), *matar* (Rs.35-40), and vegetarian numbers

(Rs.22-40). Beer comes in a teapot, so that other diners can pretend they don't know the restaurant is a den of vice. Open daily 11am-midnight.

Hotel Panchavati Restaurant, Hotel Panchavati, Station Rd. W. (tel. 28755). This passable cheapie doubles as a watering hole, giving the canteen-like atmosphere of benches and bare walls an extra edge. *Dosas* Rs.8, *utthapams* Rs.7, veg. dishes Rs.14-30. Beer Rs.37-45. Open daily 10am-9pm.

Patang Restaurant, Hotel Printravel, Station Rd. W. (tel. 29707, 29407). On the right, just after the intersection with Dr. Rajendra Prasad Rd., 1km north of the railway station. The overhead expended on features like the groovy circular doorway, the pink highlights in the alcoves, and the avant-guarde chairs has pushed up the prices a little. *Dosas* Rs.10-30, *utthapams* Rs.12-20, *thalis* Rs.33-45. Beers Rs.42-45. Open daily 7am-10:45pm.

SIGHTS

Most people treat Aurangabad as a dormitory town for the tourist hubs at Ajanta and Ellora. But it does offer some sights of its own, including some cave temples (good preparation for Ajanta and Ellora) and the Deccan's only Mughal mausoleum.

The **Bibi-Ka-Maqbara** suffers much ridicule as an inferior Taj Mahal knock-off. But Aurangzeb's milk-white monument to his wife, Begum Rabi'a Durani, deserves recognition as an important addition to the tradition of Mughal mausolea, albeit one overshadowed by its northern rival. The relatively small tomb could never have challenged the Taj even if cash shortages had not forced ungainly corner-cutting, such as the abandonment of marble for plaster after the first meter. But the building remains an ingenious compression and simplification of the Taj's plan, complete with elegant floral reliefs and ornate *jali* screens. (Open daily dawn-dusk; admission Rs.0.50.)

In the hills behind the tomb, the **Aurangabad Caves** get forgotten in the excitement about their counterparts at Ellora and Ajanta. But they remain a wonderful introduction to the promise of breathtaking sculpture all along the Maharashtrian cave trail. Split into western and eastern sections, these important examples of Buddhist art and architecture were excavated by two great dynasties during the 6th century. To get there, take a 20-min. rickshaw ride into the hills north of town or be prepared for a steep uphill bike ride. Getting a rickshaw shouldn't be too hard, but agree on a time allowance and pay upon return to the town to ensure that your rickshaw-*wallah* sticks around. Bicycles can be rented at the railway station. A wide dirt road leads out of the north side of town, right past the pearl dome and towering minarets of Bibi-Ka-Maqbara into the hills. The western caves, numbers 1 through 5, are off the dirt road atop a treacherous climb on winding stone steps. The third and most beautiful cave, supported and guarded by several wide, beautifully carved, pillars, is a *vihara,* or residence hall for the wandering Buddhist *bikshus* (monks) of the time, who gathered in monastic communities caves like these around the state. Some fragments of the original paintings depict stories from the *Jataka,* stories about the Buddha's previous incarnations upon earth. The fourth cave is a *chaitya* hall, one used for congregation and prayer, resonating with even ordinary speech to fill the space with rhythmic chant-like sound. The eastern caves, numbers 6 through 9, lie up at the end of the dirt road about 1km farther, affording an incredible view of the surrounding landscape and the silhouette of Bibi-Ka-Maqbara against the city in the distance. The seventh cave greets with lotus framed *apsaras* (celestial dancers) in stony celebration at the entrance to the crypt. The shadowed Buddha sits peacefully within the sanctuary surrounded by the frozen faces of intent listeners at his mammoth feet. Try the caves early in the morning when not many tourists are there. Beware of packs of slumbering bats who find the caves as wonderfully isolated and peaceful as tourists do. Bring a flashlight as the caves are not artificially lit and lie partly in darkness even at midday.

■ Near Aurangabad: Khaildabad and Daulatabad

On the road between Aurangabad and Ellora, buses pass through several important later sights. The Emperor Aurangzeb finally found rest from the struggle to subjugate

Maharashtra in **Khaildabad** or Rauza, a small, strongly Muslim town just over the ridge from Ellora. In a departure from the grandiose mausolea which housed all his Mughal forebears, Aurangzeb chose a modest grave funded by the receipts from his own copying of the Qur'an. The shrines of various Sufi saints nearby far outshadow it.

Further along the road, just 13km from Aurangabad, **Daulatabad** fortress crowns a tall hill. A series of sadistic despots have endowed this formidable fortress with a colorful history. In the 14th century, the Sultan of Delhi decided it was just the spot for a capital city. Rather than leave the development of a thriving city to chance, Muhammad Tughluq hit on the cunning plan of marching the whole population of Delhi 1000km across India to people his new metropolis. Needless to say, the small proportion of the deportees who did not die on the way greeted life in the Deccan with a sullen resentment unconducive to prosperity. The Sultan had to abandon his brainchild after only 17 years and march the few survivors back to Delhi. Later, Aurangzeb had the last ruler of Golconda imprisoned here 13 years before torturing him to death.

Through the first gates, spiked as usual to prevent elephant attacks, a huge, ruined city awaits the visitor. The Chand Minar victory tower, built in 1435, rises over a mosque cobbled together with columns pillaged from temples and a water tank from Daulatabad's advanced hydraulic system. Beyond, a series of steps lead up the hill past ruined palaces to the Chini Mahal, with its trace blue tiles, where the unfortunate Qutb Shahi King Abdul Hassan Tara Shah met his end. On top of the small tower next door, a cannon called Qila Shikan (Fort Breaker) points out threateningly at the horizon. From here, the defenses begin in earnest, with the crossing of the moat to enter the sheer-walled citadel. A flashlight will guide you through the pitch black maze of passages excavated from the inside of the hill. Endless stairs lead ever upwards, re-emerging into daylight and a further series of palaces coating the slope to its summit. From the top, magnificent views reveal Aurangabad and the surrounding country, through the Deccani dust. (Open daily dawn-dusk. Free.)

■ Ellora

Along with the caves at Ajanta, Ellora's Buddhist, Hindu, and Jain rock-cut temples constitute the pinnacle of an art form and the most important tourist attraction in Maharashtra. Indeed, the finest cave temples here barely resemble caves at all: the designs became so elaborate during the site's development that craftsmen ended up chiselling free-standing buildings from the cliff-face. Visitors must constantly remind themselves that these astonishing monuments are not architecture, but rather life-size sculptures masquerading as normal structures.

A mere 29km from Aurangabad (frequent buses via Daulatabad, 6am-6pm, 1hr., Rs.8), Ellora usually gets relegated to daytrip status. The main road, which runs west from the bus stand by the site entrance, conceals one budget hotel amid the trinket and cold drink stands 250m down on the right. Hard core ruin-lovers can stay at **Hotel Natraj** (tel. (02437) 41043) for Rs.100 for singles, Rs.150 for doubles with baths. Dorm beds in season cost Rs.50 in an echoing hall. Short of sodas and unsanitary *pakoras* from the street stands, hungry sightseers are caught between **Foodwala's Ellora Restaurant** by the caves (tel. 41041; *samosa* Rs.11, main dishes Rs.30-50; open daily 8am-6pm), and **MTDC's Hotel Kailas Restaurant** 100m down the road on the right (tel. 41043; breakfast Rs.65, main dishes Rs.40-70; open daily 7am-9:30pm). Many hotels and restaurants in Aurangabad offer packed lunches.

Of the 32 caves, numbers 1 through 16 give the clearest impression of Ellora's development over the centuries, culminating in the masterpiece of the **Kailas Temple** (number 16). Starting at the southernmost cave (left as you face the caves, number 1 according to ASI's reckoning) allows for a roughly chronological sequence. Caves 1-12 date from Buddhist India's twilight in the 6th to 8th centuries. The caves in this group grow increasingly elaborate and ornate in an attempt to stave off the popular revival of Hinduism evidenced by the neighboring Shiva temples whose construction began in the 7th century. Of the first nine **vihara** (monastery caves), with individual cells and statues of the Buddha and *bodhisattvas,* **Cave 5** stands out. The flat, low ridges in the floor probably served as benches to make a dining hall for the community. The stern Vajrapani (the *bodhisattva* who holds a thunderbolt) and the more forgiving Padmapani (flower-power in the form of a lotus-toting *bodhisattva*) presided over the meals from either side of the central shrine.

Cave 10, Ellora's only *chaitya* hall, echoes earlier structures at Ajanta, Karla, and elsewhere in the state. Octagonal pillars flank the walls and create an ambulatory around the *stupa,* while a window and balcony above provide illumination and a vantage from which to appreciate it. The *trompe l'oeil* beams in the ceiling imitate wooden rafters from Karla and presumably also earlier free-standing halls.

The last Buddhist gasp at Ellora, **Cave 12,** contains some beautiful sculpture on the third level. *Bodhisattvas* line the side walls, while the seven previous incarnations of the Buddha flank the main shrine. A different type of tree shades each Buddha, on the left, identifying them iconographically according to a symbology developed at Sanchi in Madhya Pradesh and other early Buddhist monuments. Traces of paint in the sanctum and chamber hint at the once bright decoration of the caves.

Caves 13-29 date from Ellora's Hindu era, which lasted late into the 9th century. These more elaborate, densely sculptured temples share many motifs: Shiva appears most often on Mount Kailasa playing dice with his wife Parvati while the demon tries frantically but futilely to dislodge him; at other times he dances with both legs bent as Nataraja, whose gyrations shook the world into being and will one day destroy it. Vishnu crops up as Narasimha, the man-lion, Varaha, the boar, and most commonly as a sleeper in the coils of a serpent, floating on the cosmic sea. From his navel grows a lotus, out of which Brahma emerges to create the world. The image of the Seven Mothers, buxom goddesses with children, flanked by Kala and Kali, emaciated momento mori, also features regularly. All of these sculptures appear in **Caves 14 and 15.** The latter also houses a depiction of Shiva emerging from a *linga,* while Brahma and Vishnu kneel before him—testimony to the supremacy of Shiva-worship among Ellora's patrons.

Ellora's Hindu epoch, and Maharashtrian rock-cut temples in general, reach their apogee in **Cave 16,** the **Kailash Temple.** This massive 8th- and 9th-century building was excavated from the top down by several generations of impeccably skilled craftsmen. The sheer scale of this vast replica of Shiva's home in the Himalayas begs belief even before you consider the technical challenge of slicing it from solid rock from the elegant *shikhara* on down. Traces of plaster and paint bear witness to further decorative complexity on top of the elaborate sculpture and architecture. (Open daily 6am-6pm. Admission Rs.50.)

The paved road down by Foodwala's restaurant leads to the remaining caves—don't let the stairs up to the left fool you. **Cave 21** repeats the iconographic scheme of Cave 14, while **Cave 29** contains perhaps the only moonie protected under UNESCO world heritage provisions in another panel of Shiva ignoring Ravana's ruckus.

Caves 30-34 date from Ellora's third and final phase of construction under Jain patrons during the 9th and 10th centuries. **Cave 32** depicts the *tirthankara* Gomatesvara concentrating so hard on his meditation that he has not noticed the vines growing on his limbs or the animals surrounding him.

■ Ajanta

Ajanta began life as remote as it remains today, as a Buddhist retreat in the 2nd century BC. The builders chose a sheer cliff-face above a horseshoe shaped valley in the Waghora River from which to excavate contemplative visions in painting and sculpture. During the 7th century AD, the monks abandoned their 29 *chaityas* and *viharas* (and the astonishingly life-like art with which they had filled them) to an even greater obscurity. Only the local tribespeople knew of the masterpieces overrun by tigers and creepers until one of those endless redcoated hunting parties which infested the forests of imperial India spied Cave 10 from the opposite ridge in 1819.

Would-be visitors no longer have to beat back the brush but they do have to suffer through long, hot, jolting **bus** rides to get here. Most visit en route between Aurangabad (108km south) and Jalgaon (58km north) on the main **railway** line. MSRTC runs a daily **tour** to Ajanta from Aurangabad at 8am for Rs.107 including guides and roundtrip transport. Otherwise, many **buses** stop at Ajanta between Jalgaon and Aurangabad, starting early in the morning and ending at 5:30pm in Aurangabad and 6:30pm in Jalgaon. You can come from one town, leave your bags at the left **luggage** at the entrance to the caves (Rs.1.50) while sight-seeing and proceed to the next in the evening. **Telephone Code:** 02438.

The omnipresent Foodwala's runs the **hotel** and **restaurant** at the caves themselves (tel. 4226). Their rooms are clean but spare with balconies and common bathrooms. Singles Rs.100. Doubles Rs.150. Their menu repeats the Ellora formula: a limited *thali* of two vegetables, *dal, papad, chapatis,* and rice retails at Rs.32 while chicken dishes will set you back Rs.50. (Open daily 8am-5:30pm.) The cold drink stands furnish the only other refreshment while the **Forest Guest House** 500m up the road offers cluttered, air-cooled rooms with a wicker-furnished and flowerful verandah for those who book in advance at the Divisional Forest Officer, Opp. Government., Engineering College, Osmanpura, Aurangabad (tel. (0240) 334701). Rs.15 per person.

The **caves** are located up the steps behind the drinks stands and over the rise. The guided tours, although interesting, rely primarily on gimmicks: "See the expression of the Buddha change when I move the light" and "see the earliest known bangs in hairdo history." On the other hand, they do guarantee decent lighting while you visit. **Cave 1,** which dates from the 5th century AD, contains some of Ajanta's most naturalistic paintings. As with all of Ajanta's art, the life-like jewelry, clothing, and domestic life materials matter more than the story here. On the left-hand wall, a king, converted to Buddhism, abandons earthly pleasures for a life of meditation. Just to the left of the rear shrine, a painting depicts the elegant Padmapani (the lotus-holding *bodhisattva*), while Vajrapani stands sentry to his right with his thunderbolt. On several capitals on the right-hand side of the hall, four deer sharing a single head gaze out contentedly at the tourists. Above them on the ceiling, the pink elephant which has become the emblem of the Indian Tourism Development Corporation romps merrily above his charges.

In **Cave 2,** paintings to the left show the dream of a six-tusked elephant which foretold the Buddha's conception, and his miraculous birth directly into the arms of his mother. In the right-hand rear corner, in a sculptural frieze of a classroom near the floor, an ill behaved student pulls the hair of the girl in front. Above to the right, the demon Hariti dances furiously while on the left his teachings have lulled a princess into a peaceful repose.

The *chaitya* hall in **Cave 9** dates from the Therevada era, during which the Buddha was not directly depicted. Instead, the *pipal*-shaped window in the façade signifies learning, while the huge *stupa* in the apse symbolizes the relics of the Buddha. The same goes for **Cave 10,** which dates from the 2nd century BC, although here millennia of sunlight and the scratchings of graffiti artists have obscured most of the symbolic paintings. In **Cave 16,** the most celebrated fresco shows yet another princess swooning in distress as her husband throws in the worldly towel. *Jataka* stories about the Buddha's earlier incarnations fill the walls of **Cave 17.** In the *vishavantara,* on the left-hand wall, a well-intentioned prince gives away his father's magic elephant, his cart and possessions, and even his wife and kids before ultimate social renunciation. On the opposite wall, confusing tales of seductive beauties and bloodthirsty demons revel in surprisingly accurate anatomical detail. The tour guides love to show off the 3-D effect created by shining their flashlights on the pearls of the princess in the upper-right-hand corner of the right wall.

The elaborate interior and exterior sculpture of **Cave 19** indicates the Buddhist response to the Hindu renaissance of the 6th century AD. Although a columned-*chaitya* hall, Cave 19 dates from the Mahayana period, during which depictions of the Buddha were permitted. The most splendid example of this freedom reclines along the left-hand wall of **Cave 26.** The sculpture shows Buddha on the verge of attaining *nirvana,* surrounded by disciples. (Open 9am-5:30pm; admission Rs.0.50, light fee Rs.5, video fee Rs.0.25.)

The path behind Cave 26 leads down the hill to a bridge. From here, intrepid visitors can climb to a **viewpoint** to relive the astonishment of the British in 1819. A second path along the river will guide the less historically minded to a waterfall and washing pool for villagers in the rainy season.

Goa

Visiting Goa, India's second-youngest state—certainly its most carefree corner—is much like crashing through the space-time continuum into an Indian-style Twilight Zone. As a Portuguese colony from 1510 until 1961, Goa spent much of the last five centuries isolated from the forces and trends that affected the rest of India, and this separateness shows. Relaxing in the shadow of Goa's tangled tropical overgrowth and its moss-covered Baroque church façades, it's easy to forget you're still in India and to imagine yourself in a palm-fringed, sun-baked Shangri-La. The quiet, gentle pace of Goa (stalled altogether in the early afternoon by the traditional siesta) attracts everyone from displaced hippies and surfers to India's elite jet set. Of course, it's not only Goa's cultural heritage or relaxed attitude that has given it such a reputation among travelers—it's the Arabian Sea, lapping at Goa's almost-unbroken 100km of beaches.

Recent statehood, conferred in 1987, belies a rich and flavorful history. In medieval times, Goa was under the rule of the Kadamba kings, who proudly claimed descent from a drop of Shiva's sweat. (They are remembered today in the decrepit vehicles of the government-run Kadamba Bus Company.) In the 15th century, Goa changed hands several times, finally ending up under Yusuf Adil Shah, the Muslim sultan of Bijapur. But in 1498, the Portuguese explorer Vasco da Gama landed on the coast of Kerala. Determined to dominate the Indian Ocean and its rich spice trade, Portugal was seeking a foothold on India's west coast. In 1510, the expeditionary Afonso de Albuquerque traipsed into Goa, massacring its Muslim residents and turning it into a Portuguese base. During the 16th century, Goa became a prosperous trading city, where Portuguese soldiers and adventurers mingled with the local population, many of whom converted to Catholicism and intermarried with Europeans. Goa was made capital of Portuguese lands in India (a loose collection of colonies on the east and west coasts which included Daman and Diu in Gujarat. Under the guidance of the Jesuits and the terror of the Inquisition, Goa also became a stronghold of Christianity in India. In 1556 the Jesuits installed in Goa the second printing press in the world outside of Europe. But by the end of the 16th century political domination by Spain and commercial competition from other European countries sent the Portuguese empire into a tailspin. Goa's fortunes fell along with it, and the next three centuries are remembered as a time of stagnation and decline. Treaties with Britain kept Goa from being absorbed into British India, and Portugal held on until 1961, when Indian troops forcibly annexed the territory. The first piece of Indian soil clutched by European colonizers was also the last to be let go.

According to some, the recent invasion of five-star tourists and hippies looking for paradise has made Goa a colony once again. But a visit to Goa need not be exploitative, and there's more to the state than its beaches and its Westernized beach culture. Goa's character and people reflect its intercultural history—you will be as likely to meet a Portuguese-speaking Roman Catholic dressed in jeans and a muscle shirt as a *lungi*-clad fisherman carrying his day's catch on his shoulder. About 40% of the state's inhabitants are Christian. Goa has one of India's highest literacy rates (over 75%), and one of India's highest income levels. Away from the beaches populated by

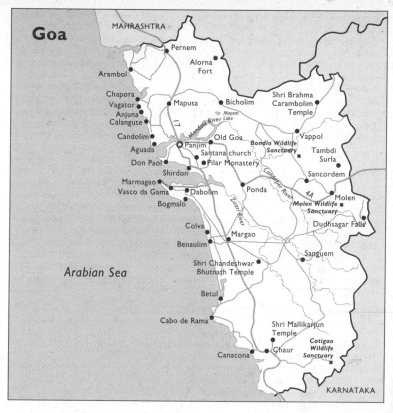

Goa

MAHRASHTRA

Pernem

Alorna
Fort

Arambol

Chapora

Vagator

Anjuna

Calangute

Candolim

Aguada

Don Paol

Mapusa · Bicholim

Shri Brahma
Carambolim
Temple

Mayem
River Lake

Old Goa

Panjim

Santana church

Pilar Monastery

Bondla Wildlife
Sanctuary

Vappol

Tambdi
Surla

Shirdon

Marmagao

Vasco da Gama · Dabolim

Bogmalo

Colva

Benaulim

Sancordem

Ponda

Molen Wildlife
Sanctuary

Molen

4A

Dudhsagar Falls

Margao

Sanguem

Arabian Sea

Shri Chandeshwar
Bhutnath Temple

Betul

Cabo de Rama

Shri Mallikarjun
Temple

Cotigao
Wildlife
Sanctuary

Canacona · Chaur

KARNATAKA

frolicking foreigners, Goa is patchworked by rice paddies, and it exports fruits, nuts, spices, iron ore, and fish.

Goa's party-packed beaches are hopping from early October to late March, with beach-fervor peaking in the weeks before and after Goa's psychedelic Christmas, when it may be difficult to find a place to stay. Things close down during the monsoon (June-Sept.), when Westerners move out and traditionally head for Manali. But the monsoon rains that cool Goa and fill its wells often cease for long stretches of sunny days. You almost can have Goa to yourself then, and at lower rates, although the choice of hotels and restaurants is limited.

GETTING THERE

Planes from all over India land frequently at **Dabolim Airport** near Vasco da Gama. There are direct flights to and from the U.K. and Germany, and flights to other locations all over India. To: Bangalore (Tues., Thurs., and Sat., 1hr., US$74); Bombay (5-6 per day, 1hr., US$59-76); Calicut (Mon. and Fri., 1hr. 15min., US$73); Cochin (1 per day, 1hr. 15min., US$90); Delhi (2-3 per day, 2½hr., US$179); Madras (Tues., Thurs., and Sat., 1½hr., US$104); Pune (Tues., Thurs., Sat., and Sun., 1hr., US$85).

Until the **Konkan Railway** is completed (see p. 620), there is no train service along the coast to Goa, although trains serve Goa from inland. Broad-gauge lines run from Bombay and Hubli to Margao. From Margao and to Vasco da Gama, the line is meter-gauge. A trip from Bombay to Margao along this route takes about 24 hours.

A unique way to reach Goa from Bombay is on one of Damania Shipping's **catamarans.** These boats, which don't look at all like romantic, lightweight, double-hulled

The Konkan Railway

Goa, as a Portuguese enclave, did not receive what is considered Britain's great gift to India: the railroad. After 35 years, the Indian government is finally working on a railroad for the Konkan coast, which would make it possible to travel by train directly from Bombay to Goa to Mangalore for the first time. Construction, however, has met many obstacles. Environmental degradation and land takings have met with bitter protests from Goans, who are quite active in protecting their natural environment. Expensive tunnels must be built; one collapsed in June 1996 killing a worker. Those in the know say that the railroad will not be completed until October 1997, although the government predicts it will be finished earlier.

sailing vessels, run from Bombay to Panjim and back Oct. 15-May 19. Prices are steep (economy class Rs.925, business class Rs.1100) but the service rocks the Arabian Sea—Bombay to Goa in seven hours. Catamarans leave Bombay at 7am and arrive in Panjim at 2pm; they leave Panjim at 3pm and arrive in Bombay at 10pm. During late December you'll have to reserve a seat at least two weeks in advance; at other times, 3-5 days is sufficient. Damania's office in Panjim is opposite the Hotel Mandovi on the Mandovi River (tel. (0832) 228711), open Mon.-Fri. 9am-5pm; Sun 10am-6pm. Damania's Bombay office is in Colaba (tel. (022) 610 2525).

For travelers on tight budgets, **buses** remain the best way to reach Goa from Bombay and from other cities. For more on bus travel, see the listings for Panjim, Mapusa, and other cities.

ORIENTATION AND TRANSPORT

Goa is roughly divided into two regions, North Goa and South Goa. The state capital, **Panjim**, is right in the middle, but is considered part of North Goa. The town of **Mapusa**, 11km north of Panjim along National Highway 17, is a smaller center for North Goa; **Margao**, 30km to the southwest of Panjim, is a hub for the south. Goa's train line from Karnataka passes through Margao on its way to **Vasco da Gama**, on the coast, where Goa's airport is located.

The beaches, also divided into northern and southern strips, are less frequented and less developed the farther you travel in either direction from Panjim, especially toward the south. Some say that one beach is pretty much like any other—they all have sand, they all have water, and they all have hippies. But in fact each has its own character. Some are strictly five-star resorts, while others cater to those with smaller wads of traveler's checks. The northern beaches begin on the north bank of the River Mandovi, across from Panjim, with the resort beaches around the hilltop ruins of **Fort Aguada**. From the ruined lookout turret, local fishermen pull in fish and frightful eels, which they drop, writhing, to the turret floor. Closest to the urban centers of Panjim and Mapusa, **Singuerim** and **Candolim** are popular with package tourists toting moneybags; the Taj Group runs a five-star complex at **Aguada** complete with its own beach. Tsunamis of hippies, soul-searchers, and surf-snorklers crashed onto the pure sandy stretches of **Calangute** in the 1960s. They soon expanded a kilometer or two up into nearby **Baga**, where a steep hill temporarily stopped the party from exploding right into **Anjuna**, now home to a crazy flea market and a hippie hip-hoppy rave scene. **Chapora** and **Vagator**, farther north, have houses available for long stays (commute from Baga and Calangute until you find one). A single, unnamed main road links all of the major beaches along the northern strip, breaking only once between Baga and Anjuna. The beach runs continuously from Aguada to Baga and the long trek can be made by foot. Continuing farther north, a ferry (for pedestrians, motorcycles, and taxis) connects **Siolem** to **Chopdem**. The as-yet-unspoiled beach realm of **Arambol** reigns here. Between the main beaches are kilometers of untouched and ignored beach.

Tourism and the Goan Environment

Goa's tourist boom has speckled the coast with huge resort hotels and smaller budget establishments, all of which consume their share of resources. Beaches not long ago imprinted only by the feet of fishermen as they pushed their boats out to sea (or as they were fished from the sea on days when the ocean was too rough) are now littered with Bisleri bottles, plastic bags, and lightbulbs. Fishermen still fish here, and people (including you, perhaps) still eat the fish they catch—only now, in addition to fish, the ocean is angrily coughing up tourist trash. Take the hint—pick up after yourself and others.

The salty Arabian Sea also deceives many travelers into thinking that Goa has plenty of water. While the monsoon brings veritable waterfalls from the sky, the rest of the year Goa is in fact very dry. The influx of travelers and tourists sucks up Goa's freshwater resources, so much so that the wells of villagers run dry or are contaminated by salty seawater pulled inland by the lowered water table. Upmarket hotels deserve most of the blame for water wastage, drilling their own wells and filling Olympic-sized swimming pools when the Arabian Sea is only a few meters away. But budget travelers also have an impact, and should try to soften it. To make that small difference, turn off the shower while soaping and scrubbing, or take a bucket bath. Bring your clothes to a *dhobi* instead of washing them in your room. Remember that the water supply to locals is often limited to only a few hours per day.

An extended stay in Goa is the best way to learn about the state's environment and what can be done for it—and many travelers enjoy prolonged stays in Goa anyway, bathed by sun, surf, coconut concoctions, and infectious mellowness. If you are considering a long stay, volunteering for any of Goa's numerous Non-Governmental Organizations (NGOs) can get you involved intimately on a local level and allow you to give back to the community. ECOFORUM in Mapusa publishes a book, *Fish Curry & Rice* (Rs.200), listing Goa's activist groups and describing the environmental situation. For more information, see **Environmentally Responsible Tourism,** p. 66.

Most beaches in South Goa are either highly developed resorts or not-at-all-developed sanctuaries of sand, stretching all the way to the border of Karnartaka and farther on south. **Margao** serves as the transportation hub of the area. The developed beaches (meaning they have some form of accommodations and restaurants) begin with the resorts of **Majorda.** Slightly south are **Colva** and **Benaulim,** reached easily from Margao. Although the travelers' scenes rages mostly in the north (at Calangute, Baga, and Anjuna), Colva and Benaulim also get a piece of the action. South of Benaulim is a 10km stretch of luxury resort beach known as **Varca** and **Cavelossim.** Further south from Colva and Benaulim is beautiful **Palolem.**

Buses to and from major cities arrive and depart about once a day from Panjim, Margao, and several other towns. Local buses grind dependably, frequently, and cheaply around Goa—but try to get on an express bus or you will halt in every village and paddy as locals hop on and off. Distances can be deceptive in Goa: traveling 30km on roads traveled also by frolicking pigs, then crossing a river by ferry, can take hours. The narrow roads braid and twist through rice paddies, buses nudge past each other shoulder to shoulder, weaving around whizzing motorbikes, pedaling bicyclists, and pedestrians. **"Tourist Vehicles"** (expensive white vans) and **taxis** are available, as are **auto-rickshaws.** Taxis can be rented for a half-day (2-4 hr. and approx. 40km) for Rs.250-300, or a whole day (not to exceed 80km) for Rs.500-600. As always, haggling is necessary. Taxis will require return fare for return journeys, even if you're not on them. **Motorcycle rickshaws** or **"pilot taxis"** (painted yellow and black) are cheaper—a licensed driver escorts a tourist on the bike's back seat. The simplest and riskiest method employed by many visitors is renting automatic Honda Kinetic **motorcycles. Motorcycles are convenient and exciting but also dangerous,** and an Indian or international driver's license is officially required. (see p. 51). Goan police have been known to enjoy raiding unlicensed bikers in the cities (Panjim, Mapusa, Margao) although license enforcement on the northern beaches is notoriously lax.

NORTH GOA

■ Panjim (Panaji)

Mellow and small for a state capital, the city of Panjim is clustered on the south bank of the Mandovi River with its 100,000 inhabitants. Panjim's Portuguese history is displayed in the mansions along its narrow streets and in the names of the colonists' descendents: Angelo, Menezes, Anthony, Lisbon. Panjim effectively became the capital of Goa in 1759, when the viceroy moved from Old Goa to reside in Yusuf Adil Shah's old palace in Panjim. In 1843 Panjim formally became the capital, and it has grown ever since. Today Panjim is cosmopolitan enough to support several motorcycle dealerships, electrical appliance stores, and two United Colors of Benetton. The people are kind enough to guide visitors around deep puddles, and are happy to engage strangers in conversation, although for beach-minded travelers Panjim is mainly a place to pass through.

ORIENTATION

Situated on the south bank of the **Mandovi River** at its rushing rendezvous with the Arabian Sea, Panjim can be easily navigated on foot. The **Ourem River** joins the Mandovi at Panjim; on the east bank of the Ourem is the **Patto** area, enclosing the newly constructed **business district** and the chaotic **bus terminal**. The rest of Panjim is west of the Ourem, including the **Fountainhas** area, whose narrow streets are lined with 300-year-old Portuguese houses. **Emidio Gracia Rd.** leads west uphill from the Ourem to **Church Square**, dominated by the white facade of the **Immaculate Conception Church.** Here, the **Municipal Garden** stretches northward almost all the way to the Mandovi River and the **Secretariat.** Past the Secretariat runs **Dayanand Bandodkar Marg (Avenida Dom Joao Castro),** which follows the bank of the Mandovi River. **18th June Rd.,** with a panorama of hotels, eateries, and shops, leads southwest from Church Sq. The thumping, thriving **town market** is in the northeast part of the city.

PRACTICAL INFORMATION

Tourist Office: Government of India Tourist Office, Communidade Building, Church Sq. (tel. 43412). Disappointing brochure selection, but you can browse their booklets for hours just to stay in the air conditioning. The friendly information officer speaks English and Portuguese. Open Mon.-Fri. 9:30am-1pm and 2-6pm, Sat. 9:30am-1pm. **GTDC,** Patto Tourist Home, Dr. Alvares Cross Rd. (tel. 226515; fax 223926). Between the traffic bridge and the footbridge on the bank of the Ourem River. Helpful, jolly staff can arrange tours to North Goa, South Goa, Bondla Sanctuary, or even a "folk music and dancing cruise" on the Mandovi River at sundown. Pamphlets can be wrung from the woodwork with patient persistence. Open 24hr. **Karnataka Tourist Information Office,** Velho Bldg. (tel. 224110), on the east edge of the Municipal Gardens. Although the staff speaks little English, they can help organize a trip to Karnataka. Open Mon.-Sat. 10am-1:30pm and 2:15-5:15pm. Closed 2nd Sat. of the month.
Currency Exchange: State Bank of India, Dayanand Bandodkar Marg (tel. 42132) across from the Hotel Mandovi. Open for exchange only Mon.-Fri. 10am-2pm and 3-4pm, Sat. 10am-noon. **Thomas Cook** on Dayanand Bandodkar Marg exchanges cash or any brand of traveler's checks at better rates than the bank's. Lost traveler's checks may be reported here for a refund. Remittances may be made by fax for the

Panjim

Mandovi River

TO MAPUSA →

Mandovi Bridge

Fishing Jetty

Ribandar Causeway

TO OLD GOA AND PONDA ↑

PATTO

Kadamba Bus Terminal

TO MERCES →

Patto Bridge

GTDC

Ourem Rd.

Ferry for Mapusa Buses

GPO

Ourem Rd.

Foot-bridge

Ourem River

Avenida Dom João Castro

G.P. Rd.

31st January Rd.

C.A. Rd.

FOUNTAIN-HAS

Secretariat

Karnataka Tourist Office

Emidio Gracia Rd.

School

Chapel of St. Sebastian

Armada Portugesa Rd.

TO AIRPORT AND MARGAO →

Customs House

Church of the Immaculate Conception

CHURCH SQ.

Government of India Tourist Office

Alliance Francaise

Dr. R.S. Rd.

Municipal Gardens

Cunha Rivara Rd.

Avenida Pe Agnelo

Damania Ferry Terminal

State Bank of India

Hotel Mandovi

Ormuz Rd.

Municipality

Phone Office

Dr. Dada Vaidya Rd.

N

Dr. Pisurleka Rd.

Central Telegraph Office

Mahalaxmi Temple

200 yards

200 meters

Ferry Ramp

Malaca Rd.

Azad Maidan

Police Headquarters

Dr. P. Shiragaonkar Rd.

Mahatma Gandhi Rd.

Central Library

Swami Vivekananda Rd.

National Parks Office

Dayanand Bandodkar Marg

Gen. Costa Alvares Rd.

18th June Rd.

Dr. Amaram Borkar Rd.

Dr. Gama Pinto Rd.

Heliodoro Salgado Rd.

Indian Airlines

Municipal Market

Gen. Bernardo Guedes Rd.

Museum

TO TALEIGAO →

Mandovi River

Children's Park

Dayanand Bandodkar Marg

TO DONA PAULA, MORMUGAO, AND MIRAMAR ↓

Dr. Brazanga Pereira Rd.

same price as wiring money. Open daily 9:30am-6pm. Closed Sun. April 1-Sept. 30. Several other banks and hotels (Hotel Fidalgo, Panjim Inn) will also change money.

Telephones: STD/ISD booths are located conveniently all over Panjim. The Tourist House has a booth that accepts calling cards without argument.

Airport: Panjim is 29km from Goa's Dabolim Airport (see **Getting There,** p. 619).

Airline Offices in Panjim: Air India, 18th June Rd. (tel. 224051), next to Hotel Fidalgo. Open Mon.-Sat. 10am-1pm and 2-4:30pm. Indian Airlines, Dayanand Bandodkar Marg (tel. 223831). Runs a shuttle (Rs.30) once daily from its office to the airport. Jet Airways (office includes Air France, TWA, Gulf Air, Air Canada), 102 Rizvi Chambers (tel. 220122). Open Mon.-Fri- 9am-5:30pm, Sat. 9:30am-1:30pm.

Buses: Kadamba Bus Terminal, Patto. To: Bombay (30 per day, most leave between 3:30-7:30pm, 18hr., express Rs.150, deluxe Rs.270); Pune (8 per day, 15hr., deluxe Rs.180); Bangalore (6 per day, 14hr., Rs.170); Mangalore (5 per day, 10hr., Rs.150); Hospet (5 per day, 10hr., Rs.150); Calangute (every 30min., 6:30am-7:15pm, 40min., Rs.3.50); Mapusa (every 15min., 6am-7:30pm, 30min., Rs.3); Margao (every hr., 7am-6pm, 1hr., Rs.6.50); Vasco da Gama (every hr., 7:30am-6pm, 1hr., Rs.6); Old Goa (every 15min., 6:30am-7pm, 20min., Rs.2.50). Advance reservations are recommended and can be made at the booking office, but for buses within Goa, tickets can be purchased on board. Shop around at the travel agencies in Panjim as they all offer slightly different services and prices.

Ferries/Catamarans: Damania Ferry Terminal, Mandovi River, across from the Hotel Mandovi (see **Getting There,** p. 619).

Local Transportation: Panjim is easily traversed by foot. **Taxis** are available for city transport as well as for trips around Goa. **Auto-rickshaws** won't want to set their meters, but offer reasonable prices. **Motorbikes** can be rented at several places; prices depend on the season and weather. **Ferries** cross the Mandovi River just downstream from the Damania Ferry Terminal (every 15min., Rs.0.75).

English Bookstore: Hotel Mandovi has an English bookstore with a translation of the *Kama Sutra* placed prominently in the window. Open Mon., Thurs.-Sun. 9am-9pm, Tues.-Wed. 9am-6pm. **Singbal's Book House,** in Church Sq., just below the Government of India Tourist Office, carries English newspapers.

Hospital: Dr. Bhandare Hospital, Fountainhas (tel. 224966). Go south on 31st January Rd., passing the Panjim Inn; bear left where the road forks and continue to the gates of the hospital. Walk-ins admitted. Specialized **clinics** (for children, venereal diseases, goats, etc.) can be found throughout the city. **Ambulance** (tel. 224096).

Pharmacy: liberally spread around the city. **Hindu Pharmacy,** 18th June Rd. (tel. 226 4134). Open 9am-9pm.

Police: Police Headquarters, 2 streets to the west of the Hotel Mandovi (tel. 223124). Visa extensions are available here, but not automatically.

Emergency: Police: 100; **Fire:** 101.

Post Office: GPO, from the traffic bridge at the Ourem River, continue along the road into Panjim. The GPO is on the left behind a wild garden. Open Mon.-Sat. 9am-5pm. Parcels stitched in canvas in the obligatory fashion may be mailed Mon.-Sat. 9:30am-1pm and 1:30-3pm. **Postal Code:** 403001.

Telephone Code: 0832—this code serves all of North Goa.

ACCOMMODATIONS

Subtle as a cat in a window, small inns offering "Boarding & Lodging" peer out from Panjim's balconies and alleyways. Some larger (and more expensive) hotels present themselves more ostentatiously. Prices are seasonal, but different inns have different ideas about exactly when the season is, so ask around. Some hotels will consent to discounts for stays longer than a few days.

Panjim Inn, 31st January Rd. (tel. 226523, 227169; fax 228136. On the left side when walking south from Emidio Gracia Rd. Set in a mansion built for a 17th-century Portuguese family, now inhabited by a Portuguese man, his big dog, and a Tibetan woman. The Panjim Inn quickly becomes home. There's no reason to leave the vine-fringed balcony and the antique furniture when the staff keeps bringing you beer in front of the TV! The in-house "Gallery Gitanjali" features local art. Hot showers, all in attached baths. June 16-Sept. 30: singles Rs.315; doubles Rs. 410. Extra person Rs.90/45. A/C Rs.135 extra. Dec. 21-Jan. 10: singles Rs.450; doubles Rs.585. Other times: singles Rs.360; doubles Rs.495. Extra person Rs.125. A/C Rs.180.

Panaji-Tourist Hotel, Dr. Alvares Costa Rd. (tel. 227103, 22396). Continue a few blocks northwest after crossing Patto Bridge. Forty rooms open off a never-ending staircase leading up from a busy, impersonal lobby with a tourist desk, rather expensive postcards, and laundry services. Institutionality brings cleanliness. Every room has attached bath, fan, and telephone. Some rooms have televisions, and some have balconies facing the Mandovi River. Mattresses are thin but soft, and clean sheets and towels are provided. The Gaylord Restaurant is below. Oct. 1-June 16: doubles Rs.250, with A/C Rs.350; triples Rs.400, with A/C Rs.450. June 17-Sept. 30: doubles Rs.200, with A/C Rs.300; triples Rs.300, with A/C Rs.400. Extra mattress Rs.40 per day.

Hotel Republica, M.G. Rd. (tel. 224630). Opposite the Secretariat. A broad staircase, teeming with history, climbs up to an office featuring books, tea, coffee, mineral water, soft drinks, bookings for airline tickets, and most importantly, "Urgent Laundry Service." The 24 rooms are less than impeccable, but many have views of the Mandovi River. Most have fans. Sheets are provided. Singles Rs.125, with bath Rs.135. Doubles Rs.150, with bath Rs.250. Triples Rs.175. Expect to pay Rs.25-75 more during season.

Elite Boarding and Lodging, 31st January Rd. Turn right from Emidio Gracia Rd.; the lodge will be on the right after a few short blocks. The Elite sports brightly lit marble-floored hallways and is almost spotless. Its friendly owner, Mario Menezes Soares, speaks English and Portuguese and loves Jesus. All rooms have fans and attached baths with showers and toilets. Doubles Rs.150-200. Triples Rs.250. Extra person Rs.25. Extra bedding Rs.25. Extra cot Rs.50. Discounts of about 50% off-season, especially for stays of 4 days or more.

Maureen Guest House (tel. 222351). Heading west on Emidio Gracia Rd., take the second left, then the second right onto a short street with the white chapel of St. Sebastian at the end. The guest house's office is on the left, and its wizened inhabitants will guide you to a yellow house. Two fairly clean rooms on the ground floor share a bath; two rooms on the first floor share another bath. The only drawback is that inhabitants of the far rooms must walk through other guests' rooms to reach the bathroom. But the little windows in the ceiling are cute, as are the schoolchildren on the office porch. Triples Rs.125. Entire floor (6 beds, and no strangers passing through) Rs.250.

Poonam Guest House, 31st January Rd. If coming from Emidio Gracia Rd., the office is tucked into an alleyway to the right. The family will escort you down the street to the guest house. Common baths. Doubles Rs.75. Prices may be higher in season.

FOOD

Panjim offers a cosmopolitan menu: visitors may choose like a Bahmani Sultan among chow mein, macaroni and cheese, South Indian snacks, Gujarati *thalis,* Punjabi *dal,* and Goan fish curry. Tucked surreptitiously into tiny balconies, alleyways, and crevices, restaurants are plentiful.

Rangoli, Ormuz Rd. (tel. 224262; fax 229971). Near Cine National. The stairs leading to the first-floor restaurant might look unstable, but the sight of the glowing silvery *thali* dishes will reassure even the most skeptical. Smiley waiters provide a constant supply of fresh *chapatis,* along with curries, chutneys, pickles, peppers, and curd. The marvelous pure-veg. Gujarati *thali* costs only Rs.35. Open daily 11am-3pm and 7-10pm.

Sher-e-Punjab (tel. 456507, 228309). On the west edge of the Municipal Gardens in the Hotel Aroma. A white-coated doorman ushers diners through glass doors into an air-conditioned interior. Bow-tied waiters spoon delicately arranged (if undersized) servings onto each plate. Rich Punjabi and tandoori cuisine. *Sabji* runs

Rs.40-75. Top off the meal with spectacular *flambé gulab jamun* (Rs.50)—if you're lucky the lights will go out. Beer and liquor available. Open daily noon-3:30pm and 6:30-11:30pm.

Hotel Venite (tel. 45573). Turn north from Emidio Gracia Rd. at the bright orange and blue Quench Corner, then head north towards the Mandovi River. A sign will direct you up a narrow staircase on the right to a hand-painted, wood-floored den of Westerners. Self-pitying Americans eat macaroni and cheese (Rs.60) in the corner. Have a beer or a *feni* (coconut or cashew, Rs.20). Portuguese, Goan, and Chinese dishes are served (fried rice Rs.60, fish curry rice Rs.75). For a special treat, try Goan desserts cooked in a "salamander" oven. Open Mon.-Sat. 9-11:30am and noon-10pm.

A Pastelaria, Dr. Dada Vaidya Rd. (tel. 225718). On the left side of Dr. Dada Vaidya Rd. heading toward the Mahalaxmi Temple from Church Sq. Another place for the homesick, with sweet delights: delectable Lindsor tortes, chocolates, slices of chocolate cake (Rs.12-18), or the whole darn cake (Rs.90-180). Enjoy tea with fresh biscuits or bread. Open Mon.-Sat. 9am-7pm, Sun. 9am-1pm.

Casa Juka (The Juicy Corner), across from the Secretariat. Small juice bar does brisk business, catering to locals and tourists from the ground floor of a 500-year-old building once used in the slave trade (according to the owner). Great nook from which to watch Panjim pass by. Serves a small selection of snacks, but their obvious forte is juices, shakes, and lassis (Rs.8-15). The water used here is purified. Regulars will urge you to try the *falooda*, "a damnably delicious delight."

Hotel Annapurna, Ormuz Rd. Two blocks up from the southwest corner of Church Sq., on the left, upstairs. Avocado-green tables with ragged benches loom under lacy curtains. Barefoot, uniformed waiters float through the dimness, bearing all varieties of snacks: tea (Rs.1.50), *samosas* (2 for Rs.5), *dosas* (Rs.8), and special *thalis* (Rs.19). Open daily 7am-9:30pm.

Goenchin, Dr. Dada Vaidya Rd. (tel. 227614). On the left if you're coming from Church Sq. "Goa's only restaurant to eat the way they do in China, with chopsticks or without." A dark mysterious air pervades the curtained, air-conditioned interior. Slightly Indianesque Chinese food, with that special viscosity in the sauce. Entrees thin your money belt at the rate of Rs.60-70 for meat dishes, Rs.45 for veg. dishes. Open daily 12:30-2:45pm, 7:30-10:45pm.

SIGHTS

Panjim itself is a sight. Walking around the city reveals an odd mixture of new concrete construction and old European homes lining angled streets wrapped with thick overgrowth. The **Fountainhas** area lingers on the west bank of the Ourem, virtually unchanged by the last centuries. One of Panjim's oldest areas, its narrow streets roll past pale Portuguese mansions. Their orange-tiled roofs shade pillared balconies and peopled verandahs from which conversations in Portuguese still sink to the street below.

The bright white **Chapel of St. Sebastian,** dating from the 1880s, stands at the end of a short street opening off 31st January Rd. The church is open daily only 6:30-8am (unless you happen to meet the priest on the road). In the darkness of the church, saints and Jesuses gaze down serenely from the walls. The life-sized crucifix that used to hang in the Palace of the Inquisition in Old Goa hangs here now, open-eyed and head unbowed. In Church Sq. stands the **Mary Immaculate Conception Church (Igreja Maria Immaculada Conceicao),** the top tier of a stack of white and blue crisscrossing staircases. The outside of the church is usually crowded with playful school kids in their uniforms (which are immaculate, but not as immaculate as Mary). The original chapel, consecrated in 1541, was the first stop for Portuguese sailors thanking God for a safe voyage. The chapel was renovated in the 17th century. Note the sign: "No one should forget that the church is a sacred place and is to be visited with due respect." This is the main place of worship for local Christians, and its musty dark interior is heavy with silence and prayer. (Open Sun. and "Days of Obligation" 10:30am-1pm and 6:15-7pm, other days 9am-1pm and 3:30-6pm.)

The **Secretariat,** on the banks of the River Mandovi, also has an intriguing history. The grand white building was constructed in the 16th century as a palace and fortress for Yusuf Adil Shah of Bijapur. The Portugese rebuilt it in 1615, and in 1759 it became the palace of the Portuguese viceroy. Just to the west of the Secretariat is the black statue of Abbé Faria with arms extended threateningly toward a cowering woman. Though he resembles a strangler, the Abbé Faria was in fact an 18th-century Goan priest who became a famous hypnotist in revolutionary France. The **Mahalaxmi Temple,** with a large open marble sacred space, can be reached by following Dr. Dada Vaidya Rd. southwest from Church Sq. Jolly temple crones ply visitors with flowers and incense.

ENTERTAINMENT

Panjim provides generously for the age-old entertainment of consuming alcohol. Local brews are sold in many small shops. Tiny bars lurk throughout the city, especially in Fountainhas. Try **Lisbon's Kwality Bar & Restaurant** on Church Sq., a place where Chinese flavor, wicker lanterns, Stevie Wonder tunes, and Goan hipsters all come together. The cashew *feni*, according to one patron, is "so strong it makes you feel like you're 12 years old again, getting into daddy's liquor cabinet."

For a little evening entertainment, both government and private companies such as Emerald Waters organize **boat rides** on the Mandovi River. These tours offer toe-tappin' electronic versions of Portuguese and Goan folk songs, as well as costumed dancers, drinks, and snacks. The cruises last about an hour and cost around Rs.55 (usually slightly more for private tours). Check one of the three English language newspapers to find what's showing at Panjim's three **cinemas:** the **Samrat** (which often shows Hollywood films) and the **Ashok** are in the same building on 18th June Rd.; the **National Theater** is behind the Hotel Aroma on Ormuz Rd. The Ashok and the National usually show Hindi films.

Ferries leaving every few minutes depart the wharf across from the Hotel Mandovi, taking locals across the River Mandovi to the **villages** opposite. Have a *chai.*

■ Old Goa (Velha Goa)

Founded as a minor port town under the Vijayanagar and Bahmani kings, Goa grew in the 16th century into an opulent capital for Portuguese India, a city with a population of 200,000 fenced in by cathedrals and palaces. Goa was a city over which European authors rhapsodized, comparing its streets and mansions to those of Lisbon. It was a center of excitement, where dispossessed Europeans came to strike it rich, Jesuit missionaries brought their wisdom and self-righteousness, imperial overlords tried to maintain control, and native Hindus tried to keep their distance. But in the 17th century, Goa's energy was sapped by epidemics, contaminated water, the terror of the Inquisition, and declining commerce. Today's Old Goa, 9km east of Panjim along the Mandovi River, is but a shadow of its former glory. Old Goa's current viceroys are not aristocratic *fidalgos,* but the conservationists of the Archaeological Survey of India, who must keep plastering the churches to keep them from crumbling in the monsoon.

At the center of Old Goa, along the main road from Panjim, the yellow **Cathedral of St. Catherine da Se** looms to the left from an expanse of green trimmed lawn. Conceived by the viceroy in 1564 as "a grandiose temple, worthy of the wealth, power, and fame of the Portuguese who dominate the seas," the vast, three-naved cathedral was 80 years in the building. One of the cathedral's twin towers was destroyed by lightning in 1775; the other may sometimes be climbed to the song of the Golden Bell or "Sino de Ouro." Scenes from the life of St. Catherine the Martyr are illustrated in grand golden carvings on the altar. Fourteen smaller altars are also set within the cavernous church. Large pillars and somber silences bestow an aura of inspiration, but be sure not to vocalize your reactions too loudly; this is still an active place of worship. Notice the fresh whitewash: guides whisper angrily that the gov-

St. Francis Xavier

Francis Xavier was born in 1506 in Navarre, Spain. After studying philosophy and theology at the Sorbonne, Xavier helped his teacher and friend Ignatius Loyola to found the Society of Jesus (the Jesuits) in 1534. Charged with the dual role of "reformer of morals and founder of missions," Xavier landed in Goa in 1542, where he spent several months engaged in social work. Xavier is said to have won converts by the thousands in India; whole villages would embrace Christianity days after his arrival. God and duty called Xavier repeatedly on missions to the rest of Asia, and he died in 1552 on the coast of Canton, China, where he was buried in a sandy grave along with lime to hasten decomposition. But this was only the beginning for Francis Xavier—he was to perform some of his greatest miracles as a corpse. When his body was disinterred after more than two months to bring the bones back to Goa, it was found to be "fresh as on the day it was buried." In 1554 the body was examined by doctors and pronounced to be miraculously preserved. During the canonization proceedings in 1622, the Pope ordered Xavier's right arm sent as evidence. Much later, during an exposition of the body, an ecstatic devotee bit off St. Francis' big toe; local legend says she died immediately. Since the canonization in 1622, St. Francis Xavier's relics (minus the arm and big toe) have been housed in the Basilica de Bom Jesus. A marble pedestal and a fence prevent pilgrims from attempting to reach the windowed casket. Every year on December 3, a festival is celebrated in honor of St. Francis' passing; every 10 years an exposition is held during which the (now slightly wilted) body is placed on view in the Se Cathedral. Over one million pilgrims are expected at the next exposition, beginning in November 2004.

ernment painted over the original brilliant greens, blues, and reds because pilgrims picked off pieces of the walls. The exquisitely carved cross in a side altar to the right of the main altar is covered with cheap wood for the same reason. Also in the Cathedral complex is the former **Convent and Church of St. Francis of Assisi**. Tread softly upon the church floor—it is paved with coats of arms marking family graves that date back as far as the 16th century. A small chapel built by eight Franciscan friars on this site was pulled down before this one was constructed in 1661. Gold ornamentation and oil paintings sill bravely adorn the walls despite the orange laterite water stains. Notice the dark hair and complexion of Mary and Jesus, similar to the dark flock of cherubs flying eternally above one of the side altars of the Se Cathedral. The attached convent is now the **Archaeological Museum** (open Sat.-Thurs. 10am-5pm), showing off portraits of the viceroys, currency from "India Portuguesa," Christian icons, and sculptures from Goan Hindu temples.

Across the road, the **Basilica de Bom Jesus,** or the Cathedral of the Baby Jesus, with its dark orange stone walls, has an air of eternity. The church's interior explodes in a profusion of gold, a testament to the wealth of the Goan Jesuit order. At the far end of the nave, above the altar, is a depiction of St. Francis Xavier embracing Christ on the crucifix. The Basilica was built between 1594 and 1605 to house the remains of St. Francis Xavier. The saint's mausoleum is set off to the right of the altar behind a curtain of stars. Inside the windowed silver casket, a lightbulb shines on St. Francis' slightly shriveled body; his right arm, which was required by the Vatican during his canonization, is missing. A doorway to the left of the mausoleum leads to a small room with historical tidbits and photographs of the relic at different stages.

To the west of the Se Cathedral, the **Church of St. Cajetan** (according to local lore) was built atop an ancient Hindu temple by Italian friars of the Order of Theatines in the 17th century. Here, the ruined **gate to Yusuf Adil Shah's collapsed palace** rises forlornly, recalling legends of pre-Portuguese Goa. Up the road toward the Mandovi River, the **Viceroy's Arch** still patiently waits to receive another incoming Portuguese viceroy, who would be handed the keys to the capital as he ceremoniously passed under the Arch. (Look for the inscription left by Governor Francisco da Gama (r. 1597-1600) in memory of his great-grandfather Vasco.) Up the hill to the west of the

Basilica de Bom Jesus are the ruins of the **Church of St. Augustine**. The 46-meter-high tower has stood stubbornly since 1602. More gravestones line the floor, and the knobby laterite alcoves have hints of carvings. Across the street is the **Church and Convent of St. Monica**.

Auto-rickshaws (Rs.150 roundtrip from Panjim), and **motorcycles** easily make the trip along the banks of the Mandovi for a full or half-day of sight-seeing in Old Goa. Buses shuttle between Old Goa and the Panjim bus terminal (every 30min., 7am-7pm, 15min., Rs.1.50). Beware of the long lunch and siesta that closes the churches at mid-day. (Churches open daily 8am-12:30pm, 3-5:30 or 6:30pm). Friendly locals frequenting the churches for earthly reasons are chock full of history and legends. These unofficial guides will elegantly and aggressively escort you, spewing secrets, and they expect to be tipped. There are **no accommodations or formal restaurants** (only tiny *dhabas*) in Old Goa.

▓ Mapusa

Mapusa (pronounced "Mapsa") clings to a hillside about 30km north of Panjim, and about 10km inland from the hopping beaches at Anjuna, Calangute, and Baga. As the main population center for North Goa, Mapusa is of interest to travelers primarily for practical reasons. Most beach-cravers coming from Bombay or Bangalore jump off the bus at Mapusa and head straight for the beach. All **buses** leaving Baga, Anjuna, and Arambol ply only to Mapusa's behemoth **bus terminal,** from where buses go to nearly every part of North Goa. To: Anjuna (every 40min., 7am-6pm, Rs.3.50.); Baga and Calangute (every 20min., 7am-7pm, Rs.4); Panjim (every 15min., 6am-8pm, Rs.3). From Panjim buses go to South Goa. Motorcycles, taxis, and auto-rickshaws also run to the beaches. If you're heading to Bombay, Bangalore, or Pune, there's no reason to go all the way to Panjim to book and catch a bus. The area around Mapusa's Kadamba Bus Terminal teems with private coach operators. To: Bombay (17hr., Rs.175); Pune (14hr., Rs.150); Bangalore (14hr., Rs.175). For **currency exchange,** the State Bank of India is to the right as you exit the front of the bus terminal. Open Mon.-Fri. 10:30am-2:30pm. Two blocks east are the **police** station (tel. (0832) 262231) and the GPO. Though the post office is open for *Poste Restante* Mon.-Sat. 9:30am-4:30pm, the post offices in tourist-saturated Anjuna and Calangute are more efficient. **Postal Code:** 403507.

If it is necessary to stay overnight in Mapusa, the **Tourist Hotel** (tel. 262794) is visible from the roundabout where the buses stop. Oct. 1-June 15: singles Rs.150; doubles Rs.200; quads Rs.240, A/C Rs.300.; A/C deluxe Rs.350. June 16-Sept. 30: singles Rs.100; doubles Rs.150; quads Rs.200, A/C Rs.250, A/C deluxe Rs. 270.

▓ Calangute and Baga

The traditional winter hangout of the backpacker set, Calangute is now densely commercialized: if you drop a rupee, it's likely to land on a guest house, a restaurant, or a Kashmiri rug shop. In season, beachside restaurants stretch along the sand from Calangute to Baga, 1km north. Just inland, a long, red dirt road lined with bars, restaurants, and places to stay links Calangute to Baga.

MGM Travels, situated on the roundabout in Calangute (tel. 273223), handles plane and Catamaran tickets, rents cars, and has fax and STD/ISD **telephone** services. Open Mon.-Sat. 9am-8pm, Sun. 9am-5pm. At **Raj Travels,** 100m from the beach (tel. 276643), you can book plane and bus tickets, rent a car, and reconfirm flights. Open Mon.-Sat. 8:30am-5pm. For currency exchange, go to the **State Bank of India,** located past the roundabout heading away from the beach, on the left (tel. 276032). The bank changes traveler's checks from American Express, Bank of America, and Citicorp; currency in U.S. and Canadian dollars, pounds sterling, French francs, and Deutschmarks. Open Mon.-Fri. 10am-2pm, Sat. 10am-noon. **Wall Street Finance** (tel. 276607), almost next door to the bank, changes currency at higher rates, but is open daily 8am-8pm. Yellow-signed STD/ISD booths offer international **telephone** service

Beach Etiquette and Trouble

In Goa, the monumental 1960s are remembered as a time of nude frolicking in the waves and drugs galore—but caravans of naked white bodies and clumps of hypodermic needles on the beach have finally exhausted the goodwill of most Goans. When you see how Indian tourists go for a dip, the women dripping wet in their full-length saris, you'll understand why nudity is now illegal and frowned upon. It's important to cover up in Goa in order to respect local sensibilities: women shouldn't go topless, and men should keep their beachwear as tame as possible too. While drugs are widely available, don't forget how strict the Indian drug laws are, and how little most Indians appreciate Westerners who use India as a place to do all the things they'd be too inhibited to do at home (see **Drugs and Alcohol,** p. 16).

Due to rapid commercialization and the fabulous amounts of wealth passing through, **theft** is also escalating to gigantic proportions in Goa. (A painted beach-cottage door in Anjuna testifies, "There is nothing left to steal.") Keep an eye on your belongings—leaving them in your hotel room is often not safe, and leaving them on the beach while you frolic in the surf is asking for trouble. Always remember to keep your passport, plane tickets, and traveler's checks with you at all times. You may want to keep some items in safe deposit boxes at banks.

around Calangute and Baga. **Buses** stop frequently near the bank (across from the **market),** and at the end of the road to the beach (wisely halting before rolling into the sea). To: Mapusa (every 20min., 7am-7pm, 30min., Rs.4); Panjim (every 15min., 6am-7:30pm, 40min., Rs.3.50); Anjuna (every hr., 7am-6pm, 30min., Rs.3) **Rama Books & Jewelry,** at the roundabout, sells and swaps English, German, and French books. Open Mon.-Sat. 9am-5pm.

Almost every building in Calangute and Baga (and especially on the road between them) has "Rooms To Let" painted on the side. Some houses are also for rent across the river north of Baga (often without running water, but with wells). Even so, in high season, an empty room may not be easy to find. **Venar Holiday Home,** halfway between Calangute and Baga on the inland side of the road, run by the world's nicest family, rents several rooms in its large house and several more in separate cottages. All have fans and 24-hour running water. Hot water is available by the bucket. An ice-cream parlor occupies what was once a guest room. All rooms are painted afresh at the beginning of the season. The family pledges to do what it can for guests, many of whom come year after year. Singles Rs.80, with attached bath Rs.100. Doubles Rs.150-200. Extra mattress Rs.20. Extra bed Rs.75. Along the main road in Baga, the **Lucky Bar & Restaurant** has rooms to let. Serving food on a cool white terrace (Rs.50 for meat dishes), Lucky rents rooms in a building toward the beach. The eight bright-blue-tiled rooms are newly renovated. Two brightly painted "cottages" are also available. All rooms have attached bath and 24-hr. running water. Doubles Rs.300, with hot water Rs.400. Triples Rs.400, with hot water Rs.500. Cottages Rs.250 for two, with extra bed Rs.300. The **Rodrigues Cottages** are located on the right side of the main road to Baga near the roundabout at Calangute. Basic rooms are strung around a courtyard, all with attached bath and toilet. The proprietress decrees "when anybody stays, it becomes clean!" Dec.-Jan.: triples Rs.100; Feb.-Nov.: triples Rs.50.

A million open-air and beachside restaurants offer basic Western-style vittles. Fresh juices abound. **The Tibetan Kitchen,** past the bus stand from Calangute Beach, down

Depad!

A good way to show your enjoyment of Goa is by shouting joyfully "*depad!*" (dee-paid!—"I enjoy it!") in Konkani. Now go, and enjoy! *Depad!*

an alleyway to the right, is one of the more unusual establishments. Along with beer, magazines, and board games, good Tibetan food is served. It's easy to get comfortable here, so sit back and enjoy those *momos*. The **Infanteria Pastry Shop,** next to the church at the roundabout in Calangute, is a great place to go when you inevitably begin to hanker for the food you like back home. The shop's repertoire includes pastries galore, doughnuts, snacks, fresh soups of the day, coffee, and even Kellogg's corn flakes. Open daily 9am-8pm.

■ Anjuna

October through March, Anjuna bustles with beach raves, full-moon parties, and everything that comes with them. A new law makes raves illegal, but they are bound to continue at the risk and price of arrest for many participants. Seaside restaurants and low cottages with red roofs run along the shore to the hill in the distance. Every Wednesday Anjuna holds its famed **flea market.** A whole cast of characters frequents the Anjuna scene, from freaks to fishermen, package tourists to Kashmiri handicraft hawkers. This is it, baby, it's a-happenin' here—as all the non-biodegradable trash attests.

Just about any expatriate need can be filled in Anjuna. **Currency exchange** is possible at M/s. Travelcash (tel. 273207), approximately 1km down the road leading away from the beach. Open Mon.-Sat. 9am-8pm, Sun. 10am-5pm. On the other side of the road is a branch of **MGM Travels** (tel. 274317), for plane tickets, reconfirmations, and car rentals. Open Mon.-Sat. 9am-6pm. **Buses** stop at the end of the road at the beach, and several places along the road away from the beach. They ply only to and from Mapusa (every 20min., 6:30am-8pm, 30min., Rs.2). **Motorcycles** can also be rented. The **police** station is located on the road away from the beach, on the left. *Poste Restante* is available at the **sub-post office** (open Mon.-Sat 9:30am-noon, 2:30-4:30pm, closed holidays). Follow the road from the beach, and it'll be on the right. **Postal Code:** 403509.

Most of the buildings on the beach are there just for travelers, built over the last decade. Facilities vary greatly. Some cottages have no running water—but who cares when you're 50m from the Arabian Sea? A few newer guest houses, built in recent years, are often booked a year or more in advance. **The Victor Guest House,** near the bus stand, has three rooms in a family house, all with attached baths, hot showers, and linen changed daily. Dec.-Jan.: doubles Rs.500. Feb.-Nov.: doubles Rs.350. **The Poonan Guest House** is also nearby.

Restaurants can be found along the beach, at the bus stand, and along the street in town. Although the food "choices" in some beach towns are monotonously Continental, Anjuna is host to a German bakery and a few other unusual culinary finds.

■ Arambol (Harmal)

Among the northernmost of Goa's beach towns, Arambol has not yet been hard-hit by development. Travelers began drifting up here several years ago as the climate around Calangute and Anjuna became less tolerant and more crowded. A beautifully unspoiled beach stretches north and south from the village. Most visitors to Arambol return year after year and rent houses for a month or several months. A few new guest houses are available for short-term stays. Over the past few years some 50 oceanside restaurants and bars, hand-painted with psychedelic suns and poems, have sprung up out of the sand, live music wafting from their balconies. Heading toward the north along the beach, travelers will discover one of Arambol's treasures, a peaceful aquamarine **freshwater lagoon,** so otherworldly one might expect to see a sparkling emerald dragon basking it. (Please do not wash your clothes here, or the aforementioned dragon will appear and smite you with fire.)

MGM Travels, next to Om Ganesh Stores in town, can help travelers with their airline needs. **Buses** connect Arambol to Panjim and Mapusa. **Taxis** can be hired for the trip, but are more expensive, and the return fare must also be paid since the driver probably won't be able to pick up passengers for the return journey. (Rs.200 each way from Panjim includes ferry fare from Siolem to Chopdem; 3 ferry boats ply continuously from 6am-10pm.) For any other facilities, travelers must take their business to smaller-but-closer Mapusa, or further-but-larger Panjim.

Houses may be rented for Rs.100-150 per night, or Rs.200-5000 per month; sizes and facilities vary as widely as the prices. Most houses are in the village, but over the last five years houses more have been built on the beach to the north. Many houses have no toilets or running water, only access to nearby wells. The **Oasis Guest House,** in town, rents rooms for Rs.100-150 with attached bath. **Om Ganesh Stores** has standard rooms with and without attached bath, and **Mrs. Naik Home** offers rooms with attached bath. Both are on the road to the beach, 500m from the splashing surf.

Where the road intersects the beach, the **Seashore Restaurant** serves up everything from Goan to Continental to Chinese cuisine. Vegetable dishes run Rs.10-15, fish and chicken Rs.20-30. Restaurants along the beach can also fill your tummy.

SOUTH GOA

■ Margao (Madgaon)

The town of Margao is South Goa's population center, claiming grandly to be the capital of Salcete Province. Now the capital of Salcete *taluk,* Margao is known to most travelers only as the gateway to the southern beaches, and few travelers stop here except to catch a bus or train. Colva and Benaulim are very close, so there's no need to stay overnight if that's where you're headed.

Margao is centered on the rectangular **Municipal Gardens,** which are brushed on their west side by **National Highway 17.** All sorts of backpackerly needs can be taken care of in Margao: traveler's checks can be magically transformed into rupees at the **State Bank of India** on the western side of the Municipal Gardens. Turn right from the GPO, then take the first left. (Open Mon.-Fri. 10am-2pm, Sat.10am-noon.) Up a side street on the other side of the Municipal Gardens, the **Bank of Baroda** performs the same service at the same rate. Open Mon.-Fri. 9:30am-1:30pm, Sat. 9:30-11:30am. Just east of the market, on Station Rd., sits the **railway station. Buses** to and from Colva and Benaulim stop frequently around the Municipal Gardens. To: Colva (via Benaulim; every hr., 7am-8pm, 25min., Rs.3.50) and Panjim (every 30min., 6am-8pm, 1½hr., Rs.6.50). Buses to and from Panjim also stop here, and at the **Kadamba Bus Stand** 2km north along the road to Panjim. This bus stand is also the place to catch buses to more bluish and faraway places such as Bombay, Pune, Bangalore, or Mangalore, or simply to another palmy Goan paradise. Worthless knick-knacks can be purchased at the Municipal Garden. Just to the south a **covered market** hustles, haggles, and churns. Other services are clustered in this area. The **Police Station** near the northern end of the Municipal Gardens, on the second left (tel. 722218). For a prayer of thanks or mercy to St. Christopher, patron saint of travelers, stop in the elaborate **Church of the Holy Spirit** as you are arriving or departing. The Church is on the north side of town. The **GPO** is posted at the northern tip of the Municipal Gardens. (Open Mon.-Sat. 10:30am-1:30pm, and 2-6:30pm.) *Poste Restante* can be received in another office nearby: coming out of the GPO hang a right, then the third left. **Postal Code:** 403601.

Most budget **accommodations** may be found between the market and the railway station along Station Rd. The **Tourist Hotel** (tel. (0834) 721966, 720470), just to the south of the Municipal Gardens, is overpriced but dependably institutional. All rooms have attached baths. Oct.1-June16: singles Rs.150; doubles Rs.200, with A/C Rs.300. June17-Sept.30: singles Rs.100; doubles Rs.150, with A/C Rs.250.

■ Colva

The smooth, flat, white sands of Colva are no longer the turf of fishermen, nor even that of hippies in palm-leaf shelters. The guest houses and guests knew a good thing when they saw it, so beach fanatics now have a wide array of accommodation and restaurants to choose from—although it's nothing compared to Calangute. Travelers here are bound to be accosted by camera-happy Bombayites and scarf-sellers charging extravagant prices. Colva doesn't appear to shut down as completely during off-season as the other beaches do, and Westerners are still to be found lounging about well into the monsoon.

The main road to Margao runs from east to west, hitting the beach at a right angle. Along this road, about 1km before the beach, is Colva Village. Near the church in the village is the **Bank of Baroda**, which gives cash advances on Visa cards. Open Mon.-Sat. 9:30am-12:30pm. Money can also be changed at less lucrative rates at Colva's larger hotels, like Silver Sands (tel. 221645), near the roundabout by the beach. Across the street, the **post office** offers *Poste Restante*. Open Mon.-Fri. 10am-1pm and Sat. 10am-12:30pm. **Postal Code:** 403708.

Buses from Margao stop at the beach about every hour between 8am and 8pm. The trip from Margao takes about 20 minutes. A **taxi** to Dabolim Airport takes about 45 minutes (Rs.250). Buses ply only to Margao and to about 1km from Benaulim. Panjim and Margao may also be reached by taxi. Official black-and-yellow **motorcycle taxis** motor between Margao, Colva, and Benaulim for Rs.20—backpacks are usually "no problem." **Auto-rickshaws** ("Hallo where you going?") are ever nearby. As in other beach towns, scooters and motorcycles may be rented.

Houses are open for long stays, but are snatched up in season (Nov.-March). Never fear—**guest houses** abound up and down the road from Margao, as well as on the cross-streets. Heading up the main road away from the beach, take the third left and a quick right to find **Hotel Tourist Nest** (tel. 723944). This 200-year old Portuguese mansion in a tangled grove is the place to be in Colva. The friendly proprietress was born in this house, and proudly hosts parties with dancing, live music and food every Saturday night. Musical instruments are provided for guests, as is French cuisine and alcohol. Scooters and airport transport are gladly arranged. A tank provides 24-hr. running water for the common bathroom. Out back are two cottages with attached baths, one with a kitchen. Doubles Rs.60-70, with discounts for longer stays (if they like you, so be nice). Cottages without kitchen Rs.300 per night, with kitchen Rs.5000 per month. The **Fisherman's Cottages** can be reached by either the first or second left coming up the main road from the beach. Watch for the sign. This freshly-whitewashed building is in view of the rolling surf, and it is actually operated by fishermen, who occasionally leave their nets in the hall. Services include 24-hr. running water and motorcycle and taxi rental. In season: doubles Rs.90. Off-season: Rs.50. Set back from the main road coming from Margao is the **La Ben Resort** (tel. 222009). It is a bit "resorty," but the rooms are immaculate and beautiful with private balconies, fans, and attached bath. There's a rooftop bar and restaurant, and it's "only 120 yards from the sea." Check-out noon. Nov. 1-Dec. 15 and Feb. 1-May 31: doubles Rs.220, with A/C Rs.375. Dec. 16-Jan. 31: doubles Rs.350, with A/C Rs.450. June 1-Oct. 31: doubles Rs.160, with A/C Rs.300. Extra mattress Rs.50.

Quite a variety of **food,** from fresh-caught seafood to barbeque and pasta, can be enjoyed in Colva. Open-air restaurants line the beach in season. The **Sea Pearl Bar and Restaurant** offers unique dishes such as "prawns pie" (Rs.65) and "cottage pie" (Rs.45)—"tourists like them because they haven't seen them before." Coriander soup (Rs.25) is very popular. (Rooms are also available for approximately Rs.200.)

■ Benaulim

About 2km south of Colva is tranquil Benaulim (been-AH-li), a village that still feels like one, hiding under a pile of tropical growth, although it won't remain this way for long if the Goa State Tourist Development Corporation has its way. Benaulim's few small guest houses and its two beachfront hotels are soon to be supplemented by a large resort.

The roads to Margao and Colva cross at the center of the village, less than 1km from the sea. This is where **buses** from Margao stop; some go on to Varca and Cavelossim. Benaulim is a 50-minute **taxi** ride from Dabolim **airport** (Rs.250). A **motorcycle** would come in handy in Benaulim—some guest houses can arrange for one, but if one can't be found, try in Colva or Margao. The Bank of Baroda here only does cash advances on Visa cards, so **currency exchange** involves a trip to Colva or Margao. To find a **post office,** travelers must go to Colva.

For those who don't fancy fashioning themselves a palm-leaf hut, two hotels sit almost on the beach, and guest houses line the road to Margao and the cross-street, about 500m back from the surf. **Houses** can be rented for long stays, but they are difficult to get in season (Nov.-March). You can reach **Kenkre Tourist Cottages** by following the road up from the beach about 500m before taking a left. The smiley, helpful proprietor has six rooms in a house, all doubles, with attached bath and 24-hr. running water. Many guests stay 3 or 4 months. In season, doubles Rs.70-80; off-season, Rs.50. The six rooms at the newly constructed **Pinto Cottages** across the street have window screens to keep out mosquitoes. Smallish but clean rooms are served by a bar and restaurant. All have attached bath with 24-hr. running water. Doubles Rs.70-80 (depending how much you plead poverty). Follow the main road up from the beach about 500m and take a right to reach **Rosario's Inn** (tel. 734167). For the price, the rooms are not very clean or large. Some rooms are upstairs from the family with shared bath, and some are in two separate buildings with attached bath. Room service brings breakfast, lunch, dinner, and cold drinks. Doubles with shared bath and double bed Rs.60. Doubles with bath and two beds Rs.150; off-season, Rs.100.

Gujarat

One of India's richest industrial regions, Gujarat has much to offer, in part because it sees fewer travelers than its neighbors Rajasthan and Maharashtra. Originally settled by the Indus Valley people in 2500 BC, Gujarat prospered under several empires including the Solanki dynasty in the 11th and 12th centuries AD, leaving its culture with a blend of Jain and Hindu influences. In 1299 the area was conquered by Muslims, who formed the Sultanate of Gujarat in 1407. For centuries now, these three religions have coexisted and influenced one another. In the 16th century, Portuguese influence was exerted in Gujarat with the capture of the ports of Diu and Daman and the subsequent imposition of European customs. At India's Independence Gujarat gained acclaim as the birthplace and operational base of Mahatma Gandhi. But Gujarat was also home to M.A. Jinnah, founder of Pakistan, and the state's proximity to Pakistan has recently resulted in communal conflicts within its borders.

Gujarat can be geographically divided into three regions with vastly differing personalities. The eastern region, containing the capital Gandhinagar, the metropolis Ahmedabad, and the commercial cities of the mainland strip, is characterized by its modern industrialization. The northwestern quasi-island of Kutch, a dry, isolated area, sits peacefully content with its traditional village lifestyle. The Kathiawad Peninsula (also known as Saurashtra), is known for lush land, rich temples, forts, palaces, and all things Gandhi.

▓ Ahmedabad

The largest city in Gujarat with 3.3 million people, Ahmedabad ranks unquestionably among the most polluted, dirty, noisy, congested, industrial, exciting, fascinating, and eccentric cities in all of Asia. Hailed as the "Manchester of the East" by many, Ahmedabad is home to booming modern industries and businesses enveloping spectacular

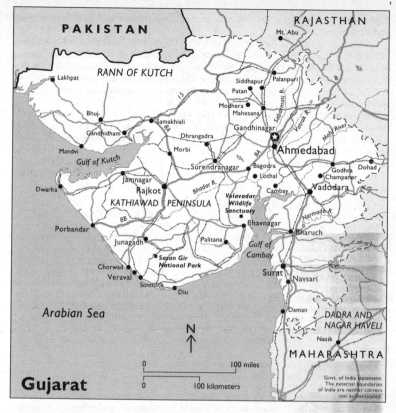

PAKISTAN

RAJASTHAN

Mt. Abu

RANN OF KUTCH

Lakhpat

Siddhapur Palanpuri

15

Patan

8

Modhera

Bhuj

Samakhiali

Mahesana

Gandhidham

Dhrangadra

Gandhinagar

Sabarmati R.

Varak R.

Mahi River

Morbi

8A

Ahmedabad

Mandvi

Gulf of Kutch

Surendranagar

Bagodra

Godhra

Dohad

Lothal

Champaner

Jamnagar

Bhadar R.

Cambay

Vadodara

Dwarka

Rajkot

KATHIAWAD PENINSULA

Velavadar
Wildlife
Sanctuary

Narmada R.

8B

Porbandar

Junagadh

Palitana

Bharuch

Bhavnagar

Gulf of
Cambay

Surat

Chorwad

Sasan Gir
National Park

Navsari

Veraval

Somnath

Diu

Arabian Sea

Daman

DADRA AND
NAGAR HAVELI

N

Nasik

MAHARASHTRA

0   100 miles
0   100 kilometers

Gujarat

Govt. of India statement:
The external boundaries
of India are neither correct
nor authenticated

mosques, temples, monuments, and museums. While definitely not a city where people come to relax, Ahmedabad's curious and at times overwhelming blend of old and new has intrigued and awestruck many a traveler.

The city was founded in 1411 by Sultan Ahmed Shah, and rapidly expanded as traders, craftsmen, and artisans flocked in. A Muslim character was decidedly established through the construction of countless mosques in the new Indo-Saracenic (Indo-Islamic) style. Through the centuries its prosperity see-sawed; in 1630 and 1812 it witnessed crippling famines that threw it into periods of decadence, from which only increasing industry helped it escape. Ahmedabad's dominance at first lay in textiles; as it grew it became a leader in more industrial fields as well, resulting in its current factory atmosphere. Nonetheless, the city has always encouraged its textile and art arenas, especially with Gandhi's establishment of an ashram in the city. Now, as the city tries harder to be competitive in international industries, the balance between old and new seems precarious.

ORIENTATION

The city is separated into two parts corresponding to new and old by the **Sabarmati River,** cutting a north-south path that is usually dry as dirt along its entire width, filled with grazing water buffalo. The **Lal Darwaja (Red Gate)** opens into the old city on the river's east side; the newer industrial and urban centers lie westward. The two parts of the city are connected by a series of five bridges—from north to south, these are **Sardar Bridge, Ellis Bridge, Nehru Bridge, Gandhi Bridge,** and **Subhash Bridge.**

The most commonly used are Ellis and Nehru connecting the middle of both the old and new cities.

Located in the east of the old city, the Ahmedabad Railway Station is quite a hike along either the entirely too busy (and inaccurately named) **Relief Road** (officially known as **Tilak Road**) or **Gandhi Road** into the center of the old city. Gandhi Rd. leads through the stone arches of the **Teen Darwaja**, through the main bazaar area to the Lal Darwaja the site of the **Local Bus Stand**. The **Central Bus Stand** is in the south past of town off of Sardar Patel Road.

The **Tourist Information Bureau** is located on the first floor of M.K. House on **R.C. Road** (the road's name changes to **Ashram Road** outside the city, but the whole thoroughfare is often referred to by the latter name), the north-south road running down the west side of the river. Ashram Rd. is a major commercial center and conveniently lined with banks and big stores. Throughout the city congestion and pollution are the norm, so it's a good idea to have a handkerchief with you to cover your nose and mouth.

PRACTICAL INFORMATION

Tourist Office: Tourist Information Bureau (Gujarat Tourism), M.K. House off Ashram Rd. (tel. 449683). Down a side-street opposite the South Indian Bank between Gandhi and Nehru Bridges. Ask rickshaw drivers for M.K. House. A helpful staff with an assortment of brochures. City maps Rs.4, Gujarat maps Rs.20. Car rentals available. Open daily 10:30am-6:10pm. **Tourist counters** at the railway station (tel. 387775) and the airport (tel. 67568) have limited information, but are helpful for travel arrangements. **Tourist office,** Ahmedabad Municipal Corporation Building (tel. 365611), intersection of Sardar Patel Rd. and R.M. Rd. Limited general information. Open Mon.-Sat. 10:30am-5:30pm. **City tours** depart from the tourist window at the Lal Darwaja Bus Stand (9:30am and 2pm, 4hr., Rs.30). The *Times of India* Ahmedabad edition has updated flight and train information on the second page.

Immigration Office: Foreigners Registration Office, Commissioners of Police, Dr. Tankeria Rd. (tel. 333887), on the left side 3km north of Lal Darwaja. Come at least 1 week before visa expiration. Open Mon.-Fri. 10am-5pm.

Currency Exchange: State Bank of India, near Lal Darwaja Bus Stand, opposite CTO (tel. 550 6800). **State Bank of Bikaner and Jaipur,** Relief Rd. (tel. 338405). **Bank of Baroda,** Relief Rd. (tel. 535 6278) and Ashram Rd. (tel. 408177). All exchange currency and traveler's checks. No Visa/MasterCard encashments. All open Mon.-Fri. 11am-3pm, Sat. 11am-1pm.

Telephones: Private STD/ISD booths are virtually everywhere in the city. Quite a good number offer fax services and/or are open 24hr. **Central Telegraph Office,** Lal Darwaja. Open 24hr. **Telecom Office,** Railway Station. STD/ISD, fax, telegraph. Open 24hr.

Airport: Ahmedabad International Airport, 10km northeast of the city center (tel. 642 5633). Taxis into the city will run you Rs.250-300, auto-rickshaws Rs.90, and buses to Lal Darwaja Bus Stand (every 30min.) Rs.4. **Air India** flies to international destinations. The office (tel. 642 5644) is near the High Court on Ashram Rd. between Gandhi and Nehru Bridges. Open Mon.-Fri. 10am-1:15pm and 2-5:15pm, Sat. 10am-1:30pm. **Indian Airlines,** Lal Darwaja (tel. 550 3061). Open daily 10am-1:15pm and 2:15-5:15pm. **Jet Airways,** Ashram Rd., 1km north of Gujarat Tourism (tel. 402519). Open Mon.-Sat. 10am-3pm. To: Bangalore (Tues.-Sun. 1 per day, 2hr., US$168); Bombay (6-8 per day, 1hr., US$50); Delhi (6-8 per day, 1½hr., US$79); Jaipur (Mon.-Tues., Thurs.-Sat. 1 per day, 1hr., US$90); Madras (Tues.-Sun. 1 per day, 3½hr., US$183).

Trains: Ahmedabad Railway Station, on the east side of town (tel. 131). Telecom center open 24hr. Tourist counter on premises. The train schedules are currently being re-worked in Ahmedabad, so check the schedules at the station before making plans. To: Bombay (*Karnavati Exp.* 2934, 5:15am, 7½hr., Rs.120/390 for 2nd/1st class; *Gujarat Mail* 9102, 10pm, 8½hr., Rs.134/390 for 2nd/1st class); Delhi (*Sarwdaya Exp.,* noon, 16½hr., Rs.221/650 for 2nd/1st class; *Ashram Exp.* 2906, 4:30pm, 17hr., Rs.210/610 for 2nd/1st class); Abu Road (*Ashram Exp.* 2906,

Sabarmati
(Gandhi)
Ashram

Subhash
Bridge

SHAHIBAG

Ashram Rd.

Calico Museum
of Textiles

Civil
Hospital

Vadaj Low
Level Bridge

DUDHESWAR

Sabarmati River

Police
Commissioner's
Office

City Rd.

HARIPURA

Balvantri Mehta Rd.

Mehta Rd.

Hathi Singh
Temple

Dada
Hari Vav

Gandhi
Bridge

Ashram Rd.

Kasturba Gandhi Rd.

Shahpur
Darwaja

Delhi
Darwaja

Dariapur
Darwaja

Tourist
Information
Bureau

Lady Vidyagauri Rd.

Rani Rupmati's
Mosque

Kalupur
Darwaja

Khanpur
Darwaja

Dr. Tankaria Rd.

Dr. Baptria Rd.

Ahmedabad
Railway
Station

MITHAKALI

Indian
Airlines

Ramanaj Sheth Rd.

GPO

Swaminarayan
Temple

Nehru Bridge

Sidi Saiyad's
Mosque

KHAS
BAZAAR

Peer Mohammedshah Rd.

Tilak (Relief) Rd.

Panchkuva
Darwaja

LAL DARWAJA

State Bank of India

Central
Telegraph
Office

Arjun Lala Rd.

Shaking Minarets
& Sidi Bashir's
Mosque

R.C. Rd.

Local Bus Stand

SEWA

Teen
Darwaja

Jumma
Masjid

Gandhi Rd.

K.T. Desai Rd.

Sarangpur
Darwaja

Ellis Bridge

Victoria
Garden

Akbarshnand Rd.

R.H. Rd.

Anandshankar Dhruv Rd.

Vivekananda Rd.

Ahmed Shah's
Mosque

Bhadra Fort &
Azamkhan's
Palace

Sardar Patel Rd.

V.S.
Hospital

Rani
Sipri's
Mosque

RAIPUR
DARWAJA

Sabarmati River

Jamalpur Rd.

Astodia
Darwaja

Central
Bus
Stand

Dayanand Rd.

Mehta Museum
of Miniatures

PALDI

Sardar
Bridge

Jagannathji Rd.

JAMALPUR

Kankaria
Lake

BEHRAMPURA

0   400 yards

0   400 meters

N

Ahmedabad

4:30pm, 5hr., Rs.52/182 for 2nd/1st class); Jaipur (*Delhi Express Mail*, 6pm, 16½hr., Rs.157/471 for 2nd/1st class; 4:30am, 20hr., Rs.187/490 for 2nd/1st class); Bhavnagar (*Shetrunji Exp.* 9810, 5:15pm, 6hr., Rs.75/260 for 2nd/1st class); Veraval via Junagadh (6 and 7:15am, 12hr., Rs.135/400 for 2nd/1st class); Rajkot (every 5hr., 6hr., Rs.76/230 for 2nd/1st class); Dwarka (7am, 10hr., Rs.134/370 for 2nd/1st class); Bhuj (*Kutch Exp.*, 1:55am, 8½hr., Rs.100/300 for 2nd/1st class). **Reservation Office** in Railway Station open Mon.-Sat. 8am-8pm, Sun. 8am-2pm.

Buses: Central Bus Stand (tel. 2144754) is for intercity buses. Government buses are rather decrepit; private buses are much more comfortable. To: Abu Road (7 and 10am, 7hr., Rs.51); Bombay (6:30, 9:30am, and noon, 11½hr., Rs. 101); Udaipur (every 3hr., 6am-10pm, 7hr., Rs.60); Bhavnagar (every hr., 6am-10pm, Rs.32); Diu via Junagadh and Una (every 2hr., 6am-9pm, 8hr., Rs.68); Jamnagar (every 3hr., 7am-7pm, 9hr., Rs.94); Rajkot (every hr., 6am-8pm, 6hr., Rs.50). Lining the road opposite the Central Bus Stand are dozens of private bus company stalls, but most are ticket agents and/or have main offices elsewhere. Few private buses depart from the Central Bus Stand; most depart from the main office of the bus company. The best companies are **Bonny Tours and Resorts,** Shefali Shopping Centre (tel. 657 6568), southwest of Ellis Bridge off Pritamrai Rd. and **Punjab Travels,** Embassy Market (tel. 211 1717), off Ashram Rd. a bit north of Gujarat Tourism. **Shrinath Travels Agency,** near the Central Bus Stand (tel. 219 4455), is good for departures to Rajasthan.

Local Transportation: Auto-rickshaws make up most of the city's chaos but they are convenient. They are metered and adjusted according to a fare card printed in Gujarati. Insist on the meter; many rickshaw drivers will try to pass a high fixed rate. If the rate still seems high after the meter adjustment, ask to see the fare card. It's worth learning Gujarati numbers if you stay for a long time in the city. **Local buses** are extensive and inexpensive, and almost as dangerous as auto-rickshaws. The **Lal Darwaja Bus Stand** (tel. 352911) is the local bus stand. Bus numbers are in Gujarati. Some useful routes: #82 and #84 cross the river and run north up Ashram Rd.; #32 runs to the Central Bus Stand and southeast to Kankaria Lake; #103 and #105 run to the airport. Fares are less than Rs.4. Air-conditioned Ambassador **taxis** can be found at the two bus stands at the Airport, at the Railway Station and at V.S. Hospital. Rs.200 to cross the city. Private **car rental** can be arranged through the Tourist Information Bureau. Trying to navigate the city on a **bicycle** is a suicidal proposition.

Luggage Storage: The railway station offers luggage storage Rs.3 for first 24hr., Rs.6 per additional 24hr.

English Bookstore: Crossword, Sri Krishna Shopping Centre, Mithakali (tel. 402238; fax 444180). West of the river between Gandhi and Nehru Bridges. Huge book collection of all types, plus magazines, newspapers, stationary, computer games, and a café. Open daily 10am-8pm. **Kitab Kendra,** near Gujarat College (tel. 405136). Good collection of paperbacks and technical books. Open Mon.-Sat. 10am-7pm. **Sastu Kitab Dhar,** Relief Rd. Good selection of paperbacks. Open Mon.-Sat. 10:30am-5pm. Numerous book stalls with smaller paperback collections line the west end of Relief Rd. as well.

Library: British Library, Bhaikala Bhawan, Law Garden (tel. 656 0693; fax 449493). An extensive book, magazine, and newspaper collection. Check-out available to members only. Nonmembers are generally allowed to browse. Open Tues.-Fri. 10:30am-6:30pm, Sat. 11:30am-7:30pm. **M.J. Public Library** at the intersection of Ellis Bridge and Ashram Rd. Decent English collection. Open Mon.-Sat. 10am-5pm.

Cultural Centers: British Library, Bhaikala Bhawan, Law Garden (tel. 656 0693; fax 449493). Organizes talks, lectures, video shows. See *Times of India* for notices. **Alliance Française,** near Gujarat College (tel. 441551). Small library with French books and newspapers. Organizes cultural activities, exhibitions, monthly programs. See *Times of India* for notices. Open Mon.-Fri. 10:30am-6:30pm, Sat. 11am-5pm.

Market: Relief Rd., Gandhi Rd., Sardar Patel Rd., Khas Bazaar, and Ashram Rd. are the main commercial areas. Fruit and vegetable stalls congregate in the Lal Darwaja and Teen Darwaja areas, but are everywhere else, too. Most stores open daily 9am-9:30pm.

Pharmacy: Pharmacies are almost everywhere because hospitals and clinics are everywhere. They are especially numerous around the 3 main hospitals (see below). Most open daily 9am-7pm, but in every cluster a few are open 24hr.
Hospital: Civil Hospital, off Khandubhai Desai Rd., Shahibagh (tel. 376351). About 3km directly north of the Railway Station. **V.S. Hospital,** near the intersection of Ashram Rd. and Ellis Bridge (tel. 657 7621). Both of these are main government hospitals. The best private hospital is **Chaturbhuj Lajpatrai Hospital,** also known as **Rajasthan Hospital,** near the Civil Hospital (tel. 786 6311). English-speaking, modern, efficient. All open 24hr.
Police: Major police stations are **Karanj,** in Teen Darwaza; **Shaherkotada,** opposite the Railway Station; **Ellis Bridge,** at the intersection with Ahram Rd. Smaller branches are scattered around.
Emergency: Police: tel. 100. **Fire:** tel. 102. **Ambulance:** tel. 102.
Post Office: GPO (tel. 550 0977). Packaging, *Poste Restante.* Large and efficient. Open Mon.-Sat. 10am-6pm. Many branch offices around town, significant ones at the Airport, at Gandhi Ashram, opposite the Railway Station, near Civil Hospital, and near V.S. Hospital. All open Mon.-Sat. 10am-5pm. **Postal Code:** 380001. **Telephone Code:** 0789.

ACCOMMODATIONS

Your stay will be a noisy one if you plan to stay anywhere reasonably near the center of the city. The best budget hotels are conveniently scattered around the west half of the city center. Most of the hotels on the east side of the city near the Railway Station and along Relief Rd. are mostly unbearable and should be avoided. If the grime of Ahmedabad is too much to bear, all the luxury hotels cluster between the Gandhi and Nehru Bridges on the east side of the river, around Khanpur Darwaja. Hotels in Gujarat are subject to a 10% luxury tax.

Hotel Balwas, 6751 Relief Rd. (tel. 550 7135). Near the Central Telegraph Office. A smart, modern place with marble-floored rooms and simple patterned furnishings. Rooms are good-sized and have balconies over chaotic Relief Rd. The restaurant is decent. Laundry, 24-hr. room service, air-conditioned lobby. All rooms have TVs, telephones, and attached baths. Check-out 24hr. Singles Rs.190, with A/C Rs.320, larger Rs.330, larger with A/C Rs.425. Doubles Rs.240, larger Rs.400, larger with A/C Rs.500. Extra bed Rs.100.
Hotel Shakunt, opposite Railway Station (tel. 211 3520). This is your best bet if you want to be near the Railway Station. A modern hotel with a pleasant terrace garden and friendly staff. Rooms are large with geometric wood panelling. All rooms have TV, telephone, and attached bath, and the hotel offers laundry, taxi rental, STD/ISD, limited room service. Check-out 24hr. Singles Rs.175, better Rs.200, with A/C Rs.300. Doubles Rs.220, better doubles Rs.250, with A/C Rs.350. Extra person Rs.60.
A-One Hotel, opposite Railway Station (tel. 214 9823). The undecorated, unfurnished, nondescript rooms are slightly larger than the beds, although they're billed as "luxuriously furnished." Check-out 24hr. Dormitory houses men only. Dorm beds Rs.40. Singles Rs.70, with bath Rs.120. Doubles Rs.200.
Hotel Good Night, Lal Darwaja, opposite Sidi Saiyad's Mosque (tel. 550 7181). Although seemingly in the middle of all the hustle, this hotel is set back from the road and is marginally quieter than the rest. Rooms are romantically dim with a painting here and there and tasteful furniture. Room service 24hr., a good air-conditioned restaurant (Food Inn), laundry, car rental, TV and telephone, and attached baths in all rooms. Check-out 24hr. Singles Rs.225, with A/C Rs.300, larger with A/C Rs.350. Doubles Rs.300, with A/C Rs.375, larger with A/C Rs.400.
Gandhi Ashram Guest House, opposite Gandhi Ashram (tel. 748 3742). If you're willing to be away from the city, the peaceful silence you'll find here is reminiscent of the ashram across the street. Rooms are eccentrically decorated with everything from busts to abstract art to nature calendars to tapestries. It's run by Gujarat Tourism, meaning the staff is well-informed about the city. Limited room service, good

veg. restaurant. Check-out 9am. Singles Rs.200, with A/C Rs.375. Doubles Rs.350, with A/C Rs.530.

Hotel Nataj, next to Ahmed Shah's Mosque (tel. 550 6048). If you're lucky enough to get a room with balcony overlooking the gardens of the mosque next door, you've got the best view in the city proper. Otherwise, rooms are large but boring. A sign in the hallway bluntly warns "Don't Spit." Limited room service, all rooms have attached baths. Check-out 24hr. Singles Rs.90. Doubles Rs.150. Extra bed Rs.30. Hot water buckets free.

Hotel Diamond, Khanpur (tel. 550 3699). Quite a good deal considering the facilities. Well-kept, clean rooms with attached baths, TVs, telephones, spotty red carpet, and bland beige bed-spreads. Limited room service. Check-out 24hr. Singles Rs.150, with A/C Rs.230. Doubles Rs.190, with A/C Rs.280. Triples Rs.260, with A/C Rs.350.

Hotel Capri, Relief Rd. (tel. 550 7143; fax 550 6646). A cheery red, white, and blue base and a grand, cool lobby suggest a gem on noisy Relief Rd., but the rooms reveal old furniture and tacky carpets. Still, the place is reasonably modern and well-kept and the staff is professional. Features a decent restaurant, 24-hr. room service, travel service, STD/ISD, fax, TVs and phones in all rooms. Check-out 24hr. Singles with bath Rs.325, with A/C Rs.375. Doubles with bath Rs.375, with A/C Rs.475.

Hotel Alif International, Khanpur (tel. 550 1270). A comparatively affordable option in the Khanpur luxury cluster, this place features 24-hr. room service, a good restaurant, travel counter, laundry service, and car rental. Rooms are very modern with TVs, telephones, attached baths, and coordinated businessy furniture. Check-out 9am. Singles Rs.295, with A/C Rs.350-460 depending on size, furniture, and location. Doubles Rs.340, with A/C Rs.475-600. Extra bed Rs.125.

FOOD

Ahmedabad is home to every imaginable type of restaurant. Khas Bazaar is a good place to go for quick and spicy stall food, and juice and ice cream stores are as common as rickshaw accidents. It's definitely worth sampling a Gujarati *thali,* which conveniently blends several local specialties in a delightful, often sweet, mix. Eating in Ahmedabad is rarely laid-back and quiet unless you head to luxury hotels or the outskirts of town.

Kalapi Restaurant, near Advance Cinema, Lal Darwaja (tel. 5507779). Dim, air-conditioned, and one of the best bargains in town. All veg., all Indian, no smoking. The food is excellent and well-presented, and generally less than Rs.25. Madrasi specialties are around Rs.15. The dessert collection is extensive and under Rs.20. Open daily 9am-10:30pm.

Chetna Dining Hall, Relief Rd. (tel. 2114278). Almost directly north of the Jumma Masjid. Your standard *thali* house—stainless steel everywhere and waiters rushing from packed table to more packed table with pots of steaming vegetables. South Indian dishes are available à la carte, but you're supposed to eat *thalis* for a cheap Rs.20. Open daily 10:30am-3pm and 6:30-10pm.

RG Pizza and Tomato's, off Chimantal Girdharlal Rd., near Law Garden (tel. 656 6129). Americana in the extreme. Neon lights, movie posters on the walls, Elvis memorabilia, plastic nouveau deco, pitchers of Coke, and thick crust pizzas (Rs.70 and up). Assorted Indian and Continental dishes also available. Open daily 10am-midnight.

Hotel Paramount, near Khas Bazaar (tel. 550 7666). The booth atmosphere is bland but dim lights and air-conditioning make it comfortable. Good seafood dishes for under Rs.40, veg. entrees under Rs.25. Open daily 9am-11pm.

Girish Ice Cream, near Law Gardens. All the young Gujarat collegiates head here and to the nearby late night eateries to get through their studies. Not coincidentally some of the best ice cream in town. Floats, shakes, sodas, popsicles, and more. Open daily until people leave.

Gopi Dining Hall, near V.S. Hospital on west side of river (tel. 76388). Just excellent enormous Gujarati *thalis.* Prepare to rub shoulders with everyone in this packed-solid den of fine stainless steel dining. Gujarati *thalis* Rs.35, Rs.30 for lunch. Open daily 10:30am-3pm and 6-11pm. Come early to make a reservation or be prepared to wait.

SIGHTS

Under the incredible noise and industry, there are still quite a number of extraordinary sights to captivate visitors. Most prominent in Ahmedabad are the dozens of **mosques,** found about every 500m in every part of the city. The **Jumma Masjid** (Friday Mosque), on Gandhi Rd., is a good place to start. Built in 1424 by Sultan Ahmed Shah I, Jumma Masjid opens into a large marble courtyard that fries the soles of your feet. A small reflecting pool surrounded by devotees stands in the center, and the magnificent mosque itself dominates at night. The gloomy structure's 15 domes are supported by 256 pillars. The carvings on the pillars and domes are detailed and predominantly Hindu. The curious black slab by the main massive archway is said to be an inverted Jain image. Remarkably, the mosque stood intact through the years, except for its two minarets which were destroyed in an earthquake in 1957. The mosque is predictably mobbed on Fridays. Through the left gate of the courtyard is the **Tomb of Ahmed Shah** and **Rani-ka-hazira,** the tomb of his queens. The cenotaphs themselves are in spacious pillared chambers and are covered with fancy gold-laced cloths. A guard can lift one for you to reveal some fine stonework. Women are prohibited from entering the chambers holding the tombs of the male members of the family.

The number two mosque in Ahmedabad is **Sidi Saiyad's Mosque,** in Lal Darwaja. It was constructed by one of Ahmed Shah's slaves in 1573, and now graces half of Gujarat Tourism's literature. The interior of the mosque is impressive, with elaborately carved ceilings and domes, but the highlight is the delicate latticework on the screens lining the upper walls. Most are floral or arboreal in nature, with windy threads of marble meandering through one another. Women are not allowed to enter, but can enjoy the screens from the gardens around. **Ahmed Shah's Mosque** on Sardar Patel Rd. is one of the oldest mosques in the city, built in 1414. It's simple compared to the big two, but in its original function as a private royal mosque, it didn't have to be too ornate. Some sections display some remarkable carvings, however. Of particular interest are the Sanskrit inscriptions and Hindu designs; these are the remains of a Hindu temple that used to stand on this spot. Across the street is **Victoria Garden,** rather bare and in need of landscaping but still a pleasant place to stroll.

Heading toward the Railway Station, on Sardar Patel Rd., **Rani Sipri's Mosque,** also known as **Masjid-e-Nagira** ("Jewel of a Mosque") was built in 1519. The central grave holds Rani Sipri, who ordered the mosque built after her son was executed for a petty crime. The mosque is known for its exquisite latticework and decorated minarets. The tomb itself is surrounded by 12 pillars under a single stylish dome. Near Sarangpur Darwaja are the famous **Shaking Minarets and Sidi Bashir's Mosque.** A huge arch supporting two giant 21-m-high minarets explains half the name. Supposedly if one minaret is shaken the other shakes as well, and this phenomena somehow acts as a shock absorber which would prevent an earthquake from destroying the construction. Apparently in the 19th century two European visitors independently shook one minaret and saw the second one shake in response. Currently, their experiment is unrepeatable, as climbing the minarets is prohibited. The mosque is less interesting than the history, with a greenish façade and colorful coverings inside. By now, even the most zealous mosque enthusiast should be satisfied. If not, **Ravi Rupamati's Mosque,** north of the city center, and **Raj Babi's Mosque,** southeast of the Railway Station, should quench your desire. Of course, dozens more of varying interest exist; just walk around and explore.

Changing religions, the **Swaminarayan Temple** on the north side of the city is well worth a visit. This Hindu temple was built in 1850 and is a barrage of bright rainbow and metallic colors, dramatically contrasting the stonework of much of the rest of the city. The temple features fine woodwork and detailed bright painting rivaling the mosques in intricacy. Paintings show figures dancing and singing, scenes from

---

The International Kite Festival

For three nights in January, the skies of Ahmedabad are peppered with kites of all styles, colors, and sizes from around the world. Enthusiasts from all over India and the world descend upon the city for the International Kite Festival, the largest kite-related happening in the world. For weeks before, shops and stalls sell huge assortments of kites and kite equipment, as experts roam the streets offering lessons on the finer points of the craft. The festival itself has a competition for kite size, originality, and beauty, and is accompanied by dancing, singing, shows, parades, and general merriment. At night the skies light up as kites are adorned with lights attached to the tails. The festival ends with a highly competitive contest in which kite strings are coated with adhesive and ground glass, turning them into razor-sharp lines. Kites are then sent flying into one another, slashing each other's lines until one emerges victorious. Meanwhile, local youngsters scour the trees for what's left of the defeated kites, hoping to find a particularly large or beautiful chunk. In 1997, the festival starts on January 14.

---

mythology, divine images, and fanciful patterned decor. The temple is dedicated to Vishnu and Lakshmi. The area is generally mobbed with musicians, worshipers, and miscellaneous guests. The **Hathi Sirjh Temple,** north of Delhi Lake, is one of a few Jain temples in the city. It was built in 1848 of white marble and is dedicated to the 15th *tirthankara*, Dharamarath. The temple's design is typically Jain, with detailed carvings of dancers and floral patterns en masse. (Open to non-Jains daily 10am-noon and 4-7:30pm.)

Gandhi's **Sabarmati Ashram,** locally called the **Gandhi Ashram,** is located on Ashram Rd. north of Gandhi Bridge. The ashram is peaceful with its reddish buildings and lush gardens. It is common to see people in quiet meditation, study, or rest. The ashram was Gandhi's base of operations from 1917 until 1930. His simple living quarters are here, as is an impressive display of his biography, philosophy, paintings, photographs, quotes, political cartoons, and stamps. The focus is on his revitalization of the Ahmedabad textile industry, which he effected through the ashram. (Open daily April-Sept. 8:30am-6:30pm; Oct.-March 8:30am-6pm. Free. A 65-minute biographical sound and light show is shown on Sun., Wed., and Fri. at 9pm, Rs.3. Buses #81, #82, #83, and #84 all come here.)

The **Calico Museum of Textiles,** Shahi Bagh, 3km north of Delhi Gate, is the premier textile museum in India and a phenomenal place to visit. Creatively set up in the *haveli* of the richest family in the city, the museum is split into two sections surrounded by beautiful peacock- and fountain-filled gardens. The first half is concerned with non-religious textiles, and features an enormous collection of textiles made from every possible fabric, in every possible style, for every possible purpose from every part of India. The white-on-white translucent shadowwork is remarkable, as are the silk embroideries so finely worked that from 2m away they appear to be paintings. Other highlights include beautiful saris (Rs.80,000 and up) made by a complicated procedure in which one mistake means beginning entirely anew, and light clothes so heavily laden with gold lace that their weight reaches over 9kg. The second half of the museum displays textiles for religious use, and features an exquisite 8-m-long pictorial scroll, a multitude of old tapestries with the Mughal Krishna image from Nathdwara, Rajasthan, and a series of rooms explaining the methods used in minute detail—every knot, stitch, thread type, dye, bead, and mirror technique imaginable. (Open Thurs.-Tues. Guided tours only at 10:30am and 2:45pm, 2½hr. Free. No photography.)

The **Mehta Museum of Miniatures,** southwest of the river in Paldi, has a large collection of miniature paintings, most relatively modern, from throughout India. (Open Tues.-Sun. 11am-noon and 3-5pm; free.) The **Shreyas Folk Museum,** west of the city, has a collection of folk work from all over Gujarat. Costumes, handicrafts, and textiles are among the items displayed. (Open Thurs.-Tues. 9am-noon and 3-5pm.) Buses #34, #35, #41, and #200 come out here. The **Tribal Research and Training Museum,** north of Ashram Rd., showcases similar crafts from regional tribal peoples and explains their customs. (Open Mon.-Fri. noon-5pm.)

Several **vavs** (step-wells) can be found in the north of town, a bit south of the Civil Hospital. The **Dada Mari Vav** is among the most impressive of the many in Gujarat. Elaborately carved walls and pillars border the steps as they descend in groups to progressively lower platforms. It's a fun place to mellowly explore, since the well dried up years ago. Visit in the morning before noon, when the sun reaches to the bottom levels and illuminates the stonework. **Mata Bhavani's Well,** a bit further north, is now converted into a temple, and is in a state of disrepair. The designs are markedly Hindu, and date from before the city's founding.

Other sights include **Bhadra Fort and Azamkhan's Palace,** near Teen Darwaja. The fort, built in 1411, is made of red sandstone and now contains offices. The view from the ramparts is decent, however. **Kankaria Lake,** to the southeast of town, provides for a pleasant stroll or picnic around the central lake with island. A moderately interesting aquarium, zoo, and children's park are also around. Buses #32, #42, #60, #152, and #153 all run there.

ENTERTAINMENT

Gujarat is a dry state, which pretty much eliminates nightlife in Ahmedabad. There are two **movie theaters** that show movies in English. **Advance Cinema** is in Lal Darwaja, and **Madhuram Cinema** is in Gheekanta, not far from Rani Roopmati's Mosque. Check the *Times of India* for listings.

■ Near Ahmedabad

Nineteen kilometers north off the road to Gandhinagar, the step-well **Adalaj Vav** ranks among the most impressive in the state. Built in 1499 by Rani Rudabai as a summer retreat, it now serves mainly as a popular relaxation spot for the locals. The gardens around are pleasant enough, but the carvings on the well are the main attraction. The walls, pillars, and platforms of this 5-story well are adorned with intricate lattices and detailed carvings of mythological scenes. The best time to visit is just before noon, when the sunlight illuminates the stonework all the way to the bottom. Buses run to here every 15 minutes from the Central Bus Stand.

Eight kilometers southwest of the city sits the suburb of **Sarkhej,** whose pacific atmosphere makes it seem much more removed than it physically is. Set on one side of an artificial lake is the tomb of Sheikh Ahmed Khattu Ganj Buksh, the spiritual mentor and unofficial advisor of Ahmed Shah. It is the largest mausoleum in the state, with a huge central dome supported by pillars and decorated with exemplary marble, brass, and wood ornamentation. Assorted mosques and mausoleums of later rulers are also around. Sultan Muhammed Beghada's mausoleum and that of his wife Rajabai are interesting as well. It is Sultan Beghada who transformed Sarkhej vastly in the 1500s, adding palaces, gardens, fountains, and courtyards to the previously solemn complex. After these additions, Sarkhej quickly became the vacation retreat of Gujarati sultans. It has declined over the years, but it is still an attractive place about which to wander peacefully. Bus #31 from Lal Darwaja makes the trip here.

The site of **Lothal,** around 90km southwest of Ahmedabad, shook the archeological community when it was discovered in 1945. Lothal is the remains of a city of the ancient Indus Valley Civilization dating from 2400 to 1900 BC. Lying in ruin are old roads, a bathhouse, a sewer, houses and shops, and a dock, suggesting Lothal was a major port city. A **museum** showcases the findings of years of excavation, including seals, jewelry, pots, toys, and weights. Of particular historical interest are the pots and toys made from red pottery, which suggest that an even older civilization once inhabited Lothal, before 4000 BC. (Open Sat.-Thurs. 10am-5pm.) To reach Lothal, take the bus to Bhavnagar, get off at Dholka, and take to a frequent bus from there.

The unassuming town of **Modhera,** 100km northwest of Ahmedabad, is home to an extraordinary Sun Temple built in 1026 by the Solanki King Bhimder I with decidedly Jain influences. As per Sun Temple norms, the temple was constructed and positioned so that at the time of the equinoxes sunlight falls directly on the image of Surya in the sanctuary—mobs of worshipers come at these times. The main pillared entry hall is adorned on the sides with 12 *adityas* representing the sun's phases through the year. The walls and pillars throughout are finely carved with classic Jain dancers, animals, mythological figures, and floral latticework. Due to earthquakes and a razing by Mahmud of Ghazni, the carvings are a bit eroded. (Open daily 8am-6pm.) Buses run to Modhera frequently from the Central Bus Stand (3hr., Rs.32) and from Mehsana, which is connected to Ahmedabad by rail.

Thirty-two kilometers northeast of Ahmedabad is **Gandhinagar,** the capital of Gujarat, the second state capital in India planned and constructed after Independence. Designed by Le Corbusier, who also laid out Chandigarh (see p. 325), the city is rather boring with its symmetry and numbered sectors. Buses run to Gandhinagar every 30 minutes.

The artificially constructed Gujarati village of **Vishalla,** 4km south of Ahmedabad, offers a night of earthy dining in village style. Eat spicy food from leaf plates and drink from clay cups as dressed-up villagers fan insect-repelling scented smoke in your face. The food is plentiful and is accompanied by live tribal music. Around are mud and thatch huts where weavers and potters make their wares. There's a museum featuring a huge collection of pots, utensils, pipes, boxes, and scales. Dinner is an expensive Rs.130, but snacks are also available. (Open daily 11am-1pm and 8-11pm.) Bus #31 comes out here.

▓ Rajkot

Rajkot is a delightfully typical Gujarati town, perhaps all the more typical for having been taken over by industry. Founded in the 16th century, it was once capital of Saurashtra state before being transformed into an important British government center. Today, its claim to fame is its relation to Mahatma Gandhi, who lived here for a short time. A few of its private colleges are also notable.

ORIENTATION

Everything of interest in Rajkot is sandwiched between the **railway station** in the north side of town and the **bus stand** in the south. The Bus Stand is on **Dharbar Road,** which darts north to a major circle that physically marks the center of the city. Right at the circle is **Lakhajiraj Road,** left leads around the Playing Fields up **Dr. Yagnik Road.** Straight ahead is **Jawahar Road,** which passes the Tourist Information Bureau, several banks, and the Jubilee Gardens. The railway station is to the northeast, on **Junction Road,** which becomes **Station Road.**

PRACTICAL INFORMATION

Tourist Office: Tourist Information Bureau, behind State Bank of Saurashtra on Jawahar Rd. (tel. 234507). Moderately helpful staff. Maps of Gujarat Rs.20. No city maps or tours. Open Mon.-Sat. 10:30am-6:10pm.

Currency Exchange: State Bank of India (tel. 226416). Follow Jawahar Rd. past the Jubilee Gardens, on the left. Currency exchange and traveler's checks. Open Mon.-Fri. 11am-3pm, Sat. 11am-1pm. **State Bank of Saurashtra,** Jawahar Rd. (tel. 226575). Currency exchange and traveler's checks. Open Mon.-Fri. 11am-3pm and 3:30-5pm, Sat. 11am-1:30pm.

Telephones: Private STD/ISD booths are throughout the city. A few have fax services. Most open daily 9am-11pm. **Central Telegraph Office:** Jawahar Rd. Open 24hr.

Airport: Rajkot Airport (tel. 53313), 4km northwest of town. **Indian Airlines,** Dharbar Rd. (tel. 27916). Open daily 10am-1pm and 2-5pm. To: Bombay (2-3 per day, 1hr., US$60); Delhi (1 per day, 6hr.); Jaipur (1 per day, 5hr.); Udaipur (1 per day, 4hr.).

Train: Rajkot Railway Station (tel. 131). To: Ahmedabad (*Saurashtra Exp.* 9216, 12:43am; fast passenger, 4:45am; *Intercity Exp.,* 6:40am; *Saurashtra Mail* 9006,

5:20pm; 6hr., Rs.80/230 for 2nd/1st class); Bhavnagar (fast passenger, 11pm, 6hr., Rs.78/228 for 2nd/1st class); Porbandar (fast passenger, 1:20pm, 5½hr., Rs.75); Veraval (fast passenger, 2:55pm; mail, 11:15am; 14hr., Rs.54); Junagadh (fast passenger, 6:15 and 8:15pm; 5hr., Rs.60). **Reservation Office** open Mon.-Sat. 8am-8pm, Sun. 8am-2pm.

Bus: Government buses run from the **Main Bus Stand** (tel. 35025) to Ahmedabad, Porbandar, Veraval via Junagadh, Jamnagar, and Bhavnagar approximately every hr., 6am-9pm. **Private bus companies** line the road opposite the Bus Stand, and run to other locations in Gujarat and Rajasthan and to Bombay. **Shiv Shakti Travels** (tel. 31144) is recommended.

Local Transportation: Unmetered **auto-rickshaws** are abundant; Rs.10 gets you around the city, Rs.20 to the airport.

Library: Lang Library, in Jubilee Gardens, has a decent English collection. Open daily 8am-8pm.

Market: The main commercial areas are throughout the old city, Lakhajiraj Rd., and along the Dharbar-Jawahar Rd. stretch. Fresh fruit and vegetable stalls abound but don't cluster. Most stores open daily 9am-9pm, although some close on Sundays.

Pharmacy: Pharmacies congregate around the Government Hospital northwest of the old city, and behind the Jubilee Gardens. Most open daily 9am-8pm.

Hospital: Government Hospital (tel. 70164). English-speaking, pretty efficient.

Police: Main Police Station, opposite Playing Fields (tel. 26659).

Emergency: Police: tel. 100. **Fire:** tel. 101. **Ambulance:** tel. 102.

Post Office: GPO (tel. 228611), west of Jawahar Rd. opposite Jubilee Gardens. *Poste Restante.* Open Mon.-Sat. 8am-6pm. **Postal Code:** 360001.

Telephone Code: 0281.

ACCOMMODATIONS

Himalaya Guest House, Lakhajiraj Rd. (tel. 31736). Enter through the shopping complex below, from the side street. Spacious but bland rooms begging for some decoration. Rooms are clean and the mattresses are soft, so few complain. Attached baths. Check-out noon. Singles with Rs.75. Doubles Rs.150. Triples Rs.225. Quads Rs.300.

The Galaxy Hotel, Jawahar Rd. (tel. 222904; fax 227053). Undoubtedly the most sophisticated place to stay in Rajkot. Rooms are large and modern and cater to the business traveler, with lounge couches and professional-looking desks, plus color TVs, telephones, and large attached baths. Travel counter, foreign exchange, laundry, and limited room service. Check-out noon. Singles Rs.260-330, with A/C Rs.420-560 depending on size. Doubles Rs.390-500, with A/C Rs.630-840. Single suites Rs.1100. Double suites Rs.1650.

Hotel Samrat International, near Bus Stand (tel. 22269; fax 322724). This modern, plant-filled hotel is the best moderately pricey business-oriented place in town after the Galaxy. Rooms are good-sized with clean carpets and a token random painting or poster. Amenities include laundry, travel service, 24-hr. room service, a fine restaurant, and TVs, telephones, and attached baths in all rooms. Check-out noon. Singles Rs.260, with A/C Rs.450. Doubles Rs.40, with A/C Rs.650. Extra bed Rs.125. 10% luxury tax.

FOOD

If you like Gujarati *thalis,* you're in luck, but it's hard to find anything else, and virtually impossible to find anything even vaguely Continental. Good ice-cream joints line Race Course Rd., and are normally mobbed by young couples every night.

Rainbow Restaurant, Lakhajiraj Rd. (tel. 23354). Under the Himalaya Guest House. A cheap eatery with a good range of veg. South Indian snacks and ice cream, plus simple pizzas. The menu features "All in Anticipation" and "Rising Higher." Sundaes such as "Going Nuts" and "Thrice Blessed" are popular. Air-conditioned upstairs. Most snacks under Rs.20. Open daily 10am-11pm.

Samarkand, in Hotel Samrat International (tel. 22269). A refreshing air-conditioned restaurant with comfortable seats and quick but impersonal service. The food is well-prepared and portions are on the large side. Indian, Continental, and Chinese cuisine, for under Rs.35. Open daily 11:30am-3pm and 7-11pm.

SIGHTS

In the heart of the promenade-worthy but otherwise not too spectacular Jubilee Gardens is the **Watson Museum.** The museum, flanked by two stone lions, is curiously dedicated to Colonel John Watson, a British political agent of the 19th century. The museum has everything from Indus Valley Civilization relics dating to 2000 BC to exquisite miniature paintings, from tribal dioramas to Rajasthani brass- and silverwork. Most peculiar is an 1899 statue of a grim Queen Victoria surrounded by portraits of Gujarati rulers. (Open Thurs.-Tues. 9am-12:30pm and 2:30-6pm. Closed the 2nd and 4th Sat. each month. Admission Rs.0.50.)

Kaba Gandhi no Delo, on Ghitaka Rd., was the residence of the Gandhi family when they moved here in 1881. It now features a small collection of photographs and relics. (Open Mon.-Sat. from 9am to noon and 3 to 6pm.)

▓ Diu

Life on the small island of Diu, also known as Div, off the southern coast of Gujarat, revolves around the twin pleasures of fish and alcohol. Diu was a Portuguese colony and important trade outpost until 1961, when India repossessed it after a bomb strike, and it is therefore considered part of a Union Territory rather than a part of Gujarat. To Gujaratis, this is a good thing, since Gujarat's prohibition laws don't apply in Diu. As a result, Gujaratis invade Diu by the thousands every weekend for mass revelry. In the same way, many tourists come to Diu to take a break from their travels. They are often surprised to find more to Diu than bars. Indeed, Portuguese influence prevails in the city, manifesting itself in the delightful, colorful buildings and churches. An impressive fort and marvelous beaches also serve to cheer up hungover revelers.

ORIENTATION

Diu Island is roughly 12km long from east to west and 3km wide. Entry into Diu is via the port town of **Una** in Saurashtra, and then past the **railway station** in the town of **Delwada** and through the little island of **Goghla,** off the northeastern tip of Diu Island. There is a **passport check** for foreigners upon entry onto Diu Island. **Diu Town** occupies the eastern tip of the island. From Diu Town, roads head west through the island past **Chakratirth Beach** and **Sunset Point,** the town of **Fudam,** the famous **Nagoa Beach,** and **Diu Airport** before ending at the west tip of the island in Varakbara. Diu Town itself is defined by a wall running north-south across the eastern tip. Entry is most common through the northern gate near the **main bus stand** along **Burden Road,** which runs through the city past the **local bus stand,** the **Main Square** with the **GPO,** the **Tourist Information Bureau,** the **Public Gardens,** and the **Police Station** before dead-ending into **Diu Fort** which marks the extreme east tip of the town and island. Entry into Diu Town through the middle **Jampa Gate** results inevitably in hopeless confusion among the tiny, winding streets of the inner old city. The southern entry into the city is along **Jallandhar Beach,** and bends up past the **St. Francis' Hospital** and **St. Thomas' Church** to meet Burden Rd.

PRACTICAL INFORMATION

Tourist Office: Tourist Information Bureau, Burden Rd. near Main Square (tel. 2653). Has maps and travel information. Make all camping arrangements here. Open Mon.-Sat. 9:30am-6pm.

Currency Exchange: State Bank of Saurashtra, near GPO. Currency exchange and travelers' checks. Open Mon.-Fri. 11am-3pm, Sat. 11am-1pm.

Telephones: Private STD/ISD booths line Burden Rd. and are scattered around the inner city as well. A handful have fax services. Most open daily 8am-11pm.

Airport: Diu Airport, 5km west of Diu Town, north of Nagoa Beach. **East-West Airlines** (tel. 2180), near the GPO, has thrice weekly flights to Bombay (US$60) and Ahmedabad (US$50). Flight departures are irregular from Diu, so check times in advance and expect delays and cancellations.

Trains: Delwada Railway Station, between Una and Goghla, 8km from Diu Town. To Veraval (6am and 1pm, 4½hr., Rs.40/122 for 2nd/1st class) and Junagadh (12:45pm, 7hr., Rs.50/168 for 2nd/1st class). Reservation office open Mon.-Sat. 8am-8pm, Sun. 8am-2pm.

Buses: Main Bus Stand, outside city walls, near bridge to mainland. From here, most buses run to Una (every hr., 6am-midnight, 40min., Rs.7). There are also infrequent buses to Ahmedabad (1 per day, 8½hr., Rs.75); Rajkot (2 per day, 6½hr., Rs.50); Veraval (2 per day, 2½hr., Rs.22). From the Una Bus Stand, in Una, there are frequent departures to most destinations in Gujarat. To: Bhavnagar (every hr., 7am-10pm, 6hr., Rs.42); Rajkot (every 2hr., 7am-10pm, 6hr., Rs.43); Veraval (every hr., 6am-11pm, 2hr., Rs.18); Ahmedabad (every 2hr., 7am-8pm, 8hr., Rs.69); Junagadh (every 1½hr., 6am-10pm, 5hr., Rs.35). **Private bus companies** are around the Main Square in Diu Town, and have comfortable minivans and buses running to all destinations in Gujarat. **RR Travels,** in the Main Square (tel. 2329), is recommended. **Avoid Sunday night buses out of Diu, which are inevitably filled with drunken Gujaratis.**

Local Transportation: Auto-rickshaws are everywhere in Diu. Rs.5 gets you around town, Rs.30 to Nagoa Beach, and Rs.60 to Una. Add Rs.20 for night travel out of Diu Town. **Local buses** leave from the **local bus stand** just west of the Main Square to Nagoa Beach (approximately every 1½hr., 7am-4:30pm, Rs.2), and back from Nagoa Beach to Diu (every 1½hr., 8am-5pm, Rs.2). Local buses also run frequently to Delwada (every hr., 6am-11pm, Rs.3). **Bicycles** can be rented from in the Main Square or near Jampa Gate for Rs.20 per day. **Mopeds** can be rented for Rs.150 per day from shops on Burden Rd. near the Public Gardens.

Market: Most markets and stores in Diu open daily 9am-9pm; many closed to some extent on Sundays. In the back of the Main Square lies the **Fish Market,** while the **Vegetable Market** is further down Burden Rd., about 200m past the Main Square on the right.

Pharmacy: A number of pharmacies congregate around St. Francis' Hospital, while fewer are scattered around town along Burden Rd. Most open daily 10am-6pm.

Hospital: St. Francis' Hospital, in St. Francis of Assisi Church, 200m north of Jallandhar Beach (tel. 102). English spoken. Open 24hr.

Police: Main Police Station, Burden Rd. (tel. 100). Past Public Gardens on left.

Emergency: Police: tel. 100. **Fire:** tel. 101. **Ambulance:** tel. 102.

Post Office: GPO, Burden Rd. in Main Square. *Poste Restante.* Open Mon.-Sat. 10am-6pm. **Postal Code:** 362520.

Telephone Code: 028758.

ACCOMMODATIONS AND FOOD

Considering that most visitors to Diu are only looking for a place to crash after a night of drinking, hotels in Diu have no incentive to be spectacular. Nonetheless, there are a number of decent ones, and the attitude throughout is mellow and relaxed. Off-season discounts are substantial, but you'll need to bargain. Most restaurants in Diu provide only bare meals, the minimum required to serve alcohol alongside, since freestanding bars are prohibited. A few restaurants around have good seafood. Catches vary by the week.

Diu Town

Hotel Mozambique, Burden Rd. (tel. 2223). A quaint, distinctly Portuguese building in the heart of the vegetable market. Rooms are big and draw in a nice breeze through the balconies with excellent seaside (or vegetable market) views. Room service 24hr. Restaurant, bar. Check-out 10am. Singles Rs.50, with bath Rs.75. Doubles Rs.80, with bath Rs.100. VIP quad with view Rs.225. None of the prices seem terribly firm.

Jay Shankar's Guest House, Jallandhar Beach. Originally just the best restaurant in town, this place now has an excellent guest house. Family-run with small, clean, homey rooms. Limited room service. The restaurant has high quality preparations of all sorts, but the seafood is what makes it stellar. Check-out 10am. Singles Rs.80. Doubles Rs.120.

Hotel Sanman, Burden Rd. (tel. 2273). A Portuguese mansion that changes its name every few years. Rooms are pretty big with good views of the northern shore and local hand-made furnishings. Limited room service, good restaurant, bar. Check-out 10am. Singles with bath Rs.100. Doubles Rs.125.

Nagoa Beach

In season only, younger crowds like to camp on Nagoa Beach. The **Oasis Camping Site** and the **Island Bar and Restaurant** both have campgrounds with equipment for rent. (Rs.150-200 per night.) Camping outside of these authorized sites is strictly prohibited. All camping enquiries or reservations are handled at the Tourist Information Bureau (see p. 646). One other accommodation option exists on Nagoa Beach.

Ganga Sagar Rest House, Nagoa Beach (tel. 2249). Rooms are small and undecorated, but clean, and the location on the beach is unbeatable. The outer courtyard faces the sea directly and is very relaxed. Limited room service, decent restaurant, bar. Check-out 8am. Singles Rs.100. Doubles Rs.125.

SIGHTS AND ENTERTAINMENT

Wandering through the labyrinthine streets is the best way to see Diu Town, especially after a few drinks at the countless bars. The old inner city is filled with painted Portuguese buildings and villas that make it almost impossible to believe you're in India. **Nagar Seth's Haveli** (ask for directions once you're in the old city) is considered the most impressive and distinctively Portuguese of the lot. Towards the Fort are Diu's three churches, also very European in architecture. **St. Paul's** is badly weathered, but it has grand ceilings and arches and excellent paintings and mass is still said here each Sunday. **St. Thomas's** is nearby, holding the **Diu Museum** with religious paintings and Catholic statues. East past the **Aquarium** is the **Diu Fort,** the most impressive structure on the island. Built in 1591, the Fort is immense and is guarded by a tidal moat. There's little to do in the fort except to wander among dozens of cannonballs and a few cannons. The views of the sea and town are beautiful, especially at sunset. The fort doubles as the island jail. Open daily from 9am to 5pm. Photography very loosely prohibited.

Travelers who are fed up with drinking might want to stop to enjoy Diu's excellent beaches. On the south side of Diu Town, **Jallandhar Beach** is small but convenient. **Chakrakirth Beach,** slightly further west, is very similar. The nearby **Sunset Point** is a favorite local hangout. Seven kilometers west of town is famous **Nagoa Beach,** the longest of the Diu beaches. Peppered with swaying palm trees, the beach exudes a feeling of mellow calm. It's rarely crowded.

Another point of interest is the town of **Vanakbana** on the west tip of Diu Island, where local fishermen can be seen in action, especially along the port. The village of **Fudam,** near Nagoa Beach, is very Portuguese and is dominated by an old church with graceful white towers.

■ Veraval and Somnath

The busy city of Veraval is the most important port in Saurashtra, home to over 1000 boats and a hand-built wooden *dhow* industry. While the docks no doubt provide for an intriguing but smelly stroll, Veraval is more interesting as a stepping stone to nearby Somnath. Known throughout Gujarat for its once-magnificent temple, Somnath is the most popular and most convenient religious vacation spot for most Gujaratis.

ORIENTATION AND PRACTICAL INFORMATION

Veraval's main **bus stand** is located on the main town thoroughfare, which runs roughly northwest-southeast, dead-ending into the port. The center of town is the intersection marked by the **Clock Tower,** 200m towards the port from the bus stand. STD/ISD **telephone** booths are concentrated here. At the Clock Tower, the left road heads northeast, passing **State Bank of India** on the right, which does not exchange traveler's checks but has other currency exchange facilities (open Mon.-Fri. 11am-3pm, Sat. 11am-1pm), and the **GPO** 2 blocks off to the right (open Mon.-Fri. 10am-5pm). This left road ends at the **railway station.** From here, all routes east lead to the one main road that bends around **Veraval Harbor,** ending up in Somnath. Its **bus stand** and the **Temple of Somnath** are 50m apart. Local buses run from Veraval to Somnath and back (every 30min., 6am-midnight, 15 min., Rs.3). An **auto-rickshaw** makes the same trip for Rs.20. Bikes can be rented in season for Rs.20 per day from opposite the Veraval bus stand is well-connected to the rest of Saurashtra. **Trains** run to Ahmedabad (*Girnar Exp.* 9845, 7:30pm, 12hr., Rs.122/370 for 2nd/1st class); Rajkot (passenger, 11:20am, 5hr., Rs.53/190) for 2nd/1st class; Delwada near Diu (passenger, 8:40am, Express 3:20pm, 4hr., Rs.38/119 for 2nd/1st class). **Buses** run to Diu (every 30min., 8am-10pm., 3hr., Rs.30); Porbandar (every 30min., 7am-10pm., 3hr., Rs.35); Junagadh (every 30min., 6:30am-11pm, 2hr., Rs.25); Bhavnagar (every hr., 7am-10pm, 3½hr., Rs.43); Rajkot (5 per day, 6hr., Rs.50). **Postal Code:** 3662265. **Telephone Code:** 02876.

ACCOMMODATIONS AND FOOD

There are only two hotels in Somnath, both of which are far preferable to the dozens located in the noisy and dirty center of Veraval. For food, you'll have to settle for standard run-of-the-mill *dhabas.*

Mayuram Hotel, opposite Somnath Bus Stand (tel. 20286). Big rooms, spotlessly maintained but on the spartan side. Still, the green bedcovers grow on you, and mosquitoes are surprisingly absent. Attached baths, travel arrangements, limited room service. Check-out noon. Singles and doubles Rs.150. Triples Rs.200. Quads Rs.250.

Sri Somnath Guest House, opposite Somnath Bus Stand. *Dharamshala*-style accommodations. The rooms are slightly larger than human-sized and offer little more than a bed, but the price is right. Check-out 24hr. Singles and doubles Rs.50. Triples Rs.80.

Hotel Kasturi, near Veraval Bus Stand (tel. 20248). On a small side street relatively away from the hustle of downtown Veraval. Rooms are fairly large with congruous furniture, a tasteful painting or three, and attached baths. Limited room service, travel arrangements. Check-out 10am. Singles Rs.90, with A/C Rs.250. Doubles Rs.175, with A/C Rs.300.

SIGHTS

Somnath is renowned throughout Gujarat for its large **Temple of Somnath,** also known as **Prabhas Patan Mandir.** The history of the temple is more interesting for the most part than the temple itself. According to a popular myth, the site of the temple was dedicated to a hallucinogenic ritual plant called *sona* which figures often in the *Vedas.* Legend has it that the temple itself was first built of pure gold by Samraj the moon god, then of silver by Ravana the sun god, then of wood by Krishna, and finally of stone by the Pandava brother Bhimdeva. Historians insist instead that the temple was built in the early 10th century AD, and are quite adamant that the temple was made of stone, not gold, silver, or wood. But at one time the temple was so rich that its coffers were stuffed with gold and jewelry and its full-time staff included hundreds of dancers and musicians. The notorious Mahmud of Ghazni raided it and destroyed it in the early 11th century, effectively starting a cycle of sacking and rebuilding that persisted until Aurangzeb's final pillage in 1706. In 1950, it was rebuilt

Mahmud of Ghazni

The first time the Temple of Somnath was destroyed, the infamous Mahmud of Ghazni was responsible. This took place in 1025, by which time the Mahmud had been raiding South Asia for almost 30 years. He began his career of temple raids in 997, and for years smashed temples and idols and stole jewels and women from throughout western India. Mahmud turned Ghazni, in Afghanistan, into one of the world's greatest centers of Islamic culture, luring many luminaries from India and elsewhere. Before his death, he annexed Punjab and added it to his empire.

The court chronicler reported (undoubtedly being generous to his ruler) that 10,000 Hindu temples were destroyed by Mahmud alone. Whatever the number, hundreds were destroyed and hundreds of people killed and wounded, fanning flames of religious hatred that have yet to be extinguished.

The court chronicler may have been exaggerating once again when he reported that 50,000 Hindus were killed and tons of gold and jewels were taken the day that Mahmud raided the Temple of Somnath. The chronicler also reports that the inhabitants of Somnath stood by peacefully, watching the charge, convinced that they were protected by Shiva, whose enormous *linga* hung suspended magnetically inside the temple's sanctum. But the *linga*'s powers of levitation didn't help—when the jewel-encrusted temple was destroyed, it too was smashed to pieces.

by Sardar Patel, who is commemorated by a statue outside the temple. Not surprisingly, very little of the original temple remains. Nonetheless, it is still very grand, and the stonework is quite elaborate in places, although the bitter sea winds seem to have gotten the better of the stone on the ocean side. Thousands of devotees are drawn here and there are avid *pujas* at 7am, noon, and 7pm.

Near the temple is the **Somnath Museum,** which holds the remains of previous temple glories—statues, paintings, latticework, stone sculptures, pottery, and more. The collection is strange and eclectic. (Open Thurs.-Tues. 9am-noon and 3-6pm, closed the 2nd and 4th Sat. each month. Admission Rs.0.50.)

Other places of interest in Somnath are the nearby temple to the east. The **Triveni Tirth** marks the intersection of the Miran, Saraswati, and Kapil Rivers and plays a role in Krishna legend. The area is home to a handful of modern temples. To the north is the **Surya Mandir,** an ancient temple of the sun, most of which was destroyed by Mahmud of Ghazni, but which still has interesting animal carvings.

■ Junagadh

The lively town of Junagadh, also known as Junagarh, less than 100km north of Diu, is surprisingly untainted by Western influences. Nestled at the base of the famous Mount Girnar, the town is filled with temples, *havelis,* mosques, and exciting bazaars. Junagadh dates from the 4th century BC when it was capital of Gujarat under the emperor Ashoka. After Ashoka's death, it passed through several hands before falling under Muslim rule, where it remained until Independence. The ruler of Junagadh at this time wanted to pass it to Pakistan, but the Hindu majority in town promptly exiled him, and Junagadh joined the Indian Union. While Junagadh is a fascinating city to visit at any time, the pilgrimage site of Mount Girnar ensures that during the Shivaratri Festival in February-March it turns into a crowded, wild, and crazy nine-day party.

ORIENTATION AND PRACTICAL INFORMATION

Due to its nonsensical layout, Junagadh is a rather difficult city to navigate, but it's so small that it's hard to get too lost. The **main bus stand** is on **Dhal Road,** the main east-west throughway, which runs through **Chittakhana Chowk,** the central bazaar area to **Uperkot Fort. Hotel Relief,** the unofficial tourist information center, is here (tel.

20280). Before Chittakhara Chowk, **Station Road** breaks north towards the **Junagadh Railway Station.** At Chittakhara Chowk, **Mahatma Gandhi Road** forks south past the **General Hospital,** the **local bus stand,** and the **City Post Office** (open Mon.-Sat. 10am-6pm) before reaching **Kalwa Chowk,** the city's south market area along the old city walls. Roughly halfway between Chittakhara Chowk and Uperkot Fort, a road branches south through **Diwan Chowk** near the **State Bank of India** (traveler's checks and currency exchange. Open Mon.-Fri. 11am-3pm, Sat. 11am-1pm). STD/ISD **telephone** booths are all over the city. **Auto-rickshaws** abound in the city; Rs.10 gets you around; Rs.25 to Mount Girnar. **Local buses** run to Mount Girnar from the local bus stand (every hr., 6am-10pm, Rs.3). **Bicycles** can be rented from several locations around Chittakhara Chowk for Rs.20 per day. Junagadh is well-connected to other cities in Gujarat. **Trains** to: Ahmedabad (*Somnath Mail* 9923, 7pm; *Girnar Exp.* 9845, 9pm, 9½hr., Rs.110/323 for 2nd/1st class); Veraval (passenger; 6:30, 9am, 2:30, and 6pm, 2hr., Rs.29/109 for 2nd/1st class); Rajkot (*Veraval-Rajkot Mail* 9837, 1:10pm, 4½hr., Rs.38/144 for 2nd/1st class); Delwada for Diu (6am, 6½hr., Rs.50/108 for 2nd/1st class). **Buses** to Rajkot (every 30min., 6am-midnight, 2hr., Rs.25); Porbandar (every 30min., 6am-midnight, 2hr., Rs.22); Veraval (every 2hr., 7am-10pm, 2½hr., Rs.30). **Private bus companies** are along Dhal Rd. and have comfortable minivans and buses to all locations in Gujarat. **Emergency: Police:** tel. 100. **Fire:** tel. 101. **Ambulance:** 102. Inconveniently located 3km southwest of town is the **GPO** (*Poste Restante.* Open Mon.-Sat. 10am-6pm). **Postal Code:** 362001. **Telephone Code:** 0285.

ACCOMMODATIONS

During Shivaratri, all hotels are booked solid; be sure to reserve well in advance if you plan to visit during these times. The Railway Station also has retiring rooms for Rs.30 (singles) and Rs.60 (doubles) per night.

Hotel Relief, Chittakhana Chowk (tel. 20280). Popular, mainly because it has assumed the role of the city's unofficial tourist information center. Average-sized rooms with tasteful decorations and furniture. Limited room service, decent restaurant with early breakfasts. Check-out 10am. Singles Rs.100, with bath Rs.125, with A/C Rs.325. Doubles Rs.125, with bath Rs.175, with A/C Rs.425.

Hotel Capital, Kalwa Chowk (tel. 21442). Let's just say that the attraction here is the price. Expect no frills of any sort. Small in-need-of-a-whitewash rooms with dingy common baths. Check-out 24hr. Singles Rs.25. Doubles Rs.40.

Hotel National, Kalwa Chowk (tel. 27891). A gem in the Kalwa Chowk spartan hotel rough. Rooms are spotless, carpeted, well-decorated, and even a bit romantic. Excellent restaurant, 24-hour room service, travel services. Check-out 10am. Singles with bath Rs.75, with bathtub and A/C Rs.225. Doubles Rs.100, with bathtub and A/C Rs.325.

FOOD

Food in Junagadh is unspectacular. Although a number of food stalls and *dhabas* are in the two main market areas (Chittakara and Kalwa Chowk), you'll find better (but still mediocre) food at hotels.

Santoor Restaurant, Mahatma Gandhi Rd. While the exterior leans towards shabby, inside you'll find a popular air-conditioned eatery. Service is quick. Indian veg. dishes are artfully presented (under Rs.30). Open daily 8am-10:30pm.

Geeda Lodge, near Railway Station. Another dingy-outside-but-great-food-inside type of place. This *thali* joint insists on keeping the stainless steel covered with gobs of steamy, spicy veggies. *Thalis* Rs.22. Open daily 11am-3pm and 6-11pm.

SIGHTS

The impressive **Uperkot Fort** stoutly sitting atop its mini-plateau in the middle of the town ranks among the best in the state. It was originally built in 319 BC, and in its colorful history was actually lost for 300 years until its rediscovery in 976 AD. It was besieged a whopping 16 times over an 800-year period; one unsuccessful siege lasted 12 years. A high stone *tripolia* gate marks the entrance of the fort and the start of the twisty cobblestone path that meanders first to the **Jumma Masjid,** built on top of a Hindu temple. It must once have been quite amazing with its 140 pillars supporting its high ceiling; now its lack of maintenance shows. Further north in the Fort are the so-called **Buddhist Caves,** dating from before 500 AD. These caves were cut into the soft rocky hillside, and are rather mystic with their faint remnants of stone carvings of flora and mythical images on the interior pillars. If the cave-exploring scene suits your fancy, check out the **Babupyana Caves,** south of the fort, and the **Khapra Kodia Caves,** north of the fort. Two *vavs,* or step-wells, are also in the fort. The **Adi Chadi Vav** has 170 steps descending into the dimness below, while the extraordinary **Navghan Kuva** has a unique 11th-century circular staircase that winds over 50m down the well. (Open daily 6am-7pm. Admission Rs.1.)

Near Diwan Chowk outside the fort is the **Durbar Hall Museum.** The collection is extensive, but pretty standard as fort city museums go. Weapons, armor, silver articles of all types, tapestries, costumes, *howdahs,* portraits, parasols, textiles, and the requisite stuffed animal or three. (Open Thurs.-Tues. 9am-12:15pm and 3-6 pm; closed the second and fourth Sat. of the month. Admission Rs.0.50.)

On Mahatma Gandhi Rd. towards the railway station is the dazzling **Mahabat Muqdara.** This mausoleum is truly impressive, with spiraling minarets and curved grand arches and numerous domes. The architecture throughout is intricate and smooth, providing for a *muqdara* quite unique in Gujarat. The interior is opulent, with carved silver doors and artifacts. Unfortunately, the **mosque** nearby clashes uneasily with this splendid structure.

Heading east towards the final destination of Mount Girnar, a granite boulder of statewide fame sits in protected modern house. The boulder is inscribed with **Ashokan edicts** dating from the 3rd century BC. These edicts, inscribed by Ashoka in Brahmi script, teach assorted moral lessons of *dharma,* tolerance, equality, love, harmony, and peace. The Sanskritic inscriptions were added later by future rulers, and are hardly as noble, referring to the floods occurring in the nearby areas.

The 1100-m extinct volcano **Mount Girnar** is about 4km east of Junagadh and has been deemed holy by several religions since 300 BC. Approximately 5000 steps wind to the summit through verdant forests alternating with sun-scorched stone outcrops. Start your climb before 7am to avoid the heat, and prepare to frequent the food and drink stalls lining the way up. One-and-a-half hours up there is a cluster of fine Jain temples. The marble **Neminath Temple,** dedicated to the 22nd *tirthankara,* who, according to legend, died on Mount Girnar, houses a black marble image of the ascetic and features typical richly detailed Jain temple carvings along pillars, domes, and arches. Some beautiful, colorful mosaic-work in several locations is rather unusual for Jain temples, but still congruous with the latticework. The nearby **Mallinath Temple** is of similar quality. Another 2000 steps seems like a lot, but it's worth the struggle to reach the peak, if only to engrave your name with chalk in the rocks along the side, along with your ascension time (claims of under two hours next to some names are hardly credible). At the top, the **Amba Mata Temple** is a small shrine that sees as many newlyweds as some hill stations because it supposedly grants a happy marriage. Smaller shrines also dot the top of the peak. The view is breathtaking.

Sakar Bagh, 4km north of Junagadh, has a **zoo** that's quite impressive by Indian zoo standards, with Gir lions, tigers, and leopards. (Open daily 9am-6pm. Admission Rs.2.) A small **museum** shelters statues, historic archeological relics, manuscripts, statues, and other miscellanea. (Open Thurs.-Tues. 9am-12:15pm and 3-6pm.)

■ Dwarka

A Hindu myth holds that Krishna set up his capital on the westernmost point on the Kathiawad peninsula after being forced to flee Mathura in Uttar Pradesh. The isolated city he established is Dwarka, now an important Hindu pilgrimage site and home to dozens of temples that pepper the crowded streets. Just about every strain of Hindu legend agrees on Dwarka's holiness. Vishnu is said to have descended as a fish and battled demons in this area. The 9th-century saint Shankara established a monastery here, marking it as the westernmost point of India, corresponding to other monasteries in the north, east, and south. Few tourists make it out to Dwarka, but those do leave quite satisfied, even though the temples are not as architecturally impressive as others further inland. Asked to explain their satisfaction, most will ascribe Dwarka's appeal to its quasi-mystic remoteness compared to most hectic cities in Gujarat. The smell of the sea blowing through Dwarka is a welcome change from urban exhaust.

ORIENTATION AND PRACTICAL INFORMATION

Dwarka is small enough to traverse on foot, even though **auto-rickshaws** abound (Rs.5 gets you anywhere). The main entry road into the city passes the **railway station,** the **police station** (tel. 100), and the **bus stand** before cutting through the town to the coast, marked by the **Dwarka Lighthouse.** Any of the tiny side streets left off the main road eventually leads to the main **Dwarkadish Temple,** which is visible from afar. STD/ISD **telephone** booths are all along the main road. From the Bus Stand, local buses run to **Okha,** which serves as the port to reach the island of **Bet Dwarka** (every hr., 6am-8pm, 1hr., Rs.5.50). Dwarka is also connected by bus to Somnath via Porbandar (6am and 6:45pm, 5hr., Rs.45) and Rajkot via Jamnagar (every 1½hr., 6am-8pm, 6hr., Rs.55). There are trains to Jamnagar (2 per day, 4hr., Rs.40/150) and to Bombay via Rajkot (5hr., Rs.60/199) and then Ahmedabad (11½ hr., Rs.137/371). **Postal Code:** 361355. **Telephone Code:** 02892.

ACCOMMODATIONS AND FOOD

There are a number of accommodations options in Dwarka, almost all catering to pilgrims. Spartan living standards are the norm. Most of these hotels are acceptable to the budget traveler, with clean well-maintained rooms and attached bathrooms. **Hotel Meera,** on the entry road into town (tel. 331), is the best choice, with spotless whitewashed rooms with attached baths, and a friendly familial staff. Check-out 24hr. Singles Rs.50. Doubles Rs.75. What makes it a great stay is the **Meera Dining Hall** to the side, with delicious bottomless *thalis* for only Rs.15. Open daily from 11am to 3pm and 6 to 11pm. The **Toran Tourist Guest House,** near the coast (tel. 313) is another good choice. Run by Gujarat Tourism, it features big well-kept rooms with coordinated furniture and a knowledgeable staff. Mosquito nets are provided. Check-out noon. Dorm beds Rs.35. Doubles with bath Rs.225. Apart from the excellent Meera Dining Hall, **food** is limited to the plentiful stalls lining the main road.

SIGHTS

The principal attraction in Dwarka is the grand **Dwarkadish Temple,** marking the center of town with its 6-story 50-m-high main spire. The exterior stonework is impressive, although a bit weathered, and is heavily dominated by spiky motifs. Sixty columns support the main structure, which houses a black marble Krishna image in a silver-plated chamber. Smaller shrines decorate the edges of the complex. The temple is open daily from 7am to 9:30pm to Hindus only, but non-Hindus can sign a release form to obtain entrance. Dreadlocked guides will take you around for Rs.30, but are entirely unnecessary.

No pilgrimage to Dwarka is complete without a visit to the tip of the peninsula, to the tiny island of **Bet Dwarka.** The island is reached through the port at Okha one hour north of Dwarka. From the port, pile onto overloaded, badly painted, pink and blue, old wood, unbalanced boats that make the 30-minute crossing every 20 minutes for Rs.2.50. The island has a number of architecturally boring temples dedicated to Krishna, where devotees come by the masses for *prasad* and *pujas*. The main temple has a central well that brings up supposedly sweet-tasting water, although it apparently draws from the surrounding salty ocean. It marks the spot of Krishna's death, according to legend. The main appeal of Bet Dwarka is its remote solitude and mysticism, eerily enhanced by its silence, broken only by howling dogs and chanting old women.

NEPAL

Rolling down from the highest, coldest mountains of the Himalaya to green hills and valleys and then to plains, Nepal is a country molded by its geography. Ridges and rivers split the country into small pockets of liveable earth, connected to one another by tenuous roads, often impassable for parts of the year. Wedged between India and China, Nepal is located on the frontier of several civilizations, its landscape refracting their many cultures, all of which come together in the country's political and social center, the Kathmandu Valley. A closed kingdom until 1951, Nepal now greets travelers with a rapidly developing tourism industry and the ubiquitous welcoming gesture of *namaste*.

ESSENTIALS

▨ Money

IRs.100=Rs.158.9
US$1=Rs.55.75
CDN$1=Rs.40.75
UK£1=Rs.85.23
IR£1=Rs.88.06
AUS$1=Rs.42.53
NZ$1=Rs.37.91
SARand=Rs.12.82

Rs.100=IRs.62.94
Rs.100=US$1.79
Rs.100=CDN$2.45
Rs.100=UK£1.17
Rs.100=IR£1.14
Rs.100=AUS$2.35
Rs.100=NZ$2.63
Rs.100=SARand7.80

Currency is measured in rupees (Rs.) which are divided into 100 paise (p.). Rupees appear in one-rupee coins and 1, 2, 5, 10, 20, 50, 100, 500, and 1000 rupee notes. Check all banknotes carefully; ripped bills will be refused by many merchants (although banks will exchange them for new ones).

The cost of living and traveling in Nepal is very low—budget tourists in Kathmandu tend to get by on about Rs.500-800 (US$9-15) per day, and when you're trekking you'll have a hard time spending more than Rs.200 (US$4) a day. It is always a good idea to take an extra few hundred dollars to Nepal with you in case of emergencies. Also, remember to budget for tips to trekking guides and porters.

▨ Getting Around

BY PLANE

Air travel is essential to Nepal's economy, providing access to northern mountainous regions where there are no roads. Travelers will find as well that air travel is important, in order to avoid long, hellish bus rides. The government-run **Royal Nepal Airlines Corporation (RNAC)** operates flights to about 35 airports and airstrips throughout Nepal. The RNAC is suffering financially and its planes are constantly used to capacity. However, privatization has recently given birth to three new airlines: Everest Air, Necon Air, and Nepal Airways. All of their prices are the same, but the new private companies are said to have better service than RNAC. All foreigners must pay for flights with foreign exchange, and prices range from US$50-160 for domestic flights.

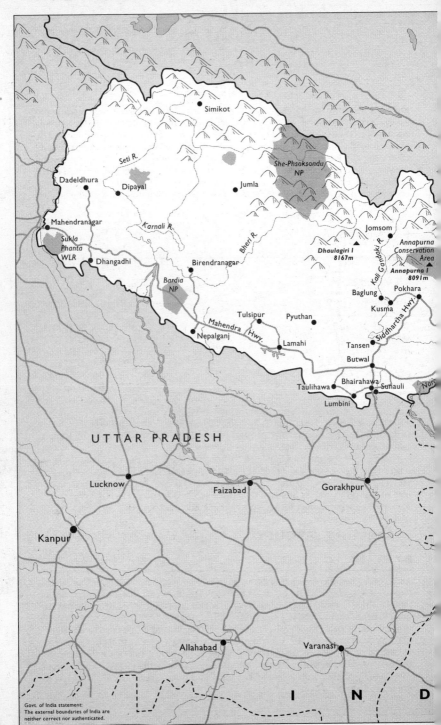

Simikot

She-Phsoksandu
NP

Seti R.

Dadeldhura
Dipayal
Jumla

Mahendranagar
Karnali R.
Jomsom

Sukla
Phanta
WLR
Bheri R.
Dhaulagiri I
8167m
Annapurna
Conservation
Area

Dhangadhi
Birendranagar
Annapurna I
8091m

Bardia
NP
Baglung
Pokhara

Kusma

Tulsipur
Pyuthan
Mahendra Hwy.

Nepalganj
Lamahi
Tansen

Butwal

Taulihawa
Bhairahawa
Sunauli

Lumbini

UTTAR PRADESH

Lucknow
Faizabad
Gorakhpur

Kanpur

Allahabad
Varanasi

I   N   D

Nepal

TIBET (CHINA)

SIKKIM

Manaslu 8163m

Langtang NP

Cho Oyu 8201m

Sagarmatha (Mt. Everest) 8848m
Lhotse 8516m
Makalu 8463m

Sagarmatha NP

Gauri Shankar 7134m

Makalu-Barun NP

Kanchenjunga 8586m

Besisahar
Gorkha
Damauli
Dumre
Mugling
Narayanghat
Bharatpur

Dhunche
Trisuli
Kodari
Chautara
Kathmandu
Bhaktapur
Patan
Dhulikhel

Nyalam
Lamosangu
Jiri
Namche
Lukla

Tumlingtar
Taplejung
Basantpur
Hile
Bhojpur
Dhankuta
Ilam
Dharan
Siliguri
Kakarbhitta

Chitwan NP

Hetauda
Amlekhganj
Birganj
Raxaul

Sindhulimadi

Koshi-Tappu WLR
Rajbiraj
Biratnagar

Janakpur
Jaleswar

Muzaffarpur

BIHAR

Patna

WEST BENGAL

I N D I A

Marsyangdi R.
Budhi Gandhaki R.
Trisuli R.
Prithvi Hwy.
Tribhuvan Hwy.
Bagmati R.
Mahendra Hwy.
Sun Kosi R.
Dudh Kosi R.
Arun R.
Tamar R.
Sapt Kosi R.

100 miles
100 kilometers

N

On the whole, air travel in Nepal is unpredictable. Bad weather prevents take-offs and landings, so long delays at the airport are the norm. During the high trekking season it might be difficult to get tickets for popular destinations such as Lukla. It is best to book plane tickets through travel agents, who can give you an idea of what's available.

BY BUS

> **Warning:** Due to poor roads, mountain weather conditions, and aggressive driving, road travel in Nepal can be dangerous.

Bus travel is widely used in Nepal, although the road conditions are poor and the hilly terrain multiplies travel time. Almost all buses are privately owned, but look out for the government **"Sajha"** buses which are safer and much more comfortable. For these you'll probably have to book tickets from the bus stand a day in advance.

Booking bus tickets can be a pain in Kathmandu or Pokhara, because the bus stands are located far from the tourist center. You might find it easier to have a travel agent make arrangements. Avoid package deals for complex bus journeys, however; these often turn out to be scams. You'll do better buying your second ticket once you arrive at your transit point. For more information, see **Getting Around by Bus** (p. 48).

BY CAR

Driving in Nepal is risky. Road conditions are poor, there are plenty of zero-visibility hairpin turns around mountainsides, and there is little infrastructure to help you if you get stuck. For more information, see **Getting Around** (p. 48). Also keep in mind that killing one of those omnipresent cows, even by accident, is punishable in Nepal by up to 20 years' imprisonment.

■ Accommodations

Much of our accommodations wisdom applies to both India and Nepal; see **Essentials: Accommodations** (p. 52). Nepal's budget lodge scene differs from India's in that it is the result of a very recent boom, and foreign tourists are its main targets. Tourist ghettoes unlike anything in India have grown up in Pokhara and Kathmandu, where fierce competition between neighboring guest houses has led to rock-bottom prices and generally better and friendlier hotels than in India. Soft beds, curtains, and clean rooms may suddenly turn out to be within your price range, and you'll find your hotel manager speaks English and wants to rent you a bike as well. More expensive hotels are only available in Kathmandu and Pokhara. **Trekking lodges** are also an important means of accommodation in Nepal. For more information about these, see **Trekking,** p. 55

■ Keeping in Touch

Most of the information about keeping in touch applies equally to India or Nepal; see **Keeping in Touch** (p. 61). The GPO in Kathmandu is by far the most reliable place in Nepal for *Poste Restante*. Tell your correspondents to underline your last name. If you can't find your mail, check under your first name. You should have to show a passport to take anything away. Stamps can be bought at post offices and at many bookshops (some will also take your mail to the post office for you).

Phones are fairly widespread in Nepal—international calls can be made from numerous STD/ISD (Standard Trunk Dialing/International Subscriber Dialing) booths, also known as "communications" booths. Some of these have fax machines too. **Nepal's country code is 977;** the city code for Kathmandu is and all of the Kathmandu Valley is 1. City codes must be preceded by a "0" if calling from within Nepal. Calling home, dial the international access code (00), the country code, the city or area code and then the number. The code is 001 for the United States and Canada, 0044 for the United Kingdom, 00353 for Ireland, 0061 for Australia, 0064 for New Zealand, and 0027 for South Africa.

■ Hours and Holidays

Although five different **calendars** are in use in Nepal, the official one used in newspapers, government offices, and on historical displays in museums is the Bikram Sambat (or Vikram Sambat) calendar, named after the legendary King Vikramaditya. Day one of this calendar was February 23, 57 BC. The year 2054 BS begins on April 13, 1997. For more information, see **Festivals and Holidays** (p. 769).

Government offices are typically open from 10am to 5pm Sunday through Thursday, closing at 3pm on Fridays, and at 4pm on weekdays in the winter (mid-Nov.-mid-Jan.). **Banks** are open from 10am to 2pm Sunday through Thursday, closing at noon on Fridays. Only embassies and international offices take Sunday off. They are usually open from 9am to 5pm Monday through Friday. **Businesses** keep much longer hours, especially in touristy areas, and may be open Saturday.

Nepal is 15 minutes ahead of Indian Standard Time, just to be different, it seems. This puts Nepalese Time at 5hr. 45min. ahead of GMT, 10hr. 45 min. ahead of North American Eastern Standard Time, and 4hr. 15min. behind Australian Eastern Standard Time. No Summer Time or Daylight Saving Time is used in Nepal, so in summer Nepal is only 4hr. 45min. ahead of British time, and 9hr. 45min. ahead of North American Eastern Daylight Saving Time.

LIFE AND TIMES

■ Geography

Snow-pinnacled heights, emerald-stepped valleys, cascading glacial rivers, river-rent gorges, thick tropical jungles—all are part of the terrain of the tiny, landlocked Kingdom of Nepal, wedged between India and Tibet on the southern slopes of the Himalaya. With eight of the world's ten highest peaks within its mere 140,797-square-kilometer area, nearly 75% of Nepal is mountain. Yet its entire cast was once submerged beneath an ancient sea. Only with the tectonic collision of India with Asia, 50-60 million years ago, did the upheaval of mountains begin. Over subsequent millennia, continued continental crunching gave rise to the mountain systems defining the region today. And the mountains continue to grow.

Nepal is customarily divided into five geographical belts running east-west across the country. The Tarai, adjacent to the Indian border, is the northernmost reach of the Indo-Gangetic Plain. Fertile, low-lying (200m elevation), hot, and humid, the Tarai once was covered with dense, malarial forest that supported wildlife but few humans. Recently deforested, the Tarai today teams with Nepal's mobile, growing population. Rising abruptly from the Tarai plain to altitudes between 1300m and 1800m, the forested Chure or Siwalik hill chain runs parallel to its neighbor further north, the Mahabharat Range. Dry climate and poor soil keeps the Chure hills sparsely populated. Intermittently separating the Chure and Mahabharat ranges are broad spindled valleys referred to as the Inner Tarai. At altitudes of 700-1000m, the Inner Tarai harbors tropical deciduous forests and wildlife similar to that once found in the Tarai, although it too is quickly succumbing to development. The Mahabharat Range rises to 3000m. With steep escarpments to the south offering natural fortification, the Mahabharat is moderately well-settled (despite its steep slopes, the range is endowed with water-retentive soils amenable to terrace cultivation), but, except along its passes, it is cut off from human traffic. The region is a transverse zone for much of Nepal's water, fissured by the deep, north-south river gorges of Nepal's three major river systems, the Karnali, Narayani, and Kosi.

NEPAL

Between the Mahabharat and the Himalaya resides the Pahar zone. At altitudes from 500-2000m, the region holds flat fertile valleys, including the Kathmandu, Banepa, and Pokhara Valleys. With accommodating climate and good crop-bearing conditions, the Pahar has been inhabited and cultivated for centuries, and today supports nearly 40% of Nepal's population. Last but not least, the Himalaya are inhabited only in scattered mountain pockets, valleys, and elevated plateaus. Human settlement gives way by 4000m, where pervasive mist and clouds inhibit any crop cultivation. Above 4000m, dense forest yields to alpine pasture, which yields in turn, at 5500m, to snowline, beyond which nothing but mountains will grow. Ten Nepalese peaks rise higher than 8000m, including Mt. Everest, at 8848m, the highest point on earth.

■ Climate

Nepal derives its overall climatic character from the monsoon regime of South Asia, yet its varied topography allows the country to entertain a dramatic sweep of climates. While the Tarai swelters in its tropical cast, altitudes higher than 5000m endure perpetually freezing temperatures. Kathmandu, at an altitude of 1331m, has a mild climate, welcoming tourists year-round with average July temperatures of 26°C, January temperatures of 10°C.

The monsoon spans a four-month period from June to September. This is also summer in Nepal, although the heat peaks in May. While most of the country is cloud-cast and beset with downpours, western Nepal, largely under rainshadow, is drier, and come August, also a wonderland of flowers. Monsoon winds discharge their greatest heft as they come upon the Annapurna range, rendering the Pokhara Valley particularly awash. The post-monsoon reprieve, from October to November, is high tourist season and the favored time for treks. The countryside is fresh, temperatures are mild, and the air is clear—the mountains are visible. December to March is too cold or snowy for most trekkers. From March to May, Nepal is characteristically hazy, dusty, and dry, and the mountains are not usually visible. For specifics about when to go, potential trekkers should see **Trekking** (p. 54).

■ People

Described in its constitution as a multilingual, multiethnic nation, the Kingdom of Nepal represents a population of 20.6 million people and over 60 ethnic, linguistic, and caste groups. Nepal owes much of its cultural heterogeneity to the difficulty of its terrain, which kept its many peoples isolated. Only over the past few centuries has the word "Nepal" has come to represent the country as a whole (formerly, a "Nepali" was an inhabitant of the Kathmandu Valley), and it is still customary among people who retain strong regional affiliations to identify themselves as *pahari, madeshi, or bhutia* (hills, plains, or northern border dwellers).

Nepali culture reflects a predominance of Indian influence, including a caste system and the Hindu faith. Most Nepalis are Hindu, speak Sanskrit-derived languages (such as Nepali), and trace Indo-Aryan ancestry. Large-scale migrations from Tibet and the east brought Tibeto-Burmese languages and Buddhist culture to Nepal, today accounting for 45% of the population. While Indo-Aryans settled mostly in southern regions and lower altitudes, where Hindus are a majority (although there are also populations of Muslims and aboriginal tribes), the Tibeto-Burmese settled mostly in higher altitudes and in the north, where Buddhist culture predominates. Distinctly Mongolian races, the highlands and northern border people retain much in common with Tibetans, and show the influence not only of Tibetan Mahayana Buddhism, but of Bön, the early religion of Tibet prior to Buddhism. Among the most recent immigrants from Tibet are the Tamangs, the most populous of Tibeto-Burmese ethnic groups, and the Sherpas, among the northernmost inhabitants of the Himalaya. Other Tibeto-Nepalese groups include the Limbus of the far eastern hills, and the Sunwar and Rai of the mid-eastern hills. In west-central Nepal, the Gurungs and Magars are thought to be among Nepal's earliest inhabitants. Although of Mongolian strain, they developed a Sanskritized language. The Newaris, the earliest known arrivals to Nepal and the original settlers of the Kathmandu Valley, today account for only 4% of the total population. Influenced by both Buddhism and Hinduism, the Newaris are the progenitors of the country's most celebrated art.

A "nation of villages," about 90% of Nepalis live in small market centers and rural settlements. Under a predominantly agricultural economy, with most people dependent on subsistence farming, population density is a function of agricultural productivity. The fertile Tarai supports Nepal's highest population density, and has become not only the country's bread-basket but also a booming industrial region. The highlands and trans-Himalayan valleys, with less than 1% of land under cultivation, remain sparsely populated, with people managing a nomadic way of life.

■ History

Nepal has been a political unit for just over 200 years, and prior to this its history is very uncertain. The Nepalese have legends to explain their origins, but these give only foggy information about how Nepal went from a collection of stone-age outposts 200,000 years ago into the collection of small agrarian Rajput kingdoms that would be unified by Prithvi Narayan Shah. Some of the answers can be found in the land itself: from the flat Tarai by the Indian border, Nepal's land rises into four ranges of hills and mountains, culminating in the Great Himalaya. The Mahabharat range, which runs through the middle of the country, has cradled Nepalese culture while consigning it to a muffin-tray of little valleys (like the Kathmandu Valley) that make transport and communication difficult. For most of its history Nepal has been divided into valley-states under local kings. The people of these hillsides were never in total isolation, for Nepal felt the influence of the great civilizations on either side: India to the south, and Tibet and China to the north. But travel was difficult, and most people clung to the land.

The lowlands of the Tarai on the Indian border have always had strong connections with India, ever since the Ganges Valley was settled around 1000 BC (although most of the Tarai was thick malarial forest until the 19th century). It was in Lumbini in the Nepalese Tarai that the Buddha was born around 560 BC.

The Early Kathmandu Valley

The Kathmandu Valley is the historical heartland of Nepal and the source of its greatest cultural traditions. The indigenous Newari people and their rulers have long exploited their position on the trade route between India and Tibet, drawing revenue from the goods passing through. Most of what is known of Nepal's early history comes from the Kathmandu Valley, and the name "Nepal" originally referred only to the Valley. The early kingdoms of Nepal never expanded far, however. They were content to guard their strategic position and control the closest adjacent lands.

The Kiratis, a dynasty with Mongol genes from the north, may have ruled the Kathmandu Valley during the first millennium BC and introduced Buddhism to the area. During the 4th or 5th century AD, the Licchavis took over, Nepal's first dynasty from the Indian plains. The Lichhavis brought with them Hinduism, establishing a longstanding pattern of a Hindu upper class ruling over Buddhist commoners. Under the Licchavis the Kathmandu Valley enjoyed an era of prosperous trade, which continued despite the petty wars and poor administration of the Thakuris, who rose to power in the 9th century. The city of Kathmandu was founded about this time.

The Malla Kingdoms

One of the most successful attempts at unity in early Nepal was the work of the Western Malla kings, who began to build a state from their base at Jumla in the 10th century. By the 14th century they ruled over all of Nepal west of Pokhara, and some parts of India and Tibet. Though they tried, the Western Mallas (also called Khasas) never conquered the Kathmandu Valley. The Muslim invasions of India sent a throng of

NEPAL

Rajput princes to Nepal looking for small states to rule, and they took over parts of the Western Malla kingdom, causing it to collapse in the late 14th century.

The Kathmandu Valley came under a new family of rulers in the year 1200, also confusingly called the Mallas (this was actually a common royal title). Though their beginnings were shaky, the Mallas ushered in the best years of Kathmandu Valley culture, and they would rule for over 500 years. Unlike earlier Hindu kings the Mallas imposed Hindu laws on the Kathmandu Valley, dividing the Buddhist Newaris into 64 occupational castes. After the death of Yaksha Malla, the greatest of the Malla kings, in 1482, the small kingdom he had ruled from Bhaktapur was split between his three children. Kathmandu, Patan, and Bhaktapur all became rival city-states. Internal competition sharpened the Malla family however. In spite of constant petty feuding over trade with Tibet they all reached new heights in urban planning and art. The great wooden-screened temples and cobbled Durbar Squares of the valley date from this time.

Unification

The Mallas were unprepared for the force that would hit them in the 18th century and expand their dominion into a proper Kingdom of Nepal. The small hill-state of Gorkha, 50km west of Kathmandu, was under the rule of the Shahs, the most ambitious of the many immigrant Rajput clans that had come to western and southern Nepal between the 14th and 16th centuries. In 1742 King Prithvi Narayan Shah ascended the throne of Gorkha, and within two years he set out to conquer Nepal's richest region, the Kathmandu Valley. After a 25-year war of attrition, the three cities of Kathmandu, Patan, and Bhaktapur surrendered in 1768-69. When Prithvi Narayan Shah invaded Kathmandu, King Jaya Prakash Malla had asked the English East India Company for help. If the company had responded, the British might have ruled Nepal since 1768. But Prithvi Narayan shunned foreign intervention, and became the founder of the modern nation of Nepal. He did not stop after conquering the Kathmandu Valley. Lusting for land, his Gorkha army proceeded to conquer the eastern Tarai and hills. Soon Prithvi Narayan implemented the closed-door policy that would keep Nepal isolated until the 1950s.

Unrest and War

Prithvi Narayan Shah was an astute ruler and he set up an exemplary government. Speaking of his kingdom as a "garden of many flowers," he respected the country's local institutions and rewarded his officials according to their merit. After his death in 1775, however, his kingdom went out of control. The throne passed to a series of infant Shahs, and the nobility battled one another to act as regent. Peasants were taxed more and more harshly. Eventually a cunning chief minister named Bhim Sen Thapa took control, and found that he could get the country to work together by launching a war. Nepal struck out to the west, annexing the Garwhal and Kumaon regions which are now part of India's Uttar Pradesh state, as well as Himachal Pradesh. But Nepal invariably mishandled its new lands, and it also got into trouble with foreign powers. In 1788-92 it fought a war with Tibet and China, and in 1814 its expansion in the Tarai provoked the calculated hostility of the English East India Company.

Although Nepal could not defeat Britain, the Anglo-Nepalese War was not the easy victory the British expected. In spite of superior numbers and weaponry the British were routed by the Nepalese soldiers, who held their hilltop forts and charged with their *khukuri* knives. It took the British two years to break through and defeat Nepal. The Treaty of Segauli they imposed in 1814 stripped Nepal of Himachal Pradesh, Garhwal, Kumaon, and the Tarai lands and fixed its eastern and western borders where they remain today. But the impression the Nepalese made on the British counted for much more. Britain was scared out of fighting Nepal again, and thus Nepal became the only South Asian kingdom to stay independent in the 19th century. A British resident came to live in Kathmandu, and the British began recruiting Nepalese soldiers for their new "Gurkha" regiments.

Stagnation and Coup d'Etat

The years following the war with Britain saw little progress. Prime Minister Bhim Sen Thapa kept the country stable by building up the army, but chaos ensued when he fell from grace in 1837. Various palace factions struggled for power. Finally on the night of September 14, 1846, a powerful minister was murdered. When the queen assembled the entire royal court in the *kot* (the army headquarters courtyard) to find the culprit, the personal guards of General Jung Bahadur, the cabinet minister for the army, surrounded the Kot and opened fire, killing thirty-two of Kathmandu's most powerful nobles. During the next few hours, due to some secret agreement, the queen appointed Jung Bahadur prime minister. He immediately began to impose his authority on the country.

The Rana Regime

Jung Bahadur took the title of "Rana," and under this name his family would keep its iron grip on Nepal for 105 years. Jung Bahadur humiliated the current king, Rajendra, and took total control for himself. He started a process of reform, encouraged by a visit to London in 1850 in which he saw the efficacy of Britain's institutions (as well as the glamor of its neo-Classical architecture). Upon his return Jung began to thoroughly rationalize Nepalese government. He did away with patronage and kept strict track of spending. Land tenure was registered; this was a victory for the common peasant, since landlords could no longer arbitrarily evict their tenants. Some of Jung's other decisions were hurtful to many people, but this made no difference to a man who was by now absolute dictator of Nepal. In 1856, Jung Bahadur had himself raised to the title of super-Minister as well as "Maharaja of Kaski and Lamjung," with a power to overrule the king. The position was made hereditary in his family.

The Indian Mutiny of 1857 was a chance for Nepal to flex its muscles and also win British support. Jung Bahadur sent 10,000 men to aid the British, and in return the British gave back the Tarai lands they had taken in 1816. The British became friendly with Nepal, and especially with the Rana regime. The British resident in Kathmandu was always keen to give Nepal "guidance" on its foreign policy, but basically Nepal remained independent, scoffing at British demands for trading rights and limiting British Gurkha recruitment.

The Rana prime ministers were at least as interested in advancing their family fortunes, however, as they were in helping the country. Jung Bahadur Rana ruled Nepal until his death in 1877. During the second half of his reign he continued his relentless policies and his pursuit of personal power, and wrapped up his family business ventures in state policy. Jung Bahadur's successors turned out to be just as venal and iron-willed but less competent. The end of the 19th century saw a plethora of halfhearted public works projects, especially bridges; while these did some good for the people, their main purpose was to impress the British.

Chandra Shamsher Rana, who ruled from 1901-29, was a better administrator than the other Ranas, yet he began his reign by building the enormous Singha Durbar palace for himself, consuming all of the national public works budget for the first three years of his rule. Some change came with the First World War, since Chandra Shamsher knew he would have to do something to please the 100,000 Nepalese Gurkha soldiers who had gone to fight for the British overseas or in India, and would return to their villages with new ideas from around the world. Chandra Shamsher enacted several serious, though belated, reforms, building bridges and roads and abolishing *sati* and slavery (Nepal had 60,000 slaves in 1924). In 1918 Tri Chandra College, Nepal's first college, was founded, and in 1923 tenant farmers were made the owners of the lands they had rented for centuries. Another major accomplishment of 1923 was the Treaty of Friendship with Britain, which formally recognized Nepal's independence. Meanwhile, however, the lowering of trade restrictions made Nepal more economically dependent on imported British and Japanese goods.

Rana Decline and Royal Restoration

Prime Minister Judha Shamsher Rana (r.1932-45) went back to ruling Nepal in military fashion, and dissatisfaction became rampant. Not even the great earthquake of 1934 shook Kathmandu like Judha's widely protested execution of four would-be revolutionaries in 1940. Indian Independence in 1947 gave Nepal a new neighbor to deal with, however, and Prime Minister Jawaharlal Nehru disapproved of the Rana regime. In 1947 the Nepali Congress was formed in the tradition of the Congress that had led India to freedom. The Ranas didn't know how to deal with these new forces. Some family members who favored democratization went to India and joined the growing anti-Rana resistance. The turning point came in 1950 when King Tribhuvan, a palace figurehead since 1911, also fled to India. Tribhuvan had now captured popular support. The king, the prime minister, and Congress leaders met in Delhi where Nehru engineered the Delhi Compromise of 1951. The Rana regime was over. The king would now preside over a government of Ranas as well as popularly elected leaders.

Panchayat Government

Major changes came to Nepal in the years after the Rana defeat. Nepal's doors were opened to foreigners, and vast improvements took place in the government's social policies. The Delhi Compromise was replaced in 1959 by a new constitution which called for a democratically elected assembly. The Nepali Congress won a large majority in the elections, and its leader, B.P. Koirala, became prime minister. But this state of affairs was fragile. King Tribhuvan had died in 1955, and his son Mahendra, who came to the throne, was much less enthusiastic about political reforms, believing Nepal wasn't developed enough to handle them. He dismissed the Congress government almost as soon as it took power and he threw its leaders in jail. In 1962 a new constitution was enacted, replacing the national assembly with a system of *panchayats,* or village councils, who would elect members to district councils which would elect a National Panchayat. Political parties were banned, and the new system, which was supposed to be a form of democracy especially suited to Nepalese traditions, was effectively a return to absolute monarchy. Mahendra opened Nepal to foreign aid donors, however, and started the long controversial process of development that is transforming Nepal today.

King Birendra, who came to power in 1972 (although for astrological reasons he wasn't crowned until 1975) fully supported the *panchayat* system. Early in his career Birendra declared Nepal a "Zone of Peace" (a declaration of neutrality which angered India) and tightened visa restrictions for foreigners. The *panchayat* system was highly contested, however, and resistance came to a head in 1979 with riots in Kathmandu and Patan. In response, Birendra called a referendum to let the people choose between *panchayats* and multiparty democracy. The *panchayats* won by the feeble margin of 55 to 45 percent, so the king's system would hang on for ten more years, assisted by censorship and police brutality. The king lost touch with the country, and the monarchy declined.

Democracy Restored

Inspired by the previous year's revolutions in Eastern Europe, and provoked by an economic blockade from India, the outlawed opposition parties banded together in 1990 to demand democracy. Protests filled the streets of Kathmandu, and when King Birendra realized his riot police and mass arrests would not quell the uprising, he gave in, lifting the ban on political parties on April 8. A week later the major parties were invited to form an interim government and write a new constitution. A parliamentary system of democracy came into effect, and Birendra became a constitutional monarch.

The May 1991 election gave a majority to the Nepali Congress, which had led the democracy movement. The Communist Party of Nepal-United Marxist-Leninist (CPN-UML) became the main opposition. The prime minister was now G.P. Koirala, the brother of the late B.P. Koirala. Although G.P. Koirala's government stabilized Nepal's democracy, most people were disappointed by his leadership. Rising inflation caused general discontent, and an agreement with India over a dam on Nepal's western frontier brought accusations of selling out to India. Unimaginative and stubborn, Koirala alienated much of his own party, and he was forced to resign in 1994 when a large chunk of the Congress backed out on him.

The ensuing elections brought the Communists to power in a minority government. Prime Minister Man Mohan Adhikary quickly launched a series of populist schemes, including the "build-your-own-village" program, which gave large cash grants to local governments to spend as they pleased. Adhikary then resigned, hoping to improve his government's standing through another election. While the king, trying hard not to meddle, approved Adhikary's call for elections, the Supreme Court ruled against this maneuver. No elections were held, and the Congress party took power by allying itself with the right-wing National Democratic Party (NDP).

Prime Minister Sher Bahadur Deuba, the new Congress prime minister, managed to bridge the factions within the Congress party and to forge solid ties with the NDP, surviving a vote of confidence in March 1996. Despite the antagonism between the two main parties, the Congress and the CPN-UML, Nepal's newborn democratic system appears to be stable. King Birendra has played his role as a constitutional monarch admirably, refraining from interfering with politics. But as the twentieth century closes, many issues for Nepal remain unsolved. The country's extreme poverty, its shortage of adequate education and health services, and its lack of industries are difficult problems to grapple with. Economic development raises environmental issues, and often puts Nepal at the mercy of foreign aid donors over which it has little control. Nepal's relations with India are another issue; although the two countries remain friendly, tensions have arisen over water rights, the migration of Nepalese workers to India, and the arrival of Bhutanese refugees into Nepal through India.

■ This Year's News

Many believe the current Nepalese government, led by Prime Minister Sher Bahadur Deuba of the Congress party, is doomed. The ambitious former prime minister G.P. Koirala is now president of the Congress party, and is seen to be undermining the prime minister's control from backstage. The Congress party's ally, the NDP, is internally fragmented, and could withdraw its support from the government. If this happens, or if Koirala succeeds in his efforts, Nepal could be in for a national election in 1997, one which Koirala stands a good chance of winning (with the Congress behind him).

The biggest issue on the government's plate for the time being is the Mahakali Treaty with India, an impending deal over a hydroelectric project on the river that forms Nepal's western border. The Communist opposition accuses the government of selling out to India, and has vowed to block the treaty.

The "people's revolutionary war" launched in western Nepal in early 1996 by the Communist Party of Nepal-Maoist appears to have been quelled by police, although tensions continue to run high in the area.

■ Government and Politics

Nepal is a constitutional monarchy with a parliamentary system of government. The king, Birendra Bir Bikram Shah, has very limited powers, although the monarchy is still said to wield some influence. Real executive power is in the hands of the prime minister (currently Sher Bahadur Deuba) who is chosen by a majority in the 205-member House of Representatives. Members of the House of Representatives are elected by universal suffrage for a term of up to five years. Nepal's judiciary and appears to be politically impartial.

The main political parties in Nepal are the Nepali Congress, now in power, and the Communist Party of Nepal-United Marxist-Leninist (CPN-UML), the main opposition party. The Congress party's government is made possible by its alliance with the

NEPAL

National Democratic Party (NDP), a relatively new right-wing party, and with the Nepal Sadhbhavana Party (NSP), a regionalist party from the Tarai.

■ Economics

Nepal is one of the poorest countries in the world. About 90% of the people live on subsistence agriculture, which is limited by the rugged terrain. Farmers in the hills must cut terraces into the slopes, so most of the country's food comes from the lowland Tarai region. Much of Nepal's arable land belongs to large landowners who demand exorbitant rents from the landless laborers who grow the crops. It is doubtful that food production can keep up with Nepal's rapidly growing population.

Due to a lack of infrastructure, Nepal's industries are embryonic. Roads are poor and do not reach all areas of the country; vast reserves of hydroelectric energy remain untapped. Nepal is landlocked, so it has no easy access to international commerce. Most of its manufactured goods must be imported from India.

Woolen rugs are Nepal's biggest export, but an important chunk of foreign cash reaches Nepal through foreign aid. This well-meant boost to Nepal's economy over the past four decades has in fact produced a plethora of complications. Donors have often introduced unsuitable technology and programs due to their ignorance of local climate conditions or customs. Development aid has also helped some parts of the country more than others, lavishing the central hills around Kathmandu while neglecting the poor mountainous regions of the far west. Grants often get siphoned back to contracting companies in the donor countries. Small-scale rural NGOs (nongovernmental organizations), are a good idea in theory, but they are unregulated and rife with corruption. Aside from these, there is the issue of neocolonialism: how much should foreign donors get to influence Nepal's affairs (or is it just a matter of making sure their money is spent well?). China and India both give aid to Nepal for blatantly political ends. And environmental destruction raises the question of whether industrial "development" is a good idea at all. Alternatives are sought that will be more in line with Nepalis' existing way of life, which is simple and usually happy without a need for a flood of consumer goods.

■ Religion

Nepal's position as a cultural crossroads between India and Tibet is clearly marked in its blend of religions. Although Nepal is a Hindu kingdom, the only country in the world with Hinduism as its state religion, most Nepalis follow some rapturous mixture of Hinduism and Buddhism, with plenty of local traditions thrown in for good measure. Asked if they are Hindu or Buddhist, many Nepalis will say they don't know or that they're "both." The fact that the Nepalese can at once follow a religion of 330 million gods and a religion that originally recognized no gods at all baffles many visitors, but it seems to work nonetheless.

In general, the mountainous northern regions of Nepal close to Tibet tend to be Buddhist, while the Tarai lands close to India are Hindu. The hilly areas in between (including the Kathmandu Valley) have gone the furthest to synthesize the two.

HINDUISM

South Asia's total cosmological system (or lack of one) began to evolve around 1500 BC when the Aryans with their Vedic sacrifices and rituals met with the local religions of the peoples they overran. The Aryans imported to India a religion of fire-sacrifices and ritualized chanting, as well as a pantheon of deities which they mixed and matched with the native peoples. Over time all of these practices came to be the quintessential religion of India, deifying everything in it. Hinduism is somewhat peculiar for most Westerners, being a blend of both monotheism and polytheism, and also heavily laden with rituals and auspicious observances. There is a general agreement that God, or the Absolute, *Brahman,* is one, but also that God has the appearance of an infinite number of forms and manifestations.

Hindu worship is usually centered on an image of the deity in question. Contrary to appearances, idols are not what is being worshipped; what is seen is the *form* of the deity. This appearance serves to help bring one's concentrated devotion fully upon the deity. This "seeing" of the god through its image is called *darshan.* The most common ritual for Hindus is *puja,* in which flowers, sweets, and other foods are offered to the deity. In Devi (Mother-Goddess) temples, animals are often sacrificed as well, especially goats, even though other Hindu sects have strong vegetarian traditions. No Hindus will kill cows, however; cows are considered sacred, and cow-slaughter is as serious an offense in Nepal as murder.

Hinduism first came to the Kathmandu Valley and other parts of the Nepalese hills around the 4th-5th centuries AD, with the advent of the Licchavi dynasty. (The Tarai has always been a part of the Ganges Valley world and has more ancient connections to Hinduism.) Also, because Hinduism was introduced to the hills by conquerors, it has long been Nepal's religion of status; Brahmins (the priestly caste) and Chhetris (Nepalese *kshatriyas;* the warrior caste) have long been at the top of society. Various Nepali Hindu legal reforms had long ago tried to work the lower-class Buddhists into an occupational caste system; the practice took hold although few Buddhists truly recognize it.

Gods and Goddesses

Shiva

Shiva is perhaps the most popular Hindu god in Nepal; he is a fitting lord for this mountainous land, since he began his career as a Himalayan wanderer. Shiva is at once terrifying and compassionate. In the Hindu trinity he has the role of destroyer, and he is most commonly depicted as an uncouth ascetic who wears live cobras and leopard skins, wields a trident, and frequents cremation grounds, riding on his bull, Nandi. He commonly appears in Nepal as Bhairava or "Bhairab," a terrible ghoulish figure who chases away demons. Yet Shiva also represents one who harnesses spiritual power, and he is worshipped through his *linga,* a simple stone shaft or phallus which symbolizes sexual or spiritual energy. Shiva is often referred to simply as "Mahadev" (Great God), and he is worshipped out of love and devotion as well as in his more terrifying aspect. Most of the *sadhus,* wandering Hindu holy men, in Nepal are Shaivas (devotees of Shiva). In his form as Pashupatinath, the benevolent Lord of Animals, Shiva is Nepal's patron deity, and Nepal is often referred to as Pashupatinath Bhumi ("Land of Pashupatinath"). The temple of Pashupatinath near Kathmandu is the most important Hindu site in Nepal.

Vishnu

The god Vishnu is also the object of a large devotional cult. A cosmic "preserver," Vishnu has repeatedly stepped in to save the universe from calamity. In Nepal he is often called Narayan; this name of Vishnu comes from his role in the Hindu creation myth, in which he sleeps on the cosmic ocean while the creator god, Brahma, sprouts from his navel. Vishnu has ten incarnations or *avatars,* three of which are very well-known. Incarnation number seven is Rama, the hero of the *Ramayana,* India's classic Sanskrit epic stressing themes of exile and devotion. The monkey-god Hanuman, the ideal servant of Lord Rama, plays a major part in the *Ramayana,* helping Rama on his quest, and is also very popular in Nepal. Vishnu's eighth incarnation was as Lord Krishna, the focus of many myths; he is both the playful cowherd who cavorts with milkmaids and the philosophical charioteer who sang out the Bhagavad Gita in the *Mahabharata* epic. Incarnation nine is the Buddha. The idea of the Enlightened One being one of the incarnations of Vishnu is obviously disregarded by most Buddhists, but it was probably evolved by early proselytizing Hindus in attempts to win them over. Nepalese Buddhists don't need this; they have many other ways of integrating the two faiths.

Goddesses

Besides Shiva and Vishnu, many Hindus worship female deities who are referred to in general as Devi, "the Goddess." The many goddesses in Hinduism are recognized as aspects of *Shakti,* a single female principle which is the dynamic force of the cosmos. Shaktism, as the Goddess cult is called, probably predates worship of the male gods, even though specific goddesses have joined the male-dominated pantheon as consorts of these gods. Shiva is married to Parvati, who also takes the form of Kali the terrible and Durga the demon-slayer, undoubtedly the most popular Hindu goddesses. Nepal's grandest festival, Dasain, is held in honor of Durga; these goddesses are benevolent mothers as well as fierce avengers. Lakshmi, the goddess of wealth, is the consort of Vishnu, and Saraswati, the goddess of learning, is the consort of Brahma the creator. Annapurna, another female deity important in Nepal, distributes food and grain. These goddesses are all considered as separate individuals but as consorts each also embodies the female aspect of each god. Due to the Tantric influence in Nepal, this female *Shakti* is often considered as the powerful and active force in the cosmos.

Ganesh

As the remover of obstacles, the elephant-headed god Ganesh is very popular in both India and Nepal. All Hindus come to him at some time or another. Known as a particularly clever figure, he may pose obstacles or remove them. His vehicle is a rat, and he is often depicted riding upon one. Ganesh is invoked whenever good fortune may be required in some undertaking, and his image is painted next to the entrances to many buildings. He is a lower-ranking deity than the others, so he can intercede with the great gods for favors. Also called Ganapati, Ganesh is the lord of the *ganas,* Shiva's attendants. He is the son of Shiva and Parvati. His mother once told him to guard her bathing spot. Shiva came along and tried to approach his wife but was readily stopped by this boy whom he did not recognize as his son. In a blind fury, he chopped off the boy's head for his refusal to let him pass. When Parvati learned of the incident, she reprimanded Shiva, and he replaced it with the head of the next creature he found, an elephant.

BUDDHISM

Lumbini, the place where the Buddha was born about 560 BC, is within the borders of present-day Nepal. Born as a prince, he was named Siddhartha Gautama, and in the first part of his life he was sheltered from the world by his father and never left the palace. The king had prevented young Siddhartha from experiencing the life of normal people in the city, and had lavished him with all sorts of comforts in the hope that he would appreciate the royal lifestyle all the more. This was due to a prophecy made by an astrologer at the boy's birth that he would either become a *chakravartin* (universal monarch) or a *buddha* (awakened one). Prince Siddhartha remained sheltered until the age of 29, when for the first time he witnessed the suffering that the rest of the world faced. He had left the palace with his attendant for the city and happened to see a sick person, a very old person, and a corpse. He immediately lost his taste for luxury, left his wife and his son, and fled south to the Indian forests where he became an ascetic, practicing austerities for seven years. Unsatisfied after these rigorous trials, he decided that they were useless, and he pursued a middle path. He had been meditating for a long time under a tree in Bodh Gaya (in Bihar, India) when he attained *bodhi* (enlightenment) and became the Buddha, the Awakened One. When he set out to teach what he had discovered, his charisma quickly won him many followers. Eventually his doctrines would return to the land of Nepal, spreading much further in the country than the Tarai area where he was born. Buddhism is now one of the country's main religious traditions.

The Buddha advocated detachment from the world. Desires arising for uncertain physical and mental things, he said, bring people suffering, because they cause one to believe in a self and an individual existence; these are only fleeting illusions. One's goal should be the end of suffering through the end of desires, thus attaining a state of *nirvana,* in which the flame of the self is blown out in blissful freedom. But how could one be motivated to attain *nirvana* without a desire for it? And then that desire would prevent its attainment. At some point on the path to *nirvana* even the desire for *nirvana* must be abandoned. The Buddha named right understanding, thought, speech, action, livelihood, effort, mindfulness and concentration (the "Eightfold Path") as the way to *nirvana.* He rejected all of Hinduism's gods and rituals, but preserved Hinduism's doctrine of *karma* and rebirth: the quest for *nirvana* could take many lifetimes. However, there is no observance of the caste system in Buddhism. In this sense, Buddhism is much more of a philosophy and a system of ethics than it is a religion. As part of the Eightfold Path Buddhism also became adamant about *ahimsa* (nonviolence).

This path of abandoning desires and worldly life seemed to put Buddhism out of the reach of most people, however, and the first Buddhists banded together in monastic communities. Lay people also supported these communities although they did not observe the central tenet of renouncing the world; their practices were more devotional and reverential, for gaining merit in order to be reborn in a more favorable position for attaining *nirvana.* The Buddhist *dharma,* though, was responsible for the conversion of the Mauryan emperor Asoka, in the 3rd century BC, and his state patronage helped to make Buddhism a mass religion in India and later to spread throughout Asia.

Buddhists in Nepal follow the Mayahana ("Great Vehicle") school, which differs in many ways from the Theravada ("Doctrine of the Elders") school. Mahayana Buddhism initially developed from a split and a disagreement over the *vinaya* (monastic rules) in the Buddhist communities. The Mahayana doctrines originally de-emphasized the individual quest for *nirvana* and instead stressed the need for acquiring discrimination and compassion for all beings. One of these doctrines was the *Prajnaparamita,* or Perfection of Wisdom. The acquisition of this *prajnaparamita* became the alternative goal in the Mahayana tradition. Also, in Mahayana Buddhism, the Buddha was no longer just an enlightened human being. Instead, he became a cosmic *bodhisattva* having many incarnations or emanations. A *bodhisattva* is one who vows to put off his enlightenment for the sake of saving all sentient beings. There are a number of *bodhisattvas* who are worshipped as well, saints on the threshold of attaining *nirvana* who altruistically remain in the world to help others attain their goal. In this development, there was also a corresponding artistic presence that emerged in the use of images and sculpture depicting many of these figures. The Mahayana school developed as a popular new sect around the first century AD and came to predominate in India, Tibet, China, and other parts of East Asia. The more orthodox Theravada school, with its emphasis on the individual quest for *nirvana,* continued in Sri Lanka and most of Southeast Asia. While Buddhism in India was subsumed by Hinduism, a particularly Indian-influenced Mahayana Buddhism remained in Nepal, and this is what is practised today. The northern mountainous areas of Nepal have the strongest Buddhist traditions, while in the hills a Hindu-Buddhist synthesis is more common.

Tibetan Buddhism

A unique form of Buddhism developed in Tibet, where Mahayana and Vajrayana ("Thunderbolt Vehicle") Buddhist traditions were mixed with the indigenous religion, Bön. Even though Buddhism was brought to Tibet through Nepal, the Tibetan tradition has returned its influence on Nepal, and due to the occupation of Tibet by China there are many real Tibetan Buddhists around as well. Prayer wheels and prayer flags, used to blow the mantra *Om Mani Padme Hum* ("Hail to the jewel in the lotus") over the mountaintops, are ubiquitous. The beliefs of Tibetan Buddhism are not very different from those of standard Mahayana Buddhism, though different rituals and imagery are used: the Buddha is divided into five "aspects" of Buddahood: the *dhyani* or meditating Buddhas, who represent the Buddha reflected in each of the five elements (earth, water, air, fire, and space). Tibetan Buddhism is also noted for its monastic tradition; it is estimated that before the Chinese invasion, 25% of Tibetans belonged to some religious order. Of the 6,000 Tibetan monasteries that were once in Tibet, only around 5 remain. The rest were destroyed in the Chinese invasion. Tibetan monasteries are headed by teachers called *lamas,* addressed by the title *rimpoche* (precious one), who are believed to have cultivated wisdom over many lifetimes transmitting their realization to their reincarnations. The reincarnation of a *lama* is usually identified by means of astrology, consulting the Tibetan oracle, and also by having the young candidtates identify the former *lama*'s possessions. The Dalai Lama, who would under normal circumstances be both the temporal and spiritual leader of Tibet, is head of the Gelug-pa sect (the most intellectual and monastic of the four main sects).

Tantra

Some forms of Tibetan Buddhism are classified as Vajrayana ("Thunderbolt Vehicle"), another sect apart from the Mahayana and Theravada schools. The major symbols of Vajrayana are the *vajra* or *dorje* (thunderbolt) and the *ghanti* (bell), representing the male element of compassion and the female element of wisdom. Vajrayana has inherited much of its cosmology from the tradition of Tantra, a medieval cult in eastern India that relished the female power of *Shakti.* The Tantric tradition espoused a non-dualistic philosophy and used specific methods to help people go beyond dualistic thought. Polar opposites were no longer seen as external objects opposed to one another. They were, rather, seen as the dual manifestations of consciousness. In this light, the true nature of desire and the mind could be realized by transcending opposites. Thus, in the Tantric tradition in India, there were rituals which prescribed the eating of meat, fish and parched grain, the drinking of alcohol, and the enjoyment of sexual intercourse as means of transcending dualities. These activities were all considered "polluting" to orthodox Hindus. Their use was considered a way to make desires go beyond desires, to realize their true nature.

The rituals of Tantra in this way also involve the releasing and harnessing of different energies in the body. This is where the Tantric association with sex, so popularly known in the West, comes from. In Tibetan Buddhism especially, the conscious release of bodily energy is prominent and heavily ritualized, especially in visualization-meditations upon female goddess figures.

There is much that Tantra has in common with other Hindu traditions such as *Shakti* and yoga, and it may be more proper to say that it is a different religion altogether. From the 7th through the 9th centuries AD in India, Tantra became quite popular throughout India as a pert of both Hinduism and Buddhism. It eventually died out in India, but its influence can be seen in Tibetan Buddhism. In line with its thunderbolt-and-bell symbolism, its sacred gestures, patterns, and mantras, Vajrayana Buddhism couples the *dhyani* Buddhas and the major *bodhisattvas* with *taras,* female consorts who have much more power and strength. These figures are often depicted engaged in sexual intercourse in Tibetan Buddhist art, symbolic of the harnessing and reconciliation of dual energies.

INDIGENOUS TRADITIONS

Aside from the great religions of Hinduism and Buddhism, Nepal has its own collection of indigenous deities. Hindus and Buddhists both worship these local heroes, regardless of the religion they claim to follow.

In the Kathmandu Valley a unique practice persists in the worship of the Kumari, a young girl recognized as an incarnation of the Hindu goddess Durga. The chosen living goddess stays secluded in a palace for her entire childhood, until she reaches puberty and then reverts to the status of a mortal. The Newaris also worship *Macchendranath,* the god born of a fish who is identified both with Lokesvara, Shiva's form as "Lord of the World," and Avalokitesvara, a *bodhisattva.* Macchendranath's towering chariot makes his festivals conspicuous. The Newari craftsmen of the Kathmandu Valley have also turned the hero Bhimsen from the Mahabharata epic into their patron deity. Also prominent in the Valley is Manjushri, the valley's creator god,

The Holy Himalaya

Since large-scale mountaineering came to Nepal in the 1950s, many climbers have halted within sight of the summit of certain mountains and returned to the bottom without actually standing on top. This is done in deference to local custom, since many peaks of the Himalaya are considered to be sacred. Looming over the land of North India, the Himalaya provide water and tremendous beauty while remaining a near-impassable barrier. It's not difficult to understand how they came to be seen as the abode of the gods. The highest points on earth, they make an easy transition between earth and heaven. The mythical Mt. Meru, believed by Hindus to be the center of the universe and the axis of all power, is located in the Himalaya. Mt. Kailasa in Tibet is considered Shiva's meditation ground, and many other mountains are homes to other gods. The deified Himalaya was the father of Shiva's wife Parvati. Many mountains in Nepal such as Gauri-Shankar and Annapurna are named after gods and share in their holiness, while others with more mundane names (such as Macchapuchare and Kanchenjunga) are sacred nonetheless, and climbers are forbidden from topping them.

who is associated with the Hindu goddess of learning, Saraswati. Manjushri used his sword to cut into the valley wall and drain out its primordial lake; he continues to use it to slice through ignorance.

Outside of the Kathmandu Valley various ethnic groups preserve many of their local beliefs in spite of the arrival of Buddhism and Hinduism. In general, these big religions have taken charge of good and evil, right and wrong, and other such concerns, while the local gods are worshiped in order to ask for good harvests and healthy children. Animal sacrifices in order to feed the gods are common. The leaders of many of Nepal's local religions are the shamans, who mediate between people and the supernatural world.

▦ Language

The official language of Nepal is Nepali, which is the mother tongue of 50% of the population and is spoken and understood by just about everyone. Formerly the language of the high-caste elite, Nepali was introduced by Prithvi Narayan Shah as a *lingua franca* for his new kingdom. Nepali is an Indic language, descended from Sanskrit like the languages of North India, and it uses the same Devanagari script that Hindi uses.

Nepal's other languages abound but each has only a small number of speakers. In the Tarai, varieties of Hindi such as Mathili and Bhojpuri are the biggest groups, while in the hills small pockets of various Tibeto-Burmese languages are found. The Newari spoken in the Kathmandu Valley is of Tibetan origin, although it has borrowed its Devanagari script and half of its vocabulary from Sanskrit. In contemporary Nepal you'll certainly also encounter Tibetan, which uses a Sanskrit-based script in spite of its foreign origin. English is widely taught in Nepali schools nowadays too, so its not difficult to get around knowing no more Nepali than the ubiquitous greeting, *namaste*, which translates literally as "I salute the God in you." For basic Nepali vocabulary, see the **Phrasebook**, p. 762.

▦ The Arts

VISUAL ARTS

In art, as in many things, Nepal has long been a crossroads for various influences. At times in its history Nepal has traded artwork with India and Tibet, absorbing their styles in the process. But whatever Nepal has taken from other countries it has adapted into styles of its own. The Newari artisan castes of the Kathmandu Valley are largely responsible for this. Art in the Tarai has been very closely connected to India, and permanent works of art in the mountainous areas are rare. The Kathmandu Valley, however, has produced one of South Asia's greatest regional styles. Unfortunately, many older works of art in the Kathmandu Valley have disappeared because they were made of wood and other short-lived materials. But many of the valley's masterpeices nevertheless remain, still to be found in their original setting.

In much the same tradition as Indian art, Nepalese art has generally been inspired by religion, executed by anonymous craftsmen, and paid for by kings. In Hindu temples, especially, originality was not the point, as a temple was meant to approximate a cosmic ideal. Personal interpretation of the ideal allowed for creativity.

Architecture

The oldest remaining structures in the Kathmandu Valley are *stupas*, sacred mounds of earth layered with plaster through the ages. *Stupas* usually mark Buddhist holy places or enclose relics, but being large hemispherical bumps, they are not very interesting architecturally (they are very durable however). Nepalese *stupas* have distinctive symbolism on the square, golden spire at their top: these *chakus* are usually painted with the eyes of Buddha, surveying the four cardinal directions, and a number "1" to represent the unity of all things. The Boudha *stupa* in the Kathmandu Valley is one of the largest *stupas* in the world. *Stupas* are usually accompanied by *chaityas*, small stone shrines that contain mantras or pieces of scripture.

The Kathmandu Valley's greatest architectural achievements have been the wood and brick pagodas, however. These buildings, which may have evolved from elaborated *chakus* on the tops of *stupas*, came to be built primarily for Hindu temples. The Hindu temple is centered on a small sanctum where an image of the deity is kept, since worshipers come to the temple one at a time. In Nepalese pagodas the sanctum is made of brick, and wooden pillars and struts on the outside support a sloping clay-tile roof. The roof, which is square, is repeated in diminishing tiers up to the pinnacle. The upper portions of the temple are not separate stories; they are deliberately empty, since nothing should be above the deity. The whole temple usually sits on a multi-level stone base with terraces, often resembling a step pyramid. The wooden doors and window frames are intricately carved. A 13th-century architect named Arniko is said to have exported the pagoda to Kublai Khan's China, from where the rest of Asia adopted it.

The Newaris also planned and built *bahals*, blocks of rooms around rectangular courtyards. These compact community units formed monasteries or blocks of houses in the cities. *Bahals* are designed to be perfectly symmetrical, with identical windows on the right and left sides; the main doors and windows usually appear along the central axis of the group.

The Rana prime ministers, who reigned from 1846 to 1951, developed a fetish for the European Neoclassical look; parts of Kathmandu's Durbar Square now seem like they belong in Trafalgar Square. The Ranas never made this style of building popular, but with their change of taste they cut off patronage for many of the Kathmandu Valley's traditional crafts, causing their decline. Most modern architecture in Nepal consists of uninspiring brick and concrete blocks.

Sculpture

Early sculpture in the Kathmandu Valley was highly influenced by North Indian stone sculpture. Newari artisans of the Licchavi period made devotional images of Vishnu and the Buddha that strongly resembled the work of the Mathura school, although they gave it a distinctly Nepali rhythm. We know from written accounts that wood sculpture was also at this time, but none of it has survived.

Stone sculpture in Nepal reached its zenith in the 7th, 8th and 9th centuries, but virtually disappeared after the 10th century. Metal became the medium of choice for medieval Nepali sculpture, under influence from eastern and southern India. In the 17th and 18th centuries, Tibet began to influence Nepalese sculpture. Newari artisans made bronze images of Tantric aspects of the Buddha which were exported to Tibetan monasteries. Many bronze sculptures usually identified as "Tibetan" were actually made in Nepal. Nepalese artists of the Malla period also created fantastic wood sculptures, usually as architectural ornaments. Wood sculpture was used to adorn temple roof struts, or most spectacularly, to make ornate wooden window grilles, often incorporating plant and animal forms.

In the last two centuries the crafts of bronze casting and woodcarving in Nepal have declined due to lack of patronage. Foreign-funded restoration projects have recently given the sculptors some business, however. Tourism has created some demand as well, although it encourages the mass-production of cheap, low quality works rather than the creation of masterpieces.

Painting

The earliest paintings from the Kathmandu Valley appear on palm leaf manuscripts; a few of these have survived from as far back as the 10th century, but most have decayed. More common in Nepal today are Tibetan *thankas*, intricate scroll-paintings of deities and *mandalas*. *Mandala* paintings, which are used as aids for meditation, represent theological ideas and must follow rigid patterns. During the medieval period a Newari style of *thanka* emerged, called a *paubha*, painted on coarser cloth than a Tibetan *thanka*, and without the landscape background that *thankas* borrowed from Chinese art. Later paintings in Nepal have been heavily influenced by the detailed miniatures of the Indian Mughal and Rajasthani styles.

MUSIC

A living cultural expression, music comes to life on the occasions of informal social gatherings as much as it adds life to Nepal's festivals. Styles and occasions for performance are as numerous as ethnic, religious, regional and tribal identities. Some sounds are as culturally and regionally grounded as the rice-transplanting songs of women in the fields, while others air the winds of distant exchange with India or Tibetan. Hindu and Buddhist religious traditions provide inspiration and performance occasions for many styles of music. The ritualistic music of the Sherpas and other Bhotiyas derives much of its character from the ancient rituals of Tibetan Buddhism, with ceremonies and rites sounding drums and winding horns preserved from ancient times. Newari Buddhist priests chant ancient Tantric verses as part of meditation exercises, and on sacred occasions such hymns often accompany monks performing esoteric ritual dances. *Bhajan* (devotional hymn singing), like a musical *puja*, is a layman version of sacred music.

The continued presence and influence of Indian classical music harkens back to the days when it was the rage in the courts of Malla kings. The Rana prime ministers were zestful patrons of Indian classical musicians also, excluding Nepali folk performers from their courts.

Music of the traditional and ubiquitous *panchai baja* (five instruments) ensembles bring jubilant accompaniment to weddings, processions, and temple rituals, with repertoires tailored to suit. The Gaines, a caste of musician-storytellers, once actively wandered the hills and dale, accompanying themselves on the *sarangi* (four-stringed fiddle), spreading news between villages. Once patronized by local chieftains to recount their glories, the musician's trade today (gainful employment only in Kirtipur in the Kathmandu Valley, in villages north of Pokhara, and in the far west), involves a repertoire of Hindu sacred songs and epics, folk ballads, and political commentary and propaganda.

Several traditional hill styles of music exist. Most popular is the *maadal*-based (double-sided drum held horizontally) *jhyaure* music of the western hills. The Jyapu farming caste developed an upbeat rhythmic style involving many percussion instruments, including the *dhime* (large two-sided drum), and the use of woodwinds to accompany nasal singing. The *selo* style, originally of the Tamangs but happily shared by others, keeps gregarious beat with the *damphu* (flat one-sided drum).

DANCE

From folk to classical, dance to drama, Hindu and Buddhist pantheons come to life in colorful recounting of the life and times of gods, saints, and heroes, of triumphs over demons, and man's relation to hearth, home, and universe. Chief exponents of classical dance, with elaborate festive masked dances, are the Newaris of the Kathmandu Valley. The performers enter into a trance to become vessels for the embodiment of gods, and sporting elaborate costumes and ornately painted papier maché masks, gyrate and gesture to the soul's delight. On the tenth day of the Dasain festival in September or October, *nawa Durga* dancers of Bhaktapur perform the vigorous dance-drama of the goddess Durga's victory over the buffalo demon. During the Indra Jatra festival dramatic dance abounds, with troupes of all kinds performing sword-scintillating Sawo Bhaku dances, the demon Lakhe dance and various Vishnu incarnation dances.

The ritualistic pulse of Tibetan Buddhism actively engages music, dance, and dramatic forms for festivals, ceremonies, and sacred rites, with performances often involving intricate, esoteric hand gestures, ritual objects, and the surprising contributions of many unusual and symbolic musical instruments. *Cham* is a dance-drama specific to Tibetans and Bhotiyas, in which monks don mask and costume to enact various Buddhist victory stories.

■ The Media

Nepal's English media is nowhere near as developed as India's. *The Rising Nepal* and the *Kathmandu Post* are daily papers published in English. *The Rising Nepal* is essentially a government mouthpiece that comes out in a Nepali edition as well. The *Post* is independent and focuses more on business; the differences are subtle. *The Independent* is a weekly newspaper that lives up to its name. The monthly magazine *Himal* covers South Asian issues intelligently and thoroughly. The *International Herald Tribune, Time,* and *Newsweek* are widely available in English-language bookshops in Kathmandu, as are several Indian papers.

Nepal has been infected with the same **satellite TV** craze currently ravaging India. Star TV beams in the BBC and/or CNN, along with rock videos, Hindi films, and American drivel. Nepal has one brand new FM **radio** station, 100 FM, which broadcasts mostly English (classic and modern rock) and a little Nepali and Hindi music from 7am-midnight.

■ Food and Drink

Dal bhat tarkari (lentils, rice, and vegetables) is the staple food for most Nepalis as it is for people in large parts of North India. Indeed, *bhat,* the word for cooked rice, is often used a synonym for *khana* (food). A great variety of rice exists in Nepal, ranging from the deliciously light Basmati to the red rice that turns pink when cooked. *Dhedo* is a rice paste often eaten by poorer families. You'll have to go looking away from the touristy restaurants if you want to try this bland staple for yourself. Food in Nepal differs little from Indian food, with the exception of some Tibetan dishes which have made their way onto the Nepali table. Ravioli-like *momo,* and *thukpa,* a soup made with noodles, are among the most popular dishes. Newari food is based largely on buffalo meat and radishes. *Choyala* is cubed buffalo meat fried with spices and vegetables.

The most popular breads in Nepal are *chapatis,* identical to their Indian counterpart. Western food is also commonly served in touristy restaurants in Nepal. Nepalis don't really eat breakfast but, again, tourist restaurants and hotels take care of this. As in India, vegetarians should have no trouble finding delicacies to their taste. Due to Hindu religious beliefs, buffalo meat is commonly served instead of beef.

Milk, or *dudh,* is an important staple of the Nepali diet that is often served hot—handy, because it is safe to drink once it has been boiled. Yogurt *(dahi)* is popular, and forms the basis for *lassis*, which are the same as in India, and the Newari delicacy *juju*, made from yogurt, cardamom and cinnamon. Most sweets are milk-based, including *burfi* and *peda* (thick, sweet, spicy milk pastes) and *kheer*, which resembles rice pudding.

Chiya (tea) is served hot with milk and lots of sugar. The coffee craze hasn't hit Nepal yet—coffee abounds but don't expect a mocha latte to meet your high Western standards. Fruit juices are yummy if overpriced and "cold drinks" (soft drinks) are a widely available alternative to tap water.

Alcohol is drunk in Nepal primarily in the form of beer, which is locally produced and quite tasty (especially when cold) and *chang,* a handmade Himalayan brew. *Raksi* is a stronger version of chang that bears a resemblance to tequila not only in taste but in impact.

■ Further Sources

General

Nepal: Profile of a Himalayan Kingdom by Leo E. Rose and John T. Scholz (1980). A country study of Nepal covering history, politics, culture, and economics; very sensibly written but now somewhat out of date.

Culture Shock! Nepal by Jon Burbank (1992). A guide to Nepali customs and etiquette especially aimed at those planning to live and work in Nepal. Advice for all sorts of social situations and business hassles.

Travel/Description

Video Night in Kathmandu by Pico Iyer (1988). A fascinating if somewhat single-minded account of the impact of western culture on Asia by the *Time* regular. Although Kathmandu made it to the title, there are also extensive chapters on India as well as other Asian countries.

History

Nepal: Growth of a Nation by Ludwig Stiller (1993). An account of the period from the unification of Nepal until 1950. One of the few histories of Nepal that doesn't slobber all over the Shah dynasty.

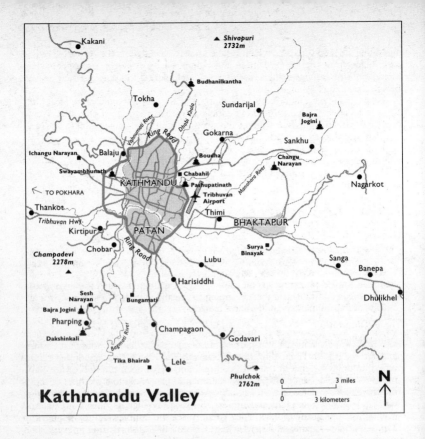

Kathmandu Valley

The Kathmandu Valley

Although Nepal is renowned for its natural beauty, the Kathmandu Valley is home the country's most spectacular artistic and architectural achievements, complemented, of course, by the backdrop of the valley's verdant hills, and, depending on the season, the awe-inspiring peaks of the Himalaya. Clusters of temples and palaces serve as living reminders of the region's rich history. The three major cities, Kathmandu, Patan, and Bhaktapur, were once individual city-states vying for control of the valley and its lucrative position on the trade route between India and Tibet. Each city boasts a Durbar Square filled with brick-and-wood architectural triumphs, including Nepal's trademark pagoda-style temples. The valley's indigenous Newari people (who speak their own Newari language, in addition to Nepali) have long been among South Asia's foremost artisans. In between the cities, the smaller, red-brick towns set amid lush farmland, are surprisingly urban, with tightly packed, multi-storyed houses. Before Nepal was unified in the 18th century, the name "Nepal" referred to this region alone, and to many the Kathmandu Valley still *is* Nepal, from the winding brick lanes of Bhaktapur to the white-washed expanse of the *stupa* at Boudha, from the sculptural extravaganza of Changu Narayan to the lush, green fields now overhung with pollution.

■ Kathmandu

To many people in the West, the word Kathmandu evokes a medieval fantasy—the capital of a mountain kingdom, lost in time and hoarding a trove of spiritual treasures. Kathmandu is second only to Shangri-La as the seat of a romanticized East, and the reason for its fame is clear to any visitor: Kathmandu is a fascinating old city, where pagodas still crowd the traffic into narrow cobbled lanes, and women look out of their carved-wood balconies onto ancient courtyards with neighborhood boys kicking soccerballs around dusty stone shrines. As in the other cities of the Kathmandu Valley, myth and history are apparent at every corner, in the form of glazed-over Ganesh shrines and old shops that have sunk into the street because the ground level has risen. But the Kathmandu of today has been paved with additional layers. Kathmandu has burst from the Middle Ages into the 1990s as the fast-growing capital of a very poor country, and it bears all the scars and trophies of economic growth and rapid Westernization. For more and more Nepalis, Kathmandu has become the Big City, a center of excitement and change. In spite of the optimism inspired here by the 1990 democracy movement, Kathmandu still faces many problems, from pollution to corrupt politicians. A persistent image of Kathmandu today is of the purse-carrying matron marching through the street while clutching her sari to her nose as she swerves to avoid an oozing trash heap. Not everything in Kathmandu is remote or mysterious; much of it is very mundane, and some of it certainly smells bad.

Founded under the name Manju-Patan in 723 AD (though this date is very uncertain), Kathmandu has not always been the valley's pre-eminent city. In Malla days, when it was also known as Kantipur, Kathmandu stood on equal terms with Patan and Bhaktapur, although it was perhaps more successful than the others at controlling the trade with Tibet. King Prithvi Narayan Shah made Kathmandu his capital when he unified Nepal in the 18th century, and it has been the hub of the Kathmandu Valley ever since. Present-day Kathmandu plays host to a plethora of diplomatic missions and foreign aid agencies, which sit comfortably behind their high walls. It feels waves of political demonstrators surge through its narrow streets. And it of course sees many tourists. They come to see the temples and to kick back in Thamel, a crazy dreamland district where Grateful Dead t-shirts hang in every shop and the restaurants primp up their display cases with cheesecakes and apple pies. For many travelers who've spent some time in South Asia, Thamel can come as a shock, and it often traps its customers in a sort of transcontinental hedonistic coma. But the capital of Nepal is more than just a pleasureland—its nooks and crannies are infinitely rewarding to explore.

GETTING THERE AND AWAY

By Air

If you're flying into Kathmandu from the east, try to sit on the right side of the plane to get a good view of the mountains; from the west, sit on the left side. Flights land at **Tribhuvan International Airport,** about 5km east of the center of town. Visas are issued upon arrival to those with photos and cash dollars (available from the exchange counter).

You'll be swarmed by touts as soon as you leave the building. The cheapest (and least convenient) way into town is by **bus,** although if you have luggage you'll probably want a **taxi.** The bus stop is right down the hill. Buses to Ratna Park (#1, frequent, 30min., Rs.3) can be prohibitively crowded if you're carrying luggage. To get to Thamel from Ratna Park, turn right after exiting the bus park, walk north along Durbar Marg all the way to the end, turn left and walk three blocks. The walk takes about 15 minutes without luggage. Alternatively, pre-paid taxis (to Thamel, Rs.200) can be arranged at a counter just before the exit or at a booth outside.

Tribhuvan Airport has a communication center from which international calls can be made, a restaurant, and a tea stall. Because planes are fairly small and this limits the number of passengers, formalities like check-in and security are much faster. How-

Kathmandu and Patan

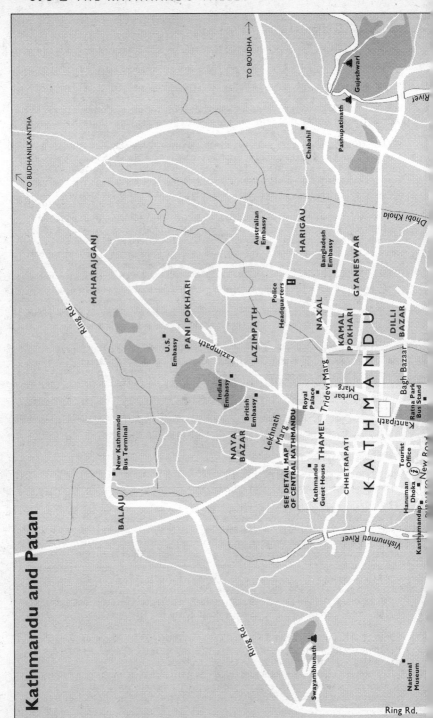

TO BOUDHA →

Gujeshwari

Pashupatinath

River

Chabahil

Dhobi Khola

TO BUDHANILKANTHA

MAHARAJGANJ

Australian
Embassy

HARIGAU

Bangladesh
Embassy

GYANESWAR

Ring Rd.

PANI POKHARI

Police
Headquarters

NAXAL

KAMAL
POKHARI

DILLI
BAZAR

U.S.
Embassy

LAZIMPATH

Lazimpath

Indian
Embassy

British
Embassy

Lekhnath Marg

NAYA
BAZAR

New Kathmandu
Bus Terminal

Royal
Palace

Tridevi Marg

Durbar Marg

THAMEL

Bagh Bazaar

Ratna Park
Bus Stand

SEE DETAIL MAP
OF CENTRAL KATHMANDU

Kathmandu
Guest House

CHHETRAPATI

K A T H M A N D U

Kantipath

Tourist
Office

i

New Road

BALAJU

Hanuman
Dhoka

Kasthamandap

Vishnumati River

Ring Rd.

Swayambhunath

National
Museum

Ring Rd.

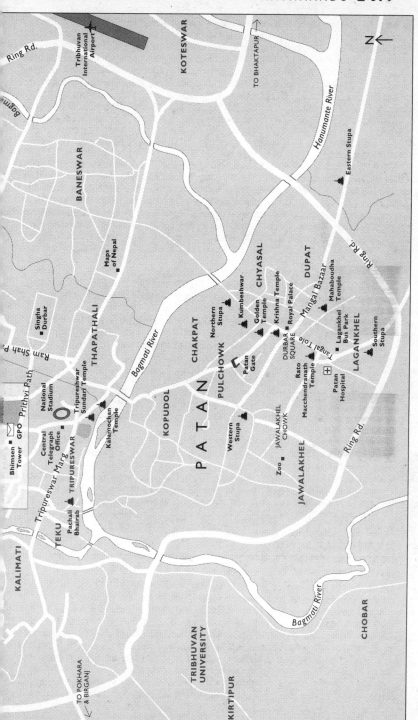

N

Ring Rd.

Bagmati

TO BHAKTAPUR →

KOTESWAR

Tribhuvan International Airport

Hanumante River

BANESWAR

Ring Rd.

Eastern Stupa

Maps of Nepal

Singha Durbar

CHYASAL

DUPAT

Kumbeshwar

Mahaboudha Temple

THAPATHALI

Golden Temple

Krishna Temple

Ram Shah Path

Bagmati River

CHAKPAT

Northern Stupa

Royal Palace

Mangal Bazaar

Lagankhel Bus Park

LAGANKHEL

National Stadium

Tripureshwar Sundari Temple

Patan Gate

DURBAR SQUARE

Southern Stupa

Prithvi Path

GPO

Bhimsen Tower

Central Telegraph Office

Tripureswar Marg

TRIPURESWAR

Kalamochan Temple

KOPUDOL

PULCHOWK

Tangal Tole

Rato Macchendranath Temple

Patan Hospital

P A T A N

Pachali Bhairab

TEKU

Western Stupa

JAWALAKHEL CHOWK

Zoo

JAWALAKHEL

Ring Rd.

KALIMATI

Bagmati River

CHOBAR

TRIBHUVAN UNIVERSITY

KIRTIPUR

TO POKHARA & BIRGANJ

ever, facilities are so basic that **even slightly bad weather invariably delays flights**—bring a book. Flying out, there is a **departure tax** of Rs.50 for domestic flights, Rs.600 to other South Asian countries, and Rs.700 to all others. Airline Offices: **RNAC,** Kantipath at New Rd. (tel. 220757, 214640); **Everest Air,** Durbar Marg (tel. 241016, 222290), **NECON Air,** New Rd. (tel. 242507, 243447); **Nepal Airways,** Maharajgunj (tel. 410786, 418494). Fares on domestic flights are virtually identical on all airlines. To: Bharatpur (US$50), Biratnagar (US$77), Janakpur (US$55), Jomsom (US$110), Lukla (US$83), Nepalganj (US$99), Pokhara (US$61). Mountain-viewing flights from Kathmandu cost US$90. To India: Bombay (Mon. and Fri. 1 per day, 2hr.20min., US$257); Calcutta (Mon.-Tues., Thurs., Sat. 1-2 per day, 1hr., US$96); Delhi (3-4 per day, 1½hr., US$142); Varanasi (Tues., Thurs., Sat.-Sun. 1 per day, 40min., US$71).

By Bus

Most buses to locations outside the Kathmandu Valley leave from the Japanese-built (but Nepali-run) **new bus park** on Ring Rd. in Gongabu, quite far from central Kathmandu. City buses drive to the new bus terminal from the old bus park at Ratna Park (every 5min., 5am-8pm, 1hr., Rs.6), with many stops along the way, including one at Amrit Science Campus, near Thamel. (Ask in Thamel for directions.) From this stop, it's a half-hour ride to the station. It's better to take a taxi (Rs.40 from Thamel or Rs.55 from New Rd.). In the departure area, a flood of ticket counter signs will confuse anyone not proficient in Nepali. Ask around. There is a 24hr. "Police Room" in the departure area, and most of the people selling tickets speak passable English. There is usually a long queue for the only telephone in the terminal. If you have to make a call, walk outside to the shops. Across the street are some modest guest houses and restaurants that cater primarily to Nepali travelers.

Buses that leave after noon are **night buses**—for these you should book a day in advance. To: Bhairahawa (25 per day, 6am-7pm, 10hr., Rs.120); Birganj (6-8 per day, 6-8pm, 8hr., Rs.125); Butwal (all buses to Bhairahawa and Lumbini, 9hr.); Dharan (10 per day, 12hr., Rs.248); Hetauda (direct 7am, 7hr., Rs.104; all buses to Birganj, Dharan, Janakpur, and Kakarbhitta pass through); Janakpur (6 per day, 5:45-7pm, 12hr., Rs.173); Kakarbhitta (9 per day, 3-5pm, 15hr., Rs.281); Lumbini (7pm, 11hr., Rs.138); Pokhara (every 30min., 6am-noon, 7hr., Rs.80; 11 per night, 6:30-7:30pm, 7hr., Rs.95); Narayanghat (almost every bus passes through, 6hr., Rs.75); Tansen (5:30pm, 12hr., Rs.140); and Tardi Bazaar (for Sauraha; every Hetauda bus except the direct passes through, 6-7hr.).

Sajha, the government bus corporation, runs fast, cheap daytime buses, which should be booked a day in advance. Blue Sajha buses are cheaper and a little faster than other buses. To: Birganj (3 per day, 7-7:45am, Rs.99); Bhairahawa (7:15am, Rs.104); Hetauda (7am, Rs.59); Janakpur (7am, Rs.138); Narayanghat (2pm, Rs.60); Pokhara (2 at 7:30am, 7hr., Rs.81); Tansen (7:30am, Rs.114). Tourist buses are minibuses with better, more comfortable seats, and clear aisles. They leave from counter #25 to Pokhara (7 per day, 7am-2pm, 7hr., Rs.150) and Gorkha (7, 8, and 9am, 6hr., Rs.85).

GETTING AROUND

By Bus

By far the cheapest way to get around the Kathmandu Valley, riding a bus is a sure way of rubbing shoulders with the locals. Just when you thought another ant couldn't possibly squeeze in, another five people and two goats climb on board. The buses and minibuses (vans with a few benches) are astoundingly dilapidated and come in all shapes and colors, with steering wheels on either side. Despite their less-than-first-class conditions, Kathmandu buses function, and they are now even painted with route numbers—a great help to visitors. In addition to a driver, every bus has at least one fare collector who prods passengers into tight spaces and directs the driver in a language of whistles and bangs on the side of the bus. Pay him as you get off. Always confirm that the bus is going to your destination. The valley bus station is known as **Ratna Park** (the name is taken from the park across the street). Buses generally leave as soon as they're "full," and standards are high. Destinations include Bhaktapur (#7, frequent, 45min., Rs.4); Boudha (#2, every 30min., 30min., Rs.3); Budhanilkantha (#5, every 30min., 1hr., Rs.6); Dhulikel (#12, every 30min., 1hr. 45min., Rs.10); Kirtipur (#21, frequent, 45min., Rs.3); Patan (#14, frequent, 20min., Rs.3); Sankhu (#4, every 30min., 1hr., Rs.7); Thimi (#10, frequent, 30min., Rs.4); and Bahaka Bazaar (#9).

By Taxi

Shiny new red, green, or yellow taxis are all metered, as are the older ones (identifiable by their black license plates). Most drivers will now use the meters, but it may take a little persuasion to get them to lift the rag they've casually draped over it. You shouldn't have to haggle over the price unless you're desperate (i.e., if it's the only cab around or you're going somewhere weird at a late hour). If the driver refuses to use the meter, get out and find another taxi. Have the fare ready to hand to the driver as soon as you arrive, or the driver might let the meter jump a notch while you rummage for change. Rates start at Rs.5 and go up in increments of Rs.1.80. Round up to the nearest rupee but don't tip. At night, rates go up over 50%, and drivers may be unwilling to go to some destinations. Taxis queue on Tridevi Marg near the entrance to Thamel.

By Trolleybus

Haggard-looking, Chinese-built electric trolleybuses creak between Kathmandu and Bhaktapur (45min., Rs.3). The first stop is on Tripureswar Marg, just south of the National Stadium. Trolleybuses tend to be less crowded than buses.

By Auto-Rickshaw

These are the same black-canopied, three-wheeled contraptions that sputter and beep their way through India. Unless you speak Nepali, their outdated meters (the proper fare is the meter reading plus 40%) might as well not exist—the drivers will not use them. From a visitor's point of view, taxis are usually a better value, since they follow their meters, and auto-rickshaw-*wallahs* tend to be stubborn bargainers. The exhaust they spew is particularly noxious, and their semi-open construction won't keep out other vehicles' waste. However, auto-rickshaws can maneuver narrow lanes more easily than cars, and are fine for short jaunts.

By Tempo

These blue vehicles are larger, sturdier versions of auto-rickshaws, seating 10 people (although you'd never guess from the outside) and run along a prescribed route. They can be flagged down anywhere along their routes; to get off, bang on the metal ceiling. Many start on Kantipath, outside the GPO. To Boudha (#2, 30min., Rs.6) and Patan (#14, 20min., Rs.4). Others gather just north of Rani Pokhari, including those that go to Budhanilkantha (#5, 45min., Rs.6).

By Rickshaw

"Hello, rickshaw?" is second only to "Hello, change money?" as the most commonly heard phrase in the streets of Thamel. These aggressive cyclists drive a hard bargain, but you may have trouble bringing yourself to haggle over a few rupees with a man or boy who is going to use his own body to move yours. The high, canopied seats and smooth pace of rickshaws make them a pleasant mode for observing Kathmandu's comparably less polluted back streets. Be aware that rickshaws are not allowed on some major streets, like Durbar Marg.

By Bicycle

Bicycles can be rented from numerous little shops in Thamel. Regular one-speeders normally cost Rs.50 per day, while Rs.80-140 is normally charged for mountain bikes. Biking is an excellent way of touring the Kathmandu Valley if you can stand the exhaust-filled air. Motorbiking (Rs.350 per day, passport must be deposited) is a great way to contribute a little more exhaust.

ORIENTATION

Kathmandu's Newari citizens once tried to keep the city compact in order to maximize farmland, but this custom has been lost now as the city spreads past its old boundaries. Nevertheless, the city is still rather small and easy to figure out. Although the city has no single center, none of the various minor centers are far apart. The two main roads are **Kantipath** and **Durbar Marg,** which run parallel to each other north-south through the middle of the city. Kantipath, to the west, has the post office and a good collection of banks; Durbar Marg, to the east, has its share of airline offices, trekking agencies, luxury hotels, and restaurants, as well as the **Royal Palace** at its north end. Between the two streets further south is the **Tundikhel** parade ground, a very flat landmark; Kantipath and Durbar Marg become one-way streets near this grassy rectangle as traffic moves clockwise around it.

Kantipath and Durbar Marg divide Kathmandu into two halves—west of Kantipath are the older, more interesting parts of the city, while the area east of Durbar Marg consists mainly of new neighborhoods. The year-round tourist carnival of **Thamel** is west of Kantipath, at the northwestern end of town (even though it might as well be in a world of its own). Thamel is joined to Kantipath and Durbar Marg by the wide avenue of **Tridevi Marg.** The area just south of Thamel is **Chhetrapati,** centered on a six-way crossing with a bandstand in the middle.

Kathmandu's old center, **Durbar Square,** filled with magnificent architecture, is also west of Kantipath, but south of Thamel and Chhetrapati. Close to the banks of the **Vishnumati River,** it is on the western edge of the city. **New Road,** which was new in 1934 when it was built out of the rubble of a great earthquake, runs east from Durbar Square to Kantipath. New Rd. is the city's top commercial district, with rows of jewellers and electronics sellers. At an angle from Durbar Sq. comes the nameless narrow lane that used to be the main trading center and cuts through the area known as **Indra Chowk,** one of Kathmandu's most interesting neighborhoods.

Tripureswar Marg is the biggest road in the southern half of town, running east-west and leading to the **Patan Bridge.** Kathmandu's twin city, Patan, lies across the **Bagmati River,** which is the southern limit of Kathmandu. A wide **Ring Road** now encircles both Kathmandu and Patan, grouping them together with the new suburbs that have grown around them. The hilltop shrine of **Swayambhunath,** across the Vishnumati from Kathmandu, has now become part of the package.

PRACTICAL INFORMATION

Tourist Office: There are 2 government-run **Tourist Information Centres:** on New Rd. just east of Durbar Sq. (tel. 220818) and at Tribhuvan Airport (tel. 470537). The **Department of Tourism** is located in Maitighar (tel. 217758). All of these hand out free maps and brochures filled with pretty pictures and broken English. Staff members are friendly and ready to assist.

Trekking Information: Himalayan Rescue Association, Tridevi Marg (tel. 418755), Hotel Tilicho, 1st fl. Focuses on Mountain safety, providing embassy registration, information on altitude sickness, and a message board for trekkers looking for companions. In the spring and fall, they offer safety talks Sun.-Fri. 2pm. **KEEP** (Kathmandu Environmental Education Project), P.O. Box 9178 (tel. 410303; fax 411533), on the ground floor of the Potala Tourist Home. Concentrates on environmental issues surrounding trekking, and sells books, maps, t-shirts, and biodegradable soap. Both have small libraries, plenty of pamphlets, log books of trekkers' advice, and helpful staff. Both open Sun.-Fri. 10am-5pm. Check bulletin boards in guest houses and restaurants for less official information.

Budget Travel: Every other shopfront in Thamel seems to be a ticket-booking, trekking, rafting, or travel agency. Some are helpful, others are shady and disappear quickly. Ask other travelers for recommendations. For bookings on tourist buses to places like Pokhara and Chitwan, most agencies offer comparable prices—check out a few to make sure you're getting the going rate. For plane tickets, go directly to the airline office (see **Getting There and Away**, p. 677).

Diplomatic Missions: Australia, Bansbari (tel. 417566), on Maharaganj, just past Ring Rd. Consular services open Mon.-Thurs. 10am-12:30pm. **Bangladesh,** Maharajgunj (tel. 414943), on Chakrapath near Hotel Karnali. Visa applications 9-10:30am. **Burma** (Myanmar), Chakupat, Patan (tel. 521788). Near Patan Gate. Visas Mon.-Fri. 9:30am-4:30pm. Apply in the morning and pick up in the afternoon; apply in the afternoon and pick up the next morning. Three photos required. Tourist visa US$10, payable in U.S. dollars or rupees. **Canada,** Lazimpath (tel. 415193), down the lane opposite Navin Books stationery shop. Open Mon.-Fri. 9am-5pm. **China,** Baluwatar (tel. 411740, visa services tel. 419053). Bring plane tickets and 1 photo. Visas Rs.480 for U.S. citizens. Ready the same day. Visas to Tibet available only to organized groups of 3 or more and not to individuals (although individuals can enter with a group and then go it alone—don't tell the officials at the Chinese embassy you plan to do this). Ready the same day. Visa dept. open Mon.-Fri. 10am-noon. **Denmark,** Baluwatar (tel. 413010). Open Mon.-Thurs. 9am-5pm. Consular services Mon.-Fri. 10am-noon. **France,** Lazimpath (tel. 412332). Past the Hotel Ambassador. Open Mon.-Fri. 9am-12:30pm. **Germany,** Gyaneswar (tel. 416832). Mon.-Fri. 9am-noon. **India,** Lainchaur (410900). Off Lazimpath just before the Hotel Ambassador. Put yourself through the week-long visa ordeal Mon.-Fri.: telex forms issued at counter B from 9:30-11am, accepted 9:30am-noon. As you fill out the duplicate forms, make sure your handwriting is big, bold, and beautiful enough to suit the man at the counter. Return a week later, check the board near counter B for your name, surrender your receipt at counter B in exchange for your approval slip. Bring the slip along with your passport, a filled-out visa application (available at the office behind counter B where you may also have to negotiate if you want a multiple entry visa) and 1 photo to counter A. Pay your visa fee (3 months Rs.1200, 6 months Rs.2300; additional Rs.1220 for U.S. citizens. Free for citizens of Afghanistan, Bangladesh, Denmark, Greece, Hungary, Mongolia, Namibia, Poland, San Marino, South Africa, Sweden, and Uruguay). Return the same day between 4:30-5:15pm to pick up your passport and visa. Check to make sure you got the visa for which you applied. Whew! Feel proud for having survived your first brush with Indian bureaucracy. For transit visas, go directly to counter A, Mon.-Fri. 9:30am-noon. **Israel,** Lazimpath (tel. 411811). Consular services Mon.-Thurs. 10am-noon. **Italy,** Baluwater (tel. 412743). Open Mon.-Fri. 10am-1:30pm. **Japan,** Pani Pokhari (tel. 414083). **Netherlands,** Bakhundole (tel. 523444). Consular services Mon.-Fri. 10am-3pm. **Pakistan,** Pani Pokhari (tel. 411421, visa services tel. 415806). Visa applications Sun.-Thurs. 10-11am. **Sri Lanka,** Kamal Pokhari (tel. 413628). Visa applications Sun.-Fri. 9am-noon. **Thailand,** Bansbari (tel. 420411). Visa applications Mon.-Fri. 9:30am-12:30pm. Visas ready in 24hr. Two photos required. One-month tourist visa Rs.450, 2 months Rs.700. **U.K.,** Lazimpath (tel. 414588). Open Mon.-Fri. 8:15am-5pm. Consular services 9am-noon. **U.S.,** Pani Pokhari (tel. 411179). Open Mon.-Fri. 8am-5pm. Consular services Mon., Wed., and Fri. 2-4:40pm, Tues. and Thurs. 8:30-11:30am.

Immigration Office: Department of Immigration, Tridevi Marg (tel. 412337, 418573), about 120m to the left as you walk from Thamel to the Royal Palace. **Trekking permits** for Annapurna, Helambu, and Everest Rs.275 per week; for Lower Dolpo Rs.550 per week. Two photos required for trekking permits. Sun.-Thurs. apply 10am-2pm, pick-up 2-5pm. Fri. apply 10am-noon, pick-up noon-3pm. Payment accepted in rupees only. There is a bank in the building itself for monetary exchanges. You can complete the process in 1 day, but at the height of the trekking season, long lines can extend the process to 2 or even 3 days—get there early. The office closes for 1 week during the Dasain holiday in Oct. Permit officials have been known to make a fuss if all the members of the group seeking permits aren't present. If your trek enters a national park (Everest and Langtang) or a conservation area (Annapurna), you will have to pay a fee of Rs.650. To pay the fees, walk across from the trekking permit building in Thamel to the Himalayan Bank building and follow the signs that say "Entry Fee Collection Centre" (tel. 233088, ext.363; open Sun.-Thurs. 10am-5pm and Fri. 10am-3pm) to the underground. The

NEPAL

collection center is to the right as you walk down a permanently stationary OTIS escalator. The process takes only a few minutes.

Currency Exchange: Legally, currency can only be exchanged at banks or government-registered agencies. Such places give encashment receipts, which you must show in order to convert leftover rupees back, and could be requested if you apply for a visa extension of over 3 months. Illegally, traveler's checks and cash can be exchanged on the **black market.** After about 30 seconds in Thamel, you'll find out how it's done. It's better to walk into a shop (most **carpet shops** change money on the side) than to be brought in by a "change money?" tout. Ask around about going rates—they may be as much as 10% better than at banks. Big, crisp bills are favored. **Nepal Bank Ltd.,** New Rd. (tel. 221185) offers the lowest commission around (.5%, good rates) for exchanging traveler's checks. You must show your Nepalese visa as well as your traveler's check purchase agreement. Open daily 7:30am-1pm and 1:30pm-7pm. There are several official exchange counters around Thamel. Western Union is represented by **Annapurna Travel and Tours,** Durbar Marg (tel. 222339, 223763, 223940; fax 222966, 220215). On the east side of the street, where it becomes one-way. Money can be wired here within 10min. Open daily 10am-5pm, but let them know if you're expecting money—hours are sometimes longer.

American Express: Yeti Travels, Hotel Mayalu, Jamal, P.O. Box 76 (tel. 226172, 227635). Mail held for traveler's check and card holders. Checks and cards replaced, and card holders can buy traveler's checks. Open Mon.-Thurs. 10am-1pm and 2-5pm, Fri. 10am-1pm and 2-4:45pm.

Telephones: Central Telegraph Office, across from the National Stadium. Open 24hr. Domestic and International calls and faxes available at the numerous STD/ISD booths sprinkled throughout the city. In Thamel, you'll only need to walk a few blocks in any direction to find one. Most offer the same rates on outgoing calls but have different deals on call-backs—shop around. **Global Communications,** Tridevi Marg (tel. 228143; fax 220143) in the shopping center across from Immigration has good rates (Rs.165 per min. to the U.S.) and charges a flat Rs.25 for calls back, which you receive in a quiet booth. The also offer fax, post, and **e-mail.** Open Sun.-Fri. 8am-8pm, Sat. 11am-5pm. International phone and fax facilities in the **GPO,** open Sun.-Thurs. 10am-5pm, Fri. 10am-4pm. Good rates, but no call-back and it's noisy.

E-Mail: More and more communications centers are adding e-mail to their facilities. You'll be charged by the kilobyte for messages sent and received. **Global Communications** (glocom@globpc.mps.com.np, glocom@globpc.wlink.com.np) has the most experience. Rs.25/50 per kilobyte to send on slow/fast satellite link; Rs.20 per kilobyte to receive.

Luggage Storage: Available at most guest houses for free or a few rupees per day.

Market: For fresh fruits and vegetables, try **Asan Tole,** in front of the Annapurna Temple, although you'll never be far from a fruit stand in any neighborhood. Watch to see what Nepalis pay for fruit and try to get the same price. Picnic and trekking supplies (and slightly cheaper mineral water) can be found in Thamel at the **Best Shopping Centre,** Tridevi Marg (tel. 410986), right where it narrows into Thamel. Open Sun.-Fri. 8am-8pm, Sat. 8am-noon. AmEx accepted. For the best simulation of a Western supermarket and its prices, head for a branch of the **Bluebird Supermarket.** The branch at Tripureswar (tel. 245726) has a department store upstairs. Open daily 10am-8pm. The other branch is in Lazimpath.

Trekking Supplies: Thamel is the place to look for trekking supplies, both new and used, to buy or rent. Don't be fooled by the phony North Face or Lowe labels. Bring boots and other essentials from home, but heavy items like sleeping bags and jackets can be rented. The quality isn't great, but items like duffle bags, pack covers, and rain gear are cheap and serviceable. Fake Teva sandals are sold on the streets of Thamel for under Rs.200, and can be a good deal. (Be sure to buy a pair with triangular plastic pieces connecting the straps, because other shapes slip out of place, and the metal can rust.) For more information, see **Trekking** (p. 54).

Library: Kaiser Library, Ministry of Education compound, corner of Tridevi Marg and Kantipath (tel. 411318). Housed in a charmingly decrepit Rana palace, the library remains as it was left by Kaiser Shamser Jung Bahadur Rana, a learned aristocrat who fell ill and died in 1964, 2 days after learning of the death of Jawaharlal Nehru. A stuffed tiger, mounted animal heads, suits of armor, and portraits are the highlights of the library. Photos of important looking men standing behind rows of freshly shot tigers and rhinos line the wall along with oil portraits of Shakespeare, Tolstoy, and George V. And there are books, too: they range from Great Men of India to pastry cookbooks. **British Council,** Kantipath (tel. 221305). The collection is aimed mostly at Nepalis learning English, but the reading room is full of British periodicals. Open Mon. and Fri. noon-7pm, Tues.-Thurs. 10am-5pm. **American Center,** Gyaneswar (tel. 415845). Gems such as *The New Yorker* and *Rolling Stone* in an A/C reading room. Open Mon.-Fri. 11am-6pm.

English Bookstore: Thamel is dotted with used book shops where you can trade 2 books for 1 or sell your books back at half price. **Pilgrims Book House,** Thamel (tel. 424942; fax 424943) deserves special mention. It houses the biggest selection of books on all things Himalayan, from Tibetan travelogues to glossy coffee-table books. Postal service, stationery, and gifts. Open daily 8am-10pm.

Pharmacy: Everywhere, especially concentrated along New Rd. **Niroj Pharma,** opposite Bir Hospital, just off Kantipath, is open 24hr. **Om Pharmacy,** New Rd. (tel. 244658) is recommended by local medical experts. Open daily 7am-9:30pm.

Hospital/Medical Services: It's best to go to a **clinic** first and if you need more care than they can provide, they'll send you to the appropriate hospital. **CIWEC Clinic,** off Durbar Marg (tel. 228531, 241732). Behind the Yak and Yeti sign, to the right. Staffed by Western doctors who charge Western prices. US$40 per consultation. Open Mon.-Fri. 9am-noon and 1-4pm, Sat.-Sun. Same hours for inoculations and lab. Call 24hr. in an emergency. **Nepal International Clinic** (tel. 412842), across from the Royal Palace, a 3-min. walk east of the main gates, down a lane to the right. Western-educated Nepalese doctors. Consultation US$30. Open daily 9am-1pm and 2-5pm. **Himalayan Internal Clinic,** Chhetrapati (tel. 216197). Western-educated doctors. Consultation US$20, follow-up US$10. **Patan Hospital,** Lagankhel, Patan (tel. 522266, 522295) has a better reputation than the government hospital in Kathmandu proper, **Bir Hospital.** The **Teaching Hospital,** Maharganj (tel. 412303, 412404) is also said to be good.

Emergency: Police: tel. 100, 226999. **Fire:** tel. 101. **Ambulance:** tel. 228094 (Red Cross). No English spoken at any of these numbers. **In a medical emergency, call a clinic to find an English speaker.**

Post Office: GPO, near Bhimsen Tower, entrance just off Kantipath. Self-service *Poste Restante* is behind the counter on the left. Open Sun.-Thurs. 10:15am-4pm (winter 10:15am-3pm), Fri. 10:15am-2pm. You can flip through the letters yourself, so even if there's nothing for you, you can read other people's postcards. A clerk may or may not ask for your passport before you make off with your mail. Stamps sold Sun.-Thurs. 7am-7pm, Fri. 7am-5pm; winter Sun.-Thurs. 8am-6pm, Fri. 8am-4pm. Cancellation: Sun.-Thurs. 10am-4pm, Fri. 10am-3pm; winter Sun.-Thurs. 10am-3pm, Fri. 10am-2pm. Many guest houses and communications centers will save you the trouble of going to the post office yourself, for a small commission. In Thamel, Pilgrims Book House is a reliable place to bring your mail. The new **Express Mail Service (EMS)** delivers within 3 days to most Asian countries as well as Australia, New Zealand, Canada, Denmark, and Italy. Open Sun-Thurs. 10am-5pm, Fri. 10am-3pm; winter Sun.-Thurs. 10am-4pm, Fri. 10am-2pm. The entrance to the **Foreign Parcel Office** is around the corner on Kantipath. Bring your open parcel to be checked by customs, then properly sewn up and sealed by the packagers who wait outside. Open Sun.-Thurs. 10am-1:30pm, Fri. 10am-1pm; winter Sun.-Thurs. 10am-1pm, Fri. 10am-12:30pm.

Telephone Code: 01.

ACCOMMODATIONS

Any mention of tourist facilities in Kathmandu must begin with **Thamel,** and that goes double for accommodations. Hanging out in the Thamel area is like hanging out in a mall—everything is within easy reach, but the experience won't broaden your horizons. Of course, Thamel's concentration of shops, restaurants, trekking agencies, and other facilities, along with its relative proximity to Durbar Sq. and the immigra-

NEPAL

tion office, make it a convenient place to stay. So try to make it just that. Use its conveniences, whether for a bed or a buffalo burger, but don't let it use you. Get out into the regular Kathmandu every once in a while. You'll find that despite the ease of Thamel, the rest of the city is actually less of a hassle, since it won't surround you with constant appeals to change money, buy hashish, or ride in a rickshaw.

Accommodations in Thamel are quickly climbing upmarket, but there are still plenty of choices in the budget range. The places below are the best budget values, whether all you want is cheap and clean or you require your own bathroom. The prices listed are for high season, but these are almost always negotiable depending on the time of year and the length of your stay. More expensive places charge 10% government tax (and many more claim to charge but don't). The following all have hot water, laundry service, luggage storage, and a noon check-out time. Bring your own towels and toilet paper unless otherwise noted. **Freak Street** is Kathmandu's original tourist ghetto, which reached its prime in the overland days of the 70s. Freak Street is less hectic than Thamel, but at most of its hotels you can tell they've been around for the last 25 years, watching lodges in Thamel steal all their business.

Thamel

Hotel Potala, Thamel (tel. 416680; fax 419317), across from K.C.'s. Not to be confused with the Potala Guest House or the Potala Tourist Home. In the center of Thamel, this place is a real find. Two clean showers and toilets on each floor. Well-ventilated rooms allow for easy eavesdropping (like it or not). Each room is different—some have fans, some have balconies, some are brighter than others, but all are well-kept. Hang out among potted plants on the roof terrace or in the lobby where the TV is even more mesmerizing than the big fish tank. Run by an exceedingly nice Tibetan family, this place is as cheery as the smiley face on its sign. Singles Rs.100-150. Doubles Rs.150-200.

Kathmandu Guest House, Thamel (tel. 413632, 418733; fax 417133). Since all directions in Thamel are given in relation to this place, you'd better figure out where it is. Live a little piece of Thamel history by staying in Kathmandu's original "budget hotel." The cheaper rooms, which are not remarkable in and of themselves, are in the old wing whose wide hallway has a worn, Rana-era charm. They are a cheap way of getting at Kathmandu Guest House's amenities: manicured gardens, a restaurant, currency exchange, ticket-booking, bicycle rental, and safe deposit. Old wing: Singles with sink US$6-8, with bath US$10. Doubles with sink US$8-10, with bath US$12. New wing: Singles US$17-25. Doubles US$20-30. Triples US$25-35 (plus 12% govt. tax). Discount of 20% for stays of over a week, 30% for over a month. AmEx/MC/V.

Pheasant Lodge, Thamel (tel. 417415). Down a short alleyway to the left of Le Bistro. Smack dab in the middle of things, separated only by a courtyard full of chirping caged birds. Basic rooms from the folks who brought you the Restaurant at the End of the Universe. The walls are smudged but the sheets are clean. A choice of common toilets—squat or sit as you please. Showers are standing room only. Often full, so try right at the noon check-out time. Singles Rs.80. Doubles Rs.150.

Hotel White Lotus, Jyatha Thamel (tel. 226342; fax 220143). The last of several guest houses at the end of a lane off Jyatha, to the right coming from Tridevi Marg. Sky-blue walled rooms vary in amenities and price, but all rooms and baths (both common and private) are clean. A dizzying spiral staircase leads to the roof garden. Towels provided. International calling available. Safe deposit. Singles US$3, with bath US$10. Doubles US$10, with bath US$10-14.

New Shangrila Guest House, Jyatha Thamel (tel. 227388, 220143). Next door to the White Lotus. Colorful floor tiles in the halls, sweet-smelling straw mats, and other decorative touches in the rooms. Ceiling fans in every room. The Belgian-Sherpa management keeps all surfaces free of grunge. Restaurant with floor seating inside, tables on the roof terrace outside. Enjoy the sounds of birds rather than auto-rickshaws in this peaceful cul-de-sac. Doubles US$5, with bath US$10. Triples with bath US$15.

Kathmandu View Guest House, Chhetrapati (tel. 244624). A few doors down from the Everest Steak House. Rooms with exposed brick walls and stone inlay are clean enough to please even the most culture-shocked tourist. Singles Rs.200. Doubles Rs.250, with bath Rs.350.

Frugal Guest House, Thamel (tel. 410875). Just north of the Kathmandu Guest House, down a lane to the right. The name says it all: simple, whitewashed rooms with cement floors around a small courtyard tucked away from the street. Despite its spartan quality, the place is cheerful. Toilets and showers are across the courtyard. Singles Rs.100. Doubles Rs.150.

Skala Guest House, Chhetrapati-Thamel (tel. 223155; fax 229459). South from the Kathmandu Guest House on the left. No frills rooms above the overgrown garden of the tasty Skala Vegetarian Restaurant. Rooms with bath are in the newer building, closer to the street; rooms without are set back further. Minimal furnishings make some rooms seem cavernous. Bathroom tiles are chipped but scrubbed. Singles Rs.100, with bath Rs.200. Doubles Rs.150, with bath Rs.350.

Fuji Guest House, Chhetrapati-Thamel (tel./fax 229234). Walking south from the Kathmandu Guest House, down the left. The simple, well-swept rooms are popular with Japanese visitors. International calling, safe deposit. A second branch on a lane off Jyotha Thamel, is scheduled to open soon. Singles US$4, with bath US$6. Doubles with shower only US$6, with bath US$9. Triples with bath US$15.

Hotel Horizon, Chhetrapati-Thamel (tel. 220904, 220927). Walking south from the Kathmandu Guest House, down a lane to the right. Set back from the street, with a greenery-fringed courtyard. All rooms have attached baths, and some have actual bathtubs. Fuzzy fake-tiger blankets and plenty of furniture make for a comfortable stay. Singles US$4. Doubles US$6-20.

Hotel Nightingale, Thamel (tel. 225038). Accessible from an alley off Thahity-Thamel to the west, or via the lane next to Pumpernickel's. Another nothing-fancy kind of place. Well-buffered from street noise, with spare rooms and plants on the roof. Singles Rs.120, with bath Rs.150. Doubles Rs.150, with bath Rs.200. Triples Rs.225, with bath Rs.250.

Prince Guest House, Satghumti-Thamel (tel. 414456; fax 415158). Follow the road where it veers left, north of the Kathmandu Guest House, and continue down the lane straight ahead. The Artist Formerly Known As would die 4 this pink and purple decor with birthday-cake moldings and wall-to-wall carpeting. Brand-new, pristine rooms with fans and attached baths complete with seat toilets and shower curtains. Rooftop garden and restaurant. Room service, safe deposit. Singles US$10-15. Doubles US$15-20.

Freak Street

Annapurna Lodge, Freak St. (tel. 247684). On the right, walking from Durbar Sq. A many-angled stairway leads to quiet, basic rooms off a balcony. Common squat toilets. Attached Restaurant Diyalo boasts a garden and a cheap menu, and shows movies. Singles Rs.100, with bath Rs.200. Doubles Rs.175, with bath Rs.250.

Himalaya's Guest House, Basantapur, Jhochhen (tel. 246555, 228718). Down a narrow, untouristy street off Freak St. to the west (right coming from Durbar Sq.). Single rooms above a coffee shop, with ratan furniture and wrinkly faux-marble linoleum flooring. Better than a lot of places on Freak St., but nothing special. Singles Rs.100. Doubles Rs.200, with bath Rs.250.

FOOD

Ironically, in the capital of a nation whose cuisine consists almost entirely of rice and lentils, a staggering array of dishes are available to visitors. From the 1954 founding of Kathmandu's first luxury hotel by Boris Lissanevitch, a charismatic Russian entrepreneur who had chandeliers and fresh fish carried in by porters, to "Pie Alley," where 1960s overlanders gathered for apple pie and hash brownies, Kathmandu has achieved an almost mythological status as an oasis of displaced delicacies. Steaks, pizza, enchiladas, french fries, and apple pie appear regularly on tourist menus. As this book went to press a Wimpy's was all set to open on Durbar Marg. Japanese, Thai, Tibetan, and Indian restaurants elbow for room in neighborhoods frequented by foreigners and wealthy Nepalis. While some of this food might taste like home (wherever you're from), much of it struggles to slough off its Nepalese flavor. "So what about Nepalese food?" asks the open-minded traveler who didn't come halfway around the world to eat blander versions of what he or she could get around the corner at home. The best bet is to get yourself invited to someone's home for a meal. Beyond that, most Nepali restaurants fall into one of two categories: very cheap hole-in-the-wall eateries marked only by a curtain (often green), and expensive tourist-oriented places that often offer set menus of Newari delicacies. For the former, ask around. As for the latter, they can actually be very good, even if the only Nepalis around are the waiters.

Thamel Area

Nepalese Kitchen, Chhetrapati (tel. 241965). "Nepal is here to change you, not for you to change Nepal," is the motto of this restaurant that one of the few to have noticed the handful of tourists in Nepal interested in eating something indigenous, although there's still a Continental menu for the apple-pie crowd. Sit under an umbrella in the garden, or inside under an upholstered ceiling, surrounded by black-and-white photo-bedecked walls. Set menus (Rs.90-175) are variations on the *dal bhat* theme, and come with or without meat. The delicious charcoal-grilled chicken with *pulao* (Rs.110) comes with plenty of chicken and flavorful rice. For dessert, try the Nepalese version of *kheer,* a rich rice pudding (Rs.30). Open daily 8am-9:30pm.

The Northfield Café, Thamel (tel. 424884), a few doors down from Pilgrims Book House. This offspring of the legendary Mike's Breakfast (see below) recently won an award for the best Mexican food (Rs.80-175) in Nepal, which isn't saying much, but the food is good, and this is the only place in town for homesick Americans to munch tortilla chips and salsa. The breakfast menu is almost identical to Mike's (no muffins, though), and the pancakes with butter and syrup are better here. The garden is lush and the classical or new age music is played at such a volume as to obliterate any traces of street noise. Open daily 7am-10pm.

Just Juice 'n' Shakes, Thamel. Down a little lane to the right, just before the zig in the zig-zag north of the Kathmandu Guest House. The *lassis,* made with frozen fruit, are thick and cold. The boy at the blender will top off your glass after you've taken a few sips. Low ratan furniture and copies of both daily English newspapers fill this tiny joint. Freshly squeezed juice, shakes, and smoothies Rs.40-60. Espresso Rs.20. Cappuccino Rs.20. Open daily 7:30am-9pm.

Pumpernickel Bakery, Thamel (tel. 240144). A Thamel institution. At breakfast time, the garden here is full and the line to order freshly baked croissants, cakes, and cinnamon rolls (Rs.6-18) runs to the street. Take off your mittens to spread creamy yak cheese on steaming buns. A small menu beyond baked goods includes sandwiches, eggs, muesli, curd, and fresh juice. Open daily 8am-6pm.

Simply Shutters Bistro, Thahity-Thamel (tel. 226015). Western food, Western setting, Western prices. A small, casually elegant dining room with gray-green walls and exposed wooden ceiling beams. The menu, which changes every few days, is written on a chalkboard. Three-course menu Rs.400. A la carte: appetizers Rs.100, main courses Rs.190-230, scrumptious desserts Rs.120. Add 10% tax. Wine by the glass. Sandwiches at lunchtime (until 5:30pm). Open Wed.-Mon. noon-9:30pm. Reservations recommended.

Tashi Deleg, Thamel. Through a narrow passageway across from Helena's. Duck in here for the good-value food, not the decor. The name means "hello" in Tibetan, and the menu includes Tibetan food (Rs.40-60) as well as Continental meat dishes and an assortment of creative veggie burgers. Open daily 7am-10pm.

Everest Steak House, Chhetrapati (tel. 217471). Carnivores delight in real, juicy, beef *(shhh!)* steaks (Rs.150-225). Stab into generous portions in wooden booth seating. Italian, Tibetan, and Mexican dishes too (Rs.950-1150). The Pokhara branch is a popular *après*-trek destination for the iron-depleted. Open daily 8am-10pm.

Le Bistro, Thamel (tel. 411170). A well-placed observation deck from which to watch the goings-on in the streets of Thamel. Downstairs, a garden and an indoor dining area provide some relief from the street. Continental, Chinese, and Indian main dishes Rs.100-150. Portions are generous: the mushroom and spinach quiche

(Rs.90) comes with potatoes, cooked veggies, and garlic bread. Open daily 7am-10pm.

The Rum Doodle 40,000½-Feet Bar and Restaurant, Thamel (tel. 414336), follow the turn in the road north of the Kathmandu Guest House, on the left. The namesake of this bar and restaurant is a silly 1956 spoof about a mountaineering expedition. The book is for sale at the bar, along with exotic cocktails and good Continental food, generous portions of which are served in the shady garden, roof terrace, floor-cushioned seating area, or in the cavernous dining room. Cardboard cut-out feet decorate the interior. Main dishes Rs.140-150, veggie dishes Rs.70-150. Save room for dessert—warm apple pie is served in big hunks (Rs.35). Open daily 11am-10pm.

Lhasa, Thamel (tel. 425185). Upstairs, just as the road turns left, north of the Kathmandu Guest House. Mostly Tibetan dishes like *momos* (Rs.40-60), spring rolls, and *thukpa*. Chow mein (Rs.30-50) and other Chinese food, too. Unusually cheap and un-Westernized for Thamel. Open daily 8am-10pm.

Skala Vegetarian Restaurant, Chhetrapati-Thamel. On the left, walking south. A thick garden and loud classical music insulate the outdoor tables from the surrounding hubbub. Set breakfasts, many of which include fresh brown bread, Rs.45-65. Names of creative veg. dishes (Rs.80-100) are inscribed by hand on the handmade-paper menus. Open daily 8am-8pm.

Durbar Marg

Nirula's, Durbar Marg (smaller branch on New Rd.). Hang here with Nepal's teenage elite if you think you're hip enough. This Indian-imported ice cream parlor/fast food joint serves 21 flavors of ice cream (different prices for different flavors) and "hot numbers" such as pizzas and "mahaburgers." Pay the cashier, then bring the receipt to the counter. Divine. Open daily 9am-10pm.

Mangalore Coffee House, Jamal Tole (tel. 231990), just off Durbar Marg, above American Express. South Indian cheap eats: *masala dosa* (Rs.25), *thali* (veg. Rs.45, non-veg. Rs.60). *Momos* and chow mein available too—we're in Kathmandu, not Karnataka. Cool off under the fans, watch the traffic go by below, and allow yourself to be titillated by poster-sized photos of not-quite embracing couples in such settings as the Taj Mahal. Open daily 9am-9pm.

Baan Thai Restaurant, Durbar Marg (tel. 243271), upstairs. Authentic Thai food in a swanky, air-conditioned setting decorated in every shade of beige. Main dishes around Rs.175, *pad thai* Rs.160. Add 10% govt. tax. Open daily noon-3pm and 6-9:30pm. AmEx/V.

Hot Breads, Durbar Marg (tel. 221331). Branches on New Rd. and in Jawalakhel. An Indian chain with sweet and savory treats from the self-serve bakery. Food tastes refreshingly processed. Mini-quiches, pizzas, croissants, doughnuts, curried vegetable patties, and buns with stuffings such as "chicken hot dog with mayonnaise" Rs.12-30. Pastries Rs.18-28. Take-out or eat here to the sounds of muzak versions of your favorite 80s hits. Pizza (Rs.60-85) and burgers (Rs.45-60) can be ordered. The selection of ice cream flavors doesn't compare to Nirula's, but there's a better choice of sundaes (Rs.50-65) with nifty names like "Pink Affair" and "Zip-a-dee-day." The cold coffee ice cream shake (Rs.55) is heavenly. Open daily 8am-9:30pm. Shop open until 10pm.

Koto Japanese Restaurant, Durbar Marg, upstairs (tel. 226025). Japanese food at moderate Nepalese prices. Simple Japanese decor with chair and floor seating, touched up with photos of Kathmandu. Set menu Rs.340. Noodle soups Rs.150-220, cold noodles Rs.170-190, rice dishes Rs.180-210. Open daily 11:30am-3pm and 6-9:30pm.

Bhanchha Ghar, Kamaladi (tel. 225172). Coming from Durbar Marg, turn left at the clocktower; the restaurant is on the left. The name of the restaurant is Nepali for "kitchen," but the food here is no ordinary *dal bhat*—this is Nepalese *haute cuisine*. Specialties include wild boar (Rs.195) and curried high-altitude mushrooms (Rs.195). The set menu is enormous, and priced to match (Rs.660), but you can easily spend half that and get plenty to eat by ordering a la carte. Lubricate your dinner with *raksi*. Set in an elegantly restored Rana house, with cushions on the floor for seats. Open daily noon-10pm.

New Road

The Bakery Café and **Nanglo Chinese Room,** New Rd., closer to the Durbar Sq. end. Downstairs, the café (behind the bakery) serves western and South Indian style fast food like pizza (Rs.45-95), burgers (Rs.42-95), fried chicken (Rs.75), *dosas* (Rs.30-50), and *idli* (Rs.30) in a candy-colored, Disneyesque courtyard. Upstairs, the Chinese Room looks like a suburban American Chinese restaurant. Main dishes around Rs.100, vegetables Rs.60, and rice Rs.20. Portions are on the small side but are well-prepared. Both places are popular with young Nepalis. Café open daily 11:30am-10pm; restaurant noon-10pm.

Naxal

Mike's Breakfast, Naxal (tel. 424303), near the police headquarters. Though somewhat diminished since its relocation to far-off Naxal, Mike's is still the mecca of Kathmandu breakfasts. Sit on mosaic-covered benches and listen to classical music in their rustling garden while you wolf down the best of Nepali American food. Pancakes Rs.35 and various waffles are excellent; *huevos rancheros* (Rs.80-125) look ugly but they're good. For a true morning of decadence here try the very popular brownie sundae (Rs.80).

SIGHTS

Kathmandu is not a huge city but it's packed with things to see. There are so many temples that a word has been coined, "templescape," to describe the city's skyline. Historical sites are just as numerous, and artistic treasures are scattered everywhere. What follows is a rundown of the highlights, since it would be impossible to hit everything in the city. The best way to tour Kathmandu is on foot, because many obscure and wonderful palaces are too easily passed by in a car or on a bike.

Durbar Square

Durbar Square ("Palace Square") is the heart of the old city. The royal family is gone from the palace here, having moved late last century to the north end of town, but that hasn't diminished Durbar Square's religious, social, and commercial importance. Many of Kathmandu's most interesting temples and historic buildings are located here, and the wide open space brings an air of bustle and alertness.

A good place to start touring the square is the **Kasthamandap** in the southwest corner. This "wooden pavilion" (supposedly built from the wood of a single tree) may be Kathmandu's oldest existing building, dating from the 14th century if not earlier (though it has been substantially altered). It was originally a *dharamshala* (rest house for travelers). It was later turned into a temple, but it still has a feeling of transience, kind of like a train platform—it has an open-air ground floor where people sit and wait (they're actually porters, waiting for loads to carry). Kathmandu gets its name from the Kasthamandap, a sign of how important trade and transportation were to this city. At the same time, the Kasthamandap is a sacred place, with an image in the center of Gorakhnath, the deified Hindu saint who watches over the Shah dynasty. There is a small Ganesh shrine at each corner, and at one corner a golden mouse points its nose at another Ganesh shrine, which has its own enclosure with metal flags. This **Maru Ganesh** (also known as Ashok Binayak) is frequently worshiped. As the remover of obstacles, Ganesh is a good god to visit before traveling.

Turn right from Maru Ganesh and walk along the row of stalls that make up the ground floor of the next pagoda. A dusty-black angelic statue of Garuda, Vishnu's man-bird vehicle, kneels before Vishnu's **Trailokya Mohan Temple.** Around on the other side of the temple great white columns stomp down on the square. Prime Minister Chandra Shamsher Rana added this wing to the main royal palace in 1908. The Rana prime ministers were infatuated with the European Neoclassical style, but the prestige of building something so *big* probably had as much to do with it. On the right, across from this façade with its fancy lampposts, there is a much more traditional-looking Kathmandu palace, with beautiful carved window frames (some shaped like peacocks) and one central window frame covered in gold. This is the **Kumari Bahal,** where the living goddess of Kathmandu, the **Kumari,** flutters, some-

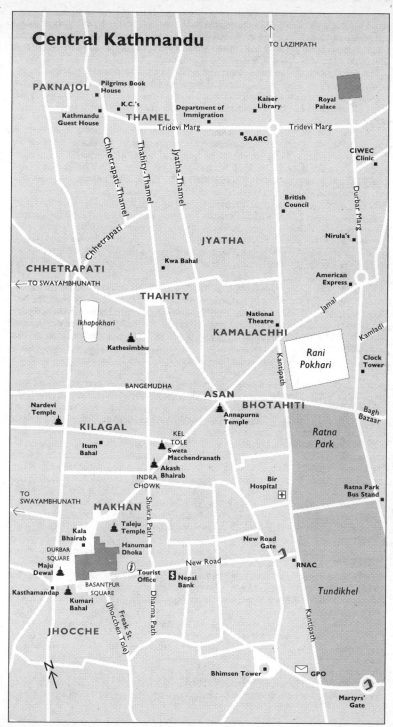

Central Kathmandu

TO LAZIMPATH

PAKNAJOL

Pilgrims Book House

K.C.'s

Kathmandu Guest House

THAMEL

Department of Immigration

Tridevi Marg

SAARC

Kaiser Library

Tridevi Marg

Royal Palace

CIWEC Clinic

Chhetrapati-Thamel

Thahity-Thamel

Jyatha-Thamel

British Council

Durbar Marg

Chhetrapati

JYATHA

Nirula's

CHHETRAPATI

TO SWAYAMBHUNATH

Kwa Bahal

THAHITY

American Express

Ikhapokhari

Jamal

National Theatre

KAMALACHHI

Kamladi

Kathesimbhu

Rani Pokhari

Clock Tower

Kantipath

BANGEMUDHA

ASAN

BHOTAHITI

Bagh Bazaar

Nardevi Temple

Annapurna Temple

KILAGAL

KEL TOLE

Sweta Macchendranath

Ratna Park

Itum Bahal

Akash Bhairab

INDRA CHOWK

Bir Hospital

Ratna Park Bus Stand

TO SWAYAMBHUNATH

MAKHAN

Shukra Path

Kala Bhairab

Taleju Temple

Hanuman Dhoka

New Road Gate

DURBAR SQUARE

Maju Dewal

New Road

RNAC

Tourist Office

Nepal Bank

Kasthamandap

BASANTPUR SQUARE

Kumari Bahal

Dharma Path

Tundikhel

JHOCCHE

Freak St. (Jhochen Tole)

Kantipath

Bhimsen Tower

GPO

Martyrs' Gate

NEPAL

times appeaing at one of the windows in the courtyard. If she doesn't appear there are plenty of touts in the square who'll offer their services in getting her to appear. Soft drinks and film are sold right in the Kumari's courtyard, but don't try to use the film to take pictures of the Kumari—this is forbidden.

Turning right on the way out of the Kumari Bahal and following the wall of the palace, one comes to a big rectangle called **Basantpur Square,** where vendors spread out their blankets with the usual trinkets. Two roads spill onto the other end of the square: straight ahead is New Rd.; in the far right corner is **Freak Street,** with its hotels and shops.

The **Maju Dewal** Shiva temple takes up the prime location in the main Durbar Square, towering over everything on its great step-pyramid. The temple was built in 1690 and it makes a well-placed observation deck for Durbar Square—its height, however, does nothing to isolate it from the fray below. You can sit here for hours watching the square, although you're bound to be hassled by "guides," "English students," and kids asking, "Do you have one coin from your country?"

Beside the Maju Dewal, the **Temple of Shiva and Parvati** rests on a skewed platform. The temple is considered unusual for being rectangular. The divine couple waves from the window above the door. Walk to the right side of the temple, past the *thanka* shops on your right which crouch under an earthquake-shattered wall of the old palace. On the left, above a huge white block, is the **Big Bell,** which rings for worship in the Degutaleju Temple east of here. All three valley cities have big bells like this one.

The road widens ahead of here, and standing before you is the column of Pratap Malla. King Pratap Malla, the brains behind the buildings in this area, prays at the top of the column towards his personal shrine in the **Degutaleju Temple.** Don't pass by the large wooden screen close to the temple without noticing the figure of **Sweta Bhairab** (White Bhairab) behind it, whose big fanged face is actually golden. At the Indra Jatra festival in August or September the screen comes off and beer pours from the mouth of this fearsome form of Shiva (devotees crowd in for a drink). On Pratap Malla's left is the **Jagannath Temple,** which has interesting roof struts—the pastel-painted gods on them have way too many arms, and at their feet strange erotic scenes go on. This is the oldest temple in the northern part of the square, dating from 1563.

The golden door to the **Hanuman Dhoka,** the old royal palace, is located in the corner next to the Jagannath Temple. The building takes its name from the statue of Hanuman lounging under a parasol to the left of the entrance (the monkey-god's face is disfigured by all the *sindur* dabbed on it). The royal family has not lived in this palace for over a century, but it is still used for royal ceremonies such as King Birendra's coronation in 1975. The art and architecture of the Hanuman Dhoka today were influenced mainly by the patronage of King Pratap Malla (r. 1641-74), although the building has evolved steadily since the time of the Licchavi kings, prior to 1200 AD. No Licchavi buildings remain, however, and the palace now has plenty of Shah-era whitewashing. Just inside the entrance is Nasal Chowk, where the nobles of the kingdom used to assemble. In 1673 Pratap Malla danced in a costume of Narasimha, Vishnu's man-lion incarnation, but he was afraid Vishnu would be angry about the stunt—the Narasimha statue just inside the palace was installed by Pratap Malla out of remorse. The main section of the palace open to the public is the **Tribhuvan Memorial Museum** (same ticket from the main door, and same hours). King Tribhuvan (r. 1911-55), who overthrew the Rana regime in 1951 and restored Nepal's monarchy, is eulogized here in a display of personal belongings. Touring through these cases full of ceremonial outfits, newspaper clippings, watches, even Tribhuvan's desk and his fishtank, you'll feel like you know the guy. The museum continues around the Nasal Chowk to the **Basantpur Tower** at the southern end. This nine-story lookout was put up by Prithvi Narayan Shah after he conquered the valley. It's open for those who want to view Durbar Square from a steeper angle. The woodcarvings at the base of the Basantpur Tower are some of the best around. The circuit around Nasal Chowk leads next to the **Mahendra Memorial Museum,** which isn't quite as impressive as Tribhuvan's, but does include a walk-through diorama that simulates one of the king's

The Living Goddess: Kumari

A Newari Buddhist girl considered to be the living embodiment of the Hindu goddess Durga, the Kumari is a perfect example of the mixing of religions in the Kathmandu Valley. Kathmandu's Kumari, the most important of the eleven in the valley, is selected at the age of four or five from the Shakya caste of gold-smiths and silversmiths. First, she must possess 32 physical characteristics such as thighs like a deer's, cheeks and chest like a lion's, eyelashes like a cow's, and body shaped like a banyan tree. Then she must remain calm in a dark room full of buffalo heads, frightening masks, and loud noises. Finally, her astrological chart must not conflict with the king's. If all these conditions are met, the Kumari is installed in the Kumari Bahal in Durbar Square, where she leads the privileged, secluded life of a goddess until she hits puberty. In the meantime, she receives *puja*-performers wearing elaborate eye make-up, jewelry, and red robes. Several times a year she is paraded about on a palanquin (during her ten-ure as Kumari, her feet may never touch the ground). During the festival of Indra Jatra, she places a *tikka* on the king's forehead as a reaffirmation of his power; he in turn bestows upon her a gold coin. As soon as the Kumari menstruates, or sheds blood any other way, the goddess's spirit is said to leave her body, and she must return to her parents' home, where the transition to the childhood of a mere mortal can be difficult. Former goddesses may have difficulty finding a hus-band later on, since men who marry them are said to die young.

The tradition of Kumari-worship can be traced back to the Middle Ages, but it was the last Malla king of Kathmandu, Jaya Prakash, who institutionalized the practice by building the Kumari Bahal in 1757. Various stories trace the Kumari's origins to Jaya Prakash's misadventures—he purportedly built the Kumari Bahal out of remorse for banishing a girl who claimed to be possessed by Durga, or for having sex with a prepubescent girl who then died. Other stories tell how Taleju, a manifestation of the goddess Durga, used to play dice with the Malla kings until one of them made a pass at her. She quit playing, but agreed to return in the form of a Newari virgin. Ironically, 11 years after making the Kumari offi-cial, Jaya Prakash was overthrown on the eve of Indra Jatra, and the victorious Prithvi Narayan Shah arrived in time to receive the *tikka* in his place.

hunts. There are more well-carved courtyards in the palace, but they're all closed to the public, and especially to foreigners—a leftover bit of Nepalese isolationism, it seems. (Open Wed., Thurs., and Sat.-Mon. 10:30am-4:30pm, Fri. 10:30am-2pm. Admission Rs.10. Photography is permitted in the courtyards and in the tower, but not in the museums.)

Outside the palace, along the wall past the Hanuman statue, there is a **stone inscription** made by Pratap Malla using words from 15 different languages. The English and French words stand out clearly, but it's said that if anyone ever manages to read the whole text (a poem dedicated to the goddess Kali) milk will gush from the spout in the middle of it.

Moving north past the palace the **Taleju Temple** emerges on the right; its three-tiered golden pagoda towers over everything else in the square. King Mahendra Malla built the temple in 1564 in honor of Taleju, his dynasty's patron goddess. At 37m, the Taleju Temple was for a long time the tallest building in Kathmandu, a singularity enforced by building codes. But in its modern growth Kathmandu has dispensed with this tradition. The temple is only open to the king and a few powerful priests. On the ninth day of the Dasain festival in October the door is opened to ordinary Hin-dus, but non-Hindus are never allowed inside.

The **Mahendreshwar Temple** is a much more accessible Hindu temple across the street from the Taleju temple. It's a popular Shiva temple, mirrors and all. Turn right through the gauntlet of Thanka shops, and on the left is a stone Garuda who has been kneeling there for over 1000 years. The Vishnu temple that once accompanied it has disappeared, but a small new one was recently built.

The police compound west of this area doesn't have anything special to see, but it's worth noting for history: this is where Jung Bahadur Rana massacred most of Nepal's nobility in 1846, inaugurating 105 years of Rana rule. If you turn back down the road to the main square, you'll be drawn by the huge and garish monolith of **Kala Bhairab** ("Black Bhairab") who dances in every color of the crayon box. Anyone who tells a lie in front of this raging destroyer of evil will supposedly vomit blood and die. To the right of Kala Bhairab's image a pair of big ceremonial drums are kept, nestled on a balcony with flowerpots. Just beyond this is the octagonal **Krishna Temple,** in which (according to the inscription) Pratap Malla had the images made to resemble him and his two wives.

North of Durbar Square

Kathmandu's most interesting little street runs northeast from Durbar Square, disrupting the whole grid system around it. This funny diagonal street doesn't have a name of its own; it takes the name of whatever area it's running through. In earlier times, it was simply the beginning of the trade route from Kathmandu to Tibet, and it was Kathmandu's top commercial area until New Rd. was built after the earthquake of 1934. The road is still a fascinating bazaar, where trays full of mangos are jostled around by passing bicycles and old women crouch next to the piles of cheap clothes they're selling. The first segment of the street, adjacent to Durbar Square, is called Makhan Tole ("Butter Place"). Butter used to be sold here, though now this area is no different from the rest of the street. The first crossroads on the street, walking away from Durbar Square, is called **Indra Chowk.** On the left side at this corner is the second-story temple of **Akash Bhairab,** a garish holy restaurant. Admire its metal gargoyles from across the street if you're not Hindu, since the usual restrictions apply. Akash Bhairab's image, a large wooden mask, is just barely visible. At the Indra Jatra festival in August or September, it is displayed here in the square.

The next crossing is Kel Tole, where on the left there's a short pillar capped with a meditating Buddha. Enter the passageway behind it to approach the **Temple of Sweta Macchendranath,** honored by local Hindus and Buddhists alike. The white-faced image is paraded around during the Macchendranath festival in March. The origin of the European-looking brass lady in the courtyard is unclear.

The pagoda in the middle of Kel Tole is dedicated to **Lunchun Lun Bun Ajima.** This goddess' bathroom-tiled sanctuary is now sunk beneath street level because the road has been repaved so many times. At **Asan Tole,** the next crossing, the road widens out and is filled with stacks of vegetables. The **Temple of Annapurna** is on the right with broad brass ribbons draped over it. The goddess of plentiful food, Annapurna's image here is simply a silver pot.

The diagonal road breaks out of its claustrophobia onto Kantipath across from the **Rani Pokhari** tank. King Pratap Malla built this pool and the temple in its center to console his wife over the death of their son. Unfortunately the green-and-yellow fence around it is locked all year except for one day in Diwali (Oct.-Nov.).

The crossing known as **Bangemudha** is near the diagonal road, west of Asan Tole. Its name means "twisted wood," and in one of the southern corners there's a twisted lump of wood stuck to the wall, with an armor of coins nailed into it. The wood is dedicated to the god of toothaches, Vaisya Dev, and nailing a coin here is supposed to relieve dental pain. The wood's contorted shape, in any case, evokes a sense of agony. On the road north from Bangemudha you'll be greeted by jawfuls of grinning teeth. This is the dentists' quarter, and their signs bear their happy symbol.

On the left side of this road a lane leads to **Kathesimbhu,** a miniature model of the Swayambhunath *stupa* west of Kathmandu. Kathesimbhu is said to have been built with leftover earth from Swayambhunath, so it shares some of Swayambhunath's power. The elderly, or any who are too weak to climb the hill to Swayambhunath, can obtain an equal blessing here. Children seem to be the most devoted visitors to Kathesimbhu, however, holding endless soccer games around its *chaityas*. Just to the north of Kathesimbhu is the crossing of Thahity Tole, with its smelly *stupa*. The 15th-century earth mound is right next to a garbage heap, and passersby hold their noses with one hand while they turn prayer wheels with the other.

The **Nardevi Temple** is conveniently located on the road that runs south from Chhetrapati to Durbar Square. Not far east from this conspicuous Kali temple on the right **Itum Bahal** appears through a gap between buildings. This long, narrow square is a favorite playground for kids, and of course it has its share of shrines too. In the far right corner there's a *chaitya* that had been broken apart by a *pipal* tree growing through it; it's now lashed together with string. Beside this is the entrance to a smaller courtyard, the **Kichandra Bahal,** which dates back to 1381. Its right side contains a primary school, right beneath a set of brass plaques depicting a demon who ate naughty children.

South from the Nardevi Temple on the road to Durbar Square there's a window worth noting, set in the second floor of an ordinary building on the left (a store occupies the first floor). It has beautifully carved wood, staggered back in several layers to a screen, and it is known as the **Desha Maru Jhayl.** It was featured several years ago on a Nepalese postage stamp. A bit further south, also on the east side of the street, is another excellent piece of woodcarving, a flimsy balcony held together by nymph-like female figures.

The current **Royal Palace,** which sits at the top of Durbar Marg, is harder to miss. Built in the 1960s, its pagoda roof does little to counter its overall impression—it resembles a swinging American Protestant church, possibly one whose services get shown on TV. One can almost imagine a cross atop the tower in front. The building is only open to the public on the 10th day of Dasain, when the king and queen offer blessings to their queued-up subjects. (The compound is now open to tourists Thurs. 11am-1pm and 2-4pm. Admission is a steep Rs.250.)

South of Durbar Square

Though they're very spread out, a few of Kathmandu's sights are on the south side of town. On the lane that runs southwest of the Kasthamandap is the **Bhimsen Temple,** dedicated to the hero-god of Newari craftsmen. The bottom floor of the temple has been entirely taken over by shops. Next to it there's a *hiti* (water-tap) in a cellar-like depression, where jugs are filled from an elephant-shaped spout.

The **Jaisi Dewal Temple** is another one of the step-pyramid kind (this one has seven steps). To get to it, continue along the road from the Bhimsen Temple until it ends, then turn left and go up the hill. This Shiva temple is painted with flowers and leopard-skin patterns, and a smooth figure of Nandi (Shiva's bull) at the base of the steps is suspended in time as he flicks his tail. Across the street from the entrance to the temple, an amazing *linga,* 2m tall and uncarved, crashes up from a *pitha.*

At a crossroads in southern Kathmandu, close to Kantipath, the **Bhimsen Tower** stands as a useful landmark. It looks something like a lighthouse with portholes, though Bhim Sen Thapa, the prime minister who built it in 1832, was probably more drawn to imitate the Ochterlony Monument in Calcutta (which is ironic, since the British put up the Ochterlony Monument to commemorate their defeat of Nepal in 1816). There's a Calcutta-Gothic wall around the tower with a locked door; unfortunately it isn't open to climbers.

The other side of Kantipath is just one big flat field—the **Tundikhel,** or parade ground, which is occasionally used for military marches and equestrian displays (the Ghora Jatra horse festival in March or April is prime time for this). Kathmandu's newer neighborhoods are located to the east of the Tundikhel. **Martyrs' Gate,** a monument to four accused conspirators who were executed after a 1940 coup attempt, sits on a circle in the middle of the road to the south of the Tundikhel.

Singha Durbar, which is out to the east of the Tundikhel, was once the greatest of the Rana palaces; alas, most of it was burned down in a mysterious fire one night in July 1974. The buttery-white building, which was meant to rival the palaces of Europe, was put up in a few frantic years from 1901-04 by Prime Minister Chandra Shamsher Jung Bahadur Rana—his monogram is on all the railings. The prime minister's household and his entire administration fit into this complex, which, with its

1700 rooms, claimed to be the largest building in Asia. Ministries and departments are lodged in what's left of the palace, but their offices are off-limits to the public.

There's a final cluster of temples on the other side of Tripureswar Marg by the banks of the Bagmati River. The area is wet and dirty, and the wind whips past some of Kathmandu's worst slums, but it's peaceful in that it's shielded from the 1990s. Cars and rickshaws can't squeeze onto the path by the river—they become just figments flying by on bridges overhead. The **Kalamochan Temple** is visible from Tripureswar Marg, close to the Patan Bridge. It has a big onion dome like a Mughal mausoleum, but its dragons and doorways are Nepali, and Jung Bahadur Rana's figure rises on a great shaft out of a turtle's back outside of it. This Macchiavellian prime minister built the temple in the mid-19th century. The ashes of the 32 noblemen he slaughtered in the Kot Massacre are supposed to be buried in the foundations. Very close to it is a three-tiered pagoda temple that's totally neglected: the **Tripureswar Sundari Temple,** which dates from 1818, is surrounded by clotheslines in its wide *bahal.*

The shrine of **Pachali Bhairab** is further downstream from these temples; just before the footbridge across the river, it's slightly inland. Music from the nearby monastery jangles down into Bhairab's square, where a golden human figure lies peacefully dead: this is a *betal,* a representation of death meant to guard against death. The small image of Bhairab is beside it, garlanded with coins, under the spreading roots of a great *pipal* tree.

The junction of the Bagmati River with the Vishnumati, at **Teku** in the southwest corner of the city, is a sacred place often used for cremations. The wailing of families echoes around the temples and *chaityas;* be sensitive about photography. A tall brick *shikhara* stands over the confluence. The riverbanks might look like a romantic scene, with buffalo munching hay in the shade, but look closely and you'll see the faded paper packages clogging the river. And the buffalo are in fact here to be slaughtered.

West of the City

The west bank of the Bishnumati River is beyond Kathmandu's traditional city limits, but it's been brought into the metropolis by the Ring Rd. around Kathmandu and Patan. Its most prominent feature is the hilltop *stupa* of **Swayambhunath,** which is over 2000 years old. Swayambhunath is the holiest place for Newari Buddhists, and it is the seat of the Kathmandu Valley's creation myth. The road from Kathmandu to Swayambhu (a 30-min. walk) certainly has a bit of a red-carpet feel to it, with the shrine looming on the hilltop ahead. At the base of the hill is a large rectangular gateway, and after that the long crooked steps start to work their way through the trees and Buddha-icons to the top. You'll be catching your breath, but right at the top of the steps is an enormous *vajra,* the eggbeater-like Tibetan thunderbolt symbol. And then there's the *stupa,* which is flattened on top like other Nepali *stupas* and whitewashed, but textured with green slime. From the golden cube on top of the *stupa* the

---

The Story of the Kathmandu Valley

According to local mythology, the Kathmandu Valley was a huge lake inhabited by snakes called *nagas.* A lotus grew out of the lake and was called *swayambhu,* or "self-created." When the *boddhisatva* of knowledge, Manjushri, went on a pilgrimage to the lotus he was dismayed to find it inaccessible to human pilgrims. So he sliced his sword into the valley, creating Chobar Gorge, from which the lake water flowed out, taking the *nagas* with it. To appease the *naga* king Karkatoka, Manjushri allowed him to live in Taudaha Lake as guardian of the monsoon. The fertile valley was now ready for its first civilization, and a shrine, the *stupa* of Swayambhunath, was built on the hill from which the lotus had grown.

According to geology, the valley was at one time filled with water, Swayambhu was an island, and the Chobar Gorge was created by an earthquake. But there's no mention of snakes.

Buddha's all-seeing eyes look out in each direction; what looks like a nose is actually a number "1" representing the unity of all things. Swayambhunath is a great place to be all-seeing, since it offers views across the valley on a clear days.

There are nine golden shrines around the *stupa*. Four of them at the cardinal points of the compass, plus one at an angle, enclose images of the *dhyani* Buddhas, who represent the Buddha's different aspects through the elements of earth, water, fire, air, and space. The four cardinal *dhyani* Buddhas also have female elements, *taras,* who occupy the shrines at the secondary points. Monkeys clamber over the many *chaityas* around the *stupa.*

There's a **Buddhist Museum** on the platform amid all the shrines; it's small and dark, but has a good assortment of Buddhist and Hindu gods in its sculpture collection. (Open Wed.-Mon. 10am-5pm. Free.) Next to the museum is a small monastery that will welcome any visitors and their donations. Around the corner and upstairs there's an **International Buddhist Library.** (Open Wed.-Mon. 11am-4pm.) The small temple in front of the monastery is dedicated to Harati, the goddess of smallpox, who could either protect or infect. It's not clear what she does now that smallpox is eradicated, although she is generally responsible for looking after children.

Behind Swayambhu is the **Natural History Museum** (tel. 271899). (Open Sun.-Fri. 10am-5pm. Admission Rs.10; camera fee Rs.10.) About 1km south of Swayambhunath, on a road that comes up from the riverside, is Nepal's **National Museum,** which isn't quite the hit it might sound like. The Art Gallery here is very good, especially in metalwork. Equally excellent carvings can be seen in their places on the Kathmandu Valley's houses and temples, but the museum allows for a closer look. The National Numismatic Museum here hardly merits the small building it occupies. The Historical Museum Building is at least as interesting as the Art Gallery, but its natural history section has an unusual abundance of stuffed deer heads, which must have come from some Rana palace. The Nepalese history section contains nothing but swords, rifles, and portraits of kings, although some of the early Nepalese-made cannons and machine guns are amusing. The museum grounds are pleasant, and the roof terrace of the Art Gallery is a good viewpoint for the surrounding valley. (Open Wed., Thurs. and Sat.-Mon. 10:30am-4pm, winter 10:30am-3pm; Fri. 10:30am-2:30pm; Rs.5, camera fee Rs.10.)

ENTERTAINMENT

When it comes to nightlife in Nepal, Kathmandu is where it's at, but that's not saying much. You'll have a choice of bars that close by 10 or 11pm, tourist-oriented cultural shows, and several casinos, some of which are open 24 hours.

Bars

Thamel's bars cater to a foreign crowd, although twentysomething Nepalis abound here as well. If you can hear over the music, these can be good places to exchange stories with returned trekkers. In addition to the following, try the Rum Doodle 40,000½-Feet Bar and Restaurant (see p. 689).

Blue Note, Chhetrapati-Thamel, just south of the intersection with the Tridevi Marg remnant. Faux-East Village vibe, authentic jazz and blues on the sound system. Free popcorn. Open daily 2-11pm.

Roadhouse Café, Chettrapati-Thamel, on the left, heading south. "Unplugged live acoustic music" 7-10pm every night except Sat.—Nepalis with guitars strum out their favorite James Taylor and John Lennon tunes in a barnlike upstairs room. Continental food (Rs.80-130). Open Sun.-Fri. noon-10:30pm.

New Orleans Café, Thamel, just north of the Kathmandu Guest House. Live jazz in the outdoor patio a few nights every week 8-10pm. Other nights (and days) enjoy the outdoor seating at one of Thamel's newest establishments. Open daily 8am-11pm.

Old Spam's Space, Thamel, in the corner where the road veers left. Thamel's original pub serves up such delicacies as vegemite and cheese sandwiches (Rs.60) and

> ### Kites
>
> During and before the festival of Dasain (Oct.-Nov.), *changga* (kites) are flown in most of Nepal. These aren't fancy kites, but nimble and highly maneuverable dogfighters. Maneuvered by a *lattai* (a circular wooden string holder) kites "fight" against each other. The idea is to use the wind to rub the kite's string against the opponent's string. The better string or the stronger wind wins out when one of the strings breaks due to friction. The winning side shouts *"Chaaeet! Chaaeet!"* ("Your string's broken!"). After the monsoon kites are flown at the festival of Dasain, to ask Indra, the god responsible for the weather, to stop the rains. Elders admonish young children who are eager to fly kites well before Dasain. The number of kites in the sky peaks on the final day of the festival. Each kite-flying group counts the number of "kills" in one day.
>
> The best dogfighting kite strings are made in India. Broken glass and strengthening materials make these strings sharp and durable. These strings easily make cuts on fingers. Kathmandu has the biggest Dasain kiting event, and people gather on rooftops with music, drink, and food in a city-wide party to watch the kites—kite flying has become a spectator sport.

bangers and mash (Rs.110). Live music (loud classic rock) Mon., Wed., Sat., 7:30-10pm. Drinks 10% off during "silly hour" 5-7pm. Open daily 8am-11pm.

Maya Cocktail Bar and **Maya Pub,** Thamel. The cocktail bar is upstairs from the Pumpernickel Bakery; the pub is next to the Blue Note. Both offer free popcorn, loud pop music, and 2-for-1 cocktails from 5-7pm. The pub is not much bigger than a walk-in closet; the cocktail bar is bigger and more swinging. There's also a branch in Pokhara.

Jesse James Bar, Thamel. At the Northfield Café, just north of the Pilgrims Book House. Free chips and salsa and an occasional live band playing in the garden. Open daily 2-10pm.

Tom and Jerry Pub, Thamel, just across from the Northfield Café, upstairs. The most bar-like of Thamel's bars, with pool tables and sports on TV. During Happy Hour (5-8pm), 10% off drinks. Open daily 4-11pm.

Cultural Shows

The following feature traditional Nepalese songs and dances, staged for a tourist audience.

Hotel de l'Annapurna, Durbar Marg. Shows daily at 7pm, Rs.220.

New Himachali Cultural Group, at the Hotel Shankar, Lazimpath (tel. 410151, 413818). In winter, shows daily at 6pm, in summer shows daily at 7pm. Rs. 350.

Hotel Sherpa, Durbar Marg, (tel. 227000). Cultural show in the restaurant Thurs.-Tues.; no charge for the show, but you're expected to eat—not cheap.

Sports

The public **swimming pool,** near the National Stadium, is open daily 10am-12:30pm and 1:30-4pm. (Admission Rs.35; Mon. is ladies' day.) The posh hotels on Durbar Marg will also let non-guests use their pools for a fee. The cheapest are the Woodlands Hotel and the Hotel Sherpa which charge Rs.300 per day.

The **tennis** court at Hotel de l'Annapurna can be used by non-guests for Rs.150 per hour. For **golf,** there's the Royal Nepal Golf Course, near the airport (tel. 472836). The National Stadium hosts soccer matches and other spectator events.

Casinos

Kathmandu now boasts the only four casinos on the Indian Subcontinent. Each one is at a luxury hotel: **Casino Royal** at the Yak & Yeti; **Casino Everest** at Hotel Everest; **Casino Anna** at Hotel de l'Annapurna; and the **Royal Nepal Casino** at the Soaltee Holiday Inn. The Everest and Soaltee run shuttle buses from major hotels. Some casinos may have special deals for those who have just arrived. Bring your plane ticket for free coupons or snacks. All but the Casino Royal are open 24 hours.

SHOPPING

If you stand still for more than 10 seconds in Thamel or Durbar Square, you're sure to be approached by a roving merchant offering jewelry, flutes, chess sets, Tiger Balm, or knives—Swiss army copies or *khukuri* style. The sheer volume of tourist trash can be off-putting, and you may be tempted to ignore it all. But what looks like junk in Kathmandu next to ten identical items might seem like a unique treasure once you get it home, to others if not to you.

Prices are almost always negotiable. Try to bargain good-naturedly, and hope that the merchant does the same. Asking a price is interpreted as intent to buy, but you can get away with just asking if you're trying to shop around. Prices and quality vary greatly, so **check out a few shops,** especially for expensive souvenirs. With most products, from wool sweaters to *thankas,* you'll be able to see the difference in quality after a little practice. Antiques, jewelry, and gems require more expertise. Many things claimed to be old are not, and travelers should be very wary of buying gems unless they really know what they're doing.

Although just about anything made in Nepal can be bought in Kathmandu, certain crafts can be found more cheaply and from a better selection in their places of origin. For woodcarving and pottery, head for Bhaktapur; for *papier maché* masks and puppets, Thimi; for metalwork, Patan; and for Tibetan crafts like *thankas,* Boudha. A lot of Indian crafts are sold in Kathmandu too, such as Kashmiri *papier maché* boxes. They're more expensive than in India, but still much cheaper than in the West. In Thamel, you'll also find much Western-style hippie clothing. Embroidered T-shirts are a Thamel specialty—skilled tailors will embroider any design you wish. Hand-knit woolens are also a good deal here.

One shop in Thamel that deserves special mention is the **Khukuri House** (tel. 536242), at the zig-zag north of the Kathmandu Guest House, near Rum Doodle's. This well-reputed knife shop is owned by a former Gurkha officer. (Open Sun.-Fri. 9:30am-7pm). **Western Nepal Crafts** (tel. 417108), on the street that leads to Thahity, north of Tridevi Marg, has a wide selection of handmade paper products. More serious and much more expensive antique shops are located on Durbar Marg.

For ready-made Indian and Nepali-style clothing, head for **Bagh Bazaar.** Saris and cloth can be found north of Indra Chowk, and the bead bazaar at the chowk is worth checking out just to see the stalls full of mutlicolored, twinkling strands of glass beads. These are the beads that married Nepalese women wear, often with an ornate gold clasp.

Moneyed Indians and Nepalis do their shopping on **New Road.** The street is lined with electronics and jewelry shops. Ready-made clothing is sold here too. Just inside the New Rd. Gate is the government-run **Cottage Industry and Handicrafts Emporium,** which happens to have the cheapest postcards in town (Rs.6).

If you're looking for maps, swing by **Maps of Nepal,** just before the Everest Hotel in Baneswar on the road to the Airport. Nepalese land-planning and political maps can make great souvenirs. (Open Sun.-Fri. 10am-7pm.)

■ Near Kathmandu: Pashupatinath

The temple complex of Pashupatinath, east of Kathmandu, is the holiest Hindu site in Nepal, dedicated to Shiva's incarnation as Pashupati, the kind and gentle Lord of Animals. All the regular business of a Hindu pilgrimage site goes on here: there are monasteries, hospices for the dying, and cremation grounds, and the narrow roads get clogged with pilgrims who come to offer flowers to Shiva and rice to the beggars. Pashupatinath is the heart of Nepali Hinduism—the king himself often comes to worship here, and he invokes Pashupati's name at the end of all his speeches. At the Shivaratri festival, which occurs in February or March (in 1997, March 7) devotees of Shiva come here to bathe and celebrate Shiva's birthday. Full-moon nights and each eleventh day after them are also good times to come here for the blessing of the Bagmati River, which Nepalis consider sacred.

The **Pashupati Temple** itself is located right on the Bagmati. A road leads directly up to it, though non-Hindus won't get any closer than the gate. The backside of the dinosaur-sized brass Nandi is visible through the entrance, but the rest of the temple is obscured. Other viewpoints in the area afford peeks over the wall at the wood and marble pagoda. The present temple was built in 1696, though earlier versions have stood here since the 5th century AD. Worshipers go inside to see the four-faced *linga*, often dancing and singing while they're at it.

Other temples are downstream from the Pashupati Temple, but there's no direct access along the river here for non-Hindus. The only recourse is to backtrack away from the river, turn left and left again, until another, bigger road leads back to the river. On the right side of this road is a group of five temples known as **Panch Dewal**, whose compound has become a social welfare center. Ahead, stone walls and *ghats* squeeze the river, making it look like a canal. Two footbridges are laid across it, and right between them on the near (west) bank is the 6th-century **Bacchareswari Temple.** The **ghats** downstream are used for cremations; if there are any cremations in progress, respect the mourning families' grief and don't zoom your camera in on their loved one's body. Picture-taking has not officially been banned, but don't behave in such a way as to make a ban necessary. At the end of this stretch of "burning ghats" is an archway, and sunk into the ground next to it is a 7th-century Buddha statue that appears to be leaning on a surfboard. Beyond this is the oval Raj Rajeshwari Temple.

Across the footbridges on the east bank of the Bagmati is a row of 11 cubic Shiva shrines. From here it's possible to see into the Pashupati Temple compound. The *ghats* immediately below it are sometimes used for VIP cremations, such as those of members of the royal family.

The steps up the hill on the east bank of the river eventually level out at a small village of Shiva temples; Nandi's figure is repeated up and down the main street. At the end of it is a temple of Gorakhnath, an 11th-century saint who is revered as a form of Shiva. The steps continue downhill to the **Gujeshwari Temple,** which is locally considered to be the place where the goddess Sati's vagina fell when she was cut into many pieces. (The Kamakhya Temple in Guwahati, India is more widely recognized as this site—see **Divine Dismemberment,** p. 404). Non-Hindus are banned from entering. The main gate to the temple, by the riverbank, is decorated with bizarre, ghoulish figures. The road downstream in front of the temple leads to a bridge, on the other side of which is a crossroads. Turn left and climb the broken stone steps up a hill; walk over the hill to return to the Pashupati Temple.

Pashupatinath is only nominally outside of Kathmandu and it's simple to get there by bike—follow Tridevi Marg away from Thamel, then turn right at the first road after Durbar Marg. When you see the Marco Polo Business Hotel, turn left, and follow the zig-zagging road east across a "Red Bridge." Eventually signs will appear showing maps of the Pashupatinath area. The #1 bus (frequent, 45min., Rs.3) also goes to Pashupatinath from Ratna Park.

■ Patan

Kathmandu's neighbor to the south, temple-filled Patan certainly lives up to its older name, Lalitpur, or "City of Beauty." But Patan has more than excellent architecture—it is also known for its crafts, especially metalwork. (The backstreets are filled with clanging and hammering sounds.) Patan is now also home to a large number of foreign aid agencies and, thanks to the Tibetan Refugee Camp in Jawalakhel, a major portion of the Tibetan carpet industry.

With only the Bagmati River lying between Kathmandu and Patan, the two cities seem to have practically merged. In spirit, however, their history as independent kingdoms is still evident. For locals and visitors alike, Patan is discernably more laidback than the capital. Pedestrians dominate over vehicles and there are no in-your-face souvenir salesmen or change-money characters (although a handful of clingy "guides" haunt Durbar Square). Even shopping is less of a hassle in Patan, with its collection of fixed-price handicrafts cooperatives, whose proceeds usually go towards a good cause.

ORIENTATION

Patan is linked to Kathmandu by a bridge over the **Bagmati River,** and is bounded to the south by the same **Ring Road** that encircles Kathmandu. Patan's main road goes by the name of whatever neighborhood it is passing through: from the bridge south to the Ring Rd. it is called **Kopundol,** then **Pulchowk,** and finally **Jawalakhel.** The old city, east of the main road, is roughly bounded by four *stupas,* one in each cardinal direction, said to date from the 3rd century BC. The eastern *stupa* lies beyond Ring Rd. **Durbar Square** is the center of the oldest part of town. Several branches lead east from the main road. From north to south, the first one leads to **Patan Dhoka** (Patan Gate), which is north of Durbar Square; the second turn-off becomes **Mangal Bazaar,** the road runs along the south end of Durbar Square; finally at **Jawalakhel Chowk,** a road leads toward **Lagankhel,** where the bus park is located.

PRACTICAL INFORMATION

Currency Exchange: Nepal Grindlays, Jawalakhel Chowk. Open Sun.-Thurs. 9:45am-3pm, Fri. 9:45am-12:30pm.

Telephones: You can find the usual smattering of STD/ISD shops in Patan; there's one in the southwest corner of Durbar Sq.

Local Transportation: Bus #14 runs frequently from **Ratna Park** in Kathmandu to the bus park in Lagankhel, a short walk directly south of Patan's Durbar Sq. (20min., Rs.3). **Blue tempos** (frequent, 20min., Rs.4) start at the **GPO** and ply the same route once they're over the bridge. A **taxi** from Thamel to Patan Durbar Sq. should cost about Rs.65.

English Bookstore: Saraswati Book Centre, Pulchowk (tel. 521599, 528017). Near the U.N. building. Open Sun.-Fri. 10am-7:30pm.

Market: Look for fruit stands in Lagankhel near the bus park. There are also several supermarkets around Jawalakhel that cater to foreign residents. For baked goods, head for the **German Bakery,** Jawalakhel Chowk. Open daily 6am-9pm.

Pharmacy: Many can be found on Mangal Bazaar, right below Durbar Sq.

Hospital: Patan Hospital, Lagankhel (tel. 522266, 522295) has a good reputation.

Post Office: Mangal Bazaar, just southeast of Durbar Square. Open Sun.-Thurs. 10:30am-2:30pm, Fri. 10:30am-1:30pm.

Telephone Code: 01.

ACCOMMODATIONS

Staying in Patan might be an appealing alternative to Kathmandu if only there were a few more choices for budget travelers.

Café de Patan, Mangal Bazaar (tel. 525499). Just southwest of Durbar Square. Only 4 clean, comfortable, and quiet rooms are available above this restaurant. Doubles Rs.300, with bath Rs.500.

Mountain View Guest House, Kumaripati (tel. 524168). A 5-min. walk towards Jawalakhel (west); on the left, behind the Campion Academy. A little removed from the older section of town. Behind a stained-glass door, above the restaurant, these new rooms are still pristine. Common bath is smartly tiled (as are, inexplicably, parts of the bedrooms). Singles Rs.200. Doubles Rs.250.

Mahendra Youth Hostel, Pulchowk Rd. (tel. 521003). Just north of Jawalakhel Chowk. Set back behind some greenery, rooms here are off a wide, dim hallway. Bunkbeds in dorms Rs.45, "special" dorms (regular beds) Rs.60. One private room with twin beds and an attached bath goes for Rs.150. Plus 10% government tax. Mahendra Youth Hostel is the headquarters of the Nepal Youth Hostels Association and offers a 10% discount for IYHF members. Open 6am-10pm. Check-out 10am.

FOOD

Again, the selection doesn't compare to that in Kathmandu, but there's still plenty to eat. A few of the tourist places around Durbar Square are good choices; other restaurants are popular with expats and locals. There are also branches of restaurant chains around Jawalakhel Chowk, such as Hot Breads and The Bakery Café.

The Third World Restaurant, Durbar Square (tel. 522187). On the western edge of the square, opposite the Patan Museum. This is the closest non-Hindus can get to the upper floors of the Krishna Mandir. Watch the action in Durbar Square from the glassed-in dining areas or in the fresh air of the roof terrace, while eating tasty food off handmade dishes. Sandwiches Rs.40-70, Continental dishes (veg. and meat) Rs.65-95, rice or noodles Rs.40-55. Open daily 9am-9pm.

Café de Patan, Mangal Bazaar (tel. 525499). Just southwest of Durbar Square. Walk through the souvenir/music shop to the ground floor dining area or the garden rooftop. Fridays and Saturdays, after 3pm, order from the Newari menu: snacks Rs.10-40, set meals Rs.70 or Rs.90. The rest of the time, choose from an unsurprising selection of Nepali, Tibetan, Chinese, and Continental dishes. Spring rolls Rs.60-75. Fried rice or noodles Rs.60-80. Open daily 8am-9pm.

Samurai Restaurant and Bar, Kupondole (tel. 521276). Next to the Hotel Himalaya. Tables and chairs on the first floor, Japanese-style floor seating upstairs—the alcove table seems reserved for Nepalese teenagers on dates. You won't be fooled into thinking you're in Tokyo, but the tempura tastes fairly authentic and the set meals are a good deal—Rs.100-150 buys a lot of food. Open daily 11am-9:30pm.

Taleju Restaurant and Bar, Mangal Bazaar (tel. 525528). On the south end of Durbar Square. Choose the angle of your view: cushioned-floor seating, tables and chairs, or the roof terrace, with spectacular views of the square. A more extensive (and a little bit more expensive) menu than the other restaurants in the area. Fried rice and noodles Rs.40-80. Vegetable curries Rs.30-65. Tandoori dishes (after 5pm) Rs.80-110. Add 10% government tax. Open daily 11am-9:30pm.

Downtown Restaurant, Pulchowk (tel. 522451). Lace curtains screen the sights but not the sounds of the busy street outside. Deservedly popular with the expat community for its extensive menu and low prices. A choice of Continental, Chinese, and especially Indian dishes, none of which is more than Rs.100. Chicken *tikka masala* (Rs.65) is rich and flavorful—*naan* (Rs.10) sops up the sauce nicely. Open Sun.-Fri. 10am-9pm, Sat. noon-9pm.

SIGHTS

As in the other cities of the valley, Durbar Square is sightseeing central. Patan's Durbar Square is particularly densely packed with temples of varying styles, and other temples are only a short walk away. In between, Patan's narrow streets offer a glimpse of daily life.

Durbar Square

One tactic for exploring Durbar Square is to start at the southern end of the **Royal Palace,** which makes up the eastern side of the square; then continue north and circle around counter-clockwise. The southernmost courtyard, **Sundari Chowk,** which contains an elaborately carved bathing tank, is not open to the public. The next courtyard, **Mul Chowk,** dating from the mid-17th century, can be entered between two curly-maned stone lions. This is a good place to pick up a self-appointed guide. The small gilded temple in the middle of the chowk is dedicated to Bidya. On the southern wall gilded statues of the Indian river goddesses **Ganga** (on a tortoise) and **Yamuna** (on a *makara,* the mythical snouted sea creature whose image often serves as a waterspout) stand on either side of the locked doorway to the **Taleju Shrine.** Peek behind the latticework to see a knife used in buffalo sacrifices. The other pagodas that rise around Mul Chowk are the **Taleju Bhawani Mandir,** the octagonal tower in the northeast corner, and the **Degu Talle Temple** on the north side, which is the tallest in the square.

The new **Patan Museum** is housed in **Keshav Narayan Chowk,** the northernmost section of the palace. Enter this most recent courtyard (built in the 18th century) through the elaborately worked golden doorway; the whitewashed shrine inside is dedicated to Narayan. The museum's permanent collection is small, but the exhibition space (beautifully restored with the help of the Austrian government and the Smithsonian Institution) is sometimes filled with an exhibit of contemporary art. If not, you can still appreciate the architecture of one of the few buildings in Patan that is actually open to the public. Wide, cushioned window seats provide an excellent lookout onto the square below. Open daily 10:30am-4:30pm. The museum was free at the time this book was researched, but current fundraising plans promise to bring an admission fee, a gift shop, and a cafeteria. Around the corner from the palace to the north is the sunken water tank known as **Manga Hiti.** The stone-carved mythical crocodile-like creatures in the tank have been spitting water since the 6th century. The adjacent pavilion, **Mani Mandap** was once used for coronations.

Diagonally across the way is the three-tiered **Bhimsen Mandir,** with a lion-topped pillar facing its recent marble facade. Merchants toss coins into the older, gilded, first floor of this temple, dedicated to the god of trade. The next temple to the left is the **Vishwanath Mandir,** a double-roofed Shiva temple, guarded by two stone elephants and originally dating from 1627. The temple collapsed in 1990, but has since been restored. The *linga* inside is said to replicate the Vishwanath linga in Varanasi, India (see p. 229). A Nandi faces the other side of the temple. Continuing south, the next temple is the stone, Indian *shikhara*-style **Krishna Mandir.** This temple stands because of its foreign design and because it is one of the few temples in Durbar Sq. still in active use. In the evenings, devotees set the building aglow with oil lamps. The upper floors (inaccessible to non-Hindus) are carved with friezes depicting scenes from the *Mahabharata* and the *Ramayana*. Vishnu's man-bird vehicle Garuda faces the temple from atop a stone pillar, serving as a reminder that Krishna is one of Vishnu's incarnations. Vishnu is the chief god of the next temple as well, the **Jagan Narayan Mandir.** Stone lions flank the front of this more Nepalese pagoda-style temple (complete with wildly erotic roof struts). The Jagan Narayan Temple is the square's oldest, built in 1565. The **Bhai Deval Mandir** squats in the southwest corner of the square, and continuing around clockwise you'll pass a **fountain** before arriving at the octagonal stone **Chyasin Deval,** which, like the other Krishna temple in the square, is built in an Indian style. Its construction is linked with the death of one of the Malla kings—whether it spontaneously appeared, or whether it was built to honor his eight wives who committed *sati* is now a matter of legendary controversy. The **Taleju Bell** next door was the first of the valley's three big bells, cast in 1736. The next temple to the north is the **Hari Shankar Mandir,** an elaborately carved three-tiered pagoda from the 18th century. The temple is jointly dedicated to Vishnu (called Hari here) and Shiva (Shankar). Circling back into the square, the stone pillar topped by a golden statue of **King Yoganarendra Malla** has its own associated legends. The king knees under the protection of a cobra's hood, and it is said that as long as the bird perched on the cobra's head remains there, the king is still alive. If the bird flies away, the elephants that guard the Vishwanath Mandir will leave their posts to drink from the Manga Hiti. Behind the pillar are some small Vishnu temples.

Beyond Durbar Square

An L-shaped circuit to the surrounding temples to the east, south and northwest skirts around the square, then returns at the north end. Continuing along Mangal Bazaar, east of Durbar Square, you'll see signs for the **Mahaboudha Temple**—the right hand turn-off is about a five-minute walk from the square. This "temple of a thousand Buddhas" is engulfed by the surrounding buildings but so clearly marked that it can't be missed. Inside the courtyard that houses it, painted arrows point the way to walk around it, and even the prayer wheels are labeled. The temple's architect was inspired by the Mahabodhi Temple in Bodh Gaya, India, where the Buddha achieved enlightenment (see p. 438). The foreign influence is obvious: the *shikhara*-style temple is covered with terra-cotta tiles, each of which carries an image of the

Buddha. Signs on the west side of the compound advertise upper floors from which tourists are welcome to take photographs (and maybe buy a little something). Turning right from the Mahaboudha, the **Uka Bahal,** the oldest monastery in Patan, is down the street. A pair of stone lions guards the former Buddhist monastery, while an arcful of brass beasts seems to have docked in the courtyard.

Follow the street parallel to Mangal Bazaar back in the direction of Durbar Square (west). The sound of metal being banged into form fills the street, which ends at the wide market street that runs south from Durbar Square. At the intersection of the two streets stands the **Ibaha Bahal,** a monastery dating from 1427 (it is Patan's second-oldest) but recently renovated with Japanese funds. There isn't much to see beyond the well-carved wooden courtyard. Further south along the same street, but on the other side, behind a water tank, is the **Minnath Mandir** with its garishly painted details including a pair of silver-painted lions. Minnath is often called *"sanno"* ("little") Machhendranath, in comparison to the deity who inhabits the temple down a short lane across the street. The **Rato Machhendranath Mandir,** a 17th-century triple-roofed pagoda with intricate, colorful roof struts, stands in the center of a big, grassy compound. A collection of brass animals (each one representing a month in the Tibetan calendar) is perched on posts facing the temple. The *rato* (red) image of Machhendranath gets to ride in a towering chariot that makes its rounds of Patan in late April. Machhendranath is another multi-purpose deity: he's the *bodhisattva* of compassion, as a Newari god he controls the rains, and he's also revered as the guru of a 7th-century saint.

Exit the compound to the south, onto a street that leads straight past Mangal Bazaar, to reach the **Golden Temple,** one of Patan's most famous structures. The temple is about a five-minute walk to the right; its entrance is on the left side of the street, marked by another pair of smiley stone lions (and a big sign that says "Golden Temple."). Also known as **Hiranyavarna Mahavihar,** this ornate, gilded temple makes up the west side of the **Kwa Bahal,** a 12th-century Buddhist monastery whose courtyard is filled by a golden shrine. No leather is allowed beyond the walkway around the edge of the courtyard. The temple's façade is elaborately worked in repoussé with images of Buddhas, *taras,* and mythological creatures. Gods are supposed to be able to slide down the *patakas,* the golden belts that hang from the roofs. Upstairs, in the northeast corner of the *bahal,* are Tibetan-style murals. A pair of stone tortoises stands on the south side of the courtyard; look for the real ones shuffling around the temple.

Continuing another minute north, the five-tiered pagoda of the **Kumbeshwar Mahadev** comes into view. The oldest temple in Patan, it only had two tiers when it was built in 1392. The three stories added later have made it one of only two free-standing five-roofed pagodas in the Kathmandu Valley (the other is the Nyatapola Temple in Bhaktapur). The deity-in-residence is Shiva, as indicated by the Nandi bull outside the temple. The water tank next to the temple inside the compound is believed to be connected to the holy Himalayan lake of Gosainkund. A pilgrim is said to have dropped a *kumbh* (pot) in the lake, which then emerged in the tank in Patan, giving the temple its name. Thousands of devotees come to bathe in the tank during the Jana Purnima festival in July or August, when high-caste Hindus change their sacred threads. One block east of the temple, the road to the right leads straight back to the northern end of Durbar Square.

Jawalakhel

The Jawalakhel neighborhood is notable for its foreign residents—both expats working for aid organizations and Tibetan refugees. Just south of Jawalakhel Chowk is the **Central Zoo.** The steep admission fee goes toward renovations. The zoo was recently painted, and some animals have been moved from depressingly small cages to bigger pens, but most are still in cages. Only the chickens have more room than they might have outside the zoo. There's a pond in the middle of the pretty grounds, and you can see that tiger (and other species) that eluded you at Chitwan. (Open

Tues.-Sun. 10am-5pm. Admission Rs.50 for foreigners, Rs.25 for foreign children 10 and under, camera fee Rs.10).

Ten minutes by foot south of the zoo, straight past the *pipal* tree, is the **Jawalakhel Handicraft Centre** (tel. 521305), part of the **Tibetan Refugee Camp.** (Open Sun.-Fri. 8am-6pm.) Established by the Red Cross and the Nepalese government in 1960, the center employs Tibetans who fled their country after 1959. Even if you're not in the market for a carpet, this is an excellent place to see how they're made. Visitors can wander freely, watching spinning and weaving. This is a good place to buy a carpet, since the money goes directly back to the workers.

SHOPPING

Patan is less hopping than Kathmandu, but there's plenty of shopping to be done. Aside from carpets (see Jawalakhel, above), metalwork makes an appropriate local souvenir. Wooden toys are also a Patan specialty—auto-rickshaws and Tata trucks make funky mementos. The **Educational Toys Centre,** on the main road in Pulchowk (tel. 525280), is a good place to look. (Open daily 9am-7pm.) Patan is full of non-profit craft outlets that sell crafts from all over the country. Many of them benefit underprivileged workers (especially women) and ensure fair wages. There's one in the old Royal Palace on Durbar Sq. and several in Kopudol, on the main road. **Sana Hastakala** (tel. 522628) opposite the Hotel Himalaya, has a particularly good selection. (Open Sun.-Fri. 9:30am-6pm, Sat. 10am-5pm.) **Dzambala Boutique** (tel. 528818) is more expensive, specializing in hand-painted silk clothing. (Open Sun.-Fri. 10am-6pm.)

▓ Kirtipur

Perched on twin hills about 5km southwest of Kathmandu, Kirtipur is a typical Newari town with its maze of narrow streets lined by tightly-packed rows of brick houses. Kirtipur also reflects the religious *masala* of the Newaris; its southeastern hill is topped by a Buddhist *stupa,* while a Hindu temple presides over the northwestern one. In addition to the town and the views afforded by its hilltop location, the fact that you might be the only tourist there (you will be greeted by more than a few stares and giggles) makes Kirtipur a pleasant excursion from Kathmandu. When Kirtipur became the first town in the Kathmandu Valley to be conquered by the Gorkha ruler Prithvi Narayan Shah in 1767, its male citizens (with the exception of accomplished wind instrument players) were punished by having their noses and lips chopped off. More recently, Kirtipur has been impinged upon by Nepal's largest university, **Tribhuvan University,** whose campus lies below the town on land once cultivated by Kirtipur farmers.

To reach Kirtipur from Kathmandu, take Bus #21 from the Ratna Park bus station (but ask to make sure it's the Kirtipur bus). Towards the end of the half-hour ride, the bus will cut through the university and head up the hill towards Kirtipur. Get off when the bus turns left at the top of the road, and look for the large painted map of the town. As you face the map, **Naya Bazaar** (New Market), Kirtipur's commercial area) is to your left. Take the stairs behind the map to the top of the hill, bearing left at the tree in the middle of the path, then right when you reach the top of the hill. A few steps lead you through a gateway up to **Chilandeo Stupa** (also called Chilanchu Vihara), a large *stupa* surrounded by four smaller ones. The whitewashed layers of the central *stupa* have chipped off over time, laying bare the brick structure underneath. Exit the compound to the right of the *stupa,* turn left and wander towards **Bagh Bhairab Mandir,** a temple dedicated to Shiva the destroyer (Bhairab) in the form of a *bagh* (tiger), but significant to Hindus and Buddhists alike. Look for the swords mounted on the upper façade, which commemorate Kirtipur's defeat by the Gorkhas—whether the weapons belonged to the conquered Newaris or the victorious Gorkhas is contestable. Bagh Bhairab is the center of Kirtipur's most important festival, which usually falls in early December. With your back to the temple, turn

NEPAL

right and meander slightly uphill to a gateway and steep set of steps leading to the **Uma-Maheshwar Mandir.** Children play among the legs and trunks of the two stone elephants that guard the temple, but their spiked backs keep the kids from climbing higher. The deities residing here are Shiva and his consort Parvati. More noteworthy than the temple itself are the views it commands: to the southwest looms one of the highest points of the Kathmandu Valley's rim; to the northeast sprawls Kathmandu (look for Swayambunath and Bhimsen Tower for orientation) and beyond, the Himalaya. To get down to Naya Bazaar and the bus back to Kathmandu, follow the street to the right of Bagh Bhairab Mandir; it turns into a path down the hill. If you do get lost, you won't be for long—Kirtipur is small, and locals will kindly point you back on track. The only noteworthy sight in Naya Bazaar is the Thai-style Buddhist temple **Nagar Mandap Srikiti Vihar.** Built with Thai funds (donors include the king of Thailand and Thai Airways) in 1989, the temple houses a reproduction of a famous Thai Buddha image. The clean, whitewashed, orange-and-green-roofed temple is surrounded by potted plants and offers a respite from the bustling bazaar above. In Naya Bazaar, fruit and biscuits are available from several **fruit stands** and **"cold stores."** There is one STD/ISD **phone** office on the west side of the street.

■ Chobar

Visitors who climb the long staircase leading up to the village of Chobar will be rewarded for their efforts by the quirky **Adinath Lokeshwar Mandir,** a Buddhist temple whose façade is covered with pots and pans. Contributions of kitchenware to the temple are said to bring good luck to the newlywed couples who provide them. Below the town, the Bagmati River flows through **Chobar Gorge,** the legendary scar left by Manjushri's sword when he drained the lake that once filled the Kathmandu Valley. The gorge is spanned by a small **suspension bridge** which was manufactured in Aberdeen, Scotland, and assembled here in 1903. Just south of the bridge, on the banks of the river, sits **Jal Binayak,** a temple dedicated to Ganesh, who is represented here in the form of a large rock protruding from the back of the temple (His vehicle, a mouse, can be found in front.) The three-tiered pagoda dates back to the 17th century. The multi-colored struts below the roof of the temple depict Ganesh, along with the usual erotica.

To get to Chobar, take bus #21 to the gates of Tribhuvan University. Get off the bus and walk back the way the bus had been heading before it turned onto the campus. Pass the Himalayan Bee Concern (for all your bee-keeping needs) on your right, then walk up the stairs at the base of the hill. You may want to stop to admire the view of the valley or just to catch your breath. Stay on the stairs all the way to the top; the temple will be directly in front of you. The walk from Chobar down to the gorge is significantly less pleasant since the landscape is dominated by a roaring, smoke-spewing cement factory. You can scamper down this side of the hill along terraced fields and further down, a wide dirt road. The gorge and temple are just to the left of the cement factory. One way of returning from the gorge is to cross the bridge and follow the road up the hill through a tiny village, then down into the valley, crossing the Nakhu River, the Ring Rd., and finally ending up in Jawlakhel in Patan. If you're relying on bottled water, make sure you have enough for the walk up to Chobar—you won't see any shops until you approach Patan.

■ Boudha (Boudhanath)

Along with Dharamsala in India (see p. 346), Boudha is one of the best places outside of Tibet to experience Tibetan culture. Its connection to Tibet stems from its location along the ancient Kathmandu-Lhasa trade route (people still pray at Boudha for safe passage through the Himalaya), but most of the Tibetan population here fled Tibet after the Chinese crackdown in 1959. Boudha is dominated by the whitewashed dome of Nepal's largest *stupa,* from which Buddha's eyes stare in four directions, and is dotted with *gompas* (monasteries) representing all four sects of Tibetan Buddhism.

Boudha is a center of Tibetan Buddhist study for Westerners as well; many stay on for months to learn *dharma* with some of the world's most renowned teachers. You'll even spot a few in maroon-and-yellow monks' robes. For the casual visitor, Boudha is a peaceful escape from the grind of Kathmandu, and the white-washed simplicity of the *stupa* cleanses eyes weary of jumbled alleyways and carved temple roof struts. Try to stay overnight, or at least through late afternoon, when Tibetan pilgrims circumambulate the *stupa* in a slow-moving, multi-colored crowd. Full and new moons are particularly auspicious times to visit the *stupa*.

ORIENTATION

Five kilometers east of Kathmandu, the **stupa** compound is entered through a **gate** on the north side of the main, east-west road. Directions to places on the main road are given locally as either "right" (west) or "left" (east) of the gate. North of the *stupa*, a main lane leads into a network of smaller lanes where most of the **gompas** are located. There are a few other small turn-offs within the compound. The *stupa* itself is entered from the north side, the opposite side from the gate. **Always walk clockwise around the stupa!**

PRACTICAL INFORMATION

Budget Travel: Several agents just outside the *stupa* gate, on the main road.

Telephones: Numerous STD/ISD outfits dot the main road and the *stupa* compound. **High Himalaya** (tel. 472051) in the *stupa* has e-mail (Rs.30 per kilobyte to send, Rs.20 to receive), as well as phone and fax. Open daily 7am-9pm.

Transportation: Buses: Bus #2 from Ratna Park (about every 30min., 30min, Rs.3) is crazily crowded, even by Nepalese standards. Watch your bag! From the GPO, blue **tempos** (#2, Rs.6) leave when they're full—and their standard for "full" is much lower than that of the minibuses. A **taxi** from Thamel costs about Rs.60.

Market: Fruit sellers gather on the main road to the left of the *stupa* gate and in the lanes behind the *stupa*. Across the street from the gate and to the left, the **Gemini Grocer** (tel. 471370) is well-stocked with Western treats and toiletries. Open daily 8am-9pm.

English Bookstore: Tibet Book Centre (tel. 471131) across the main road and to the right of the gate. Open daily 9:30am-6pm. **Dharma Book Centre** (tel. 211234) inside the *stupa*, 1 flight up. Open Sun.-Fri. 9am-noon and 1:30-6pm. Both shops sell books on Tibet and Buddhism, as well as Free Tibet/Dalai Lama paraphernalia.

Library: Ka Nying Shedrupling Monastery has a library with everything you ever wanted to know about this sect; open Wed. and Fri. 10:30am-noon, Sat. 9-10:15am.

Pharmacy: Most cluster on the main road near the *stupa* gate, and have attached clinics with morning and evening hours. For anything serious, go to Kathmandu. For **Tibetan medicine,** the Tibet Medical Centre (tel. 474025) is off the main road in Chabahil (the next town towards Kathmandu). Open Mon-Fri. 10am-noon and 2-5pm.

ACCOMMODATIONS

Most visitors to Boudha spend either a few hours or a few months, but considering the clean and peaceful lodgings available you may want to stay a few nights. Most guest houses offer discounts on long stays (two weeks or more). There are a few cheap places on the main road, but the ones in the back lanes are sheltered from the exhaust fumes and only slightly harder to find.

Lotus Guest House (tel. 472432, 472320). Off the main northern lane, at the end of the first lane to the right (east), behind the Dobsang Monastery, which runs it. Two floors of clean, windowy, basic rooms form a pea-green "L" around a manicured garden. Common baths are plentiful, with seat toilets, and toilet paper provided. Breakfast available. Singles Rs.190, with bath Rs.220. Doubles Rs.260, with bath Rs.300 (add 10% government tax; no seasonal or long-term discounts).

Dragon Guest House (tel. 479562). Off the first lane off the *stupa* as you walk around clockwise. Bear left and walk around the large monastery (or cut through if the gate is open). The Dragon is discreetly marked, just past the monastery, on the right. A tiny new place behind a tiny garden, with lots of little frills like free tea, a collection of English and Japanese books, and plastic slippers for use in the shiny-tiled bathrooms. All rooms are without bath, with motel-style furnishings. Attached veg. restaurant (main dishes Rs.35-50). Singles Rs.220. Doubles Rs.340. Quads Rs.480. 15% discount on stays of 2 weeks, 30% on 4 weeks or more.

Kailash Guest House (tel. 480741). On the right side of the main northern lane. Hawaiian print curtains cheer up the bare rooms. Terraces on each floor overlook fields and *gompas*. Singles Rs.150. Doubles Rs.175, with bath Rs.225.

FOOD

Another reason to linger in Boudha is its great selection of restaurants. Some of the touristy places have excellent views of the *stupa,* while the Tibetan holes-in-the-wall offer a more intimate, if less picturesque, glimpse of the Boudha scene. Try Tibetan *momos* (ravioli stuffed with meat or vegetables) and *thukpa* (noodle soup) in either type of establishment—but these are cheaper at the purely Tibetan places.

Steed Restaurant, on the corner of the *stupa* compound where the main northern lane starts. A blue-and-white curtain marks this blue-walled, 4-table eatery. Consult the English menu or just point at the Tibetan delicacies (Rs.10-50) on other people's plates. The portions of *momos* aren't huge, but they're yummy, and at Rs.15 a plate, you could spring for 2 courses. Open daily 6am-8:30pm.

Double Dorjee Restaurant, just off the main lane on the first eastern lane, on the right. A favorite among monks and long-term Westerners, with low tables and upholstered chairs, brightly painted walls, paper lanterns, and posters with inspirational sayings. The blackboard menu asserts that all drinking water is boiled and filtered, and veggies are soaked in potassium permangate. A Tibetan family provides slow and sweet service, so you'll have plenty of time to chat with the regulars while you wait for your food. Entrees Rs.55-100. The apple pie—available only in season—is legendary.

Stupa View Restaurant, (tel. 479044). On the north side of the *stupa*, upstairs. The menu is in German and English at this Austrian-run veg. restaurant that serves mostly Italian food without any noticeable lingering Nepali flavor. Dine on home-made pastas (Rs.110-130), pizzas with mozzarella, not yak cheese (!) (Rs.140-210), and veggie-tofu concoctions (Rs.135-200) directly in the line of Buddha's watchful gaze. Sit in the pastel-hued dining room or on the roof terrace. Open daily 9am-10pm (low season noon-9pm).

Himalayan Restaurant, next door to the Stupa View, with the same great view at less than half the price. The 7-page menu offers the usual multi-cultural assortment, including a "Nepali Mickey Mouse Salad." Main dishes Rs.25-80. Scrumptious *lassis* (Rs.25-35). Open daily 7am-9:30pm.

SIGHTS

Boudha is not only Nepal's largest **stupa,** but one of the largest in the world. Various legends tell of the *stupa*'s origins, but the 5th-century date assigned by historians is only a guess. A Tibetan myth tells of a poultry-farmer's daughter who wanted to build a *stupa.* The king granted her the area that could be covered by a buffalo skin, which she cut into strips to claim the huge lot on which it was built. The Newari version relates the construction of the *stupa* to a drought. A king tricked his son into making a blood-sacrifice to bring rain, and the remorseful pacifist prince built the *stupa* when he realized what he had done. Yet another story claims that the *stupa* was erected during such a dry time that the builders had to collect dew to form the bricks. Each segment of the *stupa*'s structure is said to correspond to one of the five elements; the three-leveled *mandala*-shaped base represents earth; the dome, water; the spire (with its thirteen steps corresponding to the thirteen steps to *nirvana*), fire; the umbrella, air; and the pinnacle, ether. Buddha's red-rimmed blue eyes gaze out from each of the four sides of the golden spire, and the "nose" in between is actually the number one in Nepali script. The *stupa* is whitewashed, then splashed with stripes of rust-colored wash to form the shape of a lotus. The *stupa's* wall is inset with niches containing prayer wheels and 108 Buddha images. At the entrance to the *stupa* itself is a shrine to the Newari goddess Ajima, protectress of children and goddess of smallpox. To the left as you enter is a room filled by two huge prayer wheels. Climb the stairs onto the *stupa* and stroll around it; the *stupa* will leave white powder on you if you sit down.

Visitors are usually welcome in the **gompas**—there is one right off the *stupa* compound and many more further afield—as long as they observe the necessary **etiquette**. Dress modestly, take your shoes off before entering the *lhakang* (main hall), walk around clockwise inside, and always ask before taking photos. If you visit a lama, present him with a white *khata* (prayer scarf). These are inexpensive and available at many shops around Boudha, where someone can show how to fold them properly. In the *lhakang*, you'll find intricate wall paintings in a rainbow of colors. Gold statues of the Buddha, other *bodhisattvas,* or the sect's founder are surrounded by offerings of food, incense, and butter-lamps.

Chyoki Nyima Rinpoche holds a teaching session in English every Saturday morning from 10:30am-noon. His **Ka Nying Shedrupling Monastery** (off the northern lane, to the west) and the **Kopan Monastery** (2km north of Boudha) are particularly accessible to Western students, and hold courses during most of the year. In monsoon season, many teachers go on tour in other parts of the world. The *stupa* is surrounded by shops. You don't need to come all the way to Boudha to buy some of the standard tourist junk available everywhere, but it is *the* place for Tibetan antiques, or cheaper souvenirs such as funky Tibetan head- and foot-gear and Buddhist prayer flags. It's also a good place to learn more about *thanka* painting. Prices are notoriously high here, so shop around and bargain hard.

Thankas

Traditional *thankas* (pronounced thang-ka, meaning "something rolled up" in Tibetan) are religious paintings on cloth that serve as aids for meditation, usually in temples or family altars. Colorful and finely detailed, they are painted in accordance with strict guidelines that dictate style and subject matter. *Thankas* may represent the Buddha surrounded by scenes from his life, *bodhisattvas,* saints, or lamas. Other forms include the wheel of life and *mandalas,* which illustrate the steps to enlightenment. *Thankas* are made by stretching cotton cloth on a wooden frame and priming it with gesso. The cloth is then rubbed smooth with a stone or shell. The outlines of the images are drawn, then colors are added in layers. If a *thanka* is made in a workshop, layers are added by increasingly skilled artists: first large blocks of color, then the setting, then any gold details, and finally the faces of the figures. A good *thanka* can take anywhere from a week to six months to create. The painting is then mounted on a frame of three colors of brocade silk, with a rod at the top for hanging and rolling. A *thanka* cannot be used, however, until it has been consecrated by a lama, who will make an inscription on the back of the painting. Most *thankas* you will see for sale have not been consecrated (although some of the same artists still make *thankas* for religious use) and many do not comply with traditional guidelines. For example, the "detailed *mandala*" form with its minute details is a style created to meet the tastes of tourists. If you are interested in buying a *thanka,* shop around first. As with any fine art, the enormous range in prices (from Rs.50-10,000) reflects the range of quality available, though a high price does not necessarily guarantee high quality. In Bhaktapur and Boudha, some workshops will let you watch artists at work.

■ Bhaktapur

The architecture of the medieval town of Bhaktapur is among the Kathmandu Valley's finest and also (thanks to a German development project in the 1970s) among its best-preserved. But the allure of Bhaktapur lies not only in its majestic temples but also in the way in which everyday life swirls leisurely around them. Men nap, children play, and women sell vegetables in the shade of magnificent pagodas, and in between the main squares there winds a network of alleys and courtyards. Located in the eastern end of the valley, Bhaktapur keeps its distance from the auto-rickshaw-bustle of its former rival kingdoms Kathmandu and Patan.

Founded in the 9th century, Bhaktapur (also known as Bhadgaon) was the capital of the Kathmandu Valley until its division into three kingdoms in 1482. Its glory faded with its conquest by the Gorkhas in 1768. A 1934 earthquake took a particularly devastating toll on the town. Despite Bhaktapur's apparent timelessness, the municipality is aware of the value of the treasures it possesses and charges foreign visitors an admission fee to fund ongoing preservation efforts.

ORIENTATION

Bhaktapur's main sights can be found in three squares strung together by a curving main street. Beginning in the west, **Durbar Square** is connected in its southeast corner to **Taumadhi Tole** by a short lane. From the northeast corner of Taumadhi Tole, the connecting street widens into Bhaktapur's commercial area and takes a right-angle turn about a quarter of the way to **Tachapal Tole,** which is about 10 minutes away by foot. North and south of this main artery are tangles of alleyways. Minibuses from Kathmandu arrive in an area that is a five-minute walk west of Durbar Square, near a large water tank called **Navpokhu Pokhari**—to your left if you follow your nose along the street that leads to the gate of Durbar Square. The trolleybus stop is a ten-minute walk south of the center of town along a road that runs perpendicular to the one on which the trolleybus runs. It ends at the southwest corner of Taumadhi Tole, crossing the **Hanumante River** about halfway.

Tourists must pay Rs.300 or US$5 at the gates to Durbar Square if they enter from the east, or as they cross the bridge coming from the south. If you wander into town by another route you will avoid these tollbooths but you may be asked for your ticket once inside. There are plans to install even more tourist checkpoints.

PRACTICAL INFORMATION

Tourist Office: Tourist Service Centre and Information Hall, Durbar Square Gate (tel. 612249). Run by the Bhaktapur Municipality, this is where you'll be asked to fork over the Rs.300 or US$5 entrance fee. In exchange, you'll get an informational pamphlet and use of an umbrella in the case of rain. Keep your ticket and use it to get in again if you leave.

Currency Exchange: Layaku Money Exchange Counter, just outside the Durbar Square gate. Good rates, 1% commission. Open daily 8am-7pm.

Telephones: There are several STD/ISD offices around town, including one just inside and one just outside the Durbar Square gate. Open daily 8am-7pm.

Buses: Minibus Park, near Navpokhu Pokhari, a large water tank. To Kathmandu's Ratna Park (#7, frequent, 45min., Rs.4). **Trolleybus Park,** south of Durbar Square. To Kathmandu (trolleybus, 45min., Rs.3). **Kamal Binayak,** in the northeast of Bhaktapur. Turn left after the pottery square east of Dattatraya Square and head north to the edge of town. To Nagarkot (every hr., 1½-2hr., Rs.10).

Local Transportation: Buses: #7 bus skirts around town from the Navpokhu Pokhari minibus park to Kamal Binayak. **Taxis** prowl outside the Durbar Square gates and across from the Minibus Park. **Bicycles** can be rented across from the cinema, near Navpokhu Pokhari. Mountain bikes Rs.60-100; regular bikes Rs.30-60 per day. Open daily 8am-6pm.

Market: Fruit and vegetable sellers gather at the bend in the main street that connects Tamadhi Tole and Tachapal Tole.

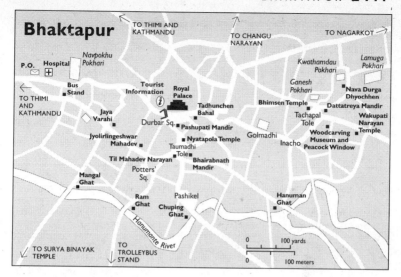

Bhaktapur

TO THIMI AND KATHMANDU

TO CHANGU NARAYAN

TO NAGARKOT →

P.O. Hospital
Navpokhu Pokhari

Kwathamdau Pokhari

Lamuga Pokhari

← Bus Stand
TO THIMI AND KATHMANDU

Tourist Information

Royal Palace

Ganesh Pokhari

Nava Durga Dhyochhen

Jaya Varahi

Tadhunchen Bahal

Bhimsen Temple

Dattatreya Mandir

Durbar Sq.

Pashupati Mandir

Tachapal Tole

Wakupati Narayan Temple

Jyolirlingeshwar Mahadev

Nyatapola Temple

Golmadhi

Woodcarving Museum and Peacock Window

Taumadhi Tole

Inacho

Til Mahadev Narayan

Bhairabnath Mandir

Potters' Sq.

Mangal Ghat

Ram Ghat

Pashikel

Chuping Ghat

Hanuman Ghat

Hanumante River

TO SURYA BINAYAK TEMPLE

TO TROLLEYBUS STAND

0   100 yards

0   100 meters

Pharmacy: There are several across from the hospital.
Hospital: (tel. 610676). Across from the Minibus Park, near Navpokhu Pokhari.
Police: (tel. 100). Just inside Durbar Square gates on the left.
Post Office: Across from the Navpokhu Pokhari minibus stop. Open Sun.-Thurs. 10am-5pm. Fri. 10am-3pm.

ACCOMMODATIONS

For many visitors to the Kathmandu Valley, Bhaktapur is just a day trip from the 'Du. But Bhaktapur is worthy of more than just an afternoon visit, and, as the growing number of guest houses in Bhaktapur indicates, it's also a very cool place to spend the night. Bhaktapur's guest houses are all conveniently located near the main squares and offer similar facilities: hot showers, laundry service, and rooftop restaurants with magnificent views of the town and the valley. Deciding which temple you want outside your window might be your greatest dilemma.

The prices below are all for the high season; off-season, try to negotiate a 20-50% discount.

Golden Gate Guest House (tel. 611099). On the left side of the street between Durbar Square and Taumadhi Tole. Spacious rooms with balconies. Views and brightness improve with the stairs. Singles Rs.100. Doubles with 1 bed Rs.150, with 2 beds Rs.200. Doubles and triples with bath Rs.500.

Bhadgaon Guest House, Taumadhi Tole (tel. 610488; fax 610481). At the southern end of the square. An unusually solid building with spiffy, slippery marble stairs, the Bhadgaon is Bhaktapur's most upscale establishment. All the rooms are sunny and have attached bathrooms; the expensive rooms have better views and bathtubs. International phone and fax. Fans and heaters available. Singles Rs.350. Doubles Rs.400, with view US$10. Triples Rs.700, with view US$20.

Pagoda Guest House, Taumadhi Tole (tel. 613248; fax 610290). Right behind the Nyatapola temple, to the left. Super-clean guest house (perhaps because it's the newest on the scene). Rooms with ceiling fans and decorative touches like Tibetan rugs and fake flowers are practically *on top* of the 5-storied pagoda. Plastic slippers provided for guests. Singles Rs.200-300, with bath Rs.500-600. Doubles Rs.400-600, with bath Rs.800-1200.

Dattatraya Guest House, Tachapal Tole. Behind and to the left of the Bhimsen Temple. Set apart from the other guest houses, the Dattatreya has unobstructed views from its roof. Funky black and white checkered linoleum floors in the rooms.

NEPAL

Possibility for long-term stays with kitchen facilities. Singles Rs.150. Doubles Rs.250. Triples Rs.300.

Traditional Guest House (tel. 611057), off the end of Durbar Square opposite the main gate, on the right. "Traditional" backpackers' scene: basic, padlocked rooms with squat toilets on attached balconies. No rooftop restaurant, but the friendly manager cooks up *dal bhat* for guests. Singles Rs.150. Doubles with 1 bed Rs.200, with 2 beds Rs.225. Triples Rs.300.

Nyatapola Rest House, Taumadhi Tole, behind the Nyatapola pagoda, to the right. If you're nostalgic for trekking teahouses you'll dig this row of 5 rooms with basket-like woven walls. Bathrooms across the courtyard. Padlocks provided. Singles Rs.100. Doubles Rs.200.

FOOD

While none of Bhaktapur's restaurants merit special mention based on their cuisine—they all offer up the usual tourist mish-mash of Nepali-Continental-Indian-Chinese—several do stand out because of their settings. (The **guest houses** have rooftop restaurants with the same scenery-to-salivary ratio, too.) One local treat, *ju ju dhau* ("king of curds") a particularly creamy, sweet yogurt, can be sampled in the restaurants straight-up, with fruit in *lassi* form, or (much less expensively) at many of the cold shops around town, where it is sold in locally made clay cups.

Café Nyatapola, Taumadhi Tole. Sight-see while you snack on the upper floor of this temple-turned-café in the center of the square. Laugh at other tourists below as they squat to fit all 5 stories of the Nyatapola pagoda into their photos. Slightly pricey (Rs.75-150 for main dishes). Open daily 8am-6pm.

Temple Town Restaurant, Durbar Square. A small garden with cages of chirping birds hanging in the trees screens the patio tables from the bustle of the square without obscuring the sights. Main dishes Rs.55-180. Open daily 8am-7pm.

Marco Polo Restaurant, Taumadhi Tole. A less romantic but cheaper alternative to the Nyatapola Café, with a cramped balcony overlooking the northwest corner of the square. Fairly extensive menu with dishes from Rs.30-80. Open daily 8am-9pm.

Café de Peacock, Tachapal Tole. Upstairs in one of the old *maths,* another historic setting with a good view of the action below. A smaller selection of expensive food than some of the other places, but again, you're paying more to sit than to eat. Mostly Western fare, Rs.70-160. Open daily 9am-9pm.

SIGHTS

Durbar Square

Bhaktapur's Durbar Square was once as temple-packed as those of Kathmandu and Patan, but the 1934 earthquake thinned it out. Just inside the gate on the left, the fierce, multi-armed couple **Bhairab** and **Ugrachandi** guard another gate. Legend has it that after the sculptor completed them in 1701, his hands were chopped off to prevent him from creating masterpieces elsewhere. To the right is a cluster of temples, the largest of which is dedicated to **Krishna.** The **Royal Palace** encloses the north side of the square, and like the square itself, it is only a fraction of what it once was. The west wing of the palace houses the **National Art Gallery** which mostly displays Newari *paubha* and Tibetan *thanka* paintings, some of which are incredibly intricate, along with other objects such as wooden book covers and stone sculptures. (Open April-Dec. Sun.-Mon. and Wed.-Thurs. 10:15am-4:45pm, Fri. 10am-2:45pm; Jan.-March Sun.-Mon. and Wed.-Thurs. 10:15am-3:45pm, Fri. 10am-2:45pm. Admission Rs.5, camera fee Rs.10.) Next door is the acclaimed, Garuda-topped **Golden Gate,** which was built in the early 18th century by King Bhupatindra Malla, who in golden form himself kneels atop a stone pillar facing the gate. A guard blocks foreigners from entering but there's plenty to admire from outside the **Fifty-Five Window Palace.** The craftsmanship of the carved wooden windows is less flashy but more impressive than that of the gate itself. Behind the king's pillar is the elephant-flanked, stone **Vatsala Durga Temple,** built in the mid-18th century in the *shikhara* style.

The small bell next to it is known as the **"Bell of the Barking Dogs,"** whose peal is said to make dogs howl (as if they needed any encouragement in Nepal). The larger **Taleju Bell** was originally used to call humans to prayer. The next temple is the **Chyasilin Mandapa,** or Octagonal Pavilion, which is actually a 1990 reconstruction incorporating fragments of the 18th-century original. The upstairs serves as a lookout point for tourists and a hang-out for local teenagers. In the eastern section of the square, around the corner of the palace, are several more temples and temple foundations, the most interesting of which is the 17th-century stone **Siddhi Lakshmi Temple,** with its procession of animals and people on either side of the stairs. Note the children on the ground level, who look like they're being dragged off to the dentist. The souvenir shops that surround this part of the square were once *dharamshalas* (pilgrims' resthouses). In a courtyard to the right off the far end of the square is **Tadhunchen Bahal,** a 15th-century monastery, holy for both Hindus and Buddhists. Back in the southeast corner of main part of the square, the **Pashupatinath Mandir** contains a 17th-century reproduction of the *linga* at Pashupatinath and is the most active of the Durbar Square temples. Check out the especially creative contortions of the couples on the roof struts.

Taumadhi Tole

Connected to Durbar Square by a short, shop-lined street, Taumadhi Tole is Bhaktapur at its best, where architectural masterpieces intermingle with daily life. Nepal's tallest pagoda, **Nyatapola,** looms majestically over the square and all of Bhaktapur. The red, five-story pagoda was built in 1702. Five pairs of stone creatures flank the stairs to the temple. Each pair of guardians is said to be ten times stronger than the one below, starting with a tremendous pair of Malla wrestlers who themselves are ten times more powerful than the average man. Next are a pair of elephants, followed by lions (often ridden by children), giraffes, and finally the goddesses Bahini (the Tigress) and Singhini (the Lioness). The image of the goddess **Siddhi Lakshmi,** to whom the temple is devoted, is locked inside the temple, accessible only to priests. The shaded upper level is a favorite local napping spot. The eastern side of the square is dominated by the comparably solid **Bhairabnath Mandir,** which was built as a single-story temple in the 17th century. A second story was added during the 18th century and the entire thing was rebuilt with the existing three stories after the 1934 earthquake. The golden image of Bhairab is miniscule in proportion to the temple as a whole. A doorway in the building at the south side of the square leads to a courtyard filled by the **Til Mahadev Narayan Mandir,** a 17th-century temple (on an 11th-century temple site) reminiscent of Changu Narayan with its pillar-mounted golden Garuda, *chakra,* and *sankha. Til* means "sesame seed," and its use in the temple's name is said to have come from a Thimi merchant who had a vision of Narayan in his stock of sesame seeds.

Tachapal Tole

A wide, curving street of shops catering to locals rather than tourists (although some of their wares make great souvenirs) links Taumadhi Tole to Tachapal Tole. The oldest square in Bhaktapur is also known as **Dattratraya Square.** The wooden buildings that enclose the square were once *maths,* residences for priests. The **Dattratraya Mandir** presides over the square from the eastern end. Built in 1427, it is the oldest surviving building in Bhaktapur, and like other famous structures in the Kathmandu Valley, is said to have been built with the wood of just one tree. A pair of newly-painted Malla wrestlers guard the entrance in jarring multi-colored contrast to the monochromatic temple, whose beauty lies in its detailed wood carvings. A gilded Garuda faces the temple from the top of a stone pillar. Dattatraya seems to be worshiped by everyone around the valley since he is considered an incarnation of Vishnu, a guru of Shiva and a cousin of the Buddha. At the opposite end of the square is the rectangular **Bhimsen Temple,** which honors the favorite god of Newari merchants. The ground floor of the temple is open for business, while the shrine is upstairs.

Behind the Dattatraya temple are two museums housed in *maths*. To the left, the **Brass and Bronze Museum** displays a collection of functional objects such as lamps, cooking pots, *hookahs*, spittoons, and ritual paraphernalia in a funky old building. Watch your head on the low doorways! Opposite in **Pujari Math** is the **National Art Gallery Woodcarving Museum** worth visiting more for its magnificent courtyard than for its minutely labeled objects. It is interesting to see carvings such as temple roof struts up close for a change. (Admission to each museum Rs.5, camera fee Rs.5. Both are open April-Dec. Sun.-Mon. and Wed.-Thurs. 10am-5pm, Fri. 10am-4pm; Jan.-March Sun.-Mon. and Wed.-Thurs. 10am-4pm, Fri. 10am-3pm.) Around the corner from the entrance to the Woodcarving Museum, on another side of Pujari Math is the famous **Peacock Window**, which is supposed to be the pinnacle of Bhaktapur wood-carving.

Other Sights

It is a pleasure just to wander through Bhaktapur. You'll stumble across many more temples and shrines. Look for craftspeople at work—the squares just east of Tachapal Tole and just south of Taumadhi Tole are both known as **Potters' Square** and you can see hundreds of pots lined up to dry in the sun or stacked up to be sold. As you lose yourself in Bhaktapur's alleys, be careful not to trip over playing children as you look up to see the carved wooden windows and onions hanging under the eaves of roofs, and to dodge the waste—water, phlegm, and chicken feet—that is sometimes flung from the windows.

ENTERTAINMENT AND SHOPPING

Bhaktapur is not big on formal entertainment. At night, look (or rather listen) for older men from the community who gather after sundown to play cymbals and drums at several of the temples. If you have three hours to spare, indulge yourself in a Hindi or Nepali film at the **cinema** near the Navpokhu Pokhari (on the street leading to Durbar Square from the Minibus Park; Rs.3-13, 3 shows per day, 4 on Sat.).

Shopping in Bhaktapur is a bigger deal. Bhaktapur is known for its **pottery** (best purchased at the Potters' Square) and **woodcarving** (available in Durbar and Tachapal Squares). The painted wooden toys such as trucks and auto-rickshaws are actually made in Patan, but the miniature carved windows and such are produced in Bhaktapur. You'll also see **papier maché masks** and marionettes but these are cheaper in Thimi where they are made. Many of the handmade **paper** products are made at the Unicef factory in Bhaktapur. Look on the street between Tachapal and Taumadhi Squares for less touristy souvenirs like *topis*, the traditional Nepalese men's hats, or saris. The black-and-red saris you'll see on local women are of the Newari *Jyapu* (farmer) caste and cost Rs.300-600.

■ Thimi

If you happen to get off the bus to Bhaktapur about three-quarters of the way from Kathmandu, you'll find yourself in Thimi, the fourth largest town in the Kathmandu Valley—which isn't saying much. Like Bhaktapur, Thimi is a pottery town and also a good place to get a taste of Newari architecture. Since Thimi has not been restored, it gives a sense of what Bhaktapur might have looked (and smelled) like before it was cleaned up by the Germans. Look down only often enough to ensure you're not stepping in the open sewers; look up and you'll be delighted by the architecture and the scenery of the surrounding valley.

Thimi stretches between the two parallel roads that run between Kathmandu and Bhaktapur. Thimi's main street connects the two roads at **Naya Thimi** ("New Thimi") in the south and **Bahakha Bazaar** in the north.

Thimi's only noteworthy temple is the 16th-century **Balkumari**, in the square just up the hill from the Naya Thimi bus stop. People pray for fertility to the goddess in residence, whose peacock vehicle faces the temple from atop a pillar. At Bisket, the Newari New Year, the square teems with men carrying images of gods on palanquins, playing drums and cymbals, and tossing orange powder everywhere. Wander the tiny streets of Thimi, allowing yourself to get lost (you'll never be too far from the main road), and you'll find courtyards full of pots drying in the sun. Witness the potters' craft as they wedge their clay by stomping on it and throw their creations on hand-powered wooden wheels. The town is dotted with tiny temples and shrines (some with erotic carvings) that are so much a part of daily life (complete with laundry hanging to dry and symbols of political parties painted on them) that you might pass them by. *Papier maché* masks, marionettes, and figurines are produced and sold in shops in Bahakha Bazaar for Rs.80-200. Visitors are rare in Thimi. Children here greet visitors with "bye-bye" instead of demanding rupees like their jaded counterparts in more touristy areas.

To get to Naya Thimi, take bus #10 or #7 (the Bhaktapur bus) from Ratna Park, or take the trolleybus. To reach Bahaka Bazaar, take the #9 Bhaktapur bus from Ratna Park. Buses are more frequent at Naya Thimi.

■ Changu Narayan

The temple of Changu Narayan, 7km north of Bhaktapur on the "shaking hill" of Changu, has a long and misty history and a pile of artistic treasures to show for it. Since the 4th century AD there has been a Vishnu shrine on Changu Narayan, the Kathmandu Valley's oldest and most sacred. The architecture of the Changu Narayan temple, a large, double-roofed pagoda, is nothing special (it was rebuilt after a fire in 1702), but it is surrounded by a profusion of large sculptures and shiny black relief panels that make those at other temples seem dinky; they are counted among Nepal's greatest artworks.

Entering the courtyard from the Bhaktapur side you'll be at the back of the **temple,** with two stone griffins facing you. Go around to the front, which is guarded by stone lions. There's a spreading brass doorway embossed with flower designs; unfortunately, the temple is closed to non-Hindus. The 7th-century golden image of Vishnu inside is so sacred that only a few favored priests can see it. On either side of the temple, pillars stand like great big candlesticks, bearing Vishnu's symbols: a discus on the left (which is teardrop-shaped here) and a conch shell on the right. The **inscription** at the base of the discus' pillar is the oldest stone inscription in the valley, dating from 454 AD. The excellent statue of Vishnu's man-bird vehicle, **Garuda,** who bows before the door wearing a cobra for a scarf, was carved about that same time. In the birdcage over Garuda's shoulder there are two more recent figures, Bupathindra Malla and Bubana Lakshmi, the king and queen of Bhaktapur who financed the temple's construction.

The best of the sculptures are beside the main temple, past Vishnu's conch emblem, on the brick pavilion of the Lakshmi Narayan temple (the one with black wooden columns). In the central relief, Vishnu as **Narasimha,** half-man and half-lion, tears a hole in the chest of a demon tangled across his lap. To the left of this, a relief shows the story of Vishnu as **Vikrantha,** who appeared before a demon king disguised as a dwarf. When the demon king granted the dwarf Vikrantha as much property as he could cover in three strides, Vishnu grew up to celestial size and stepped across the earth and the heavens, humbling the demon. The heavens swirl around him in this scene and people clutch at his toes, while his legs span the whole scene. On the platform next to the Lakshmi Narayan Temple, there's an image of Vishnu as **Narayan,** sleeping on a knotted snake, while above him a 10-headed, 10-armed version of himself rises up to the heavens, pushing aside some hurt-looking elephants. On the discus side of the courtyard there's a sculpture of **Vishnu riding Garuda** that appears on the 10-rupee note. All of these sculptures date from the Licchavi period, before the Mallas took over in 1200 AD, when stone sculpture in the valley was at its height.

Changu Narayan is about an hour's **bike** ride from Bhaktapur (the last 2km are very steep). A single **bus** sporadically runs the road between Bhaktapur and Changu Narayan (30min., Rs.5). **Trucks** going up the hill sometimes take on passengers for a totally negotiable charge; they wait at the edge of Bhaktapur where the road starts. Changu Narayan is a four-hour hike from the mountain viewpoint of Nagarkot to the east. Getting off the bus at the hairpin turn at Bhedi and walking straight along the ridge will get you there in about 1½-2 hours. Another approach is from the north side, off the road between Boudha and Sankhu, but it is trekkable only in the dry season when the Manohara river is low enough to be forded.

The inspiring view of the valley from Changu Narayan is best enjoyed over a bowl of instant noodles on the balcony of the **Changu Narayan Hill Resort** (tel. 290891), high above the road from Bhaktapur, about 500m east of Changu village. The "resort" also offers very basic accommodations if you're tempted to spend the night (double with common bath Rs.200). In the village of Changu, which dribbles down from the temple, there are a couple of other restaurants. The **Champak Restaurant** is right in the temple complex with the pilgrims' rest houses, and serves up *dal bhat* (Rs.40), fried rice (Rs.15) and chow mein (Rs.22).

▓ Dhulikhel

Just beyond the confines of the Kathmandu Valley at 1550m, Dhulikhel is a Himalayan viewpoint rivaling its neighbor to the north, Nagarkot. But unlike Nagarkot, there was actually a town of Dhulikhel before tourists came along. In fact, as evidenced by the elaborately carved wooden doorways and windows which decorate the older houses, Dhulikhel was once a prosperous market town along the main trade route between Nepal and China. The old town is still largely intact, but today Dhulikhel seems to be inhabited by more goats than people. The beautiful old buildings bulge and lean precariously (some are crumbling apart), while new ones are being assembled, giving the entire town the feeling of a construction site—it's hard to tell which buildings are going up and which are coming down. The red-brick town is most charming when seen from the distance of a roof or hilltop, against the backdrop of lush, red-soiled, terraced hillsides and the peaks of the Himalaya.

ORIENTATION AND PRACTICAL INFORMATION

Dhulikhel is just off the Arniko Highway, 32km east of Kathmandu. The #12 bus (Rs.10) leaves Ratna Park in Kathmandu about every half hour, and takes about one hour and 45 minutes to reach the small **bus park,** down from the small **hill** at the center of Dhulikhel. At the top of the hill, a bust of King Mahendra stands next to a water tank. To the right of Mahendra, the road leads northwest into the old part of town, which boasts a few temples; to the left, it heads southeast out of town toward the hill with the best view. **Telephone Code:** 011.

ACCOMMODATIONS AND FOOD

While a number of cushy hotels dot the countryside surrounding Dhulikhel (and more are on the way), the budget accommodations are in town or nearby. At the top of the heap (quite literally) is the **Panorama View Lodge,** about a 20-minute walk up the southeastern hill. The spectacular views make the trek here from the bus stand worthwhile. Follow the road to the left of the statue to the lodge's sign at the base of the hill (about 15 minutes), then take the road or the deeply eroded shortcut paths up the hill. In the new brick building, rooms are large with windows, two beds, and, except for one, attached bathrooms. Singles Rs.300. Doubles downstairs Rs.500, upstairs Rs.600. The downstairs room without a bath costs Rs.200 as a single, Rs.300 as a double. In the house opposite, two significantly more rustic rooms without baths go for only Rs.75 as singles, Rs.100 as doubles. The indoor-outdoor restaurant offers the usual curries, fried rice, and mashed potatoes at reasonable prices. From the center of town, the **Nawaranga Guest House** is a five-minute walk down the road to the left of the statue. Above the restaurant (which doubles as an "art gallery"), the Nawaranga is, according to the owner, Dhulikhel's "rock bottom" option. Common squat toilets; hot water Rs.10 a bucket. Beds in dim, low-ceilinged dorm rooms Rs.50.

Singles Rs.150. Doubles Rs.200. Good view from the roof. The **Dhulikhel Lodge** (tel. 61152) is right off the main square. Worn but clean rooms off low-ceilinged, straw-mat-covered halls. Toilets and hot showers outside across the courtyard. The lush garden out back and the floor-cushioned dining room make for a mellow stay. Singles Rs.150. Doubles Rs.250. Triples Rs.300. Quads Rs.350. Right next to the bus stop, buffered by a flight of stairs and a garden, is the **Royal East Inn**. Spare, carpeted rooms line the wide corridors. Rooms without bath have views of the mountains and the bus park. Rooms with bath are darker but quieter. Excellent views from the roof. Singles Rs.200, with bath Rs.400. Doubles Rs.300, with bath Rs.400. The snazzy restaurant has padded chairs, tablecloths, and cloth napkins, and a pricey menu of mostly Italian and Mexican food, almost identical to that of Café de la Peacock in Bhaktapur. (They're under the same ownership.) The only **restaurants** in town are the ones attached to the guest houses.

SIGHTS

The mountains are the featured attraction in Dhulikhel, but the town is worth a wander as well. In the main square, the small, brightly tiled temple is dedicated to **Harisiddhi,** and the even smaller one opposite, to **Narayan.** They are guarded by two Garudas. Further northwest, at the high point of the town, the **Bhagwati Mandir** is of more interest as a lookout than as a temple. The most popular point from which to watch the sun rise over the Himalaya is the **Kali Shrine** at the top of the southeastern hill. Walk to the Panorama View Lodge and keep going. The shrine is about 45 minutes from town.

▓ Nagarkot

Teetering at 2000m on the eastern rim of the Kathmandu Valley, Nagarkot is a popular Himalayan viewpoint from which, in the clearest weather, one can see peaks from Everest (which is just a little bump) to the Annapurna Range. The tiny town of Nagarkot was created by tourism (which continues to spur the town's expansion) so don't expect to be immersed in local culture. The ride up on the truly dilapidated local bus, however, is an authentic Nepalese experience—if you can stomach a peek out the window as the bus chugs around a hairpin turn with two inches to spare, you'll see patterned, terraced hillsides and uncultivated hills that seem draped in thick green cloth. Nagarkot gets quite chilly at night (in the hot season it's refreshingly cool) so bring warm clothes.

ORIENTATION AND PRACTICAL INFORMATION

Nagarkot consists of an ever-thickening sprinkling of guest houses along a **ridge.** At the southern end of town, close to the **bus stop,** is the new, fancy-schmancy **Club Himalaya.** The rest of Nagarkot's guest houses are off the dirt road that runs north from below this hotel. From the bus stop, a short dirt lane to the left connects the paved road from Bhaktapur to the dirt road. A few shops line the road at first; it then slopes up through a clump of pine trees before continuing along the ridge below the high point on the ridge, marked by the tiny **Mahakal Shrine.**

Local buses are supposed to leave from the Kamal Binayak bus stop in the northeast of Bhaktapur every hour, but they are in fact less frequent—just ask around for the next departure time (1½-2hr., Rs.10). To get to the bus stop, turn left after the pottery square east of Dattatraya Square and head north to the edge of town. **Tourist buses** leave from Kantipath in Kathmandu (1:30pm, 2½hr., Rs.100 one way, Rs.190 roundtrip, low season Rs.80) and return from Nagarkot at 10:30am the following day. Tickets can be booked in advance from any agency in Thamel. **Jeeps** also run from Bhaktapur for as little as Rs.20 per person after some negotiating. A **taxi** from Bhaktapur to Nagarkot costs Rs.300. **Currency exchange** is available at the Himalayan Bank Ltd. (tel. 290885) just below the Club Himalaya. (Rs.200 service charge on any amount under Rs.10,000, 2% for more; open Sun.-Thurs. 10am-3pm, Fri. 10am-noon.)

International **telephone** calls can be made from the pricier hotels (Club Himalaya, Hotel Space Mountain), but they will not let you receive a call back.

ACCOMMODATIONS AND FOOD

As Nagarkot's population of hotels expands, true budget lodges are becoming an endangered species. Prices are negotiable (especially in low season) so with a little friendly haggling there are still bargains to be found. All three of the following hotels cling to the bump in the ridge below the Mahakal Shrine. The bargain with the best name is **The Hotel at the End of the Universe** (tel. 610874), formerly the New Pheasant Lodge, one of Nagarkot's originals. Douglas Adams fans and others will want to lounge for hours soaking in mountain and valley views, at low tables on the glass-enclosed, cushioned platform in the **Restaurant at the End of the Universe,** around which the hotel's cottages are clustered. Facilities range from mud- to bamboo-walled huts, with and without bath. Hot water is coming soon, and as the End of the Universe drifts upmarket, plans to expand the restaurant are underway. Prices in high season range from Rs.200 to US$20 for doubles. The next turn-off down the road leads to the **Hotel Madhuban Village,** a collection of A-frame bamboo cottages with big windows and not much room for anything beyond the two single beds. Bathrooms are all outside, with no hot water. The glassed-in dining room affords good views. Huts go for Rs.150 as singles, Rs.200 as doubles. **The Peaceful Cottage and Café du Mont** (tel. 290877) is on the same turn-off. A skyscraper by Nagarkot standards, with a 360° view from the roof. The budget rooms are basic, without the rustic charm of the other lodges. Common baths are downstairs and outside, without hot water, which flows only to attached bathrooms. Singles Rs.200. Doubles Rs.300, with bath (and carpeting, etc.) US$20.

All of the lodges have **restaurants** with unsurprising menus and moderate prices. **The Tea House,** just below the Club Himalaya, is a restaurant only, and a snazzy one at that, with tablecloths, cloth napkins, and plate-glass windows. Uniformed waiters serve Western breakfasts and Indian and Nepali curry and rice dishes (Rs.60-150, soft drinks Rs.30). The menu also includes an "If You Insist on Continental" section. A place to splurge after you've survived the bus ride.

SIGHTS

The hip thing to do in Nagarkot is watching the sun set behind the valley and getting up to watch it rise above the hills, bathing the mountain peaks in pink light. Bring an alarm clock if you don't want to miss the dawn—guest houses don't give the most reliable wake-up calls. Fall and winter are the best times for mountain-watching, but if you're lucky, a peak or two may peek through the clouds at other seasons. Walk up to the **Mahankal Shrine** for excellent views, or find out whether the **lookout tower,** an hour's walk south of the bus stop, past the army base, is operational. It can also be fun to explore the surrounding hillsides, although many visitors to Nagarkot enjoy loafing around their lodges more than anything.

■ Sankhu

Crouched in the eastern corner of the Kathmandu Valley beyond Boudha, Sankhu is a typically toppling Newari town surrounded by farmland. The hill above the town is crowned by the **Bajra Jogini Mandir** (also spelled Vajra Yogini), a temple that attracts both Buddhist and Hindu worshipers. The 2-km walk from town starts on a dirt road to the left of the bus stop. About halfway, the road continues to the right, while a stone-paved footpath leads straight ahead. The two meet up again at the base of the long, steep stairway to the top of the hill. It's a 15min. walk to the top.

The temple of the Tantric goddess Bajra Jogini was built in the 17th century, but its site is believed to have been a holy spot since ancient times. Some say that it was Bajra Jogini who convinced Manjushri to drain the water-filled Kathmandu Valley. The temple has three gilded roofs and an elaborately-worked door hiding the goddess's image from the public. On the way up, look for other small sculptures and shrines, carved stone spouts that gush cooling water, and, halfway up the stairs, a triangular stone serving as an image of Bhairab, to whom sacrifices are made.

Bus #4 (1hr., Rs.7) departs Ratna Park in Kathmandu as soon as it is full-to-overflowing. Sankhu can also be reached by **bicycle** (the road from Kathmandu is quite flat, and beyond Boudha, fairly pollution-free) or by foot, on the way down from Nagarkot. It is also possible to walk between Sankhu and Changu Narayan in the dry season. A couple of **cold shops,** one where the dirt road ends at the bottom of the stairs, are the only source of nourishment.

■ Budhanilkantha

Eight kilometers north of Kathmandu, Budhanilkantha lies en route to the highest point on the Kathmandu Valley's rim, **Shivapuri** (2732m). Its main attraction is the temple housing the stone **Sleeping Vishnu.** The town's name has nothing to do with the Buddha (*budha* means "old" here)—the name literally means "Old Blue-Throat," referring to Shiva, whose throat turned blue after he swallowed poison that threatened to destroy the earth. The connection here between Shiva and Vishnu is a mystical one: the water on which Sleeping Vishnu floats is said to be linked to the Lake Gosainkund, which Shiva created and drank from to cool his poisoned throat. Another version tells of the image of the snoozing Vishnu appearing in the lake.

The **Jalasaya Narayan** (Sleeping Vishnu) lies 5m long on a bed formed by the multi-headed snake Ananta, whose hooded heads act as a pillow and crown. The surrounding water represents the cosmic ocean in which Vishnu was suspended when a lotus grew from his navel, creating Brahma, the creator, who brought the universe into being. Unfortunately, this serene piece of stonework can only be viewed from afar, through the red-and-yellow fence that surrounds the water tank in which Vishnu floats. If you're lucky, a gate in the fence might be open, allowing a better view. Only Hindus are allowed inside, and only priests may walk on the statue to bathe it and cover it with marigolds in *puja*.

Aside from the Hindu creation myth, the sculpture has a mythology of its own. Believed to have been carved in the 7th or 8th century from a type of black stone that it is not found in the Valley, it seems to have been dragged to the site. Two other sleeping Vishnus (at Balaju and in a private section of the Old Royal Palace) were apparently created at the same time, but all three images were lost for some years. A farmer is said to have discovered the buried Vishnu in Budhanilkantha when he struck it with his plow, causing it to spurt blood. The king of Nepal never visits the temple, a practice stemming from a dream of the 17th-century King Pratap Malla of Kathmandu, in which he was warned he would die if he laid eyes on the image. Vishnu is said to awaken from his nap at the end of the monsoon, and a festival is held in late October or early November to celebrate the occasion.

Budhanilkantha can be reached by bus from Ratna Park in Kathmandu (#5, every 30min., 1hr., Rs 6), or by blue tempo from Rani Pokhari (#5, 45min, Rs.6). The temple is just north of the bus and tempo stop. There are a few simple eateries near the temple and even an international phone booth next to the bus stop. A fancy new resort is in the works thanks to the owners of the Kathmandu Guest House, but for now, the only accommodation is the **Mount Shivapuri Lodge** "Fantasy Hill" (tel. 370232). Follow the signs from town; they point the right way, but lie about the distance—the walk takes about 30 minutes, not 15. Only three simple mint-green bedrooms in mint condition. The common bath has an upright toilet and hot water. The lodge is beautifully situated among terraced fields, but isolated from anything else. A small menu of fried rice and noodles is available. Doubles US$6.

The Central Hills

Though the central hills are the most convenient mountains to Kathmandu, they are not widely touristed. Among the broad valleys that have burrowed themselves into the world's highest peak, that of Sagamartha ("Brow of the Ocean"). In addition to the Everest trek, there are three major treks in the central hills—Langtang, Helambu, and Gosaikund. These treks can be done on their own—each is distinctly defined by the landscape and its hill people. They can also be combined in sundry ways for variations in length, difficulty, and interests. The one thing they share (and guarantee) is a voyeuristic views of the mountains.

■ The Everest Trek

Forget that it will be the most tiring part of your holiday. Just remember that you are walking to the base camp of the mountain—Sagarmatha—the pride of the Nepalese people and the highest point on earth, a feat that will guarantee you a "wow" from everyone you meet back home. The Everest trek is almost a pilgrimage—the mountain's fame seems to be the main attraction. This is not to say that the Everest trek is a bad choice—the Solu Khumbu area on the way to Everest offers a unique terrain, and the people along the way—the Tamangs, Rais, Limbus, and Sherpas—are different from the people along the Annapurna trek, and hold many local festivals during Dasain time (in October—prime trekking season). In the main villages along the Everest trek, there are weekly Saturday markets, a tradition of Eastern Nepal in which people from far and wide come together to trade. You won't want to miss the opportunity of seeing the yeti scalp in **Khumjung,** and the new monastery in **Tengboche.** Historically, the Annapurna trek has been safer than the Everest trek. The Everest trek is steeper, longer, more difficult, and less crowded. It also rises to higher altitudes than the Annapurna trek, meaning a greater danger of altitude sickness. But this should by no means deter beginners from setting off on the journey that approaches the top of the world.

ROUTES

The length and conditions of the trek to Everest allow for many variations, but most trekkers choose between four routes. There are two trailheads for the Everest trek. One is the town of **Jiri,** accessible by road. From Jiri it is about a 14-day walk to the **base camp** and **Kala Pattar** ("Black Rock"), where trekkers turn around and head back. Another possible starting point is **Lukla,** a town with its own airstrip about halfway along the trail. The walk from Jiri to the base camp and back takes 28 days and covers about 300km. But if you fly to Lukla, walk up to the base camp, and walk back to Lukla to catch a flight to Kathmandu, the trek takes only about 14 days. Many travelers fly one way, either into or out of Lukla, for a 21-day trip. There are several other less-frequented routes which require more planning and consultation.

The stretch from Jiri to Lukla is in the region known as **Solu,** an inhabited area full of green hills and terraced fields. North of Lukla at the town of **Namche Bazaar** the trail enters the mountainous and sparsely populated **Khumbu** region, which roughly coincides with Sagarmatha National Park.

PRACTICAL INFORMATION

Electricity is becoming increasingly common on the Everest trek. Jiri, Junbesi, Kenja, Khari Khola, Lukla, Manidingma, Namche Bazaar, Salari, and Tengboche are all electrified. **Currency exchange** facilities are available at Rastriya Banijya Bank (which changes U.S. dollars and traveler's checks) in Namche Bazaar. Many of the lodges along the way will also accept U.S. dollars. Take small change from Kathmandu to spend along the way, for tea houses might not have change for large bills.

There are **telephones** in Jiri, Namche Bazaar, Tengboche, on the way to Thimi (power project office), and in the Kunde Hospital. There are **police** posts in Jiri, Kinja, Lukla, Namche Bazaar, and Tengboche. Most police offices and government posts also serve as **post offices.**

The best selection of **equipment** is in Kathmandu, but there are also rental stores in Lukla and Namche. During the trekking season, **food** can be found all the way to the Gorak Shep, the location of the highest lodge. There are no lodges in Kala Pattar or at the base camp. Off-season, food can only be found up to Namche, and it is necessary to carry your own provisions any further than that. You could get tired of eating roughly the same food every day for two weeks, so take some food with you—chocolate or other goodies that you can reward yourself with. Try the yak steak and other yak delicacies that you won't find anywhere else.

GETTING THERE

To start the Everest trek, one can either fly to Lukla or take the bus to Jiri. Both methods are adventures in themselves. Getting the bus or plane tickets to the starting point might be the biggest headache of the entire trek. The bus to Jiri is one of the few that still leaves from Kathmandu's old bus station in Ratna Park. The trip takes 11 hours and costs Rs.120 one-way. Buy your ticket the day before your trip and show up a half-hour early to load your bags. On the bus, crammed, squeezed, and numb, you might start wondering whether the trek to Everest is worth the bus ride to Jiri— but hang in there. The views of terraced fields and valleys will soothe you.

Three companies have flights to Lukla. **Everest Air** flies a Soviet hand-me-down helicopter to Lukla once a day (leaves Kathmandu 9:15am; leaves Lukla 7am). **RNAC** flies a plane to Lukla twice a day (leaves Kathmandu 7 and 9:10am; leaves Lukla 8:35 and 10:45am). **Asian Airlines** has a helicopter flight to Lukla every day (leaves Kathmandu 7am; leaves Lukla 9:30am). In the trekking season, more flights are added to and from Lukla based on demand. All flights are US$83 one-way, and all travel agencies charge the same commission. Baggage allowance is 20kg.

The flight is said to take 45 minutes. Due to the weather demon, which has apparently made Lukla its home, you are extremely lucky if your flight to or from Lukla leaves only a couple of hours late. You are lucky if your flight leaves on the scheduled day at all. This could mean many hours of waiting at the airport in Kathmandu or many days of waiting in Lukla. During the trekking season, there is excess demand for flights to Lukla; off-season, flights are canceled due to insufficient demand. Call your travel agent persistently to make sure your name is on the waiting list or to make sure your flight hasn't been canceled. If everything works out as planned, then you have had your month's share of good luck.

You could be stuck in Lukla for several days—so give yourself at least two days in Kathmandu from the scheduled arrival day in Kathmandu: don't plan anything important, like an international flight. And don't get violent when you realize that long hot bath will have to wait a few more days. The people working for the airlines and your fellow trekkers in Lukla can't do anything about it. On occasion, police have been flown to Lukla to control violent would-be passengers: once, trekkers pelted the RNAC office with stones!

■ Jiri

The bus ride from Kathmandu is tiring, so many trekkers spend the night in Jiri. Swiss aid donors have developed a special liking for Jiri, and as a result Jiri has what every Nepalese town would love—electricity, running water, a 25-bed hospital, a road to the outside world, and a telephone (that's it—one telephone). Although almost no tourists would come to Jiri if it were not a trailhead for the Everest trek, Jiri has a peaceful beauty of its own. Nepalese from Kathmandu love Jiri—the air, the view of the terraced land below, and of course, the modern facilities. Most of Jiri is laid out along the road that is its lifeblood—pumping in food, manufactured goods, and determined trekkers from Kathmandu. A seven-minute walk will take you from the from the bus park at the end of the road to the outskirts of Jiri, passing everything but the hospital, the cheese factory, and the technical school.

The only **telephone** in Jiri is outside Cherdung Lodge (tel. 049-20190). Calls can be made from 6am to 8pm. Calls to Kathmandu cost Rs.7 per minute (Sat. Rs.5 per min.). International calls will be charged for at least three minutes (Rs.500-750 for first 3min., Rs.150 per each additional min.). This place will take messages for guests staying in other hotels. A **pharmacy,** Jiri Medical Mall, is right at the bus park but has limited supplies and no doctor (open 5:30am-7pm). The **hospital** is a five-minute walk on the unpaved path from the bus park, and offers outpatient care 8am-2pm. The **police station** and **post office** are 4km away on the road from Kathmandu. Four buses leave Jiri for Kathmandu daily (5:30, 6:30, 8, 10am). Tickets cost Rs.120 and go on sale at 4pm the previous day. If you happen to be in Jiri on a Saturday, a weekly market is held on the hilltop of **Naya Bazaar,** about 30 minutes away by foot.

Walk away from the bus park along to choose among the many lodges and restaurants. **Cherdung Lodge** (doubles and triples Rs.90-500), **Sagarmatha Guide Lodge** (doubles and triples Rs.50-100), and **Hotel Jiri View** (rooms Rs.60-150) are cleaner and offer better service than most.

■ The Langtang and Helambu Treks

It is said that the Langtang Valley was discovered by a lama who stumbled into it while chasing a renegade yak; this story may be true. It is said that one has to go to Annapurna or Everest to do a real trek in Nepal; this story is certainly not true. The Langtang trek, the Helambu circuit, and the Gosaikund trek represent some of the best trekking Nepal has to offer. Done on their own as short treks, or combined to make a lengthier and more challenging trek, the experience they offer is flexible, diverse, and rich. Even though the treks in the Langtang regions aren't as popular as Annapurna and Everest, their easy accessibility from Kathmandu and their multiple permutations make them very convenient.

The first expedition to the Langtang region was led by Major H.W. Tilman in 1949. The Langtang area was declared the first Himalayan National Park of Nepal in 1971. Situated in the central Himalaya, it is the closest national park to Kathmandu, and is accessible year-round. The park borders Tibet to the north and east, while the park's southern border lies only 20 miles to the north of Kathmandu.

PRACTICAL INFORMATION

The only places with **electricity** in the Langtang and Helambu regions are Dhunche, Malemchi, and Sundarijal. The only **bank** is in Dhunche; it changes U.S. dollars, but not traveler's checks. Most lodges along the way will accept U.S. dollars. Remember to take small change on the trek, because the **tea houses** won't have change for large denominations. There are **police posts** only in Dhunche, Syabru, and Taramarang, but there are also **army posts** in the park which can be contacted for help. Since the only **medical facility** in the entire Langtang and Helambu region is in Dhunche, it is a good idea to have a first aid kit with you.

If you are trekking in Helambu in the rainy season, be prepared for the difficulties and dangers of muddy paths. When the number of tourists is low or when there is too much rain or snow, tea houses close down. Those planning to trek during the low season should contact a trekking agency in Kathmandu to make sure the tea houses are going to be open.

The price of food and lodging in the Langtang National Park is fixed by the park administration (the Helambu region is not part of the park), so choose an establishment based on cleanliness and friendliness. You shouldn't bargain on prices that are fixed by the administration. Park regulations forbid the use of firewood, and you are requested to ensure that your porters and guides use alternate fuel sources. If you plan to camp on your own, take a stove and sufficient fuel with you. For more information, see **Responsible Trekking** (p. 60).

GETTING THERE

The **bus** from Kathmandu to **Dhunche,** the classic trailhead for Langtang, leaves from the new bus terminal in Gongabu. Tickets go on sale at 8am the day before; the ticket counter is open 5:30am to 5:30pm. Two buses leave daily for Dhunche, at 7 and 7:45am. Tickets cost Rs.80. Only the 7am bus goes to Syaprubensi, and tickets cost Rs.100. The trip takes four hours to Trisuli, eight hours to Dhunche, and ten hours to Syaprubensi. On the way back, tickets can be purchased two days in advance from the counter at the Thakali Hotel in Dhunche.

The road is paved from Kathmandu to Trisuli, but from Trisuli to Dhunche, the road (built by the army) is only gravel. Past Dhunche, the road to Syaprubensi is not always passable. If you take the bus to Syaprubensi, you can start your trek there and save a day of walking.

There are two ways to reach **Sundarijal,** the starting point for the Helambu trek, from Kathmandu. From Ratna Park in Kathmandu, four **buses** leave every hour from 6am to 6:30pm (75min., Rs.6) for Sundarijal. The bus makes frequent stops along the way. No tickets are required; just show up. From 5am to 6pm, four buses (Rs.6) leave for Kathmandu every hour from the bus park in Sundarijal, which is where the road ends. You can also reserve a **taxi** from Thamel to Sundarijal (Rs.400-900; bargain until the driver agrees to a fare of about Rs.550).

To go through Ganja La Pass or through Gosaikund from Dhunche to Tharepati (or vice versa), a guide is necessary. Unlike the Everest and Annapurna treks, some sections of the Langtang trek can't be done by individual, unguided trekkers. However, the Helambu circuit, the conventional Langtang trek, and the trek to Gosaikund from Dhunche can be done on your own. If you do plan to go on any of these treks without a guide, remember that you will have to spend several days in Kathmandu planning and getting the right equipment. For more information, see **Planning a Trek** (p. 55).

THE LANGTANG TREK

The Langtang trek mixes two worlds, due to its physical proximity with both Kathmandu and the Himalaya. The region it traverses is sparsely inhabited but culturally and geographically diverse. The huge fluctuations in altitude within the Langtang region also make for a great variety of vegetation. Unlike the Helambu circuit, the Langtang trek is among mountains and glaciers, and offers great views of the Himalaya (which are covered during the cloudy monsoon). The Langtang valley is surrounded by peaks such as Dorje Lokpa (6966m), Gang Chhenpo (6388m), Lantang Lirung (7246m), and Naya Kargri (5846m). Langtang village (3429m) itself is quite Tibetan, with yaks and Tibetan-style architecture. Lodges along the trek are open twelve months a year.

The trek normally starts at Dhunche (1982m), the headquarters of Langtang National Park, and a day's bus ride from Kathmandu over a tattered road. Information on the park and the trek is available at the park entrance building at Dhunche. If you didn't pay your Rs.650 park entry fee in Kathmandu, you will have to pay it here. Dhunche offers some great views of the mountains. From Dhunche there are two options: one is the classic Langtang trek, which takes you to Kyanjin Gompa (3840m), through Syabru (2100m), Chongong (also known as Lama Hotel; 2500m), Ghora Tabela (3000m), and Langtang village. This route normally takes five nights, the first at Dhunche and the fifth at Kyanjin Gompa. There are tea houses along the way, so this trek can be done without carrying tents or food. At Kyanjin Gompa you can visit the cheese factory and the *gompa,* or take sidetrips to the glaciers to the north, the Langshiska Kharka valley (4080m), and the nearby mountain of Tsergo Ri (4800m). You can then retrace your steps back to Dhunche. The trail goes downhill on the way back, so you should be able to reach Dhunche from Kyanjin Gompa in two nights, spending the third night in Dhunche. The conventional Langtang trek is comparable in difficulty to the Annapurna trek. Except for the sidetrips around Kyanjin Gompa, none of it is over 4000m, and because the ascent to Kyanjin Gompa is gradual, few people have altitude problems.

THE HELAMBU TREK

The Helambu trek is becoming increasingly popular because it's close to Kathmandu, stays below 3500m (no heavy clothing or bulky winter gear!), is possible 12 months a year, and can be done in a week. The Helambu trek is fairly easy, but doesn't have nearly as good views as Everest, Annapurna, or Langtang. (The Helambu trek also doesn't offer an opportunity for you to be the first person to photograph the yeti—go to the Langtang or Everest if you are seeking fame and fortune.) Unlike the 11-hour bus ride to Jiri or the elusive flight to Lukla at the start of the Everest trek, one only has to take a 75-minute bus ride or a shorter train ride to Sundarijal, at the perimeter of the Kathmandu valley, to start the Helambu trek. There are many tea houses along the way, open year-round, so you don't need a tent or your own food. The Helambu Sherpas are different in their cultural practices from the Sherpas in the Solu Khumbu (Everest) region due to several centuries of Tamang and Langtang Tibetan influence.

Starting at Sundarijal (1350m; the name means "beautiful water"), 21km northeast of Kathmandu, the trek goes through Pati Bhanjyan and Khutumsang, begins a clockwise loop at Tharepati, and continues on to Malemchigaon and Tarke Gyang (2480m). From Tarke Gyang, there are two ways to proceed. The more popular route passes through villages such as Kakni, Thimbu, Kiul, and Mahenkal to Taramarang. From Taramarang, you can go to Pati Bhanjyan through Batache and Thakani, thus completing the loop. From Pati Bhanjyan, you can backtrack for the first time, retracing the first day of your trek, and returning to Kathmandu through Sundarijal in one day. This loop, the **Helambu circuit**, normally requires six nights, with stays at Pati Bhanjyang on the first and sixth nights. The alternative is to leave the circuit at Tarke Gyang and continue on to Shermathang (2625m)—a day's walk. From Shermathang you can go through Malemchi and Bahunpati to reach the Arniko Highway (the road that connects Kathmandu to Tibet) at Panchkhal. From Panchkhal, buses can take you back to Kathmandu. If you are able to hitch a ride on the back of a truck from Malemchi to Panchkhal, you can go from Shermathang to Kathmandu in one long day. If you can't get a ride in Malemchi then you will have to spend a night in a lodge in Malemchi and try to get a ride the next day or walk to Panchkhal. Few people have problems with altitude sickness on the Helambu trek, so unless you choose to go slowly, you should be able to do the Helambu circuit in six nights and its Malemchi mutation in five or six nights.

There are several other starting and ending points for the Helambu circuit, including Sankhu, Nagarkot, and even Panchkhal. These, however, are less frequented than the conventional circuit beginning and ending in Sundarijal.

THE GOSAIKUND TREK

A variation of the classic Langtang trek is a trek to the Gosaikund Lake, which is believed to have been created by Lord Shiva. This lake is holy to both Hindus and Buddhists, attracting pilgrims from the entire Subcontinent. A Hindu pilgrimage here during the festival of Janai Purnima in August was attended by 15,000 pilgrims in 1995. The trek to Gosaikund is more difficult than the conventional Langtang trek or the Annapurna trek, and requires some steep climbing. The trail rises from Dhunche (1982m) to Gosaikund (4400m) in two days, so AMS can be a problem. For information on AMS, see **Trekking: Health and Safety,** p. 58.

Take the day-long bus ride to Dhunche from Kathmandu. The first day's trek, requiring steep climbing at times, will take you to **Sing Gompa** at **Chandan Bari** (3250m), where in addition to the *gompa* there is a cheese factory. The second day's trek takes you to Gosaikund Lake. Some of the climbs on the way are steep. At Laurebina Yak (3930m) there is a view of the Himalaya from Annapurna in the west to

Langtang Lirung in the east (actually not far north of Gosaikund Lake). The first lake along the trail to Gosaikund is Saraswati Kund; the second lake is called Bhairav Kund. After passing these two, you'll finally reach Gosaikund, the largest of the three lakes. Sometimes heavy snowfall will make it impossible to go from Sing Gompa to Gosaikund. People have been killed in heavy snows here, so don't take unnecessary risks. Consider taking a guide or a porter. On the trail to Gosaikund, except during the monsoon and winter, several lodges are open.

From Gosaikund, you can either walk back to Dhunche in two days and catch a bus to Kathmandu, or walk on to Tharepati to connect the Gosaikund trek with the Helambu trek. The trail from Gosaikund to Tharepati demands some steep climbing in some sections and crosses the 4610-meter **Lauribina Pass.** This route takes two days; most people stop at Ghopte for the night. There are a few lodges between Gosaikund and Tharepati. The trail is confusing so a guide is very helpful. Even a little snow makes some sections of the trail very risky, if not outright impossible. So if you plan to go from Gosaikund to Tharepati, it is best to consult a trekking agency in Thamel. You will also take precautions against AMS (see **Health and Safety,** p. 58). Several people have died on this route so be particularly cautious. If you have guides or porters with you while crossing the Lauribina Pass, make sure they, too, are properly clothed and equipped.

From Tharepati, you can continue on with the Helambu circuit, making a loop through Malemchigaon. Another option from Tharepati is to walk straight to Sundarijal through Khutumsang and Pati Bhanjyang. The Gosaikund trek can also be done backwards, starting at Sundarijal, following the Helambu circuit until Tharepati, making a left turn to Ghopte, and continuing on to Gosaikund.

CROSSING THE GANJA LA PASS

The Langtang trek and the Helambu trek are connected by the Ganja La Pass (5106m), one of the most difficult passes in Nepal. Many trekkers have run into life-threatening situations and some have died trying to cross this pass. Before attempting it, you will have to prepare for a much more difficult journey than the Helambu and Langtang treks themselves. There are many trails across the pass, so a guide is essential. Even a little snow or bad weather makes the pass very difficult, if not impossible; the pass is effectively closed from December to March. The pass can be crossed in either direction, from Kyanjin Gompa to Tarke Gyang or vice versa. You will have to carry your tents and food for the four-day crossing; you will also have to acclimatize before proceeding. If you are considering crossing the pass, get in touch with a trekking agency in Kathmandu. For your sake and theirs, make sure your guides and porters are properly clothed and equipped.

The Western Hills

Modern-day Nepal was conceived in the hills west of Kathmandu, where 250 years ago King Prithvi Narayan Shah of Gorkha had a vision of a united country. The central Himalaya, dominated by mountains such as Macchapuchhre and the Annapurna range, provide a magnificent backdrop to this part of Nepal—they have made it one of the country's most popular regions for tourism. Huddled by the side of Phewa Lake at the center of the region, Pokhara is the base for Nepal's most popular trekking routes and for the increasingly popular activity of whitewater rafting. Farther south, Tansen, the formal capital of the kingdom of Palpa, is one of the few places outside of Kathmandu Valley that is rich in Nepalese tradition and architecture.

■ Mugling

There's one pervasive theme in Mugling—buses. Without the buses, there would be no Mugling; it's where buses fuel their tanks and passengers their tummies. Almost every bus from Kathmandu stops here (now only a 4-hr. trip due to new roads).

At the bottom of several hills, Mugling summons the meeting of the Trisuli and Mershyangidi Rivers. A 10-minute stroll takes you from one end of town to another; the road then splits in two directions toward Pokhara and Narayanghat.

The only **telephone** in Mugling is in Green Mill Restaurant, on the left toward Kathmandu, at the center of town (tel. (056) 29424; open daily 6am-1am). The **transportation office**, at the junction of the roads from Narayanghat and Pokhara, has extensive information on the bus destinations and schedules (open daily 6am-7pm). Mugling's only **medical services** in the "Medical Mall" are also at this junction (open daily 7am-11pm). The **police station** is on the right as you walk down the road to Pokhara. The **post office** is on the right of the uphill that starts the road to Narayanghat (open Sun.-Thurs. 10am-5pm, Fri. 10am-3pm).

Almost every house in Mugling doubles as a restaurant and/or lodge, but don't expect menus, attached bathrooms, air-conditioning, or running hot water. **Hotel New Bijoya,** to the right towards the road to Kathmandu, has a bit of a leg up on the others (Rs.150 for the double, Rs.260 for each of 3 triples; hot water buckets Rs10). **Roopsi Restaurant, Dipa Restaurant,** and **New Bijoya Restaurant** are the best places to eat. Every restaurant serves the same food, though the Roopsi carries the only (handwritten) menus in town. Rs.75 should buy a good lunch or dinner.

Hotel du Mugling is like a piece of Kathmandu that was misplaced in Mugling. A 15-minute walk from Mugling on the road to Pokhara, this luxury hotel has 10 doubles, each equipped with attached bath (with hot and cold water) and fan. The beds are soft, the balconies offer a gentle breeze, the soothing sights and sounds of the rippling rivers are nearby. English is spoken and the restaurant (open 7am-9pm) is better than anything else around. Check-out noon. Singles US$25. Doubles US$35. Extra bed US$9. "American breakfast" US$5; lunch or dinner US$8. There's an additional 10% government tax on all prices. Contact: Hotel de l'Annapuna, Durbar Marg, Kathmandu (tel. 225242, 221711; fax 225236).

■ Gorkha

Gorkha is in the process of becoming a tourist destination. But while the museum and park (dedicated to Prithivi Narayan Shah) are being completed, and better hotels constructed, there isn't much to do in this historically important town. Known as the base from which Prithivi Narayan Shah, a direct ancestor of the present King of Nepal, set off to conquer the Kathmandu Valley and a huge chunk of present day Nepal, Gorkha preserves its history in the hilltop Gorkha Durbar, the former palace of the Shah dynasty. Situated at the end of a motorable road, Gorkha is today the link between many villages and the outside world, one of the starting points for the Annapurna trek.

ORIENTATION

Gorkha has unintentionally evolved into three distinct sections. The newest part of town ends at the bus park, the end of the pitched road, and is only 15 years old. The second section, which dates back about 100 years, starts with the unpitched road and winds uphill toward a set of stone steps. The oldest section exists at the end of the stone stairway, at the very top of the hill where the Gorkha Durbar lies.

PRACTICAL INFORMATION

Currency Exchange: Rastriya Banijya Bank (tel. 20155) is the only bank in Gorkha and is at the very end of the older part of town. Walk to the end of the narrow street then ask for directions. Exchanges most major currencies and traveler's checks. Open Sun.-Thurs. 10:30am-3pm, Fri. 10:30am-12:30pm.

Buses: Pritwi Rajmarga Bus Syndicate, at the bus park, marked by red sign. Open daily 5am-6:30pm. To: Kathmandu (6 per day, 6:15am-2:30pm, 5hr., Rs.85; less comfortable bus 7:30am, Rs.55); Pokhara (2 per day, 6 and 9:15am, 4hr., Rs.50); Birganj (4 per day, 6:30-11:20am, 8hr., Rs.76); Narayanghat (7 per day, 8:45am-2:50pm, 2hr., Rs.45; slower, less comfortable bus 2:50pm, Rs.30); Sunauli (7am, 8hr., Rs.90).

Telephones: Many shops and hotels will place international calls but the **Nepal Telecommunications booth** is cheaper (tel. 20122, 20111). Walk down the unpitched road from the bus stop about 50m and look for the yellow sign on the right. Calls to Kathmandu and Pokhara Rs.6 per min.; international calls Rs.576 for first 3min. and Rs.144 per additional min. Open daily 7am-7pm.

Hospital: Tel. 20208. Walk 5min. down from the bus park, take a left at the "Save the Children USA" sign, and walk uphill for 5min. The hospital is yellow with red lines. Out-patient care Sun.-Fri. 10am-2pm; emergency open 24hr. There are several medical stores (marked with a Red Cross sign) along the road to the bus park.

Police: The **police station** (tel. 20155) is a 7-min. walk from the bus park. Walk downhill for 5min., turn right at the blue "police" sign down the unpitched road, and take another right; the police station is the white building straight ahead.

Post Office: At the end of the older section of Gorkha. Walk right through the narrow street, past 3 stone water taps. The post office is the white-walled, rock, 2-story building. Open Sun.-Thurs. 10am-5pm, Fri. 10am-3pm.

Telephone Code: 064.

ACCOMMODATIONS AND FOOD

There are several lodges at the bus park itself but the better ones are only a short walk down the road.

Hotel Gorkha Prince (tel. 20131). Walk down from the bus park 100m; the hotel, marked by a red sign board, is to the left. Managed by 2 guys who previously ran a similar establishment in Pokhara, their experience shows! Tidy common room upstairs has 24-hr. Star TV. Room service available from rooftop restaurant. Fans, mosquito mats, and an extra bed are available free of charge. Check-out noon. In season: doubles Rs.200, with bath (with 24-hr. hot water) Rs.300. Doubles Rs.100, with bath Rs.200. Laundry Rs.5-15 per item.

Hotel Gorkha Bisauni (tel. 20107). Walk down the road 400m and follow the blue sign board to the left along an unpitched road 75m. Rooms with attached bath have mosquito mats; others get green mosquito incense. The ordinary, bench-filled restaurant is open 6am-9pm. Check-out noon. In season: doubles with bath Rs.300, with fan and better bath Rs.400, with the best bath in Gorkha Rs.500. Off-season prices reduced by Rs.100. Laundry Rs.5 per item.

Hill Top Restaurant (tel. 20181), at the bus park. Sit at an outdoor table under an umbrella, sip beer, and get a bird's eye view of the hub-bub of the bus park. With luck, you'll see a buffalo chase sheep being unloaded from the tops of buses. Open daily 6am-9:30pm.

Gorkha Prince Rooftop Restaurant, on (surprisingly enough) the roof of Hotel Gorkha Prince. Extensive menu featuring Italian, Chinese, Indian, and Nepali dishes. Open daily 5:30am-10:30pm.

SIGHTS

A 45-minute walk through the older section of Gorkha and up the stone stairway will take you to the hill-crowning **Gorkha Durbar,** where Prithivi Narayan Shah, the unifier of Nepal and a direct ancestor of the present king, was born in 1722 and crowned in 1742. After the Gorkhali army set out from Durbar to capture the Kathmandu Valley and eventually unify Nepal. Prithivi Narayan never returned to Gorkha. Instead, he established his capital city in Nuwakot in 1744, before moving it to Kathmandu after his final victory in 1768. The Gorkha Durbar is thought to have been built eight generations earlier around 1609.

Gorkha was ignored by the Shah Dynasty until 1958 when King Mahendra, the father of the present King Birendra, showed his face. In the more than 200 years of royal absence, the same families of Hindu priests continued to perform religious functions at the temples in the Durbar. The priests at the palace today are direct descendants of those who served during Prithivi Narayan's rule and earlier.

Leather shoes, belts, and cameras are not allowed inside the palace compound; as there is no repository for these items, leave them behind in Gorkha. Most of the palace compound is open to the general public, but some are restricted to Hindus, so ask the policeman on duty. The main temple and palace aren't open to the general public, but Prithivi Narayan's throne can be seen from an "eye" window. Also note the miniature statue and bull of Pashupatinath, farther to the right.

The Himalaya hover in happy hues from this hilltop. Here, you see more of the mountains than from Pokhara, but there's an even better view from the antenna-topped hill another half hour along the stone stairway. If there are no clouds, you'll be lucky enough to experience exactly the same view that one farsighted Gorkhali looked lustfully at more than two and a half centuries ago.

Just above the bus park is the **Tallo Durbar Palace,** which was built between 1835 and 1839 by King Rajendra B. Shah in a failed attempt to lure his elder son away from Kathmandu and from succession. A museum park honoring Prithivi Narayan is presently under construction around this palace and garden and expected to open to the general public sometime in 1997.

■ Pokhara

Nepal's biggest tourist destination outside of the Kathmandu Valley, Pokhara is sunk in a subtropical valley surrounded by lofty peaks and some of the world's most staggering mountain views. Pokhara Valley, like Kathmandu Valley, once collected the region's rain in a pool of water. Today, three small lakes—Phewa, Begnas, and Rupa remain. The valley's name derives from the Nepali word for pond, "pokhari." Stores of sand, gravel, and stone swim beneath the valley's topsoil and make parts of Pokhara agriculturally unproductive. The site of Pokhara was largely uninhabited because of endemic malaria and smallpox. The Gurungs, the people of the region, lived on the hilltops surrounding the valley. Only when Newari traders settled in Pokhara, trafficking salt between Kathmandu, Bandipur, and Dhankuta, did the city begin to rise on the banks of the Seti ("Milk") River. They built the Bindyabasini Temple, by far the oldest structure in Pokhara—thought to date from the 16th century. Tony Hagen, who went to Mustang in 1959, is credited by some as the first trekker in the Annapuna region. However, the tourism office has unearthed a traveler as far back as 1899, a certain Ekai Kawagachi, who is believed to have said, "In all my travels in the Himalayas I saw no scenery so enchanting as that which captured me in Pokhara." When Queen Elizabeth II visited Nepal in 1960, Her Majesty required a vehicle. When the front of her plane opened up and a car was driven out, there was tremendous excitement among the people of Pokhara—the plane had given birth not only to a car, but to a newfound interest in the region!

Development began only with the construction of two highways in the 1970s—one connecting Pokhara to Kathmandu, the other to India. As a result, Pokhara was the "hidden valley" until the 1970s when tourists and then Nepalese flocked to see the natural delights. Nowhere else is there such an abrupt change in altitude: from Pokhara to the tip of Annapurna I (the world's 10th highest mountain), a distance of only 48km, the land clambers up nearly 7200m (900-8091m). The sky, which appears cracked into white fragments in the north, is enough to make travelers blink a few times and question their depth perception. The first tourists who arrived in the 1970s were dizzied indeed, and with heads bent staring at the skyline they set up camp here. Word of the new "discovery" reached Kathmandu and spread quickly, turning this valley bazaar town into a tourist limboland. Now rooftop restaurants and souvenir shops are strewn along the banks of Phewa Tal, Nepal's second-largest lake, and the repetition of colored signs and glass is starting to rival the mountains as a dizzying

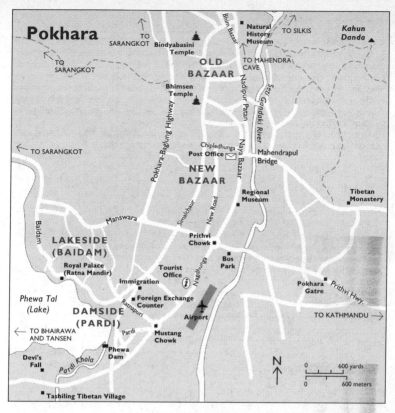

Pokhara

TO SARANGKOT
Bindyabasini Temple
TO SARANGKOT
Bhim Bazaar
Natural History Museum
TO SILKIS
Kahun Danda
OLD BAZAAR
TO MAHENDRA CAVE
Bhimsen Temple
Nadipur Patan
Setu Gandaki River
TO SARANGKOT
Pokhara-Baglung Highway
Chipledhunga
Post Office
Naya Bazaar
Mahendrapul Bridge
NEW BAZAAR
Regional Museum
Tibetan Monastery
Manswara
Baidam
Simalchaur
New Road
LAKESIDE (BAIDAM)
Prithvi Chowk
Royal Palace (Ratna Mandir)
Tourist Office
Bus Park
Immigration
Nadhunga
Pokhara Gatre
Prithvi Hwy.
Phewa Tal (Lake)
Ramapuri
Foreign Exchange Counter
Airport
TO KATHMANDU →
DAMSIDE (PARDI)
TO BHAIRAWA AND TANSEN
Pardi
Mustang Chowk
Devi's Fall
Pardi Khola
Phewa Dam
N
0 600 yards
0 600 meters
Tashiling Tibetan Village

vision. Now an important commercial and administrative center for Nepal's Western Development Region, Pokhara remains embedded in the mountains, and it is the starting point for some of Nepal's most popular treks.

ORIENTATION

Pokhara's smallish size makes it relatively easy to navigate. **Phewa Tal** (the lake) and **Pardi** (the dam) orient the whole town, and tourists gather on the low grounds by these bodies of water. Just about all the traveler's needs can be met in **Lakeside** or **Damside**. The residential and non-tourist part of town is higher up and away from the lake; its backbone is the continuation of the Siddhartha Highway from India. Under various names it forms a great north-south arc through the city. At **Prithivi Chowk** it meets the **Prithvi Highway** from Kathmandu and starts the city center; there is a bus stop here and a statue of Prithvi Narayan Shah in the roundabout. Farther north, the main road comes to the **Mahendra Pul** area, which is the heart and history of the city, and the center of the Pokhara bazaar.

Lakeside now overshadows Damside both in size and popularity. The **Nepal Grindlays Bank** is the unofficial center of Lakeside, which extends to the tourist catering businesses by the bus stop or the airport. Lakeside is a 15-minute walk from one end to the other. The maps posted at Pokhara's many corners have "you are here" markers and make excellent navigational tools.

NEPAL

PRACTICAL INFORMATION

Tourist Office: (tel. 20028). A short walk from the entrance of the airport and a 20-min. cycle ride from Lakeside. Free maps, brochures, and information. Some tourist officers are knowledgeable and speak English. Open Sun.-Thurs. 10am-5pm, Fri. 10am-3pm; from mid-Nov. to mid-Feb. Sun.-Thurs. 10am-4pm, Fri. 10am-3pm.

Budget Travel: More than 40 travel agencies are based in Lakeside or Damside, many of which are associated with the hotels and lodges. Services and prices vary little between agencies—visit more than one to find the best deal. Most open 6am-10pm during the tourist season and 8am-8pm off-season.

Currency Exchange: Lakeside and Damside each have half a dozen authorized currency exchange counters and a bank. Most accept major currencies and currency traveler's checks, as well as Visa and MasterCard. **Ambassador Money Changer** (tel. 22163), at the center of Lakeside, also accepts American Express. Open daily 7am-8pm. **Nepal Grindlays Bank** (tel. 20102, open Sun.-Thurs. 9:45am-3pm, Fri. 9:45am-12:30pm), at the center of Lakeside, sends personal checks from many countries for collection.

Immigration Office: (tel. 21167). A 20-min. bike ride or Rs.30-40 taxi ride. Follow the road out from Lakeside. At the intersection after there are no longer any tourist establishments, go straight. At the next intersection, make a sharp right; the immigration office is about 50m to the left. Takes care of visa extensions (US$1 per day), Annapurna Conservation Area entry fees (Rs.650), and trekking permits (US$5 per week for the first 4 weeks and US$10 each additional week). Applications are accepted Sun.-Thurs. 10:30am-1pm, Fri. 10am-noon; Nov. 17-Feb. 13 Sun.-Thurs. 10:30am-12:30pm; permits can be picked up Sun.-Thurs. 3-5pm, Fri. 2-3pm; Nov.17-Feb.13 Sun.-Thurs. 3-4pm. Two passport-size photos and a passport must be deposited for trekking permit applications to be picked up along with the permit later. Those who don't want to hire a cab or bike to the immigration office and stand in a queue can have a travel agency do the necessary work for them. Trekking permits have a service charge of Rs.50 per week, visa extensions Rs.100 per week. For same-day service go to the agencies before 9am.

Telephones: Just about every hotel and lodge has international calling facilities and Lakeside and Damside are teeming with 1-room **"communication" shops** which usually charge less—calls to Kathmandu Rs.180-200 per min. Prices are proportional to how fancy the facility is and how many clocks announcing time in yet fancier cities hang on its walls.

Trekking Information: Annapurna Conservation Area Project **(ACAP) Information Centre,** near Nirula's at the center of Lakeside. Look for a black-and-yellow sign board that says "Trekkers Information Centre." Free and impartial information on ACAP and general advice on treks in the Annapurna region, this center is the most authoritative source of information on treks in the Annapurna region. Cool maps and books for sale and several free pamphlets. Open Sun.-Fri. 10am-5pm. **HRA** (tel. 23318), right next to the immigration office. Offers information on altitude sickness and 1hr. programs on AMS (in season, daily 2pm). Open Sun.-Fri. 10am-5pm.

Airport: The airport is between the bus park and the section of the lake where subtropical tourist jungles grow. Cab rides from the airport to Lakeside are fixed (either Rs.80 or Rs.100—depending on how far into the tourist jungle you go). Cab rides to the airport cost Rs.40-50 and bargaining is fair game. A newer airport is under construction but the opening date keeps being pushed back into 1997. For now, settle for a very basic airport with minimal facilities. Everest Air, Necon Air, Nepal Airways, and RNAC have daily flights. To: Kathmandu (10 per day, 8:30am-3:15pm, US$61); Jomsom (3 per day, 6:30am, US$50); Manang (8:20am, US$50). Additional flights are added or canceled according to demand.

Buses: The bus park is an exotic soup of mud, garbage, various fauna, and recycled Bay of Bengal water. Cab rides from the bus park to Lakeside/Damside cost Rs.50-100. Bargain if there is only 1 taxi; if there are more, ask every driver to name his best price—the auction should drive prices down. A cab ride to the bus park from Lakeside/Damside costs Rs.40-50. The bus park is a 25-min. bike ride from Lakeside and a 20-min. bike ride from Damside. To get tickets, go right into the bus park; at the center there are 2 rooms resembling counters. Both are open daily 5am-7pm and one has a phone (tel. 20272). To ensure that you get a seat, go 1 day before to buy tickets. To: Birganj (6 per day, 5:40-10:20am, 8hr., Rs.99); Gorkha (1-2 per day, 7 and 9am, 4hr., Rs.49); Kathmandu (8 per day, 5-10:55am, 8hr., Rs.82); Narayanghat (12 per day, 9:50am-4pm, 5hr., Rs.52); Sunauli (7 per day, 5-9:30am, 8hr., Rs.105); Bhairahawa (11 per day, 5am-10:55pm, 8½hr., Rs.81; buses from here to Lumbini); Butwal (15 per day, 9:30am-5pm, 8hr., Rs.71); Tansen (2 per day, 7am and 12:40pm, 6hr., Rs.60). The travel agencies at Lakeside/Damside have a committee that operates more comfortable and more expensive buses from area hotels. Buses depart 6-9am to Narayanghat (Rs.200), Kathmandu (Rs.250), and Sunauli (Rs.200). Off-season prices are lower. Buses are added or canceled according to demand.

Local Transportation: Bikes are probably the best way to get around—when it isn't raining, that is. More than half a dozen bike rental shops are in the Lakeside and Damside (Rs.8-15 per hr., Rs.30-50 per day; motorbikes Rs.100 per hr., Rs.350-400 per day). When biking, remember that Pokhara slopes down towards the lake, making for ugly uphill but delightful downhill rides. Even the old-style **cabs** in Pokhara can do the job. Cab fares rise and bargaining power falls in season. Cab fares are hiked up after 7pm and on Sat. when many drivers brake for a break. Destinations such as the bus park, the airport and Mahendra Pul from Lakeside/Damside cost Rs.40-50 full or Rs.10 shared. Few tourists ever use the local **bus** service. A bus leaves Bahrai Chowk, the huge tree next to Moondance and Hotel Hungry-Eye, for every major location in Pokhara city (every 30min., under Rs.5). Ask locals for specifics about the bus system.

Luggage Storage: Most hotels and lodges offer luggage storage for Rs.5-10 (free off-season) and safe box storage free of charge. **Hotel the Rainbow,** near Grindlays Bark in Lakeside, will store luggage for free even in the tourist season.

Market: The Lakeside/Damside area carries most of the shopping services, including some pharmacy style shops with computerized billing systems. Pokhara locals hardly ever venture to Lakeside for shopping; they shop in the less expensive **Mahendra Pul** area.

English Bookstore: Lakeside bookshops differ in size of collection but not much in price. Most have used and new paperbacks, TinTin and Asterix comics, tourist guidebooks, and even some hardcover books. **Okinawa Book Store** (open 8am-10pm) and **Pay & Save** (tel. 23153; open 6am-11pm), both located in the center of Lakeside, have relatively large collections of books.

Pharmacy: The half-dozen small pharmacies in Lakeside and Damside carry first-aid material for trekking and have doctors available mornings and/or evenings.

Hospital/Medical Services: Most hotels and lodges can recommend a doctor or hospital. Most pharmacies on Lakeside and Damside have a part-time doctor available. **Barahi Medical Hall** (tel. 22862, open 6am-9pm) in the center of Lakeside has a doctor available 4-6pm. **Gandaki Hospital** (tel. 20066) is a 15-min., Rs.50-60 taxi ride from Lakeside and has Western doctors.

Police: The **police station** (tel. 21087) is a 10-min. cycle ride from the center of Lakeside. Past Hotel Kantipur, take a right at a blue sign board. The station is the white building about 100m down the unpitched road. The small **police post** at the entrance of the camping grounds at the end of Lakeside is open 24hr.

Post Office: The **main post office,** on the main street in Mahendra Pul, a 40-min. bike ride or a Rs.10-50 taxi ride. Ask locals for directions to this 1-story, white and red house marked "Western Regional Postal Directorate." A small 1-room "post office" at the beginning of Lakeside offers registered mail services. Come out of Lakeside, make a left turn at the first major intersection (Hotel Saino sign) and go about 200m to stone house with a sign ("Pardi Bandh Area Post Office") and a red letter box. Both post offices are open Sun.-Thurs. 10am-5pm, Fri. 10am-3pm; registered mail Sun.-Thurs. 10am-2:30pm, Fri. 10am-12:30pm. Most bookstores in Lakeside and Damside sell stamps and post letters.

Telephone Code: 061.

ACCOMMODATIONS

Do you *dam* it or do you *lake* it? Some time ago, most of the better establishments were in Damside, but in recent years development has transformed Lakeside into a haven for travel agents, bookstores, money changers, souvenir stores, cool restaurants, and entertainment opportunities. Lakeside is now the more convenient option. A 25-minute walk away, Damside is quieter, smaller, less tourist-jungle-like, a little less expensive, and more scenic.

When you get off the bus or come out at the airport, you will undoubtedly be the object of a bidding competition between young men peddling hotels. Ignore them, get into a cab, and go towards Damside or Lakeside. To select a hotel without the hassle, first have a quick bite at a restaurant and ask them to watch your pack while you hunt. Noon is check-out time at all hotels.

Lakeside

Hotel the Trans Himalaya (tel. 20917). Make a right turn next to Grindlays Bank at the center of Lakeside. Marble stairs, carved handrails, natural light, and fresh air create a luxurious atmosphere. Rooms are bigger and better furnished than any hotel in its price range, and new bathrooms have eye-catching tiles. One of the tallest buildings in Lakeside, the roof affords lake and mountain views and a cool breeze. Fans, 24-hr. hot and cold water in attached bathrooms, laundry service, free luggage storage, and mosquito coils upon request. Restaurant (open 7-11am and 4-10pm) has a large menu. Singles with bath Rs.250-300. Doubles Rs.150, with bath Rs.300-400. Triples with bath Rs.300-400. Off-season: singles with bath Rs.200. Doubles Rs.100, with bath Rs.250. Triple with bath Rs.250.

Pushpa Guest House (tel. 20332), behind Once Upon a Time at center of Lakeside. This yellow-painted establishment is well-furnished—carpets, closets, and mirrors. Clean toilets and the not-on-the-street-but-very-close location makes this guest house a good value for money. All rooms have fans, mosquito protection coils upon request, 24-hr. hot and cold water in bathrooms, laundry service, and free luggage storage. Singles Rs.100, with bath Rs.200. Doubles Rs.150, with bath Rs.300. Triples Rs.200, with bath Rs.350. Off-season: singles with bath Rs.150. Doubles Rs.100, with bath Rs.200. Triples Rs.150, with bath Rs.250.

Avocado Hotel (tel. 21183), behind Once Upon a Time. Located in the center of Lakeside, but away from the often noisy street. The views from the rooftop make for a great photo shoot. Friendly staff and well-furnished rooms with fans, mosquito coils upon request, 24-hr. hot and cold water in bathrooms, laundry service, and breakfast 7-10am. Doubles Rs.200, with bath Rs.250, with better mountain views Rs.500. Off-season: doubles Rs.80, with bath Rs.150, with view Rs.200-300.

Butterfly Lodge (tel. 22892). Make a right turn at Pyramid Restaurant, then continue 100m. A quiet garden lodge, the jungle of Lakeside seems far away. With lots of open space, the breeze is able to breathe right into the rooms. The rooftop views of the lake and mountains are pristine. Most rooms have fans, mosquito nets available, 24-hr. hot and cold water in bathrooms, laundry service, basic menu, and free luggage storage. Attractive bathroom tiles. Doubles Rs.150-200, with bath Rs.200-250. Off-season: Rs.100, with bath Rs.150.

Alka Guest House (tel. 23357), in the center of Lakeside. Admire the aesthetics of Alka: bright and clean building with fancy wooden handrails and marbled features. A tall building makes for wide views. Rooms are well-furnished. Fans, clean bathrooms with 24-hr. hot and cold water, free mosquito protection, laundry service, free luggage storage, breakfast available 6-11am. Main drawback is pollution from the street (noise and otherwise). Singles Rs.250, with bath Rs.550. Doubles Rs.250, with bath Rs.600. Triples with bath Rs.650. Off-season: singles Rs.150, with bath Rs.300. Doubles Rs.150, with bath Rs.350. Triples with bath Rs.450.

Hotel Matterhorn. Turn after Moondance; a 1-min. walk. Recently renovated, it offers 9 doubles with classy wooden beds and yet classier curtains. Clean common bathrooms have 24-hr. hot and cold water. Mosquito protection, laundry service, free luggage storage, and breakfast are available. Doubles Rs.200. Off-season Rs.125-150.

Damside

Victoria Guest House (tel. 22920), on main road of Damside. Serene lodgings with a great view, green plants, and generous furnishings, this guest house is a very good value. All rooms have fans, mosquito coils upon request, free luggage storage, but no laundry. Bathrooms have 24-hr. hot and cold water. Restaurant open 7am-9pm. Doubles Rs.350, with bath Rs.500. Off-season: doubles Rs.250, with bath Rs.300.

Super Lodge (tel. 21861), off of main road in Damside. This place has neat bathrooms, a quiet atmosphere, and 9 good value rooms. Fans, bathrooms with 24-hr. hot and cold water, mosquito coils upon request, laundry service, free baggage storage, and restaurant (open 7am-11pm). Singles Rs.150, with bath Rs.200. Doubles Rs.200, with bath Rs.350. Triples Rs.200, with bath Rs.500. Off-season: singles and doubles Rs.100, with bath Rs.150. Triples Rs.150, with bath Rs.200.

Camping Ground (tel. 21688). Near the end of Lakeside, make a left turn, 50m to the right. Bordering the lake with unobstructed views of the mountains, the location of Pokhara's only campground is ideal. Quality has recently been improved by private ownership. The shower has cool tiles and even a mirror, but the toilet is very ordinary. Despite the improved lighting, a flashlight is till necessary. Check-out 6pm. Rs.40 per tent. Hot showers Rs.50, cold showers Rs.30.

FOOD

Restaurants battle to win over your palate with delicious *puja*. As a result, some come up with delectable delicacies at incredible values. Lakeside establishments attract tourists galore, often reaching capacity during season. Many places serve up beer, snacks, and cocktails at reduced prices during Happy Hours, which are strategically arranged before dinner time. Food and fun go hand in hand here—many restaurants provide entertainment to attract more business. Some cheaper places can be found away from the center of Lakeside; otherwise prices are fairly uniform. Most restaurants boast a specialty, but also serve the usual menu variety. Many shops and stalls sell fresh fruit, trekkers' "food," expensive Swiss chocolate, and hot-out-of-the-oven bread.

Moondance, at the beginning of the center of Lakeside, next to Hotel Hungry-Eye. Named after a Van Morrison song, Moondance is reputed to play the best and most diverse music in Lakeside—and they'll honor your requests. The setting is *au naturel*—bamboo furniture, pillars, ceiling, and light shades, a brick fireplace, green plants sprouting from hardened-mud pots, a hay roof, and decorative yak tails. The combined effect is relaxing, comfortable, and addictive. Scrabble, chess, and backgammon free in the afternoons. Try their specialty pizza and be creative with the mix-n-match toppings. Most entrees Rs.85-145, most sides Rs.45-70. Beer available. Open daily 8am-11pm.

Nirula's (tel. 20779), at the center of Lakeside; look for the sign. This is *the* "fast food" joint in Lakeside—most dishes are ready in under 10min. Serving pizzas, burgers, footlongs, sundaes, and more than 25 flavors of ice cream, this Indian chain is great for a cheap bite. Open daily 10am-10pm.

7 Eleven (tel. 21565), next to the Grindlays Bank at the center of Lakeside. The name is its only Western feature. Smells of Indian dishes and sounds of Hindi and Nepali songs. Many entrees come with a generous helping of rice. The 4 musicians play film, popular, and classical songs. You can request your favorite tunes, just like the emperors of the past, except that their musicians didn't have keyboards or electric guitars. Main dishes Rs.90-150, starters Rs.50-80, beer Rs.100, cocktails Rs.100. Open daily 10am-10pm.

Maya Pub, just before the center of Lakeside. Tourists flock here, packing it to capacity even in the off-season. They play your requests and serve 2-for-the-price-of-1 cocktails during Happy Hour (5-9pm). Continental dishes are good, but tasty Mexican food is better. Beer Rs.80-85, cocktails Rs.90. Open 7am-10pm.

Once Upon A Time (tel. 22240), just before the center of Lakeside. Among the most popular restaurants in Lakeside. The host and the staff are friendly, the atmosphere homey and comfortable, and the food good. Sit upstairs under the bamboo hut and among bamboo furniture, or sit downstairs among bamboo curtains. The selection of music and the warm atmosphere make up for a food and bar menu that is less than extensive. Most entrees Rs.65-140, sides Rs.40-60, soft drinks Rs.18, beer Rs.85, most cocktails Rs.75. Open 9am-10pm.

NEPAL

SIGHTS

Most sightseeing in Pokhara is reserved for the mountains. The city itself has very few cultural attractions; it's not Kathmandu and it doesn't try to be. A large portion of the old bazaar of Pokhara burned down in 1949 in a fire that spread from a *puja* at Bindyabasini Temple, so most of the architecture is very recent. Secluded on an island right in the middle of the lake is the **Barahi Temple**—hire 1 of the colorful boats from Barahi Ghat to get there (4 people per boat, Rs.100 per hr., Rs.150 for 3hr.; with guide Rs.150 per hr., Rs.250 for 2hr.).

The lake's water flows out at the south end into the Pardi Khola, a stream which suddenly shoots down into a hole at **Devi's Fall,** 1km out of Pokhara down the road toward the Indian border. Devi's Fall is a 25-minute cycle or a Rs.100 roundtrip taxi ride from Lakeside. (Open 9am-6pm; admission Rs.6.) Rainbows are guaranteed if the sun is shining, since a powerful mist comes jumping out of the hole. Nepalis call it Patale Chhango but in English it is better known by the name of a tourist who fell in and died in the 1960s. Across the road, the refugees at the **Tashling Tibetan Village** are welcoming as they spread the usual array of jewelry and souvenirs on their tables. Farther into the village there is a shed where wool is dyed and spun for carpets and a Tibetan Children's Village for orphaned Tibetan children in Nepal.

On the road between Prithavi Chowk and Mahendra Pul, to the right, is the farm-house-like **Regional Museum** (tel. 20413) with an unimpressive collection of photographs, old weapons, and Nepali ornaments (open Wed.-Mon. 10am-5pm; admission Rs.5, camera fee Rs.5.) From Lakeside, take a taxi (Rs.50) or a bicycle (35min.). If you follow the road and turn right at Mahendrapul Bridge, you can cross the Seti Gandaki River and get to a hill-top **Tibetan Monastery,** which has good views of the Pokhara Valley. While crossing the bridge, stop and look down at the Seti gorge where the Seti river is about 46m deep. The monastery is an hour cycle and a Rs.80 one-way taxi ride from Lakeside; ask for "Madepani Gompa."

The **Natural History Museum,** at the north end of Pokhara on the Prithvi Narayan Campus, has drawers and drawers full of bugs, especially butterflies—the best collection anywhere of Nepal's lepidoptera. (Open Sun.-Fri., 10am-1pm and 2-5pm; free.) The Annapurna Conservation Area Project has an information center here with literature on ecotourism. It's a Rs.90 taxi ride or an hour uphill on a bike: stick to the road past Mahendra Pul until the sign for P.N. Campus appears on the right.

A park, also at the north end of town and on the highway to Boglung, has a long flight of steps leading up to **Bindyabasini Temple.** This temple is thought to have been built in the 16th century by Newari traders just settled in the Pokhara Valley. This temple also marks the spot from which the fire that engulfed Pokhara in 1949 escaped. The main shrine, dedicated to Kali, is accompanied by a new Shiva temple. The small Buddhist monastery at the base of the steps hints at the synthesis between Buddhism and Hinduism in Nepal. Taxis charge Rs.90 from Lakeside and cycling requires an hour of steady uphill pedaling.

At the north of Pokhara, outside city limits is a cave called **Mahendra Gufa.** Several tunnels inside the cave make for a half-hour exploration; some parts of the cave have electricity, but take a flashlight anyway. Taxis charge Rs.150; cycling there is hour and a half uphill. Admission is Rs.10.

Taxis will take you on a three-hour tour of all sights within Pokhara for Rs.500-700. Contact any travel agent or inquire with a taxi operator.

■ Near Pokhara

Phewa, Begnas, and **Rupa Lakes** were all part of the body of water that once filled the Pokhara Valley. Now, while Phewa has been garlanded by the tourism-created Lakeside, Begnas and Rupa remain untouched cousins. Begnas Lake is 13km from Mahendra Pul and is serviced by Tal buses (every hr., 1hr., Rs.7). The two-and-a-half hour cycle to Begnas will certainly loosen up your legs before the trek. Taxis charge Rs.600-1000 roundtrip and will wait for your return.

Sarangkot is one of the best places to view the mountains around Pokhara. Take a cab there for Rs.600-700 roundtrip and walk up another half hour. The three-hour walk to Sarangkot is beautiful, especially when there are clear views of Phewa Lake. Stay over in a tea house to witness the sunrise on the mountains.

The travel agencies of Lakeside and Damside have a committee that runs a day-long sightseeing bus for Rs.200. Buses leave Lakeside around 9am and return around 5pm. The bus goes to Devi's Fall, Tashling Tibetan Village, Regional Museum, Seti River Gorge, the Tibetan Monastery, Mahendra Cave, and Begnas Lake—all in one day and all for Rs.200. Contact any travel agent.

ENTERTAINMENT

Entertainment in Pokhara primarily consists of eating, drinking, listening to music, and taking in the views in Lakeside restaurants. Eating elaborate entrees is entertainment in its own right after the monotony of simple trekking foods. During the trekking season, many restaurants feature Nepali cultural shows during the evenings. On clear days, a lazy boat ride will lure you into the mountain reflections on the placid lake (Rs.100 per hr., Rs.150 per hr. with a guide).

In addition to the music madness at social eateries like **Moondance, 7 Eleven, Maya Pub,** and **Once Upon a Time,** Pokhara also has its share of social drinkeries and danceries. For those wishing to catch a glimpse of Pokhara's hippie days or just a piece of small town USA that re-emerged in Pokhara, head to **Old Blue's Night Pub** at the center of Lakeside (open 5-10pm). Pool tables, dart boards, TV sport shows, wall-space shared by Sting, Marilyn Monroe, James Dean, U2, Bob Marley, Jimi Hendrix, and the Beatles, and a yak head on a wall make for a very un-Nepali place to meet young Nepalis and tourists. Old Blue serves only beverages (soft drinks Rs.15-20, beer Rs.80-90).

The Joker Dance Place, a 100-m walk from the right turn at Nirula's, is the only place where you can shake, shake, shake. Cool disco lights, a slightly sunken dance floor, cushioned brick chairs, and a bar create a vibrant place to boogie with young Nepalese and tourists. The bar has some snacks (cokes Rs.20, cocktails Rs.100). Special dances on Fridays and on full-moon nights. (Open 6-11pm; admission Rs.200 includes complimentary beer.)

Several restaurants across the lake also have special parties. Get a boat at the Barahai Temple (Rs.20 one-way, 30min.). Most parties start around 10pm and go on until the wee hours of the morning. Boats are available to bring you back. Hard-to-miss signs advertise these parties and dances.

Pokhara Sports and Fitness Centre (tel. 20707) near Mahendra Pul has a clay tennis court, a new well-equipped gym, aerobics classes, and a wooden sauna for ten. To get there, go past the corner of the post office at Mahendra Pul and follow the map on the large blue signboard. This center is open from 6am to 8pm but members usually take over from 6 to 10am and 5 to 7pm. (For nonmembers: gym Rs.50 per hr., tennis court Rs.100 per hr., 2 rackets and 3 balls Rs.250 per hr., sauna Rs.200—call and reserve a space an hour in advance, aerobics class Rs.50.)

Pokhara Holiday Inn (tel. 20094), at Mustang Chowk, a 15-min. cycle ride from Lakeside, has a medium-sized swimming pool that is open year-round. (Sessions 9am-12pm and 1-4pm; admission Rs.100 per session.)

■ The Annapurna Trek

The Annapurna trek is by far the most popular in Nepal, and many consider it to be the most rewarding trek in the world. In the trekking season (March-May and late Sept.-Nov.), a United Nations of trekkers packs the trekking routes and tea houses along the way. Even during the snow-clad winter and monsoon-pounded summer, trekkers make their way up to or around Mt. Annapurna, named for the Hindu goddess of abundant harvests.

The construction of roads in the 1970s changed the face of the Pokhara region. For the first time, Pokhara was connected to the outside world and tourists were greeted by the holographic skyline towards the north; ever since, the Annapurna mountains, along with the mystical Maccapuchhre, have been the preferred region for personal contact with the Himalaya.

GETTING THERE

Many flights and buses connect Pokhara from Kathmandu. For more information, see **practical information** (p. 701). To get to Nayapool (Birethanti) or Phedi, take a cab from Pokhara or the bus to Baglung (every hr., 3hr., Rs.21 to Nayapool). Cabs from Lakeside to: Phedi (30min., Rs.200-300); Nayapool (2hr., Rs.500-600); Baglung bus stop (Rs.60-70). The bus ride to Pokhara and the shorter ride on the Baglung road are not as taxing as those to Jiri and Dunche (bases for Everest and Langtang), because large stretches of the road from Kathmandu to Pokhara are in better condition than they have been for 15 years, despite their state of perpetual repair.

TREKKING ROUTES

Due to the larger number of trekkers, villages, and checkposts, the Annapurna trek is safer than the Everest or Langtang trek. There are three treks in the Annapurna region. The **Annapurna Sanctuary** goes to the base camps of Machhapuchhre and Annapurna, surrounding trekkers with white peaks that appear within touching distance. The **Annapurna Circuit** trek takes you around these central Himalayan mountains, into a desert like land, and across the Thorung La Pass, the highest point (5415m) and most challenging part of the three Annapurna treks. The **Jomsom trek** reverses the last week of the Annapurna Circuit trek; it marches along the Kali Gandaki Valley, through Jomsom, and to the Hindu temple of Muktinath (also sacred to Buddhists). The Jomsom trek is the easiest of the three.

Pokhara is the natural base city for these treks. Nayapool and Phedi, the starting points for the Jomsom and Annapurna Sanctuary treks, respectively, are on the road from Pokhara to Baglung. Both are easily accessible by bus and taxi from Pokhara. The starting point for the Annapurna Circuit trek is Besisahar, north of Dumre on the road between Kathmandu and Pokhara. One does not need to go to Pokhara to start the Circuit trek, but Dumre is closer to Pokhara, so a day or two in the city can be good preparation time.

The Annapurna Sanctuary trek normally takes 10 days, the Jomsom trek seven or 13 days, depending on whether you fly or walk back from Jomsom, and the Annapurna Circuit 18 to 21 days. Rest days, day trips, and variations of the route can lengthen the trek. Many variations are possible, so get in touch with tourist office or trekking agent for more extensive information.

If you don't have the time or energy to do one of the three Annapurna treks, consider a short trek from Pokhara that either explores new routes or goes through select villages on the actual treks. Treks can range in duration from three hours to a week; consult a trekking agent in Kathmandu or Pokhara to assess your options.

One option is the four to five day loop from Pokhara to Gorepani to Gandruk and back. The six-night **Annapurna Skyland** trek requires trekkers to carry their own food and tent. Shorter options include the two- to three-night **royal trek,** the overnight trek to **Panchase** (2509m), and the six-hour trek to **Kahun Dada.**

PRACTICAL INFORMATION

Tea houses appear as often as every hour on the well-established routes of the Annapurna treks, making it convenient for individually arranged treks. Although agencies do offer organized treks, they are not at all necessary or even advantageous. Trekking independently, you still have the option of hiring a guide or porter (see **Trekking,** p. 54). Most people, especially in the trekking season, do Annapurna with only a map and trekking guidebook. This allows for flexibility and minimal cost—expect to spend Rs.300-500 per day and some planning in Kathmandu or Pokhara.

There are **health posts, post offices,** and **police check posts** in many of the villages on all three treks. The larger villages have radios which can be used to call for help in emergencies. There is **electricity** in Besisahar, Chame, Dhampus, Gandruk, Jomsom, and Tatopani. There are **banks** in Besisahar, Chame, and Tatopani. Many lodges along the way exchange U.S. dollars but rates are better in Pokhara or Kathmandu. There are **hospitals** in Jomsom and Besisahar. Scheduled flights leave from **airfields** in Manang and Jomson. There is a free **message board** in Tashi Teki Rafting's office in the center of Lakeside, Pokhara. There is a **swimming hole** next to a waterfall a little past Birethanti.

JOMSOM

Wending its way between three groups of mountains, the Jomsom trek offers some of the best views of the Himalaya. Through the Kali Gandaki valley and between the Annapurna and Nilgiri ranges to the east and Dhaulagiri to the west, the trek covers the ground of the ancient trade route between India and Tibet. Past Kalopani, strong winds blow across the flat and dry land. The tea houses in the Jomsom trek are open year-round and are reputed to be among the best in Nepal. At 3800m, Muktinath is the highest point of the trek, so very few people suffer from AMS.

It takes seven days to walk up to Muktinath. From there you can either walk back to Jomsom in a day and get a flight back to Pokhara or Kathmandu or spend (at most) another seven days backtracking to Pokhara. Take the bus from Pokhara to Nayapool, walk towards Birethani (1037m), and go through Tirkedungha (1525m) and Ulleri (2070m) to Ghorepani (2853m). Poon Hill (3193m), an hour's climb from Ghorepani, offers magnificent views of the mountain range, including Dhaulagiri to the northwest. Past the next stop at Tatopani (1189m) is the trail to what was the base camp for Maurice Herzog's 1950 ascent of Annapurna I (8091m)—the first successful ascent of an 8000m peak. Today, the Annapurna Base Camp is on the other side of the mountains. From Tatopani the trail passes through Ghasa (2000m), Kalopani (2530m), Tukche (2590m), and Marpha (2667m) to Jomsom. From Jomsom you can go to Muktinath (3800m) directly or through Kagbeni (2810m).

Past Tukche, be prepared for strong afternoon winds that blow sand and dust, making goggles and scarves necessary. Jomsom, the administrative center of the region and the last non-Tibetan area, also has an ACAP information center and a big military camp where Nepalese soldiers practice high-altitude maneuvers. The Mustang trek goes through Kagbeni. With the normal trekking permit, Kagbeni is as far north as you can go. The only lodges are in Ranipauwa (3710m), just before Muktinath, where pilgrims come to bathe by the 108 stone water taps.

The people in Ulleri are Magars, while those of the Kali Gandaki valley are Thakalis. Relative to their number in the total population of Nepal, the Thakalis are quite powerful and well off—many do business or hold high-post jobs in Kathmandu and Pokhara Valleys. The Jomsom trek is often packed with ponies carrying goods up to the far-off villages.

The flight back from Jomsom to Pokhara is far more reliable than that to Kathmandu. After 11am, strong winds make it impossible for planes to operate at Jomsom airport, and Kathmandu is often clouded over during the morning hours.

ANNAPURNA SANCTUARY

The Annapurna Sanctuary trek leaps into the lap of the almost divine circle that includes: Himchuli (6441m), Annapurna South (7219m), Varahashikhar (7647m), Annapurna I (8019m), Khangsar Kang (7485m), Tarke Kang (7193m), Gangapurna (7455m), Annapurna III (7555m), Gandravachuli (6249m), and Machhapuchhre (6993m). The tea houses up to the Annapurna Base Camp (ABC) are open almost the entire year, while the tea houses up to Himalaya Hotel (past Chhomrong) are open year-round. Farther beyond this point and at the two base camps, many tea houses close down due to excessive snow, rain, or underuse. Fortunately, tea house and lodge operators check out the trekking scene in Chhomrong and open their establishments if they anticipate trekkers. ACAP has also arranged for at least one tea house to be open at every place throughout the year. The only time that this trek is "closed" is when an avalanche blocks the approach to the base camps, a rare occurrence. If an avalanche does hit, trekkers may have to wait on the trail or at a base camp for a few days until the snow clears. The potential for AMS is greatest around Bagar (3900), just before the Machhapuchhre Base Camp. Trekkers usually acclimatize well by spending two days between Chhomrong and the base camp.

The trek can take anywhere from eight days to two weeks. Contact a travel agent or the ACAP information office in Lakeside, Pokhara for information about the different possible routes. Phedi and Nayapool (Birethanti) are the two possible starting points. Take the bus or a taxi from Pokhara to Phedi and walk to Landruk (1550m) through Dhampus (1580m) and Tolka (1710m). Continue on to Chhomrong, crossing the Nayapool (1340m). The only way to the ABC from Chhomrong is through Kuldighar (2350m), Himalayan Hotel (2680m), Hinko Cave (2960m), Deorali (3000m), Bagar (3110m), and finally Machhapuchhre Base Camp (MBC, 3480m). As you walk around Machhapuchhre, you begin to see its double peak—the famed fish tail. From MBC Machhapuchhre is barely recognizable.

Dhampus is the scene of panoramic views, but also of rampant theft activity. Be especially careful if camping, as thieves have been known to cut tents at night and steal from slumbering hikers. If staying in a lodge, be sure to lock all windows and doors. Also try not to walk alone.

Chhomrong has many good hotels, an ACAP office, a kerosene depot (with kerosene, cans, and stoves), provision shops, and even some rental stores. But don't wait until you get to Chhomrong to rent your equipment, as there is limited choice.

For overnight accommodations, Hinko Cave is a huge overhang that has been converted to a drafty dormitory—wind is rumored to blow through the walls at night. Deorali, about a half-hour farther on from Hinko, is better insulated. Potential avalanche territory starts after Hindo. After Bagar, you "enter" the sanctuary, and as you walk farther on to MBC and over snow to ABC, the mountains surround you completely. ABC has lots of snow and icy cold rivers for bathing. Wake up early to see the first rays of sun hit the mountains—a truly amazing sight.

The return trip is much easier, though the descent is taxing on the knees. From Chhomrong, you can either retrace your steps back through Landruk to Phedi, where there is transportation to Pokhara, or you can go to Ghorepani and continue on with the Jomsom trek. From Gandruk (1940m), you can go to Birethanti and catch the bus back to Pokhara from Nayapool, or hike to Gorepani and on to Birethanti; this latter route is particularly confusing, however, so ask locals for the correct trail. Gandruk is the second biggest Gurung village in Nepal (after Sikles, northeast of Pokhara) and has many lodges, some of them quite good.

ANNAPURNA CIRCUIT

The Annapurna Circuit is among the most popular treks in Nepal. The Circuit crosses the Thorung La Pass (5415m), which is the highest point that most trekkers ever go, and winds behind the Himalayan range into the Tibetan Plateau-like desert.

Although it's theoretically possible to do the Circuit clockwise—crossing Thorung La Pass west to east, it is much easier to cross it east to west. With not one tea house between Thorung Phedi and Muktinath, the west-east passage is nearly impossible to complete without having to camp out in the wild for a night. Aside from this stretch, there are tea houses all along the trail, usually spaced only an hour's walk apart. The Circuit trek is usually closed from mid-December to mid-April when the Thorung La Pass is covered in snow. As the Thorung La Pass is so high, there is significant danger of AMS. Trekkers spend the night at Thorung Phedi (4420m), cross the pass the next morning, and then settle down for the night on the other side in Ranipauwa (Muktinath). The ascent is nearly 1000m between Thorung Phedi and Thorung La Pass (5414m). If symptoms of AMS develop, immediately return to Thorung Phedi. Try again the next day, as this should be adequate time for acclimatization. Sudden bad weather can also make the pass impassable and compel trekkers back to Dumre.

The Circuit trek can be done in a span of 18 to 21 days. Dumre (440m) is 135km from Kathmandu and 65km from Pokhara, on the road between the two cities. From Kathmandu, take the bus to Pokhara; from Pokhara, take the bus to Mugling. In both cases, get off at Dumre and take local transportation to Besisahar (790m). One bus from Pokhara to Besisahar leaves early each morning from the old bus park.

From Besisahar, walk to Bahundanda (1310m), Bhulbhule (830m), and Ngadi. Cross villages including Syanje (1186m), Jagat (1250m), Chamje (1433m), Tal (1675m), Dharapani (1920m), Bargarchhap (2164m), Tyanja (2360m), and Kyupar (2590m) to reach Chame (2629m). As the administrative center of the Manang district, Chame has many facilities as well as great views of the eastern flank of Annapurna II. From Chame, continue through Pisang (3185m) and Brayga (3475m) to reach Manang (3535m). Most people spend a day acclimatizing in Manang. At Manang, you will come across the Manange people, among the most skillful traders of Nepal. There is an ACAP information center and a huge waterfall here, and during the trekking season, a Himalayan Rescue Association (HRA) health post attended by two Western doctors. From Manang, the trail goes through Letdar (4250m) to Thorung Phedi (4420m). As Thorung Phedi has only one lodge, it gets quite crowded in the trekking season, especially when snow has blocked the pass and several days of trekkers cram into the hotel. From Thorung Phedi, it is a long (8-10hr.) and difficult hike to Muktinath, crossing the Thorung La Pass. Consider staying at Phedi for a day or even retreating to Lathar. Thorung La Pass itself isn't a remarkable piece of ground at all—it is bare and ordinary, but the view from here is magnificent. Most hikers get up at 4am to cross the Pass before the sun comes out, as the heat, coupled with the high altitude makes climbing very difficult. From Muktinath, go to Jomsom to get a flight out to Kathmandu or Pokhara, or walk the Jomsom trek in reverse to Birethanti. From Gorepani, you can also go on to Gandruk and continue on with the Annapurna Sanctuary trek.

The Tarai

However Indian these hill-less lands seem, the hot, dry, flat plains of the Tarai are an integral part of Nepal. The Tarai is Nepal's food basket of Nepal, producing the vast majority of the country's rice. The flat land also makes industry, construction, and transportation easier. Until the 1950s and 60s when a massive migration of hill people (and people from bordering Indian states) cleared the land for farming and housing, the Tarai was covered with impregnable malarial jungle. Fortunately, large chunks of land like the Royal Chitwan National Park have been set aside to preserve some of the original diversity of flora and fauna. Yet there continues to be conflict between villager needs, wildlife needs, and now, tourist needs.

The neighboring towns of Narayanghat and Bharatpur form the gateway from the hills. Hetauda is the transportation hub to the east and Butwal plays a similar function to the west. The Mahendra Rajmarg, running east-west from one corner of Nepal to another, connects these cities and the whole Tarai. Lumbini in the near-west and Janakpur in the near-east are two of Nepal's main religious sites.

▨ Butwal

The city of Butwal sits where the Tarai plains end and the Mahabharat hills begin. Even before Nepalese unification, Butwal was a customs entry point for the Kingdom of Palpa. The **Mahendra Rajmarg** and the **Siddhartha Rajmarg** highways, running east-west and north-south respectively, meet at Butwal. The center of Butwal at **Traffic Chowk** is marked by a circular fluorescent-lit stand on the middle of the road and a nearly constant flow of buses. **Hospital Chowk,** 100m south of Traffic Chowk, is marked by a statue of King Mahendra.

There are three blue **police** "beat" boxes in the main squares of Butwal (police tel. 40222). **Nepal Arab Bank,** 100m north of Traffic Chowk (tel. 41059), exchanges most major currencies and traveler's checks. Open Sun.-Thurs. 10am-2:30pm, Fri. 10am-12:30pm. An authorized **money exchanger,** in the ground floor of Hotel Sid-dhartha at Traffic Chowk (tel. 40609, 41609), takes a small percentage off each trans-action. Open daily 7am-7pm. Several **"communication" shops** have opened up around Traffic Chowk. STD/ISD booths with direct dialing services are available in nearly every other shop. There are two **bus** stations in Butwal, one at Traffic Chowk, where there are box-like ticket counters, and the other immediately west. To: Bhaira-hawa (every 7min., 5am-8pm, 1hr., Rs.9) via Sunauli (70min., Rs. 11) also leave from here. **Rickshaws** operate from 4am to 10pm on set rates (Rs.4-15) that are advertised throughout the city. **Lumbini Zone Hospital** is about 50m south of Hospital Chowk (**emergency tel.** 40200). Several **medical stores** here are open 24hr. The **post office** (tel. 40059) is a 10-min. walk north from Traffic Chowk. At Nabil Bank, follow the dirt road to the left until the building on the right marked "Area Post Office Butwal." **Telephone Code:** 071.

Since most buses pass through Butwal on the way to or from Lumbini or Sunauli, you will probably have to pass through Butwal as well; but probably won't have to stay. Despite recent development, competition among hotels is only beginning to take off, so prices remain relatively high. **Hotel Royal,** Traffic Chowk (tel. 40509; fax 40732), has just opened, so its facilities are clean and in good working order. All rooms come with attached bath. Their restaurant (open daily 7am-10pm) is one of the classier ones in Butwal and serves the usual Chinese, Continental, and Indian dishes (Rs. 60-90). Singles with fan Rs.300. Doubles with air-cooling Rs.400. **Hotel Kandara,** Traffic Chowk (tel. 40175), doesn't have the royal rooms and bathrooms of Hotel Royal. Dorm beds Rs.80. Singles Rs.100, with bath Rs.250. Doubles Rs. 150, with bath Rs. 300, with air-cooling Rs.550. **Butwal Guest House,** Hospital Chowk (tel. 40228), offers less appealing furnishings, cleanliness, humidity, and smells for lower prices. Curfew 10pm. Dorm beds Rs.40. Doubles Rs.150, with bath and air-cooling Rs.250. Triples Rs.180. **Fedee Restaurant and Bar,** in Hotel Kandara (tel. 40175), has tinted windows, a dark air-conditioned room, Kwality ice cream, and light Indian music in the evening. All these make for the hippest place to eat at night in Butwal. Chinese and Indian specialties; most entrees Rs.40-80. Open daily 7am-10:30pm. **Nest Restaurant,** in Hotel Siddhartha at Traffic Chowk (tel. 40380), has Star TV. Open 7am-9:30pm.

■ Bhairahawa (Siddharthanagar)

Bhairahawa, recently but unpopularly renamed Siddharthanagar, is located is an hour's drive south of Butwal towards the Indian border, on the way to and from Suna-uli and Lumbini. The Siddhartha Ramjarg highway passes north-south through Bhaira-hawa. **Bus Chauraha** is the main square. **Bank Road,** to the west of here, leads to the main bazaar. In another square farther north, the road to Lumbini separates from the highway and heads west. The **airport** is 2km down this road.

Lumbini Money Changer, Bank Rd., 100m from Bus Chauraha (tel. 21722) changes major foreign currencies and traveler's checks. Open daily 7am-7pm. There are **"communication" shops** along Bank Rd., and STD/ISD **telephone** booths in the bazaar area. **Necon Air** (tel. 20498, 21244; open daily 9am-5pm) and **Nepal Airways** (tel. 21442, 21833; open daily 8am-6pm) have offices on the road north from Bus Chauraha. **RNAC** (tel. 20175; open daily 9am-5pm) and **Everest Air** (tel. 21777; open daily 8am-6pm) have offices in Hotel Yeti. All have flights to Kathmandu (daily, 35min., US$72). Nepal Airways flies to Nepalganj (Sat.-Thurs., US$67). The **bus counter** is at Bus Chauraha (tel. 20351; open daily 5am-8pm). Buses to Sunauli (sev-eral every hr., 10min., Rs.2) leave from Bus Chauraha; buses to Lumbini (every 30min., 7am-7pm, 70min., Rs.10) leave from a Lumbini Bus Station in the square to the north. **Jeeps** to the airport (Rs.150), Sunauli (Rs.60), and Lumbini (Rs.300) are available at Bus Chauraha from 5am to 9pm. There are jeeps to Sunauli available every hour for Rs.3, but passengers must wait until the jeep fills up. **Rickshaws** make local trips for under Rs.15. The **hospital** (tel. 20193), Bank Rd. about 130m from Bus Chauraha, is surrounded by **medical stores,** some open 24hr. There is a blue **police** "beat" box at Bus Chauraha. The **post office,** Bank Rd., 130m from Bus Chauraha (open Sun.-Thurs. 10am-5pm, Fri. 10am-3pm). **Telephone Code:** 071.

The development of nearby Lumbini has recently turned Bhairahawa into a gateway city, and posh new hotels have started appearing. **Hotel Nirvana,** southwest of the bazaar (tel. 20516, KTM tel. 225370; fax 21262), maintains three-star facilities. **Hotel Yeti,** in Bus Chauraha (tel. 20551), isn't as expensive or as elegant. **Sayapatri Guest House,** on the left of Bank Rd. (tel. 21236), is the best deal. Doubles Rs.175, with bath Rs.250. **Hotel Shambala,** farther on Bank Rd. (tel. 21837), is more expensive but all rooms have coolers, fans, 24-hr. hot and cold water, carpeting, and more than basic furniture. The restaurant here is one of the better ones in town (open 6am-9:30pm). Singles with bath Rs.475. Doubles with bath Rs.600. **Siddhartha Restaurant,** in Hotel Himalayan Inn, 500m on the road north from Bus Chauraha (tel. 20347), has a relatively large choice of Chinese, Continental, and Indian dishes, as well as a breakfast menu and a bar. Open daily 6am-9pm. **Kasturi Restaurant,** off Bank Rd. (tel. 21580), specializes in Indian food and Indian atmosphere.

■ Sunauli

The most touristed border crossing between India and Nepal, Sunauli is a three-hour bus ride from Gorakhpur in India, a ten-hour ride from Pokhara, or a twelve-hour ride from Kathmandu. Sunauli is the second most popular entry point to Nepal after Tribhuvan International Airport in Kathmandu. Entering Nepal from India, the hyper-capitalist Nepali side of Sunauli welcomes travelers with an explosion of English billboards. The limited services on the Nepali side are better than those on the Indian side. Sunauli's facilities are all in the budget range.

The **bus park** on the Indian side is at the end of Indian Sunauli. Buses go to: Varanasi (6 and 7:30pm, 9hr., IRs.120); Delhi (every hr., 6am-7pm, 24hr., IRs.225/281 for normal/express); Gorakhpur (several every hr., 4am-7pm, 2-3hr., IRs.29); Allahabad (10 per day, 4am-2:30pm, 15hr., IRs.120); Kanpur (4 per day, noon-6pm, 12hr., IRs.100); Lucknow (9hr., IRs.140, en route to Delhi). The **bus park** (main ticket counter tel. 20194) on the Nepal side is about 100m from the border. Buses to: Kathmandu (6 per day, 4:30-10:30am, 11hr., NRs.105; 4 per night, 5-8pm, 11hr., NRs.112); Bhairahawa (several every hr., 10min., NRs.2). The Kathmandu and Pokhara buses pass through Butwal, where there are connections to other Nepalese destinations. Buses to leave from the bus park.

Rickshaws charge NRs.30 for a ride across the border; unless you are burdened with heavy luggage, it makes more sense to walk. Customs officials in the two immigration posts stamp passports, a formality which should take under an hour. Nepalese visas can be obtained on the spot, but citizens of any country other than India or Nepal will need to have a visa already in order to enter India.

The Nepali **tourist office,** next to the Immigration Office on the Nepal side (tel. 20304), has free brochures about the main tourist attractions of Nepal. Open Sun.-Thurs. 10am-5pm, Fri. 10am-3pm. **Sheetal Tour and Travel** (tel. 20251), on the Nepal side, is among the few travel agents in Sunauli. Open 8am-8pm. Several authorized **currency exchangers** on the Nepal side deal with major foreign currencies and traveler's checks; most are open 7am-7pm. The one bank on the Indian side does not change foreign currencies. STD/ISD **telephone** booths cluster on the Nepal side, and are more sporadically located on the Indian side. **Telephone Codes:** Indian Sunauli 05522; Nepali Sunauli 071.

The best place to stay in Sunauli is the government-run **Hotel Niranjana** (tel. 4901) on the Indian side. A mud fort-like structure with a garden and multicolored flags, it is impossible to miss. The restaurant (open 7am-11pm) is the best on the Indian side, and serves mostly Indian dishes. Dorm beds IRs.35. Doubles with bath and air-cooling IRs.225, with bath and A/C IRs. 350. Although there are many hotels and guest houses on the Nepali side of Sunauli, competition for hard-nosed travelers is sometimes so fierce and the room rates these places have to settle for so meager that it doesn't make much sense to invest in better facilities. **Paradise Guest House** (tel. 20637), about 70m from the border, has comparatively decent facilities. Their restaurant (open 5am-noon) is cleaner and slightly more expensive than most in Sunauli. Dorm beds NRs.100. Singles with bath NRs.300. Doubles with bath NRs.400. Air-cooling NRs.50. Off-season prices are lower. **Hotel Buddha,** farther from the border on the Nepal side, is also relatively new. Dorm beds NRs.30. Doubles NRs.100, with bath NRs.300. Most restaurants have the same Chinese, Continental, and Indian dishes. **Mandro,** about 120m before the border on the Nepal side, stands out as the most popular among tourists. Open daily 5am-10pm.

▓ Lumbini

When, according to legend, Siddhartha Gautama, a prince in the Sakya royal family, was born at Lumbini in 623 BC, the site was merely a forest grove near a water tank. Siddhartha's mother, Mayadevi, was apparently on her way back from her husband's palace when she stopped for a bath in the water tank and gave birth holding a branch for support. But as soon as the newborn baby emerged, he spoke, saying, "I am the foremost of all the creatures to cross the riddle of the ocean of existence. I have come to the world to show the path of emancipation. This is my last birth and hereafter I will not be born again." This precocious boy would come to be known as the Buddha. Today, the Sacred Garden marks the spot of this event; it also contains the pillar erected by the Indian Emperor Ashoka as a token of his visit to Lumbini and as a boundary marker. The pillar cites Lumbini as Buddha's birthplace, lending legitimacy to the legend. Further evidence comes from remains of monasteries and *stupas* that date from as far back as the 3rd century BC and from accounts of two Chinese travelers who visited Lumbini in the 5th and 7th centuries. Khasa King Ripu Malla of Jumla made the last recorded visit to Lumbini in the 14th century before the location was forgotten, becoming better known as Rumnindei or Rupandehi. Lumbini was rediscovered in 1896 by a party led by Khadga Samsher and the German archeologist R.A. Fuhrer.

Since 1985, the Lumbini Development Trust has been working on an ambitious plan to turn Lumbini into an international center for Buddhist pilgrimage and research. The famous Japanese architect Mr. Kenzo Tanze designed the plan, which was estimated in 1989 to cost US$54 million. Progress has been very slow, so for the moment, Lumbini has minimal facilities. The area is populated by grass, singing birds, foxes, and young sal trees, but no humans. Current renovations to the Sacred Garden are intended to recreate the environment of Buddha's birthplace.

ORIENTATION AND PRACTICAL INFORMATION

The Sacred Garden is a five minute walk from where the bus stops. Walk past the guard house and make a left at the bunch of sign posts; the Sacred Garden appears on the right. Opposite the garden are monasteries, temples, a pilgrim rest house, and bathrooms. The Sri Lanka Rest House, the Lumbini Hokke Hotel, the temples of the various Buddhist countries, and the Eternal Flame (a 10-min. walk) are to the right of the sign posts. The temples are from one to three kilometers away. There is no local transportation in Lumbini, so moving around is very difficult.

The **information desk** at the gate leading to the Sacred Garden is often unoccupied. The **police station** (tel. 29471) is a 10-min. walk along the main road toward the village of Pahariya. There is a **phone counter** (open 6am-8pm) next to the pilgrim's home opposite the Sacred Garden. The few hotels in Lumbini also have international calling facilities. The closest airport is in Bhairahawa. Irregular buses to Bhairahawa (every hr., 7am-7pm, 70min., Rs.10) leave from the guard house before the Sacred Garden. There is a very basic free **first aid clinic** (open 8am-9pm) in the white pilgrim's home across from the Sacred Garden. **Tara Medical Centre,** about 70m into the village on the main road at the turn off for the Sacred Garden, has basic medicines. **Telephone Code:** 071.

ACCOMMODATIONS AND FOOD

The accommodations scene in Lumbini is grim. Most tourists make day trips to Lumbini and then head back to hotels in Bhairahawa. **Sri Lanka Pilgrims Rest** (tel. 20009), the "pilgrim's hotel," is 3km and a 45-min. walk from the bus stop next to the Sacred Garden. Walk past all the temples and the Korean-built research center, make a left on the main road, and take the next right. Built for Sri Lankan pilgrims, the rest house accommodates 196 people in peaceful rooms with 2-10 beds. The building's circular, communal design is centered around the dining hall (open 7am-10pm), which isn't fancy but serves good Chinese, Continental, and Indian food. Communal bathrooms only. Dorm beds on ground floor Rs.60, on top floor Rs.120. The rooms are identical, but the higher rooms supposedly get more wind. Across from the Sacred Garden are two monasteries. The yellow one to the east, **Dharmaswami Buddha Bihar,** often has rooms available in the summer when the monks go to cooler Boudha, near Kathmandu. The facilities are, well, monastic. There is a small restaurant (open 7am-10pm) attached to the monastery. The main temple (open 5am-6pm) has a big statue of Sakyamuni Buddha and during the cooler seasons has morning religious ceremonies. There's no charge, but donations are expected. The other monastery contains a pilgrim's rest house which is the white building marked **"Nepal Buddha Temple."** The rooms are little more than empty cubicles with hard straw mats, no bedding, and a single light bulb. The bathrooms suffer from neglect. The attached restaurant (open 6am-10pm) serves basic food. Donations are expected. The **Lumbini Garden Restaurant,** on the main road next to the turn to the Sacred Garden, serves decent food. The only competition to the Garden Restaurant are the monastery eateries, so its become Lumbini's only option despite its high prices. Open daily 6am-10pm.

SIGHTS

Lumbuni's **Sacred Garden** is fronted by the **Mayadevi Temple,** which is under renovation. The main Mayadevi sculpture (3rd-4th century) was moved to the building at the entrance of the garden three years ago. Renovation plans call for a new shell to be added to the original temple before the statue is reinstalled. The building at the entrance of the garden also contains several Buddha statues presented by various Buddhist countries; foreign monks often chant inside. Behind the Mayadevi temple is the **Ashokan Pillar,** erected in 249 BC. Emperor Ashoka is believed to have written the script at the bottom, while that at the top was done by King Ripu Malla in the 14th Century.

To the west of the Ashokan Pillar is the sacred **water tank** where Mayadevi is thought to have taken a bath before giving birth to Siddhartha. To the southwest of the Ashokan Pillar are red baked brick remains of monasteries, temples, and *stupas* dating from the 3rd century BC to the 9th Century AD. By the huge tree next to the water tank, the sleeping Buddha and child Buddha statues bear the red and yellow colors of traditional Hindu worship.

The large yellow temple opposite the Sacred Garden was constructed by King Mahendra and contains Buddha statues from Burma, Thailand, and Nepal. Wall paintings depict the wheel of life, four *bodhisattvas*, and the major Hindu gods welcoming Siddhartha back to Nepal after he had become a Buddha. U Thant, the late Secretary-General of the U.N., was so impressed (and perhaps frustrated?) by his 1967 visit to the temple that he donated money for the construction of several bathrooms. Temples of China, Japan, Burma, South Korea, Thailand, and Vietnam are currently under construction in Lumbini. Each country plans to send monks to live at its temple and represent its particular approach to Buddhism. The temples will be a half-hour walk from the bus stop.

■ Narayanghat and Bharatpur

The twin cities of Narayanghat and Bharatpur, located on the Mahendra Rajmarg highway in the center of Nepal, together constitute one of the nation's largest cities. Bharatpur is suburban, almost rural, and is 10 minutes west of Narayanghat, where most of the businesses, shops, hotels, and services are. The bluish hills of the Mahabharat range are garlanded by white clouds to the north, while the dark outline of the smaller Churia hills appears to the south.

A bridge crosses the **Narayani River** at the west end of town. The **Pulchowk Bus Park** is also at the west end, where buildings are plastered with neon billboards. About 120m west is **Sangam Chowk,** the central square of Narayanghat. The road that heads north from Sangham Chowk joins the highway to Pokhara and Kathmandu. **Devghat,** 20 minutes north of Naryanghat on the Narayani river, is the site of cremations and home to Hindu mystic *sadhus.*

Chitwan Sauraha Tours and Travels (tel. 21890) is located right behind the bus park at Pulchowk. (Open daily 7am-10pm.) **Nepal Bank,** 500m north of Pulchowk on the road to Pokhara and Kathmandu (tel. 20170), changes most major foreign currencies and traveler's checks. (Open Sun-Thurs. 10am-2pm, Fri. 10am-noon.) International calling services are available at STD/ISD **telephone** booths. **Rickshaws** charge Rs.20 for a two-person ride from Narayanghat to the **airport.** The offices of **Everest Air** (tel. 21093; open 6am-5pm), **Nepal Airways** (tel. 22254; open 7am-5pm), and **RNAC** (tel. 20326; open 8am-5pm) are in front of the airport. Daily flights to Kathmandu (US$50) and Pokhara (US$44). Long distance **bus** tickets are available in the box-like counters in the Pulchowk area. Buses to Kathmandu (8 per day, 7-11am, 5hr., Rs.75; several every hr. starting at 7:30pm, Rs.70) leave from just north of the bus park in Pulchowk. Buses to: Pokhara (14 per day, 5am-2:30pm, 5hr., Rs. 53) and Devghat (8, 11am, 1, and 4pm, 20min., Rs.4) leave from the Pokhara bus stop (15-min. walk or Rs.5 rickshaw ride, 5min. from Pulchowk). Buses to Tandi Bazaar (every 10min., 6am-7pm, 25min., Rs.6) leave from the Sangham Chowk area. **Rickshaws** charge Rs.12 between Narayanghat and Bharatpur. **Auto-rickshaws** also leave from west of Sangam Chowk for Bharatpur (up to 6 per hr., 6am-7pm, 10min., Rs.4). **Chitwan Taxis** (tel. 22950) have 10 white taxis and charge Rs.27 between the two twin cities, Rs.220 to Tandi Bazaar (operates 7am-7pm). The **hospital** (tel. 20111) is north of the main square in Bharatpur. There are about half a dozen **medical stores** in the Sangam Chowk area; most are open from 6am to 8pm and most have doctors available from 5 to 7pm. **Telephone Code:** 056.

For classy accommodations, try the **Safari Narayani** (tel. 20130, 20534) or **Hotel Chitwan Keyman** (tel. 20200, 22300). If you want only classy food, visit their restaurants. **Quality Guest House** (tel. 20939), a right turn from the first turn-off on the road north from Pulchowk, is a place that lives up to its name with clean rooms at decent prices. Their restaurant (open 8am-11pm) has Star TV, a bar, and serves breakfast in addition to Chinese, Continental, Indian, and Nepali fare. Singles Rs.75, with bath Rs.125. Doubles Rs.150, with bath Rs.200. Triples with bath Rs.250. Quads Rs.250. **Kailash Lodge and Restaurant,** on the right 30m east of the bus park (tel. 20469), is a moderately priced and well-run place. Singles Rs.100, with bath Rs.150. Doubles Rs.150, with bath Rs.200. Triples Rs.175. Quads Rs.200. **Pratiksha Guest House** (tel. 21566), right next to Kailash Lodge, is another good deal. Doubles Rs.150, with bath Rs.200, with air-cooling Rs.250. Triples with bath and air-cooling Rs.300. The best place to eat in town is **City Centre Restaurant and Bar** (tel. 20503); look for the sign in the Sangham Chowk area. It has the most extensive menu (Chinese, Continental, and Indian) in town, English and Hindi music, attractive furnishings, and a dutiful staff. Most entrees Rs.45-80. C.C. Special Mixed Pizza (Rs. 85) may be the spiciest pizza you'll ever eat. (Open daily 10am-10pm.)

■ Chitwan National Park

Not long ago, game hunting at Chitwan, Nepal's foremost national park, was no casual activity. In fact, the glory of the game was a rite of passage for the prince of Wales, who came to Chitwan as the guest of the incumbent Rana prime minister. Any Nepalese history book is bound to have photos of the Ranas and foreign royalty posing behind the day's kill—tigers, black bears, and deer; in the background will be the dozens of elephants that brought the foreign princes into Nepal from the outermost railway in India. Since 1846, hunting rights in Chitwan had been reserved for royalty and their guests. The royal link to Chitwan made it for a time the most popular big game hunting area in South Asia. But people that come here now point cameras rather than guns—Royal Chitwan National Park is the most protected wildlife reserve in Nepal. After malaria was eradicated from Chitwan in the 1950s, many hill people moved here and more land was cleared for cash-crop farming, resulting in a rapid loss of wildlife habitat. People living in Chitwan began to be resettled in 1964, and the area was declared a national park in 1973. Eleven years later, UNESCO designated Royal Chitwan National Park a Natural World Heritage Site.

Chitwan still provides a jungle safari experience, while catering to the needs to tourists of all budgets. Guests at the more expensive hotels inside Chitwan National Park are submerged in the jungle, while having access to good facilities and services. Some hotels provide chauffeurs to Chitwan, where they continue to pamper their guests. The most popular and most developed tourist base outside the park is Sauraha. Forty-six lodges with varying facilities and prices have planted themselves here just outside the entrance to the park. In season, demand exceeds the capacity for jungle-related activities. But regardless of where you stay or how much you pay, the hordes of tourists don't obscure the amount of wildlife from your vision. The best time to visit Chitwan is from October to May. In the monsoon, the rivers flood, many establishments are either under-staffed or closed down, and Chitwan and Sauraha fall into a slumber.

ORIENTATION

Chitwan National Park is at the center of Nepal, bordering India to the south. Narayanghat and Bharatpur form the gateway area. The **Mahendra Rajmarg** highway runs almost parallel to the northern boundary of the park. Roads head south from this highway to each of the park hotels and the few outside-park villages that also have hotels. If in **Sauraha**, the highway stop at **Tandi Bazaar** is 35 minutes east of Narayanghat. Sauraha and the entrance to the park are both 7km away from Tandi. Those without package deal transportation can take a jeep from Tandi to Sauraha. The river does not flow all the way to Chitwan, so rafters must get off at Narayanghat and take a bus to Tandi Bazaar.

During the high season, the **river** will have dried up enough for a single jeep to go the route from Tandi to Sauraha. During the monsoon, the swollen river needs to be crossed by a footbridge. Sauraha is a 15-minute walk from one end to another—to the entrance of the park, with **Sauraha Bazaar** at the center. There are two ways to the park entrance from Sauraha Bazaar. One is to follow the main gravel road past the **Tharu Village,** and make two right turns. The other is to go right and make a loop along the banks of the river. The **park entrance** is where visitors pay entry fees, book elephants, mount elephants, and see exhibits on Chitwan's history and wildlife. Canoes depart from the riverbank next to the park entrance.

PRACTICAL INFORMATION

Tourist Office: There is a National Park **entry fee** of Rs.650 covering entry to the park and river canoeing rights. This park entry permit is valid for 2 full days, enough time to do every activity Chitwan offers. There is a huge fine for being caught in the park without a valid permit. No one is allowed to enter the Park at night. In the season, the wait to get park entry permits can be 3-4 hr. but you can

Thatch Gathering

Every winter for 10 days, villagers from around the region are invited to Chitwan National Park to gather thatch. Approximately 100,000 villagers enter the park every year and remove 12,000 metric tons of grass, the total value of which comes to US$250,000. Many hotels in Sauraha have roofs made of this very grass. Grass gathering was a regular chore for the people in the region until the park was established. This grass is the material used in many fences, mats, ropes, baskets, and other household goods.

pay someone an additional Rs.50-100 to get the permit for you. The **ticket office** is at the park entrance (open daily 6-10am and 1:30-5pm; elephant ride ticket time is 6-7am and 1:30-3:30pm).

Tours: For information, see **Sights and Entertainment**, p.747.

Currency Exchange: The closest bank is in Tandi; **Nepal Bank** (tel. 60210), well-hidden 300m east on the highway, changes most major currencies and traveler's checks. Open Sun.-Thurs. 10am-3pm, Fri. 10am-12:30pm. Some hotels in Sauraha exchange currency, but at terrible rates.

Telephones: Some hotels have international calling facilities. There are several STD/ISD booths on the main road.

Buses: The **bus counter** (tel. 60134), in Tandi 15m east of the turn to Sauraha, is marked "Prithivi Rajmarg Bus Syndicate" (open daily 7am-9:30pm). From here there are **tourist buses** to Kathmandu (10 and 11am, 5hr., Rs.100-150) and Pokhara (9 and 10am, 5hr., Rs.100-150). Prices may vary with service charges. There are also cheaper buses to main Nepalese destinations that leave from here.

Local Transportation: Local bus goes from Tandi to Narayanghat, where there are connections to many destinations. **Jeeps** between Sauraha and Tandi cost Rs.300 to reserve and Rs.30 if they can pick up 10 passengers. During season, **bicycles** can be hired from three rental shops on the main road (Rs.10 per hr.). Bicycles have only one gear and often are in bad condition.

English Bookstore: Several bookstores in Sauraha Bazaar sell new and used English books. Limited selection.

Pharmacy: Several pharmacies are located in Tandi. One medical store, about 100m to the east (look for a Red Cross sign), is open 6am-10pm and has a doctor available 6-7pm.

Police: The **main police station** is a 20-min. walk from Sauraha, but the police will come to Sauraha if there is a problem. There is a police station in Tandi as well; Walk 300m east on the main highway from the turn to Sauraha and take a right at the blue "police" sign. For police complaints, go to the **Sauraha Hotel Association** office (tel. 29363). This association governs the Sauraha tourism industry. Open daily 6am-7pm.

Telephone Code: 056.

ACCOMMODATIONS

Budget travelers often find that the most difficult part of the entire Chitwan experience is getting their own transportation from Tandi Bazaar to a hotel room in Sauraha. As soon as travelers step off the bus in Tandi, they are smothered by dozens of guides eager to earn the commissions hotels pay them. A wave of the receipt from a pre-arranged package deal is enough to disperse the guides while a jeep from the appropriate hotel takes over. If you have already decided on a hotel of choice, the appropriate jeep, if currently in Tandi, will take you to Sauraha for free. Otherwise, choose the least aggressive guide to take you to Sauraha. The jeep ride is free if you stay at the hotel they take you to, and Rs.30 per person if you decide to leave.

Although hotels in Sauraha differ greatly in price, the jungle activities they offer differ very little. Everyone rides the same elephants, walks the same paths, floats on the same boats, drives in the same jeeps, and, most importantly, sees the same wildlife. Rather, the hotel rooms, food, and to some extent, the staff account for the price differentials. Cheaper places have fewer jeeps, so their guests have to walk more often. Prices fall off-season especially with skillful bargaining.

Eden Guest House (tel. 29371). At the end of Sauraha, a 10-min. walk east from the park entrance. While the walk to Sauraha may be a hassle, the isolation here makes for a quieter, more jungle-like experience. The beds and lighting are better in the newer huts, which have clean attached bathrooms, than in the older mud houses and the common doubles. The restaurant has a simple menu (open 6am-11pm). Doubles Rs.100, with bath Rs.400. Triples with bath Rs.500. Standard 2-night package deal to walk-in tourists US$60.

Hotel Wildlife Camp (tel. 29363—messages only). North of Sauraha Bazaar. The facilities here are better than similarly priced hotels. The garden is almost as pretty as the campfire, which blazes from a permanent embankment. The attractive brick houses have well-furnished rooms. All bathrooms have hot water. There's an exceptional dining hall with an unexceptional menu. Doubles with bath Rs.300-400. Standard 2-night package deal to walk-in tourists US$60-70.

Chitwan Resort Camp, main road north of Sauraha Bazaar. The cement buildings have 8 older doubles and 3 newer ones. Rooms are fairly large and well-furnished; the newer ones are more attractive and have good bathrooms. The dining room stands out for quality and the menu for quantity—in Chitwan, that is. Old doubles with bath Rs.400. Standard 2-night package deal to walk-in tourists US$60.

Jungle Tourist Camp (tel. 29363—messages only). Just north of Sauraha Bazaar. Mud houses with mud floors and thatched roof. Bathrooms have hot water. The restaurant is open 6am-8pm. Doubles Rs.150, with bath Rs.400. Standard 2-night package deal to walk-in tourists US$65-70.

FOOD

The restaurants in Chitwan simultaneously take care of food and entertainment. In season, travelers pack the restaurants in Sauraha Bazaar and create a party atmosphere. Hotel restaurants are usually not as fun as those in Sauraha Bazaar, where owners often disregard the closing time in favor of more singing, drinking, and dancing. The rooftop restaurants in Sauraha Bazaar have great sunset views. Many Chitwan restaurants have campfires during the winter. Food here can be pricey because much of it is trucked in.

Jungle View Restaurant and Bar, Sauraha Bazaar. Currently the most popular Bazaar hangout. Specializes in Italian food, with exceptional lasagna. Gorgeous rooftop views of the river, especially in the evenings. During Happy Hour (5:30-6:30pm), beer and snacks cost Rs.75. Also serving breakfast, Indian food, and some Chinese food. Most entrees Rs.70-100. Open 6:30am-10pm.

K.C.'s Restaurant and Bar, Sauraha Bazaar. This is the only place in the bazaar with Star TV. The bamboo hut rooftop has good views and a decent selection of English music. The menu is among the most extensive in Sauraha, with relatively expensive Continental, Chinese, Indian, and Italian dishes. Goodies from a "German bakery" and a wide variety of cocktails are also available. The staff is friendly and knowledgeable about getting budget deals in jungle activities. Happy Hour (4-9pm) beer and snacks Rs.75. Open 6am-11pm.

SIGHTS AND ENTERTAINMENT

Due to the risk posed by animals, especially rhinos, visitors to Chitwan National Park must be accompanied by a guide at all times. There are several ways in which to organize activities and arrange for guides. The **package tours** that are available in Sauhara organize everything from jungle activities to return transportation to anywhere in Nepal. The most popular option is two nights and three days. One money-saving alternative is to arrange individualized itineraries by booking activities through a hotel and paying by the item (plus a service charge of about Rs.300-400). Those who do not book through a hotel may undertake more hassles especially during high season when hotel guests get priority in space-limited activities. **Guide companies** provide guides for every activity in Chitwan, and generally charge less than hotels for bookings. On the other hand, hotel services are more reliable (especially for jungle walks) because they can't just pack up and leave if there is a problem. Ask other tourists for

NEPAL

Chitwan's Elephants

Just about every elephant in Chitwan is from India. There, wild elephants still roam despite a millennium-old trade of capturing and training wild elephants. With elephant roaming areas receding, and the art of elephant capture losing interest, elephant prices have skyrocketed—some cost up to one million Indian rupees. Chitwan responded by establishing the Elephant Breeding Centre in 1987. Starting with 16 elephants, the park now has 64. At the age of two, elephants begin training with both human and elephant "teachers." Each elephant has three caretakers; most caretakers are Tharu so commands are given in the Tharu language. The elephants establish relationships with these individuals, particularly the *mahout*, who is the main driver. Some elephants even play polo with their caretakers during the winter. The elephant stables, which hold between 17 and 22 elephants throughout the year, are a 10-minute walk east from the park entrance. At feeding time (which is most of the time), the elephants hint for their favorite dinner balls by throwing grass and pointing their trunks.

referrals to the better guides and companies. The number of years of experience a guide has had is stated on the guide's permit certificate. Guides' fixed salaries are quite low, so if you are happy with a guide, remember that what would be an embarrassingly small tip in the West goes a long way here.

Chitwan National Park offers protection to 56 species of mammals including the one-horned rhinoceros, Bengal tiger, leopard, sloth bear, and wild bison. There are estimated to be 470 species of mammals, over 500 species of birds, nine species of amphibians, 126 species of fish, 150 species of butterflies, and 47 species of reptiles in the park. A 1995 study guesses that 107 of the 300 tigers in Nepal are in Chitwan.

Elephant rides are the most popular activity at Chitwan. In the tourist season, demand exceeds supply, so elephants need to be booked a day in advance. The Hotel Association Office keeps the waiting list, and if necessary lotteries names at 4pm the day before. Though a typical elephant ride lasts one hour, usually only 45 minutes are spent in the jungle. Elephants depart twice a day, at 7:30am and 4:30pm. No more than eight elephants ever enter the jungle at one time. An elephant ride costs Rs.650 for the park plus a service charge (Rs.50-100) if booked through a hotel.

The **jungle drive** is a close second to the elephant ride in popularity. Because jeep rides take four to five hours they cover more of the jungle, including Kasara palace and the Gharial Conservation Project. Jeeps, unlike elephants, can't leave the road to follow animals or go through tall grass. A maximum of six 10-person jeeps leave at 7am and 1:30pm from the park entrance, following the same route (Rs.500-650). More animals can be seen in the evening (1:30pm) ride, but rhino sightings are practically guaranteed on any jungle drive.

Most **canoe rides** involve an hour of floating down the river followed by a two- to three-hour guided walk back. Two groups of canoes leave every day, at 8am and at 2pm. During season, the Hotel Association Office keeps a waiting list for the next day's trips, and if necessary, lotteries them at 4pm the day before. The canoe ride costs Rs.150 per person, and the guide usually charges an additional Rs.150-200 per person for the jungle walk back. If a hotel or agency made the bookings, there will be Rs.50-100 in service charges.

Jungle walks are ideal for jungle immersion, photography, and animal sightings, but since walkers are unarmed and have no easy getaway, they can be dangerous. A guide takes a maximum of eight people. There is only one walking path in some sections of the jungle, so they can become crowded during season. A half-day's jungle walk lasts three hours, starts at 6am or 7am, and costs Rs.250. A full-day's jungle walk lasts seven hours, starts at 6am or 7am, and costs Rs.500. There is also a two day jungle walk to **Kasara,** the headquarters of the park and the location of the museum and the Gharial Conservation Project, spending the night in Jagapur. From Kasara, you can get to Sauraha by walking or getting a ride via Bharatpur. Guides charge about Rs.300 per person, with lower prices for larger groups.

Another option is a one-hour **bicycle ride** to **Bis Hajaar Tal** ("Twenty Thousand Lakes"), outside the park to the northwest of Sauraha. The best time to leave is very early in the morning, arriving in time to see gharials, birds, and rhinos coming to the lakes. For early morning rides, bicycles need to be reserved the night before. Guides charge Rs.200-300.

Some guides are knowledgeable about birds and offer one- to two-hour bird watches. Much of that time is spent walking to and from the birdwatching lookouts. Such excursions cost Rs.50-110 per person.

The Tharus, the indigenous people of Chitwan, live in a village along the road to the park entrance. A guided Tharu Village walk covers the culture, history, and religion of the people. The walk takes nearly two hours, but less than an hour is actually spent inside the village (Rs.50-75 per person). Tharu stick dances are exuberant and easy to participate in. Tharu dance troupes perform regularly at hotels, which invite them a certain number of guests have checked in. Hotels not hosting a troupe usually make arrangements for their guests to see the dance at another hotel. Fancier hotels may charge Rs.50 for non-guests, but most allow even non-guests to watch and participate for free.

■ Hetauda

Hetauda is a transit town, the starting point of a cableway that carries cargo between the Tarai and Kathmandu, and a temporary host to buses and trucks heading to and from the Indian border at Birganj. The north-south **Tribhuvan Highway** cuts right through town; a king's statue marks the intersection with the town's main east-west drag. The **bus park** is just southwest of this section. All Birganj buses pass through Hetauda and many more buses and trucks run between the two (frequent buses, 2hr., Rs.20). The **post office,** on the western branch from the intersection, is open Sun.-Fri. 10am-5pm. There is a smattering of STD **telephone** joints in the center of town. **Fruit stands** cluster northeast of the bus park, off the western street. **Pharmacies** can also be found on the western street. **Telephone Code:** 057.

Hetauda doesn't seem to be anyone's final destination, but the **accommodations** and **food** available aren't too bad. In fact, since it's only two hours away from Birganj, it would be worth considering spending the night in Hetauda rather than at the border. **Motel Avocado** (tel. 20429, 20235, 20911; fax 20611, 20655) is on the main road, just north of town, a 10-minute walk from the bus park. Set among overgrown grounds that include the avocado trees for which the motel is named (planted by Californian volunteers in the 60s), an orchid garden, and a small menagerie of peacocks, rabbits, and deer. All rooms have attached baths with towels and toilet paper, screened windows, fans, and mosquito-zapping machines. The most expensive rooms have A/C, color TV, and phones (just like a real motel!). Singles Rs.350-1500. Doubles Rs.550-2000. Plus 10% government tax. From September to November the restaurant serves everything made of avocado; the rest of the time it's mostly North Indian food. International telephones are available. The **Lido Inn,** on the main road south of the intersection (tel. 20937), is new and clean. All rooms have attached bath (with towels) and fan. The restaurant offers the usual curry-to-chow mein options, all Rs.70 or less. Singles Rs.250-350. Doubles Rs.350-550.

■ Birganj

Birganj is the funnel through which traffic to India passes, narrowing at the border into a pot-holed, exhaust-filled passageway clogged with trucks, rickshaws, bullock-carts and tongas. The colorful gateway at the border is a failed attempt to bring cheer to the scene. The only reason to come to Birganj is to cross the border. If you're heading to India, Birganj will relieve any separation anxiety and make you glad to leave

NEPAL

Nepal. If you're coming from India, perhaps you'll appreciate that Birganj is slightly more bearable than Raxaul, the town on the Indian side of the border.

ORIENTATION AND PRACTICAL INFORMATION

> **Warning:** Crossing the border from Nepal to India, be sure to stop not only at customs but also at the Indian **immigration office,** located under the bridge to India. Most rickshaw-wallahs don't know where it is, since the majority of border-crossers (Indians and Nepalis) don't have to go there. If you don't go there on the way in to get your passport stamped, you may have trouble getting out of India since your passport will say you've never entered.

Birganj clumps for miles along the main road that leads over the Indian border. The main landmark, at the north end of town, is a **clock tower.** Buses bypass the main road and stop at the **bus park** directly east of the clock tower. There is a subtly marked **Tourist Information Centre** (tel. 22083) on the west side of the main road, well south of the clock tower. The office is tucked in a courtyard, up a flight of stairs. The staff is amiable and will happily dust off some brochures if you ask, but they don't seem to know anything more than, say, a hotel manager might. (Open Mon.-Thurs. 10am-5pm, Fri. 10am-1pm.) The **immigration office** at the border is open daily from 6am to 7:30pm. If you don't already have a Nepalese **visa** when you arrive at the border (from India), you'll need a photo and at least US$15 in cash. **The only form of payment accepted is U.S. cash dollars.** There are no exchange facilities at the border giving out U.S. dollars. The **Nepal Bank,** on the main road, south of the clock tower, will exchange Indian rupees and U.S. dollars for Nepalese rupees. (Open Sun.-Thurs. 10am-2:30pm, Fri. 10am-2pm.) The hotels will also change money and accept Indian rupees. The **post office** is on the main road, just north of the clock tower. (Open Sun.-Fri. 10am-5pm). STD/ISD **telephone** booths are easy to find—they seem to all have "Hello" in their names. **Buses** to Kathmandu leave in the morning (6-8am) and evening (6-8pm). The ride lasts about 10 hours. **Local transport** consists of rickshaws and tongas. Both cross the border into India, but only rickshaws will wait while you stop at immigration. A rickshaw from Birganj to Raxaul takes 30 minutes and costs about Rs.35 for foreigners. **Pharmacies** are plentiful along the main street at the southern end of town. **Telephone Code:** 051.

ACCOMMODATIONS AND FOOD

The two best places to stay are next door to each other, one block west of the main road, well south of the clock tower. The **Hotel Kailash** (tel. 22384) has a range of rooms, the most basic of which have fans and mosquito nets; more expensive rooms have private baths, A/C, and TVs. All baths have cold water only. Singles Rs.90, with bath Rs.180-470, with A/C Rs.850-1050. Doubles Rs.200, with bath Rs.300-550, with A/C Rs.900-1110. The **Hotel Diyalo** (tel. 22370, 21570) is more expensive but cheerier, so a better value in its price range. All rooms have attached bath, TVs, phones, and mosquito nets. Cheaper rooms have fans and cold water; more expensive rooms have A/C and hot water, and there are even some suites. Singles Rs.400-500, with A/C Rs.600-1800. Doubles Rs.450-550, with A/C Rs.650-2000 (plus 11% tax). Both hotels have dimly lit North Indian restaurants. Around the corner from the hotels, on the street to the north that leads back to the main road, is **Kanccha Sweets,** with its fly-free display cases of Indian sweets and stand-up counter at which you can partake of South Indian snacks like *masala dosa* (Rs.15).

■ Janakpur

While other Tarai towns are physically closer to India, Janakpur is Nepal's most Indian town in spirit. As the birthplace of Sita, Janakpur owes some of its Indian character to the pilgrims who flock from south of the border to pay their respects to this heroine of the Hindu epic, the *Ramayana* (see **The Ramayana,** p. 81). The *Ramayana* identifies Janakpur as the capital of Mithila, a kingdom that stretched into northern India from the 10th to 3rd century BC. Despite its ancient associations, none of the buildings are particularly old. The cityscape is dominated by the flaking onion domes and triangular roofs of its many *kuti,* pilgrims' hostels, and is broken up by artificial ponds, or *sagars,* which are used for ritual baths. The pastel colors of sacred and secular buildings glow at dawn and dusk, when cymbals and drums from the temples fill the air. The city truly comes to life during festivals, the biggest of which is Bihawa Panchami (Nov.-Dec.) which features a re-enactment of Rama and Sita's wedding.

ORIENTATION AND PRACTICAL INFORMATION

Janakpur is comprised of a network of alleyways that seem to curve imperceptibly so it's easy to get disoriented and end up walking in circles. The **bus park** is in the southwest of town, near the **telecommunications tower.** The **train station** is in the northwest. The main street, **Station Road,** runs southwest from the station, passing through **Bhanu Chowk** (named for the Nepalese poet Bhanu whose bust tops a pillar in the middle of the intersection), then bearing south past **Danush Sagar,** one of the large man-made ponds. The **tourist office,** Station Rd., north of Bhanu Chowk (tel. 20755) has mice running around on the floor and a pamphlet specifically about Janakpur. The mice do their best, but the office and the pamphlet are fairly useless. The pamphlet does contain a nice wide-angle shot of the Janaki Mandir. The **Nepal Rastra Bank,** on the southern section of the main road, is open Sun.-Thurs. 10am-2pm, Fri. 10am-noon. The **post office** is in the southwest of town (open Sun.-Fri. 10am-5pm). There are plenty of **telephone** offices around town. The **airport** is 2km south of town, and several airlines run daily flights to Kathmandu (US$77). Day **buses** to Kathmandu (10hr., Rs.137) leave at 6:30 and 7:30am. Night buses to Kathmandu (Rs.172) and other destinations leave at 6, 7, and 8pm. Buses to Kakarbhitta (8-9hr., Rs.103) leave at 6pm. There are **cycle-rickshaws,** but you can get around on **foot** easily. There is a **hospital** just west of the Janaki Mandir, and **pharmacies** along Station Rd. **Fruit stands** cluster near the southern end of Station Rd., and west of the Janaki Mandir. **Telephone Code:** 041.

ACCOMMODATIONS

Hotel Welcome, Station Rd. (tel. 20646), near the southern end of the road. Although rooms range in amenities (all have fans and nets; some have baths, TVs and A/C), none are vying for a Good Housekeeping Award. The cheaper back rooms are quieter but smoky from the kitchen's wood-burning stove. Hot water and seat toilets only in the private baths. Most of the staff speaks English, and there's an STD/ISD and fax office in the hotel. The dingy restaurant is the most popular in town and serves tasty North Indian food. Power frequently fails but returns shortly. Singles Rs.75, with bath Rs.200-400, with A/C Rs.600. Doubles Rs.150, with bath Rs.250-500, with A/C Rs.1500. Plus 10% government tax.

Anand Hotel, Station Rd. (tel. 20562). At the north end of the road, near the train station. Small, shabby but clean rooms with fans and nets. Hot water in attached baths. Stark and dimly lit restaurant downstairs. Doubles Rs.150, with bath and double bed Rs.200; with bath, A/C, TV, and twin beds Rs.300.

FOOD

Aside from the hotel restaurants, there are many sweet shops around town. The only real restaurant is the **Kwality Restaurant,** Station Rd., at the south end. Red-trimmed blue walls do little to liven the spartan atmosphere. Decent curries (veg. Rs.20-30, meat Rs.45-60) are served at low tables. Open daily from 9am to 11pm.

SIGHTS

None of Janakpur's temples are very old, but they are all very much in use. The **Janaki Mandir,** a Mughal-style wedding cake of a construction, was built in 1911 on the spot

---

Mithila Painting

Maithili women (women from the area of southern Nepal and Northern India that was once the kingdom of Mithila) have developed an artistic tradition that has been passed through generations from mother to daughter. The art consists primarily of paintings on the walls of their houses (usually made of mud-covered bamboo, with thatched roofs). The paintings often serve a ritual purpose, as part of a festival or wedding. A woman may create paintings for her future husband as part of their courtship. Stylistically, the paintings are characterized by bold outlines filled in with bright colors. Subjects vary from abstract geometric designs to scenes from daily life. Certain images have different symbolic significance; pregnant elephants, parrots, bamboo, turtles and fish represent fertility and marriage while peacocks and elephants are good luck symbols. In Mithila painting, the process and the purpose of the paintings are more important than the finished product, which may be destroyed.

---

where an image of Sita was found in 1657, and where Sita is said to have been discovered as an infant by her father. The silver image of Sita is revealed twice a day, once in the early morning and again in the evening. At other times, priests will offer *puja* for you for a contribution. Next door, to the north, is the **Ram Janaki Bibah Mandap,** which marks the place where Rama and Sita were married. Life-sized statues of the heroic couple sit inside the glass-walled pagoda. Other equally kitschy statues reside in little houses surrounding it. Foreigners pay Rs.5 to have a look, and another Rs.2 to bring in a camera. Southeast of the Janaki Mandir is the **Ram Mandir,** Janakpur's oldest (1882) and most typically Nepalese-style temple, which is the center of the Ram Navami festival. To the east of the Ram Mandir are Janakpur's largest and holiest ponds, **Dhanush Sagar** and **Ganga Sagar,** sitting side by side. West of the Janaki Mandir, on the main highway, is **Hanuman Durbar,** a small temple dedicated to Rama's monkey-god sidekick, and home to the fat, sleepy beast claimed to be the **world's largest monkey.** Just ask for the "big monkey" and you'll be pointed in the right direction.

There are a few other things to do in Janakpur aside from temple-hopping. Nepal's only **steam railway** departs from here. It's a good way to check out the surrounding countryside. Trains to Bijalpur, to the west, take one hour, leaving at 7:20am and 3pm and returning at 8:20am and 5pm. Trains to Jaynagar, over the Indian border (uncrossable for foreigners) to the east, take two hours, leave at 6:45am, 10:20am, 12:55pm, and 4:55pm, and return at 7:20am, 9:15am, 1pm and 5pm. **Get off the train before it reaches the border, or you may have trouble leaving and re-entering Nepal.**

The **Janakpur Women's Development Centre** is a delight for anyone interested in art or economic development. Located southwest of Janakpur in the village of Kuwa, the center is best reached by rickshaw (about Rs.25). Wandering back through the village, you'll see Mithila painting in place on the walls of the houses. The artists use the traditional motifs of Mithila paintings on handmade paper, papier-maché, ceramics, and textiles. The center also trains the women in literacy, mathematics, and business management. This project has given women the chance to reach levels of socioeconomic power otherwise unattainable. It's exciting to see women participating in a development project that actually works. The center's products are for sale there and at various non-profit outlets in Kathmandu and Patan. Rickshaws to Janakpur can be found on the main road. (Open Sun.-Thurs. 10am-5pm, Fri. 10am-4pm.)

■ Dharan

At the point where the landscape changes from plains to hills sits the bazaar town of Dharan, where people from the hills come to buy everything from cloth to electronics. Despite the municipality's efforts to increase tourism, the few visitors pass through more often than stay. Chatara, where rafters on the Sun Kosi finish up, is

15km west and Hile and Basantpur, in the hills to the north, are trekking trailheads. Once home to one of the British Army's Gurkha training camps, Dharan still hosts a fair share of Nepal's *khukuri*-smiths.

ORIENTATION AND PRACTICAL INFORMATION

The center of town is along the main north-south road **Bhanu Chowk,** marked by a bust of the Nepalese poet Bhanu. The main east-west street crosses the road here. **Buses** to and from the north stop at the southeast corner, while those to and from the south stop at the southwest corner.

The main street hosts numerous **travel agents,** many of them doubling as STD/ISD **telephone** booths. A branch of **Nepal Bank Ltd.** is at the next major intersection north of Bhanu Chowk (open Sun.-Thurs. 10am-3pm, Fri. 10am-noon). The closest **airport** is in Biratnagar, an hour away by private bus (Rs.100). Local buses (Rs.19) take a bit longer and stop on the main road; an auto-rickshaw from there to the airport costs another Rs.15. Nepal Airways, Necon Air, and RNAC all have several daily flights to Kathmandu. **Buses** head north to Hile via Dhankuta and go on to Basantpur (every hr., 4hr., Rs.52) and to Biratnagar (frequent, 2hr., Rs.22). A daily night bus to Kathmandu leaves around 2 or 3pm, takes 16 to 17 hours, and costs Rs.232. Other bus connections can be made at Itahari (frequent, 30min., Rs.9) at the junction of the area's two highways. The **market** at the northwest corner of Bhanu Chowk sells fruit and the nearby stores have canned goods. **Pharmacies** can be found along the main road. **Telephone Code:** 025.

ACCOMMODATIONS AND FOOD

Shristi Guest House, Chatra Line (tel. 20569). Turn left at the next intersection north of Bhanu Chowk; a 5-min. walk from the bus stands. Nothing fancy—rooms are well-maintained and all have fans. Traffic noise starts early on the road outside. Singles Rs.125. Doubles Rs.150, with bath Rs.250. **Bamboo House,** just east of Bhanu Chowk, on the left, serves veg. (Rs.20-50) and non-veg. (Rs.60) curries in a dark, bamboo-lined setting. Tandoori if you're lucky. Private booths for couples or unaccompanied women. (Open daily 7am-9:30pm.)

■ Hile

Perched above the Arun Valley at 1900m, with its spectacular mountain views and ethnic mix of Bhotiyas (people of Tibetan descent), Rais, Newaris, and Indians, cool, misty Hile has a distinctly Nepalese feel to it, unlike the hot, dusty plains of the Tarai below. Although Hile is a trailhead for treks in the Arun Valley in the clear season, it may merit a visit even for non-trekkers. The town itself consists of a row of shops boasting stacks of shiny plastic buckets and heaps of flip-flops and salt. Piles of *doka* (the cone-shaped baskets porters carry with headstraps) wait to be filled and carried off into the hills. There are a few small *gompas* but the most exciting thing to see is the Himalaya; there are great views from the hilltop just north of town, a 45-minute walk. Less spectacular but still impressive is the view from the south end of town.

Buses to and from Dharan leave hourly, take four hours and cost Rs.52. There are several trekking-style **lodges** to choose from. All are similar, but the **Hotel Gajur** has a little garden out back, and is a good place to sample *tongba,* an alcoholic drink made from fermented millet steeped like tea in hot water in a little wooden barrel.

■ Kakarbhitta

Kakarbhitta is a small trading town on the border of India and Nepal with little to distinguish as part of either country. Located on the flood plains next to the Mechi River, which constitutes the physical border between the two countries, there is more or less free traffic across the bridge. Kakarbhitta is essentially one large bazaar centered around a bus station. The main road runs east 100m to the border and west all the way to Kathmandu. A small grid of alleys to the west of the central bazaar is where Kakarbhitta's cheapest goods are found.

The **tourist office** is located on the main road next to Hotel Kathmandu. **Airline offices,** including Nepal Airlines and Everest Air (tel. 29020), are between the bus station and the border (open 7am-8pm). Kakarbhitta is the best place to catch the **bus** for Kathmandu (8-9 per day, 12:30-5pm, 16hr., Rs.258). **Rickshaws** run from the border to Panitanki in India (Rs.10), where there are buses to Siliguri (1hr., Rs.6). To reach Bagdogra Airport, get off the bus to Siliguri at Bagdogra (Rs.5) and take a rickshaw (1hr., Rs.10). At the border crossing, a Nepali visa is available (US$15 for 15 days, US$25 for 30 days, US$60 for 60 days). Open 7am-7pm. Hop out twice on the Indian side to fill out ledger books.

In town, there are a lot of hotel signs, but not many budget accommodations. Though most hotels cut deals off-season, rooms are overpriced in season. At **Hotel Lahove,** the first alley from bus station that runs parallel to the main road towards Kathmandu, Saran Bosnet has three rooms for Rs.50. **ABC Lodge,** a little farther down the next alley, has singles available for Rs.160 and doubles for Rs.225. **Hotel Kathmandu** (tel. 29008), at the far corner of the bazaar from the border, has singles for Rs.150 and doubles Rs.200. Food surrounds the central bazaar, but cleanliness varies. The kitchens are in plain sight—judge for yourself. **Restaurant Mountain View,** at the corner between the bus station and the border, has good nightly specials (open 7am-8pm; entrees Rs.15-30). Next door, **Restaurant Kathmandu** is slightly bigger, but not very cozy (open 6am-8pm; entrees Rs.15-50).

Appendix

▧ Climate

Temp in °C Rain in cm	January Temp	Rain	March Temp	Rain	May Temp	Rain	July Temp	Rain	September Temp	Rain	November Temp	Rain
Bangalore	28/15	0.4	33/19	0.6	33/21	11.9	28/19	9.3	28/19	12.9	27/17	4.6
Bombay	28/19	0.2	30/22	0.2	33/27	1.8	29/25	61.7	29/24	26.4	32/23	1.3
Calcutta	27/13	1.0	34/21	3.6	36/25	14.0	32/26	32.5	32/26	25.2	29/18	2.0
Darjeeling	08/02	1.3	14/06	4.3	18/12	21.6	19/14	79.8	18/13	44.7	12/06	2.3
Delhi	21/07	2.3	31/14	1.3	41/26	1.3	36/27	18.0	34/24	11.7	29/11	0.3
Hyderabad	29/16	0.8	36/21	1.3	40/27	2.8	31/23	15.2	31/22	16.5	29/17	2.8
Jodhpur	25/09	0.7	33/17	0.2	42/27	0.6	36/27	12.2	35/24	4.7	31/14	0.3
Kathmandu	18/02	1.5	25/07	2.3	30/16	12.2	29/20	37.3	28/19	15.5	23/07	0.8
Madras	29/19	3.6	33/22	0.8	38/28	2.5	36/26	9.1	34/25	11.9	29/22	35.6
Panjim (Goa)	31/19	0.2	32/23	0.4	33/27	1.8	29/24	89.2	29/24	27.7	33/22	2.0
Shimla	08/02	6.1	14/7	6.1	22/14	6.6	21/16	42.4	19/14	16.0	14/07	1.3
Trivandrum	31/22	2.0	33/24	4.3	31/25	24.9	29/23	21.5	30/23	12.3	30/23	20.7
Varanasi	23/09	2.3	33/17	1.4	41/27	0.8	33/26	34.6	32/25	26.1	29/13	1.5

▧ Glossary

GENERAL TERMS

adivasi	aboriginal, tribal people of India
Agni	Hindu god of fire, messenger of the gods
AIADMK	All-India Anna Dravida Munntra Kazhagam, regional party in Tamil Nadu
ahimsa	non-violence
air-cooling	low-budget air-conditioning—a fan blowing air over the surface of water
Allah	literally, "the God," to Muslims
AMS	Acute Mountain Sickness
artha	material wealth, one of the four goals of Hindu life
ashram	hermitage for Hindu sages and their students
ASI	Archaeological Survey of India
atman	Hindu concept of individual soul, the breath of Brahman
Avalokitesvara	the popular *boddhisattva* of compassion
avatar	descent of a Hindu god to earth; an incarnation
ayurveda	ancient Indian system of medicine
azan	Muslim call to prayer
bahal	Newari houses or monasteries forming a quadrangle with a central courtyard
baksheesh	tip, donation, bribe, or all of these at once
ban	forest
Bhagavad Gita	Hindu philosophical scripture sung to the hero Arjuna by the god Krishna
bhakti	personal, emotional devotion to a Hindu deity
bhang	dried leaves and shoots of the male cannabis plant
Bharat	India
bhavan	office or building
bidi	small cigarette made from a rolled-up tobacco leaf
BJP	Bharatiya Janata Party (Indian People's Party); the major Hindu nationalist party, symbolized by a lotus
bodhisattva	would-be Buddha who postpones his own enlightenment in order to help others
Bön	pre-Buddhist, animist religion of Tibet

Brahma	creator god in the Hindu "trinity," no longer commonly worshiped
Brahmin	member of the hereditary priesthood; highest of the four Hindu *varnas*
Buddha	Enlightened One
bugyal	high-altitude meadow, above the treeline
cantonment	military district in a city
caste	Hindu group that practices a hereditary occupation, has a definite ritual status, and marries within the group
chakra	Wheel of the Law in Buddhism; Vishnu's discus weapon in Hinduism
chalo	let's go
chaitya	Buddhist prayer hall or miniature *stupa*
chappals	leather sandals
chauk	market area or square
chhattri	cenotaph; cremation monument
chillum	mouthpiece of a *hookah,* or a pipe use to smoke *ganja*
chorten	Tibetan Buddhist memorial shrine
chowkidar	watchman
communalism	religious prejudice, especially between Hindus and Muslims
Congress (I)	party that has dominated Indian politics since Independence, which grew out of the Indian National Congress, the organization that pushed for Indian Independence; the party of Jawaharlal Nehru, Indira Gandhi, and P.V. Narasimha Rao, symbolized by a hand
CPM or CPI(M)	Communist Party of India (Marxist), based in West Bengal, symbolized by a hammer and sickle
CPN-UML	Communist Party of Nepal-United Marxist-Leninist, symbolized by a sun
crore	ten million (usually rupees or people), written 1,00,00,000
dacoit	armed bandit
Dalit	currently preferred term for former "untouchables"
darshan	"seeing" a Hindu deity through his or her image
deodar	tall Indian cedar tree
dham	place, often a sacred site
dharamshala	resthouse for Hindu pilgrims
dharma	a very difficult word to define; it refers to one's duty and station in life, and also to a system of morality and a way of life or religion (Hindu or Buddhist)
dhobi	washerman or washerwoman
dhoti	*lungi* with the cloth then pulled up between the wearer's legs
dhyani Buddha	meditating Buddha
DMK	Dravida Munnetra Kazhagam; regional party in Tamil Nadu
dorje	Tibetan Buddhist thunderbolt symbol
durbar	royal palace or court
Durga	Hindu goddess who slayed the buffalo demon Mahisha
Ganesha	the elephant-headed god, son of Shiva and Parvati, the Lord of Obstacles, frequently stationed at doorways and other passages
FRO	Foreginers' Registration Office

ganja	the dried leaves and flowering tops of the female cannabis plant, used for smoking
garh	fort
Garuda	Vishnu's half-man, half-bird vehicle
ghat	riverbank used for bathing, often paved with steps; also the name of the ranges of hills on the east and west coasts of the Indian peninsula
gompa	Tibetan Buddhist monastery
gopuram	trapezoidal entrance tower of a South Indian Hindu temple
GPO	General Post Office
guru	religious teacher; in Sikhism, one of the ten founding leaders of the Sikh faith
gurudwara	Sikh temple
Guru Granth Sahib	Sikh holy book
Haj	the annual pilgrimage to Mecca which all Muslims are required to make once in their lifetime
Hanuman	monkey god, helper of Rama in the *Ramayana*
harmonium	air-powered keyboard instrument
hartal	general strike
haveli	Rajasthani mansion, traditionally painted with murals
hiti	Newari water-spout
hookah	elaborate smoking apparatus in which the smoke is drawn through a long pipe and a container of water
howdah	seat for an elephant rider
imam	the leader of prayers in a mosque, or a Shi'a Muslim leader descended from Muhammad
imambara	tomb of a Shi'a Muslim imam, or a replica of one
Indo-Saracenic	architecture merging Indian styles with imported "Islamic" styles from the Middle East
Indra	early Hindu god of thunder, king of the Vedic gods
jagamohana	audience hall or "porch" of a Hindu temple
jali	geometric lattticework pattern in Islamic architecture
Janata Dal	political party based largely in Uttar Pradesh and Bihar, supported by low-caste Hindus, symbolized by a wheel
Jat	large North Indian agricultural case
jati	small Hindu caste division
jauhar	Rajput custom of mass *sati*
-ji	suffix added to names as a mark of respect
JKLF	Jammu and Kashmir Liberation Front; militant group seeking independence for Kashmir
Kali	Hindu goddess with black skin and a lolling red tongue who wears snakes and skulls
kama	physical love, one of the four goals of a Hindu's life; when capitalized, "Kama" is the Hindu god of love
kameez	loose-fitting woman's shirt
khadi	homespun, handwoven cotton cloth
Khalistan	"Land of the Pure"; name of the independent Punjab desired by Sikh separatists
khalsa	Punjabi "pure"; a Sikh who has been "baptized"
khukuri	machete-like Nepalese "Gurkha" knife
Krishna	carefree Hindu god who plays the flute and frolics with milkmaids, also the charioteer of Arjuna in the Mahabharata who sang to him the Bhagavad Gita; considered an *avatar* of Vishnu

kshatriya	member of the warrior/ruler caste, second highest of the four varnas of the Hindu caste system
kurta	long collarless shirt
lakh	one hundred thousand (usually rupees or people), written 1,00,000
Lakshmi	Goddess of fortune and wealth, often considered the consort of Vishnu
lama	Tibetan-Buddhist priest or holy man
lila	Hindu concept of divine "play," in both senses: a god (especially Krishna) sporting with his human worshipers, or a theatrical production depicting a myth (especially the *Ramayana*).
linga	stone shaft that symbolizes Shiva; while originally a phallic symbol, it has lost that meaning for most Hindus
Lok Sabha	lower house of the Indian parliament
lungi	sarong; cylinder of cloth tied around a man's waist
Macchendranath	Newari god associated with rain
maha-	great
Mahabharata	long, long, Sanksrit epic telling the story of the five Pandava brothers' struggle to regain their kingdom
mahal	palace
mahout	elephant trainer
mandala	a circle symbolizing the universe in Hindu and Buddhist art, used as an aid to meditation
mandapam	colonnaded hall leading up to a Hindu or Jain temple sanctum
mandir	Hindu or Jain temple
mantra	sacred word or chant used by Hindus and Buddhists to aid in meditation
masjid	mosque; Muslim place of worship
math	residence for Hinsu priests or sadhus
maya	the illusory world of everyday life created by the gods of Hinduism
mela	fair or festival
moksha	Hindu salvation; liberation from samsara
monsoon	season of heavy rains, usually from June to September, when moist air from the Indian Ocean is pulled over the Subcontinent by pressure systems in Central Asia.
muezzin	crier who calls Muslims to prayer from the minaret of a mosque
nadi	river
naga	Hindu aquatic snake deity
-nagar	city
Nandi	bull who is Shiva's vehicle
Narayan	Vishnu, especially when sleeping on the cosmic ocean
nawab	Muslim governor or landowner
NDP	National Democratic Party, right-wing party in Nepal
Nepali Congress	centrist party that led the movement for democracy in Nepal, symbolized by a tree
nirvana	nothingness, a blissful void, the goal of Buddhists
Om	mantra used by Hindus and Buddhists; sacred invocation
paise	1/100 of a rupee
pajama	men's baggy pants
panchayat	traditional five-member village council

Parsi	"Persian;" Zoroastrians who migrated to India after the Muslim conversion of Iran
Partition	the division of British India along religious lines to create India and Pakistan in 1947
Parvati	mountain goddess, consort of Shiva through whom his power is expressed
pitha	the circular base on which a linga sits; also a Hindu holy place associated with a goddess
prasad	food consecrated by a Hindu deity and given out to worshipers
puja	prayers and offerings of food and flowers to a Hindu deity
pujari	Hindu priest conducting ceremonies in a temple
pukkah	finished, ripe, complete
-pur	city
Puranas	"Old stories;" Hindu mythological poems
purdah	the Muslim practice of secluding women
Qur'an	"Recitation;' Muslim holy book containing Muhammad's Arabic recountings of divine revelations
Radha	milkmaid goddess, consort of Krishna
raga	melodic structure used as a base for lengthy musical improvisations
raj	government or sovereignty; when capitalized, usually refers to the British Empire in India
raja	king
Rajputs	medieval Hindu warrior-princes of central India and Rajasthan; commonly used as another word for *kshatriyas*
Rama	Hindu hero-god of the epic *Ramayana* who defeats the demon Ravana; considered an *avatar* of Vishnu
Ramayana	epic telling the story of Rama's rescue of his wife Sita from Ravana
Ramadan	holiest month in the Islamic calendar, when Muslims are required to fast between dawn and dusk
rani	queen
Ravana	villian of the epic *Ramayana*
RNAC	Royal Nepal Airlines Corporation
RSS	Rashtriya Swayamsevak Sangh (National Volunteer Corps), Hindu nationalist paramilitary organization
sadhu	ascetic Hindu holy man
sagar	sea or lake
sahib	"master," title given to English colonial bosses and still used to address Europeans
salwar	women's baggy pants worn with kameez
sambar	large, dark brown deer
samsara	the endless, painful cycle of life, death and rebirth
sangam	meeting point of two rivers; also name given to early gatherings of Tamil poets
sannyasin	"renouncer." Hindu ascetic wanderer who has given up worldly life
sant	saint, holy man
sari	six yards of cloth draped around a woman's body
sarod	fretless string instrument
Sati	Hindu goddess who landed in pieces all over India, forming Shakti pithas; considered a consort of Shiva

APPENDIX

sati	custom in which widows burned themselves on their husbands' funeral pyres
satyagraha	"truthful pleading;" Mahatma Gandhi's method of protest by non-violent non-cooperation
scheduled castes	official name for the former "untouchable" groups, whose castes are listed in a "schedule" in Indian law
scheduled tribes	aboriginal groups recognized under India law
sepoy	Indian serving in British Indian army under the Raj
Shaiva	follower of Shiva
Shakti	divine feminine power in Hinduism
Shankara	Shiva
shanti	peace
shikhara	pyramid-shaped spite on a Hindu temple
Shi'a	Muslim sect based largely in Iran, which split from the Sunnis in the 8th century AD in a succession dispute; Shi'as look to imams in Iran as their spiritual leaders
Shitala	"cool" goddess of smallpox and other fever diseases in North India
Shiva	one of the great gods of Hinduism, known as the Destroyer in the Hindu "trinity," though he has other roles as well; usually depicted as an ascetic holy man
Shiv Sena	regional Hindu nationalist party in Maharashtra
shudra	member of the laborer caste, lowest of the four Hindu *varnas*
sindur	vermillion paste used as an offering to Hindu deities
Sita	Rama's wife in the *Ramayana,* she is kidnapped by Ravana leading to the battle between Rama and Ravana
sitar	20-stringed instrument made from a gourd with a teakwood bridge
Sri	title of respect and veneration
STD/ISD	standard trunk dialing/international subscriber dialing
stupa	large hemispherical mound of earth, usually containing a Buddhist relic
Sufi	member of Islamic devotional, mystical movement
Sunni	largest Muslim sect; believes in elected leaders for the Islamic community
swadeshi	domestic goods; the Indian freedom movement called for their use rather than British imports
swaraj	self-rule; what the Indian freedom movement demanded
tabla	two-piece drum set
tal	lake
tara	Tantric female companion to a *dhyani* Buddha
tarai	foothills near the base of the Himalaya
tempo	three-wheeled motor vehicle meant to carry about six people
thanka	Tibetan scroll-painting of a *mandala,* used as an aid in meditation
tirtha	"crossing" between earth and heaven in Hinduism; while this usually means a holy place, it can also mean a holy man, *mantra,* etc.
tirthankara	one of 24 Jain "crossing-makers," a series of deities culminating with Mahavira, the founder of Jainism
tonga	two-wheeled carriage drawn by a horse or pony
topi	cap worn by Nepali men

trek	organized hike through the countryside in mountain regions
trichul	trident; symbol of Shiva and originally a symbol of the Goddess
untouchables	Hindus without caste, formerly shunned by high-caste Hindus because their touch was considered polluting. Now called scheduled castes, Dalits, or harijans.
Upanishads	speculative, philosophical Sankrit Hindu hymns composed around 800 BC.
Vaishnava	follower of Vishnu
vaishya	member of the merchant caste, third-highest of the four Hindu *varnas*
vajra	Nepali word for *dorje*
varna	broad group of Hindu castes; Brahmins, *kshatriyas, vaishyas,* and *shudras* are the four varnas
Vedas	sacred hymns in Sanskrit composed between 1500 and 800 BC, forming the basis of the Hindu religion
Vishnu	one of the Great Gods of Hinduism, known as the "Preserver" in the Hindu trinity; frequently appears on earth as an *avatar* to rescue the earth from demons
VHP	Vishwa Hindu Parishad (World Hindu Society); Hindu nationalist organization campaigning to restore Hindu temples
wallah	occupational suffix: e.g. rickshaw-*wallahs* drive rickshaws, chai-wallahs sell tea
yaksha	early Hindu nature deity
yakshi	female *yaksha*
yama	early Hindu god of death
zakat	obligatory almsgiving required of Muslims
zamindar	tax collecter or landlord in Mughal India

FOOD, DRINK, AND RESTAURANT TERMS

alu	potato
am	mango
badam	almond
baingan	eggplant
bhaji	vegetables dipped in batter and fried
bhat	rice
biryani	fried rice with vegetables or meat
chai	tea
chang	Himalayan rice wine
chapati	unleavened bread cooked on a griddle
chat	snack
cold drink	carbonated drink
dahi	yogurt
dal	lentil soup; staple dish eaten with rice
dhaba	small roadside eating place
dopiaza	with two onions
dosa	South Indian rice pancake, rolled up and stuffed with vegetables
dudh	milk
feni	alcoholic drink made from coconuts or cashews
ghee	clarified butter

gosht	mutton or goat
gulab jamun	dry milk balls in sweet syrup
halal	food prepared according to Islamic dietary rules
idli	South Indian steamed rice cakes
lassi	yogurt and ice-water drink
machli	fish
masala	a mix of spices, usually containing cumin, coriander, and cardamom
momo	Tibetan stuffed pastry similar to wontons or ravioli
murg	chicken
mutter	green peas
naan	unleavened bread cooked in a tandoor
naryal	coconut
pakoras	cheese or other foods deep-fried in chick pea batter
paneer	homemade cheese
pani	water
papadam	crispy lentil wafer
paratha	multi-layered whole-wheat bread cooked on a griddle
pan	betel leaf with stuffed with areca nut for chewing
permit room	(in Tamil Nadu) establishment with a liquor license; bar
phal	fruit
pongal	rice item garnished with black peppers and chillies
pulao	fried rice with nuts or fruit
puri	small deep-fried bread
raita	spicy salad of vegetables and yogurt
raksi	strong Himalayan liquor
roti	bread
saag	pureed spinach
sabji	vegetables
sambar	South Indian lentil soup
samosa	deep-fried pastry pyramid containing vegetables or meat
tandoor	clay oven shaped like an inverted cone
thali	complete meal served on a steel plate with small dishes of condiments
thukpa	Tibetan noodle soup
tiffin	snack or light meal
toddy	unrefined coconut liquor
utthapam	thick dosa made with onion
vadai	doughnut-shaped rice cake soaked in curd or sambar.

■ Phrasebook

English	Hindi	English	Hindi
		Phrases	
Hello.	Namaste.	How are you?	Kaisehain?
Sorry/Forgive me .	Maaf kijiyega.	Yes/no	Ha/Na
Thank you.	Shukriya.	No thanks.	Nahin, shukriya.
Good-bye.	Phir milenge.	No problem.	Koi baat nahin.
When(what time)?	Kab?	What?	Kya?
OK.	Thik hai.	Where is...?	...kahaan?

English	Hindi	English	Hindi
Who?	Kaun?	Why?	Kyon?
How much does this cost?	Iska kya daamhain?	Is...available?	Yaha...milta hai?
Go away/Leave me alone.	Chod dijiya/Tang na karo.	Stop/enough.	Bas.
I don't understand.	Samajha nahin.	please repeat.	phir se kahiye.
Please speak slowly.	Zara dhire boliye	What's this called in Hindi?	Hindi mein ise kya kehte hain?
What is your name?	Apka nam kya nai?	Help!	Bachad!
My name is...	Mera nam...hai.	My country is...	Mera desh...hai.
I like...	Mujhe...acha lagta hai.	I don't like...	Mujhe...acha nahin lagta.

Directions

(to the) right	dayne hath	(to the) left	bayan hath
How do I get to...?	...ka rasta kya hai?	How far is...?	Kitna dur hai?
near	pas mein	far	dur

Numbers

one	ek	two	do
three	teen	four	char
five	panch	six	chei
seven	saat	eight	aath
nine	naun	ten	das
eleven	gyaarah	twelve	baarah
fifteen	pandraah	twenty	bees
twenty-five	pachees	thirty	tees
forty	chaalies	fifty	pachaas
one hundred	ek sau	one thousand	ek hazar

Food

bread	dabal roti	rice	chawal
meat	naans	water	pani
vegetables	sabzi		

Times and Hours

open	khula	closed	band
What time is it?	Kitne baje hain?	morning	subah
afternoon	dopahar	evening	shaam
night	raat	yesterday	kal

APPENDIX

English	Hindi	English	Hindi
today	aaj	tomorrow	kal

Other Words

English	Hindi	English	Hindi
alone	akela	friend	dost
good	accha	bad	bura
happy	kush	sad	dukhi
hot	garam	cold	thanda

English	Bengali	English	Bengali

Phrases

English	Bengali	English	Bengali
Hello.	Namashkar.	How are you?	Kemon achhen?
Sorry/Forgive me.	Mapf korben.	No problem.	Oshubidha ney.
Thank you.	Dhonnobad.	Yes/No.	Ha/Na.
Good-bye.	Abar dekha habe	OK.	Achha/Thik.
Where is...?	...kothai?	When(what time)?	Kata?
Why?	Kano?	What?	Ki?
Who?	Ke?	Stop/enough.	Bas.
How much does this cost?	Koto taka?	Is...available?	...ase?
What is your name?	Apnar nam ki?	Go away/leave me alone.	Chede bin/Birakt korben na.
My name is...	Amar nam...	My country is...	Amar desh...
I like...	Amar...bhalo lage	I don't like...	Amar...bhalo lage na
I don't understand.	Bujhi na.	Please repeat.	Aabar bolun.
Please speak slowly	Aste aste bolun	What's this called in Bengali?	Banglay eta ke ki bole?
Help!	Sahajjo!		

Directions

English	Bengali	English	Bengali
(to the) right	dan dike	(to the) left	bam dike
How do I get to...?	...jabar rasta?	How far is...?	...koto door?
near	pashe	far	door

Numbers

English	Bengali	English	Bengali
one	ek	two	dui
three	tin	four	char
five	panch	six	choi
seven	shat	eight	at
nine	noi	ten	dosh

English	Bengali	English	Bengali
eleven	agaro	twelve	baro
fifteen	ponero	twenty	bish
twenty-five	ponchish	thirty	tirish
forty	chollish	fifty	ponchash
one hundred	ek sho	one thousand	ek hajar

Food

bread	paoruti	rice	bhat
meat	mansho	water	jol/pani
vegetables	shobji		

Times and Hours

open	khozla	closed	bandho
What time is it?	Koita baje?	morning	shokal
afternoon	dupur	evening	sondhya
night	rat	yesterday	kal
today	aj	tomorrow	kal

Etc.

alone	eka	friend	bandhu (M)/band-hobi (F)
good	bhalo	bad	kharap
happy	khushi	sad	dukhi/mon kharab
hot	gorom	cold	thandha

English	Tamil	English	Tamil

Phrases

Hello.	Namaskaram.	How are you?	Yep padi irukkai?
Sorry/Forgive me .	Mannichuko.	No problem.	Kavalai, illai.
Thank you.	Nanri.	No thanks.	Illai, véndam.
Yes/No.	Amam/Illai.	OK.	Se ri.
Good-bye.	Poittu Varén.	When(what time)?	Yepo?
Why?	Yén?	What?	Enna?
Who?	Yaru?	Where is...?	Yengai…?
How much does this cost?	Yenna vélai?	Is...available?	Trukka?
Please speak slowly.	Médhoova pésûngo.	What's this called in Tamil?	Tamille Enna?
I don't understand.	Puriyailai.	Help!	Kapathu!

English	Tamil	English	Tamil
Please repeat.	Thiruppi.	Go away/leave me alone.	Enna vidu.
I like...	Ennaku...pidikkum.	I don't like...	Ennaku...pidikkaath.
What is your name?	Unga péyar ennai?	My name is...	En peyar...
My country is...	Ennôda désham...	Stop/enough.	Porum.

Directions

English	Tamil	English	Tamil
(to the) right	valadu pakkam	(to the) left	idadhu pakkam
How do I get to...?	...eppadi pôradu?	How far is...?	...evvalavu dooram?
near	pakkam	far	dooram

Numbers

English	Tamil	English	Tamil
one	ônnu	two	rendu
three	moonu	four	naa lu
five	anju	six	aaru
seven	ézhu	eight	éttu
nine	ombôdu	ten	patthu
eleven	padinnonnu	twelve	pannandu
fifteen	payanju	twenty	iruvadu
twenty-five	irunattanju	thirty	muppadu
forty	narpadu	fifty	ambadu
one hundred	nooru	one thousand	aayiram

Food

English	Tamil	English	Tamil
vegetables	kari kai	rice	saadam
meat	maamsam	water	thanni

Times and Hours

English	Tamil	English	Tamil
open	tharandhu	closed	moodi
What time is it?	Enna néram?	morning	kaathaalai
afternoon	madyaanam	evening	saayankaalam
night	raatri	yesterday	nethikki
today	innikki	tomorrow	nazhaikki

Other Words

English	Tamil	English	Tamil
alone	thaniya	friend	nanban
good	nalladhu	bad	kéttadhu
happy	sandôsham	sad	dukham
hot	soodu	cold	aarinadhu

English	Marathi	English	Marathi

Phrases

English	Marathi	English	Marathi
Hello.	Namaste/Namaskaar.	How are you?	Kasa kaya aahey?
Sorry/Forgive me .	Maaf karaa	OK.	Achha/thik Aahey.
Thank you.	Dhanyawad.	No thanks.	Nako.
Who?	Kuon?	When(what time)?	Kehva?/Kadhi?
Why?	Kaa?	What?	Kaaya?
Where is...?	Kuthay aahey...?	Yes/No.	Ho/Naahi.
How much does this cost?	Hey kiti aahey?	Is...available?	...aahey kaa?
I don't understand.	Mala samasta hani.	Please repeat.	Parat Sangaa.
Please speak slowly.	Sowkash bolaa.	What's this called in Marathi?	Maratheet?
What is your name?	Tumhi kyon aahat ka?/ Tumsa kay kaya?	Go away/Leave me alone.	Ikerdun zaa.
My name is...	Maaza nau...aahey.	My country is...	Maza gay...aahey.
I like...	Mala...awarta aahey.	I don't like...	Mala...awardat naahi.
Help!	Madat laraa!	Stop/enough	Bas.

Directions

English	Marathi	English	Marathi
(to the) right	uz ni kar dey	(to the) left	daa vi kar dey
How do I get to...?	Mala kaa zaitsa...?	How far is...?	Kiti dur...?
near	zawal	far	dur

Numbers

English	Marathi	English	Marathi
one	ek	two	dōn
three	teen	four	char
five	paatz	six	sahaa
seven	saat	eight	aat
nine	noi	ten	dahaa
eleven	akra	twelve	baara
fifteen	tera	twenty	vis
twenty-five	panch vis	thirty	tis
forty	chaalis	fifty	paatsis
one hundred	ek shambar	one thousand	ek hazaar

Food

English	Marathi	English	Marathi
bread	chapati/bhakri	rice	bhat
vegetables	bhaji	water	pani

English	Marathi	English	Marathi
Times and Hours			
What time is it?	Kiti waazle?	closed	band
night	ratri	morning	sakarli
today	kal	yesterday	kal
tomorrow	aazudya		
Other Words			
happy	ananda	friend	mitra (M)/maitrin (F)
hot	garam	cold	thandha

English	Nepali	English	Nepali
Phrases			
Hello.	Namaste.	How are you?	Tapaii kasto gunu guncha?
Sorry/Forgive me .	Sorry (maff pau)	No problem.	Sabai theek cha.
Thank you.	Danyabad.	No thanks.	Pardaina, danyabad.
Yes/No.	Ho/Hoina.	Good-bye.	Namaste.
When(what time)?	Kahila?	What?	Ke?
Who?	Ko?	Where is...?	Kata cha...?
Why?	Kina?	OK.	Huncha.
How much does this cost?	Yo kati parcha?	Is...available?	...paincha?
Go away/leave me alone.	Tapai januus ta.	Stop/enough.	Pugyo.
I don't understand.	Buje na.	Please repeat.	Feri bhannuhos.
Please speak slowly.	Bistarai bolnuhos.	What's this called in Nepali?	Nepali ma kam ke ho?
What is your name?	Tapai ko nam ke ho?	My name is...	Mero nam...ho.
Help!	Guhar!	My country is...	Mero deas ...ho.
I like...	Man par cha...	I don't like...	Mar par dai na...
Directions			
(to the) right	daya	(to the) left	baya
How do I get to...?	...kasari njane?	How far is...?	...kati tada cha?
near	najik	far	tada
Numbers			
one	ek	two	dui
three	teen	four	char
five	panch	six	cha

English	Nepali	English	Nepali
seven	saat	eight	aathh
nine	nau	ten	daus
eleven	aegara	twelve	bahra
fifteen	pandra	twenty	biss
twenty-five	pachiss	thirty	tees
forty	chaliss	fifty	pachass
one hundred	ek saya	one thousand	ek haja

Food

bread	pau roti (bread)	rice	bhat
meat	masu	water	pani
vegetables	tarkiri		

Times and Hours

open	open	closed	closed
What time is it?	Kati bajyo?	morning	bihana
afternoon	diooso	evening	sanjha
night	rati	yesterday	hijo
today	aaja	tomorrow	bholi

Other Words

alone	eklai	friend	sathi
good	ramro	bad	na ramro
happy	kushi	sad	dukhi
hot	garni (weather)/tato	cold	chiso

■ Festivals and Holidays

There is a festival somewhere almost every day of the year in India and Nepal. Many festivals are based on religion. Hindu, Sikh, and Jain festivals correspond to the Indian lunar calendar, so the dates vary from year to year with respect to the Gregorian calendar. Islamic festivals are determined by the Islamic lunar calendar, whose years are equal to 12 lunar cycles, meaning that festivals rotate throughout the solar year. In addition, there are a number of secular holidays that recognize the political history of India and Nepal—in India these are dated according to the Gregorian calendar, and in Nepal they follow the official Vikram Sambat (or Bikram Sambat) calendar. **The following dates are for 1997 only.**

India and Nepal celebrate the **New Year's Day** (Jan. 1) of the Gregorian calendar along with much of the world. Nepalese celebrate **Prithvi Narayan Shah's Birthday** (Jan. 11) honoring the king who united the country back in the 18th century. January 11th marks the **first day of Ramadan,** the 28-day period during which Muslims fast from dawn to dusk. Starting on January 15th, the end of the South Indian harvest is celebrated at the four-day long Tamil festival **Pongal** (Makar Sankranti in Andhra Pradesh). A military parade in New Delhi is the highlight of **Republic Day** (Jan. 26), one of India's four national public holidays.

Eid-ul-Fitr (Feb. 9) is the celebratory, three-day feast at the end of Ramadan. The Hindu festival of **Vasant Panchami** (Feb. 12) honors Saraswati, the goddess of learning. **Nepal's Democracy Day** is celebrated on the 18th. **Losar,** the **Tibetan New Year** (Feb./March), is a three-day period of feasts and festivities among Tibetan and Sherpa communities.

Shivaratri (March 7) is a Hindu day of fasting and night of vigil dedicated to Shiva, whose creation dance took place on this day. **Holi** (March 24), the Hindu water festival celebrating the beginning of spring, has become a exuberant, carnival-like affair in which revelers throw colored water and powder *(gulal)* at one another.

The **New Year's Day** (April 13) celebrated in Nepal marks the beginning of the Vikram Sambat Year 2054. The Hindu festival **Ramanavami** (April 16) celebrates the birth of Rama and prompts readings of the *Ramayana* in temples all over India and Nepal. The Muslim festival of **Eid-ul-Adha** (April 18) commemorates Abraham's intended sacrifice of his son Isaac. During the lunar month of Vaisakha is **Mahavir Jayanti** (April), the Jain festival that celebrates the birthday of its founder. The Sikh festival **Baisakhi** (April 13) commemorates the day on which Guru Gobind Singh founded the Khalsa and is preceded by readings of the Guru Granth Sahib. Later in the lunar month (April/May) is one of Nepal's most celebrated festivals, **Machhendranath Rath Yatra,** which honors the rain-bringing deity of compassion.

Ras as-Sana, the Islamic New Year's Day, falls on May 8th in 1997, marking the beginning of the Islamic year 1418. The 10-day Shi'a Muslim festival of **Muharram** (May 18-28) commemorates the martyrdom of the Prophet's grandson. The festival of **Buddha Jayanti** (May 22) celebrates the day of the Buddha's birth and subsequent attainment of enlightment and *nirvana.*

The Hindu festival **Rath Yatra** (July 6) commemorates the journey that Krishna (Lord Jagannath) made to Mathura. It is widely celebrated in southern India and in Orissa, where a grandiose chariot leaves from the temple in Puri to make its stately journey. Muslims all over the world celebrate **Mawlid-un-Nabi** (July 17) the birthday of the Prophet Muhammed.

In 1997, India will celebrate the 50th anniversary of its independence from Britain; **Independence Day** (Aug. 15) is the largest national holiday. **Raksha Bandhan** (Aug. 18) is a Hindu festival that honors the sea god Varuna. The festival has become associated with brothers and sisters—girls tie protective amulets *(rakhis)* to the wrists of their brothers, who offer gifts in return. Hindus celebrate Krishna's birthday at the festival called **Janmashtami** (Aug. 24). **Indra Jatra** (Aug./Sept.) is one of the most wild and anticipated festivals in the Kathmandu Valley and includes elaborate chariot processions and dancing. During the festival **Ganesh Chaturthi** (Sept. 6), Hindus venerate Ganesh, the god of obstacles and wisdom, with elaborate idoltry. The most spectacular Ganesh Chaturthi processions occur in Bombay and all over Rajasthan. **Onam** (Sept. 14) is the Keralan harvest festival.

Indians celebrate **Mahatma Gandhi's Birthday** on October 2nd. The 10-day festival of **Dussehra** (Oct. 11-21) is associated with the vanquishing demons of Hindu epochs. Known as **Dasain** in Nepal and **Durga Puja** in West Bengal, this festival has become one of the Nepal's most celebrated and it has been embraced by most religious and ethnic groups. **Diwali** (Oct. 30-Nov. 3) is the five-day festival of lights celebrating Rama and Sita's homecoming in the *Ramayana.* In addition to the tradition of lighting oil lamps *(divas)* and firecrackers, Diwali has also become a festival of sweets; it also marks the beginning of a new financial year. The **Jain New Year** falls at the same time as Diwali.

Guru Nanak Jayanti (Nov. 14) celebrates the birthday of the founder of Sikhism. The **Pushkar Camel Festival** (Nov. 14) is one of India's most famous fairs. Held at the sacred lake in Pushkar, Rajasthan, the festival attracts bathing Hindus and features livestock parades and auctions.

Constitution Day in Nepal will fall on December 15th. **Christmas Day** (Dec. 25) is celebrated in Christian areas in India, particularly in areas of Goa and Kerala. In Nepal the **King's Birthday** (Dec. 28) is a public holiday declared by the monarch. **Ramadan** starts again on December 31st.

■ Weights, Measures, and Temperatures

1 millimeter (mm) = 0.04 inch	1 inch = 25mm
1 meter (m) = 1.09 yards	1 yard = 0.92m
1 kilometer (km) = 0.62 mile	1 mile = 1.61km
1 gram (g) = 0.04 ounce	1 ounce = 25g
1 kilogram (kg) = 2.2 pounds	1 pound = 0.55kg
1 liter = 1.06 quarts	1 quart = 0.94 liter

To convert from °C to °F, multiply by 1.8 and add 32.
To convert from °F to °C, subtract 32 and multiply by 0.55.

°C	-5	0	5	10	15	20	25	30	35	40
°F	23	32	41	50	59	68	77	86	95	104

APPENDIX

Index

Numerics

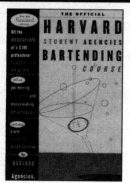

★Let's Go 1997 Reader Questionnaire ★

Please fill this out and return it to **Let's Go, St. Martin's Press,** 175 5th Ave. NY, NY 10010

Name: _____ **What book did you use?**_____

Address: _____

City: _____ **State:** _____ **Zip Code:** _____

How old are you? under 19   19-24   25-34   35-44   45-54   55 or over

Are you (circle one)   in high school   in college   in grad school
    employed   retired   between jobs

Have you used Let's Go before?   yes   no

Would you use Let's Go again?   yes   no

How did you first hear about Let's Go?   friend   store clerk   CNN
    bookstore display   advertisement/promotion   review   other

Why did you choose Let's Go (circle up to two)?   annual updating
    reputation   budget focus   price   writing style
    other: _____

Which other guides have you used, if any?   Frommer's $-a-day   Fodor's
    Rough Guides   Lonely Planet   Berkeley   Rick Steves
    other: _____

Is Let's Go the best guidebook?   yes   no

If not, which do you prefer? _____

**Which part of Let's Go do you feel needs most to be improved, if any
    (circle up to two)?**   packaging/cover   practical information
    accommodations   food   cultural introduction   sights
    practical introduction ("Essentials")   directions   entertainment
    gay/lesbian information   maps   other: _____

How would you like to see these things improved?
    _____
    _____

How long was your trip?   one week   two weeks   three weeks
    one month   two months or more

Have you traveled extensively before?   yes   no

Do you buy a separate map when you visit a foreign city?   yes   no

Have you seen the Let's Go Map Guides?   yes   no

Have you used a Let's Go Map Guide?   yes   no

If you have, would you recommend them to others?   yes   no

Did you use the internet to plan your trip?   yes   no

Would you buy a Let's Go   phrasebook   adventure/trekking guide
    gay/lesbian guide

**Which of the following destinations do you hope to visit in the next three
    to five years (circle one)?**   Australia   China   South America   Russia
    other: _____

Where did you buy your guidebook?   internet   chain bookstore
    independent bookstore   college bookstore   travel store
    other: _____